Encyclopedia of Mystery and Detection

Final problem

Encyclopedia of Mystery and Detection

CHRIS STEINBRUNNER and OTTO PENZLER

Editors-in-Chief

MARVIN LACHMAN and CHARLES SHIBUK

Senior Editors

A Harvest/HBJ Book
Harcourt Brace Jovanovich, Publishers
San Diego New York London

Reprinted by arrangement with McGraw-Hill, Inc.

LIBRARY OF CONGRESS CATALOGING IN PUBLICATION DATA

Main entry under title:

Encyclopedia of mystery and detection.

"A Harvest/HBJ book."
Reprint. Originally published: New York : McGraw-Hill, © 1976.
Bibliography: p.
1. Detectives in mass media—Dictionaries.
I. Steinbrunner, Chris. II. Penzler, Otto.
[P96.D4E5 1984] 808.83′872′0321 84-9131
ISBN 0-15-628787-0 (pbk.)

Printed in the United States of America

First Harvest/HBJ edition 1984

A B C D E F G H I J

Contributors

EDITORS-IN-CHIEF

Chris Steinbrunner

Author of *The Cinema of the Fantastic;* contributor to many books and periodicals; writer and producer of such TV specials as "The Incredible James Bond" and "The Man Who Was Sherlock Holmes"; regional vice-president of the Mystery Writers of America and editor of its journal, *The Third Degree.*

Otto Penzler

Editor of the *Ellery Queen Newsletter;* owner of one of the finest collections of detective fiction first editions and memorabilia in private hands; founder of The Mysterious Press, a publishing house specializing in mystery fiction.

SENIOR EDITORS

Marvin Lachman

Regular contributor to *The Armchair Detective* and other scholarly journals devoted to the genre.

Charles Shibuk

Author of "The Paperback Revolution" column in *The Armchair Detective* since its inception; vice-president of The Theodore Huff Memorial Film Society.

CONTRIBUTING EDITORS

Robert E. Briney

Editor of *The Rohmer Review* and of *Master of Villainy,* the biography of Sax Rohmer.

Ron Goulart

Author of *Cheap Thrills,* a history of pulp fiction, and more than 100 mystery and science fiction books and stories.

J. Randolph Cox

Reference librarian at St. Olaf College, Northfield, Minn.; authority on the detective story in the dime novel.

Allen J. Hubin

Former editor of the "Criminals at Large" column for *The New York Times;* editor of *The Armchair Detective.*

CONTRIBUTING EDITORS (cont'd.)

Daniel Morrow

Authority on radio detectives; contributor to *The Baker Street Journal* and other periodicals.

Sam Moskowitz

Editor of many science fiction anthologies and critical works including *Under the Moon of Mars*, *Masterpieces of Science Fiction*, and *Science Fiction by Gaslight*.

Norman S. Nolan

Member of the Baker Street Irregulars and the Bibliographical Society of America; noted collector of rare books.

Hans Stefan Santesson

Former editor of *The Saint Mystery Magazine;* editor of *The Locked Room Reader;* recently deceased.

PHOTOGRAPHER

Ann Limongello

Photographed all illustrations not otherwise credited.

Preface

Two titans exchange a dialogue of challenge—the master detective versus the Napoleon of crime—and the mystery story achieves its crucial confrontation. In this 1893 Sidney Paget drawing for *The Strand* magazine, the archcriminal Moriarty—who has just said, "It has been a duel between you and me, Mr. Holmes"—turns his back upon the figure of Sherlock, much like Lucifer spun away from the Archangel, and the two, frozen for all time in Paget's vision, personify the struggle of Good against Evil.

As does the mystery story.

This vigorous and universally loved literary genre charts the victories of good over evil, lights up the darkness, celebrates justice, sharpens the thinking process. It is not reading for dullards, nor for those unnoble enough not to cherish the triumph of right. Its central figure, the Detective, is a modern knight searching after strange grails; its narratives are often mystic journeys for a secular age. The authors of the *Encyclopedia of Mystery and Detection* explore the genre, its scope and its roots, its heroes and villains.

While tales of mystery go back to the beginnings of legend and literature, its modern foundations are built on the gothic novel of romance and the supernatural, on the thrillers shaped by Wilkie Collins and Charles Dickens into recognizable efforts at detection, and on the early French novels about underworld crime. But the father of the detective story is Edgar Allan Poe, the brooding American who not only fashioned the first real ratiocinator but also constructed the modern mystery.

While Poe's Dupin was pure intellect, however, Conan Doyle's colorful Sherlock Holmes became surely the most enduring figure in all the literature as well as its keenest investigator. Additionally, his creation of Professor Moriarty provided the detective with an adversary worthy of his skills, the model of many master criminals—some masked to be unmasked—to follow. The Age of the Detective had begun.

Eccentric, all-knowing, ascetic, dashing, young, old, ethnic, pugnacious, saintly, carnal, the coloration of the detective is widely varied. Philo Vance, withdrawn and superior, the timid and celibate Father Brown, the criminal Raffles, the aristocrat Lord Peter, Asiatic policeman Chan, tough Sam Spade and fellow private operatives, the enduring and prolific Ellery Queen, the spies of Greene and Fleming, cops of the 87th and other precincts, the lonely Lew Archer—all can be found in their places here. The range of the mystery story—from classic whodunit puzzles to modern narratives of suspense, from such settings as shadowy manor houses to exotic bases of espionage and intrigue—are dealt with comprehensively.There are entries, too, for significant mystery films, television mystery drama, and the melodrama theater, as well as areas such as pulps and characters from the comic pages.

Sherlock Holmes remarked to his most faithful chronicler, "I know, my dear Watson, that you share my love for all that is bizarre and outside the conventions and humdrum routine of everyday life." In a sense the master detective, to whom we owe so much, was charting the terrain of the mystery story. It is to this geography that the editors and authors of the *Encyclopedia of Mystery and Detection* hope to contribute a pioneering exploration.

THE EDITORS

Introduction

The *Encyclopedia of Mystery and Detection* is the most ambitious project of its kind yet attempted in the country's favorite literary genre. There have been a few histories of the subject, and some critical commentaries, but never before a reference work of this size.

The book was inspired to some degree by a little paperbound volume called the *Detectionary*, which was privately printed in 1972. Written by Chris Steinbrunner, Charles Shibuk, Otto Penzler, Marvin Lachman, and Francis M. Nevins, it contained 60,000 words and was a unique contribution to the reference shelf. Few copies, however, found their way into the hands of those who would have found it most valuable. When it was realized that there was a substantial demand for such a book, and that nothing equivalent was available, the present volume was launched.

The *Encyclopedia of Mystery and Detection* contains more than 300,000 words. Its 600 articles deal largely with authors, but many are devoted to detectives, crooks, and categories such as pulp magazines. We have defined mystery fiction very broadly to include the gothic romance, such as *Frankenstein* and the works of Radcliffe; some mainstream literature, by Dickens, Hugo, and Dostoevski, for example; and some pure adventure fiction, by such writers as John Buchan, H. C. McNeile, and Sax Rohmer.

The astute reader will note a certain inconsistency about who has been included, who has been omitted, and the length of the articles. Virtually everyone has a different opinion of what is significant and what is trivial. In planning this book, the editors necessarily made many purely subjective decisions, but they were also influenced by certain practical considerations. First, significance in the history of the genre was of prime importance. Obviously, Sherlock Holmes and Ellery Queen are more important than the obscure creations of some dime novelists, so the material about them is more detailed and comprehensive. Availability of information was a second consideration. Reference books abound with data about Fitzgerald, Balzac, and Dreiser, for example, so that their entries have been restricted to material relating to mystery fiction. On the other hand no standard reference guides offer much information about Will Scott, and his entry, consequently, is longer than his reputation might seem to warrant.

Still, the reader is bound to miss certain subjects and demand; "Why did you omit so-and-so?" Why indeed? The space available to us was not infinite. This is a big book, by any reasonable standard, but a line had to be drawn somewhere. If the reader insists, "But X is just as important as Y," he may be right. There are scores of borderline entries in this book, and hundreds of borderline omissions. At least 10,000 writers have turned their attention to the mystery. We have reviewed every one of even the most marginal importance. If there is an argument for their inclusion, we have heard it. No one of genuine significance, we hope, has been omitted. Some marginal writers have been included because of an idiosyncratic affection on the part of one or more of the editors. Perhaps an expanded second edition will include the missing favorite of our earnest reader.

The *Encyclopedia of Mystery and Detection* is designed for the use of scholars and librarians, who may have noticed the paucity of reference material about the subject, as well as for the mystery reader and filmgoer who may want to know more about his favorite writers, directors, books, films, detectives, and so on. Until now, there has been no single volume containing information about Charlie Chan films, Hercule Poirot cases, and Mickey Spillane works.

Every effort has been made to make this volume as accurate as possible. Almost every living writer included in the *Encyclopedia* has read his or her own entry and made corrections and emendations where necessary. In the case of major deceased writers, the entries have been seen by experts, biographers, friends, or close relatives. Additionally, many of the world's leading authorities and scholars on mystery and detective fiction have assisted in the acquisition, compilation, and emendation of information for this book.

Checklists of book titles follow the articles about some major writers and some major literary characters. These lists are arranged chronologically according to the first publication in book form of the particular title listed. Alternative English and American titles are given, with the earliest appearance being listed first, but no attempt has been made to list retitlings for paperbacks or other reprints. Omnibus volumes are not listed unless they contain significant new material. In those instances where a writer is represented with one article and his series detective with another, the books about the detective are listed under the detective's name, while those books that do not feature the series character are listed under the author's name. Thus the list of books that follows the article about John Dickson Carr does not include titles featuring Gideon Fell, Henri Bencolin, Colonel March, or Sir Henry Merrivale, as each has his own entry.

Film, television, and play sections generally provide information about the source of the plot and characters, appropriate dates, production company, director, leading players, and a brief synopsis of the plot. A film listing under an author's name generally means that a book or story has served as the basis for that film. It does not necessarily mean that the writer had a direct hand in the production, either as a screenwriter or in any other capacity. Nonmystery films have been excluded, for the most part.

Cross-references are signaled in text by the use of small capital letters. The number of these cross-references, and the equally extensive use of the main reference, or reference entry, seemed to us to obviate the inclusion of an index—which in any case would have been so huge as to require a major reduction of the text. Also, the Selective Bibliography should be useful to those readers interested in expanding their knowledge of the field.

More reference books devoted to the mystery have been published in the past decade than in all the years before. At last, it seems, critics and scholars are abandoning the simplistic snobbishness of Edmund Wilson and similar critics who denigrated the genre. Almost every great writer of the past century has turned his hand to novels and stories of mystery, crime, suspense, espionage, or detection. It is arguably the most important literary development of the twentieth century, and has attracted many of the best writers at one time or another. It is serious literature, and it is about time that it be treated with the respect and dignity it deserves.

As with any work of this magnitude, the *Encyclopedia* has come into being only because of the efforts of many interested and generous persons, particularly William Lofts, Norman Donaldson, Estelle Fox, and Nigel Morland as well as John Cocchi, Francis M. Nevins, Jacques Barzun, Christianna Brand, Professor John J. McAleer, Penelope Wallace, Frederic Dannay, John Dickson Carr, Michele S. Tempesta, Margaret Norton, John Hale, Betty Donaldson, Pat Erhardt, Joan Kahn, Robert Weinberg, Gloria Amoury, Bonnie Harris, Iwan Hedman, Ed Demchko, Cyril H. Ilott, Steven Lachman, Carol Lachman, Robert Aucott, Barbara Cronin, Resa Cronin, and John Bennett Shaw. Thanks, too, for the countless hours of manuscript editing and attention to detail by Tobia L. Worth, Olive Collen, and Beatrice E. Eckes.

New York, 1975 THE EDITORS

Selective Bibliography

In addition to standard reference works dealing with general literature and biographies, bibliographies, and critical works about individual authors, the following books have been consulted in the compilation of this work:

Barzun, Jacques, and Wendell Hertig Taylor: *A Catalogue of Crime*, Harper & Row, New York, 1971.

Butler, William Vivian: *The Durable Desperadoes*, Macmillan, London, 1973.

Chandler, Frank W.: *The Literature of Roguery*, 2 vols., Houghton Mifflin, Boston, 1907; reprinted, Burt Franklin, New York, 1958.

Glover, Dorothy, and Graham Greene: *Victorian Detective Fiction*, arr. by Eric Osborne, Bodley Head, London, 1966.

Goulart, Ron: *Cheap Thrills*, Arlington House, New Rochelle, N.Y. 1972.

Gribbin, Lenore S.: *Who's Whodunit*, University of North Carolina, Chapel Hill, N.C., 1969.

Gruber, Frank: *The Pulp Jungle*, Sherbourne, Los Angeles, 1967.

Hagen, Ordean A.: *Who Done It?* Bowker, New York, 1969.

Haycraft, Howard: *Murder for Pleasure*, Appleton-Century, New York, 1941; enl. ed. containing "The Haycraft-Queen Definitive Library of Detective-Crime-Mystery Fiction," Biblo & Tannen, New York, 1968.

———: *The Art of the Mystery Story*, containing James Sandoe, "Readers' Guide to Crime," Simon and Schuster, New York, 1946.

Hedman, Iwan: *Deckare Och Thrillers Pa Svenska 1864–1973*, Dast, Sweden, 1974.

Hubin, Allen J. (ed.): *The Armchair Detective*, magazine, White Bear Lake, Minn. 1967—.

Johannsen, Albert: *The House of Beadle and Adams*, 2 vols., University of Oklahoma Press, Norman, 1950.

La Cour, Tage, and Harald Mogensen: *The Murder Book*, T. Fisher Unwin, London, 1971.

Lofts, W. O. G., and D. J. Adley: *The Men behind Boys' Fiction*, Howard Baker, London, 1970.

Madden, Cecil (ed.): *Meet the Detective*, George Allen & Unwin, London, 1935.

Messac, Régis: *Le "Detective Novel" et L'Influence de la Pensée Scientifique*, Libraire Ancienne Honoré Champion, Paris, 1929.

Mundell, E. H., and G. Jay Rausch: *The Detective Short Story: A Bibliography and Index*, Kansas State University Library, Manhattan, 1974.

Murch, A. E.: *The Development of the Detective Novel*, rev. ed., Peter Owen, London, 1968.

Nevins, Francis M., Jr. (ed.): *The Mystery Writer's Art*, Bowling Green University Popular Press, Bowling Green, Ohio, 1970.

Quayle, Eric: *The Collector's Book of Detective Fiction*, Studio Vista, London, 1972.

Queen, Ellery: *The Detective Short Story*, Little, Brown, Boston, 1942; reprinted, Biblo & Tannen, New York, 1969.

———: *Queen's Quorum*, Little, Brown, Boston, 1951; rev. ed., Biblo & Tannen, New York, 1969.

Reynolds, Quentin: *The Fiction Factory*, Random House, New York, 1955.

Routley, Erik: *The Puritan Pleasures of the Detective Story*, Gollancz, London, 1972.

Scott, Sutherland: *Blood in Their Ink*, Stanley Paul, London, 1953.

Steinbrunner, Chris, Charles Shibuk, Otto Penzler, Marv Lachman, and Francis M. Nevins: *Detectionary*, privately printed, Lock Haven, Pa., 1972.

Symons, Julian: *The Detective Story in Britain*, Longmans, London, 1962.

———: *Bloody Murder*, Faber, London, 1972 (U.S. title: *Mortal Consequences*, Harper & Row, New York, 1972).

Thompson, H. Douglas: *Masters of Mystery*, Collins, London, 1931.

Turner, E. S.: *Boys Will Be Boys*, Michael Joseph, London, 1948; rev. ed., 1957.

Watson, Colin: *Snobbery with Violence*, Eyre & Spottiswoode, London, 1971.

A

AARONS, EDWARD S[IDNEY] (1916–1975). American mystery and short story writer. Philadelphia-born, Aarons once "covered five-alarm fires, police stations, and the morgue" in that city while employed by a newspaper. To support himself while he was in college, he also worked as a millhand, salesman, and fisherman, and held a number of other jobs. He wrote in his spare time and won a collegiate short story contest in 1933. When his first mystery novel was published (he was twenty), he decided to concentrate on writing as a career. In 1941, one week after Pearl Harbor was bombed, he enlisted in the Coast Guard, combining his patriotic duty with his lifelong love of boats.

Edward S. Aarons. [*Fred Schulze*]

In 1945 Aarons returned to school, where he met his future wife, Ruth Ives (now deceased); he subsequently married Grace Dyer.

Aarons's early work was published under the pseudonyms Edward Ronns and Paul Ayres. Most of the books were later reprinted under his own name. His nonseries novels are generally set in one of the major Eastern cities of the United States. The then-timely *The State Department Murders* (1950) takes place in Washington, D.C., where a federal employee suspected by a congressional committee of having communist leanings becomes a murder suspect. After 1956 most of his books acquired more exotic settings, as he chronicled the adventures of Sam Durell, a Yale-educated CIA agent of Cajun background. All the titles in this highly successful paperback series begin with the word "Assignment," for example, *Assignment—Burma Girl* (1961), *Assignment—The Girl in the Gondola* (1964), and *Assignment—Peking* (1969). In *Assignment–Maltese Maiden* (1972) Durrell's activities take him from North Africa to Malta. General McFee, kidnapped by villainous Chinese forces, must be rescued before he divulges top secrets. Two beautiful girls and a KGB official complicate the assignment. Aarons wrote more than 200 short stories and novelettes.

ABBOT, ANTHONY (pseudonym of [Charles] Fulton Oursler; 1893–1952). American playwright, journalist, and detective novelist; creator of Thatcher COLT. Oursler was born in Baltimore, Md., the son of William C. Oursler, a line superintendent for the United Railways and Electric Company of Baltimore. Both parents were descendants of the earliest families to settle in Baltimore.

Oursler left school before he finished the eighth grade and went to work. He was a water boy for a construction gang, an assistant on a butter and egg route, a packer in a department store, and a clerk in a law office for two years at $3 per week. He supplemented his income by performing as a magician in clubs and lodges. His family assumed that he would study law in his spare time, but he became interested in literature instead and determined to become a writer.

He worked as a cub reporter on the *Baltimore American* and then, in 1918, left for New York to join the staff of *Music Trades* as news editor; two days later he was appointed managing editor. He spent the next several years turning out stories and articles for many periodicals, including pulp magazines. In 1920 he joined the staff of MacFadden Publications and two weeks later was given full editorial power. For twenty years he served as supervising editor of all MacFadden publications including *Physical Culture, True Story,* and *True Detective.*

In the meantime Oursler had become interested in crime detection and lectured to graduating classes of the National Police Academy of the FBI. He also started to write mystery novels as Anthony Abbot, using the word "about" as the first word in most titles so that the books would be placed first on library lists (in later years he denied that this had been his intention). In the years roughly paralleling his mystery writing career, he served as editor in chief of *Liberty* (1931–1942).

Oursler spent much of his time during World War II as a radio broadcaster and in 1944 became senior editor of *The Reader's Digest.* During his literary career he wrote or collaborated on thirty books, the most famous being the highly successful *The Greatest Story Ever Told* (1949), a modern retelling of the New Testament. Started after Oursler's first trip to Palestine in 1935, it was certainly influenced by his conversion to the Roman Catholic faith in 1943. The book was acclaimed by all religions and sold over 2 million copies. Oursler also wrote *Why I Know There Is a God* (1950), *Modern Parables* (1950), *A Child's Life of Jesus* (1951), *The Greatest Book Ever Written* (1951), and the posthumously published *The Greatest Faith Ever Known* (1953).

Oursler traveled and lectured extensively in the United States and many foreign countries. He was also a screenwriter, ventriloquist, critic, psychic investigator, and undercover agent for the FBI.

He died in New York City of a heart attack. He had been married twice, and one of his four children, Will, wrote mystery novels in the 1940s. Oursler's autobiography, *Behold This Dreamer,* was published in 1964.

Anthony Abbot's detective novels were heavily influenced by S. S. VAN DINE (each author used the device of a first-person narrator—named after himself—who serves as the detective's secretary and relates his exploits) and the early Ellery QUEEN (author). A slight influence of the Freeman Wills CROFTS school of police routine can also be noted in his work.

Film

"The Perfect Case," an article Abbot wrote for *The Reader's Digest,* concerning the murder of a Connecticut priest, was made into an engrossing semi-documentary-style film entitled *Boomerang* (Twentieth Century-Fox, 1947. Dana Andrews, Lee J. Cobb. Directed by Elia Kazan).

ABBOTT, PAT AND JEAN (Creator: Frances CRANE). The most widely traveled husband and wife detective team, the Abbotts have solved mysteries throughout the world. They met while Jean Holly of Illinois was in New Mexico managing a store (in *The Turquoise Shop*). They were married at the conclusion of *The Yellow Violet,* a mystery set in San Francisco, where Pat maintains his office (he is considered the city's best detective). World War II service overseas in Marine Corps Intelligence intervened, and the couple were not reunited until Pat returned in *The Indigo Necklace,* in which they solve a murder in an ancient New Orleans mansion. Other Abbott adventures have taken them to the Florida Keys, Lexington, Ky., London, Morocco, Mexico, and Paris.

Pat Abbott, a native of Wyoming, is tall and has dark hair and green eyes. He is an expert in many areas of detective work; his well-read library includes books on ballistics, toxicology, and other subjects relevant to his work. However, he would give up this career if he could successfully pursue his hobby—painting. Jean Abbott is a pretty, dark-haired girl who is in her late twenties when she meets Pat. Fond of pets, she has a Persian cat, Toby, and later a dachshund, Pancho. Although claustrophobic, she has a tendency to wander into situations in which she is rendered unconscious and locked up by murderers who—conveniently—never kill her. Most of the Abbotts' cases are solved by Pat, whose frequent use of guesswork belies his technical competence. Jean tries very hard to assist her husband's endeavors, frequently doing her thinking in a bathtub because, as she says, "A bath always makes me very logical."

CHECKLIST

1941	*The Turquoise Shop*
1942	*The Golden Box*
1943	*The Yellow Violet*
1943	*The Pink Umbrella*
1943	*The Applegreen Cat*
1944	*The Amethyst Spectacles*
1945	*The Indigo Necklace*
1946	*The Cinnamon Murder*
1946	*The Shocking Pink Hat*
1947	*Murder on the Purple Water*
1948	*Black Cypress*
1949	*The Flying Red Horse*
1950	*The Daffodil Blonde*

1951 *Murder in Blue Street* (British title: *Death in the Blue Hour*)
1951 *The Polkadot Murder*
1953 *Thirteen White Tulips*
1953 *Murder in Bright Red*
1954 *The Coral Princess Murders*
1955 *Death in Lilac Time*
1956 *Horror on the Ruby X*
1956 *The Ultraviolet Widow*
1958 *The Man in Gray* (British title: *The Gray Stranger*)
1958 *The Buttercup Case*
1960 *Death-Wish Green*
1962 *The Amber Eyes*
1965 *The Body Beneath a Mandarin Tree*

Radio

Abbott Mysteries, based on Mrs. Crane's novels, featured the Abbotts, played by Charles Webster (later Les Tremayne) and Julie Stevens (later Alice Reinheart).

ABDULLAH, ACHMED (pseudonym of Alexander Nicholayevitch Romanoff; 1881–1945). Russian-English author of novels and short stories of adventure, fantasy, and crime. He was born in Yalta, the son of a Russian Orthodox father and a Muslim mother, and was raised in England, where he studied at Eton and Oxford. After spending many years in the British Army, he wrote numerous novels and stories, some of which drew on his experiences. He also wrote screenplays. *The Thief of Bagdad* (1924), which starred Douglas Fairbanks, was based on an original story by Abdullah; the screenplay was by Elton Thomas (a Fairbanks pseudonym).

Among Abdullah's best mystery works are *The Red Stain* (1915), *The Blue-Eyed Manchu* (1917), *The Honourable Gentleman and Others* (1919; s.s.), *The Swinging Caravan* (1925), *Steel and Jade* (1927; s.s.), and *The Bungalow on the Roof* (1931).

ABNER, UNCLE. *See* UNCLE ABNER.

ACRE, STEPHEN. *See* GRUBER, FRANK.

ADAMS, CLEVE F[RANKLIN] (1895–1949). American writer in the hard-boiled tradition, a friend and correspondent of Raymond CHANDLER and a literary disciple of Dashiell HAMMETT. Adams was born in Chicago and, until about the age of forty, worked at a wide variety of jobs, including stints as a copper miner, an art director for films, a life insurance executive, and a detective. All four professions furnished raw material for the hard-boiled mystery fiction he began to write in the mid-1930s. For about five years he wrote almost exclusively for such crime pulp magazines as *Detective Fiction Weekly* and *Double Detective.*

In 1940 he published his first book, *Sabotage,* the protagonist of which is private detective Rex McBride. Like the other tough sleuths Adams later created, McBride is slim and dark, with a wolfish, satanic look and an apparently hard shell covering a heart full of maudlin sentimentality. He has a taste for gallows humor and tall, cool women, and a constitution that is impervious to huge amounts of liquor and corporal punishment. He is a fascist ("An American Gestapo is goddam well what we need," he says in one novel), a racist (ethnic slurs appear almost as frequently as gun battles in the Adams canon), a male chauvinist, a cynic, and a hypocrite—and Adams goes out of his way to make him look stupid.

Most of Adams's plots were borrowed from Hammett; he used the same character types, mannerisms, scenes, story elements, and even dialogue over and over again. In a 1942 essay he confessed that he never worked out the end of any novel until he had written half of it—which explains why none of his plots makes much sense. His importance lies in the way he inverted Chandler's knightly image of the private eye into that of an oafish antihero, and in the readability which he learned in the pulp magazines and with which he filled all his novels. His last three novels, including the final McBride story, *Shady Lady* (1955), were published after his death.

Adams also published several pseudonymous novels: *The Vice Czar Murders,* by Franklin Charles (1941); and *Dig Me a Grave* (1942), *Death Is Like That* (1943), and *The Evil Star* (1944), by John Spain.

ADAMS, HARRIET S[TRATEMEYER]. *See* KEENE, CAROLYN.

ADAMS, HERBERT (1874–1952). English author and detective story writer. Born in London, he wrote humorous verse and short stories in his youth, and several early works were published. His first novel, *A Virtue of Necessity* (1905), was not successful. He then entered the business world, later turning to real estate. His first detective novel, *The Secret of Bogey House* (1924), was successful enough to encourage him to write fifty more novels in the genre.

Adams's chief recreation was golf; one of his major sleuths, Roger Bennion, is an excellent golfer, and the works in which he is involved, *Death off the Fairway* (1936), *The Nineteenth Hole Mystery* (1939), and *Death on the First Tee* (1957), have golfing backgrounds.

Adams also wrote a book of golfing short stories, *The Perfect Round: Tales of the Links* (1927); two romances, *Queen's Mate* (1931) and *A Lady So Innocent* (1932); and two mystery novels under the pseudonym Jonathan Gray: *Safety Last* (1934) and *The Owl* (1937).

Adams's detective novels are typical of their

time and setting, revealing much about the British ethos of the 1920s and 1930s. Although they move in a leisurely fashion, they are well plotted and well characterized. Internal evidence indicates that Adams had legal training or had done considerable research on the points of law that frequently appear in his novels.

One of his best works is *John Brand's Will* (1933; U.S. title: *The Golf House Murder*). The central problem of the first half of this work is whether Brand would have been able to sign a will as he lay dying. Adams is able to ring every variation on this theme and still interest and involve the reader until, at almost the midpoint of the story, a body is discovered in a golf house.

ADAMS, SAMUEL HOPKINS (1871–1958). American novelist and journalist. Adams's accomplishments in fields other than mystery fiction probably exceed those in it. He was an effective muckraker for several newspapers and magazines, specializing in medical stories and public health; he was the first writer to popularize those subjects. His exposé of patent medicine quackery was instrumental in bringing about the passage of the first Pure Food and Drug Act.

Born in Dunkirk, N.Y., the son of Myron and Hester Rose (Hopkins) Adams, he received B.A. and L.H.D. degrees from Hamilton College. His main interest was writing, but he admitted to the vices of fishing and "antiquing." He had two daughters by his first marriage, to Elizabeth R. Noyes in 1898; he was married to Jane Peyton Van Norman in 1915.

Adams's early research into dubious medical practices furnished him with material for his detective stories, which presented many real-life incidents in fictionalized form. Average JONES, his most famous creation, had a short life because Adams was unable to invent further mystery plots.

In addition to stories about Jones, Adams produced several other mysteries, including his first book, *The Mystery* (1905), in collaboration with S. E. White; *Flying Death* (1906); and *The Secret of Lonesome Cove* (1912). He also contributed a chapter to *The President's Mystery Story* (1935), an effort by seven mystery writers to produce a novel based on a plot idea by Franklin D. Roosevelt. Many of his stories, including "Night Bus," filmed as *It Happened One Night* (1934), were adapted for motion pictures.

Adams had an unusual solution to the problem of finding names for his characters—he took them from tombstones in country churchyards.

AIRD, CATHERINE (pseudonym of Kinn Hamilton McIntosh; 1930–). English mystery writer. Born in Huddersfield of Scottish parents, she lives in an east Kent village near Canterbury, where she acts as receptionist and dispenser for her father, a physician. She turned to writing mysteries after many years of reading them. She especially admires Josephine TEY and wrote an article for *The Armchair Detective* about Miss Tey's life and works.

The Aird books published to date have all been unusual and generally well received. The first, *The Religious Body* (1966), involved the murder of a nun. *Henrietta Who?* (1968) was selected by Allen J. HUBIN as one of the best books of the year. He and other critics were intrigued by the plight of the daughter who is told that her mother, just killed by a hit-and-run driver, had never borne children. In *A Late Phoenix* (1970) a corpse buried during the Nazi blitz twenty-five years previously is discovered—and found to have been murdered. Most of Miss Aird's mysteries are about CID Inspector Sloan, an intelligent sleuth. Other Aird titles are *A Most Contagious Game* (1967), *The Complete Steel* (1969; U.S. title: *The Stately Home Murder*), *His Burial Too* (1973), and *Slight Mourning* (1975).

ALBRAND, MARTHA (pseudonym of Heidi Huberta Freybe; 1912–). German-American author of spy novels. Although born in Rostock, Germany, Martha Albrand spent most of her youth traveling and studying throughout Europe and the Middle East, residing for long periods in Italy, England, the Netherlands, and Switzerland. Under the pseudonym Katrin Holland, she wrote fiction in Germany, where her novel *Carlotta Torrensani* (1938) became a best seller.

A voluntary exile from Nazi Germany, she settled in Great Britain but then, in 1938, moved to the United States and began writing under the Albrand pseudonym. She has also written as Christine Lambert. Despite her European background, Miss Albrand's roots are in the United States. Her great-grandfather, a Polish nobleman, renounced his title and became a missionary to the Chippewa Indians; her grandmother was the first white child born in a Chippewa settlement. Martha Albrand is the widow of Sydney J. Lamon and has lived in New York City, on a 106-acre farm in Pattenburg, N.J., and in Connecticut.

Shortly after her arrival in the United States, Martha Albrand began to write suspense novels, most of which are spy fiction. The settings, reflecting her cosmopolitan background, are usually major European cities. Her first book, the very successful *No Surrender* (1942), is about the Dutch underground during the Nazi occupation. In *Without Orders* (1943) an escaped American prisoner of war impersonates an Italian nobleman. *After Midnight* (1948), also set in Italy, deals with an American's return to that country after the war and the investigation of a murder that took place while he served with the Italian underground. *A Day in Monte Carlo*

(1959), about the Algerian rebellion, is also set in Paris and Monaco.

Although her suspense fiction has gained Miss Albrand a reputation second only to that of Helen MACINNES among authors writing primarily for a female audience, a recent book represents a radical departure: *Manhattan North* (1971) is a police procedural story set on the upper West Side of the borough. Her latest book, *Zurich A/Z 900* (1974), is about a medical invention.

ALDING, PETER. *See* JEFFRIES, RODERIC.

ALDRICH, THOMAS BAILEY (1836–1907). American poet, short story writer, novelist, playwright, and editor. Born in Portsmouth, N.H., he covered the Civil War as a correspondent and then returned to edit several periodicals, the most prestigious being *The Atlantic Monthly.* His most famous fictional works are *The Story of a Bad Boy* (1870), based on his own childhood, and *Marjorie Daw and Other People* (1873), which contains several stories with elements of mystery. *The Stillwater Tragedy* (1880) is a full-length mystery novel. *Out of His Head* (1862) contains the first short detective story written by an American to appear in book form after Edgar Allan POE's *Tales* (1845) was published. Chapters 11–14 constitute a complete detective tale involving Paul Lynde, one of the most eccentric detectives in literature. Although heavily dependent on Poe's "The Murders in the Rue Morgue" (1841), Aldrich's tale is the first variation by an American of Poe's locked-room device (*see* LOCKED-ROOM MYSTERIES) and is also the first case in which the detective is responsible for the murder.

ALEXANDER, DAVID (1907–1973). American newspaperman and author of mysteries. Born in Shelbyville, Ky., Alexander attended the University of Kentucky, where he met his future wife. A lifelong interest in horses and horse racing led him to make a career of writing about them. For more than ten years he was managing editor and columnist for the *Morning Telegraph,* a New York racing and show business newspaper. He later was racing editor of the *New York Herald Tribune* and then wrote for the *National Thoroughbred* when the *Tribune* ceased publication. His writing career was interrupted by World War II, during which he served in the U.S. Army Tank Corps.

Alexander did not publish his first mystery until he was in his mid-forties. He completed a course at the New York Institute of Criminology so that he could write authoritatively about crime. He graduated with highest honors and was offered several private detective positions, which he declined, preferring his writing career. He lived in Greenwich Village, which he used as the setting for *The Madhouse in Washington Square* (1958). Alexander's most successful books, a series featuring Bart HARDIN, had a Times Square background. The author's dedication in the first Hardin book, *Terror on Broadway* (1954): "To the old-timers on the staff of the *New York Morning Telegraph* who knew Broadway when it was the Big Street instead of a freak show," reflected his growing disenchantment with a changing area.

His short story "The Man Who Went to Taltavul's" won second prize in *Ellery Queen's Mystery Magazine's* 1956 contest. It was published along with twelve other stories in *Hangman's Dozen,* a 1961 collection. That year, too, he edited *Tales for a Rainy Day,* an anthology, for the Mystery Writers of America.

ALLEN, (CHARLES) GRANT (BLAIRFINDIE) (1848–1899). British author, philosopher, and scientist whose two most important works were literary breakthroughs. The first, *The Woman Who Did* (1895), created a sensation in Victorian England because of its candid discussion of sex (as implied in the title). The second book guarantees Allen a lasting place in the annals of mystery fiction: *An African Millionaire* (1897), a collection of stories about Colonel CLAY—the first important rogue in short crime fiction who is the hero, not a subsidiary character, villain, or antihero.

Born near Kingston, Ontario, the second son of Joseph Antisell Allen, a minister of the Church of Ireland, and Catherine Ann Grant, Allen married

Gordon Browne provided eighty illustrations for Grant Allen's collection of stories about a female detective. This is the cover of the first American edition, published by Putnam in 1899.

while still attending school (he was educated in the United States and in Europe and received a bachelor's degree from Oxford) and had to work while studying because his wife was an invalid. In 1873 he was given a professorship at a new university for Negroes in Spanish Town, Jamaica. When only a half dozen students showed up, the school was closed.

Allen returned to England and wrote several scientific and philosophical works that gave him a reputation for scholarship but little money. He turned to fiction and was rewarded with a large readership. He never enjoyed good health, however, and died at his country home at the age of fifty-one, survived by his second wife (Ellen Jerrard, whom he had married in 1873) and their son.

When Allen fell fatally ill in the fall of 1899, he had nearly finished an episodic novel and wanted to ensure that it would be completed in case he died. He called his friend Sir Arthur CONAN DOYLE, who consulted Allen's notes and discussed his intentions and then wrote the conclusion of *Hilda Wade* (1900) after Allen died.

Other Allen books with elements of mystery include *Strange Stories* (1884; s.s.), *The Beckoning Hand and Other Stories* (1887; s.s.), *This Mortal Coil* (1887), *The Jaws of Death* (1889), *Michael's Crag* (1893), *Ivan Greet's Masterpiece* (1893; s.s.), *Under Sealed Orders* (1895), *Twelve Tales* (1899; s.s.), and *Miss Cayley's Adventures* (1899; s.s.).

ALLEN, HERBERT WARNER. *See* TRENT, PHILIP.

ALLEYN, SUPERINTENDENT RODERICK (Creator: Ngaio MARSH). The detective featured in all of Dame Ngaio Marsh's novels was named by the author for Edward Alleyn, the famous actor who founded England's Dulwich College. She had visited the school's art gallery the day before she started her first book. Superintendent (formerly Inspector) Alleyn is a phenomenon of the 1930s mystery, a detective who comes to his profession from the English aristocracy. His mother, Lady Alleyn, is socially prominent, and he has all the graces necessary to move freely in "the best circles."

Alleyn, tall and lean, has good looks, a deep voice, and long-fingered hands. He impresses women whose conception of a policeman has not prepared them for a suave sleuth. His wife, Agatha Troy, is a famous British portrait painter whom he meets during his investigation in *Artists in Crime* (1938). In *Final Curtain* (1947) she receives a commission to paint an elderly patriarch who, much to the consternation of his family, is about to marry a young chorus girl. The book marks the return to England of Alleyn (called "Rory" by his wife) after three years of police duty in New Zealand. There, in a setting familiar to the author, he solves two wartime mysteries, *Colour Scheme* (1943) and *Died in the Wool* (1945); in the latter a corpse is discovered in a bale of wool.

Early in his career Alleyn is very active, relying as much on his physical prowess as on deduction to solve his cases. This is especially true of his first case, *A Man Lay Dead* (1934), in which his life is threatened by a revolutionary organization. Although never sedentary, he later becomes less active; nonetheless, in *Singing in the Shrouds* (1958) he trails a killer on a shipboard journey to South Africa. When dealing with a crime involving "high society," he is not reluctant to use his social connections to gain information. In most cases he relies on routine police procedure—and on his own perceptiveness; for example, he has the ability to spot one false word in a long speech by a criminal.

His constant companion in his investigations is Inspector Fox, whom Alleyn calls "Br'er Fox" or "Foxkin." Alleyn's early cases are chronicled by his "Watson" (*see* WATSON, DR.), journalist Nigel Bathgate of the *London Clarion*.

CHECKLIST

1934 *A Man Lay Dead*
1935 *Enter a Murderer*
1936 *The Nursing Home Murder* (written with Dr. Henry Jellett)
1936 *Death in Ecstasy*
1937 *Vintage Murder*
1938 *Artists in Crime*
1938 *Death in a White Tie*
1939 *Overture to Death*
1940 *Death at the Bar*
1940 *Death of a Peer* (British title: *A Surfeit of Lampreys*)
1941 *Death and the Dancing Footman*
1943 *Colour Scheme*
1945 *Died in the Wool*
1947 *Final Curtain*
1949 *Swing, Brother, Swing* (U.S. title: *A Wreath for Rivera*)
1951 *Opening Night* (U.S. title: *Night at the Vulcan*)
1953 *Spinsters in Jeopardy*
1955 *Scales of Justice*
1956 *Death of a Fool* (British title: *Off with His Head*)
1958 *Singing in the Shrouds*
1959 *False Scent*
1962 *Hand in Glove*
1963 *Dead Water*
1966 *Killer Dolphin* (British title: *Death at the Dolphin*)
1969 *Clutch of Constables*
1971 *When in Rome*
1972 *Tied Up in Tinsel*
1974 *Black as He's Painted*

ALLINGHAM, MARGERY (1904–1966). English social historian and mystery writer; creator of Albert CAMPION. Born in London, she grew up in Essex, part of a family prominent in English literary circles since the early nineteenth century. Her father, Herbert John Allingham, was a successful editor and writer of serials for popular magazines. Her first cousin Emily Jane Hughes also wrote for women's magazines of the day. According to Miss Allingham, "They regarded writing as the only reasonable way of passing the time, let alone earning a living." She began to write at the age of seven. *Black'erchief Dick*, a novel about smuggling and piracy on the Essex salt marshes, was published when she was a teenager. In addition to being trained in writing by her father, she was educated at the Perse High School for Girls in Cambridge. She also studied dramatic art, though her only play, *Water in a Sieve: A Fantasy in One Act*, was published but not performed.

Her career as a mystery writer began soon after her marriage in 1927 to Philip Youngman Carter (1904–1970), an artist and editor of *The Tatler*. He had, when only seventeen, designed the jacket for her first book. They divided their time between a London flat on Great Russell Street, next to the British Museum, and an Essex home at Tolleshunt d'Arcy on the edge of the marshes. This area, though only fifty miles from London, is nearly inaccessible. The residents are said to be suspicious of outsiders, and Miss Allingham once commented that she considered herself a foreigner even though she had spent most of her life there. Throughout their marriage Mr. Carter was her literary adviser and unofficial collaborator. He completed her last book, *Cargo of Eagles* (1968), after her death and wrote two additional mysteries about Campion, *Mr. Campion's Farthing* (1969) and *Mr. Campion's Falcon* (1970). Campion appeared in all her novels except her first mystery, *The White Cottage Mystery* (1928), and *Black Plumes* (1940).

The Allingham mysteries fall into two distinct periods. The earliest works are fast-moving adventures with considerable physical action. In books such as *Mystery Mile* (1929) and *Sweet Danger* (1933), Campion confronts international criminal conspiracies. Beginning with *Death of a Ghost* (1934), however, Miss Allingham wrote books in which her deft storytelling was blended with character delineation and sophisticated dialogue. Puzzles were solved as often by an understanding of human psychology as by physical clues. Her mysteries were frequently compared favorably with "mainstream" fiction, although occasionally she was criticized as being "too profound and precious" for escape fiction. Especially notable was her biting social commentary on such aspects of British life as the art world in *Death of a Ghost*, the publishing industry in *Flowers for the Judge* (1936), the theater in *Dancers in Mourning* (1937), and exclusive dress salons and country clubs in *The Fashion in Shrouds* (1938), generally acknowledged to be the best of her prewar books.

During World War II Miss Allingham virtually abandoned the mystery, devoting herself to war efforts and two works of English social history, *The Oaken Heart* (1941) and *The Dance of the Years* (1943; U.S. title: *The Galantrys*). After the war she wrote fewer books, and Campion often assumes a relatively minor role. In two volumes, *Deadly Duo* (1949; British title: *Take Two at Bedtime*) and *No Love Lost* (1954), each containing two novelettes, he fails to appear at all. In *Hide My Eyes* (1958) Campion appears almost as an afterthought toward the end of a book in which attention had been focused on a murderer and his victims. Though Miss Allingham gave Campion more to do at the end of her career, it was in the unaccustomed role of spy.

Margery Allingham.

Though her postwar work generally received poorer reviews than earlier work had, one book, *The Tiger in the Smoke* (1952), the story of a manhunt in London's underworld, received high praise. Julian SYMONS considered it her best book, and, in reviewing it, Phyllis McGinley described Miss Allingham as "sensitive enough to make human beings out of victim, criminal, and detective alike."

Film

Tiger in the Smoke. Rank (British), 1956. Donald Sinden, Muriel Pavlow, Tony Wright, Bernard Miles, Alec Clunes. Directed by Roy Baker.

In the London fog, an escaped convict, trying to elude both the police and a criminal gang, searches for treasure. Campion, who was featured in the novel, did not appear in the film.

AMBLER, ERIC (1909–). English novelist and screenwriter. Born in London, the son of Amy Madeleine and Alfred Percy Ambler, he studied engineering at the University of London but abandoned that career to write songs and sketches for vaudeville acts. He then spent several years as an advertising copywriter. In 1938, after the success of his first three novels, he gave up the directorship of a small London advertising agency. He married Louise Crombie, an American, the following year. (They were later divorced, and in 1958 Ambler married Joan Harrison, the producer of the Alfred HITCHCOCK television series and screenwriter for several Hitchcock pictures.)

Joining the Army as a private in 1940, Ambler was quickly commissioned; when he was discharged, in 1946, he was a lieutenant colonel. After serving with a combat film unit in Italy, he was named assistant director of army cinematography in the War Office, in charge of all training, educational, and morale films for the British Army. After the war, he wrote and produced several films for the J. Arthur Rank Organisation; his screenplay for the 1953 film based on Nicholas Monsarrat's *The Cruel Sea* (1951) was nominated for an Academy Award.

The modern spy story is largely a product of Ambler's groundbreaking series of pre-World War II novels. Unlike the patriotic heroes of earlier fiction (and the later James BOND thrillers and their imitators), who fearlessly battle enemy agents, Ambler's major characters are generally victims of circumstance who perform no willing acts of bravery but extricate themselves as best they can in order to survive. The political viewpoint is left wing.

Many of Ambler's early suspense novels are set in such exotic locales as Istanbul, Sofia, Belgrade, and other cities of Central Europe and the Middle East; later, he used Asian and African settings and then, again, the Middle East.

In the most famous Ambler novel, *The Mask of Dimitrios* (1939; U.S. title: *A Coffin for Dimitrios*), author Charles Latimer becomes obsessed with tracing the history of Dimitrios Makropoulos, whose sudden, squalid death is of interest to many unusual characters. Latimer's curiosity is simultaneously satisfied and intensified as he learns more about the mysterious Greek, whose career has been recorded in police dossiers in every Central European country for two decades. Colonel Haki of the Turkish police whets Latimer's appetite for information, and that information is grudgingly supplied by the equivocal Mr. Peters and by Grodek, who explains the methods used by international espionage agents.

A departure for Ambler into the standard crime story is *The Light of Day* (1962), an account of a daring robbery attempt mounted against the historic treasury of the famous Topkapi Museum. Ambler and Charles Rodda coauthored several crime novels that were published under the pseudonym Eliot Reed. In 1964 and 1975 Ambler won Edgars from the Mystery Writers of America, and he received a Gold Dagger Award from the British Crime Writers' Association in 1973.

CHECKLIST

1936	*The Dark Frontier*
1937	*Uncommon Danger* (U.S. title: *Background to Danger*)
1938	*Epitaph for a Spy*
1938	*Cause for Alarm*
1939	*The Mask of Dimitrios* (U.S. title: *A Coffin for Dimitrios*)
1940	*Journey into Fear*
1950	*Skytip* (by Eliot Reed)
1951	*Tender to Danger* (by Eliot Reed; British title: *Tender to Moonlight*)
1951	*Judgment on Deltchev*
1953	*The Schirmer Inheritance*
1953	*The Maras Affair* (by Eliot Reed)
1954	*Charter to Danger* (by Eliot Reed)
1956	*The Night-Comers* (U.S. title: *State of Siege*)
1958	*Passport to Panic* (by Eliot Reed; written wholly by Rodda; Ambler had no role in its authorship)
1959	*Passage of Arms*
1962	*The Light of Day*
1963	*The Ability to Kill and Other Pieces* (essays)
1964	*A Kind of Anger*
1967	*Dirty Story*
1969	*The Intercom Conspiracy*
1972	*The Levanter*
1974	*Doctor Frigo*

Films

Journey into Fear. RKO, 1942. Orson Welles, Joseph Cotten, Dolores Del Rio, Ruth Warwick, Everett Sloane, Agnes Moorehead. Directed by Norman Foster.

In Istanbul on business, an American gunnery expert is a witness when a magician is shot on stage during his act; Colonel Haki (Welles) tells him that Nazi agents want to kill him for what he knows about Turkey's naval arms.

Background to Danger. Warner Brothers, 1943. George Raft, Sydney Greenstreet, Peter Lorre, Osa Massen, Brenda Marshall. Directed by Raoul Walsh.

On a train headed for Ankara, a beautiful girl hands over to an American secret agent an envelope containing Russian plans for the invasion of Turkey.

The Mask of Dimitrios. Warner Brothers, 1944. Zachery Scott, Greenstreet, Lorre, Faye Emerson, Victor Francen. Directed by Jean Negulesco.

Intrigued by what Colonel Haki (Kurt Katch) of the Turkish secret police has told him about a notorious criminal whose body has just been washed up on an Istanbul beach, a timid Dutch novelist (Lorre) decides to retrace the man's life.

Hotel Reserve. RKO (British), 1944. James Mason, Lucie Mannheim, Raymond Lovell, Herbert Lom. Directed by Lance Comfort and Max Greene. Based on *Epitaph for a Spy*.

A vacationer at a resort hotel is drawn into

In Istanbul mystery writer Peter Lorre is momentarily dissuaded by Sidney Greenstreet (right) from probing into the past of a supposedly dead minor criminal named Dimitrios, in the film based on Eric Ambler's *A Coffin for Dimitrios*. [*Warner Brothers*]

intrigue when a man (who is actually a spy) borrows his camera and photographs seaside naval installations.

The October Man. Two Cities (British), 1947. John Mills, Joan Greenwood, Edward Chapman, Joyce Carey, Kay Walsh. Directed by Roy Baker. Original screenplay by Ambler, who was also the producer.

A young man who suffered brain injury in a car crash fears that he may have strangled a fashion model who lived in his rooming house.

Topkapi. United Artists (British), 1964. Melina Mercouri, Peter Ustinov, Maximilian Schell, Robert Morley, Akim Tamiroff. Directed by Jules Dassin. Based on *The Light of Day.*

An eccentric band of thieves conspires to steal a gem-encrusted dagger from Istanbul's Topkapi Museum.

Television

Epitaph for a Spy was adapted for the CBS hour-long anthology series *Climax!* in the 1950s. Ambler has been active in television and created the *Checkmate* series (seventy one-hour episodes that appeared from 1959 to 1962), in which Sebastian Cabot, a former teacher, and Doug McClure and Anthony George, his former students, formed an investigative organization in San Francisco.

AMIS, KINGSLEY. *See* BOND, JAMES; FLEMING, IAN.

ANDERSON, FREDERICK IRVING (1877–1947). American short story writer and journalist. Born in Aurora, Ill., the son of Andrew and Elizabeth (Adling) Anderson, he was a star reporter for the *New York World* from 1898 to 1908 and was later a highly paid writer for important American and British periodicals. His wife of nineteen years, Emma Helen de Zouche, died in 1937, and Anderson spent the rest of his life in virtual seclusion with his sister Mabel in East Jamaica, Vt.

Because most of his fiction appeared only in *The Saturday Evening Post* and other popular magazines, Anderson has been relegated to an undeserved obscurity. Aside from two books on farming, he produced only three volumes, which contain about one-tenth of his literary output. Written in a slow, circuitous style that can be discouraging for the impatient reader, the stories have a subtle richness that requires a careful reading of every word, lest the inevitable story between the lines be missed. Although the bemusing style sometimes found disfavor with those who preferred a snappy approach, George Horace Lorimer at *The Saturday Evening Post* and other discerning editors published his work regularly.

Among the characters in the Anderson opera are the Infallible Godahl (*see* GODAHL, THE INFALLIBLE), a master criminal, and Oliver Armiston, a writer who recounts some of Godahl's adventures. Armiston is described cryptically as the "extinct author." Deputy Parr of the New York Police Department is Godahl's adversary. The Manhattan man hunter is hopelessly outmatched when confronted with Godahl's intellect and appears equally helpless when he matches wits with Sophie Lang, an attractive and clever young lady with a penchant for jewels. Her adventures were published in book form only in England, in *The Notorious Sophie Lang* (1925).

Anderson's third book, *The Book of Murder* (1930), features Parr and Armiston pitted against assorted criminals. Whereas Parr is generally in over his head, his friend is the ideal amateur detective. No problem is too intricate for Armiston, because there is a good chance he thought of it years ago, when he still wrote mystery stories. His plots were so ingenious, and his crimes so perfect, that the underworld read his stories scrupulously and duplicated them. Frustrated by their inability to solve the crimes, the police finally had to pay Armiston *not* to write. Parr now just visits his friend and gives him all available information about an apparently insoluble problem, and Armiston arrives at a solution, often without leaving his armchair.

Other interesting Anderson characters include Orlo Sage, an "apple knocker" detective from rural New England; Morel, Parr's assistant, who has all the distinction that Park Avenue can give a man; Little Pelts, a shabby creature who looks natural only when associating with alley cats and panhandlers; and Old Ludwig Telfen, the "King of Lapidaries."

Films

The Notorious Sophie Lang. Paramount, 1934. Gertrude Michael, Paul Cavanagh, Arthur Byron, Leon Errol. Directed by Ralph Murphy.

A French thief is used as a lure to catch a notorious American adventuress, but the two fall in love and escape the clutches of the police.

The Return of Sophie Lang. Paramount, 1936. Michael, Ray Milland, Elizabeth Patterson, Sir Guy Standing. Directed by George Archainbaud.

The reformed Miss Lang is on an ocean liner traveling to the United States with her elderly benefactress when she recognizes a "distinguished" fellow passenger; he is actually a jewel thief, and he plans to involve Sophie in the disappearance of a diamond.

Sophie Lang Goes West. Paramount, 1937. Michael, Lee Bowman, C. Henry Gordon, Buster Crabbe. Directed by Charles Riesner.

Evading the police by boarding a California-bound train, the innocent Miss Lang becomes involved with some of her fellow travelers, including a brash but endearing Hollywood press agent and a desperate sultan who is carrying a valuable gem he hopes will be stolen.

ANTONY, PETER (pseudonym of Peter [Levin] Shaffer and Anthony [Joshua] Shaffer; 1926–). English playwrights and mystery novelists. The twins were born in Liverpool, the sons of Reka (Fredman) and Jack Shaffer, a realtor.

Peter graduated from Trinity College, Cambridge, in 1950, after working in the coal mines (1944–1947). He wrote many plays for radio and television in England before becoming famous for the play *Five Finger Exercise,* which was first presented in 1958 and won the New York Drama Critics Circle Award in 1960. *The Private Ear; The Public Eye,* produced in 1962, *The Royal Hunt of the Sun,* written in 1964 and produced on Broadway in 1965, a year after its London opening, and *Black Comedy,* a long one-act farce first produced in 1965, are his other major theatrical works, apart from *Equus,* which won all available dramatic awards when it was produced in New York in 1974.

Anthony had had successful careers as a barrister, advertising man, and television producer in succession before writing *Sleuth* (first produced on Broadway in 1970 and already a classic). He confides that the inspiration for the complex thriller was Agatha CHRISTIE, who he was surprised to discover is the most widely published author in the world.

Anthony and Peter collaborated on three detective novels in the 1950s, all about a shady and infallible private detective named Mr. Verity, described as "an immense man just tall enough to carry his breadth majestically. His face is sharp, smooth and teak-brown; his blue eyes small and of a startling brilliance. He has a fine chestnut Van-Dyck, an habitual cloak in winter and the expression of an

Mystery writer Wyke (Laurence Olivier) insists at gunpoint that his wife's lover (Michael Caine) put on a clown's mask (one of the many odd objects cluttering the author's country house) in the lavish Edgar-winning screen version of the play *Sleuth* by Anthony Shaffer. [*Twentieth Century-Fox*]

elderly 'Laughing Cavalier.'" He also smokes black Cuban cigars and enjoys swimming in a huge purple bathing suit purchased from a fruit merchant in Beirut many years ago. Although Verity is not wealthy, his Sussex villa is filled with sculptures and other objets d'art, acquired under dubious circumstances or with fees (which are surprisingly moderate) for his detective work. Inspector Rambler, his only friend among the official police, is a fellow member of the Beverley Club, whose purpose is to study crime as an art form.

The first case about Verity is *The Woman in the Wardrobe* (1951; by Peter Antony), a locked-room mystery in which the only person present during a murder was a helplessly bound maid. *How Doth the Little Crocodile?* (1952; published in England by Peter Antony; in 1957 in the United States by Anthony and Peter Shaffer) is a complex tale in which the Beverley Club asks Mr. Verity to solve the murders of two of its members. In the final novel in the series, *Withered Murder* (1955; by Anthony and Peter Shaffer), the victim is murdered in a room with his secretary—a few feet away—unaware of the crime. Verity uses the alias Mr. Fathom in this tale.

Plays

Anthony Shaffer's international stage success, *Sleuth*, about a mystery writer who toys diabolically with his wife's lover, has been called by at least one critic the best mystery play ever written. Peter Shaffer's *Equus* opened on Broadway in October 1974, after being much acclaimed in London. A profound, psychic thriller, it documents the psychology of a boy who blinds six horses in a single night.

Films

Sleuth. Twentieth Century-Fox (British), 1972. Laurence Olivier, Michael Caine. Directed by Joseph L. Mankiewicz.

A celebrated detective novelist, Andrew Wyke, invites his wife's paramour, young hairdresser Milo Tindle, to his gadget-filled great country house, ostensibly to propose the theft—in a sort of truce—of some jewels, but actually he is plotting murder behind his clownish facade.

The Wicker Man. Warner Brothers (British), 1974. Edward Woodward, Britt Ekland, Diane Cilento, Ingrid Pitt, Christopher Lee. Directed by Robin Hardy. Original screenplay by Anthony Shaffer.

A Scottish police officer arrives at a remote island to investigate the disappearance of a girl and finds, instead, a pagan coven.

APPLEBY, JOHN (Creator: Michael INNES). University-educated, John Appleby is one of the most erudite detectives in mystery fiction; he is especially apt at spotting obscure literary allusions. Appleby's education has been a practical one as well, for he studied modern police techniques. He is particularly suited for solving cases in an academic setting, as in *Death at the President's Lodging, Appleby Plays Chicken*, and *Hare Sitting Up*.

He also solves some sensitive cases involving murder in "the highest circles," and his abilities are recognized by his superiors. He advances rapidly through the ranks, becoming, in succession, inspector, assistant commissioner of Scotland Yard, and finally commissioner of London's Metropolitan Police. He is knighted shortly before he leaves the police for what proves to be a crime-filled retirement. In *Appleby at Allington*, as a guest at a village charity ball, he investigates the gazebo of a local estate and discovers a corpse. He is on a "bachelor" fishing trip in the short story "A Comedy of Discomfiture" (1970) when he encounters murder.

Appleby's wife is the attractive, talented sculptress Judith Raven, who brings him love, support, and, in *A Connoisseur's Case*, some real detective assistance. The Applebys' son, Bobby, is a college student when he aids his father in solving a mystery about art fraud, *A Family Affair*.

CHECKLIST

1936 *Death at the President's Lodging* (U.S. title: *Seven Suspects*)
1937 *Hamlet, Revenge!*
1938 *Lament for a Maker*
1939 *Stop Press* (U.S. title: *The Spider Strikes*)
1940 *There Came Both Mist and Snow* (U.S. title: *A Comedy of Terrors*)
1940 *The Secret Vanguard*
1941 *Appleby on Ararat*
1942 *The Daffodil Affair*
1943 *The Weight of Evidence*
1945 *Appleby's End*
1947 *A Night of Errors*
1951 *Operation Pax* (U.S. title: *The Paper Thunderbolt*)
1952 *A Private View* (U.S. title: *One Man Show*)
1954 *Appleby Talking* (s.s.; U.S. title: *Dead Man's Shoes*)
1956 *Appleby Talks Again* (s.s.)
1957 *Appleby Plays Chicken* (U.S. title: *Death on a Quiet Day*)
1958 *The Long Farewell*
1959 *Hare Sitting Up*
1961 *Silence Observed*
1962 *A Connoisseur's Case* (U.S. title: *The Crabtree Affair*)
1966 *The Bloody Wood*
1968 *Appleby at Allington* (U.S. title: *Death by Water*)
1969 *A Family Affair* (U.S. title: *Picture of Guilt*)
1970 *Death at the Chase*
1971 *An Awkward Lie*
1972 *The Open House*
1973 *Appleby's Answer*
1974 *Appleby's Other Story*

ARCHER, LEW (Creator: Ross MACDONALD). The most famous fictional private detective of the 1960s and early 1970s is admittedly largely autobiographical in conception. To Macdonald, "he is less a doer than a questioner, a consciousness in which other lives emerge. . . ." Archer is a "not unwilling catalyst for trouble" who probes the pasts of the people he investigates. He is sympathetic to the problems of the young who are seeking their identity in society and is committed to fighting those who would despoil the environment.

He was born in 1913 and was a policeman in Long Beach, Calif., until he was fired because he would not work under a corrupt police administration. He became a private investigator and has remained in that profession ever since, except for the time he spent in intelligence work during World War II. His marriage has fallen casualty to his work; his wife, Sue, divorced him because "she didn't like the company I kept." Though far from being an ascetic, he has, since his divorce, refrained from the sexual promiscuity characteristic of most fictional private detectives.

Archer's interests are varied and include reading and painting; the Japanese artist Kuniyoshi has always been one of his favorites. He is especially interested in natural history and frequently displays his ability to identify birds, trees, and flowers.

CHECKLIST

1949 *The Moving Target*
1950 *The Drowning Pool*
1951 *The Way Some People Die*
1952 *The Ivory Grin*
1954 *Find a Victim*
1955 *The Name Is Archer* (s.s.)
1956 *The Barbarous Coast*
1958 *The Doomsters*
1959 *The Galton Case*
1961 *The Wycherly Woman*
1962 *The Zebra-striped Hearse*
1964 *The Chill*
1965 *The Far Side of the Dollar*
1966 *Black Money*
1968 *The Instant Enemy*
1969 *The Goodbye Look*
1971 *The Underground Man*
1973 *Sleeping Beauty*

Films

When he reached the screen, Macdonald's private eye inexplicably underwent a name change—to Lew Harper—in an otherwise faithful adaptation of *The Moving Target*.

Harper. Warner Brothers, 1966. Paul Newman, Lauren Bacall, Julie Harris, Arthur Hill, Janet Leigh, Pamela Tiffin, Robert Wagner, Robert Webber, Shelley Winters. Directed by Jack Smight.

Private detective Lew Harper is recommended by the lawyer and personal friend of a wealthy family. The troubled household includes a scheming wife and a husband who has been kidnapped for a ransom of a half million dollars.

Ross Macdonald's Lew Archer is called Lew Harper when Paul Newman portrays the private detective in a successful screen version of *The Moving Target*, retitled *Harper*. [*Warner Brothers*]

Despite the success of *Harper*, attempts in the following years to bring *The Chill* and other Macdonald works to the screen did not succeed. Then, in 1975, Paul Newman returned to play the lonely detective in *The Drowning Pool*.

Television

After *The Underground Man* received extensive critical acclaim, it was purchased for theatrical feature release, but became instead a two-hour television film and a possible series pilot.

The Underground Man. Paramount TV, 1974. Peter Graves, Jack Klugman, Judith Anderson, Sharon Farrell, Celeste Holm, Kay Lenz, Vera Miles. Directed by Paul Wendkos.

A housekeeper and her retarded son are among those involved when private detective Lew Archer searches for a former girl friend's missing child and uncovers murders both past and present.

Archer, starring Brian Keith as the sleuth, was wholly unsuccessful in its brief run on NBC in 1975.

ARDEN, WILLIAM. See COLLINS, MICHAEL.

ARLEN, MICHAEL (1895–1956). English author. Born in Bulgaria to Armenian parents, Dikrân Kuyumjian moved to England when he was a boy. He changed his name to Michael Arlen and became an English citizen. His most famous work, *The Green Hat* (1924), earned the handsome writer fame and a half million dollars, both of which he enjoyed.

But he hated writing. Arlen spent two years in Hollywood, did nothing, and was "perfectly content." He wrote few mystery stories, the most famous being "Gay Falcon" (1940), a short story that inspired several successful motion pictures (*see* FALCON, THE). Among Arlen's other mysteries are *Hell! Said the Duchess* (1934) and *The Crooked Coronet* (1937), a short story collection that contains some elements of crime.

ARMSTRONG, ANTHONY (pseudonym of George Anthony Armstrong Willis; 1897–). English humorist, playwright, and mystery writer. Many humorous pieces by Willis were published in *The New Yorker* and in *Punch* under the pseudonymous initials "A. A." He served in the British Army during World War I and in the RAF in World War II, during which time he wrote a famous series of training manuals that transmitted instructions while recounting the misadventures of Pilot Officer Prune.

Beginning with *The Trail of Fear* (1927) Armstrong wrote a series of five fast-moving suspense novels, all of which contain the word "trail" in the title. The hero of these books, published between 1927 and 1932, is Jimmy Rezaire.

Armstrong was a popular playwright during the 1930s. His crime plays—*Well Caught* (1932), *Ten-Minute Alibi* (1933), and *Mile-Away Murder* (1937)— were all produced on the London stage. He also wrote a number of short stories, "The Case of Mr. Pelham" (1940) being the best known. In 1957 he wrote a novel based on the story, and it was televised by Alfred HITCHCOCK that year.

ARMSTRONG, CHARLOTTE (1905–1969). American poet, dramatist, and author of short stories and mystery novels. Charlotte Armstrong was born and raised in Vulcan, an iron-mining town on Michigan's Upper Peninsula. After two years at the University of Wisconsin, she moved to New York, where she received a B.A. degree from Barnard in 1925. She worked in an office and then was a fashion reporter until her marriage to advertising man Jack Lewi in 1928. While raising her three children, she continued to write and had poems published in *The New Yorker*. Her interest in the stage led her to work with local high school students in a small theater group in New Rochelle, where the Lewis resided. She wrote two plays, *The Happiest Days* (1939) and *Ring Around Elizabeth* (1941), which were produced on Broadway but ran for only seven and ten performances respectively.

Following the latter play, Miss Armstrong turned to the detective novel and soon sold *Lay On, MacDuff*, the first of three consecutive novels to feature Professor MacDougal Duff. It was with her fourth mystery, a suspense novel called *The Unsuspected*, that she achieved success. This was a controversial book, praised by many critics, notably Howard HAYCRAFT, for the author's writing skill but criticized because of her disclosure of the murderer's identity almost at the outset. Miss Armstrong went to Hollywood during the filming of *The Unsuspected*, and she and her family decided to stay in southern California, taking up residence in Glendale. She wrote many short stories and novelettes and more than twenty additional novels. She also wrote television scripts, including several that were produced by Alfred HITCHCOCK.

Suspense and peril to young and old are the characteristics of the Charlotte Armstrong mystery. A psychopathic baby-sitter appears in *Mischief*. Physical as well as psychic harm threaten a child whose dog has been poisoned in "The Enemy" (1951), a story that won first prize in the annual *Ellery Queen's Mystery Magazine* contest. Two later short stories, which received nominations for the Mystery Writers of America Edgar, "The Case for Miss Peacock" (1965) and "The Splintered Monday" (1966), deal with danger to elderly women in southern California. Among the other women threatened in Armstrong mysteries are an unattached girl in *The Dream Walker*, a new bride in the novelette *The Girl with a Secret*, and a bride-to-be in *Something Blue*. Miss Armstrong's *A Dram of Poison*, which won the Edgar as best novel, is difficult to classify; it concerns a chain of events flowing from an attempted poisoning.

In addition to enjoying great popularity among her fellow practitioners, Miss Armstrong has been a favorite of mystery readers. Reprints of her books have continued to have large sales even after her death. *Trouble in Thor*, which she published in 1953 under the pseudonym Jo Valentine was reissued in 1971 under her own name. The most autobiographical of her novels, it is set in Thor, a fictitious Michigan mine town very similar to her native Vulcan. She received many good reviews, especially from Anthony BOUCHER, who, in a much-quoted opinion, characterized Charlotte Armstrong as "one of the few authentic spell-casting witches of modern time."

CHECKLIST

1942 *Lay On, MacDuff*
1943 *The Case of the Weird Sisters*
1945 *The Innocent Flower* (British title: *Death Filled the Glass*)
1946 *The Unsuspected*
1948 *The Chocolate Cobweb*
1950 *Mischief*
1951 *The Black-eyed Stranger*
1952 *Catch-as-Catch-Can*
1953 *The Trouble in Thor* (originally published under the pseudonym Jo Valentine)

At the climax of *Don't Bother to Knock*, the mentally troubled hotel baby-sitter played by Marilyn Monroe collapses, losing all control; the film is based on a Charlotte Armstrong novel. [*Twentieth Century-Fox*]

1954 *The Better to Eat You*
1955 *The Dream Walker*
1956 *A Dram of Poison*
1957 *The Albatross* (s.s.)
1959 *The Seventeen Widows of Sans Souci*
1959 *Duo* (two novelettes)
1962 *Something Blue*
1963 *A Little Less than Kind*
1963 *The Witch's House*
1965 *The Turret Room*
1966 *I See You* (s.s.)
1966 *Dream of Fair Woman*
1967 *The Gift Shop*
1967 *Lemon in the Basket*
1968 *The Balloon Man*
1969 *Seven Seats to the Moon*
1970 *The Protégé*

Films

The Unsuspected. Warner Brothers, 1947. Claude Rains, Joan Caulfield, Audrey Totter, Hurd Hatfield. Directed by Michael Curtiz.

A famed radio narrator of mystery stories murders his secretary to cover up his thefts from his ward's inheritance but ultimately—after several more deaths—is forced into making an on-the-air confession.

Don't Bother to Knock. Twentieth Century-Fox, 1952. Richard Widmark, Marilyn Monroe, Anne Bancroft, Elisha Cook, Jr. Directed by Roy Baker. Based on *Mischief*.

At a New York hotel, a moody airline pilot starts a flirtation with a pretty but deranged baby-sitter who is contemplating harming her charge.

ASHBY, R[UBIE] C[ONSTANCE] (1899–). English novelist and mystery writer. She is the author of four mystery novels and a dozen or more other novels, many of which were published under the pseudonym Ruby Freugon.

Her first mystery, *Death on Tiptoe* (1930), is set in a castle in southern Wales and deals with the murder of a millionaire's wife and the suicide of his cousin. Of *He Arrived at Dusk* (1933), Howard HAYCRAFT said that it was "an unrepeatable blending of the ghost story and legitimate detection." The book is listed in SANDOE'S READERS' GUIDE TO CRIME. The story begins when an antique dealer, summoned to the Northumbrian moors to estimate the value of a house and its contents, discovers that the ghost of a Roman warrior slain in battle is terrorizing the neighborhood and is responsible for at least two murders.

ASHDOWN, CLIFFORD (pseudonym of R. Austin FREEMAN and John James Pitcairn, 1860–1936). Several short stories about Romney Pringle appeared under this pseudonym, mainly in *Cassell's Magazine* in 1902–1903. The first six were collected as *The Adventures of Romney Pringle* (1902), which Ellery QUEEN (author) incorrectly calls "the rarest volume of detective-crime short stories published in the 20th century." Published by Ward, Lock in London, the volume is difficult to find in the first edition, but Victor L. WHITECHURCH'S *Thrilling Stories of the Railway* (1912) and a half-dozen other works are considerably rarer. The first American edition did not appear until 1968; *The Further Adventures of Romney Pringle* was published for the first time two years later.

J. J. Pitcairn, a prison doctor, was never acknowledged by Freeman as his collaborator, his identity finally being divulged by Freeman's wife to P. M. Stone, a Freeman scholar, in 1946. Pitcairn's mother's maiden name was "Ashdown"; "Clifford" derived from Clifford's Inn, where Freeman had rooms during the 1890s. In a still-uncollected Ashdown tale, "By the Black Deep," which was published in the *Windsor Magazine* (May 1903), the authors are identified as R. Austin Freeman and Ashdown Piers.

Pitcairn also collaborated with Freeman on *The Queen's Treasure*, a novel scheduled for publication in the mid-1970s, and on a series of medicodetective stories entitled *From a Surgeon's Diary*, which ran In *Cassell's* in 1904–1905; it was published in book form in 1975.

Romney Pringle is a thief. Ostensibly a literary agent, he is, in the A. J. RAFFLES tradition, a gentleman-crook, a charming scoundrel who generally mulcts other crooks. A handsome, wholesome-looking young man, he earns enough with his questionable schemes to retire to a life of ease in Sandwich, where he spends his time cycling, reading, and cataloging his antique gem collection.

ASHE, GORDON. See CREASEY, JOHN.

ASHFORD, JEFFREY. See JEFFRIES, RODERIC.

ASIMOV, ISAAC. See SCIENTIFIC DETECTIVES.

ATKEY, BERTRAM (1880–1952). English short story writer and novelist; creator of Smiler BUNN, a not-quite-gentleman crook.

Born in Wiltshire, Atkey went to London as a teenager to write stories. After the publication of *Folk of the Wild* (1905), a collection of nature stories, he worked as assistant editor of *C. B. Fry's Magazine of Sport.* He created Bunn in 1907 and during the next several decades produced scores of stories about his character for popular magazines. His nephew Philip Atkey is the author of many crime stories about another crook, A. J. RAFFLES, under the pseudonym Barry PEROWNE.

In addition to Bunn, Atkey created several memorable series characters, including Winnie O'Wynn, a charming gold digger; Prosper Fair, an amateur detective; Dimity Gay, a different sort of gold digger; Hercules, a sportsman; Nelson Chiddenham, a crippled boy detective who has an immense knowledge of dogs and the countryside; Captain Cormorant, a widely traveled mercenary adventurer; and Sebastian Hope, a henpecked husband with a peculiar gift for disarming his wife by feeding her alibis of great verisimilitude.

Among Atkey's best mystery and crime books are *Winnie O'Wynn and the Wolves* (1921), *Harvest of Javelins* (1922), *The Midnight Mystery* (1928), *The House of Strange Victims* (1930), and *The Pyramid of Lead* (1925), which is concerned with a series of mysterious murders apparently connected with an extraordinary lead pyramid built in the sunken garden of the eccentric Lord Kern. The detective is Prosper Fair, a *nom de guerre* of the Duke of Devizes, who is also more than a little eccentric.

ATKEY, PHILIP. See PEROWNE, BARRY.

AUBREY-FLETCHER, HENRY LANCELOT. See WADE, HENRY.

AUMONIER, STACY (1887–1928). English novelist and short story writer. After successful careers as a landscape painter (he exhibited at the Royal Academy) and entertainer (he appeared at the Criterion and other prestigious theaters), Aumonier turned to writing. His short story collections contain some elements of mystery and crime. The best is *Miss Bracegirdle and Others* (1923); less well known is *Baby Grand and Other Stories* (1926).

AVALLONE, MICHAEL (ANGELO), JR. (1924–). American author. Avallone has written a great number of paperbacks of various types and under numerous by-lines—private eye thrillers, espionage, Gothic, science fiction, and supernatural novels, juvenile literature, books based on films and television programs, sex novels, and so on. The son of a sculptor, Avallone was born in Manhattan and raised in the Bronx amid sixteen brothers and sisters. He went from high school into the Army, serving as a sergeant in Europe during World War II. At the end of the war he returned to New York, determined to become a writer, and "wrote his arm off" for five years without success until "Aw, Let the Kid Hit!" was purchased for the Fall 1951 issue of *Baseball Stories.*

A year or so later Avallone created his most famous character, Ed NOON, private eye, movie and baseball enthusiast, and personal investigator for the President of the United States, who has appeared in thirty-five book-length adventures and almost a hundred short stories since his debut in *The Tall Dolores* (1953). With increased affluence Avallone moved to suburban New Jersey, where he presently resides and produces from nine to twelve paperbacks a year, spending from four days to three weeks on a book.

Unlike most prolific paperback writers, Avallone has a unique literary style, personality, and viewpoint. The key to the Nooniverse (the term collectively applied by admirers to the cases of Ed Noon) is Avallone's devotion to the film—his fanaticism even exceeds that of his detective. The plots of Noon's adventures are fantastic improvisations; the first-person-narrative style is a brain-jangling approximation of normal English; the characters are amalgams from old Alfred HITCHCOCK, Orson Welles, or Frank Capra films.

Autobiographical fragments appear in the unlikeliest places in the saga of Ed Noon. The early chapters of *The February Doll Murders* (1966) are based on Avallone's memories of combat in World War II; *Little Miss Murder* (1971) reflects his love affair with the New York Mets; the spy's shipboard diary in *London, Bloody London* (1972) re-creates some of the incidents that occurred during his cruise to Europe aboard the *Queen Elizabeth II.* But Avallone's fantasies and his fascination for the film are more important to the "Nooners" than his real life is. In *Shoot It Again, Sam* (1972), each chapter is prefaced with a line of dialogue from a vintage Hollywood epic, and each of the novel's two "books" is preceded by a full page of such dialogue. The President orders Noon to accompany the body of longtime Hollywood idol Dan Davis (based on John Wayne; his dissident son is apparently based on Peter Fonda, and one of his former wives on Lauren Bacall) on a transcontinental train ride to its final resting-place. Somewhere in eastern California, the "corpse" sits up in its coffin ("something from one of those machine-made Universal horror pictures from the last generation"), and Chinese agents raid the train, kidnap Noon, and carry him off to a replay of the film *The Manchurian Candidate* (1962). With the help of a battery of brainwashers made up to look like Clark Gable, Peter Lorre, James Cagney, and other stars from Hollywood's "Golden Age," the Chinese convince Noon that he is none other than Sam Spade (as portrayed by Humphrey Bogart, of course), and equip him with poison-needle-tipped shoes reminiscent of the ones in *From Russia, with Love* (1964), so that the next time Noon meets his employer, he can kick the presidential shin with a vengeance.

AYRES, PAUL. *See* AARONS, EDWARD S.

B

BAGBY, GEORGE. See STEIN, AARON MARC.

BAILEY, H[ENRY] C[HRISTOPHER] (1878–1961). English detective story writer and creator of Reggie FORTUNE, perhaps the most popular sleuth in England between the world wars. Although it is possible to read the Fortune stories stylistically, their philosophical viewpoint is outdated today. Bailey generally constructed his tales around an attack on social standards that have long been outmoded. There is some first-class detective work, but most of his stories seem pointless and irrelevant today, mainly because Bailey stressed social commentary so greatly.

Born in London, the only child of Henry and Jane (Dillon) Bailey, he attended University College, Oxford, and was a classical scholar at Corpus Christi College, Oxford, achieving the highest rank. His first book was a historical novel, *My Lady of Orange* (1901), published while he was still an undergraduate. Several similar volumes followed until the first book about his genteel detective, *Call Mr. Fortune,* appeared in 1920.

After leaving Oxford, Bailey wrote for the *London Daily Telegraph,* which he served as drama critic, war correspondent, and lead writer from 1901 to 1946. In 1908 he married Lydia Haden Janet; they

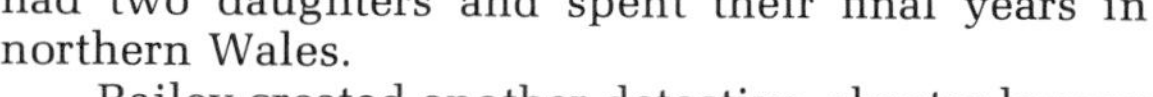

had two daughters and spent their final years in northern Wales.

Bailey created another detective, shyster lawyer Joshua CLUNK, who appeared in novels from 1930 on. Like the Fortune stories, these are filled with mild jabs at the class-conscious snobbery of English society. The British intelligentsia had begun to attack its traditional preoccupation with heredity, social standing, and educational background. Bailey, one of the intellectuals, nevertheless put Fortune into situations in which he asked about a person's school. Although Reggie often proclaims that he is of the common people, the very statement reeks of snobbery. He drives a Rolls-Royce, and his sophisticated (or condescending) speech mannerisms are reminiscent of those of Philo VANCE at his most objectionable.

Bailey's mysteries are intricate puzzles that play fair with the reader; even though Reggie is an intuitive detective, his solutions are logical and reasonable. His short stories are longer than those of other writers because of the elaborate plots and the care he takes with characterization.

BAKER, ASA. See HALLIDAY, BRETT.

BALL, DORIS BELL COLLIER. See BELL, JOSEPHINE.

BALL, JOHN (DUDLEY, JR.) (1911–). American author. Born in Schenectady, N.Y., the son of a scientist, Ball grew up in Milwaukee. He attended Carroll College in Waukesha, Wis., and later became a commercial pilot; during World War II he served for four years as a flier and flight instructor in the U.S. Army Air Corps. Long interested in music, he became, after the war, music editor and feature writer for the *Brooklyn Eagle*. Later he was a daily columnist for the *New York World-Telegram* and a broadcaster with a Washington, D.C., radio station.

He also served on the science staff of *Fortune* and lectured at New York's Hayden Planetarium before he moved to California to become director of public relations for the Institute of Aerospace Sciences. He lives in Encino, where he now devotes full time to writing. In addition to his varied occupational interests, Ball has many avocations, including the literature of Sherlock HOLMES (he is a Baker Street Irregular), Oriental culture, and the martial arts. He is active in many Oriental organizations and holds the black belt in aikido.

Ball began his mystery writing career with high honors in 1965, when his first Virgil TIBBS story, *In the Heat of the Night,* was published. It won the Mystery Writers of America Edgar as best first novel of the year and, the following year, was the recipient of the Crime Writers' Association Gold Dagger as the best non-British mystery. The film version of this work (1967) won five Academy awards, including that for best picture. *Five Pieces of Jade* (1972), a Tibbs book about Chinese politics, narcotics, and the sophisticated hobby of jade collecting, was nominated for an Edgar as best novel.

Mark One—The Dummy (1974), Ball's first non-Tibbs mystery, introduces Ed Nesbitt in an espionage thriller.

BALLARD, K. G. See ROTH, HOLLY.

BALLINGER, BILL S[ANBORN] (1912–). Following radio and advertising careers in Chicago and New York, as well as extensive travel in Europe and the Near East, Ballinger moved to southern California to take advantage of the television "boom" of the 1950s. He has written more than 150 television scripts and 8 film scripts and is the author of 29 novels of adventure and suspense. Sixteen of his books first appeared in hard-cover editions, thirteen as paperback originals. They have been reprinted in twenty-eight foreign countries in thirteen languages. Ballinger and his wife, Lucille, reside in North Hollywood.

Ballinger's earliest mysteries, *The Body in the Bed* (1948) and *The Body Beautiful* (1949), were private eye stories about Barr Breed, a Chicago detective. His first success was a nonseries book, *Portrait in Smoke* (1950), in which the new owner of a collection agency, motivated by curiosity, attempts to trace a girl named Krassy Almauniski from her origins in Chicago's slums.

A 1955 mystery, telling about a magician's pursuit of his wife's murderer, received considerable praise from critics, especially Anthony BOUCHER, who wrote, "Anyone who fears the Detective Story has exhausted itself . . . is urged to secure at once *The Tooth and the Nail,* in which Ballinger presents us with a completely new trick."

Three novels, *Portrait in Smoke, The Tooth and the Nail,* and *The Longest Second* (1957), are generally considered to be Ballinger's most successful works; they were reprinted in *Triptych* (1971), a one-volume omnibus.

Formula for Murder (1958) begins with an apparently suicidal leap from the Brooklyn Bridge and features a cerebral sleuth, Van Mars, in a classic detective story. Most of Ballinger's books of the 1960s were paperback originals. *Not I, Said the Vixen* (1965), which takes place in southern California, is a courtroom mystery about attorney Cyrus March, said to have been patterned after Earl Rogers, the famous trial lawyer. During 1965 and 1966 Ballinger also published a series of five spy novels about Joachim Hawks, a CIA agent of Spanish-Indian origin. These Ballinger books, appearing during the time of the extension of the war in Indochina, were set in Southeast Asia. *The Corsican* (1974) covers the three-decade span between 1943 and 1973 and concerns the growth of a Union Corse "family" in Corsica and Marseilles. Perhaps *49 Days of Death* (1969) is Ballinger's most innovative novel, a surprising suspense story of reincarnation based on *The Tibetan Book of the Dead*.

Ballinger has also written mysteries under the pseudonyms B. X. Sanborn and Frederic Freyer.

BALMER, EDWIN (1883–1959). American editor and author of science and mystery fiction. Born in Chicago, the son of Helen Clark (Pratt) and Thomas Balmer, he received degrees from Northwestern and Harvard Universities. He married Katharine MacHarg in 1909 (she died in 1925); they had three children. He married Grace A. Kee in 1927.

He spent a year (1903) as a reporter for the *Chicago Tribune*, then worked for various magazines, serving as editor of *Redbook* from 1927 to 1949, after which he was associate publisher for four years.

He wrote several novels on his own and collaborated with Philip WYLIE on *When Worlds Collide* (1933), *After Worlds Collide* (1933), and other science fiction and mystery novels, but his best and most important work in the mystery-detective genre was done in collaboration with William MACHARG, notably *The Achievements of Luther Trant* (1910) and *The Blind Man's Eyes* (1916). Many of Balmer's short stories were produced as plays, motion pictures, and television dramas.

BALZAC, HONORÉ DE (1799–1850). French novelist. He is the author of more than ninety novels and tales to which he gave the collective name *La Comédie Humaine (The Human Comedy),* a gargantuan project designed to present the complete social history of France. Most of his novels deal with crime and criminals, most notably the character Vautrin, based on the real-life policeman, former convict, and author François Eugène VIDOCQ. Vautrin appears in Balzac's most celebrated work, *Le Père Goriot* (1834–1835; English title: *Father Goriot*). Ironically, M. Gondureau, the police officer who captures Vautrin, has many of Vidocq's traits, as well as his official title, *Chef de Sûreté*. Balzac had no affection for the police, however, and never presented a detective sympathetically; on the other hand, criminals and murderers are often the heroes of his books.

BANGS, JOHN KENDRICK (1862–1922). American author of humorous stories, journalist, and lecturer. He worked for *Life, Harper's Monthly,* and *Literature* and wrote an endless stream of humorous poems, stories, and essays, many of which were collected in book form. His best-remembered pieces are those about the "Idiot" and his burlesques of such characters as Sherlock HOLMES and A. J. RAFFLES. Holmes appears in *The Pursuit of the House-Boat* (1897), *The Dreamers: A Club* (1899), *The Enchanted Type-Writer* (1899), and *Potted Fiction* (1908). A series of burlesques called *The Posthumous Adventures of Shylock Homes,* syndicated in American newspapers in 1903, was not published in book form until 1973, when *Shylock Homes: His Posthumous Memoirs* appeared in a limited edition of 300 copies. A son of Holmes is the title character of *R. Holmes & Co.* (1906); it is also claimed that he is the grandson of Raffles. Mrs. A. J. Van Raffles is the criminal in *Mrs. Raffles* (1905).

BARON, THE (Creator: John CREASEY as Anthony Morton). John Mannering led a double life when he was young; he was a respectable gentleman on the one hand, a flamboyant jewel thief known as "the Baron" on the other. When he married the lovely Lorna Fauntley, he changed his ways and used his skills on the side of the law as a consultant to Scotland Yard. Although he is a reputable antique dealer, owner of the posh Quinns in Mayfair, his old adversary, Superintendent Bristow, still suspects that he is capable of thievery. The series of forty-seven adventures about Mannering began with *Meet the Baron* (1937; U.S. title: *The Man in the Blue Mask*), written in six days for a "Cracksman" competition organized by two publishers who offered £1,500 for the best entry (it won).

Television

In 1965 work was begun on an internationally successful television series based on the Baron—twenty-six one-hour programs in color—with Steve Forrest as the dashing, wealthy owner of a worldwide chain of antique shops who is actually a secret agent.

BARR, ROBERT (1850–1912). British journalist, editor, and story writer. Barr is best remembered for his tales of Eugène VALMONT, a French detective.

Born in Glasgow, Scotland, Barr was taken to Toronto when he was four. He completed his education in Canada and then took a job as a reporter in Detroit, where he is said to have risked his life more than once in pursuit of news. He went to England in 1881 to edit several publications and in 1892, with Jerome K. Jerome, established *The Idler,* a vastly popular magazine for a few years until it was ruined by a lawsuit.

His numerous short stories were good, fast-moving tales that were immensely popular with mass audiences. He used the Luke Sharp pseudonym for some pieces, including a parody of Sherlock HOLMES, "Detective Stories Gone Wrong: The Adventures of Sherlaw Kombs," that appeared in *The Idler* (May 1892). It was retitled "The Great Pegram Mystery" for its subsequent book publication *(The Face and the Mask).* Among Barr's mystery novels are *From Whose Bourne* (1893), *Jennie Baxter, Journalist* (1899), and *The Girl in the Case* (1910). His mystery short story collections are *Strange Happenings* (1883), *The Face and the Mask* (1894), *Revenge!* (1896), and *Tales of Two Continents* (1920) as well as *The Triumphs of Eugene Valmont* (1906).

BARZUN, JACQUES (1907–). American literary critic and historian. Born in France, Barzun moved to the United States in 1920. He received B.A., M.A., and Ph.D. degrees from Columbia University, where he became a lecturer in history in 1927. His association with the university continued, and he became a full professor in 1945, dean of graduate faculties in 1955, provost in 1958, and university professor in 1967. He married Mariana Lowell in 1936; they have three children.

One of the leading twentieth-century historians of culture and ideas, Barzun has written extensively on art, music, and literature. A lifelong fan of crime fiction, he has written widely on the subject, showing his preference for the classic detective story. This viewpoint has been presented in his book *The Energies of Art* (1956), notably in the essay "From Phèdre to Sherlock Holmes"; his introduction to *The Delights of Detection,* a group of tales by major writers in the genre, "illustrating the art of detective fiction" (1961); and *A Catalogue of Crime* (1971; coauthored with Wendell Hertig TAYLOR), a comprehensive guide to crime literature based on notes the authors were keeping during more than fifty years of reading.

BATMAN (Creator: Bob Kane). Created for a 1939 issue of *Detective Comics,* and drawn from the Shadow (*see* SHADOW, THE) and the detectives who appeared in the PULP MAGAZINES of the 1930s, the hooded, muscular Batman, darting across the rooftops of the nighttime city in his spined batwing cape, is a mysterious avenger in a "lone battle against the evil forces in society." Actually, he is wealthy young socialite Bruce Wayne, who, years before, had seen both parents shot down by a holdup man and has vowed to devote his life to fighting crime. "Criminals are a superstitious, cowardly lot, so my disguise must be able to strike terror into their

Batman and Robin, the heroes of several hundred adventures.

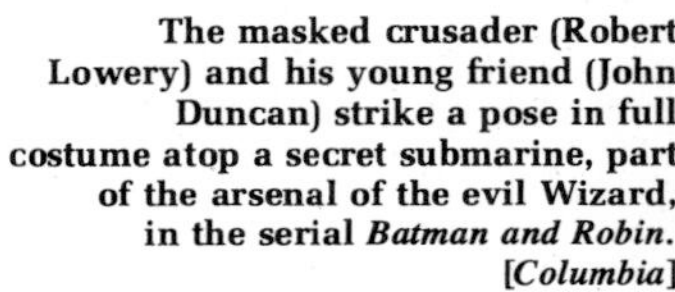

The masked crusader (Robert Lowery) and his young friend (John Duncan) strike a pose in full costume atop a secret submarine, part of the arsenal of the evil Wizard, in the serial *Batman and Robin*. [*Columbia*]

The popular heroes of melodrama endure through many decades and media. Here the masked crime fighter called Batman, inspired by the pulps and debuting in the comic pages, makes a screen appearance thirty years later. [*Twentieth Century-Fox*]

hearts. Must be a creature of the night, black, terrible. . . ." As Bruce muses, a bat flits against the window, and he knows what his costume will be. A year later, he adopts as his ward young Dick Grayson, whose parents, circus acrobats, have been killed in a fall engineered by a criminal, and the energetic duo become the team of Batman and Robin.

In a large secret cave underneath their isolated manor home, where they are looked after by an English butler, Alfred, the only living person aware of their other identities, the pair keep mementos of their past adventures and their modes of travel: the Batplane, Batmobile, and so on. Their arena is Gotham City, a metropolis overrun with exotic supercriminals such as the Penguin, who leads his gang in formal attire, wielding lethal umbrellas; the Joker, who mixes murder with bizarre puns; and Two-Face, who, driven mad when acid scars one side of his face, decides his crimes on the spin of an irregular coin. The settings for Batman's fights against crime are often industrial exhibits where giant replicas of everyday objects are displayed; many of them find their way into the Batcave as gargantuan memorabilia. Batman is unique in that he is friendly with police officialdom and is frequently called into a case by baffled Commissioner Gordon, who hurriedly floods the night sky with a searchlight that outlines a bat.

The close relationship between Wayne and his ward has been interpreted as homosexual by some psychiatrists, notably Frederic Wertham in his crusading *Seduction of the Innocent* (1953), but readers have generally regarded that accusation as alarmist. In recent years there have been attempts to modernize Batman: butler Alfred was killed off (only to be resurrected by popular demand); Bruce abandoned Wayne Manor for a penthouse apartment in town; and a maturing Robin was sent off to college—for an occasional solo adventure in the dormitories. However, the popularity of a television series based on the original stories plus the comic strip industry's vogue for cost-cutting reprints have allowed the older Batman to coexist with the modern version.

Films and Television

In his heyday Batman was the subject of two somewhat shabby film serials.

Batman. Columbia, fifteen chapters, 1943. Lewis Wilson, Douglas Croft (Robin), J. Carrol Naish, William Austin. Directed by Lambert Hillyer.

Behind an amusement park ride depicting World War II atrocities, in a headquarters that includes a hidden alligator pit, the insidious Dr. Daka (Naish) uses electronically controlled zombies in the planned Japanese conquest of the United States.

Batman and Robin. Columbia, fifteen chapters, 1949. Robert Lowery, John Duncan (Robin), Jane Adams, Lyle Talbot. Directed by Spencer Bennet.

A mysterious villain known as the Wizard has the power to stop all electric motors in Gotham and is determined to destroy the city.

In the mid-1940s Batman was occasionally a guest in Metropolis, the city of his friend Superman, and on the latter's daily radio program. In 1965, however, somewhat beyond his prime, Batman was affected by the nostalgia craze of that decade and appeared in his own extremely popular television series. Adam West was Wayne, and Burt Ward was Robin, in 120 half-hour episodes spread over three years, which, though more satiric than serious, lavishly re-created Wayne Manor and other Gotham City settings. Name stars (Liberace, Milton Berle, George Sanders, Vincent Price, Zsa Zsa Gabor) were regularly induced to portray outrageous villains. A feature film, also starring West and Ward, with expensive mountings, was also released.

Batman. Twentieth Century-Fox, 1966. West, Ward, Alan Napier (Alfred), Neil Hamilton (Gordon), Reginald Denny. Directed by Leslie H. Martinson.

Batman's four foremost foes—the Penguin (Burgess Meredith), Joker (Cesar Romero), Riddler (Frank Gorshin), Catwoman (Lee Meriwether)—combine forces against him, using a dehydrator that reduces people to flecks of dust.

After his live-action series ended, Batman starred in his own animated television program and, still later, joined forces with Superman in the animated *Super-Friends* series. In 1960 Kane created an animal cartoon pastiche, *Courageous Cat and Minute Mouse.*

BAX, ROGER. *See* GARVE, ANDREW.

BAXTER, JOHN. *See* HUNT, E. HOWARD, JR.

BECK, MARTIN (Creators: Maj Sjöwall and Per WAHLÖÖ). This thin, strong-jawed Swedish detective has spent half of his nearly fifty years in police work. Although he is not overly ambitious, his skill at examining suspects brings him frequent promotion; eventually he becomes head of the Stockholm Homicide Squad.

Beck's marriage of many years' standing is rapidly breaking up. He is bored with his teenage children and no longer in love with his once-lively blonde wife, who has allowed herself to grow lazy and fat. His long hours of work and frustrating homelife have made him perpetually tired, and his stomach is invariably upset—a condition aggravated by his addiction to coffee and cigarettes. He seems happy only when at work, or on the infrequent occasions when he has the time to build model ships.

CHECKLIST

1967	*Roseanna*
1968	*The Man on the Balcony*
1969	*The Man Who Went Up in Smoke*
1970	*The Laughing Policeman*

1970 *The Fire Engine That Disappeared*
1971 *Murder at the Savoy*
1972 *The Abominable Man*
1973 *The Locked Room*
1975 *Cop Killer*

Film

The Laughing Policeman. Twentieth Century-Fox, 1973. Walter Matthau, Bruce Dern, Lou Gossett, Anthony Zerbe, Cathy Lee Crosby. Directed by Stuart Rosenberg.

A dogged police team investigates the mass killing, by a mystery man with a machine gun, of eight passengers and the driver of a city bus, sifting through the backgrounds of each of the victims (one of them a policeman) for a possible clue. The setting was changed from Sweden to San Francisco.

BEEDING, FRANCIS (pseudonym of John Leslie Palmer, 1885–1944, and Hilary Aidan St. George Saunders, 1898–1951). Both Oxford graduates and literary men, Palmer and Saunders met and decided to collaborate while they were on the staff of the League of Nations in Geneva. Their pseudonym was, itself, a collaboration. "Francis" was chosen by Palmer, who had always wanted to be called by that name; "Beeding" was the choice of Saunders, who had once owned a home in a Sussex village of that name.

Palmer was drama critic for *The Saturday Review of Literature* and the *Evening Standard.* He wrote *The Comedy of Manners, Molière,* and other books on the theater and novels under the pseudonym Christopher Haddon.

Saunders served with the Welsh Guards in World War I and was awarded the Military Cross. During World War II he worked for the Air Ministry and was the anonymous author of *The Battle of Britain* (1940), a pamphlet that sold 3 million copies in England and was translated into twenty-five languages. He also wrote *The Green Beret* (1949), an official history of the British commandos. From 1946 to 1950 he was librarian of the British House of Commons. In discussing their collaboration, Saunders once said, "Palmer can't be troubled with description and narrative, and I'm no good at creating characters or dialogue."

The authors wrote thirty-one mysteries, including a series of seventeen spy stories about Colonel Alastair Granby, D.S.O., of the British Intelligence Service (Secret Branch). Most titles contain a number, from one to thirteen, but they are not numbered consecutively; for example, *The Six Proud Walkers* (1928) and *The One Sane Man* (1934). Francis Beeding is best remembered for *Death Walks in Eastrepps* (1931), a detective story about a series of brutal murders in a quiet English seacoast village. When the book was first published, Vincent STARRETT called it the best detective novel he had ever read. The collaboration also produced *The House of Dr. Edwardes* (1927), which was filmed by Alfred HITCHCOCK in 1945 as *Spellbound.*

BELL, JOSEPHINE (pseudonym of Doris Bell Collier Ball; 1897–). English physician and mystery novelist. Never has a mystery writer been more closely connected with the medical profession than this author has. She was born in Manchester, the daughter of a surgeon; her great-grandfathers, as well as numerous uncles and cousins, had also practiced medicine. She studied medicine at Newnham College, Cambridge, and after passing her examinations became affiliated with University College Hospital in London. She married a physician with whom she established a joint practice. They had four children; one son is a doctor, and two daughters married doctors. Dr. Bell retired from her medical practice in 1954.

She began writing mysteries in 1936, following the death of her husband. Many of her books, including her first, *Murder in Hospital* (1937), and *From Natural Causes* (1939), *Death at the Medical Board* (1944), *A Well-known Face* (1960), *No Escape* (1965), and *Death of a Con Man* (1968), have a medical background. Although doctor detectives frequently appear in the thirty-seven mysteries she has written, the one used most often is young Dr. David Wintringham. He is as adept at recognizing physical clues at the scene of the crime as he is at spotting inaccurate medical diagnoses.

Miss Bell has used a wide variety of other subjects as background for her mysteries, for example, amateur archaeology in *Bones in the Barrow* (1953), music in *The Summer School Mystery* (1950), and a wildlife sanctuary in *Death on the Reserve* (1966).

Although Miss Bell is popular in England, her works were not published in the United States until 1955. One of her most highly praised books, *Death at Half-Term* (1939), a story of murder and the theater, was not published in the United States until 1965, as *Curtain Call for a Corpse.*

She has written articles about drug addiction among the young and *Crime in Our Time* (1961), a factual account of modern crimes and criminals.

BELLAIRS, GEORGE (pseudonym of Harold Blundell; 1902–). English banker and mystery novelist. Born in Heywood, Lancashire, Blundell received a bachelor of science degree in economics from the University of London. He had a long career in banking and was manager of a large Manchester bank when he retired in 1962. He was active in charitable work and was chairman of finance and a governor of the United Manchester Hospitals before moving to the Isle of Man in 1962; his wife is a native of that island. In 1959 an honorary M.A. degree was conferred on him by Manchester University for his literary and hospital work. The Blundells have often visited France, and he has written extensively on French food and wine. For several years he contributed stories with a French background to *The Manchester Guardian.*

Bellairs wrote his first mystery in 1941 during spare moments at his air raid warden's post. He has published fifty books, fifteen of which have appeared in the United States. All except *Turmoil in Zion* (1943; U.S. title: *Death Stops the Frolic*) have been about Inspector (later Chief Superintendent) Littlejohn. The inspector is realistically drawn. In later books in the series he fears that he is getting too old and is being patronized by his younger colleagues. He resolves these self-doubts by proving that he can interpret clues as well as ever and arrive at correct solutions.

Although Littlejohn and his understanding wife, Letty, live in London's Hampstead section, their creator has permitted them to travel often to the places he loves. Several Bellairs mysteries, including *Half-Mast for the Deemster* (1953) and *Corpse at the Carnival* (1958), are set on the Isle of Man. In *Death in High Provence* (1957), the couple travels in France, where Littlejohn has worked in the past. In *Pomeroy, Deceased* (1971), Littlejohn works with the French police again. The inspector owns an original Toulouse-Lautrec, given to him as a memento of his wartime service by his associates in the Paris Police Judiciaire. He is a lover of animals, and his old English sheep dog accompanies him on several cases.

BELLOC LOWNDES, MRS. MARIE. *See* LOWNDES, MRS. MARIE BELLOC.

BENCOLIN, HENRI (Creator: John Dickson CARR). The detective created by Carr for his best-selling first novel, *It Walks by Night* (1930), Bencolin is flamboyant to the point of eccentricity. The head *(juge d'instruction)* of the Paris Police, he has also solved cases as a private detective for fees that exceed his official salary. He is a dandy and likes to sit in nightclubs drinking a glass of beer and listening to jazz, his big cigar sending clouds of bilious black smoke over his obscure corner table.

There is a legend about Bencolin, who is called the foremost police official, and the most dangerous man, in Europe. The story, in fact, which concerns his clothes, is a true one. When he is dressed in an ordinary sack suit, the wise ones know that he is interested in pleasure alone. When he wears a dinner jacket, he is involved in a case and spends his time in contemplation. But when he wears his evening clothes and carries his silver-headed walking stick with its concealed sword blade, he has tracked his prey and is about to act. Bencolin encourages a young journalist, Jeff Marle, to perpetuate this legend because he knows that Parisians like their law enforcers to be picturesque.

Bencolin appears in five novels: *It Walks by Night, Castle Skull* (1931), *The Lost Gallows* (1931), *The Waxworks Murder* (1932; U.S. title: *The Corpse in the Waxworks*), and *The Four False Weapons* (1937).

BENNETT, (ENOCH) ARNOLD (1867–1931). English novelist, dramatist, and journalist whose major works describe life in "the Potteries"—the "Five Towns" of north Staffordshire, where he lived as a boy. Virtually all his novels and plays are realistic portrayals of middle-class life, occasionally with crime and detective themes.

The Grand Babylon Hotel (1902) contains much pure detection, and *The Statue* (1908), written in collaboration with Eden PHILLPOTTS, mildly lives up to its subtitle, *A Story of International Intrigue and Mystery. The Loot of Cities* (1904), a very rare book in first edition, is a collection of six stories about detective Cecil Thorold, "a millionaire in search of joy," whose unorthodox methods include blackmailing to expose a criminal and stealing to recover stolen goods. *The Night Visitor and Other Stories* (1931) contains stories about people in a great hotel, including the adventure of the poet Lomax Harder, who kills a man for a very good reason in "Murder!" (U.S. title: "Murder").

BENSON, BEN (ca. 1920–1959). American detective story writer. Born and raised in Boston, Benson was a salesman for the Lipton Tea Company in New England before he entered the Army in 1943. A machine gun squad leader in the 38th Armored Infantry Battalion, he fought in the Battle of the Bulge and was seriously wounded in January 1945. He spent three years in Army hospitals, where he was encouraged to write by A. S. Burack, editor and publisher of *The Writer.* He sold his first story in 1947. He died of a heart attack in 1959 while strolling in Times Square; he was in New York for the awards dinner of the Mystery Writers of America.

Following considerable research into the operations of the Massachusetts State Police, Benson began two series about that organization. One, consisting of ten books, is about Detective Inspector Wade Paris. Nicknamed "Old Icewater" because of his coolness under pressure, Paris is at his calmest in *The Ninth Hour* (1956) as he attempts to free hostages taken during a prison break.

Benson's other series detective, Massachusetts

State Trooper Ralph Lindsey, is in his early twenties. His inexperience and overzealousness make him susceptible to charges of "police brutality" in *The End of Violence* (1959), one of the best-received books in the series.

Both series were well received by critics, who applauded their authenticity but complained of Paris's lack of recognizably human frailties.

BENSON, GODFREY (RATHBONE) (1864–1945). English biographer, novelist, and politician. Benson, 1st Baron Charnwood, was the author of *Tracks in the Snow* (1906), originally published under the family name and later reprinted under his title, which was conferred on him in 1911.

A graduate of Balliol College, Oxford, he began his political career in 1892, when he was elected to Parliament. He married Dorothea Mary Thorpe in 1897; they had three children. He is best known for his biographies of Abraham Lincoln and Theodore Roosevelt, as well as for his single excursion into the mystery genre. *Tracks in the Snow,* a first-person narrative of a minister-detective's attempt to solve the murder of his best friend, is listed in the HAYCRAFT-QUEEN CORNERSTONE LIBRARY.

E. C. Bentley.

BENTLEY, E[DMUND] C[LERIHEW] (1875–1956). English journalist, humorist, and detective story writer. Bentley, the creator of Philip TRENT, was once called (by John Carter) the father of the contemporary detective story. He was born in Shepherd's Bush, a suburb of London. His father was an official in the Lord Chancellor's Department, and Bentley was educated in London at St. Paul's School, where he met G. K. CHESTERTON, who became his closest friend and an important influence on his career.

At nineteen Bentley won a history scholarship to Merton College, Oxford, and quickly became involved in many activities. He was president of the Oxford Union (the famed debating society) and captain of the university's boat club. He also founded a school magazine—his first literary experience.

Bentley left Oxford to study law in London and was admitted to the bar in 1902. That year he married Violet Boileau; they had two sons; one became an engineer, the other, Nicolas, a well-known artist and illustrator who also wrote several thrillers.

Also in 1902 Bentley became involved in journalism, which was to be his lifelong career. He served for ten years on the editorial staff of the *Daily News* and then switched to the conservative *Daily Telegraph,* where he wrote editorials for the next twenty years. During this time he also wrote on a free-lance basis many works, ranging from political tracts to light verse in *Punch*.

In 1905 Bentley published *Biography for Beginners* under the pseudonym E. Clerihew. Illustrated by Chesterton, it was a volume of nonsense verse consisting of a series of four-liners called "clerihews," which became almost as popular as the limerick form. Further volumes in this vein were *More Biography* (1929), *Baseless Biography* (1939), and *Clerihews Complete* (1951).

In 1934, after a long and busy career, Bentley retired from the arduous pressures of journalism to live quietly with his wife in Paddington. He was able to devote more time to writing detective stories as well as editing an anthology, *A Second Century of Detective Stories* (1938). He also edited and wrote introductions to several volumes of short stories by Damon Runyon.

The year 1940 saw the publication of *Those Days: An Autobiography,* as well as Bentley's return to journalism, as chief literary critic (replacing Harold Nicolson) for the *Daily Telegraph*. Following the cessation of hostilities and the easing of the wartime manpower shortage, Bentley retired once again, in 1947. His wife died two years later, and he spent most of his remaining days living quietly and writing in a comfortable hotel in London.

Bentley's masterpiece, *Trent's Last Case* (1913), was called (by *The New York Times*) "one of the few classics of detective fiction." Bentley also wrote a novel (his only mystery not about Trent) entitled *Elephant's Work* (1950), about an amnesiac who urgently seeks a master criminal. It was dedicated to John BUCHAN, who had advised him to write it as early as 1916.

BENTLEY, PHYLLIS (1894–). English novelist. Born in Halifax in the West Riding of Yorkshire, Miss Bentley has written works set in that locale and has gained a reputation as a leading regional writer. She attended Cheltenham Ladies' College and received a B.A. degree from the University of London in 1914. After teaching briefly, she worked for the Ministry of Munitions in London during World War I and the Ministry of Information during World War II. The best known of her twenty novels is *Inheritance* (1932), in which she wrote of the effects of the industrial revolution. She has written about fiction and lectured on the subject during tours of the United States. She received an O.B.E. in 1970.

In the mystery field, Miss Bentley is best known for her series of short stories about an elderly spinster detective, Miss Marian Phipps. In "A Midsummer's Night Crime" (1961), Miss Phipps, a theater lover like Miss Bentley, solves a crime at the Shakespeare Festival at Stratford on Avon. In "Miss Phipps Discovers America" (1963) she is on a lecture tour of the United States.

The second story in the series, "Chain of Witnesses" (1954), won third prize in an annual contest of *Ellery Queen's Mystery Magazine*. It tells of the cumulative effect of one seemingly insignificant event (a cleaning woman's failure to appear for work) and adroitly demonstrates that "In this complex modern world . . . the lives of all of us are very subtly and intricately interwoven." This theme is also important to *Crescendo* (1958), a nonmystery novel. An earlier novel by Miss Bentley, *The House of Moreys* (1953), is a popular Gothic mystery.

BERCKMAN, EVELYN (1900–). American musician, composer, and author of plays, historical works, and mysteries. Born in Philadelphia, Miss Berckman studied piano and musical composition and has had works performed by the Philadelphia Orchestra. However, she is better known as a writer. Since 1960 she has lived in London.

Many of Miss Berckman's books reflect her interest in the past. Her highly praised first book, *The Evil of Time* (1954), is about a woman art curator investigating hidden treasures in an ancient German castle. In *The Strange Bedfellow* (1956) and *Lament for Four Brides* (1959) her heroines are archaeologists exploring ancient ruins in Germany and France respectively. *The Heir of Starvelings* (1967) is set in mid-Victorian times and displays the careful research for which her work has always been praised.

BERKELEY, ANTHONY (pseudonym of A[nthony] B[erkeley] Cox; 1893–1970). English mystery writer. A. B. Cox was a journalist with a satiric bent who once wrote a comic mystery novel; Francis Iles was a well-known mystery critic and one of the all-time mystery greats; Anthony Berkeley was a famous mystery writer. All three names were used by Anthony Berkeley Cox, whose shunning of personal publicity made his private life a notable mystery in itself.

Cox started his literary career in the pages of *Punch*, to which he contributed humorous sketches, many of which were later published as *Jugged Journalism* (1925). A career in journalism and a series of trifling comic novels followed: *Brenda Entertains* (1925), *The Family Witch* (1925), and *The Professor on Paws* (1926). *O England!* (1934) is a study of social conditions and politics in a more serious vein.

In 1925 Cox published (anonymously) his first detective novel, *The Layton Court Mystery*, written for his own amusement and that of his father, who shared his enthusiasm for the form. The financial rewards were more impressive than those of his previous literary labors, and he continued to write works in this genre for the next fourteen years.

In 1928 Cox founded London's famous Detection Club and became its first honorary secretary. In the mid-1930s he started to review nonmystery novels and some mystery fiction for the *Daily Telegraph* under the Iles pseudonym.

Cox ceased writing mystery novels in 1939 for unexplained reasons. His claim "When I find something that pays better than detective stories I shall write that" might have pertinence. One source suggests that he came into a large inheritance at this time. He continued, however, to review mystery fiction for *The Sunday Times* (London) for many years after World War II.

Cox and his wife lived in an old house in St. John's Wood. He had an office in London located near the Strand, where he was listed as one of the two directors of A. B. Cox, Ltd., a company whose specific nature and functions could not easily be determined.

The Layton Court Mystery introduces the outrageous Roger SHERINGHAM, who rapidly diagnoses an apparent case of suicide as murder and solves a locked-room problem. He then has great difficulty determining the identity of the culprit. Howard HAYCRAFT said that, with this work, Cox "brought to the detective novel an urbane and naturalistic quality that was a welcome and needed relief."

A caricature of Anthony Berkeley by George Morrow. It appears as the frontispiece of *Jugged Journalism* by A. B. Cox. Chapter 19 contains "Holmes and the Dasher," a Sherlock Holmes parody. The first edition was published in London by Herbert Jenkins in 1925.

Cary Grant is the mysterious husband bringing what may be a drugged glass of milk to the bedside of his ailing wife in *Suspicion*, Alfred Hitchcock's reworked screen version of Francis Iles's *Before the Fact*. [*RKO*]

Mr. Priestley's Problem (1927; U.S. title: *The Amateur Crime*) was signed by A. B. Cox. It details a murder hoax whose staid victim believes that he has killed a blackmailer and determines to evade the law in company with the beautiful heroine to whom he is handcuffed. *The Poisoned Chocolates Case* (1929) was the expanded version of a short story, "The Avenging Chance," written earlier that year. Many critics prefer the story to the novel and rate it among the ten best works in the genre. In the novel, a lady samples a lethal box of candy, and the Crimes Circle (founded by Sheringham) undertakes the investigation. This satire on detectives, mystery writers, and the Detection Club is often cited as the best novel signed by Berkeley and has appeared on many "best" lists. It is notable for the six possible solutions to the crime.

In 1930 Cox, proclaiming that the detective novel was changing from a puzzle of time, place, motive, and opportunity to a puzzle of character, published *The Second Shot*, in which he tried to demonstrate his theory by using the relatively unfamiliar device of telling the story from the murderer's viewpoint.

Malice Aforethought (1931), signed by Francis Iles, is the story of a caddish and cowardly doctor who murders his equally detestable wife. It was based on the true-life Armstrong case. This inverted tale received unanimous raves; filled with cynicism and irony, it was summed up by Julian SYMONS: "If there is one book more than another that may be regarded as a begetter of the post-war realistic crime novel, it is this one."

The next Iles novel, *Before the Fact* (1932), the psychological study of a potential murderer as seen through the eyes of his intended victim, was an advance over *Malice Aforethought*, especially in its shifting of the inverted point of view from murderer to victim—a device that had been anticipated in Mrs. Marie Belloc LOWNDES's *The Chink in the Armor* (1912). Haycraft commented in *Murder for Pleasure* (1941): "Not many "serious" novelists of the present era, in fact, have produced character studies to compare with Iles's internally terrifying portrait of the murderer in *Before the Fact*, his masterpiece and a work truly deserving the appellations of unique and beyond price."

Berkeley's *Murder in the Basement* (1932) concerns Sheringham's efforts to identify a corpse found in the basement of a new house and to discover the identity of the murderer. It is a prime example of the British fair-play school. *Trial and Error* (1937) tells about the hitherto insignificant Lawrence Todhunter, who discovers that he has only six months to live and determines to commit the perfect crime against the most obnoxious person he can find. Everything goes very well until an innocent man is accused of the crime and Todhunter has to turn detective to prove the innocence of the accused. A clever and often moving novel, written with great sympathy for its protagonist, it should have been signed by Iles, for its realism and its adherence to the inverted form, but the appearance in it of Ambrose Chitterwick, a character in two previous Berkeley novels, would have confirmed the widespread suspicion that Berkeley and Iles were one and the same. Of all Cox's works, *Trial and Error* and *The Poisoned Chocolates Case* are the most often reprinted.

Cox's last work, *As for the Woman* (1939), was signed by Iles and centered around a callow youth, a vain and neurotic older woman, and her sadistic husband, who form the basis of an eternal triangle. This psychological study, frank and erotic for its time, received fair reviews. Announced as the first in a series of three projected novels "about murder as the natural outgrowth of character," it never had a successor. Its mystery elements were minimal, its only concern being with adultery and revenge.

Films

Berkeley's most important screen contribution was *Before the Fact*, which was used by Alfred HITCHCOCK as the basis for *Suspicion* (1941), although the ending was changed to preserve Cary Grant's movie innocence. Earlier that year Berkeley supplied the story for another film.

Flight from Destiny. Warner Brothers, 1941. Thomas Mitchell, Geraldine Fitzgerald, Jeffrey Lynn, Mona Barrie, James Stephenson. Directed by Vincent Sherman. Based on *Trial and Error*.

A man dying of a heart ailment thinks that a good final act would be to rid the world of a person who brings only suffering to others and learns about a painter who is under the influence of a thoroughly evil woman.

BIERCE, AMBROSE (GWINETT) (1842–disappeared in 1914). American journalist, critic, poet, and short story writer. Born in Horse Cave, Ohio, he served in the Civil War. In 1871 he married Mary Ellen Day; they had two sons, one of whom, involved in a love affair, was murdered. Under the pseudonym Dod Grile, Bierce published in England several volumes of sardonic sketches, including *The Fiend's Delight* (1872) and *Cobwebs from an Empty Skull* (1874). Much of his work is cynical and often macabre, and many of his stories contain elements of mystery and crime. *Tales of Soldiers and Civilians* (1891; reprinted as *In the Midst of Life*, 1898) contains a shockingly humorous tale, "My Favorite Murder," told in the first person by the victim's perpetrator-nephew. Most of the twenty-six tales are grim, stylistically brilliant horror stories, as are some of the twenty-three pieces in *Can Such Things Be?* (1893). *The Monk and the Hangman's Daughter* (1892) is an unusual psychological document of sustained horror adapted from a German medieval romance.

BIGGERS, EARL DERR (1884–1933). American novelist, playwright, and creator of Charlie CHAN. Born in Warren, Ohio, to Robert J. and Emma E. (Derr) Biggers, he attended Harvard and graduated in 1907. His first job was on the *Boston Traveler*, for which he wrote a humorous column and occasional drama criticism, which engendered his interest in the theater. He wrote a play, *If You're Only Human* (produced in 1912), which proved unsuccessful. In 1912 he married Eleanor Ladd; they had one son. Biggers died of heart disease in Pasadena, Calif.

In 1913 Biggers published a mystery novel, *Seven Keys to Baldpate*, which was an immediate success. *Love Insurance* (1914), *The Agony Column* (1916), and *Fifty Candles* (1926) also contain elements of mystery and romance.

Earl Derr Biggers.

In the mid-1920s, while searching for an idea for a book, Biggers thought, "Sinister and wicked Chinese are old stuff, but an amiable Chinese on the side of law and order had never been used." The result was a series of six novels starting with *The House Without a Key* (1925). The adventures of Charlie Chan were extremely popular. They were quickly translated and were the basis for innumerable radio programs, comic strips, and film dramatizations that quickly exhausted the originals. Before they were published in book form, all six novels were serialized in *The Saturday Evening Post*.

Howard HAYCRAFT summed up the Chan series by saying, "They are clean, humorous, unpretentious, more than a little romantic, and . . . just a shade mechanical and old fashioned by modern plot standards. . . . His [Biggers's] detective stories are remembered less for themselves than for the wise, smiling, pudgy little Chinese they introduced. Conventional as the narratives often were, Charlie Chan's personal popularity played a part in the Renaissance of the American detective story that can not be ignored."

Plays and Films

Biggers's novel *Seven Keys to Baldpate* was adapted into a long-running Broadway play in 1913 by George M. Cohan, who also starred. It has often been revived successfully. Other, less successful, plays followed: *Inside the Lines* (1915), *A Cure for Curables* (1917), *See-Saw* (1919; a musical based on *Love Insurance*), and *Three's a Crowd* (1919).

There have been several screen versions of *Seven Keys to Baldpate*, and films based on other Biggers works have also appeared. Cohan starred with Anna Q. Nilsson in the first screen version of *Seven Keys to Baldpate*, produced by Paramount-Artcraft in 1917. It was remade in 1925 by Paramount, starring Douglas McLean; Fred Newmeyer directed. There were three sound versions of the novel as well.

Seven Keys to Baldpate. RKO, 1930. Richard Dix, Miriam Seegar, Margaret Livingston, Lucien Littlefield. Directed by Reginald Barker.

A writer makes a $5,000 bet that he can finish a story in twenty-four hours at haunted, deserted Baldpate Inn, which, to his confusion, he finds cluttered with eccentric—and criminal—strangers.

The Second Floor Mystery. Warner Brothers, 1930. Grant Withers, Loretta Young, H. B. Warner. Directed by Roy Del Ruth. Based on *The Agony Column.*

A romantic young man corresponds with a girl he knows only through a newspaper advertisement; the imaginary heroics he boasts of in his letters ultimately lead to his being accused of murder.

Inside the Lines. RKO, 1930. Ralph Forbes, Betty Compson, Montague Love, Mischa Auer. Directed by Roy Pomeroy.

Two German spies fall in love, each unaware that the other is a British double agent.

Seven Keys to Baldpate. RKO, 1935. Gene Raymond, Margaret Calahan, Walter Brennan, Henry Travers. Directed by William Hamilton and Edward Killy. A remake.

Seven Keys to Baldpate. RKO, 1947. Philip Terry, Margaret Lindsay, Jacqueline White, Eduardo Ciannelli. Directed by Lew Landers. A remake.

BLACK MASK. The most important pulp magazine published in the United States (*see* PULP MAGAZINES). Founded in 1920 by H. L. Mencken and George Jean Nathan, it published traditional thrillers and adventure fiction but is remembered today chiefly for its detective stories. The hard-boiled school of tough private detectives was begun by Carroll John DALY and his character, Race WILLIAMS, and continued with Dashiell HAMMETT, Erle Stanley GARDNER, Raymond CHANDLER, George Harmon COXE, Frank GRUBER, and other prolific writers of fast-paced, violent, cynical, yet romantic crime tales. The magazine achieved preeminence under the editorship of Captain Joseph T. Shaw (1874–1952), from 1926 to 1936. *Black Mask* survived as a viable periodical into the 1940s, but later published mainly reprints. It finally collapsed and in 1953 became part of *Ellery Queen's Mystery Magazine.* It was revived for one issue in 1974.

***Black Mask* published the best writers of hard-boiled detective fiction. This cover was painted by John Drew.**

BLACKIE, BOSTON. *See* BOSTON BLACKIE.

BLACKSHIRT (Creator: Bruce GRAEME). A gentleman cracksman who does as much crime solving as stealing, Richard Verrell is known as Blackshirt because of the costume he affects when on a job; he dresses entirely in black and even wears a black mask. During the day he is a wealthy member of high society; at night he is an audacious burglar.

Found wandering the streets as a child, he knows nothing of his real family, and his foster parents died when he was only fifteen. He had had some of his works published before he was twenty-two, and, after serving in World War I, he became a best-selling author, continuing his life of crime for adventure rather than profit. His tranquillity is shattered when his identity is discovered by a beautiful young woman who calls anonymously on the telephone and, threatening to reveal his identity, forces him to change from a thief to a kind of Robin Hood. He soon thinks of her as his "Lady of the Phone," and, by the second volume in the series, Verrell and Bobbie are married; their son has similar adventures. The first of Bruce Graeme's dozen thrillers about the cracksman is *Blackshirt* (1925 s.s.); Graeme's son, Roderic JEFFRIES, writing as Roderic Graeme, produced an additional twenty volumes about him.

BLACKWOOD, ALGERNON (1869–1951). English author of ghost stories and other supernatural and mystical works. Blackwood maintained that his great interest was in "the suggestion that the Man in the Street possesses strange powers which never manifest normally," a theory underlying his weird tales that makes them seem more realistic than many others. His *John Silence* (1908), a collection of five stories about the "Psychic Physician," is similar to William Hope HODGSON's *Carnacki, the Ghost-Finder* (1913), in which the detective is called upon to explain apparently occult crimes.

BLAISDELL, ANNE. *See* LININGTON, ELIZABETH.

BLAISE, MODESTY (Creator: Peter O'Donnell). Created in 1963 by English author Peter O'Donnell, who writes mainly for adventure magazines and comic strips, superwoman Modesty Blaise—in many ways the female counterpart of James BOND—first appeared in a daily newspaper comic strip that was syndicated widely throughout the United Kingdom, Europe, and elsewhere (she has not been successful in the United States). Her origins are obscure. A nameless postwar waif fighting for life in the back alleys of Turkey and Persia, she saves the life of an old man, sometimes called "professor," a refugee who feeds her insatiable hunger for knowledge and who wryly dubs her "Modesty." (She took her last name from the tutor of Merlin the magician.) While she is growing up, she steals for both of them—books as well as food—and learns from him; then the old man dies. Soon afterward, she is in Tangier spinning the wheel at a casino for the leader of a moderately successful gang; when he is shot down, she assumes control of his organization and, in a few years, at the age of twenty, is the notorious head of Network, a large and powerful crime organization that, uniquely, eschews drugs and vice. In Saigon she meets scruffy, earthy Willie Garvin, and he becomes her right arm, worshipfully calling her "Princess." Together they amass wealth and in a few years disband Network and retire, she to a London penthouse and he to a Thames-side pub. Sir Gerald Tarrant of British Intelligence observes that inactivity bores them and offers them the opportunity for new extralegal activity in which their intimate knowledge of the underworld can be put to use. They receive no pay and take no orders. Although they are close in the several novels (*Modesty Blaise*, 1965; *Sabretooth*, 1966; *I, Lucifer*, 1967) O'Donnell has written about the pair, the exact nature and depth of the relationship Modesty and Willie share has never been clearly explained.

Willie Garvin (Terence Stamp) lays a protective hand on Modesty Blaise (Monica Vitti), but he knows the girl can take care of herself. In this flamboyant Joseph Losey film, with Dirk Bogarde featured as an epicene villain, Modesty's coiffure can somehow instantly change shape and color. [*Twentieth Century-Fox*]

Film

Modesty Blaise. Twentieth Century-Fox (British), 1966. Monica Vitti (Modesty), Terence Stamp (Willie), Dirk Bogarde, Harry Andrews, Michael Craig, Scilla Gabel. Directed by Joseph Losey.

The British Secret Service sends Modesty to protect a fortune in gems being shipped to an Arabian sheikh in exchange for oil concessions. The considerable changes in the original character of Modesty in this film caused O'Donnell to retain film rights with a view to producing the Modesty Blaise films himself.

BLAKE, NICHOLAS (pseudonym of C. Day Lewis; 1904–1972). English poet, novelist, critic, and detective story writer. Cecil Day Lewis was born in Ireland, the only son of an Irish Protestant clergyman. He was related through his mother to the poet-playwright Oliver Goldsmith. At the age of three he was taken to England, where he was educated at Sherborne School and Wadham College, Oxford. He taught at the Summerfields School, the Cheltenham Junior School, and then Cheltenham College, from 1930 to 1935. His left-wing political views met with opposition from the college administration, and he would have been asked to leave at an earlier date had not scholar C. M. Bowra intervened on his behalf.

He made clear his adoption of communism during the 1930s, once penning a verse, "Lenin, would you were living at this hour:/ England has need of you." In *The Revolution in Writing* (1936) he claimed, "The old structure of society is incapable of dealing satisfactorily with the new developments of life." He called for a literature that was concerned with the masses and that could be a guide to action. The writer, he said, must become "a partisan in life's struggles." Disillusionment, especially following the Spanish Civil War, led him to repudiate communism. During World War II he was connected with the British Ministry of Information. By the time of *The Sad Variety* (1964) he portrayed the Russians as the villains in a spy novel.

Day Lewis became Poet Laureate in 1968; the appointment, made by Queen Elizabeth II, was regarded as final proof that he was no longer a radical. He had published twenty volumes of verse, several books of literary criticism, and an autobiography, *The Buried Day* (1960). He also frequently translated works from Latin, including *The Aeneid*. Very fond of the Irish melodies of Thomas Moore, he often sang them on BBC programs. He taught poetry at Oxford from 1951 to 1956. During the academic year 1964–1965 he was Charles Eliot Norton professor of poetry at Harvard; *The Lyric Impulse* (1965) was based on his lectures there.

His first marriage, to Constance Mary King, daughter of a Sherborne master, ended in divorce; they had two sons. He later married actress Jill Balcon, and they had a son and a daughter.

Day Lewis began writing mysteries in 1935 to supplement the income he derived from poetry. Ironically, some critics, like John Strachey, felt that he wrote better as Nicholas Blake than when he wrote "seriously" under his own name. Day Lewis never deprecated the mystery genre or his own work in it, feeling that it was a harmless release for the cruelty he believed was present in everyone. He derived great personal enjoyment from the detective story, which he once described as "the folk myth of the 20th Century." For many years, as Blake, he was a highly discriminating reviewer of mysteries for *The Spectator*.

The Blake mysteries betray their author's intellectual leanings, but despite their literary tone they are not pretentious. Critics have approved of his ability to draw characters, especially in *Minute for Murder* (1947). Nigel STRANGEWAYS, the detective who appears in seventeen of Blake's twenty novels, is considered more believable than most fictional sleuths, and the motivation upon which his other characters act is generally understandable. This is especially true in *The Beast Must Die* (1938), a great success when it was published and still frequently ranked by many among the best mysteries of all time. In it, a small boy has been killed by a hit-and-run driver, and Blake relates the father's efforts to discover the identity of the culprit and avenge his son's death.

Many of the locales used by Blake come from his own experience, and they are usually well drawn. In his first mystery, *A Question of Proof* (1935), the setting is a preparatory school similar to those at which he taught. *Malice in Wonderland* (1940; U.S. title: *The Summer Camp Mystery*) utilizes the type of proletarian resort popular in England before World War II. *Minute for Murder* mirrors the author's wartime experiences; the setting is the fictional "Ministry of Morale." Day Lewis's visit to Harvard University became a trip by Strangeways to the United States and "Cabot University" in *The Morning after Death* (1966). The theme of murder in the snow always appealed to Blake, and he used it in *Thou Shell of Death* (1936; U.S. title: *Shell of Death*), in *The Case of the Abominable Snowman* (1941; U.S. title: *The Corpse in the Snowman*), and in one of the few short stories he wrote, "A Study in White," which won third prize in *Ellery Queen's Mystery Magazine's* 1949 contest.

Topicality became a Blake strong point after *Thou Shell of Death*, which dealt, though irreverently, with a national hero not unlike the legendary Lawrence of Arabia. Blake presented the threat to England of fascism in *The Smiler with the Knife* (1939), and he later dealt with the cold war and Russian spies. His last mystery, *The Private Wound* (1968), concerned with the problems that have divided Ireland, is considered to be the most autobiographical of Blake's works in this genre.

Film

This Man Must Die. Allied Artists (French), 1969. Michel Duchaussoy, Caroline Cellier, Jean Yanne. Directed by Claude Chabrol. Based on *The Beast Must Die*.

When a hit-and-run driver kills a nine-year-old boy, the child's father vows that he will find the culprit and kill him.

BLAKE, SEXTON (Creator: Harry Blyth). British detective, the hero of more novels and stories than any other detective. Blake made his first appearance on December 20, 1893, in the adventure story "The Missing Millionaire" (signed by Hal Meredith, Blyth's pseudonym) in a boys' weekly paper called *The Halfpenny Marvel* (no. 6). The paper that became Blake's own vehicle, *Union Jack*, was launched six months later. New Blake stories continue to be produced today, and nearly 200 authors have written the approximately 4,000 tales about him (in particular, Edwy Searles BROOKS, who wrote seventy-six Blake adventures)—an even greater number than have been published about Blake's American counterpart, Nick CARTER.

Blake began as an imitation of Sherlock HOLMES and soon also resided on Baker Street. He had his own "Watson" (*see* WATSON, DR.), a boy assistant named Tinker; an ever-present landlady, Mrs. Bardell; and a non-Sherlockian member of the household, a bloodhound named Pedro.

Although Professor James MORIARTY menaces Holmes and law-abiding London, he does not appear as regularly or as menacingly as such Blake adversaries as Mademoiselle Yvonne, a semiheroine who actually loves Blake; Dr. Huxton Rymer, a mad former surgeon of Harley Street; and Prince Wu Ling, chief of the Brotherhood of the Yellow Beetle, one of many sinister Orientals (*see* ORIENTALS, SINISTER) encountered by Blake.

Blyth (1852–1898) is credited by some with naming "the most famous Englishman in the world" (as Blake is sometimes called); others maintain that the naming of the character was an editorial decision at Harmsworth, Ltd. (later Amalgamated Press, now Fleetway Publications).

Films

Blake's triumphant adventures on the British screen span many decades. In a 1909 Gaumont short, Blake (C. Douglas Carlile) disguises himself as a minister to save a heroine from "a fate worse than death." He retrieves stolen plans in *Sexton Blake v. Baron Kettler* (1912). Douglas Payne, in *The Further Exploits of Sexton Blake* (1919), with Neil Warrington as Tinker, saves a murdered scientist's kidnapped daughter aboard the S.S. *Olympic*. In 1928 Langhorne Burton is Blake, and Mickey Brantford is Tinker, in a series of short mystery films released by British Filmcraft (for example, *Sexton Blake, Gambler, The Clue of the Second Goblet, The Great Office Mystery*, and *The Mystery of the Silent Death*). Among Blake's sound screen exploits are the following.

Sexton Blake and the Bearded Doctor. Fox (British), 1935. George Curzon (Blake), Tony Sympson (Tinker), Henry Oscar, Gillian Maude. Directed by George A. Cooper.

Blake investigates the murder of a violinist and an insurance swindle.

Sexton Blake and the Mademoiselle. Fox (British), 1935. Curzon, Sympson, Lorraine Grey, Edgar Norfolk. Directed by Alex Bryce.

Blake does not stand in the way when a determined girl takes revenge on those responsible for her father's ruin.

Sexton Blake and the Hooded Terror. King (British), 1938. Curzon, Sympson, Tod Slaughter, Greta Gynt. Directed by George King.

Blake exposes a wealthy industrialist (played bravura style by British horror star Slaughter) as the maniacal leader of a nameless, hooded band of murderers.

Meet Sexton Blake. British National (British), 1944. David Farrar (Blake), John Varley (Tinker), Magda Kun. Directed by John Harlow.

Blake recovers a valuable formula for an airplane alloy.

The Echo Murders. British National–Strand (British), 1945. Farrar, Dennis Price, Pamela Stirling, Julien Mitchell. Directed by Harlow.

In order to expose a band of murderous, machine gun–wielding Nazis working secret tin mines in some sealed-off Cornish caves, Blake must fake his own death.

BLEECK, OLIVER. *See* THOMAS, ROSS.

BLOCH, ROBERT (1917–). American short story writer, novelist, and scriptwriter. Had Robert Bloch written no other work but *Psycho* (1959), which became one of the highest-grossing black-and-white motion pictures ever produced, his place in the history of crime fiction would be assured. He is, however, a most prolific writer, having published more than 400 short stories and articles and several novels, and written scripts for films and countless radio and television dramas. He is probably best known for his horror, fantastic, occult, and science fiction.

Bloch was born in Chicago, the first child of Stella (Loeb), a teacher and social worker, and Raphael A. Bloch, a bank cashier. Although his parents were German-Jewish, he received most of his religious training in a Methodist church because his parents' social life was centered there. Both parents had a great interest in the performing arts, and Bloch's first ambition was to become a comedian. He married Marion Ruth Holcombe in 1940 and took a job as an advertising copywriter two years later. Although he intended the position to be a stopgap one, his wife's tuberculosis and the birth of their daughter (1943) kept him with the company for eleven years. He has since been divorced and in 1964 married Eleanor Alexander.

As a teenager, Bloch had been influenced by H. P. Lovecraft's strange stories in *Weird Tales* magazine. He decided to become a writer, but although he sold virtually everything he wrote, starting immediately after graduation from high school, he usually received a pittance. In 1947 he wrote his first mystery novel, *The Scarf*, in the Raymond CHANDLER style. *The Kidnapper* followed in 1954 and is, aside from *Psycho*, Bloch's favorite novel. It is the story, told in the first person, of a vicious psychopathic kidnapper and is almost universally disliked by its readers for its cold honesty.

Many of Bloch's books are difficult to categorize, for they often combine elements of mystery and horror, crime and the supernatural, fantasy and science fiction. He has also written as Collier Young.

Bloch is a former president of the Mystery Writers of America (1970–1971).

CHECKLIST

The short story collections contain at least one story of mystery or crime.

1947 *The Scarf*
1954 *The Kidnapper*
1954 *Spiderweb*
1954 *The Will to Kill*
1958 *Shooting Star*
1958 *Terror in the Night* (s.s.)
1959 *Psycho*
1960 *The Dead Beat*
1961 *Firebug*
1961 *Blood Runs Cold* (s.s.)
1962 *The Couch*
1962 *Terror*
1965 *Tales in a Jugular Vein* (s.s.)
1965 *The Skull of the Marquis de Sade* (s.s.)
1966 *Chamber of Horrors* (s.s.)
1968 *The Star Stalker*

1969 *The Todd Dossier* (by Collier Young)
1972 *Night World*
1974 *American Gothic*

Films

When Bloch's novel *Psycho* was selected by Alfred HITCHCOCK to be filmed in 1960, it not only sparked a new era of screen thrillers but also made the author's name a familiar one in the genre. Since then, he has contributed much to the mystery film.

The Couch. Warner Brothers, 1962. Grant Williams, Shirley Knight, Onslow Stevens, William Leslie. Directed by Owen Crump. Bloch wrote the screenplay, based on an original story by Crump and Blake Edwards.

A personable young man makes an anonymous phone call to the police, telling them that he has killed a stranger, and then visits his psychiatrist.

The Cabinet of Caligari. Twentieth Century-Fox, 1962. Dan O'Herlihy, Glynis Johns, Dick Davalos. Directed by Roger Kay.

A young woman has a flat tire while driving her car; she seeks help at the large wooded estate of Dr. Caligari, where she is at once drugged and imprisoned. The film represents Bloch's attempt to update the surrealistic and clinical mood, but not the plot, of the German silent classic.

The Night Walker. Universal, 1964. Barbara Stanwyck, Robert Taylor, Lloyd Bochner. Directed by William Castle.

After her blind, possessive husband is supposedly killed in a fiery explosion, a terrified widow is haunted by a scarred figure who stalks her by night.

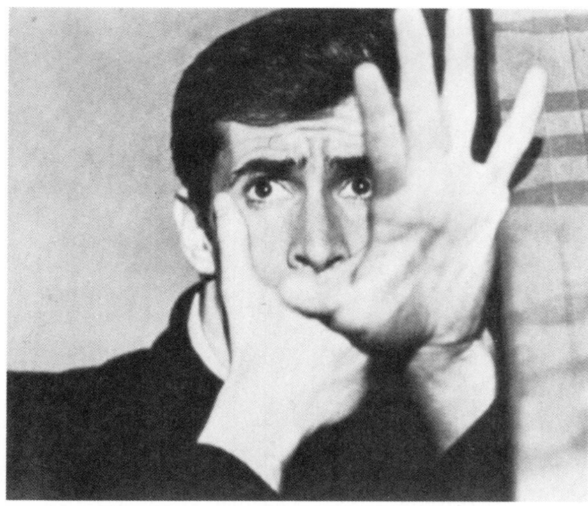

A distraught Anthony Perkins contemplates the girl stabbed to death in a shower at his run-down motel in Alfred Hitchcock's trend-setting psychological thriller *Psycho,* closely drawn from Robert Bloch's novel. [*Paramount*]

The Skull. Paramount (British), 1965. Peter Cushing, Patrick Wymark, Christopher Lee, Nigel Green, Jill Bennett. Directed by Freddie Francis. Adapted by Milton Subotsky from Bloch's story "The Skull of the Marquis de Sade."

A collector of bizarre antiques is offered the skull of De Sade, stolen from its grave; the thing begins to exert an evil influence upon its new master.

The Psychopath. Paramount (British), 1966. Patrick Wymark, Margaret Johnston, Alexander Knox. Directed by Francis.

Dolls are left at the scenes of four murders that are linked to an invalid woman and her eccentric adult son.

The Deadly Bees. Paramount (British), 1967. Suzanna Leigh, Frank Finlay, Guy Doleman. Directed by Francis. Bloch and Anthony Marriott based their script (not very closely) on *A Taste for Honey* (1941) by H. F. HEARD.

Overworked, a young singer goes for a rest to a remote British island, where she encounters a crazed resident who is training killer bees to attack.

Bloch has also specialized in such anthology mystery films as *Torture Garden* (1967), in which one of the stories is about a man (Jack Palance) who believes that he is a reincarnation of Edgar Allan POE; *The House That Dripped Blood* (1971); and *Asylum* (1972).

Television

Bloch has been very active in television, contributing many of the finest hours of *Thriller* (including Barre Lyndon's adaptation of his celebrated short story "Yours Truly, Jack the Ripper" and the chilling original television story "Wax Works") and *Alfred Hitchcock Presents.*

BLOCHMAN, LAWRENCE G[OLDTREE] (1900–1975). American journalist and author of detective fiction. Born in San Diego, the son of Haidee (Goldtree) and Lucien A. Blochman, he graduated from the University of California at Berkeley (1921) and received a certificate in forensic pathology from the Armed Forces Institute of Pathology (1952). He married Marguerite Maillard in Paris in 1926.

His journalistic career began in California; later he held positions in Japan, Hong Kong, India (Calcutta), and France before becoming a full-time freelance writer in 1928. Fluent in French, he translated about twenty books from that language into English. He worked in several branches of the United States government, held important positions with the Overseas Press Club, and was a member of the Mystery Writers of America (he was president in 1948–1949). He wrote many scripts for radio, television, and motion pictures and contributed to the *Encyclopaedia Britannica.*

Dr. Daniel Webster Coffee and his Hindu assistant, Dr. Motilal Mookerji, are depicted by Albert Orbaan on the dust wrapper of this first edition, published by Lippincott in 1964.

George Sanders here appears to be a scholarly visitor to a rare book display at a large public library, but actually he is a Nazi agent forging manuscripts in *Quiet Please, Murder*, based on a Lawrence Blochman story. [*Twentieth Century-Fox*]

Blochman's best detective fiction involves Dr. Daniel Webster Coffee, chief pathologist at Pasteur Hospital in the fictional Midwestern city Northbank. Assisted by an imperturbable Hindu, Dr. Motilal Mookerji, and by Max Ritter, "the tallest, skinniest and homeliest lieutenant of detectives on the Northbank police force (but not the most gullible)," Coffee carries out his criminal investigative work in the laboratory. The tales of the brilliant detective-doctor appeared regularly in *Collier's* for ten years, the best being collected in *Diagnosis: Homicide* (1950); a later collection was *Clues for Dr. Coffee* (1964). The only novel about him is *Recipe for Homicide* (1952), which somehow makes the details of the soup canning industry interesting. Among Blochman's mysteries that do not involve Dr. Coffee are his first mystery novel, *Bombay Mail* (1934), the first in a series about Inspector Prike; *Red Snow at Darjeeling* (1938); *Midnight Sailing* (1938); *Blowdown* (1939); *See You at the Morgue* (1941); and *Rather Cool for Mayhem* (1951).

Films

Bombay Mail. Universal, 1934. Edmund Lowe, Shirley Grey, Onslow Stevens, Ralph Forbes, Ferdinand Gottschalk. Directed by Edwin L. Marin.

A maharaja is shot on the Calcutta-to-Bombay train—the second victim of an unknown killer.

Chinatown Squad. Universal, 1935. Lyle Talbot, Valerie Hobson, Andy Devine. Directed by Murray Roth.

A tough cop, fired from the Chinatown police patrol, still continues his investigation of the murder in that sector of an agent working for Chinese revolutionaries.

Quiet Please, Murder. Twentieth Century-Fox, 1942. George Sanders, Gail Patrick, Richard Denning, Sidney Blackmer. Directed by John Larkin. Based on "Death Walks in Marble Halls."

Using a very modernistic branch of a big-city public library as transfer point, a ruthless woman sells a forged rare book to a Nazi agent.

Radio and Television

Blochman's "Red Wine" (1930), a story in which the temperature of the table wine served at a jungle outpost is a vital point, has been used several times on the radio anthology series *Escape* and on other programs. In the early 1960s a television series of hour-long mysteries called *Diagnosis: Unknown* featured Patrick O'Neal as the pathologist Dr. Coffee; Chester Morris played the police investigator.

BLOOD, MATTHEW. *See* HALLIDAY, BRETT.

BLUNDELL, HAROLD. *See* BELLAIRS, GEORGE.

BLYTH, HARRY. *See* BLAKE, SEXTON.

BODKIN, M[ATTHAIS] McDONNELL (1850–1933). Irish barrister and author of detective and mystery stories. Bodkin was appointed a judge in County Clare and also served as a Nationalist member of Parliament. His native country and years in the courtroom are recalled in the autobiographical *Recollections of an Irish Judge* (1914).

Bodkin's witty stories collected in *Dora Myrl, the Lady Detective* (1900) and *Paul Beck, the Rule of Thumb Detective* (1898) have been unjustly neglected. Beck, his first detective (when he first appeared in print in *Pearson's Magazine* in 1897, he was named Alfred Juggins), claims to be not very bright, saying, "I just go by the rule of thumb, and muddle and puzzle out my cases as best I can." He unravels several well-constructed mysteries. In *The Capture of Paul Beck* (1909) he and Dora begin on opposite sides in a case, but in the end they are married. They have a son who solves a crime at his university in *Young Beck, a Chip off the Old Block* (1911; s.s.). Other Bodkin books are *The Quests of Paul Beck* (1908; s.s.), *Pigeon Blood Rubies* (1915), and *Guilty or Not Guilty?*

BONAPARTE, INSPECTOR NAPOLEON (Creator: Arthur W. UPFIELD). A half-caste Australian child, found under a tree at the age of two weeks alongside his dead mother, was taken to a nearby mission station. Soon afterward, a matron with a keen sense of humor found him attempting to devour a thick volume on the life of the French emperor, and named him after the subject of the book.

He did very well in his studies at the mission school and attended Brisbane University, where he received an M.A. degree. He next joined the Queensland Police Department, where his skill as an expert tracker led to his rapid promotion to the rank of inspector.

Suave, slender, and handsome, with brown skin and blue eyes, he has well-kept black hair, a straight nose, and a flexible mouth. He is happily married to a girl named Marie, a half-caste like himself, and has three sons who have also received their educations at the university.

Bonaparte's success as a detective is attributed to his mixed blood. His uncanny ability to read "the book of the bush," inherited from his mother, is of incalculable value in the Australian outback; his powers of reasoning were the gift of his unknown white father. He also has vast patience.

He asks all his friends (and they are many) to call him Bony and tells them that he is the most unusual man in Australia. Despite his enormous ego and vanity, he can charm anyone. As he rolls his own cigarettes and tells his enthralled audiences about his personal history, he claims that he has never failed to bring a case to a successful conclusion and will soon be able to prove his point.

The first Bony novel and Upfield's second work, *The Barrakee Mystery*, deals with the murder of King Henry, the leader of a local aborigine tribe, on a rich homestead in the Darling River basin. A major debut for a series detective, it boasts three-dimensional characters and features an exciting flood sequence to pave the way for Bony's final deductions. *The Barrakee Mystery* did not reach the United States until 1965, when it was published as *The Lure of the Bush.*

The fourth Bony novel, *Mr. Jelly's Business*, includes disappearances as well as murder. Cited in SANDOE'S READERS' GUIDE TO CRIME, it was the first to be published in the United States. Bony was "retired" during World War II but returned in *Death of a Swagman* and *The Devil's Steps.*

An Author Bites the Dust is uncharacteristic in that Bony investigates the murder of an author turned critic in a suburb of Melbourne among more sophisticated types than are usually found in the outback. *The Mountains Have a Secret* and *Venom House* are pure thrillers.

Death of a Lake describes the effects of a drought drying up Lake Otway, which might be the final resting-place of an embezzler and £12,500. Plot, puzzle, characterizations, background, and atmosphere are blended perfectly in this work, Upfield's masterpiece.

CHECKLIST

1928 *The Barrakee Mystery* (U.S. title: *The Lure of the Bush*)
1931 *The Sands of Windee*
1936 *Wings above the Diamantina* (U.S. title: *Wings above the Claypan*)
1937 *Mr. Jelly's Business* (U.S. title: *Murder Down Under*)
1937 *Winds of Evil*
1938 *The Bone Is Pointed*
1939 *The Mystery of Swordfish Reef*
1940 *Bushranger of the Skies* (U.S. title: *No Footprints in the Bush*)
1945 *Death of a Swagman*
1946 *The Devil's Steps*
1948 *An Author Bites the Dust*
1948 *The Mountains Have a Secret*
1950 *The Widows of Broome*
1950 *The Bachelors of Broken Hill*
1951 *The New Shoe*
1952 *Venom House*
1953 *Murder Must Wait*
1954 *Death of a Lake*
1954 *The Cake in the Hat Box* (U.S. title: *Sinister Stones*)

1956 *The Battling Prophet*
1956 *The Man of Two Tribes*
1957 *Bony Buys a Woman* (U.S. title: *The Bushman Who Came Back*)
1959 *Bony and the Black Virgin*
1959 *Bony and the Mouse* (U.S. title: *Journey to the Hangman*)
1960 *Bony and the Kelly Gang* (U.S. title: *Valley of Smugglers*)
1961 *Bony and the White Savage* (U.S. title: *The White Savage*)
1962 *The Will of the Tribe*
1963 *Madman's Bend* (U.S. title: *The Body at Madman's Bend*)
1966 *The Lake Frome Monster* (completed and revised by J. L. Price and Dorothy Strange)

BOND, JAMES (Creator: Ian FLEMING). The most famous spy in literature, 007 is a patriotic English espionage agent who takes on titanic villains with unmatched fearlessness and zest. The "00" is a code number that indicates that the agent is licensed to kill in the line of duty—a prerogative Bond exercises an average of at least three times in each of his adventures.

Tall, dark, handsome, and rugged, Bond is an elegant man of the world who enjoys gambling, the best food, cognac, champagne, and other luxurious trappings of wealth—especially the beautiful women who are invariably attracted to him. He spends an inordinate amount of time engaged in sexual activities, but not so much that he does not perform his primary job.

The son of a Swiss mother and a Scottish father, Bond nevertheless feels deeply patriotic about England and is willing to endure torture and risk his life repeatedly in his efforts to smash plots engineered by Russian organizations and freewheeling supercriminals intent on world conquest. A brilliant marksman, Bond is also a superb athlete who can easily dominate three ordinary men in hand-to-hand combat with his knowledge of judo and karate. He carries a .25 Beretta automatic in his left arm holster on assignment and drives a pre-World War II Bentley outfitted with a number of ingenious lethal gadgets.

Just as the Sherlock HOLMES stories have a familiar pattern, the Bond novels have a repetitive plot structure. "M," Bond's superior, generally summons the hero to his office and tells him of a monstrous conspiracy, usually directed by or beneficial to the Soviet Union. Bond is told to destroy the organization and kill its leader. He usually finds his way into the enemy's lair, only to be captured and tortured until a beautiful woman rescues him, enabling him to complete his mission.

Bond is fallible, relying on the help of others (most frequently lusting, beautiful women) to get him out of tight situations. He was not born a superman but developed his many extraordinary abilities through the application of his mind and body. M would describe him as simply a middle-grade civil servant who somehow finds himself thrust into extremely difficult situations.

In *Dr. No*, the first film in the James Bond series, a vigorous Sean Connery as 007 invades the secret antimissile base of Dr. No and the ranks of international stardom. [*United Artists*]

The first book about Bond was *Casino Royale* (1953), in which Bond takes on the first of his archvillains, Le Chiffre, who is trying to regain misappropriated SMERSH (a Russian murder organization) funds at a gambling casino in northern France.

In *Live and Let Die* (1954) Mr. Big is called the most powerful criminal in the world. The head of the Black Widow voodoo cult, he is a high-ranking member of SMERSH. His gang ranges from New York's Harlem to the islands of the West Indies. Bond tries to prevent Mr. Big from turning over the wealth of an old pirate treasure to SMERSH.

Moonraker (1955) features 007's most formidable villain, Hugo Drax, who is intent on destroying London with a nuclear bomb. Although Drax is employed by the Soviet Union, he is aided by a covey of German scientists.

Bond fights the Syndicate in *Diamonds Are Forever* (1956) when he tries to break up a diamond-

Gert Frobe, in *Goldfinger,* portrays for the screen the Fleming villain, here fingering his target for conquest, Fort Knox. [*United Artists*]

smuggling pipeline from Africa to the United States. Bond's major assignment in *From Russia, with Love* (1957) is preventing his own assassination. The title character in *Dr. No* (1958) is employed by the Soviet Union. His assignment is to make American missiles inoperable by beaming incorrect instructions to them.

One of Bond's most fantastic adventures, *Goldfinger* (1959), pits him against his most famous adversary, the villainous Auric Goldfinger and his assistant, the seemingly indestructible Oddjob. Hired by SMERSH to steal all the gold in Fort Knox, Goldfinger might have succeeded in wrecking the world's economy but for the aid provided Bond by Pussy Galore.

For Your Eyes Only (1960) contains five short stories. *Thunderball* (1961) features Blofeld, an employee of SPECTRE, which is blackmailing Western governments with hijacked nuclear bombs. Vivienne Michel is credited with collaboration on the title page of the English edition of *The Spy Who Loved Me* (1962). She is also a character in the book—and is nearly burned to death.

SPECTRE's villainous Blofeld returns in *On Her Majesty's Secret Service* (1963) with a plot to destroy the free world by infecting it with crop and livestock pests. Bond falls in love with and marries Tracy, the daughter of Marc-Ange Draco, head of the Union Corse, in one of the shortest marriages of all time.

Blofeld again appears in *You Only Live Twice* (1964), this time as a free agent who entices his victims to commit suicide in a private garden of poison.

Cuba's Fidel Castro and the Soviet Union employ Scaramanga and assorted minor villains to damage Western sugar and other businesses in the

Caribbean in *The Man with the Golden Gun* (1965). Fleming's final book about Bond is *Octopussy and the Living Daylights* (1966; U.S. title: *Octopussy.*) The 1967 Signet paperback edition also contains "The Property of a Lady," which had made its first book appearance in *The Ivory Hammer* (1963).

There have been many burlesques, parodies, and pastiches of the James Bond stories, notably *Loxfinger* and *Matzohball*, Published by Pocket Books, and the best of the pastiches, *Colonel Sun* (1968) by Kingsley Amis, under the pseudonym Robert Markham.

A daily comic strip based on Bond's adventures, drawn in England by Horak, has been syndicated internationally for several years.

Films

Fleming's handsome secret agent was transferred—intact with attentive females, wildly inventive weaponry, and gallery of grotesque supervillains—to the screen for the first time in 1963, spawning the most successful series of thrillers of the decade and revitalizing the espionage genre, although the approach was less serious than tongue-in-cheek. The series was produced by Harry Saltzman and Albert Broccoli.

Dr. No. United Artists, 1963. Sean Connery, Joseph Wiseman, Ursula Andress, Jack Lord (the CIA's Felix Leiter), Bernard Lee (Bond's chief, "M" of "Universal Export," for the series), Lois Maxwell (M's secretary, Miss Moneypenny, for the series). Directed by Terence Young.

Bond arrives in Jamaica from London to investigate the strange disappearance of an English agent and his secretary from a normally calm listening post. Attempts are made on his life (on one occasion a poisonous tarantula is placed in his bed); he traces his adversaries to Crab Key Island, where an evil Eurasian scientist, Dr. No (Wiseman), has barricaded himself and is attempting to capture American moon missiles sent up from nearby Florida. Penetrating the base, Bond is momentarily diverted by another trespasser, Honey Wilder (Andress), who is collecting shells.

In 1973 Roger Moore, who for years had been the Saint on television, became a popular new 007. For *Live and Let Die* Bond uses a marvelous wristwatch with a hacksaw attachment to free himself in an alligator pit. Jane Seymour is the girl attached to him. [*United Artists*]

From Russia, with Love. United Artists, 1964. Connery, Daniela Bianchi, Pedro Armendariz, Robert Shaw, Lotte Lenya. Directed by Young.

SPECTRE, a worldwide organization conspiring against both the United States and the Soviet Union, attempts to eliminate Bond by sending their top agent, a tough middle-aged woman (Lenya), and a trained executioner (Shaw) to waylay him in Istanbul, where he falls into a baited trap while trying to obtain a secret Russian decoder from a Russian girl who is apparently a defector.

Goldfinger. United Artists, 1964. Connery, Gert Frobe, Honor Blackman, Shirley Eaton, Harold Sakata, Tania Mallet. Directed by Guy Hamilton.

England's gold reserves are being depleted, and European millionaire Goldfinger (Frobe) is thought

George Lazenby, in his single portrayal as 007, fires on SPECTRE chief Blofeld as both race down a Swiss mountain in bobsleds in *On Her Majesty's Secret Service.* [*United Artists*]

At his secret retreat in the Pacific, Christopher Lee, in *The Man with the Golden Gun*, engages in a duel with James Bond (Roger Moore, right). The gleaming gold weapon Lee holds can be dismantled into such innocent components as a cigarette lighter and a fountain pen. [*United Artists*]

to be responsible. When Bond romances Goldfinger's secretary (Eaton) to learn how he cheats at cards at a lush Florida hotel, the villain kills her by painting her body gold and thus keeping oxygen from entering her pores. Bond learns that Goldfinger plans an attack on Fort Knox, and in just one sexual encounter he manages to enlist the aid of a Goldfinger lieutenant, the man-hating Pussy Galore (Blackman, of the first British *Avenger* television series). He must also fight to the death the Korean Oddjob (Sakata), whose steel-rimmed hat is an axman's weapon.

Thunderball. United Artists, 1965. Connery, Claudine Auger, Adolfo Celi, Luciana Paluzzi, Rik Van Nutter (Felix Leiter). Directed by Young.

In the Bahamas, Bond utilizes novel underwater and aerial devices to stop SPECTRE aquanauts from raising two atomic bombs from a sunken NATO plane and keeps the organization from carrying out its plan to threaten to blow up American cities for £1 million ransom.

In 1967 a rival studio filmed *Casino Royale* as a wild spoof, with David Niven as an aging 007 who comes out of retirement to tangle with such international agents as Deborah Kerr, Orson Welles, William Holden, Charles Boyer, and John Huston. Peter Sellers is the inventor of a sure way of winning at baccarat; Joanna Pettet is Bond's illegitimate daughter, and Woody Allen is his inept nephew Jimmy Bond, the secret head of SMERSH. The Columbia film was the work of five directors: John Huston, Ken Hughes, Val Guest, Robert Parrish, and Joe McGrath.

You Only Live Twice. United Artists, 1967. Connery, Akiko Wakabayashi, Tetsuro Tamba, Mie Hama, Karin Dor, Donald Pleasence. Directed by Lewis Gilbert.

Assassins incapacitate Bond as he arrives in Japan searching for the American and Russian space capsules that have been captured by SPECTRE. He recovers and continues his work in secret. His quest leads him to a false lake inside a volcanic island, under which is an immense spaceship and SPECTRE's chief, Blofeld (Pleasence), an unseen presence in previous films.

Connery declined to play Bond again. Australian male model George Lazenby was assigned the role after a worldwide search.

On Her Majesty's Secret Service. United Artists, 1970. George Lazenby, Diana Rigg, Telly Savalas (Blofeld this film), Ilse Steppat. Directed by Peter Hunt.

Against the awesome splendor of the Swiss Alps, in a SPECTRE mountaintop stronghold, Bond rescues and courts the fiery daughter of a Corsican bandit (Rigg). There is a happy peasant wedding, but all of Blofeld's guns have not been stilled.

Diamonds Are Forever. United Artists, 1971. Connery (persuaded to return for a sixth and final portrayal), Jill St. John, Charles Gray (playing Blofeld and his double), Lana Wood, Jimmy Dean. Directed by Hamilton.

Diamonds are being smuggled bloodily out of South Africa and Amsterdam. Bond traces them to Las Vegas, where Blofeld and his double use the gems and an imprisoned young millionaire in a scheme for world domination. The climax occurs on an oil derrick off the California coast.

Live and Let Die. United Artists, 1973. Roger Moore, Yaphet Kotto, Jane Seymour, Clifton James, Geoffrey Holder. Directed by Hamilton.

Bond travels from New York's Harlem to New Orleans and then to a Caribbean island to tangle with voodoo, tarot cards, and a supergang of blacks trafficking in heroin.

The Man with the Golden Gun. United Artists, 1974. Moore, Christopher Lee, Britt Ekland, Maud Adams, Herve Villechaize, Clifton James, Richard Loo. Directed by Hamilton.

007 has the assignment of tracking down a missing solar energy scientist and an aristocratic international assassin, Scaramanga (Lee), who is aided by a midget named Nick Nack (Villechaize). Much of the action takes place in the Far East.

Television

In the 1950s a one-hour adaptation of *Casino Royale* was presented on *Climax!* with Barry Nelson as Bond in a dramatization that concentrated on cheating at cards. Bond has not been on television since (except as the subject of such documentary specials as *The Incredible James Bond* and in highly rated showings of some of the theatrical films), but he has inspired many imitators, for example, *Secret Agent* and *I Spy*. Fleming himself contributed the concept and pilot scripts for the successful television series *The Man from U.N.C.L.E.* (1964–1967), with Robert Vaughn as Napoleon Solo and David McCallum as Illya Kuryakin, agents serving the elderly chief Mr. Waverly (played by Leo G. Carroll) of the United Network Command for Law Enforcement.

BONETT, JOHN AND EMERY (pseudonyms of John Hubert Arthur Coulson, 1906–   , and Felicity Winifred Carter, 1906–   ). English mystery writers. This husband-wife team met while working in the offices of a publication devoted to the Spanish Civil War. John Coulson had worked in the business and banking fields. Felicity Carter had been an animator, actress, lyricist, and scriptwriter. She had also published a few short stories, and her first novel, *A Girl Must Live* (1937), about an aspiring actress, was filmed by Sir Carol Reed in England in 1939.

When they work together on a book, John Bonett does much of the plotting and research; Emery Bonett is involved for the most part with the actual writing. Their first effort, *High Pavement* (1944; U.S. title: *Old Mrs. Camelot*), signed only by Emery Bonett, is reputed to have sold more than 300,000 copies. *Dead Lion* (1949), signed by both writers, concerns the death of a famous and controversial English literary critic whose nephew investigates to determine whether murder or suicide was the cause. Six former loves of the critic are among the chief suspects. *A Banner for Pegasus* (1951; U.S. title: *Not in the Script*) is set in a small village invaded by film makers on location; it is notable for its background detail, murder problem, and romantic interludes.

The Coulsons have lived in Spain in recent years, and consequently works from this period are often set on the Costa Brava. They feature the quiet and intelligent Inspector Borges, who, in *This Side Murder* (1967; U.S. title: *Murder on the Costa Brava*), investigates a blackmail plot and murder among a group of English residents at a luxury hotel. A later work, *The Sound of Murder* (1970), finds Borges interrupting his London vacation in order to find out whether a tycoon who fell from his tenth-story apartment into a farmer's truck is the victim of accident, suicide, or murder.

BOOTHBY, GUY (NEWELL) (1867–1905). Australian novelist. Born in Adelaide, South Australia, the son of a member of the House of Assembly, he was educated in England and then returned to Australia to work as secretary to the mayor of Adelaide. After writing several unsuccessful plays, he moved to England with his wife in 1894 and wrote about fifty novels during the next eleven years. Often set in Australia, his fast-paced thrillers were very popular and generally contained elements of crime and mystery.

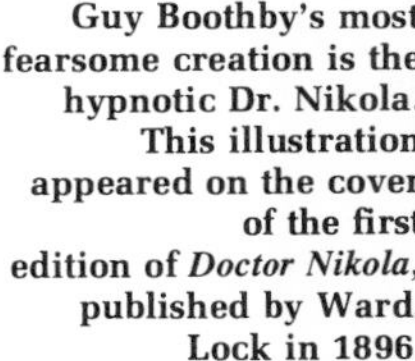
Guy Boothby's most fearsome creation is the hypnotic Dr. Nikola. This illustration appeared on the cover of the first edition of *Doctor Nikola*, published by Ward, Lock in 1896.

His best-known character is Dr. Nikola, the sinister, ruthless central figure of five novels: *A Bid for Fortune, or Dr. Nikola's Vendetta* (1895), *Doctor Nikola* (1896), *The Lust of Hate* (1898), *Dr. Nikola's Experiment* (1899), and *'Farewell, Nikola'* (1901). Accompanied by his large black cat, the unscrupulous mastermind pays well for assistance when he requires it, but he demands absolute loyalty. "I demand from you your whole and entire labour," he tells three associates at the outset of one adventure. "While you are serving me you are mine body and soul."

Among other Boothby works are *A Prince of Swindlers* (1897), featuring Simon Carne, one of the first gentleman crooks in literature, preceding A. J. RAFFLES by two years and Colonel CLAY by two months; and *My Strangest Case* (1902).

BOSTON, CHARLES K. *See* GRUBER, FRANK.

BOSTON BLACKIE (Creator: Jack Boyle). In his foreword to *Boston Blackie* (1919), the only book about the ex-convict and cracksman, Boyle wrote: "To the police and the world, he is a professional crook, a skilled and daring safecracker, an incorrigible criminal made doubly dangerous by intellect. But to me, 'Blackie' is something more—a man with more than a spark of the Divine Spirit that lies hidden somewhere in the heart of even the worst of men. University graduate, scholar, and gentleman, the 'Blackie' I know is a man of many inconsistencies and a strangely twisted code of morals." Blackie does not consider himself a criminal; he is a combatant who has declared war on society. He is married to a pretty girl named Mary, his "best loved pal and sole confidant," who knows what he does and joins in his exploits. Oddly, Blackie lives in San Francisco; Boston has nothing to do with the stories.

Most of Boston Blackie's fame came from motion pictures, radio, and television. This book, published by H. K. Fly in 1919, is the only one devoted to his adventures.

Films

The lighthearted former criminal has often been revived on the screen. His earliest appearances, in silent days, were frequently serious dramas of crime, prison, and reform.

In both *Boston Blackie's Little Pal* (1918) and *Blackie's Redemption* (1919), prison doors swing open for a pardoned Blackie, played by Bert Lytell. *The Face in the Fog* (Paramount, 1922) featured Lionel Barrymore as a wily Blackie who uses his skills to help a Russian princess, escaped from the Bolsheviks, to recover some crown jewels and also find romance with an emigrant prince. Also in that year, in *Missing Millions* (Realart), David Powell as Blackie joins with Alice Brady to rob a ship's strongbox in an act of vengeance against a hardhearted Wall Street broker who had unjustly sent the girl's father to prison. William Russell in 1923 starred as *Boston Blackie* (Fox) in a rather emotional reworking of the basic story: a convict swears to go straight after serving his prison term so that he can expose a cruel warden. Contemporary reviews called the drama both thrilling and depressing. The next year, in *Through the Dark* (Goldwyn), Blackie, now played by Forrest Stanley, is again in prison but is forced by the warden's cruelty to escape. He is aided by a young schoolgirl (Colleen Moore). Her pure love induces him to surrender, and a brave deed earns him a pardon. *The Return of Boston Blackie* (First Division, 1927), with Raymond Glenn in the title role, was another essay in rehabilitation.

For some years thereafter, through the Depression, Blackie remained inactive. Then, in 1941, Columbia revived the character and featured Chester Morris as an energetic, snappy Blackie, not so much concerned with agonizing self-reform as with utilizing his specialties just outside the law in order to better serve the cause of justice. He nearly always must elude the watchful eye of Inspector Faraday (Richard Lane), who has never been able to believe that Blackie has been rehabilitated. True, perhaps, to his prison background, Blackie has no steady girl, no permanent residence, few close friends aside from the eccentric middle-aged playboy dabbler in art Arthur Manleder (Lloyd Corrigan) and a worshipful former fellow convict appropriately named Runt (George E. Stone). As in Boyle's book, Boston is not mentioned in any of the fourteen films; Blackie could have come from anywhere.

Meet Boston Blackie. Columbia, 1941. Morris, Rochelle Hudson, Lane, Charles Wagenheim (playing Runt in this film only). Directed by Robert Florey.

A girl Blackie is tailing is shot to death on a Coney Island boardwalk. The setting allows Blackie to demonstrate his skill in legerdemain and con games.

Chester Morris (center) in a tense moment from *Meet Boston Blackie*. [*Columbia*]

Confessions of Boston Blackie. Columbia, 1941. Morris, Harriet Hilliard, Lane, Corrigan, Stone. Directed by Edward Dmytryk.

The body of a crooked art dealer is found inside the counterfeit replica of a priceless statue.

Alias Boston Blackie. Columbia, 1942. Morris, Adele Mara, Lane, Stone, Corrigan. Directed by Lew Landers.

While Blackie puts on a magic show for the inmates of the state prison, a young convict escapes, vowing revenge on the gangster who framed him.

Boston Blackie Goes Hollywood. Columbia, 1942. Morris, Lane, Stone, Corrigan, Forrest Tucker, Constance Worth. Directed by Michael Gordon.

Blackie arrives in Los Angeles at the request of hapless Arthur Manleder, who has let a pretty girl charm him out of the fabled Monterey diamond.

After Midnight with Boston Blackie. Columbia, 1943. Morris, Lane, Stone, Cy Kendall, Ann Savage. Directed by Landers.

A girl pleads with Blackie to help find her father, who she fears has been kidnapped by gangsters, along with his priceless diamonds.

The Chance of a Lifetime. Columbia, 1943. Morris, Lane, Stone, Corrigan, Jeanne Bates, Erik Rolf, Douglas Fowley. Directed by William Castle.

Blackie suggests to the Governor that prison labor be used in war plants to alleviate the wartime manpower shortage. A model convict soon makes an escape, however, and is found standing over the body of a gangster. Blackie believes him to be innocent, confesses to the murder himself, and eludes the police while he looks for the real killer.

One Mysterious Night. Columbia, 1944. Morris, Lane, Janis Carter, Stone. Directed by Oscar Boetticher, Jr.

A clerk has stolen the Blue Star of the Nile diamond from an exclusive hotel, but before Blackie can recover it, the thief is shot.

Boston Blackie Booked on Suspicion. Columbia, 1945. Morris, Lynn Merrick, Lane, Steve Cochran, Stone. Directed by Arthur Dreifuss.

Arthur Manleder asks Blackie to help him dispose of a rare first edition of Charles DICKENS's *Pickwick Papers*, which turns out to be counterfeit.

Boston Blackie's Rendezvous. Columbia, 1945. Morris, Nina Foch, Cochran, Lane, Stone. Directed by Dreifuss.

A homicidal maniac escapes from an institution, determined to find a girl whose picture he has seen in a newspaper, and leaves a trail of murdered women.

A Close Call for Boston Blackie. Columbia, 1946. Morris, Merrick, Lane, Stone. Directed by Landers.

Blackie tries to help a girl flee from her husband, a former convict, who has threatened her—and discovers that he is about to be framed for murder.

Money appears as if out of the air as turbaned magician Blackie (Chester Morris) performs before a prison audience in *Boston Blackie and the Law*. [*Columbia*]

The Phantom Thief. Columbia, 1946. Morris, Jeff Donnell, Lane, Dusty Anderson, Stone. Directed by D. Ross Lederman.

When a duped wife begs Blackie to recover the jewels she has paid as blackmail to a shady spiritualist, Dr. Nejino, several murders occur.

Boston Blackie and the Law. Columbia, 1946. Morris, Trudy Marshall, Constance Dowling, Lane, Stone. Directed by Lederman.

A woman convict escapes while Blackie is staging another prison show. Years before, she and her husband, the magician Lampau, had been involved in an unsolved robbery; later, Blackie finds them both murdered.

Trapped by Boston Blackie. Columbia, 1948. Morris, June Vincent, Lane, Patricia White, Stone. Directed by Seymour Friedman.

At a fashionable party the hostess's pearls are stolen—and Blackie finds them in his pocket.

Boston Blackie's Chinese Venture. Columbia, 1949. Morris, Lane, Maylia, Joan Woodbury, Sid Tomack (playing Runt in this film only). Directed by Friedman.

A Dutch diamond expert is sought by Blackie in a case of murder in Chinatown.

Radio and Television

"Friend to those who have no friends; enemy to those who make him an enemy" was the introduction to Blackie's radio adventures (he was portrayed first by Chester Morris and then by Richard Kollmar), in which each week he was either clearing himself of charges of jewel theft or spreading the gospel of reform among underworld cronies. The *Boston Blackie* radio show was an outgrowth of the film series. On television in the early 1950s Kent Taylor starred as *Boston Blackie.* He acquired a girl friend, Lois Collier (radio had introduced her), but his battle against the distrusting Faraday (Frank Orth) was unceasing.

BOUCHER, ANTHONY (pseudonym of William Anthony Parker White; 1911–1968). American critic, detective story and science fiction writer, editor, and anthologist. Born into a family with backgrounds in medicine, law, and the Navy, Boucher originally wanted to become an admiral, but while he was attending Pasadena High School, he decided to be a physicist. Later, at Pasadena Junior College, he again changed his mind and studied linguistics, his goal being to teach languages. He received a bachelor's degree from the University of Southern California in 1932 and a master's degree in German from the University of California in 1934, at which time he was elected to Phi Beta Kappa.

He later became sufficiently proficient in French, Spanish, and Portuguese to translate mystery stories from those languages into English, but after spending much time in acting, writing, and directing in the little theater movement while at school, he decided to become a playwright. He was unsuccessful but did manage to gain employment as theater editor of the *United Progressive News* in Los Angeles (1935–1937). He wrote a mystery novel in 1936 and sold it the following year. During the next several years he wrote a mystery novel every year, including two under the pseudonym H. H. Holmes (a famous murderer); later he signed that name to his science fiction reviews for the *Chicago Sun Times* and *The New York Herald Tribune* (1951–1963).

In the late 1930s Boucher became interested in science fiction and fantasy and, in the early 1940s, wrote stories in this genre as well as mysteries for pulp magazines, which were more remunerative than books were. After spending the years from 1942 to 1947 as a book reviewer specializing in science fiction and mysteries for the *San Francisco Chronicle,* he reviewed mysteries for *Ellery Queen's Mystery Magazine (EQMM)* for sixteen months. While employed by the *Chronicle,* he edited the anthology *Great American Detective Stories* (1945). In 1949 he cofounded and became coeditor of *The Magazine of Fantasy and Science Fiction.* He later returned to review books for *EQMM* for eleven years (1957–1968).

In 1951 Boucher began writing the "Criminals at Large" column for *The New York Times Book*

Review. He continued in this position until his death and contributed 852 columns. His mystery criticism brought him Edgar awards for 1945, 1949, and 1952 from the Mystery Writers of America (MWA).

Boucher was married, had two sons, and lived in Berkeley, Calif. His interests included Sherlock HOLMES, theological speculation, party politics, cooking, poker, cats, opera (he once conducted a radio series, *Golden Voices,* in which he played recordings and discussed opera), football, basketball, true crime (he edited *The Pocket Book of True Crime Stories,* 1943, and *True Crime Detective* magazine), and collecting old records. He was a member of MWA, which he served as national president in 1951.

Boucher (rhymes with "voucher") died of lung cancer in 1968. On learning of his death, Frederic Dannay said, "In his chosen field Tony was a Renaissance man, a complete man—writer, critic and historian. He was conscientious and a fine craftsman." *See* QUEEN, ELLERY (author).

Although Boucher's status as a critic overshadowed his reputation as a writer, his talent for inventing entertaining and well-plotted puzzles established him as one of the leading mystery writers of the late 1930s and early 1940s.

His first novel, *The Case of the Seven of Calvary* (1937), features Dr. John Ashwin, professor of Sanskrit, who acts as an armchair detective when a series of bizarre murders are committed in an academic setting, with the only clue the baffling and obscure symbol referred to in the title.

In addition to publishing four novels about Fergus O'BREEN, Boucher wrote two novels as H. H. Holmes. *Nine Times Nine* (1940), his best work, is a locked-room problem (*see* LOCKED-ROOM MYSTERIES) set against the background of a weird Los Angeles cult called the Temple of Light. It was dedicated to John Dickson CARR and solved by Lieutenant Marshall of the Los Angeles Police Department and Sister Ursula of the Sisters of Martha of Bethany. The next Holmes effort, with the same investigating team, was *Rocket to the Morgue* (1942). Its main interest is its setting among science fiction writers and fans; Boucher himself appeared in a minor role.

Much of Boucher's subsequent short fiction was of the science fiction–fantasy variety, but he occasionally published notable detective stories in *EQMM.* His Nick Noble series—written mainly in the 1940s—concerns a disgraced former policeman turned wino who sits in a cheap bar drinking sherry and trying to shoo an imaginary fly away from the tip of his nose while solving baffling crime problems brought to him by a policeman friend.

Boucher once wrote: "Good detective stories are, as I have often quoted Hamlet's phrase about the players, 'the abstracts and brief chronicles of the time,' ever valuable in retrospect as indirect but vivid pictures of the society from which they spring."

Radio

Boucher was one of the scriptwriters for the popular radio mystery series *The Case Book of Gregory Hood* and, from 1945 to 1947, wrote at least three half-hour shows each week for radio, producing many Sherlock Holmes scripts.

BOURNE, PETER. *See* GRAEME, BRUCE.

BOX, EDGAR (pseudonym of Gore Vidal; 1925–). American novelist, essayist, social, literary, and political critic, and television personality. Educated at Phillips Exeter Academy in New Hampshire, he served in the Army from 1943 to 1946. In 1960 he made an unsuccessful attempt to run for Congress. He became a member of President John F. Kennedy's Council of the Arts in 1961 and served until 1963.

Among Vidal's novels are *Williwaw* (1946), *The City and the Pillar* (1948), *The Judgment of Paris* (1952), the notorious *Myra Breckinridge* (1968), and the controversial *Burr* (1973). He has also written plays, for example, *Visit to a Small Planet* (1957) and *The Best Man* (1960), and screenplays, for the films *Suddenly, Last Summer* (1960; in collaboration with Tennessee Williams) and *The Best Man* (1964). Vidal currently resides in Italy.

In 1952 Vidal adopted the pseudonym Edgar Box and dashed off three detective novels without knowing very much about the intricate and demanding form. As detective stories, they are negligible, but Vidal compensates for his shortcomings by means of his talent as a writer and satirist, and his works are highly entertaining.

His series detective is Peter Cutler Sargeant II, a public relations specialist, former soldier, and Harvard graduate who spent several years ghostwriting for a drama critic on a newspaper before entering his current profession.

In *Death in the Fifth Position* (1952) Peter is employed by a Russian ballet company that is being picketed by a right-wing veterans' organization. On opening night, his problems are compounded when the prima ballerina falls to her death and foul play is suspected. *Death before Bedtime* (1953) concerns an ultra-right-wing senator who has presidential aspirations and is killed when a charge of gunpowder placed in his fireplace explodes. The Washington setting provides Box with a field day for his satiric thrusts. *Death Likes It Hot* (1954) revolves around a weekend party (in Long Island's exclusive Hamptons area) that includes a varied guest list and the unscheduled drowning of one of the participants.

Death before Bedtime and *Death Likes It Hot* served as the basis for two episodes in the Ellery

QUEEN (detective) television series starring George Nader in the late 1950s. The Box novels have been translated into a dozen languages and have been reprinted several times in the United States with no mention of the author's identity.

BOYLE, JACK. *See* BOSTON BLACKIE.

BRADDON, M[ARY] E[LIZABETH] (MAXWELL) (1837–1915). English novelist. Born in London, she was privately educated and later married John Maxwell, a publisher. Her first published book, *Lady Audley's Secret* (1862), was one of the most popular novels of the nineteenth century. Although some critics now regard it as the poorest of her more than eighty books, it contains the elements of crime, romance, and melodrama that characterize all her work. The three-volume first edition of *Lady Audley's Secret* is one of the great rarities of Victorian fiction, and many of her subsequent novels, also published in double- and triple-decker format, are almost as difficult to find in original bindings. Even the splendid collection of Victorian detective fiction assembled by Graham GREENE and Dorothy Glover contains only seven genuine first editions of Miss Braddon's novels. Those listed in the catalog of the collection are *Eleanor's Victory* (1863), with Gilbert Monckton as detective; *Lucius Davoren or Publicans and Sinners* (1873), with surgeon Lucius Davoren as detective; *The Cloven Foot* (1879), with surgeon George Gerrard as detective; *Wyllard's Weird* (1885), with Edward Heathcote as detective; *Thou Art the Man* (1894), with lady's companion Coralie Urquhart as detective; *Rough Justice* (1898), with Mr. Faunce of CID Bow Street as detective; and *His Darling Sin* (1899), also with Mr. Faunce. Many of Miss Braddon's works were published anonymously or pseudonymously under the name Babington White.

BRAMAH, ERNEST (pseudonym of Ernest Bramah Smith; 1868–1942). English author, creator of Max CARRADOS, the first blind fictional detective, and Kai Lung, a Chinese storyteller.

Extremely reticent, Bramah refused to divulge any details of his life. Born in a Manchester suburb as Ernest Brammah Smith (his mother's maiden name had two *m*'s), he dropped out of high school and tried farming as a profession, giving it up after losing money for three years. The experience supplied material for his first book, *English Farming and Why I Turned It Up* (1894). He switched to journalism, starting as a correspondent on a provincial newspaper, and then went to London as Jerome K. Jerome's secretary, later joining the editorial staff of Jerome's periodical, *To-day*. He soon left to edit a new publication, *The Minster;* but when it folded, he devoted his full time to writing for leading magazines. Two of his one-act plays are often produced in London. An expert numismatist, he wrote a scholarly book on the subject and used the field in a Max Carrados mystery, "The Mystery of the Vanished Petition Crown" (1927). The setting of Bramah's first book of fiction, *The Wallet of Kai Lung* (1900), is so realistic that it was believed that he had spent several years in the East (the investigations of William White have proved that he did not do so). Nevertheless, the delectably ironic mock Chinese idiom in the *Wallet* and his other Kai Lung books is usually considered his greatest achievement. In *Kai Lung's Golden Hours* (1922), the itinerant teller of tales has been accused of many crimes. In the manner of the narrator of the *Arabian Nights,* he tells fantastic tales to the judge, postponing the verdict.

Bramah's desire for privacy resulted in a long-held belief by the public that he did not exist, that he was, in fact, a well-known literary figure employing a pseudonym or, according to another myth, that he was a hoax, fabricated by several English detective story writers. To refute these rumors, Bramah wrote, in the preface to *The Specimen Case* (1924), "Either I am to have no existence, or I am to have decidedly too much: on the one hand banished into space as a mythical creation; on the other regarded askance as the leader of a double (literary) life." Photographs of Bramah show a slender, balding man with twinkling black eyes, more reminiscent of a butler or clergyman than the author of humorous tales and criminal narratives.

Ernest Bramah's stories of Kai Lung were as popular in the United States as in Great Britain. On the left is the front cover of an American gift edition of *The Wallet of Kai Lung,* published by Doran; on the right is the first-edition dust wrapper of *Kai Lung Unrolls His Mat,* published by Richards in 1928.

BRANCH, PAMELA (JEAN) (1920–1967). English mystery writer. Born on a tea plantation in Ceylon, she was educated in England at various schools along the southern coast and then went to Paris to study art. She returned to England, studied at the Royal Academy of Dramatic Art in London, and then moved to Kashmir to live on a houseboat.

Miss Branch's work is not intended for a wide audience, and many purists object to her irreverent mixture of mystery and farce. Her best works are her early ones—*The Wooden Overcoat* (1951) and *The Lion in the Cellar* (1951). Both ask the question "Where has the body gone to now?" They are somewhat like Alfred HITCHCOCK's film *The Trouble with Harry* (1955), in which a corpse keeps appearing and disappearing, but the presentation is less subtle.

BRAND, CHRISTIANNA (pseudonym of Mary Christianna [Milne] Lewis; 1907–). English detective fiction writer. Born in Malaya, she lived there and in India until she went to England to attend a convent school. After her father lost all his money, she left school to support herself at the age of seventeen, working as a governess, dress packer, receptionist in a plush nightclub, professional ballroom dancer, model in Bond Street dress shops, and secretary. She also ran a club for working girls, demonstrated gadgets at trade fairs, and worked as an interior decorator. During this ten-year period, she was "always broke and often hungry."

While working as a salesgirl, she grew to dread a fellow worker. In the intervals between selling pots and pans, she wrote the first chapters of *Death in High Heels* (1941)—to take revenge on her colleague. She left the job to marry a surgeon and later completed the book. Although she had never before written a word for publication, the novel was critically acclaimed at once.

She continued to write detective novels for fourteen years and then abandoned the form to write shorter mystery fiction. *The Three-cornered Halo* (1957) is a fantasy about an imaginary island. *Starrbelow* (1958) is an eighteenth-century mystery story published under the pseudonym China Thompson. *Heaven Knows Who* (1960) is a nonfictional account of a murder in Scotland a hundred years ago—the case of Jessie M'Lachlan. *Court of Foxes* (1969), set in Wales, is a romantic adventure about highwaymen.

Miss Brand has written many crime and horror short stories, some of which have appeared in *Ellery Queen's Mystery Magazine*. Two stories won awards from the Mystery Writers of America (MWA); one was runner-up in the MWA best short story of the year contest. Her short stories have been collected in *What Dread Hand?* (1968) and *Brand X* (1974).

Although her best mysteries feature Inspector COCKRILL of the Kent County Police, mysteries in which he does not appear have some merit. *Death in High Heels*, about murder among young ladies employed in a fashionable London dress shop, presents an evocative and accurate picture of the manners and modes of this kind of milieu. *Cat and Mouse* (1950) was chosen by Julian SYMONS for inclusion in his collection *The Hundred Best Crime Stories* (1959). Set in the rain-swept mountains of Wales, this melodrama is reminiscent of Ann RADCLIFFE's *The Mysteries of Udolpho* (1794) and similar eighteenth-century Gothic novels. A girl who has been writing to a woman's magazine suddenly finds herself involved in a terrifying situation—made no less terrifying because the author is writing tongue-in-cheek.

"You have to reach for the greatest of the Great Names (Agatha CHRISTIE, John Dickson CARR, Ellery QUEEN [author] . . .)," wrote Anthony BOUCHER, "to find Brand's rivals in the subtleties of the trade: the precise knowledge of how to plant a clue so that it is completely fair and apparently meaningless, the ability to construct an entire series of legitimate false clues to lead the over-confident reader up the garden path, the power to produce an astonishing Least Suspected Person whose guilt is as convincing as it is surprising. . . ."

Miss Brand lives in London with her husband and daughter Victoria (Tora), named after her first heroine.

BRAND, MAX. *See* FAUST, FREDERICK.

BRANDT, TOM. *See* DEWEY, THOMAS B.

BRANSON, H[ENRY] C. American detective story writer. In addition to *Salisbury Plain* (1965), a Civil War novel, Branson wrote a series of seven straightforward, unsensational, and intricate mysteries. His series detective is bearded and genial John Bent, a former doctor turned private investigator who is based in New York and smokes constantly and drinks bourbon as he investigates subtly conceived crime puzzles.

Bent's first case, *I'll Eat You Last* (1941), starts with a suspicious drowning in a small lakeside community; more fatalities occur as a killer seeks to possess a $50 million estate. In *The Pricking Thumb* (1942) a conference with a publisher sends Bent on a trip of 100 miles to a large country estate in a small town—and three murders. In *The Fearful Passage* (1945) Bent travels to a little town in upstate New York as the result of an anonymous phone call. He finds that a famous art critic and historian has been murdered. The victim's lovely young wife is in love with a young man who is a logical suspect, but everyone seems to want to protect him.

The Leaden Bubble (1949) starts with the

acquittal of a young man who was suspected by all of murdering his wife; then two more murders take place. The atmosphere of the small town—plagued by steady rain—is well defined. Bent's last recorded investigation, *Beggar's Choice* (1953), begins when a wealthy old man, suffering from a serious heart condition, dies, presumably from natural causes. The family doctor, however, suspects that his patient has been suffocated and refuses to sign the death certificate. He accuses the man's niece, who is also his heir.

Bent's other cases are *The Case of the Giant Killer* (1944) and *Last Year's Blood* (1947).

BREAN, HERBERT (1907–1973). American author, editor, and detective story writer. Born in Detroit, he was educated at the University of Michigan, where he received a B.A. degree in 1929. He married Dorothy Skeman in 1934; they had two daughters.

Brean started as a reporter and assistant bureau manager for United Press and later became a columnist, feature writer, assistant city editor, and picture editor for the *Detroit Times*. He worked for *Time*, *Life*, and *Fortune* in Detroit and became an assistant editor at *Life* in 1944; in the mid-1950s he specialized in national affairs.

He wrote *The Only Diet That Works* (1963); the best-selling *How to Stop Smoking* (1951), which sold 50,000 copies; *How to Stop Drinking* (1958); and edited *The Mystery Writers' Handbook* (1958) as well as two volumes on jazz. He lectured on mystery writing at Columbia and New York Universities and also for the Mystery Writers of America, which he served as president in 1967. Brean lived in New York City and the Virgin Islands. His interests were Dixieland jazz, antiques, cats, cooking, and Sherlock HOLMES.

Although Brean wrote only seven detective novels, most are of more than ordinary interest. His series detective, Reynold Frame, a normal and pleasant young man, is a free-lance writer and photographer. *Wilders Walk Away* (1948) is set in a small town in Vermont and concerns the mysterious disappearances, seemingly by supernatural means, of the members of a family. The book is an attractive example of the classic form, not unlike the work of John Dickson CARR. In *The Darker the Night* (1949) a Cleveland lawyer falls from the twenty-sixth floor of his New York City hotel room. Frame investigates to discover whether he has been a victim of suicide or murder.

Frame journeys to Concord, Mass., to get married, but murder, past and present, as well as some Revolutionary War ghosts and a missing manuscript, forces him to turn detective once again in *Hardly a Man Is Now Alive* (1950). Brean's best novel is probably *The Clock Strikes Thirteen* (1952). It is set on an island off the Maine coast and features a murder, a mad scientist, and a deadly bacterium that is a threat to the lives of the island's inhabitants. This effective suspense novel is the last recorded case of Reynold Frame.

A Matter of Fact (1956; British title: *Collar for the Killer*) is about a rookie policeman who becomes innocently involved in a frame-up and then risks his career to see justice done. In this inferior book Brean abandons the classic form for the police procedural novel. *The Traces of Brillhart* (1960) concerns the efforts of a magazine writer to aid a friend who was involuntarily involved in the murder of a musician—who might not be dead after all. Brean's last novel, *The Traces of Merrilee* (1966), concerns an ocean voyage disrupted by a murderer who seeks to prevent a movie actress from making a film.

BREDDER, FATHER JOSEPH (Creator: Leonard HOLTON). Although he is a priest at the Franciscan Convent of the Holy Innocentsin Los Angeles,Father Bredder looks like a truck driver or a construction worker. During World War II he was a sergeant in the Marine Corps and saw action at Guadalcanal. He was once an expert amateur boxer.

Father Bredder has several interests in addition to his calling. He is seldom happier than when he is working in the soil in his convent's garden, and he is especially proud of his roses. He enjoys fishing and sea sports. In *Out of the Depths* (1966), while fishing, he reels in a murdered scuba diver. He competes in a trans-Pacific yacht race in *A Touch of Jonah* (1968).

Bredder has often helped his friend Lieutenant Minardi, a police officer, in solving murders. However, like his coreligionist Father BROWN, he is more concerned with saving souls and securing repentance than he is in catching a killer. This religious theme is apparent in all of Bredder's cases. In the first, *The Saint Maker* (1959), he discovers a severed head in his church. In *The Secret of the Doubting Saint* (1961), he searches for a diamond reputed to have belonged to Thomas the Apostle. Bredder solves a mystery involving werewolves at a medieval castle in Portugal in *Deliver Us from Wolves* (1963). When a famous musician dies while performing with a string quartet, his rare Guarnerius violin is an important clue in *A Problem in Angels* (1970). *The Mirror of Hell* (1972) and *The Devil to Play* (1973) both explore the drug and hippie aspects of "the California scene." The latter involves the murder of a Los Angeles baseball player.

The other novels in the Bredder series are *A Pact with Satan* (1960) and *Flowers by Request* (1964).

BREEN, JON L. (1943–). American author. Although he was born in Alabama, Breen was educated in California, where he received a B.A. degree from Pepperdine College and an M.S. degree in library science from the University of Southern California. Following two years of service in the Army (including one year in Vietnam), he returned to library work and became head reference librarian at California State College in Dominguez Hills. In May 1970 he married Rita Gunson of Yorkshire, England.

A scholar of the mystery story, Breen has written articles about writers Anthony ABBOT, Lee THAYER, and Carolyn WELLS. He compiled *The Girl in the Pictorial Wrapper* (1972), an index to *The New York Times*'s reviews of original paperback novels. He has also written many humorous short stories for *Ellery Queen's Mystery Magazine*, parodying the works of S. S. VAN DINE, Ellery QUEEN (author), and John Dickson CARR, among others, and a series of sports mysteries, including "The Babe Ruth Murder Case" (1972), in which the detective is Ed Gorgon, a baseball umpire.

BRENNAN, JOSEPH PAYNE (1918–). American poet, short story writer, and librarian at Yale University. Most of Brennan's tales deal with the weird and the supernatural. His best-known character, Lucius Leffing, a private detective and psychic investigator, is a quaint old-fashioned man who fervently wishes that he had lived during Victorian times. Leffing lives in an ancient gaslit house at 7 Autumn Street in New Haven, Conn., where he consumes huge quantities of sarsaparilla. Brennan himself is Leffing's faithful companion and the chronicler of his exploits, seventeen of which were collected in *The Casebook of Lucius Leffing* (1973).

This grim dust wrapper was illustrated by Neal Macdonald for the first edition of Joseph Payne Brennan's short story collection, published in 1973 by Macabre House of New Haven, Conn.

BRINEY, ROBERT E. See ORGANIZATIONS; ORIENTALS, SINISTER.

BRISTOW, GWEN (1903–). American author of historical novels and mysteries. Born in Marion, S.C., Miss Bristow attended Judson College in Alabama and the Columbia School of Journalism in New York. She was a reporter on the *New Orleans Times-Picayune* from 1925 to 1933; in 1929 she married Bruce Manning, a reporter for the rival *New Orleans Item*. The Mannings wrote four mysteries together in New Orleans before they moved to Beverly Hills, Calif., and Manning became a film writer and producer. Two such works are *The Invisible Host* (1930) and *The Mardi Gras Murders* (1932), set in New Orleans. Miss Bristow has also published, under her own name, a trilogy of historical novels set in Louisiana: *Deep Summer* (1937), *The Handsome Road* (1938), and *This Side of Glory* (1940).

The Invisible Host was dramatized by Owen Davis in 1930 as *The Ninth Guest* and was later filmed.

BROCK, LYNN (pseudonym of Alister McAllister; 1877–1943). Irish playwright, novelist, and short story and mystery writer. Born in Dublin, McAllister served during World War I in British Intelligence and the machine gun corps. Under the pseudonym Anthony Wharton he wrote eight plays beginning with *Irene Wycherley* (1908). He also wrote numerous short stories and five novels, the first of which was *Joan of Over Barrow* (1922).

As Lynn Brock, McAllister is known for a series of mysteries about Colonel Gore. Although Jacques BARZUN and Wendell Hertig TAYLOR consider many of these books dull, they have praised *The Deductions of Colonel Gore* (1924) and *Colonel Gore's Second Case* (1926), calling the latter "a tale of incredible complexity."

BRONSON-HOWARD, GEORGE (FITZALAN) (1884–1922). American journalist, playwright, novelist, and short story writer. Born in Maryland, Bronson-Howard wrote several espionage novels and three collections of stories about Yorke Norroy, secret agent of the Department of State: *Norroy, Diplomatic Agent* (1907), *Slaves of the Lamp* (1917), and *The Black Book* (1920).

BROOKS, EDWY SEARLES (1889–1965). Prolific English author of thrillers and boys' books. Born in Hackney, London, the son of a minister, he wrote his first story while still a schoolboy. He went on to write thousands of books for several series, including the Nelson Lee Library (for which he produced 18 million words—900 stories—in 16 years). He created one of the most popular characters in the Sexton BLAKE series, Waldo the Wonderman. Seventy-six Blake adventures in the *Union Jack* (28,000 words each) were written by Brooks. He also wrote approximately sixty adult crime novels, more than forty under the pseudonym Victor Gunn. It has been estimated that Brooks published more than 36 million words during his lifetime.

Shortly before World War II, using the pseudonym Berkeley Gray, Brooks created Norman Conquest. The indomitable "1066" is a laughing desperado in the same tradition as the Saint (*see* SAINT, THE), the Toff (*see* TOFF, THE), and Bulldog DRUMMOND. He has a beautiful girl friend, Joy Everard, and lots of gimmicky devices to help him get out of tight places. The first Conquest book is *Mr. Mortimer Gets the Jitters* (1938); the last of the fifty titles, *Conquest in Ireland* (1969), was completed by Brooks's widow.

BROWN, CHARLES BROCKDEN (1771–1810). American novelist and editor. Brown is regarded as the first professional American novelist to rely solely on his literary efforts to earn a living (he failed after less than a decade). He was also the first writer to use the American Indian as a character in a work of fiction. He is chiefly remembered today for six novels, all of which are powerful Gothic romances of terror and suspense that are unusual in that they deal with human psychoses rather than the supernatural.

Much of Brown's work draws heavily on William GODWIN's *Caleb Williams* (1794), in particular, incidents and plot devices in *Ormond: or, The Secret Witness* (1799) and *Edgar Huntley: or, Memoirs of a Sleep-Walker* (1799). *Wieland: or, The Transformation* (1798), generally regarded as the first American Gothic novel, tells about a man driven to murder by a voice that he believes comes from God but is actually the work of a ventriloquist. *Arthur Mervyn: or, Memoirs of the Year 1793* (1799–1800) is about a young man who becomes involved with a criminal but later extricates himself. It effectively describes the yellow fever epidemic in Philadelphia in 1793. There is less mystery and detective interest in Brown's other two major novels, *Clara Howard: In a Series of Letters* (1801) and *Jane Talbot* (1801). All these books were published anonymously.

BROWN, FATHER (Creator: G. K. CHESTERTON). Called one of the three greatest detectives in literature (with C. Auguste DUPIN and Sherlock HOLMES) by Ellery QUEEN (author), Father Brown is a quiet, gentle, commonplace Roman Catholic priest who views wrongdoers as souls needing salvation, not criminals to be brought to justice.

He has a face "as round and dull as a Norfolk dumpling . . . eyes as empty as the North Sea . . . several brown parcels which he was incapable of collecting . . . a large shabby umbrella which constantly fell to the floor." He is even given the "harmless, human name of Brown."

Father Brown, as portrayed by Noel Syers on the dust wrapper of the first edition of *The Scandal of Father Brown*, published in London by Cassell in 1935.

He appears dull-witted before his adversaries but possesses a sharp, subtle, sensitive mind. There is no police procedure in Father Brown's life; the police, in fact, often make no appearance at all, since his sympathies lie with the criminals and he frequently allows them to go free in the hope that they will repent and reform. The kindly priest does not rely on cold logic and accumulated clues to catch his man. He uses a psychological approach, aided by his deep understanding of human nature.

Father Brown explains his method this way: "I try to get inside a man, moving his arms and legs; but I wait till I know I'm inside a murderer, thinking his thoughts, wrestling with his passions; till I have bent myself into the posture of his hunched and peering hatred. Till I am really a murderer. And when I am quite sure that I feel like the murderer, of course I know who he is."

His greatest success comes with Flambeau, who first appears as an adversary. A colossus of crime, a Frenchman of gigantic stature, incredible strength, and blazing intelligence, and a master of disguise, he is the most famous thief in Europe until he matches wits with Father Brown in "The Blue Cross" (1911). Bested, he reforms and begins his private detective agency under the priest's guidance. Flambeau's constant nemesis during his criminal days was Aristide Valentin, chief of the Paris police, an eccentric Frenchman whose success seems magical but is merely the result of "plodding logic."

Father Brown's first name remains a mystery. It is obliquely mentioned but twice in the fifty-one stories in which he appears: in "The Sign of the Broken Sword" (1911) he is referred to as "Paul"; in "The Eye of Apollo" (1911), as "the Reverend J. Brown, attached to St. Francis Xavier Church, Camberwell."

The Father Brown stories are uniformly good-humored and nonviolent, despite an abundance of

Walter Connolly as the mystery-solving priest listens to some sharp-tongued advice from Una O'Connor in a scene from *Father Brown, Detective*. [*Paramount*]

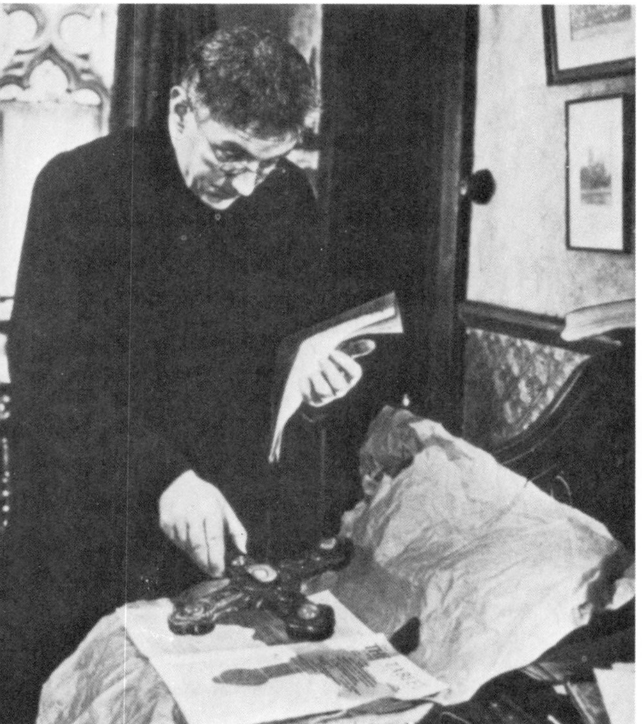

Alec Guinness, as Chesterton's eccentric prelate, must prevent the theft of a valuable jeweled cross in the film *Father Brown* (called *The Detective* in the United States). [*Columbia*]

corpses. The later tales have less and less detection, serving largely as springboards for Chesterton's religious philosophy.

The good-hearted little Essex clergyman was patterned after Father John O'Connor, a real-life priest whom Chesterton knew.

CHECKLIST

1911 *The Innocence of Father Brown* (s.s.)
1914 *The Wisdom of Father Brown* (s.s.)
1926 *The Incredulity of Father Brown* (s.s.)
1927 *The Secret of Father Brown* (s.s.)
1935 *The Scandal of Father Brown* (s.s.)
1951 *The Father Brown Omnibus* (contains all fifty-one stories, including "The Vampire of the Village," first published in book form in *Twentieth Century Detective Stories*, edited by Ellery Queen, 1948)

Films

Father Brown has appeared in films made in several countries; for example, Heinz Rühmann portrayed him in two German melodramas in the 1960s. Also, Kenneth More starred as the priest in a British television series in 1973.

Father Brown, Detective. Paramount, 1934. Walter Connolly, Paul Lukas, Gertrude Michael, Halliwell Hobbes. Directed by Edward Sedgwick.

A village priest attempts to rehabilitate a master jewel thief (Lukas) who has given him advance warning that he will steal a diamond-encrusted cross from the church.

Father Brown (U.S. release title: *The Detective*). Columbia (British), 1954. Alec Guinness, Joan Greenwood, Peter Finch, Cecil Parker, Bernard Lee, Sidney James, Ernest Thesiger. Directed by Robert Hamer.

Impish Father Brown, who returns goods stolen by light-fingered converts, crosses the English Channel to foil the theft of a sacred cross by a master criminal (Finch) disguised as a priest, and to reform him.

BROWN, FREDRIC (1906–1972). American mystery novelist and author of short stories. Born in Cincinnati, Ohio, Brown attended the University of Cincinnati and Hanover College in Indiana but never received a degree. He worked in an office from 1924 to 1936, when he left to become a proofreader and writer for the *Milwaukee Journal*. He also began writing fiction and in 1936 sold the first of more than 300 published short stories. Because of a chronic respiratory condition, he left the Midwest to live in Taos, N.Mex., and then Tucson, Ariz. He lived briefly in Los Angeles and wrote scripts for Alfred HITCHCOCK's television programs, but health considerations caused him to return to Tucson, where he settled permanently.

Fredric Brown's countless science fiction short

The shadow of a statuette of a screaming woman causes anxiety to dancer Anita Ekberg, as Phil Carey comforts her, in the film version of Fredric Brown's *The Screaming Mimi*. [*Columbia*]

stories as well as five popular novels, including *What Mad Universe* (1949) and *Martians, Go Home* (1955), give evidence of his vivid imagination. He wrote an autobiographical novel, *The Office* (1958), based upon his experiences on his first job and the people who work in his office. One of them is driven to murder.

Brown published his first mystery novel, *The Fabulous Clipjoint* (1947), after more than a decade of part-time fiction writing. It was a success, winning the Mystery Writers of America Edgar as best first novel, and permitted the author to devote full time to writing. It also introduced the nephew-uncle detective team of Ed and Am HUNTER, who appeared in six subsequent mysteries. One of them, *The Dead Ringer* (1948), and a later book not about the Hunters, *Madball* (1953), are set in a touring carnival and are based on Brown's personal experience. *Night of the Jabberwock* (1950) utilizes his newspaper background. Most of his later books are set in the Southwest and effectively portray its climate and customs; *The Far Cry* (1951) takes place in Taos, and *The Lenient Beast* (1956) and *One for the Road* (1958) are set in Arizona. *The Lenient Beast* was among Brown's most highly praised books, critics commenting with approval on his portrayal of the psychology of the aberrant as well as his handling of the problems facing a Mexican-American detective in Tucson.

CHECKLIST

Mysteries not about Ed and Am Hunter.

1948 *Murder Can Be Fun*
1949 *The Screaming Mimi*
1950 "The Case of the Dancing Sandwiches"
1950 *Here Comes a Candle*
1950 *Night of the Jabberwock*
1951 *The Far Cry*
1952 *The Deep End*
1952 *We All Killed Grandma*
1953 *Madball*
1953 *Mostly Murder* (s.s.)
1954 *His Name Was Death*
1955 *The Wench Is Dead*
1956 *The Lenient Beast*
1958 *One for the Road*
1959 *Knock Three-One-Two*
1961 *The Murderers*
1962 *The Five-Day Nightmare*
1963 *The Shaggy Dog and Other Murders* (s.s.; British title: *The Shaggy Dog and Other Stories*)

Films

Among the works by Brown that have reached the screen, perhaps the most characteristic are the following.

Crack-Up. RKO, 1946. Pat O'Brien, Claire Trevor, Herbert Marshall. Directed by Irving Reis. Based on "Madman's Holiday."

After leaving the site of a train wreck, an art expert forces his way into a museum to discover that a valuable painting is missing. Questioned by the police, he is told that there has been no crash.

The Screaming Mimi. Columbia, 1958. Anita Ekberg, Phil Carey, Gypsy Rose Lee, Harry Townes. Directed by Gerd Oswald.

An exotic dancer, attacked by a maniac, is placed in a mental hospital where she falls under the influence of an obsessed doctor who redirects her career. She is attacked again; this time, the case resembles that of another dancer who was found murdered, a statue of a screaming girl by her side.

BROWN, MORNA DORIS. *See* FERRARS, E. X.

BROWN, ZENITH JONES. *See* FORD, LESLIE.

BROWNE, HOWARD (1908–). American editor, detective fiction novelist, and screenwriter. Born in Omaha, Nebr., Browne worked in Chicago for fifteen years as an editor with Ziff-Davis (Fiction Group), gaining broad experience in pulp science and detective fiction. He left Chicago in 1951, eventually settling in California (1956), where, as a free-lancer, he wrote motion picture and television scripts. By 1973 (when he retired) he had been employed by virtually every major studio and had written more than 100 television plays for series programs ranging from *Playhouse 90* to *Columbo,* and several films, including *Portrait of a Mobster* (1961), with Vic Morrow portraying Dutch Schultz, the famous Prohibition-era gangster, *The St. Valentine's Day Massacre* (1967), with George Segal and Jason Robards, and *Capone* (1975) with Ben Gazzara.

A nonmystery, *Warrior of the Dawn* (1943), the first Browne novel, was followed by *Thin Air* (1953), which concerns the abrupt disappearance of the wife of an advertising executive just as the couple return from a Maine vacation. He summons the police, who suspect him of doing away with her; he mobilizes the members of his agency to help locate his wife. The third Browne novel, *The Taste of Ashes* (1957), features private detective Paul Pine, the hero of three earlier hard-boiled novels signed by John Evans. In *The Taste of Ashes* Pine is summoned by the head of a wealthy family to investigate some trouble involving her wild daughter. The problem seems to concern blackmail and pornography, but it becomes even more serious when one of Pine's colleagues is murdered.

Pine's first adventure (under the Evans pseudonym) is *Halo in Blood* (1946), in which a quiet funeral is attended by ministers; the story turns violent. In *Halo for Satan* (1948) a bishop hires Pine to find a disappearing visitor who owns an Aramaic manuscript worth $25 million. In *Halo in Brass* (1949) a young girl's aged parents hire Pine to find their daughter; the problem becomes more complicated when the quest leads him to the naked body of a woman with a nylon stocking around her throat. The other Evans mystery, *If You Have Tears* (1947), is an inverted tale in which a bank official falls in love with his new secretary and consequently plans to murder his wife.

Browne is a member of the Writers Guild of America and has been an active member of the Mystery Writers of America on the West Coast for several years.

BROWNING, STERRY. *See* GRIBBLE, LEONARD R.

BRULLS, CHRISTIAN. *See* SIMENON, GEORGES.

BUCHAN, JOHN (1st Baron Tweedsmuir; 1875–1940). Scottish diplomat, publisher, journalist, lawyer, and author of historical works and adventure and espionage fiction, some of which features Richard Hannay and his activities for British Intelligence.

Born in Perth, the son of a minister, Buchan attended Glasgow and Oxford Universities, winning top literary awards, and then studied law in London. He began writing professionally at an early age, publishing his first book, a biography entitled *Sir Quixote of the Moors* (1895), when he was twenty. In 1907 he married Susan Charlotte Grosvenor (they had three sons and a daughter) and the same year became a partner in the publishing firm of Thomas Nelson & Sons, Ltd., discovering E. C. BENTLEY's *Trent's Last Case* (1913) and other major works. Interested in journalism, Buchan was for a time the director of the Reuter's news agency. He became a war correspondent in France in 1915, entering military service as director of information in England two years later. Buchan's concurrent careers in business and politics were successful, and he was elected to Parliament as a Conservative in a 1927 landslide. An elder of the Church of Scotland for thirty years, he served as Lord High Commissioner of that church in London in 1933–1934. He was named Governor-General of Canada in 1935 and became 1st Baron Tweedsmuir of Enfield.

Richard Hannay is the adventurer who appears in John Buchan's best-known books. This portrait is on the dust wrapper of *Adventures of Richard Hannay,* a three-volume omnibus published by Houghton Mifflin.

More than half of his prolific literary output was biographical and historical in nature. These books were generally acclaimed for their accuracy and scholarship despite their popular approach. But it is Buchan's fiction that is most remembered today, especially the tales (he called them "shockers") involving Hannay, a heroic figure modeled after one of Buchan's military idols, General Edmund "Tiny" Ironside.

The first book in the series, *The Thirty-nine Steps* (1915), finds Hannay the object of a massive manhunt across the Scottish landscape in the days just preceding World War I—sought both by the police, who believe him to be the murderer of an American agent, and by foreign spies who want to prevent him from delivering vital information to British authorities.

In the sequel, *Greenmantle* (1916), Hannay, now a major in the army, is summoned to the Foreign Office for undercover duty. He must learn the significance of the word "Kasredin," which may be vital in determining whether or not Turkey becomes an ally of the Germans in World War I. With several aides, including the American secret service agent Blenkiron, he searches Germany and Constantinople for the driving force behind a jehad (holy war) said to be organizing in the East.

Peter Pienaar is the central character of *Mr. Standfast* (1919), a tale of counterespionage in which Hannay again works for British Intelligence. When the German villain is finally caught, he is taken into the Allied trenches and forced over the top, whereupon he is shot to death by his countrymen.

In *The Three Hostages* (1924), Hannay, living at his ease in the English countryside, is once again called upon for help, and this time is plunged into the midst of a Bolshevik intrigue. At the conclusion, Sir Richard and his adversary stalk each other for a night and a day in the misty Scottish highlands.

The Runagates Club (1928) is a collection of adventure, crime, and secret service stories, one of which involves Hannay.

Films

Buchan's *The Thirty-nine Steps* was transformed, with Robert Donat as Richard Hannay, into the definitive screen thriller in 1935 by Alfred HITCHCOCK, who for a long time has held options on *The Three Hostages*. In 1960 *"Steps"* was remade in other hands.

The Thirty-nine Steps. Twentieth Century-Fox (British), 1960. Kenneth More (Hannay), Taina Elg, Brenda de Banzie, Barry Jones. Directed by Ralph Thomas.

When a woman spy is killed in his flat, a former officer is drawn into an espionage adventure that takes him to the Scottish hills.

BUCKET, INSPECTOR (Creator: Charles DICKENS). The first detective of importance in English literature. When Bucket appeared in *Bleak House* (1852–1853), he became the prototype of the official representative of the police department: uncolorful, undramatic, and unexciting, but honest, hardworking, fair, confident, stolid, competent, and, inevitably, successful.

Possibly his most noteworthy characteristics are his tenacity and apparent ability to be omnipresent. Regardless of the furious action around him, Bucket always manages to "lurk and lounge." "Otherwise mildly studious in his observations of human nature, on the whole a benignant philosopher not disposed to be severe upon the follies of mankind, Mr. Bucket pervades a vast number of houses and strolls about an infinity of streets; to outward appearances rather languishing for want of an object." His warmth, compassion, and affection for his fellowman, however, have limits. "I am damned," he says, "if I am going to have my case spoilt by any human being in creation. Do you see this hand, and do you think I don't know the right time to stretch it out and put it on the arm that fired the shot?"

Average-looking, Bucket is stout and middle-aged, with an honest, amiable face. He generally stands with his hands behind his back, listening. His most notable physical feature is his fat forefinger, which seems invested with magic. "He puts it to his ears, and it whispers information; he puts it to his lips, and it enjoins him to secrecy; he rubs it over his nose, and it sharpens his scent; he shakes it before a guilty man, and it charms him to his destruction."

After he arrests and handcuffs an innocent suspect in *Bleak House,* Bucket returns to work and triumphantly discovers the true murderer of an unscrupulous lawyer, proudly proclaiming "I am Inspector Bucket of the Detective, I am!" Bucket's wife seems to have a natural genius for detection, and her assistance is required before Bucket is able to obtain adequate evidence to wrap up his case.

Films

Dickens's detective made his screen debut in a British silent film.

Bleak House. Ideal (British), 1920. Constance Collier, Berta Gellardi, Norman Page, Clifford Heatherley (Bucket). Directed by Maurice Elvey.

A titled lady is accused of murdering a lawyer who had been blackmailing her because of an earlier marriage and a child.

Harry J. Worth played Bucket in a 1922 British short—part of a series called *Tense Moments from Great Plays*.

BUENO, LILLIAN DE LA TORRE. *See* DE LA TORRE, LILLIAN.

BULLDOG DRUMMOND. *See* DRUMMOND, BULLDOG.

BULLITT. *See* FISH, ROBERT L.

BULLIVANT, CECIL HENRY (1882–). English author, editor, and lecturer. An expert on the English language and literature, he was on the staff of many leading British periodicals, including *Harmsworth*

(1904), *Boys Herald* (1904–1907), and *Answers* (1908). Most of his mystery and detective works are quite scarce today. The most famous is *Garnett Bell: Detective* (1920), a short story collection. Among his other works are *The Woman Wins* (1919), *Millie Lynne—Shop Investigator* (1920; s.s.), *Because of the Woman* (1922), *The Fringe of the Law* (1931), *A King of Crooks* (1932), and *The Ticket-of-Leave Man* (1935) —featuring Hawkshaw the detective. The last-mentioned book is apparently a novelization of the first melodrama to give a truly significant role to a detective, Tom Taylor's play *The Ticket of Leave Man*, which opened in London in May 1863 and in New York in November that year. The two major roles were assigned to Hawkshaw (played by J. F. Hagan) and Bob Brierly, a young man duped by forgers and jailed. When he is released, he unwittingly helps Hawkshaw catch the real villains.

BUNN, SMILER (Creator: Bertram ATKEY). A humorous crook, Bunn "makes his living off society in a manner always devious and sometimes dark, but never mean." The ingenious Bunn is described as a "condor-eyed, electric-witted and amazingly successful prowler among the perilous labyrinths of the shady side of life."

Middle-aged, fat, and wealthy, he usually steals from those who have no right to the property, thereby avoiding the possibility of confrontation with the law. His friend and partner, Lord Fortworth, also known as Henry Black or "the Squire," is regarded by Bunn as "a rum 'un."

CHECKLIST

1911	*The Amazing Mr. Bunn* (s.s.)
1916	*The Smiler Bunn Brigade* (s.s.)
1920	*Smiler Bunn—Manhunter* (s.s.)
1923	*The Man with the Yellow Eyes*
1923	*Smiler Bunn—Gentleman Crook* (s.s.)
1925	*Smiler Bunn, Byewayman* (s.s.)
1926	*Smiler Bunn—Gentleman Adventurer* (s.s.)
1929	*Smiler Bunn, Crook* (s.s.)
1931	*The Mystery of the Glass Bullet*
1939	*Arsenic and Gold*
1940	*The House of Clystevill*

BURDETT, CHARLES (b. 1815.) American journalist and historical novelist; author of *The Gambler* (1848), possibly the first American detective novel. Based on the famous Mary Rogers murder case (which also inspired Edgar Allan POE's "The Mystery of Marie Rogêt," 1842), it is subtitled *The Policeman's Story* and moralizes about the negative effects of gambling on the soul. In the preface Burdett claims that all events are true, as related to him by a member of the police department—a common practice for writers for the ensuing three decades.

BURFORD, ELEANOR. See HOLT, VICTORIA.

BURGE, MILWARD RODON KENNEDY. See KENNEDY, MILWARD.

BURGESS, (FRANK) GELETT (1866–1951). American author of juvenile fiction and humorous novels and short stories. His mystery novels, *The White Cat* (1907), *Two O'Clock Courage* (1934), and *Ladies in Boxes* (1942), are not read today. A short story collection, *The Picaroons* (1904), written in collaboration with Will Irwin and recounting adventures of various rogues, is often described as a modern version of the *Arabian Nights*. Burgess's best-known mystery work, *The Master of Mysteries* (1912), was published anonymously. It features Armenian-born Astrogon Kerby, known as Astro the Seer, who pre-

Karl Anderson and George Brehm illustrated Gelett Burgess's anonymous collection of tales about Astro the Seer, *The Master of Mysteries*, published in 1912 by Bobbs-Merrill.

tends to be a crystal ball gazer and palmist and affects such trappings as a turban, a silk robe, and a pet white lizard. The book contains two now-famous ciphers, one, from the first letter of the first word of each of the twenty-four stories: "The author is Gelett Burgess"; the other, from the last letter of the last word of each story: "False to life and false to art." There is believed to be a third cipher contained in the book, but it is not widely known.

BURKE, THOMAS (1886–1945). English novelist, essayist, and short story writer whose reputation rests on his romantic and sensational tales of Limehouse, London's Chinese ghetto.

A London native, Burke knew the city intimately and brought it to life in essays, mood pieces, and short stories, most of which had a melodramatic atmosphere of crime. His first and best crime book was *Limehouse Nights* (1916), a series of violent tales that rely on authentic background and Oriental flavor for their readability. Subtle passion and sinister murders abound, just as they do in his other volumes of crime stories: *Whispering Windows* (1920; U.S. title: *More Limehouse Nights*); *East of Mansion House* (1926); *The Bloomsbury Wonder* (1929); *The Pleasantries of Old Quong* (1931; U.S. title: *A Tea-Shop in Limehouse*); *Night Pieces* (1935); and *Dark Nights* (1943). His best novel is a fictionalized version of the murder of Weare by Thurtell and Hunt, *Murder at Elstree* (1936). "The Hands of Mr. Ottermole," based on the Jack-the-Ripper theme, was voted by Ellery QUEEN (author) and eleven other critics as "the best detective short story of all time." It was published in *The Pleasantries of Old Quong*.

Richard Barthelmess as the Chinese youth in Thomas Burke's *Broken Blossoms*. The setting is D. W. Griffith's version of Limehouse.

Thomas Burke's tales were unusual for portraying Orientals in a sympathetic way, not as sinister stereotypes. The first edition of *The Pleasantries of Old Quong* was published by Constable in 1931.

Films

A fragile masterpiece, *Broken Blossoms,* an interracial love story, set in Limehouse and ending in murder and suicide, was filmed in 1919 by D. W. Griffith with Richard Barthelmess as the Chinese youth and Lillian Gish as the daughter of a sadistic prizefighter. It was remade in 1936 in England starring Emlyn WILLIAMS and Dolly Haas and directed by Hans (later changed to John) Brahm. The film was based on "The Chink and the Child," a story published in *Limehouse Nights*.

Radio and Television

Burke's "The Hands of Mr. Ottermole," in which a reporter investigates a series of maniac slayings in the London streets, has been a huge favorite on radio anthology series for decades and, on television, has been featured on *Suspense* and *Alfred Hitchcock Presents*.

BURNETT, W[ILLIAM] R[ILEY] (1899–). American novelist whose first published book, *Little Caesar* (1929), was one of the first, and best, authentic native American crime novels.

Born in Springfield, Ohio, the son of Emily Upson Colwell (Morgan) and Theodore Addison Burnett, he had literary ambitions at an early age and produced five novels, several plays, a hundred short stories—all unpublished—before moving to Chicago, where he wrote *Little Caesar*.

Burnett, who later wrote several westerns as well as gangster stories, has been married twice, the second time to Whitney Forbes Johnstone in 1943; they had two children. He lives in southern California, where he has been an active film and television writer, winning the Writers Guild of America award for the best screenplay of 1963, *The Great Escape*. "Dressing Up" won the O. Henry Memorial Award for the best short story of 1930.

One of the most famous of all naturalistic crime novels, *Little Caesar* is the gripping tale of the rise and fall of Cesare Bandello, known as Rico, a tough Chicago gangster. The book was a Literary Guild selection and an immediate best seller. It has been translated into a dozen languages and became a significant motion picture, rocketing Edward G. Robinson to stardom and opening the gates to countless Prohibition-era films of the Chicago underworld. The story is told largely from the hoodlum's point of view, its strength deriving less from Burnett's literary style than from its swiftly paced action and the author's penetrating view of gangster life.

The same qualities made many of Burnett's other novels best sellers, particularly *High Sierra* (1940) and three novels, each complete in itself, that form a trilogy about corruption in city government: *The Asphalt Jungle* (1949), *Little Men, Big World* (1951), and *Vanity Row* (1952).

Films

Burnett's books and screenplays have had an important impact on the crime film. Some of the cinematic

Edward G. Robinson begins to assert his position as a merciless and ambitious gangster in this scene from *Little Caesar*. [*First National*]

milestones attributed to him are discussed below.

Little Caesar. First National, 1930. Edward G. Robinson, Douglas Fairbanks, Jr., Glenda Farrell. Directed by Mervyn LeRoy. A close adaptation of the novel.

Rico, a small-time gangster, ruthlessly gains control of the underworld, eliminating rivals and frightened associates—one is shot down on the church steps on his way to confession—until he, too, is stopped.

The Finger Points. First National, 1931. Richard Barthelmess, Fay Wray, Regis Toomey, Clark Gable. Directed by John Francis Dillon. Based on the actual murder of Chicago newsman Jake Lingle. An original story and screenplay by Burnett and John Monk Saunders.

A young, disillusioned, newpaper reporter joins forces with the underworld in using his stories to blackmail prominent figures.

The Beast of the City. MGM, 1932. Walter Huston, Jean Harlow, Wallace Ford, Jean Hersholt. Directed by Charles Brabin. Based on an original story by Burnett.

The dynamic police chief of a city totally in the grip of criminals learns that his brother, a bank guard, has joined the racketeers.

Scarface. United Artists, 1932. Paul Muni, Karen Morley, Ann Dvorak, George Raft. Directed by Howard Hawks. Story by Burnett; Ben Hecht, among others, wrote the original screenplay, based on the life of Al Capone.

A ruthless bootlegger with a scarred face shoots down all who stand in his way to power, but his downfall is linked to his possessive feelings about his sister.

The Whole Town's Talking. Columbia, 1935. Robinson (in a double role), Jean Arthur. Directed by John Ford. Based on a story by Burnett, originally serialized in *Collier's.*

A meek bookkeeper is troubled by a notorious gangster to whom he bears an extremely close resemblance.

Dr. Socrates. Warner Brothers, 1935. Muni, Dvorak, Barton MacLane, Robert Barrat. Directed by William Dieterle. Based on a story by Burnett, originally serialized in *Collier's.*

A penniless doctor is forced to treat the members of a gang who have been wounded in a bank robbery.

Many program films of this era were based on Burnett stories, including such crime melodramas as *36 Hours to Kill* (1936), *Some Blondes Are Dangerous* (1937), and *King of the Underworld* (1939), in which Kay Francis is a woman doctor who is forced to treat, and ultimately outwits, a gang led by Humphrey Bogart. This is a remake of *Dr. Socrates.*

High Sierra. First National–Warner Brothers, 1941. Bogart, Ida Lupino, Alan Curtis, Joan Leslie. Directed by Raoul Walsh. Burnett and John Huston wrote the screenplay, based on Burnett's novel.

A former convict, heading west, provides money for an operation to aid a crippled girl he has befriended, but a resort hotel robbery he has planned backfires, and he is trapped by the police on Mount Whitney. (The film was remade in 1955, with Jack Palance and Shelley Winters, as *I Died a Thousand Times.*)

Nobody Lives Forever. Warner Brothers, 1946. John Garfield, Geraldine Fitzgerald, Faye Emerson, George Tobias. Directed by Jean Negulesco. Based on the 1943 novel by Burnett, who also wrote the screenplay.

A confidence man falls in love with the wealthy young widow he and his gang plan to swindle out of a large sum of money.

The Asphalt Jungle. MGM, 1950. Sterling Hayden, Louis Calhern, Jean Hagen, Sam Jaffe, John McIntire, Marilyn Monroe. Directed by Huston. He and Ben Maddow adapted the novel for the screen.

An assortment of criminals carefully plot a large jewelry store robbery, but an aborted double cross changes the aftermath of the successful heist.

Burnett, who in 1940 had adapted Graham GREENE's *This Gun for Hire* (1936) for American audiences, began a busy period writing screenplays based on the works of others, for example, *The Racket* (1951), *Dangerous Mission* (1954), and *Illegal* (1955), although he occasionally still drew from his own material.

Accused of Murder. Republic, 1956. David Brian, Vera Ralston, Sidney Blackmer, Lee Van Cleef, Virginia Grey. Directed by Joe Kane. The screenplay, by Burnett and Bob Williams, was based on Burnett's *Vanity Row.*

A nightclub singer is suspected of killing a

Paul Muni is the neurotic gangster in W. R. Burnett's *Scarface*, whose career somewhat resembled Al Capone's. [*United Artists*]

gangland lawyer found shot in his own car.

Burnett also contributed to the screenplays for historical romances (for example, *Captain Lightfoot,* 1954) and westerns (for example, *Sergeants Three,* 1962). *The Asphalt Jungle* exerted a tremendous influence on the crime film genre, in both official and unofficial remakes, with numerous shifts in locale and in various guises; for instance, MGM released an Alan Ladd western (*Badlanders,* 1958), a George Sanders melodrama with an exotic Cairo Museum setting (*Cairo,* 1963), and a black ghetto "caper" film (*Cool Breeze,* 1972), all drawn from *The Asphalt Jungle.*

Television

In 1961 MGM converted *The Asphalt Jungle* into a television series of thirteen hour-long programs starring Jack Warden. The underworld viewpoint of the source was abandoned for one concerning the workings of a police department.

BURTON, MILES. See RHODE, JOHN.

BUSH, CHRISTOPHER (1888?–1973). English mystery novelist. Born in East Anglia to a Quaker family whose ancestors had lived in that part of England for more than 400 years, Bush was a schoolmaster before devoting full time to writing. Except for service in both world wars, he always lived in Sussex. Under the pseudonym Michael Home, he wrote of English rural life. His real name was Charlie Christmas Bush, and as he was illegitimate, his birth date was unrecorded. He did not know it himself, but believed it to be sometime in 1888.

Bush had a remarkably long career. His last mystery, *The Case of the Prodigal Daughter* (1968), was published forty-two years after his first, *The Plumley Inheritance* (1926). After his second, *The Perfect Murder Case* (1929), he began a series (numbering sixty-one books) about detective Ludovic Travers. The titles of all but the first five Travers books begin "The Case of the. . . ." Travers is a genial, wealthy amateur detective who acts as unofficial adviser to Superintendent Wharton of Scotland Yard for almost forty years. His specialty is breaking the "unbreakable" alibi. A typical example of his successes is *The Case of the 100% Alibi* (1934; U.S. title: *The Kitchen Cake Murder*).

Although he built a steady audience for his work, Bush had few individual critical successes. One of the more highly praised, *The Case of the Dead Shepherd* (1934; U.S. title: *The Tea Tray Murders*), concerns a suburban secondary school and its faculty. Bush drew upon his own experiences in writing this book. Similarly, his wartime Travers books, such as *The Case of the Murdered Major* (1941), *The Case of the Fighting Soldier* (1942), *The Case of the Kidnapped Colonel* (1942), and *The Case of the Corporal's Leave* (1945), were based partly on his extensive military experience.

BUTLER, ELLIS PARKER (1869–1937). American humorist and mystery and detective story writer. Butler's significant contributions to literature are the famous story *Pigs Is Pigs,* published in *The American Magazine* in 1905 and in book form in 1906, and a volume of mystery and detective stories about a humorous sleuth, *Philo Gubb: Correspondence-School Detective* (1918).

This is the only book about Ellis Parker Butler's humorous detective, Philo Gubb. It was first published in 1918 by Houghton Mifflin.

Butler was born in Muscatine, Iowa, the first of eight children. He married Ida A. Zipser in 1899; they had five children. He was a prolific writer of magazine stories, and most of his humorous books were compiled from those pieces. He was a founder of the Dutch Treat Club and the Authors League.

Gubb keeps a small-town office for his twin occupations of paperhanger and detective; on the wall is a diploma from the Rising Sun Detective Agency's correspondence school. A fan of Sherlock HOLMES, the quixotic Gubb emulates the master by wearing a deerstalker and smoking a calabash (the real Holmes, despite numerous characterizations, did not smoke a calabash). While working on his cases, he employs an enormous collection of disguises—which deceive no one; half the citizens of Riverbank greet him by name. Gubb commits a major crime during every case on which he works: the murder of the English language.

BUTLER, WALTER C. See FAUST, FREDERICK.

C

CAIN, JAMES M[ALLAHAN] (1892–   ). American author of hard-boiled crime novels. Cain has never produced a genuine detective novel—he does not like the idea of a criminal being caught in a neat ending. His stories are concerned mainly with murder and love and are told exclusively from the criminal's point of view.

He was born in Annapolis, Md., the son of James William Cain, a professor, and Rose Mallahan Cain, an opera singer. James also wanted a career in opera until he was emphatically told (by his mother) that he did not have the voice for it. His father later became president of Washington College in Chesterton, Md., where James received a bachelor of arts degree in 1910 (at the age of eighteen) and a master's degree in 1917, after teaching mathematics and English there for four years.

Cain decided to become a reporter and worked for the *Baltimore American* and the *Baltimore Sun*, with time out for a two-year term in the Army during World War I. He was encouraged by H. L. Mencken in Baltimore and later by Walter Lippmann at the *New York World*, where he wrote political columns of a relatively uncontroversial nature. There were so many taboos, said Cain, that as an independent columnist "all you could condemn was the man-eating shark, and all you could praise was your favorite flower."

His magazine articles and stories began to appear in the 1920s, and he became a best-selling author with the publication of his first and most famous novel, *The Postman Always Rings Twice*, in 1934. He had started to work on screenplays in Hollywood in 1931 and continued to write them with increasing success, artistically and financially, for seventeen years.

Throughout his life, Cain has been a victim of illness and imperfect marriages (except the last, which was happy and lasted for almost twenty years), of which there have been four: Mary Rebecca Clough (married 1920; divorced 1923); Elina Sjösted Tyszecka of Finland (married 1927; divorced 1942); actress Aileen Pringle (married 1944; divorced 1945); and Florence Macbeth Whitwell (married 1947; died 1966).

Edward G. Robinson and Fred MacMurray eye each other warily as an insurance man tries to get away with murder in Billy Wilder's film of *Double Indemnity*. [*Paramount*]

As a California writer, Cain inevitably faces comparison with Raymond CHANDLER, Dashiell HAMMETT, and, to a lesser degree, Ross MACDONALD. They are "tough-guy" writers in the same way that Steinbeck, Hemingway, and B. Traven were. The noted critic Edmund Wilson called Cain and his peers "poets of the tabloid murder" because they forced a new style of literature to be taken seriously.

Cain broke precedent with past literary works by producing a popular novel (later a play and motion picture) in which both leading characters are repulsive. After the success of *The Postman Always Rings*

Twice, he repeated the formula in *Double Indemnity*, which was published in 1943. Displaying exceptional psychological insight in these and other works, Cain was able to uncover and articulate the beginnings of the thought processes leading to the entangled schemes that ultimately result in the commission of murder.

Whereas Hammett and Chandler wrote about good-bad, soft-tough detectives who tried to unravel the mess that someone else caused by a violent or greedy act, Cain created two-dimensional characters interested in themselves and motivated by their lust for money or sex or by some form of snobbery. They

Drifter John Garfield plots murder with the young wife (Lana Turner) of his benefactor in the screen version of James M. Cain's *The Postman Always Rings Twice*. [*MGM*]

are flawed characters because they are too thoroughly evil. Cain shows them no mercy. He is, as David Madden says in his biography, "the twenty-minute egg of the hard-boiled school."

In *The Postman Always Rings Twice*, Frank Chambers, a young drifter, is dropped off at a rural diner where he is instantly attracted to Cora, the sexy young wife of the middle-aged owner, Nick Papadakis. They have a violent, passionate affair and plot to murder her husband.

There is a similar theme in *Double Indemnity*, in which an attractive woman uses her physical appeal to gain an ally. She begins an affair with an insurance agent, and they plan to kill her husband, making the murder look like an accident so that she can claim the double indemnity payment.

Mildred Pierce tells of a woman obsessed with making money in an attempt to gain the respect of her daughter. Divorced after an eleven-year marriage, she now runs a profitable bakery but has little success otherwise. Her first lover, her husband's former partner, betrays her at the earliest opportunity, and her second is quite content to accept his role of gigolo, regarding her with open contempt, an attitude adopted by Veda, Mildred's daughter. Veda, who shares her mother's lover, loathes her and looks down on her as a moneygrubber and "working woman." This contempt, however, does not prevent her from accepting the rewards of her mother's labor.

The three books mentioned above were made into highly successful films. Cain estimates that Hollywood studios earned $12 million from these motion pictures, whereas he earned a comparatively modest $100,000. As a result of these disproportionate financial benefits, he attempted to establish an American Authors' Authority to protect writers. He was unsuccessful, but the Authors League eventually adopted some features of his proposed union.

CHECKLIST

1934 *The Postman Always Rings Twice*
1937 *Serenade*
1941 *Mildred Pierce*
1942 *Love's Lovely Counterfeit*
1943 *Double Indemnity*
1943 *Three of a Kind* (contains *The Embezzler; Double Indemnity;* and *Two Can Sing* with a new title, *Career in C Major*)
1945 *Career in C Major and Other Stories* (s.s.)
1946 *Past All Dishonor*
1947 *Sinful Woman*
1947 *The Butterfly*
1948 *The Moth*
1950 *Jealous Woman*
1951 *The Root of His Evil*
1953 *Galatea*
1962 *Mignon*
1965 *The Magician's Wife*
1975 *Rainbow's End*

Films

Double Indemnity. Paramount, 1944. Fred MacMurray, Barbara Stanwyck, Edward G. Robinson. Directed by Billy Wilder.

An insurance salesman falls in love with a scheming wife and plots with her to murder her husband in a freak train accident. His boss, a claims adjuster, suspects that the "accident" had been planned.

Mildred Pierce. Warner Brothers, 1945. Joan Crawford, Ann Blyth, Zachary Scott, Jack Carson. Directed by Michael Curtiz.

An ambitious waitress gains control of a restaurant chain and becomes wealthy. Devoted to her spoiled daughter, she is discovered at the beginning of the film near the corpse of her worthless husband.

The Postman Always Rings Twice. MGM, 1946. John Garfield, Lana Turner, Cecil Kellaway, Leon Ames, Hume Cronyn. Directed by Tay Garnett.

A hitchhiker drifts into a roadside café and plans with the middle-aged owner's young wife to kill him. They are arrested, but a shrewd criminal lawyer gains their release by asking for clemency.

In 1956 Warner Brothers released a highly romanticized version of *Serenade*, featuring the vocal talents of Mario Lanza.

Television

In 1973 *Double Indemnity* was made into a two-hour television film (Richard Crenna, Samantha Eggar, Lee J. Cobb. Directed by Jack Smight); the impact of the 1944 film was far greater.

CAMPION, ALBERT (Creator: Margery ALLINGHAM). In 1900 a baby, later known as Albert Campion, was born to an aristocratic English family. Why this child, christened "Rudolph," chose not to claim his royal prerogatives was kept a secret throughout his long detective career.

Campion's Cambridge education is not evident in his early appearances. In *The Crime at Black Dudley*, he is described as "a lunatic . . . quite inoffensive . . . just a silly ass." He wears large glasses that do not hide the foolish expression of his eyes, and he announces in an idiotic high-pitched voice that he is also known by the aliases Tootles Ash and Mornington Dodd. He claims to be a con man who will do anything for a price, provided it is not vulgar or sordid. His pronouncements are apparently part of an "act" to lull criminals into a sense of false security, since there is no evidence that he has ever had a criminal career. In his early days his physical prowess and disguises (including one occasion in woman's garb) help him to solve cases.

Concurrently with the change in Miss Allingham's writing approach in *Death of a Ghost*, Campion changes. He becomes much more serious and exudes an aura of confidence that causes people in trouble to turn to him. His eyes become more thoughtful, and his fair hair begins to whiten. He is described as a "universal uncle," and it is these very avuncular qualities that cause young girls of society background to seek his aid. Though by no means restricted to sedentary activities, Campion increasingly uses his knowledge of human psychology, rather than mere physical activity, to solve crimes.

As Campion changes, so do the many characters who appear, disappear, and reappear throughout his adventures. Only the eternally brave Magersfontein Lugg, his Cockney valet, remains unchanged, having undergone his transformation before being employed by Campion. Lugg is a former burglar and Borstal inmate who has, in Campion's words, "the courage of his previous convictions." He looks after Campion's bachelor flat, located above a police station in a cul-de-sac near Piccadilly Circus.

When Lady Amanda Fitton first appears, she is a gawky teenager—interested in mechanics—whose inheritance of a royal estate at Pontisbright is threatened by a master criminal in *Sweet Danger*. She reappears in *The Fashion in Shrouds*, in which she has developed into a sophisticated engineer who designs airplanes. Love blossoms, and Amanda and Albert marry after *Traitor's Purse*, in which she helps him ward off amnesia and a plot to destroy England. Their only child, Rupert, is born during the war and is, by 1968, a graduate student at Harvard.

Not even the policemen and government officials with whom Albert Campion works remain static. Inspector Stanislaus Oates rises through the ranks to positions of great responsibility at Scotland Yard. When he retires, his place is taken by the dynamic Charlie Luke, whose career is furthered by Campion. Hard work and promotion to the rank of superintendent help Luke overcome his grief when his wife dies in childbirth. L. C. "Elsie" Corkran, destined to become head of British Intelligence, is one of the few people to know of Campion's wartime activities, a secret as closely guarded as that concerning his royal birth. The last three Campion cases tell of his adventures after he is persuaded by Corkran to take on certain delicate missions essential to British security. Even now, Albert Campion has lost none of his perceptive intelligence, and he is still remarkably fit, albeit white-haired and elderly.

CHECKLIST

- 1929 *The Crime at Black Dudley* (U.S. title: *The Black Dudley Murder*)
- 1929 *Mystery Mile*
- 1931 *Look to the Lady* (U.S. title: The Gyrth Chalice Mystery)
- 1931 *Police at the Funeral*
- 1933 *Sweet Danger* (U.S. title: *Kingdom of Death*)
- 1934 *Death of a Ghost*
- 1936 *Flowers for the Judge*
- 1937 *The Case of the Late Pig*
- 1937 *Mr. Campion: Criminologist* (s.s.)
- 1937 *Dancers in Mourning*
- 1938 *The Fashion in Shrouds*
- 1939 *Mr. Campion and Others* (s.s.)
- 1941 *Traitor's Purse*
- 1945 *Coroner's Pidgin* (U.S. title: *Pearls Before Swine*)
- 1947 *The Case Book of Mr. Campion* (s.s.)
- 1948 *More Work for the Undertaker*
- 1952 *The Tiger in the Smoke*
- 1955 *The Beckoning Lady* (U.S. title: *The Estate of the Beckoning Lady*)
- 1958 *Hide My Eyes* (U.S. title: *Tether's End*)
- 1962 *The China Governess*
- 1965 *The Mind Readers*

1968 *Cargo of Eagles* (completed by Youngman Carter)
1969 *The Allingham Casebook* (s.s.; contains eight stories about Campion)
1969 *Mr. Campion's Farthing* (by Youngman Carter)
1970 *Mr. Campion's Falcon* (U.S.title: *Mr. Campion's Quarry;* by Youngman Carter)
1973 *The Allingham Minibus* (s.s.; contains three stories about Campion)

CANADAY, JOHN. *See* HEAD, MATTHEW.

CANNING, VICTOR (1911–). English author. Born in Plymouth, Canning worked in a government office there, writing juvenile adventure stories as a sideline. His first novel for an adult audience, *Mr. Finchley Discovers His England* (1934), was highly successful, and Canning was then able to devote his career entirely to writing. Since the end of World War II, he has written suspense and spy fiction, and his works, published under his own name and under the pseudonym Alan Gould, have been popular on both sides of the Atlantic. He has traveled widely in Europe, North Africa, and the South Atlantic.

Canning has used most of the locales he has visited as settings for his books. In *The Great Affair* (1970) the action takes place in nine countries in Africa and Europe as Canning traces the adventures of Charles Nelo Sangster, a defrocked Anglican minister whose self-appointed mission is to steal diamonds so that he can sell them and turn the proceeds over to charity. Most of the Canning stories deal with international intrigue and often present one man fighting an international political or criminal conspiracy or both. In *A Forest of Eyes* (1950) engineer Robert Hudson, who goes to Yugoslavia to work, becomes involved in espionage following a friend's death. In *The Limbo Line* (1963) a retired English secret agent is called back to active duty to combat AGRIP, a Russian trade organization that has been kidnapping people and sending them behind the Iron Curtain. Rex Carver, an English private detective who loves horse races, has appeared in several Canning books; in *The Whip Hand* (1965) he battles neo-nazism.

Canning's writing skill has enabled him to overcome the implausibility of some of his plots. His books are generally fast-paced and inventive and contain generous amounts of humor. These positive features have earned him a considerable reputation. Dorothy B. HUGHES felt that he had "taken over the place Eric AMBLER held prior to World War II as the only worthy artist writing of the confidential agent." *The Reader's Digest* pronounced Canning one of the six finest thriller writers in the world.

Victor Canning.

Films

Spy Hunt. Universal, 1950. Howard Duff, Marta Toren, Philip Friend, Philip Dorn, Robert Douglas. Directed by George Sherman. Based on *Panther's Moon* (1948).

A group of spies, working against one another, search the Swiss Alps for a circus panther that has escaped with microfilm hidden in its collar.

Golden Salamander. Eagle-Lion (British), 1951. Trevor Howard, Anouk Aimée, Herbert Lom, Walter Rilla. Directed by Ronald Neame. Canning contributed to the screenplay, which was based on his novel of 1949.

An English archaeologist, in Tunis to salvage a shipment of antiques from a mined ship, is spurred to breaking a gun-smuggling ring after reading an inscription on an ancient salamander statue: "Not by ignoring evil does one overcome it, but by going to meet it."

The Assassin (British title: *Venetian Bird*). United Artists (British), 1953. Richard Todd, Eva Bartok, John Gregson, Rilla. Directed by Ralph Thomas. Screenplay by Canning, from his *Venetian Bird* (1951; U.S. title: *Bird of Prey*).

A private detective arrives in Venice to search for an Italian wartime friend, now reported dead, and learns of a political killing scheduled to take place during a gondola festival.

The House of the Seven Hawks. MGM (British), 1959. Robert Taylor, Nicole Maurey, Linda Christian, David Kossoff, Donald Wolfit. Directed by Richard Thorpe. Based on *House of the Seven Flies* (1952).

An American skipper, offered a large sum of money to transport a man from the English coast to the Netherlands, finds his passenger dead, with a map of hidden Nazi treasure taped to his chest.

Masquerade. United Artists (British), 1964. Cliff Robertson, Jack Hawkins, Marisa Mell, Bill Fraser. Directed by Basil Dearden. Based on *A Handful of Silver* (1954; British title: *Castle Minerva*).

In this tongue-in-cheek adaptation, a Foreign Office colonel hires a bungling American soldier of fortune to guard a young Near Eastern prince.

CANNON, CURT. *See* MCBAIN, ED.

CARNAC, CAROL. *See* LORAC, E. C. R.

CARNACKI (Creator: William Hope HODGSON). A psychic detective called into cases to discover or explain seemingly occult phenomena. Mr. Carnacki is generally skeptical of ghost stories but does not believe or disbelieve them "on principle." He examines each case independently and finds that many crimes attributed to supernatural causes have mundane explanations. While working on a case he employs the paraphernalia of his trade: garlic, bebe ribbons, jars of water, candles, and so on. He admits that, in the black of night, alone with his thoughts (and possibly with some "Thing from the Other World"), he is scared half to death.

After an adventure, he sends for his friends—Dodgson, Jessop, Arkright, and Taylor—lights a pipe, settles into an easy chair, and begins a narrative. When he has finished his story, he genially says, "Out you go," and the evening is concluded. Six adventures were collected in *Carnacki, The Ghost-Finder* (1913); a later American edition (1947) contains three additional stories. An American edition dated 1910 contains the first six stories condensed into one.

CARR, A. H. Z. (1902–1971). American economist and author. Born Albert Z. Carr in Chicago, he graduated from the University of Chicago with a B.A. degree, received an M.A. degree from Columbia, and also studied at the London School of Economics. Following a business career, he entered government service during World War II, working as assistant to the chairman of the War Production Board. Later, he was an economic adviser to Franklin D. Roosevelt and a special consultant to Harry S. Truman.

His writing career was a varied one. During the Depression of the 1930s he wrote romantic fiction for "slick" magazines to supplement his income. He wrote about politics and economics, and his inspirational book, *How to Attract Good Luck* (1952), appeared in five English-language editions and was also popular in Europe, where it was translated into a number of languages.

Carr once said that he turned to writing mysteries to preserve his sanity. His short stories were perennial award winners in *Ellery Queen's Mystery Magazine* contests. "The Trial of John Nobody" (1950), "Murder at City Hall" (1951), and "If a Body" (1953) won second prizes. Finally, in 1956, Carr won first prize with "The Black Kitten," a symbolic story of race relations.

Carr won the Mystery Writers of America Edgar for best first novel, posthumously, with *Finding Maubee* (1971), the story of a black policeman searching for a murder suspect on a fictional island in the Caribbean.

CARR, JOHN DICKSON (1906–). American detective story writer who has also written under the pseudonyms Carter Dickson and Carr Dickson. His ingenuity in conceiving and explaining "impossible" crimes is unchallenged; he is the most versatile author of the true detective story, which must play fair with all clues. His plots are dominated by a sense of the macabre, despite frequent scenes of almost slapstick comedy that have distressed the austere reader.

Born in Uniontown, Pa., the son of Julia and Wooda Nicholas Carr, he inherited a taste for sensationalism. His father, whom he idolized, was a lawyer who specialized in criminal cases, served a term in Congress during the first Wilson administration, and accumulated a vast library. At an early age Carr discovered Sherlock HOLMES and then Hamilton CLEEK, the Thinking Machine (*see* THINKING MACHINE, THE), Joseph Rouletabille (*see* LEROUX, GASTON), and Father BROWN, and he decided to become a detective story writer.

When he was fifteen, his parents sent him to a preparatory school, the Hill, where he first wrote

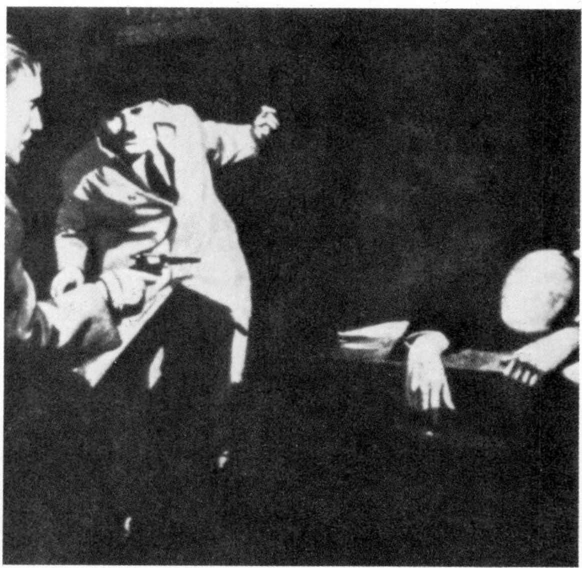

The first edition of John Dickson Carr's *The Third Bullet*, published under the Carter Dickson pseudonym by Hodder & Stoughton in 1937, is probably his scarcest book. This picture appears on the paper cover and as an internal illustration.

detective stories, and then to Haverford College, where he continued in this pursuit. By this time his favorite writer was G. K. CHESTERTON, although he never agreed with Father Brown's creator on the two subjects Chesterton said were worth arguing about: religion and politics. G. K. C. was a Roman Catholic and a liberal; Carr has always been a Presbyterian and a conservative.

After an undistinguished academic career (although Carr was proficient in literature, history, and languages, he never understood mathematics or any form of science), he was allowed to go abroad and spent a year in Paris. He disliked and avoided left-bank bohemians as much as he disliked left-wing ideas. He wrote a historical-detective chronicle but later destroyed it.

Returning to the United States, where he lived with his parents and at the home of a favorite uncle in Pittsburgh, he wrote his first detective novel, *It Walks by Night*. He took the manuscript to Eugene F. Saxton at Harper, who published it in 1930; it achieved modest success.

During another ocean crossing he met Clarice Cleaves, an English girl from Bristol. In 1932 they were married in the United States; then, because England seemed to him the ideal setting for writing detective fiction, they went to live there. Their three daughters are now married and raising families of their own.

In England Carr wrote steadily. To take care of his prodigious output, he invented a second identity for another publisher but almost gave it up in wrath at the outset. Ignoring Nicholas Wood, the pen name he had chosen, the new publisher issued his first novel for that company under the pseudonym Carr Dickson, quickly changed to Carter Dickson when Harper protested. He patterned his Carr detective, Dr. Gideon FELL, after Chesterton in the hope of creating a character everybody would like. Although not originally inspired by Winston Churchill, then a political maverick, Dickson's grumbling old Sir Henry MERRIVALE acquired Churchillian touches after critics claimed to see some resemblance.

In 1936 Carr was elected to the London Detection Club, a small prestigious group (called snobbish by many) of which Chesterton was president. G. K. C., who had no objection to Dr. Fell, had agreed to take the chair for the initiation, but his fatal illness prevented him from doing so; Carr never met him.

With novels, short stories in *The Strand*, and radio plays for the BBC, Carr was already enjoying success at the outbreak of World War II. In 1942, summoned by military authorities, he had returned to the United States; when the BBC requested his services, he was promptly sent back to London. As corporation dogsbody, he produced propaganda programs as well as a popular weekly show called *Appointment with Fear*.

After the war he wrote the official biography of Sir Arthur CONAN DOYLE from comprehensive archives produced by his friend Adrian Conan Doyle, Sir Arthur's youngest son. Then, chafing under a socialist government, he took his family and an English nurse who cherished the children until her death, "escaped Socialism"—his words—and fled to Mamaroneck, N.Y. The Carrs tried England again when the Labour party was voted out in 1951 and stayed until 1958, when they returned permanently to the United States. John and Clarice Carr now live in Greenville, S.C.

Throughout these years, the parade of detective fiction continued. Often wildly improbable, Carr's mysteries are hypnotic enough to cause some suspension of disbelief. "Never mind what they *think* of it," Gene Saxton used to say, "provided they keep on reading. And it seems they do." Carr varied this fare only with carefully researched historical novels which, in fact, were disguised detective stories. Although these novels were not in general as popular as the mysteries, one of them, *The Devil in Velvet*, sold better than any other Carr book except *The Life of Sir Arthur Conan Doyle* (1949).

Carr has created other modern detectives besides Dr. Fell and Sir Henry Merrivale: Henri BENCOLIN, the Paris *juge d'instruction* from the first novel, and Colonel MARCH of Scotland Yard. He modeled Colonel March on his close friend John

Housekeeper Barbara Stanwyck feigns friendliness to waif Leslie Caron as a young poet (Joseph Cotten) who has volunteered to help the girl looks on. We learn his famous identity at the end of *The Man with a Cloak*, a film based on John Dickson Carr's story. [*MGM*]

RHODE, another mystery writer, who in private life was Major C. J. C. Street, formerly of the British Regular Army. Not long ago he took a further step. In a detective story set against the background of London in 1869, Wilkie COLLINS, author of *The Moonstone* (1868), appears as the amateur detective who solves the mystery in *The Hungry Goblin*.

Carr regularly reviews mysteries for *Ellery Queen's Mystery Magazine*.

CHECKLIST

Mysteries not about Bencolin, Fell, March, or Merrivale.
(By John Dickson Carr)

1932	*Poison in Jest*
1936	*The Murder of Sir Edmund Godfrey* (fictionalized account of a true crime)
1937	*The Burning Court*
1942	*The Emperor's Snuff-Box*
1950	*The Bride of Newgate*
1951	*The Devil in Velvet*
1952	*The Nine Wrong Answers*
1954	*The Exploits of Sherlock Holmes* (s.s.; with Adrian Conan Doyle)
1954	*The Third Bullet and Other Stories* (s.s.)
1955	*Captain Cut-Throat*
1956	*Patrick Butler for the Defense*
1957	*Fire, Burn!*
1959	*Scandal at High Chimneys*
1961	*The Witch of the Low-Tide*
1962	*The Demoniacs*
1963	*The Men Who Explained Miracles* (s.s.)
1964	*Most Secret*
1968	*Papa Là-Bas*
1969	*The Ghosts' High Noon*
1971	*Deadly Hall*
1972	*The Hungry Goblin*

(By Carr Dickson)

1933	*The Bowstring Murders*

(By Carter Dickson)

1937	*The Third Bullet*
1939	*Drop to His Death* (with John Rhode); (U.S. title: *Fatal Descent*)
1956	*Fear Is the Same*

Films

Carr's story based on Edgar Allan POE became an important MGM film of 1951, *The Man with a Cloak*. The film was based on "The Gentleman from Paris," collected in *The Third Bullet and Other Stories*. Other notable uses of Carr material on the screen are discussed below.

Dangerous Crossing. Twentieth Century-Fox, 1953. Jeanne Crain, Michael Rennie, Carl Betz, Mary Anderson. Directed by Joseph M. Newman. A greatly expanded version of Carr's celebrated radio play *Cabin B-13*.

A new bride boards a luxury liner for a honeymoon voyage, only to have her husband disappear. It is suggested that he never existed, that she is losing her mind; but the ship's doctor (Rennie) believes that she is telling the truth.

City after Midnight. RKO (British), 1959. Dan O'Herlihy, Phyllis Kirk, Wilfrid Hyde-White, Petula Clark, Jack Watling. Directed by Compton Bennett. A flat, not fully realized, adaptation of *The Emperor's Snuff-Box*.

A valuable antique is stolen from a French resort town, and its owner murdered.

The Burning Court. Trans-Lux (French), 1963. Nadja Tiller, Jean-Claude Brialy, Perrette Pradier. Directed by Julien Duvivier.

A mystery writer (Walter Giller) and his wife (Edith Scob), descendant of a woman burned as a witch, are intrigued by the murder of a hated patriarch, descendant of the man who accused the witch.

Radio and Television

On March 16, 1943, Carr contributed a half-hour drama called *Cabin B-13*, about a terrified girl whose bridegroom has vanished aboard ship, to the CBS radio anthology series *Suspense*, to which he was a frequent contributor; it was popular and rebroadcast. In the early 1950s Carr, writing all the scripts, expanded the story for CBS into a series called *Cabin B-13*. The "cabin" was the quarters where the ship's doctor (Arnold Moss) told odd tales about intrigue and impossible crimes set in various exotic ports. Far too intelligent to win wide audience response, it was among radio's very best mystery series.

In the early 1960s the *Dow Great Mysteries* anthology program presented a television adaptation of *The Burning Court*, keeping intact both the natural and the supernatural solutions to the mystery.

CARRADOS, MAX (Creator: Ernest BRAMAH). The first and best blind detective in literature. When Carrados was a young man, he developed amaurosis as the result of an accident, and, although the appearance of his eyes was not affected, he became totally blind.

Bramah tells of Carrados's darkness " . . . but so far from crippling his interests in life or his energies, it has merely impelled him to develop those senses which in most of us lie dormant and practically unused. Thus you will understand that while he may be at a disadvantage while you are at an advantage, he is at an advantage while you are at a disadvantage." Carrados describes his own view of the situation as having unexpected compensations: "A new world to explore, new experiences, new powers awakening; strange new perceptions; life in the fourth dimension."

He was born Max Wynn but changed his name so that he could inherit a fortune from a cousin. He works with an old friend, Louis Carlyle, a disbarred solicitor who committed an indiscretion (not a crime) and is now a private investigator. He, too, has adopted a pseudonym, changing his name from Louis Calling for the sake of prudence. The exchanges between the humorless Carlyle, eager for his friend's help but unwilling to admit his bafflement, and the gentle malice of the perceptive Carrados are among the high spots of the stories.

Serving as Carrados's eyes is Parkinson, his personal attendant. Extraordinarily observant, Parkinson is nevertheless an ordinary men of strictly limited ability whose true intellect remains a mystery. "It is doubtful if anyone had yet plumbed the exact limits of the worthy fellow's real capacity," Bramah wrote. "There were moments when he looked more sagacious than any mortal man has hope of ever being, and there were times when his comment on affairs seemed to reveal a greater depth of mental vacuity than was humanly credible."

A wealthy bachelor, Carrados pursues his talent for detection whenever he pleases without accepting a fee. Supplementing his intelligence are senses he developed to read newspaper headlines with a touch of his fingers, recognize a friend he has not seen in twenty-five years by his voice, and detect a man wearing a false moustache because "he carries a five-yard aura of spirit gum." His loss of sight has never affected his splendid sense of humor, his almost overwhelming kindliness, or his strict sense of justice, which sometimes skirts the legal process and, on one occasion, causes a murderer to commit suicide.

The first adventures of the blind detective were collected as *Max Carrados* (1914), called "one of the ten best volumes of detective shorts ever written" by Ellery QUEEN (author). Two more short story collections, *The Eyes of Max Carrados* (1923) and *Max Carrados Mysteries* (1927), followed. One Carrados short story, "The Bunch of Violets," appeared in *The Specimen Case* (1924); the only Carrados novel, *The Bravo of London* (1934), is not successful, though it has many interesting Bramah touches and even—surprisingly—one or two off-color passages; the book proves that Bramah's ability rests with short fiction.

CARSON, SYLVIA. *See* HALLIDAY, BRETT.

CARTER, FELICITY WINIFRED. *See* BONETT, JOHN AND EMERY.

CARTER, JOHN FRANKLIN. *See* "DIPLOMAT."

CARTER, NICK (Creator: John R. Coryell). The young detective has appeared in more detective novels than any other character in American literature. (Only England's Sexton BLAKE has solved more cases.) Carter's first adventure was recorded in the September 18, 1886, issue of the *New York Weekly*. The actual creator of Nick Carter was Ormond G. Smith (1860–1933), son of one of the founders of Street & Smith. He provided the outline of the first

John Russell Coryell, who wrote the first three Nick Carter stories.

story to John Russell Coryell (1848–1924), who wrote it and two sequels, after which a score of writers continued the series. All the stories appeared under a pseudonym: "by the author of Nick Carter," "by Sergeant Ryan," and, finally, "by Nicholas Carter." The most prolific writer was Frederic Van Rensselaer Dey (1861–1922), who produced more than 1,000 stories, but others contributed to the saga, including Thomas C. Harbaugh (1849–1924), Eugene T. Sawyer (1846–1924), George C. Jenks (1850–1929), Frederick W. Davis (1853–1933), W. Bert Foster (1869–1929), William Wallace Cook (1867–1933), Johnston McCulley (1883–1958), John H. Whitson (1854–1936), and Thomas W. HANSHEW.

In an early Nick Carter story, the all-American detective is described this way: "Giants were like children in his grasp. He could fell an ox with one blow of his small, compact fist. Old Sim Carter had made the physical development of his son one of the studies of his life. Only one of the studies, however. Young Nick's mind was stored with knowledge—

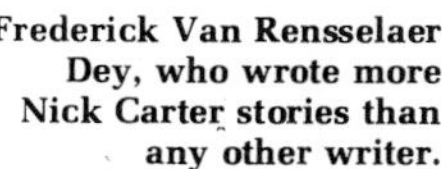

Frederick Van Rensselaer Dey, who wrote more Nick Carter stories than any other writer.

Walter Pidgeon (second from left) investigates airplane sabotage in *Nick Carter, Master Detective.* [*MGM*]

knowledge of a peculiar sort. His gray eyes had, like an Indian's, been trained to take in minutest details fresh for use. His rich, full voice could run the gamut of sounds, from an old woman's broken, querulous squeak to the deep, hoarse notes of a burly ruffian. And his handsome face could, in an instant, be distorted into any one of a hundred types of unrecognizable ugliness. He was a master of disguise, and could so transform himself that even old Sim could not recognize him. And his intellect, naturally keen as a razor blade, had been incredibly sharpened by the judicious cultivation of the astute old man."

With his faithful assistants, Chick and Patsy, Nick Carter appeared in DIME NOVELS and, later, PULP MAGAZINES for half a century. Today, his adventures are recounted in paperbacks, although he is no longer the naïve, clean-living young man of the original stories; nowadays he is a sophisticated secret agent.

Films

The French were the first to use the Nick Carter exploits in films, and he appeared in four fast-paced serials (1909–1912), all starring André Liabel. The American actor Thomas Carrigan portrayed him in a series of short films in 1920, and Edmund Lowe appeared in a second series in 1922, in some of the first roles in his career. After a lapse of nearly two decades, the dime novel detective was revived, with Walter Pidgeon featured in a series of full-length films.

Nick Carter, Master Detective. MGM, 1939. Pidgeon, Rita Johnson, Donald Meek, Henry Hull, Milburn Stone, Sterling Halloway. Directed by Jacques Tourneur.

Carter operates undercover at an aircraft factory, trying to expose a gang of spies who are stealing plans and committing sabotage and murder. He is plagued by an elderly eccentric (Meek), who, imagining himself to be a great amateur detective, becomes Carter's self-appointed assistant.

Phantom Raiders. MGM, 1940. Pidgeon, Meek, Joseph Schildkraut, Florence Rice, Nat Pendleton, John Carroll, Steffi Duna. Directed by Tourneur.

On vacation in Panama, Carter suspects a café owner of loading ships with straw, insuring the vessels as carrying valuable cargo, and then destroying them by remote control.

Sky Murder. MGM, 1940. Pidgeon, Meek, Joyce Compton, Kaaren Verne, Tom Conway, Edward Ashley. Directed by George Seitz.

In Washington, Carter is asked by a senator to uncover a fifth-column group; later a man is killed on a plane bound for New York with Carter aboard. This was the third and last time Pidgeon played Nick Carter, and the end of the MGM series.

In 1946 Nick's son Chick, portrayed by portly, fortyish Lyle Talbot, recovered a stolen diamond in the plush Century nightclub at the end of a fifteen-chapter serial, *Chick Carter, Detective* (Columbia. Directed by Derwin Abrahams). The character was based on the popular radio series, although the Chick of radio was years younger. Nick is neither seen nor mentioned.

The American actor Eddie Constantine portrayed a tough, trench-coated Nick Carter in two French films of the 1960s, *Nick Carter va tout casser* (1963) and *Nick Carter et le trèfle rouge* (1965).

Radio and Television

Debuting in 1943, *Nick Carter, Master Detective* was one of the most durable of all half-hour mystery radio programs. For years it opened in mounting surrealist hysteria: pounding on a door, a woman's shriek "Who is it?," and an officious male bawl, "Another case for Nick Carter!" Lon Clark played the master detective, and Patsy—now a girl—was Charlotte Manson. A juvenile spin-off, *Chick Carter, Boy Detective,* featuring the adventures of Nick's adopted teenage son, his friend Sue, and a grizzled cowboy guardian, Tex, became a Monday-through-Friday radio serial the same year (running from July 5, 1943, to July 6, 1945). Chick rarely had the opportunity to consult with his father.

In 1972 Robert Conrad played the detective in *The Adventures of Nick Carter* (costarring Broderick Crawford, Shelley Winters, Neville Brand), a feature film made for television and carefully set at the turn of the century. Nick is hired to investigate the disappearance of the wife of a wealthy playboy; many scenes occur in a nightclub in New York's Tenderloin. The film was the pilot for a series that did not materialize.

A pensive Nick Carter is hired by a dying millionaire (Broderick Crawford) to find his daughter-in-law in the period telefilm *The Adventures of Nick Carter;* Robert Conrad plays the title role. [*Universal*]

CARTER, PHILIP YOUNGMAN. *See* ALLINGHAM, MARGERY; CAMPION, ALBERT.

CASEY, FLASHGUN (Creator: George Harmon COXE). Jack Casey, tough photographer for the *Boston Express,* made his fictional debut in "Return Engagement" in the March 1934 issue of BLACK MASK; it was the first of dozens of Casey stories in that magazine. He is a hard drinker who enjoys a *Front Page*-type camaraderie with his cronies on the Boston newspapers. He is extremely fit (6 feet 1 inch tall, 215 pounds—"all bone and muscle"). He was a sergeant with the AEF in France during World War I, but his advancing age and a trick knee make him 4-F during World War II. His resentment at this rejection, coupled with his already hair-trigger temper, causes his violent reaction to the criminals who betray their country in *Murder for Two* (1943; originally published in Black Mask as *Blood on the Lens*).

Casey, a bachelor, lives on the second floor of an old brownstone on Marlborough Street. His editors and the Boston Police Department are easily annoyed by the frequency with which he becomes involved in murder. Ultimately, they are pacified by his ability to combine photographic scoops with the correct solution to the crime. He started his career with the *Boston Globe* but was fired when he opposed the paper's attempt to suppress one of his pictures; he later joined the *Express.*

There are six books about Casey: *Silent Are the Dead* (1942), *Murder for Two* (1943), *Flash Casey, Detective* (1946; s.s.), *Error of Judgment* (1961), *The Man Who Died Too Soon* (1962), and *Deadly Image* (1964).

Films

Women Are Trouble. MGM, 1936. Stuart Erwin, Paul

This paperback original, published by Avon in 1946, is the only short story collection about the photographer-detective.

Kelly, Florence Rice, Cy Kendall, Harold Huber. Directed by Errol Taggart.

Casey comes to the rescue when his city editor and a girl reporter whom he likes—but who is scooping him—are kidnapped from a fancy dress ball by criminals who think they know too much.

Here's Flash Casey. Grand National, 1937. Eric Linden, Boots Mallory, Howard Lang, Cully Richards, Holmes Herbert, Joseph Crehan. Directed by Lynn Shores.

Casey, the young assistant to the chief photographer on a newspaper, is innocently involved with a gang of blackmailers who are using his society pictures. Later, Casey snaps a picture of the gang leader firing a gun and rescues the society editor (a young lady) from his clutches.

Radio

Casey had a successful career on radio (in *Casey, Crime Photographer,* starring Staats Cotsworth), making his debut on CBS in 1946; the program continued for nearly a decade. He was most often to be found at the Blue Note Café, discussing a case with his girl, Anne Williams, or with Ethelbert, a sympathetic bartender, while piano music, played by the late great jazz pianist Herman Chittison, was heard in the background.

CASPARY, VERA (1899–). American novelist, screenwriter, and mystery novelist. Born in Chicago, she was the youngest of the four children of Paul Caspary, a millinery buyer for a Chicago department store, and Julia (Cohen) Caspary. From an early age she wanted to be a writer. Educated in Chicago public schools, she chose not to go to college, so that her father, then an elderly man, would not be burdened with her support. In order to get a writing job, she studied stenography and worked for eighteen months at various other jobs until she was hired by a mail-order advertising agency for which she wrote advertisements, pamphlets, and booklets on milking machines, washing tablets, and cold cream, as well as material for correspondence courses in fingerprint detection and voice culture. She founded her own mail-order ballet school, wrote a course in photoplay writing, and ran a weekly magazine for a public ballroom.

At the age of twenty-four Miss Caspary went to New York to become editor of Bernarr Macfadden's *Dance Magazine.* Her first novel, *The White Girl* (1929), is about a Negro girl who goes from Chicago to New York, where she passes for white. Her next book, *Thicker than Water* (1932), follows the lives of the members of a Portuguese-Jewish family (like the Casparys, residents of Chicago) from the turn of the century to the Depression and contains autobiographical elements. Miss Caspary's other novels of this period are *Ladies and Gents* (1929) and *Music in the Street* (1930). She turned to playwriting with *Blind Mice* (1931), in collaboration with Winifred Lenihan. That year it became a film called *Working Girls.* She wrote another play, *Geraniums in My Window* (1934), with Samuel Ornitz.

The dust wrapper of Vera Caspary's romantic mystery novel *Laura*, first published by Houghton Mifflin in 1943.

In 1932, after the failure of one of her plays, she wrote a Hollywood "original," *The Night of June 13th*. *Easy Living* (1937) is one of many other original screenplays she wrote during the next twenty-four years, the best known of which is *Les Girls* (1957). She also drew material for screenplays from books, plays, and radio scripts; *Claudia and David* (1946), *Letter to Three Wives* (1949), and *I Can Get It for You Wholesale* (1951) are the best known of these films.

During these years she lived in Norwalk, Conn., Hollywood, and Beverly Hills. In California she met and married producer I. G. Goldsmith. In World War II she went by convoy to London to work with her husband on the screenplay of her novel *Bedelia* (1945); the film was produced by one of the J. Arthur Rank subsidiaries.

Miss Caspary's first mystery novel, *Laura* (1943), was coolly received by the critics—who later wrote nostalgic rhapsodies about it. This novel and *Bedelia* typed her as a mystery writer, although she has also published nonmystery works, such as *Thelma* (1952), a novel of character.

Laura is about an unconventional detective who investigates a murder case and falls in love with the victim. Narrated by several of the main characters, it is a haunting and memorable novel and a masterpiece that Miss Caspary has never equaled.

Laura's successor, *Bedelia*, presents a pathological case history without indulging in jargon, but the heroine's villainy seems forced, and (like much of Miss Caspary's subsequent work) the story is of interest primarily to a feminine audience.

Closer to the mystery genre is *Stranger than Truth* (1946), set against the background of the magazine publishing industry; although two murders occur, the story is mainly about the theft of an idea. In technique, it resembles *Laura*. *The Weeping and the Laughter* (1950; British title: *Death Wish*) is a borderline novel that tries to investigate the causes of suicide by means of a suspense story technique. *The Husband* (1957), which was well received by the critics, is about a woman who discovers that her husband has homicidal tendencies. The theme is not unlike that of *Before the Fact* (1932) by Francis Iles (Anthony BERKELEY), but lacks that novel's power and integrity.

The very long *Evvie* (1960) is a character study of a jazz-age girl who eventually becomes a murder victim. Its evocation of the 1920s is attractive. *A Chosen Sparrow* (1964) is a Gothic tale, set in an Austrian castle, that tells of a Jewish survivor of the concentration camps who marries a former Prussian officer and discovers that he leads a double life as a homosexual. A man who has a death wish achieves his goal in a mysterious fashion in *The Man Who Loved His Wife* (1966). *The Rosecrest Cell* (1967) is a study of a group of frustrated amateur Communists who meet in a Connecticut mansion during the dramatic events of 1938 and 1939. The growing up and growing old of three sisters, members of a middle-class Chicago family, is the subject of *The Dreamers* (1975).

The career girl Laura (Gene Tierney) shows a sketch to epicene Waldo Lydecker (Clifton Webb) in the acclaimed film of Vera Caspary's suspense novel. [*Twentieth Century-Fox*]

Films

For decades Miss Caspary has provided source material and screenplays for motion pictures, in both mystery and romantic genres. In addition to the celebrated *Laura*, some of her mystery films are given below.

The Night of June 13. Paramount, 1932. Clive Brook, Lila Lee, Charlie Ruggles, Gene Raymond, Frances Dee. Directed by Stephen Roberts.

When his neurotic, suspicious wife commits suicide, a man burns her vindictive death note and finds himself accused of her murder.

Such Women Are Dangerous. Fox, 1934. Warner Baxter, Rochelle Hudson, Rosemary Ames. Directed by James Flood. Based on the Caspary story "Odd Thursday."

A young country girl, spurned by the famous writer with whom she has fallen in love, takes poison; he is charged with killing her.

Private Scandal. Paramount, 1934. Phillips

Holmes, Mary Brian, Zasu Pitts. Directed by Ralph Murphy.

A businessman makes the apparent suicide of his partner look like murder so he can collect on the insurance, unaware that it actually *was* murder.

Scandal Street. Paramount, 1938. Lew Ayres, Louise Campbell, Roscoe Karns, Porter Hall. Directed by James Hogan.

Town gossip wrongly convicts a young librarian of murder when a fellow boarder who had made advances toward her is killed.

Laura. Twentieth Century-Fox, 1944. Dana Andrews, Gene Tierney, Clifton Webb, Judith Anderson, Vincent Price. Directed by Otto Preminger.

A police officer is haunted by a young woman advertising executive, found with her head shot away. This intelligent film is augmented by an exceptional musical score (David Raksin).

Bedelia. Eagle-Lion (British), 1947. Margaret Lockwood, Ian Hunter, Barry K. Barnes. Directed by Lance Comfort.

A private detective insinuates himself on a honeymoon couple in Monte Carlo; actually, he is seeking a woman who has poisoned three husbands.

Miss Caspary also wrote the story on which *The Blue Gardenia* (1953) was based; it was directed by Fritz LANG.

Television

Miss Caspary has done television work. *Laura* has twice been a television special, once under its own title (with Lee Radziwill, and Robert Stack as detective Mark McPherson; adapted by Truman Capote) and as *Portrait for Murder* (Dana Wynter, George Sanders).

Plays

With George Sklar, Miss Caspary adapted *Laura* for the Broadway stage in 1947; it had a modest run (K. T. Stevens, Otto Kruger, and Hugh Marlowe as McPherson).

CAT AND THE CANARY, THE. *See* WILLARD, JOHN A.

CAUDWELL, CHRISTOPHER. *See* SPRIGG, C. ST. JOHN.

CECIL, HENRY (pseudonym of Henry Cecil Leon; 1902–). English jurist, humorist, and mystery writer. Born in Bayswater, he was educated at St. Paul's School and King's College, Cambridge. He was called to the bar in 1923. In 1935 he married Lettice Mabel Apperly; she died in 1950, and he married Jeanne Ovenden (née Blackmore) in 1954. During World War II he served in the Middle East. He filled the office of county court judge from 1949 to 1967, when he retired. He now lives in London.

Cecil has written numerous novels; nonfiction (*Know about English Law*, 1965); and plays (*Brothers in Law*, 1959, in collaboration with Ted Willis; and *Settled out of Court*, 1960, in collaboration with William Saroyan; both were based on Henry Cecil novels of 1955 and 1959, respectively). *Brothers in Law* was both a film and the basis of a television series that Cecil contributed to. *Alibi for a Judge*, a play based on the 1960 novel, ran in London's West End for nearly two years.

If the law is an ass, Henry Cecil does his best to prove it—in extravagant farces that turn everything upside down and prove conclusively that black is white and vice versa. In *No Bail for the Judge* (1952), a judge is tried for a murder he did not commit and is aided by a crook. (Alfred HITCHCOCK once planned to make a film from this novel with Cary Grant, but the project was not realized.) In *Much in Evidence* (1957; U.S. title: *The Long Arm*) a group of men—all bald and lame—make dubious claims against an insurance company and wind up in court. In *Settled out of Court* (1959) a convicted murderer is able to win a retrial by various means—all foul. *Unlawful Occasions* (1962) is about a gentleman who sues to get his share of a win on the football pools and lands in jail for failing to pay proper respect to the judge.

Film

Brothers in Law. Tudor (British), 1957. Richard Attenborough, Ian Carmichael, Terry-Thomas, Jill Adams. Directed by Roy Boulting. From the 1955 novel.

A young English barrister, just graduated from law school, has some legal misadventures.

CELLINI, DR. EMMANUEL (Creator: John CREASEY as Kyle Hunt; published in England under the Michael Halliday pseudonym). Psychiatrist-detective Dr. Emmanuel Cellini once had a lucrative practice in New York but now works in London. Although he always draws upon his professional background in his cases, he solves many problems intuitively or by discussing them with his wife, Felisa, formerly a ballerina but now a plump matron. The first of the eleven books in this series is *Cunning as a Fox* (1965).

CHAMBRUN, PIERRE (Creator: Judson PHILIPS as Hugh Pentecost). The resident manager of New York's foremost luxury hotel, the Beaumont, Chambrun must frequently investigate murders, or threats of violence, that could damage the hotel's reputation.

Born in France, Chambrun emigrated to the United States in his youth but returned to Europe for his professional training and joined the Resistance during World War II. After more than thirty-five years in his profession, Chambrun is an institution himself.

He is short and stocky; his most noticeable feature is his dark eyes, underlined with heavy pouches. He works very hard—often twenty hours a day to keep the Beaumont running smoothly. He never eats lunch, because he is busiest at that time, but he enjoys gourmet foods when he has more leisure. He drinks at least a half-dozen pots of Turkish coffee served in a demitasse, and chain-smokes Egyptian cigarettes. Thoroughly efficient, suave, and able to inspire devotion in his staff, he is also a fluent linguist.

Much of Chambrun's success as a hotel manager and a detective is due to his thorough knowledge of his staff, his hotel, and especially, his clients. His motto is "The Beaumont is not only a hotel, it is a way of life."

CHECKLIST

1962 *The Cannibal Who Overate*
1964 *The Shape of Fear*
1966 *The Evil That Men Do*
1967 *The Golden Trap*
1968 *The Gilded Nightmare*
1969 *Girl Watcher's Funeral*
1971 *The Deadly Joke*
1972 *Birthday, Deathday*
1973 *Walking Dead Man*
1974 *Bargain with Death*
1975 *Time of Terror*

CHAN, CHARLIE (Creator: Earl Derr BIGGERS). Detective sergeant (later inspector) of the Honolulu Police Department, Chan is very stout and yet walks with the light and dainty steps of a woman. His skin is ivory-tinted, and his cheeks are as chubby as a baby's. His hair is black and closely cut, and his slanted amber eyes have an expression of keen brightness that makes the pupils gleam like black buttons in yellow light.

The Chinese-Hawaiian-American sleuth is married, has eleven children, and lives with his family in a house on Punchbowl Hill. He wears Western clothes but speaks broken English in a stilted manner. Extremely humble, always courteous and charming, he is considered lovable by all who know him.

A student of Chinese philosophy, Chan is fond of quoting aphorisms. He is not a physically impressive figure, but his intelligence is razor-sharp. Known as the best detective on the Honolulu Police Force, he has the reputation for always getting his man.

The House without a Key (1925), the first book about Chan, is probably the best of the series. It concerns his investigation of the murder of rich, handsome, and genial Dan Winterslip, whose past was open to question. Murder on a ranch in California is the subject of *The Chinese Parrot* (1926). In spite of a bullet hole in the wall and a missing gun, the victim—a Chinese cook—has been stabbed to death. This novel is listed in SANDOE'S READERS' GUIDE TO CRIME.

Behind That Curtain (1928) starts with a murder in London and continues with a second killing in San Francisco—sixteen years later. A pair of Chinese

Warner Oland (left) as Charlie Chan in a scene from *Charlie Chan in Egypt*. [*Fox*]

Warner Oland listens attentively to satanically costumed opera singer Boris Karloff in *Charlie Chan at the Opera.* [*Twentieth Century-Fox*]

slippers embroidered with Chinese characters is the only clue to both crimes. *The Black Camel* (1929) is about famous film actress Shelah Fane, who is stabbed to death in a secluded spot on Waikiki Beach, and the public outcry that makes it imperative that Chan find the murderer immediately.

In Charlie Chan Carries On (1930) a group of people on a round-the-world tour keep encountering dead bodies, and the Chinese detective must find the culprit as the ship travels on its last lap from Honolulu to San Francisco. It is one of Chan's best cases, notable for its doom-laden shipboard atmosphere. The final Chan adventure, *Keeper of the Keys* (1932), is about a much-married prima donna whose marital and operatic careers are cut short by gunfire near romantic Lake Tahoe. This is the only Chan novel that was never filmed. The Chan stories have been reissued in paperback editions every ten years or so. In addition, Dennis Lynds (*see* COLLINS, MICHAEL) wrote a paperback original, *Charlie Chan Returns,* in 1974.

Films

Affable Chan, whose screen investigations are rivaled in number only by those of Sherlock HOLMES, has never been portrayed by a Chinese actor. But his popularity has been immense for several decades. He has been depicted as a wise, philosophical policeman who methodically pursues his quarry. Audiences have always been delighted by the almost ritualistic final assembly of suspects and Chan's accusation "*You* are *murderer!*"; his paternal patience with his Americanized offspring, who clumsily try to "help Pop," and his frequent, sage, quasi-Confucian sayings ("Bad alibi like dead fish. Cannot stand test of time"; or "If strength were all, tiger would not fear scorpion") have further endeared him to the public.

Chan's transition to the screen, however, was neither immediate nor easy. The first films based on the Chan novels altered and minimized the role of the detective. He is listed twelfth in the cast of the 1926 Pathe serial made from *The House without a Key* (Walter Miller, Allene Ray. Directed by Spencer Gordon Bennett), and is played for comedy by the Japanese actor George Kuwa. *The Chinese Parrot* (Universal, 1928. Marian Nixon, Edmund Burns), under the wildly stylized direction of Paul Leni, gave the Chan role to the Japanese star Sojin, but the film concentrates on a cursed string of pearls that brings evil to all who wear it. In the next film, *Behind That Curtain* (Fox, 1929. Warner Baxter, Lois Moran. Directed by Irving Cummings), the detective is a Scotland Yard inspector, Gilbert Emery, in a heavy drama of illicit love, blackmail, and murder that moves from desert sands to London to San Francisco. Chan (played by English actor E. L. Park) makes a token appearance at the finish, in time to shoot the villain.

Then, in 1931, Fox decided on a close adaptation of *Charlie Chan Carries On* (Warner Oland, John Garrick, Marguerite Churchill. Directed by Hamilton MacFadden) and wisely gave the Chan role to the Swedish-born Oland, who had made a career of playing Oriental villains opposite Pearl White. Nonetheless the film was still experimental;

Sidney Toler as Chan examines a murder chair and a unique method of death in *Charlie Chan in Black Magic,* a late entry in the detective series. [*Monogram*]

Sidney Toler (left) as the Oriental detective finds that death has accompanied the travelers in *Charlie Chan's Murder Cruise*. Passengers Lionel Atwill and Leo G. Carroll pay him close attention. [*Twentieth Century Fox*]

the Chinese detective appears only at the end, embarking on a round-the-world cruise on its final leg, from Honolulu to San Francisco, when a Scotland Yard friend investigating two murders that occurred during the trip is himself shot. Oland, although completely reversing his previous image, was such a success that the "Golden Age" of the screen Chan was begun.

The Black Camel. Fox, 1931. Oland, Sally Eilers, Bela Lugosi, Dorothy Revier, Robert Young. Directed by MacFadden.

While making a film on location in Hawaii, an actress is murdered after making a revelation about her past to a phoney Hindu seer (Lugosi). The black camel of the title represents death. In this film, the domestic Chan, his large family about him, is first revealed.

Charlie Chan's Chance. Fox, 1932. Oland, Ralph Morgan, H. B. Warner, Nixon. Directed by John Blystone.

A Scotland Yard detective searching in New York for a man wanted for murder in England dies of a supposed heart attack. But visitor Chan notices a dead cat in the room with the victim. Chan's eleventh son is born in Honolulu.

Charlie Chan's Greatest Case. Fox, 1933. Oland, Heather Angel, Roger Imhof, John Warburton. Directed by MacFadden. A somewhat more faithful version of *The House without a Key* than the 1926 film had been.

A much-hated man is killed; his broken arm gives Chan a vital clue.

Charlie Chan's Courage. Fox, 1934. Oland, Drue Leyton, Donald Woods, Paul Harvey. Directed by George Hadden. A remake of *The Chinese Parrot*.

Chan takes a job as a cook at a ranch in order to secretly investigate the man to whom he is to turn over a valuable string of pearls.

Charlie Chan in London. Fox, 1934. Oland, Leyton, Douglas Walton, Alan Mowbray, Mona Barrie. Directed by Eugene Forde.

Chan begins a round-the-world cruise during which he attends police conventions and similar functions; his travels serve as a device whereby the films from this point on are set in varied locales. In London, a girl begs him to clear her brother, who is about to be hanged for a murder she insists he did not commit.

Charlie Chan in Paris. Fox, 1935. Oland, Mary Brian, Erik Rhodes, John Mijan, Thomas Beck. Directed by Lewis Seiler.

A knife-throwing assassin kills a dancer at a Left Bank café. Since she was one of Chan's agents, he becomes involved in counterfeit bank stock and a chase through the Parisian sewers. Chan's son Lee (Keye Luke) makes an appearance.

Charlie Chan in Egypt. Fox, 1935. Oland, Pat Paterson, Beck, Rita Cansino (Rita Hayworth). Directed by Louis King.

On the Nile, at the site of eerie archaeological

excavations, several murders occur; one is caused by deadly vapors that seep from a violin when it is played. A mummy with a bullet in its chest is found in a tomb.

Charlie Chan in Shanghai. Twentieth Century-Fox, 1935. Oland, Irene Hervey, Jon Hall, Luke. Directed by James Tinling.

A British secret service agent calls Chan to Shanghai, rife with smuggling and gang wars, but is killed by a gun triggered when he opens up a gift. Chan is "aided" by his "number-one" son, Lee, and the warm affection between them is evident.

Charlie Chan's Secret. Twentieth Century-Fox, 1936. Oland, Charles Quigley, Astrid Allwyn, Rosina Lawrence. Directed by Gordon Wiles.

Chan arrives in San Francisco searching for a missing heir to millions who suddenly turns up—dead on the darkened floor during a séance.

Charlie Chan at the Circus. Twentieth Century-Fox, 1936. Oland, Luke, Francis Ford, Shirley Deane, John McGuire, George and Olive Brasno. Directed by Harry Lachman.

Chan and his large brood arrive at the circus to have a good time, but the detective discovers the owner strangled, supposedly by the circus ape, which had been released from its cage.

Charlie Chan at the Race Track. Twentieth Century-Fox, 1936. Oland, Luke, Helen Wood, Beck, Alan Dinehart, Gavin Muir. Directed by H. Bruce Humberstone.

As Chan's boat docks in Honolulu for a stopover, a famed racehorse owner is supposedly kicked to death by his prize steed. But Chan thinks that it is murder and accompanies the animal to a California handicap.

Charlie Chan at the Opera. Twentieth Century-Fox, 1936. Oland, Luke, Boris Karloff, Charlotte Henry, Beck, Nedda Harrigan. Directed by Humberstone. Oscar Levant composed a special opera for the film.

Famed opera singer Gravelle (Karloff) escapes from the asylum where his wife and her lover had abandoned him; soon both wife and lover are stabbed to death during the performance of an opera. Gravelle stalks the opera house in Mephistophelian costume, but Chan believes that he is innocent.

Charlie Chan at the Olympics. Twentieth Century-Fox, 1937. Oland, Luke, Katherine De Mille, Pauline Moore, Allan Lane. Directed by Humberstone.

Chan ventures to Berlin—on a dirigible—where son Lee is part of the American swimming team at the 1936 Olympics. Spies have taken a stolen device used to control airplanes by radio, and the inventor has been killed in Honolulu.

Charlie Chan on Broadway. Twentieth Century-Fox, 1937. Oland, Luke, J. Edward Bromberg, Leon Ames, Woods, Joan Marsh. Directed by Forde.

On an ocean liner returning from Europe, a girl hides her politically explosive diary in Chan's trunk. Later, she is murdered in New York's Hottentot Club, and Chan must interrupt a police banquet in his honor to sample Broadway nightlife.

Charlie Chan at Monte Carlo. Twentieth Century-Fox, 1938. Oland, Luke, Virginia Field, Sidney Blackmer, Harold Huber. Directed by Forde.

Stranded on the dark highway between Monte Carlo and Paris, Chan and son come upon a dead man in a car—a bank messenger who had been carrying a million dollars worth of bonds. Warner Oland died after this film, his sixteenth portrayal of Charlie Chan. The series continued without pause, and with no immediate lessening of quality, with Missouri-born character actor Sidney Toler in the role.

Charlie Chan in Honolulu. Twentieth Century-Fox, 1938. Toler, Phyllis Brooks, Victor Sen Yung (a new Lee Chan), Layne Tom, Jr. (Tommy, another son), Eddie Collins, John King, Claire Dodd. Directed by Humberstone.

While awaiting word on the birth of his first grandchild, Chan learns that a ship has docked in Honolulu Harbor with a murdered man on board—and $3 million missing.

Charlie Chan in Reno. Twentieth Century-Fox, 1939. Toler, Ricardo Cortez, Brooks, Slim Summerville, Kane Richmond, Yung. Directed by Norman Foster.

An old friend asks Chan to fly by China Clipper to Reno, where his wife, about to divorce him, has been accused of stabbing her rival to death. In this

A Chan offspring, Benson Fong, and the family chauffeur Birmingham (Mantan Moreland) in one of the younger Chan's frequent attempts to solve cases on his own. [*Monogram*]

Roland Winters, the final screen Charlie Chan, peers down at a dead man in *Docks of New Orleans*. [*Monogram*]

film, Yung becomes "number-two" son, James "Jimmy" Chan.

Charlie Chan at Treasure Island. Twentieth Century-Fox, 1939. Toler, Cesar Romero, Moore, Yung, Douglas Fowley. Directed by Foster.

Chan and the Great Rhandini, a flamboyant stage magician, combine forces in an attempt to expose a mysterious psychic known as Dr. Zodiac, who blackmails victims and drives them to suicide. The film is a complex mystery and is considered the best of the series.

Charlie Chan in the City of Darkness. Twentieth Century-Fox, 1939. Toler, Lynn Bari, Richard Clarke, Huber. Directed by Herbert I. Leeds.

The city is Paris, blacked out because of the Munich crisis, and Chan, stranded, becomes involved with apaches and foreign agents as he investigates the death of a millionaire munitions dealer.

Charlie Chan in Panama. Twentieth Century-Fox, 1940. Toler, Jean Rogers, Lionel Atwill, Yung, Mary Nash, Jack LaRue. Directed by Foster.

In the Panama Canal Zone, an American secret service operative is felled by a poisoned cigarette as he is about to reveal to Chan the identity of a dangerous saboteur, and the United States Fleet is scheduled to be blown up as it moves through the canal.

Charlie Chan's Murder Cruise. Twentieth Century-Fox, 1940. Toler, Marjorie Weaver, Atwill, Yung, Leo G. Carroll. Directed by Forde.

In this remake of *Charlie Chan Carries On* Chan arrives much earlier on the cruise ship, and a masked strangler has already done away with his friend from Scotland Yard.

Charlie Chan at the Wax Museum. Twentieth Century-Fox, 1940. Toler, C. Henry Gordon, Marc Lawrence, Marguerite Chapman, Yung. Directed by Lynn Shores.

Chan agrees to discuss old murder cases during a radio broadcast from an eerie waxworks whose owner secretly performs plastic surgery for the underworld and where a killer, plotting revenge against Chan, lurks.

Murder over New York. Twentieth Century-Fox, 1940. Toler, Weaver, Robert Lowery, Cortez, Melville Cooper. Directed by Lachman.

In New York for a police convention, Chan encounters yet another Scotland Yard inspector who dies (in this case poison gas is the cause) before he can identify the leader of a gang of airplane saboteurs. Chan unmasks the leader aboard a stratospheric bomber in flight.

Dead Men Tell. Twentieth Century-Fox, 1941. Toler, Sheila Ryan, Paul McGrath, George Reeves, Ethel Griffies. Directed by Lachman.

Chan's son lures him aboard a treasure hunting ship on which a "pirate ghost" is eliminating one by one the holders of pieces of a map showing the location of $6 million in bullion buried on the Cocos Islands.

Charlie Chan in Rio. Twentieth Century-Fox, 1941. Toler, Mary Beth Hughes, Victor Jory, Cobina Wright, Jr., Yung. Directed by Lachman.

Chan and son arrive in Rio de Janeiro to arrest a woman for murder but find her strangled. A psychic who uses drugged "truth" cigarettes helps Chan smoke out the killer.

Castle in the Desert. Twentieth Century-Fox, 1942. Toler, Arlene Whelan, Richard Derr, Henry Daniell, Yung, Griffies. Directed by Lachman.

Chan is invited to view the replica of an ancient Italian castle built in the middle of the Mojave Desert by a millionaire eccentric whose wife is a titled descendant of the Borgias. Several other guests are poisoned.

After twenty-seven films, Fox discontinued the series. Two years later a smaller studio, Monogram, resumed the films with Sidney Toler again in the role of Chan, though on noticeably smaller budgets.

Charlie Chan in the Secret Service. Monogram, 1944. Toler, Gwen Kenyon, Mantan Moreland (his first appearance as Chan's chauffeur, Birmingham), Benson Fong (Tommy, another son). Directed by Phil Rosen.

Chan, now a special FBI agent, investigates the death of an inventor who was in the employ of the United States government and was killed at a cocktail party attended by several suspicious foreign persons.

The Chinese Cat. Monogram, 1944. Toler, Fong, Moreland, Joan Woodbury, Weldon Heyburn, Ian Keith. Directed by Rosen.

In Washington, Chan's pursuit of jewel thieves leads him to their hideout, a dark funhouse in an abandoned amusement pier.

Charlie Chan in Black Magic. Monogram, 1944. Toler, Moreland, Frances Chan (a Chan daughter), Joe Crehan, Jacqueline DeWit. Directed by Rosen.

Just about to start his first vacation in years, Chan must solve the murder of a medium because his own daughter attended the séance at which the psychic was killed—by a bullet made of poisoned blood.

The Jade Mask. Monogram, 1945. Toler, Moreland, Janet Warren, Edith Evanson. Directed by Rosen.

Several strange residents of his household are suspected in the death of an elderly scientist. Edwin Luke is a Chan son in this film.

The Scarlet Clue. Monogram, 1945. Toler, Fong, Moreland, Helen Devereaux, Robert Homans, Virginia Brissac. Directed by Rosen.

Several murders are committed in a radio studio, by means of gas emitted from a microphone; Chan is led to stolen secret radar plans.

The Shanghai Cobra. Monogram, 1945. Toler, Fong, Moreland, Walter Fenner, Joan Barclay. Directed by Phil Karlson.

Three employees die of poisoning at the Sixth National Bank, where a priceless store of radium is kept by the government. Chan's investigation leads him to the sewers under the vaults.

The Red Dragon. Monogram, 1945. Toler, Fortunio Bonanova, Fong, Willie Best (another chauffeur, Chattanooga Brown), Carol Hughes, Barton Yarborough, Directed by Rosen.

In Mexico City, bullets fired by remote control kill several people thought to have been conspiring to obtain the plans for an improved atomic bomb.

Dark Alibi. Monogram, 1946. Toler, Fong, Moreland, Teala Loring, Joyce Compton. Directed by Karlson.

Chan is surprised to discover that several people have been convicted on the basis of forged fingerprints.

Shadows over Chinatown. Monogram, 1946. Toler, Moreland, Yung, Tanis Chandler, Mary Gordon. Directed by Terry Morse.

In San Francisco, an elderly woman asks Chan to find her missing daughter; he learns that she was once part of an escort service tied in with the rackets and murder.

Dangerous Money. Monogram, 1946. Toler, Yung, Best, Crehan, Dick Elliott, Elaine Lang. Directed by Morse.

A federal agent who, with Chan, is on board a ship sailing for Samoa is killed by a gang that smuggled currency and priceless art out of the Philippines during the Japanese invasion. Several more murders occur before the ship docks at Pago Pago.

The Trap. Monogram, 1946. Toler, Moreland, Yung, Chandler, Larry Blake, Kirk Alyn, Anne Nagel. Directed by Howard Bretherton.

A Chinese girl enlists Chan's aid when several actresses in her troupe are killed while they are rehearsing in a Malibu beach house.

After twenty-two films as Chan, Sidney Toler died. Monogram hurriedly cast actor Roland Winters in the role and continued the series. He was the sixth Chan and the last to play in a screen series.

The Chinese Ring. Monogram, 1947. Winters, Moreland, Yung, Warren Douglas, Louise Currie, Philip Ahn. Directed by William Beaudine.

A Chinese princess arrives in the United States with a million dollars. She plans to smuggle airplanes to her homeland but is murdered while in Chan's office enlisting his aid.

Docks of New Orleans. Monogram, 1948. Winters, Moreland, Yung, Virginia Dale, Carol Forman. Directed by Derwin Abrahams.

All three members of a syndicate that owns the rights to a formula for a new explosive are killed the same way: a radio tube shatters, releasing poison gas.

The Shanghai Chest. Monogram, 1948. Winters, Moreland, Yung, Tim Ryan, Deannie Best, Tristram Coffin. Directed by Beaudine.

A judge is killed by a masked man; the prints on the gun belong to a criminal whom the judge had convicted but who had been executed in prison six months earlier. Soon the district attorney and the jurors who served during the man's trial are also murdered.

The Golden Eye. Monogram, 1948. Winters, Moreland, Yung, Wanda McKay, Bruce Kellogg. Directed by Beaudine.

Chan travels to the Lazy Y dude ranch to probe attempts on the life of the owner and to discover the source of the gold coming out of the supposedly played-out Golden Eye mine.

The Feathered Serpent. Monogram, 1948. Winters, Luke (back as Lee Chan), Yung, Moreland, Robert Livingston, Nils Asther, Forman. Directed by Beaudine.

On a vacation drive in the wilds of Mexico, Chan and two of his sons become involved in the attempted murder of an archaeologist, a hidden Aztec temple, and a vast concealed treasure.

Sky Dragon. Monogram, 1949. Winters, Luke, Moreland, Noel Neill, Ryan, Iris Adrian, Elena Verdugo, Milburn Stone, Lyle Talbot. Directed by Lesley Selander.

All the passengers and crew of a plane on which Chan is traveling are drugged (the plane is on automatic pilot), and the sum of $250,000, which is being transferred under guard, vanishes. The film, an airborne locked-room mystery, was the seventeenth and last Monogram Chan film.

Radio and Television

Walter Connolly originally starred in the *Charlie Chan* radio series in 1932, and Ed Begley and Santos Ortega played the Oriental detective into the 1940s. In the late 1950s J. Carroll Naish starred in the half-hour television series *The New Adventures of Charlie Chan,* filmed in England. James Wong appeared as Chan's son. A series of half-hour cartoons called *The Amazing Chan and the Chan Clan* appeared on television in 1972. In these the detective's large brood of younger offspring tried to solve mysteries on their own, with minimal parental interference. Keye Luke supplied the voice of Charlie Chan.

Youngman Carter designed this dust wrapper for the first edition of Chandler's short story collection, published by Hamish Hamilton in 1965. Carter was Margery Allingham's husband and the author of several Albert Campion books.

CHANDLER, RAYMOND (1888–1959). American detective story writer. Born in Chicago, Chandler, when a small boy, was taken by his mother to live in England. He received a classical education at Dulwich College, London, then taught, and was a freelance journalist for *The Spectator* and the *Westminster Gazette* before returning to the United States. During World War I he went to Canada and joined the Gordon Highlanders, serving with that regiment in France, where he won two medals. He was training to be a pilot when the war ended. Returning to the United States, he settled in Los Angeles, where he was briefly a reporter for the *Daily Express* and an accountant before becoming a successful executive with various oil companies. The Depression caused a temporary collapse in the oil industry, and Chandler became insolvent. He began writing for the PULP MAGAZINES, which he had read as relaxation, and sold his first story in 1933.

He married Pearl Cecily Bowen in 1924, and although she was seventeen years older than he, they shared a love of travel, music, reading, and walking. During his wife's lengthy illness that culminated in her death in December 1954, Chandler devoted himself almost exclusively to her, neglecting his career. After she died, he wrote: "She was the beat of my heart for thirty years. . . . It was my great and now useless regret that I never wrote anything really worth her attention, no book that I could dedicate to her. I planned it. I thought of it, but I never wrote it. Perhaps I couldn't have written it. Perhaps by now she realizes that I tried, and that I regarded the sacrifice of several years of a rather insignificant literary career as a small price to pay if I could make her smile a few times more." Chandler's own health deteriorated after his wife's death, and he wrote little, drinking heavily until his own death five years later. His only book of this period, *Playback* (1958), is regarded as inferior to the rest of his work.

Chandler did not achieve fame and popularity until the publication of his first novel, *The Big Sleep,* in 1939. Before that he had written twenty novelettes for BLACK MASK and other leading magazines of the time. Twelve of these stories were reprinted in *The Simple Art of Murder* (1950). Another eight novelettes later were (in Chandler's own words) "cannibalized" to form portions of his novels. He felt uneasy about having done this and tried to prevent republication of the novelettes; they were not collected until, five years after Chandler's death, *Killer in the Rain* (1964) was published.

In his novelettes Chandler was evolving the character of his famous detective hero, Philip MARLOWE. At times the hero was anonymous; at other times he was called Carmody, Dalmas, Malvern, and Mallory. In the later novelettes he became Philip Marlowe. With each story he came closer to Chandler's conception of the fictional detective, recognizable in his novels and described by the author in his often-reprinted, self-revelatory essay "The Simple

Art of Murder" (*The Atlantic Monthly*, December 1944). Chandler saw the detective as a modern knight "in search of a hidden truth." In describing his knight's journey and character he said, "Down these mean streets a man must go who is not himself mean, who is neither tarnished nor afraid. The detective in this kind of story must be such a man. He is the hero, he is everything. He must be a complete man and a common man and yet an unusual man. He must be, to use a rather weathered phrase, a man of honor. . . . He is a relatively poor man, or he would not be a detective at all. He is a common man or he could not go among common people. He has a sense of character, or he would not know his job. He will take no man's money dishonestly and no man's insolence without a due and dispassionate revenge. He is a lonely man and his pride is that you will treat him as a proud man or be very sorry you ever saw him. He talks as the man of his age talks, that is, with rude wit, a lively sense of the grotesque, a disgust for sham, and a contempt for pettiness."

In Chandler's seven novels Marlowe remains consistent with this image, resisting the corrupting influences around him. His clients are wealthy, but money has not bought them happiness. They are vulnerable to blackmail, Marlowe's first client, the dying millionaire General Sternwood in *The Big Sleep*, being a good example. They surround themselves with the trappings of wealth—which invite theft. In *Farewell, My Lovely* (1940), it is a Beverly Hills family and their collection of imported jade; in *The High Window* (1942), the wealthy Murdocks of Pasadena and their rare coin, the Brasher Doubloon. The marriages are invariably unhappy. The successful publisher in *The Lady in the Lake* (1943) has been unfaithful to his wife; Sylvia Lennox of *The Long Goodbye* (1953) had six husbands before she was murdered. Marlowe remains steadfastly honest and loyal to his clients, immune to bribes or threats by the police. Rather than betray a client, he accepts arrest and beating by the police in *The Lady in the Lake* and *The Long Goodbye*.

Increasingly, Chandler became disenchanted with Los Angeles, the city he had once loved. In 1946 he moved to La Jolla; in *The Little Sister* (1949) he has Marlowe say in an often-quoted soliloquy: "I used to like this town. A long time ago . . . Los Angeles was just a big dry sunny place with ugly homes and no style, but good-hearted and peaceful. . . . [Now] we've got the big money, the sharpshooters, the percentage workers, the fast dollar boys, the hoodlums out of New York and Chicago and Detroit . . . the riffraff of a big hardboiled city with no more personality than a paper cup."

Part of Chandler's growing hatred of Los Angeles stemmed from his frustrating, albeit successful, career as a screenwriter. He received Academy Award nominations for *Double Indemnity* (1944), which he wrote with Billy Wilder, and *The Blue Dahlia* (1946), which he wrote alone. However, he was constantly at odds with Hollywood studio executives over their demands for changes in his material. In 1949, when Chandler was the "hottest" mystery name in the United States, he was guaranteed a sum of money if he would merely lend his name to a proposed *Raymond Chandler's Mystery Magazine*. He refused because he would have had no control over its editorial policy.

As a writer for the pulp magazines, Chandler was highly rated, but his output did not noticeably differ in either quantity or quality from that of a dozen others. His writing skills became more apparent with his first full-length book, and he was consistently praised, especially for his rendering of the sights and sounds of Los Angeles. Will Cuppy attributed to Chandler "a raw richness of simile seldom seen in a detective yarn." Howard HAYCRAFT described him as "aware, articulate, and literarily gifted" and thought that *Farewell, My Lovely* was the best hard-boiled mystery since the works of Dashiell HAMMETT. Julian SYMONS, in praising Chandler "as a very good writer," felt that he nonetheless came off second best in comparison with Hammett because of the latter's toughness and detachment. He felt that Chandler had weakened his books by permitting Philip Marlowe to become "more a piece of wish-fulfillment, and idealized expression of Chandler himself, a strictly literary conception." However, Symons mentions the esteem with which Chandler's works were held in England. W. H. Auden regarded them as "works of art" rather than escape literature. Chandler was surprised to find, while on a trip to England, that "over here I am not regarded as a mystery writer but as an American novelist of some importance."

In *A Catalogue of Crime*, Jacques BARZUN and Wendell Hertig TAYLOR devote a considerable portion of their introduction to a refutation of that portion of "The Simple Art of Murder" in which Chandler criticizes the classic detective story for its implausibility. They deny that Chandler achieved greater realism in his private eye mysteries, finding unbelievable a hero who cares little for money and perseveres despite frequent beatings and shootings. Nonetheless, they praise his work highly, especially *The Big Sleep* ("atmosphere, suspense, unexpected violence, sardonic dialogue, sharp-focus description"), *Farewell, My Lovely* ("a model of complexity kept under control"), and *The Lady in the Lake* (his "masterpiece"). The Mystery Writers of America awarded Chandler's *The Long Goodbye* the 1954 Edgar for best novel.

CHARLES, NICK AND NORA (Creator: Dashiell HAMMETT). This husband-wife team was Hammett's most popular creation, largely because of a successful series of motion pictures and long-running radio and television shows. They represent Hammett's strongest attempt at humor. Their one adventure (*The Thin Man,* 1934) is narrated in the first person by retired private detective Nick Charles (his real name—Nick is of Greek descent—is Charalambides). He is a hard-drinking, fun-loving, wisecracking, once-tough playboy—and his wife is more of the same. A former operative of the Trans-American Detective Agency of San Francisco, Nick is now married to a millionairess and is content, even anxious, to give up the rough life and concentrate on drinking. It is Nora who insists that he take on the case, and, although he just wants to be left alone and go to parties and count her money, Nick eventually enjoys the caper. Nick and Nora are a phenomenon in modern literature: a married couple who like each other. Lillian Hellman, Hammett's companion for three decades, served as the model for the fun-loving Nora.

The "thin man," incidentally, is not a reference to Nick but to a missing corpse.

"The thin man" and his wife (William Powell, Myrna Loy) join Asta, their dog, in a domestic pose. [*MGM*]

Films

The Thin Man. MGM, 1934. William Powell, Myrna Loy, Maureen O'Sullivan. Directed by W. S. Van Dyke.

Hammett's book was made into the first film of an outstanding detective series, starring William Powell and Myrna Loy who enlarged the happy lifestyle of Nick and Nora Charles for the screen. Depression audiences were delighted with the sophisticated American couple who mixed martinis and mystery and for whom living was carefree and even sexy after marriage.

The film was an instant success. The first case (like the book) concerns the disappearance of an inventor; he is "the thin man" of the title. Nick's white terrier, Asta, later discovers the charred body of the inventor in the ruins of his bombed laboratory. At the climax of the film Nick uses a wild dinner party and much drinking to close in on the guilty party. Public enthusiasm for the film triggered a sequel (cautiously offered three years later, although every other studio had rushed to produce mysteries involving similar couples in the meantime) and a curious switch of identities: William Powell, dapper but not slim, took on the name of his first case and became known throughout the subsequent series as the Thin Man.

After the Thin Man. MGM, 1936. Powell, Loy, James Stewart, Elissa Landi. Directed by Van Dyke.

Nora's cousin is accused of murdering a wayward husband, and Nick, though "retired," comes to her defense, casually tossing the murder weapon into a river and, in the end, exposing an unlikely killer.

Another Thin Man. MGM, 1939. Powell, Loy, C. Aubrey Smith, Virginia Grey. Directed by Van Dyke. Based on a Hammett story about the Continental Op (*see* CONTINENTAL OP, THE), "The Farewell Murder."

The title refers to the Charleses' newborn son, Nick, Jr., and the case revolves about an elderly munitions manufacturer who is killed on a family estate crowded with suspects.

Shadow of the Thin Man. MGM, 1941. Powell, Loy, Donna Reed, Barry Nelson. Directed by Van Dyke.

Nick goes to the races, a frequent diversion, but this time his concern is the death of a jockey. At home, he drinks milk instead of martinis at dinner to set an example for his growing son (now eight years old). The film ends with the usual domestic denouement.

The Thin Man Goes Home. MGM, 1944. Powell, Loy, Lucile Watson, Gloria DeHaven. Directed by Richard Thorpe.

The Charleses go to the peaceful hamlet of Sycamore Springs for a visit with Nick's elderly parents. A local youth is mysteriously killed, and Nick cleverly links the lad's amateur paintings with an espionage ring and stolen plans.

Son of the Thin Man. MGM, 1947. Powell, Loy, Keenan Wynn, Patricia Morison, Gloria Grahame, Jayne Meadows. Directed by Edward Buzzell.

Nick and Nora, investigating the shooting of a bandleader aboard a gambling ship, tour a great many jazz haunts in search of clues. Dean Stockwell portrays an almost fully grown Nick, Jr.

Radio and Television

In the early 1940s Nick and Nora Charles debuted on NBC radio (first played by Les Damon and Claudia Morgan); many of the half-hour scripts were written by Hammett.

Peter Lawford and Phyllis Kirk played the Charleses in *The Thin Man* television series, produced by MGM beginning in 1957. They were sophisticated and competent (Asta costarred), but the half-hour format permitted little development of either comedy or mystery. The series ran for three years (74 episodes). In 1975 Craig Stevens and Jo Ann Pflug appeared on late-night television in *Nick and Nora*.

CHARNWOOD, LORD. *See* BENSON, GODFREY.

CHARTERIS, LESLIE (1907–). American mystery story writer and creator of one of the most popular characters in crime literature—Simon Templar, the Saint (*see* SAINT, THE). Charteris sees the Saint as the embodiment of much of his idealized view of himself; his identification with the "modern Robin Hood" is shared by his readers. The author bears considerable resemblance to the Saint, being a muscular 6 feet 2 inches tall, and he often identifies himself as Templar's (inferior) twin brother. Both Charteris and the Saint enjoy the good life, with plenty of the best food and wine (Charteris wrote a column for *Gourmet* for several years); both are immaculate, even elegant, dressers (Charteris used to wear a monocle but dropped it as "an outmoded prop" about thirty years ago). The writer and his character are both good horsemen, both have airplane pilot's licenses, and both can throw knives more or less accurately (the Saint more, Charteris less). If an author can be said to base his characters on real-life people, Charteris does not seem to have strayed far in his search for a prototype.

Leslie Charteris.

Charteris was born in Singapore, the son of an Englishwoman and Dr. S. C. Yin, a physician and direct descendant of the emperors of the Shang dynasty (ca. 1766–1123 B.C.). Charteris, whose original name was Leslie Charles Bowyer Yin, learned Chinese and Malay before he could speak English. His education was provided largely by his parents and, to a lesser degree, by formal schooling, including one year at Cambridge University. Charteris decided that a life of crime would be more exciting than a conventional career, and he became an enthusiastic student of criminology, in fact and fiction. He had always enjoyed writing and considered trying to write professionally. When he was very young, he had produced his own magazine and illustrated it (by hand) with little stick figures—one of which was eventually adapted to become the internationally recognized symbol of the Saint. He wrote his first novel during his year at Cambridge and then decided not to return to his studies after it was accepted—to the disgust of his conservative father. Thereafter, he became too busy to use his knowledge of criminal techniques for any activity except writing.

Although his stories found a reasonably steady market in England, it was not a lucrative one, and Charteris thus tried his hand at a variety of jobs diverse enough to satisfy even his taste for adventure. At one time or another, he worked as a policeman, prospected for gold, drove a bus, fished for pearls, worked in a tin mine, on a rubber plantation, and in a wood distillation plant, tended bar in a country inn, was a seaman on a freighter, toured England with a carnival sideshow (his main job was to blow up balloons for dart throwers), and was a professional bridge player in a London club.

In 1926 he legally adopted the name Leslie Charteris, choosing Charteris partly because it was similar to Charles (his middle name) but mainly because of his admiration for Colonel Francis Charteris, a notorious gambler, duelist, lover, and founding member of the Hellfire Club. About this time, he began publishing his first books, *X Esquire* in 1927, *The White Rider* the following year, and, later in 1928, *Meet the Tiger*—the first Saint book. Charteris's other non-Saint mysteries are *The Bandit* (1929), *Daredevil* (1929), and *Lady on a Train* (1945).

Because his financial rewards were still meager, Charteris moved to the United States in 1932 (he became a naturalized citizen in 1946). Edgar WALLACE, the king of thrillers, died that year, and it is possible that English and American audiences were ready for a new author to take up where Wallace had left off. Whatever the reason, the Saint books were soon selling in enormous quantities. Soon, there were endless reprints, paperbacks, and foreign editions. In 1933 Charteris was hired by Paramount as a scriptwriter; he enjoyed life in Hollywood, where several moderately successful motion pictures involving the Saint were made. Templar later appeared on radio (in the 1940s), in comic strips and comic books, and on television, where Roger Moore portrayed him for six years (120 hour-long programs). *The Saint Detective Magazine* (retitled *The Saint Mystery Magazine*, then *The Saint Magazine*) was published from Spring 1953 to October 1967.

The adventures of the Saint are told in a fast, breezy style familiar to readers of PULP MAGAZINES and other popular adventure fiction. Bits of the Charteris philosophy frequently appear in the most unlikely places, for example, in the middle of a furious fistfight, but the action does not slow down. The thriller style is probably recognizably British, closer to that of Edgar Wallace than to that of Dashiell HAMMETT, just as there is a distinct difference in *The Thriller* magazine (the English magazine for which Charteris wrote) and the American BLACK MASK, which might be viewed as having placed a slightly greater emphasis on characterization and social commentary than on pure adventure.

Charteris now lives in Europe (France and the British Isles) with his fourth wife (Audrey Long, whom he married in 1952). Previously, he had married Pauline Schishkin in 1931 (divorced in 1937), Barbara Meyer (married in 1938; divorced in 1943), and Elizabeth Bryant Borst (married in 1943; divorced in 1951). He has one daughter, Patricia Ann, from his first marriage.

CHASE, JAMES HADLEY (pseudonym of René Raymond; 1906–). English author of crime novels. Born in London, he left home at eighteen to sell children's encyclopedias door-to-door; he was working for a book wholesaler when he wrote *No Orchids for Miss Blandish* (1939), one of the best-selling mysteries ever published. Dave Fenner, former reporter turned private detective, becomes involved in a case in which a kidnapped heiress has fallen into the hands of a brutal mob of gangsters. The shocking blend of violence, sex, and American gangsters sold more than 1 million copies within five years of publication.

Although Chase has produced seventy-eight additional books, Fenner appeared again only in *Twelve Chinks and a Woman* (1940). Most of his violent, action-filled thrillers are set in the United States, although he has visited only Florida and New Orleans; he uses detailed maps and a slang dictionary for background material.

Other leading Chase characters are Vic Malloy, a California private eye who appears in *You're Lonely When You're Dead* (1949) and *Figure It Out for Yourself* (1950), and Mark Girland, a former CIA agent looking for easy money and women in Paris until the head of the Paris branch of the agency calls him for help; he appears in *This Is for Real* (1965) and *You Have Yourself a Deal* (1966). As Raymond Marshall, Chase wrote about "Brick-top" Corrigan, a former commando, now a detective, who will accept any assignment, demand half the fee, and then vanish without earning it, in *Mallory* (1950) and *Why Pick on Me?* (1951); and Don Micklem, a millionaire playboy who finds himself involved, against his will, in international intrigue, in *Mission to Venice* (1954) and *Mission to Siena* (1955). Chase has also used the pseudonyms James L. Docherty and Ambrose Grant. His only short story collection is *Get a Load of This* (1941).

Films

No Orchids for Miss Blandish. Tudor (British), 1951. Jack La Rue, Linden Travers, Hugh McDermott. Directed by St. John L. Clowes.

Gangster Slim Grisson falls in love with the rich girl his gang has kidnapped, and she with him. The film is set in the United States.

Lucky Nick Cain. Twentieth Century-Fox, 1951. George Raft, Coleen Gray, Donald Stewart. Directed by Joseph M. Newman. Based on *I'll Get You for This* (1946).

On a Mediterranean vacation, an American gambler is framed by a counterfeiting ring for the murder of a U.S. Treasury agent.

The Man in the Raincoat. Kingsley (French), 1958. Fernandel, John McGiver, Bernard Blier. Directed by Julien Duvivier. A humorous telling of *Tiger by the Tail* (1954).

While his wife is away, a middle-aged clarinetist seeks out a prostitute at a friend's urging, finds her murdered, is spotted fleeing by the police, and is dubbed "the man in the raincoat."

What Price Murder. UMPO (French), 1958. Henri Vidal, Mylene Demongeot, Isa Miranda. Directed by Henri Verneuil. From a novel by Chase.

A handsome young bank clerk woos and weds a rich widow but, then, with her pretty secretary, plots her murder.

Young Girls Beware. UMPO (French), 1959. Antonella Lualdi, Robert Hossein, Michele Cordoue. Directed by Yves Allegret. From *Miss Callaghan Comes to Grief* (1941).

A convict, released from prison after serving five years (he was framed), kills his accuser—but falls in love with the woman who has witnessed the murder.

The Grissom Gang. Cinerama, 1971. Kim Darby, Scott Wilson, Tony Musante, Robert Lansing, Connie Stevens. Directed by Robert Aldrich. A violent, perverse remake of *No Orchids for Miss Blandish*.

The setting is now the Depression; a Kansas City

heiress is kidnapped by the degenerate brood of Ma Grissom (Irene Dailey).

CHESTER, GEORGE RANDOLPH (1869–1924). American novelist, film writer, and short story writer. Born in Ohio, he worked at a number of varied jobs from an early age. After his marriage to Elizabeth Bethermel ended in divorce, he married Lillian De Rimo, with whom he collaborated on several books. He spent time as a journalist, motion picture writer-director, and dramatist. He was a frequent contributor to *The Saturday Evening Post, McClure's,* and other top magazines, his most popular tales involving Get-Rich-Quick Wallingford, a genial confidence man, and Blackie Daw, his associate.

James Rufus Wallingford, a "business buccaneer," uses *nearly* legal methods to earn fortunes in business enterprises, promptly spending his money on costly food, drink, and clothes. Suave and sophisticated, with a look of affluence, he inspires confidence in potential investors in his schemes, and they are anxious to be part of his endeavors; he is equally anxious to accept their contributions. His lovely young wife, Fannie, has a vague suspicion that he is not quite honest, and she feels guilty for not trusting him.

His nefarious exploits are recounted in *Get-Rich-Quick Wallingford* (1908), *Young Wallingford* (1910), *Wallingford in His Prime* (1913), *Wallingford and Blackie Daw* (1913), all short story collections, and *The Son of Wallingford* (1921), written by Chester and his wife.

J. Rufus Wallingford inspires confidence, making it simple for him to sell shares in the Universal Covered Carpet Tack Co., the symbol of which is shown here. This illustration appears on the front cover of the first edition of *Get-Rich-Quick Wallingford,* published by Henry Altemus in Philadelphia in 1908.

Plays and Films

A very successful Broadway play was fashioned in 1910 by George M. Cohan from Chester's Wallingford stories, and it in turn inspired a film series in 1915. In 1921 Tom Gallery, in *The Son of Wallingford,* tries to escape the paternal curse—his father's name is, after all, synonymous with trickery—and be looked upon as an honest man. Wallingford (Sam Hardy) and one of his schemes (carpet-covered tacks) also appear in a Paramount feature *(Get-Rich-Quick Wallingford)* of 1921. There is also a sound-era Wallingford film.

Adventures of Get-Rich-Quick Wallingford (also known as *New Adventures of Get-Rich-Quick Wallingford*). MGM, 1931. William Haines, Ernest Torrence, Jimmy Durante, Leila Haymes. Directed by Sam Wood.

A dashing swindler is reformed by a pretty girl even though he attempts to involve her father in an impractical—to say the least—business deal.

CHESTERTON, G[ILBERT] K[EITH] (1874–1936). English artist, poet, journalist, critic, essayist, novelist, short story writer, and creator of Father BROWN, one of the most famous and unusual detectives in the genre.

Born to a wealthy Londoner and his Scottish-French-Swiss wife, Chesterton studied art and literature at University College, London. During his school years, he met E. C. BENTLEY, who became a lifelong friend. While working on various newspapers and magazines as a literary critic and contributor, he made many intellectual friends, notably Hilaire Belloc, with whom he shared religious and liberal political beliefs. His prolific pen produced literally thousands of poems, reviews, stories, and essays on literature, politics (he advocated distributism, rather than socialism, calling for the widest possible ownership of property), religion (a converted and extremely devout Catholic, he believed that religion was the world's only refuge), and any other subject that he could, by means of his diverse background, fit into his view of the cosmos. Unfailingly witty, he was a popular speaker and a beloved personality, even among those people who resented his anti-Semitism and artificial, puerile philosophy. He married Frances Blogg in 1901 and gave up the city life and literary gatherings he loved, moving to the country to please her.

Regardless of his versatility and prolificacy, Chesterton's finest and most enduring books are his mystery and detective tales. In addition to Father Brown, whose exploits border on the occult and

G. K. Chesterton, creator of Father Brown, in a silhouette by Eric Gill.

fantastic, with little pure detection, Chesterton created several interesting characters.

Horne Fisher is a gentleman detective and profound student of criminology who believes that evildoers should be brought to justice. Burning with passion for truth and honor, he is adept at ferreting out the secrets of little-publicized crimes; yet the criminals who perpetrate them are never brought to justice. His unusual exploits are collected in *The Man Who Knew Too Much.*

The Club of Queer Trades, Chesterton's first attempt at mystery fiction, is about an English club with one membership requirement: no one is eligible unless he has created a brand-new profession. Some mysterious adventures involve a man who offers himself to dinner hosts as a butt for repartee, another who provides a suitable romance for lonely souls, and the founder of the club, who earns his living by seeking new members.

In *The Man Who Was Thursday,* an allegorical novel disguised as a detective story, poet Gabriel Syme, a member of a new police force called Philosophical Policemen, is thrown into a mad, upside-down world as he becomes involved with a group of anarchists known as the Supreme Council of Seven, each member of which is named for a day of the week.

All Chesterton's novels and stories are humorous and display his kindliness and love of humanity, with his religious and social philosophy appearing at frequent intervals. His love of paradox, his whimsicality, and his sense of the absurd are evident in countless narratives.

G. K. Chesterton's *The Poet and the Lunatics* features Gabriel Gale, who "sometimes stands on his head in order to solve dreadful riddles of crime that baffle all sane research." This is the dust wrapper of the first edition, published by Cassell in 1929.

CHECKLIST

Mysteries not about Father Brown.

1905	*The Club of Queer Trades* (s.s.)
1908	*The Man Who Was Thursday*
1912	*Manalive*
1922	*The Man Who Knew Too Much* (s.s.)
1925	*Tales of the Long Bow* (s.s.)
1929	*The Poet and the Lunatics* (s.s.)
1930	*Four Faultless Felons* (s.s.)
1936	*The Paradoxes of Mr. Pond* (s.s.)

CHEYNEY, (REGINALD EVELYN) PETER (SOUTHOUSE) (1896–1951). English author, journalist, and detective. Born in London, Cheyney was trained as a lawyer but soon grew tired of legal office routine. He served in the Army in World War I and was wounded in the Second Battle of the Somme. After returning to England, he wrote songs, poems, and hundreds of short stories under various pseudonyms. He was also a journalist, newspaper editor, and owner of a detective agency, Cheyney Research Investigations.

Cheyney's first mystery novel was *This Man Is Dangerous* (1936). Thereafter, until his death, he averaged two mystery books a year, achieving excellent sales throughout the world. He is best known for his two series about English detectives Lemmy Caution and Slim Callaghan. Noted for their cruelties, Caution and Callaghan operate in the typical Cheyney crime milieu: the clubs of London's West End with their illegal drugs, gambling, and sex. Although critics generally reacted unfavorably to the excessive violence of these series, they were more appreciative of Cheyney's "Dark" series—for example, *Dark Duet* (1942) and *Dark Hero* (1946)—spy stories about Nazis and, in the postwar period, neo-Nazis.

Films

The character of Cheyney's Slim Callaghan has changed somewhat in the film versions of the stories, and he has been an engaging, though tough, screen detective.

Uneasy Terms. Pathe (British), 1948. Michael Rennie (Callaghan), Moira Lister, Faith Brook, Nigel Patrick. Directed by Vernon Sewell. Based on Cheyney's 1946 book of the same title.

Slim comes to the aid of a pretty blackmail victim accused of killing her stepfather.

Meet Mr. Callaghan. Eros (British), 1954. Derrick de Marney (Callaghan), Harriette Johns, Adrienne Corri, Belinda Lee. Directed by Charles Saunders. Based on *The Urgent Hangman* (1938).

Slim solves the murder of a rich old man.

Diplomatic Courier. Twentieth Century-Fox, 1952. Tyrone Power, Patricia Neal, Stephen McNally, Hildegarde Neff. Directed by Henry Hathaway. Based on *Sinister Errand* (1945).

An American courier is drafted by Counterintelligence to track down an important Russian document; in the course of his investigation he meets a sparkling young Indiana widow and learns that, in the world of intrigue, people are not what they seem.

Eddie Constantine, an American actor who has achieved success in French films in tough-guy roles, portrayed Cheyney's Lemmy Caution in more than eight films, finally projecting him into a mechanized police future in the surreal *Alphaville* of 1965.

CHILD, CHARLES B. (pseudonym of C. Vernon Frost; 1903–   ). English short story writer. Born in London, he began his writing career at eighteen, doing newspaper work and then contributing fictional works to the English pulp magazines. During World War II he was commissioned in the RAF and spent three years in Iraq, where he worked with the local police.

In 1946, while living in the United States, he began a series of short stories about Inspector Chafik J. Chafik of the Baghdad police, a dapper little man who has a habit of talking aloud to himself as he ponders a case. His stories, of which "Death Had a Voice" (1948) is outstanding, were popular in *Collier's*, where they originally appeared, and in *Ellery Queen's Mystery Magazine*, where most were reprinted. They have never been collected in book form.

CHILD, RICHARD WASHBURN (1881–1935). American diplomat and author of mystery and crime fiction. Born in Worcester, Mass., he is best known for two collections of short stories, *Fresh Waters and Other Stories* (1920) and *The Velvet Black* (1921). Paymaster, a criminal, appears in three stories. He has no specialty in the world of crime. "I do the thing that come along," he says.

CHILDERS, (ROBERT) ERSKINE (1870–1922). Anglo-Irish author and political activist. Born in London, he lived in Ireland until he was married. He served in the British Royal Naval Air Service during World War I and thereafter devoted his efforts to securing home rule for Ireland. A member of the Irish Republican Army, he was captured, court-martialed, and shot by a firing squad. His only work of fiction is *The Riddle of the Sands* (1903), one of the best-known espionage novels ever written. The story concerns two Englishmen who, while yachting in the Baltic, accidentally uncover a German plan to invade England by sea. The book did not appear in the United States until 1915, shortly after the outset of World War I; it was reissued in 1940 as World War II was in progress.

CHRISTIE, AGATHA (MARY CLARISSA MILLER) (1890–1976). English novelist and playwright. Agatha Christie, who created Hercule POIROT and Miss Jane MARPLE, is one of the greatest and most popular detective story writers of the twentieth century. Born in Torquay in Devon County, the daughter of Frederick Alvah Miller, an American from New York who died when she was young, she was brought up by her English mother, who encouraged the child to write poetry and short stories and guided her reading. As a child, she had the happy facility of inventing stories in her mind but did not commit them to paper. Her early efforts—she found it difficult to

Agatha Christie. [*Angus McBean, London*]

write at first—have been characterized as sad and sentimental.

When she was sixteen, she was sent to Paris to study singing, but since she was very shy, and her voice was not strong enough for opera, a vocal career was out of the question. She then went to Cairo with her mother for the winter and wrote a novel, which was never published, and short stories, some of which were published. During this period she was encouraged by a neighbor, Eden PHILLPOTTS.

In 1912 she became engaged to Colonel Archibald Christie of the Royal Flying Corps. Just after the start of World War I the couple were married. With her husband away in France, Mrs. Christie worked in the dispensary of the local Voluntary Aid Detachment hospital. She was too busy during the war to write, but she made plans to write a detective story. Mrs. Christie had read many works in the field and believed that they were an excellent means of distraction from worry. She wrote much of *The Mysterious Affair at Styles* (a Poirot story) at odd moments while at work and finished it during a two-week vacation on Dartmoor.

The manuscript was rejected by several publishers, and another publisher held it for a year before finally accepting it. The pay ($125) was small but enough to encourage Mrs. Christie, and after completing six books, she really felt she was a writer. During this period she also produced a book of poetry, *The Road of Dreams* (1925), and had a daughter, Rosalind.

The death of Mrs. Christie's mother and the impending breakup of her marriage caused her to suffer from amnesia. Her highly publicized disappearance in 1926, the result of that amnesia, increased sales but brought notoriety and unpleasantness to Mrs. Christie.

After divorcing Colonel Christie in 1928, she found it pleasant to travel abroad. In 1930 she visited Ur and met Max Mallowan, assistant to the famous archaeologist Sir Leonard Woolley; they were married in September of that year. Subsequently they spent several months each year in Syria and Iraq, and Mrs. Christie helped her husband with his photography. She found the desert conducive to writing because there were no distractions. Her novels became best sellers and were serialized in magazines and translated into more than 100 foreign languages. One of her publishers claims that sales of her mysteries have exceeded 400 million.

She has written a half-dozen romantic novels under the pseudonym Mary Westmacott and, as Agatha Christie Mallowan, wrote *Come, Tell Me How You Live* (1946), about her expeditions to Syria with her husband. She has also written plays.

Though well past eighty, Dame Agatha still produces what her publishers call "a Christie for Christmas" every year. She is also writing her autobiography, which will be published posthumously. She was made a Commander Order of the British Empire (C.B.E.) in 1956 and Dame Commander Order of the British Empire (D.B.E.) in 1971.

The Mysterious Affair at Styles (1920) concerns the investigation of the murder of a rich, elderly lady in a country house and is one of the best first mystery novels ever written. Along with Freeman Wills CROFTS's *The Cask*, also published in 1920, this novel marked the start of the "Golden Age" of the detective story. It presents Hercule Poirot as a three-dimensional human being, not the caricature he later became. *The Secret Adversary* (1922), Agatha Christie's first novel of international intrigue, stars the entertaining Tuppence and Tommy Beresford. *Poirot Investigates* (1924), her first book of short stories, is a QUEEN'S QUORUM selection.

The still controversial *The Murder of Roger Ackroyd* (1926) is Mrs. Christie's most famous, and one of her best, novels. The murder of a doctor in a small English village causes Poirot to abandon his retirement plans. Although the author's solution plays fair with the reader—the clues are there to be found—many readers and critics do not agree with that opinion. Many critics themselves are guilty of unfair play when they gratuitously reveal the ending in their discussions of the book. Mrs. Christie's use of a variation of the least-likely-suspect device is not original; in fact, critics of her subsequent work have claimed that she places too much emphasis on making her criminal the least-likely person to have committed the crime. After this volume her name became known throughout the world.

An amusing volume of short stories, *Partners in Crime* (1929), presents the Beresfords as proprietors of a detective agency, and each "case" is a spoof on such famous detectives as Father BROWN, the Old Man in the Corner (*see* OLD MAN IN THE CORNER, THE), Sherlock HOLMES, and the author's Hercule Poirot. In *The Mysterious Mr. Quin* (1930), a collection of a dozen stories tinged with fantasy, Harley Quin appears from nowhere to help his friend Mr. Satterthwaite investigate various murder problems. *Murder at the Vicarage* (1930), a story about a murder that occurs in the village of St. Mary Mead, marks the first novel about Miss Jane Marple. She had appeared earlier in short stories that were later collected in *The Thirteen Problems* (1932; U.S. title: *The Tuesday Club Murders*).

The Hound of Death (1933) is an interesting collection that contains more fantasy than mystery or detection. *The Listerdale Mystery* (1934) contains "Accident" and "Philomel Cottage"; the latter was the basis of a play and two films entitled *Love from a Stranger*. These two stories are Mrs. Christie's best works in the short form. Neither volume has been

As Barry Fitzgerald (left) reads a message from their missing host, "U. N. Owen," a puzzled group of weekend guests, isolated in a large house on a lonely island and strangers to one another, look on. The group pictured comprises Mischa Auer, Judith Anderson, C. Aubrey Smith, Louis Hayward, Roland Young, and June Duprez. Death, inspired by the lines of a nursery rhyme in Agatha Christie's *And Then There Were None*, will strike at them one by one. [*Twentieth Century-Fox*]

published in the United States, but all of the stories have appeared in various "cannibalized" collections, including *Witness for the Prosecution and Other Stories* (1948) and *The Golden Ball and Other Stories* (1971).

The A.B.C. Murders (1936) is about a serial killer who announces his apparently unmotivated killings in advance to Poirot; the only clue is a railway guide left at the scene of each crime. In the opinion of many critics, this is one of Dame Agatha's greatest detective novels. *Cards on the Table* (1936) is about a bizarre character who "collects" killers who have not been brought to justice; he is murdered while hosting a card party. Poirot is able to discover the murderer by analyzing the suspects' characters in observing their methods of playing bridge—a device first used in S. S. VAN DINE's *The "Canary" Murder Case* (1927). *Ten Little Niggers* (1939; U.S. title: *And Then There Were None*) is also about a group of criminals who have not been brought to justice; in this case, they are brought together on a deserted island and murdered one by one—to the tune of a nursery rhyme. This ingenious and harrowing suspense novel is usually cited as one of Agatha Christie's greatest works. It was a great success as a play *(Ten Little Indians)* and was filmed three times (once as *And Then There Were None* and twice as *Ten Little Indians*), with an altered ending.

N or M? (1941) features the Beresfords in a tense thriller in which they come to their country's aid in wartime by attempting to unmask a German agent concealed in a seaside boardinghouse. *Five Little Pigs* (1942; U.S. title: *Murder in Retrospect*) concerns the efforts of Poirot to solve a sixteen-year-old crime by having the suspects write down their accounts of the crime. This novel is listed in SANDOE'S READERS' GUIDE TO CRIME. *Death Comes as the End* (1944) is about a murder at Thebes in 2000 B.C. and shows the influence of the Mallowans' archaeological researches, as does *Murder in Mesopotamia* (1936), although in this case the setting is contemporary. In *The Labours of Hercules* (1947) Poirot emulates his legendary namesake in twelve modern-day detective problems. Ellery QUEEN (author) called the collection the most imaginative Poirot series and said that it was indicative of Dame Agatha's ever-increasing fertility. The motive of the murderer in *The Mirror Crack'd from Side to Side* (1962; U.S. title: *The Mirror Crack'd*) is based on a tragic incident in the life of a popular American movie actress of the 1940s; Miss Marple investigates.

Subsequent production declined slightly in quality, but not in popularity, and recent Christie titles, including the critically maligned spy thriller *Passenger to Frankfurt* (1970), have appeared on the best-seller lists with increasingly regularity. Most of her work is frequently reprinted in paper covers.

Numerous articles in newspapers and magazines testify to her popularity, which increases with new generations of readers. The secret of her success, according to fellow mystery writer Margery ALLINGHAM, is that she has entertained "more people for more hours at a time than almost any other writer of her generation."

CHECKLIST

Mysteries not about Miss Marple or Poirot.

1922 *The Secret Adversary*
1924 *The Man in the Brown Suit*
1925 *The Secret of Chimneys*
1929 *Partners in Crime* (s.s.)
1929 *The Seven Dials Mystery*
1930 *The Mysterious Mr. Quin* (s.s.)
1931 *The Sittaford Mystery* (U.S. title: *Murder at Hazelmoor*)
1933 *The Hound of Death* (s.s.)
1934 *Why Didn't They Ask Evans?* (U.S. title: *The Boomerang Clue*)
1934 *The Listerdale Mystery* (s.s.)
1934 *Parker Pyne Investigates* (s.s.; U.S. title: *Mr. Parker Pyne—Detective*)
1939 *The Regatta Mystery and Other Stories* (s.s.; contains three stories not about Miss Marple or Poirot)
1939 *Murder Is Easy* (U.S. title: *Easy to Kill*)
1939 *Ten Little Niggers* (U.S. title: *And Then There Were None*)
1941 *N or M?*
1944 *Towards Zero*
1944 *Death Comes as the End*
1945 *Sparkling Cyanide* (U.S. title: *Remembered Death*)
1948 *Witness for the Prosecution and Other Stories* (s.s.; contains eight stories not about Miss Marple or Poirot)
1949 *Crooked House*
1950 *Three Blind Mice and Other Stories* (s.s.; contains one story not about Miss Marple or Poirot)
1951 *They Came to Baghdad*
1954 *Destination Unknown* (U.S. title: *So Many Steps to Death*)
1958 *Ordeal by Innocence*
1961 *Double Sin and Other Stories* (s.s.; contains two stories not about Miss Marple or Poirot)
1961 *The Pale Horse*
1967 *Endless Night*
1968 *By the Pricking of My Thumbs*
1970 *Passenger to Frankfurt*
1971 *The Golden Ball and Other Stories* (s.s.)
1973 *Postern of Fate*

Films

In 1928, eight years after Agatha Christie's first book was published, a Tuppence and Tommy Beresford adventure was filmed in Germany (*Die Abenteuer G.m.b.H.*, based on *The Secret Adversary*), and her short story "The Coming of Mr. Quin" was made into a feature film in England.

The Passing of Mr. Quin. Strand, 1928. Stewart Rome, Trilby Clark, Ursula Jeans. Directed by Leslie Hiscott.

Is a tramp guilty of killing a woman's first husband?

A series of Hercule Poirot films followed, and, much later, Miss Marple also became a series heroine on the screen. Some of Dame Agatha's nonseries stories have also been converted into well-received films.

Love from a Stranger. United Artists, 1937 (filmed in England). Ann Harding, Basil Rathbone. Directed by Rowland V. Lee. Based on the play fashioned from the short story "Philomel Cottage,"

In an isolated cottage, a new wife realizes that her husband is a maniac who intends to kill her in the same way he has disposed of three previous wives.

And Then There Were None. Twentieth Century-Fox, 1945. Louis Hayward, Barry Fitzgerald, Walter Huston, June Duprez, Roland Young, C. Aubrey Smith, Judith Anderson, Mischa Auer.

Directed by René Clair. Based on the play *Ten Little Indians* (1944), which altered the harsh ending of the original novel, *Ten Little Niggers.*

Ten people, strangers to one another and nursing guilty secrets, are invited by a man named U. N. Owen to spend a weekend at a lonely house on an isolated island, where they are murdered one by one.

Love from a Stranger. Eagle-Lion, 1947. Sylvia Sidney, John Hodiak, John Howard, Isobel Elsom. Directed by Richard Whorf. A close American remake, now set in the early twentieth century, of the 1937 film.

Witness for the Prosecution. United Artists, 1957. Tyrone Power, Marlene Dietrich, Charles Laughton, Elsa Lanchester, Henry Daniell, Torin Thatcher. Directed by Billy Wilder. From the international stage success, which had been fashioned from the short story of that title.

A likable young drifter is accused of murdering a wealthy widow. His refugee wife, a witness for the prosecution, seems determined to testify against her husband, until a Cockney prostitute offers the defending barrister a packet of love letters that cause the wife's integrity to be suspect.

Ten Little Indians. Seven Arts, 1965 (filmed in England). Hugh O'Brian, Shirley Eaton, Fabian, Leo Genn, Wilfrid Hyde-White, Daliah Lavi, Dennis Price, Stanley Holloway. Directed by George Pollock. A remake of the 1945 film; the setting is a castle high in the Austrian Alps in the dead of winter.

In 1975, *Ten Little Indians* was again filmed, the setting this time transposed to an isolated, empty luxury hotel in the Iranian desert. The international cast featured Oliver Reed, Elke Sommer, Richard Attenborough, Gert Frobe, and the voice of Orson Welles delivering the recorded judgments of U. N. Owen. The Indian statues now have turbans. (Filmed in Iran; directed by Peter Collinson.)

Plays

Mrs. Christie's 1952 play, *The Mousetrap,* based on her novelette *Three Blind Mice* (1948), is a familiar account of a group of people trapped with an unknown murderer in a remote lodge. It has proved to be the most popular play in the English language, running for more than two decades on the London stage (ironically, it flopped in New York). In the early 1930s two stage plays featuring Poirot were presented. Frank Vosper collaborated with Mrs. Christie on an adaptation of her short story "Philomel Cottage," *Love from a Stranger,* and also starred as the Bluebeard wife murderer in the 1936 Broadway production of the play. She won international acclaim in 1944 with *Ten Little Indians,* based on the novel of 1939, and two years later adapted *Death on the Nile* (1937), a Poirot book, into a play in which Archdeacon Pennyfeather (Halliwell Hobbes), instead of Poirot, is the detective who solves the archaeological murder; the drama appeared in London as *Murder on the Nile,* on Broadway as *Hidden Horizon.* In 1953 Mrs. Christie scored another success with *Witness for the Prosecution* (from the short story of the same title), with Patricia Jessel in the demanding title role. The play won the New York Drama Critics Circle Award as the best foreign play of 1954–1955. Among her other stage plays are domestic murder dramas such as *Spider's Web* (1954) and *The Unexpected Guest* (1958).

Radio and Television

Mrs. Christie's short stories have been favorite material for anthology series. "Accident" and "Witness for the Prosecution" have been adapted often for both radio and television. *Death on the Nile* was an *Armstrong Circle Theater* hour.

CLARK, ALFRED ALEXANDER GORDON. *See* HARE, CYRIL.

CLAY, COLONEL (Creator: Grant ALLEN). The first rogue of importance in short crime fiction, preceding A. J. RAFFLES by two years. Clay's exploits are recorded in *An African Millionaire* (1897), named

A Pied Piper who attracts winged bags of money adorns the front cover of Grant Allen's *An African Millionaire,* first published in 1897 by Richards. It features the larcenous Colonel Clay.

for Sir Charles Vandrift, the Colonel's personal victim. Vandrift, a millionaire who makes his fortune in Africa, is cheated, duped, robbed, and fooled again and again by Clay. Even though Clay is known to Vandrift, who is on guard against him, the Colonel is such a master of disguise that he can almost instantly transform himself from a Mexican seer to a Scottish parson—neither of whom even slightly resembles the Colonel himself, whose fresh, clean face is the embodiment of innocence and honesty.

CLAYTON, RICHARD HENRY MICHAEL. *See* HAGGARD, WILLIAM.

CLEEK, HAMILTON (Creator: Thomas W. HANSHEW). Known as "the Man of the Forty Faces," Cleek was born with a rare physical characteristic: he has a nearly plastic face that he can contort in a remarkable variety of ways, and thus is able to set a living mask over his features and employ widely disparate disguises without having to use makeup.

In his prime, when he was the boldest criminal with whom Scotland Yard had to contend, he was called "the Vanishing Cracksman" by the newspapers, a sobriquet he despised, claiming that referring to him as "a cracksman" was analogous to calling Paganini "a fiddler." He asked journalists to refer to him as "the Man Who Calls Himself Hamilton Cleek," and in return for this consideration he promised to supply them with information as to the time and place of his next robbery. The morning after each crime, he presents a small portion of the cache to Scotland Yard as a souvenir of his performance.

Cleek has many aliases, including Lieutenant Deland, George Headland, Monsieur Georges de Lesparre, Philip Barch, Captain Burbage, and the Prince of Maurevania, a Graustarkian kingdom whose throne he spurns to marry Ailsa, for whom he also relinquishes his life of crime and turns detective. His adventures are shared by Dollops, a London street urchin.

The later novels were not written by Thomas W. Hanshew (T. W. H.) but by Mary E. Hanshew (M. E. H.), his wife, and Hazel Phillips Hanshew (H. P. H.), who drew from his notes and ideas.

CHECKLIST

1910 *The Man of the Forty Faces* (s.s.; U.S. title: *Cleek, the Master Detective*)
1913 *Cleek, the Man of the Forty Faces* (s.s.; revised edition of *The Man of the Forty Faces*)
1914 *Cleek of Scotland Yard* (s.s.)
1915 *The Riddle of the Night* (signed by T. W. H. but actually written by M. E. H. and H. P. H.)
1916 *Cleek's Greatest Riddles* (s.s.; U.S. title: *Cleek's Government Cases*)
1918 *The Riddle of the Purple Emperor* (signed by T. W. H. and M. E. H. but actually written by M. E. H. and H. P. H.)

By the time of *Cleek's Government Cases*, the once-notorious cracksman is working to combat crime. This is the front cover of the first American edition, published by Doubleday, Page in 1917.

Sinister Orientals abounded in mystery fiction in 1924, the date of this Doubleday, Page first edition. The dust wrapper credits Mary E. and Thomas W. Hanshew with the book about Hamilton Cleek, but it was actually written by Hazel Phillips Hanshew.

1920 *The Frozen Flame* (U.S. title: *The Riddle of the Frozen Flame;* signed by M. E. H. and T. W. H. but actually written by H. P. H.)
1921 *The Riddle of the Mysterious Light* (signed by M. E. H. and T. W. H. but actually written by H. P. H.)
1922 *The House of Discord* (U.S. title: *The Riddle of the Spinning Wheel;* signed by M. E. H. and T. W. H. but actually written by H. P. H.)
1924 *The Amber Junk* (U.S. title: *The Riddle of the Amber Ship;* signed by M. E. H. and T. W. H. but actually written by H. P. H.)
1925 *The House of the Seven Keys* (signed by M. E. H. and T. W. H. but actually written by H. P. H.)
1931 *Murder in the Hotel* (signed by H.P.H.)
1932 *The Riddle of the Winged Death* (signed by H.P.H.)

CLEMENS, SAMUEL LANGHORNE (1835–1910). American humorist and novelist. Born in Florida, Mo., Clemens worked as a printer, pilot on the Mississippi (the experience was the source of his famous pseudonym; the man sounding the river in shallow places called out "mark twain," meaning "by the mark two fathoms"), secretary to his brother (an employee of the Governor of Nevada), gold miner, newspaper editor, and writer and lecturer. He married the wealthy Olivia Langdon in 1870; the death of their daughter caused him to become a bitter cynic.

Samuel Langhorne Clemens, dictating his autobiography in 1905.

Regarded by many as the greatest American author because of such books as *The Adventures of Tom Sawyer* (1876), *The Prince and the Pauper* (1882), *The Adventures of Huckleberry Finn* (1884), and *A Connecticut Yankee in King Arthur's Court* (1889), Mark Twain also made major contributions to the mystery and detection field. His first published book, *The Celebrated Jumping Frog of Calaveras County and Other Sketches* (1867), about the slick stranger who filled Jim Smiley's frog with quail shot to win a bet, was selected for QUEEN'S QUORUM as an early and outstanding story of a confidence game.

More important is *Life on the Mississippi* (1883), a semiautobiographical novel incorporating a complete short story, "A Thumb-Print and What Came of It" (chap. 31), which is significant because it contains the first fictional use of fingerprints as a method of identification. *The Tragedy of Pudd'nhead Wilson* (1894) is frequently (and incorrectly) cited as the first fictional work in which fingerprints are so used. Although it appeared eleven years after the pioneering short story, it is nevertheless important because the entire plot revolves around Pudd'nhead's courtroom explanation of the uniqueness of a person's print.

Most of Twain's excursions into the mystery-detection field are humorous. *The Stolen White Elephant, Etc.* (1882) contains an out-and-out parody (the title story) featuring Inspector Blunt and his staff. In *Tom Sawyer Abroad, Tom Sawyer, Detective and Other Stories* (1896; British title: *Tom Sawyer, Detective, as Told by Huck Finn, and Other Tales,* 1897), Tom and his friend Huck Finn solve a murder and collect a $2,000 reward. According to Tage la Cour and Harald Mogensen in *The Murder Book* (1969), Twain plagiarized much of the plot from "The Vicar of Vejlbye" (1826), a short story by Steen Steensen Blicher, a Danish writer. *A Double-barrelled Detective Story* (1902) is a western that openly burlesques the omniscient powers of Fetlock Jones's uncle, Sherlock HOLMES. "A Murder, a Mystery, and a Marriage" (1945), a short story unpublished during Twain's lifetime, was printed in an unauthorized sixteen-copy edition by Lew David Feldman, a noted New York bookseller, resulting in a lawsuit by the Clemens estate. The satiric *Simon Wheeler, Detective,* unfinished at the time of Twain's death, was published in 1963 with an explanatory text by Franklin R. Rogers.

CLUNK, JOSHUA (Creator: H. C. BAILEY). Although he is a lawyer, it would be difficult to find a bigger crook in England than Clunk. The worst rascals of the underworld go to him for help, knowing that he may not get them off but certain that he will give the judge a hard fight. Other lawyers hate him, Scotland Yard wants to jail him (even though he has helped them solve several cases, if only for his own ends), and there is no judge in England who does not look forward to the day when Clunk appears before him—not as a solicitor but as a defendant. He knows so much about so many criminals that the question of whether he will die a natural death is openly debated.

The hypocritical shyster is short and plump; his smooth pale-yellow face has no wrinkles except at the corners of his large, light-gray eyes, which almost match the color of his moustache. He wears dark, conservative clothes, but he does sport a stick-pin with a large, flashy ruby in it. He sings hymns. His old enemy Scotland Yard's Superintendent Bell says, "I don't mind Clunk's always having five aces up his sleeve, but I do object to his telling me the Almighty put 'em there."

CHECKLIST

1930	*Garstons* (U.S. title: *The Garston Murder Case*)
1932	*The Red Castle* (U.S. title: *The Red Castle Mystery*)
1935	*The Sullen Sky Mystery*
1937	*Clunk's Claimant* (U.S. title: *The Twittering Bird Mystery*)
1939	*The Great Game* (also features Reggie FORTUNE)
1939	*The Veron Mystery* (U.S. title: *Mr. Clunk's Text*)
1941	*The Little Captain* (U.S. title: *Orphan Ann*)
1942	*Dead Man's Shoes* (U.S. title: *Nobody's Vineyard*)
1944	*Slippery Ann* (U.S. title: *The Queen of Spades*)
1945	*The Wrong Man*
1947	*Honour among Thieves*
1950	*Shrouded Death*

COBB, IRVIN S[HREWSBURY] (1876–1944). American author of humorous novels and short stories. Born in Kentucky, he moved to New York in 1904, and although he was not happy there, he stayed for thirty-four years and then moved permanently to California, where he sought an acting career. Cobb's best book in the mystery genre is *Faith, Hope and Charity* (1934), selected for QUEEN'S QUORUM. One of the stories features Judge Priest, who is described in *Old Judge Priest* (1916) as "a confusing muddle of broad, stooped shoulders, wrinkled garments and fat short legs." Other short story collections involving Judge Priest are *Back Home* (1912), *The Escape of Mr. Trimm* (1913), *Snake Doctor and Other Stories* (1923), *Down Yonder with Judge Priest* (1932), and *Judge Priest Turns Detective* (1937).

COBB, SYLVANUS, JR. (1823–1887). American novelist and short story writer. Born in Maine, the son of a Universalist minister, Cobb is generally considered the first American to have mass-produced fiction. One of the best-known authors of DIME NOVELS, he wrote more than 300 novels and novelettes as well as more than 1,000 short stories of a sentimental or sensational nature. His best-known mystery and adventure titles are *The Armorer of Tyre* (1895) and *The Gunmaker of Moscow; or, Vladimir, the Monk,* which was originally published in the *New York Ledger* in 1856 and often reprinted. It was dramatized by George Aiken (1830–1876). Most of his work appeared in the *Ledger* and other publications and did not appear in book form until after his death in Hyde Park.

COCKRILL, INSPECTOR (Creator: Christianna BRAND). A shrewd and irascible English detective attached to the Kent County Police. Cockrill is a little man who looks older than he really is, with bright brown eyes and a fine aquiline nose, completely unselfconscious in his shabby old mackintosh with his hat crammed down any old way on his head. Although he is widely understood to have a heart of gold, there are those who say that it is so small—and that you have to dig so deep to find it—that it is hardly worth the trouble. His fingers are stained to the color of wood because of his habit of almost constantly rolling untidy cigarettes.

Cockrill made his first appearance in *Heads You Lose* (1941). A jealous spinster declares that she "wouldn't be seen dead in a ditch" in a certain hat—and then *is* found dead in a ditch and wearing the hat—on her severed head.

Green for Danger (1944), set in a military hospital during the World War II blitz of London, has been described as "one of the truly great detective novels of all time" by Erik Routley. The victim dies on the operating table—murdered under the eyes of seven witnesses. Both the method and the motive are ingenious.

The Crooked Wreath (1946; British title: *Suddenly at His Residence*) is an outdoor locked-room mystery (*see* LOCKED-ROOM MYSTERIES). In wartime, members of a family gather at their grandfather's house in the English countryside. In a tiny lodge at the gates, surrounded by rose beds and sandy paths, the old man is murdered; there are no footprints in the sand to show how anyone could have had access to the room in which he died.

The setting for *Death of Jezebel* (1948) is a pageant at a trade show. While her knights in armor cavort below, Miss Isabel Drew, known for good reasons as "Jezebel," is strangled in full view of a thousand people and, like the biblical lady, thrown from her high tower.

London Particular (1952; U.S. title: *Fog of Doubt*) is set in a London house where, during a night of pea-soup fog, a gentleman is done to death. Since Rosie, a naughty little nymphet, has claimed him as her seducer, someone close to her must be involved. This book is remarkable in that the murder method is revealed in the last line.

In *Tour de Force* (1955) Inspector Cockrill is on an unhappy Mediterranean tour during which he finds himself languishing in a foreign jail, suspected of the murder of a fellow traveler. Miss Brand por-

Striking a casual pose with hands in pockets, Inspector Cockrill (Alastair Sim, standing in the foreground) interrogates the staff of a hospital where a suspicious death has occurred; the film is *Green for Danger*. [*Eagle-Lion*]

trayed the imaginary island with such skill that tourists have reportedly asked agencies to arrange visits there.

Film

Inspector Cockrill appeared in only one motion picture—critically hailed as among the best mystery films ever made.

Green for Danger. Independent Producers (British), 1946. Sally Gray, Trevor Howard, Rosamund John, Alastair Sim (Cockrill), Leo Genn. Directed by Sidney Gilliat.

A country mailman, injured in an air raid and taken to a hospital, is murdered on the operating table. Another murder and a cat-and-mouse game of suspicion follow.

COE, CHARLES FRANCIS (1890–1956). American author of hard-boiled detective fiction. Born in Buffalo, N.Y., Coe was a frequent contributor to PULP MAGAZINES and published more than a dozen novels, mostly with such clipped titles as *Me . . . Gangster* (1927), *Swag* (1928), *Hooch!* (1929), *Ransom* (1934), and *G Man* (1935).

COE, TUCKER. *See* WESTLAKE, DONALD E.

COFFIN, GEOFFREY. *See* MASON, VAN WYCK.

COFFIN, PETER. *See* LATIMER, JONATHAN.

COHEN, OCTAVUS ROY (1891–1959). American author of humorous Negro fiction and detective stories. Born of Jewish parents in Charleston, S.C., he graduated from Clemson College in 1911. He worked as a newspaperman before being admitted to the South Carolina bar in 1913. He was married the following year and had one son. In 1915 he abandoned the law to write fiction.

A regular contributor to *The Saturday Evening Post* and other popular magazines for many years, Cohen is chiefly noted for his Negro dialect fiction. Two of his well-known characters are unusual detectives.

Florian Slappey, known as the Beau Brummell of Birmingham, Ala., is a tall, slender, immaculately dressed sport described as "a sepia gentleman." He knows (and is known by) everybody in his hometown. He then sets out to conquer New York's Harlem. His humorous adventures are told in *Florian Slappey Goes Abroad* (1928) and *Florian Slappey* (1938).

James H. (Jim) Hanvey, who is white, is a private detective who has more friends in the underworld than in legitimate circles. Gargantuan, with several chins and short fat legs that cause him to waddle when he walks, he spends most of his time sitting with his shoes off and resting. His chief exercise is fondling a gold toothpick that hangs from a chain across his chest. He befriends criminals who have gone straight but is "the terror of crooks from coast to coast" when on a case. The stories about the gross and uncouth, if amiable, detective are found in *Jim Hanvey, Detective* (1923), "Free and Easy" in *Detours* (1927), and *Scrambled Yeggs* (1934).

Cohen was also the author of *The Crimson Alibi* (1919), a popular mystery novel and a success on the New York stage.

Play and Film

In 1920, Cohen's play *Come Seven*, starring Earle Foxe as Slappey, ran for seventy-two performances on Broadway.

Cohen's country detective, Jim Hanvey, was featured in one film.

Jim Hanvey, Detective. Republic, 1937. Guy Kibbee, Tom Brown, Lucie Kaye, Edward Brophy. Directed by Phil Rosen.

Hanvey cuts short a hunting trip to investigate the theft of an emerald necklace that was actually hidden by a young reporter friend as a publicity stunt; but before long the gems are really stolen.

COLE, G[EORGE] D[OUGLAS] H[OWARD] (1889–1959), **and M[ARGARET] I[SABEL POSTGATE]** (1893–). English economists and mystery novelists. For many years among the leaders of socialist thought in England, the Coles were also an important mystery writing team.

Douglas Cole, the son of a real estate agent, spent his youth in Ealing. He was educated at St. Paul's School and Balliol College, Oxford. He significantly affected British socialism in his innumerable articles and more than eighty books, many of which dealt with economics. His five-volume *A History of Socialist Thought* (1953) is probably his best-known work. He was a regular contributor and adviser to *The New Statesman*, a publication devoted to the left-wing reform of society. He also wrote a volume of socialist verse, *This Crooked World* (1933), and much social satire, including an "operetta" about the 1926 general strike. An eminent teacher, Cole was a pillar of the Workers' Educational Association and professor of social and political theory at Oxford. He was active in the British Labour party and influenced many of its leaders, including Hugh Gaitskell. A Guild Socialist and later a leading Fabian Socialist, he was chairman of the Fabian Society from 1939 to 1946 and from 1947 to 1951, and president thereafter, until he died.

Margaret Postgate Cole, the daughter of a professor of Latin at the University of Liverpool, is the sister of mystery writer Raymond POSTGATE. She was educated at Roedean School and Girton College, Cambridge, and taught at St. Paul's Girls' School before leaving to join the Labour movement. She has written a history of Fabian socialism, biographies of Robert Owen and Beatrice Webb, and several other biographical, historical, and social studies. She was made a Dame of the British Empire by Queen Elizabeth II. Her biography of her husband, *The Life of G. D. H. Cole*, was published in 1972. The Coles were married in 1918; they had a son and two daughters.

They once claimed that they wrote mysteries "for recreation," but it is undeniable that they wrote prolifically and achieved considerable financial success. *The Brooklyn Murders* (1923), the first Cole mystery, was the only one by G. D. H. Cole alone. He wrote it during a period of illness when he had been told by his physician not to do other work. The "Brooklyn" of the title does not refer to the New York City borough but, rather, to an English family. It introduced Superintendent Henry Wilson, a dedicated Scotland Yard investigator of great integrity who once proved a former British Home Secretary guilty of a crime. Although forced to resign by political pressure, Wilson soon became one of England's leading private detectives and later resumed his old job at Scotland Yard. He is featured in most of the Coles' thirty-three books.

Critics have commented on the extreme unevenness in the quality of the Coles' mystery output. Many books, especially the later ones, are regarded as poorly constructed, slow-paced, and generally tedious. However, some have been highly praised. Jacques BARZUN and Wendell Hertig TAYLOR regard *The Murder at Crome House* (1927) as their masterpiece, especially praising its opening. A library book is found to contain a photograph of one man about to shoot another. SANDOE'S READERS' GUIDE TO CRIME lists *Death in the Quarry* (1934), in which Wilson is aided by Everard Blatchington, a detective in several of the Coles' works. Their best short story collection is *Superintendent Wilson's Holiday* (1928), a QUEEN'S QUORUM title.

COLES, CYRIL HENRY. *See* COLES, MANNING.

COLES, MANNING (pseudonym of Cyril Henry Coles, 1899–1965, and Adelaide Frances Oke Manning, 1891–1959). English mystery novelists. London-born Cyril Coles had a background that prepared him for writing espionage and mystery fiction. Although underage in World War I, he joined the Hampshire Regiment under an assumed name. Later he became the youngest officer in British Intelligence and went on missions behind German lines from which, like his fictional creation, Tommy HAMBLEDON, he emerged unscathed.

After the war he went to Australia, where he worked on a railroad, in a garage, and for a Melbourne newspaper. In 1928 he returned to England, and the following year his collaborator-to-be, Mrs.

Manning, moved into the house next door as his father's tenant.

Mrs. Manning had already begun writing, but her one book was not a success. The collaboration, however, resulted in the popular Hambledon series, which began in 1940. Coles and Mrs. Manning also wrote three ghost novels as Francis Gaite—*Happy Returns* (1955; English title: *A Family Matter*), *The Far Traveller* (1956), and *Come and Go* (1958), which were described by Anthony BOUCHER as being "as felicitiously foolish as a collaboration of [P. G.] Wodehouse and Thorne Smith." The first Hambledon short story, "Handcuffs Don't Hold Ghosts," combined international intrigue with ghosts and the supernatural; it won a second prize in *Ellery Queen's Mystery Magazine*'s 1946 contest. In addition to his writing, Coles worked for British Intelligence until he retired from that branch in 1958. In 1959 Mrs. Manning died, and Coles continued to write alone, although he published only three novels and a volume of short stories after her death.

Although the first two Coles novels, *Drink to Yesterday* and *Pray Silence* (U.S. title: *A Toast to Tomorrow*), were published separately in 1940, they were actually one book. Boucher called them "a single long and magnificent novel of intrigue, drama, and humor." He later referred to the "good-humored implausibility" of the subsequent books of the series, which had begun on very realistic terms.

COLLECTING DETECTIVE FICTION. Just where or when the specialized pastime of collecting detective fiction began is not easily pinpointed. The genre was not recognized as an important literary form until 1928, when A. Edward Newton's list, "One Hundred Good Novels," in his book *This Book-Collecting Game* contained four titles from the mystery-detection field. Although his inclusion of these works may have indicated acceptance of the form by the general collector, the specialist was yet to be heard from.

Insofar as collecting in general is concerned, few people can exercise their interests *in vacuo*, regardless of what they collect. Although some collectors may not choose (or be able) to share their pleasures with fellow collectors, it is important for them to know that their colleagues exist. It is even more important to have sources of supply from which the collectible items can be obtained and to have authoritative reference material.

Just as 1887 and the appearance of Sherlock HOLMES marked the turning point in the writing of detective fiction, 1934 firmly established the collecting of detective fiction as a worthwhile literary pursuit, for during that year three significant works were published.

1. The first bookseller's catalog devoted exclusively to the genre, and today a little-known and rare item—*Murder, Catalogue the Seventh of Rare and Interesting Books Illustrating the Development of the Detective and Mystery Story*, George Bates, London.

2. The first lengthy discussion of the bibliographic aspects of the genre—"Detective Fiction" by John Carter, a chapter in *New Paths in Book-Collecting*, Constable, London.

3. The second catalog of works exclusively in the genre, although generally thought to have been the first—*Detective Fiction, A Collection of First and a Few Early Editions*, The Scribner Book Store, New York. Compiled by Carter, the catalog lists items primarily from his own collection, which he began in 1927.

The early days of collecting detective fiction were fruitful ones for the pioneering collector. In the relatively abundant critical and reference materials of today, the writers fondly reminisce about the plentiful supply of first editions, the unbelievably low prices, and the absence of competition in the field. These are the memories of such collectors as Carter, Frederic Dannay [Ellery QUEEN (author)], Michael Sadleir, Eric Quayle, Vincent STARRETT, and E. T. Guymon. They speak also of the important assistance through the years of such book dealers as Eric Osborne, Elkin Mathews, Bertram Rota, Ben Abramson, David A. Randall, Arthur Lovell, and Lew David Feldman.

The present state of collecting detective fiction is characterized by a short supply of really fine first editions, expectedly higher prices—often bordering on the ridiculous—and keen competition among a number of knowledgeable collectors.

The collector of detective fiction must be familiar with the literature of his interest. He must also learn the vocabulary and procedures of book collecting in general. Much of this information can be found in the works given in the bibliography at the end of this volume and by careful study of booksellers' catalogs. Most collectors limit their field of interest to, for example, Victorian detective fiction, pre-1930 novels, short story collections, one or more individual authors, the hard-boiled school, or the entries on such well-known lists as QUEEN'S QUORUM or the HAYCRAFT-QUEEN CORNERSTONE LIBRARY. Such limitation is usually important when considering space problems, as well as financial expenditure in the present high-priced market.

Probably the most difficult lesson for any collector is the importance of condition, which must be considered in relation to one's specialty. Although nothing less than first editions—with the original bindings in fine condition—in dust wrappers should be acceptable for books of the past twenty to twenty-five years, a good rebound copy of an important yellowback is a welcome acquisition for the nineteenth-century specialist. Once again, study of references, catalogs, and experience leads to the best decisions, particularly when one is trying to evaluate such dealer platitudes as "as usual for this book," a comment frequently following descriptions mentioning defects such as foxing, faded spine or cloth, and so on, and "scarce in any condition," a dealer comment usually following a description noting that the book has been shaken or bumped or has weak or cracked hinges or missing endpapers. Scarce books purchased without regard to condition must usually be replaced as a collection matures. It is usually better to be somewhat less conservative about the purchase of a really fine but high-priced copy of a book than to pass it by in the hope of finding one almost as good for less money (there is no hard-and-fast rule here, however). In the words of one well-known dealer, "You only regret the books you don't buy."

TWENTY-FIVE RARE WORKS OF DETECTIVE FICTION ARRANGED CHRONOLOGICALLY WITH ESTIMATES OF THEIR VALUES (IN SATISFACTORY COLLECTOR'S CONDITION AND WITH ORIGINAL BINDING; PUBLICATION DATES NOT APPEARING ON ORIGINAL TITLE PAGES ARE GIVEN HERE IN PARENTHESES)

Edgar Allan Poe, *Tales*, Wiley and Putnam, New York, 1845. This is not only a rare book but also a particularly complicated one from a bibliographic standpoint. The following points are believed necessary to establish a first issue: tan printed wrappers; a notice on the lower portion of the copyright page to the left of center reading in part "stereotyped by T. B. Smith, . . ., H. Ludwig, Print."; and perfect type on pages 196 and 205. Estimated value: $5,000.

"Waters" (William Russell), *The Recollections of a Policeman*, Cornish, Lamport, New York, 1852. This is the pirated but true first edition of the 1856 English title: *The Recollections of a Detective Police-Officer*, the most important detective yellowback. Estimated value: $250–$300.

Wilkie Collins, *The Woman in White*, Harper, New York, 1860. The American edition preceded the three-volume English edition (Samson Low, London) by one month. The first issue has one page of ads dated August 1860 in front and four pages of ads at the end. Estimated value: U.S.: $100–$125; English: $1,000.

Anna Katharine Green, *The Leavenworth Case*, Putnam, New York, 1878. Estimated value: $300–$350.

Fergus W. Hume, *The Mystery of a Hansom Cab*, Kemp & Boyce, Melbourne, Australia, 1886. Only two copies of the true first edition are known to exist; they are owned by the Mitchell Library, Sidney, Australia. The first British edition (1887–1888), published by the Hansom Cab Publishing Company, London, appears with various impression notices on the title page: "Fiftieth Thousand," "One Hundredth Thousand," and so on. Estimated value of first British edition: $100–$350, depending upon impression.

Sir Arthur Conan Doyle, *A Study in Scarlet*, in *Beeton's Christmas Annual*, Ward, Lock, London, (1887); pictorial wrappers. Estimated value: $2,000.

Melville Davisson Post, *The Strange Schemes of Randolph Mason*, Putnam, New York, 1896; issued simultaneously in yellow wrappers and in tan or gray decorated cloth. Estimated value: $50 cloth; $75 wrappers.

Clifford Ashdown, *The Adventures of Romney Pringle*, Ward, Lock, London, 1902; issued in both red and blue cloth. The rarity of this book (actually the work of R. Austin Freeman and Dr. John James Pitcairn) has been exaggerated. Estimated value: $250–$350.

Percival Pollard, *Lingo Dan*, Neale, Washington, D.C., 1903; red cloth. Estimated value: $200.

R. Austin Freeman, *The Red Thumb Mark*, Collinwood, London, (1907); issued simultaneously in black wrappers and in black cloth, both containing a red thumbprint on the front cover. Estimated value: $150 cloth; $300 wrappers.

William MacHarg and Edwin Balmer, *The Achievements of Luther Trant*, Small, Maynard, Boston, 1910; red cloth. Estimated value: $75.

Victor L. Whitechurch, *Thrilling Stories of the Railway*, Pearson, London, 1912; green pictorial wrappers. Estimated value: $250–$350.

Frederick Irving Anderson, *Adventures of the Infallible Godahl*, Crowell, New York, (1914); blue decorated cloth. Estimated value: $50.

G. K. Chesterton, *The Wisdom of Father Brown*, Cassell, London, 1914; blue cloth. The scarcest of the Father Brown books. Estimated value: $50–$75.

J. S. Fletcher, *The Middle Temple Murder*, Ward, Lock, London, 1918; cloth. Estimated value: $100.

Agatha Christie, *The Mysterious Affair at Styles*, John Lane, New York, 1920. Precedes the English edition (John Lane, 1921) by several months. Estimated value: $100–$150.

Vincent Starrett, *The Unique Hamlet*, privately printed, Chicago, 1920; tan boards; limited to 250 copies. Estimated value: $100.

David Durham (pseudonym of Roy Vickers), *The Exploits of Fidelity Dove*, Hodder, London, (1924), orange cloth. Estimated value: $100.

Ernest Bramah, *Max Carrados Mysteries*, Hodder, London, (1927); blue cloth. The scarcest Carrados title. Estimated value: $100.

Susan Glaspell, *A Jury of Her Peers*, Benn, London, 1927; yellow wrappers; limited to 250 signed copies. Estimated value: $150–$200.

Frances Noyes Hart, *The Bellamy Trial*, Doubleday, Page, Garden City, N.Y., 1927; orange cloth. The words "First Edition" must appear at the bottom of the copyright page. Estimated value: $50.

Dashiell Hammett, *Red Harvest*, Knopf, New York, 1929; red decorated cloth. The first edition does not contain the usual publisher's device on the copyright page. Estimated value: $50.

Ellery Queen, *The Roman Hat Mystery*, Stokes, New York, 1929; red cloth. Estimated value: $75.

C. Daly King, *The Curious Mr. Tarrant*, Collins, London, (1935); red-orange cloth. Estimated value: $250–$300.

Raymond Chandler, *Five Murderers*, Avon, New York, (1944); pictorial wrappers. Estimated value: $25–$40.

NOTEWORTHY COLLECTIONS OF DETECTIVE FICTION

The Lilly Library, Indiana University at Bloomington. The former collection of John Carter plus substantial additions.

Metropolitan Toronto Central Library, Canada. The general detective fiction collection of Arthur Baillie plus an exceptionally fine collection of Sherlock Holmes material.

Occidental College, Los Angeles, Calif. The former E.

T. Guymon collection—perhaps the finest ever assembled.

University of California at Los Angeles. The former Michael Sadleir collection, containing probably the finest yellowback collection in the world.

University of North Carolina at Chapel Hill. Approximately 5,000 volumes.

University of Texas at Austin. Approximately 8,000 volumes, including the former Ellery Queen (Frederic Dannay) and Erle Stanley GARDNER collections.

Of private collections in the United States some of the best are owned by Adrian Homer Goldstone, California; Allen J. Hubin, Minnesota; Mrs. Edward Kaye, New York; Norman S. Nolan, New Jersey; Otto Penzler, New York.

DEALERS IN DETECTIVE FICTION
(All issue catalogs or lists on a fairly regular basis)

Aardvarks Booksellers, Box 15070, Orlando, Fla., 32808.

The Aspen Bookhouse, Box 4119, Boulder, Colo., 80302.

Boulevard Bookshop, 10634 West Pico Boulevard, Los Angeles, Calif., 90064.

Diversified Books, Box 491, Peter Stuyvesant Station, New York, N.Y., 10009.

Claude Held, Box 140, Buffalo, N.Y., 14225.

Kaleidoscope Books, Box 108, Watertown, Mass., 02172.

Oswald Train, 1129 West Wingohocking Street, Philadelphia, Pa., 19140.

NORMAN S. NOLAN

COLLIER, JOHN (1901–). English poet and author of fantastic and mystery fiction. Born in London, the son of John George Collier, he was privately educated. He has spent many years in the United States, in both Virginia and Hollywood, where he has written film scripts. He married Shirley Lee Palmer, whom he met in Hollywood, in 1936. They were divorced in 1943, and in 1945, he married Margaret Elizabeth Eke.

His indescribable tales of the weird, fantastic, and mysterious fall into no standard category of fiction. They often deal with murder. The best and largest collection of his stories, *Fancies and Goodnights* (1951), was included in QUEEN'S QUORUM. Among his other mysterious short fiction collections are *Presenting Moonshine* (1941) and *The Touch of Nutmeg and More Unlikely Stories* (1943). Collier's most acclaimed fantasies are *His Monkey Wife* (1930) and *Defy the Foul Fiend* (1934).

COLLINS, HUNT. *See* MCBAIN, ED.

COLLINS, MICHAEL (pseudonym of Dennis Lynds; 1924–). American mystery writer and journalist. Born in St. Louis, Mo., he received a B.A. degree from Hofstra College in 1949 and an M.A. degree from Syracuse University in 1951.

He spent 1943–1946 in the infantry in Europe, receiving a Purple Heart and three battle stars. After working as an assistant editor at *Chemical Week*

Michael Collins. [*Dodd, Mead*]

(1951–1952), managing editor at *Chemical Engineering Progress* (1958–1961), and editor for *Chemical Equipment* (1962–1965), he began contributing short stories to such magazines as *Hudson Review, New World Writing, Mike Shayne's Mystery Magazine*, and *Alfred Hitchcock's Mystery Magazine*. One story, "No Way Out," was included in *The Best Detective Stories of the Year: 20th Annual Collection* (1965) by Anthony BOUCHER. He has also published three paperback novels, *Combat Soldier* (1962), *Uptown, Downtown* (1963), and *Charlie Chan Returns* (1974).

Michael Collins writes hard-boiled detective stories in the vein of those of Ross MACDONALD, to whom he dedicated *Act of Fear* (1967). His series detective, one-armed Dan Fortune (born Fortunowski), operates a private detective agency in New York City's Chelsea district. Slot-Machine Kelly, created by Collins for an earlier series of stories that appeared in the PULP MAGAZINES, had the same handicap and base of operation. *Act of Fear* concerns a mugged policeman, a missing boy, and a young woman who is murdered in her apartment. Fortune's debut appearance, it was awarded an Edgar by the Mystery Writers of America as the best first novel of that year.

In *The Brass Rainbow* (1968) a friend of Fortune's appeals for help, claiming that he has been framed for murdering a wealthy man while trying to collect a gambling debt. In *Night of the Toads* (1970) Fortune becomes involved on a more personal level. When a famous actor-producer makes a play for Fortune's girl friend, the detective investigates the disappearance of his enemy's former girl, hoping to find him guilty of some crime. In *Walk a Black Wind* (1971) Fortune leaves New York City for an Indian reservation and other far-off places as he investigates the murder of a rebellious girl. In a review, Newgate Callendar drew parallels between Fortune and Macdonald's Lew ARCHER. Fortune grapples with personal problems in *Shadow of a Tiger* (1972) when he is called on to investigate the death of a friend, a harmless old pawnbroker of French origin.

Lynds has also used the pseudonym William Arden, for a series of novels about Kane Jackson, who usually investigates cases involving industrial espionage, but this series is inferior to that by Collins. He also writes as John Crowe.

COLLINS, (WILLIAM) WILKIE (1824–1889). English novelist. Born in London, Collins was the son of William Collins, a noted landscape painter and member of the Royal Academy whose close friend and fellow artist David Wilkie was the future novelist's godfather. After a spotty education the seventeen-year-old sickly youth became an apprentice to a tea merchant. During his apprenticeship he wrote his first novel (reputedly *Antonina*, a historical novel of ancient Rome, first published in 1850). At one point he wanted to follow in his father's footsteps and studied art; one of his paintings was exhibited at the Royal Academy.

In 1851, after finishing his legal studies, Collins met Charles DICKENS while participating in an amateur theatrical production, and they became close friends, often collaborating on articles and stories; he also frequently contributed to Dickens's periodical *Household Words*.

Early in *The Woman in White*, Walter Hartright encounters the melancholy Anne Catherick, the title character. This illustration is from the first American edition, published by Harper in August 1860, one month before the three-volume English first edition, which was not illustrated.

Wilkie Collins.

Collins never married but spent most of his adult years with Caroline Graves, whom he is said to have met in a situation that was later immortalized as the opening scene of *The Woman in White* (1860). Collins, his younger brother, and the artist Millais were walking in a country lane one night when they heard a scream from a darkened garden and then saw a beautiful young woman dressed all in white. Obviously terrified, she raced away, with Wilkie Collins close behind. After he caught up with her, she told him an anguished story of her past several months, during which she had been held prisoner by a man. She and her daughter subsequently moved in with Collins. *The Woman in White* was not the only book suggested by this unusual encounter. Collins dealt with the stigma of the child's uncertain social position in *No Name* (1862), and in later novels he explored such themes as prostitution and marital infidelity to emphasize the suffering of women at the hands of Victorian society.

The Woman in White appears to have been based partly on Collins's alleged romantic meeting with Mrs. Graves and partly on an eighteenth-century French criminal case. The novel tells the story of a young woman, Laura Fairlie, who is the victim of a plot conceived by the villainous Count Fosco and carried out by her husband, Sir Percival Glyde, to defraud her of a large estate. When Anne Catherick, a woman resembling Laura, dies and is buried

Despite the comical appearance of Count Fosco, he is an unmitigated villain in his persecution of Laura Fairlie in *The Woman in White*. This illustration appears in the first American edition.

under her name, Laura cannot prove her own identity. She is aided by Marion Halcombe, her half sister, and the diligent detective work of Walter Hartright, a drawing instructor who falls in love with her. The unattractive Marion is the true heroine of the book, her strength and courage being largely responsible for the downfall of the unctuous, fat count and the sniveling, debt-ridden Glyde.

The book appeared in serial form in England in *All the Year Round* and in the United States in *Harper's Weekly* in November 1859 and was phenomenally successful in that form, as it was in book form the following year. Although it is frequently called a "mystery thriller," there is as much genuine detective work carried out by Hartright and Marion Halcombe as there is in Collins's second great novel, *The Moonstone* (1868), which T. S. Eliot described (wrongly) as "the first, the longest, and the best of modern English detective novels."

Although he appears in only a few sections of this famous tale about a vanishing jewel, Sergeant CUFF is one of the first and most significant detectives in English literature. Like Collins's previous classic, *The Moonstone* employs several incidents and characters from real life. One of the most famous cases in English jurisprudence was the trial of Constance Kent, who was acquitted of the Road murder in 1860. The Scotland Yard inspector Jonathan Whicher, who arrested her and gave the court his conclusions about the matter, was a well-known detective of the time whose career was seriously damaged by her acquittal. Five years later Constance Kent admitted the crime, substantiating Whicher's claims, but his reputation was already destroyed. The original trial and the later disclosure were still fresh in the public mind when Collins produced *The Moonstone* in 1868. Cuff was immediately recognizable as Whicher, and the dull-witted Superintendent Seegrave was an obvious fictionalization of the actual local police officer, Inspector Foley.

The moonstone is a great yellow diamond that John Herncastle stole from a religious idol in India. Worth a fortune, it is said to bring bad luck to everyone but the worshipers of the moon god from whose head it was taken. According to Herncastle's will, the gem is to be given to his niece, Rachel Verinder, following his death. A genial young solicitor, Franklin Blake, is assigned to transport it to her; the night after he turns it over, it disappears from her room. All clues suggest that Rachel herself took it, but her motives are vague. Rosanna Spearman, a housemaid, suspects Blake of the theft because of an incriminating stain on his nightgown that corresponds to a smudge in the room in which the crime was committed. She hides the garment and, because of her love for Blake (who loves Rachel, who, in turn, is engaged to Godfrey Ablewhite), commits suicide. A menacing contingent of three Indians, seeking the return of the gem, is never far away.

Both *The Moonstone* and *The Woman in White* are long novels with the complex plots that are the hallmark of Collins's work. He ranks with Dickens as the best popular novelist of his time, and, although his characterizations do not approach those of his friend, his carefully worked-out plots, complete with red herrings, cliff-hanging miniclimaxes, multitudinous suspicions, and evasive alibis, are superior to those of any novelist of the nineteenth century.

Several other works by Collins involve crime, mystery, and detection. *After Dark* (1856) contains several short classics, notably "A Terribly Strange Bed," in which an English gambler tells of an attempt made on his life by means of a diabolical bed that smothers its victims; "A Stolen Letter," an obvious borrowing from Edgar Allan POE's "The Purloined Letter" (1844); and "The Lady of Glenwith Grange." *The Queen of Hearts* (1859) contains the first recorded humorous detective story, "The Biter Bit"; *Little Novels* (1887) contains two mysteries among its varied contents; *No Name* (1862) features a woman detective; *Alicia Warlock, A Mystery, and Other Stories* (1875) tells of a "Dream Woman" encountered by the narrator; *Hide and Seek; or, The Mystery of Mary Grice* (1854) unravels the mysterious history of an orphan and her mother; and *The Law and the Lady* (1875) is patterned closely after the Scottish trial of Madeleine Smith and its ambiguous verdict "not proven."

Collins, whose years of bad health and heavy opium use ended with his literary reputation badly tarnished, wanted his epitaph to read: "Author of *The Woman in White* and other works of fiction."

Films

Collins's *The Moonstone* has been filmed twice, on both occasions as a lackluster old-dark-house mystery; in the silent 1915 version, Sergeant Cuff is eliminated, and in 1934 (Monogram. Directed by Reginald Barker) he is played by Charles Irwin, who tries to discover who has taken the precious, cursed gem from under the pillow of heroine Phyllis Barry.

The Woman in White was dramatized in London in 1871. Frederick Walker designed this poster for the stage production, which was more successful in England than in the United States; it lasted only three weeks in New York.

The Woman in White was first filmed by Pathé in 1917, and several versions have followed.

The Woman in White. British and Dominions (British), 1929. Blanche Sweet (in the double role of Laura and Anne), Haddon Mason, Cecil Humphreys (Glyde), Louise Prussing, Frank Perfitt (Fosco). Directed by Herbert Wilcox.

The evil Sir Percival Glyde allows his wife's double to die in her place and confines the real Laura under another identity in a madhouse so that he can take control of her fortune. The film is a period melodrama set in the 1850s.

Crimes at the Dark House. Pennant (British), 1940. Tod Slaughter, Hilary Eaves, Sylvia Marriott. Directed by George King.

In this version, the role of Glyde is amplified to fit the bravura talents of British stage actor Slaughter, known for his horror roles.

The Woman in White. Warner Brothers, 1948. Alexis Smith, Eleanor Parker (as Laura-Anne), Sidney Greenstreet (Fosco), Gig Young, John Emery (Glyde), Agnes Moorehead. Directed by Peter Godfrey.

This is the definitive film version of the novel, a lavish period production in which Fosco's villainy is more properly underscored.

Plays

Collins wrote a dramatic version of *The Woman in White* which made its London debut at the Olympic Theatre on October 9, 1871. It ran on Broadway for three weeks in 1873. The Olympic was also the stage for Collins's own adaptation of *The Moonstone,* which opened on September 17, 1877. The privately printed dramatic script for this three-act play is one of the rarest publications of nineteenth-century literature.

Television

In 1972 the BBC produced a five-hour serial production of *The Moonstone,* garrulous, but with plot and period class relationships intact.

COLLINSON, PETER. *See* HAMMETT, DASHIELL.

COLT, THATCHER (Creator: Anthony ABBOT). Abbot claimed that Colt was a composite of Grover Whalen and Theodore Roosevelt. Born to a wealthy family of high social position, Colt had ambitions of a career in either poetry or music. While attending college, he became interested in the history and science of criminology. He served with distinction in World War I and, after the war, turned to police work as a career, rising to become police commissioner of New York City.

Often called the best-dressed man in public life, Colt is a striking figure with his huge, powerful-looking body and soldier's face. Although he is in his early forties, his crisp and closely cut hair is still black. His brown eyes are somber, and his firm features reflect action and authority. He lives in a five-story gray stone mansion on West 70th Street that includes an elaborate gym, a library containing 15,000 volumes on the subject of crime, and a connoisseur's collection of fine wines.

He is regarded by those who do not know him as a rich dilettante playing at police work, but he is considered by his colleagues to be the best police commissioner since the days of Theodore Roosevelt and is noted for his strength, courage, and decision. He has been responsible for solving twelve major mysteries (several of which have remained unchronicled) during his term of office. After several romances he married Florence Dunbar and retired from his position.

Colt's keen intelligence, vast knowledge of the science of criminology, and thorough use of the resources of the Police Department are responsible for his success in solving bizarre and often seemingly impossible crimes.

His first appearance, *About the Murder of Geraldine Foster* (1930; British title: *The Murder of Geraldine Foster*), detailing the disappearance and ax murder of a doctor's secretary, was vaguely based on the Lizzie Borden and Fall River case. *About the Murder of the Clergyman's Mistress* (1931; British title: *The Crime of the Century*) starts with the discovery of a highly respectable minister and a choir singer—both dead—in a rowboat on the East River. Based on the Hall-Mills case, it has a complex formal problem that will delight admirers of the early Ellery QUEEN (author) and John Dickson CARR novels.

About the Murder of the Night Club Lady (1931; British title: *The Murder of the Night Club Lady*) deals with the murder of a wealthy socialite by unknown means on New Year's morning. *About the Murder of the Circus Queen* (1932; British title: *The Murder of the Circus Queen*) has a colorful background—the circus in Madison Square Garden. Its series of accidents culminate in the death of an aerialist. The author's interest in psychic phenomena is displayed in *About the Murder of a Startled Lady* (1935; British title: *The Murder of a Startled Lady*), in which a medium reveals a murder by means of the voice of its victim. The sequence in which a molder reconstructs the face of the unknown victim from her skull is fascinating and unique. *About the Murder of a Man Afraid of Women* (1937; British title: *The Murder of a Man Afraid of Women*) starts with the disappearance of one man while stark naked in freezing weather and the murder of another who had much to fear from the fair sex. *The Creeps* (1939; British title: *Murder at Buzzard's Bay*) concerns murder at a house party in Buzzard's Bay during a snowstorm. The mystery is solved by a retired and newly married Thatcher Colt. In Abbot's last novel, *The Shudders* (1943; British title: *Deadly Secret*), a mad scientist claims to have discovered an untraceable method of murder. He predicts his successes will culminate with the death of Police Commissioner Colt.

Films

Colt has appeared on the screen on three occasions.

The Night Club Lady. Columbia, 1932. Adolphe Menjou (Colt), Skeets Gallagher, Ruth Stevens, Nat Pendleton. Directed by Irving Cummings. Based on *About the Murder of the Night Club Lady*.

The young woman owner of a nightclub receives a threat that she will die a minute after midnight. And she does, surrounded by police.

The Circus Queen Murder. Columbia, 1933. Menjou, Greta Nissen, Donald Woods, Dwight Frye. Directed by Roy William Neill. Based on *About the Murder of the Circus Queen*.

On vacation in a small circus town, Colt cannot prevent the death of a trapeze artist when she is shot by a poisoned arrow while on the high wire.

The Panther's Claw. PRC, 1942. Sidney Blackmer (Colt), Byron Foulger, Gerta Rozen, Barry Bernard. Directed by William Beaudine. An original story by Abbot.

Members of an operatic troupe receive mysterious notes directing them to leave large sums of money in a cemetery.

Radio

Hanley Stafford—with his gravelly executive voice—played the police commissioner in the radio series *Thatcher Colt*, first heard on NBC in 1936.

COMIC ART DETECTIVES. Although humorous detectives and their adversaries—convicts, thieves, and other underworld creatures—have appeared in comic strips since this popular art form began, before the turn of the century, the first serious use of gunplay and violence occurred with the introduction of a graphic, realistic police hero, Dick TRACY, created by Chester GOULD in 1931 for the *Chicago Tribune* newspaper chain and the first modern adventure hero designed expressly for the comic strip pages. Hard-hitting and constantly innovative in his battles against a grotesque gallery of criminals and mobs, and pace-setting in his ultramodern detection methods, hawk-faced Tracy achieved instant popularity with Depression audiences hungry for the rule of law; the character has changed little during more than four decades, and enthusiasm for the strip is still widely evident.

Imitative crime strips of the 1930s were less enduring. In 1934 Dashiell HAMMETT's nameless FBI operative, Secret Agent X-9, was converted by superb artist Alex Raymond into the hero of a realistic comic strip narrative who often used underworld methods and guises in his war against spies and jewel thieves. X-9 was revitalized—and baptized—in 1967 by talented artist Al Williamson as *Secret Agent Corrigan.* Another "secret operative," numbered 48, appeared in *Dan Dunn* (created by Norman Marsh). Often accompanied by his dog, Wolf, Dan halted the evil work of the Chinese master criminal Wu Fang in the mythical American city of San Fragel. "Ace detective" Red Barry, a flame-haired policeman created by Will Gould, was involved in cases that often took him into Chinatown. *Radio Patrol,* created by Eddie Sullivan and Charlie Schmidt, explored the relationship of two uniformed cops riding in a radio-equipped and on-call police car, a novel concept for its day that was heralded as the death knell for crime but was quite outshone by Dick Tracy's battery of mechanisms (such as the wrist radio), which were slightly in advance of their time.

The second most important and durable police strip was created by Alfred Andriola. In 1938 this talented illustrator first transformed Charlie CHAN into a newspaper strip. His portrait of the Honolulu policeman was somewhat closer to the Biggers source than that presented by the film series. Five years later Andriola began *Kerry Drake.* Originally Drake was an assistant district attorney, an active crime fighter battling a Tracyesque lineup of bizarre killers (Stitches, No Face, and so on). But when his girl is murdered, a shaken Drake abandoned his career and—after some soul-searching—became a rookie cop. He has since progressed through the ranks and married the widow of a slain policeman friend (and even become the father of quadruplets). Less agile than in earlier days, he sometimes lets his private eye younger brother become the focus of the strip. Far less simplistically drawn than the Tracy strip, and much more intelligent in its writing, *Kerry Drake* during the last decades has increasingly explored the way in which ordinary people can be caught up in the crime and despair of our time.

Mysteries were regularly faced by the principal characters of adventure strips, even the young heroes of *Little Orphan Annie* (the homeless, spunky waif was fathered in 1924 by Harold Gray), the early *Terry and the Pirates* (another young orphan, discovered in China in 1934 by Milton Caniff), and *Tim Tyler's Luck* (Tim's African experiences, begun in 1931, were drawn by Lyman Young). Spies and criminals were routine adversaries in the strips *Don Winslow of the Navy* (Winslow was the dashing naval officer created in 1934 by former FBI man Frank V. Martinek), *Smilin' Jack* (Jack, a flying adventurer, took off in 1933; the comic strip was illustrated by Zack Mosley), and *Mandrake the Magician* (Mandrake's hypnotic gestures have often befuddled whole gangs of crooks. An amateur detective who has consistently worn an opera cape, top hat, and tuxedo since 1934, he was created by writer Lee Falk).

Dashiell Hammett's *Secret Agent X-9,* drawn by Alex Raymond, was a King Features comic strip. X-9's first adventure was published in two now-rare cardboard-covered volumes by McKay in 1934. This is the front cover of Volume 2.

Falk's second creation was a major comic strip innovation—a costumed crusader whose identity was concealed. To natives in the African interior the Phantom was an "immortal" (actually the gray tights costume was passed from father to son), regal Ghost Who Walks; piracy was the family nemesis. *The Phantom* comic strip first appeared in 1936. But the costumed hero assumed superpowers in 1938, when Jerry Siegal and Joe Shuster created Superman, actually an alien being from another world with incredible strengths—even the power to fly—who has dedicated himself to battling evil—in a red-and-blue outfit (also basically tights). When he is not Superman, he disguises himself as a mild-mannered, bespectacled newspaper reporter.

The Superman character was an early and incredibly successful hero of a new development of the comic art—the comic *book,* an outgrowth of the strip narrative. This illustrative means of telling an often melodramatic story swept the world during the 1940s. Called "comic books" only because of their dim origins as humorous newspaper drawings, they dealt most often with crime and those who rose against it.

The second most important costumed hero of the comic books—and perhaps the most interesting—was the caped, nocturnal BATMAN, who had no superpowers but relied only on his superb muscular skills. He was created in 1939 by Bob Kane (however, Bill Finger was responsible for many of the narrative's later attributes). He first appeared in *Detective Comics.* The multitude of costumed heroes that followed possessed either particular skills (often scientific) or very specialized superpowers. A few of the large number of such comic strips were *Captain Marvel, Spy Smasher, The Human Torch, Captain America,* and *Ibis the Invincible.* And in all of the hundreds of them, even Walt Disney's *Mickey Mouse,* and characters returned from the grave such as *The Spectre* and *The Spirit,* the "heroes" fought crooks, crime, and, in wartime, espionage agents. Although comic books are still printed today, parental concern over their excessive violence muted their popularity by the end of the 1940s.

The newspaper adventure strip has lessened in popularity as well; the impact of television on reading habits has been cited as a leading cause. However, in the 1950s and 1960s many favorite literary detectives have appeared in comic strips: *Sherlock Holmes* (see HOLMES, SHERLOCK), *Perry Mason* (see MASON, PERRY), *The Saint* (see SAINT, THE), *Nero Wolfe* (see WOLFE, NERO), *Mike Hammer* (see HAMMER, MIKE), and *James Bond* (see BOND, JAMES). Modesty BLAISE began her career in a newspaper strip that is an excellent example of the European contribution to the art.

The most important postwar detective creation was *Rip Kirby,* begun by Alex Raymond, the major force in strip illustration, in 1946 and continued after Raymond's death ten years later in the same excellent fashion by John Prentice. Kirby, a dashing and refined private eye who does not hesitate to show his intelligence, is actually allowed to wear glasses, a very novel accoutrement for heroes. With Rip Kirby on the case, the comic art detective is in distinguished hands.

CONAN DOYLE, SIR ARTHUR (1859–1930). English author, historian, doctor, spiritualist, and creator of Sherlock HOLMES, the greatest detective in literature. He was born Arthur Conan Doyle at No. 11 Picardy Place, Edinburgh, Scotland, on May 22, 1859, to Mary Foley and Charles Doyle (in later years both Arthur and his sister Annette preferred the surname Conan Doyle; Michael Conan, their father's uncle, was Arthur's godfather). The Doyles were an old aristocratic Irish family; Arthur's grandfather, John, had made the family known as both an intellectual and an artistic one. John Doyle left Dublin for London in 1815 and became an accomplished caricaturist under the pseudonym H. B. His four sons displayed similar gifts: Richard, an even more renowned artist than his father, designed the familiar cover of *Punch;* Henry, an art expert, became manager of the National Gallery in Dublin; James, the eldest, compiled the *Official Baronage of England;* and Charles, the youngest and Arthur's

Sir Arthur Conan Doyle.

father, squandered his ability as a painter and became a civil servant who paid little attention to his job, his art, or his family, leaving the raising of the children to his wife.

Arthur's romantic, idealistic spirit, so fundamental to his personality and writing, manifested itself at an early age. At school he read R. M. Ballantine, Mayne Reid, and other adventure writers of the day and was a self-styled champion of bullied younger and weaker boys. He studied first at Jesuit institutions—Hodder, a preparatory school; Stonyhurst; and Feldkirch, in Austria, for a final year—and then entered the University of Edinburgh, qualifying for a bachelor of medicine degree in 1881 and receiving a medical degree in 1885. Two of his professors were to be reborn as major characters in his fiction: Professor Rutherford, an anatomist, as Professor Challenger (in *The Lost World,* 1912, *The Poison Belt,* 1913, and *The Land of Mist,* 1926); and Dr. Joseph Bell, a surgeon, as Sherlock Holmes.

In 1879, while still in school and attempting to help pay for it, Conan Doyle wrote his first story, "The Mystery of the Sasassa Valley," and, to his amazement, sold it immediately to *Chambers' Journal.* Although his next several attempts were rejected, his initial success encouraged him to continue writing. Later in 1879 he sold his second story, "The American's Tale," to *London Society.* That year his father entered a convalescent home (where he died in 1893), and Arthur, as head of the family, assumed a heavy financial burden. In 1880, to earn money, he spent seven months as a ship's doctor on a whaler in the Arctic and, later, four months as a highly paid medical officer on an African steamer, ultimately using both experiences as background for his writings. In 1882, after a brief, unsatisfactory medical partnership with an old friend, he opened his own practice in Southsea, Portsmouth. Patients were scarce, and finding himself with much spare time, he wrote a novel entitled *The Narrative of John Smith,* presumed to be an autobiographical work, which was lost in the mails and never recovered. Two years later he began a second novel, *The Firm of Girdlestone,* which was rejected by every publisher he approached. In 1884, impressed by the tales of Émile GABORIAU and by Edgar Allan POE's character C. Auguste DUPIN, Conan Doyle tried his hand at a detective novel; the result was *A Study in Scarlet,* the first Sherlock Holmes story, published in 1887. In 1885 he wrote a historical novel, *Micah Clarke,* but it was rejected everywhere until it reached Andrew Lang at Longmans, who supported its publication in 1889.

Meanwhile, James PAYN, who was the editor of *The Cornhill Magazine,* which had published some of Conan Doyle's early short stories, recommended him to Lippincott, the Philadelphia publishing house. A dinner meeting was arranged for a Lippincott representative, Conan Doyle, and Oscar Wilde, as a result of which Wilde wrote *The Picture of Dorian Gray* (1891) for *Lippincott's Magazine* and Conan Doyle wrote *The Sign of Four* (1890), marking the second appearance of Sherlock Holmes. As Conan Doyle's literary reputation grew, his medical career drew to a close, and he spent two years writing his next novel, *The White Company* (1891), another historical piece in the vein of *Micah Clarke,* serialized in *Cornhill* in 1890–1891. The first Sherlock Holmes short story, "A Scandal in Bohemia," was published in the July 1891 issue of *The Strand,* and the subsequent Holmes series quickly became one of the most popular literary phenomena of the century. But after two dozen stories, Conan Doyle tired of the character—although Holmes had helped make his fortune—and he killed him. (The vehement protests of the public forced Conan Doyle to revive him a few years later.) Determined to concentrate on "serious" novels, he created a swashbuckling Frenchman to make his readers forget Holmes; Brigadier Étienne Gerard was thereupon added to the roster of memorable figures created by Conan Doyle.

Conan Doyle had married Louise Hawkins in 1885; they had two children, a daughter, Mary Louise, and a son, Kingsley. Mrs. Conan Doyle fell seriously ill in 1893, and for her health the family moved to Switzerland; she died in 1900. Conan Doyle was married to his second wife, Jean Leckie, in 1907.

A lover of sports and outdoor life, he is said to have introduced skis to Switzerland. He drew on his knowledge of and fondness for prizefighting in *Rodney Stone* (1896), which was written just after the first Gerard book and helped popularize the relatively unknown sport.

In 1900, eager to witness the Boer War, Conan Doyle sailed for South Africa as both a doctor and an unofficial attaché. With idealism as well as acuity, he threw himself into the midst of the fighting and later interviewed Lord Roberts and others for first-hand accounts of the battles. The resultant book, *The Great Boer War* (1900), is still the standard reference work on that moment of British history. He was knighted in 1902, ostensibly for that comprehensive and well-documented work, but actually for a small pamphlet, *The War in South Africa: Its Cause and Conduct* (1902), completed in January of that year, which he distributed at his own expense to help alter Europe's anti-British sentiment about the war.

In 1903 he unsuccessfully ran for Parliament as a Liberal Unionist, but he became even more determined to be socially effective, now with more direct methods, by championing the cause of the underdog. The two most illuminating examples of his dedication to justice arose from criminal trials that he believed had convicted innocent men and to which he devoted his total energy and his skills as a detective.

A young law student, George Edalji, half-caste son of a Staffordshire minister, was convicted of maiming horses and sentenced to seven years' imprisonment in 1903. Three years later, Conan Doyle learned of the case, was impressed with the authenticity of the defense, and investigated. He wrote a series of articles for the *Daily Telegraph* that caused a sensation when he demonstrated that Edalji was practically blind and could not have committed the crimes. Although Conan Doyle established the identity of the true criminal, no one else was charged after Edalji's release, and the innocent victim was never recompensed for his three years in prison.

An even more famous case involved Oscar Slater, a German Jew of questionable background. A few days after an elderly lady was killed and her diamond brooch stolen, Slater assumed an alias and left the country—after pawning a diamond brooch. Although the police determined that the brooches were not the same, they began extradition proceedings; Slater, however, returned to Edinburgh voluntarily and stood trial. His unshakable alibi for the night of the murder was considered unreliable because the witness was his mistress, and he was convicted on flimsy evidence in May 1909. Conan Doyle made repeated petitions, finally succeeded in getting Slater freed in 1927, and then pressed for a retrial. When it was learned that two key witnesses had been paid to give false testimony, Slater won the case and compensation of £6,000. Conan Doyle's court costs exceeded several hundred pounds, and Slater refused to pay them. Conan Doyle wrote that "it was a painful and sordid aftermath to such a story."

Conan Doyle had long anticipated England's potential problems in a war with European nations and had advocated such safeguards as a channel tunnel and a program to encourage the growth of sufficient food to make the island self-sustaining. He recommended the use of body armor and shields in warfare and was jeered at by the War Office; of course, steel helmets and tanks eventually became standard. His campaign for lifesaving equipment for sailors resulted in the saving of countless lives, and he initiated what became the 200,000-member Volunteer Force.

During the war his son Kingsley was badly wounded on the Somme and later died in London of pneumonia. This loss completed Conan Doyle's conversion to spiritualism, to which he devoted the remainder of his life. His interest in an alternate religious framework dated as far back as the Southsea days. With an ardor that verged on fanaticism, he toured Great Britain, Australia, and North America in search of converts. He went so far as to make arrangements to communicate with his second wife after his death. Conan Doyle died at Crowborough, Sussex, on July 7, 1930, leaving his wife; his daughter by his first wife, Mary Louise; and the three children of his second marriage: two sons, Adrian and Denis, and a daughter, Lena Jean ("Billy").

CHECKLIST

Books with at least one mystery not about Sherlock Holmes.

1887 *Dreamland and Ghostland* (s.s.)
1889 *Mysteries and Adventures* (s.s.)
1890 *The Captain of the Polestar and Other Tales* (s.s.)
1893 *My Friend the Murderer and Other Mysteries and Adventures* (s.s.)
1908 *Round the Fire Stories* (s.s.)
1935 *The Black Doctor and Other Tales of Terror and Mystery* (s.s.)

CONNELL, RICHARD (EDWARD) (1893–1949). Prolific American writer and author of "The Most Dangerous Game," a classic of suspense fiction.

Born in Dutchess County, N.Y., Connell attended Harvard, where he edited the *Daily Crimson* and *Lampoon*. After reporting for the *New York American*, writing advertising copy, marrying, and serving in World War I, he became a free-lance writer. He moved to Hollywood in 1925 to work on films and also began to write a wide variety of stories, many of them humorous. Several of his 300 short stories were made into films. He also wrote original stories for several films.

The short story "The Most Dangerous Game" was published in *Variety* (1925) and is often reprinted. It is the now-familiar tale of Sanger Rainsford, a big-game hunter on a trip up the Amazon who falls off his ship and saves himself by swimming to Ship-Trap Island, where he meets the sinister General Zaroff. In the middle of the dense jungle on the island Zaroff has a palatial estate—and a macabre museum. His passion for hunting has driven him to pursue the ultimate game—man—and Rainsford becomes his prey.

Connell's only detective novel is *Murder at Sea* (1929), in which reporter Matthew Kelton solves a murder on a Bermuda-bound boat only after two additional violent deaths.

Films

Connell contributed the story for Paul Muni's *Seven Faces* (1929), a nightmare fantasy set in a waxworks. Then, in 1932, his most enduringly popular work was first filmed.

The Most Dangerous Game (British title: *The Hounds of Zaroff*). RKO, 1932. Joel McCrea, Fay Wray, Leslie Banks. Directed by Ernest B. Schoedsack and Irving Pichel.

Washed ashore on a lonely island after his yacht has been wrecked, a young hunter finds himself the prey of a mad sportsman, Zaroff, who traps human beings in his domain so that he can use them as objects of a hunt.

The hunt has often been reenacted.

A Game of Death. RKO, 1945. John Loder, Edgar Barrier, Audrey Long. Directed by Robert Wise.

In this close remake, human head trophies float in jugs of water in a madman's castle.

Run for the Sun. United Artists, 1956. Richard Widmark, Jane Greer, Trevor Howard, Peter Van Eyck. Directed by Roy Boulting.

In a looser adaptation, a small plane carrying a despondent former writer and a girl crashes in the Mexican jungle. They find their way to the remote hacienda of an aristocratic Englishman and a Dutch archaeologist (actually a British traitor and a German war criminal), who pursue them with rifles and dogs through the jungle.

There have also been many unofficial uses of the story in other media. Films have been based on other Connell works as well.

F-Man. Paramount, 1936. Jack Haley, Grace Bradley, William Frawley. Directed by Edward F. Cline.

In this comedy, a simpleton, believing himself to be a federal operative, is instrumental in trapping a "most-wanted" criminal.

Brother Orchid. Warner Brothers, 1940. Edward G. Robinson, Ann Sothern, Humphrey Bogart, Ralph Bellamy. Directed by Lloyd Bacon.

A tough racketeer, wounded in a gang war, seeks refuge in a monastery and gradually accepts the way of life he finds there. He is enraged when he learns that a "protection" organization prevents the monks from selling flowers.

CONNINGTON, J. J. (pseudonym of Alfred Walter Stewart; 1880–1947). British scientist and detective novelist; creator of Sir Clinton DRIFFIELD. The first scientific investigator to recognize the existence of isobaric atoms, Stewart was the son of Professor William Stewart, dean of faculties at Glasgow University. He received his education at the Universities of Glasgow and Marburg and at University College, London. In 1901 he started his career as a teacher at Queen's University in Belfast. He was the author of *Stereochemistry* (1907) and *Recent Advances in Organic Chemistry* (1908).

He spent the years from 1914 to 1919 at the University of Glasgow lecturing on physical chemistry and radioactivity and then returned to Queen's University to become professor of chemistry and eventually chairman of his department until his retirement in 1944.

During the years at Queen's University, Stewart published *Some Physico-chemical Themes* (1922), but he also began to write works in the mystery-detection field. First he published *Nordenholt's Million*, a science fiction story appearing under the Connington pseudonym in 1923, and a novel, *Almighty Gold*, appearing in 1924. He published his first two detective novels, *Death at Swaythling Court* and *The Dangerfield Talisman*, in 1926. Stewart had begun them as a hobby, writing late at night after a full day of teaching; they were well received and were later reprinted by Penguin Books. The following year his series character, Sir Clinton, made his first appearance, and, under the Connington pseudonym, Stewart continued to write books about him for two decades.

Stewart retired from teaching in 1944 because of a heart condition, but he produced two more detective novels and a series of twelve essays, collected in *Alias J. J. Connington* (1947).

J. J. Connington might best be compared to Freeman Wills CROFTS or John RHODE with his meticulously plotted detective stories.

The Eye in the Museum (1929) is standard Connington, dealing with poisoning by digitalis and financial manipulations and concluding with a chase involving a motorboat and an automobile. The presence of the astringent Sir Clinton is dispensed with in this book, possibly the only detective novel in which the device of the camera obscura is used. The work also suggests its author's scientific and academic background.

An attempt to create a new and more sympathetic series detective than Driffield produced lawyer Mark Brand (the "Counselor"), who appears in two novels, *The Counselor* (1939) and *Four Defences* (1940), but they did not meet with the success of earlier work, nor did they come close to the popularity of Sir Clinton's exploits. Connington's work has been out of print for twenty-five years.

CONRAD, BRENDA. See FORD, LESLIE.

CONRAD, JOSEPH (1857–1924). Polish-born English novelist. Born Józef Teodor Konrad Korzeniowski, the son of a Polish nobleman, Conrad spent his early years at sea (later used as background for much of his fiction) before becoming a British citizen in 1886. He learned English and wrote in that language. Most of his novels are noted for their stylistic excellence and profound explorations of morality. In addition to such adventure tales as *Almayer's Folly* (1895), *The Nigger of the 'Narcissus'* (1897), and *Lord Jim* (1900), Conrad wrote *The Secret Agent* (1907), regarded as the first serious novel to feature a double agent. Verloc's involvement in an anarchist plot to commit an act of violence in London's Greenwich Park closely resembles an actual historical incident. It was filmed by Alfred HITCHCOCK as *Sabotage* (1936; U.S. title: *The Woman Alone*). *Under Western Skies* (1911) concerns the double agent Razumov. A short story in *A Set of Six* (1908), "The Informer," recounts the adventures of detective X. In 1924 Conrad collaborated with Ford Madox Ford in writing *The Nature of a Crime*.

CONTINENTAL OP, THE (Creator: Dashiell HAMMETT). A nameless operative for the Continental Detective Agency in San Francisco, this "hard-boiled dick" is Hammett's first important creation and one of the most significant in the literature of crime. He followed Carroll John DALY's private eye, Race WILLIAMS, in the pages of BLACK MASK by only a few months in the early 1920s to become one of the leaders of the "tough-guy" school of detective fiction.

The Op has a lot of Hammett in him, and many of his cases were based on Hammett's experiences as a Pinkerton detective, but the prime model for the tough dick was James Wright, assistant superintendent of Pinkerton's Baltimore office and Hammett's former boss.

Hammett claimed that he did not deliberately avoid giving his character a name, but: "He's more or less of a type, and I'm not sure he's entitled to a name. . . . I've worked with several of him. . . ." In most cases, the Op is described as fat and middle-aged, but he is a pro, with many years' experience, and tough, generally enjoying the violence of shooting a bad guy or smashing various parts of a hood's face or body with his bare fists.

The quiet manager of the agency, known as "the Old Man," gives the Op his orders. In his seventies, the Old Man "had no more warmth in him than a hangman's rope." Once he has his orders, the Op will give his life for a client, if necessary, and he remains loyal to his agency, however great the temptation.

In *Red Harvest*, his first book appearance, the Op fights political corruption in Personville, a town so contaminated with vice that its citizens casually call it "Poisonville." By setting warring criminal factions against one another, the Op manages to get most of them killed off and the town cleaned up.

The Dain Curse, the Op's other appearance in a novel, is, in Hammett's words, "a silly story," involving more than thirty characters leaping from one coast to the other. The Op personally shoots and stabs one man to death, helps shoot another dead, wrestles with five women, and fights off a supernatural being—bare-handed. He is involved in a jewel burglary, eight separate and distinct murders, and a seduction, is attacked with knives, guns, bombs, and chloroform, cures a girl of drug addiction by talking to her, and deals with a family curse. The many short stories involving the Continental Op are better.

CHECKLIST

1929 *Red Harvest* (revised version of a serial originally appearing in *Black Mask,* November 1927–February 1928)
1929 *The Dain Curse* (revised version of a serial originally appearing in *Black Mask,* November 1928–February 1929).
1943 *$106,000 Blood Money* (novelette combining two short stories originally published in *Black Mask* (February and March 1927) as "$106,000 Blood Money" and "The Big Knockover")
1945 *The Continental Op* (s.s.)
1945 *The Return of the Continental Op* (s.s.)
1946 *Hammett Homicides* (s.s.; contains four stories about the Continental Op)
1947 *Dead Yellow Women* (s.s.; contains four stories about the Continental Op)
1948 *Nightmare Town* (s.s.; contains two stories about the Continental Op)
1950 *The Creeping Siamese* (s.s.; contains three stories about the Continental Op)
1952 *Woman in the Dark* (s.s.; contains three stories about the Continental Op)
1962 *A Man Named Thin* (s.s.; contains one story about the Continental Op)

COOL, BERTHA, AND DONALD LAM (Creator: Erle Stanley GARDNER as A. A. Fair). The senior member of this unlikely detective team is Bertha Cool, a large gray-haired woman in her sixties. She opened her private investigation agency in 1936, when her husband, Henry Cool, died. Her twinkling eyes give her a grandmotherly appearance that is belied by her tough-mindedness and equally tough language. Her weight (as much as 275 pounds) is a constant problem. She prefers to wear loose, unconfining garments and has been described by Donald Lam as looking "like a cylinder of currant jelly on a plate" when she walks. Lam is a disbarred lawyer who has had many brushes with the police. The Cool-Lam team is formed at the outset of *The Bigger They Come* (1939), when Donald, hungry and desperately in need of work, convinces Mrs. Cool that despite his diminutive appearance (5 feet 6 inches tall and 125 pounds) he is man enough to be a detective. Though small, he is considered very attractive by most women, although Mrs. Cool's good-looking, shy secretary, Elsie Brand, generally manages to resist the Lam charms. Cool and Lam are a team through twenty-nine books, and Lam earns a full partnership in *Double or Quits* (1941), one of the most praised of the series. In this book Bertha Cool, recovering from influenza, has reduced her weight to 160 pounds—described as "solid muscle." Lam is suspected of a series of murders and almost killed before he solves the case.

Give 'Em the Ax (1944) begins with Lam's return from service in the South Pacific; he has been discharged because he contracted a tropical disease. He is welcomed back to the firm with a case of murder—and the murder weapon has been left in Donald's car. The last recorded Cool-Lam case was Gardner's posthumously published *All Grass Isn't Green* (1970), a not too highly regarded book about a missing girl and drug smuggling across the Mexican–United States border.

CHECKLIST

1939 *The Bigger They Come* (British title: *Lam to the Slaughter*)
1940 *Turn on the Heat*
1940 *Gold Comes in Bricks*
1941 *Spill the Jackpot*
1941 *Double or Quits*
1942 *Owls Don't Blink*
1942 *Bats Fly at Dusk*
1943 *Cats Prowl at Night*
1944 *Give 'Em the Ax* (British title: *Axe to Grind*)
1946 *Crows Can't Count*
1947 *Fools Die on Friday*
1949 *Bedrooms Have Windows*
1952 *Top of the Heap*
1953 *Some Women Won't Wait*
1956 *Beware the Curves*
1957 *You Can Die Laughing*
1957 *Some Slips Don't Show*
1958 *The Count of Nine*
1959 *Pass the Gravy*
1960 *Kept Women Can't Quit*
1961 *Bachelors Get Lonely*
1961 *Shills Can't Cash Chips* (British title: *Stop at the Red Light*)
1962 *Try Anything Once*
1963 *Fish or Cut Bait*
1964 *Up for Grabs*
1965 *Cut Thin to Win*
1966 *Widows Wear Weeds*
1967 *Traps Need Fresh Bait*
1970 *All Grass Isn't Green*

CORNIER, VINCENT (1898–). English author noted for his short detective stories. Born in Redcar, Yorkshire, he was a precocious writer who, at the age of fourteen, was earning 100 guineas a year by selling articles for a half guinea each. After serving as a flier during World War I, he became a newspaperman. In 1926 he tried his hand at fiction and sold his work to *Storyteller, Argosy,* and *Pearson's* magazines. He wrote stories for twenty-five years before finally publishing a novel.

An early detective story, "The Flying Hat," was published in the anonymously edited *The Best (English) Detective Stories of 1929* (1930). Jacques BARZUN and Wendell Hertig TAYLOR consider the story outstanding. It also made a vivid impression on Ellery QUEEN (author); in fact, he later resurrected a group of Cornier's stories for publication in *Ellery Queen's Mystery Magazine (EQMM).*

"The Smell That Killed" (1935; published in *EQMM,* December 1946), in a sense an anticipation of the atomic bomb, features series detective Barnabas Hildreth, a scientist similar to Dr. THORNDYKE, but fashioned in a more romantic mold, who works for British Intelligence and is called "the Black Monk."

When Queen published "The Cloak That Laughed" in his July 1947 issue, he called the Hildreth saga "one of the great series of modern detective stories." In "The Shot That Waited" (*EQMM,* September 1947) a bullet fired in 1710 somehow wounds a bank cashier in 1933. Queen called "The Stone Ear" (*EQMM,* March 1948) one of the most remarkable stories ever reprinted in *EQMM.* The final word solves all the questions raised by the preceding 7,000 words.

Cornier, encouraged by Queen's reprinting of his old stories, submitted a new story to *EQMM*'s Sixth Annual Contest; "O Time, in Your Flight" (1951) received a special award as the best short-short and was published in the December 1951 issue.

Cornier's best puzzles are as bizarre and baffling as anything written by John Dickson CARR or Queen.

CORNING, KYLE. *See* GARDNER, ERLE STANLEY.

CORNWELL, DAVID JOHN MOORE. *See* LE CARRÉ, JOHN.

CORRELL, A. BOYD. *See* MACDONALD, PHILIP.

CORYELL, JOHN R. *See* CARTER, NICK.

COULSON, JOHN HUBERT ARTHUR. *See* BONETT, JOHN AND EMERY.

COURTIER, S[IDNEY] H[OBSON] (1904–1974). Australian author, educator, and mystery novelist. Born at Kangaroo Flat, Victoria, Courtier was educated at the University of Melbourne, where he took first honors and received a certificate in education. He married Audrey Jennie George in 1932; they had three children.

Courtier taught in primary schools for a number of years and then was a principal for a dozen years in the Melbourne schools for teacher training. He served in the Australian Imperial Forces from 1942 to 1944. He wrote about 200 short stories, many of which were published in England and the United States, as well as in Australia; he used the pseudonym Rui Chestor for some of them. Courtier lectured on literature at teachers colleges, was a judge in short story contests, and was a member of the Crime Writers' Association. Long a resident of Caulfield, Victoria, he retired from teaching in 1969.

Courtier started publishing detective novels in 1950 with *The Glass Spear* and produced a book every year thereafter. The very few of his novels that were published in the United States generally concern crime problems rooted in the past. In *One Cried Murder* (1954) the members of an anthropological expedition in the remote Australian desert discover a twenty-five-year-old skeleton of a modern white man at a dig; the mystery involves blackmail and murder. This novel appears to have been influenced by the work of Courtier's fellow Australian Arthur W. UPFIELD. In *Murder's Burning* (1967) a fire patrol officer investigates the circumstances behind his best friend's death in a sudden, raging fire that destroyed a small valley town and killed several of its inhabitants a half-dozen years earlier. Lewis Ligny, the title character of *Ligny's Lake* (1971)—and an individual with highly distinctive features—is seen by a casual acquaintance at a boxing match; the man then discovers that Ligny had been reported drowned twelve hours earlier while fishing 500 miles away. The acquaintance determines to investigate, in spite of family and government obstacles and objections.

COX, A. B. *See* BERKELEY, ANTHONY.

COXE, GEORGE HARMON (1901–). American scriptwriter and author of mystery novels and short stories. Born in Olean, N.Y., Coxe attended high school in nearby Elmira. After one year each at Purdue and Cornell Universities, he left school and worked in a lumber camp and an automobile factory before going into newspaper work. He was employed by papers in California, Florida, and New York before going to Cambridge, Mass., where he worked for an advertising agency from 1927 to 1932.

In 1932 Coxe decided to abandon his advertising career and return to writing. Ten years earlier he had sold an article about his college days to *The American Boy* and two detective stories to *Detective Story* magazine. He wrote the detective stories because "as a kid I used to read mysteries. . . . It was easier for me to think up something that had a gimmick and crime is a universal subject." Eventually, during a highly successful career writing for the PULP MAGAZINES, he was to write sports, love, adventure, and sea stories. The first of his more than sixty hard-cover mysteries was published in 1935.

From 1936 to 1938 he was a contract writer for MGM in Hollywood, sharing screen credit on one script, *Arsène Lupin Returns* (1938). He returned to MGM in 1945 and received billing as coauthor of *The Hidden Eye,* for which he also wrote the original story. He wrote an audition script for the radio series featuring his famous fictional creation Flashgun CASEY. For two years he wrote a radio series, *The Commandos,* for CBS. He also wrote television scripts, including a play for the *Kraft Television Theater* that appeared in 1957.

During the 1940s Coxe wrote many stories, usually nonmysteries, for such "slicks" as *Collier's, The American Magazine,* and *The Saturday Evening Post.* Many of them had a war background and reflect considerable firsthand research by Coxe, who visited military bases and also made a tour of the Pacific theater as a special correspondent.

Coxe has spent most of his adult life in New England. He married Elizabeth Fowler in 1929 while working in Cambridge, and they had two children, a son and a daughter. His most famous detectives, Casey and Kent MURDOCK, are Boston news photographers; Coxe himself is much interested in photography. Since 1941 the Coxes have lived in Old Lyme, Conn., but they often winter on Hilton Head Island, S.C.

They have also traveled extensively in the South and the Caribbean, and Coxe has used the latter area for many nonseries mysteries including *Murder in Havana* (1943) and *One Minute Past Eight* (1957). *Inland Passage* (1949) is about a crime-filled journey up the rivers of the United States, from Florida to the Northeast. *One Way Out* (1960), a suspense story about newspaperman Rick Marston, captures much of the flavor of New Orleans.

Most critics have reviewed Coxe's work favorably. Jacques BARZUN and Wendell Hertig TAYLOR had noted the frequency with which Kent Murdock stories depend upon the theft of incriminating pictures that the detective-photographer has taken (e.g., *The Charred Witness,* 1942, and *The Hollow Needle,* 1948). However, they have been attracted to many Coxe books, most notably *The Groom Lay Dead* (1944), the story of murder at a wedding party in upstate New York, praising its "ingenious murder" and calling it "well motivated and suitably unraveled." Anthony BOUCHER commented that Coxe was the "professional's professional." The Mystery Writers of America presented him with their Grand Master Award in 1963.

CRAIGIE, GORDON. *See* DEPARTMENT Z.

CRANE, BILL (Creator: Jonathan LATIMER). A private detective who works and lives in Chicago, Crane frequently travels to places like New York and Florida in the course of his cases. He is thirty-four years old but looks only thirty and is a quiet and modest person whose clear-skinned face is often sun-tanned. He smokes cigarettes and drinks anything—and often. His brown tweed suits are rumpled and creased because he falls into a drunken sleep anywhere. He is aided in his investigations by his friends Tom O'Malley and Doc Williams. During his last case he became engaged to lovely Ann Fortune.

In his first adventure, *Murder in the Madhouse* (1934), there is an unusual location for a series of murders that start out with Crane's incarceration in a mental institution. *Headed for a Hearse* (1935) concerns Crane's efforts to save a man, convicted of murdering his wife, from the electric chair. Christopher Morley thought that this book was better than Dashiell HAMMETT's *The Thin Man* (1934). It contains controversial material on social issues that was deleted when it was reissued by the Dell Great Mystery Library in 1957. *The Lady in the Morgue* (1936), Latimer's most popular success, begins with the discovery of a nude blonde hanging from her bathroom door; the pace becomes frantic when the body disappears. James SANDOE cited this novel in SANDOE'S READERS' GUIDE TO CRIME and called it a "sample of the rye-soaked, zany-cum-sex school."

The Dead Don't Care (1938), set in the Florida sunshine, involves a series of threatening letters and another good-looking girl—found murdered in a well-guarded room. In Crane's last case, *Red Gardenias* (1939), he investigates a death threat made

Preston Foster as detective Bill Crane (extreme left) tries to trap a killer in the climactic confrontation of the film *Lady in the Morgue*. He mingles with people in all walks of life, but here his companions are in evening dress. [*Universal*]

against the family of an industrial magnate by someone willing to prove he is not joking.

Films

The films about Bill Crane are good portraits of a tough, resilient, hard-drinking private detective in a dark Depression world. Crane drinks too much and naps at every opportunity. Identifying and categorizing the various kinds of liquor is his passion (his expertise calls to mind Sherlock HOLMES's acuity in identifying cigar ash). Often he is unsteady, but his mind is sharp.

The Westland Case. Universal, 1937. Preston Foster, Frank Jenks, Carol Hughes, Barbara Pepper, Astrid Allwyn, Theodore Von Eltz. Directed by Christy Cabanne. Based on *Headed for a Hearse.*

Just one week before an attorney is to be electrocuted for the murder of his wife, Crane is assigned to save him.

The Lady in the Morgue. Universal, 1938. Foster, Jenks, Patricia Ellis, Tom Jackson. Directed by Otis Garrett. Based on the 1936 novel.

Crane goes to the morgue to identify the body of a girl found hanged in a midtown hotel; he thinks that she may be the missing daughter of a client, but the corpse has disappeared and the morgue attendant murdered.

The Last Warning. Universal, 1938. Foster, Jenks, Frances Robinson, Joyce Compton, Raymond Parker, Robert Page, E. E. Clive. Directed by Al Rogell. Based on *The Dead Don't Care.*

Crane moves from the metropolis (New York has been the setting of his first two screen mysteries) to Raymond CHANDLER country, Los Angeles, where one by one, the members of a rich, troubled family are being kidnapped and murdered by someone who calls himself "the Eye."

CRANE, FRANCES (1896–   ). American author of short stories and mystery novels. Born Frances Kirkwood in Lawrenceville, Ill., she has used that town as a home base during a much-traveled life and has written most of her books there. For many years she and her husband lived in Europe, where she wrote short stories, almost 100 of which were published in *The New Yorker*; others appeared in *Harper's Magazine* and *Harper's Bazaar.* The Cranes have one daughter, born in Berkeley, Calif., in 1921.

Among Mrs. Crane's mystery works are twenty-six novels about a popular husband and wife detective team, Pat and Jean ABBOTT. A color is used in the title of almost every Abbott book, and the settings are cities Mrs. Crane has visited. The first book in the series, *The Turquoise Shop* (1941), describes the meeting of the Abbotts in Taos, N.Mex. In *The Golden Box* (1942) Pat Abbott arrives in his wife's hometown, "Elm Hill" (fictional Lawrenceville), in time to solve a murder. Other books are set in New Orleans, Paris, and Key West. *The Flying Red Horse* (1949) is a story of love and death among Dallas oil millionaires. The setting for *The Ultraviolet Widow* (1956) is the ruins of an ancient city in the Mexican jungle.

San Francisco, the city in which Pat Abbott's detective office is located, is Mrs. Crane's most often used setting. *The Yellow Violet* (1942) tells of a spy hunt there that postpones the Abbotts' wedding a number of times. In reviewing *Thirteen White Tulips* (1953), Bay Area resident Anthony BOUCHER praised the "splendid (and very accurately reported) eating in San Francisco restaurants" described therein. However, of *Death-Wish Green* (1960), set in the city's North Beach area during its beatnik days, Boucher said that the book "captures its geography accurately and its spirit not at all."

Although some of her early books received good reviews, Frances Crane was generally more popular with American readers than with American critics because of "HAD-I-BUT-KNOWN" SCHOOL tendencies in her work. She also had a wide audience in England, where the *Evening Standard* once generously referred to her as "America's Agatha CHRISTIE."

CREASEY, JOHN (1908–1973). English author of mystery, crime, suspense, and detective novels. Creasey was the most prolific writer in the genre, with close to 600 books published under twenty-eight pseudonyms.

Born in Southfields, Surrey, the seventh of nine children of Ruth and Joseph Creasey, a poor coach maker, he attended several schools without distinction and took clerical, factory, and sales jobs until he had a book published in 1932. He had accumulated 743 rejection slips. He was married four times,

John Creasey. [*Mark Gerson*]

had three children, and spent his later years living alternately in England and in Arizona. A political activist, he founded the All Party Alliance in England, which advocated a government composed of the best men of all parties. He was an unsuccessful campaigner for a seat in Parliament.

Creasey created many memorable series characters under familiar pseudonyms, including the George GIDEON books (by J. J. Marric); the Toff series (*see* TOFF, THE); the Roger WEST series; the Dr. PALFREY series; the DEPARTMENT Z series; the Patrick DAWLISH books (by Gordon Ashe); the Mark Kilby series (by Robert Caine Frazer); the Liberator series, the Bruce Murdoch series, and other books (by Norman Deane); the Baron (*see* BARON, THE) series (by Anthony Morton); the Superintendent Folly series and other books (by Jeremy York); the Dr. Emmanuel CELLINI series (by Kyle Hunt, published in England under the Michael Halliday pseudonym, which was also used for many suspense novels not published in the United States). A comprehensive listing of all titles is given in *John Creasey, Master of Mystery*, Harper & Row, New York, 1972.

Creasey was so prolific that his publishers could not keep up with his output. Consequently, there are many manuscripts scheduled for publication in the future, with ample titles to ensure at least a score of new books during the years following his death.

CRIME DOCTOR, THE (Creator: Max MARCIN). Based on a long-running radio program that began in 1940, *The Crime Doctor* film series featured a crime specialist, a medical detective named Dr. Robert Ordway. Most of his cases involved the mentally aberrant, and all of his solutions were based on psychiatry. He made his debut just when psychiatry was enjoying its first important vogue as a dramatic device, and he was ready to solve any problems with glib Freudian generalities, some of them extremely suspect.

Films

The Crime Doctor. Columbia, 1943. Warner Baxter, Margaret Lindsay, John Litel. Directed by Michael Gordon.

In the initial film of the series, Dr. Ordway (Baxter) is the respected head of a parole board and a noted criminal psychiatrist, although there is amnesia in his past. A convict whose parole has been denied reveals that Ordway was once the leader of a gang—and had disappeared with the proceeds of a payroll robbery. A blow on the head helps Ordway remember both his evil past and the location of the hidden money. Happily, his subsequent good works and regeneration exonerate him—and he settles down to a lifetime of bizarre cases.

The Crime Doctor's Strangest Case. Columbia, 1943. Baxter, Lynn Merrick, Lloyd Bridges, Reginald Denny. Directed by Eugene Forde.

A former convict is accused of murdering a millionaire in a case that is not, in spite of the title, particularly strange.

Shadows in the Night. Columbia, 1944. Baxter, Nina Foch, George Zucco. Directed by Forde.

A distraught young heiress tells Dr. Ordway that a ghost haunts her sleep, insisting the she jump from her cliffside home into the ocean. Ordway discovers that hypnotic gas, piped through vents, is causing her dreams.

Crime Doctor's Courage. Columbia, 1945. Baxter, Hillary Brooke, Jerome Cowan. Directed by George Sherman.

A dance team, made up of a husband and wife who have seemingly occult powers, involves Dr. Ordway in the murder of a friend.

Crime Doctor's Warning. Columbia, 1945. Baxter, Litel, Dusty Anderson. Directed by William Castle.

Two models who have posed for a young artist, another victim of amnesia, are discovered murdered. A third model is missing, and Dr. Ordway sets out to find her.

Crime Doctor's Man Hunt. Columbia, 1946. Baxter, Ellen Drew, William Frawley. Directed by Castle.

A war veteran tells Dr. Ordway about his irrational fear of a certain part of the city; later Ordway finds his body there. The heiress to whom the victim had been engaged is certain that he was killed by her jealous twin sister, who is often missing for long periods of time.

Just Before Dawn. Columbia, 1946. Baxter, Adelle Roberts, Martin Kosleck, Mona Barrie. Directed by Castle.

Solicitous psychiatrist Dr. Ordway (Warner Baxter) listens as Ellen Drew tells of the disappearance of her mysterious twin sister in *Crime Doctor's Man Hunt.* [*Columbia*]

The Crime Doctor investigates: Warner Baxter in *Crime Doctor's Courage*. [*Columbia*]

A Paris trip involves Warner Baxter (center) as Dr. Ordway in a baffling series of murders in *Crime Doctor's Gamble*. [*Columbia*]

Dr. Ordway administers to a stricken diabetic at a party, using the sick man's own hypodermic—but the needle contains poison rather than insulin. Ordway later pretends to be blind in order to trap the guilty person.

The Millerson Case. Columbia, 1947. Baxter, Nancy Saunders, Clem Bevans. Directed by George Archainbaud.

On a backwoods hunting trip, Dr. Ordway discovers that someone has used a local typhoid outbreak to cover up a poisoning and then killed the district doctor when he became suspicious. In the end the unmasked killer feigns insanity but is no match for the sharp-witted Ordway.

Crime Doctor's Gamble. Columbia, 1947. Baxter, Micheline Cheirel, Roger Dann, Steven Geray. Directed by Castle.

On a vacation in Paris, Ordway is invited by his old friend Inspector Morell to look into the case of a young man accused of murdering his own father during a quarrel over a girl.

Crime Doctor's Diary. Columbia, 1949. Baxter, Stephen Dunne, Lois Maxwell, Adele Jergens. Directed by Seymour Friedman.

A convict whom Ordway had helped to get paroled finds himself caught in the intrigues of the music-recording business and framed for murder.

CRIME HATERS. *See* DAWLISH, PATRICK.

CRIME WRITERS' ASSOCIATION. *See* ORGANIZATIONS.

CRISPIN, EDMUND [pseudonym of (Robert) Bruce Montgomery; 1921–]. English musician and detective novelist. Of Scots-Irish parentage, Crispin was educated at Merchant Taylors' School and St. John's College, Oxford, where he read modern languages and numbered Kingsley Amis and Philip Larkin among his friends. Since the age of fourteen he has been a pianist, organist, and conductor; he is a serious composer as well as a writer.

He spent two years as an assistant master in a public school and traveled around Europe, particularly Germany, before World War II. After establishing an enviable reputation as a master of detective fiction with eight novels and a collection of short stories published during a nine-year period (1944–1953), he ceased production until the 1970s. He has also written film scripts and radio plays and edited a number of anthologies, mainly science fiction. Since 1967 he has been mystery fiction reviewer for *The Sunday Times* (London).

Montgomery has written the scores for many British films, including the famous *Carry On Nurse* (1959). For relaxation, he composes requiem masses. He is unmarried and lives in Devon.

Crispin has published only one mystery book not entirely about Gervase FEN, a short story collection in which two of the sixteen cases do not involve the Oxford professor who solves Crispin's other mysteries. *Beware of the Trains* (1953) exhibits his mastery of the short form. Ellery QUEEN (author) listed it in QUEEN'S QUORUM, and Anthony BOUCHER called the stories "models of fairplay trickery"; yet it took nine years for this book to find an American publisher.

In less than a decade Crispin proved himself a modern master through his ability to construct baffling puzzles, his sense of humor, his master detective (Fen), and his ability to entertain. Julian SYMONS says: "Crispin's work is marked by a highly individual sense of light comedy, and by a great flair for verbal deception rather in the [Agatha] CHRISTIE manner. If he never gives the impression of solid learning that can be sensed behind [Michael] INNES's frivolity, he is also never tiresomely literary. At his weakest he is flippant, at his best he is witty, but all his work shows a high-spiritedness rare and welcome in the crime story."

Recent attempts to revive Crispin's works in paper covers have met with indifference in the United States, but in England both hard-cover and paperback reprints have been highly successful.

CROFTS, FREEMAN WILLS (1879–1957). Irish engineer and detective story writer. Crofts, the creator of Inspector FRENCH, was the first mystery writer to regularly use the step-by-step methods of police routine in detective fiction. Many readers and critics maintain that he has never been equaled in his particular sphere.

Crofts was born in Dublin of English stock. His father was a doctor attached to the British Army who died while on foreign service. His mother later married Archdeacon Harding of the Church of Ireland, and the boy was raised in Northern Ireland. Educated at Methodist and Campbell Colleges in Belfast, at seventeen he became a civil engineering pupil apprenticed to his uncle, Berkeley D. Wise, chief engineer of the Belfast and Northern Counties Railway. In 1899 he became a junior construction engineer, rose to be district engineer, and, ten years later, transferred to Belfast to become chief assistant engineer for the line with which he had started his apprenticeship.

Freeman Wills Crofts.

In 1912 Crofts married Mary Bellas Canning, the daughter of a bank manager. In 1919, after suffering a severe illness, he spent the endless hours of his long convalescence in writing a story to amuse himself. He found this occupation enjoyable and later sent the story, *The Cask* (1920), to a London firm that secured publication. It was acclaimed as a classic, was translated into many languages, and within two decades had sold more than 100,000 copies. Crofts immediately started work on a successor and continued to turn out about a book a year until 1929, when he was forced to stop working for a while because of poor health.

He and his wife moved to Guildford in Surrey—the scene of several of his novels—and he retired to write and pursue his hobbies of music (as organist and conductor), gardening, carpentry, and travel. In 1939 he was elected a Fellow of the Royal Society of Arts.

He continued to write a mystery novel almost every year until his death. In addition, he produced about fifty short stories; thirty radio plays for the BBC; true crime works; a play, *Sudden Death* (1932); a juvenile mystery, *Young Robin Brand, Detective* (1947); and a religious work, *The Four Gospels in One Story* (1949).

The Cask is concerned with the discovery of gold coins and a corpse in a cask that has been shipped to London. Inspector Burnley of Scotland Yard investigates, and Monsieur Lefarge of the Sûreté picks up the trail; but private investigator Georges La Touche brings the case to a satisfactory solution. Both this novel and Agatha CHRISTIE's *The Mysterious Affair at Styles* were published in 1920 and marked the advent of the "Golden Age" of the detective story. About the 1967 reissue, Anthony BOUCHER stated, "This book astonished me by being even better than I remembered it. Possibly the most completely competent first novel in the history of crime, it is the definitive novel of alibis, timetables—and all the absorbing hairsplitting of detection so beloved by Jacques BARZUN and, I trust, traditional men."

Crofts's other mysteries that do not involve Inspector French, his greatest detective, are *The Ponson Case* (1921), *The Pit-Prop Syndicate* (1922), *The Groote Park Murder* (1923), and *The Mystery of the Sleeping Car Express* (1956), a collection of ten stories, six of which are not about French.

Attempts to reprint Crofts's works in paperback editions in the United States have not been successful. On the other hand, one-third of his novels have been reprinted frequently by Penguin Books in England.

CROOK, ARTHUR (Creator: Anthony GILBERT). This attorney-detective was created in 1936 as the author's reaction to the aristocratic sleuths then in vogue. A "vulgarian," he often speaks Cockney English and wears bright clothes. When his red car, "which looks as if it had been manufactured from old tin cans," is destroyed in *Is She Dead, Too?* Crook buys an equally bright (yellow) Rolls-Royce. He habitually drives all cars at excessive speeds.

Crook is a burly beer-drinking man with red-brown hair and a red face under the brown bowler he favors. He has a loud voice. The saying most closely associated with him is: "My clients are *never* guilty." Yet, when the police fail to see his point, he is not willing to wait for a trial to prove his clients' innocence. The quick-witted attorney roams the English countryside or the London fog looking for the clues he needs to uncover the true murderer.

CHECKLIST

1936 *Murder by Experts*
1937 *The Man Who Wasn't There*
1937 *Murder Has No Tongue*
1938 *Treason in My Breast*
1939 *The Bell of Death*
1939 *The Clock in the Hatbox*
1940 *Dear Dead Woman*
1941 *The Vanishing Corpse* (U.S. title: *She Vanished in the Dawn*)
1941 *The Woman in Red*
1942 *Something Nasty in the Woodshed* (U.S. title: *Mystery in the Woodshed*)
1942 *The Case of the Tea-Cosy's Aunt* (U.S. title: *Death in the Blackout*)
1943 *The Mouse Who Wouldn't Play Ball* (U.S. title: *Thirty Days to Live*)
1944 *A Spy for Mr. Crook*
1944 *He Came by Night* (U.S. title: *Death at the Door*)
1944 *The Scarlet Button*
1945 *Don't Open the Door* (U.S. title: *Death Lifts the Latch*)
1945 *The Black Stage*
1946 *The Spinster's Secret* (U.S. title: *By Hook or by Crook*)
1947 *Death in the Wrong Room*
1947 *Die in the Dark* (U.S. title: *The Missing Widow*)
1948 *Lift Up the Lid* (U.S. title: *The Innocent Bottle*)
1949 *Death Knocks Three Times*
1950 *Murder Comes Home*
1950 *A Nice Cup of Tea* (U.S. title: *The Wrong Body*)
1951 *Lady Killer*
1952 *Miss Pinnegar Disappears* (U.S. title: *A Case for Mr. Crook*)
1953 *Footsteps behind Me* (U.S. title: *Black Death*)
1954 *Snake in the Grass* (U.S. title: *Death Won't Wait*)
1955 *Is She Dead, Too?* (U.S. title: *A Question of Murder*)
1956 *And Death Came Too*
1956 *Riddle of a Lady*
1957 *Give Death a Name*
1958 *Death against the Clock*
1959 *Third Crime Lucky* (U.S. title: *Prelude to Murder*)
1959 *Death Takes a Wife* (U.S. title: *Death Casts a Long Shadow*)
1960 *Out for the Kill*
1961 *She Shall Die* (U.S. title: *After the Verdict*)
1961 *Uncertain Death*
1962 *No Dust in the Attic*
1963 *Ring for a Noose*
1964 *Knock, Knock, Who's There?* (U.S. title: *The Voice*)
1964 *The Fingerprint*
1965 *Passenger to Nowhere*
1966 *The Looking Glass Murder*
1967 *The Visitor*
1968 *Night Encounter* (U.S. title: *Murder Anonymous*)
1969 *Missing from Her Home*
1970 *Death Wears a Mask* (U.S. title: *Mr. Crook Lifts the Mask*)
1971 *Tenant for the Tomb*
1972 *Murder's a Waiting Game*
1973 *A Nice Little Killing*

CROW, ANDERSON (Creator: George Barr MCCUTCHEON). In Tinkletown, N.Y., the entire police force is represented by Crow, who is Town Marshal, Fire Chief, Chairman of the Board of Health, Commissioner of Streets, Truant Officer, Commander of the local GAR, turnkey of the Tinkletown hoosegow, and member in good standing of three detective agencies (with a nickel-plated star to prove it). With total authority in the region, the dignified lawman must employ extraordinarily effective methods—no crimes have been committed in Tinkletown for years. His humorous adventures are recounted in *The Daughter of Anderson Crow* (1907) and *Anderson Crow, Detective* (1920), a collection of short stories.

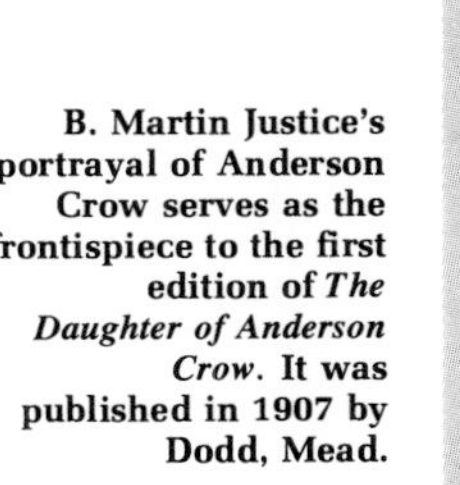

B. Martin Justice's portrayal of Anderson Crow serves as the frontispiece to the first edition of *The Daughter of Anderson Crow*. It was published in 1907 by Dodd, Mead.

CUFF, SERGEANT (Creator: Wilkie COLLINS). When Superintendent Seegrave fails to solve the mysteries of *The Moonstone* (1868), Sergeant Cuff is called into the case, preceded by his reputation as the finest police detective in England. A hardworking professional, he solves his cases with perseverance and energy rather than genius. His hobby—and passion—is roses, and when he is preoccupied, he whistles "The Last Rose of Summer"; when he retires, he settles in a little cottage to grow them.

His physical appearance is not calculated to impress the casual observer. According to a character in the single novel in which he appears, Cuff is "a grizzled, elderly man, so miserably lean that he looked as if he had not got an ounce of flesh on his bones in any part of him. He was dressed all in decent black, with a white cravat around his neck. His face was as sharp as a hatchet, and the skin of it was as yellow and dry and withered as an autumn leaf. His eyes, of a steely light grey, had a very disconcerting trick when they encountered your eyes as if they expected something more from you than you were aware of yourself. His walk was soft, his voice was melancholy, his long lanky fingers were hooked like claws. He might have been a parson, or an undertaker, or anything else you like, except what he really was."

Sergeant Cuff was based on the real-life detective Jonathan Whicher, who solved the Constance Kent case, which Collins drew upon when he wrote *The Moonstone.*

Lady Verinder shocks Sergeant Cuff in this scene from *The Moonstone*, the only novel in which he appears. The illustration is taken from page 91 of the first American edition.

Sergeant Cuff resembles a parson and retains the calm of an undertaker as he is pinned to the wall by Betteredge. This illustration is from the first American edition of *The Moonstone*, published by Harper in 1868.

CULVER, KATHRYN. *See* HALLIDAY, BRETT.

CURTISS, URSULA (1923–   ). American novelist. Born Ursula Reilly, she is the daughter of mystery novelist Helen REILLY and artist Paul Reilly. In 1944, following her husband's death, Helen moved with her daughters to New York City, where Ursula wrote advertising copy for Gimbel's and Macy's before marrying John Curtiss in 1947. The Curtiss family lived in Massachusetts until 1960, when the asthmatic condition of one of their five children caused their move to New Mexico.

Mrs. Curtiss's first novel, *Voice Out of Darkness* (1948), won first prize in Dodd, Mead's annual contest. This book and her subsequent ones combine the elements of the suspense novel and the modern Gothic, with detection relegated to the background. Frequently, family relationships and young women or children in peril are featured. In *The Wasp* (1963) a young New England woman's fear of wasps is pivotal; the author has admitted that she, too, is terrified of these insects. Most of the Curtiss novels published after 1960, including *Hours to Kill* (1961), *The Forbidden Garden* (1962), and *Don't Open the Door* (1968), are set near Albuquerque, N.Mex.

D

D. A., THE. *See* SELBY, DOUG.

DALE, JIMMIE (Creator: Frank L. PACKARD). A brilliant crook who has three aliases: the Gray Seal, a gentleman safecracker who leaves a gray seal behind as his mark of identification; Larry the Bat, a member of the underworld who "slouched through New York's gangland"; and Smarlinghue, an artist who has fallen from better days. A sparkling sophisticate and member of one of New York's most exclusive clubs, Dale is a modern Robin Hood; he commits illegal acts (in his case he cracks safes) to correct injustices. Like his namesake, O. HENRY's Jimmy Valentine, he learned about safes from his father's business, which manufactured them. And like BLACKSHIRT, who appeared a few years later, he is blackmailed by a beautiful woman.

Jimmie Dale, alias the Gray Seal, was a popular American crook of the type usually found in England (Blackshirt, Cleek, the Saint, and Raffles, for example). This illustration appears on the dust wrapper of the first edition of *Jimmie Dale and the Phantom Clue*, published by Doran in 1922; it was designed by A. D. Rahn.

Dale's adventures were recorded in a series of extremely popular and often-reprinted thrillers: *The Adventures of Jimmie Dale* (s.s.; 1917), *The Further Adventures of Jimmie Dale* (s.s.; 1919), *Jimmie Dale and the Phantom Clue* (1922), *Jimmie Dale and the Blue Envelope Murder* (1930), and *Jimmie Dale and the Missing Hour* (1935).

As early as 1916, a silent serial entitled *Jimmie Dale Alias the Gray Seal* appeared.

DALY, CARROLL JOHN (1889–1958). American author of hard-boiled detective fiction. Born in Yonkers, N.Y., the son of Mary L. (Brennan) and Joseph F. Daly, he attended preparatory schools and the American Academy of Dramatic Arts. His passion for the theater led him to take jobs as an usher, a projectionist, and an actor; finally, he became the owner and operator of the first film theater on the Atlantic City boardwalk. He married Margaret G. Blakely in 1913; they had one son.

Throughout his long writing career Daly contributed to many PULP MAGAZINES, notably BLACK MASK, for which he created Race WILLIAMS, the first popular "hard-boiled dick" and the prototype of Mickey SPILLANE's Mike HAMMER. Williams was essentially an extension of Daly's first *Black Mask* sleuth—and the first fictional tough private eye—Three-Gun Mack, who was known for both tough talk and a quick trigger finger.

Daly was the most popular *Black Mask* writer; an editor once stated that, when Race Williams appeared on the cover, sales rose 15 percent. At the height of his popularity, Daly lived a hermitlike existence in White Plains. Later, unable to sell his fiction, he moved to California and wrote comic books. His short stories and novels were violent, fast-paced action thrillers that lacked the strength of characterization so evident in the work of his more gifted contemporaries. A fast-working writer whose work was often crude and sloppy, he nevertheless had a flair for storytelling that kept him among the most highly paid writers for three decades.

After Williams, Daly's best-known detective is Vee Brown, who was created for magazines competing with *Black Mask*. A frail-looking little man, Brown is quicker on the draw than the most experienced gangster. When not working on a case, he writes popular songs, using his real name, Vivian. In *Emperor of Evil* (1936), he tangles with Vincent van Houton, an apparently respectable member of society who is actually a human devil, the head of the Black Death organization, and so successful at concealing his identity that the police refuse to believe in his guilt. Although van Houton never makes a mistake or is brought to justice, Brown manages to rid the world of this menace.

DALY, ELIZABETH (1879–1967). American mystery writer, the creator of Henry GAMADGE. Born in New York City, the daughter of Joseph Francis Daly, a justice of the Supreme Court of New York County, and Emma Barker Daly, she was a niece of Augustin Daly, a famous playwright and producer of the 1890s. She was educated at Miss Baldwin's School and Bryn Mawr College, where she received the B.A. degree in 1901. She received the M.A. degree from Columbia in 1902.

She returned to Bryn Mawr in 1904 and for three years was a reader in English and tutored in English and French. She also coached and produced amateur plays and pageants. In addition to her interest in the theater, Miss Daly was an omniverous reader. At sixteen she had written light verse and prose—some of which found its way into the pages of *Life, Puck,* and *Scribner's Magazine*. However, this interest was soon replaced by activities in amateur theatricals.

Her youthful fondness for games and puzzles led to Miss Daly's lifelong interest in detective fiction; one of her favorite authors was Wilkie COLLINS. In the late 1930s she made some unsuccessful attempts to write in this genre. It was not until 1940 that her first detective novel, *Unexpected Night,* was published. Fifteen works produced during the following twelve years received popular and critical acclaim. Also during this period Miss Daly wrote *The Street Has Changed* (1941), a novel of manners spanning forty years in the theater as seen through the eyes of a retired actress.

As a mystery writer, Miss Daly was a careful craftsman and usually wrote four drafts of each of her books. She also considered that, at its best, the detective novel was a high form of literary art.

In 1960 Miss Daly received an Edgar from the Mystery Writers of America for her meritorious body of work. She was also praised by Agatha CHRISTIE, who considers Miss Daly her favorite American mystery writer.

DANE, CLEMENCE. *See* SIMPSON, HELEN.

DANIEL, GLYN E[DMUND] (1914–). British archaeologist, educator, television personality, mystery writer, and reviewer. Born in Lampeter, in southern Wales, to John and Mary Jane Daniel, he was educated at Barry County School; University College, Cardiff; and St. John's College, Cambridge, where he took first-class honors with distinction, archaeological and anthropological tripos. Further study at St. John's, mainly on scholarships, brought him an M.A. degree in 1938 and a Ph.D. degree in 1939. He has been a fellow of St. John's since 1938 and a lecturer in archaeology since 1948. In 1974 he became head of the Department of Archaeology at Cambridge.

During World War II he served as an intelligence officer in the RAF and was in charge of photo interpretation. In 1943 he achieved the rank of wing commander, served in India and Southeast Asia, and was mentioned in dispatches.

After the war he lectured at Edinburgh and Birmingham Universities, at the British Academy, and on radio and television. He has written many articles in archaeological journals and has edited *Ancient People and Places* and *Antiquity* since 1958. Daniel has written about twenty books on his specialty, including *The Three Ages* (1942), *A Hundred Years of Archaeology* (1950), and *Archaeology and the History of Art* (1970). His role as moderator on a television series, *Animal, Vegetable, Mineral,* in the mid-1950s brought him national fame.

Daniel believes that detective stories are one of the best forms of light entertainment but that they must not be taken too seriously—especially his own. His detective, Sir Richard Cherrington, is vice-president of Fisher College, Cambridge, as well as professor of prehistory—and an enthusiastic amateur detective in his spare time. He first appears in *The Cambridge Murders* (1945), which was originally published under the pseudonym Dilwyn Rees. It starts when the body of a porter is found lying across a path between two college buildings on the last day of the term; the mystery becomes more complicated when the unpopular dean suddenly vanishes. Daniel's only other mystery is *Welcome Death* (1954).

DANNAY, FREDERIC. *See* QUEEN, ELLERY (author).

DA SILVA, CAPTAIN JOSÉ (Creator: Robert L. FISH). This tall, dark Brazilian detective in his late thirties has a college degree in criminology and has been a Rio de Janeiro policeman for about fifteen years. Da Silva's bravery is beyond question; he has risked his life on several occasions. Yet, he has a great fear of flying and must fortify himself with alcohol in advance. In his role as liaison officer between the Brazilian police and Interpol he works with his friend Wilson, an American agent whose nondescript appearance disguises a detective adept at karate and even picking pockets. They combine to hunt down an escaped Nazi in *The Fugitive* and a would-be assassin who wants to stop the meeting of the OAS in *Always Kill a Stranger*.

CHECKLIST

1962	*The Fugitive*
1963	*Isle of the Snakes*
1963	*The Shrunken Head*
1965	*The Diamond Bubble*
1965	*Brazilian Sleigh Ride*
1967	*Always Kill a Stranger*
1968	*The Bridge That Went Nowhere*
1969	*The Xavier Affair*
1971	*The Green Hell Treasure*
1975	*Trouble in Paradise*

DAVIOT, GORDON. *See* TEY, JOSEPHINE.

DAVIS, DON. *See* HALLIDAY, BRETT.

DAVIS, DOROTHY SALISBURY (1916–). American author of mystery novels and short stories. Born in Chicago, Mrs. Davis grew up on farms near that city. She attended Holy Child High School in Waukegan and graduated from Barat College in Lake Forest. She worked on a WPA writers' project, in advertising, and as a librarian before beginning to write fiction in the late 1940s. She is married to an actor, Harry Davis; they live in Snedens Landing, N.Y.

In her mysteries Mrs. Davis has attempted to express her hatred of violence and her sympathy for the underdog. Often, her protagonists are undergoing crises of religious faith. This is especially true of *A Gentle Murderer* (1951), which most critics cite as containing characterization and insight seldom found in the mystery, and of *The Pale Betrayer* (1965), *Where the Dark Streets Go* (1969), and *The Little Brothers* (1973), all with New York City settings. She also received high praise for *Enemy and Brother* (1967) and *God Speed the Night* (1968), set in Europe.

Mrs. Davis's second book, *The Clay Hand* (1950), is set in the coal mine area of Kentucky and deals sympathetically with poverty in Appalachia. Drawing upon her own experiences, she has written two mysteries set in Illinois college towns, *A Town of Masks* (1952) and *Shock Wave* (1972). The latter tells of politics and race riots at a university where a world-famous scientist has been killed.

Dorothy Salisbury Davis's considerable reputation is based as much on her short stories as on her novels. She won second prizes in *Ellery Queen's Mystery Magazine* contests for "Spring Fever" (1952), "Backward, Turn Backward" (1954), and "By the Scruff of the Soul" (1963). She won a third prize for "Born Killer" (1953), a penetrating psychological study of a Wisconsin farmboy. A 1964 short story, "The Purple Is Everything," received a Mystery Writers of America Edgar nomination, as have five of her books.

DAVIS, GORDON. *See* HUNT, E. HOWARD, JR.

DAVIS, NORBERT. *See* PULP MAGAZINES.

DAVIS, RICHARD HARDING (1864–1916). American journalist, dramatist, short story writer, and novelist. Born in Philadelphia, the son of Rebecca Harding Davis, the pioneer naturalistic novelist, Davis became the most successful reporter of his time. He published twenty-five plays, several novels, and eleven short story collections. His best mystery tale is *In the Fog* (1901), which contains three connected short stories in the style of Robert Louis STEVENSON's *New Arabian Nights* (1882). There is a double surprise ending.

DAWLISH, PATRICK (Creator: John CREASEY as Gordon Ashe). A huge man with a group of hard-hitting friends, Dawlish is drawn into a series of vicious crimes. Deciding to settle them on his own, he often runs into trouble with the law, in the person of Chief Inspector Trivett. The outbreak of World War II finds Dawlish a powerful figure in MI5, Britain's Intelligence Corps, fighting the Nazis as a modern-day Scarlet Pimpernel (*see* SCARLET PIMPERNEL, THE). After the war and enforced retirement, he tries to settle down into a normal, peaceful life, but trouble seems to seek him out, and he is unable to resist helping anyone in difficulty. Suddenly offered a job as deputy assistant commissioner for crime at Scotland Yard, he specializes in crimes that cross national borders and becomes England's delegate to a worldwide anticrime organization known as the Crime Haters.

There are fifty books in the Patrick Dawlish series, beginning with *The Speaker* (1939); the last fifteen, beginning with *The Crime Haters* (1960), are about his activities with that group.

DAY LEWIS, C. *See* BLAKE, NICHOLAS.

DEAD ENDS, DEPARTMENT OF. *See* DEPARTMENT OF DEAD ENDS.

DEANE, NORMAN. *See* CREASEY, JOHN.

DEBRETT, HAL. *See* HALLIDAY, BRETT.

DECOLTA, RAMON. *See* WHITFIELD, RAOUL.

DEE, JUDGE (Creator: Robert VAN GULIK). The fictional detective Judge Dee Jen-djieh (the surname

The cover of this collector's item is an original design by Robert van Gulik. Executed as a block print in the ancient Chinese process of *t'ao-pan*, or printing in colors from wooden blocks, it was struck from nine different blocks. This first edition, published in English by the Toppan Printing Company of Tokyo in 1949, is limited to 1,200 copies, signed by the translator.

Robert van Gulik drew six illustrations "in the Chinese style" for this book. A scarce paperback original, it was first published in Kuala Lumpur, Malaya, by the Art Printing Works in July 1961. This is the front cover of the first edition.

precedes the personal name in Chinese) is based on the historical Ti Jen-chieh (630–700), an important Chinese detective who rose to become an influential statesman in the T'ang dynasty.

In his younger days Dee serves as a magistrate in various provincial cities: Peng-lai (663–665), Han-yan (665–668), Poo-yang in Kiangsu Province (668–670), Lan-fang on the western frontier (670–676), and Pei-chow in the far north (676). He solves many complicated criminal cases—including murder—and his name becomes famous throughout China.

At the end of the year 676 Dee is appointed president of the Metropolitan Court of Justice in the imperial capital by the Emperor and, through his intelligence and statesmanship, is able to exercise a beneficent influence on the court.

While engaged in a criminal case, Judge Dee often does much of the investigation himself and frequently resorts to disguises or traveling incognito among the common people. He is assisted by his trusted adviser, Hoong Liang, and his lieutenants, Ma Joong, Chiao Tai, and Tao Gan, who frequently bring him important information and vital clues.

Judge Dee is also a family man with three wives and several sons who travel with him to his various outposts. They are wise enough to leave him alone as he ponders the solution of a mystery while stroking his full black beard or caressing his long side whiskers and indulging in innumerable cups of his favorite beverage—tea.

Dee's inspiration, Ti Jen-chieh, was so successful as a real-life detective that many Chinese detective stories (predating those of Edgar Allan POE) were based on his cases. Van Gulik, however, used actual criminal cases as the basis of some of his stories about the Chinese detective. Most of the books contain three intertwined cases for the judge to solve.

The first Judge Dee work was *Dee Goong An*, a seventeenth- or eighteenth-century Chinese detective novel that van Gulik translated and had published in 1949. He then proceeded to write a number of original works about the seventh-century judge. *The Chinese Bell Murders* was published first and follows the pattern of *Dee Goong An*. It appeared first in Japan (in Japanese), was published in England in 1958, and reached the United States in 1959. This delayed publishing pattern is also true of several of van Gulik's subsequent works, including some in the early 1960s that first appeared in Malaya in English. Although van Gulik had written *The Chinese Maze Murders* first, it was not published until after *The Chinese Bell Murders* appeared; it reached England and the United States in 1956 and 1957. It contains a locked-room problem (see LOCKED-ROOM MYSTERIES) and a discussion of local religions.

Judge Dee illuminates a medieval Chinese mystery in his television feature debut. [*ABC-TV*]

Among the problems in *The Chinese Lake Murders* are the murder of a prostitute, a dead bride whose body vanishes, and a plot to overthrow the empire. The ingenious plot of *The Chinese Nail Murders* involves a brilliant dying-message clue. In *The Chinese Gold Murders* Judge Dee arrives at Peng-lai in 663 to assume the duties of the former magistrate, who has been murdered; his first problem is to find the killer.

The Haunted Monastery finds Judge Dee and his family and retainers stranded because of a broken axle and a howling storm. He has to spend the night solving three murders and a problem of impersonation before he can proceed on his journey the following day. He vacations incognito in a neighboring province in *The Lacquer Screen*, but problems involving blackmail, the suicide of a banker, and the murder of a beautiful woman claim his attention. Van Gulik's attempt to maintain three distinct plots, in the Chinese tradition, is strained in *The Emperor's Pearl*.

The Willow Pattern occurs in about the year 677, when Dee is lord chief justice of the empire. He has several cases to solve, but even more serious is the deadly threat of the plague on the horizon. *Murder in Canton*, set in 680, with Dee now the president of the Metropolitan Court in imperial China, concerns troublesome Muslims, a missing imperial censor, and a pair of lovely Persian twins.

Judge Dee at Work illustrates van Gulik's ability in writing short stories. Of interest are the endpapers, which give an accurate and complete chronology of Judge Dee's adventures.

CHECKLIST

1949	*Dee Goong An (Criminal Cases Solved by Judge Dee)*
1951	*The Chinese Bell Murders*
1951	*The Chinese Maze Murders*
1953	*The Chinese Lake Murders*
1957	*The Chinese Nail Murders*
1958	"New Year's Eve in Lan-fang" (s.s.)
1959	*The Chinese Gold Murders*
1961	*The Red Pavilion*
1961	*The Haunted Monastery*
1962	*The Lacquer Screen*
1963	*The Emperor's Pearl*
1965	*The Willow Pattern*
1965	*The Monkey and the Tiger* (two novelettes)
1966	*Murder in Canton*
1966	*The Phantom of the Temple*
1967	*Necklace and Calabash*
1967	*Judge Dee at Work* (s.s.)
1968	*Poets and Murder*

Film

In 1974 the seventh-century Chinese magistrate-detective appeared in a feature made for television, investigating the disappearance of three young girls, in a case involving a killer bear and a one-armed lady. *Judge Dee in the Monastery Murders* starred Khigh Dhiegh.

deFORD, MIRIAM ALLEN (1888–1975). American author and journalist. Born and raised in Philadelphia, Miss deFord moved to California, where she was a public stenographer and an insurance claims adjuster before embarking on a writing career during which she worked as a newspaper reporter (thirty-five years as a labor reporter) and wrote poetry and both factual and fictional works on crime. *The Overbury Affair: The Murder That Rocked the Court of King James I,* which tells of the imprisonment and poisoning in the Tower of London of the courtier who was once the favorite of James I, won the Mystery Writers of America (MWA) Edgar as best fact-crime book of 1960. In 1965 an MWA Award went to *Murderers Sane and Mad*. Another factual crime book, *The Real Bonnie and Clyde,* was published in 1968, when the author was in her eightieth year, and in 1970 *The Real Ma Barker* was published.

Although Miss deFord never published a mystery novel, she was a prolific author of short stories. Seventeen stories were collected in 1967 in *The Theme Is Murder*. Often prizewinners in *Ellery Queen's Mystery Magazine* contests and frequently anthologized, these stories display considerable variety in both subject matter and approach. "Farewell to the Faulkners" (1946) presented the reader with the necessary facts and then asked him to assume the role of detective. In "The Mystery of the Vanished Brother" (1950), a story set in Philadelphia in 1841, the detective is Edgar Allan POE. "The Judgement of En-Lil" (1954) is another historical detective story, but in this case the action takes place in 1850 B.C., and the characters are Sumerians living along the banks of the Euphrates. In "De Crimine" (1952), Cicero is the detective. The question raised and resolved in "A Case for the U.N." (1964) is that of jurisdiction over a murder committed on a plane in flight over the Atlantic. But the setting of the deFord story often considered her best is prosaic; "Walking Alone" (1957) is about an innocent bystander who sees a crime committed.

DE FOREST, JOHN WILLIAM (1826–1906). American author of travel and historical books and novels. He was born in Connecticut and traveled extensively abroad. He served as a captain in the Union Army and used the experience as the basis for *Miss Ravenel's Conversion from Secession to Loyalty* (1867), the first realistic novel about the Civil War. *The Wetherel Affair* (1873) is one of the earliest American murder mysteries. It features the adventures of young Mr. Edward Wetherel as he successfully woos the beautiful Nestoria Bernard and prevents nefarious double-dealing with an enormous estate.

DEIGHTON, LEN (1929–). English author of espionage thrillers. Born in London, Deighton was educated at the Royal Academy of Art and has held a variety of jobs—he has worked as an assistant pastry cook at the Royal Festival Hall (which resulted in his syndicated column on cooking and *Len Deighton's Cookstrip Cook Book,* 1965), as a waiter in Piccadilly, in advertising in London and New York, as a teacher in Brittany, as a magazine artist, and as a news photographer. He has also been employed in the RAF's Special Investigation Branch.

Deighton's vast knowledge of exotic locales and military history is evident in the realistic details (he even includes footnotes and appendixes) of his complex spy novels—most of which involve a young man of the working class in Burnley who dislikes and distrusts everyone in authority. He is nameless in the books but is popularly known as Harry Palmer because he was given that name in the films drawn from the stories. Although Deighton claims that he prefers a small, devoted audience rather than a large one, his suspenseful accounts of the cold war have become highly successful and popular as books and as films. Julian SYMONS calls the author "a kind of poet of the spy novel."

Deighton has produced six espionage novels: *The Ipcress File* (1962), *Horse under Water* (1963), *Funeral in Berlin* (1964), *The Billion Dollar Brain* (1966), *An Expensive Place to Die* (1967), and *Spy Story* (1974).

Films

Deighton's unflamboyant—and involuntary—British intelligence agent has appeared in three deft spy films (played by Michael Caine and called Harry Palmer).

The Ipcress File. Universal (British), 1965. Caine, Nigel Green, Guy Doleman, Sue Lloyd. Directed by Sidney J. Furie.

To stay out of jail after his black market activities have been uncovered, Palmer is drafted into British espionage; he discovers that a behind-the-Iron-Curtain brainwashing cell is actually located in the heart of London and unmasks a particularly well-entrenched double agent.

Funeral in Berlin. Paramount (British), 1966. Caine, Eva Renzi, Paul Hubschmid, Oscar Homolka. Directed by Guy Hamilton.

Reluctant Palmer is assigned to help a top Russian officer defect to the West from his Berlin post by smuggling him out in a coffin, only to discover that the funeral will not be a simple one.

Billion Dollar Brain. United Artists (British), 1967. Caine, Karl Malden, Ed Begley, Homolka, Françoise Dorléac. Directed by Ken Russell.

Michael Caine portrays a British counterspy groggily preparing a solo breakfast in *The Ipcress File,* from the Len Deighton book. [*Universal*]

Palmer, now an unsuccessful private detective, grudgingly allows himself to be lured back into the British Secret Service; he becomes involved with virus-laden eggs and a violently anti-Communist American multimillionaire who is planning a computer-directed private invasion of Latvia carried out by an army of tanks moving across a frozen sea.

de la TORRE, LILLIAN (1902–). American playwright and author of mystery fiction. Born Lillian de la Torre Bueno in New York City, she graduated from White Plains High School in 1916 and from the College of New Rochelle in 1921. She received master's degrees from Columbia University in 1927 and Radcliffe College in 1933. Since 1932 she has been married to George S. McCue, professor of English at Colorado College (now retired).

A student of history and crime and a devotee of the theater, Miss de la Torre combined these interests in her one-act play *Goodbye, Miss Lizzie Borden* (1948). In the field of true crime, she has written such mystery books as *Elizabeth Is Missing* (1945), about the notorious Elizabeth Canning case, *Villainy Detected* (1947; an anthology of eighteenth-century crime), *The Heir of Douglas* (1952), and *The Truth about Belle Gunness* (1955).

Her reputation as a writer of fiction is largely based on the series in which the famous eighteenth-century lexicographer Dr. Samuel Johnson appears as a detective. Miss de la Torre's decision to write the stories followed an argument in which she had defended the detective story, pointing out that a good fictional detective has many of the attributes possessed by Johnson. She also observed that Johnson had his perfect "Watson" (*see* WATSON, DR.) in his chronicler, James Boswell. She has written 26 stories about Dr. Johnson, most originally appearing in *Ellery Queen's Mystery Magazine*. "The Stroke of Thirteen" won a second prize in the magazine's 1953 contest. The Johnson stories were collected in *Dr. Sam: Johnson, Detector* (1946) and *The Detections of Dr. Sam: Johnson* (1960). Anthony BOUCHER, in praising the first of these volumes, said, "These magical eighteenth century pastiches, conceived and written with an ideal blend of scholarly precision . . . [comprise] probably the most attractive book of detective shorts ever published."

DEPARTMENT OF DEAD ENDS (Creator: Roy VICKERS). An obscure branch of Scotland Yard. The Department of Dead Ends has the unenviable task of trying to solve those crimes everyone else has given up on. Trivial details, meaningless clues—all "dead ends"—are stored in this department, which, wrote Vickers, "does not grope for points missed in the investigation [but] keeps an eye open for any unusual occurrence to any of the persons who were once in the orbit of the unsolved murder." With what sometimes appears to be luck, Detective Inspector Rason manages to find a link between a murderer and some trifle that once seemed to have no significance.

The Department of Dead Ends stories are the inverted type invented by R. Austin FREEMAN in *The Singing Bone* (1912): the reader sees the crime committed, is present when the incriminating clue is finally discovered, and follows the police methods leading to arrest. The accurate representation of criminal procedure gives the stories the realistic quality of documentary accounts of true-life crimes. Rason, who had so little success when pitted against the brilliant female crook Fidelity DOVE, describes his function as "a fool kept at Scotland Yard on the principle of setting a fool to catch a fool."

The department's unusual cases are recorded in *The Department of Dead Ends* (1947; the British edition of 1949 contains largely different stories, and their number has been increased); *Murder Will Out* (1950); and other collections.

DEPARTMENT OF QUEER COMPLAINTS. *See* MARCH, COLONEL.

DEPARTMENT Z (Creator: John CREASEY). A lantern-jawed Scotsman, Gordon Craigie, presides over the counterespionage arm of British Intelligence, known as Department Z. Employing a widely varied group of patriotic agents, Craigie guards England's security before and during World War II, after which his group merges with Dr. PALFREY's Z5 organization and engages in fantastic battles with mad scientists intent on world conquest. The first of the twenty-eight novels in the Department Z series, *The Death Miser*, appeared in 1932; the last, *The Black Spiders*, in 1957.

DERLETH, AUGUST (WILLIAM) (1909–1971). Versatile and prolific American author who produced more than 130 books and countless short stories, poems, essays, reviews, and anthologies.

Born in Sauk City, Wis., he spent virtually his entire life there. In 1940 he and Donald Wandrei founded Arkham House, a firm that soon became the leading publisher of horror and supernatural fiction; a subsidiary, Mycroft and Moran, published mysteries, chiefly the adventures of Solar PONS.

Called a "one-man fiction factory" (he began writing at thirteen, was first published at fifteen, and subsequently produced nearly 1 million words a year), Derleth claimed that he was the "most versatile and voluminous writer in quality writing fields." Among his nonmystery works are a long series of novels, short stories, and verse about Sac Prairie, a mythical Midwestern town, as well as nature books and poems, biographies, juvenile works, and supernatural stories.

In addition to the Sherlock HOLMES pastiches featuring Pons, he wrote mysteries about Judge Ephraim Peck, a kindly, good-humored dispenser of justice in Sac Prairie, notably *Murder Stalks the Wakely Family* (1934; British title: *Death Stalks the Wakely Family*) and *No Future for Luana* (1945). Under the Tally Mason pseudonym, he wrote an unusual collection of crime stories, *Consider Your Verdict* (1937), in which the reader is challenged to find the flaws in witnesses' statements at coroners' inquests.

DETECTION CLUB, THE. *See* ORGANIZATIONS.

DEVINE, D[AVID] M[cDONALD] (1920–). Scottish author of detective novels. Born in Greenock, Devine was educated at the University of Glasgow, where he received an M.A. degree with honors in 1945, and at the University of London, where he received an LL.B. degree with honors in 1953. He has served as secretary and registrar at St. Andrews University and now lives at Melvaig, St. Andrews, with his wife (the former Betsy Findlay Munro), whom he married in 1946, and daughter. He plays golf, bridge, and cricket, and enjoys travel, music, and other authors' mystery novels.

He used the name D. M. Devine for his first six novels and then, on the advice of his publisher (Collins Crime Club), used Dominic Devine for the rest; his American publishers have been Walker, Doubleday, and Dodd, Mead.

Devine's first book, *My Brother's Killer* (1961), deals with the murder of a lawyer who is later suspected of having been a blackmailer—and with his brother's efforts to clear his name and find his murderer.

The second novel, *Doctors Also Die* (1962), is similar in plot to the first but involves partners in the medical profession. Critic Anthony BOUCHER, in reviewing this book, called Devine "one of the most promising new writers in the old tradition of solid whodunit, with sound construction, skilled misdirection and admirably firm plotting."

The Royston Affair (1964) is an ingenious, exciting story about a firm of family solicitors. *His Own Appointed Day* (1965) concerns a girl's attempts to solve the murder of her younger brother. *Devil at Your Elbow* (1966) is set in a small English university where the dean of the law school is obliged to solve a murder and a blackmail case amid rumors of an old scandal and the installation of a new chancellor.

The Fifth Cord (1967) deals with a series of apparently unrelated murders. The problem is to discover the link between the murders and stop the killer before he can claim more victims. One of Devine's best works, it was made into a film in Italy.

The Sleeping Tiger (1968) is a low-keyed but absorbing mystery in which a mouse turns into a man. *Death Is My Bridegroom* (1969), set in a new English university, involves a student march, protesting the expulsion of a student for theft, that ends in murder on the campus. At the outset of *Illegal Tender* (1970), a girl who works in the town clerk's office announces that she has made a discovery and intends to inform the police. When a murder takes place, the secrets of the small Scottish town are probed, and a clever killer who has much to lose is revealed. *Dead Trouble* (1971) is a study of a scheming young man and an old man who has something to hide. *Three Green Bottles* (1972) is a novel of psychological suspense about partners in a medical practice.

DEVINE, DOMINIC. *See* DEVINE, D. M.

DEWEY, THOMAS B[LANCHARD] (1915–). American detective novelist. Born in Elkhart, Ind., Dewey traveled widely in the Midwest when he was a child; he lived in Ohio, Michigan, and Illinois and attended school in Kansas and Iowa. Shortly after World War II, Dewey, his wife, and their small son moved to Hollywood, where he has worked in advertising, written stories for *Ellery Queen's Mystery Magazine*, *Argosy*, and *Cosmopolitan*, and published thirty-four mystery novels, including two under the pseudonym Tom Brandt and one as Cord Wainer. He is now a member of the English faculty at Arizona State University.

Dewey's early books, beginning with his first, *Hue and Cry* (1944; British title: *The Murder of Marion Mason*), concern amateur detective Singer Batts, a Shakespearean scholar and bibliophile who owns a hotel in the fictional town of Preston, Ohio. Another Dewey creation, Pete Schofield, is one of the few fictional private detectives who is married. He has been featured in ten mysteries, including *Too Hot for Hawaii* (1960), *The Golden Hooligan* (1961; British title: *Mexican Slayride*), and *Nude in Nevada* (1965).

The private detective known only as MAC (his full name, Mac Robinson, is perhaps revealed in *The Love-Death Thing*, 1969) is Dewey's most famous character and the hero of fifteen novels. Although most of the Mac books are set in the Midwest, three late works in the series take place in California. Dewey has painted Mac as a tough but unusually sympathetic sleuth, one who expresses the author's obvious concern for the problems of the young. *The Mean Streets* (1955) was considered by Dorothy B. HUGHES to be "the best fictional account yet on juvenile delinquency." The youths attracted by the early "hippie" culture, especially a young folk singer and his girl friend, gain the detective's sympathy in *A Sad Song Singing* (1963). *The Love-Death Thing* and *The Taurus Trip* (1970) show Dewey's concern for

California youth trapped by the addiction and crime of the drug culture.

DEY, FREDERIC VAN RENSSELAER. *See* CARTER, NICK.

DICKENS, CHARLES (1812–1870). The greatest of all English novelists, many of whose books have strong elements of crime, mystery, and detection.

Born in Portsea, Dickens was the second of eight children of a housekeeper and a naval clerk who was sent to Marshalsea Prison because of his debts. Charles, forced to earn his own living at the age of twelve, worked in a factory—an experience he later described in *David Copperfield* (1849–1850). His father suddenly received a legacy, and Charles was able to return to school for three years, after which he took jobs as a solicitor's clerk and reporter (a stenographer, not a writer, in the mid-nineteenth century) for the *Morning Chronicle*.

His first published work was a sketch in the *Monthly Magazine* that appeared in 1833 and was signed "Boz." It was followed by similar pieces in the *Evening Chronicle* (illustrated by George Cruikshank and collected in *Sketches by Boz* in 1836). He was in love with Mary Hogarth (on whom he based his character Little Nell); but since she was too young to be married, he married her older sister, Catherine. The following year (1837) Mary died. Although they never loved each other, Catherine and Charles had ten children, and their marriage lasted twenty-two years, until Dickens publicly flaunted his affairs and accused his wife of being insane.

With the publication of *The Posthumous Papers of the Pickwick Club* in 1836–1837, Dickens's fortune was assured, and he wrote tirelessly for the rest of his life, producing some of the most beloved and famous novels in the English language, peopling them with aptly named characters who have given their names to the language (Fagin, Micawber, Scrooge, Mrs. Nickleby, Sydney Carton, Mr. Pickwick, et al.). He also lectured and gave public readings from his works and edited the successful *Household Words* and its successor, *All the Year Round*, from 1849 until his death. Despite poor health, he never stopped working and died while he was working on *The Mystery of Edwin Drood* (1870), the first six chapters of which indicate that it might have been one of the greatest of all mystery novels. The second half of the tale has been written by numerous other authors in an attempt to complete one of the most tantalizing mysteries in literature. Four different conclusions appeared the year Dickens died, and one volume, purported to be the work of Dickens himself, was taken down through a medium.

Drood is a young engineer engaged to marry Rosa Budd; but, when they realize that they do not love each other, they agree to remain only friends. John (Jack) Jasper, Drood's uncle and guardian, is in love with the pretty Rosa, but she fears Jasper, an opium addict, and falls in love with Neville Landless, who returns her love. One day, Jasper reports that Drood and Landless (who hates Rosa's former fiancé) were seen near the river the previous night. After a brief search, Drood's watch and tie are found. Although his body is not discovered, Landless is suspected of murdering him, and Jasper tells Rosa that he has enough evidence to hang her lover. An obviously disguised white-haired stranger named Datchery arrives and sits hour after hour behind his open door, making a chalk mark every time he hears Jasper's name. At this point, the novel ends, leaving unexplained the identity of Datchery and the killer of Drood—if in fact, Drood has been murdered.

A silhouette of Charles Dickens by Auguste Édouart.

Most of Dickens's books touch to some degree on the work of the police and the activities of criminals. Factual sketches of the Bow Street Runners and the Detective Force appeared in his periodicals, and his first book, *Sketches by Boz*, contained similar material; in addition, his long, episodic novels often include characters working on one side of the law or the other.

Oliver Twist (1837–1838) presents an entire

lineup of criminals dominated by the infamous Fagin. Mr. Brownlow investigates Oliver's history in a performance worthy of any detective, finally confronting Monks with his evidence, witnesses, and clues, and explaining every mystery with impressive thoroughness.

The entire plot of *Barnaby Rudge* (1840; contained in the periodical *Master Humphrey's Clock*, 1840–1841) revolves around two murders. The title character is born on the night of the supposed murder of his father, who has murdered his employer, Reuben Haredale, and the gardener whose mutilated body is mistaken for his own. Benefiting from this case of mistaken identity, the elder Rudge remains a fugitive from justice but finally returns twenty-two years later. In an extraordinary sidelight, Edgar Allan POE read the first installment of this long, complex novel and accurately predicted virtually every path the plot would follow, including several subplots and difficulties facing the author. After seeing Poe's essay, Dickens is reported to have stated incredulously, "The man must be the devil himself!"

Hunted Down (1859) is a story about murder. The manager of a life insurance company, Mr. Sampson, suspects that one of his clients has murdered one niece and is poisoning another. Aided by a colleague, Mr. Meltham, the sweetheart of the murdered girl, Sampson is able to prove the guilt of the uncle. This story is a fictionalized account of the case of Thomas Griffiths Waineright, who murdered his sister-in-law for her insurance of £18,000 and was subsequently discovered to have poisoned other people as well.

The London police force also played prominent roles in *Great Expectations* (1861) and *Our Mutual Friend* (1864–1865), but the most important of all Dickens's contributions to the mystery genre is *Bleak House* (1852–1853), which introduced Inspector BUCKET, the first significant detective in English literature. In this tale of forgery, blackmail, drugs, and murder, a complex series of inheritance cases involving the Jarndyce fortune drags through the courts for generations, consuming the entire estate. The heirs, who have spent their lives waiting for the distribution of the fortune, are destroyed by the outcome, and one of them commits suicide. The entanglements of a large cast of characters are finally resolved by the accidental discovery of a will, but too late to help any of them.

Douglass Montgomery and Heather Angel are star-crossed lovers in Hollywood's attempt to provide a solution to Dickens's *The Mystery of Edwin Drood*. [*Universal*]

Films

Many of Dickens's works that have reached the screen have contained elements of mystery, murder, imprisonment, the theft of name or fortune, and so on. Hollywood made an interesting attempt to film—and finish—*Drood*.

The Mystery of Edwin Drood. Universal, 1935. Claude Rains, Heather Angel, Douglass Montgomery, David Manners. Directed by Stuart Walker.

The audience is aware from the first that the addicted choirmaster Jasper (Rains) plans to murder his nephew because he stands in the way of an impassioned love.

This version, however, had been anticipated by a primitive (1909) British silent with scenes in "an opium den" and "Jasper's study."

Plays

There were two major stage versions of *The Mystery of Edwin Drood*. On November 4, 1871, London's Surrey Theatre presented a hasty adaptation by W. Stephens. J. Comyns Carr also adapted the unfinished novel; that drama had its London premiere performance in January 1908.

DICKINSON, PETER (1927–   ). English poet and novelist. Born in Africa, the son of a civil servant, Dickinson spent his early childhood in South Africa and Rhodesia. He won a scholarship to Eton and studied classics there and at Cambridge University. After graduation he became an assistant editor at *Punch* but eventually left to devote his full time to writing satirical verse, juvenile thrillers, and detective stories. He is married, has four children, and lives in London.

Dickinson's first mystery, *Skin Deep* (1968; U.S. title: *The Glass-sided Ants' Nest*), attracted considerable attention, especially for its depiction of a New Guinea tribe settled in the heart of London by a wealthy sponsor. The British Crime Writers' Association selected it as best novel, and the Mystery Writers of America nominated it for an Edgar in the same category.

The first five Dickinson novels are about aging,

unglamorous Superintendent Pibble, who has a talent for solving bizarre cases. Even after he retires, as in *The Lizard in the Cup* (1972), Pibble's talents are in demand. In that case he journeys to the Greek islands to help a businessman friend who has become involved with the Mafia, political revolutionaries, drugs, and a mosaic from an ancient monastery. The remaining Dickinson titles are *A Pride of Heroes* (1969; U.S. title: *The Old English Peep Show*), *The Seals* (1970; U.S. title: *The Sinful Stones*), *Sleep and His Brother* (1971), *The Green Gene* (1973), *The Poison Oracle* (1974), and *The Lively Deed* (1975).

DICKSON, CARR. *See* CARR, JOHN DICKSON.

DICKSON, CARTER. *See* CARR, JOHN DICKSON.

DIETRICH, ROBERT. *See* HUNT, E. HOWARD.

DiMARCO, JEFFERSON (Creator: Doris Miles DISNEY). Born in a Boston tenement, DiMarco is now a successful claims adjuster for the Commonwealth Insurance Company of that city. He is a scrupulously honest man whose loyalty to Commonwealth is reflected in the zeal with which he investigates fraudulent insurance claims. Not especially impressive in appearance (he is short and has gray hair and an expanding waistline), he is resigned to his bachelor status.

If DiMarco has any weakness, it is his tendency to become emotionally involved with the people he is investigating. In *Dark Road* (1946), he makes the mistake of falling in love with a woman who has killed her husband, a Commonwealth policyholder. However, in *Method in Madness* (1957; British title: *Quiet Violence*), his pity for a lonely old woman in a nursing home leads him to investigate her death and discover a murderer.

DiMarco's other adventures are recounted in *Family Skeleton* (1949), *Straw Man* (1951; British title: *The Case of the Straw Man*), *Trick or Treat* (1955; British title: *The Halloween Murder*), *Did She Fall or Was She Pushed?* (1959), *Find the Woman* (1962), and *The Chandler Policy* (1971).

DIME NOVELS. Originally, a series of paper-covered books called Beadle's Dime Novels published between 1860 and 1874 by Irwin Pedro Beadle (1826–1882); popularly, the term refers to any work of sensational fiction published in paper covers in the United States between 1860 and 1915. Irwin Beadle, his older brother Erastus (1821–1894), and their partner, Robert Adams (1837–1866), were not the first to publish cheap paper-covered novels, but they were the first to publish them regularly and continually at a fixed price. The firm later became known as Beadle and Adams and remained in existence until 1898. Many of their titles were reprinted by other publishers after that date.

The format of a dime novel varied from a 4- by 6-inch or 5- by 7-inch book of 96 to 250 pages (sometimes more) to the 8½- by 11-inch, or larger, "nickel weeklies" (sometimes called "broadleaves") of 32 to 64 pages. The folio "story papers" were not dime novels themselves but contained serials and shorter works reprinted as dime novels. Some dime novels were illustrated throughout, but most had only a single cover illustration of an action scene designed to attract the customer. Originally black and white, these illustrations were printed in color by 1897. The earliest editions were printed on rag-content paper, the later ones on newsprint or wood pulp paper.

The earliest dime novels were tales of frontier life in America [Beadle's Dime Novels No. 1 was Mrs. Ann S. Stephens's (1813–1886) *Malaeska: The Indian Wife of the White Hunter,* published in June 1860], but as the cities grew, the frontier hero was replaced by the urban hero, often a detective.

Thousands of titles were published by such major firms as George P. Munro (1825–1896), Frank Tousey, Street & Smith, and J. S. Ogilvie; Beadle and Adams published 3,158 titles, excluding reprints. Hundreds of thousands of copies were sold during the Civil War, and many more afterward.

The stories were patriotic; they promoted rugged individualism and praised moral fiber. They made up in action and melodramatic dialogue what they may have lacked in literary style. Some of the more prolific writers contributed heroes to American folklore; for example, Edward L. WHEELER's frontier highwayman, Deadwood Dick; Gilbert Patten's (pseudonym of William George Patten, 1866–1945) sports hero, Frank Merriwell; and Horatio Alger's (1834–1899) enterprising young men. Ned Buntline (Edward Z. C. Judson, 1821–1886) and Colonel Prentiss Ingraham (1843–1904) made a legend of Buffalo Bill. Lu Senarens (1863–1939) wrote stories about young inventor Frank Reade, inspiring Jules Verne's later books.

The earliest reported dime novel detective story was Kenward Philip's *The Bowery Detective* (*New York Fireside Companion* serial, 1870; reprinted in *Old Sleuth Library,* no. 64, 1894). The first series detective was Old Sleuth himself, in Harlan Page Halsey's *Old Sleuth, the Detective* (*New York Fireside Companion* serial, 1872; reprinted in *Old Sleuth Library,* no. 1, 1885).

The first dime novel weekly devoted exclusively to detective stories was *Old Cap. Collier Library* (April 9, 1883–September 9, 1899), published by Norman L. Munro. Old Cap. Collier appeared in only a handful of stories, but his name was signed to many more. This series offered 10-cent editions of the works of Émile GABORIAU along with original stories about Old Broadbrim, the Quaker Detective,

Sergeant Sparrow, Gideon Gault, Dave Dotson, Dick Danger, and Old Thunderbolt. There were two editions, one with an illustrated cover, another without.

The *New York Detective Library* (June 7, 1883–April 1, 1898), published by Frank Tousey, also featured scores of detectives but by 1885 had begun publishing stories about James Brady (Old King Brady) by a "N.Y. Detective" (Francis W. Doughty). His serial adventures in the story paper *Boys of New York* were often reprinted in the *New York Detective Library*. One of the most plausible and realistic of dime novel detectives, Brady may also have been the first detective in fiction to have a continuing arch-enemy—Jesse James.

The *Old Sleuth Library* (1885–1905) was intended to be a weekly but became a quarterly. Published by George Munro, it featured, in addition to stories about the title character, the adventures of Iron Burgess, Manfred the Metamorphosist, Old Electricity, and Red Light Will.

The first dime novel weekly to feature the adventures of one detective hero exclusively was Street & Smith's *Nick Carter Library* (August 8, 1891–December 26, 1896). It was succeeded by the *Nick Carter Weekly* (January 2, 1897–September 7, 1912) and *Nick Carter Stories* (September 14, 1912–October 2, 1915). The last became the pulp magazine *Detective Story* (October 5, 1915–Summer 1949).

Among the other publications that fed the public demand for cheap detective fiction were *Old Sleuth Weekly, Secret Service* (Old King Brady again, this time with Young King Brady), *Young Sleuth Library, Shield Weekly, Old Broadbrim Weekly, Young Broadbrim Weekly,* and the short-lived (nine issues) *Dick Dobbs Detective Weekly*. In addition, there were *Old Sleuth's Own,* the *Secret Service Series,* the *New Secret Service Series,* the *Shield Series* (and the *Shield Detective Series*), and the *Eureka Detective Series*. The *Magnet Library* and the *New Magnet Library* published original novels and reprinted material from the weeklies. The *Magnet Library* (Street & Smith, 1897–1933) published works by Gaboriau, Edgar Allan POE, Sir Arthur CONAN DOYLE, Maurice LEBLANC, and Fergus HUME as well as the Felix Boyd stories by Scott Campbell (Frederick William Davis, 1858–1933), from *The Popular Magazine*. The character most in evidence was Nick CARTER.

The importance of the dime novel to the development of the American detective story has been underestimated and little understood. Its contributions may lie more in the field of social history than in literature, but later detective works cannot be fully appreciated without a consideration of the "paperback originals." Their existence is proof of the fascination that tales of crime and mystery held for the growing nation. Twentieth-century detective fiction did not just spring onto the reading table; a generation of slim books with lurid cover illustrations was responsible for the popular notions about how detectives work and had thus provided the impetus.

J. RANDOLPH COX

"DIPLOMAT" (pseudonym of John Franklin Carter; 1897–1967). Born in Fall River, Mass., he was one of seven children of an Episcopalian clergyman. Carter graduated from Yale in 1920 and became a newspaperman; from 1923 to 1928 he was on the staff of *The New York Times*. He moved to Washington, D.C., and was an economic specialist in the State Department from 1928 to 1932. He then became a correspondent for *Liberty* magazine and later a radio commentator with the National Broadcasting Company. As Jay Franklin he wrote a newspaper column, "We, the People," and a number of works of fiction and nonfiction. A close friend and confidant of President Franklin D. Roosevelt, he served as Undersecretary of Agriculture from 1934 to 1936 and during World War II did special intelligence work for the White House.

Carter wrote more than twenty books, including biographies of Fiorello La Guardia and Drew Pearson. His mysteries, all signed by "Diplomat," called upon his intimate knowledge of international and national politics. They concern Dennis Tyler, the Harvard-educated chief of the fictional U.S. Bureau of Current Political Intelligence. In the first "Diplomat" mystery, Tyler solves the murder of an undersecretary in the State Department as chemical warfare and a pacifist plot threaten the United States government.

There are seven "Diplomat" mysteries: *Murder in the State Department* (1930), *Murder in the Embassy* (1930), *Scandal in the Chancery* (1931), *The Corpse on the White House Lawn* (1932), *Death in the Senate* (1933), *Slow Death at Geneva* (1934), and *The Brain Trust Murder* (1935).

DISHER (Creator: Will SCOTT). A precursor of Nero WOLFE, Disher is a vast, spacious figure whose bulk sweeps the sky, blots out the sun, and is guaranteed to fill any chair he is offered. His fat face is usually frowning, but on occasion a small curly smile makes it seem bright. The waterfall of his hair frequently cascades down into his eyes, and he must push it back. He wears a monocle, which he polishes frequently and uses to lend emphasis to his words.

Disher is always tired. He never walks when he can ride, and never rides when he can pay others to ride for him. His chief occupations are smoking expensive cigars and talking about himself for an hour or two. Then he will probably yawn, close his eyes, and fall asleep.

He is not modest. A policeman once accused him of withholding information, and he replied, "Life is too short for me to tell you all I know." At the successful conclusion of one of his cases, Disher remarks, "It is the most boring thing in all the world, of course, but I am always right." There are few great detectives in this world. Disher claims that he himself was born great, and that since he knew everything, there was nothing else for him to do but become a detective.

His first adventure, *Disher-Detective* (1925; U.S. title: *The Black Stamp*), concerns an elaborate conspiracy. The victims receive a letter bearing a black stamp—and then vanish into thin air. *Shadows* (1928) centers about the proverbial weekend party at an estate; Disher must investigate such odd incidents as ringing bells, mysterious footsteps, and a suspicious limping man. Disher's last investigation, *The Mask* (1928), starts with a masked figure entering an inn. After the person leaves, it is found that a crime has been committed. The problem is taken to Disher, who promptly identifies the masked figure but investigates further.

DISNEY, DORIS MILES (1907–1976). Born in Glastonbury, Conn., Doris Miles attended high school there and then worked in a Hartford insurance office prior to her marriage in June 1936 to George J. Disney. Their only daughter, Elizabeth, was born in 1943, the year Mrs. Disney's first book was published. She continued her writing while her husband was away during World War II, serving in the Navy. Subsequently, as a widow, she was able to support herself through her increasingly prolific writing. For many years a Connecticut resident, she now lives in Fredericksburg, Va.

Mrs. Disney's New England background has been reflected in most of her mysteries, and she has portrayed the lives of the suburban middle class with what Anthony BOUCHER called an "acid etching of the everyday." Her most famous series character is Jefferson DIMARCO, an insurance claims investigator. Her research into the investigatory activities of the U.S. Postal Department led to three well-received mysteries about Postal Inspector David Madden: *Unappointed Rounds* (1956; British title: *The Post Office Case*), *Black Mail* (1958), and *Mrs. Meeker's Money* (1961).

Children are potential victims in several Disney novels, including *Shadow of a Man* (1965), *The Magic Grandfather* (1966; British title: *Mask of Evil*), and *Two Little Children and How They Grew* (1970; British title: *Fatal Choice*). An earlier novel, *Family Skeleton* (1949), was dedicated "to Elizabeth Disney, age five, in spite of whom this book was written." Elizabeth was also the dedicatee of *The Hospitality of the House* (1964; British title: *Unsuspected Evil*) and was referred to as the author's "consultant." The story is told from the viewpoint of a college girl who is terrorized during a visit to a school friend in upstate New York.

Although recent reviews by Newgate Callendar in *The New York Times* have been unfavorable, critics have usually praised Mrs. Disney's work. Occasionally, they have questioned her approach in books they otherwise considered satisfactory. They objected in *Appointment at Nine* (1947) to the withholding of a vital piece of evidence. *Straw Man* (1951) starts as a suspenseful detective puzzle, but, without apparent reason, Mrs. Disney discloses the identity of the murderer midway through the book.

Possibly her best-known book is *Do Not Fold, Spindle or Mutilate* (1970; British title: *Death by Computer*), also a successful television film.

DISNEY, DOROTHY CAMERON (1903–). American mystery novelist. Born in Indian Territory, which became part of the state of Oklahoma, Miss Disney was the daughter of a government employee with the Dawes Commission, which partitioned Indian lands. After six years at several colleges she obtained a degree from Barnard College in New York. She then had such varied occupations as stenographer, nightclub hostess, advertising copy writer, and movie extra.

In 1929 she began writing fiction for newspaper syndicates, then proceeded to contribute stories to magazines, and, finally, in 1936 published her first mystery novel, *Death in the Back Seat*. She received critical approval for the atmosphere of *The Balcony* (1940), set in an old mansion in the Deep South. Though classifying her as firmly in the "HAD-I-BUT-KNOWN" SCHOOL, Howard HAYCRAFT believes that she writes far too well to need such devices.

DIXON, FRANKLIN W. *See* HARDY BOYS, THE.

DOCHERTY, JAMES L. *See* CHASE, JAMES HADLEY.

DOMINIC, R. B. *See* LATHEN, EMMA.

DONOVAN, DICK (pseudonym of Joyce Emmerson Preston Muddock; 1843–1934). English journalist and detective story writer. Born in Southampton, Muddock traveled extensively throughout Asia, the Pacific, and Europe as a special correspondent for the *London Daily News* and the *Hour* and as a contributor to other journals. In his autobiography, *Pages from an Adventurous Life* (1907), he regrets the popularity of his more than fifty detective volumes, preferring his other work.

Generally regarded as his best mysteries are such novels as *The Man from Manchester* (1890), *The Mystery of Jamaica Terrace* (1896), and *Whose Was the Hand?* (1901), the only detective novel published under his own name (although *From the*

Two typical Dick Donovan short story collections. These first editions are cloth; many of his books were issued in printed boards simultaneously with the cloth issue. Both volumes were published by Chatto & Windus in 1899.

Bosom of the Deep, 1886, which he also published under his own name, contains elements of crime and mystery).

Far more popular, however, was the endless stream of short stories that regularly appeared in *The Strand* for many years. These melodramatic tales feature the physically active Donovan boastfully recounting his adventures with sinister secret societies, supervillains, and innocent people who commit crimes while hypnotized or under the influence of powerful drugs. More than a dozen volumes featured Donovan as the detective, beginning with *The Man-Hunter: Stories from the Note-Book of a Detective* (1888) and including *Caught at Last!* (1889), *Tracked and Taken* (1890), *A Detective's Triumphs* (1891), *Link by Link* (1893), *From Clue to Capture* (1893), *Found and Fettered* (1894). Among the most popular later collections were *The Chronicles of Michael Danevitch of the Russian Secret Service* (1897), *The Records of Vincent Trill of the Detective Service* (1899), *The Adventures of Tylor Tatlock: Private Detective* (1900), and *The Triumphs of Fabian Field: Criminologist* (1912).

DOSTOEVSKI, FYODOR MIKHAILOVICH (1821–1881). Russian novelist. Born in Moscow, he became one of the most important and influential writers of the modern era. He suffered from epilepsy throughout most of his adult life and was in constant financial difficulty, partly because of his addiction to gambling, until the publication of *The Brothers Karamazov* (1879–1880), a novel of crime and sensation as well as a religious document and a critique of socialism. In this book, as in *Crime and Punishment* (1866), the psychological aspects of murder are of greater consequence than the act itself, or its detection. In *Crime and Punishment*, a poor young student, Raskolnikov, plans and commits the murder of a greedy pawnbroker. Caught in the act, he kills the old woman's sister as well. After successfully making his escape, Raskolnikov begins to question his motives and, after a long period of mental anguish, turns himself in to the shrewd police inspector, Petrovich, who had suspected him from the first. The interrogation, the confession, and the banishment to Siberia are all necessary steps in the murderer's repentance. The great German philosopher Friedrich Nietzsche is said to have developed his idea of *Übermensch* (superman) after reading *Crime and Punishment*.

A dogged police lieutenant (Frank Silvera) brings a young murderer (George Hamilton) close to the breaking point in *Crime and Punishment, U.S.A.*, a 1959 reworking of the Dostoevski classic in an American setting. [*Allied Artists*]

DOVE, FIDELITY (Creator: Roy VICKERS). An angelic-looking girl whose ethereal beauty has made slaves of several brilliant men, Fidelity Dove is one of the most inventive and successful of all crooks. With her "gang," consisting of a lawyer, a businessman, a scientist, and other devoted servants, the exquisitely beautiful Fidelity rights the wrongs committed against those unable to help themselves, generally turning a handsome profit. She always wears gray, partly because the color goes well with her violet eyes, and partly because it reflects her strict, puritanical life. Detective Inspector Rason, her frustrated adversary, who later has more success when he joins the DEPARTMENT OF DEAD ENDS, calls her "the coolest crook in London, and then some."

Her brilliantly conceived crimes are recorded in *The Exploits of Fidelity Dove* (1924), published under the pseudonym David Durham; it is one of the rarest mystery books published in the twentieth century. The book was reissued in 1935 with the same title but under Vickers's name.

DOVER, INSPECTOR WILFRED (Creator: Joyce PORTER). Little explanation has been given for this detective's comparatively high position as a chief inspector at Scotland Yard other than the report that he was "kicked upstairs." Certainly, he has none of the attributes of the sleuth; he is fat, dishonest, lazy, and inefficient. His main interests are sleeping and cadging as many free meals and drinks as possible. He constantly complains, his woes ranging from his ill-fitting false teeth to his many gastrointestinal ailments. Dover occasionally stumbles upon the correct solution to a crime; just as often, he takes credit for the good ideas provided by his long-suffering assistant, Sergeant MacGregor.

There are seven Dover novels: *Dover One* (1964), *Dover Two* (1965), *Dover Three* (1966), *Dover and the Unkindest Cut of All* (1967), *Dover Goes to Pott* (1968), *Dover Strikes Again* (1973), and *It's Murder with Dover* (1973).

DOWNES, QUENTIN. See HARRISON, MICHAEL.

DOYLE, SIR ARTHUR CONAN. See CONAN DOYLE, SIR ARTHUR.

DRACULA, COUNT (Creator: Bram STOKER). The most famous vampire in literature. Dracula lives in Transylvania, appearing only between sundown and sunup; he spends the rest of the time sleeping in a coffin. Deathless, he perpetuates his existence by sucking the lifeblood from the throats of living people. The old nobleman is a curiosity to his neighbors, since he is never seen to eat or drink, and even the most blasé of them are impressed by the fact that he has no reflection in a mirror.

Although it is now impossible to think of Dracula without envisioning Bela Lugosi, in his first appearance, in *Dracula* (1897), he is a tall, thin man with a long white moustache. He always dresses in black. His hands are unusually coarse, with hair growing in the middle of the palms; his long fingernails end in sharp points. He has enormous strength in his grip, and the touch of his hand is as cold as ice—"more like the hand of a dead man." His thin-lipped mouth is cruel-looking, and he has exceptionally sharp white teeth that protrude somewhat over his lips, which are such a bright red that they appear to be covered with fresh blood. His pointed ears contribute to his satanic appearance.

In *Dracula*, the perceptive Dr. Van Helsing (Edward Van Sloan) exposes a mirror inside a cigarette case to the infamous vampire, brought to the screen in 1931 by Bela Lugosi. [*Universal*]

In *Dracula*, the last great Gothic novel, an English solicitor, Jonathan Harker, visits the master of Castle Dracula to transact business. After several unusual experiences, such as finding his host lying in a coffin, apparently dead, and seeing phantomlike women walking about the castle, Harker realizes that he is a prisoner whose strength is being drained.

After the count moves to London, great numbers of people are found dead with two small puncture marks on their throats. Dr. Van Helsing warns a skeptical public that a vampire is responsible; he then sets out to destroy it.

A little-known book, *Dracula's Guest and Other Weird Tales* (1914), contains a previously unpublished episode in the life of the sinister count.

The fictional Dracula is said to have been based on a real-life character, the fifteenth-century Romanian prince Vlad the Impaler (1431–1476).

Play and Films

As early as 1922 Count Dracula was the inspiration for a German film classic, F. W. Murnau's (1889–1931) *Nosferatu*, a freely adapted version (the name was changed so that royalty payments could be avoided) in which the vampire is a bloated, corrupt demon who darts from his home in the Carpathians to the German port city of Bremen, bringing with him hordes of rats to spread pestilence and death. He is stopped by the goodness and self-sacrifice of the hero's wife and, in the first rays of the morning sun, turns into a wraith. Nosferatu is played by Max Shreck. In 1927 the Hungarian actor Bela Lugosi

(1882–1956) achieved great fame in the title role of a play based on *Dracula,* dramatized by Hamilton Deane and John L. Balderston; he later starred in frequent revivals of the play, both in the United States and England, until his death. (It is a stock favorite to this day.) In 1931 he repeated the role in the screen version, which was based more on the stage drama than on the novel. John Carradine played the count in two 1945 films, and Christopher Lee successfully revived the character for England's Hammer Studios in 1958.

DREISER, THEODORE (1871–1945). American novelist, one of the most prominent of the naturalistic school of fiction. He began his career as a journalist and then tried writing novels. He had abysmal luck with *Sister Carrie* (1900) but fared better with his second book, also about a fallen woman, *Jennie Gerhardt* (1911). In 1927 Dreiser visited the Soviet Union and thereafter became active in left-wing causes, which preoccupied him until his death.

His major contribution to the crime genre is *An American Tragedy* (1925), a realistic study based on the real-life murder of Grace Brown at Big Moose Lake in the Adirondacks by Chester Gillette in 1906. Clyde Griffiths, the protagonist, seduces a factory worker but wants to marry Sondra Finchley, a wealthy member of the town's aristocracy. When the factory girl tells him that she is pregnant and expects him to marry her, the social-climbing Griffiths fears that his relationship with Sondra will end; he plans to murder the girl. He takes her rowing but lacks the courage to implement his plan; ironically, she is drowned accidentally. He is arrested, tried, and convicted of murder. Somehow, Dreiser believed that he had written an indictment of American capitalism.

Play and Films

Patrick Kearney adapted Dreiser's book for the stage, and it was extremely popular. Two film versions have been produced. In 1931 Josef von Sternberg made a vigorous motion picture starring Phillips Holmes, Sylvia Sidney, and Frances Dee. George Stevens remade it in 1951 as *A Place in the Sun,* starring Montgomery Clift, Elizabeth Taylor, and Shelley Winters.

DRESSER, DAVIS. *See* HALLIDAY, BRETT.

DREW, NANCY (Creator: Carolyn KEENE). The teenage detective heroine of fifty-two novels (and more planned), aimed at readers in the eight-to-thirteen age group, solves crimes that generally take place in old dark houses, secret passages, and underground caves; many are set in foreign countries. Highly intelligent and extraordinarily brave, Nancy ventures into situations that would cause Mike HAMMER

A curious teenager finds herself in trouble: Bonita Granville in *Nancy Drew and the Hidden Staircase.* [*Warner Brothers*]

to think twice. Since her first appearance, in *Secret of the Old Clock* (1930), more than 60 million copies of her adventures have been sold.

Her best friends and constant companions are George, a "slender, boyish-looking girl with close-cropped brown hair," and Bess, who is pretty, a little plump, and more fearful than Nancy and George. Nancy's boyfriend, Ned, attends an out-of-town college but is often present to help solve a mystery. Her mother is dead, but her father, Carson Drew, an eminent attorney, often helps his daughter at critical moments. He, in turn, gives her cases allied with his work.

Films

The pert youngster has starred in several screen mysteries.

Nancy Drew, Detective. Warner Brothers, 1938. Bonita Granville (Nancy), Frankie Thomas, Jr., John Litel, Dick Purcell. Directed by William Clemens.

Nancy is suspicious when an elderly lady who had promised her school a large endowment suddenly disappears.

Nancy Drew, Reporter. Warner Brothers, 1939. Granville, Thomas, Litel, Mary Lee, Dickie Jones. Directed by Clemens.

Nancy, working on a newspaper as part of a school assignment, is sure that a girl held for murder after an inquest is innocent.

Nancy Drew, Trouble Shooter. Warner Brothers, 1939. Granville, Thomas, Litel, Charlotte Wynters. Directed by Clemens.

Nancy tries to help one of her father's friends, who has been accused of murder.

Nancy Drew and the Hidden Staircase. Warner Brothers, 1939. Granville, Thomas, Litel. Directed by Clemens.

Nancy aids two elderly sisters whose homestead has been threatened when she discovers a secret passage.

DRIFFIELD, SIR CLINTON (Creator: J. J. CONNINGTON). The chief constable of his district, Driffield is in his mid-thirties, a thin and ordinary-looking individual with a shrewd and penetrating glint in his eye. His face is sun-tanned, his mouth firm; he has a closely clipped moustache. He is a neat, if unimaginative, dresser, and his hands and teeth give evidence of great care. There is a slightly cynical air about him.

Driffield is a chess enthusiast and collects books on crime. His memory is excellent, and he usually notices the important characteristics of uninteresting people. He is also fond of matching wits with criminals. He is usually assisted by his friend, chess partner, and "Watson" (*see* WATSON, DR.), Wendover, a rich landowner and justice of the peace, whom he continually addresses as "Squire."

Sir Clinton has been known to be rude and tactless on occasion and is often abrupt when questioning people. One critic has characterized him as efficient but essentially unlikable.

Driffield and Wendover make their debut in Connington's third detective novel, *Murder in the Maze* (1927), which features an unusual background and the murders of the twin Shandon brothers (fraternal incidents occur in several subsequent books).

The Sweepstake Murders (1931) concerns the killing of a group of people—mainly unattractive—who hold shares in a winning sweepstakes ticket, and it also presents considerable material about photography. This novel is listed in SANDOE'S READERS' GUIDE TO CRIME.

The Castleford Conundrum (1932), one of Connington's best novels, is about a weak and unhappy husband whose problems are partially solved by the murder of his unsympathetic but wealthy second wife—until he becomes the chief suspect. Ballistics plays an important role in this novel.

CHECKLIST

1927 *Murder in the Maze*
1927 *Tragedy at Ravensthorpe*
1928 *The Case with Nine Solutions*
1928 *Mystery at Lynden Sands*
1929 *Nemesis at Raynham Parva* (U.S. title: *Grim Vengeance*)
1931 *The Boathouse Riddle*
1931 *The Sweepstake Murders*
1932 *The Castleford Conundrum*
1934 *The Ha-Ha Case* (U.S. title: *The Brandon Case*)
1935 *In Whose Dim Shadow* (U.S. title: *The Tau Cross Mystery*)
1937 *A Minor Operation*
1938 *For Murder Will Speak* (U.S. title: *Murder Will Speak*)
1938 *Truth Comes Limping*
1941 *The Twenty-one Clues*
1942 *No Past Is Dead*
1944 *Jack-in-the-Box*
1947 *Common Sense Is All You Need*

DRUMMOND, BULLDOG (Creator: H. C. MCNEILE). A gentleman adventurer who finds peace dull after his demobilization following World War I, Captain Hugh Drummond continues to defend England from its enemies. His major adversaries are Germans and Russians, but his most notable encounters involve Carl Peterson, an archvillain who will accept anyone as an ally if doing so will help him realize personal goals.

Intensely patriotic, Drummond will do anything for his country: break the law, risk his life (and that of Phyllis, his lovely wife), and commit acts of violence against those foreign devils who would do the same if given the opportunity. He is often contemptuous of the police and others who allow the law to interfere with justice.

Drummond does not think in terms of politics, finding England's enemies on the right as well as on the left. He does not play favorites and has little patience with either extreme. "Years ago," he said once, "we had an amusing little show rounding up Communists and other unwashed people of that type. We called ourselves the Black Gang, and it was great sport while it lasted."

Physically, Drummond has the qualities necessary to handle the situations in which he finds himself. Six feet tall, quite broad and muscular, he is an excellent boxer and "a lightning and deadly shot with a revolver." Not even his greatest admirers call him handsome, but he has a cheerful sort of ugliness that inspires the confidence of other men. His best feature is his eyes, which reveal the strength of character that makes him a true sportsman and adventurer—hard-playing and hard-fighting but clean-living and unwaveringly fair and honest.

Regulars in the Drummond coterie include Tenny, his valet; Algie, his aristocratic friend; and Colonel Neilson, a Scotland Yard policeman.

In his first adventure, *Bulldog Drummond*, he discovers that Peterson is behind a Russian plot to overthrow the British government by means of a ruinous general strike, supported by several prominent Englishmen who plan to lead the new social system.

Jack Hulbert (left, standing) seems quite undisturbed as gangsters hold a gun on him in *Bulldog Jack*. [*Gaumont-British*]

The Final Count finds Peterson as the brains behind an incredible plot to rule the world. Robin Gaunt, a scientist, has perfected the deadliest poison ever devised; it is capable of bringing instantaneous death to multitudes. Fearing that it will fall into the wrong hands (namely "Russia, ruled by its clique of homicidal, alien Jews"), Gaunt is prepared to turn it over to Great Britain when he is kidnapped—with his sample of the lethal liquid.

Peterson has been killed, but in *The Female of the Species* his mistress attempts to turn the tables on Drummond, kidnapping his wife.

Gerard Fairlie, a friend of McNeile and a fellow author, continued the Bulldog Drummond stories after McNeile died.

CHECKLIST

(By H. C. McNeile, "Sapper")

1920 *Bulldog Drummond*
1922 *The Black Gang*
1925 *The Third Round* (U.S. title: *Bulldog Drummond's Third Round*)
1926 *The Final Count*
1928 *The Female of the Species*
1929 *Temple Tower*
1932 *Return of Bulldog Drummond* (U.S. title: *Bulldog Drummond Returns*)
1933 *Knockout* (U.S. title: *Bulldog Drummond Strikes Back*)
1935 *Bulldog Drummond at Bay*
1937 *Challenge*

(By Gerard Fairlie)

1938 *Bulldog Drummond on Dartmoor*
1939 *Bulldog Drummond Attacks*
1945 *Captain Bulldog Drummond*
1947 *Bulldog Drummond Stands Fast*
1949 *Hands Off Bulldog Drummond*
1951 *Calling Bulldog Drummond*
1954 *The Return of the Black Gang*

Films

McNeile's dashing former army officer has had a healthy and varied screen career. English matinee idol Carlyle Blackwell first played him in 1922 (*Bulldog Drummond,* Hodkinson Pictures) in a close, exciting adaptation of the first novel in which Hugh ends the schemes of a band of criminals who operate a sanatorium in order to rob their patients. Three years later Jack Buchanan was a two-fisted Drummond in *The Third Round.* Among later English Drummonds were Ralph Richardson, who in 1934 not only starred in *The Return of Bulldog Drummond* but was the eccentric villain in *Bulldog Jack,* a comedy-melodrama about an inept playboy impersonating Hugh, and John Lodge, who starred in *Bulldog Drummond at Bay* (1937; directed by Norman Lee), in which Hugh battles with a munitions gang masquerading as workers for peace, blasts his way out of a gas-filled room, and proposes to a British secret service agent (Dorothy Mackaill). But the most memorable of the early Drummonds was Ronald Colman, a popular young actor made even more famous by the role.

Bulldog Drummond. United Artists, 1929. Colman, Joan Bennett, Lilyan Tashman, Montague Love, Claude Allister (Algie). Directed by F. Richard Jones.

Again, Hugh and his beautiful Phyllis meet as outlined in McNeile's basic novel and play; Drummond rescues the girl's uncle, who is imprisoned in the private hospital run by archcriminal Carl Peterson.

Temple Tower. Fox, 1930. Kenneth MacKenna, Marceline Day, Henry B. Walthall, Cyril Chadwick (Algie). Directed by Donald Gallagher.

Hugh (MacKenna) fears that a girl's life is in danger behind the locked gates of Temple Tower, a mysterious building complete with secret passageways, located on an estate set deep in a forest.

Bulldog Drummond Strikes Back. United Artists, 1934. Colman, Loretta Young, Warner Oland, C. Aubrey Smith. Directed by Roy Del Ruth.

Lost in a fog, Hugh stumbles into a "murder mansion"—with sliding panels, disappearing corpse, and kidnapped heroine—owned by an evil foreign prince (Oland).

Bulldog Drummond Escapes. Paramount, 1937. Ray Milland, Heather Angel, Porter Hall, Sir Guy Standing (Colonel Neilson of Scotland Yard), Reginald Denny (Algie), E. E. Clive (valet Tenny). Directed by James Hogan. Based on the play *Bulldog Drummond Again.*

This is the third version of the Drummond-Phyllis meeting, and it has uncommon charm. When Hugh climbs through the window of the old manor where the girl has been kept drugged and a prisoner, she pleads, "Captain Drummond, don't stay, you are in the most frightful danger!"

Walter Pidgeon, as a Drummond called out of retirement in *Calling Bulldog Drummond,* finds himself tied up next to an attractive undercover operative (Margaret Leighton) in the same predicament. [*MGM*]

Bulldog Drummond Comes Back. Paramount, 1937. John Howard (assuming the Drummond role for the next seven films), Louise Campbell (Phyllis), John Barrymore (Colonel Neilson), J. Carroll Naish. Directed by Louis King. Based on *The Female of the Species.*

A maddened widow, Irena Soldanis (Helen Freeman), plots vengeance against Hugh for killing her husband; she makes off with Phyllis into fog-shrouded Limehouse, with Hugh and Neilson—the latter assuming various disguises—in pursuit, led on by crazed limerick clues.

Bulldog Drummond's Revenge. Paramount, 1937. Howard, Campbell, Barrymore, Denny, Clive, Frank Puglia. Directed by King. Based on *The Return of Bulldog Drummond.*

Hugh boards the train ferry from Dover to Calais to follow a man who has stolen a powerful explosive. As in most of the films in the series, he promises Phyllis that he will abandon his adventurous ways after he marries her. Their ever-impending wedding is a subtheme of every film.

Bulldog Drummond's Peril. Paramount, 1938. Howard, Campbell, Barrymore, Denny, Clive, Porter Hall, Halliwell Hobbes. Directed by Hogan. Based on *The Third Round.*

A synthetic diamond given to Hugh and Phyllis as a wedding gift is purloined by the head of the Metropolitan Diamond Syndicate. Drummond is off on a chase from Switzerland to London.

Bulldog Drummond in Africa. Paramount, 1938. Howard, Angel (returning as Phyllis), H. B. Warner (Neilson for the remainder of the series), Naish. Directed by King. Based on *Challenge*.

Hugh and Algie start out on another chase when they learn that an international spy has kidnapped Colonel Neilson and transported him by plane to a lion-guarded courtyard near Morocco.

Arrest Bulldog Drummond! Paramount, 1938. Howard, Angel, Warner, Denny, Clive, George Zucco. Directed by Hogan. Based on *The Final Count*.

Hugh and his friends travel to a British-held tropical island to corner a villain who has transported a powerful death ray there from London after killing its inventor.

Bulldog Drummond's Secret Police. Paramount, 1939. Howard, Angel, Warner, Denny, Clive, Leo G. Carroll. Directed by Hogan. Based on *Temple Tower*.

On the eve of his wedding Hugh is told that the Drummond family residence, the Tower, contains secret passageways and a treasure.

Bulldog Drummond's Bride. Paramount, 1939. Howard, Angel, Warner, Denny, Clive, Eduardo Ciannelli. Directed by Hogan.

A master bank robber engineers a traffic snarl on High Regent Street and hides in Hugh's soon-to-be occupied honeymoon flat. Later his explosives nearly—but not quite—sabotage Hugh's wedding to Phyllis in a small French town.

Bulldog Drummond at Bay. Columbia, 1947. Ron Randell, Anita Louise, Terry Kilburn. Directed by Sidney Salkow.

Drummond (played by the Australian Randell), now less romantic and unmarried, and with a boy assistant (Kilburn), rescues a young Scotland Yard man who has been abducted with a fortune in gems.

Bulldog Drummond Strikes Back. Columbia, 1947. Randell, Gloria Henry, Kilburn, Anabel Shaw. Directed by Frank McDonald.

Drummond has difficulty deciding which of two girls is the actual heiress to a fortune.

The Challenge. Twentieth Century-Fox, 1948. Tom Conway, June Vincent, Richard Stapley, Eily Malyon. Directed by Jean Yarbrough.

A murdered ship captain leaves clues to the location of his buried treasure hidden in the model of a ship.

Thirteen Lead Soldiers. Twentieth Century-Fox, 1948. Conway, Helen Westcott, Maria Palmer, John Newland. Directed by McDonald.

A set of eleventh-century toy soldiers, its owners murdered, leads Drummond to more secret treasure, this time belonging to ancient kings and discovered behind a fireplace.

Calling Bulldog Drummond. MGM, 1951. Walter Pidgeon, Margaret Leighton, Robert Beatty, David Tomlinson (Algie). Directed by Victor Saville.

An aging Hugh is called from retirement to combat up-to-the-minute crooks who use radar to steal gold bullion—and finds some romantic moments with a lady undercover agent (Leighton).

For the next decade Drummond remained in seclusion, too old-hat for the changing times. Then the popularity of the James BOND films inspired a virile, "mod" version of the adventurer.

Deadlier Than the Male. Universal, 1967. Richard Johnson, Elke Sommer, Sylva Koscina, Nigel Green (Carl Peterson), Suzanna Leigh, Steve Carlson. Directed by Ralph Thomas.

Lloyd's of London insurance investigator Drummond pursues the evil Peterson, who, with an international band of girl assassins (headed by Sommer and Koscina) is attempting to control the world's oil. The confrontation takes place in a Mediterranean villa where Drummond and Peterson do battle on a gigantic chessboard. Algie and Tenny are gone, replaced by Hugh's American nephew (Carlson).

Some Girls Do. Universal, 1971. Johnson, Daliah Lavi, Beba Loncar, James Villiers (Peterson this film), Robert Morley. Directed by Thomas.

Peterson is aided in his sabotage of England's new supersonic air strength by another deadly girl team (actually programmed robots). One of their victims is an eccentric chef named Miss Mary (Morley).

Radio, Television, and Plays

"Out of the fog, out of the night, and into his American adventures steps Bulldog Drummond . . ." began a popular half-hour radio series of the 1940s (George Coulouris and Ned Wever were among the actors who portrayed Drummond). *Bulldog Drummond* was first heard on Mutual in 1941. It did not, however, closely resemble McNeile's original creation. Robert Beatty played Hugh for British television.

Bulldog Drummond by "Sapper" and Gerald du Maurier opened in London in 1921; that year it opened on Broadway, with A. E. Matthews as Drummond. *Bulldog Drummond Again*, by "Sapper" and Gerard Fairlie, was presented on the London stage in 1936. In October 1974 an English group called the Low Moan Spectacular brought to Broadway *Bullshot Crummond*, which they called "a satiric reminder." Captain Hugh Bullshot Crummond was played by Alan Shearman.

DU BOISGOBEY, FORTUNÉ (HIPPOLYTE-AUGUSTE) (1821–1891). French author of sensational mystery thrillers. He freely borrowed from Émile GABORIAU, in both style and subject, and even used Gaboriau's famous detective, Monsieur LECOQ, as a character in *La vieillesse de Monsieur Lecoq* (1878; U.S. title: *The Old Age of Lecoq, the Detective*, 1880). In England, where the story was the first in a long series of successful paperbacks called Boisgobey's Sensational Novels, it was first published in

1885. Possibly the best of the series, which included more than thirty titles, is *Le crime de l'Opéra* (1880; U.S. title: *The Crime of the Opera House,* 1881).

DUDLEY-SMITH, TREVOR. *See* HALL, ADAM.

DUKE, WINIFRED (d. 1962). English novelist, historian, and author of true-crime stories. Born in Liverpool, where her father was a church canon, she was educated privately at the Belvedere School. She then moved to Edinburgh and spent the rest of her life in and around the city, which provided the setting for most of her novels.

An interest in true crime, possibly spurred by the writings and presence in Edinburgh of William Roughead, led her to write a series of forty novels of varying degrees of basis in fact. Her earliest works were *The House of Ogilvy* (1922), *The Wild Flame* (1923), and *The Laird* (1925).

Her true-crime book *Madeleine Smith: A Tragi-Comedy* (1928) was followed by several volumes in the Notable British Trials series, including *The Trial of Harold Greenwood* (1930), *The Trial of Field and Gray* (1939), and *The Trial of Frederick Nodder* (1950). Shorter true-crime cases appeared in *Six Trials* (1934) and *The Stroke of Murder* (1937).

Research on the Harold Greenwood volume also provided material for a fictional version of that criminal's life entitled *Bastard Verdict* (1931), usually cited as Miss Duke's best work. It was published in the United States in 1934. The sequels and successors to this book are *The Dark Hill* (1932), *The Sown Wind* (1932), *Finale* (1933), *These Are They* (1933), *Magpie's Hoard* (1934), and *Long Furrows* (1936), all of which continue to detail the family saga of the protagonist of *Bastard Verdict;* fact, however, soon evolved into fiction as the series proceeded.

Skin for Skin (1935), the psychological study of a murderer, is based on the famous Julia Wallace case and adheres to the facts with scrupulous devotion and attention to detail. Unlike *Bastard Verdict,* it is of moderate length and moves rapidly to its conclusion. It is included in SANDOE'S READERS' GUIDE TO CRIME. Miss Duke's last novel was *The Dancing of the Fox* (1956).

DULUTH, PETER (Creator: Patrick QUENTIN). A famous theatrical producer who stumbles into detective work by accident, Duluth has often found himself or his friends and relatives in need of his ability to solve crimes. In his first adventure, *A Puzzle for Fools,* on the verge of a breakdown caused by alcoholism, Duluth commits himself to a mental institution where he solves two murders on the premises—with the aid of friendly psychiatrist Dr. Lenz and actress Iris Pattison, a victim of melancholia, whom he later marries. Subsequent mysteries occur in the theatrical setting that Duluth knows well, several involving his wife, his older brother Jake, and his nephew.

In *Black Widow* Duluth loans his apartment to a young woman. When Mrs. Duluth returns from vacation and finds their tenant dead, Peter becomes the logical suspect. Lieutenant Trant (from the Q. Patrick stories) is assigned to the official investigation. *My Son, the Murderer* is narrated by Jake, whose business partner is murdered. Jake's son is the chief suspect. Peter's role (in his last appearance) is minimal, as is the part played by Trant, who goes on to dominate most of the succeeding Quentin novels.

CHECKLIST

1936	*A Puzzle for Fools*
1938	*Puzzle for Players*
1944	*Puzzle for Puppets*
1945	*Puzzle for Wantons*
1946	*Puzzle for Fiends*
1947	*Puzzle for Pilgrims*
1948	*Run to Death*
1952	*Black Widow* (British title: *Fatal Woman*)
1954	*My Son, the Murderer*

Films

Homicide for Three. Republic, 1948. Warren Douglas (Duluth), Audrey Long (Iris), Grant Withers, Stephanie Bachelor. Directed by George Blair. Based on *Puzzle for Puppets.*

While on a honeymoon during a thirty-six-hour leave, a young naval lieutenant discovers that his uniform has been stolen; an unknown person wearing it is soon seen murdering two women.

Black Widow. Twentieth Century-Fox, 1954. Van Heflin (Peter), Gene Tierney (Iris), Ginger Rogers, George Raft, Peggy Ann Garner, Reginald Gardiner. Directed by Nunnally Johnson.

While Iris is away, Peter lets a pretty, young aspiring writer use their apartment as a study during the day; Iris returns to find the girl dead. She had been pregnant, and suspicion quickly falls on Peter.

du MAURIER, DAPHNE (1907–). English author of romantic fiction. Born in London, she is a member of an illustrious family. Her great-great-grandmother was a Regency courtesan protected by the Duke of York. Her grandfather was the famous artist George du Maurier, who produced his first novel, *Peter Ibbetson* (1891), at the age of fifty-six and then wrote *Trilby* (1894), which added the name of a character, Svengali, to the language. Her father was Gerald du Maurier, an actor who dominated the British theater in the first quarter of the twentieth century; her mother was Muriel Beaumont, also an accomplished actress. Her older sister, Angela, who played Wendy in *Peter Pan,* is also a writer. The youngest of the three sisters, Jeanne, is an artist. In 1932 Miss du Maurier married Lieutenant Colonel Frederick Arthur Montague Browning II, who was

The shy new mistress of Manderley wavers under the frosty stare of her housekeeper; Joan Fontaine and Judith Anderson in Alfred Hitchcock's version of Daphne du Maurier's *Rebecca*. [*United Artists*]

knighted for his distinguished service during World War II. They had three children; Browning died in 1965. Miss du Maurier is also known as Lady Browning or Dame Daphne, since she was made a Dame of the Order of the British Empire by Queen Elizabeth II for her literary distinction.

Although all her fiction is widely read, by far the best known of Miss du Maurier's work is *Rebecca* (1938), one of the most popular novels ever written, with several million copies printed. The opening line, "Last night I dreamt I went to Manderley again," is perhaps the most recognizable in twentieth-century literature. This romantic tale of suspense is set in a sinister but beautiful old house—a fictionalized portrait of Menabilly, a seventeenth-century mansion, overlooking the sea from the rugged coast of Cornwall, that was Miss du Maurier's home for a quarter of a century. The plot, centering on a lovely, beleaguered young heroine, apparently at the mercy of a strange husband and inscrutable servants, is now a staple of hundreds of Gothic romances, but little claim to originality was made even when *Rebecca* first appeared. The "second wife" and her problems in a cold or hostile environment are familiar ingredients to readers of *Jane Eyre* (1847), by Charlotte Brontë, to which *Rebecca* is often compared, and *Vera* (1921), by Elizabeth (Countess Russell). Plagiarism suits brought by contemporary writers against Miss du Maurier were subsequently dropped when the widespread popularity of the theme was established. It is the masterful treatment of this familiar situation that made *Rebecca* a classic book, and the Alfred HITCHCOCK film of 1940 equally well regarded in its genre.

Among other works by Miss du Maurier in the mystery-suspense field are *Jamaica Inn* (1936), *My Cousin Rachel* (1951), *The Scapegoat* (1957), and *The House on the Strand* (1969). Her short story collections contain some of her most famous work, and many of the tales have been the basis of films, notably "The Birds" from *The Apple Tree* (1952; U.S. title: *Kiss Me Again, Stranger*) and stories from *The Breaking Point* (1959) and *Don't Look Now* (1971).

Miss du Maurier's unusual method of producing fiction allows her characters to "find her," she says, without her having to search for them. She finds a setting that interests her, does the necessary research for the historical background, and then takes endless, solitary walks in the country, during which she meticulously plans every detail of the story. When she finally gets to the typewriter, according to her editor, "she may produce the manuscript of a novel in two or three months. It's all there in her head, as if she were transcribing from a tape recorder."

Films

Hitchcock has been an enthusiastic admirer of Miss du Maurier and has directed *Jamaica Inn* (1939) and *The Birds* (1963) as well as *Rebecca*. Other works by Miss du Maurier have reached the screen.

My Cousin Rachel. Twentieth Century-Fox, 1952. Olivia de Havilland, Richard Burton, John Sutton, George Dolenz. Directed by Henry Koster.

A young Englishman falls hopelessly in love with the mysterious widow of his older cousin, even though he suspects that she may have murdered her husband.

The Scapegoat. MGM (British), 1959. Alec Guinness, Bette Davis, Nicole Maurey, Pamela Brown. Directed by Robert Hamer, who, with Gore Vidal (Edgar BOX), coauthored the script.

A meek and lonely English schoolmaster on a motor tour of France is forced to take on the identity of his "look-alike," a debauched French aristocrat who later proposes a scheme for murder.

Don't Look Now. Paramount (British), 1973. Donald Sutherland, Julie Christie, Hilary Mason, Massimo Serato. Directed by Nicholas Roeg.

During a gray winter in Venice, with bodies floating in the canals, a troubled English architect and his wife meet a blind psychic who says that she has "seen" the couple's dead young daughter.

Some of Miss du Maurier's nonmysteries were also made into films, among them *Frenchman's Creek* (1944) and *Hungry Hill* (1947).

DUNSANY, LORD (1878–1957). Irish dramatist,

poet, novelist, and short story writer, most of whose works deal with fantasy and the supernatural in an often unique blend of humor and the macabre.

Edward John Moreton Drax Plunkett, 18th Baron Dunsany, was born in London of Irish parents. He was educated at Cheam School, Eton, and the Royal Military Academy at Sandhurst, and then served in the Boer War, World War I, and World War II (in the Home Guard). In 1904 he married Lady Beatrice Villiers; they had one son. Dunsany devoted most of his life to hunting, traveling, cricket, and other sports, his prolific literary output being produced in short, rapid spurts.

William Butler Yeats produced Dunsany's first successful play, *The Glittering Gate,* at Dublin's Abbey Theater in 1909. It is a fantasy about two dead burglars who, realizing that they cannot get into heaven in the usual fashion, simply jimmy the gates. *The Little Tales of Smethers and Other Stories* (1952) contains twenty-six stories of murder, detection, and fantasy, the first nine of which are accounts of how Mr. Linley solves unusual crimes, narrated by Smethers, a simpleminded relish salesman. The most famous of the stories is the classic "Two Bottles of Relish," which first appeared in a 1934 anthology, *Powers of Darkness: A Collection of Uneasy Tales.*

This tableau of menace from Universal's *Mystery of Marie Rogêt,* which deals with the staged disappearance and eventual murder of a profligate Paris actress, is quite extraneous to the Poe source. [*Universal*]

DUPIN, C. AUGUSTE (Creator: Edgar Allan POE). The first fictional detective of importance and the model for virtually every cerebral crime solver who followed.

Presented without physical description, the Chevalier Dupin seems less human than his successors because Poe wanted to stress the supreme importance of the intellect, unencumbered with emotional considerations—a character, in short, who is Poe's idealization of himself.

Detesting daylight, Dupin prefers to sit behind closed shutters in a room lighted only by "a couple of tapers which, strongly perfumed, threw out only the ghastliest and feeblest of rays." He frequently remains in his room, a small library at the rear of No. 33 Rue Dunot, Paris, for a month or more without allowing a visitor. From this sanctuary he sometimes comes out at night to walk the dark, gas-lit streets and enjoy "the infinity of mental excitement" afforded by observation.

Dupin is poor, but he considers this condition unimportant as long as he has enough for necessities and his one luxury—books. He is "of an excellent—indeed of an illustrious—family." Poe, who would have liked to have had such a background, provides him with an ancestry equal to his intellect and creativity.

Young, scholarly, eccentric, romantic, aristocratic, arrogant, and apparently omniscient, Dupin has only one companion—the anonymous friend who chronicles his adventures. His devoted assistant is intellectually far inferior to Dupin, his role establishing a precedent that was subsequently almost universally followed by authors of works about fictional detectives. His slow wit serves as an excellent foil for the hero's cerebral processes, providing a handy technical tool by which to explain Dupin's feats of mental gymnastics to readers.

An omniverous reader, Dupin once admitted writing "certain doggerel" reminiscent of the limerick form. He smokes heavily, enjoying a quiet meerschaum with his friend. His green spectacles improve his shortsighted vision and also enable him to observe people intently, and yet surreptitiously.

Although he likes Monsieur G———, prefect of the Paris police, he holds the official police and their methods in open contempt—an attitude much copied in succeeding literature.

Only three stories (collected in *Tales,* 1845) display the powers of observation and deductive skills of Dupin. Often cited as the first detective story, "The Murders in the Rue Morgue" (1841) is certainly the most important of the three and introduced Dupin to the public. In this now-familiar tale—the first "impossible" crime—two women are found brutally murdered in a sealed room (*see* LOCKED-ROOM MYSTERIES). When a man who once helped him is arrested for the crime, Dupin decides to investigate. He reads newspaper accounts, visits the

Dr. Mirakle (Bela Lugosi) rails at his trussed-up captive, a woman of the Paris streets, because her blood is "impure"; he therefore cannot mate her experimentally with his carnival gorilla. In this strange adaptation of Poe's *Murders in the Rue Morgue*, the doomed prostitute is played by Arlene Francis in her first screen role. [*Universal*]

scene, examines the bodies, and deduces the identity of the killer.

"The Mystery of Marie Rogêt" (1842), unlike the thriller in which Dupin first appeared, is an example—the first in literature—of the pure "armchair detective" approach to the solution of a crime. Newspaper accounts of a murder are reprinted, and Dupin's running commentary to his friend is also given. This story, based on the actual case of Mary Cecilia Rogers, was published in three installments in *Snowden's Ladies' Companion* while investigations were still under way. Since the crime was never solved (in spite of Poe's declaration that he had deduced the actual events, an assertion often accepted today), there is no definite ending, merely Dupin's (Poe's) theory of the line of inquiry that the police would find most beneficial. New evidence appeared as Poe worked, and he had to make several changes in the final installment to authenticate his original speculations. This murder case provided the plot for what was probably the first American detective novel, *The Gambler* (1848), by Charles BURDETT.

Dupin's final exploit, in "The Purloined Letter," first appeared in *The Gift: 1845*, an annual publication that was actually published in October 1844. The best of the Dupin tales, it combines the action-thriller style of the first with the purely analytical and deductive exercise of the second. In this prototype of the modern spy story, a potentially embarrassing document is stolen from "the royal apartments" by a minister too powerful to be arrested without proof. The police thoroughly search his rooms every night for months without success until, in frustration, they ask Dupin for help. He visits the Minister's residence and spots the letter at once; it is in such an obvious place that everyone overlooked it. After receiving an enormous reward, Dupin hands the elusive letter to the stunned Monsieur G——— without explanation.

An English author, Michael HARRISON, wrote a good series of pastiches about Poe's detective for *Ellery Queen's Mystery Magazine*, collected as *The*

Exploits of the Chevalier Dupin (1968). The British edition, entitled *Murders in the Rue Royale* (1972), contains five additional stories.

Films

Poe's stories about the famous detective have been brought to the screen in various guises.

Murders in the Rue Morgue. Universal, 1932. Bela Lugosi, Leon Waycoff (Dupin; Waycoff later changed his name to Leon Ames), Sidney Fox. Directed by Robert Florey.

Medical student Pierre Dupin is certain that Dr. Mirakle (Lugosi), the owner of a large ape named Eric, which he exhibits in carnivals and with which he converses, has been murdering streetwalkers and other women to further his experiments in mingling the blood of animals and human beings. The mother of Dupin's sweetheart is one of the gorilla's victims, and the girl herself is carried off.

Mystery of Marie Rogêt. Universal, 1942. Maria Montez, Patric Knowles (Dupin), John Litel, Lloyd Corrigan, Maria Ouspenskaya. Directed by Phil Rosen.

The disappearance and murder of a celebrated French actress are investigated by Inspector Gobelin (Corrigan) and his friend Dr. Paul Dupin, chief medical officer of Paris, who makes this offhand comment on how an autopsy he has performed proved that the corpse was an English girl who had not been in France more than twenty-four hours: "A very simple thing for a chemist. You see, the Chinese subsist mainly on rice and vegetables. The English are known to be beef eaters, and so you see we are what we eat."

Phantom of the Rue Morgue. Warner Brothers, 1954. Karl Malden, Claude Dauphin, Patricia Medina, Steve Forrest (Dupin). Directed by Roy Del Ruth.

The deranged head of the Paris zoo (Malden) trains a giant ape to kill women in the streets of gaslit Paris to avenge the death of his wife (actually he had driven her to suicide); young Paul Dupin, a medical student with a bent for psychology, reasons that the killer was an animal who responded to the tinkling of bracelet bells all the victims wore.

Murders in the Rue Morgue. American International, 1971 (filmed in Spain). Jason Robards, Christine Kaufmann, Herbert Lom, Adolfo Celi, Michael Dunn, Lilli Palmer, Maria Perschy. Directed by Gordon Hessler.

The members of a Parisian Grand Guignol theater, whom we briefly see staging a play involving a murderous gorilla, are killed one after another by acid, supposedly the victims of a man long dead. Inspector Vidocq (Celi) investigates. Dwarfs and premature burials are borrowed from other Poe sources, but Dupin and all traces of the original story are omitted.

Young medical student Dupin (Steve Forrest) observes an exchange of pleasantries between the secretly mad head of the Paris zoo (Karl Malden) and a police inspector (Claude Dauphin) in *Phantom of the Rue Morgue.* [*Warner Brothers*]

DURBRIDGE, FRANCIS (1912–). English author of mystery novels, plays, and radio, television, and film scripts; creator of Paul TEMPLE. In addition to publishing more than two dozen mystery novels under his own name, mostly about Temple and Tim Frazer, his other series detective, Durbridge has collaborated on many novels with James D[ouglas] R[utherford] McConnell (1915–) under the joint pseudonym Paul Temple. Durbridge's 1939 novel *Paul Temple and the Front Page Men* is an adaptation of the play he had written with Charles Hatton. *A Man Called Harry Brent* (1970) is his novelization of a British television series.

DURHAM, DAVID. See VICKERS, ROY.

E

EBERHART, MIGNON G[OOD] (1899–   ). American mystery novelist. Born Mignon Good in Lincoln, Nebr., she attended Wesleyan University for three years before she married Alinson C. Eberhart. She traveled extensively throughout the world with her husband. She once covered a trial for a newspaper but was fired when her editor said that he "no longer wanted to impose" on her. She subsequently restricted her efforts to fictional crime; her fifty-two mysteries have earned her a loyal following.

Mrs. Eberhart's first five books were about the detective team of Sarah Keate, a middle-aged spinster nurse, and Lance O'Leary, a promising young police detective in an unnamed Midwestern city. This unlikely duo functions very effectively, despite Miss Keate's penchant for stumbling into dangerous situations from which she must be rescued. She is inquisitive and supplies O'Leary with considerable information. He, to quote his partner, "has a way of having eyes in the back of his head and ears all around." The second book in the series, *While the Patient Slept* (1930), won $5,000 in a Doubleday, Doran best mystery of the year contest. Nurse Keate returned in two solo appearances, *Wolf in Man's Clothing* (1942) and *Man Missing* (1954).

Miss Eberhart's other detectives are an attractive young mystery story writer, Susan Dare, whose adventures were collected in *The Cases of Susan Dare* (1934), and Mr. Wickwire, an elderly New York banker, who has appeared in short stories as yet uncollected.

Films

Mrs. Eberhart's Nurse Keate had an active screen career during the 1930s.

While the Patient Slept. First National, 1935. Aline MacMahon (Keate), Guy Kibbee (Lance O'Leary), Allen Jenkins, Henry O'Neill, Lyle Talbot. Directed by Ray Enright.

The son of a wealthy invalid is killed when he tries to steal a statue of a small elephant from his dying father's room.

The Murder of Dr. Harrigan. First National, 1936. Kay Linaker (renamed Nurse Sally Keating and now younger), Ricardo Cortez, Robert Strange, Mary Astor. Directed by Frank McDonald. Based on *From This Dark Stairway.*

Both the chief surgeon and the director of a private hospital are murdered during a quarrel over a new ether formula.

Murder by an Aristocrat. First National, 1936. Marguerite Churchill (Keating), Talbot, William Davidson, Stuart Holmes. Directed by McDonald.

Called in to tend a member of a distinguished family who has been accidentally shot, Nurse Keating discovers that a deliberate attempt was made on her patient's life.

The Great Hospital Mystery. Twentieth Century-Fox, 1937. Jane Darwell (an older Keating), Sally Blane, Thomas Beck. Directed by James Tinling.

A hospital patient, witness to murder and in fear for his own life, pretends to die.

The Patient in Room 18. Warner Brothers–First National, 1938. Ann Sheridan (Keating), Patric Knowles (O'Leary), Rosella Towne. Directed by Crane Wilbur.

A wealthy hospital patient is killed, and radium is stolen; Detective O'Leary, in the hospital recovering from a nervous breakdown, takes charge of the investigation over the protests of his nurse.

Mystery House. Warner Brothers–First National, 1938. Dick Purcell (O'Leary), Sheridan (Keating), Anne Nagel, Sheila Bromley. Directed by Noel Smith.

When the daughter of a supposed suicide summons to her home all the people who had been there the night her father died, two deaths occur; a private detective and her aunt's nurse solve the murders.

In addition to the Nurse Keate films, another important Eberhart work has been transferred to the screen.

The White Cockatoo. Warner Brothers, 1935. Jean Muir, Cortez, Minna Gombell, Walter Kingsford. Directed by Alan Crosland.

An American orphan living in a French hotel waits for her brother to arrive with the family inheritance; she is unaware that the hotel's owners plan to kill her and substitute another girl in her place.

EGAN, LESLIE. *See* LININGTON, ELIZABETH.

EGREMONT, MICHAEL. *See* HARRISON, MICHAEL.

87TH PRECINCT, THE (Creator: Ed MCBAIN). Although the author specifically states that the 87th Precinct is not located in New York City, the mythical island of Isola is clearly Manhattan. The most prominent member of the squad is Detective Steve Carella, whose beautiful wife, Teddy, is a deaf-mute.

Other members of the squad are Lieutenant Peter Byrnes; Detective Cotton Hawes, a giant of a man with a white streak in his hair; Detective Meyer Meyer, whose father thought it would be amusing to give his son the same first name and surname; Detective Andy Parker, a braggart with few redeeming social qualities; Desk Sergeant Dave Murchison; Alf Miscolo, the clerk; and Detective Bert Kling, the youngest member of the squad.

CHECKLIST

1956 *Cop Hater*
1956 *The Mugger*
1956 *The Pusher*
1957 *The Con Man*
1957 *Killer's Choice*
1958 *Killer's Payoff*
1958 *Lady Killer*
1959 *Killer's Wedge*
1959 *'Til Death*
1959 *King's Ransom*
1960 *Give the Boys a Great Big Hand*
1960 *The Heckler*
1960 *See Them Die*
1961 *Lady, Lady, I Did It!*
1962 *Like Love*
1962 *The Empty Hours*
1963 *Ten Plus One*
1964 *Ax*
1965 *He Who Hesitates*
1965 *Doll*
1966 *Eighty Million Eyes* (s.s.)
1968 *Fuzz*
1969 *Shotgun*
1970 *Jigsaw*
1971 *Hail, Hail, the Gang's All Here!*
1972 *Sadie When She Died*
1972 *Let's Hear It for the Deaf Man*
1973 *Hail to the Chief*
1974 *Bread*

Films

Several of McBain's 87th Precinct novels have been transferred to the screen, often with a change of locale.

Cop Hater. United Artists, 1958 (filmed in New York City). Robert Loggia, Gerald O'Loughlin, Ellen Parker, Shirley Ballard. Directed by William Berke.

Within a few weeks two police detectives have been killed in Manhattan's 87th Precinct; when his own partner is the next victim. Steve Carelli (this film) begins to suspect the murderer is not a crazed cop hater but someone trying to cover up a specific target by killing several people.

The Mugger. United Artists, 1958 (filmed in New York City). Kent Smith, Nan Martin, James Franciscus, Leonard Stone. Directed by Berke.

A dance hall girl is killed, the eleventh victim in a series of recent muggings but the first fatality; a police psychiatrist (Smith) believes that the killer and the mugger are two different people.

High and Low. Continental Distributing (Japanese), 1963. Toshiro Mifune, Kyoko Kagawa, Tatsuya Nakadai. Directed by Akira Kurosawa. Based on *King's Ransom*, but with Japanese locations and police methods.

In Tokyo, an industrial tycoon desperately raising cash to gain control of the firm that is planning to oust him is stunned to learn that he must use the money to rescue his kidnapped young son.

Without Apparent Motive. Twentieth Century-Fox, 1972 (filmed in Nice). Jean-Louis Trintignant, Dominique Sanda, Erich Segal. Directed by Philippe Labro. Based on *Ten Plus One*, transposed to European settings.

A mad sniper is on the loose on the French Riviera; only when his mistress is one of the victims does a police detective stumble upon the link between all the targets and the sniper's bizarre motive.

Fuzz. Twentieth Century-Fox, 1972 (filmed in Boston). Burt Reynolds, Yul Brynner, Raquel Welch, Tom Skerritt. Directed by Richard A. Colla. 87th Precinct doings transposed to Boston; the screenplay by Evan Hunter (McBain).

A rapist, some teens who are setting sleeping vagrants afire, and spectacular political extortion attempts by a luxury-loving supercriminal called "the Deaf Man" (Brynner) are all in a precinct's day's work.

Television

For two seasons (1961–1962) the personnel of the 87th Precinct starred in thirty one-hour television programs, based on the McBain novels. Robert Lansing was Detective Carella, Gena Rowlands was his deaf-mute wife, Teddy, and Gregory Walcott was Detective Havilland.

ELLIN, STANLEY (BERNARD) (1916–   ). American mystery writer whose short tales of crime and horror have become instant classics.

Born in New York City, Ellin graduated from

John Barrymore, Jr., portrays a distraught teenager determined to avenge his father's beating in *The Big Night*, a film based on a book by Stanley Ellin. [*United Artists*]

Brooklyn College, worked as a boilermaker's apprentice, steelworker, dairy farmer, teacher, and "pusher" for a newspaper distributor, and served in the Army during World War II before becoming a full-time writer. His wife, Jeanne, is, he says, "a brilliant, remorseless and objective critic." They have one child, Susan.

Ellin writes only about one short story a year, working in a slow, painstaking way. After mulling over an idea, sometimes for weeks, he laboriously writes and rewrites each page, sometimes a dozen times, before he is satisfied.

Brilliant and imaginative, his stories rarely fall within the bounds of detective fiction; yet each of his first seven stories won a prize in the prestigious annual contests conducted by *Ellery Queen's Mystery Magazine*, beginning with "The Specialty of the House" (1948), one of the finest crime stories of modern times. It is a macabre tale about Sbirro's, an inconspicuous little New York restaurant that occasionally serves its guests lamb Amirstan, a delicious dish that is the delight of gourmets.

In addition to two short story collections, *Mystery Stories* (1956) and *The Blessington Method* (1964), Ellin has published several novels, including *Dreadful Summit* (1948), *The Key to Nicholas Street* (1952), *The Eighth Circle* (1958), *House of Cards* (1967), *The Valentine Estate* (1968), *The Bind* (1970; British title: *The Man from Nowhere*), *Mirror, Mirror on the Wall* (1972), and *Stronghold* (1974).

He has won three Edgars, two for best short story of the year ("The House Party," 1954, and "The Blessington Method," 1956) and one for best novel of the year (*The Eighth Circle*, 1958). He received Le Grand Prix de Littérature Policière in 1975 for the French edition of *Mirror, Mirror on the Wall*.

Films

The Big Night. United Artists, 1951. John Barrymore, Jr., Preston Foster, Joan Loring, Howard St. John. Directed by Joseph Losey. Based on *Dreadful Summit.*

A confused boy, after seeing his bartender father beaten by a violent-tempered sports columnist, sets out during one night of confrontation to kill the man.

Leda. Times Films (French), 1961. Madeline Robinson, Antonella Lualdi, Jean-Paul Belmondo. Directed by Claude Chabrol. Based on *The Key to Nicholas Street.*

A middle-aged husband, living unhappily with his family in a French country house, turns his romantic attentions toward a young woman neighbor, who is found murdered.

Nothing but the Best. Royal Films (British), 1964. Alan Bates, Denholm Elliott, Harry Andrews, Millicent Martin. Directed by Clive Donner. Based on the story "The Best of Everything" (1952).

An ambitious young man, determined to get ahead, offers to share his flat with a discredited aristocratic type if the latter will groom him in the social graces; his lessons over, he kills his tutor.

House of Cards. Universal, 1968. George Peppard, Inger Stevens, Orson Welles, Keith Mitchell. Directed by John Guillermin. Based on the 1967 novel.

Down on his luck, an American drifter in Paris is hired as a tutor and is drawn into a fascist plot to overthrow the French government.

Television

Much of Ellin's shorter work has frequently been used by television anthology series. An example is "The Specialty of the House," presented by Alfred HITCHCOCK, who had initially claimed that network pressures prevented him from doing so.

EUSTACE, ROBERT. *See* MEADE, L. T.; SAYERS, DOROTHY L.

EUSTIS, HELEN (1916–). American novelist. Born in Cincinnati, Ohio, Miss Eustis attended Smith College in Massachusetts, where she won an award for creative writing. She has written only two novels but has also translated works, including mysteries, from French to English. She is married to press photographer Martin Harris.

The author's considerable reputation is based entirely on her first novel, *The Horizontal Man* (1946), the story of the murder of a professor at Hollymount, a fictional college much like her own alma mater. It received the Mystery Writers of America Edgar for best first mystery novel. Her only other book, *The Fool Killer* (1954), deals with a rural American folk legend and received an indifferent critical reception.

Film

The Fool Killer. Allied Artists, 1968. Anthony Perkins, Edward Albert, Salome Jens. Directed by Servando Gonzalez.

A twelve-year-old runaway boy meets a strange wanderer who may be the legendary avenger who kills fools with a hatchet.

EVANS, JOHN. *See* BROWNE, HOWARD.

F

FAIR, A. A. *See* GARDNER, ERLE STANLEY; COOL, BERTHA, AND DONALD LAM.

FAIRLIE, GERARD. *See* DRUMMOND, BULLDOG.

FALCON, THE (Creator: Michael ARLEN). In the story that bears his name, Gay Stanhope Falcon describes himself as hard-boiled, unlike the suave character that appears on the screen. He is tall, with a long, slim, dark face and deep-set, penetrating eyes. He earns his living by keeping his mouth shut and handling dangerous assignments. In "Gay Falcon" (1940), he breaks into the bedroom of beautiful Diana Temple and burglarizes her safe, confident that she will not call the police. He takes his haul to an insurance company, the officials of which are happy to see the stolen jewelry on which claims of a quarter of a million dollars have been paid during the past few years.

Tom Conway allows a gallant gesture to begin his interrogation of Barbara Hale in *The Falcon in Hollywood.* [*RKO*]

Films

The sophisticated adventurer (his first "real" name in his screen escapades is Gay Lawrence) was the only American series detective to die on the screen—in order to advance the career of George Sanders, who felt limited by the continuing role of the debonair semiscoundrel. Gay's brother Tom takes over as the Falcon (coincidentally, Sanders's role was shouldered by his brother, Tom Conway).

The Gay Falcon. RKO, 1941. Sanders, Wendy Barrie, Allen Jenkins, Gladys Cooper. Directed by Irving Reis.

The Falcon promises his fiancée not to aid any more damsels in distress but instead to enter the safe family brokerage firm; soon, however, at the behest of a pretty girl, he is in pursuit of jewel thieves who are crashing society balls. At the end of the film, he decides that sleuthing, not marriage, is to his taste.

A Date With the Falcon. RKO, 1941. Sanders, Barrie, James Gleason, Jenkins, Mona Maris. Directed by Reis.

The Falcon is about to leave town with another fiancée, to meet her family, when he learns that the inventor of an artificial diamond, which cannot be distinguished from the "real thing," has been kidnapped by a gang of criminals.

The Falcon Takes Over, RKO, 1942. Sanders, Lynn Bari, Gleason, Helen Gilbert, Ward Bond. Directed by Reis. The first screen use of Raymond CHANDLER's *Farewell, My Lovely* (1940), trimmed to suit the Falcon.

A hulking hood who has just killed a nightclub

owner forces the Falcon to find an old girl friend, named Velma, who has disappeared.

The Falcon's Brother. RKO, 1942. Sanders, Conway, Jane Randolph, Don Barclay, Amanda Varela, George Lewis. Directed by Stanley Logan.

Photographs in a magazine are a code message instructing Nazi agents to assassinate a South American diplomat. Gay's brother Tom joins him in exposing the spy ring, and when Gay dies heroically at the end of the film, Tom swears that he will carry on his work.

The Falcon Strikes Back. RKO, 1943. Conway, Harriett Hilliard, Randolph, Edgar Kennedy, Rita Corday, Directed by Edward Dmytryk.

The Falcon has been knocked unconscious in a cocktail bar—which vanishes, as do some war bonds. The trail leads to a large country hotel, where, while an elaborate puppet performance of *Scheherazade* is staged, several murders occur.

The Falcon in Danger. RKO, 1943. Conway, Jean Brooks, Elaine Shepard, Amelita Ward, Ed Gargen. Directed by William Clemens.

A large airliner crash-lands at an airport, but no one is found on board. The Falcon discovers that a fortune in securities is also missing.

The Falcon and the Co-Eds. RKO, 1943. Conway, Brooks, Corday, Isabel Jewel, George Givot. Directed by Clemens.

A complicated case of jealousy and murder unfolds for the Falcon at an exclusive girls' school.

The Falcon Out West. RKO, 1944. Conway, Barbara Hale, Carole Gallagher, Joan Barclay, Lyle Talbot. Directed by Clemens.

A wealthy Texan dies of snake poisoning while celebrating in a New York nightclub; the Falcon follows the man's fiancée, a model, back to the old Panhandle homestead.

The Falcon in Mexico. RKO, 1944. Conway, Maris, Martha Vickers, Nestor Paiva. Directed by William Berke.

A Mexican girl pleads with the Falcon to recover a recent portrait of herself, but the owner of the gallery in which it hangs is murdered, and the artist has supposedly been dead for fifteen years.

The Falcon in Hollywood. RKO, 1944. Conway, Hale, Veda Ann Borg, John Abbott, Sheldon Leonard. Directed by Gordon Douglas.

A movie studio is the interesting background for nearly all the action as the Falcon, on a visit to Hollywood, probes why the eight investors in a motion picture are being killed off one by one.

The Falcon in San Francisco. RKO, 1945. Conway, Corday, Sharyn Moffett, Faye Helm, Robert Armstrong. Directed by Joseph H. Lewis.

Heading west by train, the Falcon takes charge of a seven-year-old girl when her nurse is murdered; at the climax of the film, the sleuth is on board a ship that is about to explode.

The Falcon's Alibi. RKO, 1946. Conway, Corday, Vince Barnett, Jane Greer, Elisha Cook, Jr. Directed by Ray McCarey.

Stolen jewels and several murders implicate the Falcon; but he suspects the announcer of an all-night radio show.

The Falcon's Adventure. RKO, 1946. Conway, Madge Meredith, Robert Warwick, Myrna Dell. Directed by Berke.

The Falcon must take a formula for synthetic diamonds to Florida when the inventor is killed.

The Devil's Cargo. Film Classics, 1948. John Calvert (the third and last screen Falcon; for legal reasons, the Falcon's real name is changed to Michael Waring), Rochelle Hudson, Roscoe Karns, Talbot. Directed by John F. Link.

A man in prison, accused of murder, asks the Falcon's help just before he dies of poisoning.

Appointment with Murder. Film Classics, 1948. Calvert, Catherine Craig, Jack Reitzen, Talbot. Directed by Jack Bernhard.

The Falcon, an insurance investigator, tracks down stolen paintings and finds murder.

Search for Danger. Film Classics, 1949. Calvert, Dell, Albert Dekker, Douglas Fowley. Directed by Don Martin.

A gambler who disappears with a large betting sum leads the Falcon to two deaths.

Radio and Television

The Falcon—named Mike Waring—was portrayed by many actors during a long radio career that began on Mutual in 1945 and continued through the late 1940s: James Meighan, Les Damon, Berry Kroeger, Les Tremayne, and George Petrie. He was revived on television for a season during the mid-1950s with Charles McGraw as a gravel-voiced, tough Mike Waring in *The Adventures of the Falcon*.

FARJEON, B[ENJAMIN] L[EOPOLD] (1838–1903). English novelist. Born in London, he lived for a while in Australia and New Zealand, where he was coeditor of the *Otago Daily Times*, the first daily newspaper in that country. He returned to England to pursue a career as a novelist and playwright with considerable success. Many of his romantic novels are sensational and melodramatic mysteries. Newspaper reporters do most of the crime solving, despite the presence of several official lawmen, in *Great Porter Square* (1885) and *Samuel Boyd of Catchpole Square* (1899). The young "special crime reporter" from *The Evening Moon*, in search of a "scoop," solves the first mystery, and Dick Remington, an intelligent young girl, and Inspector Robson of Scotland Yard collaborate on the solution to the second. Perhaps the scarcest Farjeon mystery novel is *Devlin the Barber* (1888). *The Evening Moon*'s crime reporter returns in *The Mystery of M. Felix* (1890); in this novel, he is given a name—Robert Agnold.

FATHER BROWN. *See* BROWN, FATHER.

FAULKNER, WILLIAM (1897–1962). American novelist and short story writer whose tales of the South are chronicles of morbidity and perversion that sometimes contain elements of mystery, crime, and detection.

Born in Mississippi, he spent virtually his entire life in that state and used it as the background for his fiction. He did, however, work in Hollywood for Warner Brothers and other studios, writing some of the dialogue for Raymond CHANDLER's *The Big Sleep* (1946) and several screen plays. He won the Nobel Prize for Literature in 1949.

After writing several books that received little critical or popular attention, he wrote a melodramatic thriller, *Sanctuary* (1931), a bestial tale of human evil peopled with prostitutes, half-wits, and moonshiners. It became a best seller and a popular motion picture.

"Uncle" Gavin Stevens, the shrewd attorney of Yoknapatawpha County, investigates the crime in *Intruder in the Dust* (1948), in which a Negro is accused of murder. The case soon transcends his guilt or innocence, dealing with the larger moral problems of justice itself. The six tales in *Knight's Gambit* (1949) again feature Stevens, a corncob-pipe-smoking Phi Beta Kappa from Harvard who has an unorthodox approach to criminal investigation. "I am more interested in justice and human beings than in truth," he says. "In my time I have seen truth that was anything under the sun but just, and I have seen justice using tools I wouldn't want to touch with a ten-foot fence-rail."

William Faulkner.

Like those of another popular American detective of the South, UNCLE ABNER, Stevens's adventures are related by a nephew, Chick Mallison.

Films

The Story of Temple Drake. Paramount, 1933. Jack LaRue, Miriam Hopkins, William Gargan, Irving Pichel. Directed by Stephen Roberts. Based on *Sanctuary*.

A girl and a college youth on a drunken spree are kidnapped by a gangster; the boy is killed and the girl raped, but she remains with her seducer because of his physical appeal.

Intruder in the Dust. MGM, 1949. David Brian, Claude Jarman, Jr., Juano Hernandez. Directed by Clarence Brown.

In the deep South, a boy helps his uncle Gavin, a lawyer, clear a hapless Negro framed for the murder of a local lumberman.

Sanctuary. Twentieth Century-Fox, 1961. Lee Remick, Yves Montand, Bradford Dillman. Directed by Tony Richardson.

In the South of the 1920s, a belle overcome by moonshine falls for a dashing gangster and at his urging takes a room in a New Orleans house of prostitution.

FAUST, FREDERICK (1892–1944). American author of westerns and mysteries and the creator of Dr. Kildare. Faust was best known by his Max Brand pseudonym. Born in Seattle, Wash., he was a prolific contributor of virtually every kind of fiction to both the PULP MAGAZINES and the "slicks." Under three pseudonyms he published six mysteries in book form: *Cross over Nine* (1935) and *The Night Flower* (1936) as Walter C. Butler; *Secret Agent Number One* (1936), *Spy Meets Spy* (1937), and *The Bamboo Whistle* (1937) as Frederick Frost; and *Six Golden Angels* (1937) as Max Brand. A series of humorous detective stories published only in *Detective Fiction Weekly* (1935–1936) involve two police sergeants who compete with each other: Angus Campbell, a dour Scotchman, and Patrick O'Rourke, a happy-go-lucky Irishman. Other Faust mysteries published in magazines did not appear in book form until recently. *The Granduca* (1973), for instance, was published as a book thirty-seven years after its magazine debut.

FEARING, KENNETH (FLEXNER) (1902–1961). American writer noted for the dynamic quality of his poetry. Born in Oak Park, Ill., he was the son of attorney Harry L. Fearing and Olive (Flexner) Fearing. He left home to attend the University of Wisconsin and graduated in 1924. He then worked as a newspaper reporter in Chicago and also had such varied odd jobs as salesman, mill hand, and clerk.

After moving to New York City, he was

Kenneth Fearing. *[Photo by Arni]*

extremely active as a commercial free-lancer, using various pseudonyms, and he wrote highly praised poetry later collected in *Angel Arms* (1929), *Poems* (1935), *Collected Poems* (1940), and other volumes. Fearing claimed that he had been influenced by poets ranging from Villon to Keats and that he wrote in the Walt Whitman tradition. He won Guggenheim fellowships in 1936 and 1939. He also worked for *Time* magazine.

An early marriage produced one son and ended in divorce. Fearing married painter Nan Lurie in 1945. He wrote several novels including *The Hospital* (1939) and *Clark Gifford's Body* (1942), a fantasy-thriller, set in a mythical country, that depicts fifth-column seizures of public property and is told in documentary form. *The Generous Heart* (1954) and *The Crozart Story* (1960) are both thrillers.

By the end of the 1930s critics thought that Fearing's poetry had begun to falter (nonetheless, before his death in 1961, his poems were published occasionally in *Poetry* and *The New Yorker*). On the other hand, his fiction was becoming popular and reaching wide audiences.

Dagger of the Mind (1941) is set in a summer artists' colony. One of the characters plans the perfect crime, only to become the victim of someone else's plot. It is an unconventional performance; Raymond CHANDLER called it "a savage piece of intellectual double-talk." Much more satisfactory is *The Big Clock* (1946), a breathless tale of pursuit in which the megalomaniac publisher of a *Time*-like magazine commits a murder that is inadvertently witnessed by an unknown underling. The publisher arranges to have his best crime reporter head the search for the missing witness (now the chief suspect), but the hunter and the hunted turn out to be identical. *The Loneliest Girl in the World* (1951) is a minor work about a double suicide and its investigation by the heroine.

Film

The Big Clock. Paramount, 1948. Ray Milland, Charles Laughton, Maureen O'Hara, Elsa Lanchester. Directed by John Farrow.

The ruthless publisher of *Crimeways* magazine kills his unhappy mistress in a fit of rage and attempts to pin the crime on a stranger seen leaving her apartment. He gives the manhunt assignment to his ace reporter, who secretly is that stranger.

FELL, DR. GIDEON (Creator: John Dickson CARR). The great 250-pound detective was modeled after G. K. CHESTERTON, the creator of Father BROWN and a boyhood idol of Carr. At times, Fell resembles a madman, making no attempt to control his eccentricity; yet he somehow retains his dignity. The only cases for which he can muster any enthusiasm are those involving "miracles"—impossible crimes which have an aura of the supernatural about them but which he ultimately solves with a reasonable explanation.

In *The Man Who Could Not Shudder*, Gideon Fell is described this way: "Vast and beaming, wearing a box-pleated cape as big as a tent, he sat . . . with his hands folded over his crutch stick. His shovel hat almost touched the canopy overhead. His eyeglasses were set precariously on a pink nose; the black ribbon of these glasses blew wide with each vast puff of breath which rumbled up from under his three chins, and agitated his bandit's moustache. But what you noticed most was the twinkle in his eye. A huge joy of life, a piratical swagger merely to be hearing and seeing and thinking, glowed from him like steam from a furnace. It was like meeting Old King Cole or Father Christmas."

Fell enjoys more than one glass of beer, savors his tobacco, likes to build houses of cards, and, although he enjoys telling jokes, is constantly surprised when other people laugh at them. Unlike most members of his profession, he enjoys mystery stories.

CHECKLIST

1933	*Hag's Nook*
1933	*The Mad Hatter Mystery*
1934	*The Blind Barber*
1934	*The Eight of Swords*
1935	*Death Watch*
1935	*The Hollow Man* (U.S. title: *The Three Coffins*)
1936	*The Arabian Nights Murder*
1937	*To Wake the Dead*

1938 *The Crooked Hinge*
1939 *The Black Spectacles* (U.S. title: *The Problem of the Green Capsule*)
1939 *The Problem of the Wire Cage*
1940 *The Man Who Could Not Shudder*
1941 *The Case of the Constant Suicides*
1941 *Death Turns the Tables* (British title: *The Seat of the Scornful*)
1944 *Till Death Do Us Part*
1946 *He Who Whispers*
1947 *Dr. Fell, Detective* (s.s.)
1947 *The Sleeping Sphinx*
1949 *Below Suspicion*
1954 *The Third Bullet and Other Stories* (s.s.; contains three stories about Fell)
1958 *The Dead Man's Knock*
1960 *In Spite of Thunder*
1963 *The Men Who Explained Miracles* (s.s.; contains two stories about Fell)
1965 *The House at Satan's Elbow*
1966 *Panic in Box C*
1967 *Dark of the Moon*

FEN, GERVASE (Creator: Edmund CRISPIN). Professor of English language and literature at the University of Oxford, Fen is about forty years old, tall, and very thin. His clean-shaven face is ruddy and usually cheerful. His dark hair is carefully plastered down with water, but it manages to break out into disaffected fragments toward the crown. He wears an overlarge raincoat, and his hats have been pronounced "extraordinary."

Fen's wife is an ordinary and sensible little woman, and the marriage is happy. Fen is the proud owner of a disreputable-looking red roadster—in spite of his limited vehicular skills.

The erudite professor suffers from a lack of patience and is often despondent when he has overcommitted himself and cannot meet his obligations. However, he radiates goodwill and boundless enthusiasm and dashes around with more energy than discretion as he tries to solve mysteries in a highly undonnish manner.

Fen claims to be "the only literary critic turned detective in the whole of fiction." His first adventure, *The Case of the Gilded Fly* (1944; U.S. title: *Obsequies at Oxford*), was written in two weeks and was highly acclaimed. Set in Oxford in a little theater group, it concerns the mysterious death of an attractive but unloved actress. *Holy Disorders* (1945) is set in the cathedral town of Tolnbridge; the elements of murder, espionage, and witchcraft are well blended.

The Moving Toyshop (1946) is about a poet who, immediately upon stumbling across a corpse in a room above a toyshop, is knocked unconscious. When he comes to, he finds corpse and toyshop missing and a grocery store in their place. The influence of John Dickson CARR can be detected in this baffling puzzle. *Swan Song* (1947; U.S. title: *Dead and Dumb*), with its operatic setting and its humor, especially that involving Fen's car, is entertaining but a minor work. *Love Lies Bleeding* (1948) concerns three murders and a quest for a long-lost priceless Shakespearean manuscript. The book is included in the HAYCRAFT-QUEEN CORNERSTONE LIBRARY.

In *Buried for Pleasure* (1948) Fen's efforts to gain a seat in Parliament are complicated by the poisoning of a now-respectable lady whose former profession was the oldest one, and by the murder of a police inspector who was once Fen's classmate. The novel also introduces Inspector Humbleby, who aids in later Fen investigations.

Frequent Hearses (1950; U.S. title: *Sudden Vengeance*) describes a film studio's attempt to make a movie about the life of famed poet Alexander Pope, but the director, his sister, and the leading lady are not going to be present at the first screening. Crispin's film-making experience lends a note of authenticity to the proceedings. *The Long Divorce* (1951), Fen's last full-length adventure (to date), mixes equal amounts of crime and romance with controlled humor.

Fourteen of the sixteen cases in *Beware of the Trains* (1953) involve Fen.

FERRARS, E[LIZABETH] X. (pseudonym of Morna Doris Brown; 1907–). English novelist and mystery story writer. Born Morna Doris MacTaggart in Rangoon, Burma, to a Scottish father and an Irish-German mother, she grew up in England, taking a diploma in journalism in 1928 at London University. She wrote several novels under her own name before she began to write mysteries in 1940, at which time she adopted her mother's maiden name as her pseudonym. Also in 1940, she married Professor Robert Brown, a botanist. The Browns have lived in many English college cities, but Edinburgh is their home.

Although she has written more than thirty books, Mrs. Brown has not gained great fame in the mystery field. She has not had a series detective in most of her books, though young Toby Dyke does appear in several. She has written short stories in which there is an amateur detective, a garrulous old curmudgeon named Jonas P. Jonas. In discussing her *Enough to Kill a Horse* (1955), Jacques BARZUN and Wendell Hertig TAYLOR describe Mrs. Brown as having "a sound enough grasp of motives and human relations and a due regard for probability and technique, but whose people and plot are so standard. . . ."

FISH, ROBERT L. (1912–). American parodist and detective story writer. A native of Cleveland, Fish was in his late forties when, in 1960, his first mystery story was published. Since then, he has become a successful and prolific writer. When he

Somewhat younger and with a name different from that of his Robert L. Fish inspiration, the police lieutenant in *Bullitt* (Steve McQueen) must stop an escaping murderer in a crowded airport as passengers scatter for safety. [*Warner Brothers*]

submitted the story "The Adventure of the Ascot Tie," a Sherlock HOLMES parody, to *Ellery Queen's Mystery Magazine*, he was living in Brazil with his wife and two teenage daughters. He had been a consulting engineer to the Brazilian plastics industry for ten years. Fish's hero is called "Schlock Homes," and his assistant is "Dr. Watney"; they operate from 221B Bagel Street. The first twelve stories in the series were collected in *The Incredible Schlock Homes* (1966). A second collection, *The Memoirs of Schlock Homes*, appeared in 1974.

Under the pseudonym Robert L. Pike, Fish has written police procedural novels and short stories about Lieutenant Clancy of the New York Police Department's 52d Precinct. He used another ichthyological pen name, A. C. Lamprey, for "Gumshoe Glossary," a series of comic definitions of criminological terms which appeared in *Ellery Queen's Mystery Magazine*. In 1963, under his own name, Fish completed *The Assassination Bureau, Ltd.*, a spy novel left unfinished by Jack London. He has also written a popular series of novels about a Rio de Janeiro policeman, Captain José DA SILVA. A more recent series, beginning with *The Hochmann Miniatures* (1967), introduced Kek Huuygens. Labeled "the world's greatest smuggler," he has never been caught, although he is alleged to have smuggled "everything from an original Bach cantata to a two-ton Indian elephant." The other books in this series are *Whirligig* (1970), *Tricks of the Trade* (1972), and *The Wager* (1974).

Critics have been divided in their opinions on the Schlock Homes stories. They are liked by Ellery QUEEN (author), Vincent STARRETT, Dorothy B. HUGHES, and Anthony BOUCHER, who believed that they were "the best parody-pastiches of Sherlock Holmes now being written," but Jacques BARZUN and Wendell Hertig TAYLOR have found them to be "distressing" and "indifferent." There has been greater unanimity about the well-received Da Silva series. The first of these stories, *The Fugitive* (1962), dealing with Nazis who have escaped to South

America, gained Fish the Mystery Writers of America Edgar for best first novel. The 1968 movie *Bullitt,* based on *Mute Witness* (1963), written under the Pike pseudonym, also won an Edgar, as did a short story, "Moonlight Gardener" (1971), originally published in *Argosy.*

Films

Lieutenant Clancy undergoes radical changes in his only film—he is portrayed as a much younger man by Steve McQueen, and his name is changed to Bullitt.

Bullitt. Warner Brothers, 1968. McQueen, Robert Vaughn, Jacqueline Bisset, Robert Duvall. Directed by Peter Yates.

A police lieutenant is chosen by an opportunistic politician to guard a racketeer who is about to testify before a crime committee, but the hoodlum is shot down.

The Assassination Bureau was made into a film in England in 1969, with Diana Rigg, Telly Savalas, Oliver Reed, and Curt Jurgens; it was directed by Basil Dearden. It bears little relation to the book.

FISHER, STEVE (1912–). American author of mysteries and film scripts. Born Stephen Gould Fisher, he went to New York from California in the 1930s, hoping to become a writer. He had already spent four years in the Navy, writing over 200 stories and articles for Navy publications. He settled in Greenwich Village and became a friend of fellow writer Frank GRUBER, who described their struggle to become successful writers for the PULP MAGAZINES in

Promoter Victor Mature and Betty Grable come across the body of Betty's sister (Carole Landis), a girl Mature had been grooming for stardom, in the screen version of Steve Fisher's *I Wake Up Screaming.* [*Twentieth Century-Fox*]

The Pulp Jungle (1967). After finally being published in the leading pulp magazine, BLACK MASK, Fisher turned to such "slicks" as *Collier's*, *Liberty*, and *Cosmopolitan*. He then went to Hollywood, where he became a highly successful screenwriter, numbering among his many credits *The Lady in the Lake* (1946), based on Raymond CHANDLER's novel; *Dead Reckoning* (1947), which starred Humphrey Bogart; and *Susan Slept Here* (1954). He also wrote many scripts for television series and anthology programs, receiving five Emmy Award nominations. He is still an active television writer.

Fisher's first novel, *Spend the Night* (1935), which he describes as "a dreadful book," was published under the pseudonym Grant Lane. As Stephen Gould, he wrote two books, *Murder of the Admiral* (1936) and *Murder of the Pigboat Skipper* (1937), which draw upon his Navy experience for background, as do two nonmysteries, *Destroyer* (1941) and *Destination Tokyo* (1943), published under his own name.

His most famous mystery, *I Wake Up Screaming* (1941), is set in a Hollywood studio and concerns the murder of a promising young movie star. An earlier work, the short story "If Christmas Comes" (1937), also used a film studio locale and prompted Ellery QUEEN (author) to write (when he reprinted it in *Ellery Queen's Mystery Magazine*, 1944): "Fisher packs more emotion, more heart, into his yarns than most contemporary writers of the detective story."

The only other Stephen Gould book by Fisher is *Homicide Johnny* (1940). Other novels under the Fisher name include *Satan's Angel* (1935), *The Night before Murder* (1939), *Winter Kill* (1946), *Giveaway* (1954), and *The Big Dream* (1970).

Films

I Wake Up Screaming. Twentieth Century-Fox, 1941. Betty Grable, Victor Mature, Carole Landis, Laird Cregar. Directed by H. Bruce Humberstone.

On a bet, a sports promoter builds a pretty waitress into a celebrated cover girl but is ultimately accused of her murder and hounded by a relentless police detective.

The film was remade by Twentieth Century-Fox in 1953 as *Vicki*, with Jeanne Crain, Elliott Reid, Jean Peters, and Richard Boone and directed by Harry Horner.

FITZGERALD, F. SCOTT (1896–1940). A giant of modern American literature whose contribution to the mystery genre is negligible. However, his first published work was a murder story, "The Mystery of the Raymond Mortage," written when Fitzgerald was thirteen years old and first published in September 1909 in *Now and Then*, the publication of St. Paul Academy. The plot is flawed in that the young author neglected to bring the mortage of the title into the story in any way. It was reprinted by Random House in 1960 in a rare pamphlet limited to 750 copies.

FLANAGAN, THOMAS (1923–). American mystery story writer. Born in Greenwich, Conn., Flanagan attended Amherst and received an M.A. degree from Columbia University. He served on an LST in the Pacific during World War II.

His first short story, "The Fine Italian Hand," a historical mystery set in Renaissance times, was selected as the best first story in the 1948 contest of *Ellery Queen's Mystery Magazine (EQMM)*. "The Cold Winds of Adesta," chosen best story in the 1951 *EQMM* contest, was the first of several stories about Major Tennente, an honest policeman in a corrupt foreign dictatorship.

FLEMING, IAN (LANCASTER) (1908–1964). English journalist, secret service agent, and author of novels featuring literature's most famous spy—James BOND, the notorious 007.

Born in London, the son of Evelyn Beatrice (Ste. Croix Rose) and Valentine Fleming, a major and a

Ian Fleming. This portrait by Amherst Villiers was used as the frontispiece to the limited edition (250 copies, numbered and signed) of *On Her Majesty's Secret Service*, published by Cape in 1963.

Conservative member of Parliament, Ian was the younger brother of Peter Fleming, also an author. He was educated at Eton, the Royal Military Academy at Sandhurst, the University of Munich, and the University of Geneva. After serving as the Moscow correspondent for Reuter's, he spent several years working as a banker and stockbroker. But, in 1939, he returned to Moscow, ostensibly as a reporter for the *London Times* but actually (and unofficially) as a representative of the Foreign Office. He also performed secret service work as a personal assistant to the Director of Naval Intelligence. From 1949 to 1964 he was the foreign manager of Kemsley (later Thompson) Newspapers. In 1952 he married Anne Geraldine Charteris (formerly Lady Rothermere); they had one son, Caspar.

Fleming wrote several books of various types, for example *Chitty-Chitty-Bang-Bang* (1964), a juvenile; *The Diamond Smugglers* (1957), true accounts of gem smugglers; and *Thrilling Cities* (1963), essays on his favorite cities around the world. The works for which he will be remembered, however, are the enormously popular tales of 007, the superspy. Much of Fleming's personality and appearance—although idealized—is to be found in Bond. John Pearson, Fleming's biographer, described the handsome, buoyant writer as a modern-day Lord Byron: "tall, saturnine, hollow-cheeked, his face lopsided with its magnificently broken nose."

During World War II Fleming approached author William Plomer and told him that he wanted to write a thriller. Plomer thought that his idea was good but that the hero ought to be a series character. Fleming frankly acknowledged that he had no literary pretensions; he simply wanted to make money. By the time he died, he had reportedly earned $2.8 million from the books alone. In the decade since his death, none of the fourteen Bond books has gone out of print; they still sell in huge numbers, in both hard cover and paperback; and the motion pictures based on them have grossed some of the largest sums in cinematic history. The popularity of the adventures of 007 skyrocketed in the United States when it was learned that President John F. Kennedy was an avid fan, and the films boosted book sales.

Fleming's years with British Intelligence make his novels more authentic than other espionage stories. In his introduction to *From Russia, with Love* (1957), Fleming wrote that "a great deal of the background to this story is accurate. SMERSH . . . exists and remains today the most secret department of the Soviet government. . . ."

Fleming eventually tired of his superhero, calling the books "trivial piffle." Some critics call them snobbish and bigoted (the villains are always foreigners, usually Russian); they are in fact old-fashioned fairy tales told in a contemporary setting. The forces of Good have superhuman strengths—physically, intellectually, and morally—and the forces of Evil are almost nonhumanly ruthless and vicious. As in the great myths of another age, Good emerges triumphant.

FLEMING, OLIVER. *See* MACDONALD, PHILIP.

FLETCHER, J[OSEPH] S[MITH] (1863–1935). English author. Born in Halifax, Yorkshire, he went to London at the age of eighteen to become a journalist and writer, contributing articles on country life for the next decade under the pseudonym Son of the Soil. He also wrote dialect poetry, biography, historical fiction, and nonfiction books which, combined with his mysteries, totaled more than 100 volumes by the time of his death in Dorking, Surrey.

Although popular in England, Fletcher was relatively unknown in the United States until President Woodrow Wilson read and applauded *The Middle Temple Murder* (1918), in which a young newspaperman decides to improve his paper's circulation by investigating the murder of an unknown man and publishing his findings. As the case progresses, he finds himself enmeshed in a problem involving many people he knows. Fletcher's only other novel demonstrating comparable skill is *The Charing Cross Mystery* (1923), in which Hetherwick, a young barrister, becomes involved in a double murder. Riding a late-night train to his rooms, he becomes curious about two men in the smoking compartment. Just as the train pulls into Charing Cross, one of the men drops dead. The next day the other is found dead in his ghetto flat.

Fletcher's best-known detectives are Roger Camberwell, in *The Murder of the Ninth Baronet* (1932), *The Ebony Box* (1934), *The Eleventh Hour* (1935), and other works; and the title characters of two of his many short story collections, *The Adventures of Archer Dawe, Sleuth-Hound* (1909) and *Paul Campenhaye: Specialist in Criminology* (1914); Campenhaye also appears in three stories in *The Massingham Butterfly and Other Stories* (1926).

FLYNT, JOSIAH (pseudonym of Josiah Flynt Willard; 1869–1907). American hobo and author of crime fiction. Born in Appleton, Wis., he left college for an itinerant life, riding freight cars, stealing a horse and buggy (then escaping from jail after being arrested), and tramping around Europe. His largely autobiographical works deal with crime and criminals in a sympathetic manner. *The Powers That Prey* (1900), a collection of short stories coauthored by Flynt and Francis Walton (pseudonym of Alfred Hodder, 1866–1907), records incidents that support the authors' contention that the "Under World" of criminals and the "Upper World" of policemen are in league out of necessity. In *Notes of an Itinerant Policeman* (1900) Flynt recounts his purportedly

The first edition of this young criminal's biography was published by Dodd, Mead in 1903.

true adventures as a law-enforcement officer who lived among tramps and criminals. *The Rise of Ruderick Clowd* (1903) is a novel about a young man driven to a life of crime.

FOOTNER, (WILLIAM) HULBERT (1879–1944). Canadian-American author, actor, and playwright. Born in Hamilton, Ontario, the son of Frances Christine (Mills) and Harold John Footner, he received a high school education in New York City before beginning a journalism career in New York and then in Alberta. He married Gladys Marsh in 1916; they had five children. He was living in Maryland at the time of his death.

His first books were mystery-adventure novels set in the Northwest. Soon he began writing detective stories and thrillers involving Amos Lee Mappin, an amateur detective who resembles Dickens's Mr. Pickwick, in *The Death of a Celebrity* (1938), *The Murder That Had Everything* (1939), and *Orchids to Murder* (1945), among many others; and Madame Rosika Storey, a stunningly beautiful young woman who describes herself as "a practical psychologist—specializing in the feminine." Her adventures are recorded in *The Under Dogs* (1925), *Madame Storey* (s.s.; 1926), *The Velvet Hand* (s.s.; 1928), *The Viper* (1930; three stories, two from *The Velvet Hand*), *Easy to Kill* (1931), *The Casual Murderer* (s.s.; 1932), *The Almost Perfect Murder* (s.s.; 1933), and *Dangerous Cargo* (1934).

FORBES, STANTON (pseudonym of DeLoris [Stanton] Forbes; 1923–   ). American mystery writer. Born DeLoris Stanton in Kansas City, Mo., the author grew up and attended schools in Wichita, Kans. She did newspaper work in Oklahoma and Louisiana before moving to Wellesley, Mass., where she was associate editor of the *Wellesley Townsman* until her retirement in April 1973. She is married to William J. Forbes and has three children, one by an earlier marriage.

Mrs. Forbes's earliest mysteries were short stories published under the name Dee Forbes. With a fellow Wellesley resident, Helen Rydell, she wrote her first four mystery novels under the joint pseudonym Forbes Rydell. Her first book alone, *Grieve for the Past* (1963), earned her a best mystery runner-up scroll from the Mystery Writers of America. Her series detective, Knute Severson of the Boston police, was created under her Tobias Wells pseudonym. In *Dead by the Light of the Moon* (1967) he investigates a murder committed during the Northeastern power blackout of November 1965.

FORD, COREY. *See* VANCE, PHILO.

FORD, ELBUR. *See* HOLT, VICTORIA.

FORD, LESLIE (pseudonym of Zenith Jones Brown; 1898–   ). Born in Smith River, Calif., she was the youngest of eleven children of an Episcopal clergyman. All the children were named for biblical characters or early Christian martyrs; Zenith is a short form of her given name, Zitzenith, which, in turn, is a variation of the spelling of Nazephatha, the name of David's mother. She grew up in Tacoma, Wash., and married Ford K. Brown after her graduation from the University of Washington. They have one daughter, Janet, who is a New York City attorney.

While the Browns were in England on his Guggenheim fellowship in 1928, Mrs. Brown wrote her first mystery. The book, *Murder of an Old Man*, was published in England in 1929 under the pseudonym David Frome; it has never been published in the United States.

Brown became professor of English at St. John's College in Annapolis, Md., on their return to the United States in 1931, and they have lived there since. During the World War II period Mrs. Brown wrote about military nurses under another pseudonym, Brenda Conrad. She is very active in Historic Annapolis, a group seeking to preserve the antiquities and homes of that city.

Under the Frome pseudonym she wrote a highly successful series about a Welshman, Evan PINKERTON. Her publisher persuaded her also to write a series of mysteries set in the United States. In 1931 she took the name Leslie Ford and in 1937 introduced her most popular sleuths, Grace LATHAM and Colonel John Primrose, who had previously appeared in several novelettes published in magazines.

The Ford books are set in many different cities,

Mrs. Brown's life and travels being the source of the authentic detail. This is especially true of Georgetown, where Mrs. Latham and Colonel Primrose live, and Annapolis, scene of the nonseries mysteries *By the Watchman's Clock* (1932) and *Date with Death* (1949). *The Town Cried Murder* (1939) is set in restored colonial Williamsburg, Va. The author spent six weeks in San Francisco shortly after the bombing of Pearl Harbor doing research for *Siren in the Night* (1943), a mystery about a murder during an air raid alert. The *Philadelphia Murder Story* (1945) tells of murder at the headquarters of *The Saturday Evening Post*, which serialized most of her books. The locale was suggested by the magazine's editors.

The Ford mysteries, always extremely popular, have been reprinted and remain available in paperback editions. However, they were often criticized because of the "had-I-but-known" excesses of the narrator, Grace Latham (*see* "HAD-I-BUT-KNOWN" SCHOOL). The Colonel's fortuitous habit of turning up all over the world in time to rescue Mrs. Latham was questioned.

A late book, *Trial by Ambush* (1962; British title: *Trial from Ambush*), represented a radical, but successful, departure for Mrs. Brown. It did not use a series detective and dealt, albeit circumspectly, with rape and abnormal psychology.

FORESTER, C[ECIL] S[COTT] (1899–1966). English novelist; author of the Horatio Hornblower series. Born in Cairo, Egypt, the son of George F. and Sarah (Troughton) Forester, he spent part of his early childhood traveling in Corsica, Spain, and France. He was brought up in a London suburb and educated at the lower school of Dulwich College and then at the college itself (1910–1917). Forester studied medicine at a hospital in London, but his lack of commitment caused him to turn from medicine to writing.

In 1917 he contributed verse to *Nash's* magazine and the *English Review*, but it was not until the publication of his first novel, *Payment Deferred* (1926), that he achieved success.

In 1926 Forester married Katherine Belcher (they had two sons). They spent their honeymoon sailing in a dinghy called the *Annie Marble*, after a character in *Payment Deferred*, and toured England, France, and Germany. Soon afterward they published two travel books.

Forester also wrote *The Gun* (1933), *The General* (1936), and other novels and covered the Spanish Civil War in 1936–1937 and Prague during the Nazi occupation as a newspaper correspondent. *The Happy Return* (1937; U.S. title: *Beat to Quarters*), *Flying Colours* (1938), and *A Ship of the Line* (1939) introduced Captain Horatio Hornblower.

In 1934 Forester wrote a play, *Nurse Cavell*, with mystery writer C. E. Bechhofer Roberts and the following year produced the romantic thriller *The African Queen*.

Although Forester disliked Hollywood, he settled in Berkeley, Calif., in the early 1940s, spending time also in England and New York. In 1944 he and his wife were divorced; three years later he married Dorothy Foster. At this time, a serious attack of arteriosclerosis left him a semi-invalid.

Payment Deferred is a gripping account of a man who murders his nephew for financial gain and prospers until his conscience takes over. It is of historic interest and importance in that it stands midway between those of the "originators" of the inverted tale, Mrs. Marie Belloc LOWNDES and R. Austin FREEMAN, and the later work of Francis Iles (Anthony BERKELEY), who, with his followers, gave new life and dimension to the form and began to deemphasize the detective story in favor of the modern crime novel.

Plain Murder (1930) is another inverted tale that, although skillful and amusing, lacks the intensity of its predecessor. It concerns the efforts of three advertising men to avoid dismissal from their jobs and contains two murders and a near miss.

Play and Film

In 1931 Jeffrey Dell fashioned a successful stage play from *Payment Deferred*, starring Charles Laughton and Elsa Lanchester; it has become a stock favorite. The following year a film was also based on the novel.

Payment Deferred. MGM, 1932. Laughton, Ray Milland, Maureen O'Sullivan, Dorothy Peterson. Directed by Lothar Mendes.

A bank clerk, desperate for money and hounded by his wife, murders his nephew for the cash the latter is carrying and buries the body in his garden.

FORTUNE, REGGIE (Creator: H. C. BAILEY). Although generally called "Mr.," Reginald Fortune is actually a practicing physician and surgeon who acts as special adviser to Scotland Yard on medical matters. His associates at the Yard are the bitter, if grudgingly respectful, chief of the CID, Stanley Lomas, and the openly admiring and devoted Superintendent Bell, Lomas's assistant.

Reggie was born in a London suburb near the end of Victoria's reign, the only son of a middle-class doctor. His schooling at Charterhouse and Oxford, completed with little distinction, was understood to be preparation for a career in his father's footsteps. An amiable and popular student, he displayed an extraordinary interest in a variety of peculiar subjects. He went to a London hospital and concentrated on pathology but soon gave it up to begin general practice at his birthplace. When two criminal cases came to his attention early in his career, he was

The aristocratic Reggie Fortune was probably the most popular detective in England between World Wars I and II. This illustration appears on the dust wrapper of the first American edition of *Case for Mr. Fortune,* published for the Crime Club by Doubleday, Doran in 1932.

Reggie Fortune looks more handsome and less cherubic than usual in this illustration, which appears on the dust wrapper of the first edition of *Mr. Fortune Wonders,* published by Ward, Lock in 1933.

unable to ignore his calling.

Plump and younger-looking than his years, Reggie is a gourmet who enjoys virtually all fine food and drink—except port and whiskey. He has blond hair and round, full cheeks that appear never to have been shaved; the look of candor and innocence in his blue eyes has contributed to his being christened "Cherub" by an irreverent young lady.

Reggie enjoys life and feasts on its pleasures—unless they happen to include hunting or any activity that attracts great crowds. He loves his wife (who has complained once or twice about the difficulties of being married to a small boy) and is happiest in his laboratory or garden. He is bighearted, especially toward children. Although his genteel benevolence seems overly mannered, he can be tough physically as well as intellectually. He solves crimes by having, as he says, a "simple faith in facts" plus "no imagination"—he just believes in evidence.

Reggie has an "old-fashioned" mind, described thus by Bailey in the introduction to *Meet Mr. Fortune,* an omnibus volume published in 1942. "Insofar as this refers to morals it means that he holds by the standard principles of conduct and responsibility, of right and wrong, of sin and punishment. He does not always accept the law of a case as justice, and has always been known to act on his own responsibility in contriving the punishment of those who could not legally be found guilty or the immunity of those who were not legally innocent."

Some people find Reggie's speech mannerisms grating. A middle-aged, cherubic doctor uttering such phrases as "Oh, my aunt!" or "My dear chap! Oh, my dear chap!" can be almost as offensive as the man who points to the end-of-day crowds leaving their offices and says, "Look at 'em, all glad they're alive and lettin' live and goin' home to enjoy it. Same like me. The common people of whom I am the chief." Reggie drives a Rolls-Royce.

CHECKLIST

1920	*Call Mr. Fortune* (s.s.)
1923	*Mr. Fortune's Practice* (s.s.)
1925	*Mr. Fortune's Trials* (s.s.)
1927	*Mr. Fortune, Please* (s.s.)
1929	*Mr. Fortune Speaking* (s.s.)
1930	*Mr. Fortune Explains* (s.s.)
1932	*Case for Mr. Fortune* (s.s.)
1933	*Mr. Fortune Wonders* (s.s.)
1934	*The Shadow on the Wall*
1935	*Mr. Fortune Objects* (s.s.)
1936	*A Clue for Mr. Fortune* (s.s.)
1937	*Black Land, White Land*
1938	*This Is Mr. Fortune* (s.s.)
1939	*The Great Game* (also features Joshua CLUNK)
1940	*The Bishop's Crime*
1940	*Mr. Fortune Here* (s.s.)
1942	*No Murder* (U.S. title: *The Apprehensive Dog*)
1943	*Mr. Fortune Finds a Pig*
1944	*The Cat's Whiskers* (British title: *Dead Man's Effects*)
1946	*The Life Sentence*
1948	*Saving a Rope* (U.S. title: *Save a Rope*)

FRANCIS, DICK (1920–). Welsh jockey and mystery writer. Born near Tenby, Francis helped run his father's hunting stable when he was fifteen. Since then, except for World War II service as a bomber pilot, he has been associated with the sport of steeplechase racing. He became champion jockey in 1954 and raced under the Queen Mother's colors for four years. He had a 10-length lead in the 1956 Grand National when his mount, Devon Loch, collapsed in the stretch. When Francis retired in 1957, he had been in 2,305 races and had compiled the excellent record of 345 wins, 285 seconds, and 240 thirds.

Dick Francis began his series of suspense novels in 1962, and his first novel, *Dead Cert*, was an immediate success. He used his intimate knowledge of horse racing to produce what has often been called the best series of sports mysteries ever written. His books have explored almost every aspect of the sport, although most often the viewpoint has been that of a jockey or an airplane pilot. In *Odds Against*, his hero is Sid Halley, a crippled former jockey who is now a private detective investigating a scheme that could destroy racing in England. In *For Kicks* an amateur detective poses as a stableboy to investigate an apparently foolproof method of fixing races. The protagonist in *Flying Finish* is a man who transports horses from one country to another.

Following his retirement from the track, Francis became racing correspondent for the *Sunday Express*. His protagonist in *Forfeit*, James Tyrone, holds a similar position with a fictional paper, the *Sunday Blaze*. Francis's only work of nonfiction, *The Sport of Queens* (1957), is his autobiography.

That Dick Francis could write about his sport with clarity and authenticity was not overly surprising. That he would be able to generate so much suspense in each book that *The Atlantic Monthly* called him "the best thriller writer going" was less expected. Critics have also praised his inventiveness and tight plotting. Virtually the only fault noticed in his work is the tendency, pointed out by Jacques BARZUN and Wendell Hertig TAYLOR, to create heroes of unbelievable stoicism and pit them against criminals of equally extreme villainy.

For Kicks received a runner-up award from the British Crime Writers' Association in 1965. *Forfeit* was presented with the Mystery Writers of America Edgar as the best novel of 1969.

CHECKLIST

1962 *Dead Cert*
1964 *Nerve*
1965 *Odds Against*
1965 *For Kicks*
1966 *Flying Finish*
1967 *Blood Sport*
1969 *Forfeit*
1969 *Enquiry*
1970 *Rat Race*
1971 *Bonecrack*
1972 *Smokescreen*
1973 *Slayride*
1974 *Knockdown*
1975 *High Stakes*

FRANKAU, GILBERT (1884–1952). English novelist and short story writer. After completing his studies at Eton, he entered the cigar business with his father and married Dorothea Drummond Black; they had two daughters, one of whom became the popular novelist Pamela Frankau. There were later wives and, by his own admission, many other women in his life.

Frankau wrote two novels of suspense and espionage, *The Lonely Man* (1932) and *Winter of Discontent* (1941; U.S. title: *Air Ministry, Room 28*), but his best detective adventures appear in his short story collections, *Concerning Peter Jackson and Others* (1931), *Wine, Women, and Waiters* (1932), *Secret Services* (1934), and *Experiments in Crime* (1937).

FRANKENSTEIN (Written by: Mary SHELLEY). The most famous Gothic novel ever written. *Frankenstein* is a weird and fantastic story, unrealistic and horrible, yet poignant and memorable.

Dr. Victor Frankenstein, a brilliant young scientist, discovers the secret of life and creates an 8-foot giant from parts of cadavers obtained from dissecting rooms, butcher shops, and hospitals. The gentle monster's grotesque appearance frightens all who see him. Rebuffed by man when he seeks only friendship, the monster vows vengeance and kills Victor's young brother. Succumbing to his threats of random killing, Victor creates a female companion for the monster, but at the last moment his conscience causes him to destroy it. The enraged monster tells Victor that he will regret his action and kills Henry Clerval, a friend and fellow scientist, and Victor's bride, Elizabeth, on her wedding night. Promising vengeance of his own, Victor chases the monster into the polar regions but dies before he can avenge the murders. The unrepentant monster claims that Victor deserved his punishment for creating a hideous creature without soul, friend, or love.

First published in three volumes in 1818, *Frankenstein: or, The Modern Prometheus,* has never been out of print.

Films

Mary Shelley's bizarre tale of an inhuman creation attracted film makers as early as 1910, but it swept the cinematic world during the 1930s. Universal Studios decided upon a Gothic version of the novel, to be filmed in its extensive back-lot European village, and ultimately gave the project to its most promising British directorial import, James Whale (1896–1957). Whale chose an unknown for the role

A distraught and vengeful creature menaces the bride (Mae Clarke) of Victor Frankenstein in a landmark Gothic masterwork. [*Universal*]

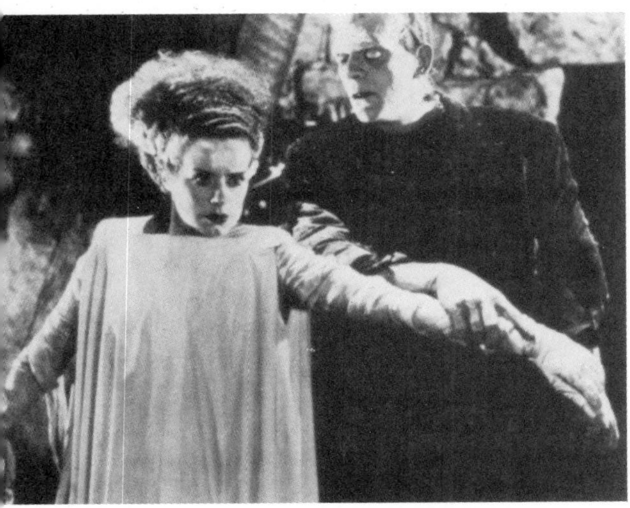

Boris Karloff with Elsa Lanchester in *The Bride of Frankenstein.* [*Universal*]

of the monstrous creation, a gaunt but cultured English actor named Boris Karloff (1887–1969), who had spent more than a decade of a not very substantial career in bit and character parts. Though he was not considered important enough to be invited to the film's premiere, Karloff became a major star, and the character he played became a deathless figure of the screen. He played the monster twice more, and he has had numerous imitators.

FRAZER, ROBERT CAINE. *See* CREASEY, JOHN.

FREEDGOOD, MORTON. *See* GODEY, JOHN.

FREELING, NICOLAS (1927–). Mystery novelist. Though born in London, Freeling lived in France throughout his childhood. He attended the University of Dublin and lived in the Netherlands before returning to France. For fifteen years he worked in the hotel business, and he recounted his experiences in his 1970 autobiography, *The Kitchen.*

He wrote his first mystery, *Love in Amsterdam* (1962), partly in reaction to his own experience of being arrested and unjustly accused of theft. He admits to having been influenced in his writing by Georges SIMENON, and many critics have found similarities between Freeling's series detective, Inspector VAN DER VALK, and Simenon's Jules MAIGRET. Freeling has been praised for his characterizations and his authentic descriptions of rural and urban Dutch locales. His tendency to insert political discussions has been found intrusive by some critics. Freeling's *The King of the Rainy Country* won the Mystery Writers of America Edgar as best novel in 1966.

FREEMAN, R[ICHARD] AUSTIN (1862–1943). English physician and mystery writer; creator of Dr. THORNDYKE, the world's premier scientific detective.

Born in London's Soho district, the son of Ann Maria (Dunn) and Richard Freeman, a tailor, the future author was originally named Richard; he added the "Austin" later. He received medical training at Middlesex Hospital Medical College and was immediately accepted as a member of the Royal College of Surgeons. Professing no particular religious faith, he married a Catholic, Annie Elizabeth Edwards, in 1887; they had two sons. A few weeks after the wedding, he arrived in Accra on the Gold Coast of Africa as assistant colonial surgeon. His time on the Dark Continent produced hard work, little money, ill health, and, seven years after he was invalided out in 1891, a critically acclaimed, if unremunerative, travel book, *Travels and Life in Ashanti and Jaman* (1898). He returned to England to establish an eye-ear-nose-throat practice, but his health forced him to give up medicine (except for temporary posts and, during World War I, in the ambulance corps).

R. Austin Freeman.

Aside from creating his brilliant detective, Thorndyke, Freeman made a great contribution to the literature of mystery fiction with his invention of the "inverted" detective story. In *The Singing Bone* (1912; s.s.), which introduces the form, the reader is a witness to the crime, the suspense of the chase thereby being eliminated. Interest centers not on *whether* the criminal will be caught, but on *how.*

Freeman's first book of fiction was in the crime genre. It was entitled *The Adventures of Romney Pringle* (1902) and was a collaborative effort published under the name Clifford ASHDOWN. Within a few years he was devoting full time to writing, producing, in 1905, a nonmystery, *The Golden Pool,* and, in 1907, *The Red Thumb Mark,* the classic novel that introduced Dr. Thorndyke to the public. Short stories about the well-conceived detective followed in *Pearson's Magazine,* and a fabulously successful career was under full sail.

In addition to the Pringle stories, Freeman wrote about other rogues, among them, Danby Croker and his immoral friend, Tom Nagget. They look like twins, except that Croker's hair is blond and Nagget's black. By coloring their hair, they are able to impersonate each other and often do so in some nefarious schemes, collected in *The Exploits of Danby Croker* (1916). The tales about Mr. Shuttlebury Cobb are little better, Freeman himself describing *The Surprising Experiences of Mr. Shuttlebury Cobb* (1927) as a "resuscitated potboiler." Still another collection about a villain (of sorts), although more serious, is *The Uttermost Farthing* (1914; British title: *A Savant's Vendetta*). In these connected episodes, Professor Humphrey Challoner's wife has been killed by an unknown burglar. Her husband devotes the rest of his life to luring members of that disreputable profession to his house, killing them, and forming a collection of their skeletons and shrunken heads. *Flighty Phyllis* (1928) is a series of connected episodes about a young girl, Phyllis Dudley, who finds herself in several unusual circumstances, perhaps not surprisingly, in her role as a transvestite. *The Great Portrait Mystery* (1918) contains nine stories involving Thorndyke, and five others.

FRENCH, INSPECTOR (Creator: Freeman Wills CROFTS). A Scotland Yard detective, Inspector Joseph French stands below medium height and is comfortable-looking rather than stout. His face is clean-shaven, and his expression is kindly. His eyes are dark blue and often twinkle. Usually dressed in tweeds and often wearing a bowler hat, he is easygoing and leisurely and looks like a man who could enjoy a good dinner and a good story in the smoking room afterward.

Happily married, French often discusses his cases with his wife, who has been known to give him worthwhile suggestions. He is fond of good food and enjoys traveling during his vacations, and, indeed, since he is not fond of office routine or paperwork, he prefers to travel away from London while engaged in the investigation of a case.

French is often referred to as "Soapy Joe" by his companions in the Criminal Investigation Department. Having served for more than thirty years and never having failed to bring a case to a successful conclusion, he has received promotions to chief inspector and superintendent for his meritorious service. Though French appears to be pleasant and unaggressive, he is not only a patient and thorough investigator but a formidable man-hunter who specializes in destroying so-called unbreakable alibis.

Inspector French's Greatest Case (1924) introduces the redoubtable sleuth, who investigates a baffling murder and robbery; the head clerk of a Hatton Garden diamond firm has been found lying beside an open safe. In *Sir John Magill's Last Journey* (1930) a wealthy linen manufacturer disappears while on a trip to Belfast. The presence of much material about trains and timetables reflects Crofts's personal experience. An abrupt departure from Crofts's previous work, *The 12:30 from Croyden* (1934) is an inverted tale about Charles Swinburn's plan to kill his rich uncle on a plane. We follow Swinburn as he conceives his perfect crime, executes it, tries to evade the penalty of the law, and hears the jury's verdict. The narrative then switches to Inspector French, who wraps everything up in the last two chapters by telling how he was able to solve the case. Most of Crofts's previous work had stressed plot and was the product of a mind trained in mathematics and engineering, but in this work he delved deeply into character to produce a masterpiece of the inverted form. Crofts never repeated this performance in a novel-length work, confining his subsequent use of the inverted form to short stories, as in the collection *Many a Slip* (1955). However, he did concern himself with greater depth of characterization in such later novels as *Golden Ashes* (1940) and *Silence for the Murderer* (1948).

Crofts's last major novel, *Death of a Train* (1946), concerns a vital shipment of radio valves to the British forces in North Africa during World War II and the breach of security that endangers their delivery. The first quarter of the novel races breathlessly along, culminating in a thunderous train wreck (Crofts's work as a railway engineer is again in evidence). French risks his life for his country and is eventually rewarded by promotion to the rank of superintendent.

CHECKLIST

1924 *Inspector French's Greatest Case*
1926 *Inspector French and the Cheyne Mystery* (U.S. title: *The Cheyne Mystery*)
1927 *Inspector French and the Starvel Tragedy* (U.S. title: *The Starvel Hollow Tragedy*)
1928 *The Sea Mystery*
1929 *The Box Office Murders* (U.S. title: *The Purple Sickle Murders*)
1930 *Sir John Magill's Last Journey*
1931 *Mystery in the Channel* (U.S. title: *Mystery in the English Channel*)
1932 *Death on the Way* (U.S. title: *Double Death*)
1932 *Sudden Death*
1933 *The Hog's Back Mystery* (U.S. title: *The Strange Case of Dr. Earle*)
1934 *The 12:30 from Croyden* (U.S. title: *Wilful and Premeditated*)
1934 *Mystery on Southampton Water* (U.S. title: *Crime on the Solent*)
1935 *Crime at Guildford* (U.S. title: *The Crime at Nornes*)
1936 *The Loss of the Jane Vosper*
1936 *Man Overboard!*
1937 *Found Floating*
1938 *Antidote to Venom*
1938 *The End of Andrew Harrison* (U.S. title: *The Futile Alibi*)
1939 *Fatal Venture* (U.S. title: *Tragedy in the Hollow*)
1940 *Golden Ashes*
1941 *James Tarrant, Adventurer* (U.S. title: *Circumstantial Evidence*)
1941 *The Losing Game* (U.S. title: *A Losing Game*)
1942 *Fear Comes to Chalfont*
1943 *The Affair at Little Wokeham* (U.S. title: *Double Tragedy*)
1945 *Enemy Unseen*
1946 *Death of a Train*
1947 *Young Robin Brand, Detective* (juvenile)
1948 *Murderers Make Mistakes* (s.s.; although dated 1947, this volume was not published until the following year)
1948 *Silence for the Murderer*
1951 *Dark Journey* (British title: *French Strikes Oil*)
1955 *Many a Slip* (s.s.)
1956 *The Mystery of the Sleeping Car Express* (s.s.; four of the ten stories are about French)
1957 *Anything to Declare?*

FREUGON, RUBY. See ASHBY, R. C.

FREYBE, HEIDI HUBERTA. See ALBRAND, MARTHA.

FREYER, FREDERIC. See BALLINGER, BILL S.

FROME, DAVID. See FORD, LESLIE.

FROST, C. VERNON. See CHILD, CHARLES B.

FROST, FREDERICK. See FAUST, FREDERICK.

FU MANCHU, DR. (Creator: Sax ROHMER). The ultimate villain, a Chinese master criminal of untold wealth, intellect, and occult powers whose goal is world conquest.

The Boxer Rebellion at the turn of the century had aroused fears of a "Yellow Peril," and Rohmer recognized that popular literature was ready for an Oriental archcriminal. His research for an article on Limehouse had divulged the existence of a "Mr. King," an actual figure of immense power in the Chinese district of London. His enormous wealth derived from gambling, drug smuggling, and the organization of many other criminal activities. The apparent head of powerful tongs and their many unsavory members, Mr. King was never charged with a crime, and his very existence was in question. One foggy night, Rohmer saw him—or someone who might have been him—from a distance; his face was the embodiment of Satan. This was Fu Manchu, the Devil Doctor.

Fu Manchu is a diabolical fiend who ruthlessly seeks to become emperor of the world. In addition to possessing degrees from three European universities, he has vast knowledge of the occult and of secrets of chemistry, medicine, and physics unknown to Western man. He also commands the tongs of Asia and is master of the secret sects of the East—Dacoits, Hashishin, Phansigars, and Thugs.

Fu Manchu is believed to be a Chinese noble descended from members of the Manchu dynasty.

Evil incarnate and the ultimate sinister Oriental as portrayed on the dust wrapper of the first English edition of *Emperor Fu Manchu*, published in London by Herbert Jenkins.

Warner Oland (right) is the very portrait of Oriental villainy in *The Return of Dr. Fu Manchu.* [*Paramount*]

The most sinister villain in history, the Devil Doctor is nevertheless bound by the code of a gentleman: his word is inviolate.

Fu Manchu's constant adversary is Sir Denis Nayland Smith, who, with his companion, Dr. Petrie, seems hopelessly overmatched against the ubiquitous doctor. Vaguely connected with Scotland Yard, Smith was knighted for his efforts to thwart Fu Manchu, although he would admit that the honor was not earned by superior intellect. His life is frequently saved by luck and even more often by the beautiful Kâramanèh, once a slave in Fu Manchu's power and later Petrie's wife.

Late in his career, Fu Manchu temporarily abandons his attempt to conquer the world and joins forces with the West to defeat the growing threat of communism.

With infinite attention to detail, Rohmer deliberately gave an impossible name to his villain, "Fu" and "Manchu" both being Chinese surnames. The name was hyphenated in the first three books.

Tall and slender, Fu Manchu generally wears a yellow robe or a black one with a silver peacock embroidered on the front. He wears a black cap on his smooth skull. Often portrayed with what is now known as a "Fu Manchu moustache," he is in fact clean-shaven so as not to interfere with his disguises—he is a master of disguise. His eyes are his most notable physical feature: long, magnetic, and true cat-green—so piercing and compelling that their gaze is often sensed even before his presence is made known.

Rohmer once wrote that, just after he had created his character, he had an extraordinary experience. Fu Manchu appeared in his bedroom. He asserted his independence of the author, telling him of his plans for world conquest: "I, the Mandarin Fu Manchu, I shall go on triumphant. It is your boast that you made me. It is mine that I shall live when you are smoke."

The vitality of Fu Manchu is demonstrated by the fact that it is almost impossible to hear a mention of a sinister Oriental without instantly calling to mind the Devil Doctor. *See also* ORIENTALS, SINISTER.

CHECKLIST

1913 *The Mystery of Dr. Fu-Manchu* (U.S. title: *The Insidious Dr. Fu-Manchu*)

1916 *The Devil Doctor* (U.S. title: *The Return of Dr. Fu-Manchu*)

1917 *The Si-Fan Mysteries* (U.S. title: *The Hand of Fu-Manchu*)

1919 *The Golden Scorpion* (Fu Manchu is present but unnamed)

1931 *Daughter of Fu Manchu*

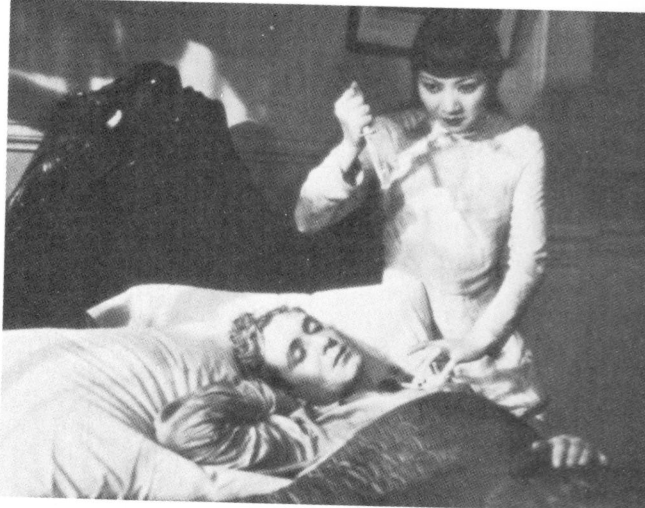

Anna May Wong, in the title role of *Daughter of the Dragon*, attempts to avenge the death of her father, Dr. Fu Manchu, by taking the life of the scion (Bramwell Fletcher) of the hated Petrie family. Her hand falters, and love blossoms for a time. [*Paramount*]

1932	*The Mask of Fu Manchu*
1933	*Fu Manchu's Bride* (British title: *The Bride of Fu Manchu*)
1934	*The Trail of Fu Manchu*
1936	*President Fu Manchu*
1939	*The Drums of Fu Manchu*
1941	*The Island of Fu Manchu*
1948	*Shadow of Fu Manchu*
1957	*Re-Enter Fu Manchu* (British title: *Re-Enter Dr. Fu Manchu*)
1959	*Emperor Fu Manchu*
1970	*The Secret of Holm Peel and Other Strange Stories* (s.s.; contains "The Eyes of Fu Manchu")
1973	*The Wrath of Fu Manchu* (s.s.)

Films

Rohmer's insidious doctor made an early screen debut, in 1923, in a series of short British films with Harry Agar Lyons as a rather rigid Fu Manchu and Fred Paul as Denis Nayland Smith; the rather close adaptations of episodes from the Rohmer source include fungi cellars and coughing horrors. Nearly all the Fu Manchu cinematic exploits that followed do not stray far from the source that inspired them.

The Mysterious Dr. Fu Manchu. Paramount, 1929. Warner Oland, Jean Arthur, Neil Hamilton, O. P. Heggie. Directed by Rowland V. Lee. Based on *The Insidious Dr. Fu-Manchu.*

During the Boxer Rebellion, "foreign devils" kill Fu Manchu's wife, and the doctor vows revenge. Soon he is in England eliminating all the white officers who took part in suppressing the uprising. Ultimately he is exposed by Scotland Yard and drinks poisoned tea. (Warner Oland, whose performance was called "bloodcurdling," is the screen's premier sinister Oriental; later he "atones" by portraying Charlie CHAN.)

The Return of Dr. Fu Manchu. Paramount, 1930. Oland, Arthur, Hamilton, Heggie. Directed by Lee.

The poisoned tea was merely a potion; the "dead" Fu Manchu escapes through a panel in the side of his coffin and continues his revenge. Finally, the Yard reports that he has been torn to pieces by one of his own bombs in a secret Thames-side den—but one can never be sure.

Daughter of the Dragon. Paramount, 1931. Oland, Anna May Wong, Sessue Hayakawa, Bramwell Fletcher, Frances Dade. Directed by Lloyd Corrigan. Loosely based on *Daughter of Fu Manchu.*

The Petrie family, Fu Manchu's hated enemies, are warned that he has been seen again. The Chinese doctor is shot, but before he dies, he makes his daughter—a dancer—vow to carry out his revenge on the last of the Petries. The two young people, however, begin a tragic love affair.

The Mask of Fu Manchu. MGM, 1932. Boris Karloff, Karen Morley, Lewis Stone, Jean Hersholt, Charles Starrett. Directed by Charles Brabin.

Now sinisterly civilized, Fu Manchu—doctor of medicine, science, philosophy—and his evil daughter (Myrna Loy) seek the lost tomb of Genghis Khan. Warns Nayland Smith: "Once Fu Manchu puts the mask of Genghis Khan across his yellow face and takes that scimitar into his hands, all Asia rises!"

Boris Karloff as Dr. Fu Manchu in a scene from *The Mask of Fu Manchu.* [*MGM*]

Drums of Fu Manchu. Republic serial, fifteen chapters, 1940. Henry Brandon (Fu Manchu), William Royle, Robert Kellard. Directed by William Witney and John English. From incidents in several Rohmer novels.

Fu Manchu and his daughter (Gloria Franklin) again seek the Khan's tomb and scepter, this time directing their activities mainly from California's Chinatowns.

For many years Fu Manchu remained silent, the changing attitudes toward the Chinese forcing him from the screen. Then, in 1965, an elaborate new series began, the first in color and in period, featuring the towering British horror star Christopher Lee as the evil doctor, with Dublin filling in as London of the 1920s. Later films in the series used locations in Spain, Brazil, and Turkey.

The Face of Fu Manchu. Seven Arts (British), 1965. Lee, Nigel Green, Howard Marion Crawford, Karin Dor, Joachim Fuchsberger. Directed by Don

Christopher Lee is the evil Oriental genius in *The Face of Fu Manchu.* [*Seven Arts*]

Sharp. An original story.

Fu Manchu, aided by his daughter (Tsai Chin) and called by Nayland Smith "cruel, callous, brilliant, the most evil and dangerous man in the world," demonstrates a poison gas by destroying all life in a remote English village. Eventually tracked to a monastery in Tibet, the doctor is supposedly killed in an explosion, but over the smoke his voice snarls: "The world has not heard the last of Fu Manchu!"

The Brides of Fu Manchu. Seven Arts (British), 1966. Lee, Douglas Wilmer (replacing Green as Nayland Smith), Crawford, Chin, Heinz Drache. Directed by Sharp. An original story.

At his secret headquarters, Fu Manchu holds as captives twelve girls from powerful political and industrial families whom he forces to collaborate with him in his electronic conquest of the world.

The Vengeance of Fu Manchu. Seven Arts (British), 1967. Lee, Wilmer, Crawford, Chin, Tony Ferrer, Wolfgang Kieling, Horst Frank. Directed by Jeremy Summers. An original story.

Fu Manchu arranges to have Nayland Smith accused of the murder of his pretty Chinese servant and, at an Interpol convention, plots to have all the police chiefs of the world replaced by doubles under his control.

Kiss and Kill. Commonwealth (British), 1970. Lee, Richard Greene (replacing Wilmer as Smith), Crawford, Chin, Maria Rohm. Directed by Jess (Jesus) Franco. An original story.

The evil doctor sends out infected girls to plant kisses of death upon the world's leaders. Among the first victims is Nayland Smith, who is unaccountably merely blinded, remaining so for most of the film.

The Castle of Fu Manchu. Commonwealth (British), 1972. Lee, Greene, Crawford, Chin. Directed by Franco. An original story.

Fu Manchu plots to control the world's waterways—especially such routes as the Suez and Panama Canals—with a device that can create icebergs in the Caribbean; he is finally traced to Istanbul, where he has seized as headquarters a Turkish national monument, the Anatolian Castle.

Radio and Television

The satanic doctor appeared in several successful radio series in both the United States and England during the 1930s; most memorable were the serial dramatizations presented on *The Collier Hour* and drawn from *Collier's* magazine. NBC once made a pilot telefilm with John Carradine as Fu Manchu and Sir Cedric Hardwicke as Nayland Smith, but a program never materialized. In the early 1950s Republic released for television a series of thirteen half-hour programs featuring a corpulent, less vigorous Fu Manchu (Glen Gordon) in the somewhat reduced circumstances of a television budget, leavened in large measure by action stock footage from the studio's files.

FULLER, TIMOTHY. *See* MARQUAND, JOHN P.

FUREY, MICHAEL. *See* ROHMER, SAX.

FUTRELLE, JACQUES (1875–1912). American journalist and author of detective stories featuring the Thinking Machine (*see* THINKING MACHINE, THE).

Born in Pike County, Ga., the son of Linnie (Bevill) and Wiley H. H. Futrelle, he became a theatrical manager and worked for the *Boston American*, in which many of his fictional works first appeared. He married L. May Peel in 1895. Futrelle died heroically when the *Titanic* sank. His wife, also a writer, survived.

Although he wrote several light romantic novels and stories, his detective fiction is most remembered today. In addition to the tales about Professor Van Dusen (the Thinking Machine), Futrelle wrote several crime and mystery novels, notably *The Diamond Master* (1909), a story about a plot to force natural diamonds off the market by manufacturing synthetic gems on a large scale; and *My Lady's Garter* (1912), the tale of the Countess of Salisbury's disappearing garter and the mysterious identity of the Hawk, a gentleman thief.

G

GABORIAU, ÉMILE (1832–1873). French novelist of sensational mystery and detective stories featuring Monsieur LECOQ.

Born in Saujon, he spent seven years in the cavalry before becoming secretary, assistant, and ghost-writer to Paul Féval, an author of criminal romances for *feuilletons* (serial leaflets of French daily newspapers). Gaboriau gathered material in police courts, morgues, and prisons for Féval and then—in 1859—began work on his own serialized novels. After writing seven romantic works, he produced *L'Affaire Lerouge* (1866; U.S. title: *The Widow Lerouge*, 1873; British title: *The Lerouge Case*, 1881), introducing Lecoq in the first of several detective novels that quickly became immensely popular.

Gaboriau moved ahead of his contemporaries by focusing attention on the gathering and interpreting of evidence in the detection of crime, rather than on the previously emphasized sensational commission of it. The *roman policier* he invented was instantly copied by scores of prolific French hacks, most of whom followed a standard pattern: a brutally murdered victim is found; a police officer demonstrates his ingenuity in solving the crime, which inevitably is connected with old family scandals; the villain is usually a handsome nobleman, often of illegitimate birth.

Films

File 113. Hollywood Pictures, 1932. Mary Nolan, Clara Kimball Young, George E. Stone, June Clyde, Lew Cody (Lecoq). Directed by Chester M. Franklin.

A banker's wife, in order to conceal secrets concerning her daughter's birth, is blackmailed into giving a crook jewels and money.

There had been two silent versions, one in 1915 and one in 1917, the latter called *Thou Shalt Not Steal*.

GAITE, FRANCIS. *See* COLES, MANNING.

GAMADGE, HENRY (Creator: Elizabeth DALY). Tall, in his thirties, with blunt features and a colorless but amiable face, Gamadge has grayish-green, intelligent eyes. His hair is mouse-colored. He habitually twists his mouth to one side when he smiles and turns his eyes upward when he thinks deeply. He wears clothing of excellent material and cut, but his poor posture keeps him from looking well dressed. His good physique has been marred by long hours spent pouring over old volumes in his scholarly researches. He is charming and genteel, and most people consider him a well-mannered and relaxed young man.

Born in New York City, he lives and works in an old residence in the East 60s with his wife and son, and a cat named Martin. He is assisted by Harold Bantz, whom he had helped when Bantz was a destitute youth.

Bibliophile and author, Gamadge is a consultant on old books, manuscripts, autographs, and inks. He is also an amateur detective whose cases frequently require him to use his bibliographic skills.

The first Gamadge case, *Unexpected Night* (1940), was a runner-up in the Mary Roberts RINEHART Mystery Novel Contest and deals with a conspiracy to obtain a huge legacy; it contains three murders. *Deadly Nightshade* (1940) is about murder by poisoning. Its successor, *Murders in Volume 2* (1941), is one of Miss Daly's best and concerns a girl who claims to be the reincarnation of a governess who had mysteriously vanished more than 100 years ago. She vanishes herself, as does a volume from a collection of Lord Byron's poems. This novel was one of two Daly works listed in SANDOE'S READERS' GUIDE TO CRIME.

The House without the Door (1942) starts with the inexplicable disappearance of a young woman from her home. It was loosely based on the Dorothy Arnold case. In *Evidence of Things Seen* (1943) Clara Gamadge is on vacation in the Berkshires, awaiting her husband's return from a war assignment. She is merely puzzled by an apparition that appears on a hill at sunset but terrified when murder strikes by apparently supernatural means. A marked railroad timetable leads to murders in a dignified old New York family in *Arrow Pointing Nowhere* (1944). One of Miss Daly's best works, it was also cited by Sandoe. *The Book of the Dead* (1944) touches on theatrical matters when a clue to a baffling murder is provided by a marked copy of *The Tempest* in a collection of Shakespeare's plays.

The serenity of a rose garden is rudely shattered by a rifle bullet in *Any Shape or Form* (1945). In *The Wrong Way Down* (1946) an elderly caretaker goes to mail some letters but uses the wrong door, trips over a low railing, and falls to her death in the street below. Although she appears to have died accidentally, Henry Gamadge suspects something more sinister. *Night Walk* (1947), set in the village of Fraser Mills, contains two murders and a mysterious prowler who is trapped by the bibliophilic sleuth in the local library. In *The Book of the Lion* (1948) a lost Chaucerian manuscript triggers an investigation into the mysterious death of a famous expatriate poet and playwright whose private papers mention the missing manuscript. A widow being held incommunicado in a Hudson River mansion, threatened with commitment to a mental institution by her in-laws, is the subject of *Death and Letters* (1950). She manages to send Gamadge a clue in a crossword puzzle. *The Book of the Crime* (1951), Miss Daly's last mystery novel, concerns both impersonation and a murder that is solved by Gamadge's bibliographic skill.

The other novels about Gamadge are *Nothing Can Rescue Me* (1943), *Somewhere in the House* (1946), and *And Dangerous to Know* (1949).

GARDNER, ERLE STANLEY (1889–1970). American author of detective fiction. One of the best-selling writers of all time, Gardner was born in Malden, Mass., on July 17, 1889. Because his father was a mining engineer, he traveled often when he was a child, his residences including the Klondike, Oregon, and California. After completing high school in Palo Alto, Calif., he briefly attended Valparaiso University in Indiana, later claiming, "I was kicked out for slugging a professor."

As a teenager he did some professional boxing and also promoted unlicensed matches, placing himself in danger of criminal prosecution. Out of these legal difficulties he developed an interest in the law and took a job as a typist with an Oxnard, Calif., law firm. In 1911, after having read law for an average of fifty hours a week for three years, he was admitted to the California bar. From 1911 to 1918 he practiced in Oxnard, gaining a considerable local reputation as a champion of the underdog through his defense of penniless Mexican and Chinese clients. Gardner won almost all of these cases, tirelessly researching forgotten statutes or legal precedents and conducting devastating cross-examinations of hostile witnesses. Regarding his success before juries, a former law partner said of the stocky, plain-looking Gardner, "Erle didn't try for the dapper, slick-lawyer look. The jurors probably considered him as ordinary as themselves, which suited him just fine."

Then, for several years, he left his law practice and worked as a tire salesman so that he could earn more money. However, in 1921, missing the courtroom, he joined a Ventura, Calif., law firm. Soon afterward, he began to write fiction, hoping that writing might bring him economic success and freedom to travel and pursue his hobbies. For a number of years Gardner followed a hectic schedule, spending a full day in court and several hours in the law library afterward, and then working until the early hours of the morning writing at least 4,000 words of fiction each day. In 1923 he sold his first mystery to a pulp magazine. Between 1923 and 1932 he wrote millions of words and sold hundreds of stories; since he used pseudonyms, a magazine often published several of his works in the same issue. He wrote variously as Charles M. Green, Robert Parr, Kyle Corning, Les Tillray, Charles J. Kenny, and Carleton Kendrake. Several of his early stories appeared in magazines such as *Breezy Stories* and *Snappy Stories*, but soon his work was appearing regularly in BLACK MASK, *Argosy*, and other prestigious PULP MAGAZINES. Although most of his stories were mysteries, he also wrote westerns for *Sunset*, *Cowboy Stories*, *West*, and *Outdoor Stories*. In 1932, the year he finally took a vacation, an extended trip to China, he earned the unprecedented amount of $20,525 solely from his magazine sales.

That year Gardner began submitting the manuscript of his first novel, *The Case of the Velvet Claws* (1933). After being rejected by several publishers, it was accepted by William Morrow & Company, the firm that subsequently published the original hardcover editions of all Gardner's books. Thayer Hobson, then president of Morrow, suggested (and Gardner agreed) that Perry MASON, the hero of the first book, should become a series character.

The Mason series was an immediate success, and Gardner, who had been spending several days a week on his law practice, was now able to devote himself exclusively to writing. He began the lifelong search for places where he could write and avoid everyone but the business associates and friends he chose to have nearby. At first he wrote in a house trailer parked in a lonely spot in the desert. Then he began acquiring the parcels of Southwestern real estate that were to provide the hideouts he was seeking. The nucleus of the "Gardner fiction factory" was his thousand-acre Rancho del Paisano at Temecula, Calif., 100 miles southeast of Los Angeles. The ranch had more than a dozen guest cottages and house trailers and supported a staff of twenty employees, all of whom supposedly called Gardner "Uncle Erle." Among them were six secretaries working full time transcribing the novels, nonfiction, and correspondence he dictated. Gardner's executive secretary was Mrs. Agnes Jean Bethell, a divorcée whom he employed in 1930. Mrs. Bethell's sisters, Peggy and Ruth, also worked as secretaries for him. It was said that Della Street, Perry Mason's secretary, was a composite of the three sisters. Gardner married Mrs. Bethell in 1968, shortly after the death of his first wife, the former Natalie Talbert, from whom he had been separated since the early 1930s. They had been married in 1912 and had one daughter, Grace, now Mrs. Alan R. McKittrick.

A man of wide interests, Gardner was well read in such diverse fields as psychology, criminology, forensic medicine, and penology. He was proud of his friendships with many of the country's leading experts in these fields and often dedicated his books to them. He was intensely interested in the problems of prison conditions and a strong advocate of reform. In 1948 he founded the Court of Last Resort, a private organization dedicated to helping men believed to have been unjustly convicted. The group secured the release of many prisoners. A 1952 book (*Court of Last Resort*) describing its work earned Gardner the Mystery Writers of America Edgar for best fact crime book. Through the years he also covered many famous criminal trials, including those of Sir Harry Oakes and Dr. Sam Sheppard, for the newspapers.

Gardner was also greatly interested in natural history, archaeology, and geology. He was an excellent photographer and a crack shot with pistol and rifle, although he gave up hunting twenty years before his death because he felt that the odds were weighted too heavily against the animals. The country in which Gardner most frequently pursued his interests was Mexico, especially the area of Baja California. Among his nonfiction books were *Hunting the Desert Whale* (1960), *Hovering over Baja* (1961), and *Host with the Big Hat* (1970). In the last, he wrote of his investigation of the archaeologically controversial Julsrud Collection of artifacts in Acámbaro, Mexico.

Gardner was frequently asked why he wrote mysteries. In an often-quoted response he said, "I write to make money, and I write to give the reader sheer fun. People derive a moral satisfaction from reading a story in which the innocent victim of fate triumphs over evil. They enjoy the stimulation of an exciting detective story.

"Most readers are beset with a lot of problems they can't solve. When they try to relax, their minds keep gnawing over these problems and there is no solution. They pick up a mystery story, become completely absorbed in the problem, see the problem worked out to a final and just conclusion, turn out the light and go to sleep. If I have given millions that sort of relaxation, it is reward enough."

Erle Stanley Gardner.

In the 1960s, alarmed at recent trends in American literature, he told *The New York Times*, "I have always aimed my fiction at the masses who constitute the solid backbone of America. I have tried to keep faith with the American family. In a day when the prevailing mystery story trends are toward sex, sadism and seduction, I try to base my stories on speed, situation and suspense."

Before he created Perry Mason, Gardner had used many series characters in the pulp magazines; they are now largely forgotten. Among them were lawyers Ken Corning and Peter Wennick; Speed Dash, the human fly; Sidney Zoom and his police dog, Rip; Ed Jenkins, the Phantom Crook; Hard Rock Hogan; Senor Arnaz de Lobo; confidence men Lester Leith and Paul Pry; and the Patent Leather Kid. Many of Gardner's pulp magazine stories are listed chronologically in *Erle Stanley Gardner: A Checklist* (1968), by E. H. Mundell. After his success in hard covers with Mason, Gardner wrote about other sleuths, including Sinophile Terry Clane of *Murder up My Sleeve* (1937) and wily seventy-year-old Gramp Wiggins of *The Case of the Smoking Chimney* (1943), who lives in a house trailer. More famous are District Attorney Doug SELBY and the team of Bertha COOL and Donald Lam, whom he created under the pseudonym A. A. Fair. Unlike most of his work, which is basically humorless, the Cool-Lam series is marked by bright, often funny dialogue.

Regardless of the detective about whom Gardner

wrote, each book gives evidence of certain clearly identifiable characteristics of his style. There is a minimum of description and a maximum of dialogue. This tendency was carried to its logical conclusion in the lengthy courtroom interrogations of the Mason series. Gardner's heroes are not averse to breaking the exact letter of the law to secure what they consider to be true justice. They share a hatred of pomposity. Villains or deserving victims are often self-important, wealthy individuals who can usually be identified because Gardner has given them two last names—for example, Harrington Faulkner.

Mason's clients often have something to hide, and, although they are ultimately proved innocent, this makes them appear suspect. The Gardner detective wages a vigorous investigation, ultimately breaking down a seemingly airtight case. The Mason books contain many variations on the theme of a switch (or the possibility of a switch) of physical evidence, including such objects as tape recordings in *The Case of the Green-eyed Sister* (1953); guns in *The Case of the Restless Redhead* (1954); artificial eyes in *The Case of the Counterfeit Eye* (1935); people in *The Case of the Substitute Face* (1938); and even animals, for example, dogs in *The Case of the Howling Dog* (1934); birds in *The Case of the Perjured Parrot* (1939); and horses in *The Case of the Fan-Dancer's Horse* (1947).

In Gardner's work clues often take second place to crisp dialogue and hectic action, the latter element clearly revealing the author's early writing for pulp magazines. In his first case, *The Case of the Velvet Claws*, Mason is indistinguishable from most private detectives of his time. Although identified as an attorney, he seldom gives legal advice and never appears in court. The stress is on action; the people are ordinary and the setting nondescript. Later books place the action in Los Angeles, but there is little local color. Crime and motivation throughout the series tend toward the commonplace, as if Gardner wanted most of his readers to identify with his characters. It was a rare Gardner book that had the exotic elements found in *The Case of the Grinning Gorilla* (1952), *The Case of the Stuttering Bishop* (1936), or *The Case of the Sleepwalker's Niece* (1936), which raises the question of whether one who walks in his sleep is legally responsible for any criminal actions he commits.

Even after Gardner's death, his books have not lost their immense popularity with the reading public. More than 200 million copies have been sold in the United States alone, and his works have been translated into at least thirty languages. In an authorized biography, *The Case of Erle Stanley Gardner* (1947), Alva Johnston spoke approvingly of his subject as "a prose industrialist" and "the Henry Ford of detective mysteries." Howard HAYCRAFT called him, in a less complimentary vein, "the king of the time-killers." Critics generally agreed that the early Gardner books were the best, and even those once favorable admitted increasing disenchantment with his later work. Yet Gardner was, as Francis M. NEVINS wrote in a eulogistic essay, "one of the great natural storytellers," a writer who left behind "over a quarter of a century of rich creative work which will be read and reprinted and reread as long as the art of storytelling is cherished."

Television

In 1957 Gardner's *Court of Last Resort* was transformed into a television series of twenty-six half-hour programs, with Lyle Bettger as the chief investigator for a seven-man court that tried to clear—and free—wrongfully convicted prisoners.

GARVE, ANDREW (pseudonym of Paul Winterton; 1908–). English journalist and mystery writer. Born in Leicester and educated at the London School of Economics and the University of London, he worked for *The Economist* (1929–1933) and the *London News Chronicle* (1933–1946) as a reporter, lead writer, and foreign correspondent. His tour of duty in Moscow (1942–1945) furnished him with material for several mystery novels, for example, *Murder in Moscow* (1951; U.S. title: *Murder Through the Looking Glass*) and *The Ashes of Loda* (1965), as well as nonfiction books such as *Report on Russia* (1945) and *Inquest on an Ally* (1948). Winterton's interests, traveling and sailing, are often reflected in his mystery fiction. In addition to using the Garve pseudonym, he writes as Roger Bax and Paul Somers. A founding member of the Crime Writers' Association, he served as its first joint secretary.

Winterton's first novel, *Death Beneath Jerusalem* (1938), published under the Bax pseudonym, is a tale of suspense, set in Palestine, that is now difficult to obtain. Other Bax efforts, *Disposing of Henry* (1947) and *Blueprint for Murder* (1948; U.S. title: *The Trouble with Murder*), are interesting but slightly erratic examples of the inverted tale. *A Grave Case of Murder* (1951), also by Bax, is a rare example of a Garve novel that is pure detection, and a Russian-based thriller, *Came the Dawn* (1949; U.S. title: *Two if by Sea*), served as the basis for the film *Never Let Me Go* (1953), with Clark Gable.

A series of four novels—*Beginner's Luck* (1958), *Operation Piracy* (1958), *The Shivering Mountain* (1959), and *The Broken Jigsaw* (1961)—were published under the Somers pseudonym and concern the exploits of a young reporter who competes with a more experienced woman journalist on a rival paper—with predictable results. Although some detection occurs in this series, the emphasis is on thrills and suspense.

As Andrew Garve (Winterton's best-known pseudonym), he has written a long series of successful suspense novels. The first, *No Mask for Murder* (1950; U.S. title: *Fontego's Folly*), is set in the West Indies and concerns the efforts of a newly arrived doctor to operate a leper colony while frustrated by a series of unrelated murders. The setting of *A Hole in the Ground* (1952) is a cave situated under an atomic power plant. Garve's spelunking expertise is much in evidence. *The Megstone Plot* (1956) is about a complicated scheme to defraud a newspaper; a lawsuit, claiming that the paper has falsely accused an individual of treachery, is the device used by the conspirators. The film *A Touch of Larceny* (1960), with James Mason, was based on this book.

In *The Narrow Search* (1957) a father kidnaps his daughter from his estranged wife and her new boyfriend. Their search for the child through a group of inland waterways gives Garve ample opportunity to display his sailing knowledge. So, too, does *A Hero for Leanda* (1959), whose protagonist proves his worth to the heroine by means of his navigational skills. *The Sea Monks* (1963) is set in a lighthouse invaded by a gang of vicious juvenile delinquents. During a howling hurricane, described with all of Garve's narrative skill, the problems are resolved. *Frame-Up* (1964) is about the murder of an artist and the efforts of the police to solve the crime. One of Garve's rare detective stories, it was described by Anthony BOUCHER as "a flawless specimen of the most classic form" and "a modern gem in the grand old genre."

Garve returned to the inverted form with *Murderer's Fen* (1966; U.S. title: *Hide and Go Seek*), about the efforts of an ambitious young man to get rid of the girl he has "gotten in trouble" so that he can marry for money and live comfortably for the rest of his life. *The Long Short Cut* (1968) is more lighthearted than the usual Garve work and tells of the efforts of a young couple to smuggle a man out of England in spite of the fact that the police are looking for him. *The Ascent of D-13* (1969) is about two men who must climb a dangerous mountain to find and destroy a secret weapon before it falls into enemy hands.

GAULT, WILLIAM CAMPBELL (1910–). American author of sports and mystery fiction. A transplanted Milwaukeean, Gault has lived in southern California for many years. He started his career writing sports fiction for PULP MAGAZINES during the 1930s. For many years he has been one of the most popular authors of sports novels (mostly about automobile racing and football) for teen-age boys.

Gault's first mystery work was "Marksman," a short story that appeared in the September 1940 issue of *Clues*. He wrote hundreds of mystery stories for the pulp magazines before publishing his first novel, *Don't Cry for Me*, winner of the Mystery Writers of America Edgar as best first mystery of 1952. *The Bloody Bokhara* (British title: *The Bloodstained Bokhara*), also published in 1952, is set in Milwaukee and concerns Armenian rug dealers in that city. Most of Gault's books since 1952 have a southern California setting. *The Canvas Coffin* (1953) has a boxing background. *Ring Around Rosa* (1955) is the first novel about private detective Brock "the Rock" Callahan, a former guard on the Los Angeles Rams, who also appears in *Day of the Ram* (1956), about the murder of a football player. In *The Convertible Hearse* (1957), Callahan investigates murder and the local used-car "industry." Callahan is noted for his stubborn honesty and cynicism about southern California and its trappings. He is similar in these respects to Gault's other series private detective, Joe Puma, who first appears in *End of a Call Girl* (1958). Gault's last mystery novel was *Dead Hero* (1963). A new novel about Callahan is unpublished thus far.

GETHRYN, ANTHONY (Creator: Philip MACDONALD). Born about 1885, the son of an English squire and a Spanish actress-dancer-painter, Anthony Ruthven Gethryn attended Oxford University, where he excelled at sports as well as academic subjects. He developed an early and intense affection for painting, writing, and riding horses. During World War I he rose from private to colonel, a title he retains in civilian life. After being wounded (he always limps slightly) and then serving in the British Secret Service, he retires to a quiet pastoral life, only to have the peace disturbed by two elements: a new wife, Lucia, and a local murder that the official police have been unable to solve.

Gethryn's first appearance is in *The Rasp* (1924), in which at one point he is the prime murder suspect. The body in the study is that of a Cabinet minister; the unusual murder weapon is a rasp. In *The Link* (1930) the chief clue in the murder of Lord Grenville is a bit of silver sand. Lady Grenville and a veterinary surgeon (who narrates the tale) are principals. Another tiny clue, a forgotten shopping list, is the central item in *The Nursemaid Who Disappeared* (1938; U.S. title: *Warrant for X*), a suspenseful tour de force in which the villain is neither seen nor heard. *The List of Adrian Messenger* (1959) begins in England and concludes in California. Messenger writes ten names on a slip of paper and turns it over to a friend at Scotland Yard. When the people named are found dead, apparently accident victims but evidently murdered, Gethryn has the seemingly impossible task of finding the connection among them and tracking down the diabolical killer.

CHECKLIST

1924 *The Rasp*
1928 *The White Crow*
1930 *The Noose*
1930 *The Link*
1931 *Persons Unknown* (British title: *The Maze*)
1931 *The Choice* (U.S. title: *The Polferry Riddle*)
1931 *The Crime Conductor*
1931 *The Wraith*
1932 *Rope to Spare*
1933 *Death on My Left*
1938 *The Nursemaid Who Disappeared* (U.S. title: *Warrant for X*)
1952 *Something to Hide* (s.s.; British title: *Fingers of Fear;* contains six stories, one, "The Wood for the Trees," about Gethryn)
1959 *The List of Adrian Messenger*

Films

The Rasp. Fox (British), 1931. Claude Horton (Gethryn), Phyllis Loring, James Raglan, C. M. Hallard. Directed by Michael Powell. Based on the 1924 novel.

Gethryn investigates a case involving a body found in a study.

The Nursemaid Who Disappeared. Warner Brothers (British), 1939. Arthur Margetson (Gethryn), Peter Coke, Leslie Brook, Coral Browne, Martita Hunt. Directed by Arthur Woods. Based on the 1938 novel.

A playwright and a detective join forces to foil a kidnapping.

23 Paces to Baker Street. Twentieth Century-Fox (British), 1956. Van Johnson, Vera Miles, Cecil Parker. Directed by Henry Hathaway. A considerably altered version of *Warrant for X* in which Gethryn does not appear.

A blind young American playwright in London, embittered by his handicap, is drinking in a pub when he overhears a conversation about a kidnapping plot; but no one will believe him.

The List of Adrian Messenger. Universal (British), 1963. George C. Scott (Gethryn), Dana Wynter, Kirk Douglas, Clive Brook, Herbert Marshall, with cameo appearances by Tony Curtis, Burt Lancaster, Robert Mitchum, Frank Sinatra. Directed by John Huston. Based on the 1959 novel.

A murderer in various disguises is eliminating those who stand in his way to a fortune. A writer, suspicious, shows Gethryn a list of victims before he, too, is killed when a bomb rips apart the passenger plane on which he is traveling.

GHOTE, INSPECTOR GANESH (Creator: H. R. F. KEATING). Homicide expert for the Bombay CID, Inspector Ghote (pronounced "go-tay") is nonetheless a man much beset by doubts. Somewhat dominated by his wife, he invariably gives the impression, at work, of being prone to become the victim of tough superiors, tough criminals, and influential witnesses. Yet, this usually naïve (occasionally shrewd) policeman always comes through with the correct solution. In *Inspector Ghote Hunts the Peacock* he is in London to deliver a paper at an international conference on drug smuggling, and he is delighted with the city, although his stay is marked by many embarrassments before his ultimate triumph. In *Inspector Ghote Plays a Joker* he investigates the killing of a number of flamingos at the Bombay Zoo. Ghote's compassionate nature is evident in *Inspector Ghote Trusts the Heart,* in which the son of a poor man, mistaken for a rich man's child, is kidnapped.

Inspector Ganesh Ghote was portrayed by Zia Mohyeddin in *Hunt the Peacock,* a 1969 production on a British Broadcasting Corporation program. [*BBC*]

CHECKLIST

1964 *The Perfect Murder*
1966 *Inspector Ghote's Good Crusade*
1967 *Inspector Ghote Caught in Meshes*
1968 *Inspector Ghote Hunts the Peacock*
1969 *Inspector Ghote Plays a Joker*
1970 *Inspector Ghote Breaks an Egg*
1971 *Inspector Ghote Goes by Train*
1972 *Inspector Ghote Trusts the Heart*
1974 *Bats Fly Up for Inspector Ghote*

GIBSON, WALTER B. (1897–). American magician and author of mystery novels about the Shadow (*see* SHADOW, THE), the most famous superhero to appear in PULP MAGAZINES and on radio. While working on the *Philadelphia Public Ledger* as a young man, Gibson wrote many articles on magic and attracted the attention of Howard Thurston and Harry Houdini, two of the world's greatest magicians, who engaged him to write books and articles on magic that were published under their names. He enjoyed writing, and, after being encouraged by Sir Arthur CONAN DOYLE, he wrote mystery fiction.

The character of Lamont Cranston, the Shadow, appeared in the spring of 1931 with the first issue of *The Shadow* magazine, which contained a novel, *The Living Shadow*, by Maxwell Grant—the pseudonym used by Gibson for 283 novels about the Shadow (including one published under his own name, *Return of the Shadow*, 1963). The magazine quickly became popular and expanded from a quarterly to a biweekly, with Grant writing 1 million words a year for the next fifteen years, after which other authors wrote some of the stories (also under the Maxwell Grant name). After 325 issues, the magazine ceased publication with the Summer 1949 issue. *The Shadow* radio program, which began in 1936, was based on the magazine stories.

In addition to the many adventures about the Shadow and the ghosted books for others, Gibson has written more than thirty books on magic under his own name, as well as numerous works about games, puzzles, psychic subjects, and true crime.

GIDEON, GEORGE (Creator: John CREASEY as J. J. Marric). Commander (formerly Superintendent) Gideon of Scotland Yard is a massive, slow-moving policeman with large, soft, pale-blue eyes with sleepy-looking lids, a gentle voice, and a pale face. It is difficult to anger him, but when "G. G. is on the warpath," his subordinates stay far away. Nothing infuriates him as much as crimes involving child abuse or murder, desecration of a church, or dishonesty by a colleague or other policemen. His cases are excellent examples of police procedure.

Gideon's Day, the first of the twenty-one books about the reassuring policeman, appeared in 1955.

Creasey derived the pseudonym for this series from his own initial, J(ohn), and that of his wife J(ean), and from his sons' first names, Mar(tin) and Ric(hard).

Film

In 1958 John Ford filmed *Gideon's Day* in authentic London locales.

Gideon of Scotland Yard (British release title: *Gideon's Day*). Columbia (British), 1958, Jack Hawkins, Dianne Foster, Anna Massey, Anna Lee, Andrew Ray, Howard Marion-Crawford, John Loder. Directed by Ford.

Chief Inspector Gideon starts his day badly with a traffic ticket and goes on to tackle such "typical" police problems as bribery, an escaped and murderous madman, and a payroll robbery. He must also deal with the romantic problems of his daughter (Massey).

Television

In 1965 John Gregson portrayed Commander Gideon in a series of twenty-six hour-long programs made in England and called *Gideon, C.I.D.*

GIELGUD, VAL (HENRY) (1900–). English mystery writer and former BBC official. The elder brother of actor Sir John Gielgud, he was educated at Rugby School and Trinity College, Oxford. His varied early career included acting, secretarial work for a member of Parliament, and a job as subeditor for a comic paper. He joined the *Radio Times* in 1928 and in 1929 was appointed head of sound drama for the BBC, a position he held for thirty-five years.

Gielgud has written novels (*Black Galantry*, 1928, and *Gathering of Eagles*, 1929), thrillers (*Imperial Treasure*, 1931, *The Broken Men*, 1932, and *Gravelhanger*, 1934; U.S. title: *The Ruse of the Vanished Woman*); plays (*Away from It All*, *Party Manners*, *Iron Curtain*, and *The Bomb Shell*); nonfiction (*Outrage in Manchukuo*, 1937, *The Red Account*, 1939, *Beyond Dover*, 1940, *Radio Theatre*, 1946, and *British Radio Drama, 1922–1956, A Survey*, 1958); radio plays; film scripts (including a collaboration on the screenplay of his mystery *Death at Broadcasting House*); and three autobiographies (*Years of the Locust*, 1946, *One Year of Grace*, 1950, and *Years in a Mirror*, 1965).

Married five times, he has one son. He was awarded the Order of the British Empire in 1942 and was made a Commander of the British Empire in 1959. He had resided in London until his retirement in 1964, when he moved to Sussex and devoted his time to writing mystery novels.

Death at Broadcasting House (1934; U.S. title: *London Calling*) draws heavily on Gielgud's background: a radio actor is killed in the middle of a broadcast. Plot, puzzle, characterizations, and setting are blended expertly; the result is a minor masterpiece and Gielgud's best novel. *Death as an Extra* (1935) starts promisingly enough when a villainous film director is shot while a scene is being photographed. An investigation is begun, but at this point the novel becomes a thriller and, then, hastily returns to the detective form for an ill-considered last-minute solution to the murder. *Death in Budapest* (1937) is a travelogue that deals with the murder of an opera singer during a performance witnessed by a convention of professional detectives as well as several fictional sleuths. Gielgud wrote these three novels in collaboration with Holt Marvell (pseudonym of Eric Maschwitz); they all feature Inspector Simon Spears—a young and promising member of the CID.

The title of *Cat* (1956) is an acronym formed from the initials of the protagonist. The first few pages deal with a crime, its discovery, and the punishment of its perpetrator. The rest of this inverted tale traces the life of the "hero" and the events leading up to the crime. The milieu of *The Goggle-Box Affair* (1963; U.S. title: *Through a Glass Darkly*) is British commercial television; the death of an executive looks like suicide, but foul play is suspected. *A Necessary End* (1969) is about murder on board a ship.

Many of Gielgud's novels have not been published in the United States, among them three recent works: *The Candle-Holders* (1970), *The Black Sambo Affair* (1972), and *In Such a Night . . .* (1974).

GILBERT, ANTHONY (pseudonym of Lucy Beatrice Malleson; 1899–1973). English author of novels and short stories. Although her mother wanted her to be a schoolteacher, Miss Malleson succeeded in fulfilling her own ambition and became a novelist. At first she wrote nonmystery fiction as Anne Meredith; she even wrote an autobiography, *Three-a-Penny* (1940), under that name. She saw John WILLARD's play *The Cat and the Canary* (Broadway debut in 1922), became thriller-conscious, and, in 1927, as Anthony Gilbert, published her first mystery, *The Tragedy at Freyne*. For many years Gilbert's identity was kept secret, and most readers assumed that the author was a man.

The detective in the early Gilbert novels, like *The Body on the Beam* (1932), is generally Scott Egerton, a rising young British political leader. He was dropped with the introduction of Arthur CROOK, an enormous success from the time he first appeared, in *Murder by Experts* (1936). The only Crook short story, "You Can't Hang Twice" (1946), won a second prize in *Ellery Queen's Mystery Magazine*'s contest. Although all Gilbert novels after 1936 were about Crook, Miss Malleson continued to write such nonseries stories as "The Mills of God" (1969), a crime story about abortion. When it was published, before the "permissive" era, Ellery QUEEN (author) called it "a poignant, and at moments heartbreaking, story that few writers in the field would have dared to attempt."

Jacques BARZUN and Wendell Hertig TAYLOR, in writing about her frequent use of women (especially the elderly) and children in peril, believed that she stretched villainy "beyond credence." Later books such as *Missing from Her Home* (1969) and *Death Wears a Mask* (1970; U.S. title: *Mr. Crook Lifts the Mask*) are typical of this type of story. In the former, a nine-year-old girl vanishes while on a trip to the supermarket. In the latter, Crook's client stumbles upon a body while out feeding her wild cats.

Most critics have been more favorable than Barzun and Taylor. At the time when Gilbert's true identity was still unknown, the reviewer for the *News Chronicle* of London said: "I know of no author of this type of tale who is more skilled at making a good story seem brilliant by sheer force of writing and clear perception of his own characters."

GILBERT, MICHAEL (FRANCIS) (1912–). English lawyer and detective story writer. A noted lawyer and one of the finest of the post-World War II generation of detective story writers, Gilbert was born in Billinghay, Lincolnshire, to Bernard Samuel Gilbert and Berwyn Minna (Cuthbert) Gilbert, both writers. He was educated at St. Peter's, Seaford, Blundell's School, and London University, where he was influenced to study law by his uncle, Sir Maurice Gwyer, who was Lord Chief Justice of India. Because of lack of funds, he was obliged to teach at the Cathedral School in the Close at Salisbury and while thus engaged received his law degree in 1937.

During World War II he served as a gunner with the Hon. Artillery Company, Twelfth Regiment, and saw action in North Africa and Italy. Captured by the Germans in January 1943, he was imprisoned near Parma in northern Italy, where, by chance, he read Cyril HARE's legal mystery *Tragedy at Law* (1942), an experience that had later personal and professional repercussions. Gilbert managed to escape when Italy surrendered, and he rejoined his regiment in the field.

Returning home after the war, he completed his legal training and joined Trower, Still & Keeling in 1947. The same year Gilbert married Roberta Mary Marsden; they have two sons and five daughters.

Gilbert has risen to become a partner in his law firm and at one time was Raymond CHANDLER's legal adviser and drew up his will. He writes while commuting from his home in Kent to his office in Lincoln's Inn. Gilbert's favorite form is the short story, and he has written hundreds of them, many appearing in *Ellery Queen's Mystery Magazine (EQMM)*. He has written mystery dramas (*A Clean Kill*, 1960, and *The Shot in Question*, 1963) and true-crime novels (*The Claimant*, 1957, based on the Tichborne case); edited *Best Detective Stories of Cyril Hare* (1959); and is editor of Hodder & Stoughton's Classics of Adventure and Detection.

His first detective novel, *Close Quarters* (1947), is about a murder in a locked room in the precincts of Melchester Cathedral. It introduces Inspector Hazelrigg, one of Gilbert's series detectives. A bit dull, it had to await American publication until 1963, when its author's fame had spread. The mildly satiric *Smallbone Deceased* (1950) is set in a lawyer's office and concerns the discovery of a body in a safe-deposit box. *Death Has Deep Roots* (1951) is a long courtroom novel in which an attempt is made to determine whether a girl murdered her lover. Gilbert's law background is much in evidence.

Death in Captivity (1952; U.S. title: *The Danger Within*) is set in an Italian prisoner-of-war camp, an ingenious locale for a murder; the formal problem is well blended with the prisoners' attempt to escape. Another excellent novel, *Fear to Tread* (1953), concerns the efforts of gangsters to commit various robberies against the British Railways system. *Sky High* (1955; U.S. title: *The Country-House Burglar*) is about an anxious mother whose son cannot seem to readjust to postwar conditions and might be responsible for a series of spectacular neighborhood robberies that culminate in an explosion and murder. A tale of international intrigue, *Be Shot for Sixpence* (1956) has an unpleasant hero and much double-dealing.

Blood and Judgment (1959) starts with the discovery of a woman's body near a reservoir by three little boys who are collecting wood for a Guy Fawkes bonfire. It features Detective Sergeant Patrick Petrella, who had appeared in Gilbert's short stories, and is the author's first attempt at the police procedural novel. Anthony BOUCHER selected it as one of the best mystery novels of 1959.

After the Fine Weather (1963) is a novel of intrigue and suspense, with the visiting sister of a vice-consul stationed in Austria as the eyewitness to an assassination who identifies the wrong man. *The Crack in the Teacup* (1966) concerns corruption on a local council and is an attempt by Gilbert to return to form after a series of so-so works. Boucher thought that it was one of the best mystery novels of 1966 and called it a "quietly nonviolently tense and absorbing story of municipal corruption, British style." *Game Without Rules* (1967), a group of short stories (mostly reprinted in *EQMM*), is about counterintelligence agents Calder and Behrens. Ellery QUEEN (author) selected this volume for QUEEN'S QUORUM and stated that, after W. Somerset MAUGHAM's *Ashenden* (1928), it was the best volume of spy stories ever written.

Other examples of Michael Gilbert's work in the short form are *Stay of Execution* (1971) and a paperback volume, *Amateur in Violence* (1973), which contains a novelette and ten short stories selected and edited by Queen, who had published them in his magazine. Petrella and Hazelrigg are both featured.

Among Gilbert's later novels are *The Etruscan Net* (1969; U.S. title: *The Family Tomb*), about art objects in Florence after the flood, and *The Body of a Girl* (1972), which begins with the discovery of a body and proceeds by exploring the motives of many of the local citizens and the police as well.

Queen wrote: "Mr. Gilbert is the 'compleat professional': he is in complete control of his material . . . his storytelling. His plots have their origins in first-hand knowledge of law, war, and living, nourished by a fertile imagination that never fails him; and through his varied backgrounds and experiences he has come to know people. And as critics have pointed out, he writes often with droll, dry wit, and always with compassion."

GODAHL, THE INFALLIBLE (Creator: Frederick Irving ANDERSON). The ultimate criminal, the perfect intellect that never fails to consummate a contemplated crime. Unlike A. J. RAFFLES, who relies on wit, charm, intuition, whim, and good luck to pull off a caper, Godahl has a scientific approach to jobs. His computerlike mind assesses every possibility in terms of logic and probabilities; his successes are triumphs of pure reason, the inevitable victory of superior intellect. More colorful than the Thinking Machine, he has a similar approach to problems—albeit on the opposite side of the law (*see* THINKING MACHINE, THE).

Godahl has never even been suspected of a crime, much less caught; his perfection is known only to Oliver Armiston, a writer who has recorded some of his exploits. The intellectual superior of any adversary, Godahl has one fear—of the afflicted, that is, the blind, the deaf, and so on. He believes that the loss of any sense heightens the sensitivity of those that remain, giving the individual an advantage unavailable to a normal person.

Godahl's uninterrupted successes have made him rich, and he is a member of the Pegasus Club (which has a membership of fifty millionaires).

Only six stories about Godahl appeared in *The Saturday Evening Post*. They were later collected as *Adventures of the Infallible Godahl* (1914).

GODEY, JOHN (pseudonym of Morton Freedgood; 1912–). American author. Born in Brooklyn, he has spent most of his life in New York except for an eleven-year period in Connecticut. He attended the College of the City of New York and New York University and held a variety of jobs before serving in the infantry during World War II. He has worked in public relations and publicity for many film companies, including United Artists, Twentieth Century-Fox, and Paramount. His short stories and articles have been published in *Cosmopolitan, Collier's, Esquire,* and other magazines. As Freedgood, he has published *The Wall-to-Wall Trap* (1957), a novel about suburbia. He also wrote a book of reminiscences of his New York childhood, *The Crime of the Century and Other Misdemeanors* (1973).

John Godey. [*Courtesy of G. P. Putnam's Sons*]

The Godey mysteries have always relied heavily on humor. *A Thrill a Minute with Jack Albany* (1967) and *Never Put Off till Tomorrow What You Can Kill Today* (1970) are farcical mysteries about a bungling, unemployed actor, Jack Albany. The former was filmed as *Never a Dull Moment* (1968), with Dick Van Dyke in the title role; the latter is a lampoon of television and right-wing extremists.

Godey's 1973 mystery, *The Taking of Pelham One Two Three*, a best seller for many weeks, is the story of the hijacking of a New York subway train. It was a Book-of-the-Month Club selection, was picked for *The Reader's Digest* Condensed Book Club, and was made into a major motion picture in 1974, starring Walter Matthau.

GODWIN, WILLIAM (1756–1836). English novelist and radical political theorist. Born in Wisbech and raised in Norfolk, Godwin studied for the ministry and was a clergyman for five years before becoming an atheist. Influenced by the French Revolution, he espoused an anarchist philosophy that opposed all laws, including those regulating marriage, believing that man could live in harmony without laws or institutions. Nevertheless, he married the pregnant Mary Wollstonecraft in 1797; their daughter, Mary SHELLEY, was the author of FRANKENSTEIN. Godwin's wife died as a result of giving birth, and he married again in 1801.

Things as They Are; or, The Adventures of Caleb Williams (1794), Godwin's best-known book, is generally regarded as the first novel of crime and detection. Because of his political beliefs, however, the viewpoint is the reverse of that of virtually all subsequent detective fiction. In the genre as we know it, the law is regarded as good; in *Caleb Williams,* it is totally evil, demonstrating the injustice of any system in which all men are not equal, that is, in which one man may be victimized by another.

Tyrell, a brutal squire, comes into conflict with Ferdinando Falkland, a benevolent neighbor, and is soon found murdered. Suspicion is immediately directed at Falkland, but he is acquitted, the blame shifting to a man named Hawkins and his son when their knife is proved to be the murder weapon. After they are tried and executed, Falkland becomes extremely eccentric. Caleb Williams, his secretary, is convinced that his employer is, in fact, the murderer. Although Williams's curiosity prompts him to attempt to discover evidence to prove his theory, he is loyal to his employer and has no intention of betraying him. But the fearful Falkland has Williams arrested for stealing, and, when the poor young man escapes, has his agents chase him from one hiding place to another. Finally, in desperation, the persecuted Williams charges his employer with murder, drawing a confession from him.

The tale is told in three books, and Godwin was probably the first author to write the last section first and the first section last. In March 1796 *Caleb Williams* was adapted for the stage by George Colman the Younger (1762–1836) under the title *The Iron Chest* and was extremely successful as the first melodrama of its kind.

GORDONS, THE (Mildred [Nixon] Gordon, 1912– , and Gordon Gordon, 1912–). American husband-wife writing team. The Gordons met while they were attending the University of Arizona. Each has been active in journalism. He worked for the Hearst newspapers and also edited the *Tucson Daily Citizen;* she wrote for United Press and edited *Arizona Magazine.* During World War II, while Gordon was an FBI agent, his wife turned to mystery writing. She published *The Little Man Who Wasn't There* in 1946.

The Gordons' highly successful mystery collaboration began in 1950 with *The FBI Story,* which was dedicated to J. Edgar Hoover. Many of their subsequent books are also about FBI agents and clearly call upon Gordon's experiences. The hero in *Case File: FBI* (1953) and *Operation Terror* (1961) is a quiet, reserved, and contemplative agent, John Ripley. He and all FBI agents depicted by the Gordons are invariably brave and self-sacrificing. The authors have received praise for their realistic description of FBI routine and their fast-paced narratives. Although their early works were not noted for their humorous qualities, later books such as *Undercover Cat* (1963) and *Undercover Cat Prowls Again* (1966) have corrected that deficiency.

Films

Experiment in Terror. Columbia, 1962. Glenn Ford, Lee Remick, Ross Martin, Stefanie Powers. Directed by Blake Edwards. Based on *Operation Terror.*

An FBI man in San Francisco is contacted by a terrified bank teller. A criminal is trying to force her to embezzle $100,000 by threatening her and her young sister.

That Darn Cat. Buena Vista, 1965. Hayley Mills, Dean Jones, Dorothy Provine, Roddy McDowall, Neville Brand, Elsa Lanchester. Directed by Robert Stevenson. Based on *Undercover Cat.*

A Siamese cat wanders into a neighborhood apartment where bank robbers are holding a woman teller prisoner. When the animal returns to its pretty owner with a wristwatch on its neck, the girl communicates with the FBI.

GOTHIC NOVELS. *See* "HAD-I-BUT-KNOWN" SCHOOL.

GOULD, ALAN. *See* CANNING, VICTOR.

GOULD, CHESTER (1900–). American artist

and creator of Dick TRACY, the incorruptible comic strip hero. Born in Oklahoma, the son of a newspaper publisher, he moved to Chicago to finish his education at Northwestern University. While working as a commercial artist, he submitted his first comic strip idea to Captain Joseph Medill Patterson of the *Chicago Tribune–New York News* syndicate. From 1921 to 1931 many of his ideas were rejected until he conceived a plainclothes detective who would fight criminals on their own terms—using fists and guns when necessary. The strip and the character were originally named "Plainclothes Tracy," but Patterson suggested the shorter first name—the best-known slang term for detective. The strip was created for the *Chicago Tribune* syndicate and first appeared on October 4, 1931. It is estimated that 800 newspapers throughout the world now carry it, with a total readership of 100 million.

The inspiration for Dick Tracy, and the probable reason for the enormous success of the strip, was the era of Prohibition lawlessness and the American public's frustration at the inability of law enforcement agencies to deal with the situation. As Gould said, "I decided that if the police couldn't catch the gangsters, I'd create a fellow who would."

Bruce Graeme's Blackshirt was portrayed as a cracksman even after he began to devote his energies to fighting crime. This stark illustration appears on the dust wrapper of the first American edition, published by Lippincott in 1936, of *Blackshirt the Audacious*.

GOULD, STEPHEN. *See* FISHER, STEVE.

GRAEME, BRUCE (pseudonym of Graham Montague Jeffries; 1900–). English author of adventure and mystery fiction and creator of BLACKSHIRT, a daring cracksman.

Graeme's private education was interrupted during World War I, when he volunteered for the Queen's Westminster Rifles. He returned from the war to become a free-lance journalist, short story writer, and film writer-producer. In 1925 he married Lorna Helene Louch; they have a daughter and a son, Roderic JEFFRIES, who continued the Blackshirt series after Graeme tired of it.

While working as a literary agent in 1922, Graeme submitted his first novel to a publisher but it was rejected. He later wrote a 10,000-word Blackshirt story that was quickly bought by a magazine which commissioned seven more. T. Fisher Unwin used the eight Blackshirt stories to launch a new series of cheap "novels" in 1925. More than 1 million copies of *Blackshirt* were sold during the next fifteen years; its successor, *The Return of Blackshirt* (1927), also a collection of stories, did as well.

Graeme has also written about several other series characters: Theodore I. Terhune, a genial young bookseller, in *Seven Clues in Search of a Crime* (1941), *A Case of Books* (1946), and others; and Superintendent Stevens of Scotland Yard and Inspector Pierre Allain of the Sûreté ("France's finest detective and fiercest lover"), who team up in *A Murder of Some Importance* (1931), *The Imperfect Crime* (1932) and many other books. Stevens soloes in *Epilogue* (1933), an intelligent attempt at a solution to Charles DICKENS's unfinished novel, *The Mystery of Edwin Drood* (1870). Graeme also writes under the pseudonym Peter Bourne, and, as David Graeme, he produced four novels about Monsieur Blackshirt—historical fiction featuring a swashbuckling seventeenth-century ancestor of Blackshirt.

GRAEME, DAVID. *See* GRAEME, BRUCE.

GRAEME, RODERIC. *See* JEFFRIES, RODERIC.

GRAINGER, FRANCIS EDWARD. *See* HILL, HEADON.

GRANT, AMBROSE. *See* CHASE, JAMES HADLEY.

GRANT, LANDON. *See* GRIBBLE, LEONARD R.

GRANT, MAXWELL. *See* GIBSON, WALTER B.

GRAY, BERKELEY. *See* BROOKS, EDWY SEARLES.

GREEN, ANNA KATHARINE (1846–1935). American writer, variously regarded as the "mother, grandmother, and godmother of the detective story" because of her authorship of *The Leavenworth Case* (1878)—usually considered to be the first detective

There are two states of the front cover of Anna Katharine Green's *A Difficult Problem;* the one on the left is the earlier.

novel written by a woman (the less-well-known novel *The Dead Letter*, by Seeley REGESTER, was published in 1867).

Born in Brooklyn, N.Y., the daughter of Katharine Ann (Whitney) and James Wilson Green, a well-known criminal lawyer, she was educated at Ripley Female College in Poultney, Vt. She married Charles Rohlfs, a furniture designer and manufacturer, and spent most of her life in Buffalo, N.Y., with him and their three children.

Her ambition was to write poetry. She published a volume of verse, *The Defense of the Bride and Other Poems* (1882), and a drama in verse, *Risifi's Daughter* (1887), but her first book, *The Leavenworth Case*, was fiction, and virtually all the rest of her work was in the mystery-detective genre. Her father's career undoubtedly provided her with the background for the plot of *The Leavenworth Case;* the book's subtitle, *A Lawyer's Story*, reveals its intent. It was instantly successful and is one of the best-selling detective novels ever written. Mrs. Rohlfs later produced a successful dramatic version in which her husband appeared. Her first and most famous detective is Ebenezer GRYCE, who solves the Leavenworth case and subsequent ones, but she also wrote books involving lady detectives Violet Strange and Amelia Butterworth, Gryce's able assistant.

Most of Mrs. Rohlfs's novels have substantial love-story qualities and melodramatic flourishes, but there is genuine detective work—both investigative and deductive—throughout. Plot construction is the greatest strength of her works, the complex story lines being carefully devised to heighten suspense until the logical denouement.

CHECKLIST

Mysteries not involving Ebenezer Gryce.

1881 *The Sword of Damocles*
1883 *X.Y.Z.: A Detective Story* (s.s.)
1886 *The Mill Mystery*
1887 *7 to 12: A Detective Story* (s.s.)
1890 *The Forsaken Inn*
1891 *The Old House and Other Stories* (s.s.)
1892 *Cynthia Wakeham's Money*
1893 *Marked "Personal"*
1894 *Miss Hurd: An Enigma*
1895 *Doctor Izard*
1899 *Agatha Webb*
1900 *A Difficult Problem* (s.s.; five of the stories are not about Gryce)
1902 *Three Women and a Mystery* (s.s.)
1903 *The Filigree Ball*
1905 *The House in the Mist* (s.s.)
1905 *The Millionaire Baby*
1905 *The Amethyst Box*
1906 *The Woman in the Alcove*
1906 *The Chief Legatee* (British title: *The Woman of Mystery*)
1907 *The Mayor's Wife*
1910 *The House of the Whispering Pines*
1910 *Three Thousand Dollars*
1913 *Masterpieces of Mystery* (s.s.)
1914 *Dark Hollow*
1915 *The Golden Slipper and Other Problems for Violet Strange* (s.s.)
1916 *To the Minute and Scarlet and Black* (s.s.)
1923 *The Step on the Stair*

GREEN, CHARLES M. *See* GARDNER, ERLE STANLEY.

GREEN HORNET, THE (Creators: Fran Striker and George W. Trendle). Popular radio and comic book hero. With his faithful Japanese sidekick, Kato, Britt Reid, publisher of *The Daily Sentinel*, fights crime as a semifugitive from the law. He shoots his victims with a gas gun that only stuns them until the police arrive. His trademarks are his extraordinary automobile, the Black Beauty, and his Green Hornet seal, which he always leaves at the scene of his adventures. Reid is reported to be the grandnephew of the Lone Ranger. The first *Green Hornet* radio program was broadcast over the Mutual network in 1938, with Al Hodge in the title role.

The Green Hornet was featured in two movie serials by Universal in 1940. Van Williams as Reid and Bruce Lee as Kato starred in twenty-six half-hour episodes of a 1966–1967 television series.

GREENE, GRAHAM (1904–   ). English author who prefers to call his novels of crime and intrigue "entertainments." He was born in Berkhamsted, Hertfordshire, the son of Marion Raymond (Greene)

Orson Welles as Harry Lime, the enigmatic figure in Graham Greene's *The Third Man*, filmed in the streets and sewers of postwar Vienna. [*Selznick Releasing*]

and Charles Henry Greene (cousins); Graham's mother was a first cousin of Robert Louis STEVENSON. After graduating from Oxford, he worked on the London *Times* for three years. He married Vivien Dayrell-Browning in 1927; they have a son and a daughter. During World War II Greene served with the Foreign Office, assigned to special duty in West Africa. After the war, his connections with the United States became shaky when his visa was delayed because of his four-week provisional membership in the Communist party at the age of nineteen.

Strongly imbued with his profound belief in Catholicism, Greene's fiction focuses attention on the endless problem man faces in relation to God. His interest in abnormal psychology and his fascination with the struggle between good and evil led naturally to his exploration of these themes in the crime novel. Unlike many mystery-adventure novelists, Greene is less concerned with the action of the plot—the events—than he is with the people involved—their motivations, emotions, and inner turmoil.

Although Greene separates his entertainments (espionage thrillers) from his more serious novels with their somber religious overtones, the two types are less distinct than he might wish them to be. This overlapping of categories is best exemplified in the book often considered his best crime novel, *Brighton Rock* (1938). Although Greene lists it among his serious books, the title page of the first American edition bears the words "an entertainment."

Pinkie, a seventeen-year-old Catholic boy raised in a slum, becomes the leader of a mob. When a journalist is killed on crowded Brighton Beach during a bank holiday, the coroner calls it "natural death." The only person who suspects the truth is a large, cheerful, vulgar woman the journalist had picked up on the day of his murder. She believes in right and wrong, she says, and begins a private investigation. The apparently totally evil Pinkie has married a sixteen-year-old girl who is as good as he is bad. The woman tries to save the girl from the lad, whose love of crime is so intense that he needs no sexual passion, drink, or even friendship.

Arthur Raven, the paid assassin in *A Gun for Sale* (1936; U.S. title: *This Gun for Hire*), is a repulsive character, but, by the time his case history is unfolded, he is seen as a helpless, pathetic figure. After Raven murders a Socialist minister, nearly precipitating the inevitable war, Inspector Mather trails and corners him. Although Mather's fiancée reveals the hidden humanity in the killer, he has been doomed from the outset.

The Third Man, written directly for the film, appeared in a condensed version in *The American Magazine* in 1949. After the release of the popular motion picture that year, the original film treatment was published in the form of a short novel in 1950. American novelist Rollo Martins is in postwar Vienna to meet his friend Harry Lime. He learns that Lime is dead, the victim of a mysterious accident. Two witnesses to the accident tell him what they saw but also tell him about a third witness—someone who knows what really happened. As Martins searches for the third man, his own life becomes jeopardized . . . until he learns the truth about his friend.

CHECKLIST

1929 *The Man Within*
1930 *The Name of Action*
1932 *Stamboul Train* (U.S. title: *Orient Express*)
1934 *It's a Battlefield*
1935 *England Made Me* (U.S. title: *The Shipwrecked*)
1935 *The Basement Room* (s.s.)
1936 *A Gun for Sale* (U.S. title: *This Gun for Hire*)
1938 *Brighton Rock*
1939 *The Confidential Agent*
1940 *The Power and the Glory* (U.S. title: *The Labyrinthine Ways*)
1943 *The Ministry of Fear*
1947 *19 Stories* (s.s.)
1948 *The Heart of the Matter*
1950 *The Third Man*
1951 *The End of the Affair*
1954 *21 Stories* (s.s.; revision of *19 Stories,* with two stories removed and four added)
1955 *The Quiet American*
1955 *Loser Takes All*
1958 *Our Man in Havana*
1961 *A Burnt-out Case*
1966 *The Comedians*
1969 *Travels with My Aunt*
1973 *The Honorary Consul*

Films

Many of Greene's best-selling thrillers have served as the source of films, and furthermore he has written several original screenplays. His major motion pictures are listed below.

Orient Express. Fox, 1934. Norman Foster, Heather Angel, Ralph Morgan, Roy D'Arcy. Directed by Paul Martin.

On board that famous train, leaving Ostend for Istanbul, the hero falls in love with a penniless dancer who he discovers has fainted from hunger; later he realizes that she is connected with a Communist agent who is also on the train.

This Gun for Hire. Paramount, 1942. Alan Ladd, Veronica Lake, Robert Preston, Laird Cregar. Directed by Frank Tuttle.

A ruthless young killer is hired by an effete, middle-aged fifth columnist to assassinate an opponent but is rewarded with marked bills; the novel was transposed to American locales, in a screenplay to which W. R. BURNETT contributed.

The Ministry of Fear. Paramount, 1944. Ray Milland, Marjorie Reynolds, Carl Esmond, Hillary Brooke. Directed by Fritz LANG.

Released from an insane asylum—he had killed his incurably ill wife—and waiting for a train, a man wins a cake at a charity bazaar and becomes involved in a murder at a séance and an incredible spy ring.

Confidential Agent. Warner Brothers, 1945. Charles Boyer, Lauren Bacall, Peter Lorre, Victor Francen, Wanda Hendrix, George Zucco. Directed by Herman Shumlin.

A Spanish Loyalist agent goes to England to prevent coal from being sold to the fascists, finds himself a murder target, uncovers Loyalist traitors, and reluctantly falls in love with the coal magnate's daughter.

The Man Within. (U.S. title: *The Smugglers*). Eagle-Lion (British), 1947. Michael Redgrave, Jean Kent, Richard Attenborough, Joan Greenwood, Francis L. Sullivan. Directed by Bernard Knowles.

In this period tale of Sussex smuggling, a frail young sailor, unjustly whipped, is persuaded to betray his fellow crew members who have been transporting brandy illegally.

Brighton Rock. Pathe (British), 1947. Attenborough, Carol Marsh, Hermione Baddeley, William Hartnell. Directed by John Boulting.

The tough teen-age leader of a Brighton seaside gang marries a childlike, devout waitress to prevent her from serving as a witness against him.

The Fugitive. RKO, 1947. Henry Fonda, Dolores Del Rio, Ward Bond, Pedro Armendariz, J. Carroll Naish. Directed by John Ford. Based on *The Labyrinthine Ways.*

In a Mexico where religion has been outlawed, a despairing, drink-sodden village priest is hunted by a sadistic revolutionary.

The Fallen Idol. Selznick (British), 1948. Ralph Richardson, Michele Morgan, Bobby Henrey, Sonia Dresdel. Directed by Carol Reed. Greene wrote the screenplay, based on his short story "The Basement Room."

Tragedy results when a neglected nine-year-old boy lies to protect a butler whom he hero-worships and believes has killed his shrewish wife.

The Third Man. Selznick (British), 1949. Joseph Cotten, Alida Valli, Orson Welles, Trevor Howard. Directed by Reed. Screenplay by Greene.

An American writer arrives in Vienna to solve conflicting reports about the death of an old friend in a street accident and also learns that the man had been callously black-marketing penicillin.

The Heart of the Matter. Associated Artists (British), 1953. Howard, Elizabeth Allan, Maria Schell, Denholm Elliott, Peter Finch. Directed by George More O'Farrell.

A deputy police commissioner in a dispiriting British colony in West Africa, harboring deep guilt because of an extramarital affair, allows himself to be

Graham Greene's most popular works are the thrillers he describes as entertainments; he regards as his best works those he describes as novels. That almost-arbitrary division is best illuminated by *Brighton Rock,* labeled an entertainment by Viking, his American publisher, and a novel by Heinemann, his English publisher. This is the dust wrapper of the first American edition of 1938, which reportedly precedes the English publication date by a few days.

blackmailed into aiding a diamond-smuggling operation.

The Stranger's Hand. DCA, 1954 (filmed in Italy). Richard Basehart, Howard, Valli, Eduardo Cianelli. Directed by Mario Soldati. Greene contributed the original idea and, with John Stafford, produced the film.

A schoolboy (Richard O'Sullivan) meets his father, a major (Howard), in Venice, but the latter is kidnapped by enemy agents because he has tried to interfere in a political abduction.

The End of the Affair. Columbia, 1955. Deborah Kerr, Van Johnson, John Mills, Peter Cushing. Directed by Edward Dmytryk.

In this tale of adultery and vows of faith, a shabby private detective (Mills) is hired by a bewildered, distraught husband.

Across the Bridge. Rank (British), 1957. Rod Steiger, Bill Nagy, Noel Willman. Directed by Annakin. From the story of the same name, first published in *Nineteen Stories*.

A shady international financier crosses into Mexico and, after placing his identification papers on his "double," tosses the man off a train; the victim, however, is a political assassin and is traveling with a dog, which the financier subsequently adopts.

Short Cut to Hell. Paramount, 1957. Robert Ivers, Georgann Johnson, William Bishop, Jacques Abuchon. Directed by James Cagney (his only directorial effort).

In this remake of *This Gun for Hire*, the assassination is carried out to silence the people who know about faulty construction work. Again, the setting is California.

The Quiet American. United Artists, 1958 (filmed in Saigon). Audie Murphy, Redgrave, Claude Dauphin, Giorgia Moll. Directed by Joseph L. Mankiewicz, who also wrote the screenplay.

An English journalist covering the Indochina war is responsible for the murder of an idealistic young American during the Chinese New Year celebration; the victim's fervent belief in a "Third Force" may have caused him to instigate terrorist activities. The film, which changed the intent of the novel to some extent, was repudiated by Greene.

Our Man in Havana. Columbia, 1959 (filmed in Cuba). Alec Guinness, Burl Ives, Maureen O'Hara, Ernie Kovacs, Noel Coward, Richardson, Jo Morrow. Directed by Reed. Greene wrote the screenplay, based on his novel.

A bumbling vacuum cleaner salesman is approached by the wry chief of the British Caribbean espionage network to be its man in Havana. He enthusiastically sends to London the plans for secret installations in the hills—they are actually vacuum cleaner designs.

The Comedians. MGM, 1967 (filmed in Africa). Richard Burton, Elizabeth Taylor, Guinness, Peter Ustinov, Paul Ford, Lillian Gish, James Earl Jones, Cicely Tyson. Directed by Peter Glenville. Screenplay by Greene, from his 1966 novel.

At the height of Haiti's political unrest, a hotel owner (Burton) returns to the island with three fellow passengers and soon abandons his cynicism and attempts to aid a rebel group.

Travels with My Aunt. MGM, 1972. Maggie Smith, Alec McCowen, Lou Gossett, Robert Stephens, Cindy Williams. Directed by George Cukor.

At his mother's funeral, a mild-mannered bank teller reencounters his elderly but flamboyant Aunt Augusta, who convinces him to accompany her on an international journey across several borders that involves—he later discovers—smuggling and other illegal activities.

England Made Me. Hemdale (British), 1973. Finch, Michael York, Hildegard Neil, Michael Hordern. Directed by Peter Dufell.

A vagabond idealist is drawn into intrigue by his domineering sister, mistress of a ruthless financier (Finch) whose empire is toppling. The setting of the novel has been transferred from Stockholm to an obvious prewar Nazi Germany.

Radio and Television

Greene's novels and stories have not been extensively used in either medium. In the late 1940s abbreviated versions of *The Confidential Agent* and *Orient Express* were presented on the CBS-radio half-hour anthology series *Escape*. For one season, in 1950, Orson Welles starred in *The Lives of Harry Lime*, a series of British-made half-hour radio adventures drawn from the title character of *The Third Man*, now more a globe-trotting rogue sometimes devoting his efforts to good causes. Although most of the settings were European, Lime extended his confidence trickery as far afield as India. There was also a television series entitled *The Third Man* (1960), starring Michael Rennie as Lime. In late 1961 a CBS television special presented Sir Laurence Olivier as the hunted Mexican priest in an impressive version of *The Power and the Glory*.

A series of short stories under the title *Shades of Greene* was televised in England in the fall of 1975.

GREX, LEO. *See* GRIBBLE, LEONARD R.

GREY, JOHN W. *See* REEVE, ARTHUR B.

GREY, LOUIS. *See* GRIBBLE, LEONARD R.

GRIBBLE, LEONARD R[EGINALD] (1908–). English detective novelist. Since he published his first book in 1929, Gribble, a prolific writer, has written or edited more than 200 books under his own

The same dust wrapper appears on the English and American editions of this short story collection by Leonard R. Gribble. Jenkins published the London edition in 1956; Roy, the New York edition in 1957.

name and many pseudonyms, including Leo Grex, Louis Grey, Landon Grant, Dexter Muir, and Sterry Browning. An intimate friend of many of Scotland Yard's leading detectives, he has used their exploits in writing such true-crime books as *Famous Feats of Detection and Deduction* (1934), *Adventures in Murder* (1955), *Murders Most Strange* (1959), *Such Women Are Deadly* (1965), and *They Conspired to Kill* (1975).

Most of Gribble's novels have featured the imaginative but cautious policeman, Anthony Slade of Scotland Yard. Two of the most popular ones are about soccer. In *The Arsenal Stadium Mystery* (1939) a member of the opposing team is murdered while playing in a game against the famous Arsenal professional team. *They Kidnapped Stanley Matthews* (1950) is a story of what might happen if the most famous soccer player of his time were kidnapped.

GRUBER, FRANK (1904–1969). American screenwriter and author of detective and western stories. Born in Elmer, Minn., the son of Susanna (Reisinger) and Joseph Gruber, he worked on trade journals and taught writing in New York City before becoming a full-time free-lance writer. He married Lois Mahood; they had one son.

PULP MAGAZINES were attaining unprecedented popularity when he determined to write for them. For years, though, his stories were accepted only occasionally, and he was virtually penniless; but he wrote an enormous number of words (about 600,000 a year during most of his career) and eventually became one of the top-paid writers in the United States. His trials and tribulations are recorded in *The Pulp Jungle* (1967), an autobiographical work. He produced more than 300 short stories that were published in 50 different magazines, more than 60 novels, about 70 film scripts, 150 television scripts, and countless miscellaneous works. His books, translated into twenty-four languages, have had combined sales exceeding 90 million copies.

Among Gruber's many memorable characters is Oliver Quade, a man whose photographic memory is responsible for his nickname, the "Human Encyclopedia." With his straight man, Charlie Boston, he hawks a one-volume *Compendium of Human Knowledge*, and his memory for obscure facts helps him solve some strange mysteries. Ten short tales about him, most of which originally appeared in BLACK MASK, were collected in *Brass Knuckles* (1966).

Johnny Fletcher is an amateur detective who teams up with Sam Cragg in a series of popular novels. Johnny is the brains of the team; Sam is the brawn. Unable to sell many copies of their muscle-building book, *Every Man a Samson*, they are constantly broke and have more trouble dodging bill collectors than they have solving crimes. Their first case, *The French Key*, was written in seven days and appeared on every published list of "best mysteries" in 1940.

The title character of *Simon Lash, Private Detective* (1941) is a connoisseur of rare editions—as was Gruber.

Gruber also published books as Stephen Acre, Charles K. Boston, and John K. Vedder, and wrote magazine pieces under such house names as C. K. M. Scanlon and Tom Gunn.

Films

Although Gruber made a career in Hollywood writing screenplays, many of them westerns, three of his mystery novels served as the source of motion pictures.

The French Key. Republic, 1946. Albert Dekker, Mike Mazurki, Marjorie Manners, Selmer Jackson. Directed by Walter Colmes.

Johnny Fletcher's clowning (he is played by Albert Dekker) outside a hotel window causes some concern to his partner, Sam Cragg (Mike Mazurki). Fletcher is demonstrating entry and egress from cheap hotel rooms sealed with a French key, a door lock clogged with wax by the management to keep a tardy-paying guest from his belongings. The film *The French Key* is based on the book by Frank Gruber, who drew on his experiences as a struggling writer in New York. [*Republic*]

Johnny Fletcher and Sam Cragg (Dekker and Mazurki), locked out of their hotel room with the management's wax "French" key, climb through the window of an adjoining room and discover a corpse.

Accomplice. PRC, 1946. Richard Arlen, Veda Ann Borg, Edward Earle. Directed by Colmes. Based on *Simon Lash, Private Detective.*

Simon Lash (Arlen), private eye, is asked by an old flame to track down her husband, a bank manager, and at an old mink ranch unearths his body.

Twenty plus Two. Allied Artists, 1961. David Janssen, Jeanne Crain, Dina Merrill, Agnes Moorehead, Brad Dexter. Directed by Joseph M. Newman. Based on Gruber's 1961 book of the same title.

In a complicated plot, a private detective who specializes in finding missing heirs links a woman who vanished years ago to the murder of a movie star's fan mail secretary.

GRYCE, EBENEZER (Creator: Anna Katharine GREEN). A stolid, competent, hardworking policeman with many characteristics reminiscent of those of Sergeant CUFF and Inspector BUCKET, Gryce made his first appearance in *The Leavenworth Case* (1878). There is no eccentricity about him, and no lack of dignity, but he nevertheless feels that his profession does not allow him to be considered a gentleman.

Everett Raymond, the gentlemanly lawyer who relates the Leavenworth case, assists Gryce in acquiring information from people who move in the social circle that Gryce shuns. The socially sensitive detective also employs a subordinate, "Mr. Q," to perform some of the less dignified and more menial chores—such as scuttling across roofs to peek through windows, listening at doors, and collecting obvious clues.

The middle-aged Gryce is portly and gentle, inspiring confidence and affection, especially among the women involved in his cases. Like Sherlock HOLMES (who did not appear until nine years later), Gryce is able to speak knowledgeably about such esoteric subjects as various grades of writing paper and the type of ash each would make if burned and the "science of probability."

The Leavenworth Case has many elements that have become clichés in detective fiction. Rich old Mr. Leavenworth is murdered in his luxurious library just as he is about to sign a new will. A dignified, if suspicious, butler, a ballistics expert, and a long coroner's inquiry—complete with minute medical evidence—are components of this novel, which has been inaccurately described as the first American detective novel. As Gryce uncovers clues, and expert witnesses prove the cause and time of death, each of the Leavenworth daughters falls under suspicion.

In several other cases Gryce uses Amelia Butterworth to serve a function similar to that performed by Mr. Raymond. She is one of the earliest female detectives, and her social standing gives her entrée to certain people and situations that Gryce—incomprehensibly—feels are above him.

CHECKLIST

1878	*The Leavenworth Case*
1880	*A Strange Disappearance*
1883	*Hand and Ring*
1888	*Behind Closed Doors*
1890	*A Matter of Millions*
1895	"The Doctor, His Wife, and the Clock" (s.s.)
1897	*That Affair Next Door*
1898	*Lost Man's Lane*
1900	*A Difficult Problem* (s.s.; one story, "The Staircase at the Heart's Delight," involves Gryce)
1900	*The Circular Study*
1901	*One of My Sons*
1911	*Initials Only*
1917	*The Mystery of the Hasty Arrow*

Films

The Leavenworth Case was first made into a film in 1923; a sound version appeared in 1936. Neither film was a close adaptation.

The Leavenworth Case. Republic, 1936. Donald Cook, Norman Foster, Erin O'Brien-Moore. Directed by Lewis D. Collins.

By whistling a certain tune, the owner of a monkey trains the animal to enter a room and turn on the gas jet; several murders result.

H

"HAD-I-BUT-KNOWN" SCHOOL. Term referring to the type of mystery and suspense fiction first popularized by Mary Roberts RINEHART with the publication of *The Circular Staircase* (1908). In the countless imitations of this novel, by both Mrs. Rinehart and others, a beautiful heroine invariably and inevitably finds herself involved in a situation she has been warned to avoid. To prove how courageous—or pigheaded—she can be, she risks her life but is saved at the last instant—usually by her lover. These novels are told in retrospect, with the heroine saying, or implying, "Had I but known then what I know now, these terrible murders would not have occurred." The heroine rarely behaves in a way that bears much relation to common sense, and she seldom uses good judgment. She never has an explanation for her actions—nor can the reader ever determine one. In recent years, variations of this type of fiction have been called "Gothic novels," although they bear little resemblance to the Gothic novels of such masters as Ann RADCLIFFE or Mary SHELLEY. These novels are generally regarded as "feminine" because of the readership they have. Among the practitioners of the most successful "HIBK" novels are Dorothy Cameron DISNEY, Mignon G. EBERHART, Leslie FORD, and Mabel SEELEY.

HAGGARD, WILLIAM (pseudonym of Richard Henry Michael Clayton; 1907–   ). English civil servant and mystery novelist; creator of Colonel Charles RUSSELL. Born in Surrey and educated at Lancing and Christ Church, Oxford, Clayton entered the Indian Civil Service in 1931 and became a magistrate and sessions judge. After serving in the Indian Army during World War II, he received further education at the Staff College at Quetta and was promoted to the General Staff as an intelligence officer. In 1945 Clayton was assigned to Whitehall for less arduous tasks. He became an official of the Board of Trade and controller of enemy property in 1957.

William Haggard is one of the current masters of the spy-intrigue novel. But, unlike such contemporaries as Ian FLEMING and Donald HAMILTON, he is unsensational and subtle. He uses overt violence infrequently and, when he does, gains impact through contrast. His witty, urbane style may not appeal to those readers who prefer simple and direct spy stories.

Haggard's forte is the depiction of characters caught on the horns of an insoluble dilemma (frequently a moral one); they usually have much to lose regardless of the decision they make. They are the prominent, highly placed people one would expect to find in Haggard's tales, which deal with espionage in the highest political and diplomatic circles.

Closed Circuit (1960) is an unusual Haggard book in that it does not involve Russell. The heir to a large estate in a Latin American country seeks help from the British Foreign Office in claiming an inheritance that is threatened by an old family enemy who is now the dictator of that country.

Julian SYMONS summed up the Haggard works: "The operations of Colonel Russell . . . are marked by a feeling for aristocratic attitudes, linked less with birth than with behavior, that is unique in the modern spy story. Haggard is a Right Wing romantic of the [John] BUCHAN kind . . . who has an agreeable streak of realism. Russell is capable of getting on perfectly well, on a basis of *Realpolitik,* with his Soviet opposite number, but cannot bear the pettifogging liberal equivocation of his own country's politicians. *The Arena* (1961) and *The Unquiet Sleep* (1962) are among the best of his books, which are all cunningly plotted, although the motivations of his characters seem at times to be of Jamesian complexity."

HALIFAX, DR. CLIFFORD. *See* MEADE, L. T.

HALL, ADAM (pseudonym of Elleston Trevor; 1920–   ). English novelist, especially well known for his spy thrillers. Born Trevor Dudley-Smith in Bromley, Kent (he changed his name legally to Elleston Trevor), he was educated at Sevenoaks and appren-

Elleston Trevor, better known as Adam Hall. *[Jean-Pierre Trevor]*

ticed as a racing driver upon leaving school in 1938. He served in the RAF during World War II and began to write professionally after the war was over. He married Jonquil Burgess in 1946; they have one son.

Hall is the author of a number of novels, many of which have been used as film sources, including *Dead on Course* (1951; under the pseudonym Mansell Black), *The Big Pick-Up* (1955; film title: *Dunkirk*), the Trevor novel *The Pillars of Midnight* (1957; film title: *80,000 Suspects*), and *The Flight of the Phoenix* (1964; by Trevor). Other novels have been sold to motion-picture companies but have not yet been filmed (*Chorus of Echoes*, 1950; a Mansell Black novel, *Sinister Cargo*, 1952; a Trevor novel, *Gale Force*, 1956; *Heat Wave*, 1957, under the pseudonym Caesar Smith; a Trevor novel, *The V.I.P.*, 1959; and *The Freebooters*, 1968).

His best-known spy novel, *The Berlin Memorandum* (1965; U.S. title: *The Quiller Memorandum*), was awarded an Edgar by the Mystery Writers of America and the French Grand Prix de Littérature Policière. It was also a Book-of-the-Month Club selection in the United States and a Book Club choice in England. Anthony BOUCHER, reviewing it in *The New York Times Book Review*, said: "This is a grand exercise in ambivalence and intricacy, tense and suspenseful at every moment, with fascinatingly complex characters, unusual plausibility in detailing the professional mechanics of espionage, and a genuine uncompromising tough-mindedness comparable to [John] LE CARRÉ's."

This book was followed by *The Ninth Directive* (1966)—Quiller in Bangkok; *The Striker Portfolio* (1969)—the mysterious crashes of the German Starfighters; *The Warsaw Document* (1971)—set in Poland; *The Tango Briefing* (1973)—in the Sahara Desert; and *The Mandarin Cypher* (1975).

Time magazine has referred to Adam Hall as "the most successful literary double agent now in the business."

Film

The Quiller Memorandum. Twentieth Century-Fox (British), 1967. George Segal, Alec Guinness, Max von Sydow, Senta Berger, George Sanders. Directed by Michael Anderson.

A British intelligence officer speculates about the death of his predecessor and the rise of neonazism in Berlin. In 1975 these characters served as the basis for a British television miniseries.

HALLIDAY, BRETT (pseudonym of Davis Dresser; 1904–). American author of private eye novels. Though Chicago-born, Dresser spent his childhood in Texas, where, at the age of fourteen, he ran away from home and joined the Army, serving in the cavalry at Fort Bliss in El Paso. Discharged at sixteen, when his true age was discovered, he finished high school but then took to wandering throughout the Southwest and Mexico, working in construction camps and oil fields. He returned to school (Tri-State College in Indiana) and received a certificate in civil engineering. He then resumed his travels, working as an engineer and surveyor.

In 1927 Dresser began to write, and, despite an initial lack of success, he continued to do so, especially when the Depression made it difficult to find engineering work. Using various pseudonyms (Matthew Blood, Peter Shelley, Anthony Scott, Sylvia Carson, Kathryn Culver, and others), he wrote dozens of mystery, western, love, adventure, and sex stories for the PULP MAGAZINES. His first mystery, *Mum's the Word for Murder*, was published in 1938 under the pseudonym Asa Baker. The following year he published, after four years of rejections, the first novel about Michael SHAYNE, the detective who brought him lasting fame and success. Later he published another book by Baker, and others by Don Davis, Anderson Wayne, and Hal Debrett (a joint pseudonym with Kathleen Rollins), but none achieved the success of the Shayne series. Dresser based the detective on a man he had met while working in Mexico on an oil tanker.

Dresser was a founding member of the Mystery Writers of America; he is also a member of the Western Writers of America. He has edited many books, including *Murder in Miami* (1959) and *The Best Detective Stories of the Year: 16th Annual Collection* (1961).

He has edited *Mike Shayne's Mystery Magazine* and was the owner of a publishing firm, Torquil & Company, whose books were distributed by Dodd, Mead. His wives have all been writers. He was formerly married to Helen MCCLOY and Kathleen Rollins. His current wife, Mary Savage, has written several books, including a mystery, *A Likeness to Voices* (1963).

There have been more than sixty Shayne novels, and many novelettes. Most take place in Miami, where the detective has his office. Dresser has never explored the city in depth in the series; indeed, he has been at his best in those books in which Shayne leaves Miami. In such "foreign" locales, he reveals his personal views more readily, as in *A Taste for Violence* (1949), in which Shayne fights a corrupt police force and unfair management practices in a Kentucky mining town, and in *The Violent World of Michael Shayne* (1965), set in Washington, D.C., amid an atmosphere of lobbying, bribery, and political corruption. Dresser's most unusual setting was the annual frontier festival in Central City, Colo., visited by Shayne in *Murder Wears a Mummer's Mask* (1943). He used his Army days in El Paso for *Murder Is My Business* (1945), a novel about illegal drugs and AWOL soldiers crossing the Mexican border.

Dresser also drew upon his Southwestern experiences for a distinguished group of crime stories Ellery QUEEN (author) has called his "engineering stories." Set in Texas and/or Mexico, they vividly convey a picture of construction crews working in intense heat to meet deadlines. Among them are the frequently anthologized "Human Interest Stuff" (1946) and "Extradition" (1948), winner of a second prize in *Ellery Queen's Mystery Magazine* contest.

The Halliday private detective stories contain more legitimate detection than the reader has come to expect from other works in this subgenre. Anthony BOUCHER frequently praised the author's ability to "play fair" with the reader in presenting clues. Jacques BARZUN and Wendell Hertig TAYLOR noted that the Halliday plots were "complicated but often adroitly worked out." They also commented that, in Halliday's stories, unlike other private eye tales, sex is "somewhat surprisingly underplayed."

HALLIDAY, MICHAEL. *See* CREASEY, JOHN.

HALSEY, HARLAN PAGE. *See* DIME NOVELS.

HAMBLEDON, TOMMY (Creator: Manning COLES). Thomas Elphinstone "Tommy" Hambledon served British Intelligence in Germany during World War I, and his adventures in that hostile country are recounted in *Drink to Yesterday*. He is in a German hospital, suffering from amnesia, in *Pray Silence*. His ability to speak German (he had taught modern languages at Chappell's School in England) helps him become accepted, and he rises rapidly in the Nazi party. On the eve of World War II he is, as Klaus Lehmann, chief of police of Berlin when his memory returns. He returns to England, but in his fifth adventure, *Green Hazard*, he is again in Germany, posing as Herr Professor Ulseth, inventor of a new, powerful explosive.

Hambledon is medium-sized, unexceptional in appearance, with blue eyes and blond hair. When not in disguise, he favors tweeds and carries a camera, "the very picture of a harmless tourist." He loves good food and wine but can dine simply when the need arises. He is friendly and easy to talk to and has an excellent sense of humor. Beneath the relaxed surface is a total dedication to career and country. He has said, "If a country is worth living in, it is worth fighting for."

CHECKLIST

1940 *Drink to Yesterday*
1940 *Pray Silence* (U.S. title: *A Toast to Tomorrow*)
1941 *They Tell No Tales*
1943 *Without Lawful Authority*
1945 *Green Hazard*
1946 *The Fifth Man*
1947 *A Brother for Hugh* (U.S. title: *With Intent to Deceive*)
1947 *Let the Tiger Die*
1948 *Among Those Absent*
1949 *Not Negotiable*
1949 *Diamonds to Amsterdam*
1950 *Dangerous by Nature*
1951 *Now or Never*
1952 *Night Train to Paris*
1952 *Alias Uncle Hugo*
1953 *A Knife for the Juggler*
1954 *Not for Export* (U.S. title: *All That Glitters*)
1955 *The Man in the Green Hat*
1956 *The Basle Express*
1956 *Birdwatcher's Quarry* (British title: *The Three Beans*)
1957 *Death of an Ambassador*
1958 *No Entry*
1960 *Nothing to Declare* (s.s.)
1960 *Crime in Concrete* (U.S. title: *Concrete Crime*)
1961 *Search for a Sultan*
1963 *The House at Pluck's Gutter*

HAMILTON, (ARTHUR DOUGLAS) BRUCE (1900–). English educator and mystery writer. Educated at Westminster and University College, London, he became a history master and later a principal in Barbados, serving as president of the Barbados Arts Council in 1958–1959. Hamilton has written plays and historical and political works; edited *The Brighton Murder Trial, Rex v. Rhodes* (1937); and written the biography of his younger brother, Patrick HAMILTON, *The Light Went Out* (1972).

In addition, he has written ten mystery novels, half of which are now difficult to locate. The others are highly individualistic works.

To Be Hanged (1930) starts as a character study but promptly turns into a tale of police routine. *Traitor's Way* (1939) is a chase novel in the best tradition of Geoffrey HOUSEHOLD. *Let Him Have Judgment* (1948; U.S. title: *The Hanging Judge*) is a long courtroom novel called a masterpiece by Erle Stanley GARDNER. *Too Much of Water* (1958), an excellent example of the classic form, is set on a ship headed for Barbados with a serial murderer on board.

Middle Class Murder (1937; U.S. title: *Dead Reckoning*) is an outstanding work in the inverted form. The protagonist is a dentist in a small Sussex town who has prospered and married well enough to rise to the upper stratum of the middle class. His reasonably happy existence is shattered by a tragic accident that maims and disfigures his wife. Everything goes downhill from there—until he meets an attractive and wealthy woman and starts to wonder how he can get rid of his wife.

The first half of the book is a fascinating portrait of a murderer who conceives and executes the perfect crime, culminating in a coroner's inquest and a favorable verdict. The second half shows the threads beginning to unravel as the dentist's errors begin to reveal themselves; his struggles to hide his guilt end in a debacle.

HAMILTON, DONALD (BENGTSSON) (1916–). American mystery and western novelist; creator of Matt HELM. Born in Uppsala, Sweden, he arrived in the United States at the age of eight. He studied chemistry at the University of Chicago and received a B.S. degree in 1938. After serving for four years in the Naval Reserve as a chemist, he became a free-lance writer and photographer (1946).

Hamilton married Kathleen Stick in 1941; they have two sons and two daughters. He lives in Santa Fe, N. Mex., and is a member of the Mystery Writers of America, the Western Writers of America, and the Outdoor Writers Association of America. He has written articles on hunting, yachting, and photography for various magazines, and is the author of *Donald Hamilton on Guns and Hunting* (1970). He has also published a series of paperback westerns, for example, *Smoky Valley* (1954), *Mad River* (1956), *The Man from Santa Clara* (1960), and *Texas Fever* (1960). Another western, *Ambush at Blanco Canyon*, serialized in *The Saturday Evening Post*, was published as *The Big Country* (1957), and was later made into a film starring Gregory Peck and Charlton Heston.

An early Hamilton work, *Date with Darkness* (1947), is an outstanding example of the counterspy novel. Most of his mystery novels were originally published in paperback editions, but they have been reviewed and praised by nearly all critics and frequently reprinted. His best novel is probably *Line of Fire* (1955), the chief elements of which are an assassination, firearms, the politics of a mythical state, and the psychological problems of impotence.

HAMILTON, (ANTHONY WALTER) PATRICK (1904–1962). English novelist and playwright. Born in Sussex, he attended school in Hove and went on stage at seventeen, acting in small parts, and was assistant stage manager for Andrew Melville, a noted melodramatist. Finding a theatrical career precarious, Hamilton learned typing and shorthand by correspondence and then moved from suburban Chiswick to London to find employment.

He began writing novels and produced *Monday Morning* in 1925. His second work, *Craven House* (1926), was praised in England and the United States for its reproduction of the atmosphere of middle-class Chiswick. Critics thought that his style was reminiscent of that of Charles DICKENS. *Twopence Coloured* (1928), a romance of the theater world, was followed by *The Midnight Bell* (1929), *The Siege of Pleasure* (1932), and *The Plains of Cement* (1934). Hamilton received acclaim for his dialogue, his insight into character, and his talent for creating suspense.

Hamilton was also a notable playwright. *Angel Street* was chosen by Burns Mantle as one of the best plays of the 1941–1942 season in the United States. A later play, *The Duke in Darkness* (1943), is forgotten. In 1939 he wrote two plays for radio, *Money with Menaces* and *To the Public Danger.* Hamilton died in Sheringham, Norfolk.

As a mystery writer, Hamilton is best known for *Hangover Square* (1942), which is set in the squalid Earl's Court section of London. Its protagonist is a schizophrenic whose problems are complicated by his doglike devotion to a worthless trollop who is two-timing him. Grim and powerful, this work is possibly the most valid fictional treatment and psychological study of the criminally insane.

Plays and Films

Hamilton's play *Rope*, based on the Loeb-Leopold case, opened in London in March 1929 and was presented on Broadway, as *Rope's End*, later that year. It was a modest success, but *Angel Street*, starring Judith Evelyn and Vincent Price in a 1941 production, was an extraordinary one, with more than a thousand performances to its credit. The London production, entitled *Gas Light*, had opened in December 1938. Using innovative camera techniques, Alfred HITCHCOCK based his film *Rope* (1948) on the earlier play. Other films based on Hamilton's work have been produced.

Angel Street (British title: *Gaslight*). British National (British), 1940. Anton Walbrook, Diana Wynyard, Frank Pettingell. Directed by Thorold Dickinson.

This English version of the play is an early work by a gifted director.

Gaslight (British title: *Murder in Thornton Square*). MGM, 1944. Ingrid Bergman, Charles Boyer, Joseph Cotten, Angela Lansbury. Directed by

College professor James Stewart (left) has a duel of wits at a party with two students, John Dall and Farley Granger (standing right), who have hidden the body of a classmate they have just murdered, in Alfred Hitchcock's *Rope*, from the Hamilton play. Note the unusually panoramic New York skyline in virtually a one-set film shot (except for reel changes) in one apparently continuous camera take. [*Warner Brothers*]

George Cukor. Based on the play.

In an atmosphere of brooding terror, a sinister husband slowly drives his wife insane in order to gain time to find jewels hidden in the London town house where, years before, he had murdered the tenant.

Hangover Square. Twentieth Century-Fox, 1945. Laird Cregar, Linda Darnell, George Sanders. Directed by John Brahm. Set in gaslit London, the film is a distortion of Hamilton's psychological novel.

An erratic composer, given to murderous lapses, kills the cabaret singer with whom he has become infatuated and tosses her body onto a Guy Fawkes Day bonfire.

HAMMER, MIKE (Creator: Mickey SPILLANE). Probably the toughest of all private detectives, Hammer never hesitates to kick a bad guy in the groin, gouge him in the eye, shoot him in the guts, or break several of his bones. When finished, he has no regrets because he knows that his victim deserved it. Called a fascist, a paranoid, and even a latent homosexual, Hammer is simply a "hard-boiled dick" who never backs away from physical contact—violent with villains, tender with beautiful women. Of all the voluptuous females with whom he comes in contact, the most dazzling is Velda, his dark-haired assistant-secretary–girl friend.

Hammer first appears in *I, the Jury* (1947). The man who saved his life in the war, and lost his arm in the process, is murdered, and Hammer vows vengeance. A gorgeous psychiatrist pursues Mike while he hunts the killer. Eschewing the legalities of

Biff Elliot is a grim Mike Hammer in *I, the Jury*. [*United Artists*]

a trial, he shoots the murderer. The stunned killer asks Hammer, "How could you?" He answers, "It was easy."

Vengeance Is Mine! (1950) is a behind-the-scenes view of the fashion world. Juno, an incredibly beautiful sex queen, chases, and is chased by, Mike. *My Gun Is Quick* (1950) again shows Hammer avenging the murder of a friend—a redheaded streetwalker he met the night before. Before killing the murderer, Hammer spends two pages telling him what is about to happen. In *One Lonely Night* (1952) he is pitted against a Communist cell. In *Kiss Me, Deadly* (1952), Hammer burns the villain to death, watching the body as it is consumed by roaring flames.

CHECKLIST

1947	*I, the Jury*
1950	*Vengeance Is Mine!*
1950	*My Gun Is Quick*
1951	*The Big Kill*
1951	*One Lonely Night*
1952	*Kiss Me, Deadly*
1962	*The Girl Hunters*
1964	*The Snake*
1966	*The Twisted Thing* (written in 1947 but previously unpublished)
1967	*The Body Lovers*
1970	*Survival . . . Zero!*

Films

Spillane's raw, tough private eye lost little time in conquering the screen. A few years after his sensational literary debut, he appeared in a three-dimensional film treatment of the book.

I, the Jury. United Artists, 1953. Biff Elliot (Hammer), Preston Foster, Peggy Castle. Directed by Harry Essex.

Mike becomes involved in a number of brawls and seamy rackets, and with a beautiful lady psychiatrist, when he vows revenge for the murder of an Army friend who once saved his life.

Kiss Me Deadly. United Artists, 1955. Ralph Meeker (Hammer), Albert Dekker, Paul Stewart, Juano Hernandez, Wesley Addy, Marian Carr, Maxine Cooper, Cloris Leachman. Directed by Robert Aldrich.

Mike gives a lift to a girl (Leachman), who is obviously in trouble, on a lonely country road; thugs waylay them and force the car over a cliff, killing the girl. Mike's trail of vengeance ultimately leads him and his secretary, Velda (Maxine Cooper), to the root of several deaths: an insulated container holding valuable radioactive material—a Pandora's box that, when opened, causes a catastrophe, in this case, a conflagration. The ending of this richly individualistic film *noir* by producer-director Aldrich leaves unresolved the question of whether Mike and Velda escape alive.

My Gun Is Quick. United Artists, 1957. Robert

Mike Hammer, as played by Ralph Meeker, does not let an amorous moment distract him from the revolver in *Kiss Me Deadly*. [*United Artists*]

Mickey Spillane portrays his own creation in *The Girl Hunters;* Hammer discusses Communist infiltration with columnist Hy Gardner, playing himself. [*Colorama*]

Bray (Hammer), Whitney Blake, Jan Chaney, Richard Garland. Directed by Phil Victor.

The traditional murder of a destitute B-girl whom Mike has befriended points him to a gem collection stolen years before overseas, a nightclub deaf-mute also marked for death, and a rich, beautiful divorcée.

The Girl Hunters. Colorama, 1963 (filmed in England though set in New York). Spillane (the author portraying his creation), Shirley Eaton, Lloyd Nolan. Directed by Roy Rowland.

Hammer is pulled out of a seven-year binge caused by the disappearance and probable death of his secretary-lover Velda at the hands of the Dragon, a Red assassin, by the news she may still be alive. Newspaper columnist Hy Gardner, playing himself ("I hate those Commie punks as much as you do"), tells Mike about another Dragon victim, a murdered senator, and Mike briefly falls in love with the senator's beautiful but ultimately treacherous widow.

Radio and Television

In the early 1950s, Mickey Spillane's "That Hammer Guy" was heard on the Mutual Broadcasting System network.

Darren McGavin played a no less intense but less pugilistic detective in *Mickey Spillane's Mike Hammer* teleseries (1957–1958); there was an attempt at mild metropolitan realism, with footage of Mike passing in front of familiar New York landmarks, but the series was shot mainly on Hollywood back lots.

HAMMETT, DASHIELL (1894–1961). American detective novelist and short story writer, the most important member of the hard-boiled school of fiction. Only Carroll John DALY preceded him in writing tough-guy detective fiction for BLACK MASK magazine, which developed the first truly original American style of detective fiction.

Samuel Dashiell Hammett was born in St. Mary's County on the eastern shore of Maryland, the son of Richard Thomas and Annie Bond Dashiell (an Americanized version of the French De Chiel, with the accent on the second syllable). He dropped out of school at thirteen and knocked around in various jobs before landing a spot with the Pinkerton National Detective Agency in Baltimore. He worked for the agency in several cities, notably San Francisco, and used this experience extensively in his fiction. He won his first promotion by catching a man who had stolen a ferris wheel; was assigned to shadow gangster Nick Arnstein; and was involved in the famous Fatty Arbuckle rape case, in which the ruined actor had to appear in court three times to prove his innocence. Hammett used several of his cases as plots for his stories, which were peopled with characters he had encountered. His eight years as a Pinkerton operative enabled him to give an authenticity to his stories that no other writer of his stature could match.

When World War I erupted, he joined the Army and served as a sergeant in the Motor Ambulance Corps until he contracted tuberculosis and was hospitalized. After the armistice, he resumed his job with Pinkerton, but the difficult work took its toll of his health. He returned to the hospital, where he met nurse Josephine Annas Dolan; they were married in 1920 and had two children. After quitting his detective job, he filled his days writing advertising copy and his nights with liquor. He was separated from his wife and children and started to write detective stories.

His first efforts were published under the name Peter Collinson. In the underworld argot of the time, a "Peter Collins" was a nobody. Hammett added the "on" to make the name, literally, "nobody's son." He created the Continental Op (*see* CONTINENTAL OP, THE), the nameless San Francisco detective who quickly became one of the most popular characters in *Black Mask.*

In the years that followed, Hammett's hard-boiled detective stories appeared regularly in the foremost PULP MAGAZINES, but his best were published in *Black Mask,* where he shared top billing with Daly, Erle Stanley GARDNER, and the other big names. His first four novels were serialized in its pages prior to book publication, and there were dozens of short stories. *Red Harvest* burst on the scene in November 1927 (to February 1928), followed immediately by another Continental Op thriller, *The Dain Curse* (November 1928 to February 1929). Then came the *Maltese Falcon* (September 1929 to January 1930), which made Sam SPADE one of the most

Dashiell Hammett, taken from the front of a four-page promotional brochure issued by Knopf.

famous detectives of the twentieth century. Hammett's personal favorite, *The Glass Key,* introduced Ned Beaumont in March 1930 (to June 1930).

This story of political corruption (one of Hammett's favorite themes) represents an attempt to depart from the routine detective hero. Beaumont is much like Hammett: tall and slim, he wears a moustache, is a heavy drinker, has suffered from tuberculosis, is a compulsive gambler, and is cynical but loyal to friends and ideals. Hammett's most complex character, Beaumont is also the most enigmatic. His relationship with politician Paul Madvig, his boss, is confusing and unsatisfying because neither the character nor the author ever reveals a trace of genuine emotion. The fraudulent mask of total, inhuman self-control is never pulled aside.

With the success of *The Maltese Falcon,* Hammett got a call from Hollywood and was offered a job as a screenwriter. Although he had never had much regard for the movie industry, the Depression caused him to decide to move from New York to California, where he met Lillian Hellman and began a love affair that lasted until his death three decades later. The famous playwright was then in her mid-twenties and married (she was divorced in 1932; Hammett did not officially obtain his divorce until 1937). He helped her learn how to write. Ironically, his own writing career virtually ended a few years later, for, after he went to Hollywood, he published only a few short stories and *The Thin Man* (1934). The semi-humorous exploits of Nick and Nora CHARLES were the most financially successful of all Hammett's books, inspiring numerous films and a radio and television series.

In January 1934 an original comic strip of crime and adventure appeared. Hammett wrote, and Alex Raymond drew, *Secret Agent X-9,* which chronicled the violent adventures of an FBI agent. Raymond later became famous for his own *Flash Gordon* strip. Mel Graff took over the writing in 1939 and toned down the character. He also gave him a name: "X-9" died, and "Phil Corrigan" was born.

Aside from Hollywood assignments of varying importance, and working with Miss Hellman on her plays, Hammett directed his energies mainly toward political causes. He supported the Loyalist forces during the Spanish Civil War and devoted himself to other left-wing political activities from that point on. In 1951 he was a trustee of the Civil Rights Congress, which had provided bail for four Communists who were to stand trial for conspiracy against the United States government. The four jumped bail, and, when Hammett refused to name the contributors to the fund, he was convicted of contempt and served five months in jail. Two years later, he was called before Senator Joseph McCarthy's subcommittee. He refused to say whether he was a member of the Communist party, even to Miss Hellman, with whom he lived, off and on, for thirty years. She did not share his radical politics, and they argued often. She wrote: "Certainly he was a Marxist, but he was a very critical Marxist, often contemptuous of the Soviet Union . . . and often witty and bitingly sharp about the American Communist Party, but he was, in the end, loyal to them. A great deal about communism worried him."

There was strong anti-Hammett sentiment in the United States for several years, but a changing political climate helped to reverse those feelings before his early tuberculosis and decades of alcoholism caught up with him.

Because of Hammett's immediate and enormous success, his style has been imitated for half a century, and many stories, situations, characters, even sentences, that seem trite in his work today were vigorously new and alive on the pulp pages of *Black Mask.* As Raymond CHANDLER said, Hammett "gave murder back to the kind of people that commit it for reasons, not just to provide a corpse"—professional killers, bums, low-level politicians, and the hardworking, everyday people whose passions were just beneath one layer of skin.

CHECKLIST

Mysteries not about Nick and Nora Charles, the Continental Op, or Sam Spade.

1931 *The Glass Key*
1934 *Secret Agent X-9* (two volumes, each containing half of the first X-9 adventure)
1945 *The Adventures of Sam Spade and Other Stories* (s.s.; contains four stories not about Spade)
1946 *Hammett Homicides* (s.s.; contains two nonseries stories)
1947 *Dead Yellow Women* (s.s.; contains two nonseries stories)

A youthful Lloyd Bridges played the title role in *Secret Agent X-9*, a 1945 Universal serial based on Dashiell Hammett's comic strip character. Keye Luke and Jan Wiley also starred. [*Universal*]

1948 *Nightmare Town* (s.s.; contains two nonseries stories)
1950 *The Creeping Siamese* (s.s.; contains three nonseries stories)
1952 *Woman in the Dark* (s.s.; contains four nonseries stories)
1962 *A Man Named Thin and Other Stories* (s.s.; contains seven nonseries stories)
1966 *The Big Knockover* (s.s.; contains first appearance of the unfinished novel *Tulip*)

Films

In 1930 *Red Harvest* was used, unrecognizably, as the basis of a Paramount comedy-medodrama about bootleggers, *Roadhouse Nights* (Charles Ruggles, Helen Morgan, Jimmy Durante. Directed by Hobart Henley). In addition to the Nick and Nora Charles series, based on *The Thin Man*, and the films based on *The Maltese Falcon* (with Sam Spade), other motion pictures have been drawn from Hammett material.

City Streets. Paramount, 1931. Gary Cooper, Sylvia Sidney, Paul Lukas. Directed by Rouben Mamoulian. Adapted by Max MARCIN from Hammett's original story for the film, "After School."

A young gangster, in the beer rackets out of necessity, defies his boss in order to save the life of a girl.

Woman in the Dark. RKO, 1934. Ralph Bellamy, Fay Wray, Melvyn Douglas. Directed by Phil Rosen. Based on the 1933 short story of the same name.

A former convict, on parole, is confronted by a strange girl, dressed in an evening gown, who asks for his aid.

Mister Dynamite. Universal, 1935. Edmund Lowe, Jean Dixon, Minor Watson, Esther Ralston. Directed by Alan Crosland. Based on Hammett's original story for the film, "On the Make."

A private detective investigates the mysterious murder of a concert pianist in San Francisco.

The Glass Key. Paramount, 1935. George Raft, Edward Arnold, Claire Dodd. Directed by Frank Tuttle.

Political aide Ned Beaumont (Raft) stands by his boss in a complex tale of corrupt politics as seen from the inside.

The Glass Key. Paramount, 1942. Alan Ladd, Brian Donlevy, Veronica Lake. Directed by Stuart Heisler. A remake.

The Fat Man. Universal, 1951. J. Scott Smart, Rock Hudson, Jayne Meadows, Emmett Kelly. Directed by William Castle.

In this film, inspired by the radio series, rotund investigator Brad Runyon interrupts his gourmet dining to look into the mysterious death of a dentist whose last patient was a missing former convict involved in an armored car robbery.

Radio

The success of the radio series based on *The Thin Man* resulted in a spin-off series called *The Fat Man*. Private detective Brad Runyon, a character vaguely based on the Continental Op, made his debut on ABC in 1945. At the opening of each program, he stepped on a penny scales and informed the audience that his weight was 237 pounds and that his fortune was danger.

HANAUD, INSPECTOR (Creator: A. E. W. MASON). The first official policeman of importance in twentieth-century detective fiction, Inspector Gabriel Hanaud is a rotund, middle-aged member of the Sûreté. Unlike most of his contemporaries, he has no major eccentricities, apart from keeping Mr. Ricardo, his wine-loving companion and the chronicler of his tales, in the dark about a case until it is solved.

Although Hanaud has a strong sense of justice and deep respect for the law, he maintains an attitude of lightheartedness—even when circumstances seem inappropriate. Motivated by humanistic values, he gives others a feeling of security. Instead of being frightened by his presence, one person at the scene of the crime at the Villa Rose is so comfortable with him around that she says, "I feel as if I had a big Newfoundland dog with me."

Like most French detectives in English literature, Hanaud is a comic character, though not as broadly drawn as Eugène VALMONT or Henri BENCOLIN, or even Hercule POIROT, a Belgian. He has no unusual mental capabilities; he employs the methods of the average astute policeman, claiming that his chief skill is to seize the skirts of chance and cling tightly to them.

The first adventure in which Hanaud appears is *At the Villa Rose* (1910), in which he defends the reputation of a beautiful Englishwoman who is involved in the murder of her employer. Greed and jealousy motivate the villain to throw suspicion on the innocent girl in this intricate tale, which is loosely based on an actual French murder case. The next full-length problem for Hanaud occurs in *The House of the Arrow* (1924), in which another innocent young girl, this time the victim's niece, is accused of murder. Both novels are classics, combining ingenious plots with good characterization, authentic French background, and pleasant humor. Hanaud's pleasure at Ricardo's bafflement does not interfere with his commitment to protect potential victims. He may be ruthless with the murderer, but his sympathetic treatment of the other characters makes Hanaud one of the most likable and human of all detectives.

Other Hanaud novels are *The Prisoner in the Opal* (1928), *They Wouldn't Be Chessmen* (1935), and *The House in Lordship Lane* (1946). There are also three short stories about Hanaud: "The Affair at the Semiramis Hotel," a rare booklet published by Scribner in 1917, later collected in *The Four Corners of the World* (1917) with twelve stories not about Hanaud; "The Man from Limoges," a complete short story contained in a novel not about Hanaud, *The Sapphire* (1933); and "The Ginger King," which was printed in *The Strand* (August 1940) and *Ellery Queen's Mystery Magazine* (August 1950). A story called "The Healer" was never published; Mason expanded it to the full-length novel *They Wouldn't Be Chessmen*.

Probably the least-remembered novel about Inspector Hanaud is *They Wouldn't Be Chessmen*, a story about a master criminal who attempts to use people as chess pieces. This is the dust wrapper of the first edition, published by Hodder & Stoughton in 1935.

Films

At the Villa Rose. Stoll (British), 1920. Manora Thew, Langhorne Burton, Teddy Arundell (Inspector Hanaud). Directed by Maurice Elvey.

On the Riviera, an English girl is accused of murder when her rich companion is discovered dead.

At the Villa Rose. Twickenham (British; U.S. title: *Mystery at the Villa Rose*), 1930. Norah Baring, Austin Trevor (Hanaud), Richard Cooper. Directed by Leslie Hiscott. A remake.

The House of the Arrow. Twickenham (British), 1930. Denis Neilson Terry (Hanaud), Benita Hume, Cooper. Directed by Hiscott.

In a great old house in France, there are rumors of foul play when a wealthy woman dies and leaves her fortune to an adopted niece.

At the Villa Rose. Associated British Picture (British), 1939. Keneth Kent (Hanaud), Judy Kelly, Walter Rilla. Directed by Walter Summers. A remake, entitled *House of Mystery* in the United States.

The House of the Arrow. Associated British Picture (British), 1940. Kent (Hanaud), Diana Churchill. Directed by Harold French. A remake, entitled *Castle of Crimes* in the United States.

The House of the Arrow. Associated British Picture (British), 1953. Oscar Homolka (Hanaud), Yvonne Furneaux, Robert Urquhart. Directed by Michael Anderson. A more elaborate remake.

Play

Mason wrote a dramatic version of *At the Villa Rose*, which made its stage debut in London on July 10, 1920.

HANSHEW, THOMAS W. (1857–1914). American-English mystery writer whose works, with their stilted prose and melodramatic plots, are not widely read today, although the stories about Hamilton CLEEK, known as "the Man of the Forty Faces," have ingenious action lines and a certain nostalgic appeal. Hanshew's best-known books record the adventures of Cleek, but among his other mysteries are *Beautiful but Dangerous* (1891), *The World's Finger* (1901), *The Mallison Mystery* (1903), *The Great Ruby* (1905), *The Shadow of a Dead Man* (1906), and *Fate and the Man* (1910). He also was one of the numerous authors who wrote pseudonymous novels featuring Nick CARTER.

HARBAGE, ALFRED B. *See* KYD, THOMAS.

HARDIN, BART (Creator: David ALEXANDER). Hardin, the editor of the *Broadway Times,* a fictional racing–show business daily, lives in an apartment above a Times Square flea circus and wanders around the nearby streets at all hours. A former Marine and war hero, Hardin is known for his generosity and his love of gambling and Irish whiskey.

In his first case, *Terror on Broadway* (1954), the murderer of several attractive show girls writes to Hardin announcing his crimes in advance. Although the editor-detective is interested in a "hot" news story, he also wants to apprehend the killer, who is causing panic among the denizens of his beloved "Great White Way." In this and seven other cases, he helps Lieutenant Romano of the Homicide Bureau.

HARDY, ARTHUR SHERBURNE (1847–1930). American novelist, short story writer, and scientist. After graduating from the U.S. Military Academy, he spent a year in the Army before becoming a professor of civil engineering at Iowa College; he later taught at Chandler Scientific School and Dartmouth. After working as editor of *Cosmopolitan Magazine,* he entered the diplomatic service, serving in Persia, Greece, Switzerland, and Spain. Hardy published many novels and stories, but only two works are mystery fiction. The philosophical and gentle Inspector Joly is featured in *Diane and Her Friends* (1914), a collection of short stories selected for QUEEN'S QUORUM; Hardy's only mystery novel is *No. 13, Rue du Bon Diable* (1917).

HARDY BOYS, THE (Creator: Edward L. Stratemeyer as Franklin W. Dixon; *see* KEENE, CAROLYN). These teen-age brothers solve mysteries either on their own or with their detective father. Friends frequently help out, particularly fat, good-natured Chet Morton. The boys have a car and a boat, nicknamed *Sleuth,* and often use their father's private plane while solving complicated mysteries at home and abroad. The first nine books about the Hardy Boys were written by Stratemeyer, the others (now numbering fifty-four), by the Stratemeyer Syndicate; total sales exceed 50 million. Walt Disney has presented the brothers on television.

HARE, CYRIL (pseudonym of Alfred Alexander Gordon Clark; 1900–1958). English lawyer, judge, and mystery writer; creator of Francis PETTIGREW. Born in Mickleham, Clark spent most of his formative years in the country, where he learned to hunt, shoot, and fish, but he was never an avid sportsman. He was educated at Rugby, where he won a prize for English verse. He also attended New College, Oxford, where he received a coveted first in history. Family tradition dictated a legal career, and Clark was called to the bar in 1924. He joined the chambers of famed lawyer Ronald Oliver and practiced in the civil and criminal courts in and around London.

Clark was married in 1933 and settled in *Cyril* Mansions, Battersea. At the time, he was employed in *Hare* Court, Temple. These names—as well as a far from adequate income—suggested the pseudonym he used in his literary endeavors.

Clark's first efforts were short, flippant sketches for *Punch;* later stories and articles were published in *Illustrated London News* and *The Law Journal.* In 1936 he wrote his first full-length detective novel, *Tenant for Death.* The following year, while embroiled in defending a suspected larcenist in court, he was informed that the book had been accepted for publication. *Tenant for Death* (1937) was called an engaging debut by Jacques BARZUN and Wendell Hertig TAYLOR in *A Catalogue of Crime.* It concerns the disappearance of a financier named Ballantine, who turns up as a strangled corpse in an empty and obscure house in South Kensington.

During the early days of World War II Clark toured as a judge's marshal, an experience that provided the basic material for *Tragedy at Law* (1942). In 1942 he was employed as a civil servant in the office of the Director of Public Prosecutions. He served with the Ministry of Economic Warfare during the last part of the war. This position served as the inspiration for *With a Bare Bodkin* (1946).

Clark reached the summit of his profession in 1950, when he was appointed county court judge in his native Surrey. He traveled the circuit trying civil cases and spent his spare time writing fiction.

Aside from his judicial career and his too-infrequent detective stories, Clark was a noted public speaker whose services were always in demand by widely varying groups. His occupation and numerous outside activities, plus his inability to use a typewriter and "constitutional and incurable indolence," curtailed his literary production to nine novels and a group of short stories.

Both *Tenant for Death* and *Death Is No Sportsman* (1938) are typical of their period; they feature Inspector Mallett of Scotland Yard—an investigator not unlike Freeman Wills CROFTS's Inspector FRENCH. *Suicide Excepted* (1939), an improvement over Hare's previous work, concerns three amateur detectives who try to change a verdict of suicide to murder and features Inspector Mallett in a supporting role. It also has a wholly unexpected ending.

Tragedy at Law (1942) introduced Francis Pettigrew. Hare's favorite novel, it is a lovingly detailed study of a judge on a second-rate circuit who falls on the wrong side of the law. Further complications ensue when a murder is committed toward the end of the novel. Usually cited as Hare's masterpiece, it received rave reviews. Legal novelist Henry CECIL stated, "This book is acknowledged by many lawyers to be the classic detective story with a legal background. It has stood the test of time. . . ."

In *An English Murder* (1951) members of a typical English Christmas party are snowbound in a castle—with death as an uninvited guest. A Czech refugee, Dr. Bottwink, is obliged to help Scotland Yard solve three baffling murders. The book is a model of the English "fair-play" school, and a "must" for Agatha CHRISTIE fans. Lighter in tone than his previous work, it is unexpected from Hare.

Hare wrote four more Pettigrew novels. The *Best Detective Stories of Cyril Hare,* a collection selected by Michael GILBERT, was published after his death (1959). This volume of thirty crime stories contains an introduction by Gilbert that is a fine memorial tribute by a fellow lawyer and mystery writer.

HARRINGTON, JOSEPH (1903–). American journalist and mystery writer. Born in Newark, he began his career as a newspaperman at the age of fourteen by working as a copyboy for the *New York American* and was a reporter for many years until he became a free-lance writer. He is married, has two children, and currently resides on the Gulf Coast of Florida.

Harrington's newspaper experience served to acquaint him with many real detectives. "As individuals they varied a lot but they all had certain traits in common—an incredible tenacity, infinite patience, and an unlimited capacity for hard and often dull work. To them there was no such thing as a good clue, or a bad one. A clue was a clue; something to be pursued to the very end, hopeless or not. I never knew of a real-life mystery that they cracked by any other means."

Harrington drew upon his experiences in three novels that are models of the police procedural school of "ambulatory" detection. His series detective, Sergeant (later Acting Lieutenant) Francis X. Kerrigan, walks a lot and rings many doorbells. Eventually he gets the right answers. His creator says that he is "no smarter than the reader, just a lot more dogged, and a good workman." He is assisted by detective Jane Boardman, who is helpful and learns much about her profession under Kerrigan's tutelage.

The Last Known Address (1965) is an account of a search for a missing witness whose previous residence is two years out of date, with no leads to his current location. Anthony BOUCHER, writing in *Ellery Queen's Mystery Magazine,* cited this novel as one of the best mysteries of the year. *Blind Spot* (1966) concerns the efforts of Kerrigan and Boardman to uncover fresh evidence in the case of a young woman who has been convicted of murdering her lover, in order to prove that she is the victim of a miscarriage of justice. Boucher was impressed by this novel and stated, "I am tempted to call him [Harrington] the most truly procedural of all police-procedure novelists. He also has an admirable plot here, with a nicely tricky psychological point." In *The Last Doorbell* (1969) the detective and his assistant must locate and capture an insane kidnapper-murderer who has the odd penchant of writing letters to the family of his victim.

Joseph Harrington.

HARRIS, HERBERT (1911–). Prolific English short story writer. Harris has been listed in the *Guinness Book of World Records* since 1969 as England's most prolific short story writer. His 3,500 stories (mostly crime, suspense, and detection) have been published in twenty-six countries and translated into nineteen languages. The stories have appeared

Herbert Harris.

in every major mystery magazine and in many anthologies. They have also been presented on radio and dramatized in England and other countries. Harris founded *Red Herrings*, the news bulletin of the British Crime Writers' Association (CWA), in 1956 and edited it for nine years. He was awarded the CWA's Special Merit Award in 1965 and was its chairman in 1969–1970. He has published several mystery novels: the first was *Who Kill to Live* (1962); the most recent, *The Angry Battalion* (1973).

HARRISON, MICHAEL (1907–). English writer of mystery fiction. Harrison has written more than fifty books on such diverse topics as history, archaeology, cybernetics, advertising, and collecting stamps and coins. He has written fiction as Quentin Downes and Michael Egremont. Under the latter name he published a novel in 1936 based on the famous film *The Bride of Frankenstein*.

Under his own name Harrison published a biography, *Peter Cheyney: Prince of Hokum* (1954). He also wrote *In the Footsteps of Sherlock Holmes* (1960), which so successfully evoked the London of Holmes's time that he was given a special award by the Baker Street Irregulars. His article "A Study in Surmise" (*Ellery Queen's Mystery Magazine*, February 1971) was described by Ellery QUEEN (author) as "perhaps the most important Sherlockian scholarship in forty years." His pastiches of Edgar Allan POE's famous detective, C. Auguste DUPIN, were collected in *The Exploits of the Chevalier Dupin* (1968); the British edition, entitled *Murders in the Rue Royale* (1972), contains five additional stories.

HART, FRANCES (NEWBOLD) NOYES (1890–1943). American detective novelist. Born in Silver Spring, Md., the daughter of Janet Thurston (Newbold) and Frank Brett Noyes, she married Edward Henry Hart in 1921; they had two daughters.

Her first mystery was the classic courtroom novel *The Bellamy Trial*, serialized in *The Saturday Evening Post* in 1927 and highly successful in book form later that year. This leisurely, rambling, humorous book is based on the famous Hall-Mills murder case of the time. All the action takes place in a courtroom, and the atmosphere of a trial is conveyed realistically. Seen through the eyes of a pair of newspaper reporters, the trial involves two wealthy members of Long Island society, Stephen Bellamy and Mrs. Susan Ives, who the state contends were having a clandestine affair. Circumstantial evidence indicates that they were discovered by Mrs. Bellamy and subsequently murdered her. After the charming young couple present their side of the story from the witness box, public sympathy swings their way.

Mrs. Hart's second mystery novel, *Hide in the Dark* (1929), tells how a ten-year-old mystery is resolved during a fun-filled house party attended by the thirteen March Hares, but only after a murder occurs. This novel is credited with popularizing the parlor game "Murder." *The Crooked Lane* (1934) is a love story, involving Karl Sheridan and Tess Stuart, in which legitimate scientific detection results in an unusual denouement.

Film and Play

The Bellamy Trial. MGM, 1929. Leatrice Joy, Betty Bronson, Edward Nugent, George Berraud, Margaret Livingston. Directed by Monta Bell.

A determined district attorney tries to prove that two lovers are guilty of stabbing the man's wife to death.

Mrs. Hart, in collaboration with Frank E. Carstarphen, adapted the story for the Broadway stage in 1931.

HASTINGS, GRAHAM. *See* GRAEME, BRUCE.

HASTINGS, MACDONALD (1909—). English editor, news correspondent, and mystery novelist. Hastings's years at Stonyhurst, a famous Roman Catholic public school, are described in his autobiography, *Jesuit Child* (1971), which he wrote after he left the church. He has had a varied literary career, having written children's adventure stories, edited magazines, written extensively for the British Broadcasting Corporation, and been a war correspondent. He also served in all three branches of the British armed services during World War II. Following the war he became editor of *The Strand* and also began writing mystery novels. He is married and has a son and two daughters.

His reputation in the mystery field is based upon a series of five novels about Montague Cork, general manager of the Anchor Insurance Company, an elderly man with an uncanny ability to spot false claims. In the last Cork book the detective attempts to recover £1 million in stolen jewelry. Drawing from his own experience, the author provides a satirical look at British television.

CHECKLIST

1951	*Cork on the Water*
1953	*Cork in Bottle*
1955	*Cork and the Serpent*
1957	*Cork in the Doghouse*
1966	*Cork on the Telly* (U.S. title: *Cork on Location*)

HAWKSHAW. *See* BULLIVANT, CECIL HENRY.

HAWTHORNE, JULIAN (1846–1934). American author. Born in Boston, the son of Nathaniel Hawthorne, he was a prolific writer who averaged three or four books a year and produced many poems, articles, and stories for more than twenty years. He published three collections of mystery and crime stories: *Prince Saroni's Wife* (1884), *David Poindexter's Disappearance and Other Tales* (1888; British title: *David Poindexter's Disappearance Etc.*, 1888, which contains two stories not included in the American edition), and *Six Cent Sam's* (1893). A series of novels was based on the real-life adventures of a famous New York City policeman, Inspector Byrnes, among them, *A Tragic Mystery* (1887), *An American Penman* (1887), *The Great Bank Robbery* (1887), and *Section 558; or, the Fatal Letter* (1888).

HAYCRAFT, HOWARD (1905–). American editor and mystery critic. After attending the state university in his native Minnesota, Haycraft went to New York in 1929 and began a long association with the H. W. Wilson Company, publishers of library indexes and reference books. He became vice-president in 1940 and in 1953 was elected president, succeeding Halsey W. Wilson, the firm's founder. He has been chairman of the board since 1967.

After many years of work involving the visually handicapped, Haycraft was appointed to the President's Committee on Employment of the Handicapped. In 1966 he received the first American Library Association Francis Joseph Campbell Medal for contributions to library service for the blind. He is married to Molly Costain, who is the daughter of the late historical novelist Thomas Costain and a novelist in her own right.

Haycraft has helped compile many of the Wilson publications, including *Twentieth Century Authors* (1942). He has edited many anthologies of mystery works, beginning with *The Boys' Sherlock Holmes* in 1936. However, his fame in the genre rests with two landmark books. The first, *Murder for Pleasure: The Life and Times of the Detective Story* (1941), was the first book *about* detective fiction as a literary form to be published in the United States. In it, Haycraft provided a history, brief biographies of leading writers, a critique based on his extensive reading, and much valuable speculation on the future directions of the detective story. Following military service during World War II, Haycraft published *The Art of the Mystery Story* (1946), an anthology of fifty-three essays by leading mystery writers and critics, covering all aspects of the field.

Haycraft served as president of the Mystery Writers of America in 1963 and has received two Edgars—the first in 1947 for best mystery reviews, and a Special Award in 1975 for "distinguished contribution to mystery criticism and scholarship."

HAYCRAFT-QUEEN CORNERSTONE LIBRARY. In *Murder for Pleasure* (1941), Howard HAYCRAFT offered a collection that he called "A Readers' List of Detective Story 'Cornerstones'." He subsequently brought the list up to date, and, at a still later time, Ellery QUEEN (author) took a broader view of the genre and added titles. The complete list of 167 volumes, entitled "The Haycraft-Queen Definitive Library of Detective-Crime-Mystery Fiction: Two Centuries of Cornerstones, 1748–1948," is now regarded as the finest of its kind.

HEAD, MATTHEW (pseudonym of John Canaday; 1907–). American art critic and mystery novelist. Born in Fort Scott, Kans., Canaday grew up in Texas in the Dallas–San Antonio area. He was senior art critic of *The New York Times* and has written *Mainstreams of Modern Art: David to Picasso* (1959) and *Embattled Critic: Views on Modern Art* (1962). A noted gourmet, he became restaurant reviewer for the *Times* in 1974. As Matthew Head, he published seven mystery novels between 1943 and 1955. The three most popular of these were set in Brazzaville and feature Dr. Mary Finney, a medical missionary, as the detective. In her first appearance, *The Devil in the Bush* (1945), she and her friend Emily Collins, a fellow missionary, solve a murder during a native revolt in the Congo.

HEARD, GERALD. *See* HEARD, H. F.

HEARD, H[ENRY] F[ITZGERALD] (1889–1971). English social historian and author of science and mystery fiction. Born in London, he studied at Cambridge University and then turned to writing essays and books on historical, scientific, religious, mystical, cultural, and social subjects, signing these works Gerald Heard—the name under which all his nonfiction appeared. He moved to the United States in 1937, heading a commune in California for many years, and appeared as a character in several Aldous Huxley novels, notably as William Propter, a mystic, in *After Many a Summer Dies the Swan* (1939).

A Taste for Honey (1941), Heard's first mystery novel, introduces Mr. Mycroft, a tall, slender gentleman who has retired to Sussex to keep bees—just as Sherlock HOLMES did. Since the two detectives have physical similarities, there has been speculation that Mr. Mycroft is actually Holmes, living under an assumed name to assure anonymity. Sydney Silchester, the narrator of this pseudoscientific detective novel, is a strange man who has two passions—solitude and honey. He obtains the latter from Mr. and Mrs. Heregrove, the village beekeepers. One day he discovers the lady's body, black and swollen from bee stings. After the coroner's inquest, Silchester turns to Mr. Mycroft for a fresh supply of honey, and the aged detective warns him of Heregrove's killer bees. Silchester is skeptical . . . until he faces a horrible death.

Mr. Mycroft also appears in *Reply Paid* (1942) and *The Notched Hairpin* (1949). *Murder by Reflection* (1942) is an unusual murder mystery involving mirrors. *The Great Fog and Other Weird Tales* (1944) contains an ingenious science fiction–murder story, "The Crayfish," and other fantastic mysteries. Heard's best-known mystery short story, "The President of the U.S.A., Detective" (1947), won First Prize in *Ellery Queen's Mystery Magazine's* contest.

Film and Television

In 1966 Robert BLOCH adapted *A Taste for Honey* into a contemporary screenplay called *The Deadly Bees*. Boris Karloff played Mr. Mycroft, the retired detective of the story, in a production on television's *Elgin Hour* in the 1950s.

HECHT, BEN (1893–1964). American novelist, playwright, short story writer, and film writer. Born in New York, he moved to the Midwest, where he became one of the leaders of the "Chicago school" of writers. With Charles MacArthur (1895–1956), Hecht wrote a brilliant play, *The Front Page* (1928), drawing on his extensive background as a newspaper reporter, and many of the greatest films of the prime days of Hollywood, including *Gunga Din* (1939), *Wuthering Heights* (1939), *Spellbound* (1945), *Notorious* (1946), and *Kiss of Death* (1947). In addition to the mystery novels *The Florentine Dagger* (1923), which was filmed in 1935, and *I Hate Actors!* (1944), Hecht published short story collections that contain many tales of crime, murder, and detection, notably *Broken Necks and Other Stories* (1924; expanded edition, 1926), *The Champion from Far Away* (1931), *Actor's Blood* (1936), and *The Collected Stories of Ben Hecht* (1945).

Hecht's first screen story, *Underworld* 1927), directed by Josef von Sternberg, was the first gangster film; its tremendous popularity paved the way for countless successors.

HELM, MATT (Creator: Donald HAMILTON). The American equivalent of James BOND, Helm is a free-lance writer, mainly of western novels, and a photographer of hunting and fishing subjects. He worked for a secret military organization during World War II and learned the fine arts of spying and killing. His code name was Eric.

After the war Helm resumed his peacetime occupations and was married, but in the early 1960s he was summoned by his former chief, known only as "Mac," to serve his country and undertake a special mission.

Helm accepted, but the price he had to pay was the breakup of his family. Later, his wife remarried. In subsequent missions Helm travels (with various beautiful girls) in his beloved old pickup truck all over the United States, and his assignments take him to other areas of the world, such as Canada, Mexico, Hawaii, Scotland, and Scandinavia.

Death of a Citizen, the first book in the Matt Helm series, tells of his return to his wartime profession of spy and killer. Anthony BOUCHER called this novel "a harsh and sometimes shocking story, told with restraint, power, and conviction." The series seemed to hit its peak with numbers six through eight of the saga; these stories are more credible than previous episodes are, but they are embellished with frightening overtones that hold the reader in suspense until the final page. *The Ambushers* involves a Castro-type potential dictator who must be eliminated, an eagerly sought Nazi war criminal, and a deadly atomic missile. *The Shadowers* concerns Helm's efforts to save a beautiful space scientist from assassination by marrying her. The plot contains, in addition to the Helm spy-adventure story, a detective puzzle. In *The Ravagers* Helm's mission is to see that secret plans get into the right hands—but this time they are destined for the Soviet Union. All this is set against a long chase across Canada.

Boucher summed up the Helm saga when he said, "Donald Hamilton has brought to the spy novel the authentic hard realism of [Dashiell] Hammett; and his stories are as compelling, and probably as close to the sordid truth of espionage, as any now being told." The entire Helm series is reprinted at frequent intervals.

CHECKLIST

1960	*Death of a Citizen*
1960	*The Wrecking Crew*
1961	*The Removers*
1962	*The Silencers*
1962	*Murderers' Row*
1963	*The Ambushers*
1964	*The Shadowers*
1964	*The Ravagers*
1965	*The Devastators*
1966	*The Betrayers*
1968	*The Menacers*
1969	*The Interlopers*
1971	*The Poisoners*
1973	*The Intriguers*
1974	*The Intimidators*
1975	*The Terminators*

Films

In the 1960s singer-actor Dean Martin starred in four film distortions of Hamilton's professional spy in an attempt to present on film, as in the books, a glib, easygoing American counterpart to Bond's tongue-in-cheek derring-do. As in the Bond films, girls abound, the inventions are fantastic, and the menace is global.

The Silencers. Columbia, 1966. Dean Martin, Stella Stevens, Daliah Lavi, Victor Buono, Arthur O'Connell, Robert Webber, James Gregory (Matt's chief, head of ICE, Organization for Intelligence and Counter-Espionage), Cyd Charisse. Directed by Phil Karlson.

Dean Martin (center) as Matt Helm and a frightened Ann-Margret search for a missing scientist in *Murderers' Row*. [*Columbia*]

Former spy Helm is pulled out of a happy retirement photographing girls when enemy agents attempt to divert an American missile so that it will turn back on its atomic testing grounds in New Mexico and spread destruction. An important bit of computer tape is passed from one pretty girl to another to keep Helm occupied.

Murderers' Row. Columbia, 1966. Martin, Ann-Margret, Karl Malden, Camilla Sparv, Gregory, Beverly Adams (Helm's assistant Lovey Kravezit in films one through three). Directed by Henry Levin.

Helm stages his own funeral in order to proceed under cover to the French Riviera, where a master spy has kidnapped a scientist and his formula so that he can destroy Washington, D.C., in the first stage of a plan to conquer the world. Matt joins forces with the scientist's energetic daughter.

The Ambushers. Columbia, 1967. Martin, Senta Berger, Janice Rule, Gregory, Albert Salmi, Kurt Kasznar, Adams. Directed by Levin.

An experimental flying saucer sent up in a test flight by American scientists is brought down mysteriously somewhere in Mexico. Matt enters that country posing as a tourist-photographer, with a "wife" as cover, while assorted representatives of foreign powers kill one another off.

The Wrecking Crew. Columbia, 1968. Martin, Elke Sommer, Sharon Tate, Nancy Kwan, Nigel Green, Tina Louise. Directed by Karlson. Screenplay by William P. MCGIVERN.

Matt must single-handedly save the American and British economy by making certain that a gold shipment en route to London via Denmark arrives safely.

Television

In 1975, an ABC pilot film became a series starring Tony Franciosa as Helm. The film also featured Patrick Macnee, Ann Turkel, and Loraine Stephens as Helm's lawyer–girl friend, Kronsky. Helm becomes involved with a black market ring supplying munitions to a mercenary group attempting to take over an African nation. Buzz Kulick directed.

HEMYNG, (SAMUEL) BRACEBRIDGE (1841–1901). English author of DIME NOVELS. Born in London, he followed in his father's footsteps and became a barrister, but, unsuccessful in this career, he turned to writing and produced the first book in a long series about Jack Harkaway, a popular boys' adventure hero. Hemyng arrived in the United States in 1874 and began writing for the *Police Gazette*. His short story collection *On the Line and Danger Signal* appeared about 1890. His most famous novel is *Called to the Bar* (1885), chapters 17 and 18 of which are complete short stories about Sergeant Stoppford, a London detective.

HENNISSART, MARTHA. *See* LATHEN, EMMA.

HENRY, O. (pseudonym of William Sidney Porter; 1862–1910). American short story writer. Porter was born in Greensboro, N.C., the son of Mary Jane Virginia (Swaim), who died when he was three, and Algernon Sidney Porter, a physician. He moved to Texas for reasons of health when he was twenty, working first on a ranch and then as a bookkeeper and bank teller in Austin. He eloped with Athol Estes in 1887. While writing for the *Houston Daily Post,* he was indicted for embezzlement of the Austin bank. Instead of standing trial, he fled to New Orleans and then to Honduras, South America, and Mexico, where he learned of his wife's grave and ultimately fatal illness. When he returned to Texas to see her, he was arrested and sentenced to five years in the Ohio State Penitentiary, where he met a friendly guard named Orrin Henry, whose name is believed to have inspired Porter's pseudonym. Soon after his release he settled in New York, which he called Bagdad-on-the-Hudson, and married Sarah Lindsay Coleman in 1907. Three years later he was dead from (reports conflict) tuberculosis or his long-standing habit of consuming 2 quarts of whiskey a day.

O. Henry produced more than 600 original stories during his career, his most prolific period being the years in New York. Humorous, often ironic, but never bitter, they are often disdained today because of their sentimentality, but many remain among the best and most popular short stories ever written. His innumerable imitators have never equaled O. Henry's skill in creating the surprise, or twist, ending—the hallmark of his work.

In 1918 the Society of Arts and Sciences established the O. Henry Memorial Award for the best short story published each year. The *O. Henry Memorial Award Prize Stories,* an anthology published annually, is a symbol of prestige in the form.

Many of O. Henry's tales deal with mystery, crime, and detection. One of the most famous mystery plays in the American theater, *Alias Jimmy Valentine,* was based on "A Retrieved Reformation" (published in *Roads of Destiny,* 1909). In this now-familiar tale, Valentine, a charming young burglar, gives up his career when he falls in love. The best safecracker in the country, he is the only man who can open the bank vault in which his sweetheart's sister has been accidentally locked. He is prepared to open the safe when he notices the detective who has been stalking him for a year. If he opens it, he will give away his profession and identity; if he does not, the girl will die.

The Gentle Grafter (1908) features criminals Jeff Peters and Andy Tucker and was included in QUEEN'S QUORUM. Other O. Henry collections in which at least one mystery-detective story appears are *Waifs and Strays* (1906); *The Four Million* (1906); *Heart of the West* (1907); *The Voice of the City* (1908); *Roads of Destiny* (1909); *Strictly Business* (1910); *Whirligigs* (1910); *Sixes and Sevens* (1911), which contains two parodies of Sherlock HOLMES; and *Rolling Stones* (1912), with two parodies of François Eugène VIDOCQ. *Cops and Robbers* (1948), a paperback with a new introduction by Ellery QUEEN (author), contains reprints.

Plays and Films

O. Henry's reformed crook, Jimmy Valentine, has had a healthy stage and screen career, beginning with the successful Broadway run in 1910 of *Alias Jimmy Valentine,* adapted by Paul Armstrong from "A Retrieved Reformation," with H. B. Warner as Jimmy. A 1921 stage revival starred Otto Kruger. Robert Warwick was the first screen Valentine, in 1915; the film used the basic "child in the safe" story, as did most subsequent films based on the character.

Alias Jimmy Valentine. Metro Pictures, 1920. Bert Lytell, Wilton Taylor. Directed by Maxwell Karger.

A master crook who has reformed because of his love for a girl and is now a bank manager is still being tracked down by a police detective. He has just convinced the detective that he is not the nimble-fingered safecracker the latter has been seeking when he learns that a child has accidentally been locked in a bank vault.

Alias Jimmy Valentine. MGM, 1928. William Haines, Lionel Barrymore (Detective Doyle), Leila Hyams, Karl Dane, Tully Marshall. Directed by Jack Conway. A close remake of the 1920 film.

The Return of Jimmy Valentine. Republic, 1936. Roger Pryor, Charlotte Henry, J. Carroll Naish. Directed by Lewis D. Collins.

A newspaper reporter writes a series of stories speculating on whether the legendary safecracker Valentine is still alive; he thinks that he has found him, now a respected elderly banker (Robert Warwick) living in a small town. A gangster, however, has followed the reporter to the town.

Affairs of Jimmy Valentine. Republic, 1942. Dennis O'Keefe, Ruth Terry, George E. Stone. Directed by Bernard Vorhaus.

An employee of the advertising agency used by the *Jimmy Valentine* radio program offers $100,000 to anyone who can locate the real Valentine, thereby precipitating several murders. The reformed criminal is now a middle-aged newspaper editor (Roman Bohnen).

Radio and Television

There have been many unofficial renderings of the Valentine dilemma, and the story was frequently dramatized on radio and early television anthology series, especially *The O. Henry Playhouse* (1956), a series of half-hour plays in which Thomas Mitchell, portraying the author, told about Valentine and other O. Henry characters.

HERITAGE, MARTIN. *See* HORLER, SYDNEY.

HERMAN, HENRY. *See* MURRAY, DAVID CHRISTIE.

HEWITT, MARTIN (Creator: Arthur MORRISON). The first popular detective to follow in the footsteps of Sherlock HOLMES. As unlike the master physically as he is similar to him in method, Hewitt is stout, of average height, with a round, smiling face and an amiable nature. He is relatively colorless, and he usually resolves his spectacular cases by means of his skill in statistical and technical matters, with "no system beyond a judicious use of ordinary faculties."

The most popular detective after Sherlock Holmes was Martin Hewitt. This is the front cover of a series of reprint editions published by Ward, Lock in London around 1900.

As a lawyer's clerk, he had been so successful in collecting evidence for his employer's clients that he decided to establish a private detective agency. His office, in an old building near the Strand, has a plain ground-glass door on which appears the single word "Hewitt." A journalist friend, Brett, chronicles his cases.

Like the Holmes short stories, those about Hewitt first appeared in *The Strand* and were illustrated by Sidney Paget.

Four volumes of short stories contain all the exploits of Martin Hewitt: *Martin Hewitt, Investigator* (1894), *The Chronicles of Martin Hewitt* (1895), *The Adventures of Martin Hewitt* (1896), and *The Red Triangle* (1903).

HEXT, HARRINGTON. *See* PHILLPOTTS, EDEN.

HEYER, GEORGETTE (1902–1974). English author of historical novels and mystery stories. Educated at seminaries, Miss Heyer attended lectures on history by Professor Forbes at Westminster College. She wrote her first novel, *The Black Moth: A Romance of the 18th Century,* when she was seventeen; it was published in 1921. In 1925 she married George Ronald Rougier and lived in East Africa until 1928, when she moved to Yugoslavia for a year. The couple had one son.

Miss Heyer's fame rests largely upon a series of about forty historical novels that have been highly praised for their re-creation of Regency days in London. Among her more widely known works are *The Devil's Cub* (1932), *The Spanish Bride* (1940), *The Reluctant Widow* (1947), *Arabella* (1949), *The Quiet Gentleman* (1951), and *Cotillion* (1953).

Miss Heyer wrote a dozen mystery novels. She was noted for her ability to plot simon-pure detective novels and for her light and humorous touch. *Why Shoot a Butler?* (1933) is an early effort that starts with the protagonist, a lawyer, discovering a dead body sitting in a car next to a very beautiful young lady who claims complete innocence. *The Unfinished Clue* (1934) takes place during a typical country house party, complete with an obnoxious host who ends up with a Chinese dagger in his back.

Death in the Stocks (1935) brought wide fame to Miss Heyer when it was published in the United States as *Merely Murder.* It is about another stabbing victim—whose body is found in the village stocks. Superintendent Hannasyde investigates, and his successor in later novels, Sergeant (later Inspector) Hemingway, is also present. In *A Blunt Instrument* (1938), a body is discovered, obviously the victim of foul play; but where is the weapon of the title? This novel has been highly praised for its excellent puzzle, its strict adherence to the rules of fair play, and its plot and characters. Another unpleasant host, this time of a country Christmas party, becomes the victim of a knife-wielding killer in *Envious Casca* (1941). Inspector Hemingway deals with numerous equally unpleasant relatives as he tries to solve this baffling locked-room murder.

HIBBERT, ELEANOR BURFORD. *See* HOLT, VICTORIA.

HIGHSMITH, PATRICIA (1921–). American suspense novelist and short story writer. Born in Fort Worth, Tex., Miss Highsmith attended public schools in New York City and graduated from Barnard College. Shortly thereafter, her short story "The Heroine" was published in *Harper's Bazaar* and was selected by Herschel Brickell as one of the twenty-two best stories that appeared in American magazines in 1945. Like many of her short stories, this one straddles the border between mystery and nonmystery fiction. A collection of her short fiction was published in 1970 as *The Snail-Watcher and Other Stories*. Miss Highsmith has lived in England and, more recently, in France for the past fifteen years.

Her first suspense novel, *Strangers on a Train* (1950), was an immediate success. Critics and public alike were intrigued with the plot device of two potential murderers exchanging victims in order to provide alibis. A subsequent book, *Deep Water* (1957), was highly praised in Europe, where her works have always received far greater acclaim than in the United States. The London *Sunday Times* called it one of her "most brilliant analyses of psychosis in America." The British Crime Writers' Association selected *The Two Faces of January* as the best foreign novel of 1964. *The Talented Mr. Ripley* (1955) was awarded the Grand Prix de Littérature Policière as the best foreign mystery, translated into French, of 1957. In this book, in *Ripley under Ground* (1970), and in *Ripley's Game* (1974), the amoral Mr. Ripley, art collector, con man, and murderer, appears. The Highsmith novels frequently explore the relationship between two people brought together by a crime. Although some critics have thought that these relationships are unrealistic, Julian SYMONS believes that Miss Highsmith is "the writer who fuses character and plot most successfully . . . the most important crime novelist at present in practice."

Films

Somewhat changed, *Strangers on a Train* became the basis of a memorable Alfred HITCHCOCK film in 1951.

Purple Noon. Times Films (French), 1961. Alain Delon, Marie Laforêt, Maurice Ronet. Directed by René Clément. Based on *The Talented Mr. Ripley*.

A handsome young opportunist, idling in European resorts with a rich American school friend, kills him and assumes his identity.

Enough Rope. Artixo (French), 1966. Gert Fröbe, Ronet, Marina Vlady, Robert Hossein, Yvonne Furneaux. Directed by Claude Autant-Lara. Based on *The Blunderer* (1954).

An unhappy husband, intrigued by newspaper accounts of a wife murderer whom the police cannot arrest, decides to duplicate the crime—but someone else kills the wife first.

Once You Kiss a Stranger. Warner Brothers, 1969. Paul Burke, Carol Lynley, Martha Hyer, Peter Lind Hayes, Philip Carey, Stephen McNally. Directed by Robert Sparr. A reworking of *Strangers on a Train*.

The relationship is now a male-female one; a bizarre girl offers to rid a golf pro of his chief competition if he kills her psychiatrist (her "father image").

HILL, HEADON (pseudonym of Francis Edward Grainger; 1857–1924). English author of romantic, mystery, and detective fiction. Among his many mystery novels are *Guilty Gold* (1896), about Inspector Heron of Scotland Yard; *By a Hair's Breadth* (1897), featuring a female detective, Laura Metcalf; *Caged: The Romance of a Lunatic Asylum* (1900), with Sergeants Trevor and Godbold; and *The Perils of the Prince* (1901), with Montague Wardrop of the Foreign Office. His short story collections about Sebastian Zambra are some of the rarest first editions in the genre: *Clues from a Detective's Camera* (1893), *Zambra, the Detective: Some Clues from His Notebook* (1894), and *The Divinations of Kala Persad and Other Stories* (1895), which contains two tales about Zambra and four about Persad and Mark Poignand. *Radford Shone* (1908) is another rare collection.

HILTON, JAMES (1900–1954). English novelist. Born in Leigh, Lancashire, he was raised in London and graduated from Christ's College, Cambridge University. He wrote his first novel, *Catherine Herself* (1920), while still a teenager, but he had little financial success until the publication of *Goodbye, Mr. Chips*. Hilton wrote this touching story of an old English schoolmaster in just four days for the Christmas 1933 issue of the *British Weekly*. Beginning in 1934, it appeared in American magazines and in book form in both England and the United States; a special illustrated edition was published, and stage and film adaptations followed, making "Mr. Chips" one of the most famous and beloved characters in English literature. *Lost Horizon* (1933), an adventure-fantasy pushed to the status of a best seller by the popularity of *Goodbye, Mr. Chips*, added a word to the English language: "Shangri-la," the mythical Tibetan land that is now synonymous with Nirvana or paradise. *Random Harvest* (1941), the moving story of an amnesiac, is the third of Hilton's best-known and still widely read novels.

Under the pseudonym Glen Trevor, Hilton wrote one of the classic detective novels of the 1930s, *Murder at School* (1931); it was published in 1933 in the United States as *Was It Murder?* by James Hilton. Young Colin Revell is an "old boy," now a private detective, who returns to Oakington School to investigate the curious death of a student named Marshall. Everyone is relieved and satisfied when Revell confirms the theory that Marshall was killed accidentally by a falling gas pipe. When the student's older brother dies six months later by diving into an empty swimming pool, Revell returns to the school, his credulity strained by another apparent accident.

Films

In addition to his many distinguished romantic dramas, Hilton contributed mystery works to the screen.

We Are Not Alone. Warner Brothers–First National, 1939. Paul Muni, Jane Bryan, Flora Robson. Directed by Edmund Goulding. From Hilton's novel of 1937.

The small son of an unhappily married man innocently puts poison tablets into an aspirin bottle; when the shrewish wife dies, the father is accused of murder—along with a women he has befriended—and a sensational trial begins.

Rage in Heaven. MGM, 1941. Robert Montgomery, Ingrid Bergman, George Sanders. Directed by W. S. Van Dyke II. Christopher Isherwood and Robert Thoeren based the screenplay on Hilton's 1932 novel.

Secretly insane, a rich young man plots to destroy the family friend who he wrongly imagines is having an affair with his wife, going so far as to have his own suicide look like murder so that the man will be hanged.

HITCHCOCK, ALFRED (1899–). English film director, a master of suspense and mystery. Hitchcock began his career as a title artist, eventually graduating to directing. Among his early films were well-handled thrillers, a genre in which he came to specialize. The films he directed in the 1930s were among the best English motion pictures ever made. In 1940 he arrived in Hollywood and began a long series of great, stylish suspense films.

Films

All of Hitchcock's films are individualistic (a characteristic is his brief appearance in each) and often innovative. Many are landmark films of the mystery cinema.

The Lodger (subtitle: *A Story of the London Fog*). Gainsborough, 1926. Ivor Novello. Based on the 1913 novel by Mrs. Marie Belloc LOWNDES.

An elderly English couple rents an upstairs room to an eccentric stranger; meanwhile, the Avenger, a Jack the Ripper type of killer, stalks the London streets.

Blackmail. British International, 1929. John Longdon, Anny Ondra, Cyril Ritchard.

A detective's girl commits murder; black-

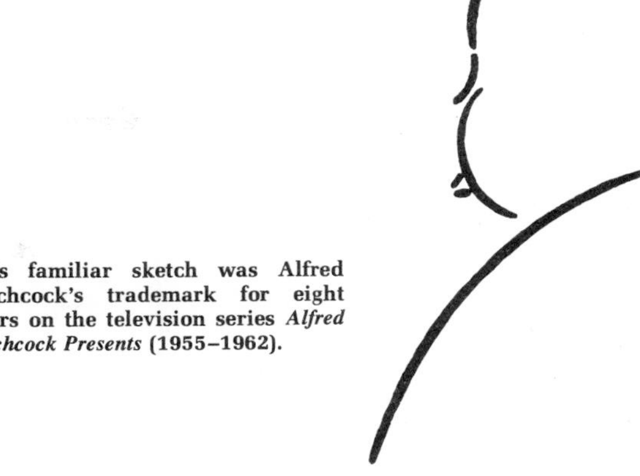

This familiar sketch was Alfred Hitchcock's trademark for eight years on the television series *Alfred Hitchcock Presents* (1955–1962).

Alfred Hitchcock explains that a "MacGuffin" is the plot device, or gimmick, of his films, such as secret plans, a stolen gem, or documents; they are unimportant in themselves but must be vitally important to the characters. Hitchcock suggests that the term might have originated in Scotland, where two men were on a train. The first asks, "What's that package in the baggage rack?" The other answers, "Oh, that's a MacGuffin." The first one asks, "What's a MacGuffin?" The other man replies, "It's an apparatus for trapping lions in the Scottish Highlands." The first man says, "But there are no lions in the Scottish Highlands." And the other answers, "Well, then, that's no MacGuffin." A MacGuffin is actually nothing at all.

Newsmen George Sanders and Joel McCrea (center, left to right), joined by Laraine Day and assorted police, have pursued a political assassin to the Dutch countryside, where he has disappeared by a deserted windmill: Alfred Hitchcock's sweeping melodrama of the uncertain days before World War II, *Foreign Correspondent.* [*United Artists*]

Ingrid Bergman and Cary Grant uncover a deadly secret concealed in a bottle in her husband's wine cellar in *Notorious,* Alfred Hitchcock's romantic espionage thriller set in postwar Brazil. [*RKO*]

mail follows in Hitchcock's (and England's) first sound film.

Murder. British International, 1930. Herbert Marshall, Norah Baring, Phyllis Konstam, Miles Mander. Based on the 1929 novel *Enter Sir John* by Helen SIMPSON and Clemence Dane.

This is Hitchcock's first "whodunit," and a rare film.

Number Seventeen. British International, 1932. Leon M. Lion, John Stuart, Anne Grey, Donald Calthrop, Barry Jones. Based on the play by Jefferson Farjeon.

A detective pursues, across the English countryside, a gang of thieves who have stolen a valuable necklace.

The Man Who Knew Too Much. Gaumont-British, 1934. Leslie Banks, Peter Lorre, Edna Best, Nova Pilbeam.

An ordinary couple become involved in international intrigue and an assassination attempt at Albert Hall; their daughter is kidnapped to ensure their silence. The climax is a re-creation of the Sydney Street siege.

The Thirty-nine Steps. Gaumont-British, 1935. Robert Donat, Madeleine Carroll, Lucy Mannheim, Godfrey Tearle. Based on the 1915 novel (considerably tightened) by John BUCHAN.

At a music hall a former officer is contacted by a mysterious woman who is later stabbed in his rooms; he soon finds himself pursued by both spies and the police—a favorite Hitchcock device.

The Secret Agent. Gaumont-British, 1936. Robert Young, Carroll, John Gielgud, Lorre. From W. Somerset MAUGHAM's Ashenden stories.

A British agent is assigned to kill a German spy.

Sabotage (U.S. title: *The Woman Alone*). Gaumont-British, 1936. Sylvia Sidney, Oscar Homolka, John Loder. From Joseph CONRAD's *The Secret Agent* (1907).

A London housewife realizes that her immigrant husband is an anarchist and that he has sent her young brother to deliver a parcel containing a bomb.

Young and Innocent (U.S. title: *The Girl Was Young*). Gainsborough–Gaumont-British, 1937. Pilbeam, Derrick De Marney, Percy Marmont. From Josephine TEY's *A Shilling for Candles* (1936).

A young woman pursues a murderer—a blinking man—on her own.

The Lady Vanishes. Gainsborough, 1938. Michael Redgrave, Margaret Lockwood, Paul Lukas, Dame May Whitty. From the Ethel Lina WHITE novel *The Wheel Spins* (1936).

On a train speeding through Central Europe, a young English girl is worried about a new acquaintance, an older woman. Her friend has disappeared, and no one on the train remembers having seen her.

Jamaica Inn. Mayflower–Associated British, 1939. Charles Laughton, Maureen O'Hara, Robert Newton, Emlyn WILLIAMS, Banks. From Daphne DU MAURIER's novel of 1936.

In this period melodrama, an English girl staying at a coastal inn suspects the local squire of being the head of a murderous band of cutthroats and shipwreckers.

Jane Wyman (left) and Marlene Dietrich in a scene from *Stage Fright*. [*Warner Brothers*]

Montgomery Clift (center) and Karl Malden (foreground) in a scene from *I Confess*. [*Warner Brothers*]

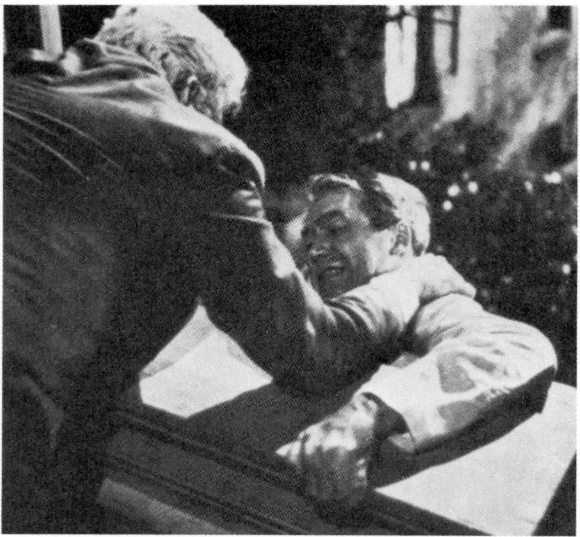

In *Rear Window*, the prying, disabled James Stewart is finally visited and attacked by the murderer (a white-haired Raymond Burr) he has observed through his window. The killer is about to push him through the window in Alfred Hitchcock's elaborate version of the Cornell Woolrich short story. [*Paramount*]

Rebecca. United Artists (a David O. Selznick production), 1940. Laurence Olivier, Joan Fontaine, George Sanders, Judith Anderson, Nigel Bruce. Hitchcock's first American film, based on Daphne du Maurier's popular romance of 1938.

A nameless heroine marries a brooding widower and is taken to his great estate, Manderley, filled with ghostly reminders of Rebecca, his dead first wife.

Foreign Correspondent. United Artists, 1940. Joel McCrea, Laraine Day, Marshall, Sanders, Albert Basserman, Robert Benchley, Edmund Gwenn. Very loosely based on a real-life journalist's experiences.

A young, aggressive American reporter, newly assigned to a European post, finds himself thrust into a world of spies and political assassinations, in the last days before the start of World War II.

Suspicion. RKO, 1941. Cary Grant, Fontaine, Sir Cedric Hardwicke, Bruce, Whitty. Loosely based on *Before the Fact* (1932) by Francis Iles (Anthony BERKELEY); the ending was revised.

A plain, retiring English girl marries a charming scoundrel, aware of his faults and sure of his love, but gradually begins to suspect that circumstances are forcing him to plot to murder her. (Miss Fontaine won an Academy Award for her role in this film.)

Saboteur. Universal, 1942. Robert Cummings, Priscilla Lane, Otto Kruger, Norman Lloyd, Alan Baxter. An American attempt at *The Thirty-nine Steps,* even to the handcuffed-to-the-heroine device, climaxing atop the Statue of Liberty.

A factory worker avenges the death of his friend by tracking down—cross-country—the spy ring that was responsible.

Shadow of a Doubt. Universal, 1943. Teresa Wright, Joseph Cotten, MacDonald Carey, Henry Travers, Hume Cronyn.

A young California girl begins to suspect that her visiting Uncle Charlie is a lonely-hearts killer. The warm small-town setting makes this the most distinctly "American" of Hitchcock's films; it is also his personal favorite.

Lifeboat. Twentieth Century-Fox, 1944. Tallulah Bankhead, John Hodiak, William Bendix, Walter Slezak. Based on an original story by John Steinbeck, who also contributed to the screenplay.

The survivors of a torpedoed ship huddle in a lifeboat (the film's only setting), dominated by a Nazi submarine commander whom they have rescued.

Spellbound. United Artists, 1945. Ingrid Bergman, Gregory Peck, Michael Chekhov, Leo G. Carroll. Based on *The House of Dr. Edwardes* (1927) by Francis BEEDING. Screenplay by Ben HECHT.

An amnesia victim is suspected of having murdered the man he is impersonating, a famous psychiatrist who was in charge of an asylum. His disordered subconscious, haunted by clues to the real killer, is illustrated by abstract dream sequences created by Salvador Dali.

Notorious. RKO, 1946. Grant, Bergman, Claude Rains, Louis Calhern, Madame Leopoldine Konstantin. Based on an original idea by Hitchcock. Screenplay by Hecht.

The notorious daughter of a convicted spy is asked by the United States government, to which she is loyal, to infiltrate a Nazi spy colony in Rio and marry its mother-dominated chief.

The Paradine Case. RKO, 1947. Peck, Laughton, Alida Valli, Ann Todd, Louis Jourdan, Charles Coburn, Ethel Barrymore. Based on Robert Hichens's novel of 1933.

A famous young barrister is asked to defend a mysterious, seductive widow accused of murdering her husband—and finds himself falling in love with her.

Rope. Warner Brothers, 1948. James Stewart, John Dall, Farley Granger, Joan Chandler, Hardwicke. Based on the play *Rope's End* (1929; British title: *Rope*) by Patrick HAMILTON.

Two college youths kill a fellow student for thrills and engage in a cat-and-mouse game with a former professor as they host a party while the corpse is still concealed in their apartment. Hitchcock unfolds the drama in what appears to be one continuous camera take.

Stage Fright. Warner Brothers, 1950. Jane Wyman, Marlene Dietrich, Michael Wilding, Richard Todd, Alastair Sim, Dame Sybil Thorndike,

Kay Walsh, Joyce Grenfell, Patricia Hitchcock (the director's daughter). Based on Selwyn JEPSON's Eve Gill character, mainly from *Man Running* (1948; U.S. title: *Outrun the Constable*).

A young girl, a drama student at the Royal Academy, joins the efforts being made to keep a desperate friend from being charged with the murder of the husband of a famous but arrogant musical comedy actress.

Strangers on a Train. Warner Brothers, 1951. Robert Walker, Granger, Ruth Roman, Leo G. Carroll, Patricia Hitchcock, Marion Lorne. Raymond CHANDLER contributed to the screenplay, based on the 1950 novel of the same title by Patricia HIGHSMITH.

An unhappily married tennis pro is approached by an unstable young man who offers an easy solution: he will murder the pro's spouse if, in return, the athlete will do away with the father the young man detests.

I Confess. Warner Brothers, 1953. Montgomery Clift, Anne Baxter, Karl Malden, Brian Aherne, O. E. Hasse, Dolly Haas. Based on the Paul Anthelme play *Our Two Consciences*.

Under the seal of the confessional, a killer reveals his deed to a priest who is later accused of the murder but can say nothing to clear himself.

Dial M for Murder. Warner Brothers, 1954. Ray Milland, Grace Kelly, Robert Cummings, John Williams, Anthony Dawson. Based on the play by Frederick M. P. KNOTT, which first appeared on Broadway in 1952.

A husband hires a seedy former classmate to kill his rich wife, but the plot misfires when the woman, in self-defense, turns on her attacker—and finds herself imprisoned for premeditated murder.

Rear Window. Paramount, 1954. Stewart, Kelly, Wendell Corey, Thelma Ritter, Raymond Burr, Judith Evelyn. Based on the William Irish (Cornell WOOLRICH) story "It Had to Be Murder" (1942), retitled "Rear Window" for its first book publication, in *After-Dinner Story* (1944).

A news photographer, confined to a wheelchair because of a broken leg, amuses himself by sitting at his window and, from across a courtyard, spying on the people living in the apartment building that faces his. Gradually, he suspects that he has uncovered a murder.

To Catch a Thief. Paramount, 1955. Grant, Kelly, Jessie Royce Landis, Williams. From the 1952 novel by David Dodge.

A headstrong American heiress visiting the Riviera begins a romance with a dashing reformed cat burglar, even though the resort area is rocked by a series of spectacular jewel thefts.

The Trouble with Harry. Paramount, 1955. John Forsythe, Shirley MacLaine, Gwenn, Mildred Natwick, Mildred Dunnock. Based on a 1950 John Trevor Story novel.

In this bizarre black comedy, several residents of a Vermont community attempt to hide a body.

The Man Who Knew Too Much. Paramount, 1956. Stewart, Doris Day, Brenda de Banzie, Bernard Miles, Daniel Gelin. A remake, though much more elaborately done, of the 1934 film.

The Wrong Man. Warner Brothers, 1957. Henry Fonda, Vera Miles, Anthony Quayle. Based on a true story.

The film is an almost documentary-style account of a New York musician falsely arrested for armed robbery.

Vertigo. Paramount, 1958. Stewart, Kim Novak, Barbara Bel Geddes, Tom Helmore, Henry Jones. Based on the novel *The Living and the Dead* (1956) by Pierre Boileau and Thomas Narcejac.

A detective's fear of heights keeps him from preventing the suicide of a friend's neurotic wife,

Eva Marie Saint dangles from Mount Rushmore, clinging to Cary Grant in an attempt to flee some spies in the climactic chase from Hitchcock's *North by Northwest*. [*MGM*]

and she hurls herself from a mission tower. Later, he sees a girl on a San Francisco street and becomes convinced that the suicide victim has returned from the dead.

North by Northwest. MGM, 1959. Grant, Eva Marie Saint, James Mason, Landis, Leo G. Carroll, Martin Landau.

This is the ultimate chase film—across country, from the United Nations in Manhattan to the Presidents' faces carved on Mount Rushmore. An urbane New York advertising executive is bewildered to learn that he has been mistaken by an enemy spy ring for a counterespionage agent—who, in fact, does not exist. Fleeing killers who are intent upon eliminating him, the hero finds both danger and romance on the run.

Psycho. Paramount, 1960. Anthony Perkins, Janet Leigh, Miles, John Gavin, Martin Balsam. Based on the 1959 novel by Robert BLOCH.

A secretary who has absconded with $40,000 to aid her lover stops in her flight—and is later stabbed to death—at a lonely motel run by a psychotic young man dominated by the shadowy figure of his knife-wielding mother. A cinematic milestone, this film inspired a decade of psychopathic terror films.

The Birds. Universal, 1963. Rod Taylor, Tippi Hedren, Suzanne Pleshette, Jessica Tandy, Ethel Griffies. Based on a story by Daphne du Maurier (contained in *The Apple Tree,* 1952). Screenplay by Evan Hunter (*see* MCBAIN, ED).

In this cryptic nonmystery, for unknown, apocalyptic reasons, numerous flocks of birds attack the population of a small coastal town in California.

Marnie. Universal, 1964. Sean Connery, Hedren, Diane Baker, Louise Latham, Martin Gabel, Mariette Hartley. Based on the 1961 novel by Winston Graham.

A rich young man falls in love with a girl who he realizes is a neurotic and a compulsive thief who is afraid of sex. Not until after his marriage to her does he—in a dramatic encounter with her slattern mother—discover the cause of Marnie's problem.

Torn Curtain. Universal, 1966. Paul Newman, Julie Andrews, Lila Kedrova, Hansjoerg Felmy, Tamara Toumanova.

A young American scientist pretends to defect to East Berlin in order to contact an antimissile expert and return with his secrets to the United States.

Topaz. Universal, 1969. Frederick Stafford, Dany Robin, John Vernon, Karin Dor, Forsythe. Based on the 1967 novel by Leon Uris.

A spy scandal rocks Washington; against an international setting (Copenhagen, Harlem, Havana, and Paris) a diplomat tries to ferret out a spy ring whose code name is Topaz, which has been passing secrets to the Russians.

Frenzy. Universal, 1972. Jon Finch, Alec McCowen, Barry Foster, Anna Massey, Barbara Leigh-Hunt, Vivien Merchant. Screenplay by Anthony Shaffer (*see* ANTONY, PETER), from the book *Goodbye Picadilly, Farewell Leicester Square* (1966) by Arthur La Bern.

A down-on-his-luck former RAF pilot is accused of a series of London sex murders—the victims are raped and strangled—when first his former wife and then his girl friend are killed. The murderer is actually a Covent Garden friend of the suspect.

Publications

Beginning in the mid-1950s Hitchcock became the nominal editor of a series of popular anthologies of mystery short stories and of a successful periodical, *Alfred Hitchcock's Mystery Magazine.*

Television

Since the mid-1950s Hitchcock has made steady contributions to television, mainly as the host (but only occasionally the director) of an eight-year series, *Alfred Hitchcock Presents,* his pithy introductions rivaling in popularity the brief, ingenious "cameo" appearances he had devised for himself in nearly all his feature films. Stories by virtually every modern writer in the genre were adapted for the series, which was sufficiently innovative to occasionally defy television codes by allowing the criminal to remain unpunished at the end of the story (although Hitchcock usually provided a cautionary wink at the audience in his summing-up). Indeed, he increasingly took liberties, for many of the titles he collected in the anthology *Stories They Wouldn't Let Me Do on TV,* such as Stanley ELLIN's indelicate tale, "Specialty of the House" (1948), ultimately appeared on his program. In 1963, the series was lengthened and retitled *The Alfred Hitchcock Hour;* it went off the air in 1965.

HOCH, EDWARD D. (1930–). American novelist and short story writer. Born in Rochester, N.Y., he attended the University of Rochester before serving in the Army (1950–1952). He wrote in his spare time, while doing advertising work, until 1968, when he became a full-time writer. He is married to the former Patricia McMahon and resides in Rochester.

Hoch has written only four novels. The first, *The Shattered Raven* (1969), is about murder at an annual Mystery Writers of America (MWA) awards dinner. *The Transvection Machine* (1971) and *The Fellowship of the Hand* (1973) combine mystery and science fiction. His most recent novel is *The Frankenstein Factory* (1975).

He has, however, published almost 400 short stories and created four major series characters. "The Oblong Room," a story about Captain Leopold, won the MWA Edgar as best short story of 1967. Simon

Ark, a mystical detective, claims to be 2,000 years old and solves crimes involving the supernatural, although he uses rational means. Eight of the Ark stories were collected in *The Judge of Hades* (1971) and *City of Brass* (1971).

The fourteen stories in a 1971 collection, *The Spy and the Thief*, are about Hoch's two other major protagonists, Rand and Velvet; each character appears in seven tales. Rand, the spy of the title, is a cipher expert in charge of England's Department of Concealed Communications. Nick Velvet steals only unusual objects, such as a tiger from a zoo, water from a swimming pool, and, in an uncollected story, "The Theft of the Meager Beavers" (1969), a major league baseball team.

Hoch's novels have been greeted indifferently by critics, but his short stories are highly regarded.

HOCKABY, STEPHEN. *See* MITCHELL, GLADYS.

HODGSON, WILLIAM HOPE (1875–1918). English writer of ghost stories and creator of CARNACKI, the ghost-finder. Born in Essex, the son of a clergyman, Hodgson left home at an early age to spend eight years at sea, traveling around the world three times. He was living in the south of France with his wife when World War I erupted. He returned to England, received a commission, and was killed in action.

Most of Hodgson's stories deal with the weird and the occult, the best being eerie tales about the sea. In addition to his novels and short stories of the supernatural, he wrote a series of crime stories about a shady smuggler, collected in *Captain Gault: Being the Exceedingly Private Log of a Sea-Captain* (1917).

This gloomy illustration for the first American edition of William Hope Hodgson's *Carnacki, The Ghost-Finder,* published by Mycroft & Moran in 1947, was designed by Frank Utpatel.

HOLDING, ELIZABETH SANXAY (1889–1955). American author of mystery and suspense novels. Born and brought up in Brooklyn, N.Y., Elizabeth Sanxay married George E. Holding, an Englishman, in 1913. They traveled widely in South America and the West Indies and spent a number of years in Bermuda, where he was an official of the British government. The couple had two daughters and a number of grandchildren. When Holding left government service, they moved to New York City.

During a 1949 interview, Mrs. Holding said that she had begun writing as soon as she could spell words like "dog" and "cat." She commented, "When I was a girl going upstairs to bed I thought to myself as a fiction writer would: 'The little girl slowly climbed the stairs, pausing on the fifth step to peer over the banister.'" Before turning to mysteries, she wrote romantic fiction. Her first magazine story was published in 1920, and a series of successful romantic novels appeared during the 1920s. *Miasma* (1929) was her first mystery; it was followed by almost twenty books through *Widows Mite* (1953). Her mysteries were seldom detective stories, although *The Strange Crime in Bermuda* (1937), a book reflecting her own experiences on that island, does involve detection. "People Do Fall Downstairs" (1947), the first of her three prizewinning stories for *Ellery Queen's Mystery Magazine,* also stressed detection and was also set on an island, albeit a fictional one, Puerto Azul, in the Caribbean.

Anthony BOUCHER once wrote: "Back in the early thirties before anybody ever heard of 'psychological novels of suspense,' Elizabeth Sanxay Holding was writing them, and brilliantly." Raymond CHANDLER said, "For my money she's the top suspense writer of them all." James SANDOE characterized her work as "half-understood horrors viewed in a nightmare of uncertainties." Her characterizations and storytelling ability caused some critics to ignore plot absurdities, for example, amnesia as a plot device in *Net of Cobwebs* (1945). Her characters are often caught up in confusing personal relationships. In *The Blank Wall* (1947) a teen-age daughter's affair with a married man causes her mother concern and danger. *The Virgin Huntress* (1951) tells of the relations of a spoiled young man with a wealthy middle-aged woman and the jealousy of the woman's niece.

HOLMES, GORDON (pseudonym of Louis TRACY and M. P. SHIEL). Eight mystery and detective novels appeared under this name, the first written by Tracy alone. The rest were, according to Shiel, "conceived" by Tracy, with Shiel concocting the actual plot and writing the first half and Tracy writing the second half. Although inferior to the individual work of both authors, the books are fast-paced and ingenious, with a style of their own. The Gordon Holmes novels are: *A Mysterious Disappearance*

(1905), *The Arncliffe Puzzle* (1906), *The Late Tenant* (1906), *By Force of Circumstances* (1909), *The de Bercy Affair* (1910; later retitled *The Feldisham Mystery*), *The House of Silence* (1911; British title: *The Silent House*, by Louis Tracy), *No Other Way* (1912; published in England as by Louis Tracy), and *The House 'Round the Corner* (1919). The last title initially appeared in 1915 under Tracy's name; the texts of the two books are identical.

HOLMES, H. H. *See* BOUCHER, ANTHONY.

HOLMES, SHERLOCK (Creator: Sir Arthur CONAN DOYLE). The tall, slender, hawk-nosed detective is possibly the most famous literary creation of all time. In his deerstalker hat and Inverness cape, he is instantly recognizable in every corner of the world, particularly because of the popularity and excellence of the actors who have portrayed him on stage and screen and the artists who have illustrated his adventures (especially Sidney Paget and Frederic Dorr Steele).

A romanticized depiction of Sherlock Holmes; note Moriarty hovering in the background. Thomas Beecham painted it for a paperback reprint edition.

Sherlock (he was nearly named Sherrinford) was born on January 6, 1854, on the farmstead of Mycroft (the name of his older brother) in the North Riding of Yorkshire. He solved his first case (eventually titled "The *Gloria Scott*") while a twenty-year-old student at Oxford. Following graduation, he became the world's first consulting detective—a vocation he followed for twenty-three years.

In January 1881 he was looking for someone to share his new quarters at 221B Baker Street, and a friend introduced him to Dr. John H. Watson (*see* WATSON, DR.). Before agreeing to share the apartment, the two men aired their respective shortcomings. Holmes confessed, "I get in the dumps at times, and don't open my mouth for days on end." He also smokes a vile shag tobacco and conducts experiments with loathsome-smelling chemicals. He failed, however, to mention an affection for cocaine. Although he ruefully noted his fondness for scratching away at the violin while in contemplation, he proved to be a virtuoso who could calm his roommate's raw nerves with a melodious air. Watson's admitted faults include the keeping of a bull pup, a strong objection to arguments because his nerves cannot stand them, a penchant for arising from bed "at all sorts of ungodly hours," and an immense capacity for laziness. "I have another set of vices when I'm well," he said, "but those are the principal ones at present." They became friends, and Watson chronicled the deeds of his illustrious roommate, often to the displeasure of Holmes, who resented the melodramatic and sensational tales. He believed that the affairs, if told at all, should be put to the public as straightforward exercises in cold logic and deductive reasoning.

Holmes possesses not only excellent deductive powers but also a giant intellect. Anatomy, chemistry, mathematics, British law, and sensational literature are but a few areas of his vast sphere of knowledge, although he is admittedly not well versed in such subjects as astronomy, philosophy, and politics. He has published several distinguished works on erudite subjects: *Upon the Distinction between the Ashes of the Various Tobaccos; A Study of the Influence of a Trade upon the Form of the Hand; Upon the Polyphonic Motets of Lassus; A Study of the Chaldean Roots in the Ancient Cornish Language;* and, his magnum opus, *Practical Handbook of Bee Culture, with Some Observations upon the Segregation of the Queen.* His four-volume *The Whole Art of Detection* has not yet been published. When he needs information that his brain does not retain, he refers to a small, carefully selected library

William Gillette as Sherlock Holmes.

of reference works and a series of commonplace books. Since Holmes cares only about facts that aid his work, he ignores whatever he considers superfluous. He explains his theory of education thus: "I consider that a man's brain is like an empty attic, and you have to stock it with such furniture as you choose. A fool takes in all the lumber of every sort that he comes across, so that the knowledge which might be useful to him gets crowded out, or at best is jumbled up with a lot of other things, so that he has a difficulty in laying his hands upon it. . . . It is a mistake to think that that little room has elastic walls and can distend to any extent. Depend upon it there comes a time when for every addition of knowledge you forget something you knew before."

An athletic body complements Holmes's outstanding intelligence. He seems even taller than his 6 feet because he is extremely thin. His narrow, hooked nose and sharp, piercing eyes give him a hawklike appearance. He often astonished Watson with displays of strength and agility; he is a superb boxer, fencer, and singlestick player. He needed all his strength when he met his nemesis, the ultimate archcriminal Professor James MORIARTY, in a struggle at the edge of the Reichenbach Falls in Switzerland. The evenly matched adversaries, locked in battle, fell over the cliff; both were reported to be dead. All England mourned the passing of its great keeper of the law, but in 1894, after being missing for three years, Holmes returned. He had not been killed in the fall, after all, but had seen a good opportunity to fool his many enemies in the underworld. He had taken over the identity of a Danish explorer, Sigerson, and traveled to many parts of the world, including New Jersey, where he is believed to have had an affair with Irene Adler (who will always be *the* woman to Holmes), and to Tibet, where he learned the secret of long life from the Dalai Lama.

When Miss Adler (the famous and beautiful opera singer Holmes first meets in "A Scandal in Bohemia") died in 1903, he retired to keep bees on the southern slopes of the Sussex Downs with his old housekeeper, Mrs. Martha Hudson. He came out of retirement briefly before World War I, but his life since then has been quiet.

Holmes has outlived the people who have participated at various times in his adventures. In addition to Mycroft, Watson, Moriarty, Irene Adler, and Mrs. Hudson, the best-known auxiliary personalities in the stories include Billy the Page Boy, who occasionally announces visitors to 221B; Mary Morstan, who becomes Mrs. Watson; the Baker Street Irregulars, street urchins led by Wiggins, who scramble after information for Holmes's coins; Lestrade, an inept Scotland Yard inspector; Stanley Hopkins, a Scotland Yard man of greater ability; Gregson, the "smartest of the Scotland Yarders," according to Holmes; and Colonel Sebastian Moran, "the second most dangerous man in London."

The first story written about Sherlock Holmes, *A Study in Scarlet*, originally appeared in *Beeton's Christmas Annual* for 1887 and subsequently was

John Barrymore (left) played Holmes in the 1922 film, opposing a determined-looking Moriarty (Gustav von Seyffertitz). [*Goldwyn*]

Basil Rathbone as Sherlock Holmes.

published in book form in London by Ward, Lock & Company in 1888; the first American edition was published by J. B. Lippincott Company in 1890. Holmes is called to assist Scotland Yard on what Inspector Tobias Gregson calls "a bad business at 3, Lauriston Gardens." An American, Enoch J. Drebber, has been murdered, and Yard men can point to only a single clue, the word "Rache" scrawled upon the wall in blood. They believe it to be the first letters of a woman's name, Rachel, but Holmes suggests that it is the German word for "revenge." Soon, the dead man's private secretary, Stangerson, is also found murdered; the same word is written in blood nearby. A long middle section of this novel, dealing with Mormons, is an unusual flashback.

The Sign of Four first appeared simultaneously in the English and American editions of *Lippincott's Magazine* for February 1890. Spencer Blacket published the first English book edition in the same year; P. F. Collier published the first American book edition in 1891. Calling at 221B Baker Street for help is Mary Morstan, a fetching young lady by whom Watson is totally charmed; ultimately, he marries her. She is the daughter of a captain in the Indian Army who had mysteriously disappeared ten years earlier and had never been heard from again. Four years after the disappearance, Miss Morstan received an anonymous gift, a huge, lustrous pearl, and received another like it each year thereafter. Holmes and Watson accompany her to a tryst with the eccentric Thaddeus Sholto, twin brother of Bartholomew Sholto and the son of a major who had been Captain Morstan's only friend in London. Holmes sets out to find a fabulous treasure and is soon involved with the strange Jonathan Small and Tonga.

"A Scandal in Bohemia" first appeared in *The Strand* in July 1891; its first book appearance was in *The Adventures of Sherlock Holmes* (1892). The first published short story in which Holmes appears features the detective in an uncharacteristic battle of wits with a lady and with no real crime to be solved. The King of Bohemia has had a rather indiscreet affair with the beautiful Irene Adler, who threatens to create an international scandal when he attempts to discard her and marry a noblewoman. Holmes is hired to obtain possession of a certain unfortunate photograph before it can be sent to the would-be bride's royal family. Holmes is outwitted, and he never stops loving Irene for fooling him.

In *The Hound of the Baskervilles* (1902), Sir Charles Baskerville, of Baskerville Hall, Dartmoor, Devon, has been found dead. There are no signs of violence at the scene, but his face is incredibly distorted with terror. Dr. James Mortimer enlists the aid of Holmes to protect the young heir to the estate, Sir Henry Baskerville. Watson goes to the grim moor to keep an eye on Sir Henry but is warned to return to London by a neighbor, Beryl Stapleton, the beautiful sister of a local naturalist, who hears a blood-chilling moan at the edge of the great Grimpen Mire and identifies it as the legendary Hound of the Baskervilles, calling for its prey.

The Conan Doyle stories about Holmes number sixty; more than that number have been written by other authors, however. Even Conan Doyle wrote a parody of his characters, "How Watson Learned the Trick," first published in *The Book of the Queen's Doll's House* in 1924. *The Seven-Per-Cent Solution* (1974) by Nicholas Meyer was a longtime best seller. Among the most famous pastiches are those by H. F. HEARD, whose Mr. Mycroft is a pseudonymous Holmes; the tales of August DERLETH, whose Solar PONS is "the Sherlock Holmes of Praed Street"; and "The Unique Hamlet" (1920), by Vincent STARRETT, in which the great detective appears under his true name. Other names (and guises) under which Holmes has appeared are Herlock Sholmes and Holmlock Shears [in Maurice LEBLANC's *The Exploits of Arsène Lupin*, 1907 (see LUPIN, ARSÈNE), and *The Fair-haired Lady*, 1909]; Picklock Holes (in R. C. Lehmann's *The Adventures of Picklock Holes*, 1901); Shylock Homes (in John Kendrick BANGS's series of stories in American newspapers in 1903, reprinted as *Shylock Homes: His Posthumous Memoirs*, 1973; Bangs also wrote many parodies of Holmes using the detective's real name, as in *The Pursuit of the House-Boat*, 1897; *The Enchanted Type-Writer*, 1899; and *R. Holmes & Co.*, 1906, in which the hero is the son of Sherlock Holmes and the grandson of A. J. RAFFLES); Shamrock Jolnes (by O. HENRY in two stories in *Sixes and Sevens*, 1911); Hemlock Jones (by Bret Harte in "The Stolen Cigar Case" in *Condensed Novels: Second Series*, 1902); Schlock Homes in many stories by Robert L. FISH; Sherlaw Kombs (by Robert BARR in "The Great

Pegram Mystery" in *The Face and the Mask,* 1894); and Shirley Holmes, the daughter of Sherlock (in "The Adventure of the Queen Bee" by Frederick Arnold Kummer and Basil Mitchell, a four-part serial in *Mystery* magazine in 1933). Other writers who have written of Holmes (calling him Sherlock Holmes, "The Great Detective," or some scrambled version of his name) are Mark Twain (*see* CLEMENS, SAMUEL LANGHORNE; *A Double-barrelled Detective Story,* 1902); Stephen Leacock ("Maddened by Mystery: or, The Defective Detective" in *Nonsense Novels,* 1911; and "An Irreducible Detective Story" in *Further Foolishness,* 1916); James M. Barrie ("The Adventure of the Two Collaborators" in Conan Doyle's *Memories and Adventures,* 1924). Holmes has also been called on to solve the unfinished novel by Charles DICKENS, *The Mystery of Edwin Drood,* in pastiches by Andrew Lang, Edmund Pearson, and Harry B. Smith. Ellery Queen's anthology *The Misadventures of Sherlock Holmes* (1944) is a comprehensive collection of stories featuring Holmes by writers other than Conan Doyle; it also contains a reliable bibliography of parodies, burlesques, and pastiches written to that date.

CHECKLIST

Books about Holmes by Conan Doyle.

1887 *A Study in Scarlet*
1890 *The Sign of Four*
1892 *The Adventures of Sherlock Holmes* (s.s.)
1894 *The Memoirs of Sherlock Holmes* (s.s.)
1902 *The Hound of the Baskervilles*
1905 *The Return of Sherlock Holmes* (s.s.)
1915 *The Valley of Fear*
1917 *His Last Bow* (s.s.)
1927 *The Case Book of Sherlock Holmes* (s.s.)

Films

Holmes's incredible cinematic career has spanned every decade of the medium; he is the most beloved and enduring of all screen detectives, and more actors have portrayed him that any other literary figure. There are more than a hundred films about him; thus his major achievements are discussed here.

In 1903 Holmes entered motion pictures with the brief *Sherlock Holmes Baffled* (American Mutoscope), in which unheralded actors present a screen-trickery vignette involving a vanishing Baker Street visitor. Soon Holmes was the central figure in several short series films, portrayed by Forrest Holger-Madsen in Denmark and M. Treville in France; he faces such extra-Canonical opponents as a gorilla, A. J. Raffles, and Arsène Lupin! There were careful short adaptations of the stories, and the heroic detective character was even parodied in slapstick by the 1910s. Longer translations of *A Study in Scarlet* (1914) and *The Valley of Fear* (1916) appeared in England, with James Braginton as Holmes in the former and H. A. Saintsbury in the latter; there was a French version in 1915 of *The Hound of the Baskervilles* (a German version followed two years later). In 1916 the great William Gillette brought his enormously successful stage play to the new medium—and enjoyed his only screen role as Holmes.

Sherlock Holmes. Essanay, 1916. Gillette, Marjorie Kay (Alice Faulkner). Directed by Arthur Berthelet.

A dispirited detective is revitalized when he rescues a girl from the clutches of the evil Professor Moriarty. At the end of the film, the elderly Holmes proposes.

Six years later, John Barrymore, at the height of his dramatic powers, tackled the role in a more elaborate vehicle that extended the Gillette play but still retained its romantic interest and its climactic confrontation between Holmes and Moriarty—even to the ruse by which Billy the Page Boy delivers a second revolver to the detective.

Sherlock Holmes. Goldwyn, 1922. Barrymore, Roland Young (Watson), Carol Dempster (Alice), Reginald Denny, William Powell. Directed by Albert Parker.

Barrymore, who seized the opportunity to disguise himself as the grotesque Professor Moriarty (Gustav von Seyffertitz), was criticized for over-reaching.

In 1921, in England, the British actor Eille Norwood began an extraordinary series of Holmesian impersonations in nearly fifty films during a two-year period. Hubert Willis played Watson, and mystery specialist Maurice Elvey produced and directed the lot, mainly close—but short and perfunctory—adaptations of the Conan Doyle stories. Norwood, though unexciting and diminutive, is still fondly remembered for his portrayal. In 1929 Germany's Richard Oswald, who had directed the 1917 version, cast the American actor Carlyle Blackwell in *Der Hund von Baskervilles,* the last silent Holmes film.

The sound period ushered in several Holmesian interpretations. Debonair Clive Brook, regarded as the perfect screen Englishman, is a straight-backed, stiff-lipped detective in *The Return of Sherlock Holmes* (Paramount, 1929. Directed by Basil Dean), in which he and Watson (H. Reeves-Smith) encounter an evil Moriarty (Harry T. Morey) aboard an ocean liner. Moriarty has kidnapped the fiancé of Watson's grown daughter. The following year, in the portmanteau showcase *Paramount on Parade* (1930; various directors), Brook, as Holmes, joins Powell's Philo VANCE in being done in by Dr. FU MANCHU (Warner Oland) in a spoof skit. He played the detective one more time.

Sherlock Holmes. Fox, 1932. Brook, Reginald Owen (Watson), Ernest Torrence (Moriarty), Miriam Jordan (Alice). Directed by William K. Howard. The climax is taken from "The Red-headed League" (1891).

Evil Germanic prisons and carnivals underscore Moriarty's importation of American gangster methods to London and attempts to frame Holmes for the murder of a Scotland Yard man. The detective again romances Alice Faulkner.

Other Holmeses of the period included Raymond Massey in a heavy version of the 1892 story "The Speckled Band" (British and Dominions Studios, 1931), with Athole Steward as Watson and Lyn Harding as the villainous Roylott; brisk, rather short Robert Rendel in a British *Hound of the Baskervilles* (Gainsborough, 1932), with Frederick Lloyd as Watson; rotund, somewhat bland Reginald Owen, who was Watson to Brook's Holmes (also in 1932) and the only man to play both roles, in *A Study in Scarlet* (World Wide, 1933), with Warburton Gamble as the good doctor, Alan Mowbray as Lestrade, and Anna May Wong as an extraordinary Oriental villainess in essentially a rich old-dark-house melodrama. In Germany there was another version of the *Hound* (1937). Matinee idol Hans Albers, in *Der Mann der Sherlock Holmes War* (UFA, 1937), plays a cocky private detective who impersonates the more famous investigator and has an encounter with Conan Doyle! But the definitive Holmes of the early 1930s was England's Arthur Wontner, called by Vincent Starrett "the veritable fathomer of Baker Street in person." He played a wry, mature, but authoritative detective in five British films.

The Sleeping Cardinal (U.S. title: *Sherlock Holmes' Fatal Hour*). Twickenham, 1930. Wontner, Ian Fleming (Watson), Phillip Hewland, Leslie Perrins. Directed by Leslie S. Hiscott. Loosely based on "The Final Problem" (1893) and "The Empty House" (1903).

Holmes investigates the mysterious deaths of two night watchmen—one of the largest bank in London, the other in Berlin.

The Missing Rembrandt. Twickenham, 1932. Wontner, Fleming, Francis L. Sullivan (Baron von Guntermann), Miles Mander. Directed by Hiscott. An elaboration of "Charles Augustus Milverton" (1904).

The Sign of Four. World Wide, 1932. Wontner, Ian Hunter (Watson for this one film), Isla Bevan, Ben Soutten (Jonathan Small). Directed by Graham Cutts. A close version of this novel of revenge.

The Triumph of Sherlock Holmes. Real Art, 1935. Wontner, Fleming, Lyn Harding, Leslie Perrins, Jane Carr. Directed by Hiscott. A faithful rendering of *The Valley of Fear*.

There are interesting attempts at "American" flashbacks and an in-person climactic appearance at Birlstone Manor of Moriarty (Harding).

Silver Blaze (deceptively released in the United States as *Murder at the Baskervilles*). Twickenham, 1937. Wontner, Fleming, Harding. Directed by Thomas Bentley. Based on "Silver Blaze" (1893).

Moriarty becomes involved with the theft of a racehorse.

Wontner was the best of the many Holmes figures of the 1930s, but only one extraordinary interpretation was to dominate the following decade. At a Hollywood cocktail party Twentieth Century-Fox studio head Darryl F. Zanuck suddenly turned to British actor Basil Rathbone—who had previously played lovers and rogues and even Philo Vance—and declared that he would make a perfect Holmes. Plans were immediately made for an elaborate production of *Hound,* in period—the first Holmes film to be deliberately set in Victorian times. Blustery British character actor Nigel Bruce was chosen as a portly, older Watson.

The Hound of the Baskervilles. Twentieth Century-Fox, 1939. Rathbone, Bruce, Richard Greene (Sir Henry Baskerville), Wendy Barrie, Morton Lowry, Lionel Atwill, John Carradine. Directed by Sidney Lanfield.

A lavish, faithful chronicle of the happenings at Baskerville Hall and fog-laden Grimpen Mire.

The Adventures of Sherlock Holmes. Twentieth Century-Fox, 1939. Rathbone, Bruce, Ida Lupino, Alan Marshal, George Zucco (Moriarty), Terry Kilburn (Billy the Page Boy). Directed by Alfred Werker. Credited as from the Gillette play, but there is no resemblance.

Holmes becomes involved in a family curse; South American bolas are used as a murder weapon, and Moriarty steals the Crown Jewels from the Tower of London (at one point Holmes disguises himself as a music hall entertainer).

Fox then abandoned the series, but in 1942 Universal reunited the pair for twelve more films, less expensive but competent programmers. The studio did not use period settings, and Holmes and Watson faced such contemporary problems as wartime spies and sabotage. Muting this transition were the Victorian atmosphere of the London in which Holmes detected and a carefully worded explanation after the opening credits of the first few films: "Sherlock Holmes is ageless, invincible and unchanging. In solving significant problems of the present day he remains—as ever—the supreme master of deductive reasoning."

Sherlock Holmes and the Voice of Terror. Universal, 1942. Rathbone, Bruce, Evelyn Ankers, Thomas Gomez, Reginald Denny, Henry Daniell, Mary Gordon (Mrs. Hudson, the role for which she was born, throughout the series). Directed by John Rawlins. Credited to "His Last Bow" (1917).

Holmes, summoned by Britain's Inner Council, must expose "The Voice of Terror," who, in a series of terrifying wartime broadcasts, gloats over the destruction achieved by Nazi saboteurs.

Sherlock Holmes and the Secret Weapon. Universal, 1942. Rathbone, Bruce, Kaaren Verne, Atwill

(Moriarty), Dennis Hoey (the definitive Lestrade through the series). Directed by Roy William Neill. The code of "The Adventure of the Dancing Men" (1903) is used in the plot.

Moriarty kidnaps a young Swiss scientist and—using torture—tries to extract from him his new bombsight invention.

Sherlock Holmes in Washington. Universal, 1943. Rathbone, Bruce, Daniell, Majorie Lord, Zucco. Directed by Neill.

Holmes and Watson hurry to wartime Washington in pursuit of a stolen microfilm concealed in a matchbook and unwittingly passed from smoker to smoker.

Sherlock Holmes Faces Death. Universal, 1943. Rathbone, Bruce, Hillary Brooke, Milburn Stone, Arthur Margetson, Halliwell Hobbes. Directed by Neill. A considerable, but very interesting, reworking of "The Musgrave Ritual" (1893).

Holmes learns of an ancient family ritual as murder strikes at Musgrave Manor.

Spider Woman. Universal, 1944. Rathbone, Bruce, Gale Sondergaard (Adrea Spedding), Directed by Neill. Uses bits from *The Sign of Four* and "The Final Problem" (1893).

A series of "pajama suicides" leads Holmes to a patrician adventuress, a pygmy, deadly spiders, and the shooting gallery of a carnival.

The Scarlet Claw. Universal, 1944. Rathbone, Bruce, Kay Harding, Arthur Hohl, Gerald Hamer, Paul Cavanagh. Directed by Neill. Based on no story from the Canon, and the best film in the Universal series.

While attending a Canadian psychic convention (sic), Holmes and Watson are drawn to the small village of La Morte Rouge, in whose fog-shrouded marshes a century-old glowing monster has been seen again—and a killer lurks in a variety of disguises.

The Pearl of Death. Universal, 1944. Rathbone, Bruce, Ankers, Mander, Rondo Hatton. Directed by Neill. Suggested by "The Six Napoleons" (1904).

The grotesque "Creeper" (Hatton) begins a series of horrible murders in which the victims are surrounded by smashed china.

The House of Fear. Universal, 1945. Rathbone, Bruce, Aubrey Mather, Gavin Muir, Cavanagh, Holmes Herbert. Directed by Neill. Suggested by "The Five Orange Pips" (1891).

One by one, the members of "The Good Comrades" club, all of whom reside at a manor called Drearcliff, suffer mutilation deaths after receiving letters containing orange pips.

The Woman in Green. Universal, 1945. Rathbone, Bruce, Brooke, Daniell (Moriarty), Cavanagh, Matthew Boulton (Inspector Gregson). Directed by Neill. Draws bits from "The Adventure of the Empty House" (1903).

Basil Rathbone as a modern-dress Sherlock Holmes (center) finds himself trapped by a cheerful Spider Woman, in one of the programmer Holmes films of the 1940s. [*Universal*]

A blackmail ring headed by Moriarty and the treacherous Lydia Marlowe (Brooke) uses hypnosis to instigate a series of "finger murders"—the fingers are sent to Scotland Yard.

Pursuit to Algiers. Universal, 1945. Rathbone, Bruce, Marjorie Riordan, John Abbott, Martin Kosleck, Hamer, Rosalind Ivy, Rex Evans. Directed by Neill.

Holmes and Watson guard the young heir to the throne of Rovenia as they accompany him (he is impersonating the doctor's nephew) on a dangerous sea journey to his homeland.

Terror by Night. Universal, 1946. Rathbone, Bruce, Alan Mowbray, Renee Godfrey, Billy Bevan, Hobbes. Directed by Neill.

On the night train speeding from London to Edinburgh, several deaths occur, and Watson's old school chum (Mowbray) is revealed as Colonel Sebastian Moran.

Dressed to Kill. Universal, 1946. Rathbone, Bruce, Patricia Morison, Edmond Breon, Frederic Worlock, Harry Cording. Directed by Neill.

In one of three music boxes made in Dartmoor Prison, a £5 Bank of England plate lies concealed.

In addition, Rathbone and Bruce (and the elaborately detailed Baker Street interior) made a quick cameo appearance, along with other Universal stars, in the Olsen and Johnson comedy *Crazy House,* in 1943.

After portraying the great detective for eight years, Rathbone declined to associate himself further with the role, declaring that no actor in history had ever been so fearfully typed. He was never able to shed, however, the public's identification and worship of him as Holmes. Indeed, it was more than a decade before anyone else dared attempt the role in a major film.

The Hound of the Baskervilles. Hammer Films (British), 1959. Peter Cushing (Holmes), André Morell (Watson), Christopher Lee (Sir Henry), Ewen Solon, Marla Landi, Francis De Wolff, Miles Malleson, John le Mesurier. Directed by Terence Fisher.

In this distorted version of the events and relationships on the moor, Cushing is a short, nervous Holmes in a nonetheless elaborate period film, the first Holmes motion picture made in color.

Three years later, in Germany, Christopher Lee, who previously had played Sir Henry Baskerville and was later to play brother Mycroft, donned the deerstalker. (English horror great Lee, who has also portrayed Count DRACULA, Fu Manchu, and the creation of FRANKENSTEIN, is the only actor to have impersonated three central figures in the Canon.)

Sherlock Holmes und das Halsband des Todes (released in the United States, dubbed, as *Sherlock Holmes and the Deadly Necklace*). CCC-Criterion (German), 1962. Lee (Holmes), Thorley Walters (Watson), Hans Söhnker (Moriarty), Senta Berger, Ivan Desny, Leon Askin. Directed by Fisher. Drawn from incidents in *The Sign of Four* and, especially, *The Valley of Fear.*

There are some especially interesting confrontations between Holmes and the professor, who emerges unscathed at the finish of the film. An announced sequel was never made.

Four years later, American producer Herman Cohen, working in England, fashioned a clash between the detective and Jack the Ripper and chose dashing Shakespearean actor John Neville as an unusually youthful and agile, but not miscast, Holmes, Donald Houston as a very solid Watson, and Robert Morley as a mobile, dyspeptic Mycroft—the first appearance of Holmes's brother on the talking screen. Initially called *Fog*, the film gives a chilling view of the Victorian London ghettos in which the Ripper stalked.

A Study in Terror. Columbia (British), 1965. Neville, Houston, Morley, Frank Finlay (Lestrade), Anthony Quayle, John Fraser, Barry Jones, Cecil Parker, Barbara Windsor, Adrienne Corri, Georgia Brown. Directed by James Hill.

Holmes ends the Ripper's career but does not publicly reveal his identity.

Ellery QUEEN (author) scripted a "movie edition" book of this film, inserting alternating chapters in which Ellery QUEEN (detective) theorized over a

Watsonian manuscript outlining the events that he had just discovered.

The American director Billy Wilder had for years planned to do his own version of the Holmesian saga, bringing to light new cases and providing intimate insights based upon the discovery of Watson's dispatch box (with more writings locked inside) in a London bank vault. His film touched upon two daring themes: Holmes's professional failures, and his suspect sexual makeup. Just as radical was the casting of Christopher Lee as a *lean* Mycroft, the right hand of Queen Victoria—who also makes an appearance. Robert Stephens is the high-strung, misogynist detective.

The Private Life of Sherlock Holmes. United Artists, 1970. Stephens, Colin Blakely (Watson), Lee, Irene Handl (Mrs. Hudson), Genevieve Page, Clive Revill, Tamara Toumanova, Stanley Holloway, George Benson (Lestrade). Directed by Wilder.

Holmes copes not too successfully with spies, sea monsters, midgets, and canaries; despite his lack

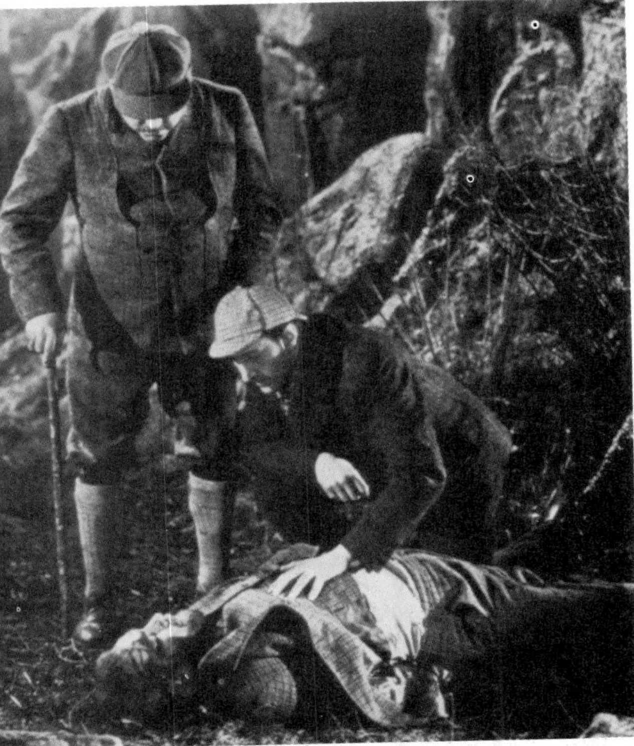

(opposite) Stewart Granger, the newest in a long line of cinematic Sherlock Holmeses, stands (holding the lantern at right) on the very edge of Grimpen Mire, on the Baskerville moorland, where, in the picture above, Basil Rathbone knelt three decades earlier.

of interest in women, he is provided with a love affair to melt his heart.

Slightly outside the mainstream is *They Might Be Giants* (Universal, 1971. Directed by Anthony Harvey), in which George C. Scott, an eccentric lawyer suffering from the delusion that he is Sherlock Holmes, is assigned a lady psychiatrist named Watson (Joanne Woodward); together they drive out reality.

Plays

Conan Doyle adapted his short story "The Speckled Band" into a play of the same name (first produced on Broadway in 1910; first published in 1912). The plot closely follows the original story: Miss Julia Stoner cries out to her sister, "O, my God! Helen! It was the band! The speckled band!" The frightened and perplexed Helen asks Holmes to come to Stoke Moran to solve the riddle. Here, the bizarre is ordinary, as a cheetah and a baboon freely roam the grounds, strange whistles sound in the night, and a sinister bully, Dr. Grimesby Roylott, is omnipresent.

In 1922, William Gillette, the great stage actor who had portrayed Holmes approximately 1,300 times for more than a generation, published *Sherlock Holmes: A Drama in Four Acts.* Gillette had wired Conan Doyle for permission for Holmes to consummate his romance with Alice Faulkner ("May I marry Holmes?"); the celebrated author, by then abandoning his creation, replied that Gillette could marry or murder the detective or do what he liked. Gillette's monumental stage dramatization made its debut in 1899 and was revived continually for three decades thereafter. The detective's cool confrontation with Moriarty provided rich drama for author-star Gillette and a format for the film and stage clashes that followed.

Less rash dramatists in the 1920s and the 1930s fashioned repertoire and even puppet plays from the Sacred Writings. There was, in fact, on Broadway in 1936, a daughter for the Master, Shirley Holmes, in *The Holmeses of Baker Street* (written by Basil Mitchell). In 1953 Ouida Rathbone prepared for her husband a play called *Sherlock Holmes* (his return to the role after an avoidance of several years), based on "The Final Problem," "A Scandal in Bohemia," and "The Bruce Partington Plans" (1908). Although interestingly cast (Thomas Gomez was Moriarty and Jarmila Novotna was an Irene Adler to turn Holmes's eye) and not without spectacle—in one scene a hotel balcony overlooks the Reichenbach Falls—the play lasted only three performances. Somewhat more successful—lasting nearly a year—was Jerome Coopersmith's 1965 *Baker Street;* Fritz Weaver was a tuneful detective, and Martin Gabel, as an evil Moriarty, employed dancing minions. Inga Swenson, as Irene Adler, had opportunity to demonstrate her vocal talents and to intrigue Holmes. In 1974 England's Royal Shakespeare Company staged an extremely successful revival of the Gillette landmark play. That fall the production began an equally heralded tour of the United States with John Wood as Holmes—the 109th actor to play him on film or the professional stage (by Wood's own count).

Radio and Television

Starting in 1930 Holmes was a radio staple. William Gillette was the star of a special dramatization of his play (the role was repeated later by Orson Welles). A somewhat pompous Richard Gordon was the first series impersonator; by far the most endearing voice belonged to Rathbone, who, with Nigel Bruce, occupied radio's Baker Street for some years after the success of their first films as Holmes and Watson. Many of the programs were based on stories in the Canon, although some were originals; many of the scripts were written by Anthony BOUCHER, others by Leslie CHARTERIS. Invariably the format had Watson, now quietly retired to a California cottage (!), recalling long-ago adventures to an announcer-visitor and extolling the sponsor's product. Other actors who played Holmes were Tom Conway, Ben Wright, and John Stanley; in the late 1950s a singularly faithful and well-produced BBC radio series with John Gielgud as Holmes (and Ralph Richardson as Watson and Orson Welles as Moriarty) began an endlessly successful American syndication, playing on local American radio stations for more than a decade, although only thirteen half-hour programs were recorded.

In 1955 one of the first successful television series (thirty-nine half-hour programs) to be filmed in Europe was *The Adventures of Sherlock Holmes,* with a pallid, too youthful Ronald Howard (son of Leslie) in the title role, overshadowed by H. Marion Crawford's robust portrayal of Watson (he was later to play a very Watsonian Dr. Petrie in a Fu Manchu film series). There have been other Holmesian appearances in anthology programs, including Alan Napier as the detective in a *Story Theater* version of "The Speckled Band," and Rathbone, returning to the role on CBS's *Suspense* in the 1950s, in an adaptation of a pastiche written by Adrian Conan Doyle, Sir Arthur's son, and John Dickson CARR. During that same period, Rathbone often donned deerstalkers for television variety program burlesques. And also in the 1950s, in a series of cultural programs called *Omnibus,* Rex STOUT (with tongue in cheek) presented a curious dramatization of "The Red-Headed League," claiming that the adventure actually occurred while Holmes briefly lived in the Gramercy Park section of New York City.

Holmes has been particularly active on British television. Both Douglas Wilmer and Peter Cushing are among the actors who have played the master detective in Holmesian presentations. (The Cushing series, of the 1960s, set against elaborate period backgrounds, was criticized for inserting too much violence as the everyday occurrence of Victorian times.) In 1972, for American television, British actor Stewart Granger portrayed a silver-haired, stocky Holmes in a well-mounted but somewhat abbreviated new version of *The Hound of the Baskervilles* done as a television feature.

The Hound of the Baskervilles. Universal, 1972. Granger, Bernard Fox (Watson), William Shatner (Stapleton), Sally Ann Howes, John Williams, Anthony Zerbee, Jane Merrow, Alan Callio (Lestrade). Directed by Barry Crane. The pilot for a projected television series that did not materialize.

HOLT, VICTORIA (pseudonym of Eleanor Burford Hibbert; 1906–   ). English author of Gothic and romantic fiction. Born in London, the daughter of Alice (Tate) and Joseph Burford, she was privately educated. Following her marriage to G. P. Hibbert, she continued to live in London when not traveling.

Mrs. Hibbert is a prolific writer, with scores of books to her credit; she has used several pseudonyms, including Elbur Ford, Kathleen Kellow, and Ellalice Tate, as well as her own name, Eleanor Burford. Her most successful work (and she earns more than $300,000 a year) has been signed by Victoria Holt. The books are fairly standard Gothic thrillers—largely ignored or derided by critics but read avidly by the public, especially women. She admits that her work is not profound, calling it "pure entertainment," but her chief concern is her reading audience. "It's nicer to be read," she says, "than to get nice reviews."

When she first adopted the Victoria Holt pseudonym, her true identity was kept secret by Doubleday, and there was speculation that Daphne DU MAURIER had written the popular Holt books because they had the sense of atmosphere to be found in *Rebecca* (1938).

Among her best sellers are *Mistress of Mellyn* (1960), *Bride of Pendorric* (1963), *The Legend of the Seventh Virgin* (1965), and *The King of the Castle* (1968).

HOLTON, LEONARD (pseudonym of Leonard Patrick O'Connor Wibberley; 1915–   ). A native of Ireland, Leonard Wibberley has traveled extensively since his youth. He has lived in England, the British West Indies, Canada, Portugal, and the United States, where, during World War II, he was in charge of employee relations in a shipyard that produced Liberty ships. Later, he was American correspondent for the *London Evening News* and a reporter on the *Los Angeles Times.* In 1954 he decided to devote full time to writing books. Using his own name, the Holton pseudonym for mysteries, and the pseudonyms Christopher Webb and Patrick O'Connor, he has written over ninety books, including more than fifty juvenile works. He has also written several plays. His most popular work, *The Mouse That Roared* (1955), is about a tiny European country named Grand Fenwick that invades the United States with twenty longbowmen; it was also a very popular motion picture starring Peter Sellers. Also successful was *Meeting with a Great Beast* (1971), an account of a man suffering from terminal cancer. More recently, *The Last Stand of Father Felix* (1974) deals with Father Felix Borowski's problems in the former Portuguese colony of Blemi in the 1950s.

As Leonard Holton, he has published ten detective novels about Father Joseph BREDDER, a Los Angeles priest. All of the books have an underlying spiritual theme. The television series *Sarge* drew some of its inspiration (but none of its plots) from the Father Bredder series, and Wibberley received a royalty for each episode. There were thirteen one-hour episodes, televised in 1971, following a successful two-hour pilot film starring George Kennedy the previous year.

Many of Wibberley's interests are reflected in his books. In the Bredder novel *A Touch of Jonah* (1968), the San Pedro-to-Honolulu yacht race (in which the author has participated) provides a frame for the story. A rare Guarnerius violin provides a clue in *A Problem of Angels* (1970); Wibberley not only plays the viola and the violin but also constructs these instruments. *The Devil to Play* (1973) deals with professional baseball (his son Christopher plays ball professionally).

HOMES, GEOFFREY (pseudonym of Daniel Mainwaring; 1901–). American mystery novelist and screenwriter. Born in California, the son of a state forest ranger, he was educated at Fresno State College. He tried teaching for a year and then entered journalism, becoming a copyboy and reporter (for ten years) on the *San Francisco Chronicle.* He switched to publicity work and went to Hollywood to work for Warner Brothers. He changed jobs again when he went to Paramount to be a scenarist.

Among Mainwaring's screen credits are *Out of the Past* (1947), based on his own novel *Build My Gallows High* (1946); *The Lawless* (1950); *The Phenix City Story* (1955); the excellent *Invasion of the Body Snatchers* (1956), from Jack Finney's science fiction novel *The Body Snatchers* (1955); and *Baby Face Nelson* (1957).

The Homes novels are cool and detached examples of the "medium-boiled" school and are intelligently written and plotted. The early ones, such as *The Man Who Murdered Himself* (1936), *The Doctor Died at Dusk* (1936), and *The Man Who Didn't Exist* (1937), all feature tall, good-looking newspaperman Robin Bishop, who, unlike many other members of his profession, is not hard-boiled and does not make wisecracking jokes. His wife, Mary, is sometimes involved in his investigations. Later works, such as *Finders Keepers* (1940), concern the investigations of Humphrey Campbell, who works for a missing persons bureau. He is a rough, tough, skirt-chasing private eye who plays the accordion and drinks nothing stronger than milk.

HOPLEY, GEORGE. *See* WOOLRICH, CORNELL.

HOPWOOD, AVERY. *See* RINEHART, MARY ROBERTS.

HORLER, SYDNEY (1888–1954). English mystery novelist. Born in Leytonstone, Essex, Horler grew up in Bristol, where he attended the Colston School. His parents wanted him to become a schoolteacher, but he refused and left school to become a copyreader for the *Bristol Evening News;* later he wrote copy and became a reporter. Subsequently, he wrote for other papers in Manchester, Birmingham, and London. On the eve of World War I Horler began to write fiction, but he ceased this activity when he enlisted. At first he was a payroll clerk, but then, because of his journalistic experience, he was commissioned a second lieutenant assigned to writing propaganda for Air Force Intelligence. Because of his poor eyesight, he never saw combat.

"Horler for Excitement" appeared on the dust wrapper of the Hodder & Stoughton best sellers of the 1930s. This short story collection was first published in 1930.

Following the war Horler (now married) gave up journalism and became a reader for several magazines. He began to write and sell sports fiction, mostly about football and boxing. His first novel was *Goal* (1920). Four years later, he wrote his first mystery, *The Mystery of No. 1,* and it was published in 1925. Encouraged by its success, he became a full-time mystery writer, with much of his prolific output serialized in the popular British periodicial *News of the World.* He wrote of his working methods in *Writing for Money* (1932) and *Excitement: An Impudent Autobiography* (1933).

Horler wrote more than 150 books, and the advertising slogan "Horler for Excitement" became well known throughout England, for it appeared on all the Hodder & Stoughton books, issued in bright yellow covers.

His most famous series character is the Honorable Timothy Overbury "Tiger" Standish, son of the Earl of Quorn—a hearty, two-fisted, soccer-playing superhero similar to Bulldog Drummond (*see* DRUMMOND, BULLDOG). Tall, strong, and impeccably dressed, he is endowed with, as Horler once said, "all the attributes of a thoroughly likable fellow . . . he likes his glass of beer, he is a confirmed pipe-smoker, he is always ready to smile back into the face of danger." The virile patriot appears in *Tiger Standish* (1932), *Tiger Standish Comes Back* (1934), *The Lady with the Limp* (1944), and other books.

Horler also wrote about Ian Heath, British secret service agent, in *The Curse of Doone* (1928) and other books. Gerald Frost, known as "Nighthawk," another series character, is an outraged cracksman who steals jewelry from society ladies of questionable virtue, using their own lipsticks to scrawl the word "wanton" on their pillows as they sleep. He appears in *They Called Him Nighthawk* (1937), *The Return of Nighthawk* (1940), *Nighthawk Strikes to Kill* (1941), and four other works.

Horler also wrote as Peter Cavendish and Martin Heritage.

HORNUNG, E[RNEST] W[ILLIAM] (1866–1921). English author of crime and mystery stories and creator of A. J. RAFFLES, the greatest of all fictional thieves.

Born in Middlesbrough, Yorkshire, Hornung suffered from poor health and, at eighteen, moved to Australia in the hope that the climate would be beneficial. He remained there less than three years but absorbed the physical surroundings and atmosphere, using them as the background for many books. When he returned to England, he married Constance Doyle, the sister of Sir Arthur CONAN DOYLE. He never enjoyed full health but served in World War I anyway, going to France to organize a library and rest hut under the auspices of the YMCA. His combat-zone adventures are described in *Notes of a Camp-Follower on the Western Front* (1919). Hornung's only son, called Oscar (his real name was Arthur, for his uncle and godfather), served in France and was killed by a shell. Shortly after the war Hornung accompanied his wife to Saint-Jean-de-Luz and contracted a fatal chill.

Hornung was an authority on cricket and, despite poor eyesight and health, was an excellent player, as was his most famous creation, Raffles. The exploits of the amateur cracksman, the subjects of Hornung's best and most famous books, are not, however, his only contribution to the literature of crime and detection.

Because of the circumstances of the colonization of Australia, stories of nineteenth-century life there often deal with crime, convicts, and bushranging, and Hornung's are some of the best of the kind. *The Boss of Taroomba* (1894) is the story of a girl who, together with a German piano tuner, defends her ranch against an attack by bushrangers (escaped convicts living in the bush). *The Rogue's March* (1896) is a serious novel about convicts in a chain gang in New South Wales. Cole, a gold miner on Black Hill Flats, performs some detective work in *Dead Men Tell No Tales* (1899). *The Belle of Toorak* (1900; U.S. title: *The Shadow of a Man*), describes how a former convict is protected by a young man who believes the felon to be his father. *Stingaree* (1905) is a collection of ten stories about Tom Erichsen, a cultivated New South Wales bushranger who has some of Raffles's characteristics. He is a "man of birth and mystery, with an ostentatious passion for music, and as romantic a method as that of any highwayman of the Old World." Other romantic novels of crime and adventure in Australia are *A Bride from the Bush* (1890), *Under Two Skies* (1892), *Tiny Lutrell* (1893), *Irralie's Bushranger* (1896), *My Lord Duke* (1897), *Some Persons Unknown* (s.s.; 1898), and *At Large* (1902).

In the more civilized setting of England, Hornung's best-known non-Raffles book is *The Crime Doctor* (1914), a collection of stories about Dr. John Dollar, one of the first detectives to solve crimes using psychological means. Max Marcin created a psychiatrist-detective for radio in 1940. Also known as the Crime Doctor, Robert Ordway has no connection with Hornung's Dr. Dollar (*see* CRIME DOCTOR, THE).

The hero of *Young Blood* (1898) comes into conflict with a villain and a swindler as he tries to live down his father's disgrace. The English clergyman in *Peccavi* (1900) has committed a crime and endures a tragic penance. Although a man believes the woman guilty of murdering her first husband, he marries the heroine of *The Shadow of a Rope* (1902), only to fall under suspicion for the crime. *The Camera Fiend* (1911) concerns a precocious seventeen-year-old asthmatic schoolboy who discusses "psychophotography" with the title character ("the camera fiend") and is forced to deal with a series of intricate crimes, aided in his solutions by Mr. Eugene Thrush. *Old Offenders and a Few Old Scores* (1923), a posthumous collection with an introduction by Conan Doyle, contains various kinds of crime tales.

HOUSEHOLD, GEOFFREY (1900–). English author of adventure and suspense novels that often deal with international intrigue. Born in England, he moved to Romania, then to Spain, and finally to the United States in time for the Depression. He supported himself with hack writing for two years and then returned to England, where he now resides with his second wife, the former Ilona M. J. Zsoldos-Gutman, whom he married in 1942. They have three children.

Household received some acclaim when the long short story "The Salvation of Pisco Gabar" was published in *The Atlantic Monthly* in 1936 (it appeared as the title story of a collection published in 1938); but his future as a writer was assured with the publication, first, of *The Third Hour* (1937) and, then, of his first thriller and best book, *Rogue Male*, in 1939. This is a psychological thriller about a wealthy young sportsman who goes hunting for an unnamed European dictator (presumably Hitler). He is captured while stalking his prey, tortured, and thrown over a cliff, apparently to his death. He survives, however, and escapes to England, only to find himself in jeopardy again.

Other Household books with elements of crime, mystery, and intrigue include *The High Place* (1950), *A Rough Shoot* (1951), *A Time to Kill* (1951), *Watcher in the Shadows* (1960), *Olura* (1965), and *Dance of the Dwarfs* (1968).

Films

In 1941 Fritz LANG presented a classic chase thriller, *Man Hunt*, based on *Rogue Male*.

Shoot First (British release title: *A Rough Shoot*). United Artists (British), 1953. Joel McCrea, Evelyn Keyes, Herbert Lom, Marius Goring, Roland Culver. Directed by Robert Parrish. Based on the 1951 novel.

A U.S. Army colonel stationed in England shoots at a poacher trespassing on his rented hunting grounds and discovers that he has apparently killed a British secret service agent.

HOWARD, GEORGE BRONSON. *See* BRONSON-HOWARD, GEORGE.

HUBIN, ALLEN J. (1936–). American scientist, editor, and reviewer. After receiving a B.S. degree from Wheaton College in Illinois in 1958 and an M.S. degree from the University of Minnesota in 1961, Hubin joined the 3M Company. He lives and works in the Minneapolis–St. Paul area and has been a research chemist and patent specialist for his employer. He is married and has five children.

A longtime reader and collector of mystery fiction (he owns about 22,000 volumes), in 1967 Hubin founded *The Armchair Detective*, the first journal devoted to all aspects of the genre. He has continued as editor of this quarterly, which regularly attracts articles, checklists, and reviews from the leading scholars in the field. In 1968 he replaced Anthony BOUCHER as mystery reviewer for *The New York Times Book Review* and continued in that assignment until 1971. He has edited several of the annual *Best Detective Stories of the Year* and updated the section on the post-World War II mystery for the 1973 edition of *Encyclopaedia Britannica*.

HUGHES, DOROTHY B[ELLE] (1904–). American author and reviewer of mystery works. Born Dorothy Belle Flanagan in Kansas City, Mo., she attended the University of Missouri, Columbia University, and the University of New Mexico. Early in her writing career she worked on newspapers and wrote poetry. *Dark Certainty*, a book of poems published in 1931, won an award in the Yale Series of Younger Poets competition. She settled in Santa Fe, N.Mex., following her marriage to Levi Allen Hughes, Jr., of that city. They have three children. In 1939 she published *Pueblo on the Mesa: The First Fifty Years of the University of New Mexico*. The following year she launched her career as a mystery novelist and reviewer.

In 1950 the Mystery Writers of America awarded Mrs. Hughes an Edgar for her reviews, which have appeared in the *Albuquerque Tribune*, the *Los Angeles Times*, and *The New York Herald Tribune*. Mrs. Hughes's *The So Blue Marble* was the first in a series of suspense stories that won her some of the best reviews of the 1940s. Will Cuppy called the book "impressive in wallop and so irresistible in manner." For Anthony BOUCHER, it was "an unforgettable experience in contemporary sensation fiction." James SANDOE, writing of two subsequent books, *The Blackbirder* and *The Delicate Ape*,

A young Indian girl (Wanda Hendrix) offers her services as guide to a gangster (Robert Montgomery) on a grim mission of vengeance in New Mexico in the screen treatment of Dorothy B. Hughes's *Ride the Pink Horse*. [*Universal*]

called them "superlatively skillful tales of pursuit and escape."

With the end of World War II Mrs. Hughes turned her attention to postwar social problems. *Dread Journey* is a suspense story about a famous movie star terrorized on a cross-country luxury train. An important observer of (and participant in) the events is James Cobbett, an articulate, intelligent Negro pullman car attendant. *Ride the Pink Horse* is as important for its descriptions of the three cultures that have fused in New Mexico as it is for its story. Against the setting of Santa Fe's annual fiesta, Mrs. Hughes tells of the collision of Indian, Spanish, and "Anglo" societies and also explores in depth the mind of a murderer.

At one time a very prolific writer (she published eleven books in seven years), Mrs. Hughes has written only three books since 1947. *The Candy Kid* deals with drug smuggling across the border between the United States and Mexico. *The Davidian Report* is a routine spy story. After a hiatus of more than ten years, she published *The Expendable Man,* a book Boucher thought was her best. Set in Phoenix, it provided what he called "unrelenting suspense, deft trickery, firmly penetrating treatment of individual and social problems."

CHECKLIST

1940 *The So Blue Marble*
1940 *The Cross-eyed Bear*
1941 *The Bamboo Blonde*
1942 *The Fallen Sparrow*
1943 *The Blackbirder*
1944 *The Delicate Ape*
1944 *Johnnie*
1945 *Dread Journey*
1946 *Ride the Pink Horse*
1946 *The Scarlet Imperial*
1947 *In a Lonely Place*
1950 *The Candy Kid*
1952 *The Davidian Report*
1963 *The Expendable Man*

Films

Three major works by Mrs. Hughes have reached the screen.

The Fallen Sparrow. RKO, 1943. John Garfield, Maureen O'Hara, Walter Slezak. Directed by Richard Wallace.

An American veteran of the Spanish Civil War, tortured in a prison camp, goes to New York to avenge the death of the man who had helped him to escape and thinks that he recognizes, in the friend's old haunts, the crippled, evil camp supervisor, now a Nazi espionage agent.

Ride the Pink Horse. Universal, 1947. Robert Montgomery, Thomas Gomez, Wanda Hendrix. Directed by Montgomery.

A tough crook wanders into a New Mexico town during fiesta time, intent on blackmailing a vacationing crime czar who has killed his pal; he is befriended by a wistful Indian girl and the native operator of a shabby carrousel.

In a Lonely Place. Columbia, 1950. Humphrey Bogart, Gloria Grahame, Martha Stewart. Directed by Nicholas Ray.

A short-tempered Hollywood screenwriter cannot come to grips with the fact that he is wrongly suspected of the murder of a hatcheck girl he was the last to see alive.

HUGO, VICTOR (-MARIE) (1802–1885). French novelist, poet, and dramatist, arguably the greatest romantic novelist of all time. His most famous works are *Notre Dame de Paris* (1831; English title: *The Hunchback of Notre Dame*) and *Les Misérables* (1862), a long account of the trials of Jean Valjean. A poor, honest peasant, Valjean steals a loaf of bread to feed his sister's starving family and is arrested. Sentenced to five years in prison, he is caught trying to escape and is given an additional nineteen years, escaping again, now as a hardened criminal. With the help of a kindly bishop, he changes his name but is recognized by the relentless detective on his trail, Javert. Valjean flees, a sympathetically drawn victim of society with a one-dimensional hunter constantly in his wake. The flight and pursuit through the slums and sewers of Paris constitute one of the most realistic and memorable scenes in literature. The novel was selected for the HAYCRAFT-QUEEN CORNERSTONE LIBRARY.

Films

There have been many cinematic versions of *Les Misérables.* Silents were released in the United States in 1909 and 1918, in France in 1913 and 1925, and in England in 1922. A sound version appeared in France in 1934, and the following year Fredric March and Charles Laughton starred in the classic, which was remade in 1952 with Michael Rennie and Robert Newton. There was an Italian version in 1946 and, in 1957, another French production, starring Jean Gabin and Bernard Blier.

HULL, RICHARD (pseudonym of Richard Henry Sampson; 1896–1973). English crime novelist; disciple of Francis Iles (Anthony BERKELEY). Born in London, the son of Nina (Hull) and S. A. Sampson, he was educated at Rugby and was awarded a mathematical scholarship on leaving but was prevented from entering Trinity College, Cambridge, by World War I. He obtained a commission after entering the Army on his eighteenth birthday, served with an infantry battalion and the Machine Gun Corps, and spent three years in France. At the end of the war he was articled to a firm of chartered accountants and remained with the company for several years, during which time he passed his qualifying examinations.

After he was unsuccessful in an attempt to set up a private practice, he decided to try writing, having read Iles's *Malice Aforethought* (1931), which was to have a great influence on his subject matter and style. With the success of his first novel, *The Murder of My Aunt,* Sampson devoted himself to writing and published a book a year for almost a decade, after which his output continued at a slower pace.

Sampson had retained an interest in the Army after the war and remained on the active list of his original battalion until 1929, when he retired; he kept in touch, however. On September 1, 1939, he was recalled to service but was released as a major in July 1940 because of his age. He quickly found employment in the Admiralty as a chartered accountant and investigated costs of government contracts. He remained in this position until the mid-1950s. Sampson never married and most of the time lived in a London club.

The Hull novels "have a peculiarly acid 'bite' to them that is quite original. . . . Someone characterized them as 'brilliantly vicious,' and they do expose the capacity of the human mind for self-delusion as mordantly, at times, as anything from the pen of Iles, Hull's avowed master. They are all written, 'for preference,' in the first person. To one of his most despicable villain-narrators, in fact, the author has given the name Richard Henry Sampson—a singularly effective method of underlining the 'but for the grace of God' quality," wrote Howard HAYCRAFT.

The Murder of My Aunt details the mainly unsuccessful efforts of a worthless young man to kill his aunt for financial gain, until he hits upon what he believes to be the perfect scheme. Hull's finest novel, it bears comparison with the major accomplishments of Iles, C. E. VULLIAMY, and other practitioners of the inverted form. Haycraft called it "a classic of its kind, an intellectual shocker par excellence."

In *Keep It Quiet* the wife of a club chef places perchloride of mercury in a bottle labeled essence of vanilla. Through further accident, the poison finds its way to the club's dinner table—with disastrous results. The secretary of the club tries to hush up the incident and leaves himself open to a blackmailer's designs.

Murder Isn't Easy, in a more conventional vein, anticipates Vera CASPARY's *Laura* (1943) by telling the story of the murder of a company director from a variety of viewpoints. *Excellent Intentions* tells a straightforward detective story by means of courtroom scenes. The judge, realizing the basic worthlessness of the victim and the unselfish motives of the murderer, is able to temper justice with mercy. *My Own Murderer* concerns an elaborate conspiracy to have an unwitting substitute take the place of a murderer and pay the supreme penalty. (This is the novel with the Richard Henry Sampson character.)

Later work by Hull is more conventional. When asked why he specialized in unpleasant characters, Hull replied that there was more to say about them and that he found them more amusing.

CHECKLIST

1934 *The Murder of My Aunt*
1935 *Keep It Quiet*
1936 *Murder Isn't Easy*
1936 *The Ghost It Was*
1937 *The Murderers of Monty*
1938 *Excellent Intentions* (U.S. title: *Beyond Reasonable Doubt*)
1939 *And Death Came Too*
1940 *My Own Murderer*
1941 *The Unfortunate Murderer*
1946 *Left-handed Death*
1947 *Last First*
1949 *Until She Was Dead*
1950 *A Matter of Nerves*
1950 *Invitation to an Inquest*
1953 *The Martineau Murders*

HUME, FERGUS[ON] (WRIGHT) (1859–1932). English author of mystery and romantic fiction. Hume was born in England; his family subsequently returned to its native New Zealand, where he attended the University of Otago, studying to be a barrister. Of his more than 130 novels, the only one remembered today is the first, *The Mystery of a Hansom Cab* (1886), the best-selling detective novel of the nineteenth century.

The first edition, published in Melbourne at Hume's own expense, is perhaps the rarest book in the genre, with only two copies known to exist. After earning a small amount from its sale, he sold all rights to a group of English investors called the Hansom Cab Publishing Company for £50. Appearing in paper covers, it quickly sold nearly 350,000 copies. Subsequent editions and American publications boosted sales past the half-million mark.

In *Mortal Consequences* (1972), Julian SYMONS recounts Hume's explanation of how *The Mystery of a Hansom Cab* came to be written: "I enquired of a leading Melbourne bookseller what style of book he sold most of. He replied the detective stories of [Émile] GABORIAU had a large sale; and as, at this time, I had never ever heard of this author, I bought all his works and . . . determined to write a book of the same class; containing a mystery, a murder, and a description of low life in Melbourne. This was the origin of the 'Cab'."

Hume was a hack writer whose other books did not sell well; in fact, his work is largely unreadable. Of most interest are *The Piccadilly Puzzle* (1889), *The Lone Inn* (1894), *The Crimson Cryptogram* (1900), *The Millionaire Mystery* (1901), and his two short story collections, *The Dwarf's Chamber* (1896)

Fergus Hume's *The Mystery of a Hansom Cab* was first published in Melbourne, Australia, by Kemp & Boyce in 1886. This paper-covered edition, published by the Hansom Cab Publishing Company in London in 1887, although usually described as the first edition, is actually the second edition, of which 340,000 copies were issued in little more than a year.

and *Hagar of the Pawn-Shop* (1898), which features Hagar Stanley, a beautiful gypsy who solves mysteries.

HUNT, E[VERETTE] HOWARD, JR. (1918–). American secret agent and author of detective and spy fiction. A 1940 graduate of Brown University, Hunt was a film scriptwriter and editor for the *March of Time* and a correspondent for *Life* before World War II. From 1948 to 1970 he was connected with the U.S. State Department and served in Washington and many world capitals including Paris, Vienna, Tokyo, and Montevideo. These assignments frequently involved "covers" for his activities with the CIA. In 1971 he became a consultant on President Richard M. Nixon's White House staff. In 1973 he was convicted of six counts of conspiracy in connection with the June 1972 break-in at the Democratic party national headquarters at the Watergate residential complex in Washington. Hunt had married Dorothy Wetzel in 1949; they had four children. In December 1972 Mrs. Hunt died in a plane crash; she had been raising money for his defense.

Hunt had published six nonmystery novels during the 1940s; the first two, *East of Farewell* (1942) and *Limit of Darkness* (1944), were based on his wartime experiences. Although these books received generally good reviews, they were not financially successful, and Hunt concentrated on his CIA career, writing private eye and spy novels in his spare time. Of Hunt's private detective Chris Powell, in *Lovers Are Losers* (1953), Anthony BOUCHER said: "His ruthless methods of executing private justice make Mike HAMMER look like a staunch upholder of law and order." Hunt also wrote as Gordon Davis, John Baxter, Robert Dietrich, and David St. John. As Dietrich, he wrote a dozen paperbacks about Steve Bentley, an accountant-troubleshooter who lives in Washington. As St. John, he wrote about Peter Ward, a graduate of Brown University whose Washington law practice is a cover for CIA activities.

HUNT, KYLE. *See* CREASEY, JOHN.

HUNTER, ALAN (JAMES HERBERT) (1922–). English poet and detective story writer. Born in Norwich, Hunter has continued to reside there except for his World War II service (1940–1946) as a leading aircraftsman in the RAF. His first book, a volume of poetry entitled *The Norwich Poems* (1945), was published while he was still on active duty. Before devoting full time to writing, Hunter was a poultry farmer and a bookseller. He is primarily known for his Superintendent Gently novels, a series well liked in England, though largely ignored in the United States.

Gently is a patient man whom one English reviewer called "our native rival to [Georges] SIMENON." Anthony BOUCHER praised "the brilliant questioning of Gently, who is probably the best interrogator in the business today." The detective's trademarks are his pipe and the peppermint creams that he chews continuously.

Gently Floating (1963), about the murder of a boatbuilder, involves Gently in his creator's hobby, sailing. The first book in the series, *Gently Does It* (1955), was dramatized by Mrs. August Belmont as *That Man Gently* and was produced in Harlow, England, in November 1961.

HUNTER, ED AND AM (Creator: Fredric BROWN). The Hunter detective team is formed in *The Fabulous Clipjoint* (1947) when Am (Ambrose) leaves his carnival job, goes to Chicago, and helps his young nephew Ed catch a murderer. The boy's father (Am's brother) has been killed. In *The Dead Ringer* (1948) the Hunters are traveling with a "carny" through the Midwest and become involved in the murder of the troupe's midget. By the time of *Death Has Many*

Doors (1951) they have left show business, served an apprenticeship with a large Chicago detective agency, and have their own small private investigation operation in that city.

Middle-aged Am is usually cheerful; he looks like a cherub, albeit one with a scraggly brown moustache. His nephew is handsome and brashly optimistic, and tends to fall in love with murder suspects. They frequently go to the movies; Ed claims that he does his best thinking about cases there.

There are four additional Hunter cases: *The Bloody Moonlight* (1949; British title: *Murder in the Moonlight*), *Compliments of a Fiend* (1950), *The Late Lamented* (1959), and *Mrs. Murphy's Underpants* (1963).

HUNTER, EVAN. *See* MCBAIN, ED.

HUXLEY, ELSPETH (JOSCELINE GRANT) (1907–). English writer, a cousin by marriage to Aldous and Julian Huxley. Born in Kenya, the daughter of Major Josceline Grant, she described her childhood in that African country in two autobiographical volumes, *The Flame Trees of Thika* (1959) and *The Mottled Lizard* (1962). She studied agriculture at Reading University in England and Cornell University in the United States.

In 1929 she became press officer for the Empire Marketing Board. Two years later she married Gervas Huxley, a tea expert, and traveled widely with him in Australia, New Zealand, Ceylon, Africa, and the United States. During World War II she worked for the BBC and the Colonial Office. In 1959 she was a member of the Monckton Commission, which advised the British government on the future of the Federation of Rhodesia and Nyasaland; this experience served as background material for *The Merry Hippo* (1963; U.S. title: *The Incident at the Merry Hippo*).

Mrs. Huxley has written biographies; travel books such as *The Sorcerer's Apprentice, Four Guineas, Forks and Hope,* and *Their Shining Eldorado;* six novels; *Back Street New Worlds, a report on immigrants in England;* and *Brave New Victuals,* a report on modern factory farming methods. Her latest books are biographies of David Livingstone and Florence Nightingale.

Her husband wrote a number of historical biographies before his death in 1971. She has a married son and now lives in Wiltshire.

Mrs. Huxley's first mystery novel, *Murder at Government House* (1937), introduces Superintendent Vachell, who also appears in her next two mysteries. She relied heavily on her professional background in writing this book, which is cited in SANDOE'S READERS' GUIDE TO CRIME.

Murder on Safari (1938) is usually regarded as Mrs. Huxley's best detective novel. At first a mildly satiric picture of a big-game safari, it turns serious when jewels belonging to a titled lady are stolen. *Death of an Aryan* (1939; U.S. title: *The African Poison Murders*) involves Nazis, romance, and detection.

The Merry Hippo concerns the attempts by a royal commission to draft a new constitution for the protectorate of Hapana. Problems ensue when the vice-chairman of the group eats a poisoned sandwich, and another member must play the role of detective to solve the crime. Mrs. Huxley's most recent detective novel is *A Man from Nowhere* (1964).

HYNE, C[HARLES] J[OHN] CUTCLIFFE (WRIGHT) (1866–1944). English author and creator of a famous fictional sea captain, the fiery Captain Kettle. Born in Gloucestershire, the son of a clergyman, he graduated from Clare College, Cambridge, where he was a superb athlete. He traveled to every part of the world, later using his extensive journeys as realistic background for his stories.

Although Hyne wrote several mystery novels, including *Honour of Thieves* (1895), which features Captain Kettle in his first adventure (as a magazine serial, the story was entitled *The Giant Sea Swindle*), he produced a memorable detective, Mr. Horrocks, in a series of short stories. The first five published stories about him appeared in *The Derelict* (1901); these five, and "The Looting of the Specie-Room," were included in *Mr. Horrocks, Purser* (1902), which also contains eleven stories that do not involve Horrocks. Other Hyne collections with elements of mystery and crime are *Paradise Coal-Boat* (1897) and *Man's Understanding* (1933).

I

I LOVE A MYSTERY (Creator: Carleton E. Morse). Having previously won renown for *One Man's Family,* scriptwriter Morse used a totally different milieu in another highly successful radio series, entitled *I Love a Mystery.*

Radio

Three young adventurers—two Americans, Jack Packard and Texan Doc Long, and an Englishman named Reggie York—meet in an Oriental prison during the Japanese attack on Shanghai; they escape and agree to meet the following New Year's Eve in a San Francisco bar. At their reunion, they decide to form the A-1 Detective Agency. Their bizarre cases ("No job too tough, no mystery too baffling") constituted the radio program *I Love a Mystery,* the pronoun referring to the audience, the heroes, and the creator.

Chivalrous to the extreme, but watchful and suspicious where women were concerned, Jack, Doc, and Reggie gave no thought at all to marriage and settling down. Instead, they tackled lost tribes and murderous thugs, helped girls in distress, prowled around old dark houses haunted by the cries of a phantom baby (as well as an ax murderer), and, always with infectious high spirits, went all over the world—to locales like fog-bound Chinatown and Bury-Your-Dead, Ariz.—in search of mystery and adventure.

The program began in 1939 and continued, first as a serial and then as a half-hour series, for five years; it was revived in 1949 for three more years.

Films

In 1945 Columbia began a series of three films drawn from the radio series, all directed by Henry Levin. Contract player Jim Bannon was a rugged, acceptable Jack Packard, and Barton Yarborough (who originated the role on radio) was a good-natured, drawling Doc ("honest to my grandmaw, Son!"). Reggie was eliminated.

I Love a Mystery. Columbia, 1945. Bannon, Yarborough, Nina Foch, George Macready, Carole Matthews. Based on one of the most successful sequences in the radio serial, "The Head of Jonathan Monk."

Millionaire Monk believes that a peg-legged man wants his head because he is the image of the long-dead leader of a secret Oriental cult; the leader's body has been preserved, but the head is beginning to deteriorate.

The Devil's Mask. Columbia, 1946. Bannon, Yarborough, Anita Louise, Michael Duane, Mona Barrie, Paul Burns.

In the wreckage of a South American plane, police find a package containing a shrunken human head—that of a missing explorer—and in its braids a coded message that leads to a murder in a museum.

The Unknown. Columbia, 1946. Bannon, Yarborough, Karen Morley, Robert Wilcox, Jeff Donnell, Wilton Graff.

The film was loosely based on the "Faith, Hope and Charity Sisters" radio sequence, though reduced to one girl, who returns to the isolated family home she had left years before and hears a baby's wail in the night and an ax-wielding murderer moving along hidden passageways.

Television

In the late 1960s Universal made a "mystery" telefeature in the camp style then briefly popular. It was not released until 1973, hopes that it would serve as a pilot for a television series being dim.

I Love a Mystery. Universal, 1973. Les Crane (Jack), David Hartman (Doc), Hagen Beggs (Reggie), Ida Lupino, Jack Weston, Don Knotts, Karen Jensen (Faith), Deanna Lund (Hope), Melodie Johnson (Charity). Directed and written by Leslie Stevens.

Jack, Doc, and Reggie, now private investigators of the mid-twentieth century, have their headquarters in a 727 jet. They are hired by a government official (Terry-Thomas, seen only on the plane's telescreen) to locate a missing billionaire. They head for the man's island castle, where his three daugh-

Doc (David Hartman), Reggie (Hagen Beggs), and Jack Packard (Les Crane) are confronted by an aggressive Ida Lupino in the television feature *I Love a Mystery*. [*Universal*]

ters are frightened by a phantom baby's cry, and his domineering wife, Randolph [sic] (Lupino), conducts human survival experiments in her private gladitorial arena, complete with hungry lions.

IAMS, JACK (1910–). American mystery novelist. Born Samuel H. Iams (rhymes with "crimes"), he is descended from Celtic stock and spent most of his formative years in Waynesburg, Pa. He first tried his hand at writing comic novels, three of which were published with fair success. In 1942 he joined the Office of War Information (OWI) and spent an uncomfortable but otherwise happy year in Brazzaville, French Equatorial Africa (now Congo-Brazzaville), with the Free French Forces. This experience was later used as background for his first mystery novel, *The Body Missed the Boat* (1947), which details the murder, under rather peculiar circumstances, of an American consul in Brazzaville. Iams was subsequently assigned by the OWI to Lisbon, as press attaché, and to Brussels.

In November 1945, shortly after the end of World War II, Iams returned to the United States and settled in Bay Head, N.J. At the suggestion of his original publisher, he produced a series of seven mystery novels, in a humorous vein, between 1947 and 1952. One of the best and most popular of this group was *Death Draws the Line* (1949), set in a cartoon strip factory.

ILES, FRANCIS. *See* BERKELEY, ANTHONY.

INNES, MICHAEL (pseudonym of John Innes Mackintosh Stewart; 1906–). British novelist, scholar, and author of mystery fiction. Born near Edinburgh, Stewart is the son of a Scottish professor. He attended Edinburgh Academy and Oriel College, Oxford, where he won the Matthew Arnold Memorial Prize in 1929 and honors in English. From 1930 to 1934 he taught at the University of Leeds, where he met his wife, who was then a young medical student. Mrs. Stewart later became a physician and the mother of their five children. For the next decade Stewart was professor of English at Adelaide University in South Australia. Returning to England in 1946, he taught at Queen's University in Belfast until 1948 and since 1949 has been a member of the faculty of Christ Church, Oxford.

Under his own name he has achieved a considerable reputation as a novelist and scholar. He has written a dozen works of nonmystery fiction, including a collection of short stories appropriately titled *The Man Who Wrote Detective Stories* (1959). His *Eight Modern Writers* (1963) was the final volume in the *Oxford History of English Literature.* He has also published biographies of Rudyard Kipling (1966) and Joseph Conrad (1968).

The first Michael Innes mystery was written in 1934 during the author's long sea voyage to Australia. Subsequent books have been written between semesters or, during the academic year, by two hours' daily writing before breakfast. In a 1964 essay for *Esquire,* "Death as a Game," Innes described his writing methods and also commented on the reading of detective stories, which he recognizes as addictive. He feels that he has escaped this compulsion—by writing such works himself. He regards characterization in depth, one of the hallmarks of serious fiction, as inimical to the mystery. His cardinal principle in writing detective stories has been to regard them solely as escape literature and never to allow real problems or feelings to intrude on his characters.

Death at the President's Lodging (1936) was Innes's first mystery and the first of twenty-nine books about his detective, John APPLEBY. When it was published in the United States, it was called *Seven Suspects* to avoid having readers think that the book dealt with their chief executive. The setting is "St. Anthony's," a fictional English college much like an Oxford college, and the subject is murder among the senior dons. This book established the characteristics of the Innes approach: erudition, including frequent literary allusions and quotations; complex, albeit unrealistic, plotting; and humor, often at the expense of one segment of society—in this case the academic community.

The author's reputation took hold with his second book, *Hamlet, Revenge!* (1937), and the *Times Literary Supplement,* which had touted him highly as a newcomer, said that he already was "in a class by himself among writers of detective fiction." He displayed his expertise regarding Shakespeare by using a performance of *Hamlet* as the setting for murder. A decade later he used *Othello* in a similar way in "Tragedy of a Handkerchief," which won second prize in *Ellery Queen's Mystery Magazine's* short story contest. Innes also received great praise for his third book, *Lament for a Maker* (1938), the story of the mysterious laird of Erchany Castle, which fully utilizes the author's imagination as well as his Scottish ancestry.

Few of the author's subsequent books have achieved the popularity of his early work, although he has continued to have a sizable audience. Critics, including so strong an original supporter as Howard HAYCRAFT, felt that the quotations no longer served a legitimate purpose in the story and frequently descended to the level of being "showoffish." Furthermore, they felt that what had once been a successful attempt to fuse satire with the mystery novel had deteriorated into strained attempts at humor.

IRISH, WILLIAM. *See* WOOLRICH, CORNELL.

IRWIN, WILL. *See* BURGESS, GELETT.

J

JACOBS, W[ILLIAM] W[YMARK] (1863–1943). English short story writer whose horror classic "The Monkey's Paw" is considered one of the most terrifying stories ever written. Born in Wapping, London, the son of a wharf overseer, he wrote scores of humorous stories about the seashore and seamen and several moderately successful plays.

Several of his short story collections contain elements of mystery and detection, notably *The Lady of the Barge* (1902), which contains three detective stories in addition to "The Monkey's Paw," and *Sea Whispers* (1926), which contains two classic murder tales, "His Brother's Keeper" and "The Interruption."

JAMES, P[HYLLIS] D. (1920–). English mystery writer. Born in Oxford, she was educated at Cambridge Girls' High School. Her brief marriage to a doctor produced two daughters but ended with his death, after a long illness, in 1944. To earn a living, she entered the field of hospital administration and worked for the Hospital Service from 1949 to 1968, when she became a senior civil servant in the Home Office, where she currently works in the criminal department. A fellow of the Institute of Hospital Administrators, Miss James lives in London; both her daughters are married, and she has four grandchildren.

Miss James began writing as a hobby and has published six detective novels since her debut in 1962 with *Cover Her Face*. Not unlike Ngaio MARSH, she presents plots, puzzles, characterizations, and backgrounds with great skill. Her major sleuth, Inspector (later Chief Superintendent) Adam Dalgliesh, is an attractive human being, intelligent and perceptive, as well as a poet. *Shroud for a Nightingale* (1971) is set in a nurses' training school and concerns a student nurse who is murdered while on the job. It received a scroll from the Mystery Writers of America as one of the five best mysteries of that year. A short story, "Moment of Power," won first prize in a Crime Writers' Association contest sponsored by *Ellery Queen's Mystery Magazine* in 1967; it was published in the July 1968 issue.

JARRETT, CORA (HARDY) (1877–19?). American author of novels and short stories. Born in Norfolk, Va., she received a B.A. degree from Bryn Mawr in 1899 and also studied at the Sorbonne and Oxford before teaching English and Greek. She married Edwin Jarrett, a civil engineer from New York City; they had two sons and a daughter.

Mrs. Jarrett is best remembered for two books included in SANDOE'S READERS' GUIDE TO CRIME (1946). *Night over Fitch's Pond* (1933), a "borderline" mystery with psychological overtones, was published under her own name. *Pattern in Black and Red* (1934) appeared under the pseudonym Faraday Keene, as did a short story, "The Little Dry Sticks" (1930), which critic Viola Brothers Shore rated among the ten best of all time.

JEFFRIES, GRAHAM MONTAGUE. *See* GRAEME, BRUCE.

JEFFRIES, RODERIC (1926–). English lawyer and author of mysteries. The son of mystery writer Bruce GRAEME, Jeffries, using the pseudonym Roderic Graeme, has continued the series about BLACKSHIRT, the gentleman-adventurer created by his father. A nonpracticing barrister, Jeffries has had considerable success with children's books (mysteries and stories about automobile racing) and with radio and television adaptations for the BBC. He lives with his wife and two children in a seventeenth-century farmhouse near Romney Marsh in Kent.

Jeffries's books reflect what Anthony BOUCHER has called his "unusually acute insight into the mechanics of law and detection and into the minds of lawyers, policemen, and criminals." Under his own name, and as Jeffrey Ashford, Graham Hastings, and Peter Alding, he has written courtroom mysteries that have been highly praised for their trial scenes, such as *Evidence of the Accused* (1961) and *A Traitor's Crime* (1968), as well as police procedurals, such as *Counsel for the Defense* (1961) and *The Investigations Are Proceeding* (1961; U.S. title: *The D.I.*), both under the Ashford pseudonym.

JEPSON, SELWYN (1899–). English writer, the only son of novelist Edgar Jepson. Educated at St. Paul's School, he served when very young in the British Army at the end of World War I and again throughout World War II, rising to the rank of major, in Military Intelligence and Special Operations Executive. He made his debut as a mystery novelist in 1922 with *The Qualified Adventurer.*

During the early stages of his career he wrote more than 150 short stories on varied themes for leading magazines in England and the United States. He also wrote screenplays for British film makers in the 1930s. Among his original scripts are *For the Love of You* (1932) and *The Riverside Murder* (1935); adaptations include *The Scarab Murder Case* (1936), based on S. S. VAN DINE's novel of 1930, and *Toilers of the Sea* (1936), based on Victor HUGO's novel of 1866, which he also codirected.

Jepson currently lives in Hampshire, where he writes novels and radio and television plays. His chief recreations are painting and furniture making.

In much of Jepson's work in the thriller category, justice is meted out, but not necessarily obviously, for it is often a poetic justice, arising out of the circumstances of a crime, or a secret justice, resulting from the efforts of a hero or heroine to bring it about against all the odds.

His novel *Keep Murder Quiet* (1940) is a minor masterpiece. In this modern variation on the Hamlet theme, a young man named Roger Spain finds that his father has been brutally murdered and vows vengeance on the killer. There seem to be no clues, but by persistent effort and luck he follows a thread of evidence that leads slowly but inexorably to his unknown nemesis. This novel, cited in SANDOE'S READERS' GUIDE TO CRIME, has been compared by various critics to Philip MACDONALD's *Warrant for X* (1938; English title: *The Nursemaid Who Disappeared*), which is similar in method if not in theme.

Jepson's most famous character is Eve Gill, the heroine of a half-dozen novels, including *The Golden Dart* (1949) and *The Hungry Spider* (1950). She was the heroine of an Alfred HITCHCOCK film, *Stage Fright* (1950), based on *Man Running* (1948; U.S. title: *Outrun the Constable*).

JESSE, F[RYNIWYD] TENNYSON (1889–1958). English novelist, dramatist, and criminologist. The daughter of Reverend Eustace Tennyson d'Eyncourt Jesse and grandniece of poet Alfred, Lord Tennyson, she first studied art but turned to journalism when she was twenty, working for *The Times* and the *Daily Mail,* as well as contributing book reviews to the *Times Literary Supplement* and the *English Review.* In 1914 she went to New York and worked briefly on *Metropolitan Magazine.* At the start of World War I she became an unaccredited war correspondent and later worked for the Ministry of Information and the National Relief Commission, then headed by Herbert Hoover. She was also a visitor for the Red Cross in small frontline hospitals in France.

In 1918 she married Harold Marsh Harwood, a dramatist. They enjoyed sailing and flying and lived all over the world, including the United States. At the outbreak of World War II they were living in St. John's Wood, London.

Miss Jesse wrote several nonfiction books and many novels, including *The Milky Way* (1913), *Beggars on Horseback* (1915), *Secret Bread* (1917), *The White Riband* (1921), *Tom Fool* (1926), *Moonraker* (1927), *The Lacquer Lady* (1929), *Act of God* (1936), and *The Alabaster Cup* (1950).

Avowing that her chief passion was murder, Miss Jesse edited a number of cases (Madeleine Smith, Timothy John Evans, and John Reginald Halliday Christie) for the *Notable British Trials* series. Her *Murder and Its Motives* (1924) is a pioneering work that surveys the subject in a long introduction and then continues with illustrative case studies.

Solange Fontaine, who has a "strange gift of sensing a moral flaw," is the heroine of F. Tennyson Jesse's *The Solange Stories*. This rather modern portrait is taken from the dust wrapper of the first American edition, published by Macmillan in 1931.

She also wrote two notable mystery books. *The Solange Stories* (1931; s.s.) contains an introduction in which Miss Jesse discusses and defines detective stories. Her detective, a young Frenchwoman, is named Solange Fontaine. She is, we are told, "gifted by nature with an extra-spiritual sense that [warns] her of evil." Ellery QUEEN (author) included the book in his QUEEN'S QUORUM.

A Pin to See the Peepshow (1934), partially based on the famous Thompson-Bywaters case of 1922, is a long and richly detailed account of the heroine's life that culminates in her husband's accidental murder and a long trial. Julian SYMONS once wrote, "In this sound, long, well-organized novel, Miss Jesse . . . excelled particularly in showing the romantic Julia Almond, whose life became in the end an enveloping web of fantasy. Miss Jesse transformed undoubted murder to dubious accident with a weakening of artistic effect, but through the change she looked forward to that questioning of the ultimate justice done by the law which is one feature of the modern crime novel." Miss Jesse and her husband dramatized this novel with limited success. It encountered censorship difficulties in England and could be presented only in private clubs. It was poorly received and had a brief New York run in 1953. It was televised in England and shown on educational television in the United States in 1975.

JOHNS, VERONICA PARKER (1907–). American businesswoman and author of short stories and mystery novels. Since 1964 Mrs. Johns has operated a New York City store, Sea Shells Unlimited. In pursuit of this combined hobby-business, she has traveled throughout Africa, England, and the Caribbean, and she has written *She Sells Sea Shells* (1968), an autobiographical work telling of her new career. She is a member of the New York Shell Club.

Mrs. Johns had written a number of short stories and five mystery novels before her business interests became paramount. Three of her stories, "Homecoming" (1952), "The Gentleman Caller" (1955), and "Mr. Hyde-de-Ho" (1956), won second prizes in contests held by *Ellery Queen's Mystery Magazine*. Her most popular novel, *Murder by the Day* (1953), introduced Webster Flagg, a black actor turned butler because there were few roles for members of his race, in the role of the detective.

JOHNSON, OWEN (McMAHON) (1878–1952). American novelist and short story writer. Born in New York, he graduated from Yale, the setting for his most famous novel, *Stover at Yale* (1911). He also wrote the very popular boys' books *The Tennessee Shad* (1911) and *The Varmint* (1910). His mystery novels are *Max Fargus* (1906) and *The Sixty-first Second* (1913). Probably his best mystery fiction is in *Murder in Any Degree* (1913), particularly the story "One Hundred in the Dark."

JONES, AVERAGE (Creator: Samuel Hopkins ADAMS). The handsome young advertising adviser modestly prefers the near-acronym "Average" to his full given name: Adrian Van Reypen Egerton. He is a member of and resident at the exclusive Cosmic Club, which is also inhabited by a variety of experts in widely diverse professions. Jones maintains a remarkable sense of humor throughout a series of unusual adventures, which often have medical backgrounds. The cases were collected in *Average Jones* (1911). Jones meets a premature retirement, owing to Adams's inability to invent further plots.

JUNKIN, HARRY W. *See* SAINT, THE.

K

KANE, BOB. *See* BATMAN.

KANE, HENRY (1918–). American author. Born in New York City, he was a lawyer for a number of years before he turned to writing. His first detective novel, *A Halo for Nobody,* was published in 1947, and he has since written many novels, short stories, television plays, and nonmystery novels, such as *The Virility Factor* (1972).

Kane's stories usually feature private eye (Richard) Peter Chambers, who is young and good-looking and has an eye for the ladies. His profession is financially rewarding, and he is able to indulge his tastes for good food, drink, and jazz. His earlier cases represented serious and straightforward attempts by Kane to invade the Dashiell HAMMETT–Raymond CHANDLER field; they were sufficiently relaxed, however, for humor to enter the proceedings. Chambers narrates his own cases and frequently talks too much as he gets involved in word games. One wonders whether he will win the girl before he captures the criminal, or vice versa.

Kane's work is not all frivolous, and he has written excellent short stories and novelettes, as well as strict detective puzzles such as *Too French and Too Deadly* (1955; British title: *The Narrowing Lust*), featuring an intricate locked-room problem, and *Unholy Trio* (1967), which involves Chambers with a group of fascists and murder.

He has written many non-Chambers works, including a series of three novels (*The Midnight Man,* 1965; *Conceal and Disguise,* 1966; and *Laughter in the Alehouse,* 1968), featuring former Inspector McGregor of the New York City Police Department, who has retired and become a private eye; he seems to be an older, wiser, and more conservative version of Peter Chambers.

Kane's current writing alternates between long, straightforward novels aimed at the best-seller lists and a series of "X-rated" Chambers novels that contain long, explicit, and periodically spaced passages on sex.

KANTOR, MacKINLAY (1904–). American journalist, novelist, and short story writer. Born in Webster City, Iowa, he began selling hard-boiled detective stories to the PULP MAGAZINES at an early age. His fiction covers a wide range of subjects, but his best work is associated with the Civil War, notably *Andersonville* (1955), which won the Pulitzer Prize. *Signal Thirty-two* (1950), one of the best police procedural novels ever written, is set in New York City's 23d Precinct, which includes penthouses for the rich and reeking slums for the poor. It centers on three policemen and follows the development of a rookie. In 1948 Kantor had received permission from the acting commissioner of police (Thomas Mulligan) to accompany the police on all their activities to gather background information, which is evident in the realistic style and language of the novel.

Midnight Lace (1948) is a suspenseful tale of a young woman terrorized by an anonymous telephone caller. It was filmed in 1960 with Doris Day and Rex Harrison. Four of the forty stories in *Author's Choice* (1944) are crime and detection tales. *It's about Crime* (1960) contains eleven stories of crime and the underworld. Both volumes contain "Rogue's Gallery," which originally appeared in *Collier's* in 1935. Kantor believes that this is his most frequently reprinted short story; it has been translated into several languages and collected in many anthologies.

KEATING, H[ENRY] R[EYMOND] F[ITZWALTER] (1926–). English novelist. Born in Sussex, he attended the Merchant Taylors' School before joining, in 1942, the BBC's Engineering Department as a youth-in-training. He was drafted into the Army in 1945 and served until 1948, when he entered Trinity College in Dublin. He became a journalist, working successively on the *Wiltshire Herald, Swindon Evening Advertiser, London Daily Telegraph,* and *The Times* (London). He married actress Sheila Mitchell in 1953; they have four children. Keating left *The*

H. R. F. Keating. [*Fay Godwin*]

Times in 1960 and devoted himself to writing mysteries and occasional nonmystery novels, supplementing his income by working as a free-lance journalist. He has reviewed mysteries for *The Times* since 1967.

Keating's early mysteries, *Death and the Visiting Firemen* (1959), *Zen There Was Murder* (1960), and *A Rush on the Ultimate* (1961), though praised, were considered too surrealistic by some reviewers. He achieved success with *The Perfect Murder* (1964), the first novel about Inspector Ganesh GHOTE of the Bombay CID, which won the Crime Writers' Association best mystery novel award and a special award from the Mystery Writers of America. In 1970 he won the short story competition for British crime writers organized by *Ellery Queen's Mystery Magazine* with "The Shell-Collector."

KEELER, HARRY STEPHEN (1890–1967). American author of zany, complicated intrigue-farces, most of which were published as mystery novels, although in fact they are almost a genre in themselves. Keeler was born in Chicago, growing up there in a rooming house for theater people that his widowed mother managed. He worked his way through high school, obtained an electrical engineering degree from Armour Institute of Technology (later Illinois Institute of Technology) in 1912, and spent much of his time during the next two years working in South Chicago as an electrician in a steel mill and writing a few short stories on the side. Between 1914 and 1924 he wrote and sold dozens of long novelettes and magazine serials. In 1919 he became editor of *10-Story Book* magazine, a position he held until 1940. Also that year he married Hazel Goodwin, a writer, who later "collaborated" (in a unique way) with her husband on his novels. His first book, *The Voice of the Seven Sparrows*, was published in 1924 and was followed by more than fifty books, each wilder and more outlandish than the one before. His novels became so idiosyncratic that most of his readers gave up on him, and by 1948 he had lost his American and English publishers; after the publication of his last English-language novel, *Stand By—London Calling* (1953), he wrote directly for translation into Spanish and Portuguese. His wife died in 1960; three years later Keeler married Thelma Rinaldo, who had been his secretary in the 1920s. At his death more than a dozen novels were awaiting publication in Spain.

Keeler was the inventor of the "webwork novel," lengthy and full of bizarre elements so interrelated that eventually every absurd complication makes perfect sense—within the author's zany frame of reference. The raw material for his novels reposed in a huge filing cabinet filled with thousands of old newspaper clippings. When Keeler was ready to begin a new book, he picked out a handful of clippings at random, interweaving them into the plot, no matter how disconnected they might be. His favorite devices for tying plot elements together were lunatic laws, bizarre religious tenets, wacky wills, crackpot contracts, and—most common of all—coincidences piled one on top of another.

The novels Keeler published between 1924 and the mid-1930s were set in Chicago, and most were expanded from his magazine fiction. *Sing Sing Nights* (1927) deals with three authors who are about to be electrocuted. The Governor offers a blank pardon to one of them, and the writers agree to a game of "Arabian Nights": each will tell an impromptu story to the uneducated death house guard; the teller of the tale the guard judges to be the best will be pardoned. Most of the book consists of the three stories told to the guard—actually three unrelated Keeler novelettes written years before—intercut with discussions about the nature of the storytelling.

By the mid-1930s Keeler had exhausted his backlog of magazine stories, and his books became even more bizarre. He wrote a 1,500-page novel that was published in three volumes during an eighteen-month period. Another book, 135,000 words long, has a first-person narrator who blithely assumes dozens of identities in his search for an escaped lunatic millionaire—who turns out to be the narrator himself. Later novels frequently included individual stories written by Hazel Goodwin Keeler and spliced into the text, the way, in earlier days, Keeler had included his own short stories in his novels and attributed them to characters in the books.

KEENE, CAROLYN (pseudonym of Edward L. Stratemeyer, 1862–1930, and, later, his daughter Harriet S. Adams). American author of books for boys and girls; creator of Nancy DREW.

Edward L. Stratemeyer.

Harriet S. Adams.

Stratemeyer was born in Elizabeth, N.J. At an early age he wrote DIME NOVELS under various pseudonyms and edited several Horatio Alger novels after that author's death. He later created most of the popular American series of children's books, writing more than 400 during his lifetime. In 1906 he founded the Stratemeyer Syndicate, which has published a prodigious number of long and short stories for boys and girls—to date, about 1,200 books. Stratemeyer supplied the plot outlines and edited the tales himself—about 700 before his death. His two daughters continued to run the syndicate until 1942, when one of them became an inactive partner; Mrs. Harriet S. Adams is now head of the organization.

The most successful series produced by Stratemeyer and the Syndicate involve such characters as Tom Swift, the Rover Boys, the Bobbsey Twins, the Hardy Boys (see HARDY BOYS, THE), Ted Scott, Bomba the Jungle Boy, the Pioneer Boys, Dave Porter, the Dana Girls, Kay Tracy, and Nancy Drew (Stratemeyer wrote three of the novels about the teen-age girl detective; Harriet S. Adams wrote the rest).

It is impossible to estimate the total number of volumes sold by Stratemeyer (under forty-six pseudonyms) and the Syndicate, but sales since 1930 are reported to have exceeded 100 million.

KEENE, FARADAY. *See* JARRETT, CORA.

KELLEY, MARTHA (PATSY) MOTT. *See* QUENTIN, PATRICK.

KELLOW, KATHLEEN. *See* HOLT, VICTORIA.

KEMELMAN, HARRY (1908–). American author of detective short stories and novels. Born in Boston, Kemelman graduated from Boston University in 1930; he also received an M.A. degree from Harvard Graduate School. During the Depression he owned a hardware store and was a teacher. In 1942 he entered government service, becoming wage administrator for the Boston Port of Embarkation. He was a wage analysis consultant after the war and began writing fiction while waiting for clients. He is presently assistant professor of English at the State College of Boston. He and his wife, Anne, live in Marblehead, a Boston suburb, and have three children.

Kemelman's first short story, "The Nine-Mile Walk," was selected as one of the best first stories in *Ellery Queen's Mystery Magazine*'s 1947 contest. In it, a crime is reconstructed solely from a chance remark. It is truly an example of armchair detection, for the detective who overhears the comment never visits the scene of the crime. The detective is Nicky Welt, an arrogant (but always right) English professor who lectures his friend, the district attorney of "Suffolk County," Mass., while solving his cases. There have been eight Nicky Welt stories, collected in *The Nine-Mile Walk* (1967).

It is doubtful whether the Welt stories would have been collected had not Kemelman, in 1964, become one of the few mystery writers to win best-seller status, with his first book about Rabbi David SMALL, *Friday the Rabbi Slept Late.* It received five printings; its sequel, *Saturday the Rabbi Went Hungry* (1966), ten. Both were alternate selections of the Book-of-the-Month Club. Kemelman, describing the suburban New England scene he knows so well, discovered a hitherto unsuspected reader interest in synagogue politics and in the idea of a rabbi as a detective.

Jewish lore is an important part of the series about Rabbi Small, especially in *Saturday,* in which murder occurs on Yom Kippur, the Jewish Day of Atonement. Passover is the setting for *Sunday the Rabbi Stayed Home* (1969); in *Monday the Rabbi Took Off* (1972) Small visits Israel.

Harry Kemelman. [*William Charles Studios*]

Kemelman won the Mystery Writers of America Edgar for best first novel with *Friday*. In reviewing it, Anthony BOUCHER said, "If a series is in prospect, this could be the most important debut of a detective in recent years." As the series has developed, subsequent reviews have stressed that, although the portrayals of suburban Jews and Judaism have continued to be excellent, the mystery elements have moved into the background.

KENDRAKE, CARLETON. *See* GARDNER, ERLE STANLEY.

KENDRICK, BAYNARD H[ARDWICK] (1894–). American mystery writer. Born in Philadelphia, he was educated at the Tome School, Port Deposit, Md., and the Episcopal Academy in Philadelphia. He married Edythe Stevens in 1919. Following her death, he married Jean Morris in 1971. He has traveled in Europe and the Middle East and has lived in almost every part of the United States. A lawyer and certified public accountant, he has been a secretary for a door company in Florida (1921–1927), president of the Trades Publishing Company in Philadelphia (1927–1928), and general manager of a New York City hotel chain (1930–1931). In 1932 he switched to free-lance writing. His first mystery novel, *Blood on Lake Louisa*, was published in 1934, and he continued to produce this type of work through the mid-1960s.

In World War I Kendrick was the first American to enlist in the Canadian Army—exactly one hour after that country declared war—and served in the Canadian Expeditionary Forces. During World War II he was a consultant to the staff of the Old Farms Convalescent Hospital for Blinded Veterans (for a dollar a year). Long interested in the problems of the blind, Kendrick is an acknowledged expert on the subject. He once served as the only sighted adviser to the Blinded Veterans Association; he was its organizer and chairman of its board of directors and holds honorary life membership card number one. He received a plaque for this work from General Omar Bradley in July 1946.

Kendrick's experiences provided him with the source material for a nonmystery novel, *Lights Out* (1945; filmed as *Bright Victory* in 1951), and for his series about blind detective Captain Duncan MACLAIN.

One of the founding fathers of the Mystery Writers of America, Kendrick carries membership card number one. He served as the organization's first president and was given the special award of Grand Master in 1967.

Kendrick lives in Florida and, in recent years, has devoted much time to working with Cuban refugees, an activity that provided background material for his last mystery, *Flight from a Firing Wall* (1966), selected by *The Reader's Digest* as one of its condensed books. His historical novel *Flames of Time* was a Literary Guild selection in 1948.

Florida also provides the setting for one of Kendrick's earliest novels, *The Iron Spiders* (1936), which features his first series detective, deputy sheriff Miles Standish Rice, noted for his height (he is 6 feet tall, 3 inches shorter than his creator) and his insatiable hunger. He tries to capture a multiple murderer who leaves spiders at the scene of his bizarre crimes, but his investigation is hampered by voodoo and a tropical storm in the Florida Keys.

Kendrick, one of the outstanding American mystery writers when he was at the height of his powers in the late 1930s and 1940s, could write, plot, and create puzzles and characters with the best of his contemporaries. Many of his earlier novels were reprinted in paper covers, but few of the post-1945 novels were ever made available in this format. Nearly all the Maclain tales have appeared serially in the *Chicago Tribune–New York Daily News* syndicate, as well as in *Redbook* and *The American Magazine*.

KENNEDY, CRAIG (Creator: Arthur B. REEVE). One of the earliest and most popular SCIENTIFIC DETECTIVES. At the height of his fame, Kennedy was known as the "American Sherlock HOLMES." Scientific "miracles" are commonplace in his cases; for example, such technical marvels as lie detectors, gyroscopes, and a portable seismograph that can differentiate between the footsteps of different individuals were all accurately predicted. Like Holmes, Kennedy is a chemist who uses his knowledge to solve cases. He is also one of the first detectives to use psychoanalytic techniques. He is a professor at Columbia University but also earns fees for his work as a consulting detective. A man of action as well as thought, he is a master of disguise and often uses a gun when circumstances require it. Inspector Barney O'Connor of the New York Police Department frequently asks for unofficial help from Kennedy. Walter Jameson, Kennedy's roommate, is a newspaper reporter who chronicles his adventures and also tries to solve cases on his own, with a predictable lack of success.

CHECKLIST

1912 *The Silent Bullet* (s.s.; British title: *The Black Hand*)
1913 *The Poisoned Pen* (s.s.)
1914 *The Dream Doctor* (s.s.)
1915 *The War Terror* (s.s.; British title: *Craig Kennedy, Detective*)
1915 *Gold of the Gods*
1915 *The Exploits of Elaine*
1916 *The Social Gangster* (s.s.; British title: *The Diamond Queen*)
1916 *The Ear in the Wall*

This illustration appeared on the front cover of *The Black Hand,* the English title of the first Craig Kennedy book. It was published in 1912 by Eveleigh Nash.

1916 *The Romance of Elaine*
1916 *The Triumph of Elaine*
1917 *The Treasure Train* (s.s.)
1917 *The Adventuress*
1918 *The Panama Plot* (s.s.)
1919 *The Soul Scar*
1921 *The Film Mystery*
1923 *Craig Kennedy Listens In* (s.s.)
1924 *Atavar*
1925 *The Fourteen Points* (s.s.)
1925 *The Boy Scouts' Craig Kennedy* (s.s.)
1925 *Craig Kennedy on the Farm* (s.s.)
1926 *The Radio Detective*
1926 *Pandora*
1932 *The Kidnap Club*
1934 *The Clutching Hand*
1935 *Enter Craig Kennedy* (four connected novelettes written by Ashley Locke from unsold short stories by Reeve)
1936 *The Stars Scream Murder*

Films

Kennedy made his first film appearance in a 1915 Pathé serial, *The Exploits of Elaine.* Although Elaine—popular Pearl White—is the nominal central character, it is her friend Kennedy (Arnold Daly) who does battle against the mysterious Clutching Hand. Clutching Hand, seeking Elaine's inheritance, is extraordinarily scientific himself, wielding death rays and creating poison-kiss epidemics; in one episode, Kennedy brings a dead girl back to life with "Dr. Leduc's method of electric resuscitation," a machine he wheels out of a corner of his well-equipped laboratory. There were two sequels featuring both Elaine and Kennedy: *The New Exploits of Elaine* (1915) and *The Romance of Elaine* (1916).

Kennedy uses the wireless and x-rays and is shot with phosgene bullets and trapped in a vacuum room in a fifteen-chapter serial of 1919, *The Carter Case* (subtitled *The Craig Kennedy Serial*). Herbert Rawlinson played the detective. In 1926, Kennedy (Jack Mower) was a subordinate character in the ten-chapter serial *The Radio Detective,* coming to the aid of the hero (Jack Daugherty), an inventor and devoted Boy Scout leader whose radio wave discovery is a gangsters' target. Overshadowed by both another inventor and a scout troop. Kennedy retired for ten years, emerging only when challenged by an old villain.

The Clutching Hand. Stage and Screen, 1936 (fifteen-chapter serial). Jack Mulhall, Marion Shilling, Yakima Canutt, Ruth Mix, Mae Busch, Robert

This surrealistic dust wrapper appeared on the next-to-last Craig Kennedy book; it was published in 1935 by Macauley.

Frazier. Directed by Albert Herman.

The director of a large industrial corporation announces the discovery of synthetic gold and is kidnapped by the unknown Hand. The hooded villain contacts his many (numbered) agents by way of television as he sits before multileveled monitors; the electronic and video tape gimmickery rampant throughout the serial and upon which the solution depends is really extraordinarily sophisticated for its day.

Television

In the early days of television (1952) Donald Woods starred in *Craig Kennedy, Criminologist,* a series of twenty-six half-hour programs.

KENNEDY, MILWARD (pseudonym of Milward Rodon Kennedy Burge; 1894–1968). English civil servant, journalist, mystery writer, and reviewer. Educated at Winchester and New College, Oxford, he served during World War I in the Military Intelligence Directorate of the War Office and was awarded the Croix de Guerre. He worked for the Ministry of Finance in Cairo (1919–1920) and then the International Labour Office in Geneva (1920–1924), becoming director of that organization's London office (1924–1945). He also served as director of the United Kingdom's Information Office in Ottawa in 1943 and 1944. At the end of World War II he became London editor of the *Empire Digest* (1945–1949) and was active for many years as a mystery fiction reviewer for *The Sunday Times* (London). He retired in the 1960s to west Sussex. He had been married twice (in 1921 and 1926) and had one son.

Kennedy wrote twenty mystery novels between 1929 and 1952. Most were of the police routine variety, but several recounted the adventures of titled aristocrat Sir George Bull, a professional private investigator (*Bull's Eye,* 1933, and *Corpse in Cold Storage,* 1934). Kennedy drew on his wartime experiences in Canada for a spy story, *Escape to Quebec* (1946).

Death to the Rescue (1931), dedicated to his friend and fellow mystery writer Anthony BERKELEY, is atypical of Kennedy's work. It concerns the leading citizen of a small town who believes that his unpleasant neighbor is actually a long-vanished silent film star. Further probing uncovers a suspicious railway accident and a murder that had both occurred just before the actor vanished. The citizen, who tells of these events in his diary, decides to investigate further; the results are completely unexpected.

In *The Murderer of Sleep* (1932) there is a house party in a small Welsh village called Sleep; there is also a serial murderer who is not above disposing of a man of the cloth.

KENNY, CHARLES J. *See* GARDNER, ERLE STANLEY.

KERSH, GERALD (1911–1968). English novelist and short story writer. Born in Teddington-on-Thames, Kersh once described himself as having been "a morose and tearful child" who wrote his first story when he was eight, publishing it in a "limited edition of one copy." He worked as a baker, a nightclub bouncer, a salesman, and a professional wrestler before gaining fame as a writer. Kersh served with the Coldstream Guards in World War II until an injury forced him to leave the service and become a war correspondent. Although he became a successful writer, he left England after the war to escape what he considered confiscatory taxation on his earnings. He settled in the United States, first in New York City and then in Cragsmoor, N.Y.

His most famous novel, *Night and the City,* a story of London's underworld, was published in England in 1938 but did not appear in the United States until 1946. He wrote hundreds of short stories including, in the mystery field, a series about Karmesin, a rogue who narrates his own adventures and who was called by Ellery QUEEN (author) "either the greatest criminal or the greatest liar of all time." Typical of these clever stories of uncertain endings is "Karmesin and the Crown Jewels" (1954), in which Karmesin may have stolen the jewels from the Tower of London.

KING, C[HARLES] DALY (1895–1963). American psychologist and detective story writer. King's slim output of seven books in nine years nearly established him as a master. He was born in New York City and educated at Newark Academy and Yale University, where he graduated as a Phi Beta Kappa. He served as a second lieutenant in the field artillery during World War I and received a commission as a captain in the Reserve, which he resigned in 1926. He then became a partner in a cotton and woolen business for five years and treasurer in an advertising agency for two years.

King decided to resume studying and received his master's degree in psychology from Columbia University in 1928 and his Ph.D. degree from Yale for an electromagnetic study of sleep. He practiced psychology and wrote *Beyond Behaviorism* (1923) *Integrative Psychology* (1931; in collaboration), *The Psychology of Consciousness* (1932), and the posthumous *States of Human Consciousness* (1963).

In the 1930s King divided his time between Summit, N.J., and Somerset, Bermuda, where he wrote his detective novels. With the advent of World War II he ceased writing fiction, but he continued his work in psychology until his death.

As a mystery writer, King is an enigmatic figure. At times he is brilliant, writing with the verve and assurance of a master. At other times he is as frustrating as the old club bore who tells the same stories over and over again. King is undoubtedly the only mystery writer to have inserted a fifteen-page treatise on economic theory into a detective novel—for absolutely no reason.

King was not adept in conveying—or sustaining—atmosphere. His powers of characterization were weak, and he reveals little about his series detective, Michael Lord (who appears in all the King novels), except that he is reasonably young and is a special officer attached to the staff of the police commissioner of New York City, where he rises to the rank of inspector. Lord's intelligent "Watson" (see WATSON, DR.), Dr. L. (for Love) Rees Pons, is a plump integrative psychologist. King's major strength, however, lies in his plots. At his best, he can concoct puzzles that are as baffling and bizarre as those of Ellery QUEEN (author) and John Dickson CARR, and as devious as those of Agatha CHRISTIE.

Obelists at Sea (1932) is concerned with a shipboard murder that is investigated by four psychologists in the light of their varying persuasions. All are proved wrong. The pace is leaden, the characters cardboard, and the satire mild. An obelist is defined in this novel as a person of little or no importance; but King changed his mind about this definition in *Obelists en Route* (1934), in which he said that the word refers to one who views with suspicion. This work, less cluttered than its predecessor, deals with murder on a moving train.

King's high point is *Obelists Fly High* (1935), in which a famous surgeon, racing by airplane to save the life of his influential brother, is threatened with murder. This novel contains an epilogue in the beginning and a prologue at the end that clear up the mystery.

King's only collection of short stories, *The Curious Mr. Tarrant* (1935), was included in QUEEN'S QUORUM, in which the book was referred to as containing "the most imaginative detective short stories of our time." This collection (like several of King's novels) was published only in England and is one of the rarest volumes of twentieth-century detective fiction.

Careless Corpse (1937), subtitled *A Thantophony*, concerns a murder that occurs during a musical performance being held in a remote castle. *Arrogant Alibi* (1938) has two murders and nine suspects, all with perfect alibis. The scene is the 1937 flood in Hartford, Conn. A final and romantic effort, *Bermuda Burial* (1940), is little more than a travelogue of King's beloved Bermuda.

KING, RUFUS (1893–1966). American detective story writer. Born in New York City, King divided his time mainly between that city and an upstate farm near the Canadian border. He also lived in Florida. He was educated in a private school (Dodsworth) and at Yale, but he was working in a Paterson, N.J., silk mill when he joined the Army in 1916, becoming a cavalryman on patrol duty along the Mexican border. When the United States entered World War I, he became a first lieutenant in the 105th Field Artillery and saw action in the Meuse-Argonne offensive in France, where he was awarded the Conspicuous Service Cross. After the war he went to sea as a wireless operator and spent some time beachcombing along the Buenos Aires waterfront; he once claimed that he learned there how to live on 6 cents a day. He returned to the United States and began to write. During the 1920s he created, for magazine publication, dandyish Reginald De Puyster, said to be the wealthiest detective of all time—he inherited more than $20 million from his father. In *Murder by the Clock* (1929) King introduced his most famous character, Lieutenant VALCOUR, who was featured in eleven novels. The series was originally very popular with readers, although critical reception was more subdued.

When King abandoned Valcour, he turned to a tough New York City private detective, Cotton Moon, who appears in only one book, *Holiday Homicide* (1940). Thereafter, King's novels received less public and critical acceptance, and he returned to the short story. In 1941 he published *Diagnosis: Murder*, a collection of short stories about a medical detective, Dr. Colin Starr. Ellery QUEEN (author) was highly favorable toward these tales of a fictional small-town (Laurel Falls, Ohio) doctor who suspects that many "natural" deaths are actually murder—and proves that he is right.

At sixty-one, King began publishing, in *Ellery Queen's Mystery Magazine*, a series of twenty short stories, all of which are set in the "Gold Coast" of Florida, between Miami and Fort Lauderdale. The detective in most of the stories is Stuff Driscoll, a young criminologist in the local sheriff's office; they were collected in three volumes, *Malice in Wonderland* (1958), *The Steps to Murder* (1960), and *The Faces of Danger* (1964). Although critics generally thought that these stories were clever, they noted the almost complete lack of action in some of them.

Films and Plays

In addition to the Valcour film mysteries, King's *Museum Piece No. 13* (1946) was brought to the screen by Fritz LANG in 1948 as *Secret Beyond the Door*. For a very successful Broadway run, King coauthored (with theatrical producer Earl Carroll) "a musical mystery play," *Murder at the Vanities*, in 1933, featuring Bela Lugosi as a misdirecting menace. A year later, without Lugosi, the stage play became a film. Also in 1934, *Invitation to Murder* appeared on Broadway, starring Humphrey Bogart, Gale Sondergaard, and Walter Abel; it ran for fifty-four performances.

Murder at the Vanities. Paramount, 1934. Jack Oakie, Victor McLaglen, Kitty Carlisle, Carl Brisson,

Gertrude Michael. Directed by Mitchell Leisen.

On opening night of a musical two murders occur backstage; the leading man and the wardrobe mistress—secretly his mother—are suspected.

Among other films based on King works is *The Hidden Hand* (Warner Brothers, 1942), an old-dark-house mystery in which an eccentric elderly lady sheltering her brother (who has escaped from an asylum) fears that her nephews are trying to kill her.

In the 1930s King enjoyed modest success with such Broadway stage melodramas as *I Want a Policeman*.

KITCHIN, C[LIFFORD] H[ENRY] B[ENN] (1895–1967). English author, lawyer, and detective novelist. Born at Harrogate, he was educated at Clifton and at Exeter College, Oxford. He served in France (1916–1918) during World War I. Called to the bar (Lincoln's Inn) in 1924, he practiced law and wrote many nonmystery novels, including *Streamers Waving* (1925), *The Sensitive One* (1931), *Olive E.* (1937), *Birthday Party* (1938), *The Auction Sale* (1949), *The Secret River* (1956), *Ten Pollitt Place* (1957), and *The Book of Life* (1960). His best book is a mystery, *Death of My Aunt* (1929), about Malcolm Warren, a young stockbroker who appears in four of Kitchin's crime novels. He is summoned to the country by his rich aunt to advise her about her investments. She dies under mysterious circumstances, and Warren (who is first-person narrator) is suspected and must clear himself by finding the guilty party. His concern with his own aesthetic sensibilities tends to divert the reader's interest from the crime problem.

KNOTT, FREDERICK M. P. (1918–   ). English-American playwright. Born in China of English parents while his father was teaching at a Chinese university near Hankow. Knott went to school in China until he was ten and was then educated in England, graduating from Cambridge University with a degree in law. After more than six years in the British Army (1939–1946) he was retired as a major. In 1947 he joined the Rank Organisation as a trainee screenwriter and became a member of the Associate Branch of the (British) Screenwriters, of which he was elected chairman for 1950.

During the year, while free-lancing, he wrote his first stage play, *Dial M for Murder*. The history of the play is complicated. Six London producers turned it down in 1951, and Knott returned to screenwriting. Then, early in 1952, the BBC offered to put it on its Sunday night television series, and Knott converted it into a 90-minute TV play. The adaptation took two days. It was produced live on March 23, 1952, and although it received unanimous rave reviews, there was still no interest shown by London stage producers; Knott finally sold the film rights to a London film company headed by Sir Alexander Korda. A few days after the deal had been concluded, James P. Sherwood, a stage producer who had a lease on the Westminster Theatre, had to cancel the production of one play and decided to produce *Dial M for Murder* in its place. After only two and a half weeks' rehearsal, it opened on June 19, 1952, to critical acclaim.

Grace Kelly, in horror, contemplates the assailant she has just killed in Alfred Hitchcock's screen version of the Knott stage success *Dial M for Murder*. [*Warner Brothers*]

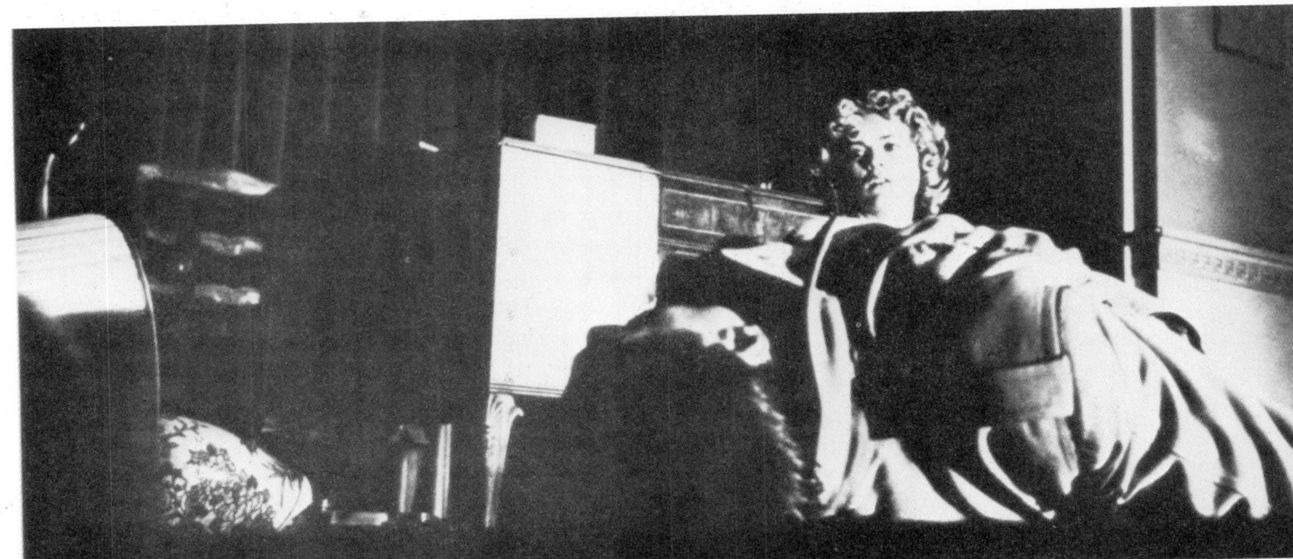

Maurice Evans read the script while the play was in rehearsal and offered to star in it on Broadway. In the film contract with Korda, however, a clause prohibited the play from being staged anywhere in the world for a full year after the release of the film. Plans were already underway to make the film, with Knott writing the screenplay. Finally, Sherwood and Evans managed to negotiate an agreement lifting this restriction, and *Dial M for Murder* began its run of 552 performances on Broadway in October 1952 at the Plymouth Theater.

During the following five years, the play was produced in over thirty countries and was translated into twenty-five languages.

Shortly after the Broadway opening, Korda sold the film rights to Warner Brothers, who made it in 3-D, with Alfred HITCHCOCK producing and directing, and Knott writing the screenplay under Hitchcock's supervision. It was never shown in 3-D to the public because, by the time it opened (1954), 3-D had been abandoned.

Knott emigrated to the United States in 1954.

His next Broadway play, *Write Me a Murder,* opened at the Belasco Theater in October 1961 and ran for 196 performances. Knott won a special Edgar Allan Poe award from the Mystery Writers of America (*see* ORGANIZATIONS) for his play, just as he had for *Dial M for Murder.*

In February 1966, Knott's terrifying drama, *Wait until Dark,* opened at the Barrymore Theater. It became extremely popular, running for eleven months on Broadway and two years in London. Its Broadway star, Lee Remick, was nominated for a Tony award as best actress. The film rights had been bought by Warner Brothers prior to its Broadway debut for a then-record sum for a preproduction deal for a play. The film was highly successful, opening in November 1967. An Academy award nomination for best actress went to Audrey Hepburn for her performance as the blind girl who is threatened in her apartment by a trio of criminals (Alan Arkin, Richard Crenna, and Jack Weston) because she is the unknowing custodian of a doll filled with heroin. Mel Ferrer produced and Terence Young directed the film.

Frederick Knott married Ann Francis Hillary in 1953; they have a son, Anthony, born in 1959.

KNOX, MONSIGNOR RONALD A[RBUTHNOTT] (1888–1957). English detective story writer and influential Catholic apologist. The son and grandson of Anglican bishops, he began his literary career, writing Latin and Greek epigrams, at the age of ten. Educated at Eton and Balliol College, Oxford, where he was an outstanding student, he was president of the Union and the recipient of several scholarships and a first in Greats. He was a fellow and lecturer at Trinity College, Oxford, for two years and then took holy orders and served as Anglican chaplain of the college for five years.

In 1917, he was converted to Roman Catholicism and ordained a priest two years later, becoming Catholic chaplain at Oxford in 1925 and domestic prelate to the Pope in 1936. In the summer of 1939 he retired from his duties at Oxford and moved to Shropshire to prepare a new translation of the Vulgate. His version of the New Testament was published in 1944, the Old Testament in 1949 and 1950. During World War II Father Knox headed a committee that provided Catholic books for servicemen. In 1946 he moved to Mells, Somerset (where he resided until his death). In 1950 he was elected a Fellow of the Royal Society of Literature.

Knox wrote many books, essays, and magazine articles, and a collection of his sermons was published. He was a member of the Detection Club, and his essay "Studies in the Literature of Sherlock Holmes" (*see* HOLMES, SHERLOCK), published in *Essays in Satire* (1930), was responsible for an upsurge in Holmesian scholarship.

His first mystery novel, *The Viaduct Murder* (1925), starts as a lighthearted, mildly satiric tale as a group of golfers discover a dead body, but it becomes more serious as the investigation proceeds. A man insured by a large policy from the Indescribable Insurance Company dies when the gas valves in his room are not operated properly. Was it accident, suicide, or murder? Miles Bredon investigates for the company in Knox's second novel, *The Three Taps* (1927). *The Footsteps at the Lock* (1928) concerns two cousins who take a canoe trip. Only one returns. He had the motive, the means, and the opportunity to make his cousin "disappear." He also has a perfect alibi. *Still Dead* (1934) is about a Scotsman who kills a child with his car while under the influence of alcohol but is acquitted of wrongdoing. Soon afterward he is found dead. *The Body in the Silo* (1933; U.S. title: *Settled out of Court*) starts with the cadaver of the title and ends with a second victim. *Double-Cross Purposes* (1937) concerns financial skulduggery as an interested group of people search for treasure on an island located in a Scottish river. This is the last novel from Knox, who stopped writing detective stories because of pressure from his church superiors.

In *The Best English Detective Stories of 1928* (1929), which Knox coedited with H. Harrington, he wrote an introduction and stated his "ten commandments" of fair-play detection that must be obeyed by all writers who aspire to the form. These rules, rather than his fiction, represent Knox's most important contribution to the form.

KORZENIOWSKI, JÓZEF TEODOR KONRAD. *See* CONRAD, JOSEPH.

KRUMGOLD, JOSEPH (1908–). American film producer and director and author. Born in Jersey City, N.J., and educated at New York University, Krumgold has had a long and varied career in Hollywood that began in 1928, when he worked as a press agent for MGM. He has served as assistant producer, producer, writer, and director and is noted for television documentaries and such critically acclaimed documentary films as *Mr. Trull Finds Out* (1940), *Sweeney Steps Out* (1942), *The Autobiography of a Jeep* (1943), and *Tomorrow We Fly* (1941), which was nominated for an Academy award.

He has also written several books about boys and their problems growing up in today's society, among them, *And Now Miguel* (1953), which was the basis of a 1966 film, and *Onion John* (1959). Both were awarded Newbery Medals for distinguished contributions to American literature for children.

Krumgold wrote one mystery novel, *Thanks to Murder* (1935), about a former Latin teacher who goes to New York to become a detective as the first step in a dubious scheme to be part of a more carefully ordered universe that is soon to come.

KRUSE, JOHN. *See* SAINT, THE.

KURNITZ, HARRY. *See* PAGE, MARCO.

KUTTNER, HENRY (1914–1958). American author of detective novels and science fiction. Born in Los Angeles, Kuttner studied English and psychology at the University of Southern California. He wrote science fiction under his own name and mysteries as Lewis Padgett (in collaboration with his wife, C[atherine] L. Moore). *The Brass Ring* (1946) and *The Day He Died* (1947) received critical approval. He used his own name, however, in his series about Michael Gray, a psychoanalyst-detective. Kuttner was commended for his handling of physical and psychological clues in the last book in this series, *Murder of a Wife* (1958), which was published shortly before his death.

KYD, THOMAS (pseudonym of Alfred B[ennett] Harbage; 1901–). American educator, Shakespearean scholar, and detective story writer. Born in Philadelphia, he was educated at the University of Pennsylvania, where he received a B.A. degree in 1924, an M.A. degree in 1926, and a Ph.D. degree in 1929. He became an instructor in English at that institution in 1924, was eventually promoted to professor, and left in 1947 to join the faculty of Columbia University as professor of English and comparative literature. In 1952 he went to Harvard, where he remained until 1970.

Harbage has lectured extensively throughout the United States and Canada and is the author of many volumes on Elizabethan drama and Shakespeare. He married Eliza Finnesey in 1926; they have four children.

Harbage has written four mystery novels. *Blood Is a Beggar* (1946) starts with the murder of a college professor in a classroom darkened while a film is being shown. The chief of police assigns detective Sam Phelan to investigate despite opposition because Sam was born "on the wrong side of the tracks" and is not the academic type. Phelan's common sense enables him to solve a difficult case. *Blood of Vintage* (1947) is an intricately plotted tale about a socialite killed by a rifle shot. The murder of a burlesque queen in an old theater is the subject of *Blood on the Bosom Devine* (1948). *Cover His Face* (1949) is about an American scholar who is in England looking for letters written by Dr. Johnson but discovers, instead, a corpse in a rural cottage.

KYLE, SEFTON. *See* VICKERS, ROY.

L

LACY, ED (pseudonym of Len Zinberg; 1911–1968). American author of short stories and mystery novels. Born in New York City, where he lived most of his life and died, Zinberg used the city as the setting for most of his twenty-eight books. He also wrote hundreds of short stories for magazines as diverse as *Esquire, The New Yorker, Collier's,* and *Ellery Queen's Mystery Magazine.* During World War II he was a correspondent for *Yank.* His boxing novel, *Walk Hard, Talk Loud* (1940; signed by Len Zinberg), was adapted for the Broadway stage in 1944.

Lacy first gained attention in the mystery field with *The Best That Ever Did It* (1955), an unusual "big-caper" mystery. *Room to Swing* (1957), which earned Lacy the Mystery Writers of America Edgar as best novel, was the most famous of the many novels and short stories in which he, a white man, wrote sympathetically of blacks. The hero is Toussaint Moore, a young private detective whose first big case takes him from Harlem to the South and into confrontations with racial prejudice.

LAM, DONALD. *See* COOL, BERTHA, AND DONALD LAM.

LAMPREY, A. C. *See* FISH, ROBERT L.

LANE, DRURY [Creator: Ellery QUEEN (author) as Barnaby Ross]. When deafness forces this aged, wealthy Shakespearean actor to leave the stage, he retires to the Hamlet, a castle overlooking the Hudson River, and proceeds to re-create an Elizabethan community. He surrounds himself with old friends from the theater and dresses them in costumes befitting Shakespearean roles. His most important retainer is Quacey, a hunchback who was his loyal wigmaker and makeup man for more than forty years.

Lane's detective career begins when, without ever leaving his home, he arrives at the correct solutions to cases that have baffled the New York City Police Department. One of the unsolicited letters he sends to the authorities causes New York District Attorney Bruno and Inspector Thumm to ask his assistance in solving the murder of an unscrupulous stockbroker on a 42d Street trolley (*The Tragedy of X,* 1932). They receive his help in three other cases, the last of which, *Drury Lane's Last Case* (1933), involves the theft of Shakespearean manuscripts from the fictional Britannic Museum on New York City's Fifth Avenue. The other cases involving Lane are *The Tragedy of Y* (1932) and *The Tragedy of Z* (1933).

LANE, GRANT. *See* FISHER, STEVE.

LANG, FRITZ (1890–). Austrian-born director who achieved his earliest successes in the German cinema and continued his work in the United States. Although Lang has been responsible for landmark science fiction (*Metropolis,* 1926) and westerns (*The Return of Frank James,* 1940; *Western Union,* 1941), he is most closely associated with dark tales of crime and supercriminals and has won critical acclaim for his contributions to the genre. While still in Germany, he began the Dr. MABUSE series; in the United States, he brought Graham GREENE's *The Ministry of Fear* to the screen; and he is renowned for other achievements in the mystery film field.

Films

The Spiders. Decla (German), 1919. A two-part serial written by Lang. Part I: *The Lake of Gold;* Part II: *The Diamond Ship.* Carl de Vogt, Ressel Orla, Lil Dagover. Two additional sections scripted by Lang were never filmed.

A secret organization seeks world domination.

Spione (Spies). UFA (German), 1928. Rudolph Klein-Rogge, Gerda Maurus, Willy Fritsch. Based on a novel by Thea von Harbou, then Lang's dynamic, politically active wife.

International spies, both Caucasian and Oriental, clash with a master criminal who operates under various disguises. The settings include a large bank

Brooding terror accompanies Joan Bennett, a newlywed who explores her husband's strange mansion in Fritz Lang's *Secret Beyond the Door*. [*Universal*]

and a derailed railroad locomotive.

M. Nero (German), 1931. Peter Lorre, Otto Wernicke (Inspector Lohmann), Ellen Widmann. Screenplay by Von Harbou, original story by Von Harbou and Lang, based on newspaper accounts.

A twisted child murderer (Lorre in his first screen role) roams through a German town, while police and criminal gangs hunt him down.

Five years later Lang, having fled Nazi Germany, directed his first American film.

Fury. MGM, 1936. Spencer Tracy, Sylvia Sidney, Walter Abel, Bruce Cabot.

An innocent young man is accused of a kidnapping; an aroused mob sets fire to the prison in which he has been placed.

You Only Live Once. United Artists, 1937. Henry Fonda, Sidney, Barton MacLane, William Gargan.

A petty criminal, framed and imprisoned for murder, escapes and shoots the priest who is bringing him the news that he has been cleared.

You and Me. Paramount, 1938. Sidney, George Raft, Robert Cummings.

A young man and woman, each keeping a prison record secret from the other, marry—and falter.

Man Hunt. Twentieth Century-Fox, 1941. Walter Pidgeon, Joan Bennett, George Sanders, John Carradine, Roddy McDowall. A superb cinematic elaboration of Geoffrey HOUSEHOLD's *Rogue Male* (1939).

A British game hunter on a European holiday decides to stalk Hitler as a bloodless exercise; he is captured by the Führer's guards. He manages to escape but is pursued first to London and then deep into an English wood by ruthless German agents, who "play the game to win."

Hangmen Also Die. United Artists, 1943. Brian Donlevy, Anna Lee, Walter Brennan, Dennis O'Keefe, Gene Lockhart.

A Nazi occupation officer in Czechoslovakia is assassinated by a Czech surgeon who then slips into the underground movement.

The Woman in the Window. Paramount, 1944. Edward G. Robinson, Bennett, Raymond Massey, Dan Duryea. Based on *Once Off Guard* (1942), by J. H. WALLIS.

A middle-aged professor, his family away, finds himself forced to kill a man he encounters in the apartment of a woman he has met just by chance; he decides against calling the police.

Scarlet Street. Universal, 1945. Robinson, Bennett, Duryea, Margaret Lindsay, Rosalind Ivan. Based on the French novel and play *La Chienne* by Georges de La Fouchardière in collaboration with André Mouézy-Éon.

A timid and artistic cashier falls hopelessly in love with a femme fatale who exploits both him and his paintings and drives him to an act of violence.

Cloak and Dagger. Warner Brothers, 1946. Gary Cooper, Lilli Palmer, Robert Alda, Vladimir Sokoloff. Based on the real-life experiences of Lieutenant Michael Burke.

A scientist is asked by the OSS to go on a mission behind enemy lines, and is soon surrounded by vicious foreign agents and underground heroes.

Secret Beyond the Door. Universal, 1948. Michael Redgrave, Bennett, Anne Revere. Based on *Museum Piece No. 13* (1946) by Rufus KING.

After a whirlwind courtship, a New York girl marries a brooding architect who, in an upstate mansion, re-creates rooms in which murder has been committed.

House by the River. Republic, 1950. Louis Hayward, Jane Wyatt, Lee Bowman, Dorothy Patrick. Based on the 1920 novel of the same name by A. P. Herbert.

A mystery author allows his own writings to betray him after he strangles his maid and silences his crippled brother.

Rancho Notorious. RKO, 1952. Marlene Dietrich, Arthur Kennedy, Mel Ferrer, Gloria Henry.

Seeking revenge for the murder of his fiancée, a cowpoke infiltrates a ranch run by a woman as a secret refuge for outlaws.

The Blue Gardenia. Warner Brothers, 1953. Anne Baxter, Richard Conte, Ann Sothern, Raymond Burr, Jeff Donnell. Based on a story by Vera CASPARY.

A columnist tricks a girl into confessing that she beat to death with a poker an overly amorous artist—but then becomes uncertain about her guilt.

The Big Heat. Columbia, 1953. Glenn Ford, Gloria Grahame, Lee Marvin, Jocelyn Brando, Alexander Scourby. Based on the 1952 novel by William P. MCGIVERN.

His wife killed in a car explosion meant for him, a rogue cop sets out to destroy—using one of the underworld's discarded mistresses—the organization which has corrupted even the ranks of the police.

Human Desire. Columbia, 1954. Ford, Grahame, Broderick Crawford, Edgar Buchanan. Émile Zola's *La Bête Humaine* (1890) transposed to American settings and somewhat altered.

A young railroad engineer, returned from service in Korea, is seduced by the young wife of a coarse yardmaster who has already committed one murder.

Moonfleet. MGM, 1955. Stewart Granger, Sanders, Joan Greenwood, Viveca Lindfors, Jon Whiteley. Freely taken from J. Meade Falkner's 1898 adventure novel of the same title.

A young orphan boy (Whiteley) attaches himself to a dashing rogue in a tale of smuggling, gypsies, and corrupt aristocracy along the eighteenth-century Cornish coast.

While the City Sleeps. RKO, 1956. Dana Andrews, Ida Lupino, Sanders, Rhonda Fleming, Vincent Price, John Drew Barrymore, Thomas Mitchell, Howard Duff, Sally Forrest, James Craig. Based on *The Bloody Spur* (1953) by Charles Einstein.

The executives of a powerful newspaper syndicate vie with one another in cutthroat fashion to be the first to capture an unknown psychopath—actually a mother-dominated delivery boy—who has been killing young girls.

Beyond a Reasonable Doubt. RKO, 1956. Andrews, Joan Fontaine, Sidney Blackmer, Barbara Nichols.

A mystery writer deliberately allows himself to be framed for a murder by circumstantial evidence in order to test judicial procedure; at the last minute, his confidant, a newspaper owner who has the evidence to clear him, is killed in a car crash.

Beyond a Reasonable Doubt was Lang's last American film. In 1958, at the request of the German film industry, he returned to that country, first to direct a period adventure epic (*Das indische Grabmal*, filmed in two parts with extensive location settings in India) and, finally, to direct an elaborate postwar adventure of Dr. Mabuse (*The Thousand Eyes of Dr. Mabuse*, 1960).

LATHAM, GRACE, AND COLONEL JOHN PRIMROSE (Creator: Leslie FORD). Although they are unmarried and middle-aged, this female-male detective team achieved great popularity. At the time of their first meeting, at a Chesapeake Bay summer colony in *Ill-met by Moonlight*, Colonel Primrose is fifty-one years old, and Grace Latham is thirty-eight. He is short and plump, a West Point graduate who had to retire from the Army because of wounds he received during World War I. He has become a consulting detective and frequently takes on special assignments for the government. His personal aide, and constant companion in war and peace, is Sergeant Phineas T. Buck, who anxiously protects his employer's bachelor status from "designing females."

Grace Latham, the object of Sergeant Buck's concern, was left a widow with two young sons when her lawyer husband was killed in a plane crash. Born and raised in Washington, D.C., she lives on P Street in Georgetown. The Colonel lives nearby.

Primrose, who relies on clear thinking to solve his cases, finds Grace charming and delightful but decries her lack of objectivity. In *Siren in the Night* they still shake hands, and he calls her "Mrs. Latham" or "my dear" in a formal manner. By *Honolulu Story* he has proposed but has been refused. At the conclusion of *Washington Whispers Murder*, however, it appears that marriage may be imminent.

CHECKLIST

- 1937 *Ill-met by Moonlight*
- 1937 *The Simple Way of Poison*
- 1938 *Three Bright Pebbles* (Primrose is absent in this case)
- 1939 *Reno Rendezvous* (British title: *Mr. Cromwell Is Dead*)
- 1939 *False to Any Man* (British title: *Snow-white Murder*)
- 1940 *Old Lover's Ghost*
- 1941 *The Murder of a Fifth Columnist* (British title: *The Capital Crime*)
- 1942 *Murder in the O.P.M.* (British title: *The Priority Murder*)
- 1943 *Siren in the Night*
- 1944 *All for the Love of a Lady* (British title: *Crack of Dawn*)
- 1945 *The Philadelphia Murder Story*
- 1946 *Honolulu Story* (British title: *Honolulu Murder Story*)
- 1947 *The Woman in Black*
- 1948 *The Devil's Stronghold*
- 1953 *Washington Whispers Murder* (British title: *The Lying Jade*)

LATHEN, EMMA (pseudonym of Mary J. Latsis and Martha Hennissart). Although the two Boston businesswomen who write as Emma Lathen have requested that their publishers not reveal information about them, some facts are known. Their real names appear in the *Catalog of Copyright Entries: Books and Pamphlets*. They met while they were both graduate students at Harvard, discovered that each read mysteries, and began to write them as a logical extension of their hobby. Mary Latsis, an attorney, and Martha Hennissart, an economic analyst, prefer that their true names and business affiliations not be widely circulated, for fear that their clients will begin to think their business matters might become subjects for Lathen mysteries, all of which have business settings. They arrived at their pseudonym by using the first parts of their real names: "M" of "Mary" and "Ma" of "Martha," and "Lat" of "Latsis" and "Hen" of "Hennissart." They have also written mysteries as R. B. Dominic.

All the Lathen books (sixteen since 1961) feature John Putnam THATCHER, who, as senior vice-president of the Sloan Guaranty Trust Company, is drawn into the investigation of murders that threaten the soundness of his bank's investments.

Since their first book was published, the authors have consistently received rave reviews. *The Times* (London) commented: "She is a sort of Jane Austen of the detective novel, crisp, detached, mocking, economical." Discussing the authors' hold over the reader, despite their use of business technicalities, Anthony BOUCHER modestly remarked on their "extraordinary ability to clarify the most intricate financial shenanigans so that even I can understand them."

LATIMER, JONATHAN (WYATT) (1906–). American writer of hard-boiled mystery novels. Born in Chicago, he is the namesake of a great-great-grandfather who had been attached to George Washington's staff during the Revolutionary War. Educated at Mesa (Arizona) Ranch School and Knox College in Galesburg, Ill., where he received a B.A. degree in 1929, he became a newspaperman for the *Chicago Herald-Examiner* and, later, for the *Chicago Tribune* (1930–1935). He spent the immediate prewar years as a scriptwriter in Hollywood for Paramount and MGM. After serving at sea with the Navy (1942–1945), he returned to Hollywood to work for RKO and Paramount. His numerous screenplays include the second version of Dashiell HAMMETT's *The Glass Key* (1942), Kenneth FEARING's *The Big Clock* (1948), and Cornell WOOLRICH's *The Night Has a Thousand Eyes* (1948). Later, he wrote numerous scripts for the Perry MASON television series (1960–1965). Latimer married Ellen Baxter Peabody in 1937; he married his second wife, Ann Hanzlik, in 1954. He currently resides in La Jolla, Calif.

A successor to Hammett in the hard-boiled field, Latimer wrote a series of five novels about private detective Bill CRANE that came close to capturing the mood, characterization, and atmosphere of Hammett's works. However, he imbued them with his own cynical, wry, slightly grotesque, and bawdy sense of humor. His longest and most serious work, *The Search for My Great Uncle's Head* (1937), was published under the pseudonym Peter Coffin.

Latimer's postwar work is skillful, but the prewar qualities that made him an individual writer seem to have vanished. His best work of this period, *Sinners and Shrouds* (1955), begins when the protagonist, a Chicago newspaperman, wakes up one morning, with a hangover, to discover an undraped female corpse in his room.

LATSIS, MARY J. *See* LATHEN, EMMA.

LAWLESS, ANTHONY. *See* MACDONALD, PHILIP.

LAWRENCE, HILDA (ca. 1906–). American author of mysteries. Born Hildegarde Kronmiller in Baltimore, she is the daughter of former Maryland Congressman John Kronmiller. After a finishing-school education in Rochester, N.Y., she moved to New York City, where she worked in the publishing field and also wrote for radio. Her marriage to playwright Reginald Lawrence ended in divorce.

A mystery fan, Mrs. Lawrence claimed that she began writing mysteries when she could not find enough good ones to read. Her first book, *Blood upon the Snow* (1944), was a success and had four hard-cover printings. It introduced detective Mark East and was praised as a subtle horror story. East is also the detective in *A Time to Die* (1945) and in her last novel, *Death of a Doll* (1947), the story of murder at a very proper New York residence house for out-of-town working girls. Although by 1947 she had established a considerable reputation (Howard HAYCRAFT called her "far and away the most exciting new talent in the American mystery field today"), she never wrote another novel.

LEBLANC, MAURICE (1864–1941). French playwright, novelist, and short story writer; creator of the popular rogue Arsène LUPIN.

Born in Rouen, he was educated in France, Germany (Berlin), and England (Manchester) and studied law before becoming a hack writer and police reporter for French periodicals. His sister Georgette—a famous actress and singer—was the mistress of Maurice Maeterlinck, the noted dramatist, and it is possible that this relationship influenced Leblanc's work; some critics claim that his plays are his most polished literary productions.

In 1906 Leblanc's previously undistinguished career skyrocketed when he was asked to write a short story for a new journal and produced the first Lupin adventure. His subsequent success and worldwide fame culminated in his being made a member of the French Legion of Honor.

Reading his fiction today, one is generally impressed with the fast pace and diversified action, although it borders on burlesque, and the incredible situations and coincidences are difficult to accept.

le CARRÉ, JOHN (pseudonym of David John Moore Cornwell; 1931–). English author of espionage fiction. Born in Poole, Dorsetshire, he attended Bern and Oxford Universities. He served as an intelligence officer following World War II and, after teaching at Eton, joined the Foreign Service and was assigned to Bonn, the setting of *A Small Town in Germany* (1968). The financial rewards of *The Spy Who Came in from the Cold* (1963) allowed him to resign his civil service job, admit that his real name is Cornwell, and devote full time to writing.

Le Carré's spy novels are not romantic tales of adventure and sex, in the James BOND tradition. His characters are weary victims of the espionage establishment of both sides of the cold war—not supermen, but antiheroes trying to play the game according to the rules and blundering into situations in which they are merely pawns. Told with the insight and precision of one who has firsthand knowledge of the system, le Carré's stories reveal spies to be largely incompetent social misfits who have been dragged into a degrading life-style. His messages are clear: authority is destructive; "our" side and "their" side are equally doomed and evil; individual agents have no power (over themselves or the system); and the only way to get out of the cold is to die. Alec Leamas, the central figure in *The Spy Who Came in from the Cold,* willingly becomes a martyr, even though he dies for a cause with which he has no sympathy.

The first espionage novel by le Carré was *Call for the Dead* (1960), featuring George Smiley, who has a more traditional detective role in *A Murder of Quality* (1962). *The Looking Glass War* (1965) is the story of an unimportant espionage department in London and its self-serving efforts to train a Pole named Leiser for an obviously unnecessary assignment in East Germany.

Le Carré's *Tinker, Tailor, Soldier, Spy* (1974) describes Smiley's efforts to unearth, and neutralize the effect of, a Russian agent operating inside the British Secret Service.

Films

The Spy Who Came in from the Cold. Paramount, 1965. Richard Burton (Alec Leamas), Claire Bloom, Oskar Werner, Peter Van Eyck, Rupert Davies (George Smiley). Directed by Martin Ritt.

British Intelligence's Berlin agent is assigned to get a former Nazi counterspy chief out of East Germany; he is unaware that he is a pawn in the behind-the-scenes maneuvering of East-West espionage forces.

The Deadly Affair. Columbia, 1967. James Mason (Smiley; the name was changed to Charles Dobbs in the film), Simone Signoret, Maximilian Schell, Harry Andrews, Kenneth Haigh, Lynn Redgrave. Directed by Sidney Lumet. Based on le Carré's novel *Call for the Dead.*

A secret service agent investigates when an anonymous letter questions the loyalty of a member of the British Foreign Office; he can find nothing irregular. When the man is found dead—an apparent victim of suicide—the agent is sure that he has been murdered.

The Looking Glass War. Columbia, 1970. Christopher Jones, Ralph Richardson, Paul Rogers, Anthony Hopkins, Pia Degermark, Anna Massey.

Directed by Frank R. Pierson.

A young amateur is sent into East Germany by the powers at British Intelligence, but when their scheme does not work out, they leave him to die.

LECOQ, MONSIEUR (Creator: Émile GABORIAU). Introduced as a minor detective who had a shady past before becoming a member of the Sûreté, Lecoq soon becomes the best and most famous detective in the world, though Sherlock HOLMES describes him (perhaps unjustly) as "a miserable bungler."

His career roughly parallels the life of François Eugène VIDOCQ, who also joined the Sûreté after a life of crime. When he was young, Lecoq had to discontinue his legal studies when his father died, and he was forced to take menial jobs, during which time he contemplated illegal methods of gaining wealth. He then joined the French police force and, in addition to becoming a master of disguise, developed valuable crime-fighting techniques, such as using plaster to make impressions of footprints and devising a test of when a bed had been slept in.

Lecoq plays only a minor role in his first case, *L'Affaire Lerouge* (1866; U.S. title: *The Widow Lerouge*, 1873; British title: *The Lerouge Case*, 1881). In this novel, originally serialized in 1863, Gevrol, chief of the Detective Police, is in charge, but the major detection is provided by Père Tabaret, known as "Tir-au-clair," an amateur who explains his methods to the young Lecoq. In a later adventure, *Monsieur Lecoq* (1869; British title: *Lecoq the Detective*, 1881), Lecoq has clearly become the central figure in the case. Tabaret remains to lend a hand, but the ambitious Lecoq, jealous of Gevrol's position, treats the head of the Sûreté with contempt and ridicule. Perhaps Lecoq's most famous case is *Le Dossier No. 113* (1867; U.S. title: *File No. 113*, 1875; British title: *Dossier No. 113*, 1883). He also appeared in *Le Crime d'Orcival* (1867; U.S. title: *The Mystery of Orcival*, 1871). This was followed by *Les Esclaves de Paris* (1868; U.S. title: *The Slaves of Paris*, 1882) and a posthumously published long short story, *Le Petit Vieux des Batignolles* (1876; U.S. title: *The Little Old Man of Batignolles*, 1880).

LEE, FLEMING. See SAINT, THE.

LEE, GYPSY ROSE. See RICE, CRAIG.

LEE, MANFRED B. See QUEEN, ELLERY (author).

LE FANU, JOSEPH SHERIDAN (1814–1873). Irish author of mystery and supernatural fiction. Born in Dublin, he was privately educated until he entered Trinity College, Dublin. He was a nonpracticing barrister in 1839 when he bought two newspapers and combined them to form the *Evening Mail*, which he owned, edited, and wrote columns for until his death, using it to further the causes of the Conservative party. After the death of his beloved wife in 1858, Le Fanu, a giant of Irish society, withdrew from his many activities and began writing the supernatural stories for which he is remembered.

His most famous novel is *Uncle Silas: A Tale of Bartram Haugh* (1864), which introduced one of the great villains of literature. The white-haired, marble-faced Uncle Silas is described as being "like an apparition in black and white, bloodless, fiery-eyed." *The House by the Churchyard* (1863) also deals with murder and criminals but is more involved with supernatural happenings and ghosts. Two impressive villains appear in *Wylder's Hand* (1864), which contains a problem similar to that in *The Thin Man* (1934) by Dashiell HAMMETT, as Julian SYMONS points out in *Bloody Murder* (1972; U.S. title: *Mortal Consequences*). *Checkmate* (1871) is an almost-pure detective story that introduces new elements to the form. The criminal has employed plastic surgery to alter his appearance. When Paul Davies, a former detective, learns that Walter Longcluse has committed several murders while retaining his place in society, he blackmails him but leaves his information with David Arden, whose brother was murdered eight years earlier. Arden sets out to track down the killer, finally proving his guilt with dental records and other medical evidence.

At his best, Le Fanu ranks with Wilkie COLLINS as a creator of well-constructed plots. At his worst, he is long-winded—he had to fill the many pages of three-decker novels—and displays the weakest elements of the romantic, melodramatic Gothic novel a half century after the form fell from favor.

LEON, HENRY CECIL. See CECIL, HENRY.

LE QUEUX, WILLIAM (TUFNELL) (1864–1927). English author of novels and short stories of mystery, crime, and international intrigue. Born in London, he worked during the Balkan War as a correspondent for the *London Daily Mail* (1912–1913) and is reputed to have also been employed for many years as a member of the British Secret Service. A pioneer expert in wireless transmission, mainly as it related to espionage activity, Le Queux seems to have spent the major portion of his life in behind-the-scenes patriotic activities for England. He began writing stories about secret agents largely to finance his work for British Intelligence, which required much traveling and personal contact with royalty and other high-ranking people.

His first book, *Guilty Bonds* (1890), deals with political conspiracy in Russia and was banned in that country. During the next two decades he wrote scores of espionage stories and novels that anticipated almost every development in that form until the works of Eric AMBLER appeared. The earliest tales

William Le Queux. This is the frontispiece of his official biography, *The Real Le Queux,* by N. St. Barbe Sladen, published in 1938 by Nicholson & Watson.

warned of the menace presented by France, and the later ones portrayed Germany as the enemy. In *England's Peril* (1899) a member of Parliament is betrayed and murdered by his wife, who is in love with the chief of the French Secret Service. In *The Great War in England in 1897* (1894) the Russians join the French in invading England. It is often claimed that Le Queux accurately predicted World War I in *The Invasion of 1910* (1905) and *Spies of the Kaiser* (1909), in which the threat of invasion by the Germans is described. In *The Bomb Makers* (1917), Le Queux recounts "some curious records concerning the craft and cunning of Theodore Drost, an enemy alien in London, together with certain revelations regarding his daughter Ella."

Among Le Queux's more than 100 books are several short story collections about criminals, including *The Count's Chauffeur* (1907), about Count Bindo di Ferraris; *The Lady in the Car* (1909), about "Prince Albert of Hesse-Holstein," who masquerades as the Kaiser's nephew; *"Cinders" of Harley Street* (1916), about Dr. Villiers Beethom-Saunders; and *The Secret Telephone* (1920), about Henri Martin. *The Crimes Club* (1927) is a collection of stories about the detective work of ten members of that organization.

Perhaps Le Queux's best collection is *Mysteries of a Great City* (1920), a QUEEN'S QUORUM selection.

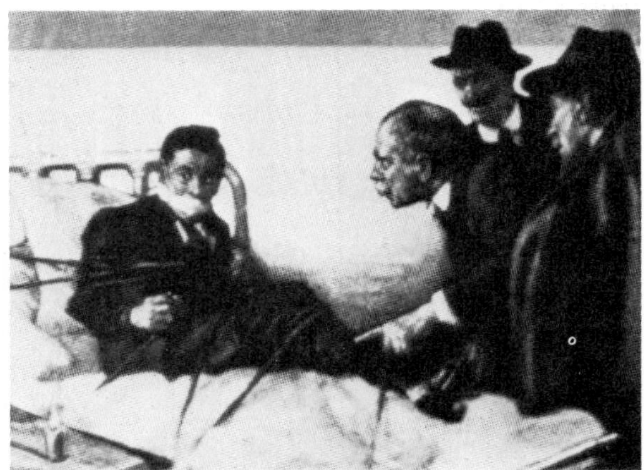

This illustration appears on the dust wrapper of the first edition of William Le Queux's *The Luck of the Secret Service,* published by Pearson in London in 1921. It is subtitled *Being the Startling Adventures of Claud Heathwaite, C.B., of His Britannic Majesty's Foreign Office, Related by Himself and Edited by William Le Queux.*

LEROUX, GASTON (1868–1927). French journalist, dramatist, and author of mystery-adventure-detective thrillers. His extensive career as a crime reporter and war correspondent provided the background for his popular novels, which were largely typically French stories of sensational melodrama.

Gaston Leroux's most famous detective is Joseph Rouletabille, who solves the puzzle in *The Mystery of the Yellow Room.* This is the frontispiece of the first American edition, published by Brentano's in 1908.

Leroux wrote one of the most famous thrillers of all time, *The Phantom of the Opera* (1911), also successful in several films. His many novels about Chéri-Bibi and Hardigras were eagerly read adventure-mysteries, but his best work features Joseph Rouletabille, a young police reporter–amateur detective.

Introduced as a precocious teenager in *Le Mystère de la Chambre Jaune* (1907; U.S. title: *The Mystery of the Yellow Room,* 1908), Rouletabille virtually takes over the investigation of an apparently impossible crime from the official police. Although many elements of this locked-room mystery seem familiar to readers of *The Big Bow Mystery* (1892) by Israel ZANGWILL, some critics still consider the Leroux book one of the best and most important titles in the history of the genre. Among the superior features of the novel are the author's willingness to be more fair with the reader than most

Striding majestically down the great marble stairway of the Paris Opera House, the Phantom of the Opera disguises himself as the Red Death during a masked ball. Lon Chaney portrays Erik in the stunning 1925 film production of the Leroux novel. [*Universal*]

writers of French crime novels are. Rouletabille has his Watson (*see* WATSON, DR.)—the reverential Sainclair, who is exasperated by the energetic reporter's many flashes of insight (all of which he keeps to himself). The least-likely-person device employed in this novel is now a classic. The sequel, and the only other well-known tale involving Rouletabille, is *Le Parfum de la Dame en Noir* (1907; U.S. title: *The Perfume of the Lady in Black,* 1909). Less successful than the previous work, it relies heavily on coincidence and sensationalism.

A dramatized version of *The Mystery of the Yellow Room,* produced in 1912, was highly successful.

Films

The Mystery of the Yellow Room was filmed in France several times, especially during the silent screen period. Lorin Baker played Joseph Rouletabille in an American version (Realart, 1919), discovering who made an attempt on the life of a girl who was in a locked room. Similarly, Chéri-Bibi has twice reached the French screen (the second time portrayed by Pierre Fresnay in 1937); in the United States he has been portrayed only by John Gilbert.

The Phantom of Paris. MGM, 1931. Gilbert, Leila Hyams, Lewis Stone, Jean Hersholt, C. Aubrey Smith. Directed by John S. Robertson.

The magician Chéri-Bibi is convicted of murdering his beloved's father; he escapes from prison, and when the man he suspects dies four years later, he assumes the killer's identity to prove his guilt.

The most extensive use of a Leroux character on the screen, however, has been of mad Erik haunting the Paris Opera.

The Phantom of the Opera. Universal, 1925. Lon Chaney, Mary Philbin, Norman Kerry. Directed by Rupert Julian.

Lurking in the subterranean passages under the Paris Opera House, occasionally terrorizing and even murdering stragglers above, the hideously scarred, masked Erik, once a prince of an Oriental land, falls in love with a young understudy.

The Phantom of the Opera. Universal, 1943. Nelson Eddy, Claude Rains, Suzanna Foster. Directed by Arthur Lubin.

Disfigured by acid hurled at him during a dispute over a concerto he had written, a musician (Rains) retreats into the depths of the Paris Opera.

The Phantom of the Opera. Hammer (British), 1962. Herbert Lom, Heather Sears, Edward de Souza, Michael Gough. Directed by Terence Fisher.

In the sewers under an *English* opera house, a man in a one-eyed mask (Lom), cared for by a dwarf, protests the theft of his lifework; he is musician Professor Petrie, in a relocated, period version of the Leroux novel.

The story was converted into a contemporary New York electronic rock palace setting in 1974 as *Phantom of the Paradise,* starring William Finley, directed by Brian de Palma, and released by Twentieth Century-Fox.

A mask covering his acid-scarred face, the Phanton of the Opera (Claude Rains) lurks in the passages under the Paris Opera House in the lavish 1943 production. [*Universal*]

LEVIN, IRA (1929–). American playwright and novelist. Born in New York City, the son of Beatrice (Schlansky) and Charles Levin, he graduated from New York University in 1950. He married Gabrielle Aronsohn in 1960 (divorced 1968); they have three children.

Levin's best-known work is the contemporary Gothic horror story *Rosemary's Baby* (1967), in which a New York couple face the unendurable terror of the commonplace gone wrong when Rosemary believes that a witches' coven wants her unborn child.

A Kiss Before Dying (1953), Levin's first novel, is a suspense classic. A charming but deranged young college student coolly plans to marry the youngest daughter of a rich copper magnate. When she becomes pregnant, he knows that the family will disinherit her, so he kills her and sets out to win the hand of her sister. A third daughter provides the greatest challenge to his scheme of marrying into the Kingship fortune.

The versatile Levin has also written song lyrics, television scripts, and seven Broadway shows, including a 1955 adaptation of Mac Hyman's novel *No Time for Sergeants* (1954). He has written two other novels, *This Perfect Day* (1970), a story of the future, and *The Stepford Wives* (1972), a tale of terror set in the suburbs.

Films

A Kiss Before Dying. United Artists, 1956. Robert Wagner, Jeffrey Hunter, Virginia Leith, Joanne Woodward, George Macready, Robert Quarry. Directed by Gerd Oswald.

A rich young girl in a college town is certain that her pregnant sister did not jump from a high building but was murdered; her suspicions fall on the wrong fellow student.

Rosemary's Baby. Paramount, 1968. Mia Farrow, John Cassavetes, Ruth Gordon, Sidney Blackmer, Maurice Evans, Ralph Bellamy. Directed by Roman Polanski.

A frail young wife, some months pregnant, slowly realizes that her husband is in league with a coven of witches living in their apartment building.

The Stepford Wives. Columbia, 1974. Katharine Ross, Paula Prentiss, Peter Masterson, Nanette Newman, Tina Louise, Patrick O'Neal. Directed by Bryan Forbes.

A young feminist moves to a quiet suburban Connecticut community and wonders darkly why all the wives seem models of contentment and perfect accomplishment.

Plays

Levin has made brave attempts at the mystery stage. His *Interlock (1958)—"a psychological melodrama"*—and his 1965 musical, *Drat! The Cat!*, a spoof of cops-and-robbers melodrama starring Lesley (Ann) Warren, had only a few performances. More recently, his chilling *Veronica's Room* (1973) enjoyed slightly greater success.

A coven of strange people surrounds a confused and exhausted Mia Farrow in a scene from the film made from Ira Levin's *Rosemary's Baby*. [*Paramount*]

LEWIS, ALFRED HENRY (1858–1914). American editor and author. Born in Cleveland, Ohio, he used the pseudonym Dan Quin and the character "Old Cattleman" to relate the Wolfville stories, the first of which appeared in the *Kansas City Times* in 1890; there were six volumes of stories in the series, beginning with *Wolfville* (1897). Lewis founded *The Verdict* magazine in 1898 and edited it until his death. His *Confessions of a Detective* (1906), selected for QUEEN'S QUORUM, is a collection of realistic detective tales about Inspector Val, a "hickory knot" of a man.

LEWIS, C. DAY. *See* BLAKE, NICHOLAS.

LEWIS, MARY CHRISTIANNA (MILNE). *See* BRAND, CHRISTIANNA.

LEWIS, MONK (1775–1818). English novelist, poet, dramatist, and diplomat. Matthew Gregory Lewis is best known as "Monk" Lewis because of his sensational Gothic novel *Ambrosio: or, The Monk* (1795), which was published to enormous public furor when he was twenty. It is the story of an abbot, Ambrosio, and a young noblewoman, Matilda, who, disguised as a monk, enters the monastery to be with the eloquent holy man. She soon reveals her passion, and Ambrosio yields, going from one crime to another until he is caught and condemned to death by the Inquisition. Following the example of Matilda (actually a demon in disguise), he first bargains with the devil for his life and then repents and is finally slain by Lucifer. Terror, murder, blood, and other staples of the Gothic romance are also well in evidence in Lewis's other novels, *The Bravo of Venice* (1804) and *Feudal Tyrants* (1806). Although loud and often-repeated charges of immorality were leveled at Lewis because he described situations and incidents that were generally only alluded to in other Gothics of the time, he was essentially a gentle man who collaborated with Sir Walter Scott on a collection of ballads, *Tales of Wonder* (1801), and translated from German and Spanish sources *Tales of Terror* (1807) and *Romantic Tales* (1809).

LININGTON, ELIZABETH (1921–   ). American author of historical and mystery novels. Born in Aurora, Ill., Miss Linington went to California as a child. Her family settled in Hollywood, where she attended public schools, graduating from Herbert Hoover High School and, later, from Glendale College. She began writing while still in high school, but her first book was not published until 1955. That book, *The Proud Man,* was a historical novel about Shane O'Neill, prince of Ulster in sixteenth-century Ireland. She subsequently published four more historical novels between 1956 and 1958; one of them, *The Anglophile* (1956), appeared under the pseudonym Egan O'Neill. She then wrote what she considered to be her best historical novel but could not get it published because, as she subsequently told an interviewer, "It was on the national patriotism theme, but the leftist liberal publishers wouldn't buy it, so I swore I wouldn't write another historical until they published that." She turned to mystery fiction.

The major interest in her life, in addition to writing, is her membership in the John Birch Society. She has been active as a contributor and organizer and has written a book for the organization. She sees the detective story in political and philosophical terms, calling it "the morality play of our time . . . it deals with basics; with truth versus lie, law and order versus anarchy, a moral code versus amorality."

Miss Linington published her first mystery in 1960 and since then has written more than forty under her own name and three pseudonyms. All have been police procedural novels except *Nightmare* (1961), the only book she wrote as Anne Blaisdell. Her first book published under the Dell Shannon pseudonym (*Case Pending,* 1960) launched her most popular series detective, Lt. Luis MENDOZA. As Lesley Egan, she has written a series about Detective Sergeant Andrew Clock of the Los Angeles Police Department. These books are concerned equally with an amateur detective, a Talmud-quoting lawyer named Jesse Falkenstein. Clock is engaged to Falkenstein's sister, and when, in *Some Avenger, Rise!* (1966), the policeman is accused of a crime, his prospective brother-in-law is ready to defend him and search for a mass murderer.

Also under the Lesley Egan pseudonym, Miss Linington has written a series about Vic Varallo, who made his debut in *A Case for Appeal* (1961) as captain of the police force of Contera, a fictional small town in California. He is thirty-three when he transfers to the Glendale Police Department as a rather old "rookie," but he is experienced and hard-working and rises to the rank of detective in cases such as *Detective's Due* (1965), which tells of his search for a rapist.

Under her own name, the author has written about the detective squad at Hollywood's Wilcox Avenue police station. Foremost in a large cast of characters is Sergeant Ivor Maddox, a dedicated policeman whose major problem is that most women he meets (especially criminal suspects) fall in love with him. He eventually combines business and pleasure by falling in love with Policewoman Sue Carstairs, a member of his squad. Maddox is a fan of mystery fiction and has made a convert of his subordinate Detective César Rodriguez, who reads detective stories during every free moment. Mystery fiction, in particular Agatha CHRISTIE's *The A.B.C. Murders* (1936), is important to *Greenmask* (1964), the first Wilcox Avenue book.

A prolific author, Miss Linington has written

about three books a year, but since she spends only about two weeks on each book, she is able to spend considerable time on political activities and on other interests. She has admitted that she has no direct knowledge of the methods of the Los Angeles Police Department and that many of her ideas come from true detective magazines. Allen J. HUBIN reflected the viewpoint of her many fans when he called her the "Queen of the Procedurals."

LINKS, J. G. *See* WHEATLEY, DENNIS.

LOCKED-ROOM MYSTERIES. Stories of crimes, generally murder, perpetrated in apparently sealed rooms or other "impossible" situations.

When Dr. Gideon FELL delivers the classic lecture in John Dickson CARR's *The Hollow Man* (1935; U.S. title: *The Three Coffins*) on the number and types of crimes that could be committed in a "hermetically sealed" room (from which no murderer could have escaped for the simple reason that no murderer had actually been in the room), he is drawing on precedents established by Israel ZANGWILL in *The Big Bow Mystery* (1892). Since the publication of that short novel, many other writers have been intrigued by the plot possibilities suggested by Zangwill.

Obviously thinking of Melville Davisson POST's UNCLE ABNER story "The Doomdorf Mystery" (1918), Dr. Fell suggests that, in some circumstances, a case of apparent murder is actually no more than a series of lethal coincidences.

Another type of locked-room murder is the one committed by a hidden mechanical device. This demands a degree of inventiveness on the part of the murderer to which a real-life person could seldom rise. A devious extension of this device can be achieved by the individual bent on suicide. If one were to stab oneself with an icicle, or poison oneself with a substance unknown to forensic medicine, it would be presumed that murder had been committed, for no weapon would be found inside the locked room. This method is recommended for pointing the finger of suspicion at relatives one wishes to inconvenience.

A subtle method of murder—from a legal standpoint—is to influence the victim to kill himself or herself. The only prerequisites are an allegedly haunted room that is locked from the inside and an individual (the victim) burdened with guilt. It helps if the prospective victim is prone to hearing voices—voices that combine with a guilty conscience in urging that the only possible expiation for past sins is suicide. The idea is to convince the target that he or she is going mad and that the only option remaining is to die before it is too late.

Another popular method of committing a locked-room murder is to use gas—introduced, perhaps, from outside the room; the victim, often a ghost from the past who has returned most inconveniently, is effectively eliminated.

A deceptive type of locked-room crime has commonly been perpetrated by someone who can "confirm" that he was physically outside the room; the blame falls on someone who is known to have been near the victim. As Dr. Fell notes, in some of G. K. CHESTERTON's Father BROWN stories, illusion and staged effects have been notoriously dependable tools of the imaginative murderer.

There is also the possibility that—all evidence to the contrary—the victim could have been murdered later than it seems. Tinkering with clocks is not necessary—merely the withholding of a vital clue while the criminal attempts to make his getaway.

Laboriously planned crimes of this locked-room type are more likely to be found in English detective fiction than in American works. The detectives most likely to bring their deductive powers to such cases are Lord Peter WIMSEY, Albert CAMPION, Superintendent Roderick ALLEYN, Nigel STRANGEWAYS, and Sir Henry MERRIVALE. American exceptions to this rule include Ellery QUEEN (detective) and cases recorded by Anthony BOUCHER, Edward D. HOCH, and Clayton RAWSON.

When locked-room crimes were at the peak of their popularity (mainly between the world wars), fictional murderers were more concerned with the technique of the crime than the actual murder itself. The taking of a person's life demanded a certain ritual procedure, choreographed against an almost Wagnerian background. In that age, murder was a private affair. It had not yet become a way of life, or something to be investigated while attempting to cope with nymphomaniacs and indulging in pseudo-Freudian jabberwocky. Today, the age is more violent, more impatient; perhaps that is why the device of a murder committed in a hermetically sealed room (or its equivalent) is used less frequently than it once was.

HANS STEFAN SANTESSON

LOCKRIDGE, FRANCES. *See* LOCKRIDGE, RICHARD.

LOCKRIDGE, RICHARD (1898–). American novelist and drama critic. Born in St. Joseph, Mo., Lockridge attended Kansas City Junior College and the University of Missouri. His studies were interrupted by service in the Navy (1918). During 1921–1922 he was a reporter for the *Kansas City Kansan* and then the *Kansas City Star*. In 1922, the year he married Frances Louise Davis, he joined the *New York Sun*, becoming its drama critic in 1928. In 1932 he published *Darling of Misfortune: Edwin Booth*, a biography of the famous actor. During the 1930s he frequently wrote for *The New Yorker*, and his short stories and sketches won him praise as the archetypal contributor to that magazine. During World War II Lockridge returned to the Navy, serving as a public relations officer.

Lockridge's series of nonmystery stories about a publisher and his wife, originally published in *The New Yorker*, were collected in *Mr. and Mrs. North* (1936). A year later, Mrs. Lockridge, a frequent reader of mysteries, decided to write one herself, but she became bogged down. Her husband, also an avid mystery reader, suggested that she use his creations as the main characters. She provided the plot, and he did the actual writing. The result, *The Norths Meet Murder* (1940), established the characters of Mr. and Mrs. NORTH, who were to become one of the most famous husband and wife detective teams in fiction. The Lockridges lived in Greenwich Village at the time, and the book was praised for capturing the atmosphere of the prewar Village. Later books in the series dealt with other aspects of New York life. In *Death on the Aisle* (1942) a Broadway "angel" is found in a theater, stabbed to death with an ice pick. *Murder within Murder* (1946) is about a murder committed at the 42d Street branch of the New York Public Library. A natural history museum is the setting for *Dead as a Dinosaur* (1952), in which a famous mammalogist is murdered, and the weapon apparently is a battle-ax several thousand years old. Devoted cat lovers, the Lockridges wrote many nonfiction works about these animals (their favorite being *Cats and People*, 1950); they usually included at least one cat in their North novels.

There was considerable critical approval for the North series, especially the early books. "Civilized" was the word most often applied, and many critics credited the Lockridges with having popularized the use of humor in the mystery, though they were not the first to do so. They also popularized the idea of a husband and wife detective team and had many less successful imitators. Although the North books continued to sell, their adherence to a formula brought some critical disenchantment. Referring to the tendency of Pam North to require rescue from danger, Howard HAYCRAFT said in 1946, "Someday I'd like to read a North story in which Mrs. North does *not* wander alone and unprotected into the murderer's parlor in the last chapter." There are twenty-seven books in the North series; the last, *Murder by the Book*, was published in 1963, the year Frances Lockridge died.

Lockridge is now married to Hildegarde Dolson, a Pennsylvania-born writer who had written a dozen books before launching her own career as a mystery writer. The couple live in Tryon, N.C.

Lockridge has been responsible for three other mystery series, two of which he began with the first Mrs. Lockridge and has continued alone. *Think of Death* (1947) launched a series about Captain (now Inspector) Merton Heimrich of the New York State Police. Most of the action takes place in the suburban counties of Westchester, Putnam, and Dutchess. The Lockridges had lived in this area after they left New York City. *With Option to Die* (1967), by Richard Lockridge alone, successfully combined a murder mystery with the story of right-wing opposition to racial integration in Westchester County. The Heimrich books have featured the policeman's courtship of Susan Faye, a young widow with a small son. Although the series has been generally well received, a number of critics have expressed annoyance at Heimrich's tendency to start most of his sentences with "Now . . ."

With his first wife, Lockridge began a series in 1956 about a diffident New York police detective, Nathan Shapiro. By the time of *Die Laughing* (1969), in which Shapiro investigates the murder of a famous actress, he has been promoted to lieutenant but, typically, cannot understand why he has received the promotion. He is no more confident in *Preach No More* (1971), a case involving the murder of a successful evangelist under strange circumstances. The third series, written by Lockridge alone, is about Bernie Simmons of the New York District Attorney's office; it began with *Squire of Death* (1965).

LONDON, JACK. See FISH, ROBERT L.

LONE WOLF, THE (Creator: Louis Joseph VANCE). Michael Lanyard was raised as Michael Troyon, a virtual slave and drudge in a disreputable Paris

Francis Lederer as Michael Lanyard eavesdrops in *The Lone Wolf in Paris*. [*Columbia*]

hotel. Forced to lie, steal, and cheat at an early age, he once tried to rob an accomplished thief named Bourke, who liked the darkly handsome youth and did not report him for the attempted theft. Instead, he taught him the skills necessary to be the master criminal he had always dreamed of being. In addition to schooling the lad in such practical subjects as mathematics, explosives, gem appraisal, art, and social graces, Bourke taught him the "three cardinal principles of successful cracksmanship: know your ground thoroughly before venturing upon it; strike and retreat with the swift precision of a hawk; be friendless. And the last of these is the greatest." Lanyard learned his lessons well and became the Lone Wolf—a respected, sophisticated gentleman by day; a brilliant, daring thief by night.

Lanyard first appeared in 1914, in *The Lone Wolf*, in which members of the underworld, resentful because of his success and independence, threaten to reveal his identity unless he becomes a member of their "pack." His vows of solitude are in jeopardy when he meets and falls in love with the beautiful Lucy Shannon.

CHECKLIST

1914	*The Lone Wolf*
1918	*The False Faces*
1921	*Alias the Lone Wolf*
1921	*Red Masquerade*
1923	*The Lone Wolf Returns*
1931	*The Lone Wolf's Son*
1933	*Encore the Lone Wolf*
1934	*The Lone Wolf's Last Prowl*

An extremely formal Warren William as the Lone Wolf attempts to break into a safe while Ida Lupino looks on in *The Lone Wolf Spy Hunt*. The setting is Washington. [*Columbia*]

Films

Michael Lanyard, whose habit of working alone not only gained him a nickname but added an expression to the language, has long been active and charming on the screen (with almost no exceptions, the cinematic Lone Wolf is a reformed jewel thief). Dashing Bert Lytell first began amassing gems for the good of society in *The Lone Wolf* (Selznick, 1917), and Henry B. Walthall assumed the role in *The False Faces* (Paramount, 1919). *The Lone Wolf's Daughter* (Hodkinson, 1919) was the first of several films to use Lanyard's motherless young offspring as a romantic subtheme. In 1924 Lanyard (played by Jack Holt), in another film entitled *The Lone Wolf* (Associated Exchange), is in Paris and, on orders from the American Embassy, is trying to steal plans on how to stop an airplane in flight. A girl he thinks is a crook turns out to be a secret service operative, and they are married.

The Lone Wolf Returns. Columbia, 1926. Lytell, Billie Dove. Directed by Ralph Ince.

Lanyard, a "silk hat" thief, falls in love with a girl he meets while he is burglarizing a house during a masked ball, and reforms.

Alias the Lone Wolf. Columbia, 1927. Lytell, Lois Wilson. Directed by Edward H. Griffith.

Aboard ship, Lanyard helps a French girl recover jewelry stolen by crooks; at the end he reveals that he is a secret service agent!

The Lone Wolf's Daughter. Columbia, 1929. Lytell, Gertrude Olmstead, Charles Gerrard.

Lanyard is detailed by Scotland Yard to watch a band of notorious jewel thieves; the girl he loves sees him open a safe and mistakes his intentions.

Last of the Lone Wolf. Columbia, 1930. Lytell, Patsy Ruth Miller. Directed by Richard Boleslavsky.

This is a Graustarkian melodrama in which Lanyard helps a queen retain her crown jewels and throne in spite of sinister court intrigue.

Cheaters at Play. Fox, 1932. Thomas Meighan, Charlotte Greenwood, William Bakewell, Ralph Morgan. Directed by Hamilton MacFadden.

En route from Europe a reformed Lone Wolf discovers on board ship that an old flame, who had married millions, has lost her jewels and that his long-lost son may have stolen them.

The Lone Wolf Returns. Columbia, 1936. Douglas, Gail Patrick, Tala Birell. Directed by Roy William Neill. A remake of the 1926 film.

About to steal some jewels, Lanyard meets a young lady (Patrick) at a costume ball, falls in love, and reforms. Other thieves frame him for a robbery.

The Lone Wolf in Paris. Columbia, 1938. Lederer, Frances Drake, Olaf Hytten, Walter Kingsford. Directed by Albert S. Rogell.

In his Paris hotel room, Lanyard finds a princess who pleads with him to steal back her stolen crown jewels, which she needs for a coronation.

The Lone Wolf Spy Hunt. Columbia, 1939. William, Ida Lupino, Rita Hayworth, Ralph Morgan. Directed by Peter Godfrey. A remake of *The Lone Wolf's Daughter*, with a screenplay by Jonathan LATIMER.

Retired in Washington, a widower with a young daughter (Virginia Weidler) and courted by the daughter (Lupino) of a senator, the Lone Wolf is forced by spies to steal government antiaircraft plans. In this urbane, witty film, the obligatory masked ball has a surrealistic motif.

The Lone Wolf Strikes. Columbia, 1940. William, Joan Perry, Robert Wilcox. Directed by Sidney Salkow.

Lanyard helps recover the famous Jordan necklace for the daughter of a murdered friend. The Lone Wolf's hapless manservant Jamison, played by Eric Blore, has become a regular in the series.

The Lone Wolf Meets a Lady. Columbia, 1940. William, Jean Muir, Victor Jory, Warren Hull. Directed by Salkow.

A troubled girl begs the Lone Wolf for help; not only has a priceless heirloom been stolen, but her husband, whom she thought dead long ago, has been found murdered in her apartment. Naturally, Lanyard is soon suspected of having killed him.

The Lone Wolf Keeps a Date. Columbia, 1940. William, Frances Robinson, Bruce Bennett. Directed by Salkow.

On a flight from Cuba, the young woman sitting next to Lanyard reveals to him that she is carrying $100,000 in ransom money.

The Lone Wolf Takes a Chance. Columbia, 1941. William, June Storey, Henry Wilcoxon. Directed by Salkow.

The inventor (Lloyd Bridges) of a burglar-proof baggage car used by the government to ship currency plates has been kidnapped by a gang of counterfeiters. Inspector Crane (Thurston Hall), who, in many of the films, is Lanyard's nemesis, suspects that the Lone Wolf is involved.

Secrets of the Lone Wolf. Columbia, 1941. William, Ruth Ford, Roger Clark, Jory. Directed by Edward Dmytryk. Story and screenplay by Stuart PALMER.

A group of French patriots have arrived in the United States by private yacht with the famed Napoleon jewels, which they plan to sell to raise money for the Resistance; Lanyard must make the yacht burglar-proof.

Counter-Espionage. Columbia, 1942. William, Hillary Brooke, Forrest Tucker. Directed by Dmytryk.

In wartime London, Lanyard rescues the daughter of the head of British Intelligence from a Nazi spy ring.

One Dangerous Night. Columbia, 1943. William, Marguerite Chapman, Mona Barrie, Birell, Margaret Hayes, Ann Savage. Directed by Michael Gordon.

Valet Jamison's light-fingered ways (he has stolen a purse to keep in practice) lead Lanyard to the body of a blackmailer who had several women victims.

Passport to Suez. Columbia, 1943. William, Savage, Sheldon Leonard, Bridges. Directed by Andre de Toth.

Arriving in spy-filled Alexandria, Lanyard discovers that Jamison's son, a young lieutenant, has become innocently involved in the theft of defense plans for the Suez Canal.

The Notorious Lone Wolf. Columbia, 1946. Gerald Mohr (Lanyard), Janis Carter, John Abbott. Directed by D. Ross Lederman.

Upon his return from military duty overseas (explaining a three-year absence from the screen), Lanyard is accused of stealing a sapphire from a museum; two Indian potentates are offering a huge reward for its return.

The Lone Wolf in Mexico. Columbia, 1947. Mohr, Sheila Ryan, Jacqueline de Wit, Nestor Paiva. Directed by Lederman.

Lanyard becomes involved in jewel theft, blackmail, and murder at a luxurious Mexico City casino.

The Lone Wolf in London. Columbia, 1947. Mohr, Nancy Saunders, Evelyn Ankers, Queenie Leonard, Alan Napier. Directed by Leslie Goodwins.

Scotland Yard suspects Lanyard of the theft of two jewels known as the Eyes of the Nile; his investigations lead him to a musical comedy star.

The Lone Wolf and His Lady. Columbia, 1949. Ron Randell (the ninth screen Lone Wolf), June Vincent, Alan Mowbray (Jamison in this film only), William Frawley. Directed by John Hoffman.

Lanyard is promptly arrested when the world's third-largest diamond is stolen from an exhibit he is covering on special assignment for a newspaper.

Television

Louis Hayward starred in a television series, first called *The Lone Wolf* and later syndicated as *Streets of Danger*, in the mid-1950s. The opening scene featured the Lanyard crest, a wolf's-head medallion.

LORAC, E. C. R. (pseudonym of Edith Caroline Rivett; 1894–1958). English detective novelist who also wrote as Carol Carnac. The author formed the more famous of her two pseudonyms by using her initials and, for the surname, the first part of her middle name, spelled backward. Her first novel was *The Murder on the Burrows*, published in 1931. She produced about two novels a year until her death.

Many of the detective novels written by Carol Carnac seem intended for a feminine audience, but some—especially those featuring Inspector Julian

Rivers—have a wider appeal. In *Upstairs, Downstairs* (1950) Rivers investigates a difficult case concerning the death of a clerk in a medical research center. The murder was cleverly planned and involved an automatic elevator.

The Lorac novels, on the other hand, usually feature the sober Scottish Chief Inspector Robert Macdonald. His early cases, such as *Bats in the Belfry* (1937), are routine, but several works of the early 1950s are noteworthy for their beautifully described rural settings and warmly shrewd observations of character. *Policeman in the Precinct* (1949; U.S. title: *And Then Put Out the Light*) probes the effect of malicious gossip on the perpetrator of a crime as Macdonald investigates what appears to be a simple case of heart failure due to electrocution. Stressing plot and character, this is one of the few Lorac novels to have been reprinted in paperback in recent years. In *Murder in the Mill-Race* (1952; U.S. title: *Speak Justly of the Dead*), set on the Devonshire moor, a hypocritical and overbearing woman is struck on the head and thrown into a millrace. In *Crook o' Lune* (1953; U.S. title: *Shepherd's Crook*) Macdonald goes to Lancashire to purchase a farm for his retirement years, but a fire and some sheep stealing quickly turn the detective's attention back into investigative channels.

LOVESEY, PETER (1936–). English educator and detective story writer. Educated at the University of Reading, Lovesey majored in English and is currently head of the General Education Department at Hammersmith and West London College. He lives in Surrey with his wife and two children.

Lovesey conceived the idea of writing detective stories set in the Victorian era and embarked on a series that features Sergeant Cribb and his assistant, Constable Thackeray. He does most of his research for these works in the National Newspaper Library at Colindale in north London. His wife, Jackie, an avid mystery fan, helps him with the plots. She holds a degree in psychology and is currently studying Chinese at the School of Oriental and African Studies.

Lovesey's first novel, *Wobble to Death* (1970), won the Panther-Macmillan First Crime Novel Competition from among a group of 250 entrants; he received a prize of £1,000. The story, which takes place in 1879, concerns a six-day walking race, called a "wobble," staged in an agricultural hall at Islington. It starts with the accidental death of one of the major contestants and the suicide of his remorseful manager, but there is more to these deaths than meets the eye. *The Detective Wore Silk Drawers* (1971), set in 1880, concerns the highly dangerous and illegal sport of bareknuckle boxing. It starts with the discovery of a headless corpse, continues with a policeman's efforts to penetrate a shady organization, and concludes with a twenty-six-round boxing match.

Abracadaver (1972), which takes place in 1881, is about a series of almost fatal but ridiculous accidents that occur to various music hall performers. *Mad Hatter's Holiday* (1973) moves to the coastal resort of Brighton. The discovery of a severed hand in the crocodile tank of the aquarium leads to more grisly finds on the beach. Cribb and Thackeray pursue their suspect across the Sussex downs to the Devil's Dyke in an exciting climax.

The Tick of Death (1974) is based on a historical event, the dynamiting of London in 1884 that caused the destruction of part of Scotland Yard. Sergeant Cribb infiltrates a gang of Irish-American extremists who are planting the "infernal machines" and is soon in danger of his own life.

LOWNDES, MRS. MARIE (ADELAIDE) BELLOC (1868–1947). English author of historical, romantic, and crime fiction and plays. The daughter of a French barrister, Louis Belloc, and an English mother, Marie Belloc was a member of a distinguished family. Her brother was the famous writer Hilaire Belloc; her great-great-grandfather was Joseph Priestley, the chemist who discovered oxygen; her grandmother was the translator of Harriet Beecher Stowe's *Uncle Tom's Cabin* (1852) in France; and her husband, Frederic Sawrey Lowndes, was a well-known journalist for the London *Times*.

She began writing at sixteen, although her first novel was not published until many years later, and she claimed to have written virtually every day of her life. A perfectionist, she rewrote constantly and painstakingly, and yet she produced a large number of books. Although she is chiefly remembered for her crime and suspense thrillers, her major ability was character development; she was overwhelmingly concerned about the relationships between her male and female characters, with particular emphasis on sexual matters (which were, however, discreetly handled).

Most of Mrs. Belloc Lowndes's novels are based on historical events. *The Lodger* (1913), which draws heavily on the Jack-the-Ripper murders, is the best. Originally a short story, written in 1911, it is now a full-length classic that has never been out of print. Mr. Sleuth, a gentle man as well as a gentleman, takes rooms in Mr. and Mrs. Bunting's lodging house. Inexplicably, Mrs. Bunting becomes more and more terrified of him as the series of brutal Ripper murders continues to horrify London. A psychological suspense thriller rather than a tale of detection, it is more a "why-done-it" than a "who-done-it"—the essential viewpoint of Mrs. Belloc Lowndes's best work.

The Chink in the Armour (1912) anticipates Francis Iles (Anthony BERKELEY) in some respects.

A bereaved widow listens attentively at the inquest; Joan Fontaine portrays the amoral title role in a cinematic version of Marie Belloc Lowndes's *Ivy*. [*Universal*]

Another tale of psychological terror, it presents a cunning murder plot—as told from the point of view of the unsuspecting intended victim. *Lizzie Borden: A Study in Conjecture* (1939) is a fictionalized account of the motives involved in that famous case, with passionate love offered as the explanation. The prologue and epilogue are factual.

Films

The classic delineation of the Jack-the-Ripper case, *The Lodger*, has intrigued a variety of film makers. The first official adaptation was by Alfred HITCHCOCK in 1926; the stranger in the upstairs room (Ivor Novello) turns out to be unlike the one in the novel. Other versions of *The Lodger* were produced.

The Lodger (U.S. title: *The Phantom Fiend*). Twickenham (British), 1932. Novello, Elizabeth Allan, Jack Hawkins. Directed by Maurice Elvey.

Again, the eccentric stranger renting upstairs (Novello) is suspect; the film ends with mob violence.

The Lodger. Twentieth Century-Fox, 1944. Laird Cregar, Merle Oberon, George Sanders, Sir Cedric Hardwicke, Sara Allgood. Directed by John Brahm.

London is terrorized by Jack the Ripper, and an elderly couple suspect the fastidious, unorthodox pathologist to whom they have rented a room.

The Man in the Attic. Twentieth Century-Fox, 1953. Jack Palance, Constance Smith, Byron Palmer, Rhys Williams, Frances Bavier. Directed by Hugo Fregonese.

In this close remake of the 1944 version, the lodger again tries to do away with the elderly couple's niece, a dance hall girl, because of the evil of her beauty.

Films have also been based on other Lowndes novels.

Letty Lynton. MGM, 1932. Joan Crawford, Robert Montgomery, Nils Asther, Lewis Stone. Directed by Clarence Brown. Based on the 1931 novel *Letty Lynton*.

Distraught when her former lover refuses to return intimate letters to her, a girl prepares poisoned wine for her own suicide; but when he drinks it instead, she is accused of his murder.

Ivy. Universal, 1947. Joan Fontaine, Patric Knowles, Herbert Marshall, Hardwicke. Directed by Sam Wood. Based on *The Story of Ivy* (1927).

Her husband's fortune gone, a beautiful, amoral woman decides to poison him so that she can advance herself unhampered.

LUPIN, ARSÈNE (Creator: Maurice LEBLANC). Known as the "Prince of Thieves," Lupin is France's greatest criminal, rivaling the Englishman A. J. RAFFLES and the American the Infallible Godahl (see GODAHL, THE INFALLIBLE), although his style differs from theirs.

A brilliant rogue, he pursues his career with carefree élan, mocking the law for the sheer joy of it, rather than for purely personal gain. Young, handsome, brave, and quick-witted, he has a joie de vivre uniquely and recognizably French. His sense of humor and conceit make life difficult for the police, who attribute most of the major crimes in France to him and his gang of ruffians and urchins.

Like most French criminals and detectives, Lupin is a master of disguise. His skill is attested to by the fact that he once became Lenormand, chief of the Sûreté, and, for four years, conducted official investigations into his own activities. He employs numerous aliases, including Jim Barnett, Prince Renine, Le Duc de Charmerace, Don Luis Perenna, and Ralph de Limezy; his myriad names, combined with his brilliant disguises, make it nearly impossible for the police to identify him (the reader of his exploits sometimes encounters a similar difficulty).

After a long criminal career of uninterrupted successes, Lupin begins to shift position and aids the police in their work—usually for his own purposes and without their knowledge. Toward the end of his career, he becomes a full-fledged detective, and although he is as successful in his endeavors as ever before, his heart does not seem to be in it.

The first book about him is *Arsène Lupin: Gentleman-Cambrioleur* (1907; U.S. title: *The Exploits of Arsène Lupin*, 1907; reissued as *The Extraordinary Adventures of Arsène Lupin, Gentleman-Burglar*, 1910; British title: *The Seven of Hearts*, 1908). One of the stories, "Holmlock Shears Arrives Too Late," is a parody of Sherlock HOLMES. The second book in the series, and the worst, is *Arsène Lupin contre Herlock Sholmes* (1908; British

Charles Korvin as a formally attired Arsène spies on an heiress (Ella Raines) he is trying to help in the 1944 *Enter Arsène Lupin*. [*Universal*]

title: *The Fair-haired Lady*, 1909; reissued as *Arsène Lupin versus Holmlock Shears*, 1909; reissued again as *The Arrest of Arsène Lupin*, 1911; U.S. title: *The Blonde Lady*, 1910; reissued as *Arsène Lupin versus Herlock Sholmes*, 1910). Other short story collections about Lupin are *The Confessions of Arsène Lupin* (1912), *The Eight Strokes of the Clock* (1922), and *Jim Barnett Intervenes* (1928; U.S. title: *Arsène Lupin Intervenes*). Among the best of the novels are *813* (1910), in which Lupin, accused of murder, heads the police investigation to clear himself by finding the true killer; and *The Hollow Needle* (1910), in which Lupin is shot by a beautiful girl and falls in love with her, vowing to give up his life of crime. Among the other Lupin novels are *The Crystal Stopper* (1913), *The Teeth of the Tiger* (1914), *The Golden Triangle* (1917), and *The Memoirs of Arsène Lupin* (1925; British title: *The Candlestick with Seven Branches*).

Films

There are many early screen versions of Arsène Lupin's basic conflicts with the Paris police, both in the United States (starting in 1917) and in Europe. *The Teeth of the Tiger* (Paramount, with David Powell) of 1919 is an old-dark-house murder melodrama, with sliding panels, secret passageways, and serial-like thrills. Wedgewood Newell portrays Lupin in *813* (Robertson-Cole, 1920), impersonating a police officer to clear himself of a murder charge. There are several later European Lupins, notably French, in films even until the 1950s. The most important American Lupin films are given below.

Arsène Lupin. MGM, 1932. John Barrymore, Lionel Barrymore, Karen Morley, John Miljan. Directed by Jack Conway. Based on the play by Leblanc and Francis de Croisset.

When the silk-hatted Lupin announces that he

will steal a famous painting from the Louvre under the nose of the police and does so, a pretty lady crook is used by the chief of detectives to lure him into a trap.

Arsène Lupin Returns. MGM, 1938. Melvyn Douglas, Warren William, Virginia Bruce, Monty Woolley, E. E. Clive. Directed by George Fitzmaurice.

The signature of Arsène Lupin, long thought dead, is scrawled across a safe from which a necklace has been stolen; the real Lupin, innocent and now living as a country gentleman, is as perplexed as the police are.

Enter Arsène Lupin. Universal, 1944. Charles Korvin, Ella Raines, J. Carrol Naish, Gale Sondergaard, Miles Mander. Directed by Ford Beebe.

International thief Lupin, on a train from Istanbul to Paris, steals an emerald from a young heiress but returns it when he begins to suspect that the girl's aunt and uncle plan to murder her.

LUSTGARTEN, EDGAR (MARCUS) (1907–). English novelist and criminologist. Born in Manchester, the only child of a successful lawyer, Lustgarten attended Manchester Grammar School and Oxford University, where his gift of oratory gained him the presidency of the Union. Soon after graduation he was called to the bar; he established a flourishing practice in Manchester. He was married in 1932.

Lustgarten's early interest in writing led him to produce short plays, features, and song lyrics, all under a pseudonym, for radio broadcast. With the start of the war he gave up his law practice, moved to London, and spent five years working with the BBC staff in counterpropaganda.

As the pressure of work declined in the last days of the war, he tried his hand at writing a novel; the very successful *A Case to Answer* was the result. Turning his full attention to writing, he specialized in true and fictional crime works. He has since served in many capacities at and written material for the BBC and ATV, including a series on famous trials for the BBC.

Lustgarten's true-crime books, *Verdict in Dispute* (1949), *Defender's Triumph* (1951), *The Woman in the Case* (1955), and *The Business of Murder* (1968), have established him as the foremost contemporary analyst of the subject. He currently resides in London and claims that, although he can write anywhere, it is a slow and painful process, and he can manage to produce only about 600 words a day.

A Case to Answer (1947; U.S. title: *One More Unfortunate*) deals with the trial of a young businessman for the sordid murder of a Soho prostitute. Its documentary realism provided a contrast to most English or American legal mysteries of the time, and its climax strongly implied not only that the verdict was unfair but that the entire British judicial system was less than perfect. *Game for Three Losers* (1952) concerns an elaborate plot to blackmail a highly regarded member of Parliament whose prospects seem bright. The politician's attempt to expose this scheme results in disaster for all, and the outcome is an indictment of a legal system that fails to protect the innocent and, moreover, punishes them along with the guilty.

LYALL, GAVIN (TUDOR) (1932–). English thriller writer. Born in Birmingham, the son of an accountant, he was educated at King Edward's School in Birmingham and at Pembroke College, Cambridge University, where he received a B.A. degree with honors. He served in the RAF (1951–1953) as a pilot.

After working for *Picture Post* (1956–1957), he became a television director for the BBC in 1958 and then returned to journalism, working for the *Sunday Times* and later becoming aviation editor for the paper. In 1963 he turned to free-lance writing. His articles on many subjects, including flying and motoring, have been published in such magazines as the *Spectator, Lilliput*, and *Everybody's*. Lyall lives in London with his wife, the former Katharine Whitehorn, whom he married in 1958.

Lyall has used material from his own background in a series of literate thrillers that have been critically acclaimed and popular with readers in the United States and in England. His first novel, *The Wrong Side of the Sky* (1961), was suggested by a conversation Lyall had had with a British European Airways pilot, and the setting was drawn from his honeymoon trip to the Greek islands and from his experiences as a journalist in Libya. His second novel, *The Most Dangerous Game* (1963), is a spy story that, like its predecessor, involves flying and includes a manhunt that compares favorably with the one in the Richard CONNELL story of the same name. It was a runner-up in the Crime Writers' Association (CWA) contest for best novel of that year. *Shooting Script* (1966) is an accurate view of film making in the Caribbean that includes several aerial sequences. *Midnight Plus One* (1965) concerns a pilot's efforts to fly his millionaire employer from Brittany to a business meeting in Liechtenstein while evading the French police, who want the employer on a false charge of rape. The CWA considered this book to be the best crime novel of 1965 and, in addition, presented Lyall with an award in 1970 for editing the organization's series of Crime Background Pamphlets.

LYNCH, LAWRENCE L. (pseudonym of Emma Murdock Van Deventer). American detective novelist. Her series of thrillers, originally published in Chi-

The English editions of Lawrence Lynch books, with their picturesque covers, are often more sought after than the American first editions. The first English edition of *The Last Stroke* was published by Ward, Lock in 1897.

cago and frequently reprinted in England, and widely read there, includes *Shadowed by Three* (1879), featuring private detective Francis Ferrars; *The New Detective Story: The Diamond Coterie* (1884), with Neil J. Bathurst, private investigator; *A Mountain Mystery; or, The Outlaws of the Rockies* (1886), with Stanhope of the Mounties; *Against Odds* (1894), with Carl Masters of the Chicago Police Department; *No Proof* (1895), with Kenneth Jasper, a young criminal lawyer turned private detective; and *The Last Stroke* (1896), also with Ferrars.

LYNDE, FRANCIS (1856–1930). American novelist and short story writer. Although Lynde was born in Lewiston, N.Y., his fiction accurately portrays the American West. His mystery novels include *Blind Man's Buff* (1928) and *Young Blood* (1929), but his best and most famous work is a short story collection, *Scientific Sprague* (1912). The six stories are about Calvin Sprague, a government chemist who is sent west to test soils but finds time to solve railroad mysteries for his friend Richard Maxwell, the new general superintendent of the Nevada Short Line. The stories are universally praised for their authentic portrayal of railroading.

LYNDS, DENNIS. *See* COLLINS, MICHAEL.

M

MABUSE, DR. (Creator: Norbert Jacques). The enduring European master criminal was brought to the screen by director Fritz LANG in Germany in 1922, with a screenplay written by his wife, Thea von Harbou, based on a novel by Jacques.

Films

Dr. Mabuse, the Gambler. UCO (Germany), 1922 (released in two sections a few months apart, called *The Great Gambler* and *Inferno*). Rudolf Klein-Rogge (Mabuse), Aud Egede Nissen, Alfred Abel, Bernhard Goetzke (Prosecutor von Wenk), Paul Richter.

Mabuse, a supercriminal, often in disguise and portraying several personages in turn, constantly spins webs to entrap weak, unwary victims in the clubs, cabarets, séance chambers, and dark alleys of a Germany increasingly given to decadence. A plodding public prosecutor, Von Wenk, finally ferrets out and raids Mabuse's secret headquarters, even though Mabuse had used hypnosis (a favorite weapon) to make Von Wenk attempt to destroy himself. His gang of thieves, counterfeiters, and murderers caught, Mabuse collapses, his mind gone.

The great success of Mabuse caused Lang to use the character eleven years later.

The Testament of Dr. Mabuse. Nero (Germany), 1933. Klein-Rogge, Otto Wernicke (Inspector Lohmann, a police figure carried over from Lang's 1931 film, *M*), Oscar Beregi, Gustav Diessl, Vera Liessem. Screenplay by Von Harbou.

Mabuse is in an asylum run by the respected Dr. Baum (Beregi), scribbling volumes of mad plans for dominating society by spreading terrorism. Ultimately Mabuse dies, but not before he hypnotizes Baum, causing him to take over his plots and identity. Concealed behind a screen, Baum directs new criminal gangs. Finally caught by a bulldog policeman, he too goes insane.

Clashes with Minister Goebbels over the film and its anti-Nazi overtones caused Lang to hurriedly leave Germany. After nearly three decades in the United States, he was invited by officials of the German film industry to direct once more in that country. His second project after his return was a Mabuse film.

The Thousand Eyes of Dr. Mabuse. CCC Films (Germany), 1960. Peter van Eyck, Dawn Addams, Wolfgang Preiss, Gert Fröbe (Superintendent Krass), Werner Peters.

A television reporter is killed at a traffic intersection while waiting in his car for the light to change (Lang had first used the device in the 1928 *Spies*), an event predicted by a bearded, blind clairvoyant, Cornelius (Preiss): "I see dark clouds—murder." At the lush Hotel Luxor, secretly invested with electronic eyes and ears, a young American millionaire rescues a distraught girl from a high ledge and

News photographer Daliah Lavi observes policeman Gert Fröbe, on the trail of a supposedly long-dead master criminal, in the 1961 German thriller *The Return of Dr. Mabuse*. [*CCC Films*]

falls in love with her. She is actually the minion of an unknown mastermind, a criminal who exploits the dead Mabuse's plans and is his spiritual heir, and who wishes to extend—by her marriage—his influence to the United States.

The Thousand Eyes of Dr. Mabuse was Lang's last film, but other German directors continued the series. Through all the popular sequels, the Mabuse papers inspire new supercriminals and madmen, all fervent followers of the long-dead evil genius, and most often played, sometimes in disguise, by German actors Wolfgang Preiss and Walter Rilla.

The Return of Dr. Mabuse. CCC Films (Germany), 1961. Fröbe (Inspector Lohmann), Lex Barker, Daliah Lavi, Preiss. Directed by Harald Reinl.

The unknown Mabuse figure takes over a prison, to use convicts in his scheme for world domination.

The Invisible Dr. Mabuse. CCC Films (Germany), 1962. Fröbe, Senta Berger, Helmut Schmid, Directed by Reinl.

The Mabuse figure, in seeking a formula for invisibility, terrorizes a young ballerina who nightly performs a curious dance that ends with her being guillotined.

The Testament of Dr. Mabuse. CCC Films (Germany), 1962. Fröbe, Senta Berger, Helmut Schmid, Preiss, Rilla. Directed by Werner Klinger. An exact reworking of the 1933 film, except that, now, the mantle is worn by another.

The madhouse scribblings of a new Mabuse figure (Preiss) intrigue a new asylum chief, Professor Pohland (Rilla).

Scotland Yard versus Dr. Mabuse. CCC Films (Germany), 1963. Van Eyck, Sabine Bethmann, Peters, Klaus Kinski, Rilla. Directed by Paul May. Based on a novel by Bryan Edgar Wallace.

Professor Pohland, inspired by Mabuse, goes to England to acquire an electronic device that can enslave minds. He sends out telepathic orders to thirteen political leaders—and the mother of a young Scotland Yard man.

Death Rays of Dr. Mabuse. CCC Films (Germany), 1963. Van Eyck, Leo Genn, O. E. Hasse, Yvonne Furneaux, Yoko Tani, Preiss, Rilla, Robert Beatty. Directed by Hugo Fregonese.

At the coast of Malta, Pohland seeks a death-ray mirror that can destroy any city on earth. The underwater scuba sequences, with frogmen en masse, are remarkably similar to those in the James BOND film *Thunderball* two years later. At the finale, a dying Pohland mutters, "It was not me; it was Mabuse—he used my body."

By the mid-1960s the postwar Mabuse series (most of the scripts had been written by Ladislas Fodor) had disappeared, German audiences turning to the similar but more diverse thrillers based on Edgar WALLACE books.

MAC (Creator: Thomas B. DEWEY). Until *The Love-Death Thing*, this private detective is known only as Mac; in this book he signs a hotel register as "Mac Robinson."

As a product of Chicago's tenements, Mac joined the city's police force but was dismissed when he solved a case that the mob preferred to remain unsolved. He becomes a private detective and eventually gains a reputation as the best in Chicago. Nonetheless, he maintains a modest combination office-apartment near Michigan Boulevard on the North Side. Although he has a good relationship with Donovan, his mentor on the police force, he is resentful of most policemen, especially those of dubious honesty. He is a lonely man but never so sorry for himself that he cannot become involved in the problems of others. His sympathy for the young is well known, but in fact he helps most underdogs, regardless of whether he might earn a fee. In *Deadline* he leaves his Chicago office to reopen a murder investigation in a hostile, small downstate Illinois town; his client waits on death row. After being summoned to southern California on two cases, Mac decides to settle there permanently in *The Taurus Trip*. In *The King Killers* he is involved in the murder of a leader of a Neo-Nazi movement. He goes to Los Angeles in *The Love-Death Thing* to find the missing daughter of a Chicago businessman who suspects—correctly—that his child has become the prey of drug pushers.

CHECKLIST

1947	*Draw the Curtain Close*
1953	*Every Bet's a Sure Thing*
1954	*Prey for Me*
1955	*The Mean Streets*
1956	*The Brave, Bad Girls*
1958	*You've Got Him Cold*
1959	*The Case of the Chased and the Unchaste*
1962	*How Hard to Kill*
1963	*A Sad Song Singing*
1964	*Don't Cry for Long*
1965	*Portrait of a Dead Heiress*
1966	*Deadline*
1967	*Death and Taxes*
1968	*The King Killers* (British title: *Death Turns Right*)
1969	*The Love-Death Thing*
1970	*The Taurus Trip*

McALLISTER, ALISTER. *See* BROCK, LYNN.

McBAIN, ED (1926–). American mystery-detective novelist. Born in New York, the son of Marie (Coppola) and Charles Lombino, he legally changed his name from Salvatore A. Lombino to Evan Hunter (after attending Evander Childs High School and Hunter College, although he claims that there is no connection between the schools and his pseudonym, that the suggestion that such a connec-

Police psychiatrist Kent Smith searches the city streets for an elusive attacker of women in *The Mugger*, a realistic screen version of an Ed McBain work. [*United Artists*]

tion exists is the result of gossip). He married Anita Melnick in 1949; they had three children. He is now married to the former Vann Hughes Finley.

Hunter held several jobs briefly, including teaching at two vocational high schools in 1950. The experiences provided him with the background for his most famous book, *The Blackboard Jungle* (1954), a grim picture of violence and racial tension in New York secondary schools. Also under the Evan Hunter by-line, he published *The Jungle Kids* (1956; expanded edition published in England as *The Last Spin and Other Stories*, 1960), a collection of stories about teenagers and crime—street gangs, drug addiction, Russian roulette, the menace of a mugger, the sex murder of a baby-sitter.

For paperback publication he wrote *I Like 'Em Tough* (1958), a short story collection, and *I'm Cannon—For Hire* (1958) under the Curt Cannon by-line. These first-person accounts involve a tough former private eye who lives in the Bowery and freely describes himself as a derelict. "I sleep on park benches when I don't have the money for a bed," he says, and "I drink twenty-five hours out of twenty-four."

As Ed McBain, he produces the long series of novels about the 87th Precinct (see 87TH PRECINCT, THE), which present social problems at the street level. These starkly realistic police procedural tales have a range of subjects and approaches—from intangible terror to physical brutality to slapstick humor—that is unmatched in versatility for this subgenre. The only McBain novels not about the 87th Precinct are *The Sentries* (1965) and *Where There's Smoke* (1975).

Hunter has also written scripts for television and films, including the screenplay for Daphne DU MAURIER's story "The Birds" (an Alfred HITCHCOCK film). He completed Craig RICE's novel *The April Robin Murders* (1958) when she died suddenly. As Hunt Collins, he published *Cut Me In* in 1954, and, as Richard Marsten, he produced five paperback novels with mystery-detective themes in the 1950s.

McCLOY, HELEN (WORRELL CLARKSON) (1904–). American author of mystery novels and short stories. Miss McCloy's father, William C. McCloy, was managing editor of the *New York Evening Sun* for eighteen years. She received a Quaker education at the Friends' School in Brooklyn and completed her education in Europe. She remained abroad to write about politics and art for American and European newspapers and magazines. Having read Sherlock HOLMES as a young girl, she retained an interest in mysteries and began to write them in the late 1930s after her return to the United States. She was once married to mystery writer Brett HALLIDAY; they have a daughter and a granddaughter. She lives in Boston, where, in 1971, she helped found a New England chapter of the Mystery Writers of America (MWA). She became the first woman president of MWA in 1950; three years later she received the Edgar award for mystery criticism.

Miss McCloy's first novel, *Dance of Death* (1938), and many of her subsequent books have been about psychiatrist-detective Dr. Basil WILLING. *Cue for Murder* (1942) conveys the atmosphere of early World War II and has also been praised for the "intricate clueing" in its story of murder onstage during a Broadway revival of Sardou's *Fédora*. *The One That Got Away* (1945) made more "best" lists than any other mystery that year, critics applauding its Scottish setting and its characterizations. A non-Willing mystery, *Panic* (1944), is set in a remote cottage in the Catskills and is notable for its use of cryptoanalysis. Miss McCloy invented a variation of Vigenère's "unbreakable cipher" for this book.

Miss McCloy had published only one short story before she entered the first contest held by *Ellery Queen's Mystery Magazine (EQMM)*, in 1946, but she won second prize with "Chinoiserie," a story set in Peking during the early 1860s. In "The Other Side of the Curtain," a 1947 *EQMM* third-prize winner, an anonymous psychiatrist plays an important role, but it was not until her 1948 second-prize winner that Basil Willing first appeared in a short story. That story, "Through a Glass, Darkly," was a retelling of the legend of the Doppelgänger and was expanded into a novel of the same name in 1950. In "The Singing Diamonds," winner of a special prize awarded by *EQMM* in 1949, Willing investigates reports of flying saucers; it became the title story of a 1965 collection of works by Miss McCloy.

McCONNELL, JAMES D. R. *See* SURBRIDGE, FRANCIS.

McCUTCHEON, GEORGE BARR (1866–1928). American romantic novelist and dramatist. Born near Lafayette, Ind., the son of Clara (Glick) and John Barr McCutcheon, he ran away from Purdue University to join a touring theatrical company and then worked as a reporter and city editor for several years. In 1904 he married Marie (Van Antwerp) Fay, a widow.

His first published book, *Graustark* (1901), is a highly romantic tale of a mythical Balkan kingdom; it sold a million copies and was an equally successful play. Although McCutcheon had sold the rights for only $500, his publisher voluntarily paid him royalties. His only detective books involve Anderson CROW.

MacDONALD, JOHN D[ANN] (1916–). American author of short stories and mystery novels. Born in Sharon, Pa., he moved to Utica, N.Y., when he was twelve. He received a B.S. degree from Syracuse University and an M.B.A. degree from the Harvard School of Business Administration. In 1937 he married Dorothy Mary Prentiss, an artist. Their only child, John Prentiss MacDonald, resides in Christchurch, New Zealand.

After several relatively unsuccessful years in business, MacDonald entered the Army, serving from 1940 to 1946. He was with the OSS in the China-Burma-India theater and had achieved the rank of lieutenant-colonel by the time he was discharged. He began writing short stories for his wife because Army censorship restricted his personal letters to her. She sold his first story, "Interlude in India," to *Story Magazine* while he was still in the service.

John D. MacDonald.

After he returned to the United States, he continued to write, selling sports, science fiction, adventure, fantasy, and mystery stories to the PULP MAGAZINES under his own name and such house names as Scott O'Hara, John Lane, Peter Reed, John Wade Farrell, Henry Rieser, and Robert Henry. Also during this period, he sold stories to such "slicks" as *Liberty, Collier's, Cosmopolitan,* and *Esquire*.

In 1949 he moved to Florida, where proximity to the water permitted him to pursue his hobby, boating, which he has used as background for many of his books. He is also interested in travel and true crime; his book on the famous Coppolino trial, *No Deadly Drug,* was published in 1968.

The once-flourishing pulp magazine market had dwindled by 1950, its place gradually taken by paperback originals. MacDonald's first mystery novel, *The Brass Cupcake,* was published as a paperback in 1950 and was followed by more than fifty other mysteries, making him probably more renowned than any other writer of paperback originals. Most of his books, including his highly successful Travis MCGEE series, are set in Florida. Using his business background, MacDonald has integrated various aspects of the state's economic life into his mysteries. In *A Key to the Suite* (1962), he presents a devastating view of a Miami Beach hotel hosting a convention. In *Pale Gray for Guilt* (1968) McGee is pitted against "Tech-Tex," a large business conglomerate trying to destroy the life and business of one of his friends, the owner of a small marina-motel.

In many mysteries MacDonald explores human psychology in considerable depth. *The Executioners* (1958) is about a peaceful man who is transformed into a potential murderer when his family is threatened by the psychopath he once sent to jail. In *The Last One Left* (1967), a book nominated for the Mystery Writers of America (MWA) Edgar, the physical and psychological traumas experienced by refugees from Castro's Cuba are considered.

MacDonald's narrative abilities have gained him considerable praise, ranging from Julian SYMON's discussion of the "efficiency of the plotting" to Richard Condon's description of him as "the great American storyteller." However, since his books appear mainly in paperback editions, they often are not reviewed. Anthony BOUCHER, one of the critics who reviewed MacDonald from the start, said of an early work, *Dead Low Tide* (1953): "The writing is

Unable to contain his anger, Gregory Peck lashes out at the ex-convict (Robert Mitchum) who has been stalking him and his family in the film version of John D. MacDonald's *Cape Fear*. [*Universal*]

marked by sharp observation, vivid dialogue, and a sense of sweet warm horror." Referring to MacDonald's ability to portray American society and mores, Boucher called him "the John O'Hara of the crime-suspense story."

MacDonald is one of the few writers whose work is the subject of a continuing publication. Since March 1965 the *JDM Bibliophile* has been published by Len and June Moffatt of Downey, Calif. In 1972 the MWA honored its former president (1962) with its Grand Master Award for his lifelong contribution to the mystery. He also received the French Grand Prix de Littérature Policière in 1964 and the Benjamin Franklin Award for the best American short story in 1955.

Films

Man-Trap. Paramount, 1961. Jeffrey Hunter, David Janssen, Stella Stevens. Directed by Edmond O'Brien. Based on a story by MacDonald.

A former Marine, bored, and troubled with an alcoholic wife, is persuaded by an Army buddy to recover from a South American delegate $3 million that supposedly belongs to his boss.

Cape Fear. Universal, 1962. Gregory Peck, Robert Mitchum, Polly Bergen, Martin Balsam, Jack Kruschen, Telly Savalas, Barrie Chase. Directed by J. Lee Thompson. Based on *The Executioners*.

A lawyer is terrorized by a sadistic, brutal former convict whom he had helped put in prison for a sex crime eight years earlier; finally, he must take the law into his own hands.

MACDONALD, JOHN ROSS. *See* MACDONALD, ROSS.

MacDONALD, PHILIP (1896?–). Anglo-American author of detective fiction. Little is known about his personal life except that he is the grandson of the Scottish poet and juvenile novelist George MacDonald. He served in Mesopotamia with a British cavalry regiment during World War I and has maintained a lifetime interest in horses, ranging from training them for military service to fancy riding and jumping at horse shows. In 1931 he and his wife, novelist F. Ruth Howard, moved to Hollywood, where they raised prizewinning Great Danes and where he was an active scenarist, with the 1940 film version of Daphne DU MAURIER's novel *Rebecca* (1938) among his credits.

His first detective novel, *The Rasp* (1924), introduced his famous semiofficial detective, Anthony GETHRYN, to the public. The novels in which Gethryn appears, as well as MacDonald's other mysteries, have one essential point in common—they are scrupulously fair to the reader, with no clues hidden or neglected. MacDonald's philosophy on the subject is: "The ideal detective story is a sort of competition between the author and reader."

Dr. Alcazar, a combination seer-detective-rogue, although less well known than Gethryn (appearing in only three short stories), is a more original character. MacDonald has also written mysteries as Martin Porlock (*Mystery at Friar's Pardon*, 1931; *Mystery at Kensington Gore*, 1932; and *X. v. Rex*, 1933, U.S. title: *The Mystery of the Dead Police*); with his father, Ronald MacDonald, as Oliver Fleming (*Ambrotox and Limping Dick*, 1920; and *The Spandau Quid*, 1923); and as Anthony Lawless (*Harbour*, 1931). Other non-Gethryn mystery novels include *Rynox* (1930; U.S. title: *The Rynox Murder Mystery*), *R.I.P.* (1933; U.S. title: *Menace*), and *Guest in the House* (1954). He collaborated with A. Boyd Correll to produce *The Dark Wheel* (1948).

Some critics consider MacDonald's short stories to be superior to his novels; they have won five second prizes in the annual contests held by *Ellery Queen's Mystery Magazine*. The best have been collected in *Something to Hide* (1952; British title: *Fingers of Fear*), which won the Mystery Writers of America Edgar for the year's best book of short stories; *The Man Out of the Rain and Other Stories* (1955); and *Death and Chicanery* (1962).

Films

MacDonald has been a prolific Hollywood screenwriter and has written the screenplays for several Charlie CHAN and Mr. MOTO films. *The Lost Patrol* (RKO, 1934), in which British soldiers lost in the desert are shot down, one by one, by unseen Arab marauders, has been remade several different ways, including as a western. MacDonald's major screen mysteries, aside from those involving Gethryn, are discussed below.

The Mystery of Mr. X. MGM, 1934. Robert Montgomery, Elizabeth Allan, Lewis Stone, Ralph Forbes. Directed by Edgar Selwyn. Based on *The Mystery of the Dead Police.*

Nicholas Revel (Montgomery), a diamond thief, decides to give Scotland Yard some unofficial help when a baffling series of murders of policemen occurs.

The Menace. Paramount, 1934. Gertrude Michael, Paul Cavanagh, Berton Churchill, Ray Milland, Halliwell Hobbes. Directed by Ralph Murphy. Based on *R.I.P.*

Three people on vacation in East Africa insist that a friend leave his post at a new dam to join them for a party; the dam gives way, and the distraught friend commits suicide. A year later, in California, his brother announces that he will kill the trio.

The Hour of 13. MGM (British), 1952. Peter Lawford, Dawn Addams, Roland Culver, Derek Bond. Directed by Harold French. Also based on *The Mystery of the Dead Police,* but set in Edwardian times.

Eleven British policemen have been killed by a maniac called "The Terror," and, to clear his own name, a suave young jewel thief decides to give Scotland Yard a hand—especially since he has caught a glimpse of the commissioner's pretty daughter.

MacDONALD, RONALD. *See* MACDONALD, PHILIP.

MACDONALD, ROSS (pseudonym of Kenneth Millar; 1915–). American novelist and mystery writer. One of the few mystery writers also regarded as a major American novelist, Millar was born in Los Gatos, Calif., but when he was an infant, his parents returned to their native Canada, separating soon afterward. He was brought up by his mother, who was in ill health, and they lived with her relatives in various parts of Canada. Millar graduated from Kitchener Collegiate Institute in Ontario in 1932 and then attended the University of Western Ontario. When his mother died, he left school for a year and traveled throughout England, France, and Germany. Shortly after he returned to Canada, he married Margaret Sturm (*see* MILLAR, MARGARET), whom he had known in school there.

After Millar graduated from Western Ontario, the couple moved to Ann Arbor, where he attended the Graduate School of the University of Michigan, receiving a Phi Beta Kappa key and a doctorate in English literature; his dissertation was on Coleridge. He also taught at the university before serving in the Navy during World War II, most of the time as a communications officer aboard an escort carrier in the Pacific.

Ross Macdonald. [*Alfred A. Knopf*]

While her husband was in the Navy, Margaret Millar settled in Santa Barbara, Calif., where they still live. Their only daughter, Linda, died of a stroke in 1970 at the age of thirty-one. The Millars are both keen observers of wildlife, especially birds, and helped found the Santa Barbara branch of the National Audubon Society. Committed to preserving the ecology of their region, they have led demonstrations against industrial encroachment, especially following the 1967 oil spills that damaged local beaches.

In 1941 Margaret Millar published her first mystery, and her husband's own interest in the genre was reawakened. He had read mysteries as a young boy and had even written a Sherlock HOLMES parody, "The South Sea Soup Company, about "Herlock Sholmes." In 1944 he published *The Dark Tunnel,* the first of four mysteries that appeared under his own name, the others being *Trouble Follows Me* (1946), *Blue City* (1947), and *The Three Roads* (1948). When he realized that his books could be confused with those of his wife, whose own career as a mystery writer was flourishing, he adopted the pseudonym John Ross Macdonald; the last name had been his father's middle name. However, he was now being confused with another rising writer, John D. MACDONALD. Thus Millar made his final name change, shortening his pseudonym to Ross Macdonald. All his earlier works have been reprinted under that name.

Millar's early mysteries contain many autobiographical elements. *The Dark Tunnel,* which he wrote while teaching at Michigan, is set at fictional Midwestern University and deals with the threat of nazism, a concern of the author's since his prewar travels in Germany. The protagonist of *Trouble Follows Me* (1946) is a Navy officer who follows a murder trail from Hawaii to Detroit and then to San Diego. In his fifth mystery, *The Moving Target* (1949; originally published under the pseudonym John Macdonald), Millar created his famous private detective, Lew ARCHER, who he admits is partly an autobiographical creation—"I'm not Archer, exactly, but Archer is me"—and whom he has featured in all but two of his subsequent books: *Meet Me at the Morgue* (1953; British title: *Experience with Evil*) and *The Ferguson Affair* (1960).

Millar continues to use the mystery as his chosen medium for conveying his views on life in the United States. He is aware of the potential in the mystery for complicated plots, and he views "plot as a vehicle of meaning. It should be as complex as contemporary life, but balanced enough to say true things about it." As a result, well integrated into his plots are subjects seldom considered seriously in the mystery genre, including race relations, ecology, and the "generation gap."

Blacks have figured prominently in *Trouble Follows Me* and in the Archer novels *The Ivory Grin* (1952) and *The Barbarous Coast* (1956). Millar's description of the black community in Detroit in the aftermath of the 1943 race riots in *Trouble Follows Me* was ahead of its time, and since then he has consistently depicted blacks as real people, not stereotypes.

Early in his career Millar showed his awareness of California's natural beauty and his sadness at the spoilage of its air and water. By the late 1960s he thought of writing about "an ecological crime" threatening an entire city. In *The Underground Man* (1971) a man-made forest fire threatens part of the city that is the fictional counterpart of Millar's Santa Barbara. In 1964 a real fire was brought under control only 200 yards from Millar's home, as he waited on his roof, water hose in hand, to extinguish sparks. When he wrote *The Underground Man,* he rejected the idea of using the 1967 oil spill off Santa Barbara, but in *Sleeping Beauty* (1973) he did integrate this "crime" into his plot.

Since *The Galton Case* (1959) the dominant theme in the Macdonald mysteries has been the search by children for their "lost" fathers. Millar admitted that this book, written after a period of psychotherapy, marked "a personal and, especially, a professional, watershed." There is much autobiography in this book, in which Archer travels to Canada to trace a father missing more than twenty years.

As this theme recurs (perhaps too frequently) in subsequent Macdonald books, it is often accompanied by another, the problem of communication between parent and child. In books such as *The Chill* (1964), *The Far Side of the Dollar* (1965), *The Instant Enemy* (1968), *The Goodbye Look* (1969), and *The Underground Man,* young people reject their parents' affluence and seek their own identity by running away or taking drugs. Their parents often react as does the mother in *The Underground Man* who says of her daughter, "As you can see, we gave her everything; but it wasn't what she wanted."

Although Millar's writing skill was quickly recognized, Howard HAYCRAFT believed that he relied too heavily on psychology, and Raymond CHANDLER thought that he depended too much on simile. To Julian SYMONS, his use of metaphor and simile was uneven, though occasionally vivid. By the 1950s, after Archer had been introduced, Anthony BOUCHER said that Millar was a better novelist than either Dashiell HAMMETT or Chandler and had developed the private eye novel into a medium in which an author could write about "people with enough feeling to be hurt and enough complexity to do wrong." Richard SALE said that Macdonald had "become the best writer we have about California."

Since 1969 Millar has been accepted as an important American novelist. Glowing front-page reviews in *The New York Times Book Review* and a cover article in *Newsweek* helped his books to become best sellers. During the 1960s Boucher invariably selected a Macdonald book for his annual "best" list. The Crime Writers' Association selected *The Chill* as runner-up for best novel in 1964, and in 1965 the organization selected *The Far Side of the Dollar* as the best.

McGEE, TRAVIS (Creator: John D. MACDONALD). A combination detective-thief, McGee makes a living by recovering stolen property. Although he works outside the law, his "victims" are invariably criminals. McGee's standard "contract" permits him to keep half of what he recovers, but profit is not his only motivation. A man of deep loyalty to his friends, he has been described by Jacques BARZUN and Wendell Hertig TAYLOR as "more the private avenger than the private eye." Loyalty has compelled him to leave Florida for the big cities he detests. In *Nightmare in Pink,* he goes to New York to help the sister of a wartime friend; in *One Fearful Yellow Eye,* he journeys to Chicago, in winter, to aid a former girl friend whose husband was defrauded of $600,000 before his death.

McGee lives on a Fort Lauderdale–based boat, *The Busted Flush,* which he won in a card game. His neighbor and assistant in many adventures is Meyer, a highly successful economist. Although far from being an ascetic, McGee does not seek casual relationships with women. However, befitting his role as a modern knight-errant, he often encounters women who are in severe emotional distress and forms a liaison that permits him to administer practical sex therapy. This practice began in his first case, *The*

Deep Blue Good-By, in which he befriends an attractive girl who has been abused by a psychopath.

CHECKLIST

1964	*The Deep Blue Good-By*
1964	*Nightmare in Pink*
1964	*A Purple Place for Dying*
1964	*The Quick Red Fox*
1965	*A Deadly Shade of Gold*
1965	*Bright Orange for the Shroud*
1966	*Darker than Amber*
1966	*One Fearful Yellow Eye*
1968	*Pale Gray for Guilt*
1968	*The Girl in the Plain Brown Wrapper*
1969	*Dress Her in Indigo*
1970	*The Long Lavender Look*
1972	*A Tan and Sandy Silence*
1973	*The Scarlet Ruse*
1973	*The Turquoise Lament*
1975	*The Dreadful Lemon Sky*

Film

Darker than Amber. National General, 1970. Rod Taylor (McGee), Suzy Kendall, Theodore Bikel, Janet MacLachlan, William Smith, Jane Russell. Directed by Robert Clouse.

From his houseboat on the Florida Keys, McGee rescues a girl who was tied onto an anchor and tossed into the water; later, her would-be killers try again—and succeed. Miffed, McGee plots an elaborate vengeance with the dead girl's double.

McGIVERN, WILLIAM P[ETER] (1924–). American author of mystery novels and screenplays. Born in Chicago, McGivern began his career by writing mysteries for the PULP MAGAZINES and then directed his attention to such "slick" publications as *The Saturday Evening Post.* He also wrote radio scripts and television scripts for a crime series, *San Francisco International Airport.* After writing *The Road to the Snail* (1961), he began to spend much time in Hollywood, where he has written more than 100 hours of prime-time television films and several major feature films, including *The Wrecking Crew* (1968), based on Donald HAMILTON's 1960 novel about Matt HELM, and the John Wayne feature *Brannigan* (1975).

McGivern is married to Maureen Daly, a well-known short story writer and editor.

Most of McGivern's twenty-two novels have been published in more than a dozen foreign countries. A practitioner of the hard-boiled school of detective fiction, he received good reviews for his first book, *But Death Runs Faster* (1948), from Will Cuppy, James SANDOE, and other respected critics. Still better were the reviews for his best-known novel, *The Big Heat* (1952), about which Anthony BOUCHER wrote: "It's a powerful story, powerfully told, with depths of perception rarely to be found in the gangsters-and-corruption melodrama."

The novel is an excellent treatment of McGivern's favorite theme—the crooked cop—used

Robert Taylor buys information from an underworld informer, in the screen version of the William P. McGivern novel *Rogue Cop.* [*MGM*]

also in *Rogue Cop* (1954). He is fascinated by crooked cops because, he says, "the frustration of our society forms a powerful thrust for people to take the law into their own hands and, while this is a tempting indulgence, I have tried to make it plain in my books that it never really works. The law, imperfect and erratic as it may be, is still our best shield against the jungle."

McGivern's later works have foreign locales, usually Spain or Morocco, although Rome provides the background for the counterespionage activities of a young American engineer in *Margin of Terror* (1953). His only short story collection is *Killer on the Turnpike and Other Stories* (1961), a paperback original. He has also written, under the pseudonym Bill Peters, *Blondes Die Young* (1952), which features a Mike HAMMER-like private eye who literally prays for the chance to kill his quarries before the police can arrest them.

Films

In 1953 Fritz LANG turned McGivern's *The Big Heat* into a classic crime film.

Rogue Cop. MGM, 1954. Robert Taylor, George Raft, Janet Leigh, Anne Francis, Steve Forrest. Directed by Roy Rowland.

A crooked police detective turns against the syndicate that pays him when his younger, honest patrolman brother is killed by gangsters.

Hell on Frisco Bay. Warner Brothers, 1955. Alan Ladd, Edward G. Robinson, Joanne Dru, Fay Wray. Directed by Frank Tuttle. Based on *The Darkest Hour* (1955).

A former cop, released from San Quentin after being framed for manslaughter, is determined to avenge himself on the San Francisco rackets boss who railroaded him.

Odds against Tomorrow. United Artists, 1959. Robert Ryan, Harry Belafonte, Shelley Winters, Ed Begley, Gloria Grahame. Directed by Robert Wise. Based on McGivern's 1957 novel.

Prejudice tears apart three men—a former cop, a psychopathic racist, and a Negro—who have reluctantly joined forces to rob a small upstate New York bank.

The Caper of the Golden Bulls. Avco-Embassy, 1967. Stephen Boyd, Yvette Mimieux, Walter Slezak, Vito Scotti. Directed by Russell Rouse. Based on McGivern's 1966 novel.

A reformed bank robber, now living under an assumed name in Spain—after using stolen money to restore a French cathedral he had accidentally bombed during the war—is blackmailed into cracking a bank vault during a fiesta.

McGUIRE, (DOMINIC) PAUL (1903–). Australian author, diplomat, and mystery writer. The son of James and Mary McGuire, he was educated at Christian Brothers' College, Adelaide, and was a Tinline scholar in history at the University of Adelaide and a Workers Educational Association and University Extension lecturer for several years. He married Frances Margaret Cheadle in 1927. McGuire lectured extensively in the United States and Canada from 1936 to 1940 and again in 1946. He achieved the rank of commander in the Royal Australian Navy (Reserve) during World War II. He has served as a delegate to the United Nations (1953), Minister to Italy (1953–1957), Ambassador to Italy (1957–1959), and Special Ambassador and Envoy Extraordinary to the Holy See for the funeral of Pope Pius XII and the coronation of Pope John XXIII (1958). He was made a Commander of the British Empire (1951), a Knight Grand Cross of St. Sylvester (1959), and a Commendatore in the Order of Merit of Italy (1967). He has retired from Her Majesty's Australian Diplomatic Service.

Paul McGuire. [*Antoine-Kershaw Studios*]

His nonmystery books include *The Two Men* (1932), *The Poetry of Gerard Manley Hopkins* (1935), *Westward the Course!* (1942), *The Three Corners of the World* (1948; U.S. title: *Experiment in World Order*), and *There's Freedom for the Brave* (1949).

McGuire's first mystery novel, *Murder in Bostall* (U.S. title: *The Black Rose Murder*), appeared in 1931. Although he then wrote fifteen more mysteries, he published none after 1940. James SANDOE called two of his books "brilliant, mordant and sensitive."

Daylight Murder (1934; U.S. title: *Murder at High Noon*) begins with the discovery, in a haystack, of a body—the financial editor of a newspaper who had been missing for eight months. Blight, a reporter, joins the police investigation. *Burial Service* (1938; U.S. title: *A Funeral in Eden*) is set on an out-of-the-way, idyllic island whose serenity is shattered early one morning when a very unpopular stranger is found dead on the beach, his skull fractured. A tempest of suspicion causes the pasts of many of the characters to be uncovered, and a turmoil of fear reigns until the murderer is revealed. McGuire's reputation is assured by this highly regarded novel. His last mystery, *The Spanish Steps* (1940; U.S. title: *Enter Three Witches*), received rave reviews, but, except for a chase scene around an Italian estate, little happens until one of the characters is murdered near the end. "The book was finished as World War II began," says McGuire, "and we were obviously going to have an appalling slaughter. I thought that, for once, we might have a murder story without a murder. But when I took it to my London publisher, he said, 'But you can't have a murder story without a body.' So we dragged the lake and fetched up a body in the last two hundred words."

McGuire's other mysteries are: *Three Dead Men* (1931), *The Tower Mystery* (1932; U.S. title: *Death Tolls the Bell*), *Murder by the Law* (1932), *Death Fugue* (1933), *There Sits Death* (1933), *Murder in Haste* (1934), *7:30 Victoria* (1935), *Born to Be Hanged* (1935), *Prologue to the Gallows* (1936), *Threepence to Marble Arch* (1936), *Cry Aloud for Murder* (1937), and *W.1.* (1937).

His wife has also written a mystery novel, *Time in the End* (1963), based on events of World War II in the Pacific, with an authentic naval background.

William Oberhardt illustrated the first edition of *The Achievements of Luther Trant*, a scarce short story collection. It was published by Small, Maynard in 1910.

MacHARG, WILLIAM (BRIGGS) (1872–1951). American journalist and author of mystery fiction. Born in Dover Plains, N.Y., the son of Frances Eunice (Briggs) and Williams Storrs MacHarg, he attended the University of Michigan and then worked as a reporter for the *Chicago Tribune* before becoming a fiction writer. A frequent contributor to *The Saturday Evening Post, Collier's,* and other well-paying magazines, he produced several highly regarded novels and detective fiction books, both in collaboration with Edwin BALMER and on his own.

The most important book by Balmer and MacHarg is *The Achievements of Luther Trant* (1910). The stories in this collection represent the first use in fiction of the new science of psychology as a method of crime detection, and one of them, "The Man Higher Up," features the first fictional appearance of the lie detector.

Another MacHarg-Balmer collaboration is *The Blind Man's Eyes* (1916), in which an attempt is made on the life of Basil Santoine, a nationally famous blind lawyer. Traveling with him on a transcontinental train, and serving as his "eyes," are his daughter and his private secretary—one of whom must be involved in the attempted murder. When the train is snowbound in the Rockies, the criminal cannot escape, and Santoine sets out to solve the mystery.

The Affairs of O'Malley (1940) contains thirty-three very short, crisp stories about one of the smartest of "dumb cops," O'Malley, who begins each case by saying that it cannot be solved—and then proves himself wrong. Unlike MacHarg's other stories, these realistic tales approach the hard-boiled type of modern crime story.

MACHEN, ARTHUR (1863–1947). British actor, journalist, essayist, and author of supernatural fiction. His best-known occult fiction, stories filled with the mood and background of demonology, witchcraft, and spiritual terror, are *The Great God Pan and the Inmost Light* (1894), the partly autobiographical *The Hill of Dreams* (1907), and *The Terror* (1917). His major contribution to the mystery-detective form is *The Three Imposters* (1895), a series of thirteen loosely connected episodes about Dyson and Phillipps, amateur detectives who spend most of their time listening to mysterious tales of murder, terror, and the macabre.

MacINNES, HELEN (1907–). Scottish-American author. Miss MacInnes graduated from the University of Glasgow and also studied at University College in London. She was married in 1932 to critic-educator Gilbert Highet, and they lived at Oxford, where he was a don, until they moved to New York City in 1937, when Highet was invited to lecture at Columbia University. The Highets have one son, born in 1933. They have become citizens of the United States and have traveled extensively, visiting many parts of the country.

Miss MacInnes did not begin her first novel until 1939, although she had long wanted to write a thriller. Family obligations and acting in amateur theatricals had previously kept her from writing. The protagonists of her first book, *Above Suspicion*, are, as the Highets had been, an Oxford don and his wife. The fictional couple is sent by the British Foreign Office to prewar Nazi Germany to find out whether a British spy is still alive. Most of Miss MacInnes's subsequent books have dealt with espionage and the threat of nazism or communism, or both. Her early books, set during World War II, included *Assignment in Brittany*, in which a British agent is parachuted into France to spy on the Nazis' coastal defenses. With the advent of the cold war, Miss MacInnes, who writes from a politically centrist viewpoint, began to portray Communists as villains. *I and My True Love* is a story of an anti-Communist Czech diplomat in Washington, D.C., and his love for an American woman. In *The Venetian Affair* and *The Double Image*, two young Americans, a newspaperman and a historian, traveling in Europe become involved in cold war intrigue. In *The Salzburg Connection* an American attorney in Austria finds himself combating the rise of neo-nazism. The fact that the villains in the MacInnes books are invariably totalitarians reflects her belief that "to me, both as a writer and as a citizen of a free country, the most important thing is the survival of freedom in the world."

Her work has frequently been praised for accurate physical descriptions and evocation of the atmosphere of such cities as Washington, Rome, Paris, Venice, and Salzburg. Lewis Gannett once described her as having "a poet's eye for landscape." With the exception of Poland, the setting for *While Still We Live*, she has always depicted locales she has visited. The details of her historical, political, and social backgrounds give evidence of her careful research.

Miss MacInnes has written sixteen novels, which have sold, in the United States alone, almost 20 million copies. Despite occasional objections that her books are slow and talky and her villains not sufficiently villainous, critical appraisal has generally been highly favorable.

CHECKLIST

1941 *Above Suspicion*
1942 *Assignment in Brittany*
1944 *While Still We Live* (British title: *The Unconquerable*)
1945 *Horizon*
1947 *Friends and Lovers*
1949 *Rest and Be Thankful*
1951 *Neither Five nor Three*
1953 *I and My True Love*
1955 *Pray for a Brave Heart*
1958 *North from Rome*
1960 *Decision at Delphi*
1963 *The Venetian Affair*
1966 *The Double Image*
1968 *The Salzburg Connection*
1971 *Message from Málaga*
1974 *The Snare of the Hunter*

Films

Assignment in Brittany. MGM, 1943. Jean Pierre Aumont, Susan Peters, Signe Hasso, Richard Whorf. Directed by Jack Conway.

A heroic Free French officer poses as a quisling to locate a secret Nazi submarine base hidden by an innocent-looking village on the Brittany coast.

Above Suspicion. MGM, 1943. Fred MacMurray, Joan Crawford, Basil Rathbone, Conrad Veidt, Reginald Owen. Directed by Richard Thorpe.

Just before the war, an American professor at Oxford and his bride are asked by the British Foreign Office to use their Continental honeymoon as a cover to contact an agent in Nürnberg who has information about Germany's magnetic mines.

The Venetian Affair. MGM, 1967. Robert Vaughn, Elke Sommer, Felicia Farr, Karl Boehm, Luciana Paluzzi, Boris Karloff. Directed by Thorpe.

An American diplomat in Venice sets off an explosion to kill himself and all the delegates to a peace conference; a former CIA man is reinstated in order to find out why.

McINTOSH, KINN HAMILTON. See AIRD, CATHERINE.

McKEE, INSPECTOR CHRISTOPHER (Creator: Helen REILLY). Following service in World War I, McKee joined the New York City Police Department and, by the mid-1940s, had risen to head its Manhattan Homicide Squad. He is a tall man with a "gaunt head, sardonic mouth, and penetrating eyes." With his teeth usually clamped on a cold pipestem, he gives the appearance of "dourness." Although his clothes are well made, his inevitable gray tweeds make him blend easily into the background.

Totally dedicated to his work, McKee has even

forgotten Christmas because of a case. Although he is occasionally capable of warmth in the presence of people he likes, he often appears to be brusque because he feels that he has little time for the social amenities. His attitude toward murderers and blackmailers is one of implacable hatred. Even when relaxing, taking long walks, or riding the open-top Fifth Avenue buses of the 1930s, McKee has the habit of professionally observing people.

The inspector has his detractors, probably because of his "fatal gift of being too often in the right." They call him lucky but ignore the astuteness, keen observation, and long hours of hard work behind each McKee triumph. In most cases he has worked closely with his assistant, fellow bachelor, and friend, Inspector Todhunter. Although they work primarily out of Centre Street, they have concluded local cases in such far-flung locations as upstate New York (*Mourned on Sunday* and *The Farmhouse*), British Columbia (*Compartment K*), Cape Cod (*The Canvas Dagger*), and New Mexico (*Follow Me* and *The Day She Died*).

CHECKLIST

1930 *The Diamond Feather*
1931 *Murder in the Mews*
1934 *McKee of Centre Street*
1934 *The Line-Up*
1936 *Mr. Smith's Hat*
1936 *Dead Man Control*
1939 *Dead for a Ducat*
1939 *All Concerned Notified*
1940 *Murder in Shinbone Alley*
1940 *Death Demands an Audience*
1940 *The Dead Can Tell*
1941 *Mourned on Sunday*
1941 *Three Women in Black*
1942 *Name Your Poison*
1944 *The Opening Door*
1945 *Murder on Angler's Island*
1946 *The Silver Leopard*
1947 *The Farmhouse*
1949 *Staircase 4*
1950 *Murder at Arroways*
1951 *Lament for the Bride*
1952 *The Double Man*
1953 *The Velvet Hand*
1954 *Tell Her It's Murder*
1955 *Compartment K* (British title: *Murder Rides the Express*)
1956 *The Canvas Dagger*
1958 *Ding-Dong Bell*
1959 *Not Me, Inspector*
1960 *Follow Me*
1961 *Certain Sleep*
1962 *The Day She Died*

MacKINTOSH, ELIZABETH. *See* TEY, JOSEPHINE.

MACLAIN, CAPTAIN DUNCAN (Creator: Baynard H. KENDRICK). Tall, dark, strikingly handsome, and immaculately dressed and groomed, Captain Maclain moves with astonishing ease and self-assurance in spite of his total blindness. Although injured while serving as an intelligence officer during World War I, Maclain has been able, through ceaseless effort, to master his handicap by developing his other senses. He turned to the profession of private detective—and has found that his resources are often challenged to their utmost.

Maclain lives in a penthouse apartment twenty-six stories above 72d Street and Riverside Drive in New York City. His hobbies are reading (his braille books), listening to his Capehart phonograph, and putting together massive jigsaw puzzles. He has taught himself to shoot, guided only by sound. He is assisted by his best friend and partner, Spud Savage; his secretary, Rena—who is married to Spud; and his Seeing Eye dogs, the gentle Schnucke and the not so gentle Dreist.

Maclain's debut appearance is in *The Last Express,* which starts with a murder in a nightclub and reaches a climax in a tense hunt for a killer in a deserted subway tunnel under New York City's financial district. *The Whistling Hangman* concerns the apparent suicide of a fatally ill millionaire who jumps from his hotel balcony. Yet, the verdict is death by hanging. The title of *The Odor of Violets* is counterpointed by the fumes of gasoline at the scene of the murder of a beautiful girl who has been decapitated. A madman has left traces of his favorite perfume at the scene of his misdeed. In *Blind Man's Bluff,* Maclain tries to investigate a series of murders, set in a bank building, that seem impossible to solve.

Death Knell opens at a cocktail party; all the guests are enjoying the fun until a very attractive young woman enters and an ominous silence falls upon the scene. This unpopular individual is soon found dead of a gunshot wound, and Duncan Maclain is drawn into the investigation. In *Out of Control,* Kendrick is more concerned with suspense and thrills than with his customary detection; Maclain pursues an extremely dangerous and deranged murderess through the picturesque but treacherous mountains of Tennessee. *You Die Today* concerns Maclain's efforts to help a blind client adjust to postwar life. *Reservations for Death* is about a millionaire steel tycoon who prefers anonymity and is willing to commit murder to preserve it. An incident involving an attempt by a bomb expert to blow up a plane in midflight is very timely today.

CHECKLIST

1937 *The Last Express*
1937 *The Whistling Hangman*
1941 *The Odor of Violets*
1943 *Blind Man's Bluff*

1945 *Death Knell*
1945 *Out of Control*
1947 *Make Mine Maclain* (three novelettes)
1952 *You Die Today*
1954 *Blind Allies*
1957 *Reservations for Death*
1958 *Clear and Present Danger*
1960 *The Aluminum Turtle* (British title: *The Spear Gun Murders*)
1961 *Frankincense and Murder*

Films

The Last Express. Universal, 1938. Kent Taylor, Dorothea Kent, Don Brodie, Addison Richards, Paul Hurst. Directed by Otis Garrett.

Private detective Maclain, who is not blind in this film, uncovers corruption in the district attorney's office involving the theft of incriminating papers. The title refers to the abandoned subway station in which the papers are found.

Eyes in the Night. MGM, 1942. Edward Arnold, Ann Harding, Donna Reed, Reginald Denny, Katherine Emery. Directed by Fred Zinnemann. Based on *The Odor of Violets.*

Blind detective Maclain is visited by a woman whose stepdaughter is involved in murder and espionage; he solves the case with the help of his Seeing Eye dog.

The Hidden Eye. MGM, 1945. Arnold, Frances Rafferty, Ray Collins, Paul Langton, William Phillips. Directed by Richard Whorf. George Harmon COXE and Harry Ruskin, drawing on Kendrick's character, wrote the screenplay.

Heavily perfumed notes hinting at a betrayal in faraway Sumatra are found at the scenes of murder of several members of one family; Maclain and his dog are called into the case, and later both are kidnapped.

Television

In the early 1970s a series called *Longstreet,* starring James Franciscus, featured a blind insurance investigator purportedly based on Maclain.

McMULLEN, MARY (1920–). American designer and author. Born Mary Reilly in Yonkers, N.Y., she is the daughter of Helen REILLY and the sister of Ursula CURTISS. Her father was the artist Paul Reilly, and she studied art, worked as a fashion designer, and spent more than twenty years doing advertising work. She is married to Alton Wilson.

Miss McMullen wrote her first mystery novel, *Stranglehold* (1951; British title: *Death of Miss X*), to prove a point to the other members of her mystery-writing family. The setting is an advertising agency, and heroine Eve Fitzsimmons, a young copywriter, solves the mystery of the nude corpse found in the firm's boardroom. *Stranglehold* was awarded the Mystery Writers of America Edgar as best first novel of 1951. Miss McMullen's second mystery, published twenty-three years after *Stranglehold,* is *The Doom Campaign* (1974). It was followed by *A Country Kind of Death* (1975).

McNEILE, H[ERMAN] C[YRIL] (1888–1937). English author of crime and adventure fiction; creator of Bulldog DRUMMOND.

The son of Captain Malcolm McNeile of the Royal Navy, he studied at the Royal Military Academy and joined the Army at nineteen, serving twelve years in the Royal Engineers until his retirement as a lieutenant colonel in 1919. He wrote many military adventure stories while in the service and produced the first Drummond book the year after his return to civilian life, using the pseudonym "Sapper," which was derived from the military slang term for an engineer.

After McNeile's death from a war-related illness, the Drummond series was continued by Gerard Fairlie, his friend, fellow novelist, biographer, and partial model for the adventurous hero (much of McNeile is also to be found in Drummond: enjoyment of the camaraderie of military friends, loud talk and laughter in bars and clubs, fondness for vintage port, unquenchable enthusiasm for adventure).

Most of McNeile's works are fast-paced action tales, satisfying their audience with skillfully used violence, romance, and cliff-hanging melodrama rather than characterization, stylistic subtleties, or realistic story lines. The "good guys" are clearly heroic; the "bad guys," inevitably foreigners, have no redeeming qualities. The forces of good, despite the scheming and brutal acts of their adversaries, invariably emerge triumphant.

In addition to the many novels about Drummond, McNeile wrote several tales featuring a similar character, Jim Maitland, including *The Island of Terror* (1930; U.S. title: *Guardians of the Treasure*) and *Jim Maitland* (1932), as well as short story collections involving other detectives, agents, and adventurers: *The Dinner Club* (1923), *Out of the Blue* (1925), *Word of Honour* (1926), *The Saving Clause* (1927), *The Finger of Fate* (1930), *Ronald Standish* (1933), and *Ask for Ronald Standish* (1936).

MAIGRET, JULES (Creator: Georges SIMENON). The French equivalent of Sherlock HOLMES had become so popular in the fourth year of his literary life that his creator's attempts to retire and abandon him were doomed to failure (Maigret has recently retired and is now living in a country house in Meung-sur-Loire with Madame Maigret).

Maigret is 5 feet 11 inches tall, heavy-set, and broad-shouldered. His heavy features, always clean-shaven, reflect his bourgeois origin. His suit is well-cut and made from good material, and his hands are

Jean Gabin as Inspector Maigret interrogates Annie Girardot when several women die in a district where she lives. [*Lopert Films*]

clean and well cared for. He usually wears a heavy overcoat with a velvet collar and a bowler hat, and he keeps his hands in his pockets constantly. He does not resemble the popular conception of a policeman.

In his younger days, before he was married, Maigret signed up at the Quai des Orfèvres after an unsuccessful attempt to study medicine and pounded a beat for two years. He was promoted to patrolling railway stations, then worked for the vice squad, and finally was assigned to detective work in large department stores. He later rose through the ranks, becoming a superintendent and finally a *commissaire* (commissioner); however, many early translators of his exploits promoted him to the rank of inspector when he was only a "detective" or "detective sergeant."

In Maigret's first recorded cases he is about forty-five. In books published four decades later, he has almost reached the mandatory retirement age of fifty-five. He lives with his wife in a shabby but much-loved apartment on the Boulevard Richard-Lenoir and tries to go home for lunch whenever possible. His chief recreation is taking walks with his wife after dinner or going to the movies. A pipe smoker, he has a collection of fifteen different ones at his office.

Maigret is unique in that he does not use the methods of ratiocination favored by most fictional detectives; rather, he is an intuitive detective. When investigating a crime, he places himself at the scene and establishes a daily routine. He walks the streets, goes into cafés to drink something—usually beer or calvados, sometimes marc, pernod, or an aperitif—and asks numerous questions. In the meantime, his subordinates, Inspectors Lucas, Janvier, Lapointe, and Torrence, do the background research.

As Maigret acclimatizes himself in his new environment, he learns much about the actors in the crime he is investigating. Finally, he discovers the guilty person, or his formidable physical presence so overwhelms the criminal that he is driven to seek Maigret out and confess.

Maigret is a greathearted human being known for his compassion for his fellowman; his most notable characteristic is his infinite patience.

The Death of Monsieur Gallet, the first Maigret novel to be published, concerns the mundane killing of a commercial traveler in a hotel room near the Loire. Although *The Strange Case of Peter the Lett* was the first book Simenon wrote about Maigret, it was the fifth to be published. It concerns a body found in the bathroom of an express train as it enters the Gare du Nord and Maigret's attempts to establish the true identity of the victim. The sixth book, *The Crossroad Murders*, is about a diamond merchant from Antwerp whose body is found in an unidentified car at a small garage near Paris. Maigret is stalemated until he is a witness to the shooting of the murdered man's widow. One of Simenon's closest approaches to the true detective novel, this book is also more conventional than most Maigret stories.

A Battle of Nerves concerns the double murder of a wealthy American widow and her maid. When a delivery boy is convicted on circumstantial evidence, Maigret is unimpressed and continues the investigation. In the meantime, the murderer and Maigret engage in a psychological battle of wits, à la *Crime and Punishment*, until his conscience (and Maigret) forces the criminal to confess. This theme appears in other Maigret stories and in many of Simenon's nonseries crime novels. The Maigret novels issued after 1942 place less stress on atmosphere and psychology, however, and favor plot and dialogue.

CHECKLIST

1931 *M. Gallet Decédé* (U.S. title: *The Death of Monsieur Gallet*, 1932; British title: *The Death of Monsieur Gallet*, in *Introducing Inspector Maigret*, 1933)

1931 *Le Pendu de Saint-Pholien* (U.S. title: *The Crime of Inspector Maigret*, 1932; British title: *The Crime of Inspector Maigret*, in *Introducing Inspector Maigret*, 1933)

1931 *Le Charretier de La "Providence"* (U.S. title: *The Crime at Lock 14*, in *The Shadow in the Courtyard and the Crime at Lock 14*, 1934; British title: *The Crime at Lock 14*, in *The Triumph of*

Inspector Maigret, 1934)

1931 *Le Chien Jaune* (British title: *A Face for a Clue*, in *The Patience of Maigret*, 1939; U.S. title: *A Face for a Clue*, in *The Patience of Maigret*, 1940)

1931 *Pietr-le-Letton* (U.S. title: *The Strange Case of Peter the Lett*, 1933; British title: *The Strange Case of Peter the Lett*, in *Inspector Maigret Investigates*, 1933)

1931 *La Nuit du Carrefour* (U.S. title: *The Crossroad Murders*, 1933; British title: *The Crossroad Murders*, in *Inspector Maigret Investigates*, 1933)

1931 *Un Crime en Hollande* (U.S. title: *A Crime in Holland*, in *Maigret Abroad*, 1940; British title: *A Crime in Holland*, in *Maigret Abroad*, 1940)

1931 *Au Rendez-Vous des Terre-Neuvas* (British title: *The Sailors' Rendezvous*, in *Maigret Keeps a Rendezvous*, 1940; U.S. title: *The Sailors' Rendezvous*, in *Maigret Keeps a Rendezvous*, 1941)

1931 *La Tête d'un Homme* (British title: *A Battle of Nerves*, in *The Patience of Maigret*, 1939; U.S. title: *A Battle of Nerves*, in *The Patience of Maigret*, 1940)

1931 *La Danseuse du Gai-Moulin* (British title: *At the Gai-Moulin*, in *Maigret Abroad*, 1940; U.S. title: *At the Gai-Moulin*, in *Maigret Abroad*, 1940)

1932 *La Guinguette à Deux Sous* (British title: *Guinguette by the Seine*, in *Maigret to the Rescue*, 1940; U.S. title: *Guinguette by the Seine*, in *Maigret to the Rescue*, 1940)

1932 *L'Ombre Chinoise* (British title: *The Shadow in the Courtyard*, in *The Triumph of Inspector Maigret*, 1934; U.S. title: *The Shadow in the Courtyard*, in *The Shadow in the Courtyard and The Crime at Lock 14*, 1934)

1932 *L'Affaire Saint-Fiacre* (British title: *The Saint-Fiacre Affair*, in *Maigret Keeps a Rendezvous*, 1940; U.S. title: *The Saint-Fiacre Affair*, in *Maigret Keeps a Rendezvous*, 1941)

1932 *Chez les Flamands* (British title: *The Flemish Shop*, in *Maigret to the Rescue*, 1940; U.S. title: *The Flemish Shop*, in *Maigret to the Rescue*, 1941)

1932 *Le Fou de Bergerac* (British title: *The Madman of Bergerac*, in *Maigret Travels South*, 1940; U.S. title: *The Madman of Bergerac*, in *Maigret Travels South*, 1940)

1932 *Le Port des Brumes* (British title: *Death of a Harbour-Master*, in *Maigret and M. Labbé*, 1941; U.S. title: *Death of a Harbour-Master*, in *Maigret and M. Labbé*, 1942)

1932 *Liberty Bar* (British title: *Liberty Bar*, in *Maigret Travels South*, 1940; U.S. title: *Liberty Bar*, in *Maigret Travels South*, 1940)

1933 *L'Écluse No. 1* (British title: *The Lock at Charenton*, in *Maigret Sits It Out*, 1941; U.S. title: *The Lock at Charenton*, in *Maigret Sits It Out*, 1942)

1934 *Maigret* (British title: *Maigret Returns*, in *Maigret Sits It Out*, 1941; U.S. title: *Maigret Returns*, in *Maigret Sits It Out*, 1942)

1942 *Maigret Revient* (untranslated; contains *Cécile Est Morte*, *Les Caves du Majestic*, and *La Maison du Juge*)

1944 *Signé Picpus* [contains *Signé Picpus* (British title: *To Any Lengths*, in *Maigret on Holiday*, 1950; not published in the United States) and *L'Inspecteur Cadavre* and *Félicie est Là* (both untranslated)]

1944 *Les Nouvelles Enquêtes de Maigret* (s.s.; untranslated; various short stories from this volume and subsequent short story collections have been included in *The Short Cases of Inspector Maigret*, 1959, and in *Ellery Queen's Mystery Magazine*)

1947 *La Pipe de Maigret, et Maigret se Fâche* (untranslated)

1947 *Maigret à New-York* (U.S. title: *Maigret in New York's Underworld*, 1955; not published in England)

1947 *Maigret et L'Inspecteur Malchanceux* (s.s.; untranslated; title changed to *Maigret et L'Inspecteur Malgracieux* in second edition and in all subsequent printings)

1948 *Maigret et son Mort* (British title: *Maigret's Special Murder*, 1964; U.S. title: *Maigret's Dead Man*, 1964)

1948 *Les Vacances de Maigret* (British title: *A Summer Holiday*, in *Maigret on Holiday*, 1950; U.S. title: *No Vacation for Maigret*, 1953)

1949 *La Première Enquête de Maigret* (British title: *Maigret's First Case*, 1958; U.S. title: *Maigret's First Case*, in *Maigret Cinq*, 1965)

1949 *Mon Ami Maigret* (British title: *My Friend Maigret*, 1956; U.S. title: *The Methods of Maigret*, 1957)

1949 *Maigret Chez le Coroner* (untranslated)

1950 *Maigret et la Vieille Dame* (British title: *Maigret and the Old Lady*, 1958; U.S. title: *Maigret and the Old Lady*, in *Maigret Cinq*, 1965)

1950 *L'Amie de Madame Maigret* (U.S. title: *Madame Maigret's Own Case*, 1959; British title: *Madame Maigret's Friend*, 1960)

1950 *Maigret et les Petits Cochons sans Queue* (s.s.; untranslated)

1950 *Les Mémoires de Maigret* (British title: *Maigret's Memoirs*, 1963; not published in the United States)

1951 *Un Noël de Maigret* (s.s.; untranslated)

1951 *Maigret au "Picratt's"* (British title: *Maigret in Montmartre*, in *Maigret Right and Wrong*, 1954; U.S. title: *Inspector Maigret and the Strangled Stripper*, 1954)

1951 *Maigret en Meublé* (British title: *Maigret Takes a Room*, 1960; U.S. title: *Maigret Rents a Room*, 1961)

1951 *Maigret et la Grande Perche* (British title: *Maigret and the Burglar's Wife*, 1955; U.S. title: *Inspector Maigret and the Burglar's Wife*, 1956)

1952 *Maigret, Lognon et les Gangsters* (U.S. title: *Inspector Maigret and the Killers*, 1954; British title: *Maigret and the Gangsters*, 1974)

1952 *Le Révolver de Maigret* (British title: *Maigret's Revolver*, 1956; not published in the United States)

1953 *Maigret et L'Homme du Banc* (untranslated)

1953 *Maigret a Peur* (British title: *Maigret Afraid*, 1961; not published in the United States)
1953 *Maigret se Trompe* (British title: *Maigret's Mistake*, in *Maigret Right and Wrong*, 1954; U.S. title: *Maigret's Mistake*, in *Five Times Maigret*, 1964)
1954 *Maigret à l'École* (British title: *Maigret Goes to School*, 1957; U.S. title: *Maigret Goes to School*, in *Five Times Maigret*, 1964)
1954 *Maigret et la Jeune Morte* (British title: *Maigret and the Young Girl*, 1955; U.S. title: *Inspector Maigret and the Dead Girl*, 1955)
1954 *Maigret Chez le Ministre* (British title: *Maigret and the Minister*, 1969; U.S. title: *Maigret and the Calame Report*, 1970)
1955 *Maigret et le Corps sans Tête* (British title: *Maigret and the Headless Corpse*, 1967; U.S. title: *Maigret and the Headless Corpse*, 1968)
1955 *Maigret Tend un Piège* (British title: *Maigret Sets a Trap*, 1965; U.S. title: *Maigret Sets a Trap*, 1972)
1956 *Un Échec de Maigret* (British title: *Maigret's Failure*, 1962; U.S. title: *Maigret's Failure*, in *A Maigret Trio*, 1973)
1957 *Maigret s'Amuse* (British title: *Maigret's Little Joke*, 1957; U.S. title: *None of Maigret's Business*, 1958)
1958 *Maigret Voyage* (British title: *Maigret and the Millionaires*, 1974; U.S. title: *Maigret and the Millionaires*, 1974)
1958 *Les Scrupules de Maigret* (British title: *Maigret Has Scruples*, 1959; U.S. title: *Maigret Has Scruples*, in *Versus Inspector Maigret*, 1960)
1959 *Maigret et les Témoins Récalcitrants* (British title: *Maigret and the Reluctant Witnesses*, 1959; U.S. title: *Maigret and the Reluctant Witnesses*, in *Versus Inspector Maigret*, 1960)
1959 *Une Confidence de Maigret* (British title: *Maigret Has Doubts*, 1968; not published in the United States)
1959 *The Short Cases of Inspector Maigret* (s.s.; not published in England; the stories are taken from various short story volumes previously published only in France)
1960 *Maigret aux Assises* (British title: *Maigret in Court*, 1961; not published in the United States)
1960 *Maigret et Les Vieillards* (British title: *Maigret in Society*, 1962; U.S. title: *Maigret in Society*, in *A Maigret Trio*, 1973)
1961 *Maigret et le Voleur Paresseux* (British title: *Maigret and the Lazy Burglar*, 1963; U.S. title: *Maigret and the Lazy Burglar*, in *A Maigret Trio*, 1973)
1962 *Maigret et les Braves Gens* (untranslated)
1962 *Maigret et le Client du Samedi* (British title: *Maigret and the Saturday Caller*, 1964; not published in the United States)
1963 *Maigret et le Clochard* (British title: *Maigret and the Dosser*, 1973; U.S. title: *Maigret and the Bum*, 1973)
1963 *La Colère de Maigret* (British title: *Maigret Loses His Temper*, 1965; U.S. title: *Maigret Loses His Temper*, 1974)
1964 *Maigret et le Fantôme* (untranslated)
1964 *Maigret se Défend* (British title: *Maigret on the Defensive*, 1966; not published in the United States)
1965 *La Patience de Maigret* (British title: *The Patience of Maigret*, 1966; not published in the United States)
1967 *Maigret et l'Affaire Nahour* (British title: *Maigret and the Nahour Case*, 1967; not published in the United States)
1967 *Le Voleur de Maigret* (British title: *Maigret's Pickpocket*, 1968; U.S. title: *Maigret's Pickpocket*, 1968)
1968 *Maigret à Vichy* (British title: *Maigret Takes the Waters*, 1969; U.S. title: *Maigret in Vichy*, 1969)
1968 *Maigret Hésite* (British title: *Maigret Hesitates*, 1970; U.S. title: *Maigret Hesitates*, 1970)
1968 *L'Ami d'Enfance de Maigret* (British title: *Maigret's Boyhood Friend*, 1970; U.S. title: *Maigret's Boyhood Friend*, 1970)
1969 *Maigret et le Tueur* (British title: *Maigret and the Killer*, 1971; U.S. title: *Maigret and the Killer*, 1971)
1970 *Maigret et le Marchand de Vin* (British title: *Maigret and the Wine Merchant*, 1971; U.S. title: *Maigret and the Wine Merchant*, 1971)
1970 *La Folle de Maigret* (British title: *Maigret and the Madwoman*, 1972; U.S. title: *Maigret and the Madwoman*, 1972)
1971 *Maigret et l'Homme tout Seul* (U.S. title: *Maigret and the Loner*, 1975; not published in England)
1971 *Maigret et l'Indicateur* (British title: *Maigret and the Flea*, 1972; U.S. title: *Maigret and the Informer*, 1973)
1972 *Maigret et Monsieur Charles* (British title: *Maigret and Monsieur Charles*, 1973; not published in the United States)

Films

Maigret has had a varied screen career; he has been portrayed by such actors as Pierre Renoir and Harry

Inspector Maigret, depicted on a commemorative stamp issued by Nicaragua in 1972 to celebrate the fiftieth anniversary of Interpol.

Baur in French-made films since 1932. His only American film appeared in 1949.

The Man on the Eiffel Tower. RKO, 1949 (filmed in Paris). Charles Laughton (Maigret), Franchot Tone, Burgess Meredith, Robert Hutton, Jean Wallace. Directed by Meredith.

Inspector Maigret is certain that a nearsighted knife grinder is not the murderer of an elderly woman recluse; he begins a cat-and-mouse game in the Paris streets with the real killer. The film was based on *A Battle of Nerves*.

Although other French Maigrets followed, Jean Gabin most closely adhered to the character Simenon created.

Inspector Maigret. Lopert (French), 1958. Gabin, Annie Girardot, Oliver Hussenot, Jean Desailly. Directed by Jean Delannoy.

Several attractive women are murdered in one section of Paris; the killer not only eludes Maigret but taunts him. The film was based on *Maigret Sets a Trap*.

Gabin portrayed Maigret in two more films, and Italy's Gino Cervi and Germany's Heinz Rühmann also starred in films about the French detective.

Television

In 1970 Rupert Davies portrayed Maigret in a British television series; Ewen Solon was his assistant Sergeant Lucas.

MAINWARING, DANIEL. *See* HOMES, GEOFFREY.

MAITLAND, ANTONY (Creator: Sara WOODS). An urbane English barrister, Maitland is the protégé of his uncle, the famous Sir Nicholas Harding, Q.C. Maitland shares not only Sir Nicholas's chambers at the Inner Temple but also, with his pretty wife, Jenny, Harding's spacious house in London's Kempenfeldt Square.

Maitland uses solid deduction and adroit cross-examination of witnesses to prove the innocence of his clients and reveal the guilty. In *The Taste of Fears* the past—Maitland's World War II experiences as a British secret agent working with the French Resistance—has an important bearing on the present.

CHECKLIST

1962 *Bloody Instructions*
1962 *Malice Domestic*
1963 *The Taste of Fears* (U.S. title: *The Third Encounter*)
1963 *Error of the Moon*
1964 *Trusted Like the Fox*
1964 *This Little Measure*
1965 *The Windy Side of the Law*
1965 *Though I Know She Lies*
1966 *Enter Certain Murderers*
1966 *Let's Choose Executors*
1967 *The Case Is Altered*
1967 *And Shame the Devil*
1968 *Knives Have Edges*
1968 *Past Praying For*
1969 *Tarry and Be Hanged*
1970 *An Improbable Fiction*
1971 *Serpent's Tooth*
1971 *The Knavish Crows*
1972 *They Love Not Poison*
1973 *Yet She Must Die*
1973 *Enter the Corpse*
1974 *Done to Death*

MALLESON, LUCY BEATRICE. *See* GILBERT, ANTHONY.

MALONE, JOHN J. (Creator: Craig RICE). Although he later becomes famous in his own right, Malone begins his career as the friend of a madcap couple, press agent Jake Justus and his socially prominent bride-to-be, Helene Brand. Malone is a Chicago lawyer whose marginal practice reflects his greatest interest—whiskey, rather than the law. His "Personal" file usually contains a bottle of rye; if it is empty, Malone heads for his favorite spot, Joe the Angel's City Hall Bar.

Despite his seeming irresponsibility, Malone has been able to inspire great loyalty in many people, including the Justuses, Maggie Cassidy, his long-suffering and seldom-paid secretary, and Captain Daniel von Flanagan of the homicide squad. Later, Malone forms an unlikely detective team with Stuart PALMER's Hildegarde WITHERS, spinster schoolteacher.

Malone repays some of this loyalty in *Trial by Fury* (1941), in which Jake and Helene, on their honeymoon in Wisconsin, are accused of murder. They call Malone, who leaves his customary urban haunts to rescue them. When sober, Malone is capable of real emotion, as in "His Heart Could Break" (1943), in which he determines why his client in the Illinois State Prison death house hanged himself, although Malone had uncovered enough evidence for a new trial.

CHECKLIST

1939 *Eight Faces at Three*
1940 *The Corpse Steps Out*
1940 *The Wrong Murder*
1941 *The Right Murder*
1941 *Trial by Fury*
1942 *The Big Midget Murders*
1943 *Having Wonderful Crime*
1945 *The Lucky Stiff*
1948 *The Fourth Postman*
1957 *My Kingdom for a Hearse*
1957 *Knocked for a Loop* (British title: *The Double Frame*)
1958 *The Name Is Malone* (s.s.)

1963 *The People vs. Withers and Malone* (s.s.; written with Stuart Palmer)
1967 *But the Doctor Died*

Films

Having a Wonderful Crime. RKO, 1945. Pat O'Brien (Malone), George Murphy (Jake Justus), Carole Landis (Helene), Leonore Aubert, George Zucco. Directed by Eddie Sutherland.

Malone accompanies newlywed friends Helene and Jake to a vacation resort after seeing a magician do a disappearing act and fail to reappear.

The Lucky Stiff. United Artists, 1949. Brian Donlevy (Malone), Dorothy Lamour, Claire Trevor, Irene Hervey, Robert Armstrong. Directed by Lewis R. Foster.

Malone arranges with the Governor to secretly exonerate a convicted cabaret singer headed for the electric chair so that she can "haunt" members of a protection racket. (The Justuses do not appear.)

James Whitmore, as Malone, meets Hildegarde Withers—renamed Mrs. O'Malley—in *Mrs. O'Malley and Mr. Malone* in 1950.

MANCHU, FU. *See* FU MANCHU, DR.

MANNING, ADELAIDE FRANCES OKE. *See* COLES, MANNING.

MANNING, BRUCE. *See* BRISTOW, GWEN.

MARCH, COLONEL (Creator: John Dickson CARR as Carter Dickson). Scotland Yard assigned Colonel March to head the Department of Queer Complaints (known officially as D-3) because it was said that nothing could surprise him—a valuable attribute when one's only function is solving impossible crimes. March smokes a large-bowled pipe and is a big, amiable man whose bland blue eyes, sandy hair, and generous moustache combine to make him look like a comic book caricature of a retired colonel. He has a vast store of virtually useless information that serves him well in his bizarre cases. March's assistant is Inspector Roberts, who, as Captain Roberts, once served under the colonel.

The Department of Queer Complaints (1940) contains seven stories about March; *The Men Who Explained Miracles* (1963, by John Dickson Carr) contains two.

Television

In 1953 Boris Karloff starred in *Colonel March of Scotland Yard,* a television series of twenty-six half-hour programs based on the puzzles of Carr's Department of Queer Complaints.

MARCIN, MAX (1879–1948). German-American playwright and producer; creator of Dr. Ordway, the psychiatrist-detective known as the Crime Doctor (*see* CRIME DOCTOR, THE). Born in the province of Posen, Germany (now Poznań, Poland), he was taken to the United States when he was a child. He was the author of *The House of Glass* (1915), with George M. Cohan, and other successful plays. Marcin created Benjamin Ordway for radio in 1940 and wrote the popular thrillers; the doctor's name was changed to Robert Ordway for the films.

MARKHAM, ROBERT. *See* BOND, JAMES.

MARLOWE, DAN J[AMES] (1914–). American businessman, newspaperman, politician, and mystery writer. Born in Lowell, Mass., Marlowe studied at the Bentley School of Accounting and Finance in Boston. He had a successful business career in accounting, insurance, and public relations but gave it up in 1957, when his wife died, to pursue a lifelong ambition to become a writer. Since 1960 he has lived in Harbor Beach, a small Michigan town on Lake Huron. He has been active in political and civic affairs, serving on the city council and for a term as mayor pro tem. He has also written a weekly column appearing in many Michigan newspapers as well as occasional book reviews for the *Detroit Free Press.* He writes magazine articles and fiction under his own name and as Jaime Sandaval.

Marlowe has been one of the most prolific and popular writers of paperback originals. His first five books, beginning with *Doorway to Death* (1959), are about New York detective Johnny Killain. *The Name of the Game Is Death* (1962), which is not one of the Killain series, gained Marlowe considerable critical acclaim and even national publicity. In his review Anthony BOUCHER said: "This is the story of a completely callous and amoral criminal (bank robber and murderer), told in his own self-justified and casual terms, tensely plotted, forcefully written, and extraordinarily effective in its presentation of a viewpoint quite outside humanity's expected patterns."

A fan letter and phone call about the book from a notorious bank robber, Albert Nussbaum, was traced to Marlowe by the FBI and was considered a factor in the eventual capture of Nussbaum's partner, Bobby Wilcoxson. Marlowe has remained in touch with Nussbaum during the latter's imprisonment, and he has aided his rehabilitation and writing career.

Earl Drake, who appeared in *The Name of the Game Is Death,* became a series character in *One Endless Hour* (1968) and has appeared regularly. He has changed his name (originally "Chet Arnold") and, by altering his appearance through plastic surgery, is now truly "the man with nobody's face." A Drake book, *Flashpoint* (1970; later retitled *Operation Flashpoint*), won the first Mystery Writers of America best paperback mystery award.

MARLOWE, PHILIP (Creator: Raymond CHANDLER). Along with a handful of others, Marlowe has come to epitomize the private eye in detective fiction. More thoughtful than his brethren, who rely on guns and fists, he has a college education and can quote Browning, Eliot, and Flaubert. He relaxes by solving chess problems and enjoys classical art and symphonies; he dislikes abstract expressionist painting and atonal music.

Marlowe clearly has not chosen his occupation for the money it can bring him. His one-man detective agency is only marginally successful. He will not knowingly accept a client who is dishonest. When he discovers that a $5,000 check that he received as a fee represents "tainted money," he places it in his office safe—uncashed. Trouble, as Marlowe has said, is his business, but it is a business chosen out of a desire to restore some decency to the world about him. Unswervingly loyal to those clients he will serve, Marlowe accepts arrest rather than betray their interests. In *The Lady in the Lake* and *The Long Goodbye,* he is brutally beaten by corrupt policemen but stoically answers their punishment with flippant remarks.

He is a good detective, his introspective qualities serving him equally well in his work and in his chess games. His milieu, Los Angeles, is a city he knows intimately, from the mansions of Beverly Hills to the changing areas of Central Avenue and downtown Bunker Hill. He speaks Spanish, a distinct asset in some parts of the city.

A man of about forty, Marlowe has been described as tall, with gray eyes, a thin nose, and "a jaw of stone." A lonely, though not ascetic, man, Marlowe falls in love late in his literary life with a thirty-six-year-old millionairess, Linda Loring, whom he meets in *The Long Goodbye.* Their marriage is described at the beginning of the Marlowe novel *The Poodle Springs Mystery,* which Chandler left unfinished at his death. Marlowe refuses to stay permanently at Linda's Palm Springs estate; nor will he accept her offer to set him up in business or settle a million dollars on him. He prefers to remain a private detective, saying: "I'm a poor man married to a rich wife. I don't know how to behave. I'm only sure of one thing—shabby office or not, that's where I became what I am. That's where I will be what I will be. . . . For me there isn't any other way."

CHECKLIST

1939 *The Big Sleep*
1940 *Farewell, My Lovely*
1942 *The High Window*
1943 *The Lady in the Lake*
1949 *The Little Sister*
1950 *The Simple Art of Murder* (s.s.; these stories were reprinted from previous collections, with the detectives' names changed to Marlowe for this volume)
1953 *The Long Goodbye*
1958 *Playback*
1965 *The Smell of Fear* (s.s.; contains "The Pencil," the only short story originally written about Marlowe)

Dick Powell, the first actor to portray detective Philip Marlowe by name on the screen, comes upon a corpse in *Murder My Sweet,* a film based on Raymond Chandler's *Farewell, My Lovely.* [*RKO*]

Films

At first, Chandler's detective contributed his cases to the films of others. In 1942 *Farewell, My Lovely* was shortened and became a vehicle for the Falcon entitled *The Falcon Takes Over* (see FALCON, THE). That year, too, the search for a rare coin in *The High Window* became the basis of a Michael SHAYNE mystery (*Time to Kill*). Two years later Dick Powell, anxious to shed his musical comedy image, was the first to portray the moody, introspective Marlowe.

Murder My Sweet. RKO, 1944. Powell, Claire Trevor, Anne Shirley, Mike Mazurki, Miles Mander, Otto Kruger. Directed by Edward Dmytryk. Based on *Farewell, My Lovely.*

A convict fresh out of prison hires detective Marlowe to locate his long-lost girl friend. The case leads to a wealthy, turbulent family, a sinister psychiatrist, a jewel robbery, and murder. The film won the first Edgar award given by the Mystery Writers

Humphrey Bogart as Philip Marlowe tries to bring client Martha Vickers to her senses in the tough screen treatment of Raymond Chandler's *The Big Sleep*. [*Warner Brothers*]

of America for best mystery film of the year.

The Big Sleep. Warner Brothers, 1946. Humphrey Bogart, Lauren Bacall, Martha Vickers, Louis Jean Heydt, Elisha Cook, Jr. Directed by Howard Hawks.

An elderly millionaire calls Marlowe to his steamy hothouse and hires him to free his mentally unbalanced, drug-addicted daughter (Vickers) from the clutches of a dealer in pornographic books; the dealer is murdered. Another daughter (Bacall), heavily in debt to gamblers, tries to protect her sister by ending Marlowe's investigation. A rich, complex plot, full of outré characters and, contrary to the title, an exhilarating screen experience.

Lady in the Lake. MGM, 1946. Robert Montgomery, Audrey Totter, Leon Ames, Lloyd Nolan. Directed by Montgomery. Screenplay by Steve FISHER.

The camera itself plays Marlowe, as director-star Montgomery tells his story in a subjective narrative; the camera is the detective's—and the spectator's—eyes, and the audience sees Marlowe only when his face is reflected in a mirror and at the end of the film. He is hired to locate the missing wife of a publisher and finds a woman's body at the bottom of a mountain lake.

The Brasher Doubloon. Twentieth Century-Fox, 1947. George Montgomery, Nancy Guild, Florence Bates, Fritz Kortner. Directed by John Brahm. A version of *The High Window*.

A tougher Marlowe discovers a missing rare coin that leads him to two murders, and to the shadowy past of a frightened, insecure girl who is certain that, some years earlier, she pushed a man from a high building.

Marlowe. MGM, 1969. James Garner, Gayle Hunnicut, Rita Moreno, Carroll O'Connor. Directed by Paul Bogart. Based on *The Little Sister*.

In this rather bright adaptation, Marlowe is drawn into the family troubles of a blackmailed movie starlet whose younger sister has traveled from the Ozark hills to cause mischief and murder.

The Long Goodbye. United Artists, 1973. Elliott Gould, Nina van Pallandt, Sterling Hayden, Mark Rydell. Directed by Robert Altman.

A seedy, bemused, and uncertain Marlowe of the 1970s wonders what drove his best friend (Jim Bouton)—who may or may not have killed his wife—to Mexico and suicide. As the confused plot unfolds, Marlowe is allowed to shoot a man down.

In 1975 Robert Mitchum portrayed Marlowe in a close, brooding adaptation of *Farewell, My Lovely*, carefully located in 1940s Los Angeles.

Radio and Television

A tough Marlowe appeared in his own weekly half-hour radio series. Van Heflin, then Gerald Mohr, who is more closely associated with the role, starred in *The Adventures of Philip Marlowe*, which began on CBS in 1949. Dick Powell played Marlowe once again, in a one-hour adaptation of *The Long Goodbye* on *Climax!* Five years later, Phil Carey starred as the detective in a brief season (twenty-six episodes) of half-hour television adventures, *Philip Marlowe*.

MARPLE, MISS JANE (Creator: Agatha CHRISTIE). The most famous spinster sleuth in detective fiction. Vaguely based on the author's own grandmother—a sheltered and Victorian lady not unacquainted with the depths of human depravity—Miss Marple is tall and thin and has china-blue eyes. She once wore a lace fichu and gloves and, during much of her investigative work, used bird glasses. Not noted for her admirable character, she was prone to gossip. Time, however, has mellowed Miss Marple, and she is now presented as a grandmotherly English gentlewoman.

Born in the village of St. Mary Mead, she still resides there in a small house. She is about eighty and has grown frail in recent years. Unable to do much gardening or go for long walks, she still enjoys knitting. She lives on a small fixed income that is generously augmented by her nephew, Raymond West, a best-selling novelist.

In the later works, too, Miss Marple's character has been probed in depth by her creator, and the reader can see that she is attempting to keep up with the times but that she deplores the disappearance of a more genteel era. Miss Marple is a shrewd student of human nature, and her keen intelligence, unmarred by the years, her insight, and her ability to draw analogies between current mysteries and past events in St. Mary Mead are responsible for her unfailing success.

CHECKLIST

1930 *Murder at the Vicarage*
1932 *The Thirteen Problems* (s.s.; U.S. title: *The Tuesday Club Murders*)
1939 *The Regatta Mystery and Other Stories* (s.s.; one of the nine stories is about Miss Marple)
1942 *The Body in the Library*
1942 *The Moving Finger*
1950 *Three Blind Mice and Other Stories* (s.s.; four of the nine stories are about Miss Marple)
1950 *A Murder Is Announced*
1952 *They Do It with Mirrors* (U.S. title: *Murder with Mirrors*)
1953 *A Pocket Full of Rye*
1957 *4:50 from Paddington* (U.S. title: *What Mrs. McGillicuddy Saw!*)
1960 *The Adventure of the Christmas Pudding and Other Stories* (s.s.; one of the six stories is about Miss Marple)
1961 *Double Sin and Other Stories* (s.s.; two of the eight stories are about Miss Marple)
1962 *The Mirror Crack'd from Side to Side* (U.S. title: *The Mirror Crack'd*)
1964 *A Caribbean Mystery*
1965 *At Bertram's Hotel*
1971 *Nemesis*

Films

The late Margaret Rutherford portrayed the elderly but indefatigable amateur sleuth in a series of four British films.

Murder She Said. MGM, 1962. Rutherford, Arthur Kennedy, Muriel Pavlow, James Robertson Justice, Ronald Howard, Thorley Walters, Stringer Davis (Miss Marple's elderly librarian friend, a character added to all the films and portrayed by Miss Rutherford's husband). Directed by George Pollock. Based on *4:50 from Paddington*.

While traveling on a train, Miss Marple witnesses a murder on another train that passes by and, in order to trace the crime, poses as a maid on an elderly invalid's estate.

Murder at the Gallop. MGM, 1963. Rutherford, Robert Morley, Flora Robson, Charles Tingwell, Davis. Directed by Pollock. Based on the Hercule POIROT novel *After the Funeral* (1953).

Miss Marple is convinced that the death of an elderly recluse was actually murder and, in order to uncover the killer, becomes a member of a riding lodge.

Murder Most Foul. MGM, 1964. Rutherford, Ron Moody, Tingwell, Davis, Megs Jenkins. Directed by Pollock. Based on the Poirot novel *Mrs. McGinty's Dead* (1952).

Miss Marple, a juror in a mistrial, is certain that the accused is innocent of the murder of a former actress and, to prove her theory, joins a third-rate repertory troupe.

Murder Ahoy! MGM, 1964. Rutherford, Lionel Jeffries, Tingwell, Davis, Francis Mathews. Directed by Pollock. An original story and screenplay.

A trustee of an organization that maintains a moored ship as part of a youth program, Miss Marple uncovers murder, poisoning, and a Fagin-like school for young criminals.

Miss Marple also makes a quick appearance in the Poirot mystery film *The Alphabet Murders* (1966), based on the novel *The A.B.C. Murders* (1936).

Margaret Rutherford as Agatha Christie's aged Miss Marple scrutinizes a nautical corpse in *Murder Ahoy!* [*MGM*]

Television

Lancashire actress Gracie Fields portrayed a wide-eyed Jane Marple in a 1956 *Goodyear Playhouse* dramatization of *A Murder Is Announced*.

MARQUAND, JOHN P[HILLIPS] (1893–1960). American novelist; creator of Mr. MOTO. Born in Wilmington, Del., the son of Margaret (Fuller) and Philip Marquand, he graduated from Harvard in 1915, taking a job as a reporter for the *Boston Transcript*. After serving as an officer in World War I, he worked for the *New York Tribune* and then wrote advertising copy. In 1922 he married Christina Davenport Sedgwick; they had two children and were divorced in 1935. Two years later he married Adelaide Ferry Hooker; they had a daughter.

The Saturday Evening Post published his short stories for many years, and the Mr. Moto novels were serialized in its pages. Although most of his earliest novels are mysteries, he won the 1937 Pulitzer Prize for a social satire, *The Late George Apley*, which, like his later work, is a cynical appraisal of the New

England social scene of which he was a part.

Marquand appeared as the murder victim in Timothy Fuller's *Three-thirds of a Ghost* (1941), a crime novel set in Boston. Many other well-known figures of the area populate the humorous book.

MARRIC, J. J. *See* CREASEY, JOHN.

MARSH, NGAIO (1899–). New Zealand author of detective fiction. She was born Edith Ngaio (pronounced *ny'o*) Marsh in Christchurch, New Zealand; her famous middle name is the Maori word for a local flowering tree. However, Ngaio Marsh is a descendant of an ancient English family; her maternal grandfather was among the early colonizers of New Zealand. She attended St. Margaret's College, receiving an Anglo-Catholic education, and the Canterbury University College School of Art.

Although Miss Marsh originally intended to be a painter, she changed her mind and decided to become a playwright. Her mother had loved the theater but chose not to make her career in it, considering that way of life to be too bohemian. Miss Marsh submitted what she later conceded was "a terrible romantic drama" to Allan Wilkie, actor-manager of the touring English Shakespeare Company. He rejected it but offered her a place as an actress in his troupe, and she toured with that company and others for two years. She then worked as a writer, producer, and director for various amateur theatrical groups until 1928, when she went to England. In London she helped found an interior decorating shop that was highly successful until the Depression. Miss Marsh had been writing since she was a teenager and had had many pieces published in the *Christchurch Sun*, but it was not until 1932 that she wrote her first mystery.

She was called home to New Zealand because of her mother's fatal illness and remained there to keep house for her father. During World War II she drove a hospital bus. She also produced Shakespearean plays at Canterbury University College and worked with the drama society there for many years. Upon her father's death in 1949 she returned to England to help form the British Commonwealth Theatre Company, a group that later toured Australia and New Zealand with great success.

Ngaio Marsh.

Miss Marsh has continued to divide her time between England and New Zealand. She limits the number of mysteries she writes, preferring to spend at least half of each year directing theater groups, although that work is much less remunerative than her writing. Her autobiography, *Black Beech and Honeydew*, published in 1965, is devoted mainly to recollections of her family life in New Zealand and her theatrical experiences and makes only casual references to her career as a mystery writer. She was made a Dame of the British Empire in 1966.

All the Marsh books have featured the urbane Superintendent Roderick ALLEYN as the detective. In the first, *A Man Lay Dead* (1934), a traditional English country weekend is interrupted by a murder as the guests play the "Murder Game," the "corpse" proving to be real. In the second book, *Enter a Murderer* (1935), a murder is committed onstage in full view of witnesses. It is the first of many mysteries set in what Howard HAYCRAFT has called the "typical Marsh-milieu" of theater and art. The London theater figures prominently in *Opening Night* (1951; U.S. title: *Night at the Vulcan*), in *Killer Dolphin* (1966; British title: *Death at the Dolphin*), and in the novelette *I Can Find My Way Out* (1946), which was awarded third prize in the first contest held by *Ellery Queen's Mystery Magazine*. In *Overture to Death* (1939) a murder is committed as a pianist plays a Rachmaninoff prelude. In *Swing, Brother, Swing* (1949; U.S. title: *A Wreath for Rivera*) a jazz pianist is murdered. Many of Miss Marsh's books, including *Artists in Crime* (1938) and *Final Curtain* (1947), touch on the art world and painters.

Dame Ngaio has used many biographical elements in her mysteries. A serious illness and convalescence led to her only collaboration, *The Nursing Home Murder* (1935), written with her friend and physician, Dr. Henry Jellett. *Death of a Peer* (1940; British title: *A Surfeit of Lampreys*) tells of Roberta Grey, a young New Zealander in London. The author has admitted that the Lampreys are close friends with whom she stayed during her first trip to England. In the book the head of the fictional family is stabbed to death in an elevator.

In *Murder for Pleasure* (1941) Haycraft included Dame Ngaio (along with Margery ALLINGHAM, Michael INNES, and Nicholas BLAKE) in a list of writers who had brought the English detective novel to "full flower." He pointed out that, despite her powers of characterization, her books are more novels of manners than of character. She depends upon police procedure more than her contemporaries, who are concerned with the psychology of their characters. Haycraft, in praising her sense of drama, felt that it was also her weakness; she tends to substitute dialogue for action.

Dame Ngaio has stated that "the mechanics in a detective novel may be shamelessly contrived, but the writing need not be so." Julian SYMONS has applauded the "ease and elegance" of her style, but he has been disappointed in books such as *Opening Night,* which begins with what he considers a brilliant picture of backstage theatrical intrigue. He deplores her failure to resolve the problems in terms of character, maintaining that she emphasizes, instead, the investigation and interrogation of suspects.

MARSHALL, ARCHIBALD (1866–1934). English author of popular fiction. After graduating from Trinity College, Cambridge University, he studied for the ministry but then married and began writing fiction. He founded the publishing firm of Alston Rivers (which published Arnold BENNETT's now rare book *The Loot of Cities,* 1904) and published his own novel *The House of Merrilees* (1905) after other English publishers rejected it. *The Mystery of Redmarsh Farm* was a popular serial in the London *Daily Mail* before it was published in book form in 1912. His short story collection *The Terrors and Other Stories* (1913) contains two crime and mystery tales, "'Gentleman Jim'" and "The Llanryll Mystery."

MARSHALL, RAYMOND. *See* CHASE, JAMES HADLEY.

MARSTEN, RICHARD. *See* MCBAIN, ED.

MARTINEAU, INSPECTOR HARRY (Creator: Maurice PROCTER). The head of A Division, Criminal Investigation Department, in the town of Granchester (that is, Manchester), England, Chief Detective Inspector Martineau is a big man with a rock-hard but handsome face and gray eyes. He is married and has spent more than twenty years in police service. Liked and admired by most people for his fairness and dedication to his profession, he has an awesome reputation among the members of the underworld and is feared by them.

Martineau's efficient subordinates and his thorough knowledge of both the underworld and the methods of police routine have been responsible for his continuing successes.

Martineau debuts in *Hell Is a City,* in which he is obliged to capture an old childhood enemy who is now an escaped convict. In later adventures, less emphasis is placed on Martineau's personal life, although much attention is focused on his subordinates and their problems. Throughout the series, though, Martineau spends much time and effort trying to get evidence to put Dixie Costello, the most important criminal in Granchester, behind bars; he is usually frustrated at the last moment.

Two Men in Twenty integrates the police procedural novel with elements of the big caper as alternating sections deal first with a gang of safecrackers who are planning their biggest haul and then with the police who are trying to track them down.

Honest, hardworking Inspector Martineau is accused of blackmail by one of Granchester's most prominent citizens in *Hideaway*, and he must prove his innocence while bringing a group of hijackers to justice.

CHECKLIST

1953 *Hell Is a City* (U.S. title: *Somewhere in This City*)
1955 *The Midnight Plumber*
1958 *Man in Ambush*
1958 *Killer at Large*
1960 *Devil's Due*
1961 *The Devil Was Handsome*
1962 *A Body to Spare*
1963 *Moonlight Flitting* (U.S. title: *The Graveyard Rolls*)
1964 *Two Men in Twenty*
1965 *Death Has a Shadow* (U.S. title: *Homicide Blonde*)
1966 *His Weight in Gold*
1966 *Rogue Running*
1967 *Exercise Hoodwink*
1968 *Hideaway*

MASON, A[LFRED] E[DWARD] W[OODLEY] (1865–1948). English playwright and author of many novels of adventure, mystery, and detection, some of which feature the highly respected Inspector HANAUD.

Born in London, Mason received an M.A. degree at Oxford and then began a theatrical career, serving as a soldier in a production of George Bernard Shaw's *Arms and the Man* (1894). He soon turned to writing and produced several first-rate historical and adventure novels, the first being *A Romance of Wastdale* (1895). His masterpiece, *The Four Feathers,* was published in 1902. He spent four years in the House of Commons (1906–1910) and led a vigorous life, even when old, devoting vast amounts of time and energy to traveling, sailing, climbing, and cricket. Most of his prodigious output was both popular and critically well received, for his style was smooth, his characters believable, his moods convincing, and, above all, his stories excellent. Meticulous about realistic detail, Mason often used personal experiences in his books. His tenure in Parliament resulted in a political novel; his role as civilian chief of British Naval Intelligence during World War I provided material for novels of espionage and intrigue; and his travels in the Mideast served as authentic background for other adventure tales.

Several of Mason's books were adapted into successful plays and motion pictures. The pattern for *The Witness for the Defence,* a love story woven into a melodramatic crime tale, was reversed, however; this unusual mystery was already a stage hit when Mason novelized it in 1913. Other mystery works are *The Four Corners of the World* (1917), a short story collection that contains one Hanaud adventure, "The Affair at the Semiramis Hotel"; *The Winding Stair* (1923); *No Other Tiger* (1927); *The Sapphire* (1933), a novel that contains a chapter entitled "The Man from Limoges," which has little to do with the rest of the book and is a Hanaud short story, complete in itself; *Dilemmas* (1934), short stories of crime and mystery; and *The Secret Fear* (1940).

Film

Mason has been well served by the mystery screen, beginning in 1919, when Paramount released *The Witness for the Defense,* with Elsie Ferguson as the girl forced by her father's illness into a loveless marriage with a wealthy man and then placed on trial for manslaughter. There have also been several films involving Hanaud.

MASON, PERRY (Creator: Erle Stanley GARDNER). The most famous attorney in fiction is the hero of more than eighty novels, some of which have been published since his creator's death. Internal evidence in the Mason series indicates that the lawyer was born in 1891. He is described as a big man, but he is not heavy. Although he says that he has no time for sports or exercise, he remains fit and performs well in situations involving physical danger. He has long legs, broad shoulders, and piercing eyes in a rugged face. His thick, wavy hair and excellent speaking voice make him attractive to many women.

The woman in his life is Della Street, the most famous secretary in fiction. In *The Case of the Stuttering Bishop,* Della says: "I wouldn't want to live unless I could work for a living." Knowing that Mason would not permit his wife to work, she has, on five separate occasions, refused his proposal of marriage. However, she has remained steadfastly loyal, risking her life and freedom on his behalf; she has been arrested five times while performing her job. The other characters with whom Perry Mason comes into contact have also gained notoriety. Paul Drake is the private detective who does the lawyer's investigative work. He is invariably at Mason's side in periods of stress, although he frequently complains that the work is bad for his digestion. Hamilton Burger is the district attorney whose office has never successfully prosecuted one of Mason's

Raymond Burr as Perry Mason, depicted on a commemorative stamp issued by Nicaragua in 1972 to celebrate the fiftieth anniversary of Interpol.

clients. In half of these situations, the client was arrested through the efforts of Lieutenant Arthur Tragg, the attorney's implacable (albeit friendly) foe.

Operating out of a large office suite at Seventh Street and Broadway in downtown Los Angeles, Mason has built a considerable reputation. His loyalty to his clients, even those who lie to him, is legendary. If he is interested in a case, he will accept a client regardless of his ability to pay. However, as he said in *The Case of the Perjured Parrot,* "I never take a case unless I am convinced my client was incapable of committing the crime charged." He will not hesitate to use extralegal methods to secure evidence in preparing his cases. Analysis of his record indicates that he has committed such clear violations of the law as assault and battery (*The Case of the Velvet Claws*), breaking and entering (*The Case of the Empty Tin*), reckless driving (*The Case of the Silent Partner*), and illegal wiretapping (*The Case of the Fiery Fingers*). Although he is invariably well prepared, he is so skilled in courtroom procedure that he can think "on his feet" and ask just the right question to befuddle a witness, embarrass a prosecutor, and exonerate a client.

Mason provided the final evidence that tied up the loose ends of *The President's Mystery Story,* a novel suggested by Franklin Delano Roosevelt and written by six popular mystery novelists. First serialized in *Liberty* magazine (beginning on November 16, 1935), it was published in book form in 1936. Gardner's concluding chapter did not appear until the book was reprinted in 1967, when the book was retitled *The President's Mystery Plot.*

CHECKLIST

1933 *The Case of the Velvet Claws*
1933 *The Case of the Sulky Girl*
1934 *The Case of the Lucky Legs*
1934 *The Case of the Howling Dog*

1934 *The Case of the Curious Bride*
1935 *The Case of the Counterfeit Eye*
1935 *The Case of the Caretaker's Cat*
1936 *The Case of the Sleepwalker's Niece*
1936 *The Case of the Stuttering Bishop*
1937 *The Case of the Dangerous Dowager*
1937 *The Case of the Lame Canary*
1938 *The Case of the Substitute Face*
1938 *The Case of the Shoplifter's Shoe*
1939 *The Case of the Perjured Parrot*
1939 *The Case of the Rolling Bones*
1940 *The Case of the Baited Hook*
1940 *The Case of the Silent Partner*
1941 *The Case of the Haunted Husband*
1941 *The Case of the Empty Tin*
1942 *The Case of the Drowning Duck*
1942 *The Case of the Careless Kitten*
1943 *The Case of the Buried Clock*
1943 *The Case of the Drowsy Mosquito*
1944 *The Case of the Crooked Candle*
1944 *The Case of the Black-eyed Blonde*
1945 *The Case of the Golddigger's Purse*
1945 *The Case of the Half-wakened Wife*
1946 *The Case of the Borrowed Brunette*
1947 *The Case of the Fan-Dancer's Horse*
1947 *The Case of the Lazy Lover*
1948 *The Case of the Lonely Heiress*
1948 *The Case of the Vagabond Virgin*
1949 *The Case of the Dubious Bridegroom*
1949 *The Case of the Cautious Coquette* (novel and two s.s.)
1950 *The Case of the Negligent Nymph*
1950 *The Case of the One-eyed Witness*
1951 *The Case of the Fiery Fingers*
1951 *The Case of the Angry Mourner*
1952 *The Case of the Moth-eaten Mink*
1952 *The Case of the Grinning Gorilla*
1953 *The Case of the Hesitant Hostess*
1953 *The Case of the Green-eyed Sister*
1954 *The Case of the Fugitive Nurse*
1954 *The Case of the Runaway Corpse*
1954 *The Case of the Restless Redhead*
1955 *The Case of the Glamorous Ghost*
1955 *The Case of the Sunbather's Diary*
1955 *The Case of the Nervous Accomplice*
1956 *The Case of the Terrified Typist*
1956 *The Case of the Demure Defendant*
1956 *The Case of the Gilded Lily*
1957 *The Case of the Lucky Loser*
1957 *The Case of the Screaming Woman*
1957 *The Case of the Daring Decoy*
1958 *The Case of the Long-legged Models*
1958 *The Case of the Footloose Doll*
1958 *The Case of the Calendar Girl*
1959 *The Case of the Deadly Toy*
1959 *The Case of the Mythical Monkeys*
1959 *The Case of the Singing Skirt*
1959 *The Case of the Waylaid Wolf*
1960 *The Case of the Duplicate Daughter*
1960 *The Case of the Shapely Shadow*
1961 *The Case of the Spurious Spinster*
1961 *The Case of the Bigamous Spouse*
1962 *The Case of the Reluctant Model*
1962 *The Case of the Blonde Bonanza*
1962 *The Case of the Ice-cold Hands*
1963 *The Case of the Mischievous Doll*
1963 *The Case of the Step-Daughter's Secret*
1963 *The Case of the Amorous Aunt*
1964 *The Case of the Daring Divorcee*
1964 *The Case of the Phantom Fortune*
1964 *The Case of the Horrified Heirs*
1965 *The Case of the Troubled Trustee*
1965 *The Case of the Beautiful Beggar*
1966 *The Case of the Worried Waitress*
1967 *The Case of the Queenly Contestant*
1968 *The Case of the Careless Cupid*
1969 *The Case of the Fabulous Fake*
1970 *The Case of the Crimson Kiss* (s.s.; one of the five stories is about Mason)
1971 *The Case of the Crying Swallow* (s.s.; one of the four stories is about Mason)
1972 *The Case of the Irate Witness* (s.s.; one of the four stories is about Mason)
1972 *The Case of the Fenced-in Woman*
1973 *The Case of the Postponed Murder*

Films

Mason, much smoother on the screen than in his tough early novels, has opportunity in every film for richly dramatic courtroom oratory and a climactic revelation of the guilty party—invariably not the defendant—who immediately crumbles and confesses hysterically.

The Case of the Howling Dog. Warner Brothers, 1934. Warren William, Mary Astor, Gordon Westcott, Helen Trenholme (Della Street). Directed by Alan Crosland.

William, whose courtroom style could be likened to that of John Barrymore, is a Mason with flair, trying his best to defend a client charged with murdering her husband, who had turned a ferocious dog on her.

The Case of the Curious Bride. Warner Brothers, 1935. William, Margaret Lindsay, Allen Jenkins, Donald Woods. Directed by Michael Curtiz.

Mason postpones a European vacation to help a distraught newlywed whose first husband—supposedly dead—is blackmailing her (later he does die). After solving the case, Mason proposes to Della (Claire Dodd), suggesting that the interrupted trip be their honeymoon.

The Case of the Lucky Legs. Warner Brothers, 1935. William, Genevieve Tobin (Della), Patricia Ellis, Lyle G. Talbot. Directed by Archie L. Mayo.

The pretty winner of a beauty contest consults Mason when the promoter of the contest runs off with the cash prizes; Mason finds him stabbed.

The Case of the Velvet Claws. Warner Brothers, 1936. William, Winifred Shaw, Gordon Elliott, Dodd (Della). Directed by William Clemens.

Mason and Della are married just an hour when a socialite insists, at gunpoint, that he defend her of the charge of shooting her husband.

The Case of the Black Cat. Warner Brothers,

1936. Ricardo Cortez, Gary Owen, June Travis (the new Della, still unmarried). Directed by William McGann. Based on *The Case of the Caretaker's Cat.*

There is a feline witness to a murder Mason investigates.

The Case of the Stuttering Bishop. Warner Brothers, 1937. Donald Woods (Mason in this film), Ann Dvorak, Robert McWade, Anne Nagel. Directed by Clemens.

In the last Perry Mason film, an Australian bishop implores Mason to help him find a young girl who is unaware that she is an heiress, but Mason is curious about the churchman's crippling stammer.

Radio and Television

During the 1940s Mason had a successful career on radio, especially in a Monday-through-Friday afternoon serial, with John Larkin best remembered as the lawyer and Joan Alexander as a cool Della. *Perry Mason* was first heard on CBS radio in 1943.

But Perry has been most memorable in television's courtrooms, in an Emmy-winning portrayal by Raymond Burr. The *Perry Mason* series, which began in 1957, lasted a full decade; among the other members of the cast were Barbara Hale as Della, William Hopper as investigator Paul Drake, and William Tallman as District Attorney Burger, Mason's constant antagonist. Many of the more than 200 cases were based on Gardner novels.

The unflagging popularity of the series prompted the debut, in 1973, of *The New Perry Mason,* a series of hour-long programs, with Monte Markham in the title role and Sharon Acker as Della. A freer, more personal approach allowed the lawyer and his secretary to appear in scenes outside the confines of court and office. Albert Stratton was Paul Drake, Harry Guardino was the district attorney, and Dane Clark was Lieutenant Tragg, replacing the elderly Ray Collins of the old series. Generally criticized as lacking the impact of the earlier series, *The New Perry Mason* was short-lived.

MASON, RANDOLPH (Creator: Melville Davisson POST). One of the great rogues in mystery fiction, Mason is a crooked lawyer whose name was carried on by an honest one, Perry MASON. In the Randolph Mason cases Post created an original form of crime story. In the past, criminals had concerned themselves with eluding capture, but in these narratives, the avoidance of punishment is paramount.

The totally unscrupulous Mason is a Virginia-born New York lawyer who, early in his career, recognizes that justice and the law are unrelated. In his introduction to *The Strange Schemes of Randolph Mason* (1896), his first collection of stories about Mason, Post wrote: "The law provides a Procrustean standard for all crimes. Thus a wrong, to become criminal, must fit exactly into the measure laid down by the law, else it is no crime; if it varies never so little from the legal measure, the law must, and will, refuse to regard it as criminal, no matter how injurious a wrong it may be. There is no measure of morality, or equity, or common right that can be applied to the individual case." Since it is such a simple matter to circumvent the law, Mason decides to profit from his legal education.

Mason once explained his amoral philosophy: "No man who has followed my advice has ever committed a crime. Crime is a technical word. It is the law's term for certain acts which it is pleased to define and punish with a penalty. What the law permits is right, else it would prohibit it. What the law prohibits is wrong, because it punishes it. The word moral is a purely metaphysical one."

Hated and feared by other attorneys, Mason was once one of the country's great criminal lawyers, until giant corporations recognized his genius and paid him to find ways of complying with the letter of the law while violating its spirit with impunity.

Since Mason's cases were all based on actual legal loopholes, moralists feared that they would serve as handbooks for the villainous. In "The Corpus Delicti" (the first story in *The Strange Schemes of Randolph Mason*), for instance, Mason suggests only one possible legal solution to his client's problem: he must kill his wife. The story spurred a much-needed change in criminal procedure.

The second collection of tales is *The Man of Last Resort: or, The Clients of Randolph Mason* (1897); in the final volume, *The Corrector of Destinies* (1908), a reformed Mason works on the side of justice.

MASON, TALLY. *See* DERLETH, AUGUST.

MASON, (FRANCIS) VAN WYCK (1901–). American historical novelist and author of international intrigue books featuring Hugh NORTH. Born in Boston, the son of Erma (Coffin) and Francis Payne Mason, he graduated from Harvard and entered military service, logging twenty-six years of active and reserve duty. He traveled much and planned a diplomatic career, but became a full-time writer in 1928, contributing regularly to the best popular fiction magazines. He married Dorothy Louise Macready in 1927; they had two children. She died in 1958, and he married Jeanne-Louise Hand later that year. He now lives in Bermuda.

In addition to the many tales involving North, Mason has written several best-selling historical novels, juvenile novels, and other fiction under the pseudonyms Frank W. Mason and Ward Weaver. His uniformly polished style has a smoothness often associated with "slick" magazine fiction.

In collaboration with H. Brawner, he wrote two mysteries as Geoffrey Coffin, *Murder in the Senate*

(1935) and *The Forgotten Fleet Mystery* (1936). *The Castle Island Case* (1937) is an unusual book for which Henry Clay Gipson provided numerous photographic clues.

MASTERSON, WHIT. *See* MILLER, WADE.

MASUR, HAROLD Q. (1912–). American lawyer and author of detective fiction. Masur is the creator of Scott Jordan, an attorney who also solves crimes while defending clients. Jordan lives in a New York hotel, loves records, and is one of the few bachelor private eyes who does not spend most of his time in bed with beautiful woman clients. His best adventures are *Bury Me Deep* (1947), *Suddenly a Corpse* (1949), *You Can't Live Forever* (1951), *The Last Gamble* (1958), and *Make a Killing* (1964), in which he becomes involved in the complex, behind-the-scenes financial jungle of the motion picture world.

Masur has served as president of the Mystery Writers of America (1973–1974) and, beginning in 1973, as counsel to the organization. His most recent novel is *The Attorney* (1973).

MATHERS, HELEN (BUCKINGHAM) (1853–1920). English novelist. Born in Somerset, she married a surgeon, Henry Reeves, in 1876. She wrote many sentimental, romantic, and melodramatic novels, several with strong elements of mystery and crime. Hugo Hold, a Scottish barrister, solves the problem in *Murder or Manslaughter* (1885), and the first-person narrator serves as the detective in *Blind Justice* (1890). *The Land o' the Leal* (1878) contains two unrelated novelettes, *As He Comes up the Stair* and *Stephen Hatton*, both of which tell about people who have been wronged—an innocent woman convicted of murdering her husband and his gypsy sweetheart, and a man whose alleged victim is found alive after he has been executed.

MAUGHAM, W[ILLIAM] SOMERSET (1874–1965). English dramatist, novelist, and short story writer. Born in Paris, Maugham suffered from tuberculosis and a pronounced stammer, a physical affliction he treated semiautobiographically in *Of Human Bondage* (1915), with its clubfooted hero. Raised by a strict clergyman uncle in Kent after his parents died, he studied accounting and medicine, qualifying as a physician. He wanted to be a writer, however, and produced countless unsuccessful works for ten years until a play, *Lady Frederick*, triumphed in 1907. He married Lady Wellcome in 1915; they had one daughter and were divorced in 1927.

During World War I Maugham first served with an ambulance unit but was soon transferred to the Intelligence Department and traveled to Russia. In World War II he served with the British Ministry of Information in Paris. He bought a villa in southern France in 1928 and made it his permanent home until his death.

Although Maugham gained fame initially as a playwright, nowadays his short stories are considered his best work, along with four of his novels: *Of Human Bondage*; *The Moon and Sixpence* (1919), the story of an unconventional artist in the South Pacific, based on Paul Gauguin's life; *Cakes and Ale* (1930), about a famous novelist, regarded as a contemptuous treatment of Thomas Hardy and Sir Hugh Walpole; and *The Razor's Edge* (1944), in which an idealistic American veteran searches for a satisfying way of life. Maugham's sharp, clear style and profound understanding of human nature are responsible for his reputation as one of the great fiction writers of the twentieth century.

Maugham's experiences with British Intelligence provided him with material for *Ashenden; or, The British Agent* (1928), a series of connected episodes about World War I. A well-known writer, Ashenden meets a British colonel, known to the Intelligence Department only as R., who asks him to work as a secret service agent. It is thought that his profession will allow him to travel freely without causing suspicion and that his knowledge of European languages will prove useful. The last advice R. gives to him before his first assignment impresses Ashenden: "If you do well, you'll get no thanks and if you get into trouble you'll get no help."

Ashenden admires goodness in others but has learned to live with evil. His interest in other people goes no further than the scientist's feeling for experimental rabbits. They are source material for future books, and he is as realistic about their bad points as he is about their good qualities. Never bored, he believes that only stupid people require external stimulation to be amused; a man of intellect can avoid boredom by using his own resources.

Regarded as the first realistic look at the life of a spy, *Ashenden* shows that secret agents are simply ordinary people in unusual circumstances, not dashing heroes whose lives are filled with beautiful blondes, secret societies, and cliff-hanging adventures.

Several of Maugham's novels and short stories contain elements of crime and mystery, notably the often-anthologized "The Footprints in the Jungle" (published in *Ah King*, 1933), in which the head of the Malayan police narrates a story about a case that he was unsuccessful in solving—and does not seem unhappy about his failure.

Films

Many of Maugham's works have reached the screen, but few in the mystery genre. Most important are the Ashenden stories, transformed into the film *The*

Secret Agent by Alfred HITCHCOCK in 1936, and *The Letter*.

The Letter. Paramount, 1929. Jeanne Eagels, O. P. Heggie, Reginald Owen, Herbert Marshall. Directed by Jean De Limur. Based on Maugham's extremely successful stage play, produced in 1927.

Acquitted of shooting her lover by claiming self-defense, an unfaithful wife must recover an incriminating letter. The film was remade in 1940, starring Bette Davis.

MAXWELL, M. E. BRADDON. *See* BRADDON, M. E.

MAYO, ASEY (Creator: Phoebe Atwood TAYLOR). The "Codfish Sherlock" is, in the words of Nicholas BLAKE, an "eccentric original." A former sailor who made his first voyage on one of the last clipper ships, he lives in Wellfleet on Cape Cod, where he is handy-man-chauffeur for the local tycoon but finds time to solve murders.

He is tall but unimpressive in appearance, for he walks with his lean frame hunched over. Variously called "wily, ornery, and homespun," he relies on his profound, albeit practical, knowledge of human nature for success as a detective. "Common sense" has been the tobacco-chewing Mayo's hallmark since *The Cape Cod Mystery*, in which he solved the murder of a celebrated novelist during an uncommonly warm Cape Cod weekend.

CHECKLIST

1931	*The Cape Cod Mystery*
1932	*Death Lights a Candle*
1933	*The Mystery of the Cape Cod Players*
1934	*The Mystery of the Cape Cod Tavern*
1934	*Sandbar Sinister*
1935	*The Tinkling Symbol*
1935	*Deathblow Hill*
1936	*The Crimson Patch*
1936	*Out of Order*
1937	*Octagon House*
1937	*Figure Away*
1938	*The Annulet of Gilt*
1938	*Banbury Bog*
1939	*Spring Harrowing*
1940	*The Deadly Sunshade*
1940	*The Criminal C.O.D.*
1941	*The Perennial Boarder*
1942	*3 Plots for Asey Mayo* (novelettes)
1942	*Six Iron Spiders*
1943	*Going, Going, Gone*
1945	*Proof of the Pudding*
1946	*Punch with Care*
1946	*The Asey Mayo Trio* (novelettes)
1951	*Diplomatic Corpse*

MEADE, L[ILLIE] T[HOMAS] (pseudonym of Elizabeth Thomasina Meade Smith; 1854–1914). English author of girls' books and mystery and detective fiction. Credited with more than 250 semijuvenile

***The Sanctuary Club*, one of L. T. Meade's most famous short story collections, was reprinted in a popular series of Victorian fiction that is highly sought after by collectors for its colorful covers. Published by Ward, Lock in London around 1900, the books are often misrepresented as first editions.**

works, she also produced several important books in the mystery genre, including a prodigious number of short stories, many of which originally appeared in *The Strand*.

One historic volume contains the first series of stories about a female criminal. Madame Koluchy, the thoroughly evil leader of an Italian criminal organization, matches wits with Norman Head, philosopher and recluse, in *The Brotherhood of the Seven Kings* (1899). The first series of medical mysteries published in England is *Stories from the Diary of a Doctor* (1894; second series, 1896), which Miss Meade wrote in collaboration with Dr. Clifford Halifax (pseudonym of Dr. Edgar Beaumont), who also serves as the detective.

Robert Eustace (pseudonym of Dr. Eustace Robert Barton), who also collaborated with Dorothy L. SAYERS on *The Documents in the Case* (1930), coauthored many stories with Miss Meade. They worked together on *The Brotherhood of the Seven Kings* and also on *A Master of Mysteries* (1898), which features John Bell; *The Gold Star Line* (1899), with detective George Conway; and *The Sanctuary Club* (1900), which involves amateur detectives Dr. Henry Chetwynd and Dr. Paul Cato, an unusual health club, and a series of murders apparently caused by supernatural means.

Even more sinister than Madame Koluchy is Madame Sara, the villainess of *The Sorceress of the Strand* (1903)—and a specialist in murder.

MENDOZA, LT. LUIS (Creator: Elizabeth LININGTON as Dell Shannon). The tastes of this detective, a member of the Los Angeles Police Department, run to foreign cars and expensive, custom-made clothes. He is independently wealthy, having inherited a fortune from a grandfather, and remains a policeman because he enjoys solving puzzles and would like to bring order to the chaos he sees around him.

In his first appearance, *Case Pending*, he tries to find the connection between two corpses; in both cases, one of the victim's eyes was deliberately mutilated. In *Extra Kill* he investigates murder, pornography, and a Hollywood spiritualist's racket at the "Temple of Mystic Truth." The usually suave Mendoza is aroused to anger as he hunts down the murderers of policemen in *The Death-Bringers* and *Chance to Kill*.

CHECKLIST

1960	*Case Pending*
1961	*The Ace of Spades*
1962	*Extra Kill*
1962	*Knave of Hearts*
1963	*Death of a Busybody*
1963	*Double Bluff*
1964	*Root of All Evil*
1964	*Mark of Murder*
1965	*The Death-Bringers*
1965	*Death by Inches*
1966	*Coffin Corner*
1966	*With a Vengeance*
1967	*Chance to Kill*
1967	*Rain with Violence*
1968	*Kill with Kindness*
1969	*Schooled to Kill*
1969	*Crime on Their Hands*
1970	*Unexpected Death*
1971	*Whim to Kill*
1971	*The Ringer*
1972	*Murder with Love*
1972	*With Intent to Kill*
1973	*No Holiday for Crime*
1973	*Spring of Violence*
1974	*Crime File*
1975	*Deuces Wild*

MERCER, CECIL WILLIAM. *See* YATES, DORNFORD.

MEREDITH, HAL. *See* BLAKE, SEXTON.

MERLINI, THE GREAT (Creator: Clayton RAWSON). Professional magician and amateur detective. Merlini was born in a Barnum and Bailey circus car about the turn of the century. He was married in 1919. After working as a carnival and circus magician for four years, he formed his own show and toured the world for several years before opening his Times Square magic store in 1939.

Free-lance writer Ross Harte chronicles his adventures (Merlini silently coauthors); his friendly rival is Inspector Homer Gavigan of the New York City homicide squad, an intelligent man who is nevertheless baffled by Merlini's ability to solve apparently impossible "locked-room" murders.

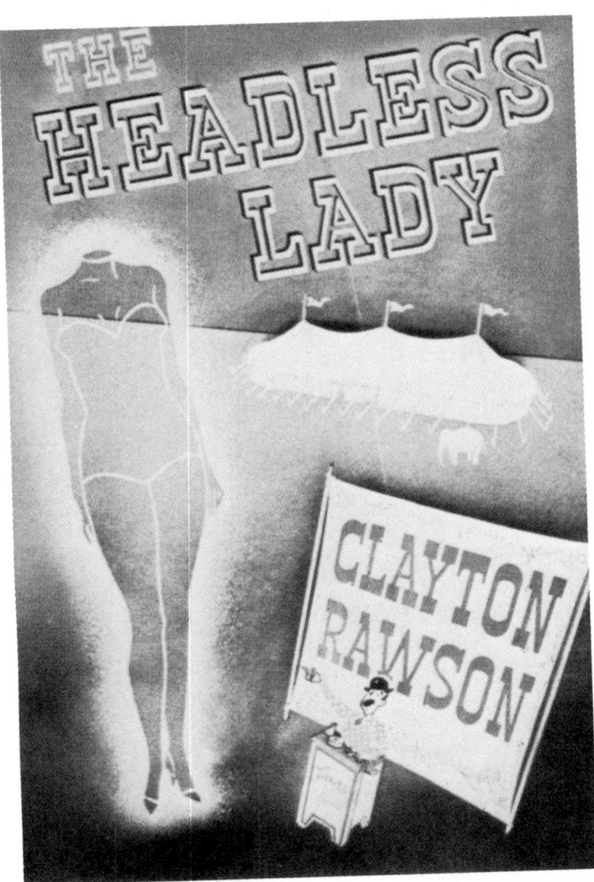

Clayton Rawson wrote the book and also designed the dust wrapper for *The Headless Lady*, first published in book form by Putnam in 1940. The Great Merlini is the detective in the novel, which originally appeared as a serial in *Detective Fiction Weekly* as *The Case of the Deadly Clown*.

Merlini's first case, *Death from a Top Hat* (1938), concerns multiple murder; magicians are the victims, and some of their colleagues are the leading suspects. Conjurers, fortune tellers, escape artists, mediums, sleight-of-hand experts, mentalists, and others of that ilk prove too formidable for the official police, so Merlini's expertise is required. In the aptly titled *The Footprints on the Ceiling* (1939), magic seems to be the cause of the footprints on the ceiling of a room in which a man was murdered. In *The Headless Lady* (1940) Merlini seeks a ruthless killer who performs his deadly tricks under the circus Big Top. The fourth and last Merlini book, *No Coffin for the Corpse* (1942), shows how the retired prestidigitator solves the murder of a multimillionaire neurotic who was apparently killed by a man everybody "knew" was dead and buried.

Films

Although Merlini has had a cinematic career, he has appeared in "disguise."

Miracles for Sale. MGM, 1939. Robert Young, Florence Rice, Frank Craven, Henry Hull, Lee Bowman. Directed by Tod Browning. Based on *Death from a Top Hat.*

A young former magician, now a successful manufacturer of devices used in stage illusions (the Merlini character, called Mike Morgan and played by Young), allows a frightened girl to involve him in the bizarre ritual murders of two fellow practitioners of magic. He unmasks the killer during an elaborate stage act, in which the girl is to "catch" a rifle bullet with her teeth.

In the Michael SHAYNE film *The Man Who Wouldn't Die* (1942), based on *The Footprints on the Ceiling,* Merlini is now Shayne. The detective consults a professional magician for help in solving a mystery involving the "buried-alive" stunt.

MERRILL, P. J. *See* ROTH, HOLLY.

MERRIMAN, PAT. *See* PEROWNE, BARRY.

MERRION, DESMOND (Creator: Cecil John Charles Street as Miles Burton; *see* RHODE, JOHN). This former intelligence agent served in the British Admiralty during World War I and became interested in detective work as a result of his wartime experiences. In frequent demand by Scotland Yard, he helps (and bickers with) his friend Inspector Henry Arnold of the Criminal Investigation Department.

Merrion is married but dashes off at the drop of a hat to investigate baffling murder cases. He has a vivid imagination and is whimsical and lighthearted. He is fond of driving his car and smokes a lot of cigarettes.

Merrion's career as a private detective is interrupted by World War II, in which he serves as a captain in the intelligence branch of the Admiralty once again. With the cessation of hostilities in 1945, Merrion returns to his position as unofficial consultant to Scotland Yard.

CHECKLIST

The following works are about Merrion or Arnold or, most often, both.

1930 *The Secret of High Eldersham*
1931 *Menace on the Downs*
1931 *The Three Crimes*
1932 *The Death of Mr. Gantley*
1933 *Death at the Crossroads*
1933 *Fate at the Fair*
1933 *Tragedy at the Thirteenth Hole*
1934 *The Charabanc Mystery*
1934 *To Catch a Thief*
1935 *The Milk-Churn Murder* (U.S. title: *The Clue of the Silver Brush*)
1935 *The Devereux Court Mystery*
1936 *Death in the Tunnel* (U.S. title: *Dark Is the Tunnel*)
1936 *Murder of a Chemist*
1936 *Where Is Barbara Prentice?* (U.S. title: *The Clue of the Silver Cellar*)
1937 *Death at the Club* (U.S. title: *The Clue of the Fourteen Keys*)
1937 *Murder in Crown Passage* (U.S. title: *The Man with the Tattooed Face*)
1938 *Death at Low Tide*
1938 *The Platinum Cat*
1939 *Death Leaves No Card*
1939 *Mr. Babbacombe Dies*
1940 *Murder in the Coalhole* (U.S. title: *Written in Dust*)
1940 *Mr. Westerby Missing*
1940 *Death Takes a Flat* (U.S. title: *Vacancy with Corpse*)
1941 *Death of Two Brothers*
1941 *Up the Garden Path* (U.S. title: *Death Visits Downspring*)
1942 *This Undesirable Residence* (U.S. title: *Death at Ash House*)
1943 *Dead Stop*
1943 *Murder, M.D.* (U.S. title: *Who Killed the Doctor?*)
1944 *The Four-ply Yarn* (U.S. title: *The Shadow on the Cliff*)
1944 *The Three-Corpse Trick*
1945 *Not a Leg to Stand On*
1945 *Early Morning Murder* (U.S. title: *Accidents Do Happen*)
1946 *The Cat Jumps*
1946 *Situation Vacant*
1947 *Heir to Lucifer*
1947 *A Will in the Way*
1948 *Death in Shallow Water*
1948 *Devil's Reckoning*
1949 *Death Takes the Living* (U.S. title: *The Disappearing Parson*)
1949 *Look Alive*
1950 *Ground for Suspicion*
1950 *A Village Afraid*
1951 *Beware Your Neighbor*
1951 *Murder out of School*

1952 *Murder on Duty*
1953 *Heir to Murder*
1953 *Something to Hide*
1954 *Murder in Absence*
1954 *Unwanted Corpse*
1955 *A Crime in Time*
1955 *Murder Unrecognized*
1956 *Death in a Duffle Coat*
1956 *Found Drowned*
1957 *The Chinese Puzzle*
1957 *The Moth-Watch Murder*
1958 *Bones in the Brickfield*
1958 *Death Takes a Detour*
1959 *Return from the Dead*
1959 *The Smell of Smoke*
1960 *Legacy of Death*
1960 *Death Paints a Picture*

MERRIVALE, SIR HENRY (Creator: John Dickson CARR as Carter Dickson). "The Old Man" is Carr's personal favorite detective. He is loud and vulgar and shouts (never-quoted) obscenities at the drop of a guard, embarrassing the dignified personages around him, although the lovely young heroines generally seem less offended than do various clerks, lawyers, and poor, doddering Inspector Humphrey Masters of Scotland Yard, who is invariably confused by the crime at hand and convinced that supernatural powers are at work. Like his contemporary Dr. Gideon FELL, Merrivale usually works on "locked-room" murders and similar "impossible" crimes.

H. M. is bald-headed, pigeon-toed, and barrel-shaped, and scowls evilly while clamping a cigar between his teeth. He holds one of the oldest baronetcies in England—a cause of disgust to those who consider the dignity of the nobility a matter of importance. In appearance and unorthodox personality, Merrivale is a conglomerate; he was not inspired by Churchill but developed some of his traits in later years.

CHECKLIST

1934 *The Plague Court Murders*
1934 *The White Priory Murders*
1935 *The Red Widow Murders*
1935 *The Unicorn Murders*
1936 *The Magic Lantern Murders* (U.S. title: *The Punch and Judy Murders*)
1937 *The Peacock Feather Murders* (British title: *The Ten Teacups*)
1938 *The Judas Window*
1938 *Death in Five Boxes*
1939 *The Reader Is Warned*
1940 *Nine—And Death Makes Ten* (British title: *Murder in the Submarine Zone*)
1940 *And So to Murder*
1941 *Seeing Is Believing*
1942 *The Gilded Man*
1943 *She Died a Lady*
1944 *He Wouldn't Kill Patience*
1945 *The Curse of the Bronze Lamp* (British title: *Lord of the Sorcerers*)
1946 *My Late Wives*
1948 *The Skeleton in the Clock*
1949 *A Graveyard to Let*
1950 *Night at the Mocking Widow*
1952 *Behind the Crimson Blind*
1953 *The Cavalier's Cup*
1954 *The Third Bullet and Other Stories* (s.s.; by John Dickson Carr; contains one story about Merrivale)
1963 *The Men Who Explained Miracles* (s.s.; by John Dickson Carr; contains one story about Merrivale)

MERWIN, SAMUEL. *See* WEBSTER, H. K.

MILLAR, KENNETH. *See* MACDONALD, ROSS.

MILLAR, MARGARET (1915–). Canadian-American author. Born Margaret Sturm in Kitchener, Ontario, Canada, she majored in classics at the University of Toronto but left in 1938, before completing her degree, to marry an American, Kenneth Millar (Ross MACDONALD). Since the end of World War II the Millars have lived near Santa Barbara, Calif., where they have become active conservationists and helped found a chapter of the National Audubon Society. In 1965, for her "outstanding achievements as a writer and citizen," the *Los Angeles Times* selected her to receive a Woman of the Year award. Mrs. Millar's observations on the wildlife in the canyons near her home were collected in *The Birds and the Beasts Were There* (1968), her only nonfiction book. The Millars' only child, Linda, died in 1970.

In 1941, while confined to bed for a heart ailment, Mrs. Millar read mysteries omnivorously and then, against doctor's orders, wrote a detective novel. Her first three books featured as detective a tall, whimsical psychiatrist who was appropriately named Paul Prye. Two later novels, *Wall of Eyes* and *The Iron Gates*, are about Inspector Sands of the Toronto Police Department. A lonely, compassionate man of drab appearance, Sands is once described as having "a face that looked as if he had slept in it."

Following *The Iron Gates,* which received excellent reviews, Mrs. Millar wrote three nonmystery novels, *Experiment in Springtime* (1947), *It's All in the Family* (1948), and *The Cannibal Heart* (1949), which were greeted with relative indifference by the critics. She wrote only one other nonmystery, *Wives and Lovers* (1954).

Her mysteries continued to receive very favorable reviews. *Vanish in an Instant*, which is set in midwinter at the fictional college town of Arbana, Mich., was especially well received. *Beast in View* won the Mystery Writers of America Edgar as best mystery novel of 1955. *A Stranger in My Grave* is most effective on several counts. It concerns a young woman who has a recurring nightmare in which she sees her own grave. One day she actually does see the grave she has dreamed about. The book introduces Mrs. Millar's first private detective, Steve Pinata, who is in the tradition of the California sleuths created by Raymond CHANDLER and her husband. *The Fiend*, also in the realm of abnormal psychology, deals with a borderline mental case who has a past history of assault and is suspected of attacking a nine-year-old girl.

Most of the Millar mysteries since 1950 have been set in California, and that state's phenomena are often in evidence. *How Like an Angel* is about a religious cult called the True Believers. A private detective named Quinn searches among their members for a missing husband. *Beyond This Point Are Monsters* includes many insights into the life of the Chicano in the San Diego region.

CHECKLIST

1941	*The Invisible Worm*
1942	*The Weak-eyed Bat*
1942	*The Devil Loves Me*
1943	*Wall of Eyes*
1944	*Fire Will Freeze*
1945	*The Iron Gates* (British title: *The Taste of Fear*)
1950	*Do Evil in Return*
1952	*Rose's Last Summer*
1952	*Vanish in an Instant*
1955	*Beast in View*
1957	*An Air That Kills* (British title: *The Soft Talkers*)
1959	*The Listening Walls*
1960	*A Stranger in My Grave*
1962	*How Like an Angel*
1964	*The Fiend*
1970	*Beyond This Point Are Monsters*

MILLER, BILL. *See* MILLER, WADE.

MILLER, WADE (pseudonym of Robert Wade, 1920– , and Bill Miller, 1920–1961). There were many parallels in the lives of these mystery writers. Miller's birthplace was Garrett, Ind.; Wade was born in San Diego, Calif. After Miller was taken to California as a child, he met Wade at San Diego's Woodrow Wilson Junior High School, and they began to collaborate on school newspapers, plays, and radio and film scripts. While at San Diego State College, they edited the *East San Diego Press*, the largest-circulation weekly newspaper in that town. They were separated during World War II; although both were Air Force sergeants, Miller served in the Pacific and Wade in Europe. They continued collaborating, by mail, on their first mystery, *Deadly Weapon*, published in 1946, soon after they were discharged. Each had a home near San Diego and was married. Miller had a son and daughter; Wade, two sons and two daughters.

Deadly Weapon, published under the joint pseudonym Wade Miller, begins with a murder in a San Diego burlesque theater. Their second book, *Guilty Bystander* (1947), is the first in a series of six novels about San Diego private detective Max THURSDAY. A short story, "Invitation to an Accident," won second prize in *Ellery Queen's Mystery Magazine*'s 1955 contest. As Dale Wilmer, they wrote *Memo for Murder* (1951) and *Dead Fall* (1954), the latter a novel of spying and murder at a California aircraft plant.

In 1955 they adopted another pseudonym, Whit Masterson, which Wade continues to use in writing alone. *All Through the Night* (1955) is a popular suspense novel about the kidnapping of a girl (played by Natalie Wood in the film version, *A Cry in the Night*, 1956). *A Hammer in His Hand* (1960) was one of the first mysteries to use a policewoman as protagonist.

Wade has written two books under his own name; one of them, *Knave of Eagles* (1969), is about an adventurer sent to Cuba to bring back a major league baseball player who has been prevented from leaving by the Castro government. Wade also has nine solo Whit Mastersons to his credit.

On a professional level, the Wade Miller collaboration was one of the most successful and prolific in mystery fiction; it produced thirty-three novels, two screenplays, 200 radio scripts, and countless novelettes and short stories.

MILNE, A[LAN] A[LEXANDER] (1882–1956). English author of juvenile literature, verse, plays, essays, short stories, and novels. Born in London, he graduated from Cambridge University in 1903 and began a journalistic career, eventually becoming assistant editor of *Punch* (until the onset of World War I). He married Dorothy (Daphne) de Sélincourt, a writer, in 1913; they had a son, Christopher Robin, who was immortalized in the children's books about Winnie-the-Pooh, the works for which A. A. Milne is best known.

His one true detective novel, *The Red House Mystery* (1922), is one of the most important of the 1920s, for it introduces the jolly, "what fun!" approach to crime in the person of Antony Gillingham, a slightly zany amateur detective whose nickname is "Madman." After a fifteen-year absence in Australia, Robert—Mark Ablett's black-sheep brother—returns to England and is shot to death. Inexplicably, Mark disappears from his home, the red house of the title, even though it is believed that he must have shot his brother in self-defense. Since the local police are baffled, the lighthearted Gillingham and Bill Beverley, who narrates the adventure, set about to solve the case.

In addition to this classic tale, described by Alexander Woollcott as "one of the three best mystery stories of all time," Milne made other contributions to the genre. *The Fourth Wall* (1928; U.S. title: *The Perfect Alibi*) was a popular play; the audience saw the murder committed and then witnessed every logical step taken to uncover and apprehend the culprit. *Four Days' Wonder* (1933) is a humorous satire on crime. *A Table near the Band* (1950) contains two skillful mystery stories, "Portrait of Lydia" and "Murder at Eleven." He also wrote an early parody of Sherlock HOLMES, "The Rape of the Sherlock," published in *Vanity Fair* magazine (London).

MITCHELL, GLADYS (1901–). English schoolteacher and author of detective novels. Born in the village of Cowley in Oxford, she attended University College, London, and then taught in elementary schools for more than twenty-five years. At first she taught out of financial necessity, but then, during World War II, she continued because of the teacher shortage. She published her first mystery in 1929 and since then has published almost fifty books under her own name and as Stephen Hockaby.

Miss Mitchell's enthusiasms, the works of Sigmund Freud and witchcraft, are clearly reflected in her books. Her series detective, Dame Beatrice Bradley, psychiatric consultant to the British Home Office, resolves many of her cases with explanations of the murderer's psyche, and the supernatural figures prominently in her investigations. *Watson's Choice* (1955) uses the Sherlock HOLMES canon as the basis for a party game that ends in murder. Four of Miss Mitchell's novels, *Laurels Are Poison* (1942), *When Last I Died* (1942), *Sunset over Soho* (1943), and *The Rising of the Moon* (1945), are included in SANDOE'S READERS' GUIDE TO CRIME.

MOFFETT, CLEVELAND (LANGSTON) (1863–1926). American journalist, dramatist, novelist, and short story writer. Born in Boonville, N.Y., the son of Mary (Cleveland) and William H. Moffett, he graduated from Yale and then spent many years in Europe as a correspondent for several New York newspapers. Even after he returned to live in the United States, many of his settings and characters were French; he died in Paris.

Among his best-known works are *True Tales from the Archives of the Pinkertons* (1897), semifictionalized accounts of cases handled by the famous detective agency; *Through the Wall* (1909), listed in the HAYCRAFT-QUEEN CORNERSTONE LIBRARY; *The Bishop's Purse* (1913; written with Oliver Herford, 1863–1935), a humorous tale of robbery and impersonation set in England; *The Seine Mystery* (1925), featuring the amateur detective work of an American journalist in Paris; and *The Mysterious Card* (1896), one of the most significant works of its kind. Originally published as two entirely separate short stories in *The Black Cat*, an American magazine, the tale is

The first edition of Cleveland Moffett's *The Mysterious Card*, perhaps the world's most familiar shaggy-dog story, is rarely seen with a dust wrapper. It was published in 1896 by Small, Maynard.

perhaps the first to use a now-familiar device: an innocent person meets with anger, suspicion, horror, and persecution when he asks other people to translate a message written on a card in a strange language. Color blindness is used as a clue (another possible first). The second part of the story, called "The Mysterious Card Unveiled," is a fantastic attempt at a supernatural explanation of the Jack the Ripper murders, using the Jekyll-Hyde theme. As a publisher's gimmick when the book was first published, this part was sealed; the purchaser was promised a refund if the book was returned, seal unbroken, to the bookseller.

MOFFITT, JACK. See STOCKTON, FRANK R.

MONTGOMERY, (ROBERT) BRUCE. See CRISPIN, EDMUND.

MORIARTY, PROFESSOR JAMES (Creator: Sir

Professor Moriarty is one of twenty-five characters taken from Conan Doyle's books to appear in this series of cigareete cards. Similar to bubble-gum cards, these cards were given away with packs of Turf cigarettes. The series was printed by Alexander Boguslavsky.

Arthur CONAN DOYLE). The "Napoleon of Crime" is considered the most dangerous man in London by Sherlock HOLMES, his archrival and sinister adversary. Only Moriarty, known to the rest of the world as merely a mild-mannered mathematics professor, has sufficient intellect to challenge Holmes, who

Edgar W. Smith (1894–1960), commissionaire of the Baker Street Irregulars and founder of *The Baker Street Journal,* used this portrait of Professor Moriarty for the 1953 pamphlet *The Napoleon of Crime,* published by Pamphlet House, Summit, N.J. It is derived from Sidney Paget's depiction.

sees him as a great spider in the center of a giant web of crime that touches every part of the city. Holmes calls him "a genius, a philosopher, an abstract thinker"—a man so brilliant that no one, not even the officials at Scotland Yard or Dr. WATSON, Holmes's friend and associate, recognizes Moriarty for the master criminal he is. After battling inconclusively for several years, the two giants on opposite sides of the law finally engage in a physical battle at the edge of the Reichenbach Falls in Switzerland, Moriarty losing his life and Holmes escaping miraculously. T. S. Eliot wrote a poem, "Macavity: The Mystery Cat," in which the feline is identified as the "Napoleon of Crime." Suspicions that Moriarty survived the plunge over the cliff were confirmed with the publication of John Gardner's *The Return of Moriarty* (1974) and *The Revenge of Moriarty* (1975).

MORLAND, NIGEL (1905–). English author and editor. Born in London, he briefly attended school, but, tiring of this, he decided to educate himself. He was first employed as a packer on the *London Daily Mail* and then went on to various jobs—in printing, bookbinding, and advertising, as a door-to-door salesman, mortuary assistant, copyboy, and so on. His lifelong friend Edgar WALLACE helped him begin his careers in journalism and writing. He took a job as a cub reporter in China, covering crime stories, and worked on various Far Eastern newspapers, studying (as an unpaid assistant) forensic medicine as a sideline. Later he wrote screen, radio, and television adaptations, wrote dialogue, and edited, in various capacities, publications ranging from *Doctor* and the *Edgar Wallace Mystery Magazine* to *News-Review*. He began to write potboilers at full speed (totaling more than 300), including about a dozen ghost-written books, and achieved notice with his first thriller about Palmyra Evangeline Pym, deputy assistant commissioner of Scotland Yard.

Morland has written a number of textbooks, including *An Outline of Scientific Criminology* (1950) and *An Outline of Sexual Criminology* (1966). He writes or edits an occasional book nowadays, but his main interest is *The Criminologist,* which he has edited since 1966; currently, he is also editor of *Forensic Photography* and *The International Journal of Forensic Dentistry*. He has been married three times, to Peggy Barwell, Pamela Hunnex, and Jill Wilson Harvey, and has one daughter and two sons.

Among the titles in the long series about the indomitable Mrs. Pym of Scotland Yard are *The Corpse on the Flying Trapeze* (1941), *Dressed to Kill* (1947), *The Lady Had a Gun* (1951), *A Bullet for Midas* (1958), and *The Dear, Dead Girls* (1961).

Morland also wrote under the pseudonyms Mary Dane, John Donavan, Norman Forrest, Roger Garnett, Neal Shepherd, and Vincent McCall.

MORRISON, ARTHUR (1863–1945). English dramatist, journalist, art expert, fiction writer, and creator of Martin HEWITT, a famous private detective whose methods closely resemble those of Sherlock HOLMES.

Born near London, Morrison worked for several journals until the publication of *Tales of Mean Streets* (1894), which, like *A Child of the Jago* (1896) and *To London Town* (1899), were fictional illustrations of life in the slums of London. The impact of these naturalistic novels and stories of crime and poverty in London's East End was instrumental in initiating many vital social reforms, particularly with regard to housing.

An art connoisseur and owner of one of the great private collections of English and Oriental masters, Morrison wrote the monumental *The Painters of Japan* (1911), still a standard reference tool.

Morrison's best fiction can be clearly divided into the straight detective stories about Hewitt, for which he had little enthusiasm, and the atmospheric tales of the London slums, which sold well in their day and have greater vitality than his other work. Other books related to the mystery genre are *The Dorrington Deed-Box* (1897), short stories about the unscrupulous Dorrington, a con man and thief who occasionally earns his money honestly—as a private detective; *Cunning Murrell* (1900), a fictionalized account of a witch doctor's activities in early-nineteenth-century rural Essex; *The Hole in the Wall* (1902), a story of murder in a London slum, and of the effects of that environment on its inhabitants; and *The Green Eye of Goona* (1903; U.S. title: *The Green Diamond*), an adventure tale, ending in murder, in which the object of a chase is the fabulous gem eye of an Indian idol.

MORSE, CARLETON E. See I LOVE A MYSTERY.

MORTON, ANTHONY. See CREASEY, JOHN.

MOTO, MR. (Creator: John P. MARQUAND). The soft-spoken, overly polite Mr. I. O. Moto is Japan's number-one secret service agent. His diminutive stature belies great physical strength which, combined with expertise in judo, makes him capable of killing an adversary with little difficulty.

Mr. Moto's impeccable English is spoken softly, his *s*'s hissing through shiny, gold-filled teeth. He says: "I can do many, many things. I can mix drinks and wait on tables and I am a very good valet. I can navigate and manage small boats. I have studied at two foreign universities. I also know carpentry and surveying and five Chinese dialects. So very many things come in useful. . . ."

Moto closely resembles an earlier Oriental detective, Charlie CHAN. In his first case, *No Hero* (1935; British title: *Mr. Moto Takes a Hand*), he assists Commander James Driscoll, a young American flier in the Far East who holds the balance of power in the Pacific in his hands. It is not difficult to understand why the adventures of an espionage agent whose sympathies lay with the Japanese termi-

Peter Lorre (left) plays the Oriental detective with a minimum of makeup, in *Mysterious Mr. Moto*, [*Twentieth Century-Fox*]

nated in 1941. Mr. Moto reappeared in *Stopover: Tokyo* (1957), which deals with the struggle for political supremacy in postwar Japan.

The other Mr. Moto novels are *Thank You, Mr. Moto* (1936), *Think Fast, Mr. Moto* (1937), *Mr. Moto Is So Sorry* (1938), and *Last Laugh, Mr. Moto* (1942).

Films

The unobtrusive Japanese secret agent was portrayed brilliantly by Peter Lorre in eight films during a two-year period. With very little facial change beyond thick eyeglasses and flattened hair, the Hungarian Lorre was able to suggest the pleasant and subservient—but secretive and cunning—Moto perfectly.

Think Fast, Mr. Moto. Twentieth Century-Fox, 1937. Lorre, Virginia Field, Thomas Beck, Lotus Long. Directed by Norman Foster.

Alone, Moto travels from San Francisco's Chinatown across the Pacific (on a steamer from which he throws an adversary overboard) to Shanghai, in pursuit of a gang of diamond smugglers.

Thank You, Mr. Moto. Twentieth Century-Fox, 1937. Lorre, Beck, Pauline Frederick, Jayne Regan, Sidney Blackmer. Directed by Foster.

A Chinese prince kills himself when the dowager queen is murdered by enemies of the throne who are looking for some ancient scrolls that show the location of Genghis Khan's treasure. There are other deaths, and Moto dispatches two of the villains himself, before he manages to burn the scrolls. The setting is Peiping.

Mr. Moto's Gamble. Twentieth Century-Fox, 1938. Lorre, Keye Luke, Lynn Bari, Harold Huber. Directed by James Tinling.

Moto attends a prizefight after which the loser dies of poison; he is "aided" in his investigation by Charlie Chan's son Lee! (The film was begun as a Chan vehicle but was changed when Warner Oland, who had portrayed Chan many times, died.)

Mr. Moto Takes a Chance. Twentieth Century-Fox, 1938. Lorre, Rochelle Hudson, Robert Kent, J. Edward Bromberg. Directed by Foster.

A famous aviatrix on a round-the-world solo flight crashes in an Asian jungle—deliberately—in order to spy on a politically ambitious rajah. Moto is there, too, pretending to be an archaeologist, and often disguised as a white-bearded hermit priest who lives in a jungle temple.

Mysterious Mr. Moto. Twentieth Century-Fox, 1938. Lorre, Henry Wilcoxon, Mary Maguire, Erik Rhodes, Leon Ames. Directed by Foster, who coauthored the original screenplay with Philip MACDONALD.

Moto "escapes" from Devil's Island in order to penetrate an international league of assassins and unmask its leader. In London's murky Limehouse, Moto saves the life of a fragile Oriental girl and, disguised as a sputtering German art critic, attends a gallery opening so that he can rescue a young millionaire marked for death.

Mr. Moto's Last Warning. Twentieth Century-Fox, 1939. Lorre, Ricardo Cortez, Field, John Carradine, George Sanders, Robert Coote. Directed by Foster, who coauthored the original screenplay with MacDonald.

In Port Said, international conspirators, plotting to blow up both the English and French fleets, put Moto into a sack and toss him off a dock; he cuts himself loose underwater.

Mr. Moto in Danger Island. Twentieth Century-Fox, 1939. Lorre, Jean Hersholt, Amanda Duff, Warren Hymer. Directed by Herbert I. Leeds. Based on *Murder in Trinidad* (1933) by radio commentator–mystery novelist John W. VANDERCOOK.

The Danger Island of the title is Puerto Rico, and it proves to be exceedingly dangerous for Moto as he journeys there on the trail of diamond smugglers.

Mr. Moto Takes a Vacation. Twentieth Century-Fox, 1939. Lorre, Joseph Schildkraut, Lionel Atwill, Field, John King. Directed by Foster, who coauthored the original screenplay with MacDonald.

In the East, a young archaeologist unearths the legendary crown of the Queen of Sheba, and Moto, apparently on a holiday, declares that he will accompany the find back to the United States. The crown is placed on display in a burglar-proof museum, but Moto senses the presence of a master jewel thief, long thought dead, who is preparing a final great coup.

Mr. Moto Takes a Vacation was the last film in the series; the growing popular feeling against Japan brought an end not only to the Moto books but also to the Oriental's American screen career. In *Stopover: Tokyo* an older, more communicative Moto returned; during the war he had been involved with the Japanese secret police. In the film (1957) based on the book, the Moto character was eliminated.

The Return of Mr. Moto. Twentieth Century-Fox, 1965. Henry Silva, Suzanne Lloyd, Terrence Longdon. Directed by Ernest Morris.

In this attempt to revive Moto, in the wake of the James BOND thrillers, he is young and muscular, a member of Interpol, and much more aggressive. He follows a trail of murders from London to the Middle East and oil intrigue.

MOTTEN, D. R. *See* SAINT, THE.

MOYES, PATRICIA (1923–). Anglo-Irish author and detective story writer; creator of Henry TIBBETT. Born in Bray, Ireland, the daughter of Marion (Boyd) and Ernst Pakenham-Walsh, a judge in the Indian Civil Service, she was educated at Overstone School in Northamptonshire, England (1934–1939). She served in the radar section of the Women's Auxiliary Air Force between 1940 and 1945 and became a flight officer. After the war she acted as secretary to Peter Ustinov Productions, Ltd. (1947–1953), and was the assistant editor for *Vogue* in London (1954–1958). She married John Moyes, a photographer, in 1951 (divorced 1959). In 1962 she married John S. Haszard, an official of the International Court of Justice, now with the International Monetary Fund in Washington, D.C.

Miss Moyes wrote the screenplay for *School for Scoundrels* (1960), with Alastair Sim; published a juvenile novel, *Helter-Skelter* (1968); and translated Jean Anouilh's *Léocadia* as *Time Remembered*. She has also written a lighthearted autobiography centered on her two Siamese cats, *After All, They're Only Cats . . .* (1973). She currently resides in a small house in Georgetown. Her interests are skiing, sailing, good food and wine, and travel.

Vivian Mort of the *Chicago Tribune* once stated that Miss Moyes has "put the who back in whodunit." Although the remark is now a cliché, it is indeed applicable to Miss Moyes, one of the finest practitioners in the classic form.

MUDDOCK, JOYCE EMMERSON PRESTON. *See* DONOVAN, DICK.

MUIR, DEXTER. *See* GRIBBLE, LEONARD R.

MURDOCH, BRUCE. *See* CREASEY, JOHN.

MURDOCK, KENT (Creator: George Harmon COXE). Reflecting his creator's newspaper background and interest in photography, Kent Murdock is picture chief for the *Boston Courier-Herald* and the most highly paid photographer in that city. From the time of his debut, in *Murder with Pictures,* his vocation is an important factor in the crimes he solves. Quick to be on the scene of a crime, Murdock takes pictures that frequently are the vital evidence that will determine the guilty party. Thus he or his film—or both—are often the object of the criminal's attention. In *The Fifth Key* he is drugged and then photographed lying beside a nude female corpse; it is only with great difficulty that he extricates himself from this situation. A case of mistaken identity occurs in *Eye Witness,* in which Murdock, on a secret photographic assignment, is arrested for murdering *himself.*

At ease in a bar or a drawing room, Murdock is more cultured than his fellow Boston photographer Flashgun CASEY, with whom he is often compared. During World War II Murdock sees combat and receives the Purple Heart for head and thigh wounds. He is then given an assignment as museum and monument officer in the fine arts division of the American military government in Europe. *The Jade Venus,* Murdock's first case after he returns to the United States, involves him in the recovery of stolen art treasures. By this time he is free to become involved with attractive females, his wife, who was featured in *Mrs. Murdock Takes a Case,* having been conveniently eliminated.

CHECKLIST

1935 *Murder with Pictures*
1936 *The Barotique Mystery*
1937 *The Camera Clue*
1939 *Four Frightened Women*
1939 *The Glass Triangle*
1941 *Mrs. Murdock Takes a Case*
1942 *The Charred Witness*
1945 *The Jade Venus*
1947 *The Fifth Key*
1948 *The Hollow Needle*
1949 *Lady Killer*
1950 *Eye Witness*
1951 *The Widow Had a Gun*
1953 *The Crimson Clue*
1954 *Focus on Murder*
1957 *Murder on Their Minds*
1958 *The Big Gamble*
1960 *The Last Commandment*
1963 *The Hidden Key*
1965 *The Reluctant Heiress*
1969 *An Easy Way to Go*

Film

Murder with Pictures. Paramount, 1936. Lew Ayres (Murdock), Gail Patrick, Joyce Compton, Paul Kelly, Onslow Stevens. Directed by Charles Barton.

A criminal lawyer, having just won the acquittal of a notorious gangster, is shot to death while surrounded by newspaper reporters taking photographs.

MURRAY, DAVID CHRISTIE (1847–1907). English journalist, lecturer, and novelist. Born in West Bromwich, Staffordshire, he became a police reporter at an early age and continued in journalism throughout much of his life. In later years he lectured extensively on behalf of Alfred Dreyfus. His novels are written in a journalistic style, reflecting his background, and his years in court provided many plots and incidents for his mystery and crime novels, notably *He Fell among Thieves* (1891), written with Henry Herman, and *A Race for Millions* (1898), which features Inspector Prickett of Scotland Yard. Murray's only collection of detective stories is *The Investigations of John Pym* (1895).

MYSTERY WRITERS OF AMERICA. *See* ORGANIZATIONS.

N

NEBEL, FREDERICK. *See* PULP MAGAZINES.

NEVINS, FRANCIS M., JR. (1943–). American lawyer, editor, critic, and author. Born in Bayonne, N.J., Nevins graduated from the Law School of New York University and was admitted to the New Jersey bar in 1967. After Army service in Oklahoma and work as a poverty lawyer, he began teaching at St. Louis University Law School.

Interested in the mystery since he was thirteen, Nevins has written many book reviews and articles and edited two books. *The Mystery Writer's Art* (1970) is an anthology of essays written between 1949 and 1970 and dealing with such subjects as the mystery film, the work of various writers, and historical trends in the genre. *Nightwebs* (1971) is a collection of fifteen stories by Cornell WOOLRICH that had never previously been reprinted. The book includes a complete checklist of Woolrich's work compiled by Nevins, Harold Knott, and William Thailing.

Nevins is the author of *Royal Bloodline: Ellery Queen, Author and Detective* (1974), a book about the lives and works of Frederic Dannay and Manfred B. Lee, for which he won an Edgar [*see* QUEEN, ELLERY (author)]. He has contributed short stories to *Ellery Queen's Mystery Magazine*, including a series about an amateur detective, law school professor Loren Mensing. His first Mensing novel, *Publish and Perish*, appeared in the fall of 1975.

NIELSEN, HELEN (BERNIECE) (1918–). American novelist and scriptwriter. Born on a farm in Warren County, Ill., she moved with her family to Chicago in 1928. Prior to World War II she worked in commercial art and interior decorating. She was also briefly a dressmaker and an assistant costumer for a Shakespearean repertory company. In 1942 she moved to southern California and spent the war years working in factories that produced the B36, the P80, and other planes. She did not regard any of these jobs as permanent because she "never intended to be anything but a writer."

She calls politics her great love and is active in California Democratic party circles. In 1963 she took a night flight to Washington, D.C., to be present at the funeral of John F. Kennedy. In 1968 she was at the Ambassador Hotel in Los Angeles, celebrating Robert Kennedy's primary victory, when he was shot. She has written that she has never completely recovered from that experience.

Miss Nielsen professes her love of Los Angeles despite the smog, which she detests. She lives in Laguna Beach in a house with an ocean view and has traveled extensively, in Mexico, Scandinavia, and Greece. She has written television scripts for the Perry MASON, Alfred HITCHCOCK, Checkmate, and other TV series, as well as nonmystery fiction under the pseudonym Kris Giles.

Miss Nielsen's early mystery work drew upon her Midwestern background. *The Crime Is Murder* (1956) takes place during the annual musical festival of a small northern Michigan city. The protagonist is a young writer. An earlier book, *Gold Coast Nocturne* (1952), is set in the wealthy sections of Chicago. Most of her recent work has had a Los Angeles background.

Miss Nielsen has generally received favorable critical attention. Jacques BARZUN and Wendell Hertig TAYLOR praised *The Crime Is Murder*, and Anthony BOUCHER was impressed with her work—especially *Woman Missing* (1961), a paperback collection of five short stories she had written for *Manhunt* and *Alfred Hitchcock's Mystery Magazine* during 1959–1960. She has also written extensively for *Ellery Queen's Mystery Magazine*. The crime in her 1959 story "Won't Somebody Help Me?" has its roots in the unemployment problem in "the promised land" of southern California.

NOLAN, WILLIAM F. (1928–). American artist and author of short stories, mysteries, and science fiction. Born in Missouri, he attended the Kansas City Art Institute before moving to southern California in 1947 to pursue a career as a cartoonist and commercial artist. In 1956 he became a full-time writer and has sold more than 500 articles and short stories. He also has written thirty-one books, including nine about automobile racing. One of these, *Adventure on Wheels* (1959), was cited by the American Library Association in 1960 as "one of the outstanding books of the year for Young Adults." Nolan lives in Los Angeles with his wife, Kam, who is also a professional writer.

Nolan's mysteries have appeared in most of the leading magazines in the field and in numerous anthologies. He has written two novels, *Death Is for Losers* (1968) and *The White Cad Cross-Up* (1969), about Los Angeles private eye Bart Challis. Nolan's *Space for Hire* (1971), blending science fiction and the mystery, received a Mystery Writers of America (MWA) nomination for best paperback original novel. Earlier, he had received an MWA scroll for his nonfictional *Dashiell Hammett: A Casebook* (1969).

NOON, ED (Creator: Michael AVALLONE, Jr.). This New York private eye–private spy possesses much of the past as well as the likes and dislikes of his creator. He has likewise aged with his creator; he was in his late twenties during his first book-length case, *The Tall Dolores* (1953), and in his late forties by *The Moon Maiden* (1974). Noon was born in Manhattan and raised in the Bronx, spent the early part of World War II at Fort Riley, Kans., and went overseas with a unit that saw much combat in Europe. In his early cases, his combined office and home is "the mouse auditorium"—one room in a run-down office building on West 56th Street. With time and affluence, Noon moved to Central Park West and dressed up his office with modern business furniture, a lovely black secretary–sex partner, and a red, white, and blue telephone on which he receives occasional assignments from the White House. Throughout his adventures, Noon remains the ultimate movie and baseball "nut," the quintessential "cockeyed optimist," the last true believer in the Hollywood myths of the late 1930s and the early 1940s, when he was an adolescent. Or, as he describes himself in *Shoot It Again, Sam* (1972): "Strong, tough, Manhattan-cynical but underneath still a small boy. A movie lover. Cried when dogs got run over, helped little old ladies across the street, works for principle and integrity. Not an antihero. He believes the home team will win the old ball game in the ninth, that nice guys will not finish last, and when the climax comes, the Good Guys will always beat the Bad Guys. He grew up that way, through the Depression years, a second World War, and all the time he dreamed in a million darkened movie houses. He embraced the word Hero; he believed there was no other way for a man to be."

NORTH, HUGH (Creator: Van Wyck MASON). In one of the early adventures in which the lean, handsome, pipe-smoking intelligence agent appears, *The Washington Legation Murders* (1935), North is a captain in Military Intelligence. He quickly rises to major, apparently skips lieutenant colonel, and has been a full colonel for decades. North believes in living life to its utmost—whether he is involved with beautiful women or with the riskiest assignments. Of his thirty cases, the best known are *The Seven Seas Murders* (1936; four novelettes), *The Singapore Exile Murders* (1939), *Saigon Singer* (1946), and *Dardanelles Derelict* (1949).

Radio

Staats Cotsworth played Major North in *The Man from G-2*, an international spy adventure series that made its radio debut on ABC in 1945.

NORTH, MR. and MRS. (Creators: Frances and Richard LOCKRIDGE). This famous husband and wife team made its detective debut in 1940 in *The Norths Meet Murder*, the first in a series of twenty-six mystery books and many radio and television dramas. In their first case, Pamela, accompanied by her husband, Jerry, finds a corpse in the vacant Greenwich Village studio she plans to use for a party.

Throughout the series, Mr. North, a publisher, is usually busy examining prospective manuscripts. His wife has little to do (except care for their cats) and seems to fill her days finding bodies and looking for murderers. This happens whether they are in

Gracie Allen attempts an unorthodox method of removing handcuffs from husband William Post, Jr., in the film version of the stage comedy *Mr. and Mrs. North*. [*MGM*]

New York or on vacation (in an upstate New York cabin, in *Murder Out of Turn;* on a Caribbean-bound cruise ship, in *Voyage into Violence;* or in the Florida Keys, in *Murder by the Book*). When not directly involved in a murder case, Pam and Jerry relax by playing tennis and devoting attention to their beloved cat, Martini, and her daughters, Gin and Sherry, who are eventually replaced by a series of other cats in the North household. Their adventures are usually shared by Lieutenant (later Captain) Bill Weigand, a Homicide Squad detective who has considerable social charm. Weigand and his wife, Dorian, are close personal friends of the Norths. The policeman's loyal assistant is Detective Sergeant Aloysius Clarence Mullins.

CHECKLIST

1940	*The Norths Meet Murder*
1941	*Murder Out of Turn*
1941	*A Pinch of Poison*
1942	*Death on the Aisle*
1942	*Hanged for a Sheep*
1943	*Death Takes a Bow*
1944	*Killing the Goose*
1945	*Payoff for the Banker*
1946	*Murder Within Murder*
1946	*Death of a Tall Man*
1947	*Untidy Murder*
1948	*Murder Is Served*
1949	*The Dishonest Murderer*
1950	*Murder in a Hurry*
1951	*Murder Comes First*
1952	*Dead As a Dinosaur*
1953	*Death Has a Small Voice*
1953	*Curtain for a Jester*
1954	*A Key to Death*
1955	*Death of an Angel*
1956	*Voyage into Violence*
1958	*The Long Skeleton*
1959	*Murder Is Suggested*
1960	*The Judge Is Reversed*
1961	*Murder Has Its Points*
1963	*Murder by the Book*

Play and Film

The sleuthing team was brought to the Broadway stage by Owen Davis in 1941, in a competent, humorous whodunit with Peggy Conklin and Albert Hackett as Pam and Jerry. Long-running (and a stock favorite since), it was soon made into a film, with the same title.

Mr. and Mrs. North. MGM, 1941. Gracie Allen, William Post, Jr., Paul Kelly (Lieutenant Weigand), Rose Hobart, Virginia Grey, Tom Conway. Directed by Robert B. Sinclair.

Scatterbrained Pam North, welcoming her publisher husband home from a business trip with a drink, discovers a corpse in the liquor cabinet.

Radio and Television

In 1942 a radio series (also called *Mr. and Mrs. North*) of half-hour adventures made its debut on NBC, with Alice Frost and Joseph Curtin, who became one of the most endearing, and enduring, mystery-solving couples in the medium. Later, the television counterpart, with Richard Denning and Barbara Britton, mixed murder with comedy in fifty-seven half-hour programs that began in 1953.

O

O'BREEN, FERGUS (Creator: Anthony BOUCHER). This private detective, who runs a one-man agency in Los Angeles, is very Irish—his hair is bright red, and he has the reputation of being a wild man.

Born about 1910, he never knew his mother, and his father was an alcoholic whose interests did not extend to his children. His older sister, Maureen, had the responsibility of bringing up Fergus and did a more than satisfactory job.

O'Breen has been described as "cocksure," "curious," "brash," and "colorful" (he has the habit of referring to himself as "The O'Breen"). All these qualities seem to be the instinctive camouflage of a man who, in another age, might have been a bard, a crusader, or possibly a prophet. He is moderately successful in a financial sense, and his clients, usually pleased with his efforts, speak highly of him and call him a thoroughly nice young man.

His hobbies are reading, cooking, football, and classical music. His allergy to cats makes him sneeze exactly seven times. Many of his cases are set in Hollywood and are often brought to his attention by his sister, the head of publicity at Metropolis Pictures and one of the smartest career women in the industry.

The first O'Breen story, *The Case of the Crumpled Knave* (1939), deals with the murder of an elderly inventor whose anti-gas weapon could be of incalculable value during wartime. *The Case of the Baker Street Irregulars* (1940), cited as one of Boucher's best by James SANDOE, who called it "a cheerful Sherlockian frolic," is about a movie studio's plan to film a HOLMES story. *The Case of the Solid Key* (1941) concerns a little theater group whose managing director is found dead in a locked room. O'Breen's last book-length case, *The Case of the Seven Sneezes* (1942), is set on an island off the California coast and concerns a silver wedding anniversary party during which murder repeats a pattern from twenty-five years ago. One of the eleven stories in *Far and Away* (1955) also features O'Breen.

O'CONNOR, PATRICK. See HOLTON, LEONARD.

O'DONNELL, PETER. See BLAISE, MODESTY.

OFFORD, LENORE GLEN (1905–). American reviewer and author of mystery fiction. Mrs. Offord, who lives in Berkeley, Calif., is the wife of Harold R. Offord, division chief in charge of forest diseases for the U.S. Forest Service. Her hobby is reading mysteries, and since 1950 she has also reviewed them for the *San Francisco Chronicle.*

The author's own mysteries, including *Murder on Russian Hill* (1938), *Skeleton Key* (1943), and *Glass Mask* (1944), have frequently been set in and around San Francisco. The detective in most of her works is a mystery writer, Todd McKinnon, who lives in Berkeley with his wife and daughter. In *Walking Shadow* (1959) the McKinnons attend the annual Shakespeare Festival in Ashland, Oreg., where their daughter, Barby, is appearing. It was not at all surprising that this book was praised for its authenticity, for the Offords spent many years in Ashland, where their own daughter, Judith, was a performer.

O'HIGGINS, HARVEY J[ERROLD] (1876–1929). American novelist, playwright, and short story writer. Born in London, Ontario, Canada, the son of Isabella (Stephenson) and Joseph P. O'Higgins, he began a career as a newspaperman, only to abandon it in 1901 (the year of his marriage) for the more lucrative fees of free-lance writing. He made two notable contributions to the detective story.

The Adventures of Detective Barney (1915) is a collection of seven stories about Barney Cook, a typical American boy and the most believable young detective in American literature. Barney was also the subject of *The Dummy,* a play coauthored by O'Higgins and Harriet Ford and produced in 1914. The play bore some similarity to one of the stories, "The Kidnappers." All the plots were based on a series

Barney Cook is probably the least offensive boy detective in criminal fiction. Seven stories about him were collected in *The Adventures of Detective Barney.* Henry Raleigh's illustration appeared on the dust wrapper of the first edition, published by Century in 1915.

of factual articles O'Higgins had written about the Burns Detective Agency.

Detective Duff Unravels It (1929), published posthumously, was selected for QUEEN'S QUORUM and offered as the most significant collection of its decade because it represents the first serious approach to psychoanalytical detection. The dust wrapper of the first edition describes John Duff's methods: "Every crime is committed in two places. It is committed at the scene of the crime, where the police investigate it, but what is far more important, it is also committed in the mind of the criminal. The old-fashioned detective followed the first trail, but Detective Duff tracked the psychological trail of the criminal through a labyrinth of haunting fears and hidden repressions and veiled passions. Duff. . . discovered the guilty ones by the warm, believable tracing of a human being's motives."

This short story collection was published posthumously in 1929, the year of O'Higgins's death. The dust wrapper of the first edition, published by Liveright, was designed by Politzer.

OLD MAN IN THE CORNER, THE (Creator: Baroness Emmuska ORCZY). Among the first and greatest of all "armchair detectives." The nameless Old Man in the Corner is able to solve complex cases without leaving his chair in a London tea shop. Polly Burton, a young reporter for the *Evening Observer,* brings details of apparently insoluble cases to him, and he uses his deductive powers and giant intellect to unravel them, nervously tying and untying complicated knots in a piece of string as he talks. He claims, "There is no such thing as a mystery in connection with any crime, provided intelligence is brought to bear upon its investigation." He solves the most baffling crimes with ease, but only when "it resembles a clever game of chess, with many intricate moves which all tend to one solution."

Unlike most detectives, he is usually sympathetic toward the criminal; his attitude may be explained by the denouement of "The Mysterious Death in Percy Street," in which the anonymous Old Man attributes the murder to "one of the most ingenious men of the age, who will never be caught," thereby pointing a strong finger of suspicion at himself.

The first stories about the shabby, retiring Old Man appeared in magazines in 1901. The second series of stories became the first to be published in book form, as *The Case of Miss Elliott* (1905). The initial series appeared as *The Old Man in the Corner* (1909; U.S. title: *The Man in the Corner*). The final adventures of the enigmatic solver of mysteries were published as *Unravelled Knots* (1925). Before this book was released, the stories were published by Doran in 1924 and 1925 in a series of slim volumes, each containing one or two stories, all of which are now virtually unavailable.

Films

In 1924 a British series of short films was based on *The Old Man in the Corner.* The eccentric old man (Rolf Leslie) tells a girl reporter (Renee Wakefield) how he solved such curious crimes as *The Kensington Mystery, The Brighton Mystery, The Northern*

H. M. Brock illustrated the stories about the Old Man in the Corner. Reference to his age was dropped for the first American edition, published by Dodd, Mead in 1909.

Mystery, The York Mystery, and so on. There were twelve episodes in all.

O'NEILL, EGAN. *See* LININGTON, ELIZABETH.

OPPENHEIM, E[DWARD] PHILLIPS (1866–1946). English author of novels and short stories of mystery, crime, and international intrigue. Born in Leicester, he left school at an early age to work in his father's leather business. After working all day, he wrote until late at night and had about thirty books published before he sold the business when he was forty. While on a business trip to the United States in 1890, he met and married Elise Hopkins of Boston; they had one daughter. His wife remained with Oppenheim throughout his life, despite the author's frequent and highly publicized infidelities abroad and aboard his luxurious yacht. After he began devoting full time to writing, he produced more than 100 additional volumes, ultimately publishing 116 novels and 39 short story collections. Five novels appeared under the pseudonym Anthony Partridge.

In 1898 he published *The Mysterious Mr. Sabin,* calling it "the first of my long series of stories dealing with that shadowy and mysterious world of diplomacy." Virtually all his tales deal with wealthy people and are filled with fantastic anecdotes of luxurious living. Unlike some writers who attempt to provide mass audiences with the vicarious pleasures of enormous wealth, Oppenheim wrote from firsthand knowledge. He spent winters on the Riviera, entertaining more than 250 people at grand parties, and was a well-known figure in high society.

Known as "the Prince of Storytellers" (Robert Standish used the epithet as the title of his biography of Oppenheim, published in 1957), Oppenheim earned vast amounts of money from his novels and short story collections. Many of them are rather similar to one another, and his creative process—especially in later years—reflected his casual attitude toward them. After dictating a story to one of a succession of pretty secretaries, he allowed her to edit it before it was submitted to the publisher. Oppenheim made little effort to create memorable characters; the plot is the major factor in his tales, possibly exceeded in importance only by the description of life among the rich. The women, elegant and beautiful, seem unreal and uninteresting. The men are often heroic, especially Sir Everard Dominey, the disgraced aristocrat in *The Great Impersonation* (1920), who overcomes his alcoholism when England needs him to outwit the Germans.

Edmund Lowe is suspected of having a second identity in the 1935 film version of E. Phillips Oppenheim's classic, *The Great Impersonation.* [*Universal*]

Among the most popular and successful of Oppenheim's novels are *A Maker of History* (1905), *The Double Traitor* (1915), *The Evil Shepherd* (1922), *The Treasure House of Martin Hews* (1928), and *Envoy Extraordinary* (1937). His autobiography is *The Pool of Memory* (1939).

Films

Aside from his most famous work, *The Great Impersonation*, Oppenheim's screen material, especially in the early silent period, was concerned with vamps and stolen passion. Among his best melodrama films are the following.

The Great Impersonation. Paramount, 1921. James Kirkwood stars in a double role.

An English nobleman and a German master spy exchange places in the South African jungle in the days before August 1914.

Midnight Club. Paramount, 1933. George Raft, Clive Brook, Helen Vinson. Directed by Alexander Hall and George Somnes.

Scotland Yard suspects that a certain English lord is the leader of a gang of jewel thieves but is unaware that their convincing alibis are due to the use of doubles.

The Great Impersonation. Universal, 1935. Edmund Lowe, Valerie Hobson, Spring Byington. Directed by Alan Crosland.

During World War I, an English nobleman falls ill while on safari in East Africa; a German who is his double plots to kill him and take his place in London. His demented wife is not certain which man returns.

The Great Impersonation. Universal, 1942. Ralph Bellamy, Evelyn Ankers, Kaaren Verne, Henry Daniell. Directed by John Rawlins.

This remake is set in World War II. A ruthless German baron in Africa plans to take over the identity of his double, a decadent English aristocrat.

One of the least physically attractive detectives in literature is Baroness Orczy's Skin o' My Tooth, the unconventional lawyer-detective. His nickname is equally unappealing. This is the dust wrapper of the first American edition, published by Doubleday, Doran for the Crime Club in 1928.

ORCZY, BARONESS EMMUSKA (1865–1947). Hungarian-English artist, playwright, and author of romantic novels and short detective stories.

Born in Tarna-Örs, Hungary, she was the only child of Baron Felix Orczy, a well-known composer and conductor, and his wife, Emma. She spoke no English until she was fifteen, although all her manuscripts are in that language. While enrolled at the Heatherley School of Art in London, she met her future husband, Montagu Barstow. She went on to become a highly regarded artist, and several of her paintings were exhibited at the Royal Academy.

She produced a series of stories about the Old Man in the Corner beginning in 1901 in the *Royal Magazine* (*see* OLD MAN IN THE CORNER, THE). After attempting unsuccessfully to get her novel about the Scarlet Pimpernel (*see* SCARLET PIMPERNEL, THE) published, she and her husband transformed it into a play that became a popular success—even though the critics were not enthusiastic. Later works about the famous effete English adventurer, and other historical novels of love and swashbuckling adventure, enjoyed wide readership without critical acclaim.

In addition to the works about her two best-known characters, she produced several volumes recording the exploits of other interesting detectives. Lady Molly Robertson-Kirk heads the "Female Department of Scotland Yard." After five years on the job, she finally proves the innocence of her husband, a convicted murderer in Dartmoor Prison. Her cases are collected in *Lady Molly of Scotland Yard* (1910). Monsieur Fernand, a secret agent during the days of Napoleon, is the hero of the title in *The Man in Grey* (1918), which consists of semihistorical narratives of intrigue and detection. Patrick Mulligan, whose unsavory nickname is used as the title of another collection, *Skin o' My Tooth* (1928), is one of the first in a long line of unscrupulous lawyers who go to extreme lengths to solve mysteries and exonerate clients.

ORGANIZATIONS. Through the years, mystery and detective fiction writers and aficionados have formed many clubs, societies, associations, and organizations, with varying degrees of prestige and success.

In the United States the most important is the Mystery Writers of America (MWA). Founded in 1945, it was established to "promote and protect the interests and to increase the earnings of mystery story writers; to maintain and improve the esteem and recognition of mystery writing to the publishing industry and among the reading public; to disseminate helpful and rewarding information among the membership, and to foster the benefits of stimulating association with others having this common interest and uncommon talent."

Edgar Allan Poe Awards (Edgars) are presented at the MWA awards dinner in New York City each spring; special Edgars and Ravens are also awarded at this time. National headquarters is located at 105 East 19th Street, New York City; the five regional chapters of the nonprofit organization are located in New York, Boston, Chicago, San Francisco, and Los Angeles. The MWA publishes a newsletter, *The Third Degree,* distributed free to all members, and an annual anthology of short stories, the proceeds of which go to the organization; the first anthology appeared in 1946.

The British counterpart of the MWA, the Crime Writers' Association (CWA), was founded in 1953 by John CREASEY and Nigel MORLAND. Its aims are essentially the same as those of the MWA. Since 1955 the CWA's Annual Critics Awards (Gold Daggers) have been given to the authors of the outstanding novels of the year. Unlike the MWA, which forms committees to decide prizewinners, the CWA plays no part in the selection process; a panel of leading critics votes on the nominees.

The first important mystery writers' organization, the Detection Club (generally referred to as the London Detection Club), was founded by Anthony BERKELEY in 1928. G. K. CHESTERTON was its first "Ruler," serving until his death in 1936, after which E. C. BENTLEY occupied the chair. The smallest and most prestigious of the major organizations, it was customarily referred to as "snobbish." Curiously, one of its most active members for many years was John Dickson CARR, an American. Unlike the other organizations of mystery writers, the Detection Club had honorary membership requiring an election procedure. The organization occasionally published anthologies, with proceeds going to the club. *The Floating Admiral* (1932) was a novel written by "Certain (13) Members of The Detection Club"; each member involved wrote a chapter and left problems for the next contributor. Berkeley's *The Poisoned Chocolates Case* (1929) features the Detection Club and its members. Dorothy L. SAYERS wrote: "If there is any serious aim behind the avowedly frivolous organisation . . . it is to keep the detective story up to the highest standard that its nature permits. . . ."

In addition to the general organizations for mystery writers and readers, associations have been formed by devotees of individual writers.

The Edgar WALLACE Society was organized by his daughter, Penelope. Originally called the Edgar Wallace Club, it sends newsletters to members quarterly; the first issue appeared in January 1969. Dues are £1 per year. Miss Wallace's address is 4 Bradmore Road, Oxford, OX2 6QW, England.

Robert E. Briney publishes *The Rohmer Review* two or three times a year for members of the Sax ROHMER Society, who maintain a strong interest in the exploits of Dr. Fu Manchu (*see* FU MANCHU, DR.). The address is 4 Forest Avenue, Salem, Mass., 01970.

The largest following of any detective character in the world accords suitable reverence to Sherlock HOLMES. The Baker Street Irregulars (BSI), named for the street urchins Holmes used on several cases, was founded in 1934 by Christopher Morley, Vincent STARRETT, and Edgar Smith, who went on to become

The Edgar, the Edgar Allan Poe Award given annually by the Mystery Writers of America.

One group of Sherlock Holmes devotees, the Scandalous Bohemians of New Jersey, issued this sterling silver coin for collectors.

editor of the *Baker Street Journal,* a quarterly publication devoted entirely to Sherlockian studies. The first issue appeared in January 1946, and the thirteenth and last of the original (old) series in January 1949. The new series, in a slightly less ambitious format, began appearing in January 1951 and is still published regularly. The editor now is Dr. Julian Wolff, 33 Riverside Drive, New York, N.Y., 10023. Subscriptions are $10 per annum.

A horse race in New York, the Silver Blaze (named after the equine character in a Holmes adventure) is an annual event attended by members of the BSI. At the annual BSI dinner in New York City in January, Holmes scholars are honored by investiture with the Irregular Shilling.

In England, the Sherlock Holmes Society of London (5 Manor Close, Warlingham, Surrey CR3 9SF, England) publishes the *Sherlock Holmes Journal* twice a year for members. Subscriptions are $7.50 a year.

Among the many other Sherlock Holmes organizations (Scion Societies) are the Five Orange Pips (Westchester County, N.Y.), Mrs. Hudson's Lodgers (Cleveland), the Brothers Three of Moriarty (Santa Fe, N.Mex.), the Noble Bachelors (St. Louis), the Priory Scholars (New York), the Greek Interpreters (East Lansing, Mich.), the Hounds of the Baskerville [sic] and Hugo's Companions (both Chicago), the Cornish Horrors (Connecticut and Rhode Island), the Sons of the Copper Beeches (Philadelphia), the Red Circle (Washington, D.C.), the Scandalous Bohemians (New Jersey), the Norwegian Explorers (Minneapolis–St. Paul), and the Speckled Band of Boston.

ORIENTALS, SINISTER. The sinister Oriental, whether as an individual menace or as the mastermind of a large criminal organization, was a staple of thriller fiction for many years. Throughout most of the nineteenth century, the Orient impinged on Western consciousness mainly as the source of a lucrative trade in porcelain, silks, jade, and delicate graphic art. But, then, the China trade declined, the Open Door policy was imposed on a reluctant nation, and news of increasing military and political ferment filtered out to the West. Perhaps most significant of all, sizable colonies of Chinese immigrants settled in New York, London, and other large cities, bringing their traditions and culture into direct contact with Western society. The more superficial and sensational aspects of this contact became grist for the mill of popular fiction.

Early treatment of Orientals in fiction focused either on China's growing military power or on the supernatural-mystical aspects of Chinese philosophy and legends. The military aspect is exemplified by *The Yellow Danger* (1898) by M. P. SHIEL. This tale, about an Oriental invasion of Europe under the leadership of a warlord named Yen How, was published at the outset of the Boxer Rebellion. The supernatural touch is apparent in *The Yellow Hand* (1904) by Allen Upward (1863–1926), in which a Chinese sorcerer terrorizes the inhabitants of an East Anglian manor house; and more colorful Chinese wizardry plays a role in the fantastic novel *The Maker of Moons* (1896), by Robert W. Chambers (1865–1933).

The "traditional" sinister Oriental *par excellence* is, without doubt, the devilish Dr. FU MANCHU, created by Sax ROHMER. Fu Manchu made his first appearance in 1912, shortly after the overthrow of the Manchu dynasty in China. For the next three decades, a host of colleagues and imitators thronged the pages of mystery-adventure fiction.

During this era, probably the best-known Oriental villain after Fu Manchu was Wu Fang, the creation of prolific thriller writer Roland Daniel (William Roland Daniel; 1880–1969). Wu Fang's exploits are told in a series of novels that appeared, appropriately enough, in *The Thriller* and then in book form. Among the titles are *Wu Fang* (1929), *Wu Fang's Revenge* (1934), *The Son of Wu Fang* (1935), and *The Return of Wu Fang* (1937). The stories are not mere copies of Rohmer's but stem in large part from the author's own fascination with all things Chinese. Less well known, but equally interesting, is the dwarfish deaf-mute Chu-Sheng, who lends color and menace to such novels as *The Dancing Dead* (1933), *Shadow of Chu-Sheng* (1933), and *Yellow Magic* (1934), by Eugene Thomas.

Edgar WALLACE tried his hand at an Oriental criminal in *The Yellow Snake* (1926). Nigel Vane, in *The Menace of Li-Sin,* offered a tale about Prince Li-Sin's vengeance on the thieves who stole the jewel-filled Black Idol of Buddha from the Inner Temple of Tsao Sun. Anthony Rud (1893–1942), with eyes firmly fixed on the Rohmerian original, and tongue not far from cheek, presented *The Stuffed Men* (1935), in which the villain Wun Wey threatens the heroes with such delicacies as the Fungus Vat and the Saffron Horror.

With the advent of World War II and China's alliance with the West, Chinese master criminals were quietly eased out of popular fiction. They never recovered their earlier role. Later years produced only the rather pallid villain of Ian FLEMING's *Dr. No* (1958), or such ludicrous lending-library fare as Thane Leslie's *Yu-Malu the Dragon Princess* (1962). Leslie attempted to meld Rohmer's Sumuru with James BOND; his success can be gauged from the obligatory Monte Carlo gambling sequence in which all the atmospheric French phrases are misspelled.

In addition to appearing in hard-cover books, Oriental villains occurred frequently in British boys' magazines. Tong wars, opium smuggling, and Oriental masterminds played frequent roles in the stories Edmund Snell (1889–   ) and John G. Brandon (1879–1941) wrote for *The Thriller*, and the same magazine published Rohmer's *Yu'an Hee See Laughs* (1932) as an eighteen-part serial, under the title *The Slaver*. Of equal interest is a group of novels published in *Aldine Detective Tales*, second series (1922–1923), chronicling the battles of detective Dixon Brett against the mandarin Fan Chu Fang. The stories, among them *The Case of the Mandarin's Mask* and *The Whispering Death*, were written by Jack Wylde, a pseudonymous author whose prose contains startling textual similarities to the work of R. Austin FREEMAN—to such an extent that it has been conjectured that "Wylde" was Freeman.

Wu Fang is an omnipresent Oriental villain. Norman Marsh wrote this illustrated tale, based on the newspaper comic strip. It was published by Whitman in 1938.

Perhaps the most congenial home for fictional Oriental villains was in the American PULP MAGAZINES of the 1920s and 1930s. Scarcely one of the major pulp characters failed to encounter his share of evil Chinese opponents, and the faithful pulp reader was presented with such novels as *The Curse of the Mandarin's Fan*, by Paul Chadwick (writing under the name Brant House, in *Secret Agent X*, February 1938), *Scourge of the Yellow Fangs*, by Norvell W. Page (1904–1961; writing as Grant Stockbridge, in *The Spider*, April 1937), and *The Golden Master*, by Walter B. GIBSON (as Maxwell Grant, in *The Shadow*, September 15, 1939)—the first of four novels in which the Shadow (see SHADOW, THE) battled against master villain Shiwan Khan, a descendant of Genghis Khan.

Mystery Adventure Magazine published a series of stories about an archfiend named Wo Fan, bylined Bedford Rohmer—perhaps a case of a writer borrowing more than mere plot details from an earlier model!

Among the most direct copies of Fu Manchu were the novels published in two short-lived pulp magazines issued by Popular Publications. *The Mysterious Wu Fang* (no relation to Roland Daniel's character) lasted for seven issues, from September 1935 to March 1936. Each issue featured a novel by prolific pulp writer Robert J. Hogan (whose other pulp magazine works included *G-8 and His Battle Aces*). The main ingredients of the stories were a plenitude of monstrous insects and snakes, intricate torture devices, and an unimaginative fidelity to Rohmer's original characters and plots. It may have been pressure from Rohmer's agents that led to the suspension of the magazine. If so, the publishers retooled with amazing rapidity, for their next offering, *Dr. Yen Sin*, appeared only two months later, in May 1936. The novels featured in the new magazine were the work of Donald E. Keyhoe (1897–   ), a writer who later earned a measure of fame during the flying saucer craze of the 1950s. Again, the plots and personnel differed little from the original model (after all, why change a winning combination?). Dr. Yen Sin was variously known as the Yellow Doctor and the Crime Emperor and was the head of a vast organization called the Invisible Empire (not unlike Fu Manchu's Si-Fan organization). He dispatched his enemies by means of the *shi muh*, the Corpse Flower of Tibet, or visited upon them the curse of the Dragon's Shadow, which caused physical degeneration, madness, and death. The main claim to novelty was the character of the hero, Michael Traile, "the Man Who Never Slept," who was in many ways a more interesting personage than Yen Sin was. The magazine ceased publication after three issues.

Fu Manchu himself remains the most durable of all fictional Oriental villains. In addition to his role in Rohmer's novels, he has appeared in affectionate pastiches in August DERLETH's Solar PONS stories ("The Adventure of the Camberwell Beauty," in *The Return of Solar Pons,* 1958, and others) and in *The Rainbow Affair* (1967), a Man from U.N.C.L.E. novel by David McDaniel (1939–). He has also been subjected, through the years, to large numbers of less affectionate parodies—and he has survived all of them.

ROBERT E. BRINEY

OSBOURNE, FANNY VAN DE GRIFT. *See* STEVENSON, ROBERT LOUIS.

OSBOURNE, LLOYD. *See* STEVENSON, ROBERT LOUIS.

OURSLER, FULTON. *See* ABBOT, ANTHONY.

P

PACKARD, FRANK L[UCIUS] (1877–1942). Canadian-American novelist and short story writer; creator of Jimmie DALE. Born in Montreal, the son of Americans Frances (Joslin) and Lucius Henry Packard, he studied at McGill University and in Belgium and then went to the United States as a civil engineer in 1898. He married Marguerite Pearl Macintyre in 1910; they had three sons and a daughter. His early fiction was about railroads, but he is remembered chiefly for his crime stories about Dale. Among his other mysteries are *The Locked Book* (1924), *Shanghai Jim* (1928), *Tiger Claws* (1928), and *The Hidden Door* (1933).

Films

In 1919 *The Miracle Man* (1914) was filmed for the first time, with Lon Chaney as a fake cripple named "Frog," a confidence man who misdirects the ministrations of a faith healer (the film was remade in 1932 with Chester Morris). In 1920 William Faversham starred in *The Sin That Was His* (based on the novel of 1917) and portrayed a hardened gambler who assumes the identity of a priest to save himself from being convicted for a murder he did not commit.

PADGETT, LEWIS. *See* KUTTNER, HENRY.

PAGE, MARCO (pseudonym of Harry Kurnitz; 1909–1968). American playwright, film script writer, and mystery novelist. New York City–born, Kurnitz attended the University of Pennsylvania and later was a book and music reviewer for the *Philadelphia Record.* As Harry Kurnitz, he wrote a number of popular Broadway plays and movie scripts. As Marco Page, Kurnitz was a successful mystery author prior to his theater and film career. His first mystery, *Fast Company* (1937), a story of murder in the world of rare books, won Dodd, Mead's Red Badge Award. *The Shadowy Third* (1946) was praised by critics for its plot, pace, and knowledgeable use of a symphony hall as a setting for murder. The novel *Reclining Figure* (1952) deals with art objects and their forgery. Page adapted it for Broadway in 1954.

Films

Kurnitz wrote more than forty scripts for films, including such mysteries as *Witness for the Prosecution* (1957) and *How to Steal a Million* (1966).

Fast Company. MGM, 1938. Melvyn Douglas, Florence Rice, Claire Dodd, George Zucco, Louis Calhern. Directed by Edward Buzzell. Based on Page's 1937 novel; Page also worked on the screenplay.

A rare-book salesman, amateur sleuth on the side, joins his wife in trying to prove a young former convict innocent of killing a rich bookshop owner.

A Shot in the Dark. United Artists, 1964. Peter Sellers, Elke Sommer, George Sanders, Herbert Lom. Directed by Blake Edwards. Screenplay by Kurnitz, based on his 1961 stage adaptation of the French farce by Marcel Achard.

A bungling French police inspector refuses to believe that an attractive maid is guilty when murder strikes a wealthy home, even though she was found with a smoking gun in her hand. (A 1941 film with the same title was written by Frederick Nebel and has no connection with Page's work.)

PAIN, BARRY (ERIC ODELL) (1864–1928). English author and journalist. Born in Cambridge, the son of a draper, he was educated at Sedburgh and Cambridge University, where he edited the university magazine, *Granta.* Following graduation, he succeeded Jerome K. Jerome as editor of *To-day,* an important literary periodical. He wrote novels and humorous stories of working-class life and several short stories about mystery, crime, and detection.

His best collection is *The Memoirs of Constantine Dix* (1905), which recounts the adventures of a lady thief. *One Kind and Another* (1914) contains four stories from a group called "Detection without Crime," about Horace Fish. Other short story collections with some elements of crime and mystery are

Stories and Interludes (1892), *Stories in the Dark* (1901), *Stories without Tears* (1912), and *The Problem Club* (1919).

PALFREY, DR. (Creator: John CREASEY). Leader of a secret underground group that owed its allegiance to the Allies during World War II. After the war, Dr. Stanislaus Alexander Palfrey and his Z5 organization change their targets from Nazis and Japanese to mad scientists seeking to conquer the world. Although the original Palfrey works were spy stories, the later ones are allegories, as Creasey points out the dangers of propaganda (in *The Plague of Silence,* 1958), indifference (in *The Sleep,* 1964), and overpopulation (in *The Famine,* 1967). The first of the thirty-four volumes in the Dr. Palfrey series was *Traitor's Doom* (1942). *See also* DEPARTMENT Z.

PALMER, JOHN LESLIE. *See* BEEDING, FRANCIS.

PALMER, STUART (HUNTER) (1905–1968). American mystery novelist and film script writer. Born in Baraboo, Wis., Palmer was a descendant of colonists who settled in Salem, Mass., in 1634. Educated at the Chicago Art Institute and the University of Wisconsin, he later held a wide variety of jobs including iceman, sailor, publicity man, apple picker, newspaper reporter, taxi driver, advertising copy writer, poet, editor, and ghost-writer.

Palmer was six years old when he wrote his first story, but he had to wait fourteen years before selling a short story to *College Humor.* He began writing mystery stories in 1931, when *The Penguin Pool Murder* introduced the popular spinster-sleuth Hildegarde WITHERS.

Omit Flowers (1937; British title: *No Flowers by Request*) deals with a Christmas party highlighted by a mysterious death by fire and is seasoned with a group of money-hungry heirs. This tense puzzle is solved—unexpectedly—by the black sheep of the family.

With the appearance of the film version of *The Penguin Pool Murder* in 1932, and the successful series of Hildegarde Withers films that followed, Palmer gained employment as a scriptwriter. Most of his thirty-seven scripts were mysteries featuring the Falcon, the Lone Wolf, and Bulldog Drummond (see DRUMMOND, BULLDOG; FALCON, THE; LONE WOLF, THE).

Palmer enlisted in the Army in World War II and served as a training-film instructor in the field artillery school and liaison officer for the Army and Hollywood's war effort. He was noted for his exceptional reading speed and his collections of bawdy limericks and penguin statuettes. His personal trademark was a picture or drawing of a penguin.

PARR, ROBERT. *See* GARDNER, ERLE STANLEY.

PARTRIDGE, ANTHONY. *See* OPPENHEIM, E. PHILLIPS.

PATRICK, Q. *See* QUENTIN, PATRICK.

PAUL, ELLIOT (1891–1958). American news correspondent and mystery writer. Born in Malden, Mass., Paul was a librarian and newspaperman in nearby Boston. He also worked in irrigation fields in Idaho and Wyoming before serving as a sergeant with the AEF in France during World War I. Following the war he remained in Europe as a correspondent for a number of American newspapers. He wrote fiction and worked as an editor but gained real prominence with his nonfictional *The Life and Death of a Spanish Town* (1937), in which he told of the effect of the Civil War on a Spanish island in the Balearics where he had lived for five years. During the rest of his European career he lived in Paris, and when World War II forced his return to the United States, he wrote *The Last Time I Saw Paris* (1942), a book of reminiscences of the city he loved.

As a mystery writer, Elliot Paul was one of the few who consistently attempted to inject humor into his books. His detective hero, Homer Evans, is, like his creator, an American living in Paris. Evans surrounds himself with unpredictable bohemians in *Hugger-Mugger in the Louvre* (1940) and *Murder on the Left Bank* (1951), books dealing in a light fashion with theft and murder in the Parisian art world. In *Waylaid in Boston* (1953) the Boston-born Evans returns to the scene of his (and Paul's) youth for breakneck dashes through corpse-laden bars and hotels. Music frequently plays an important role in Paul's mysteries, especially *Mayhem in B-Flat* (1940), since Evans (like Paul) is an expert on jazz and classical music. Perhaps Paul's best-known mystery is *The Mysterious Mickey Finn; or, Murder at the Café du Dôme* (1939).

PAYN, JAMES (1830–1898). English novelist and editor. Born in Cheltenham, he began writing at an early age, contributing to Charles DICKENS's *Household Words.* He served as editor of *Chambers's Journal* and the *Cornhill Magazine* (1883–1896) and also wrote numerous novels. His best mystery and detective works are *Lost Sir Massingberd* (1864) and *Found Dead* (1869). Payn inspired E. W. HORNUNG to write crime fiction (according to a letter from Hornung to Payn) but may be forever condemned for rejecting Sir Arthur CONAN DOYLE's first Sherlock HOLMES adventure, *A Study in Scarlet* (1887), while editor of *Cornhill.* Payn later dedicated *The Disappearance of George Driffell* (1896) "To Conan Doyle, from his friend."

PEMBERTON, SIR MAX (1863–1950). English novelist and editor. Born in Birmingham, he was edu-

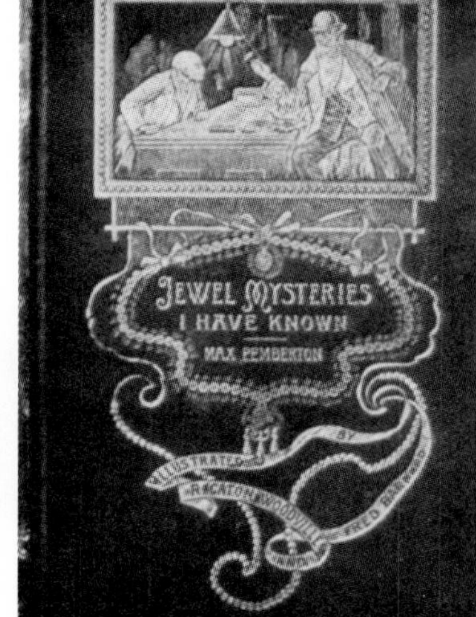

Max Pemberton's *Jewel Mysteries I Have Known* was published in markedly different bindings by his English and American publishers, but they are both striking. The Ward, Lock edition (left), illustrated by R. Caton Woodville and Fred Barnard, was published in 1894. The illustrator of the Fenno edition is not credited; it was published in 1904.

cated at Cambridge and became a successful author and editor almost immediately. After editing *Chums* for two years, he became the editor of the popular *Cassell's Magazine* (1894–1906). He also founded the London School of Journalism and directed the Northcliffe newspaper chain. In 1928 he was knighted. Pemberton's most successful plays and novels were historical adventures, but he also wrote many mystery and crime stories.

In *A Gentleman's Gentleman* (1896), a valet who is a rogue is employed by a gentleman who is also a rogue; theirs is one of the first teams of crooks in literature, anticipating A. J. RAFFLES and Bunny by three years. *Jewel Mysteries I Have Known: From a Dealer's Note Book* (1894) features Bernard Sutton, a jewel dealer, in ten tales about unique, exotic gems. Also of interest are *The Diary of a Scoundrel* (1891), *The Mystery of the Green Heart* (1910), and *John Dighton: Mystery Millionaire* (1923).

PENTECOST, HUGH. *See* PHILIPS, JUDSON.

PEROWNE, BARRY (pseudonym of Philip Atkey; 1908–   ). English author of crime, adventure, and mystery stories, notably a long series of adventures about A. J. RAFFLES, the amateur cracksman.

Born in the New Forest area of Wiltshire, Perowne left school before he was fourteen to work for a manufacturer of carnival equipment. The experience served as background material for his writings about the carnival showmen who, with their families and caravans, took up winter quarters in the factory yards. After working as secretary for Bertram ATKEY, his uncle, Perowne edited two magazines that published humorous and romantic fiction and wrote stories for several other magazines as well as 30,000-word paperback originals about Dick Turpin, the highwayman, and Red Jim, the first air detective. By agreement with the E. W. HORNUNG estate, he revived Raffles (using the Perowne pseudonym) for *The Thriller,* a popular British magazine, converting the sophisticated cracksman into a two-fisted adventurer whose escapades were placed in a contemporary setting. He married Bertram Atkey's daughter in 1933 (they had one daughter and were divorced in 1948). In 1940 he joined the Army, serving three years in the infantry and three more in the intelligence corps. Beginning in 1950 he wrote Raffles stories that have a turn-of-the-century background and flavor and that many critics consider superior to Hornung's works. Many were published in *Ellery Queen's Mystery Magazine*; fourteen of the best were collected in *Raffles Revisited* (1974).

As Philip Atkey, he wrote *Blue Water Murder* (1935), *Heirs of Merlin* (1945), and *Juniper Rock* (1952), a mystery-romance, set in Corsica, about a man who has amassed a fortune as a smuggler in the Mediterranean. He devises an ingenious method of legalizing his ill-gotten gains so that he can use the funds to restore his family estate—only to have his scheme backfire.

Night Call (1937) was written under the pseudonym Pat Merriman; his other books carry the Barry Perowne by-line: *Arrest These Men!* (1932), *Enemy of Women* (1934), *Ladies in Retreat* (1935), *Ask No Mercy* (1937), *I'm No Murderer* (1938), *The Girl on*

Barry Perowne.

Zero (1939), *The Whispering Cracksman* (1940; U.S. title: *Ten Words of Poison*), *Blonde without Escort* (1940), *Gibraltar Prisoner* (1942; U.S. title: *All Exits Blocked*), *Rogue's Island* (1950), and *A Singular Conspiracy* (1974), a crime fantasy based upon an apocryphal meeting between Edgar Allan POE and Charles Baudelaire, the French poet and translator of Poe's macabre tales, who desperately needs a plan that will enable him to regain control of his patrimony.

The first collection of Raffles stories in sixty-nine years is *Raffles Revisited*, Barry Perowne's volume of pastiches published by Harper in 1974. Richard Rosenblum illustrated the volume and designed this dust wrapper.

PERTWEE, MICHAEL. *See* SAINT, THE.

PETERS, BILL. *See* MCGIVERN, WILLIAM P.

PETTIGREW, FRANCIS (Creator: Cyril HARE). After receiving high academic honors and entering the legal profession with spectacular promise, Pettigrew encounters a series of personal difficulties and sheer bad luck that mitigate against his expected success. The years roll by, and he becomes an unsuccessful, aging, and frustrated lawyer who has to accept work that is beneath him—if he is lucky enough to get it at all. Pettigrew, whose eyes are as dull as his mind is keen, is able to unravel several murder cases and in the course of one of them (*With a Bare Bodkin*, 1946) meets Eleanor Brown, a young woman half his age (who has "financial expectations"), and achieves a happy marriage with her.

Pettigrew makes his debut in *Tragedy at Law* (1942), an unorthodox novel in which he matches wits with Inspector Mallett. *With a Bare Bodkin* finds Pettigrew once again Mallett's adversary when a murder is committed with a spiked paper holder in a government office. It is more conventional than *Tragedy at Law*, and not unlike Nicholas BLAKE's *Minute for Murder*, which was published the following year. *When the Wind Blows* (1949; U.S. title: *The Wind Blows Death*) details Pettigrew's investigation of the death of England's foremost violinist, who had been scheduled to play with the local music society.

The remaining Pettigrew adventures are recorded in *The Yew Tree's Shade* (1954; U.S. title: *Death Walks the Woods*), in *He Should Have Died Hereafter* (1958; U.S. title: *Untimely Death*), and in two of the thirty stories in *Best Detective Stories of Cyril Hare* (1959).

PHANTOM OF THE OPERA, THE. *See* LEROUX, GASTON.

PHILIPS, JUDSON (PENTECOST) (1903–). American mystery writer; creator of Pierre CHAMBRUN. Born in Massachusetts, the son of an opera singer and an actress, he traveled widely throughout Europe as a child. While a sophomore at Columbia University, he wrote his first short story, "Room Number Twenty-three" (1925). His detective character in that story, James W. Bellamy, was based on his roommate, James Warner Bellah, who also became a successful writer.

Philips wrote prolifically for PULP MAGAZINES. A founding member of the Mystery Writers of America, he served as its third president. He was given the special award of Grand Master in 1973 for distinction in the novel and the short story. He also founded the Sharon (Conn.) Playhouse in 1950. He currently resides in Canaan, Conn. (scene of several of his short stories), with his second wife, actress Norma Burton, and his teen-age son.

A competent and prolific writer, Philips has created many series detectives and has concocted good detective puzzles.

His first novel to attract attention was *Cancelled in Red* (1939), which deals with murder within the philatelic set. Published under the pseudonym Hugh Pentecost, who was actually Philips's granduncle and a prominent lawyer of the 1890s in New York, it won first prize in Dodd, Mead's mystery competition that year.

As Pentecost, Philips created such series detectives as Inspector Luke Bradley (*I'll Sing at Your Funeral*, 1942), columnist Grant Simon (*The Obituary Club*, 1958), bearded artist John Jericho (*Dead Woman of the Year*, 1967), public relations man Julian Quist (*Don't Drop Dead Tomorrow*, 1971), and Uncle George Crowder, who has appeared in a series of short stories in *Ellery Queen's Mystery Magazine* and in *Around Dark Corners* (1970), a short story collection.

Under his own name, Philips has only created one important series detective, Peter Styles, a one-legged magazine columnist and crusader against injustice who has appeared in most of the recent books. One of the best Styles novels is *Hot Summer Killing* (1969), which details the columnist's efforts to prevent the blowing up of Grand Central Station during rush hour.

As Pentecost, Philips is usually concerned with crime and detection, but under his own by-line, he usually stresses thrills and suspense.

Philips's novels are frequently reprinted, and one paperback publisher is bringing back the exploits of his best and most famous sleuth, Chambrun, who, as resident manager of New York's top luxury hotel, is constantly troubled by crimes of violence. The Styles books (by Philips) and those about Jericho (by Pentecost) are also being reissued in soft covers.

PHILLPOTTS, EDEN (1862–1960). English novelist, poet, dramatist, and short story writer. Born in Mount Aboo, India, he spent most of his life in England, mainly in Devon. After studying acting in London, he worked for an insurance company for ten years, meanwhile writing fiction. He married Emily Topham in 1892 (she died in 1928); they had two children. In 1929 he married Lucy Robina Webb.

In addition to writing numerous plays (some in collaboration with his daughter, Adelaide), much conventional nature poetry, and frequent essays and nonfiction books, Phillpotts was the author of more than 150 novels. Generally regarded as the best are the long series of "Dartmoor novels," often compared with Thomas Hardy's "Wessex novels," and his many mystery and suspense tales, written under his own name and the pseudonym Harrington Hext.

Among the most unusual is *The Grey Room* (1921), in which a quiet country house is the setting for a bizarre series of deaths. Unsuspecting victims meet their ends in this macabre room because a poison, secreted in the mattress of a beautiful antique bed, is released by the body heat of the individual sleeping in the bed. *The Red Redmaynes* (1922) involves the efforts of a snuff-taking American detective, Peter Ganns, to solve a case concerning the calculated extermination of a family. Phillpotts's first published book, *My Adventure in the Flying Scotsman: A Romance of London and North-Western Railway Shares* (1888), is a rare short novel.

The best-known mysteries that appeared under the Hext pseudonym are *The Thing at Their Heels* (1923), in which a Radical clergyman is the villain, and *Who Killed Diana?* (1924; U.S. title: *Who Killed Cock Robin?*), in which even the victim's identity is questionable. Cock Robin and Jenny Wren are nicknames for twin daughters of an English archdeacon.

Perhaps the two greatest contributions to the mystery genre made by Phillpotts do not actually involve his writing. Since he was accepted as a major writer of fiction, his name lent prestige to the roster of mystery and detective writers. Also, his well-publicized encouragement of the youthful Agatha CHRISTIE appears to have been instrumental in her subsequent development.

PIDGIN, CHARLES FELTON (1844–1923). American novelist and short story writer. Born in Roxbury,

The front cover of *The Further Adventures of Quincy Adams Sawyer and Mason Corner Folks* by Charles Felton Pidgin features an interesting depiction of an early automobile. This is one of the many elaborate bindings made by L. C. Page, a Boston publisher.

Mass., he was paralyzed in one leg while still a youth and was nearly blind from middle life onward. His first novel, *Quincy Adams Sawyer: or, Mason's Corner Folks* (1900), a quaint account of rural life in Massachusetts, introduced his most popular character. Its sequels were two short story collections with elements of detection, *The Further Adventures of Quincy Adams Sawyer and Mason Corner Folks* (1909) and *The Chronicles of Quincy Adams Sawyer, Detective* (1912), which was written in collaboration with John M. Taylor, whose name does not appear on the cover.

PIKE, ROBERT L. See FISH, ROBERT L.

PINKERTON, A. FRANK. See PINKERTON, ALLAN.

PINKERTON, ALLAN (1819–1884). Scottish-American detective and author of quasi-fictional narratives of crime. Born in Glasgow, the son of a police sergeant, he moved to Chicago in 1842. His discovery and capture of a gang of counterfeiters led to his position as deputy sheriff of Cook County. In 1850 he resigned from the Chicago Police Department to open a private agency specializing in railway theft cases. The Pinkerton National Detective Agency soon became the most successful organization of its kind.

Cases from the agency's archives served as source material for several books on murder, crime, and detection, published under Pinkerton's name. The cases are highly sensationalized, and it is difficult to separate fact from fiction. Among the widely read books of the period, recognized by the symbol of the agency on the covers (an open eye with the motto "We Never Sleep"), are *The Expressman and the Detective* (1874), *Claude Melnotte as a Detective and Other Stories* (1875), *The Mollie Maguires and the Detectives* (1877), *The Spy and the Rebellion* (1883), and *Thirty Years a Detective* (1884).

This open eye is the symbol of the Pinkerton National Detective Agency, and "We Never Sleep" is its motto. The symbol appeared on the covers of most of Allan Pinkerton's books.

Later novels, written by A. Frank Pinkerton (Allan's son), appeared under the overall title "The Frank Pinkerton Detective Series" and included *Dyke Darrel, the Railroad Detective; or, The Crime of the Midnight Express* (1886) and *Jim Cummings; or, The Great Adams Express Robbery* (1887). The text of the latter book is virtually identical to that of *Jim Cummings; or, The Crime of the 'Frisco Express* (1887), by Francis Farrars, which preceded the volume bearing Pinkerton's name. It is not known whether Farrars was a pseudonym of A. Frank Pinkerton; therefore, the Pinkerton volume may have been plagiarized.

PINKERTON, EVAN (Creator: Leslie FORD as David Frome). "Rabbity" is the word most frequently applied to Mr. Pinkerton, a timid little widower from Wales. When his miserly and domineering wife died, she left him £75,000 and a freedom he had never previously had.

Although he still wears his old-fashioned bowler hat, celluloid collar, and string tie, he indulges himself by going to the movies three times a week. He also helps his friend, Scotland Yard Inspector J. Humphrey Bull, whom he has known since the days when Bull, a police constable at the time, occupied a room in Mrs. Pinkerton's boarding house. Their cases usually begin with Pinkerton stumbling upon a dead body. Pinkerton's solutions (he often stumbles onto them also) aid his friend, who is officially assigned to the case.

CHECKLIST

1930 *The Hammersmith Murders*
1931 *Two Against Scotland Yard* (British title: *The By-Pass Murder*)
1932 *The Man from Scotland Yard*
1933 *The Eel Pie Murders* (British title: *The Eel Pie Mystery*)
1934 *Mr. Pinkerton Goes to Scotland Yard* (British title: *Arsenic in Richmond*)
1934 *Mr. Pinkerton Finds a Body* (British title: *The Body in the Turl*)
1935 *Mr. Pinkerton Grows a Beard* (British title: *The Body in Bedford Square*)
1936 *Mr. Pinkerton Has the Clue*
1937 *The Black Envelope* (British title: *The Guilt Is Plain*)
1939 *Mr. Pinkerton at the Old Angel* (British title: *Mr. Pinkerton and the Old Angel*)
1950 *Homicide House* (British title: *Murder on the Square*)

PITCAIRN, JOHN JAMES. See ASHDOWN, CLIFFORD.

PLUNKETT, EDWARD JOHN MORETON DRAX. See DUNSANY, LORD.

POE, EDGAR ALLAN (1809–1849). American poet, critic, editor, short story writer, and acknowledged inventor of the detective story—regarded by many as the greatest American writer of the nineteenth century. Although Poe's creation of the first significant fictional detective, C. Auguste DUPIN, and his invention of the short detective story, may be his most important contribution to literature, his finest works are his tales of terror and the supernatural.

Born in Boston, the son of an English-born actress, Elizabeth (Arnold) Hopkins, and David Poe, Jr., an actor from Baltimore, Edgar was the second of three children, orphaned at an early age when both parents died of tuberculosis in Richmond, Va., in 1811. Edgar was taken into the home of a wealthy childless couple, John Allan, a merchant, and his wife, who loved the boy as if he were her own. Never legally adopted, Edgar nevertheless took Allan's name.

Poe received a classical education in England (1815–1820) and then enrolled at the University of Virginia. His gambling debts infuriated Allan, who refused to permit him to remain in college. Forced into a business he hated, Poe ran away to join the Army (as Edgar A. Perry). Within a few months, he published his first book, *Tamerlane and Other Poems* (1827), by "A Bostonian."

Mrs. Allan died in 1830, and Poe's guardian promptly remarried. Responding to her final wishes, Allan bought Poe out of the Army and got him a commission to West Point, from which the unhappy young man was immediately expelled for deliberately missing classes and drills. The second Mrs. Allan was jealous of her charming and brilliant stepson, and he was soon thrown out of the house and eventually disinherited.

Poe's second volume of poetry, *Al Araaf* (1829), was as financially unsuccessful as his first, and *Poems* (1831) fared no better. He moved to Baltimore to write stories, winning a prize for "The MS. Found in a Bottle" (1833), and was offered a job with a prominent Richmond magazine, the *Southern Literary Messenger*.

Before taking the job, he married his cousin Virginia, the thirteen-year-old daughter of his father's sister, Mrs. Clemm, for whom Poe possibly felt more affection than he did for his bride, and who accompanied the couple wherever they went. After two years with the magazine, Poe moved with his family to New York, where they lived in desperate poverty for years, a circumstance that contributed to the premature death (at twenty-four) of Virginia in the family's cottage at Fordham (now part of the borough of the Bronx, New York City).

As literary critic and editor, he doubled the circulation of *Burton's Gentleman's Magazine*, *Graham's Magazine*, and other periodicals, but his periods of employment were brief—possibly because of alcoholism but also because his strong views and arrogance often enraged his employers.

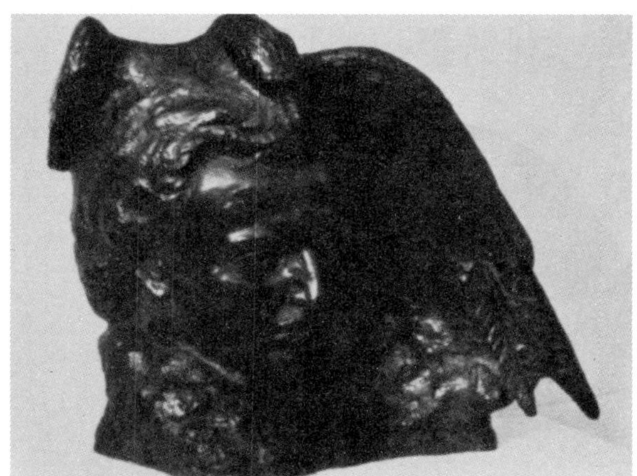

Bust of Edgar Allan Poe by Olaf Bjorkman.

He always worked at a furious pace, excelling at every job he undertook, but was never fully understood or appreciated by his contemporaries, receiving neither the acclaim he knew he deserved nor the financial rewards he needed for himself and his fragile young wife.

After Virginia died in 1847, he pursued several wealthy widows interested in literature and was engaged, or quasi-engaged, to more than one, including the poet Sarah Helen Whitman and Elmira Royster (then the widowed Mrs. Shelton), his first and most intense love. He was making marriage plans when he went to a birthday party, toasted the guest of honor, and (it is believed) began a drinking spree that left him lying in a Baltimore gutter. Taken to a hospital, he died in delirium a few days later and was buried in Baltimore, next to Virginia and her mother.

According to most Poe scholars, the above biographical points seem to be true, but the most learned of them, Thomas O. Mabbott, disagrees with majority opinion on many issues. Some scholars claim that Poe was not an alcoholic but that a single glass of wine was enough to drive him into maniacal rages. Whether or not he used drugs is widely debated. His reasons for marrying Virginia are obscure, and it is suggested on one hand that she provided him with the emotional and physical outlets he needed, and on the other that she died a virgin. Months, even years, of his life remain unaccounted for, and there are rumors that he wrote a novel. The degree to which he retained his sanity at given stages is often questioned.

Poe's personality seems clearly defined; by all accounts he was never humble, and his enforced poverty and consequent humiliations tormented him

Robert Walker, Jr., portrays the tortured author caught in the nightmares of his own bizarre stories in *The Spectre of Edgar Allan Poe*. [*Cinerama*]

more than they would have affected a less proud man.

The romantic poets of England clearly influenced Poe's fiction as well as his verse. His creation of the detective short story owes much to the French criminal-cum-detective François Eugène VIDOCQ, whose *Mémoires* (1828–1829) were published when Poe was in his twenties.

When Poe created Dupin to perform feats of ratiocination (a word Poe invented), he did not call him a detective because neither the word nor the position existed. Dupin appeared in only three stories, for the versatility of the writer proved the undoing of the detective. The stories met with moderate success (attributed by Poe to their original flavor rather than to any literary excellence), and there was little demand for more of the same. Poe quickly tired of the form and returned to his more effective, if less original, themes of the occult and the macabre.

In addition to the three stories involving Dupin, Poe wrote two legitimate mystery stories. Essentially a puzzle story, "The Gold Bug" (1843) relies on the deciphering of a cryptogram for its solution. Legrand, like Sherlock HOLMES in a later story, "The Adventure of the Dancing Men" (1903), breaks a code based on the predominance of the letter e in the English language. A scrap of paper left by Captain Kidd, the pirate, and a lost treasure on a strange island are the ingredients of this tale, to which Robert Louis STEVENSON's *Treasure Island* (1883) owes much.

In the semihumorous "Thou Art the Man" (1844), "Old Charley" Goodfellow discovers the body of his friend, the wealthy Barnabas Rattleborough. Evidence, including bloodstained clothing and a knife, points an accusing finger at the murdered man's dissolute nephew. Later, in a grotesque conclusion, the true murderer confesses when the putrefying corpse unexpectedly appears, rises to a sitting position, and confronts his killer with the words "Thou art the man." This murder mystery employed such precedent-setting devices as false clues left by the guilty man, the use of ballistics, and the least-likely person as murderer.

In these five tales Poe anticipated virtually every possible type of detective-mystery-crime story: sensational thriller ("The Murders in the Rue Morgue," 1841); straight analytical exercise and fictional treatment of a real-life crime ("The Mystery of Marie Rogêt," 1842); classic detective story and secret agent tale ("The Purloined Letter," 1844); puzzle story revolving around the breaking of a code ("The Gold Bug," 1843); and a small-town murder mystery solved by the narrator ("Thou Art the Man," 1844). All except the last were published in *Tales* (1845), now one of the rarest books of American literature.

Films

Poe's tales of mystery have frequently, but often not closely, been translated to the screen. Poe himself has been the central figure in several film romances—the only mystery writer to be so treated. D. W. Griffith directed an early short motion picture called *Edgar Allan Poe* (Mutoscope and Biograph, 1909), in which the author sees "The Raven" (his poem of 1845) bought for a pittance and his young wife die. In *The Raven* (American Eclair Company, 1912), while Poe composed several tales and poems, "dream" sequences from the works were shown. In another film called *The Raven* (Essanay, 1915) the distinguished American actor Henry B. Walthall portrayed Poe, unsuccessful as a writer, witness to his wife's death, and, at the end of the film, dead himself. Aspects of Poe's life were the subjects of later films, too.

The Loves of Edgar Allan Poe. Twentieth Century-Fox, 1942. John Shepperd (later Shepperd Strudwick, as Poe), Linda Darnell, Virginia Gilmore, Jane Darwell. Directed by Harry Lachman.

A somber, Gothic-type account of Poe's struggles and marriage in which the writer is encouraged by Charles DICKENS (Morton Lowry) to feud with his publishers over copyright matters and is blacklisted. The film ends with Poe's death in a Baltimore hospital.

Man with a Cloak. MGM, 1951. Joseph Cotten. Barbara Stanwyck, Louis Calhern, Leslie Caron. Directed by Fletcher Markle. Based on "The Gentleman from Paris," a story by John Dickson CARR.

An alcoholic poet living in the New York of the 1840s prevents a wealthy invalid's fortune from falling into the hands of a housekeeper who has hastened his death. At the climax the viewer learns from a rain-splattered signature that the poet (Cotten) is Poe.

The Spectre of Edgar Allan Poe. Cinerama, 1974. Robert Walker, Jr., Cesar Romero, Tom Drake, Carol Ohmart. Directed by Mohy Quandour.

Poe (Walker) becomes disturbed when his sick wife, Lenore, is nearly buried alive; she is placed in a sanitorium, where several murders then occur. The film script was loosely based on one aspect of Poe's life and offered a fantastic "explanation" of why the strange fate of Poe's first love drove him to write tales of the macabre.

Despite Poe's popularity with scenarists, his introspective, brooding tales have often been misused. In feature-length films his stories of mystery and the supernatural have almost always been expanded and altered, at times beyond recognition. Short films have invariably fared better. *The Tell-tale Heart,* a short film based on the 1839 story, was released by MGM in 1941. Directed by Jules Dassin and starring Joseph Schildkraut, it was the fourth screen version of the story and won an Academy award. "The Fall of the House of Usher" (1839) has inspired a number of abstract and experimental short films. Some of the more significant films derived from Poe's works are listed below.

Unheimliche Geschichten (Terrible Stories; U.S. title: *The Living Dead).* German Universal, 1932. Richard Oswald directed three interrelated episodes in the story of the capture of a maniac, fairly routine adaptations of "The Black Cat" (1843), in which a deranged man walls up his wife, and "The System of Dr. Tarr and Professor Fether" (1845). The final story deserts Poe for Robert Louis STEVENSON's "The Suicide Club" (1878).

The Black Cat. Universal, 1934. Boris Karloff, Bela Lugosi, Jacqueline Wells, David Manners. Directed by Edgar Ulmer.

Although the film did not use specific details from the tale upon which it was supposedly based, the story, about a clash between good and evil in a war-ravaged fortress in the Balkans—a struggle that culminates in a black mass—is a brooding masterpiece that incorporates much of Poe's mood and images.

The Crime of Dr. Crespi. Republic, 1935. Erich Von Stroheim, Dwight Frye, Harriet Russell. Directed by John H. Auer. Suggested by "The Premature Burial" (1844).

The head of a clinic operates on the man who had stolen the woman he loved, injecting him with a drug that causes paralysis; the patient is then buried alive.

The Raven. Universal, 1935. Lugosi, Karloff, Irene Ware, Lester Matthews. Directed by Louis Friedlander.

Dr. Richard Vollin (Lugosi), a retired surgeon, is so steeped in the works of Poe that he sometimes seems to be the embodiment of some of Poe's characters: "The raven is my talisman; death is my talisman!" When a patient, a young woman, does not return his love, he invites her and her friends to spend a weekend at his home, a sinister manor filled with instruments of torture reminiscent of those in Poe stories such as "The Pit and the Pendulum" (1843). "Poe," he cries, "you are avenged!"

The Black Cat. Universal, 1941. Basil Rathbone, Hugh Herbert, Broderick Crawford, Gale Sondergaard, Alan Ladd. Directed by Albert S. Rogell.

The film revolves around a routine gathering to read a will in an ominous mansion; walled-in cats and strange burial devices are the only traces of Poe.

Manfish. United Artists, 1956. John Bromfield, Victor Jory, Lon Chaney, Jr. Directed by W. Lee Wilder. Loosely based on "The Gold Bug" and "The Tell-tale Heart."

In the Caribbean, a mysterious professor joins a sailor in a search for sunken pirate treasure and then kills his partner.

In 1960 American International, a small studio specializing in melodrama, achieved great success with a lush color version of "The Fall of the House of Usher" and proceeded to produce—often teaming star Vincent Price and producer-director Roger Corman—a series of elaborate color adaptations of Poe works, which, although they expanded the original stories, were truer to the spirit of the tales than most of the previous films had been.

Deranged surgeon Bela Lugosi (left), so steeped in admiration for Poe that his home is filled with torture appliances reconstructed from the writer's stories, has with relish turned upon a wanted criminal (Boris Karloff) whose face he has just disfigured. The film is attributed, quite without basis, to *The Raven.* [*Universal*]

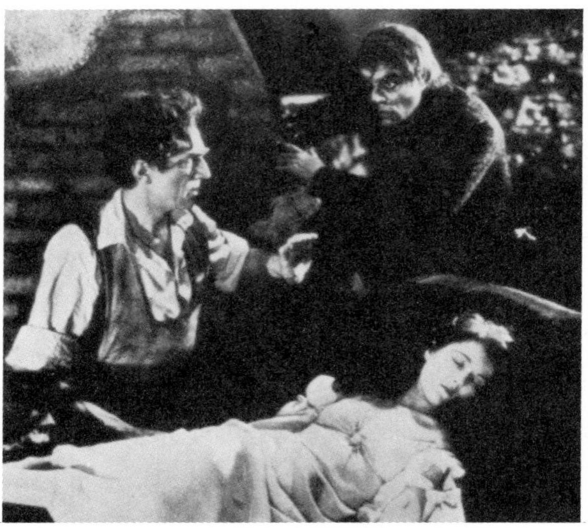

The maniacal Dr. Mirakle (Bela Lugosi, left) is about to begin his experiments on the blood of another victim brought to his secret laboratory in the nightmarish 1932 version of Poe's *Murders in the Rue Morgue*. [*Universal*]

House of Usher. American International, 1960. Price, Mark Damon, Myra Fahey. Directed by Corman.

The last of a long line of Ushers tells his sister's suitor that their ancestors' evil deeds have made the family mansion evil. The girl appears to die, but the young man fears that she is suffering from catalepsy.

The Pit and the Pendulum. American International, 1961. Price, John Kerr, Barbara Steele, Luana Anders. Directed by Corman.

A young Englishman arrives at a Spanish castle to learn that his sister, married to a deranged count, had become ill and had been entombed, perhaps alive, in the structure's lower depths next to an ancient torture chamber.

The Premature Burial. American International, 1962. Ray Milland, Hazel Court, Heather Angel. Directed by Corman.

On the eve of his wedding, a man terrified of catalepsy builds a tomb from which he can escape should he be buried prematurely. Persons whom he trusts take advantage of his fear.

Tales of Terror. American International, 1962. Price, Rathbone, Peter Lorre, Debra Paget. Directed by Corman.

An anthology of three Poe stories: "Morella" (1835), in which a man (Price) is haunted by his wife's death in childbirth; "The Black Cat," a comedy treatment with Lorre as a drunken wife murderer; and "The Facts in the Case of M. Valdemar" (1845), about a man (Rathbone) who staves off death for a time with hypnosis.

The Raven. American International, 1963. Price, Lorre, Karloff, Hazel Court, Jack Nicholson. Directed by Corman.

The time is the Middle Ages. A magician, mourning the death of his wife, learns from a raven (the raven is a man who has had a spell cast on him) that she is actually alive and in the castle of a master sorcerer. The film is a black comedy about a magic duel.

The Haunted Palace. American International, 1963. Price, Paget, Chaney, Frank Maxwell. Directed by Corman. A curious combination of a mood poem by Poe and, more significantly, of H. P. Lovecraft's "Case of Charles Dexter Ward."

A two-hundred-year-old metaphysician invades the body of a descendant and calls on beings from another world to help him in taking revenge on a town.

Masque of the Red Death. American International, 1964. Price, Court, June Asher, David Weston, Patrick Magee. Directed by Corman. From Poe's 1842 short story.

A medieval prince, in league with the devil, holds a masked ball while a plague spreads throughout the countryside, but Death mingles with the guests at the castle. Filmed in England, with a trace of Ingmar Bergman imagery, this is perhaps the best of all the Corman-Poe dramas.

The Tomb of Ligeia. American International, 1965. Price, Elizabeth Shepherd, John Westbrook. Directed by Corman. Suggested by the poem.

A widower, living amid the ruins of an abbey, is haunted by the memory of his first wife and a sinister black cat.

Having exhausted the eminent author's major works, American International nonetheless continued the series with *The Oblong Box,* 1969, from the 1844 story, grafting conventional horror tales of witch-hunts and maniac revenge to Poe's less familiar titles. The company concluded its interest in Poe suitably when, in 1969, it imported (from Les Films Marceau-Cocinor in Paris) an ambitious attempt by three of Europe's most respected directors to wed the techniques of the art film to horror-fantasy material by Poe.

Spirits of the Dead. American International, 1969. Vincent Price narrated (off-screen) the three stories. "Metzengerstein" (1832), directed by Roger Vadim, tells about a young man (Peter Fonda) who has perished in a stable fire and returns from the dead as a huge black horse to haunt his cousin, a decadent aristocrat (Jane Fonda) who had set the fire deliberately. "William Wilson" (1839), directed by Louis Malle, is about a wicked young man (Alain Delon) who, after abusing an opponent whom he has bested at cards (Brigitte Bardot), turns upon the mysterious double who has pursued him all his life.

"Never Bet the Devil Your Head" (1845), directed by Federico Fellini, is about an alcoholic has-been actor (Terence Stamp) who goes to a frenzied Rome studio to film a western but is haunted by a vision of a young, white-clad girl.

Radio and Television

Poe's introspective narratives of terror and the supernatural have lent themselves particularly well to the radio anthology program; "The Tell-tale Heart" and "The Black Cat" were favorites of the medium's "Golden Age." Interestingly, during the revival of dramatic radio that began in 1973, an hour-long adaptation of "The Fall of the House of Usher" was one of the successes of the network *Mystery Theater*. Similarly, Poe's tales were popular during the early days of the television half-hour anthology show. A version of "The Cask of Amontillado" (1846) was shown on *Suspense*, featuring Bela Lugosi and set in wartime Paris.

POGGIOLI, PROFESSOR HENRY (Creator: T. S. STRIBLING). Born in Boston in 1888, Poggioli graduated from Cornell with an M.D. degree and a Ph.D. degree in psychology, which he then taught at Ohio State University. As a specialist in the criminal mind, he is often asked to help solve curious cases in such exotic locales as Haiti, Martinique, and other islands of the West Indies. Professor Poggioli is strongly attracted to beautiful women, but he refuses to marry because he believes that men and women want different things from that relationship. His unorthodox crime-solving method—trial-and-error deduction—leads to humorous but successful conclusions.

Professor Henry Poggioli, Ph.D., strolling on the shore of a Caribbean island while on a sabbatical leave, as depicted on the endpapers of the first edition of *Clues of the Caribbees*, published in 1929 by Doubleday, Doran.

Poggioli's first five adventures appeared in *Clues of the Caribbees* (1929). In "The Governor of Cap Haitien" he serves as "the great American voodoo inspector," demonstrating to the natives that voodooism is only a superstition. In "A Passage to Benares" he is accused of committing murder as part of a psychological experiment. His later adventures were published in *Ellery Queen's Mystery Magazine* and *The Saint Detective Magazine*.

POIROT, HERCULE (Creator: Agatha CHRISTIE). One of the most celebrated detectives in English crime fiction. Poirot is a Belgian who was forced to flee to England after the German invasion of his homeland in 1914. He had served as a policeman with honor and distinction before retiring in 1904.

After the war he remains in England and becomes a private inquiry agent (the American term is "private detective"). He shares a home with his old friend Captain Hastings at 14 Farraway Street in London. The not-overly-bright captain acts as Poirot's Watson (*see* WATSON, DR.) and chronicles his early adventures. When Hastings marries and moves to Argentina in the 1930s, Poirot moves to Whitehaven Mansions, a "modern" block of flats whose geometrical appearance and proportions indulge his passion for "method" and "order." His needs are served by his faithful manservant, Georges, and his efficient secretary, Miss Lemon. He is now about eighty and semiretired but has been known to investigate occasional murder cases brought to him by his friend Mrs. Ariadne Oliver, a rather scatterbrained lady detective novelist.

Monsieur Poirot is short—only 5 feet 4 inches tall—but his ego is enormous. His egg-shaped head is slightly bent to the left, and his hair seems suspiciously dark for one of his age. When he is excited, his eyes look green. His pride and joy is his luxuriant moustache, which is waxed and twirled into points at the ends. He wears small black patent leather shoes and has carried a cane for many years because of a leg injury he received during World War I. He smokes fancy cigarettes and is an immaculate dresser. His use of the English language leaves much to be desired, and, during his early years in England, he constantly used French phrases.

Although Poirot seems to be a comic figure, his reasoning power is immense and he proudly boasts of his "little grey cells." He has been known to make an occasional mistake—whereupon he says, "I am a triple imbecile"—but his energy and supreme belief in his own ability oblige him to state that he is the only detective in the world who could possibly solve his case. He dies in *Curtain*, the last Poirot novel, which was written in the 1940s but remained unpublished until 1975.

Hercule Poirot (the Belgian detective is portrayed by Tony Randall) is baffled by a series of seemingly unrelated deaths in *The Alphabet Murders,* as the gout-afflicted Hastings of the Secret Service (Robert Morley) listens to a dissertation. [*MGM*]

CHECKLIST

1920 *The Mysterious Affair at Styles*
1923 *Murder on the Links*
1924 *Poirot Investigates* (s.s.)
1926 *The Murder of Roger Ackroyd*
1927 *The Big Four*
1928 *The Mystery of the Blue Train*
1929 "The Under Dog" (published with "Blackman's Wood" by E. Phillips OPPENHEIM; the book is entitled *Two New Crime Stories*)
1932 *Peril at End House*
1933 *Lord Edgware Dies* (U.S. title: *Thirteen at Dinner*)
1934 *Murder on the Orient Express* (U.S. title: *Murder in the Calais Coach*)
1934 *Murder in Three Acts* (British title: *Three-Act Tragedy*)
1935 *Death in the Clouds* (U.S. title: *Death in the Air*)
1936 *The A.B.C. Murders*
1936 *Murder in Mesopotamia*
1936 *Cards on the Table*
1937 *Dumb Witness* (U.S. title: *Poirot Loses a Client*)
1937 *Death on the Nile*
1937 *Murder in the Mews* (s.s.; U.S. title: *Dead Man's Mirror*)
1938 *Appointment with Death*
1938 *Hercule Poirot's Christmas* (U.S. title: *Murder for Christmas*)
1939 *The Regatta Mystery and Other Stories* (s.s.; five of the nine stories are about Poirot)
1940 *Sad Cypress*
1940 *One, Two, Buckle My Shoe* (U.S. title: *The Patriotic Murders*)
1941 *Evil under the Sun*
1942 *Murder in Retrospect* (British title: *Five Little Pigs*)
1946 *The Hollow*
1947 *The Labours of Hercules* (s.s.)
1948 *Taken at the Flood* (U.S. title: *There Is a Tide*)
1948 *Witness for the Prosecution and Other Stories* (s.s.; one of the nine stories is about Poirot)
1950 *Three Blind Mice and Other Stories* (s.s.; three of the eight stories are about Poirot)
1951 *The Under Dog and Other Stories* (s.s.)
1952 *Mrs. McGinty's Dead*
1953 *After the Funeral* (U.S. title: *Funerals Are Fatal*)
1955 *Hickory, Dickory, Dock* (U.S. title: *Hickory, Dickory, Death*)
1956 *Dead Man's Folly*
1959 *Cat among the Pigeons*
1960 *The Adventure of the Christmas Pudding and Other Stories* (s.s.; five of the six stories are about Poirot)
1961 *Double Sin and Other Stories* (s.s.; four of the eight stories are about Poirot)
1963 *The Clocks*
1966 *Third Girl*
1969 *Hallowe'en Party*
1972 *Elephants Can Remember*
1975 *Curtain*

Films

Five years after *The Murder of Roger Ackroyd* was published, it was made into a film in England, with character actor Austin Trevor as Poirot, a role he played two more times.

Alibi. Twickenham, 1931. Trevor, Franklin Dyall (Roger Ackroyd), Elizabeth Allan. Directed by Leslie Hiscott.

A country doctor serves as Poirot's assistant as the Belgian detective investigates a supposed suicide on a wooded estate.

Black Coffee. Twickenham, 1931. Trevor, Richard Cooper (Captain Hastings), Adrianne Allen, Allan, Melville Cooper (Inspector Japp). Directed by Hiscott. Based on the 1931 play.

Poirot probes the theft of a secret formula.

Lord Edgware Dies. Real Art, 1934. Trevor, Jane Carr, Cooper, John Turnbull (Japp). Directed by Henry Edwards. Based on the 1933 novel.

Poirot must ascertain who murdered an elderly lord and attempted to poison an actress at her own dinner party.

More than three decades later, MGM, which had previously used two Poirot novels for screen mysteries featuring Miss Jane MARPLE, cast American actor-comedian Tony Randall as a heavily made-up Poirot in a version of *The A.B.C. Murders* filmed in England.

The Alphabet Murders. MGM, 1966. Randall, Anita Ekberg, Robert Morley, Maurice Denham, Guy Rolfe, James Villiers. Directed by Frank Tashlin.

While on a holiday in England, Poirot is curious about a series of seemingly unrelated murders: an

Albert Finney (standing, center) as the moustached Hercule Poirot interrogates an international cast of suspects in the dining car of a snow-stalled train in the 1974 adaptation of *Murder on the Orient Express*. [*EMI*]

aqua-clown drowned in a swimming pool, a girl killed in a bowling alley by a dart, and so on. A bungling British Intelligence agent (Morley) is assigned to protect the Belgian detective, and he and Miss Marple (Margaret Rutherford) briefly cross paths.

Murder on the Orient Express. EMI (British), 1974. Albert Finney (Poirot), Lauren Bacall, Martin Balsam, Ingrid Bergman, Jacqueline Bisset, Jean-Pierre Cassel, Sean Connery, John Gielgud, Wendy Hiller, Anthony Perkins, Vanessa Redgrave, Rachel Roberts, Richard Widmark, Michael York. Directed by Sidney Lumet.

An international all-star cast portrays the passengers on a train on which death and conspiracy are to be found.

Plays

Michael Morton adapted *The Murder of Roger Ackroyd* for the British stage. Called *Alibi*, it was the basis for the 1931 film about Poirot and murder at a country house. It was presented in the United States in 1932, starring Charles Laughton and Jane Wyatt, and retitled *The Fatal Alibi*. Mrs. Christie featured Poirot in her original play *Black Coffee*, which opened in London in 1931 and was filmed later that year.

Radio and Television

Martin Gabel portrayed Hercule Poirot in a 1961 *General Electric Theater* half-hour program. Harold Huber played the title role in the short-lived radio series *The Adventures of M. Hercule Poirot*.

POLLARD, (JOSEPH) PERCIVAL (1869–1911). American author and literary critic. Born in Greifswald, Pomerania (now in East Germany), of German-English parents, he arrived in the United States in 1885. He wrote several novels and volumes of criticism. *Lingo Dan* (1903), one of the rarest first editions of crime fiction and a QUEEN'S QUORUM selection, recounts the adventures of the first American murderer in a series of short stories. He is also a thief, con man, and tramp—and very patriotic.

PONS, SOLAR (Creator: August DERLETH). When Sir Arthur CONAN DOYLE stopped writing about Sherlock HOLMES, Derleth asked his permission to write pastiches of the master. Receiving no opposition, he created Solar Pons, later known as "the Sherlock Holmes of Praed Street." The first short story appeared in 1929.

Pons resembles Holmes; he wears an Inverness cape and a deerstalker hat and employs Holmes's old-fashioned methods of detection, using the classic skills of observation, deduction, and ratiocination. Pons began his practice in 1907, trying to fill the gap created by Holmes's absence from London. Although successful, he is not Holmes, and he amiably recognizes that he does not fill the master's shoes.

His companion, Dr. Lyndon Parker, records his adventures. Factual essays about Pons, Parker, and their milieu are in *Praed Street Papers* (1965) and *A Praed Street Dossier* (1968).

CHECKLIST

1945 *"In re: Sherlock Holmes": The Adventures of Solar Pons* (s.s.)
1951 *The Memoirs of Solar Pons* (s.s.)
1952 *Three Problems for Solar Pons* (s.s.)
1958 *The Return of Solar Pons* (s.s.)
1961 *The Reminiscences of Solar Pons* (s.s.)
1965 "The Adventure of the Orient Express" (s.s.)
1965 *The Casebook of Solar Pons* (s.s.)
1968 *Mr. Fairlie's Final Journey*
1968 "The Adventure of the Unique Dickensians" (s.s.)
1973 *The Chronicles of Solar Pons* (s.s.)

Solar Pons, August Derleth's popular detective, is known as the Sherlock Holmes of Praed Street. This illustration appears on the dust wrapper of *The Return of Solar Pons*, published by Mycroft & Moran in 1958. Frank Utpatel is the artist.

POOLE, INSPECTOR JOHN (Creator: Henry WADE). Poole is middle-sized, and has dark-brown hair and a pleasant face. There is often a twinkle lurking in his steady gray eyes. He has good manners and is noted for his tact and judgment.

Poole had a college education, received training at police school, and quickly rose from the ranks to become the youngest inspector in New Scotland Yard's famed Criminal Investigation Department (CID).

His career starts in 1929 and reaches its climax in 1953, when he is promoted to the rank of chief inspector in *Too Soon to Die*, which concerns a family's attempt to avoid the financial ruin that paying exorbitant inheritance taxes will bring. Poole soon must solve a murder.

CHECKLIST

1929 *The Duke of York's Steps*
1931 *No Friendly Drop*
1933 *Policeman's Lot* (s.s.; seven of the thirteen stories are about Poole)
1934 *Constable Guard Thyself!*
1936 *Bury Him Darkly*
1940 *Lonely Magdalene*
1953 *Too Soon to Die*
1954 *Gold Was Our Grave*

PORLOCK, MARTIN. *See* MACDONALD, PHILIP.

PORTER, JOYCE (1924–). English mystery novelist. A native of Cheshire, Miss Porter attended King's College, University of London. From 1949 until 1963 she served as an officer in the Women's Royal Air Force (WRAF). She began writing after her retirement from the service, achieving immediate success with a series of novels and novelettes about Inspector Wilfred DOVER of Scotland Yard. She deliberately sought to inject humor into the Dover series as well as into nonseries works such as her spoof on spy fiction, *Sour Cream with Everything* (1966). Part of that book is set in the Soviet Union, which Miss Porter has visited; she has also traveled extensively by car throughout the United States.

Joyce Porter's first book, *Dover One* (1964), received widespread praise for its humor and excellent construction. However, such critics as Julian SYMONS and Jacques BARZUN and Wendell Hertig TAYLOR have felt that the novelty of a bumbling detective antihero has worn thin, the character of Dover not having varied since he first appeared.

PORTER, WILLIAM SYDNEY. *See* HENRY, O.

Enid Schantz designed this portrait of Melville Davisson Post for the dust wrapper of *The Methods of Uncle Abner*.

POST, MELVILLE DAVISSON (1869–1930). American lawyer and author who created several memorable characters, including UNCLE ABNER and Randolph MASON.

Born in Romines Mills, W.Va., the son of Florence May (Davisson) and Ira Carper Post, he grew up in the rural environment that he later used for the setting of his best stories. After graduating from West Virginia University, he practiced criminal and corporate law for eleven years and became active in Democratic politics. He married Ann Bloomfield Gamble in 1903 (she died in 1919). Post died at the age of sixty-one after falling from a horse.

Regarded by some critics as the best American short story writer since Edgar Allan POE, he was the most commercially successful magazine writer of his day. His technical skill in plotting a tale is conceded even by those who do not consider his work of great literary value. He believed that the primary purpose of fiction was to entertain the reader, and his fast-paced, suspenseful tales are reminiscent of those of O. HENRY, the master of the well-plotted story. Charles A. Norton's *Melville Davisson Post: Man of Many Mysteries* (1973) is at once a biography of the author and an analysis and bibliography of his work.

Credited with creating a new "formula" for the mystery story, Post avoided the repetition of the traditional tale by developing the mystery and its solution simultaneously, substantially speeding up the action. His works, which generally have a strong moral tone (except for the early Mason tales), carefully combine the ratiocination of Poe's tales with the dramatic flair of the French writers.

In addition to Uncle Abner and Mason, Post created several interesting detectives. Sir Henry Marquis, chief of the Criminal Investigation Department of Scotland Yard, appears in *The Sleuth of St. James's Square* (1920) and *The Bradmoor Murder* (1929; British title: *The Garden in Asia*). A middle-aged Englishman with short-cropped gray hair, Marquis seems more like a typical outdoorsman than a policeman. Although a Londoner, he directs secret service operations in Asia, and many of his cases take place in distant countries, including the United States.

Monsieur Jonquelle, Prefect of Police of Paris (1923) recounts the adventures of a monocled Frenchman who battles crime in every corner of the world.

Another character, named Walker, is introduced in "The Reward" in *The Sleuth of St. James's Square*. Powerfully built and very young, he falls under the influence of a pair of expert train robbers. The first six episodes of *Walker of the Secret Service* (1924) are a compressed novel, at the end of which Walker has clearly reformed and, with the aid of a girl, is inducted into the Secret Service.

In *The Silent Witness* (1930) Colonel Braxton is a lawyer in old Virginia. Often aided by Dabney Mason, the gallant gentleman solves crimes committed by the greedy. An ancient concept guides him: the human mind is incapable of producing a false set of facts that consistently fit into reality. "At some point," Post writes, "there would appear a physical fact to destroy it. This silent witness . . . was always standing in the background to be called by anyone who had the acumen to discover it."

Other mysteries by Post are *The Gilded Chair* (1910); *The Nameless Thing* (1912), a rare short story collection; and a collection of seventeen crime, mystery, and adventure tales, *The Mystery at the Blue Villa* (1919).

POSTGATE, RAYMOND (WILLIAM) (1896–1971). English author. Born in Cambridge, Postgate was educated at the Perse School, Liverpool College, and St. John's College, Oxford. A classical scholar and economist, he was also a newspaper editor and a contributor to the *Encyclopaedia Britannica* (1929 edition). A noted food and wine connoisseur, he founded and edited *The Good Food Guide to Britain* (1950–   ; published biennially). His sister, Margaret Cole, was married to G. D. H. Cole (see COLE, G. D. H., AND M. I.); Postgate and his brother-in-law, both Socialists, collaborated on *The History of the*

English Common People (1938). Postgate was married to Daisy Lansbury; they had two sons. He wrote a biography of her father, George Lansbury, a member of Parliament and leader of the Labour party (1931–1935). Postgate also wrote many other works, including some of a historical nature, and he published translations from Greek, Latin, and French.

Of the three mysteries he wrote, he is best remembered for his first, *Verdict of Twelve* (1940), a highly successful book in which the progress of a murder trial is followed through the reactions of the jurors. It was selected for inclusion in the HAYCRAFT-QUEEN CORNERSTONE LIBRARY.

POTTS, JEAN (1910–). American author of mysteries and short stories. Born in St. Paul, Nebr., Miss Potts was a newspaperwoman in her hometown after she graduated from Nebraska Wesleyan University in Lincoln. She moved to New York City to pursue a writing career and has had short stories published in *McCall's, Woman's Day, Family Circle, Cosmopolitan,* and *Ellery Queen's Mystery Magazine.* Her first novel, *Go, Lovely Rose,* was awarded the Mystery Writers of America Edgar as best first novel of 1954. It is a fictionalization of a famous murder case, the 1902 killing of a housemaid, Rose Harsent, in Suffolk, England.

Miss Potts's early books, including *Go, Lovely Rose, The Man with the Cane* (1957), and *Lightning Strikes Twice* (1958), are set in small Midwestern towns. Other ones, such as *Death of a Stray Cat* (1955), *The Evil Wish* (1962), *The Only Good Secretary* (1965), and *The Trash Stealers* (1968), tell of young career women involved in murder. Lenore Glen OFFORD, praising Miss Potts's ability to write mysteries about recognizable people, referred to her "peculiar genius for portraying people who might live in the next block from you."

POWELL, CHRIS. *See* HUNT, E. HOWARD.

PRESBREY, EUGENE. *See* RAFFLES, A. J.

PRICHARD, HESKETH (VERNON HESKETH) (1876–1922). English author. Although born in India, he was taken to England by his widowed mother (Kate Ryall Prichard) while he was still an infant. He spent much of his life traveling and hunting, using his outdoor experiences as background for his short story collection, *November Joe: The Detective of the Woods* (1913; the American edition preceded the English edition by one month), which recounts the adventures of possibly the only backwoods detective in literature. Prichard collaborated with his mother on many works, most notably those about Don Quebranta Huesos. The first Don Q story was published in *Badminton Magazine* (January 1898). The first two books about the grim Spaniard,

Hesketh Prichard's most famous characters are Don Q, an abbreviation of the nickname Don Quebranta Huesos, or the bone smasher, and November Joe, the backwoods detective. The illustration on the left appears on the front cover of *Don Q in the Sierra,* published by Lippincott in 1906; the one on the right is on the front cover of the first edition of *November Joe,* published by Houghton Mifflin in 1913.

who is vicious toward the rich and evil but kind to the poor and good, were collections entitled *The Chronicles of Don Q* (1904) and *New Chronicles of Don Q* (1906; U.S. title: *Don Q in the Sierra*); the last was a novel, *Don Q's Love Story* (1909). These books were signed by K. and Hesketh Prichard. Douglas Fairbanks played the adventurous rogue in *Don Q, Son of Zorro* (1925), and Fred Terry portrayed him on the London stage in 1921.

PRIESTLEY, DR. LANCELOT (Creator: John RHODE). This mathematician's grim-visaged face shows both intelligence and the unmistakable stamp of the English aristocrat. Because of his poor vision, he wears strong glasses. He lives and works in a house on Westbourne Terrace in London with his daughter, April, and his secretary, Harold Merefield (pronounced Merryfield), who is also his son-in-law.

Dr. Priestley, once a professor who held a chair of applied mathematics at a famous English university, was forced to resign his position after a heated and acrimonious disagreement with the university authorities. Fortunately, he possessed considerable means and was able to spend his time writing books on abstruse mathematical subjects and debunking various widely held but false theories through strict application of logic.

The remorseless logician's chief form of recreation is solving crime problems as if they were impersonal exercises in pure logic. They are frequently brought to him by Inspector (later Superintendent) Hanslet and Inspector James Waghorn of Scotland Yard. He has been known to call these problems "the very breath of life to me" but seems completely indifferent to the human element or to any question of justice.

The aging professor is dry and academic, seldom betraying any sense of humor. He once took an active part in his investigations, but toward the end of his career, he does not bother to leave his house to visit the scenes of the various crimes.

Dr. Priestley has an aversion to the telephone and hardly ever uses it. He is noted as a genial host—especially if his guests have a mystery for him to solve.

CHECKLIST

1925 *The Paddington Mystery*
1926 *Dr. Priestley's Quest*
1927 *The Ellerby Case*
1928 *The Murders in Praed Street*
1928 *Tragedy at the Unicorn*
1929 *The House on Tollard Ridge*
1929 *The Davidson Case* (U.S. title: *Murder at Bratton Grange*)
1930 *Peril at Cranbury Hall*
1930 *Pinehurst* (U.S. title: *Dr. Priestley Investigates*)
1931 *Tragedy on the Line*
1931 *The Hanging Woman*
1932 *Mystery at Greycombe Farm* (U.S. title: *The Fire at Greycombe Farm*)
1932 *Dead Men at the Folly*
1933 *The Motor Rally Mystery* (U.S. title: *Dr. Priestley Lays a Trap*)
1933 *The Claverton Mystery* (U.S. title: *The Claverton Affair*)
1933 *The Venner Crime*
1934 *The Robthorne Mystery*
1934 *Poison for One*
1934 *Shot at Dawn*
1935 *The Corpse in the Car*
1935 *Hendon's First Case*
1935 *Mystery at Olympia* (U.S. title: *Murder at the Motor Show*)
1936 *Death at Breakfast*
1936 *In Face of the Verdict* (U.S. title: *In the Face of the Verdict*)
1937 *Death in the Hop Fields* (U.S. title: *The Harvest Murder*)
1937 *Death on the Board* (U.S. title: *Death Sits on the Board*)
1937 *Proceed with Caution* (U.S. title: *Body Unidentified*)
1938 *Invisible Weapons*
1938 *The Bloody Tower* (U.S. title: *Tower of Evil*)
1939 *Death Pays a Dividend*
1939 *Death on Sunday* (U.S. title: *The Elm Tree Murder*)
1940 *Death on the Boat Train*
1940 *Murder at Lilac Cottage*
1941 *Death at the Helm*
1941 *They Watched by Night* (U.S. title: *Signal for Death*)
1942 *The Fourth Bomb*
1943 *Dead on the Track*
1943 *Men Die at Cyprus Lodge*
1944 *Death Invades the Meeting*
1944 *Vegetable Duck* (U.S. title: *Too Many Suspects*)
1945 *Bricklayer's Arms* (U.S. title: *Shadow of a Crime*)
1946 *The Lake House* (U.S. title: *The Secret of the Lake House*)
1946 *Death in Harley Street*
1947 *Nothing but the Truth* (U.S. title: *Experiment in Crime*)
1947 *Death of an Author*
1948 *The Paper Bag* (U.S. title: *The Links in the Chain*)
1948 *The Telephone Call* (U.S. title: *Shadow of an Alibi*)
1949 *Blackthorn House*
1949 *Up the Garden Path* (U.S. title: *The Fatal Garden*)
1950 *The Two Graphs* (U.S. title: *Double Identities*)
1950 *Family Affairs* (U.S. title: *The Last Suspect*)
1951 *Dr. Goodwood's Locum* (U.S. title: *The Affair of the Substitute Doctor*)
1951 *The Secret Meeting*
1952 *Death in Wellington Road*
1952 *Death at the Dance*
1953 *By Registered Post* (U.S. title: *The Mysterious Suspect*)
1953 *Death at the Inn* (U.S. Title: *The Case of the Forty Thieves*)
1954 *The Dovebury Murders*
1954 *Death on the Lawn*
1955 *Domestic Agency* (U.S. title: *Grave Matters*)
1955 *Death of a Godmother* (U.S. title: *Delayed Payment*)
1956 *An Artist Dies* (U.S. title: *Death of an Artist*)
1956 *Open Verdict*
1957 *Robbery with Violence*
1957 *Death of a Bridegroom*
1958 *Murder at Derivale*
1958 *Death Takes a Partner*
1959 *Licensed for Murder*
1959 *Three Cousins Die*
1960 *Twice Dead*
1960 *The Fatal Pool*
1961 *The Vanishing Diary*

PRIESTLEY, J[OHN] B[OYNTON] (1894–). English novelist, dramatist, and essayist. Priestley is not regarded as a mystery writer, although he wrote *The Old Dark House* (1928; published in England as *Benighted* the previous year), a tale of terror and suspense subsequently made into a successful film. The basic plot has been imitated so frequently that it is now one of the great clichés of mystery novels and films, but it was truly terrifying when Priestley wrote it: a group of people, thrown together in an eerie old mansion and unable to leave because of a storm, are terrorized by its strange inhabitants.

Priestley is best known for his long, traditionally English novels, such as *The Good Companions* (1929) and *Angel Pavement* (1930), both of which were enormously successful, and for his popular, experimental plays. His other contributions to the literature of crime are *I'll Tell You Everything* (1933; in collaboration with Gerald Bullett), *Blackout in Gretley* (1942), *Saturn over the Water* (1961), *The Shapes of Sleep* (1962), and *Salt Is Leaving* (1966).

Films

Priestley has made notable contributions to the film

melodrama, but one stands out as a celebration of its type and a statement of its theme. Terror in old dark houses had long been a thriller staple, but Priestley fashioned fear into a masterpiece.

The Old Dark House. Universal, 1932. Boris Karloff, Melvyn Douglas, Charles Laughton, Gloria Stuart, Raymond Massey, Ernest Thesiger. Directed by James Whale.

One stormy night several people find themselves stranded at the manor house of the ancient, degenerate Femm family.

Tom Poston and Robert Morley starred in a 1963 version, directed by William Castle, that retained nothing from Priestley's book but the title.

Other Priestley mystery works have reached the screen.

Dangerous Corner. RKO, 1934. Virginia Bruce, Conrad Nagel, Douglas. Directed by Phil Rosen. From the Priestley play of the same name, which opened in London in 1932; Priestley and Ruth Holland novelized it in 1933.

At a house party, a twist in time—seemingly caused by a burst radio tube—causes friends to make dangerous revelations about embezzlement, an accidental killing, and other secrets.

Laburnum Grove. Associated Talking Pictures (British), 1936. Edmund Gwen, Cedric Hardwicke, Victoria Hopper. Directed by Carol Reed. From the Priestley play of the same name, which began a successful run in London in 1933.

A middle-aged suburban father cheerfully reveals to his family that he is a forger.

An Inspector Calls. Watergate (British), 1954. Alastair Sim, Arthur Young, Eileen Moore, Bryan Forbes. Directed by Guy Hamilton. From the Priestley play, which premiered in London in 1946.

Paying an unexpected visit, a strange inspector demonstrates to a respectable family how they all share responsibility for the death of a shopgirl.

PROCTER, MAURICE (1906–1973). English mystery novelist. Born in Nelson, Lancashire, and educated at the Nelson grammar school, Procter was expected by his family to enter the teaching profession, but at fifteen he ran away and joined the Army. His parents had to enlist the aid of a local member of Parliament to have him released. When Procter reached the age of consent, he promptly joined the police. He spent the next nineteen years serving with the Halifax Borough Police in Yorkshire, where, he said, "I walked 5,000 miles a year and my weight fell to nine stone." He also gained the experience that served him well in later years, when he became an outstanding practitioner of the police procedural novel.

In 1946 Procter resigned from the police department and that year published a critical novel about his former colleagues called *No Proud Chivalry*. *Each Man's Destiny* (1947) deals with the same subject. His first mystery novel, *The Chief Inspector's Statement* (1949), was published in the United States in 1951 as *The Pennycross Murders*.

Procter retired to Halifax and, later, the country, with his wife (former Winifred Blakey, whom he had married in 1933) and son and spent four and a half hours a day writing about the men of the fictional Granchester Police Department, in his Inspector Harry MARTINEAU series. His hobbies included music, gardening, and travel.

Procter's long tenure with the police enabled him to depict the men and officers credibly, and their methods of fighting crime are described with a rare authenticity. He established himself as a master of the police procedural novel, ranking with John CREASEY's J. J. Marric in England and Hillary WAUGH and Ed MCBAIN in the United States.

Although most of Procter's mystery novels are about Martineau, he also wrote some nonseries mysteries, notably *The Chief Inspector's Statement*, which concerns the investigation of the sex murders of two little girls, complicated by the police inspector's romance with a local girl. Anthony BOUCHER praised Procter's understanding of the character of the villain and the type of police work necessary to capture him. *I Will Speak Daggers* (1956; U.S. title: *The Ripper*), about a wanton murderer, is an unusual Procter work in that it is a classic detective novel.

PROPPER, MILTON M[ORRIS] (1906–?). American detective novelist. In many ways Propper is the American counterpart of Freeman Wills CROFTS, in that he writes the type of police routine stories that were common in England in the 1920s and 1930s but were more rare on the opposite side of the Atlantic.

Propper was adept at devising puzzles and plots but not as good a prose stylist as Crofts was and could not create a fully three-dimensional character. His first novel, *The Strange Disappearance of Mary Young* (1929), introduces Tommy RANKIN, of Philadelphia's Homicide Bureau. At the end of a ride on a scenic railway, a young girl remains in the front seat. When a guard finds a knife in her heart, the police are summoned to ascertain her identity and capture the murderer. In *The Boudoir Murder* (1931; British title: *And Then Silence*) the Philadelphia scene is well handled; the tale is typical of its period, and there is an impressive motor chase climax. *The Election Booth Murders* (1935; British title: *Murder at the Polls*) starts out with the murder of a reform party's choice for the office of district attorney as he enters a booth to cast his ballot. A couple of suspects flee the scene of the crime, and another good motor chase follows, which ends with their capture by the police. However, when two additional murders occur, Rankin and the police exert all their efforts to ensure clean government for their city.

PULP MAGAZINES Seven by ten inches in size, with bright glossy covers and usually 120 untrimmed wood pulp pages, the first pulp magazines appeared in the late nineteenth century, but their heyday was roughly the two decades between the world wars. Street & Smith's somewhat sedate *Detective Story,* which appeared during the World War I period, was the first pulp magazine devoted entirely to crime fiction. In the 1920s BLACK MASK, *Detective Fiction Weekly,* and *Clues* were established, followed in the 1930s by *Dime Detective, Thrilling Detective, Spicy Detective, Crimebusters,* and a multitude of others. Although they featured every sort of detective, from Scotland Yard inspector to masked avenger, the major contribution of the pulp magazines to mystery fiction was the private eye. The tough private investigator was born in the early 1920s, in the pages of *Black Mask.* The chief contributors to his growth and development were Carroll John DALY, Dashiell HAMMETT, Frederick Nebel, Raoul WHITFIELD, and Erle Stanley GARDNER.

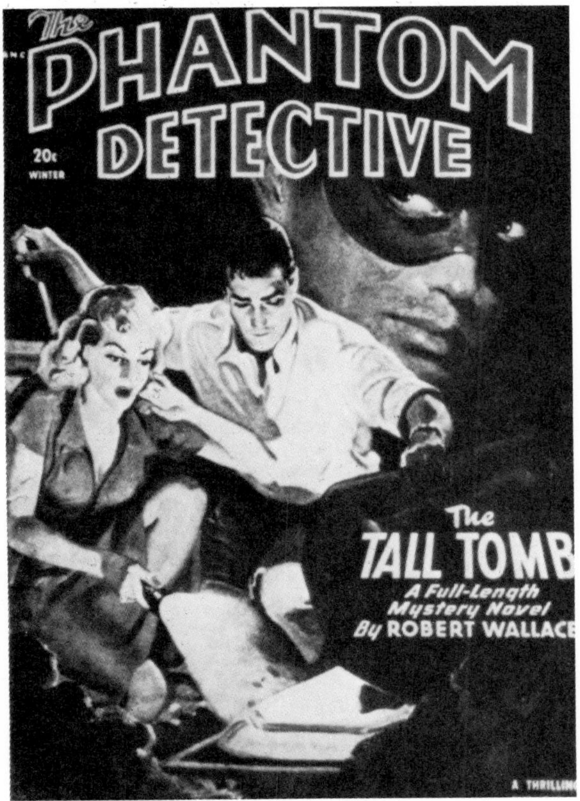

The Phantom Detective **published the exploits of playboy millionaire Richard Curtis Van Loan for twenty years; the first issue was dated February 1933; the last of 170 issues, Summer 1953. All the stories were signed by Robert Wallace, a house name, but the creator was D. L. Champion.**

Daly was the pioneer contributor to the pulp detective category. A former movie projectionist and theater manager, and the least gifted of the above-mentioned authors of hard-boiled detective stories, he tried to develop a convincing tough private operative who narrated his own adventures. By June 1923, after a few false starts, he had the character roughed out and named. He was Race WILLIAMS, who introduced himself thus: "I'm what you might call a middleman—just a half-way house between the cops and the crooks. . . . I do a little honest shooting once in a while—just in the way of business—but I never bumped off a guy that didn't need it."

Fortunately for the survival of the private eye, Hammett also began writing during that era. He introduced his fat, nameless operative for the Continental Detective Agency in the early 1920s, also in *Black Mask,* and in 1929 Sam SPADE appeared. Nebel, Gardner, and Whitfield produced a variety of hard-boiled detectives—private investigators, tough cops, wisecracking newsmen, even fugitive crooks. Most of the detectives of this school shared certain attitudes and qualifications. They usually stayed away from small towns, working for detective agencies or on their own in large cities—New York, Chicago, Detroit, Miami, and Los Angeles, which *Black Mask* called the New Wild West. Many of them shared, too, a distrust of police and politicians. They could patiently collect evidence, but they could also cut corners, something the law could not do. They were linked, particularly during the Depression years, with reality, with the real crimes of the urban world, and with the real smell and feel of the mean streets.

Black Mask faced no real competition in the tough detective field until the 1930s. The strongest competitor then was *Dime Detective.* Inaugurated in 1932 as part of Popular Publications' low-priced line, the magazine was at first a disparate blend of private eye stories and old-dark-house melodramas. By the mid-1930s, under the editorship of Kenneth S. White, it was almost completely given over to the kind of story Captain Joseph T. Shaw (1874–1952) had pioneered in *Black Mask.* After Shaw left *Black Mask* in 1936, many of his contributors began working for White's magazine. Most notable among them was Raymond CHANDLER, whose works had first appeared in *Black Mask* in 1933. In the early 1940s *Black Mask* itself was sold to Popular Publications, and thus White edited not only the imitation but the

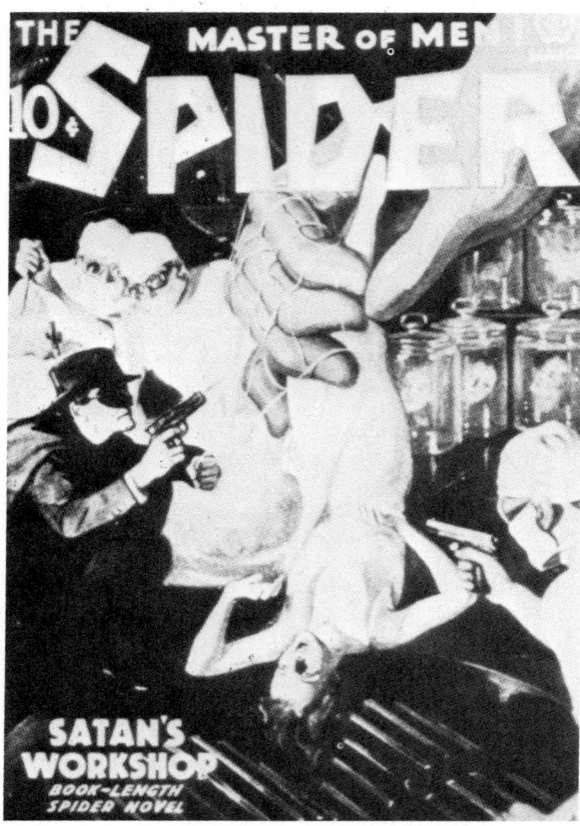

One of the most popular pulp fiction superheroes, the Spider was created by R. T. M. Scott (pseudonym of Reginald T. Maitland), who wrote the first two novels for the magazines. The remainder of the 118 tales were produced by Grant Stockbridge (pseudonym of Norvell Page). The first issue appeared in October 1933; the last, in December 1943.

"real thing." Eventually almost all the detective pulp magazines featured private eye stories.

As detective titles multiplied during the 1930s, numerous able writers began working for the pulp magazines. Their work, in all but a few cases, has not survived the cheap paper magazines it appeared in. Hammett, Chandler, and Gardner continue in print, but few of their contemporaries, even the gifted ones, fared as well. The names Eric Taylor, Paul Cain (pseudonym of Peter Ruric), W. T. Ballard, John K. Butler, Roger Torrey, Norbert Davis, and H. H. Stinson do not produce a shock of recognition now. Yet they all did effective work—hard-boiled, vernacular, cynical, and full of action.

Another type of detective that abounded in the wood pulp magazines of the 1930s was the mystery man, the cloaked and masked type of crime fighter. The leader of the pack was the Shadow (*see* SHADOW, THE), who came to the attention of the public in *The Shadow* magazine in the spring of 1931. The Shadow novels, which appeared twice a month at the height of their popularity in the mid-1930s, were credited to Maxwell Grant. Most of them, about 280, were written by Walter B. GIBSON. After the Shadow came a horde of other avenging detectives—the Spider, the Phantom Detective, the Whisperer, the Avenger, the Green Lama, the Black Bat, the Ghost, the Black Hood, the Masked Detective, and so on. These Depression-era sleuths owe something to the mystery men who flourished in the early years of the century, in the pulp magazines and in the silent movie serials. It may be significant that their memory has faded less than that of the hard-boiled detectives of the pulp magazines.

RON GOULART

PUNSHON, E[RNEST] R[OBERTSON] (1872–1956). English playwright and mystery novelist. Punshon went to work in an office in his native London at the age of fourteen but was successful neither at this endeavor nor in his subsequent attempt at wheat farming in Canada. His literary career began more hopefully with the winning of a prize, and it continued with a play, many short stories and novels, and radio plays for the BBC. His study of the Landru ("Bluebeard") case was included in *The Anatomy of Murder* (1937), edited by Helen SIMPSON, who also contributed to the book. He also was a frequent reviewer of mysteries.

Punshon's best-known fictional works are a series of short stories and novels about Bobby Owen, an Oxford graduate who becomes a police constable when the Depression leaves him jobless. The Owen novels have often used various aspects of the entertainment industry. At the outset of *Information Received* (1933), one of the wealthiest men in England is thrown into terror when he is given free tickets to a performance of *Hamlet*. *Death of a Beauty Queen* (1935) centers around a beauty contest designed to bolster receipts at a movie theater.

QUEEN, ELLERY (author) (pseudonym of Frederic Dannay, 1905– , and Manfred B[ennington] Lee, 1905–1971). American mystery novelists and editors; creators of Ellery QUEEN (detective). The Brooklyn-born cousins made Ellery Queen world-famous as author, detective, and editor. Dannay used his real name, Daniel Nathan, for an autobiographical novel, *The Golden Summer* (1953), which told about his boyhood in Elmira, N.Y. The family returned to New York City, where he was graduated from Boys High School. Although he never went to college, at the time he started his mystery writing career he was, at twenty-three, a copywriter and an art director for an advertising agency.

Lee was originally named Manford Lepofsky and grew up in New York City. He attended New York University and was writing publicity and advertising material for a motion picture company when he and his cousin began their collaboration. Both Nathan and Lepofsky changed their names as young men.

Attracted by a $7,500 first prize in a mystery novel contest sponsored by *McClure's* magazine, they submitted *The Roman Hat Mystery* in 1928. However, just before they were awarded first prize, the publisher went bankrupt, and *Smart Set*, the magazine that took over *McClure's* assets, awarded the prize to a mystery they thought would have greater appeal to women readers. The Frederick A. Stokes Company decided to publish the first Queen novel in book form, and this publication proved to be a major historical event in the genre.

The contest had required that all entries be submitted under a pseudonym, and the authors chose "Ellery Queen" because it seemed unusual and memorable to them. They also decided to give their main character the same name, hoping that readers would remember the author's name more easily if it appeared throughout the book. Their books (and their detective) quickly became extremely popular.

After three novels about Queen, they adopted another pseudonym, Barnaby Ross, and began, in *The Tragedy of X* (1932), a series of four mysteries whose detective is retired Shakespearean actor Drury LANE. After *Drury Lane's Last Case* (1933), Queen was the detective in all their mysteries except the novels *The Glass Village* (1954) and *Cop Out* (1969) and the novelette *Terror Town* (1956).

Their success led to contracts with Columbia, Paramount, and MGM, for which they wrote, in Hollywood, during the mid-1930s, although they never received any screen credits. For nine years, beginning in 1939, they wrote the scripts for the *Ellery Queen* radio series. To increase publicity for their ventures, Dannay and Lee lectured throughout the country. Both were masked, and Dannay, appearing as Barnaby Ross, presented an intricate crime puzzle, challenging Lee, as Ellery Queen, to solve the mystery. After due deliberation, Queen detailed the correct solution—the whole procedure having been, of course, well rehearsed.

The cousins, especially Dannay, had long been interested in detective fiction as literature and had wanted to edit a magazine of quality mystery stories, not restricted to any particular subgenre. *Mystery League*, which they founded and edited in 1933, had the requisite quality but failed after four issues when the publisher went bankrupt. However, after Dannay's long convalescence from a 1940 automobile accident that almost took his life, they interested publisher Lawrence E. Spivak of Mercury Press, and *Ellery Queen's Mystery Magazine (EQMM)* appeared in the fall of 1941. The magazine has always been the "child" of Dannay, who amassed the world's greatest library of mystery short stories (now at the University of Texas). In the magazine's early days he relied on this collection to reprint stories not otherwise easily available to American readers. He also adopted a policy of encouraging new authors; many mystery writers, among them James YAFFE, Lillian DE LA TORRE, Harry KEMELMAN, Stanley ELLIN, and Robert L. FISH, had their first stories published in

Frederic Dannay.

EQMM. Established writers also contributed stories, and many became prizewinners in the magazine's thirteen annual contests (1946–1957; 1962). Ellery Queen achieved his goal so well that Anthony BOUCHER could say accurately: "*EQMM* has published every important crime writer who ever wrote a short story." Dannay also purposely sought out and published stories by nonmystery writers that are nonetheless about crime or detection. Thirty Pulitzer and twelve Nobel Prize winners appeared in *EQMM*, including John Steinbeck, Arthur Miller, Sinclair Lewis, Bertrand Russell, Edna St. Vincent Millay, and Pearl Buck.

Ellery Queen has edited over seventy anthologies, including such landmark collections as *101 Years' Entertainment* (1941), the definitive anthology of detective short stories, commemorating the one-hundredth anniversary of Edgar Allan POE's first detective story; *Sporting Blood* (1942; British title: *Sporting Detective Stories*), an anthology of mysteries that have as their background a major sport or hobby; *The Female of the Species* (1943; British title: *Ladies in Crime*), mysteries in which a woman is either the detective or the criminal (Women's Lib more than thirty years ago); and *The Misadventures of Sherlock Holmes* (1944), an anthology of Holmesian parodies and pastiches that was suppressed shortly after publication because of the threat of legal action by the estate of Sir Arthur CONAN DOYLE.

A feature of the first two decades of *EQMM* was the introductions to the stories, which were brief essays on detective fiction. Some of them were collected in *In the Queens' Parlor* (1957). Among other important critical works are *The Detective Short Story: A Bibliography* (1942) and QUEEN'S QUORUM (1951).

Dannay lives in Larchmont, N.Y. His second wife, Hilda, died in 1972; there are two sons. Lee was survived by his second wife, the former radio actress Kaye Brinker; they had five children. They lived on a 65-acre estate in Roxbury, Conn., that Lee, a nature lover, had declared a game preserve.

Because of the well-advertised differences in their personalities, there has been considerable interest in the modus operandi of the Dannay-Lee collaboration. They had in common a Jewish heritage and a dislike of nonfictional violence. Dannay is a quiet, scholarly introvert, inclined to be a perfectionist. Lee was impulsive and assertive, given to explosiveness and earthy language. They steadfastly refused to disclose specific details regarding their collaborative methods but admitted that they often disagreed violently. However, they believed that their clashing personalities ultimately improved their product. Dannay once said, "We're not so much collaborators as competitors. It has produced a sharper edge."

Ellery Queen was influenced by his predecessor S. S. VAN DINE, whose Philo VANCE exemplifies the erudite detective who solves crimes that are out of the ordinary. Although Queen as detective is at least as knowledgeable in as many subjects as Vance is, he (and his creator) is less inclined to digress and lecture his fellows on obscure topics. The first nine book-length stories about Queen have a geographical adjective in the title, and all deal with murder in bizarre situations. A Broadway theater during the performance of a play is the setting for murder in *The Roman Hat Mystery*. A department store window and a hospital operating room are the locales for *The French Powder Mystery* (1930) and *The Dutch Shoe Mystery* (1931). A crowded trolley car, a ferry, and a railroad train are used in *The Tragedy of X*, and the Washington Square mansion of the eccentric "Mad Hatter" family is the setting of *The Tragedy of Y* (both published in 1932 under the Barnaby Ross pseudonym). The victims in *The Egyptian Cross Mystery* (1932) are all crucified, the first on Christmas Eve. The first corpse in *The Chinese Orange Mystery* (1934) is found with all his clothes turned around and everything on the scene reversed—the rug upside down, pictures facing the wall, and so on. The first victim in *The Spanish Cape Mystery* (1935) is found nude, except for an opera cape, on a deserted beach.

These early books established one of the characteristics of the Queen mystery—"playing fair" with the reader by providing him with all the clues with which the detective solves the murder. In each of the first eleven Queen books the action is stopped after all pertinent facts have been presented, and a "challenge to the reader" is issued.

Queen is also known for his many variations on the theme of "the dying message," whereby the victim, immediately before his death, provides the critical clue to his murder, either in writing or through an object he holds in his hand.

Halfway House (1936) proved to be a transitional book that ended the sequence of titles containing a geographical name. It tells of the murder of a man who maintained separate residences and identities in New York and Philadelphia. Relying more heavily on psychology than any previous Queen title had, the story involves some probing into the mind of Queen the detective.

This trend toward more "serious" detective novels was temporarily diverted by events in the personal and literary lives of Ellery Queen. Prior to Dannay's accident and work on *EQMM*, they worked in movies and radio. A series of juvenile mysteries were also published at this time, signed by Queen. *The Devil to Pay* and *The Four of Hearts* (both 1938) are set against a Hollywood background, as Ellery Queen, like his creators, struggles unhappily as a film writer.

Calamity Town (1942) is generally regarded as the best Queen novel. It places Ellery Queen, using the pseudonym Ellery Smith so that he can write a book in peace and quiet, in Wrightsville, a small, fictional New England town. Queen (as author and detective) explores in depth the town's attitudes and mores and the relationships among the members of the town's oldest families. He also provides a typically intricate crime problem and a picture of Ellery, in love, as a more believable sleuth.

Subsequent mysteries vary considerably in theme (as well as quality), but many represent an attempt to fuse elements of the nonmystery novel with mystery fiction. Noteworthy is *Cat of Many Tails* (1949), concerning a series of apparently unconnected crimes in New York City during a summer heat wave. Although his plotting is less complex than in his early books, Queen provides a very effective portrait of a city undergoing mass hysteria as the population wonders where "the Cat" will strike next.

The Glass Village appears to be the authors' reaction to the social and political climate of the early 1950s. When a leading citizen of a small New England town is murdered, the outsider who does not conform to local patterns of behavior is assumed to be the murderer. In *And On the Eighth Day* (1964), Ellery has wandered into Quenan, an isolated religious community in the California desert where the people lead a simple life. Murder in this apparently crime-free "Eden" is the catalyst for a tricky puzzle. It also provides Queen with an opportunity to use religious symbolism, which has provoked considerable debate.

Best known for their thirty-nine novels, the authors have written many short stories and novelettes. Seven volumes have been gleaned from this short fiction, beginning with *The Adventures of Ellery Queen* (1934), eleven short stories in which Queen solves mysteries in typically bizarre settings;

Manfred B. Lee.

for example, "The Adventure of the Three Lame Men" is about the investigation of three cripples who kidnap a prosperous banker from his love nest; "The Adventure of the One-Penny Black" concerns the theft of a rare stamp, originally initialed by Queen Victoria; and the final story in the volume, "The Adventure of the Mad Tea Party," tells of the events during a strange Long Island house party that parallel those of *Alice in Wonderland*.

The New Adventures of Ellery Queen (1940) contains nine stories, four of which have sports backgrounds. In one of them, the frequently anthologized "Man Bites Dog," Ellery solves a murder while he watches a World Series game between the Yankees and the Giants. In *Calendar of Crime* (1952) a crime is committed during each month of the year, usually on a national holiday.

Howard HAYCRAFT, in *Murder for Pleasure* (1941), called Queen's books "as adroit a blending of the intellectual and dramatic aspects of the genre, of meticulous plot-work, lively narration, easy, unforced humor, and entertaining personae, as can be found in the modern detective novel. They represent the detective romance at its present-day skillful best." To him, Queen's only flaw is "an occasional tendency to too-great intricacy."

The "ingenuity" of the Queen novels has been cited by James SANDOE, Jacques BARZUN and Wendell Hertig TAYLOR, and Julian SYMONS, who also described the "relentlessly analytical treatment of every possible clue and argument. Judged as exercises in rational deduction, these are certainly among the best detective stories ever written." However, Symons felt that Queen had achieved these positive qualities at the expense of "feeling for the people in his story."

Ellery Queen's popularity with his fellow writers has gained him an unprecedented total of five Mystery Writers of America Edgars and the organization's special award, the Raven. His success with mystery readers is reflected in the sales of the Queen books, close to 150 million. He is one of the few authors to be the subject of a journal of critical evaluation, *The Queen Canon Bibliophile* (renamed *The Ellery Queen Review,* published from 1968 to 1971). A full-length study by Francis M. NEVINS, *Royal Bloodline: Ellery Queen, Author and Detective* (1974), was the recipient of an Edgar from the MWA.

Boucher, recognizing Ellery Queen's many roles (detective, novelist, short story writer, editor, anthologist, bibliographer, and encourager of new mystery writers), said in an oft-quoted description: "Ellery Queen *is* the American Detective Story."

QUEEN, ELLERY (detective) [Creator: Ellery QUEEN (author)]. Shortly after his debut, Ellery Queen was dubbed "the logical successor to Sherlock HOLMES" because of his mental agility and acute observation of detail. He is a somewhat arrogant young man (internal evidence in the Queen books indicates that he was born in 1905) when he first appears, in 1929 in *The Roman Hat Mystery*. Although he is a writer, he spends little time early in his career working at his profession. He appears to have unlimited time to collect rare books and help his father, Inspector Richard Queen, solve difficult cases. Ellery is very close to his father, whom he accompanies on a Canadian vacation in *The Siamese Twin Mystery* and to a Chicago police convention in *The Egyptian Cross Mystery*. However, he is often condescending toward the older man and, during his youth, inclined to show off his erudition.

Age smooths some of Ellery's rougher edges as the series progresses, and he works harder at his writing, often struggling to meet a publisher's deadline. He is under contract in Hollywood in *The Devil to Pay* and *The Four of Hearts* and complains bitterly because he has never been given any film assignments. He returns to New York and begins another career, as a private detective (Ellery Queen, Inc.), in *The Dragon's Teeth* but goes back to Hollywood to write films for the Army during World War II. His social conscience develops with the years, especially in connection with crime and juvenile delinquency on the West Side of Manhattan, where he and his father maintain an apartment on West 87th Street. When all of New York City is terrorized by a killer in *Cat of Many Tails*, he accepts the unpaid post of special investigator to the mayor until he solves the series of murders.

When Ellery leaves New York, he most frequently goes to the fictional New England town of Wrightsville. He finds that its rural setting revitalizes him as a writer, although the town's peaceful exterior is belied by the frequency with which he must solve murders there.

Women have always found Ellery Queen attractive, noticing his "devastatingly" silver eyes and his

Sergeant Velie (James Burke) and Ellery's father, Inspector Queen (Charlie Grapewin), are investigative regulars in the series. The scene is from *Ellery Queen, Master Detective*. [*Columbia*]

A body tumbles from a magician's trunk; Ellery (Ralph Bellamy) is startled in *Ellery Queen's Penthouse Mystery*. [*Columbia*]

tall, slim figure usually dressed in elegant tweeds. At first aloof, he increasingly seeks feminine company. He has had romantic episodes with Hollywood columnist Paula Paris, with his secretary, Nikki Porter, and with several other women, but none of these relationships has been permanent.

Ellery Queen's forte as a detective is his ability to juggle mentally all the clues, timetables, motives, and personalities in a complex murder case and arrive, with unassailable logic, at the only possible solution.

CHECKLIST

1929	*The Roman Hat Mystery*
1930	*The French Powder Mystery*
1931	*The Dutch Shoe Mystery*
1932	*The Greek Coffin Mystery*
1932	*The Egyptian Cross Mystery*
1933	*The American Gun Mystery*
1933	*The Siamese Twin Mystery*
1934	*The Adventures of Ellery Queen* (s.s.)
1934	*The Chinese Orange Mystery*
1935	*The Spanish Cape Mystery*
1936	*Halfway House*
1937	*The Door Between*
1938	*The Devil to Pay*
1938	*The Four of Hearts*
1939	*The Dragon's Teeth*
1940	*The New Adventures of Ellery Queen* (s.s.)
1942	*Calamity Town*
1943	*There Was an Old Woman*
1945	*The Case Book of Ellery Queen* (s.s.)
1945	*The Murderer Is a Fox*
1948	*Ten Days' Wonder*
1949	*Cat of Many Tails*
1950	*Double, Double*
1951	*The Origin of Evil*
1952	*Calendar of Crime* (s.s.)
1952	*The King Is Dead*
1953	*The Scarlet Letters*
1955	*Q.B.I.: Queen's Bureau of Investigation* (s.s.)
1956	*Inspector Queen's Own Case*
1958	*The Finishing Stroke*
1963	*The Player on the Other Side*
1964	*And On the Eighth Day*
1965	*The Fourth Side of the Triangle*
1965	*Queens Full* (s.s.)
1966	*A Study in Terror* (British title: *Sherlock Holmes vs. Jack the Ripper*)
1967	*Face to Face*
1968	*The House of Brass*

1968 *Q.E.D.: Queen's Experiments in Detection* (s.s.)
1970 *The Last Woman in His Life*
1971 *A Fine and Private Place*

Films

The distinguished American detective has not always been accurately portrayed on the screen, although his first film adventure was based on a book written that very year.

The Spanish Cape Mystery. Republic, 1935. Donald Cook, Helen Twelvetrees, Berton Churchill, Frank Sheridan. Directed by Lewis D. Collins.

A corpse is found on a beach wearing a cape and little else. The setting is the lonely Spanish Cape; Ellery is erudite.

The Mandarin Mystery. Republic, 1937. Eddie Quillan, Charlotte Henry, Rita Le Roy, Wade Boteler, Franklin Pangborn. Directed by Ralph Staub. Partly based on *The Chinese Orange Mystery*.

A young, cocky Ellery (Quillan) tackles a case of a missing valuable stamp and finds murder.

After a hiatus of almost four years, Ellery returned to the screen, the recent success of his weekly radio series having made him and his associates familiar to millions. Ralph Bellamy's touches of urbanity and scholarship made him a very acceptable Ellery, and Charley Grapewin was an inspired old Inspector Queen. James Burke was Sergeant Velie throughout the series, and Nikki Porter, a character created for radio, made the transition to the film and was portrayed well by Margaret Lindsay.

Ellery Queen, Master Detective. Columbia, 1940. Bellamy, Lindsay, Grapewin, Burke, Michael Whalen, Marsha Hunt. Directed by Kurt Neumann.

An account (one of three versions ultimately chronicled) is given of the first meeting between Ellery and Nikki, a determined girl who wants to become a mystery writer. She finds herself in danger when she becomes involved in a weird case of suicide and murder that begins with the discovery of the body of the patriarch of a health-faddist empire; no weapon is found nearby. At the end of the film, girl-shy author Ellery offers her a job typing his manuscripts.

Ellery Queen's Penthouse Mystery. Columbia, 1941. Bellamy, Lindsay, Anna May Wong, Eduardo Ciannelli, Frank Albertson. Directed by James Hogan.

Soon after a ventriloquist returns from China with a fortune in jewels to sell to raise money for the war there, he disappears from his penthouse apartment. Ellery finds his body in a trunk, but the gems are gone.

Ellery Queen and the Perfect Crime. Columbia, 1941. Bellamy, Lindsay, Spring Byington, H. B. Warner, Douglas Dumbrille. Directed by Hogan.

Ellery investigates the death of another tyrannical father, whose stock manipulations had ruined even his friends and servants and who had alienated his own son.

Ellery Queen and the Murder Ring. Columbia, 1941. Bellamy, Lindsay, Mona Barrie, Paul Hurst, George Zucco, Blanche Yurka. Directed by Hogan. A compressed version of *The Dutch Shoe Mystery*, published ten years earlier.

Ellery poses as a patient when the elderly woman owner of Stack Memorial Hospital is strangled on the operating table.

A Close Call for Ellery Queen. Columbia, 1942. William Gargan, Lindsay, Ralph Morgan, Kay Linaker, Edward Norris, Micheline Cheirel. Directed by Hogan.

Ellery, somewhat gruffer and less intellectual in the person of Gargan, investigates the case of two murdered blackmailers whose target was a retired businessman. The man's two grown daughters are missing. Nikki takes an active solo hand in the case.

A Desperate Chance for Ellery Queen. Columbia, 1942. Gargan, Lindsay, John Litel, Lillian Bond, Jack LaRue. Directed by Hogan.

Ellery and Nikki head for San Francisco to seek out a banker, missing for more than a year and thought dead, who had disappeared just when a large sum of money was embezzled from his bank.

Enemy Agents Meet Ellery Queen. Columbia, 1942. Gargan, Lindsay, Gale Sondergaard, Gilbert Roland, Sig Rumann. Directed by Hogan.

Ellery and his friends are aboard a New York-bound train carrying an Egyptian mummy case and trailed by Nazi spies; the case contains diamonds smuggled out of occupied Holland.

Ten Days' Wonder. Levitt-Pickman, 1972. Orson Welles, Marlene Jobert, Anthony Perkins, Michel Piccoli. Directed by Claude Chabrol.

A millionaire eccentric lives alone and in the past, while his troubled son wakes up in strange hotel rooms covered with blood—not his own. In this moody screen version of the landmark novel, Ellery is not present; the two murders that occur are solved by a friend and former professor of the young man (Piccoli).

Radio and Television

Dannay and Lee claimed to have pioneered the radio detective program format with their *Ellery Queen* show; they approached the networks with the idea of a weekly detection series in 1939 and volunteered to write the first sponsorless shows without a fee. *Ellery Queen* made its debut on CBS that year. In an innovative approach, they interrupted the dramatization before the climax so that Ellery could ask his guests—well-known civic or theatrical personalities—to solve the case; their efforts were nearly always in vain. Then the program would proceed, and the correct solution be given. In his long radio life (all the scripts for the weekly radio programs

William Gargan assumes the role of the master detective later in the series; here he is eavesdropping on a phone call to Nikki in *A Desperate Chance for Ellery Queen.* [*Columbia*]

were written by Dannay and Lee) of nine years, Ellery was portrayed by Hugh Marlowe, Larry Dobkin, Carlton Young, and Sidney Smith. The adventures of Ellery Queen were revived on television beginning in 1950—in both half-hour and hour-long series programs—featuring Richard Hart, Lee Bowman, Hugh Marlowe, George Nader, and Lee Philips, titled variously *Ellery Queen, The Adventures of Ellery Queen,* and *Murder Is My Business.*

In 1971 a television feature, a pilot for a series that did not materialize, was released.

Ellery Queen: Don't Look Behind You. Universal, 1971. Peter Lawford, Harry Morgan, E. G. Marshall, Coleen Gray. Directed by Barry Shear. Based on *Cat of Many Tails.*

Ellery tries to uncover the motive linking a series of seemingly senseless murders. The film transformed old Inspector Queen into Ellery's uncle rather than his father, no doubt because actor Harry Morgan was only nine years older than Lawford.

In 1975 Jim Hutton portrayed Ellery, with David Wayne as his father, in a successful NBC telefeature set in the 1940s. It was based on *The Fourth Side of the Triangle.* David Greene directed the pilot, which became a series that fall.

QUEEN'S QUORUM. The 125 most important volumes of short stories published in the crime-detective genre from 1845 to 1967, selected by Ellery QUEEN (author). The first book edition of *Queen's Quorum* was published in 1951 by Little, Brown, with extensive annotations. It was reprinted in 1969 by Biblo & Tannen, with supplements bringing the list up to date.

QUEER COMPLAINTS, DEPARTMENT OF. *See* MARCH, COLONEL.

QUENTIN, PATRICK. Pseudonym of four authors in a complicated collaboration that eventually created the Peter DULUTH series. Richard Wilson Webb first collaborated with Martha (Patsy) Mott Kelly (Mrs. Stephen Wilson) as Q. Patrick. Webb then wrote one book himself and two with Mary Louise Aswell until he collaborated with Hugh Callingham Wheeler; they used the Q. Patrick, Patrick Quentin, and Jonathan Stagge pseudonyms. Webb left the collaboration in the early 1950s, and Wheeler used Patrick Quentin until 1965.

Wheeler (1912–   ) was born in Hampstead, London, and educated at Clayesmore School and the University of London, where he received a B.A. degree with honors in 1933. Like Webb, he moved to the United States (in 1934) and eventually became a citizen. During World War II he served in the U.S. Army Medical Corps. After the war he spent much time traveling and lived in an eighteenth-century farmhouse in Monterey, Mass. His interests include music, modern painting, and gardening. Wheeler collaborated and wrote on his own more than thirty books under the three pseudonyms.

In later years Wheeler turned to playwriting. He has written *Big Fish, Little Fish* (1961), *Look: We've Come Through* (1961), and *We Have Always Lived in the Castle* (1966; from the novel by Shirley Jackson) and has supplied the books for such musical shows as *A Little Night Music* (1972), for which he won a Tony Award and the New York Drama Critics Circle Award, the 1973 revival of *Irene*, and *Candide* (1974), for which he also won Tony and Drama Critics awards. His film credits include *Something for Everyone* (1970), Graham GREENE's *Travels with My Aunt* (1972), and *Cabaret* (1972).

The early Q. Patrick works are typical English mysteries of the period. *S.S. Murder* (1933) details the cruise of a luxury liner to South America, with death seeking new victims amid the claustrophobic confines of the ship. This work is cited in SANDOE's *Readers' Guide to Crime*, as is *The Grindle Nightmare* (1935). Later Patrick novels were set in the United States and featured Lieutenant Timothy Trant of the New York City Homicide Squad. Trant also appeared in the last novels signed by Patrick Quentin.

The Jonathan Stagge series features Dr. Hugh Westlake, a general practitioner in a small Eastern town, and his precocious teen-age daughter, Dawn. These stories contain the atmosphere of terror, combined with strong hints of the supernatural, that is present in the early works of John Dickson CARR. In *The Stars Spell Death* (1939; British title: *Murder in the Stars*) Dr. Westlake goes for a walk in the woods and stumbles upon a wrecked car with a corpse inside. A hasty search reveals a suit and identification belonging to Dr. Westlake. *Turn of the Table* (1940) starts with a séance that accurately predicts a murder. The killer has vampiric tendencies—and a special interest in Dr. Westlake's throat. In *The Yellow Taxi* (1942) a girl appeals for help because she is afraid of the vehicle that was involved in the death of a friend. Dr. Westlake, doubting the girl's story, prescribes sleeping pills; then he finds the cab parked in his driveway.

The Ordeal of Mrs. Snow and Other Stories (1961), by Patrick Quentin, contains a good title novelette and eleven short stories. Many of the stories were winners in the annual short story contests held by *Ellery Queen's Mystery Magazine*. These well-plotted and well-characterized crime studies (the portraits of children are especially good) were written by both Wheeler and Webb and originally signed by Q. Patrick. They have been reprinted in many anthologies, and the collection was included in QUEEN'S QUORUM.

Film

The Man in the Net. United Artists, 1959. Alan Ladd, Carolyn Jones, Diane Brewster, Charles McGraw, Tom Helmore, John Lupton. Directed by Michael Curtiz. Based on Quentin's 1956 novel of the same name.

An artist moves to Connecticut, hoping that the change will help his alcoholic wife. When he returns from an overnight trip, she is missing, and her body is later discovered buried under the barn floor; he is accused of her murder.

R

RADCLIFFE, ANN (WARD) (1764–1823). English author of Gothic novels. Born in London, the only daughter of Ann (Oates) and William Ward, she received no formal education. Two years after her marriage to William Radcliffe, she published her first novel, *The Castles of Athlin and Dunbayne: A Highland Story* (1789).

The Mysteries of Udolpho (1794), one of the milestones in the history of the Gothic novel, is little different from her other fictional works or, indeed, from most other Gothics. It is set in a castle that has sliding panels and dark hidden passageways; a beautiful heroine is persecuted by a series of murder threats, abductions, and other terrors. In a significant break with preceding works of this type, Mrs. Radcliffe ultimately offers rational explanations of the apparently supernatural events that have occurred. As usual, the heroine emerges unscathed, her tormentors vanquished.

In *The Italian; or, The Confessional of the Black Penitents* (1797), Mrs. Radcliffe employs a device still widely used in detective fiction. In conversations, the more intelligent, perceptive person explains events to the slower, confused, but curious listener (with whom the reader can identify).

These novels and others are set in Italy, which Mrs. Radcliffe never visited. Her chief ability is in setting a mood of horror and providing realistic descriptions of brooding, macabre, romantic landscapes. All her fiction was published in an eight-year period, during which she earned fabulous sums as a best-selling author. Having no further stories to tell, she then quit writing abruptly. She shunned publicity and was rumored to have died or to have been committed to an insane asylum; in fact, she lived quietly, traveling extensively with her husband.

RADIO DETECTIVES. From the inception of radio in 1920, there is no record of a successful detective series until the *Sherlock Holmes* program in 1930. Then, however, the floodgates opened, and during the next three decades scores of popular detective heroes appeared; many justly sank into oblivion (*see* HOLMES, SHERLOCK).

The first popular programs were based on characters that had become famous in books and stories: Charlie CHAN, Philo VANCE, Nero WOLFE, Philip MARLOWE, Sam SPADE, Michael SHAYNE, Bulldog DRUMMOND, and BOSTON BLACKIE. *The Fat Man* was a logical successor to Dashiell HAMMETT's *The Thin Man*.

Soon, radio created its own characters. The series *Richard Diamond, Private Detective,* starring Dick Powell, with Ed Begley a regular as Lieutenant Levinson, originated on NBC in 1949. There were a number of lead players on *Yours Truly, Johnny Dollar,* including Charles Russell and Edmond O'Brien. Johnny was an insurance investigator who itemized his expenses throughout the program and, at the end, signed off: "Yours truly, Johnny Dollar." First heard on CBS in 1950, the series lasted into the 1960s.

Adventurer-detectives included the Lone Wolf (*see* LONE WOLF, THE), the Crime Doctor (*see* CRIME DOCTOR, THE), the Saint (*see* SAINT, THE), the Falcon (*see* FALCON, THE), and Rocky Fortune, a soldier of fortune who frequently solved crimes, played by Frank Sinatra in the early 1950s. *Let George Do It* concerned a casual shamus named George Valentine (played by Bob Bailey). Two heroes who traveled around the globe to right wrongs were Ken Thurston, in *A Man Called X* (played by Herbert Marshall, beginning on ABC in1944), who could usually be found at the Café Tambourine in Cairo, and Steve Mitchell (played by Brian Donlevy), on *Dangerous Assignment,* which made its debut on NBC in 1950.

Among the programs about tough private detectives were *Martin Kane, Private Eye,* starring William Gargan and first heard over the Mutual network in 1949, and *Pat Novak, for Hire,* played by Jack Webb. When the series about this San Francisco sleuth ended, Webb played in another one, *Johnny Modero, Pier 23,* about a waterfront character who

An entry in Columbia's *The Whistler* series of the mid-forties, film dramas based on the radio program. Nearly always, aging Richard Dix played the main character in differing stories of strange fate. This film is *Mysterious Intruder* (1946). [*Columbia*]

took assorted odd jobs, including detective work.

Some offbeat radio detectives were Father BROWN, Hercule POIROT, and Mr. Keen, in *Mr. Keen, Tracer of Lost Persons,* first heard on NBC's Blue network in 1937. The theme song for this show was "Someday I'll Find You." *Tales of Fatima* starred Basil Rathbone, who played himself as an actor-detective and also delivered the commercials for Fatima cigarettes. I LOVE A MYSTERY combined mystery with voodoo, science fiction, fantasy, and comedy.

Husband and wife teams were popular, with Nick and Nora CHARLES in *The Thin Man, Mr. and Mrs. North* (see NORTH, MR. AND MRS.), and Pat and Jean ABBOTT in *Abbott Mysteries.*

Many daytime soap operas often wove murder mysteries into their plots. *Front Page Farrell,* first heard over Mutual in 1941, was one example. Among those who played the title role were Richard Widmark, Carleton Young, and Staats Cotsworth. Many newspapermen were detectives in their own right. Flashgun CASEY, also played by Cotsworth, appeared for many years in *Casey, Crime Photographer.* He was joined by Steve Wilson of the *Illustrated Press* on *Big Town,* which was sponsored by Rinso soap when Edward G. Robinson played Wilson. Other crime fighters with newspaper backgrounds were Clark Kent of the *Daily Planet* on *Superman* and Britt Reid of the *Daily Sentinel* on *The Green Hornet* (see GREEN HORNET, THE) series. *The Orange Lantern* featured Botak, a Javanese adventurer. *The Blue Beetle,* with another color-oriented title, was a mystery-adventure series.

A popular newspaper-detective program was *Big Story,* which retold true front-page stories. The reporter involved received an award for his detective work. Other true-crime series were *True Detective Mysteries, Official Detective, Famous Jury Trials,* and *Wanted.*

Similar in spirit were some programs featuring policemen and detectives on the government payroll. *This Is Your FBI* took its stories from the files of the Bureau. *The FBI in Peace and War* did not have the "official seal of approval" from the Bureau but was just as popular. Its theme was taken from "Love for Three Oranges" by Prokofiev, and it was sponsored by Lava soap. A closely related program was *Gangbusters.* Its loud opening—sirens, machine gun fire, whistles, and marching feet entering jail cells—added a phrase to the vernacular: "coming on like gangbusters."

Dragnet, with its familiar theme song and realistic touches, was a popular radio series before it became a top-rated television program. Jack Webb played Joe Friday. Originally sponsored by Fatima cigarettes, it gained Chesterfield's sponsorship when it became more popular. It first aired on NBC in 1949. The following year, CBS introduced a San Francisco–based crime drama, *The Line-Up. G-Man, T-Man* (with Dennis O'Keefe), and *Under Arrest* were other police shows. The long-running *Mr. District Attorney* was first broadcast in 1939. Each program opened with the line "And it shall be my duty . . . ."

Karl Swenson played *Mr. Chameleon,* a police detective of many disguises, much like the title character of *Toma,* a television series of the early 1970s. It first aired in 1948 on CBS.

Several "men of magic" tried their hands at detective work. In the early 1930s, Chandu (of the film *Chandu the Magician*) traveled to exotic locales to fight crimes involving bizarre adversaries. Mandrake continued his comic strip adventures on radio (in *Mandrake the Magician*). Similar programs were *Thurston, the Magician, Blackstone, the Magic Detective, Omar the Mystic,* and *The Strange Dr. Karnac. The House of Mystery* concerned an unusual detective who proved each week that some apparently unnatural set of circumstances could be easily and logically explained.

There were few female detectives. Aside from the distaff halves of husband and wife teams, women were featured on *Policewoman,* based on actual police files; *Pretty Kitty Kelly,* a serial; and *Meet*

Miss Sherlock, a weekly half-hour series. In the last (a short-lived program), Peter Blossom kept asking the heroine to marry him, but she was always too busy solving mysteries.

Among other mystery and crime programs were *Chick Carter, Boy Detective, Rogue's Gallery* (with Dick Powell), *Alias Jimmy Valentine* (based on the O. HENRY character), *Peter Quill* (with Marvin Miller as a scientist-detective-adventurer), *Perry Mason* (see MASON, PERRY), *Ellery Queen* (see QUEEN, ELLERY, detective), *Fu Manchu* (see FU MANCHU, DR.), *Nick Carter, Master Detective* (see CARTER, NICK), *Inner Sanctum* (originally called *The Squeaking Door*), *I Deal in Crime* (with William Gargan), *Highway Patrol* (later a popular television series), *Hannibal Cobb* (with Santos Ortega in the title role), *Eno Crime Club* (later called *Crime Clues*, with Spencer Dean, man hunter, played by Edward Reese), *Twenty Thousand Years in Sing Sing, The Whistler, Thatcher Colt* (see COLT, THATCHER), *Treasury Agent, Dr. Kenrad's Unsolved Mysteries* (which starred Stanley Peyton), Dick Tracy (a long-running serial based on the comic strip; see TRACY, DICK), *Cloak and Dagger* (with its two series characters, the Hungarian Giant and Impy the Midget), *Crime Fighters, The Case Book of Gregory Hood* (with many actors in the lead role, including Gale Gordon and Martin Gabel), *Call the Police, Calling All Cars, Calling All Detectives* (listeners were awarded prizes for solving the mysteries), *Suspense* (the most popular episode was "Sorry, Wrong Number," with Agnes Moorehead; among the other stars were Orson Welles, Ida Lupino, Cary Grant, Lucille Ball), *The Strange Dr. Weird* (a fifteen-minute series), *Special Agent* (with insurance investigator Alan Drake), *Scotland Yard's Inspector Burke* (featuring Basil Rathbone in one of his many detective series), *The Man from G-2* (Hugh NORTH), *Murder and Mr. Malone* (written by Craig RICE and starring Frank Lovejoy), *Murder Will Out* (with Gargan), *The Mysterious Traveler* (who told listeners, "I take this same train every week at this time" and suggested that they keep a "hypo" handy for emotional emergencies), *Mystery Theater* (with Alfred Shirley as Inspector Hearthstone of the Death Squad; the original name of the series was *Mollé Mystery Theater*, for its shaving cream sponsor; it was finally called *Hearthstone of the Death Squad*), *Ned Jordan, Secret Agent* (a railroad detective), *The Black Hood* (about a rookie policeman who acquired magical powers when he donned the "black hood"), *The Black Museum* (hosted by Orson Welles), *The Black Castle* (fifteen-minute tales narrated by the Wizard), *Lights Out, Junior G-Men* (kids battling crime), *Jeff Regan* (another Jack Webb series), and, the most successful and famous of all original radio detectives, *The Shadow* (see SHADOW, THE).

DANIEL J. MORROW

RAFFLES, A. J. (Creator: E. W. HORNUNG). The greatest cracksman in the literature of roguery. Raffles could have succeeded at any career, but he chose a life of crime. Once, penniless and desperate in Australia, he realized that his only salvation was to steal. He had intended the robbery, forced on him by necessity, to be his only such experience, but he had "tasted blood" and loved it. "Why settle down to some humdrum, uncongenial billet," he once asks Bunny Manders, his devoted companion, "when excitement, romance, danger and a decent living were all going begging together? Of course, it's very wrong, but we can't all be moralists, and the distribution of wealth is very wrong to begin with."

In England, his fame as one of the finest cricket players in the world, combined with his charming personality, brilliant wit, and remarkably handsome appearance, makes him a welcome guest at the homes of the country's wealthiest families. He is comfortable in these surroundings, wearing evening clothes as if he were born in them, and is delighted to make the acquaintance of owners of fabulous fortunes.

No criminal can match Raffles for courage and the ability to stay cool under the most difficult circumstances. In fact, he seems to relish situations that would unnerve many men, enjoying the thrill of the sport as much as the reward that waits behind the door of a safe. He plans most of his escapades down to the finest detail, but he is also capable of acting on the spur of the moment and pulling off a crime almost as a joke. Although he sometimes steals merely for sport, he usually has a motive—to help a needy friend, to keep the creditors from his door, or to right a wrong that the law was unable to handle.

He lives alone in expensive rooms in the Albany, with his friend Bunny just a short distance away, and has other expensive tastes, such as smoking Sullivan cigarettes. Living by his wits and skill

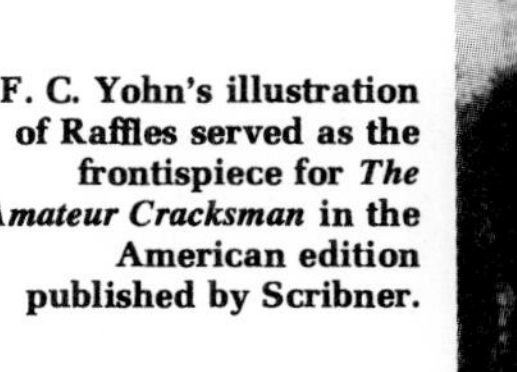

F. C. Yohn's illustration of Raffles served as the frontispiece for *The Amateur Cracksman* in the American edition published by Scribner.

Kyrle Bellew, a matinee idol of the American theater, starred in *Raffles, the Amateur Cracksman,* which began its Broadway run of 168 performances at the Princess Theater on October 27, 1903.

Ronald Colman as Raffles in the 1930 motion picture. [*United Artists*]

The 1940 film *Raffles* starred David Niven as A. J. Raffles, shown here with Dame May Whitty (seated) and Olivia de Havilland. [*United Artists*]

Ronald Colman as Raffles with Kay Francis. [*United Artists*]

A scene from *Raffles* with (left to right) Olivia de Havilland, Dudley Digges, and David Niven. [*United Artists*]

as a thief, he seems quite happy with his hedonistic life of absolute luxury.

This is the Raffles who appeared in three short story collections and one novel by Hornung. Hornung and Eugene Presbrey also collaborated on a successful drama, *Raffles, the Amateur Cracksman: A Play in Four Acts,* produced in London with Sir Gerald du Maurier in the title role; in the United States, in 1903, a handsome matinee idol, Kyrle Bellew, played Raffles.

A somewhat different character, also named Raffles, appeared on the scene in 1932, when Barry PEROWNE revived the gentleman jewel thief as a contemporary two-fisted adventurer in a long series for *The Thriller.* World War II ended the life of the magazine and, temporarily, of Raffles. Beginning in 1950 Perowne again wrote tales about the amateur cracksman (for *Ellery Queen's Mystery Magazine* and *The Saint Mystery Magazine*), but this time the adventures occur in the late Victorian and early Edwardian times in which they belong. Here too, Raffles pursues a hedonistic way of life, but he is now more socially aware; he commits crimes primarily to correct injustices, and personal profit is a secondary motivation. His ethical standards are a little higher than they were when Hornung recounted his exploits. Fourteen of the best tales were collected in *Raffles Revisited*, with an introduction by Otto Penzler.

The fixed point in all the stories is Bunny, Raffles's former schoolmate who, in those days, had idolized "A. J." When he and Raffles meet again as adults, Bunny has attempted suicide to avoid financial disgrace. Raffles saves his life and steals enough to get Bunny out of debt, earning his undying devotion in the process. Bunny hates the illegal life and often tries to dissuade his friend from committing a crime, but, once involved, he is fearless and loyal. Bunny is typically English in appearance and is less than brilliant, but his journalistic background enables him to chronicle Raffles's adventures in a lively style.

CHECKLIST

(By E. W. Hornung)

1899 *The Amateur Cracksman* (s.s.)
1901 *The Black Mask* (s.s.; U.S. title: *Raffles: Further Adventures of the Amateur Cracksman*)
1905 *A Thief in the Night* (s.s.)
1909 *Mr. Justice Raffles*

(By Barry Perowne)

1933 *Raffles after Dark* (U.S. title: *The Return of Raffles*)
1934 *Raffles in Pursuit*
1934 *Raffles under Sentence* (s.s.)
1936 *She Married Raffles*
1937 *Raffles vs. Sexton Blake*
1939 *The A.R.P. Mystery*
1939 *They Hang Them in Gibraltar*
1940 *Raffles and the Key Man*
1974 *Raffles Revisited: New Adventures of a Famous Gentleman Crook* (s.s.)

Films

Raffles appeared in a short American film as early as 1905 and was featured in an Italian serial by 1911. In 1917 John Barrymore starred in *Raffles, the Amateur Cracksman* (Hiller-Wilk), and in 1925 another film with the same title (released by Universal) featured House Peters as the daring thief, "a gentleman by birth," who takes only from the rich.

Raffles. United Artists, 1930. Ronald Colman, Kay Francis, Bramwell Fletcher, David Torrence, Alison Skipworth.

Raffles promises to reform, but a dear friend comes to him for aid. He needs a large amount of money in a hurry, and the only answer is for Raffles to steal a necklace during a country weekend party.

The Return of Raffles. Williams and Pritchard (British), 1932. George Barraud, Camilla Horn, Claud Allister (Bunny). Directed by Mansfield Markham.

Again reformed, Raffles attends a house party, where he is framed for the theft of a necklace actually stolen by a gang.

Raffles. United Artists, 1940. David Niven, Olivia de Havilland, Douglas Walton, Dame May Whitty, Dudley Digges. Directed by Sam Wood.

At the now-familiar weekend party, Raffles agrees to steal a necklace to help the brother of the girl he loves, but a gang beats him to it.

Television

In 1973 England's Hammer Film Studios announced that its entry into television production would include a series based on Raffles and set in the turn-of-the-century era.

Play

The Return of A. J. Raffles, a comedy by Graham GREENE, was produced by the Royal Shakespeare Company. It opened in London in December 1975.

RANDOLPH, GEORGIANA ANN. *See* RICE, CRAIG.

RANKIN, TOMMY (Creator: Milton M. PROPPER). A detective in Philadelphia's Homicide Bureau, Rankin is medium in height and stocky, with broad shoulders. He has firm features with sensitive nostrils, thin, determined lips, and a square jaw. His eyes are dark and clear; his forehead is high and topped by curly brown hair.

He started his career on the police force by pounding a beat in the heart of the underworld. He acquired a reputation for absolute fairness to everyone—including crooks—and gained the experience that, combined with common sense, enabled him to rise from the ranks at an early age.

Rankin is not a brilliant detective, but he posesses a down-to-earth, logical mind. His reputation is built on a foundation of solid achievement, the result of his determination and perseverance.

CHECKLIST

1929 *The Strange Disappearance of Mary Young*
1930 *The Ticker Tape Murder*
1931 *The Boudoir Murder* (British title: *And Then Silence*)
1932 *The Student Fraternity Murder* (British title: *Murder of an Initiate*)
1934 *The Divorce Court Murder*
1934 *The Family Burial Murders*
1935 *The Election Booth Murder* (British title: *Murder at the Polls*)
1936 *One Murdered, Two Dead*
1937 *The Great Insurance Murders*
1938 *The Case of the Cheating Bride*
1939 *Hide the Body!*
1940 *The Station Wagon Murder*
1941 *The Handwriting on the Wall*
1943 *The Blood Transfusion Murders*
1947 *Murder in Sequence*
1949 *You Can't Gag the Dead*

RAWSON, CLAYTON (1906–1971). American magician and author of detective stories featuring the Great Merlini, a professional magician and amateur detective (*see* MERLINI, THE GREAT).

Born in Elyria, Ohio, the son of Clarence D. and Clara (Smith) Rawson, he graduated from Ohio State University and married Catherine Stone the same year (1929); they had four children. One of the nation's most famous illusionists, Rawson was a member of the Society of American Magicians. Before turning to writing, he was an artist, specializing in magazine illustration and advertising. He also served as editor of *True Detective Magazine*, Ziff-Davis Publications, Unicorn Books, Simon and Schuster's Inner Sanctum Mysteries, and *Ellery Queen's Mystery Magazine* (1963–1971). He was a member of the Mystery Writers of America and the British Crime Writers' Association.

In addition to his novels and short stories about Merlini, he wrote four novelettes as Stuart Towne, all about Don Diavolo. All were originally published in *Red Star Mystery* magazine in 1940; two were collected in *Death out of Thin Air* (1941)—*Death from the Past* (originally *Ghost of the Undead*) and *Death from the Unseen* (originally *Death out of Thin Air*).

RAYMOND, RENÉ. *See* CHASE, JAMES HADLEY.

REACH, ANGUS (BETHUNE) (1821–1856). British author and journalist. Born in Inverness, Scotland, the son of a solicitor, he moved to London and joined the staff of the *Morning Chronicle* in 1842. A crime reporter, he knew the detectives and the methods and argot of criminals and used this knowledge as a source for *Clement Lorimer; or, The Book with the Iron Clasps*, one of the earliest novels of crime and detection. The first of six monthly parts appeared in paper wrappers in October 1848, the last in March 1849. Illustrated by George Cruikshank, the work was an immediate success and appeared in a cloth-bound edition in 1849. A tale of poisoning, murder, abduction, and many other crimes, it is the first book on record to have used the word "sleuthhound" to describe a detective.

REEDER, MR. J. G. (Creator: Edgar WALLACE). A timid, gentle man, John G. Reeder was once connected with Scotland Yard. He next served for many years with Bankers Trust and then was a member of the public prosecutor's office. Although he is the most benign of men, he thinks of himself as "vicious" and credits his success in detection to his "criminal mind," which sees the wrong in everything.

Reeder's extraordinary memory for faces has been an invaluable aid in his career as one of England's leading experts in solving bank robberies and forgery and counterfeiting cases. Small and middle-aged, he has muttonchop whiskers, wears steel-rimmed pince-nez and an old-fashioned flat-topped derby, and carries a resolutely furled umbrella—rain or shine, day or night—in the handle of which is a concealed knife blade. The overt milksop also carries a well-oiled revolver in an inner pocket. He prefers meditating in his private library to action, and does not seem to be capable of intense human emotions. On one occasion, he told a romantic policeman: "Love is a very beautiful experience—I have frequently read about it."

Reeder's cases may be found in *The Mind of Mr. J. G. Reeder* (1925; U.S. title: *The Murder Book of J. G. Reeder*, 1929), *Red Aces* (1929), and *The Guv'nor and Other Stories* (1932; U.S. title: *Mr. Reeder Returns*), all short story collections; and in the novels *Room 13* (1924) and *Terror Keep* (1927).

Films

Red Aces. British Lion (British), 1929. Janice Adair, Geoffrey Gwyther, Nigel Bruce. Screenplay and direction by Wallace. Based on the title novelette of *Red Aces* (1929).

A banker is framed for murder in the screen introduction of Mr. Reeder (George Bellamy).

Mr. Reeder in Room 13 (U.S. title: *Mystery of Room 13*). National (British), 1938. Gibb McLaughlin (Reeder), Sara Seeger, Sally Gray. Directed by Norman Lee. Based on *Room 13* (1924).

Wallace's elderly detective exposes a gang that uses a shabby room as a base.

The Mind of Mr. Reeder. (U.S. title: *The Mysterious Mr. Reeder*). Grand National (British), 1939.

Will Fyffe (Reeder), Kay Walsh (Peggy Gillette), Ronald Shiner (Sam). Directed by Jack Raymond.

The disarming old sleuth unmasks a mystery forger.

The Missing People. Grand National (British), 1939. Fyffe, Walsh, Shiner, Lyn Harding, Patricia Roc. Directed by Raymond. Based on a story in *The Mind of Mr. Reeder.*

Mr. Reeder discovers the insurance fraud behind the drowning of old women.

REES, DILWYN. *See* DANIEL, GLYN E.

REEVE, ARTHUR B[ENJAMIN] (1880–1936). American author of mystery fiction, mainly featuring scientific detective Craig KENNEDY. Born in Patchogue, N.Y., the son of Jennie (Henderson) and Walter F. Reeve, he graduated from Princeton University in 1903 and went on to study law, which he never practiced, becoming a journalist instead. Reeve became interested in scientific crime detection when he wrote a series of articles on the subject, and he subsequently created Kennedy, the most popular detective in America for several years. Much of that vast popularity was due to silent film serials, written by Reeve, about a young heroine named Elaine who constantly finds herself in the clutches of villains, only to be rescued at the last moment by the white-coated Kennedy.

Reeve's mysteries were the first by an American to gain wide readership in Great Britain. They are not read much today, for pseudoscientific methods and devices that were of great interest then are all outdated; many of them never had a solid technical basis in the first place. Reeve's major achievement was his application of Freudian psychology to detection two decades before psychoanalysis gained substantial public acceptance. During World War I he was asked to help establish a spy and crime detection laboratory in Washington, D.C.

Reeve wrote only four mysteries not involving Kennedy: *Guy Garrick* (1914), *Constance Dunlap: Woman Detective* (1916; s.s.), *The Master Mystery* (1919; a novel based on a motion picture serial starring Harry Houdini; written with John W. Grey), and *The Mystery Mind* (1920; a novel based on a motion picture serial about hypnosis; also written with Grey).

REGESTER, SEELEY (pseudonym of Mrs. Metta Victoria Fuller Victor; 1831–1886). American writer of romantic and humorous fiction; author of the first American detective novel written by a woman, *The Dead Letter* (1867). Born in Erie, Pa., she published her first novel, *The Last Days of Tul; A Romance of the Lost Cities of Yucatan* (1846), when she was only fifteen. She wrote many DIME NOVELS for the firm of Beadle and Adams, beginning with *Alice Wilde* (August 1, 1860). *The Dead Letter,* one of the most important detective novels published in the United States, is often overlooked, and credit is given to Anna Katharine GREEN as the first woman detective novelist in the country. The long-disputed identity of Seeley Regester contributed to the neglect of the author.

REILLY, HELEN (1891–1962). American detective novelist. Born Helen Kieran, she was the daughter of Dr. James M. Kieran, president of Hunter College, and grew up in New York City. Her brother, John Kieran, is a famous naturalist and erstwhile panelist on the radio program *Information Please.* Another brother, James Kieran, wrote one mystery, *Come Murder Me* (1952). She was married to artist-cartoonist Paul Reilly; they had four daughters, two of whom, Ursula CURTISS and Mary MCMULLEN, have written mysteries. Most of Mrs. Reilly's books featured Inspector Christopher MCKEE, whom Ursula Curtiss called her "rather sinister godfather."

After living in Westport, Conn., for many years, Mrs. Reilly returned to New York City in 1944, when her husband died. She and her daughters occupied a house on East Tenth Street in Greenwich Village and maintained a summer home at North Truro on Cape Cod. In 1960 she moved to New Mexico with the Curtiss family, although Ursula later said that her mother "always missed New York. She was a born and bred New Yorker."

Mrs. Reilly began writing mysteries at the urging of a family friend, author William McFee. She wrote during an era when most women writing mysteries belonged to the "HAD-I-BUT-KNOWN" SCHOOL. Because her books were straightforward procedural novels about the Manhattan Homicide Squad, readers occasionally thought that a man, using a woman's pseudonym, had written them. She was one of the few "outsiders" permitted to review the Homicide Squad's files. An early book, *The File on Rufus Ray* (1937), has been called "the ultimate in police procedurals." It contained facsimiles of the evidence mentioned in the book, for example, telegrams, a button left at the scene of the crime, glossy photographs of suspects, and even cigarette ashes in a small envelope. Prohibitive costs caused the series to be discontinued, and the author resumed her popular McKee series. Her work was often serialized in *The Saturday Evening Post, Collier's,* or *Woman's Home Companion.* She wrote more than thirty books under her own name, as well as three under the pen name Kieran Abbey.

In 1941 Howard HAYCRAFT praised her McKee stories as "among the most convincing that have been composed on the premise of actual police procedure." He also mentioned her avoidance of the "had-I-but-known" approach. With the emphasis in the mystery shifting to suspense rather than detection in the 1940s, she too began to create heroines who have a propensity for getting into dangerous situations from which McKee must rescue them. This is characteristic of *The Opening Door* (1944), *The Farmhouse* (1947), *The Canvas Dagger* (1956), and *Follow Me* (1960).

RHODE, JOHN (pseudonym of Cecil John Charles Street; 1884–1964). English mystery writer. Street was extremely reticent, and his name is not in most standard references. A career army officer, he attained the rank of major. His interests were politics and criminology, and he was a member of London's famous Detection Club.

Street was a prolific writer with 140 mysteries to his credit. He also wrote such volumes as *The Administration of Ireland* (1921), *Ireland in 1921* (1922), *Rhineland and Ruhr* (1923), *Hungary and Democracy* (1923), *East of Prague* (1924), and *The Treachery of France* (1924) and biographies of Lord Reading (1928) and Thomas Masaryk (1930). His true-crime study, *The Case of Constance Kent* (1928), was well received. Street's work was not considered sufficiently interesting by film makers, with the exception of *The Murders in Praed Street* (1928), which was freely adapted as *Twelve Good Men* and eliminated Dr. Lancelot PRIESTLEY. Street, however, produced a novel, *Mademoiselle from Armentières* (1927), based on a famous English silent war film.

Street spent thirty-seven years of his life producing four detective novels a year. He died in an Eastbourne hospital near his home at Seaford.

Street wrote his first mystery novel, *A.S.F.* (1924; U.S. title: *The White Menace*), under the pseudonym John Rhode. A thriller about cocaine traffic, it was followed by two other thrillers: *The Double Florin* (1924), in which an impecunious young aristocrat battles the Bolshevik menace, and *The Alarm* (1925). *The Paddington Mystery* (1925) introduces Dr. Priestley, who proves the innocence of Harold Merefield, who, in turn, later becomes his secretary and son-in-law. *Dr. Priestley's Quest* (1926) and *The Ellerby Case* (1927) followed, and then came *The Murders in Praed Street*, one of Rhode's most popular works, often cited as his best. In a case involving a series of apparently unrelated and bizarre murders, Dr. Priestley almost becomes one of the victims. *The House on Tollard Ridge* (1929) is about the murder of a wealthy recluse whose wayward son is blamed for the crime.

In 1930 Major Street could not contain his prolific output and adopted another pseudonym, Miles Burton. He established Burton's date of birth as 1903. The closely guarded secret of this dual identity was not revealed until the late 1960s. The first Burton title was *The Hardway Diamonds Mystery* (1930); the second was *The Secret of High Eldersham* (1930), a tale of witchcraft that introduces Desmond MERRION, who detects and bickers through most of the Burton works with his friend Inspector Henry Arnold of Scotland Yard.

In comparing the works written by Street under the two pseudonyms, Jacques BARZUN and Wendell Hertig TAYLOR stated: "Burton's tend to be wittier and less dependent on mechanical devices, as well as more concerned with scenery and character. They are often less solid too, the outcome being sometimes pulled out of a hat rather than demonstrated." Burton's work is duller than Rhode's, and, although Merrion is a competent investigator, he lacks the flair and interesting qualities of Dr. Priestley, one of the most impressive detectives in British mystery fiction.

Two of the best 1930s Rhode novels are *Mystery at Greycombe Farm* (1932; U.S. title: *The Fire at Greycombe Farm*), in which a corpse is found after a fire in a barn housing cider barrels, and *Invisible Weapons* (1938), about a murder committed in a locked cloakroom with a weapon that cannot be identified. *Hendon's First Case* (1935), about the death of a chemist, marks a change in Rhode's work. It introduces Inspector James Waghorn, a college-educated and police school–trained detective of considerable intelligence. His superior officer, Superintendent Hanslet, had played a supporting role to Dr. Priestley in earlier stories. As the years pass, Waghorn becomes more experienced in crime investigation, and his role becomes greater. On the other hand, Priestley, an active investigator in earlier cases, becomes more sedentary in the 1940s, and his appearances briefer.

The 1940s saw good work with such books as *Death in Harley Street* (1946), which deals with a clever scheme of revenge and features Dr. Priestley at the height of his powers, and *The Telephone Call* (1948; U.S. title: *Shadow of an Alibi*), a retelling of the Julia Wallace case.

Rhode collaborated with Carter Dickson (John Dickson CARR) on *Drop to His Death* (1939; U.S. title: *Fatal Descent*), in which the crime is committed in an elevator; the book is set in a pulp magazine publishing house.

Critics have praised Rhode for his clever and carefully worked-out, frequently baffling, plots but they have found his work to be talky, tedious, and unexciting—especially toward the end of his career. Rhode is not a master of characterization (with the exception of Dr. Priestley) or atmosphere.

Film

Twelve Good Men. Warner Brothers (British), 1936. Henry Kendall, Nancy O'Neil, Joyce Kennedy. Directed by Ralph Ince. From *The Murders in Praed Street* (1928).

A convict escapes from prison to eliminate the

twelve men of the jury that put him behind bars.

RICE, CRAIG (pseudonym of Georgiana Ann Randolph; 1908–1957). American mystery novelist and film script writer. Born in Chicago, Craig Rice spent most of her life in that city, where she did radio and public relations work, and in Los Angeles. Although she was the subject of a profile (and cover portrait) in the January 28, 1946, issue of *Time* magazine, many questions about her remain. Neither the origin of her pseudonym nor the exact number of husbands she had is known. She was married at least four, and possibly as many as seven, times; her last husband was Lawrence Lipton. She had three children.

She began writing mysteries after attempting, unsuccessfully, to write novels, poetry, and music. Although she wrote under several names, her most famous series, about John J. MALONE, was published under the Rice pseudonym. Also as Craig Rice, she wrote about Bingo Riggs and Handsome Kusak, itinerant sidewalk photographers who graduate to being con men and solve murders out of self-preservation. Typical of their cases is *The Thursday Turkey Murders* (1943), in which, en route to Hollywood, they acquire a turkey farm in Iowa where several hundred thousand dollars is reputedly hidden.

She wrote one book, *To Catch a Thief* (1943), as Daphne Sanders, and three novels as Michael Venning, about Melville Fairr, a colorless New York private detective ("the little man in gray") who is especially adept at probing criminal psychology. As Craig Rice, she wrote *Home Sweet Homicide* (1944), a semi-autobiographical mystery novel about a crime writer distracted by murder and her three children.

In Hollywood Craig Rice worked on two film scripts for the Falcon series (*see* FALCON, THE), one in collaboration with mystery writer Stuart PALMER. They later combined their detectives, her John J. Malone and his Hildegarde WITHERS, in a series of short stories collected in *The People vs. Withers and Malone* (1963). Two of the stories, "Once upon a Train" (1950) and "Cherchez la Frame" (1951), won second prizes in *Ellery Queen's Mystery Magazine* contests.

Her association with George Sanders, who had starred as the Falcon, led her to ghostwrite his *Crime on My Hands* (1944), a mystery novel in which Sanders solves a series of murders in a film studio. She was also publicity agent for Gypsy Rose Lee and published two successful murder mysteries, *The G-String Murders* (1941) and *Mother Finds a Body* (1942), under that famous burlesque dancer's name.

A longtime devotee of true-crime cases, Craig Rice edited *Los Angeles Murders* (1947), a book about famous crimes in that city; she also wrote *45 Murderers* (1952), which contains brief true-crime accounts.

Craig Rice is best remembered for her attempts (generally successful) to infuse comedy into the detective novel.

Films

The Underworld Story. United Artists, 1950. Dan Duryea, Herbert Marshall, Gale Storm, Gary Moore, Howard da Silva. Directed by Cyril Endfield. Originally called *The Whipped* and based on a Rice story.

A blacklisted big-city news reporter uses gangster money to buy a half interest in a small-town paper and senses a great story when a local tycoon tries to railroad a maid for his daughter-in-law's death.

Home Sweet Homicide. Twentieth Century-Fox, 1946. Randolph Scott, Lynn Bari, James Gleason, Peggy Ann Garner, Connie Marshall, Dean Stockwell. Directed by Lloyd Bacon.

A young widow, supporting her three children by writing mystery novels, uncovers murder when her offspring hear gunshots from a neighboring house. The youngsters are delighted when a bachelor police detective seems interested in their mother.

RIDDELL, JOHN. *See* VANCE, PHILO.

RINEHART, MARY ROBERTS (1876–1958). American author who created a new type of detective novel, now usually maligned as being of the "HAD-I-

John Lavalle painted this portrait of Mary Roberts Rinehart in 1947.

BUT-KNOWN" SCHOOL, in which a pretty heroine finds endless methods of getting into dangerous situations.

She was born to a poor family in Pittsburgh, the daughter of Cornelia (Gilleland) and Thomas Beveridge Roberts, a dreamer and unsuccessful inventor who committed suicide just as Mary was finishing nursing school. There she met Dr. Stanley Marshall Rinehart; they were married in 1896 and had three sons within five years. After her husband's death (1932) she lived alone in a luxurious, eighteen-room Park Avenue apartment.

Early in their marriage Mrs. Rinehart and her husband were in debt because of unsuccessful stock market investments, so she began to write, selling forty-five stories during the first year (1903) and earning the considerable sum of $1,842.50. The editor of *Munsey's Magazine* suggested that she write a crime serial. The first story, *The Man in Lower Ten,* was quickly followed by *The Circular Staircase,* which was later the first to be published in book form.

Best sellers ever since, Mrs. Rinehart's murder mysteries are generally violent, with the initial killing serving as a springboard to subsequent multiple murders. Her tales are unfailingly filled with sentimental love and humor—unusual elements in crime thrillers in the first decades of the twentieth century. Detection is less evident than in the works of her predecessors, which generally concentrated on the methods of eccentric sleuths. Mrs. Rinehart's stories involve ordinary people entangled in a terrifying situation that could happen to anyone. The heroines, however, generally have bad judgment and dubious intelligence. Warned never—*never*—to enter the attic, for instance, they are certain to be found there within a few pages, to be rescued at the last instant by their lovers. These heroines often have flashes of insight—just too late to prevent additional murders.

The statement (or a variation of it) "Had I but known then what I know now, this could have been avoided," which often creeps into her books, has given a name to a school of writing that has produced innumerable followers.

Mrs. Rinehart's most famous characters are Miss Letitia Carberry (Tish), a slapstick figure who gets involved in whacky situations, rarely of a genuine detective nature; and Nurse Adams, an obviously autobiographical creation affectionately called "Miss Pinkerton" by the official police because of her uncanny ability to become embroiled in criminal activities. She is introduced in *Miss Pinkerton* (1932; British title: *The Double Alibi*).

Mrs. Rinehart described some of her best-known books this way: *The After House* (1914), in which "I kill three people with one axe, raising the average number of murders per crime book to a new high level"; *The Red Lamp* (1925; British title: *The Mystery Lamp*), in which "a murder is committed every time the sinister red lamp goes out"; *The Album* (1933), in which "the answer to four gruesome murders lies in a dusty album for anyone to see"; *The Wall* (1938), in which "I commit three shocking murders in a fashionable New England summer colony"; *The Great Mistake* (1940), "a murder story set in the suburbs, involving a bag of toads, a pair of trousers and some missing keys"; and *The Yellow Room* (1945), in which "I used my Bar Harbor house . . . the yellow bedroom on the second floor, and the linen closet near the back stairs."

Mary Roberts Rinehart's most popular character, Nurse Adams, was nicknamed Miss Pinkerton by the district attorney's office. This illustration appears on the dust wrapper of the first edition of *Miss Pinkerton*, published by Farrar & Rinehart in 1932.

In *The Circular Staircase* (1908), Miss Cornelia Van Gorder, a middle-aged spinster, takes a summer house with her niece and nephew. A series of eerie events follow as a bank defaulter tries to retrieve stolen securities hidden there, until the terrifying mysteries are solved by the aunt. Mrs. Rinehart and Avery Hopwood adapted the novel into a play entitled *The Bat* (1920), which instantly became one of the most successful mystery dramas ever produced; it was translated into many languages and grossed a total of several million dollars. In addition to the films based directly on *The Bat,* countless imitations, both on the stage and on the screen, have appeared. It was novelized in 1926.

Plays and Films

By 1915 *The Circular Staircase* had served as the basis of a film by Selig. The Broadway production of

Agnes Moorehead portrays a famous writer of mysteries who is plunged into real-life crime when she rents a summer house in a 1959 screen version of Mary Roberts Rinehart's *The Bat.* [*Allied Artists*]

The Bat, with Effie Ellsler as the imperious Miss Van Gorder, ran for two years; the play was revived in 1953, with Lucile Watson as Miss Van Gorder and Zasu Pitts as the maid, Lizzie. Another Rinehart play, *The Breaking Point,* fared less well in 1923.

In its turn, *The Bat* became a source for films. The first, in 1926, was a silent film that faithfully told of the events that occurred in the Long Island manor with its secret room and hidden proceeds from a bank robbery. Louise Fazenda, as the dim-witted, screaming Lizzie, received top billing. A sound feature was released by United Artists in 1930, with the title *The Bat Whispers* (Chester Morris, Una Merkel, DeWitt Jennings, Maude Eburne. Directed by Roland West). The gloomy opening scene is a bank robbery engineered by the black-shrouded archcriminal, the Bat. Chester Morris—playing the detective who goes to Miss Van Gorder's house to investigate—turns to the audience after the surprise finale and requests them not to reveal the identity of the Bat.

Miss Pinkerton. First National, 1932. Joan Blondell, George Brent, Holmes Herbert, Ruth Hall. Directed by Lloyd Bacon.

A bored young hospital nurse, craving excitement, accepts a position looking after a sick old woman whose nephew has been murdered; a dashing young policeman asks her to keep her eyes open, dubbing her "Miss Pinkerton." Soon afterward, someone substitutes poison for the old woman's sleeping powder.

The Nurse's Secret. Warner Brothers, 1941. Lee Patrick, Regis Toomey, Julie Bishop, Virginia Brissac, Clara Blandick. Directed by Noel Smith.

In this remake of *Miss Pinkerton,* the eerie shadows of the old house to which Nurse Adams is assigned are retained.

The Bat. Allied Artists, 1959. Agnes Moorehead, Vincent Price, Gavin Gordon, John Sutton, Darla Hood. Directed by Crane Wilbur.

In the third film based on the play, Miss Van Gorder (Moorehead), an author of mysteries, moves with her maid (Lenita Lane) into a summer home, "The Oaks," where strange happenings occur.

Television

The Zasu Pitts stage version of *The Bat* was brought to television in 1953 after the play closed. In the same year a handsomely mounted version of *The Circular Staircase* was performed on CBS-TV's *Climax!* In 1960 Helen Hayes played Cornelia opposite Jason Robards, Jr., in *The Bat* on the *Dow Great Mysteries* series.

RIVETT, EDITH CAROLINE. *See* LORAC, E. C. R.

RODDA, CHARLES. *See* AMBLER, ERIC.

ROGERS, JOEL TOWNSLEY (1896–). American mystery writer. In Rogers's first detective novel, *Once in a Red Moon* (1923), a murder on shipboard finally brings the story into focus. The book seems to be a pulp magazine writer's idea of a romantic novel, or a romantic novelist's idea of what a pulp magazine story should be, or something that Harry Stephen KEELER might have thought up on the spur of the moment.

The Red Right Hand (1945) concerns a peculiar-looking, insane killer, called Corkscrew, who has committed at least one "impossible" crime and sawed off his victim's hand in the bargain. He also has his eye on several other potential victims. Reprinted periodically, it is sensational fiction at its best. Its opening passage is dazzling.

The Stopped Clock (1958), an expanded version of an earlier novelette, is a series of flashbacks racing through the mind of a former film star who is dying from a beating administered by one of her former husbands. Critic Anthony BOUCHER mentioned its fair but tricky puzzle and its overuse of coincidence and stated: "It's all about twice as long as the average suspense novel, five times as intricate and ten times as exciting."

ROHLFS, ANNA KATHARINE GREEN. *See* GREEN, ANNA KATHARINE.

ROHMER, SAX (pseudonym of Arthur Henry Sarsfield Ward; 1883–1959). English novelist, short story writer, and creator of the Chinese master criminal Dr. FU MANCHU. Although he wrote more than fifty books, Rohmer is remembered primarily for the thirteen novels featuring the famous Oriental Devil Doctor and his fantastic battles of wits with Sir Denis Nayland Smith.

Born Arthur Henry Ward in Birmingham, Rohmer had an unusual childhood. His Irish father, William Ward, was a hardworking office clerk. His mother, Margaret Mary Furey, was an alcoholic. Often delirious, she imagined herself to be a descendant of Patrick Sarsfield, the famous seventeenth-century Irish general. The name "Sarsfield" appealed to Rohmer, and he adopted it at the age of eighteen. In 1910, at his wife's urging, he began using the Sax Rohmer pseudonym for his fiction and soon used it exclusively, even in his private life.

Sax Rohmer.

Although he read widely in such areas as Egyptology and occultism, Rohmer had little interest in school and attended only sporadically. A free spirit, he also failed dismally at any job that required set hours, so he determined to be a writer. As a young man, he literally papered his wall with rejection slips. "In order to complete the color scheme," he said, "I sent the same manuscript to the same magazine three times. But the third time they lost it."

Deeply interested in "the Unknown" and a witness to several occult happenings, he joined such societies as the Hermetic Order of the Golden Dawn, whose other members included W. B. Yeats, Aleister Crowley, and Arthur MACHEN. His early stories concentrated on the occult and the mysterious East, which embraced Egypt in those days.

A newspaper assignment sent Rohmer to Limehouse, London's Chinatown, the great crowded repository for thousands of Chinese—many of whom had fled their native land under dubious circumstances. It was an area that few Caucasians dared enter, even in daylight, but Rohmer explored it nightly for months in search of "Mr. King," said to rule the criminal elements of the district. According to Rohmer, King became the model for Fu Manchu.

Success did not bring wealth to Rohmer. Most of his life, in fact, was far from luxurious, largely because of his erratic personality. When a royalty check arrived, he and his wife, Elizabeth, often spent it on a frivolity while remaining half-starved and in debt. Rohmer could never handle money, and this carelessness cost him dearly. His first agent was a scoundrel and cheated Rohmer of much of his royalties for fifteen years. Another financial arrangement, as late as 1955, nearly ruined him (and probably hastened his death); a lucrative American motion picture contract brought him $8,000—after a hard court battle—instead of the $4 million reported in newspapers. At the time, he and Elizabeth lived in a small, unheated New York City apartment, too poor to afford a taxi to the courthouse for their battle with another unscrupulous lawyer.

Rohmer had met Rose Elizabeth Knox, a beautiful entertainer, in 1905 and married her four years later. Despite several crises, they remained together for the next fifty years. The handsome author had several affairs, easily discovered by his wife because he was too absentminded to hide indiscreet letters. Elizabeth was an invaluable asset, often provoking fights so that Rohmer, usually good-humored, would be in the malevolent mood that, for him, was the right frame of mind for writing his sinister stories. She then locked him in his room until he produced a satisfactory amount of work.

In addition to Fu Manchu, Rohmer created Sumuru, the female counterpart of the evil doctor, and wrote occult novels, science and fantasy fiction, detective stories, and mystery and adventure fiction.

He mentioned "Mr. King" by name in *The Yellow Claw*, which, along with *Dope*, helped clean up Limehouse and bring about government action on drug traffic.

Rohmer combined occultism and detection in the tales about Moris Klaw, collected in *The Dream Detective*. Klaw's psychic intuition becomes activated when he visits the scene and then sleeps on his "odically sterilized" red cushion. After absorbing the atmosphere of the crime and dreaming about its circumstances, he can point out the guilty person. Klaw describes himself as "an old fool who sometimes has wise dreams." He is assisted by his beautiful daughter, Isis.

When he began *Fire-Tongue* in 1920, Rohmer wrote himself into a corner. Resolving to produce an exceptional detective story, he began with no solution in mind. He carefully wrote the first three chapters to eliminate any potential solution to the crime. Rohmer apparently did his work too well and could

Shirley Eaton (center) poses with some of her devoted lieutenants, women determined to dominate the world in *The Million Eyes of Su-Muru*, based on the Sax Rohmer novels of distaff villainy. [*American International*]

think of no way out of his own trap. His consequent difficulties in keeping up with the scheduled publication of the serial in *Collier's* seem to have caused a rift in his relations with the editors of that magazine; it was seven years before they accepted another of his novels for serialization. In his own account of the episode, Rohmer credited his friend Harry Houdini with providing the idea that resolved the plot difficulties. It was the only time Rohmer used this unorthodox method of story construction.

Readers are not always aware of one aspect of Rohmer's stories: Although his tales are often fantastic, they are wholly accurate with regard to background material. If a 7-inch poisonous millipede appears in a story, the reader can be sure that the insect actually exists. Even Fu Manchu is based on fact, and many bizarre tales were based on historical events that took place in China, related to Rohmer by an old Limehouse merchant.

Charges that Rohmer was a racist are difficult to refute, unless one takes into account the times in which he wrote. Until World War II the average Englishman had never seen an Oriental. Victorian attitudes of white supremacy prevailed until then, and tales of the "mysterious East" and "sinister Orientals" were accepted as accurate. In London, Limehouse was populated with the most undesirable Oriental characters, who were thought to represent their race. With the Boxer Rebellion and a later increase in drug traffic between the Far East and Britain, it was not unnatural for a writer to reflect the viewpoints of most of his countrymen.

Although prolific, Rohmer was not a hack who ground out words to meet deadlines. He always needed money, so he wrote much, but generally with care and pride, taking time to rewrite and polish, often pacing the room nervously, searching his mind for *le mot juste*.

The products of Rohmer's pen were as varied as they were plentiful. He spent many years as a writer of songs and comedy sketches for well-known entertainers; wrote musical and dramatic plays and newspaper and magazine articles on a variety of subjects; ghosted an "autobiography" of a well-known music hall comedian; and wrote a standard reference book on the occult, *The Romance of Sorcery* (1914). The checklist contains all his fiction—with the exception of the Fu Manchu works—much of which is borderline mystery.

CHECKLIST

Books not about Fu Manchu.

1910 *Pause!* (s.s.; written with George Robey and published anonymously)
1914 *The Sins of Séverac Bablon*
1915 *The Yellow Claw*
1916 *The Exploits of Captain O'Hagan* (s.s.)
1918 *Brood of the Witch Queen*
1918 *Tales of Secret Egypt* (s.s.)
1918 *The Orchard of Tears*
1919 *The Quest of the Sacred Slipper*
1919 *Dope*
1919 *The Golden Scorpion*
1920 *The Dream Detective* (s.s.)
1920 *The Green Eyes of Bâst*
1920 *The Haunting of Low Fennel* (s.s.)
1921 *Bat-Wing*
1921 *Fire-Tongue*
1922 *Tales of Chinatown* (s.s.)
1924 *Grey Face*
1925 *Yellow Shadows*
1927 *Moon of Madness*
1928 *She Who Sleeps*
1929 *The Emperor of America*
1930 *The Day the World Ended*
1932 *Yu'an Hee See Laughs*
1932 *Tales of East and West* (s.s.; British edition)
1933 *Tales of East and West* (s.s.; U.S. edition; altered contents)
1935 *The Bat Flies Low*
1936 *White Velvet*
1939 *Salute to Bazarada and Other Stories* (s.s.)
1943 *Seven Sins*
1944 *Egyptian Nights* (s.s.; U.S. title: *Bimbâshi Barûk of Egypt*)
1949 *Hangover House*
1950 *Nude in Mink* (British title: *Sins of Sumuru*)
1950 *Wulfheim* (by Michael Furey)
1951 *Sumuru* (British title: *Slaves of Sumuru*)
1952 *The Fire Goddess* (British title: *Virgin in Flames*)
1954 *The Moon Is Red*
1954 *The Return of Sumuru* (British title: *Sand and Satin*)
1956 *Sinister Madonna*
1970 *The Secret of Holm Peel and Other Strange Stories* (s.s.)

Films

In addition to the endlessly popular Fu Manchu films, a distaff Rohmer villain has reached the screen.

The Million Eyes of Su-Muru (British title: *Sumuru*). American-International (British), 1967. Frankie Avalon, George Nader, Shirley Eaton (Su-Muru), Wilfrid Hyde-White, Patti Chandler. Directed by Lindsay Shonteff. A composite of themes from the Sumuru novels.

Two Americans on vacation in Italy investigate the murder of the chief security officer of a nation called Sinonesia and discover, at a remote, mysterious villa, a secret worldwide organization of beautiful women from all nations seeking to enslave the globe's most influential men.

ROLLS, ANTHONY. *See* VULLIAMY, C. E.

ROMANOFF, ALEXANDER NICHOLAYEVITCH. *See* ABDULLAH, ACHMED.

RONNS, EDWARD. *See* AARONS, EDWARD S.

ROSS, BARNABY. *See* QUEEN, ELLERY (author).

ROTH, HOLLY (1916–1964). American mystery fiction writer. Born in Chicago, she grew up in Brooklyn but spent considerable time as a child in London, where her father owned a business. She originally worked as a model and then did newspaper and magazine work before she began to write mysteries. Her death occurred under mysterious circumstances; she fell off a small sailing vessel while fishing in the Mediterranean, and her body was never recovered.

Married to Joseph Franta, Miss Roth used the pseudonyms K. G. Ballard and P. J. Merrill as well as her own name for her works. As Holly Roth, she published one of her most popular books, *The Content Assignment* (1954), about an English journalist who travels from Berlin to London to New York in his search for a female American agent who has disappeared.

RUNYON, (ALFRED) DAMON (1884–1946). American journalist and author of humorous short stories.

The dust wrapper of Damon Runyon's most famous book was designed by Arthur Hawkins. The first edition was published by Frederick A. Stokes in 1931.

Born in Kansas, he became a reporter and spent time in cities in every part of the country before he settled on New York's Broadway, where he adapted the slang and the shady characters of the underworld for his prose. Bookies, con men, robbers, bootleggers, prostitutes, and murderers populate his stories, but they are generally presented as having hearts of gold. His most famous book, *Guys and Dolls* (1931), was selected for QUEEN'S QUORUM and gave its name to a popular musical play and film. All of Runyon's story collections have elements of crime. He collaborated with Howard Lindsay (1889–1968) on a play, *A Slight Case of Murder* (1935). He moved to Hollywood to write films. *Little Miss Marker* (1934), which featured Shirley Temple in her first starring role and was a most sympathetic portrayal of bookies, was based on his short story.

RUSSELL, COLONEL CHARLES (Creator: William HAGGARD). Russell is the head of England's Security Executive, a military intelligence organization that operates on the highest level of international political diplomacy. The colonel is not particularly tall, but he has a soldierly and faintly donnish air about him. His mouth appears slightly sardonic beneath an admirably tended moustache. He fought with bravery and distinction in World War I and served in India afterward.

Urbane, with an erect and elegant figure, he has spent most of his lifetime serving his country's interests in a patient and unobtrusive manner. In times of crisis he makes decisions with cool shrewdness—the political fate of nations hanging in the balance.

Although forced into mandatory retirement at the age of sixty-five, Colonel Russell has no hesitation in undertaking further difficult assignments for his friends or country. His first case, *Slow Burner*, deals with a nuclear secret in danger of being turned over to an enemy power by a traitor from among a group of top atomic scientists. *The Arena* is about a shaky firm of merchant bankers threatened with a merger by an unimpressive new firm. The repercussions of this minor power struggle extend to the highest levels of national policy. A new tranquilizer, unstable and addictive to its users, all in sensitive positions of power, is the subject of *The Unquiet Sleep*; a government scandal could wreak havoc on the party in power. In *The High Wire* an engineer in London unwittingly becomes involved in a spy plot that ends in Switzerland in a stalled funicular car. *The Antagonists* concerns a famous scientist, residing in England, who is a danger to a rival power. Another major power, formerly friendly to England, intervenes and tries to obtain the scientist for its own purposes; Russell is given the "assignment."

CHECKLIST

1958	*Slow Burner*
1959	*Venetian Blind*
1961	*The Arena*
1962	*The Unquiet Sleep*
1963	*The High Wire*
1964	*The Antagonists*
1965	*The Powder Barrel*
1965	*The Hard Sell*
1966	*The Power House*
1967	*The Conspirators*
1968	*A Cool Day for Killing*
1969	*The Doubtful Discipline*
1970	*The Hardliners*
1971	*The Bitter Harvest* (U.S. title: *Too Many Enemies*)
1973	*The Old Masters* (U.S. title: *The Notch on the Knife*)
1975	*The Scorpion's Tail*

RUSSELL, JOHN (1885–1956). American novelist, short story writer, journalist, and explorer. Born in Davenport, Iowa, he joined the staff of the *New York Herald* and then explored in South America, Asia, and the South Seas. He used his experiences as background for much of his fiction, most notably *The Red Mark* (1919), a short story collection selected for QUEEN'S QUORUM. It was retitled *Where the Pavement Ends* in 1921. A more traditional collection of crime stories is *Cops and Robbers* (1930; U.S. title: *Cops 'n Robbers*), thirteen tales including Russell's favorite of the more than 1,000 short stories he published during his lifetime. "The Man Who Was Dead."

RUSSELL W[ILLIAM] CLARK (1844–1911). English author of sea stories. At the age of thirteen, he went to sea with the merchant navy and became his generation's leading writer of adventure stories set on the high seas. His first novel was *John Holdsworth, Chief Mate* (1875); his most famous, *The Wreck of the Grosvenor* (1877). In later years he lost the use of his legs; he died an invalid.

His best-known mystery novel is *Is He the Man?* (1876), published in three volumes. The first American edition, entitled *The Copsford Mystery; or, Is He the Man?*, did not appear until 1896. The detective role is played by the retired Colonel Kilmain.

Dr. WATSON makes a great point of mentioning the high regard in which he holds the works of Russell.

RUSSELL, WILLIAM. *See* "WATERS."

RYDELL, HELEN. *See* FORBES, STANTON.

RYDELL, STANTON. *See* FORBES, STANTON.

S

SAINT, THE (Creator: Leslie CHARTERIS). Simon Templar is known as the Saint because, however nefarious his schemes may be, his motives are absolutely pure. He bears a striking physical resemblance to Charteris, but on a much grander scale. Although his creator and most of his readers see something of themselves in Templar, only a man with his unbounded love of romance could behave the way he does. The Saint once discussed his philosophy of adventure, the raison d'être of his life, this way: "I'm mad enough to believe in romance. And I'm sick and tired of this age—tired of the miserable little mildewed things that people racked their brains about, and wrote books about, and called life. I wanted something more elementary and honest—battle, murder, sudden death, with plenty of good beer and damsels in distress and a complete callousness about blipping the ungodly over the beezer. It mayn't be life as we know it, but it ought to be."

The Saint is a modern-day Robin Hood—as Robin Hood really was, not as modern legend perpetuates him. Like the bandit of Sherwood Forest, the Saint attempts to right injustices perpetrated against those unable to help themselves. And also like Robin Hood, the Saint steals only from criminals and rascals, and there are no limits to the methods he will use to help their innocent victims. He has broken the law so often that his constant adversary, Chief Inspector Claud Eustace Teal of Scotland Yard, is thrilled when Templar moves to New York, where he becomes the special headache of Inspector John Fernack. But the Saint has also helped official law-enforcement agencies with some of their biggest problems, wreaking his own brand of justice when legal means are impossible. In this sense, he has emulated the Four Just Men of Edgar WALLACE, who also bring criminals to justice when the law is powerless to act against them.

This simple stick figure is internationally recognized as the symbol of the Saint.

Templar, physically well equipped for his adventurous life, is a muscular and athletic 6 feet 2 inches tall and is an expert at many sports, including fighting, knife throwing, automobile racing, horseback riding, and flying; in fact, he has almost all the skills one might need in any emergency. His intellect is no less enviable, for he possesses a vast amount of specialized knowledge in diverse fields and is able to converse in several languages.

A spectacular dresser, he patronizes the most elegant tailors in London. He appreciates the good life, from the best wines to the finest foods. In a rugged, masculine sort of way, he is handsome, and women are instantly attracted to him, as he is to them—he frankly admits that his interest in women is not platonic. Although he enjoys the company of many beautiful women, he returns most often to Patricia Holm, who was present in his first adventure, *Meet the Tiger,* and many early exploits.

Whenever the Saint is involved in a case, he leaves his calling card so that his adversaries know whom they are up against. The card bears no name, just a small stick figure that is instantly recognized by police and criminals alike. Inspector Fernack describes the drawing this way: "I'm not much on art, but it looks to me like this guy Templar ain't so

Louis Hayward (center) is pugnacious in *The Saint in New York.* [*RKO*]

hot either. But the idea's there. See that figger; the sort of things kids draw when they first get hold of a pencil—just a circle for a head, and a straight line for a body, and four more for the arms and legs, but you can see it's meant to be somep'n human. An' another circle floating on top of the head. When I was a kid I got took to a cathedral once . . . and there were a lot of paintings of people with circles round their heads. They were saints or somep'n and those circles were supposed to be halos. . . ."

CHECKLIST

1928 *Meet the Tiger*
1930 *The Last Hero*
1930 *Enter the Saint* (three novelettes)
1930 *Knight Templar* (U.S. title: *The Avenging Saint*)
1931 *Featuring the Saint* (three novelettes)
1931 *Alias the Saint* (three novelettes)
1931 *She Was a Lady* (U.S. title: *Angels of Doom*)
1931 *Wanted for Murder* (U.S. title of *Featuring the Saint* and *Alias the Saint*)
1932 *The Holy Terror* (three novelettes; U.S. title: *The Saint vs. Scotland Yard*)
1932 *Getaway*
1933 *Once More the Saint* (three novelettes; U.S. title: *The Saint and Mr. Teal*)
1933 *The Brighter Buccaneer* (s.s.)
1934 *The Misfortunes of Mr. Teal* (three novelettes)
1934 *Boodle* (s.s.; U.S. title: *The Saint Intervenes*)
1934 *The Saint Goes On* (three novelettes)
1935 *The Saint in New York*
1936 *Saint Overboard*
1937 *The Ace of Knaves* (three novelettes)
1937 *Thieves' Picnic*
1938 *Prelude for War*
1938 *Follow the Saint* (three novelettes)
1939 *The Happy Highwayman* (s.s.)
1940 *The Saint in Miami*
1942 *The Saint Goes West* (three novelettes)
1943 *The Saint Steps In*
1944 *The Saint on Guard* (two novelettes)
1946 *The Saint Sees It Through*
1948 *Call for the Saint* (two novelettes)
1948 *Saint Errant* (s.s.)
1953 *The Saint in Europe* (s.s.)
1955 *The Saint on the Spanish Main* (s.s.)
1956 *The Saint around the World* (s.s.)
1957 *Thanks to the Saint* (s.s.)
1958 *Señor Saint* (s.s.)
1959 *The Saint to the Rescue* (s.s.)
1962 *Trust the Saint* (s.s.)
1963 *The Saint in the Sun* (s.s.)
1964 *Vendetta for the Saint*
1967 *The Saint on TV* (two novelettes: *The Death Game*, original story by John Kruse, teleplay by Harry W. Junkin, adapted by Fleming Lee; *The Power Artist*, original teleplay by Kruse, adapted by Lee); final revision by Charteris.
1968 *The Saint Returns* (two novelettes: *The Gadget Lovers*, original teleplay by Kruse, adapted by Lee; *The Dizzy Daughter*, original story by D. R. Motten, teleplay by Leigh Vance, adapted by Lee); final revision by Charteris.
1968 *The Saint and the Fiction Makers* (original teleplay by Kruse, adapted by Lee, final manuscript revision by Charteris)
1969 *The Saint Abroad* (two novelettes: original teleplays by Michael Pertwee, adapted by Lee, final manuscript revision by Charteris)
1970 *The Saint and the People Importers* (by Lee); final revision by Charteris.
1970 *The Saint in Pursuit*
1974 *Catch the Saint* (two novelettes by Norman Worker and Lee)
1975 *Catch the Saint* (two novelettes by Worker and Lee)

Films

"The Robin Hood of Modern Crime" waited for more

George Sanders as Simon Templar, with perennial heroine Wendy Barrie, in *The Saint in Palm Springs.* [*RKO*]

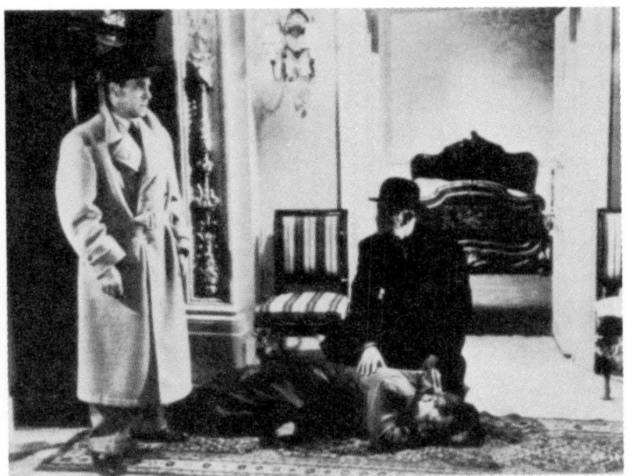

Louis Hayward (left) returns to the Simon Templar role, uncovering violence in a London setting, in *The Saint's Girl Friday*. [*RKO*]

than a decade before making the transition into films. Louis Hayward starred in both his first and his last cinematic adventures, but George Sanders played the suave Simon Templar most often.

The Saint in New York. RKO, 1938. Hayward, Kay Sutton, Jonathan Hale, Jack Carson. Directed by Ben Holmes. Based on the 1935 novel.

In his auspicious debut, Simon, an international adventurer known for his daring in dealing single-handedly with crime, is called to Manhattan by a citizens' committee to cope with six of the city's most vicious gangsters, most of whom he cheerfully kills off.

The Saint Strikes Back. RKO, 1939. Sanders, Barrie, Hale, Jerome Cowan, Neil Hamilton, Barry Fitzgerald. Directed by John Farrow. Based on *Angels of Doom.*

The Saint helps a girl who exists on the fringes of the underworld clear the name of her dead father—a policeman who had been accused of graft.

The Saint in London. RKO, 1939. Sanders, Sally Gray, David Burns, Gordon McLeod. Directed by John Paddy Carstairs. Based on the Charteris short story "The Million Pound Day."

In London to ferret out spies, Simon learns that a foreign ambassador is in danger and hides him in a boardinghouse. The ambassador is killed anyway, and the Saint must track down the murderers.

The Saint's Double Trouble. RKO, 1940. Sanders, Helene Whitney, Hale, Bela Lugosi. Directed by Jack Hively.

Gangster Duke Plato (also played by Sanders), the Saint's double, commits two murders and leaves Templar's calling card at the scene. One of his victims is a professor who was an old friend of Simon's. Lugosi plays a cheap crook.

The Saint Takes Over. RKO, 1940. Sanders, Barrie, Hale, Paul Guilfoyle. Directed by Hively. Script revision by Charteris.

Simon tries to clear one of his friends, police inspector Fernack (Hale), of false bribery charges, but his chief underworld suspects are being killed one by one.

The Saint in Palm Springs. RKO, 1941. Sanders, Barrie, Guilfoyle, Linda Hayes. Directed by Hively. Original story outline by Charteris.

Simon is asked to deliver an inheritance—three rare stamps worth $65,000 apiece—to a girl in Palm Springs. Shortly after he arrives, the stamps are taken from him and three people die.

The Saint's Vacation. RKO, 1941 (filmed in England with an all-British cast). Hugh Sinclair, Gray, Arthur Macrae, Cecil Parker. Directed by Leslie Fenton. Based on *Getaway.*

The Saint's peaceful vacation in Dover is interrupted by a bothersome girl reporter and by spies looking for the plans for a valuable sound detector.

The Saint Meets the Tiger. Republic, 1943 (filmed in England). Sinclair, Jean Gillie, McLeod, Clifford Evans. Directed by Paul Stein. Slightly based on *Meet the Tiger.*

A man dying on the Saint's doorstep sends him to a small Cornish coastal village where, in an elaborate swindle, a gang led by "the Tiger" is using gold stolen from a bank to seed a defunct mine.

The Saint's Girl Friday. RKO, 1954 (filmed in England). Hayward, Naomi Chance, Sidney Tafler, Charles Victor, Jane Carr, Diana Dors. Directed by Seymour Friedman.

A socialite lady friend of an older, more serious Saint crashes her car into the Thames; officially, her death is considered an accident, but the Saint thinks otherwise. His investigation brings him to an illegal gambling casino on a river barge.

Radio and Television

Several actors, including Tom Conway, Brian Aherne, and Vincent Price, portrayed Templar during a radio series, *The Saint,* which began on NBC in 1944 and continued through the 1940s. In 1963 England's ITC produced a weekly hour-long *Saint* television series starring a vigorous Roger Moore as Simon. Internationally successful, the program lasted three seasons.

ST. JOHN, DAVID. *See* HUNT, E. HOWARD.

SALE, RICHARD (1911–). American author, film director, and mystery writer. Born in New York City and educated at Washington and Lee University (1930–1933), he started writing short stories and, later, serials for magazines. His more than 350 stories have been published in periodicals ranging from

Much of Richard Sale's early mystery fiction was aimed at such pulp magazines as *Super-Detective*.

the PULP MAGAZINES to *The Saturday Evening Post.* One of his stories is listed on the honor roll of the *Best Short Stories of 1935*.

Sale married Mary Anita Loos in 1940; they have three children. He began working for the film industry in 1944, joining Paramount as a writer, and has been employed by many studios since. Among his credits are *Mr. Belvedere Goes to College* (1949), *A Ticket to Tomahawk* (1950; he also directed), *Suddenly* (1954), and *Abandon Ship* (1957). Sale has also worked as a producer-director-writer for CBS and has published a nonmystery novel about Hollywood, *The Oscar* (1963). He lives in Newport Beach, Calif.; his hobbies include fishing and hunting.

Not Too Narrow, Not Too Deep (1936) is about a group of ten convicts who escape from a penal colony in South America and are joined by a stranger who controls and guides them by means of a strange and supernatural power. It was filmed as *Strange Cargo* in 1940, with Clark Gable, Joan Crawford, and Peter Lorre. *Lazarus No. 7* (1942; British title: *Death Looks On*) concerns a group of Hollywood writers and a murderer with a unique motive.

The recent *For the President's Eyes Only* (1971) recounts the adventures of a James BOND type of hero who attempts to defeat a group of specialists in international blackmail.

SAMPSON, RICHARD HENRY. *See* HULL, RICHARD.

SANBORN, B. X. *See* BALLINGER, BILL S.

SANDAVAL, JAIME. *See* MARLOWE, DAN J.

SANDERS, DAPHNE. *See* RICE, CRAIG.

SANDERS, GEORGE. *See* RICE, CRAIG.

SANDOE, JAMES (1912–). American teacher, anthologist, and critic. While professor of bibliography and English literature at the University of Colorado, Sandoe also reviewed mysteries for *The New York Herald Tribune*. He lectured on the psychological thriller at *Poetry Magazine's* 1946 Modern Art Series. That lecture, entitled "Dagger of the Mind," was printed in the magazine's June 1946 issue and reprinted in Howard HAYCRAFT's *The Art of the Mystery Story* (1946), along with SANDOE'S READERS' GUIDE TO CRIME, an annotated checklist.

He compiled *Murder Plain and Fanciful* (1948), an anthology of true-crime articles and fiction, some of which is based on actual crimes. Jacques BARZUN and Wendell Hertig TAYLOR called it a "virtually perfect anthology." They also praised as "a model of incisive criticism" Sandoe's *The Hard-boiled Dick* (1952; privately published pamphlet, reprinted in *The Armchair Detective*, vol. 1, no. 2, January 1968). Sandoe also compiled and wrote the introduction for *Lord Peter* (1972), a collection of stories about Lord Peter WIMSEY.

Sandoe has won two Edgars for criticism, one while he was writing for the *Chicago Sun-Times*, the other during his tenure at *The New York Herald Tribune*.

SANDOE'S READERS' GUIDE TO CRIME. In an attempt to point out the responsibility of university libraries to collect detective fiction, James SANDOE published a suitable list in the *Wilson Library Bulletin* of April 1944, entitled "The Detective Story and Academe." It was updated and revised for publication in Howard HAYCRAFT's *The Art of the Mystery Story* (1946), a collection of critical essays.

SANXAY, ELIZABETH. *See* HOLDING, ELIZABETH SANXAY.

"SAPPER." *See* MCNEILE, H. C.

SAUNDERS, HILARY AIDAN ST. GEORGE. *See* BEEDING, FRANCIS.

SAYERS, DOROTHY L[EIGH] (1893–1957). English author. Born at Christchurch Cathedral Choir School, Oxford, she was the only child of the headmaster. She learned Latin at the age of seven and fluent French from her governess. A brilliant scholar at Somerville College, Oxford, she took top honors in medieval literature and received her degree in 1915—one of the first Englishwomen to do so.

In 1916 she published *Opus I*, a volume of poems in a series of works by "unknown" poets published by Blackwell. She was an editor of the periodical *Oxford Poetry* from 1917 to 1919, and her second book of verse, *Catholic Tales and Christian Songs*, was published in 1918.

Although her interest in religious literature continued until her death, she was forced to seek more remunerative forms of writing and became a copywriter for England's largest advertising agency, S. H. Benson, in London. She conceived the idea of her famous detective, Lord Peter WIMSEY, in 1920 and, three years later, published her first mystery story. After completing the last of her mystery novels, she wrote *The Zeal of Thy House* (1937), a religious play about William de Sens, the twelfth-century architect of Oxford's Cathedral Choir School. The following year, expressing her faith in the Anglican Church, Miss Sayers published a pamphlet, *The Greatest Drama Ever Staged*. Writing of the Divine Incarnation, which she called "this terrifying drama of which God is the victim and hero," she asked, "if this is dull, then what, in Heaven's name, is worthy to be called exciting?" Her 1939 religious play, *The Devil to Pay*, dealt with Faustian themes.

In 1947 Dorothy Sayers announced that she would write no further detective stories. Annoyed by interviewers who asked, she once replied, "I wrote the Peter Wimsey books when I was young and had no money. I made some money, and then stopped writing novels and began to write what I had always wanted to write." She spent the last decade of her life translating Dante and lecturing on religion, philosophy, and medieval literature. Her translation of the *Divine Comedy* was commissioned by the English publisher Penguin. *Hell* was published in 1949, *Purgatory* in 1955, and *Paradise* (completed by Barbara Reynolds after Miss Sayers's death) in 1962. She also wrote two books about Dante, *Introductory Papers on Dante* (1954) and *Further Papers on Dante* (1957).

In her biography, *Such a Strange Lady* (1975), Janet Hitchman reveals that Miss Sayer secretly gave birth to a son in January 1924. Two years later she married a ne'er-do-well journalist and barfly, Oswold Atherton (né Oswald Arthur) Fleming (1881–1950); the couple adopted Dorothy's boy in 1934, but he was reared elsewhere by a cousin. The need to provide for his support was evidently an important reason for the continuation of the Wimsey series.

Whose Body? (1923), her first mystery, introduces Lord Peter Wimsey, an aristocratic amateur detective, as he is about to leave to attend a sale of rare books. His mother asks him to help a friend who has inconveniently discovered a corpse in his bathtub. Lord Peter complies, deputizing Bunter, his incredibly efficient manservant, to attend the sale on his behalf. The second Sayers mystery, *Clouds of Witness* (1926), established her popularity. A murder has occurred at one of the Wimsey family homes; Lord Peter's sister is a suspect, but his older brother has been accused of the crime. As Lord Peter seeks the murderer, the climax of the case takes place in the House of Lords, where the elder Wimsey, as a member of the peerage, must stand trial.

Collaborating with Robert Eustace (pseudonym of Dr. Eustace Robert Barton), Miss Sayers published her only non-Wimsey mystery, *The Documents in the Case*, in 1930. Written largely in the form of a series of letters, it tells of a poisoning in which a synthetic substance with the characteristics of a deadly toadstool is prepared and administered. In *Strong Poison* (1930) Miss Sayers introduced Harriet Vane, a mystery writer on trial for allegedly killing her lover. Wimsey falls in love with her as he seeks the evidence to prove her innocent. Miss Vane discovers a body while she is hiking at the outset of *Have His Carcase* (1932). She and Lord Peter are successful in their detective work, but it is obvious that Peter's major efforts are concentrated on attempts (unsuccessful) to get Harriet to marry him.

Miss Sayers temporarily abandoned the Wimsey-Vane romance to produce two of her most famous detective novels. She drew on her own career for *Murder Must Advertise* (1933), which involves a killing at a London advertising agency. *The Nine Tailors* (1934) is set in the East Anglian fen country she knew from childhood. With its strongly religious background, it is the only Sayers mystery to give evidence of the author's other major interest. Miss Sayers's foreword begins with her famous defense: "From time to time complaints are made about the ringing of church bells. It seems strange that a generation which tolerates the uproar of the internal combustion engine and the wailing of the jazz band should be so sensitive to the one loud noise that is made to the glory of God."

Harriet Vane returns in *Gaudy Night* (1935), this time as the major character of the book. The setting is Miss Vane's alma mater, a women's college at Oxford closely resembling Miss Sayers's own Somerville. Invited to attend a class reunion, Miss Vane (with the eventual help of Lord Peter) remains to investigate a series of strange events. Originally intended as a nonmystery novel, the book explores the role of women in society, especially the academic community. It also permitted Miss Sayers to choose a "plot that should exhibit intellectual integrity as the one great permanent value in an emotionally unstable world."

The author termed *Busman's Honeymoon* (1937) "A Love Story with Detective Interruptions,"

Dorothy L. Sayers.

presumably because it deals with problems of marital adjustment as much as it does with the murder that interrupts the honeymoon of Peter and Harriet. Originally written as a play in collaboration with Muriel St. Clare Byrne, it was later converted into a novel.

Three volumes of short stories were published during Miss Sayers's lifetime. *Lord Peter Views the Body* (1928) contains twelve Wimsey tales. *Hangman's Holiday* (1933) also has a dozen stories, but only four are about Wimsey. Six of the remaining tales are about Montague Egg, a wine salesman who is an amateur detective on the side. The third volume, *In the Teeth of the Evidence* (1939), has two stories about Wimsey and five about Egg. Among the ten nonseries stories in this volume are two that have been frequently anthologized, "Suspicion" and "The Leopard Lady." An omnibus volume, *Lord Peter* (1972), contains all previously collected Wimsey stories and, in addition, two stories, "Striding Folly" and "The Haunted Policeman," that had never appeared in any volume by Miss Sayers. The second printing of *Lord Peter* marked the first appearance in a collection of "Talboys," the last Wimsey story—written in 1942 and discovered three decades later by the author's heir. It was printed in a limited-edition pamphlet in 1972, just prior to its publication in the collection.

Miss Sayers read widely in the detective genre and produced three landmark anthologies, published in 1928, 1931, and 1934. Of her introduction to the second omnibus, Jacques BARZUN and Wendell Hertig TAYLOR said: "This 16-page essay must rank as one of the very best discussions of the genre ever penned. Every page is crammed with shrewd observations. . . ." In 1936 a smaller but also excellent anthology appeared under her editorship: *Tales of Detection*.

Regarding her fiction, critics have frequently commented on Miss Sayers's self-professed goal of producing a book "less like a conventional detective story and more like a novel." She later refined this objective in 1937, declaring that she tried to make the detective novel "more a novel of manners than a crossword puzzle." This was especially apparent in her last two books, *Gaudy Night* (1935) and *Busman's Honeymoon* (1937), in which the elements of detection were underplayed. John Strachey wrote, in 1939, that she "has now almost ceased to be a first-rate detective story writer, and has become an exceedingly snobbish popular novelist." Julian SYMONS summarized the dichotomy of opinion regarding Miss Sayers, pointing out that to her admirers "she is the finest detective story writer of the 20th century; to those less enthusiastic, her work is long-winded and ludicrously snobbish."

In *Murder for Pleasure* (1941) Howard HAYCRAFT wrote of Miss Sayers's work, "No single trend in the English detective story of the 1920s was more significant than its approach to the literary standards of the legitimate novel. And no author illustrates the trend better than Dorothy Sayers, who has been called by some critics the greatest of living writers in the form. Whether or not the reader agrees with this verdict he cannot, unless he is both obtuse and ungrateful, dispute her preeminence as one of the most brilliant and prescient artists the genre has yet produced." Conceding that her last two books were failures, falling into the "dangerous no-man's-land which is neither good detection nor good legitimate fiction," Haycraft praises her willingness to experiment, saying, "Her very errors do her honor."

SCARLET PIMPERNEL, THE (Creator: Baroness Emmuska ORCZY). Sir Percy Blakeney, a foppish Englishman whose dual identity is known only to his devoted wife and to his archenemy, Chauvelin, serves as an espionage agent during the days of the French Revolution. He made his initial appearance, in the romantic play *The Scarlet Pimpernel*, on the London stage in January 1905. The work was a collaborative effort by Baroness Orczy and Montague Brastow (her husband). A novel with the same title was also published in 1905. Many novels featuring Sir Percy were published during the next several decades, including *The Elusive Pimpernel* (1908), *Sir Percy Hits Back* (1927), and *The Way of the Scarlet Pimpernel* (1933).

His success inspired this doggerel: "We seek him here . . . / We seek him there . . . / Those Frenchies seek him . . . / everywhere./ Is he in heaven?/ Is he in h-ll?/ That demmed elusive Pimpernel!" The Scarlet Pimpernel takes his name from a wildflower that blossoms and dies in a single night.

Films

The first version of *The Scarlet Pimpernel* was released by Fox Films in 1917, but the most memorable Pimpernel appeared almost two decades later.

The Scarlet Pimpernel. United Artists (British), 1935. Leslie Howard, Merle Oberon, Raymond Massey. Directed by Harold Young.

A courageous English baronet, seemingly a fop,

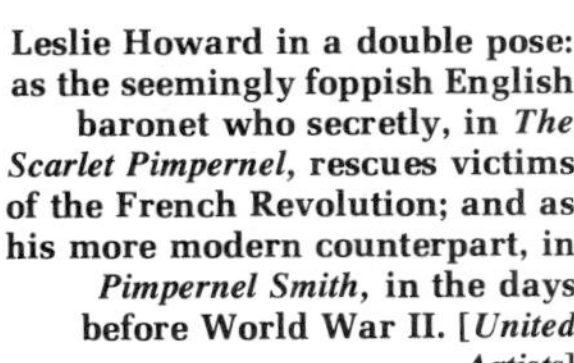

Leslie Howard in a double pose: as the seemingly foppish English baronet who secretly, in *The Scarlet Pimpernel,* rescues victims of the French Revolution; and as his more modern counterpart, in *Pimpernel Smith,* in the days before World War II. [*United Artists*]

masquerades as "the Scarlet Pimpernel" to rescue French aristocrats from the guillotine during the revolution.

There have been countless unacknowledged uses of the basic Pimpernel character under other names. Of the official sequels, one is updated to contemporary settings.

The Return of the Scarlet Pimpernel. United Artists (British), 1938. Barry K. Barnes, Sophie Stewart, James Mason. Directed by Hans Schwartz.

Robespierre, annoyed that so many aristocrats have been liberated by the Pimpernel, lures him once more across the English Channel by kidnapping his wife.

Pimpernel Smith (U.S. release title: *Mister V*). United Artists (British), 1941. Howard, Francis X. Sullivan, Mary Morris. Directed by Howard.

Just before World War II, Professor Horatio Smith, a gentle British archaeologist touring with his students in Germany, secretly rescues intellectuals from concentration camps . . . until a Gestapo general uncovers his identity.

The Elusive Pimpernel. London Films (British), 1950. David Niven, Margaret Leighton, Jack Hawkins, Cyril Cusack. Directed by Michael Powell and Emeric Pressburger.

The film centers on the familiar Pimpernel exploits at the tumbrils (the same title and story were used for a British silent film in 1919, with Cecil Humphreys as Sir Percy).

SCHERF, MARGARET (1908–). American mystery novelist. Born in West Virginia, Miss Scherf attended elementary school in New Jersey and Wyoming and high school in Montana. After spending three years at Antioch College in Ohio, she went to New York to work in magazine and book publishing. She has been a free-lance writer since 1939. After she returned to Montana, she became active in Democratic party politics, serving in the State Legislature during the 1965 session. In 1966 *Harper's Magazine* published her article about her experience in government, entitled "One Cow, One Vote." She married Perry E. Beebe in 1965; they spend their winters in an old Arizona mining town.

Miss Scherf has written more than twenty adult mysteries as well as three mysteries for children and one novel, *Wedding Train* (1960), about the early days in Kalispell, Mont., where her grandfather was a pioneer. Her mysteries combine humor and crime. A slow-moving clergyman, Martin Buell, is the detective in several Montana stories, for example, *Always Murder a Friend* (1948), *Gilbert's Last Toothache* (1949), *The Elk and the Evidence* (1952), *The Cautious Overshoes* (1956), and *The Corpse in the Flannel Nightgown* (1965).

She has also written about Henry and Emily Bryce, a husband and wife team who paint furniture for Manhattan decorators. Among their adventures are *The Gun in Daniel Webster's Bust* (1949), *The Green Plaid Pants* (1951), and *The Diplomat and the Gold Piano* (1963; British title: *Death of the Diplomat*).

A retired pathologist, Dr. Grace Severance, makes her first appearance as a detective in *The Banker's Bones* (1968), set in a small Arizona town where the natives and the "winter people" mingle. Dr. Severance appears again in *The Beautiful Birthday Cake* (1971) and *To Cache a Millionaire* (1972), in which a man resembling a notorious financial genius disappears from his casino-motel in Las Vegas. Las Vegas is also the setting for *If You Want a Murder Well Done* (1974), in which Dr. Severance does not appear.

SCIENTIFIC DETECTIVES. The popularity of the scientific detective, introduced by Sir Arthur CONAN DOYLE with his creation of Sherlock HOLMES, made inevitable an imitation of his approach and an exaggeration of the creation and his methods of solving crimes scientifically that caused many detective stories to border on science fiction.

When "The Man in the Room," by Edwin BALMER and William MACHARG was published in the May 1909 issue of *Hampton's Magazine*, the editor claimed to have introduced with Luther Trant the "psychological detective," an apparently "new" form of detective story. The scientific instruments used in solving crimes in that story, and in subsequent ones, in effect resulted in a form of science fiction.

So closely did Arthur B. REEVE imitate the Luther Trant formulas in the first story in his Craig KENNEDY series, "The Case of Helen Bond," published in the competing *Cosmopolitan* magazine in December 1910, that he used the same plot and the same device for recording the lapsed time in a subject's reply to an association test that Balmer and MacHarg had used in "The Man in the Room." Reeve became ever more scientific until his 1915 novel, *The War Terror*, which contains an excellent description of a kidney machine.

The enthusiastic reader response to the Kennedy series sparked still further imitators; one of the most successful was the "psychological detective" of Max Rittenberg in *The Strange Cases of Dr. Xavier Wycherly*, which began in the March 1911 issue of *The London Magazine*. A few of the titles—"The Man Who Lived Again," "The Voice from the Other World," "The Man Who Was Three Years Ago"—suggest their appeal. Dr. Wycherley solved crimes by picking up residual thought waves in the rooms in which they had been emitted, through the aid of a special drug. The series also ran in *The Blue Book* in the United States, beginning with the June 1911 issue.

The character of Proteus Raymond was created by Michael White for Street & Smith's *Top-Notch Magazine* in 1911. A chemical criminologist in one of the most imaginative novelettes in the series, *The Viper of Portland* (February 15, 1912), utilizes radioactive saturnium rays to vaporize the bodies of the dead.

Many other scientific characters involved in detection appeared, but their numbers were held in check by Reeve's endless series of Craig Kennedy stories for a number of magazines. One such casualty was Stoddard Goodhue, who introduced Dr. Goodrich—"*the new* scientific detective. . . . His stories give us the scientific truths of the future in the guise of fiction"—with "The Phantom Auto" in the December 1921 issue of *Everybody's Magazine*. But after five stories, Reeve also began writing for *Everybody's*, and Dr. Goodrich disappeared from the scene.

The greatest exponent of the scientific or science fiction detective story was Hugo Gernsback (1884–1967), publisher of *Electrical Experimenter*, an early radio and popular science publication. His first story was "The Educated Harpoon," by Charles Wolfe, in which a man is stabbed to death on the sixteenth floor of his skyscraper office by a radio-controlled model airplane guided into an open window; it was published in the April 1920 issue. It introduced detective Joe Fenner, who appeared thereafter almost monthly in Gernsback's *Science and Invention* (a continuation of *Electrical Experimenter*). Gernsback published many science fiction detective stories by other authors in that magazine, including "A Subconscious Murderer," by Nellie E. Gardner, in which the hypnobioscope (Gernsback's own invention) was used to commit the crime. Gernsback published a substantial number of science fiction and wireless detective stories in another of his magazines, *Radio News*.

When Gernsback launched the first science fiction magazine, *Amazing Stories*, dated April 1926, he reprinted five Balmer and MacHarg Luther Trant stories; one was awarded the cover. He reprinted Wolfe's "The Educated Harpoon" and ran stories featuring six different scientific detectives: Merlin Moore Taylor's Robert Goodwin; A. Hyatt Verrill's (1871–1954) Curtis Thorne; W. F. Hammond's Fiske Errell; Charles Cloukey's David S. Harris; Edward S. Sears's Milton Jarvis; and, the most remarkable, the laconic Taine of San Francisco, creation of David H. Keller, M.D. (1880–1967), a completely colorless master of disguise. The plots were 100 percent science fiction. Taine made his debut with four stories in the Summer 1928 *Amazing Stories Quarterly*, in which Negroes turn themselves white in the first step toward conquering the white world.

The only magazine that even approached publishing the number of science fiction detective stories published by Gernsback was *Detective Fiction Weekly* (later *Flynn's Weekly*). Particularly noteworthy was a series by (Wilfred) Douglas Newton in which Odoric Dyn seeks to conquer the world and is thwarted by the efforts of detectives Raphel Phare and Martin Sondes.

With the issue dated January 1930, Gernsback launched the first magazine in history devoted entirely to science fiction and scientific detective stories, entitled appropriately *Scientific Detective Monthly* (later changed to *Amazing Detective Tales*). Reeve was his editorial consultant, and the magazine ran reprints of stories about Kennedy, Trant, R. Austin FREEMAN's Dr. Thorndyke (see THORNDYKE, DR.), and S. S. VAN DINE's Philo VANCE. However, after a few issues, most of the stories were new; among them were yarns about Taine of San Francisco.

The most unusual new detective was the Electrical Man (Miller Rand), created for the May 1930 issue by Neil R. Jones. Rand's clothes were completely electrified by radio waves, and would stun any man who touched him.

After ten issues Gernsback sold his rights to Wallace R. Bamber, publisher of *Far East Adventure Stories*, who eliminated all scientific detectives and carried straight action detective stories for the few issues he published.

Argosy included some outstanding science fiction detective stories from 1928 on; especially noteworthy was Garrett Smith's "You've Killed Privacy," in which closed-circuit television is used to guard against criminals; Erle Stanley GARDNER's "The Human Zero" (December 19, 1931), in which men vanish from locked rooms and no body is ever discovered; and Murray Leinster's (pseudonym of William Fitzgerald Jenkins, 1896–1975) enthralling series beginning with "The Darkness on Fifth Avenue" (November 30, 1929), in which criminals scientifically create artificial blackness as a cover for crime.

Fine scientific detective stories continued to appear in Gernsback's science fiction magazines, as well as in *Argosy* and *Detective Fiction Weekly* and, later, in *Amazing Stories, Fantastic Adventures,* and *Thrilling Wonder Stories*. But the real breakthrough for the modern science fiction detective yarn began with "Needle," by Hal Clement (pseudonym of Harry C. Stubbs, 1922–   ) in John W. Campbell's *Astounding-Science Fiction* in 1949, in which an alien space detective must discover which of the billions of human beings is host to his quarry; and it continued with "The Demolished Man," by Alfred Bester (1913–   ) in Horace Gold's *Galaxy Science Fiction* in 1952, based on the puzzle of how one could get away with murder in a world in which detectives can read minds. The apex of modern science fiction detective stories was reached with Isaac Asimov's (1920–   ) "The Caves of Steel" in *Galaxy Science Fiction* in 1953, in which the human detective Lije Baley must compete with the robot detective R. Daneel Olivaw in solving interplanetary crime.

SAM MOSKOWITZ

SCOTT, ANTHONY *See* HALLIDAY, BRETT.

SCOTT, WILL (WILLIAM MATTHEW) (1894?–1964). English author and artist. Born in Leeds, Yorkshire, he began his professional career as a free-lance caricaturist and cartoonist, worked as an art editor and critic, and contributed humorous features to *Everyweek* magazine. For health reasons, he moved to Herne Bay, Kent, in 1920, with his family. He founded the Herne Bay Mask Players, an amateur theatrical company, writing and producing plays for it between 1931 and 1939.

Scott produced more than 2,000 short stories during his lifetime (some under the pseudonym William Watt), selling them to *Pan, John Bull, The Strand* magazine, *Ellery Queen's Mystery Magazine,* and countless others. About 1952, at the suggestion of his small grandson, Scott began writing children's stories; the fourteen adventures of the Cherry family have been translated into four languages.

The anonymously edited *The Best (English) Detective Stories of the Year 1929* (1930) included Scott's "Clues." Some of the many stories about Giglamps, a combination hobo-detective-rogue, were published in *Giglamps*. The best and most popular of Scott's works, however, were the three novels involving DISHER, one of the first fat detectives.

The most successful London productions of Scott's plays were *Queer Fish, Married for Money,* and *The Limping Man,* which was also frequently broadcast by the BBC and was filmed in 1953. Later rewritten as the Disher novel *Shadows* (1928), it is about a former American soldier (Lloyd Bridges in the film) who returns to England to renew a romance with an English girl, only to find that she is involved with racketeers.

Geoffrey Williamson, former editor of *John Bull,* wrote of Scott (in the *Herne Bay Press*) that "his style was distinctive, especially notable for economy of expression and pleasing flashes of incisive and discerning wit. If he had O. HENRY's fertility of invention, he also possessed Saki's gift of brevity and more than a dash of G. K. CHESTERTON's love of paradox and the bizarre."

SEELEY, MABEL (HODNEFIELD) (1903–   ). American mystery novelist. Born in Minnesota, where she has spent most of her life, she studied writing with Mary Ellen Chase at the University of Minnesota in Minneapolis. Her husband taught at a high school in that city, as well as at the university, and she was an advertising copywriter for a Minneapolis department store before her first novel was published in 1938.

The Listening House (1938), her highly successful first mystery, was marked by many of the autobiographical elements expected in initial efforts. The heroine, a department store copywriter in "Schilling City," a fictional Midwestern state capital, encounters murder at the cheap lodging house in which she lives. Later Seeley books explore many aspects of Minnesota life. *The Crying Sisters* (1939) is set at a lake resort. The habits and speech patterns of the Norwegian immigrants among whom Mrs. Seeley grew up are discussed in *The Whispering Cup* (1940). *The Chuckling Fingers* (1941), set in the forests of northeastern Minnesota, contains many descriptions of the region's natural beauty and references to its Paul Bunyan and Indian legends. *Eleven Came Back* (1943), another mystery with elements of the outdoors, is set in the Grand Tetons of Wyoming; one of a dozen participants in a midnight horseback ride is murdered.

To mystery critics sated in the late 1930s with the worst excesses of the "HAD-I-BUT-KNOWN" SCHOOL, Mabel Seeley was regarded, in Howard HAYCRAFT's words, as the "white hope" of the American "feminine" detective story. She was praised by Haycraft for her use of realistic Midwestern backgrounds and her ability to create suspense, and by James SANDOE, who called *The Listening House* "a terrifying reply to those who object to the HIBK-school." However, the critics eventually came to believe that she never lived up to her potential.

SELBY, DOUG (Creator: Erle Stanley GARDNER). Gardner created many lawyer protagonists, but only Selby, the D. A., prosecutes criminals, although he spends more time solving murders than he does in court. He successfully ran as reform candidate for district attorney of California's fictional Madison County in 1936, and it was said that some voters selected him because of his curly hair, penetrating eyes, and good looks. In his first case, *The D. A. Calls It Murder,* he correctly contends that the mysterious little clergyman found dead in the Madison Hotel was murdered. Selby's unofficial assistant in most cases is Sylvia Martin, a beautiful and alert reporter on the *Clarion,* who loves him. Complications are provided by an attractive lawyer, Inez Stapleton, who has also set her sights on Selby. Selby's opponent is often "old A. B. C." (Alphonse Baker Carr), a wily local criminal attorney.

CHECKLIST

1937 *The D. A. Calls It Murder*
1938 *The D. A. Holds a Candle*
1939 *The D. A. Draws a Circle*
1940 *The D. A. Goes to Trial*
1942 *The D. A. Cooks a Goose*
1944 *The D. A. Calls a Turn*
1946 *The D. A. Breaks a Seal*
1948 *The D. A. Takes a Chance*
1949 *The D. A. Breaks an Egg*

Television

The crusading district attorney appeared in a two-hour telefilm, a possible series pilot.

They Call It Murder. Twentieth Century-Fox, 1971. Jim Hutton, Lloyd Bochner, Jessica Walter, Leslie Nielsen, Nita Talbot, Jo Ann Pflug.

In an episode based on *The D. A. Draws a Circle,* the D. A. investigates a drowning in a pool that is somehow connected to a car that went off a cliff, a large insurance claim, and a complicated switch of identity.

SHADOW, THE (Creator: Walter B. GIBSON as Maxwell Grant). The character most associated with pulp melodrama originally was an anonymous, wickedly mirthful narrator (once played by Orson Welles) of a series of radio mysteries that began in the late 1920s, wise to all the byways of evil and known only as "the Shadow." Street & Smith (*see* PULP MAGAZINES) soon began to issue a magazine, *The Shadow,* and attempted to flesh out its shadowy character by making him a black-cloaked, nearly omniscient stalker of underworld crime, a dread figure with many other secret identities (one of them being that of millionaire explorer Lamont Cranston), who, each week, would creep through the corridors of Mutual Broadcasting (many were on the lookout for him, the magazine often related, but he was never seen) to do his regular radio show.

Gradually, the Shadow's number of alter egos was reduced by his chronicler, Maxwell Grant, into a single identity—Cranston—and the radio series made full use of the medium by not merely suggesting that the Shadow blended into the darkness but,

This sinister portrait of the Shadow appeared on the cover of the first edition of *The Living Shadow*, published in 1931 by Street & Smith.

rather, declaring that he had learned "in the East" the power to cloud men's minds so as to become invisible. Only his "friend and companion" Margot Lane was aware of his hypnotic skill.

Films

The Shadow Strikes. Grand National, 1937. Rod La Rocque, Lynn Anders. Directed by Lynn Shores.

In the first Shadow film, "based on the Street & Smith story *The Ghost of the Manor*, by Maxwell Grant," a debonair criminologist misnamed Granston seeks to avenge his lawyer father's death at the hands of gangsters by occasionally—and without much enthusiasm—donning a cloak and black felt hat for a personal tangle with criminals. Only his meek manservant, Henry (Norman Ainsley), is aware that he is the Shadow. The mystery is of the murder mansion variety—a rich victim's many heirs, and those to whom they owe gambling debts, are all suspected of shooting him.

International Crime. Grand National, 1938. La Rocque. Directed by Charles Lamont.

This time, the Shadow appears sans disguise. With neither cape nor hat brim, he is a crime reporter who crusades against espionage agents and prewar fifth columnists. His scatterbrained secretary is named Phoebe Lane.

The Shadow. Columbia serial, 1940. Victor Jory, Veda Ann Borg. Directed by James Horne.

The best screen realization of the pulp magazine character, this fifteen-chapter serial featured stern, hawk-nosed Victor Jory as a Shadow magazine cover come to life. Margot Lane makes her first screen appearance, as do such Shadow aides as Harry Vincent, and Cranston employs a second secret identity, as an Oriental, Lin Chang. The Shadow's nemesis is the criminal mastermind known as the Black Tiger, who is determined to destroy and conquer the city; curiously, it is the Tiger who knows the secret of invisibility (his skills are more electronic than hypnotic). The Cobolt Club, exclusive gathering spot for the city's leading figures, and a familiar location in the pulp magazine stories, also appears in the serial; the Tiger has infiltrated the organization.

The Shadow Returns. Monogram, 1946. Kane Richmond, Barbara Reed, Tom Dugan, Joseph Crehan. Directed by Phil Rosen.

This is the first of three Monogram Shadow features that were released during 1946, with the same basic cast and directors. Kane Richmond is an aggressive and entertaining cloaked Cranston, not too busy for an occasional time-out with Margot, and taxi driver Shrevvie (George Chandler), recruited from the pulp magazine adventures, assists. The eerie opening scene takes place in a cemetery, and the action occurs mainly within the familiar walls of a murder mansion. In this film the Shadow discovers gems that contain secret formulas and also uncovers a "murder method" that causes the victims to fall from balconies.

Richard Derr, as Lamont Cranston, the Shadow, indulges in mystic exercises with Mark Daniels (left), his mentor, in *Bourbon Street Shadows* (also released as *Invisible Avenger*). [*Republic*]

Behind the Mask. Monogram, 1946. Richmond, Reed, Dugan, Crehan. Directed by Phil Karlson.

Lamont must interrupt his wedding to Margot because someone dressed in the Shadow's cloak has murdered a vicious newspaper columnist.

The Missing Lady. Monogram, 1946. Richmond, Reed, Dugan, Crehan. Directed by Karlson.

An art dealer is killed, and the jade statuette of a woman is stolen, in a case that leads the Shadow deep into the underworld.

Bourbon Street Shadows (Invisible Avenger). Republic, 1958 (filmed in New Orleans). Richard Derr, Mark Daniels, Helen Westcott. Directed by James Wong Howe and John Sledge.

The Shadow investigates the death of a friend, a Dixieland musician, and links the murder to the exiled president of Santa Cruz, who is hiding from his ruthless twin brother. In this film Cranston has the power to become invisible, having learned how to cloud men's minds from an Oriental mystic named Jogendra (Daniels) who has accompanied him to New Orleans.

SHAFFER, PETER AND ANTHONY. *See* ANTONY, PETER.

SHANNON, DELL. *See* LININGTON, ELIZABETH.

SHARP, LUKE. *See* BARR, ROBERT.

SHAW, JOSEPH T. *See* BLACK MASK; PULP MAGAZINES.

SHAYNE, MICHAEL (Creator: Brett HALLIDAY). Miami's most famous private detective began his literary career in 1939. Evidence in the Shayne saga places him in New York in 1935, working as a detective for the Worldwide Agency. Following the death of his young wife, Phyllis, in 1943, Shayne temporarily deserts Miami, setting up an office in New Orleans.

Mike Shayne is a rugged 6-foot 1-inch redhead who, though adept at the cerebral side of detection, is best known as a two-fisted operative, always extricating himself from danger. At his best in *A Taste for Violence,* Shayne settles a long-lasting Kentucky coal mine strike, cleans up a corrupt government, catches a murderer, and accepts an appointment as reform police chief for six months.

Shayne's loyalty extends not only to his clients but also to the people who have appeared in so many of his books: his secretary, Lucy Hamilton; his friend Timothy Rourke, reporter for the *Miami Daily News;* Will Gentry, chief of Miami detectives. When Shayne crosses the causeway to Miami Beach, however, he is generally met with hostility by Peter Painter, chief of detectives (later police chief) there. Although Shayne rescues the officious Painter from the kidnappers in *Murder in Haste,* there is little improvement in their relationship. In one unusual case, the man Shayne helps is Brett Halliday. In *She Woke to Darkness* Halliday is visiting New York City, attending the annual Mystery Writers of America awards dinner, when he becomes a murder suspect. Shayne travels from Miami to find the murderer and rescue the man who relates his adventures.

As Shayne enters his fourth decade as a detective, he is as rugged as ever, although his hair is graying. He drinks much brandy—preferably Martell's—and has a new interest—football. In *Violence Is Golden* he is watching a game at the Orange Bowl when an attempt is made on his life. His client in *Fourth Down to Death* is the Miami Dolphins; his fee, if he is successful, stock in the team.

CHECKLIST

1939 *Dividend on Death*
1940 *The Private Practice of Michael Shayne*
1940 *The Uncomplaining Corpses*
1941 *Tickets for Death*
1941 *Bodies Are Where You Find Them* (in Great Britain, published in *Michael Shayne Investigates*)
1942 *The Corpse Came Calling* (in Great Britain, published in *Michael Shayne Investigates*)
1943 *Murder Wears a Mummer's Mask* (in Great Britain, published in *Michael Shayne Takes a Hand*)
1943 *Blood on the Black Market* (in Great Britain, published in *Michael Shayne Takes a Hand*)
1944 *Michael Shayne's Long Chance*
1944 *Murder and the Married Virgin*
1945 *Murder Is My Business*
1945 *Marked for Murder*
1946 *Blood on Biscayne Bay*
1947 *Counterfeit Wife*
1948 *Blood on the Stars* (British title: *Murder Is a Habit*)
1948 *Michael Shayne's Triple Mystery* (three novelettes)
1949 *A Taste for Violence*
1949 *Call for Michael Shayne*
1950 *This Is It, Michael Shayne*
1951 *Framed in Blood*
1951 *When Dorinda Dances*
1952 *What Really Happened*
1953 *One Night with Nora* (British title: *The Lady Came by Night*)
1954 *She Woke to Darkness*
1955 *Death Has Three Lives*
1955 *Stranger in Town*
1956 *The Blonde Cried Murder*
1957 *Weep for a Blonde*
1957 *Shoot the Works*
1958 *Murder and the Wanton Bride*
1958 *Fit to Kill*
1959 *Date with a Dead Man*
1959 *Target: Mike Shayne*
1959 *Die Like a Dog*
1960 *Murder Takes No Holiday*
1960 *Dolls Are Deadly*
1960 *The Homicidal Virgin*
1961 *Killer from the Keys*
1961 *Murder in Haste*
1961 *The Careless Corpse*
1962 *Pay-Off in Blood*
1962 *Murder by Proxy*
1962 *Never Kill a Client*
1963 *Too Friendly, Too Dead*
1963 *The Corpse That Never Was*
1963 *The Body Came Back*
1964 *A Redhead for Mike Shayne*
1964 *Shoot to Kill*
1964 *Michael Shayne's Fiftieth Case*
1965 *The Violent World of Michael Shayne*
1966 *Nice Fillies Finish Last*
1966 *Murder Spins the Wheel*
1966 *Armed . . . Dangerous . . .*
1967 *Mermaid on the Rocks*
1967 *Guilty as Hell*
1968 *So Lush, So Deadly*
1968 *Violence Is Golden*
1969 *Lady Be Bad*
1970 *Six Seconds to Kill*
1970 *Fourth Down to Death*
1971 *Count Backwards to Zero*
1971 *I Come to Kill You*
1972 *Caught Dead*
1973 *Kill All the Young Girls*
1973 *Blue Murder*
1974 *Last Seen Hitchhiking*
1974 *At the Point of a .38*

Films

Shayne was the liberated screen investigator of the 1940s, more assured, less dour than the breed had been during the previous decade.

Michael Shayne, Private Detective. Twentieth Century-Fox, 1941. Lloyd Nolan, Marjorie Weaver, Douglas Dumbrille, Walter Abel. Directed by Eugene Forde. Based on *The Private Practice of Michael Shayne.*

A practical joke of Shayne's backfires when the blood-soaked body of a racketeer is found inside the car owned by a girl he has been hired to watch.

Sleepers West. Twentieth Century-Fox, 1941. Nolan, Lynn Bari, Mary Beth Hughes, Louis Jean Heydt, Don Douglas. Directed by Forde. Based on *Sleepers East* (1933) by Frederick Nebel.

Shayne is on the San Francisco–bound express guarding an important witness (Hughes) at a murder trial; also aboard are a private detective who has been paid to kill Shayne's charge and a girl reporter (Bari) who was once in love with Mike.

Dressed to Kill. Twentieth Century-Fox, 1941. Nolan, Hughes, Sheila Ryan, William Demarest. Directed by Forde.

As Shayne is leaving the marriage license bureau with his girl (Hughes), he hears a scream and turns his attention to a double murder during which two guns were fired but only one shot was heard. At the end of the film, Shayne has been stood up.

Blue, White and Perfect. Twentieth Century-Fox, 1941. Nolan, Hughes, George Reeves, Helen Reynolds, Steven Geray. Directed by Herbert I. Leeds.

German spies smuggle uncut diamonds out of the country, and Shayne follows the gems on board a ship heading for Honolulu.

The Man Who Wouldn't Die. Twentieth Century-Fox, 1942. Nolan, Weaver, Reynolds, Paul Harvey, Henry Wilcoxon. Directed by Leeds. Based on the 1939 novel *The Footprints on the Ceiling,* by Clayton RAWSON.

On the grounds of a sinister mansion, at night, a body is placed in a pit. Shayne learns that the supposed victim was one of the few professional magicians to have mastered the "buried-alive" trick.

Just Off Broadway. Twentieth Century-Fox, 1942. Nolan, Weaver, Janis Carter, Phil Silvers, Richard Derr. Directed by Leeds.

Shayne gets a sixty-day jail sentence for violating courtroom rules when, as a juror, he solves the murder of a witness who is killed while testifying during a trial.

Time to Kill. Twentieth Century-Fox, 1942. Nolan, Heather Angel, Ethel Griffies, Ralph Byrd, Richard Lane. Directed by Leeds. Based on Raymond CHANDLER's Philip MARLOWE mystery *The High Window* (1942).

A rare coin is missing, and Shayne suspects the owner's high-strung secretary—who is sure that she has committed murder.

Murder Is My Business. PRC, 1946. Hugh Beaumont (the second screen Shayne), Cheryl Walker, George Meeker, Lyle Talbot, Ralph Dunn. Directed by Sam Newfield.

Shayne is hired by a wealthy woman to cope with a playboy who is trying to blackmail her; soon both the client and the playboy are murdered.

Larceny in Her Heart. PRC, 1946. Beaumont, Walker, Gordon Richards, Dunn, Paul Bryar. Directed by Newfield.

Shayne postpones a vacation with his girl (Walker) when a civic leader asks him to locate his stepdaughter. The girl's double is killed in Shayne's office, but the real missing daughter is actually locked in a madhouse—to which Shayne has himself committed.

Blonde for a Day. PRC, 1946. Beaumont, Kathryn Adams, Cy Kendall, Marjorie Hoshelle, Sonia Sorel. Directed by Newfield.

Shayne involves himself in a series of neighborhood apartment murders when he tries to uncover why one of his friends, a newspaperman, was shot. He tangles with some dangerous ladies.

Three on a Ticket. PRC, 1947. Beaumont, Walker, Dunn, Gavin Gordon, Douglas Fowley, Louise Currie. Directed by Newfield.

A private investigator dies in Shayne's office, a baggage ticket in his pocket.

Too Many Winners. PRC, 1947. Beaumont, Trudy Marshall, Claire Carlton, Byron Foulger, Grandon Rhodes. Directed by William Beaudine.

A blackmailer offers to sell Shayne information about how racetrack pari-mutuel tickets are being forged.

Radio and Television

Jeff Chandler starred as Mike Shayne in a brief weekly radio series, *Michael Shayne, Private Detective.* In 1960 Richard Denning portrayed Shayne for a season in thirty-two hour-long television programs set in Miami.

SHELLEY, MARY (1797–1851). English novelist, known mainly as the author of *Frankenstein: or, The Modern Prometheus* (1818) and as the wife of the poet Percy Bysshe Shelley (*see* FRANKENSTEIN). Born in London, Mary Shelley was the daughter of William GODWIN and Mary Wollstonecraft, the first radical feminist, who died a few days after giving birth. A month before her seventeenth birthday, Mary Wollstonecraft Godwin eloped with Shelley, who was a friend of Godwin. Shelley was twenty-one years old and married; his wife committed suicide two years later, and he and Mary were then able to be married. Suffering severe depression because of her mother's death (for which she blamed herself) and the early deaths of her first three children, she wrote *Frankenstein* when she was twenty. Deeply influenced by the genius of her husband and his friends (especially Lord Byron), she never again produced a work of the excellence she achieved in this tale of Dr. Victor Frankenstein and his monster, although she wrote several other books, including *Valperga: or, The Life and Adventures of Castruccio, Prince of Lucca* (1823), a medieval Italian romance; *The Last Man* (1826); and the autobiographical *Lodore* (1835). After her husband died (1822), she remained nearly impoverished for twenty years, turning down numerous offers of marriage from Edward Trelawny, Washington Irving, John Howard Payne, and others because, she said, "I want to be Mary Shelley on my tombstone."

SHERINGHAM, ROGER (Creator: Anthony BERKELEY). Born in 1891 in a small provincial town near London, Sheringham obtained a small scholarship to one of the old and snobbish public schools and in 1910 went up to Merton College, Oxford, where he studied history and the classics. Adept at rugby and punting, he also excelled at golf. He graduated just in time to serve in World War I and was slightly wounded twice. After short careers in business, teaching, and farming, Sheringham dashed off a novel as a lark. Accepted by a publisher, it became an overnight best seller. Further novels and work in crime journalism followed, although Sheringham was aware of his literary shortcomings, cheerfully sneering at his reading public.

A little below average height and stocky, he has a round face and is usually engaged in smoking a short-stemmed pipe with a large bowl, drinking beer, or talking—usually nonsense.

Sheringham is rude, vain, loquacious, and offensive. As he became more popular, an attempt was made to smooth over his rough edges and have him conform to the more conventional picture of a great detective. A. B. Cox (Anthony Berkeley) said that Sheringham was "founded on an offensive person I once knew because in my original innocence I thought it would be amusing to have an offensive detective. Since he has been taken in all seriousness, I have had to tone his offensiveness down and pretend he never was." Sheringham is very fallible, as evidenced by his incorrect solution to *The Poisoned Chocolates Case*.

CHECKLIST

1925 *The Layton Court Mystery*
1926 *The Wychford Poisoning Case*
1927 *Roger Sheringham and the Vane Mystery* (U.S. title: *The Mystery at Lovers' Cave*)
1928 *The Silk Stocking Murders*
1929 *The Poisoned Chocolates Case*
1930 *The Second Shot*
1931 *Top Storey Murder* (U.S. title: *Top Story Murder*)
1932 *Murder in the Basement*
1933 *Jumping Jenny* (U.S. title: *Dead Mrs. Stratton*)
1934 *Panic Party* (U.S. title: *Mr. Pidgeon's Island*)

SHERLOCK HOLMES SOCIETY OF LONDON. *See* ORGANIZATIONS.

SHIEL, M[ATTHEW] P[HIPPS] (1865–1947). English author of fantastic fiction and mysteries and creator of Prince ZALESKI, one of the most original and bizarre detectives in literature.

Shiel was born in the West Indies, the first son (after eight daughters) of a Methodist preacher. On his fifteenth birthday, Shiel's Irish father had him crowned king of Redonda, a small island that no government had bothered to claim. He attended King's College, London, and then studied medicine at St. Bartholomew's, but he quickly abandoned his interest in that career and turned to literature. He married a Spanish beauty, Carolina García Gómez, who died five years later; fifteen years after her death, he married Mrs. Lydia (Fawley) Jewson, described as resembling his first wife and his mother; they separated in 1929. Raised in a religious atmosphere, he was devout, if unorthodox, and created his own religion. He devoted the last part of his life to writing a biography of Jesus Christ.

Shiel's unusual literary style is archaic, picturesque, complex, ornate—and impossible to take in heavy doses. His vocabulary is immense, and he eschews simple words for obscure ones. One critic said that Shiel's characters seem intoxicated, but drugged seems to be a more applicable term—the suggestion is possibly equally valid in reference to their creator.

His first book, *Prince Zaleski* (1895; s.s.), was followed by a long series of indescribably fantastic

M. P. Shiel, in a drawing by Neil Austin.

novels, many of which have elements of mystery and detection, notably *The Rajah's Sapphire* (1896), *The Weird o' It* (1902), *Unto the Third Generation* (1903), *The Lost Viol* (1905), *How the Old Woman Got Home* (1927), *Dr. Krasinkski's Secret* (1929), and *The Black Box* (1930). *The Pale Ape* (1911) is a rare collection of stories including an adventure of Cummings King Monk, another bizarre detective.

Shiel collaborated with Louis TRACY on several mystery-detective novels, published under the pseudonym Gordon HOLMES.

SILVER, MISS MAUD (Creator: Patricia WENTWORTH). One of the most popular spinster detectives, Miss Silver is an elderly former governess who has retired on a small, fixed income. Tired of a shabby existence and gifts of clothing from her niece, she becomes a private investigator, and by the time of her debut in print, she has built up a considerable reputation. She is described as "a little person with no features, no complexion, and a great deal of tidy mouse-coloured hair done in a large bun at the back of her head." She knits while interviewing her clients, and she frequently says, "Pray, proceed," to encourage them as they tell their tale of woe. Scotland Yard inspectors have not been ashamed to ask for, and receive, her free assistance.

Although Maud (sometimes called "Maudie") Silver is a moralist who has a penchant for helping young lovers in distress, she is not an intuitive detective. She depends upon pure logic to solve problems such as that in *The Brading Collection*, in which the owner of a very valuable collection of jewels, all of which are connected with the famous crimes of history, is murdered. Maud Silver was one of the few detectives in literary history popular enough to have a fan club.

CHECKLIST

1928 *Grey Mask*
1937 *The Case Is Closed*
1939 *Lonesome Road*
1941 *In the Balance* (British title: *Danger Point*)
1943 *The Chinese Shawl*
1943 *Miss Silver Deals with Death* (British title: *Miss Silver Intervenes*)
1944 *The Clock Strikes Twelve*
1944 *The Key*
1945 *She Came Back* (British title: *The Traveller Returns*)
1946 *Pilgrim's Rest*
1947 *The Latter End*
1947 *Wicked Uncle* (British title: *The Spotlight*)
1948 *The Eternity Ring*
1948 *The Case of William Smith*
1949 *Miss Silver Comes to Stay*
1949 *The Catharine Wheel*
1950 *The Brading Collection*
1950 *Through the Wall*
1951 *The Ivory Dagger*
1951 *Anna, Where Are You?*
1952 *Watersplash*
1952 *Ladies' Bane*
1953 *Out of the Past*
1953 *The Vanishing Point*
1954 *The Silent Pool*
1954 *The Benevent Treasure*
1955 *Poison in the Pen*
1955 *The Listening Eye*
1955 *The Gazebo*
1956 *The Fingerprint*
1958 *The Alington Inheritance*
1961 *The Girl in the Cellar*

SIM, GEORGES. *See* SIMENON, GEORGES.

SIMENON, GEORGES (JOSEPH CHRISTIAN) (1903–). Belgian mystery writer; creator of Jules MAIGRET. One of the most prolific of all writers, with more than 200 novels to his credit, Simenon is also a master of the psychological novel. He was born in Liège to a middle-class family of Breton and Dutch stock. His father made a meager living as an insurance salesman, and his mother took in university students as boarders. His plans to enter either the church or the Army—whichever would offer the most spare time for writing—were thwarted by the elder Simenon's death, and Georges had to leave school at sixteen to earn a living. His first job, as an apprentice to a baker, did not interest him, but he then obtained a job in a bookstore and was able to spend long hours reading. He did not stay there very long, though, for he soon became a cub reporter on the *Gazette de Liège*, covering the police court beat. One month later he had his own column (it continued for three years), and he also began to write short stories and novels. He wrote a novel, *Au Pont des Arches*, in ten days. Published in 1920 (when Simenon was seventeen), it remains untranslated.

After Simenon received military training in the cavalry, he emigrated in 1923 to Paris, where he produced about 300 stories by writing 80 pages a day—under many pseudonyms, including Christian Brulls, Jean du Perry, and Georges Sim. He earned enough to buy a car and a yacht and to hire a chauffeur.

Realizing the triviality of his early efforts, Simenon wanted to write more serious works. His solution, to travel about and meet interesting people, led him to spend much time aboard his yacht, the *Ostrogoth*, cruising and writing. Tentative efforts to produce a detective hero finally resulted in a 60,000-word novel, *The Strange Case of Peter the Lett*, written in September 1929, near Delfzijl, in the Netherlands, and featuring Maigret (published in 1931). He turned out eighteen more Maigret novels, at the rate of one a month, but became weary of the character and abandoned him in favor of more serious work.

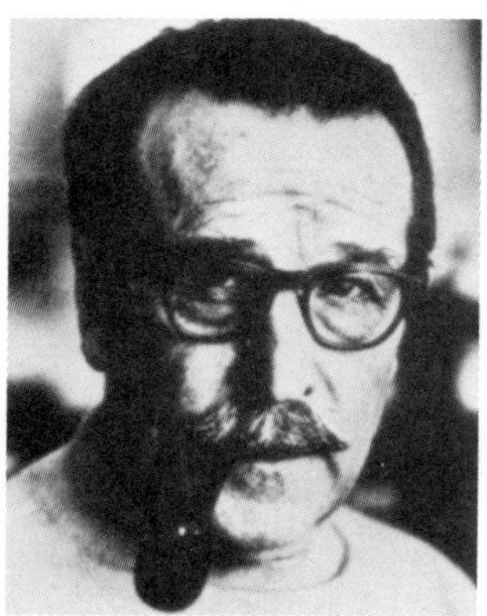

Georges Simenon. [*Horst Tappe*]

In the meantime, the Maigret series had become enormously popular, and by the end of the first year of publication (1931) had been translated into eighteen languages. Maigret soon became as popular in France as Sherlock HOLMES had become in England and the United States. Maigret did not sell very well in England and the United States, however, until publishers issued the stories two to a volume. Additional translations and film (and later television) adaptations brought added fame and wealth to Simenon, but he had lost interest in Maigret. For the next decade he wrote a series of probing psychological novels—among other works—of about 60,000 words each. André Gide called him "perhaps the greatest and most truly 'novelistic' novelist in France today."

Simenon was able to write a book in three or four days when he was young, but he later restricted his output to about a dozen books a year when he began to strive for quality. He immersed himself in his protagonist and the environment of the story to the total neglect of all other matters, writing out a chapter a day for eight to eleven days until he had a completed manuscript. He claimed that he could not write longer works because he was unable to tolerate this degree of identification much longer than two weeks. The manuscript would be put away for a week, and then Simenon would spend two or three days going over and "touching it up" slightly before mailing it to his publisher.

In the early 1940s Simenon returned to Maigret as a form of relaxation from more strenuous literary efforts. Several short stories from this period were later translated and published in *Ellery Queen's Mystery Magazine.*

During the war (1939–1945) Simenon lived in unoccupied France and organized aid for refugees from Paris. In 1948 the semiautobiographical *Pedigree*, a 544-page novel that many critics consider to be his best work, was published.

Simenon spent the next decade in the United States, in New York, Arizona, Florida, California, and Connecticut. By the 1950s his production had slowed to six novels a year, Maigret appearing in only one or two of them. Simenon returned to Europe in 1955 and spent much time in travel. He, his wife, and four children finally settled in a small village near Lausanne, Switzerland, and he slowed his pace to four volumes per year. Notebooks he kept from 1960 to 1963 were published as *When I Was Old* (1970), later translated for publication in the United States in 1971. In early 1973 Simenon announced that, owing to ill health, he would give up writing because he wanted to live his own life and not in the skin of his characters.

The early and better Maigret novels are unpopular with many mystery readers because they do not involve elaborate feats of ratiocination, although they do have some psychological insight and exemplify Simenon's forte—the evocation of atmosphere with a few deft strokes of the pen. He has had some influence on the type of police procedural novel that is popular today, and his influence on current Continental mystery writers has been enormous. If Simenon is to be judged in this genre, it must be as an author of crime, not detective, stories.

Of Simenon's non-Maigret books, there are three historically important volumes of short stories that were published beginning in 1932: *Les 13 Énigmes*, *Les 13 Mystères*, and *Les 13 Coupables*. The last-mentioned was included in QUEEN'S QUORUM, and Alexander Woollcott regarded all three volumes highly. Except for the few that appeared in early issues of *EQMM*, most of these stories have not been translated.

One of Simenon's important full-length novels, *The Man Who Watched the Trains Go By* (1938), is the story of a dull family man from Holland, Kees Popinga, who embezzles his firm's money, kills a cabaret dancer, and flees to Paris, where he engages in, and loses, a battle of wits with the police, carried out through the newspapers. Simenon characters find that confession is good for the soul. In *The Girl in His Past* (1951), a murderer tells all to a psychiatrist. In *Act of Passion* (1947), the tortured protagonist feels compelled to write a full account of his crimes to a judge. In the full-length *The Snow Was Black* (1948), regarded as one of Simenon's best works, the central character has committed every possible despicable act; he kills a German guard in occupied France and, through torture and death, achieves expiation for his crimes.

Films

Temptation Harbour. Monogram (British), 1947. Robert Newton, Simone Simon, William Hartnell. Directed by Lance Comfort.

A railroad worker finds a suitcase full of money and decides to keep it—to give his motherless daughter a measure of security. The film was based on the novel *Newhaven-Dieppe,* which was published in *Affairs of Destiny* (1942).

Midnight Episode. Triangle (British), 1950. Stanley Holloway, Leslie Dwyer, Reginald Tate. Directed by Gordon Parry.

A tramp and his discovery—a discarded wallet—help the police trap a killer. The film was based on the novel *Monsieur La Souris* (1938).

Paris Express (British title: *The Man Who Watched the Trains Go By*). Compton (British), 1953. Claude Rains, Marta Toren, Marius Goring, Anouk Aimée, Herbert Lom. Directed by Harold French.

A trusted clerk steals money from his firm and flees on the Paris train. Based on the 1938 novel.

A Life in the Balance. Twentieth Century-Fox, 1955. Ricardo Montalban, Anne Bancroft, Lee Marvin, Jose Perez. Directed by Harry Horner.

During Mexico City's Independence Day celebrations, a ten-year-old boy becomes the hostage of a homicidal maniac.

The Bottom of the Bottle. Twentieth Century-Fox, 1956. Van Johnson, Joseph Cotten, Ruth Roman. Directed by Henry Hathaway. Based on the novel *Le Fond de la Bouteille* (1949; English title: *The Bottom of the Bottle*).

A convict who has escaped from prison turns up one rainy night at his wealthy brother's ranch, a posse close behind.

The Snow Was Black. Continental (French), 1956. Daniel Gelin, Marie Mansart, Valentina Tessier. Directed by Luis Saslavsky. Based on the 1948 novel.

During the occupation of France, a black marketeer kills an old woman so that he can steal antique clocks for a Nazi general.

Love Is My Profession. Kingsley International (French), 1959. Jean Gabin, Brigitte Bardot, Edwige Feuillère, Franco Interlenghi. Directed by Claude Autant-Lara. Based on *In Case of Emergency* (1956).

A prostitute involved in a minor jewelry-store holdup asks a famous lawyer to help her, offering her body as a fee.

The Passion of Slow Fire. Trans-Lux (French), 1962. Jean Desailly, Alexandra Stewart. Directed by Édouard Molinaro. Based on the novel *La Mort de Belle* (1952; English title: *Belle*).

A girl boarding with a college instructor and his wife is murdered; he is a suspect and, though innocent, comes to realize how dull his life has been.

SIMPSON, HELEN (DEGUERRY) (1897–1940). British playwright and author of mystery novels and short stories. Born in Sydney, Australia, Miss Simpson went to France to complete her education and then studied music at Oxford. She lived alternately in England and Australia and married Denis J. Browne, an Australian surgeon. They had one daughter, Clemence, named for Miss Simpson's close friend and collaborator, Clemence Dane (pseudonym of Winifred Ashton; 1888–1965). While recovering from surgery in a London hospital in October 1940, Miss Simpson died when German bombs struck the building.

She wrote her first novel, *Reprisal* (1925), on a bet, completing it in three weeks. With Clemence Dane, she wrote two mysteries with a theatrical background, *Enter Sir John* (1928) and *Re-enter Sir John* (1932). The amateur detective in these "novels of character" is Sir John Saumarez, famed actor-manager. The two authors also collaborated on a play, the light comedy *Gooseberry Fool,* which was successfully produced in London in 1929.

Miss Simpson was also the sole author of several short stories and novels, including *The Prime Minister Is Dead* (1931), a suspenseful story of British politics and sports. In addition, she wrote novels chronicling Australian history, including *Boomerang* (1932) and *Under Capricorn* (1937).

SIMS, GEORGE R[OBERT] (1847–1922). English poet, novelist, playwright, journalist, and short story writer. Born in London, he was educated at Hanwell College and Bonn University and then worked as a journalist. He married Florence Wykes in 1901. Most of his work, including plays and poetry, was devoted to describing the difficult life of the poor.

Sims's most important contribution to crime and detective fiction is *Dorcas Dene, Detective* (1897; another collection of stories, bearing the same title, was published in 1898). These tales involve one of the first female detectives, Dorcas Dene (nee Lester), an actress who leaves the stage to earn money as a detective when her young artist husband becomes blind. The pretty Mrs. Dene quickly becomes one of the most successful detectives in England.

Sims's best-known novels are *The Mystery of Mary Ann* (1907) and *The Case of George Candlemas* (1890), in which Sir Arthur Strangeways answers personal advertisements and finds himself in many peculiar circumstances resulting from his desire to be a detective. Among Sims's numerous short story collections are *Rogues and Vagabonds* (1885), *Tales of Today* (1889), *Dramas of Life* (1890), *Tinkletop's Crime and Other Stories* (1891), *My Two Wives and Other Stories* (1894), *Life Stories of Today* (1896), *Biographs of Babylon* (1902), *The Mysteries of Modern London* (1906), and *The Death Gamble* (1909; stories based on real-life insurance crimes).

SJÖWALL, MAJ. *See* WAHLÖÖ, PER.

SMALL, RABBI DAVID (Creator: Harry KEMELMAN). The rabbi's training in *pilpul,* the hairsplitting Talmudic logic, ideally suits him for his role as detective. It has been said that he "can see the third side of any question." Detection is an avocation; Small's main concern is his congregation in Barnard's Crossing, a fictional Massachusetts town. However, since his debut, his solutions to murder have been an important factor in his retaining his position. Each time his contract comes up for renewal, he is opposed by some members of his temple because he is regarded as *too* honest and lacking in some of the social graces. In *Friday the Rabbi Slept Late* he is a suspect himself when a pregnant girl is found murdered in the temple parking lot.

Although a young man, Small is regarded by some as old-fashioned. In *Sunday the Rabbi Stayed Home* he confronts rebellious youths, exponents of the drug culture, and an anti-Semitic black militant. His good friend throughout the series, Hugh Lanigan, Barnard's Crossing's police chief, is a Catholic. In addition to discussing murders, Small and Lanigan have engaged in many truly ecumenical discussions of religion. Because he is absentminded, the rabbi is fortunate to have a very practical wife, Miriam, the mother of his young son, Jonathan.

CHECKLIST

1964 *Friday the Rabbi Slept Late*
1966 *Saturday the Rabbi Went Hungry*
1969 *Sunday the Rabbi Stayed Home*
1972 *Monday the Rabbi Took Off*
1973 *Tuesday the Rabbi Saw Red*

SMITH, CAESAR. See HALL, ADAM.

SMITH, ELIZABETH THOMASINA MEADE. See MEADE, L. T.

SMITH, ERNEST BRAMAH. See BRAMAH, ERNEST.

SNOW, C[HARLES] P[ERCY] (1905–). English novelist and physicist. Lord Snow (he was knighted in 1957 and made a life peer in 1964) is best known for his series of novels (beginning with *Strangers and Brothers,* published in 1940) that portray English life from 1920 to the present as viewed through the eyes of one central character, Lewis Eliot. Snow's first book, however, was a witty detective novel, *Death under Sail* (1932), which features the arrogant Detective Sergeant Aloysius Birrell, who has read virtually everything written about factual and fictional crime, and the more helpful Finbow, a civil servant on leave from Hong Kong. A small group of people are cruising on a yacht off the coast of England when the captain is found with a bullet in his heart. The holiday makers are forced to stay together in a primitive local cottage until the shrewd psychological insight of Finbow unravels the mystery.

SOMERS, PAUL. See GARVE, ANDREW.

SPADE, SAM (Creator: Dashiell HAMMETT). When private detective Sam Spade appeared in *The Maltese Falcon,* a five-part serial beginning in BLACK MASK magazine in 1929 and a best-selling book in 1930, one of the most famous detectives in American literature was born. He knows every cop and every hood in San Francisco (which he calls "my burg"), and they know and respect him, because he is part of both their worlds. He is idealistic, if not honest, and breaks the law frequently, but usually to help bring a criminal to justice. He is the ultimate "hard-boiled dick," able to laugh at loaded guns, cops, gangsters, politicians, and seductive women.

He has the face of a pleasant Satan, marked by a recurring series of V's. He has a long, bony jaw, a jutting V of a chin under a more flexible V of a mouth. His nostrils pull back to form another V, smaller than the others. His yellow-green eyes are nearly horizontal, but the Vs begin again with the thick eyebrows that rise outward from twin creases above his hooked nose. His pale-brown hair grows down from high flat temples to a V point on his forehead. He keeps his lips tightly closed when he smiles, and all the V's grow longer. Casper Gutman, his fat adversary in *The Maltese Falcon,* calls him "wild, astonishing, unpredictable, amazing." Incredibly, for a man of action, he does not carry a gun.

The Maltese Falcon, called the best American detective novel by some critics, opens with Spade accepting a case from Brigid O'Shaughnessy, a statuesque redhead masquerading as a Miss Wonderly. Almost immediately, his partner, Miles Archer, is killed. Spade hated him and has been having an affair with his wife, but feels duty-bound to find his killer. He becomes involved with an odd assortment of characters, each searching for a statue of a black bird, about a foot high, said to be worth a fortune.

Most of the characters in *The Maltese Falcon* were modeled on people Hammett had known as a Pinkerton agent, but Spade had no prototype. He was, said Hammett, "idealized . . . in the sense that he is what most of the private detectives I've worked with would *like* to have been." The typical private eye wants "to be a hard and shifty fellow," continues Hammett, "able to take care of himself in any situation, able to get the best of anybody he comes in contact with."

Sam Spade also appeared in three short stories collected in *The Adventures of Sam Spade and Other Stories* (1944).

Films

The Maltese Falcon, which introduced Spade to the 1930s, a period he perfectly mirrored, was filmed no less than three times in ten years. The third version is an American classic.

Called by many the finest private eye film ever made, *The Maltese Falcon* (1941) was director John Huston's first effort. Here, Humphrey Bogart (left) discusses the falcon with the cast of villains: Peter Lorre, Mary Astor, and Sydney Greenstreet. [*Warner Brothers*]

The Maltese Falcon. Warner Brothers, 1931. Ricardo Cortez, Bebe Daniels, Dudley Digges, Una Merkel, Thelma Todd. Directed by Roy Del Ruth.

Sam Spade and his partner are hired by a frightened girl to trail a man; the partner is killed. Sam learns that the girl is in league with crooks and is trying to find a statue of a black falcon that is worth a fortune; he suspects that she is a murderer.

Satan Met a Lady. Warner Brothers, 1936. Warren William (playing the Spade character, more debonair and unprincipled and renamed Ted Shayne), Bette Davis, Alison Skipworth, Arthur Treacher, Marie Wilson. Directed by William Dieterle.

A private detective is hired by three crooks to locate a horn filled with jewels; he plans on double-crossing the trio and selling the horn himself but is sidetracked by the murder of his partner, who he suspects was killed by one of the three crooks. In this version, the "fat man" crook is played by a hulking, domineering old woman (Skipworth).

The Maltese Falcon. Warner Brothers, 1941. Humphrey Bogart, Mary Astor, Sydney Greenstreet, Peter Lorre, Elisha Cook, Jr., Jerome Cowan. Directed by John Huston.

This film, which closely follows the Hammett novel (adapted by director Huston), is the definitive detective film. A dour, haunted Spade probes his partner's puzzling murder through dark streets and cheap rooms, dealing with eccentric criminals (Greenstreet as the immense Gutman and Lorre as the homosexual Joel Cairo reaped a decade of top-billed melodrama roles from this one film) who pursue a falcon statue from Malta that has a fortune in gems hidden in its base. At the end, the statue is empty, and so is Sam's triumph in turning in his partner's killer. There has never been another Sam Spade film.

Radio

Howard Duff portrayed a less driven Spade in a popular weekly radio series, *Sam Spade,* debuting on CBS in 1946; each broadcast was a telephone report of a new case to secretary Effie (Lurene Tuttle). Closely identified with the program was its hair-tonic sponsor—and the recurring jingle "Get Wildroot Creme Oil, Charlie. . . ." When Hammett encountered political difficulties, the radio Spade vanished, but he was replaced by a remarkably similar character, in his own brief weekly series, *Charlie Wild, Private Eye.*

SPILLANE, MICKEY (1918–   ). American mystery novelist. Born Frank Morrison Spillane in Brooklyn, N.Y., he was raised in a tough neighborhood in Elizabeth, N.J. In an unusual reversal of the

Anthony Quinn (right) is the amnesiac hero of Spillane's *The Long Wait,* seeking clues to his identity from town leader Charles Coburn. [*United Artists*]

ordinary sequence, he began writing for "slick" magazines in 1935 and, after some success, turned his talents to the PULP MAGAZINES. As a comic book writer, he was one of the originators of superheroes Captain Marvel and Captain America, among others. During World War II he trained pilots and flew combat missions for the Air Force. After the war he wrote more comic strip and magazine stories, was a trampoline performer for the Ringling Brothers, Barnum and Bailey circus, and later worked with federal agents to break a narcotics ring (he still has the scars from two bullet wounds and a knife stab as mementos). He became a Jehovah's Witness in 1952. In 1965 he married his second wife, Sherry, a beautiful blonde model featured on the dust wrapper of *The Erection Set* (1972).

Spillane and his major hero, Mike HAMMER, are alike in many ways. Both men are big, strong, tough, and direct. The resemblance is close enough so that Spillane himself posed for dust wrapper photographs and starred in the motion picture version of *The Girl Hunters*.

The cliché that Spillane's novels are filled with sex and violence is an oversimplification. The violence is undeniably there, often perpetrated by one of his heroes. Sex, however, is generally described only in the vaguest, most euphemistic terms. The sex passages would not shock schoolchildren today, although the early works were more explicit than most of their contemporaries. Lacking all literary pretension, Spillane claims that he writes only for the money. As Norman Mailer pointed out, however, that is not the question; the significant point is whether it is done well, and the enormous success of Spillane's work indicates that its appeal does not rest merely on public interest in sadism. Of all American writers, only Erle Stanley GARDNER has had greater sales, and Spillane has produced only a fraction as many books. At one time, a list of the top ten best-selling American fictional works of the twentieth century contained the first seven Spillane novels.

This public enthusiasm has rarely been shared by critics, who almost uniformly condemn the brutality of his characters. Occasionally, however, they grudgingly admit to the power of Spillane's work—an honest, incisive, accurate, gripping, and realistic (and often romantic) style that propels the reader along with the action. The objectivist philosopher and novelist Ayn Rand compared reading Spillane to hearing a military band in a public park. There is no phoniness in Spillane—the man, the stylist, or the storyteller—and all his books are highly readable. There is also a clear-cut morality about his heroes that is absent in most contemporary novels. Hammer, Tiger Mann, and the others are honest and incorruptible, despite the illegal acts they often commit. When they break a villain's arm, or shoot him in the stomach, he has invariably deserved the treatment, and no whining self-remorse follows the retribution. Although Hammer's philosophy has been compared to James BOND's, he has a stronger sense of morality and will risk his life for what he believes to be right—even if "right" is an abstract ideal to which he has no personal commitment.

Mann, the hero of later Spillane books, spends most of his time and effort fighting (and killing) Russian agents. A lone wolf in the espionage field, he is as tough and ruthless as Hammer—and just as attractive to sexy women. Mann appears in *Day of the Guns* (1964), *Bloody Sunrise* (1965), *The Death Dealers* (1965), and *The By-Pass Control* (1966).

Other Spillane mysteries are *The Long Wait* (1951), *The Deep* (1961), *Me, Hood!* (1963; contains two novelettes, *Me Hood!* and *Return of the Hood*), *Killer Mine* (1964; contains two novelettes, *Killer Mine* and *Man Alone*), *The Flier* (1964; contains two novelettes, *The Flier* and *The Seven-Year Kill*), *The Delta Factor* (1967), *Tough Guys* (1970), *The Erection Set* (1972), and *The Last Cop Out* (1973).

Films

Aside from his cinematic success with Hammer, Spillane has had other works translated to the screen.

The Long Wait. United Artists, 1954. Anthony Quinn, Charles Coburn, Peggy Castle, Gene Evans. Directed by Victor Saville. Based on the 1951 novel.

An amnesia victim, searching for clues to his identity, learns that he may have been responsible for a two-year-old murder and bank robbery.

The Delta Factor. ACF, 1970. Christopher George, Yvette Mimieux, Diane McBain. Directed by Tay Garnett.

A privateer captured in Caribbean waters is forced by the CIA into rescuing a scientist from an impregnable fortress in which he has been imprisoned by the dictator of a banana republic.

Spillane has always been a very visible author; in the first few years of his success he appeared on several television variety programs (notably *The Milton Berle Show*) in parodies of his tough, trench-coated private eye. In 1954 he portrayed himself in a mystery film (he solved the mystery), the only mystery writer other than Edgar Allan POE to be a central character in a feature film, and the only mystery author to portray himself.

Ring of Fear. Warner Brothers, 1954. Clyde Beatty, Pat O'Brien, Spillane, Sean McClory, Marian Carr, Jack Stang. Directed by James Edward Grant. One of the writers of the original screenplay was Philip MACDONALD.

A homicidal maniac (McClory), nursing a grudge, joins the Clyde Beatty Circus and sabotages it. Clyde calls in his old friend Spillane to find out who is responsible.

In 1963 Spillane became the first mystery author

Author Mickey Spillane (left) portrays himself caught up in a circus mystery in *Ring of Fear*. [*Warner Brothers*]

to portray his own creation in a feature film, starring as Mike Hammer in *The Girl Hunters*. Previously, Ellery QUEEN (author) had assumed the identities of Queen and Barnaby Ross in a lecture tour debate.

SPRIGG, C[HRISTOPHER] ST. JOHN (1907–1937). English poet, Marxist theorist, and detective story writer. Sprigg received early training as a writer on the *Yorkshire Observer* and then founded a technical journal, *Aircraft Engineering*, and published several books on that subject. *Illusion and Reality: A Study of the Sources of Poetry* (1937) revealed that Sprigg's views on poetry were similar to those of C. Day Lewis (Nicholas BLAKE), W. H. Auden, Stephen Spender, and Christopher Isherwood. His volume *Poems* was published posthumously in 1939, as were *The Crisis in Physics* (1939), *Studies in a Dying Culture* (1938), and *Further Studies in a Dying Culture* (1949). Sprigg joined the British Battalion of the International Brigade in December 1936 and was killed in action in Spain the following March.

He wrote seven detective novels during a five-year span in a short, hectic life. He was one of the few authors to care enough about the form to publish his detective works under his own name while reserving the pseudonym Christopher Caudwell for his more serious or scholarly books.

Crime in Kensington (1933; U.S. title: *Pass the Body*) is about the murders of the owners of a private hotel. These crimes are investigated by Charles Venables, a newspaper columnist and resident of the hotel, and Inspector Bray. Venables and Bray return for brief but telling appearances in *The Perfect Alibi* (1934), which starts with the discovery of a corpse in a locked garage that has burned down. The victim has also been shot, and there is no trace of either the key or the gun in the ruins of the garage; furthermore, the alibis of the obvious suspects are unimpeachable.

In *Death of an Airman* (1934) a pilot takes his plane out for a spin, crashes, and then becomes the victim of foul play. The first half of *The Corpse with the Sunburned Face* (1935) is standard: a stranger is found dead in a small English village, and the police investigate. But in the second half of the book the setting is Africa, and the narrative assumes fantastic, if not supernatural, proportions as the detective nearly loses his life during the course of a peculiar native ceremony.

STAGGE, JONATHAN. *See* QUENTIN, PATRICK.

STARK, RICHARD. *See* WESTLAKE, DONALD E.

STARRETT, (CHARLES) VINCENT (EMERSON) (1886–1974). American journalist, bibliophile, essayist, poet, novelist, and distinguished scholar of detective fiction and Sherlock HOLMES for a half century.

Born in Toronto, Starrett was taken to Chicago when he was a child and lived there most of his life, although his extensive travels took him to virtually every major city in the world. Despite his desire to become an illustrator, he first worked as a reporter for several Chicago newspapers. He produced innumerable essays, biographical and bibliographical works, and critical studies of a wide range of authors and is regarded as one of the twentieth century's three or four outstanding writers about books and bookmen. He conducted the famous "Books Alive" column in the *Chicago Tribune* for many years.

Starrett's finest work is probably the erudite study *The Private Life of Sherlock Holmes* (1933). In addition to his many nonfiction books and articles, he wrote several mystery and detective books. In *The Unique Hamlet* (1920), generally conceded to be the best Holmes pastiche ever written, the great detective deals with the loss of the ultimate Shakespearean rarity, an inscribed first edition of *Hamlet*. Starrett's short story collections in the mystery genre are *Coffins for Two* (1924); *The Blue Door* (1930), which contains stories about theft, murder, and blackmail and features, among other characters, Jimmie Lavender and G. Washington Troxell, antiquarian bookdealer and amateur detective; *The Case Book of Jimmie Lavender* (1944), with the whimsical amateur detective who "looks more like an actor or an army officer" investigating cases set mainly in the Chicago of the gangster era (the dust wrapper of the first edition incorrectly spells the hero's name "Jimmy"); and *The Quick and the Dead* (1965), ten macabre tales of grim horror.

Starrett's detective novels are *Murder on "B" Deck* (1929), featuring Walter Ghost as an amateur detective who solves the crime by waiting for answers to cablegrams; *Dead Man Inside* (1931); *The End of Mr. Garment* (1932); *The Great Hotel Murder* (1935); *Midnight and Percy Jones* (1936); and *The Laughing Buddha* (1937). He edited *World's Great Spy Stories* (1944), which is listed in SANDOE'S READERS' GUIDE TO CRIME.

In his autobiography, *Born in a Bookshop* (1965), Starrett admits to being a Dofab—Eugene Field's word—which is a "damned old fool about books." Peter Ruber's *The Last Bookman* (1969) contains a biographical sketch of Starrett, plus tributes by many well-known writers.

Film

The Great Hotel Murder. Fox, 1935. Edmund Lowe, Victor McLaglen, C. Henry Gordon, Henry O'Neill. Directed by Eugene Forde.

A hotel detective reluctantly joins forces with a mystery writer to solve the murder of a guest who has been found poisoned.

STEEVES, HARRISON R[OSS] (b. 1881–d.?). American author, critic, and educator. Steeves was born in New York City and educated at Columbia University, where he received a B.A. degree in 1903, an M.A. degree in 1904, and a Ph.D. degree in 1913. He became an assistant and lecturer in English in 1905 at his alma mater, rising to assistant professor in 1913, associate professor in 1919, full professor in 1926, and, finally, head of the English department, until his retirement to emeritus status in 1949.

His marriage to Jessie Hurd (1906) produced two children; it ended in divorce in 1947. Steeves married Edna R. Leake that year. After his retirement, he lived in Cornish, N.H.

Like S. S. VAN DINE, Steeves read mystery stories while recuperating from a long illness. He thought that he could write a mystery as good as—if not better than—the ones he had read. Many revisions followed his first draft, and aid was extended by Mark Van Doren, Bennett Cerf, and others. The result was *Good Night, Sheriff* (1941), a minor masterpiece listed in SANDOE'S READERS' GUIDE TO CRIME. The story, about the sordid murder of a farmer's wife, has a small cast of characters and few possible motives, but Steeves manages to point the finger of suspicion in many directions as a life insurance claims adjustor investigates the crime with the aid of the local sheriff, who is brighter than he appears.

STEIN, AARON MARC (1906–). American detective novelist. Born in New York City, Stein attended the Ethical Culture School there before enrolling at Princeton University, where he graduated in 1927 with a B.A. degree in classics and archaeology. He worked for the *New York Evening Post* from 1927 to 1938 as a reporter, art critic, and columnist. After spending a short time as contributing editor at *Time* (March 1938–January 1939), he decided to devote his full time to writing fiction. During World War II he spent a year at the Office of War Information and more than two years in the Army as a Chinese-language specialist and Japanese code cryptanalyst.

Stein's prolific career as a fiction writer began with *Spirals* (1930), the first of three nonmystery novels he wrote during his spare time when he was a newspaperman. The author of more than eighty mysteries, Stein uses two pseudonyms as well as his own name. As George Bagby, he has written a series about New York Police Inspector Schmidt, capable of brilliant deduction but so colorless in personality that he is best remembered for complaining about his aching feet. One of the best books in the series is *The Body in the Basket* (1954), set in Madrid.

Stein uses the pseudonym Hampton Stone for his series about New York Assistant District Attorney Jeremiah X. "Gibby" Gibson. The unusual New York settings, frequent doses of humor, and unusual titles (for example, *The Swinger Who Swung by the Neck*, 1970) have caused most critics to call this series Stein's best work. *The Murder That Wouldn't Stay Solved* (1951), a mystery about a New York hotel killing (and an early attempt to deal with homosexuality in the mystery), received very high praise.

Under his own name Stein has written two series, one about American archaeologists Tim Mulligan and Elsie Mae Hunt, whose adventures invariably occur in foreign settings such as Mexico (*Days of Misfortune*, 1949). In the other, more recent, series, Stein's hero has been a tough engineer, Matt Erridge, who also investigates crimes in remote areas of the world.

STEVENSON, ROBERT LOUIS (1850–1894). Scottish author, many of whose works are in the mystery-crime-suspense field.

Born in Edinburgh, the son of Margaret Isabella (Balfour) and Thomas Stevenson, an engineer, he was christened Robert Lewis Balfour but adopted his more familiar name at eighteen. Ill constantly, he received a spotty education. He discontinued his engineering studies at the University of Edinburgh because of lack of interest, and, although he later passed his bar examinations, he never practiced law. Stevenson moved several times because of his lung disease, and he was living in a French artists' colony in 1876 when he fell in love with Fanny Van de Grift Osbourne, a woman ten years his senior with three children from an unhappy marriage. Three years after their meeting, he followed her to California, where a traveling accident made him a virtual invalid for the rest of his life. They were married in 1880, returning to Europe to live in Scotland, Switz-

Robert Louis Stevenson.

Boris Karloff in a version of Mr. Hyde. [*Universal*]

erland, and France. After returning to the United States for another year, the Stevensons sailed for the South Seas in 1888 and, two years later, settled in Samoa, where he spent the rest of his life.

Stevenson wrote some of the most famous and popular books for boys in all literature, notably *Treasure Island* (1883), *Prince Otto* (1885), *Kidnapped* (1886), *The Black Arrow* (1888), and *The Master of Ballantrae* (1889), as well as the still-beloved volume of poems for young people, *A Child's Garden of Verses* (1885). He ventured into the mystery-crime field at every stage of his literary career, beginning with a collection of stories, *New Arabian Nights* (1882), that were models of romantic roguery, among them such classic tales as "The Suicide Club" and "The Pavilion on the Links." Three years later he produced *More New Arabian Nights* in collaboration with his wife; one of the stories in this collection, "The Dynamiter," is often reprinted.

In 1886 Stevenson published *The Strange Case of Dr. Jekyll and Mr. Hyde,* a macabre allegory once described as the only crime story in which the solution is more terrifying than the problem. In this classic tale of a dual personality, Dr. Henry Jekyll, a brilliant doctor and chemist, is obsessed with the concept of one person possessing two separate and distinct personalities. Experimenting with drugs, he is able to prove his theory, committing the vilest acts of unremitting evil at night as "Mr. Hyde," only to return to respectability as Dr. Jekyll the next day.

The Wrong Box (1889), which Stevenson wrote in collaboration with his stepson, Lloyd Osbourne, was originally titled *A Game of Bluff*. In this humorous crime story, two nephews watch over their aged uncle so that he can live long enough to inherit the fortune they expect to acquire when he passes on. When they discover a corpse they believe to be his, they attempt to prevent the revelation of his death by shipping the body from one place to another in a zany series of improbable stratagems. Lawyer-detective Michael Finsbury earnestly (and helplessly) tracks the decaying body.

Stevenson and Osbourne also collaborated on *The Wrecker* (1892), an adventure tale involving pirate treasure, opium smuggling, sabotage, murder, and business swindles involving bankruptcy and fraudulent insurance claims; the narrator is also the investigator.

Treasure Island and *Kidnapped* have elements of mystery; "The Body-Snatcher" (1895) is an eerie thriller; and *The Merry Men and Other Fables* (1887) contains a good murder story, "Markheim," in which an antique dealer is brutally stabbed to death.

Films

Stevenson's Dr. Jekyll has been one of the screen's most interesting characters, and his historical

Fredric March's transformation into a lustful, degenerate Mr. Hyde won him an Oscar in the 1932 interpretation of the Stevenson classic. [*Paramount*]

In a composite photograph Spencer Tracy portrays both Dr. Jekyll and Mr. Hyde; for this 1941 production Tracy relied more heavily on menacing gestures than on makeup for the latter character. [*MGM*]

romances, for example, *Treasure Island, Kidnapped,* and *The Black Arrow,* have often been filmed. Among the films based on his mystery works are the following.

Trouble for Two. MGM, 1936. Robert Montgomery, Rosalind Russell, Louis Hayward, Reginald Owen. Directed by J. Walter Ruben. Based on "The Suicide Club."

The heir to the throne of a European kingdom, visiting incognito in London, falls in with the morbid, death-seeking members of a gambling club.

The Body Snatcher. RKO, 1945. Boris Karloff, Henry Daniell, Bela Lugosi, Russell Wade. Directed by Robert Wise. Based on the short story.

The head of a Scottish medical school is forced to hire grave robbers to supply him with corpses for dissection; the body snatchers soon turn to murder.

The Strange Door. Universal, 1951. Charles Laughton, Karloff, Sally Forrest, Richard Stapley, Paul Cavanagh. Directed by Joseph Pevney. From "The Sire de Maletroit's Door," which first appeared in the January 1878 issue of *Temple Bar;* it was collected in *New Arabian Nights.*

In seventeenth-century France, a young man invades a castle—full of secret passageways, torture chambers, and crushing walls—ruled by a madman.

The Wrong Box. Columbia (British), 1966. John Mills, Ralph Richardson, Michael Caine, Peter Cook, Dudley Moore, Nanette Newman, Peter Sellers, the Temperance Seven. Directed by Bryan Forbes. From the 1899 novel.

In this black comedy, the conniving heirs of two elderly brothers, who stand to inherit a large trust fund, are befuddled by a mix-up in corpses.

Stevenson's probing, tortured physician was an early film subject. By the 1910s Jekyll had already endured several short screen treatments portrayed by Alwin Neuss (1910), James Cruze (1912), King Baggot (1913), and others. He has made many subsequent appearances, among them those discussed below.

Dr. Jekyll and Mr. Hyde. Paramount, 1920. John Barrymore, Nita Naldi, Martha Mansfield, Brandon Hurst, Louis Wolheim. Directed by John S. Robertson.

Barrymore's electrifying dramatics were put to good use in the transformation sequences; he achieved the changeover by twisting his face grotesquely and clawing his hands. Added to the Stevenson source was philosophical discourse from Oscar Wilde's *The Picture of Dorian Gray* (1891).

Nearly simultaneously Louis B. Mayer released a version set in New York, with Sheldon Lewis as a frenzied, maniac Jekyll-Hyde darting down alleys, attacking women, and setting fires. The ending is a dream. That year, too, German actor Conrad Veidt starred as a doctor with twin personalities in *Der Januskopf,* directed by F. W. Murnau.

Dr. Jekyll and Mr. Hyde. Paramount, 1932. Fredric March, Miriam Hopkins, Rose Hobart, Holmes Herbert. Directed by Rouben Mamoulian.

March's sexual, ape-like Hyde, combined with director Mamoulian's vibrant, fascinating camera work, brought the actor an Academy award for the role.

Dr. Jekyll and Mr. Hyde. MGM, 1941. Spencer Tracy, Ingrid Bergman, Lana Turner, Ian Hunter, Donald Crisp. Directed by Victor Fleming.

Tracy's snarling Hyde is an ugly sadist; Freudian symbolism is added to the transition.

Numerous subsequent films employed the Jekyll-Hyde theme to a greater or lesser degree. Among the more interesting are *Son of Dr. Jekyll* (1951), with Louis Hayward; *Daughter of Dr. Jekyll* (1957), with Gloria Talbott; *Abbott and Costello Meet Dr. Jekyll* (1953), with Boris Karloff; *House of Fright* (1960; British title: *The Two Faces of Dr. Jekyll*); *The Nutty Professor* (1963), with Jerry Lewis; and *Dr. Jekyll and Sister Hyde* (1972).

Radio and Television

Dramatizations of the Jekyll-Hyde story have often been used on anthology radio. In the days of early (live) television, Basil Rathbone appeared on CBS's

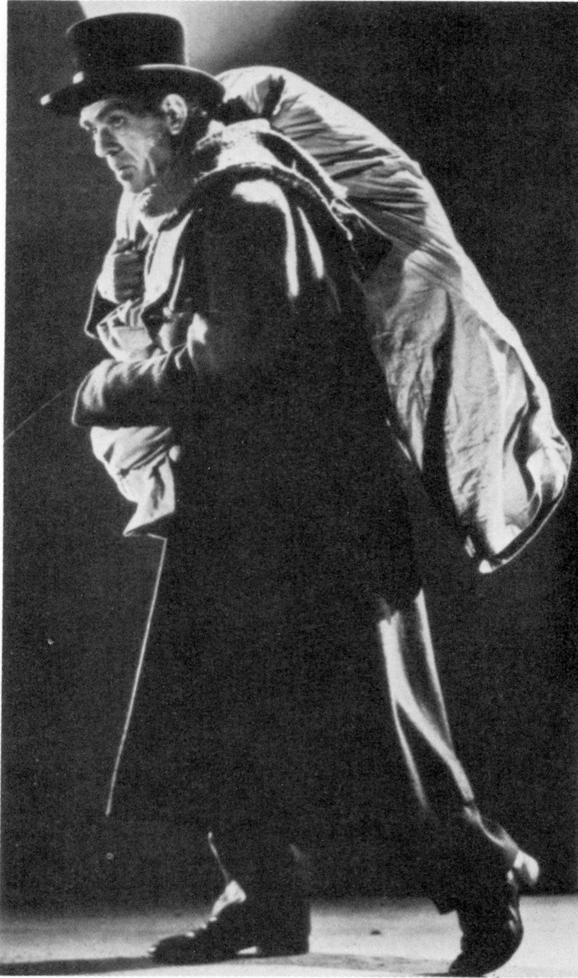

Boris Karloff is the grave robber of the title role in the 1945 version of Stevenson's *The Body Snatcher*. [*RKO*]

Suspense as a distinguished experimenter whose transformations were achieved by having Hyde played by another actor (seen only briefly). In 1967 Jack Palance was an extraordinarily fine Jekyll in a two-hour telefilm (with Canadian exteriors serving as gaslit London) that won an Edgar award from the Mystery Writers of America. In 1973 Kirk Douglas starred in a difficult musical adaptation of Stevenson's work.

Plays

T. R. Sullivan adapted *Dr. Jekyll and Mr. Hyde* for the London stage with Richard Mansfield in the title role. It opened at the Lyceum on August 4, 1888. Henry Irving played the lead in J. Comyns Carr's adaptation, which made its debut at the Queen's Theatre on January 29, 1910.

STEWART, ALFRED WALTER. *See* CONNINGTON, J. J.

STEWART, JOHN INNES MACKINTOSH. *See* INNES, MICHAEL.

STEWART, MARY (FLORENCE ELINOR RAINBOW) (1916–). English author. Born in Sunderland, Durham, the daughter of Mary Edith (Matthews) and Frederick Albert Rainbow, a clergyman, she attended the University of Durham, achieving first-class honors. She lectured there on English literature until 1956. In 1945 she married Frederick Henry Stewart; they live in Scotland, where he is head of the Geology Department of the University of Edinburgh. She was elected a Fellow of the Royal Society of Arts in 1969.

Lady Stewart's first books were "suspense novels" that have a pronounced romantic element and a strong sense of locale. Her talent as a storyteller combined with the high quality of her prose have

Peter McEnery, an English boy accused of stealing some jewels, joins Hayley Mills in trying to find the real thieves in the Walt Disney screen version of Mary Stewart's *The Moon-Spinners*, set on the island of Crete. [*Buena Vista*]

assured best-seller status for her work.

Among her best books are *Nine Coaches Waiting* (1959), *My Brother Michael* (1960), *The Ivy Tree* (1961), *The Moon-Spinners* (1962), *Airs above the Ground* (1965), and *The Gabriel Hounds* (1967). She is also the author of four short radio dramas, *Lift from a Stranger, Call Me at Ten-thirty, The Crime of Mr. Merry,* and *The Lord of Langdale* (all produced in 1957–1958).

After *The Gabriel Hounds,* she wrote a short novel (not yet published in the United States) called *The Wind off the Small Isles,* which showed a change of approach that in turn led to two Arthurian novels, *The Crystal Cave* (1970) and *The Hollow Hills* (1973), which have brought her recognition in a new field.

Film

The Moon-Spinners. Buena Vista, 1964. Hayley Mills, Eli Wallach, Peter McEnery, Joan Greenwood, Irene Papas, Pola Negri. Directed by James Neilson.

A teen-age English girl and her aunt, traveling through Crete, are refused rooms at the quaint Hotel Moon-Spinners because the brother of the woman owner is planning a jewel robbery.

STOCKTON, FRANK (FRANCIS) R[ICHARD] (1834–1902). American author of juvenile and popular fiction. Born in Philadelphia, he began writing at an early age—first magazine stories for children and then humorous novels, stories, and sketches. His most famous work is the classic riddle story "The Lady or the Tiger?" Stockton read the story (originally "The King's Arena") at a party, and it received such an enthusiastic response that he expanded it and sold it to *Century Magazine* (November 1882); it was later the title story of his collection *The Lady, or the Tiger?* (1884). In this now familiar tale, a handsome youth falls in love with the king's daughter, who returns his love. His audacity is discovered, and he is condemned. In the king's arena are two doors: behind one is a ferocious tiger that will surely kill him; behind the other is a beautiful maiden who will marry him. The king's daughter discovers where each will be placed and directs her lover to the door on the right. The detective for this story is every person of the millions who have read it, for with his last sentence Stockton asks: "And so I leave it with all of you: Which came out of the opened door—the lady, or the tiger?" Stockton wrote a sequel to his famous story—"The Discourager of Hesitancy. A Continuation of 'The Lady, or the Tiger?'" which first appeared in book form in *The Christmas Wreck and Other Stories* (1886)—but it also failed to answer the question and had little popularity. In the September 1948 issue of *Ellery Queen's Mystery Magazine,* Jack Moffitt's "The Lady and the Tiger" finally solves the problem. His solution was collected in *The Queen's Awards, 1948* (1948).

STOKER, BRAM (1847–1912). British author and theatrical manager whose novel *Dracula* (see DRACULA, COUNT) is the most famous vampire story ever written.

Born Abraham Stoker in Dublin, the son of Charlotte Matilda Blake Thornley and Abraham Stoker, he was a sickly child who hovered near death for months and did not leave his bed until he was seven. He grew to be a giant, however, and excelled in athletics at Dublin University, where he also received many scholastic honors. He spent a tedious decade in his first job, as a civil servant at Dublin Castle, and then, for five years, was the (unpaid) drama critic of the *Dublin Mail* while holding several other positions in journalism. After a brief legal career, he took employment with the celebrated English actor Sir Henry Irving, serving as his secretary and business manager for twenty-seven years. He handled all the actor's correspondence, estimated at fifty letters a day—about a half million in all.

In spite of that energy drain, Stoker managed to produce several full-length books before Irving died in 1905; thereafter, his books appeared at a faster rate—seventeen in all. Most of his works are tales of horror and the supernatural, but he also wrote a few volumes of mystery and crime, including *The Mystery of the Sea* (1905) and *Dracula's Guest and Other Weird Tales* (1914), which includes a previously unpublished segment of *Dracula*—a complete story in itself.

His most famous work is the long novel about the mysterious Count Dracula, published in 1897. An instant success, it later became a stage hit as well, with Bela Lugosi, in the title role, curdling the blood of audiences; his later film version is a classic.

Other vampire stories may have influenced Stoker. Perhaps the earliest is the vampire tale in the *Arabian Nights' Entertainments.* The most notable of the books that preceded Stoker's was *The Vampyre* (1819), by Dr. John Polidori, the physician of Lord Byron (who is often inaccurately cited as the author). Polidori's tale was written as a result of the same friendly challenge that inspired Mary SHELLEY to write FRANKENSTEIN. A later appearance of a bloodsucking character was in Thomas Preskett Prest's *Varney the Vampire* (1847), an almost endless story that was published in 220 "penny dreadful" parts.

Stocker's *Dracula* was written in a style invented by Wilkie COLLINS for *The Woman in White* (1860); events are related in journals and diaries and in the words of the different characters, the reader gaining an insider's view of the thoughts of the leading figures.

STONE, HAMPTON. *See* STEIN, AARON MARC.

Rex Stout.
[*The Viking Press*]

STOUT, REX (TODHUNTER) (1886–1975). American detective story writer and creator of Nero WOLFE, possibly the best, probably the most eccentric, and certainly the largest detective in America.

Almost anyone who thinks of it at all assumes that Stout bore a physical resemblance to his most famous character; his name probably contributed to the misapprehension. In fact, they could not have been more unalike physically. Whereas Wolfe weighs a seventh of a ton, Stout was always a stringy 150 pounds—after dinner. He had a scraggly beard that someone once suggested had been "stolen from a billy goat," and he was unafraid of a hard day's work, even at an advanced age.

Stout, one of nine children, was born in Noblesville, Ind., but very shortly thereafter his parents, Lucetta Elizabeth (Todhunter) and John Wallace Stout, a Quaker and a teacher, moved west to Kansas with their family. By the time he was four years old, he had read the Bible twice, and he had read more than a thousand classics before he was ten. His public education was good enough for him to become the state spelling champion by the time he was thirteen; he was always proud of the fact that he was a superb speller. After two years as a yeoman in the Navy (on Theodore Roosevelt's yacht) he sold some poetry to *Smart Set* but got a job as a clerk in a cigar store after the checks stopped coming. He had about thirty jobs in six states during the next four years; then he began selling numerous articles and stories to the popular magazines of the day, including *Munsey's*.

He married Fay Kennedy in 1916 (divorced in 1931) and invented a school banking system that he helped install in 400 cities throughout the United States. This lucrative enterprise lasted ten years and enabled him to travel extensively in Europe. While in Paris, he wrote his first book, *How Like a God* (1929), a psychological study that was well received but is difficult reading today, and three other novels. He returned to the United States and began writing detective novels. In 1932 he married Pola Hoffman in New York.

Stout's first detective novel, *Fer-de-lance*, appeared serially in *The Saturday Evening Post* and in book form in 1934. It featured Nero Wolfe and his confidential assistant, Archie Goodwin, and was an instant success, as was its successor, *The League of Frightened Men* (1935). Both books have earned a place in the HAYCRAFT-QUEEN CORNERSTONE LIBRARY.

Stout had seen the palace of the Bey of Tunis and was so impressed that he wanted his own house to resemble it. He built the fourteen-room structure himself, aided by nine men and "three and a half boys," all amateurs, just to be sure that he could have exactly what he wanted.

He was active in many semipolitical activities and, like another great mystery writer, Dashiell HAMMETT, espoused many liberal causes during the 1930s and after World War II. He wrote propaganda and made speeches for preparedness, Lend-Lease, and the draft during the war. He edited *The Illustrious Dunderheads* (1942), an analysis of congressional isolationists; was one of the more militant members of the Fight for Freedom; served as master of ceremonies for the Council of Democracy's radio program *Speaking of Liberty;* was chairman of the Writers War Board and president of the Authors Guild, the Authors League of America, and the Mystery Writers of America.

Although Stout and Wolfe did not resemble one another in appearance, they were intellectually akin, though Wolfe appeared to be apolitical. They both had a strong affection for the English language and knew how to use it gracefully, correctly, and humorously. Wolfe may spend a ritualistic four hours a day with his orchids, but Stout spent twice that much time some days working in his huge garden, where he grew prizewinning strawberries and other vegetation. Like the detective, Stout was a gourmet, although not a fanatic about food. He could eat a hot dog; Wolfe would rather starve.

Criticism has sometimes been leveled at Wolfe's recorded cases because the plots have occasionally been flawed, the reader being placed at a disadvantage because of a reliance on Wolfe's intuitive flashes. But the real strength of the stories is the Wolfe-Goodwin relationship, their repartee, the humor, which is unequaled in any sustained series in literature, and the ambience of their life-style. The reader has never been more comfortable in any lodging in crime fiction except 221B Baker Street, and the floor plan of Wolfe's brownstone is better known than that of any other house in the United States, save perhaps 1600 Pennsylvania Avenue.

As the author approached ninety, his output slowed, but did not stop. Some years ago, he wrote about other detectives, but later he concentrated on Wolfe and Archie Goodwin.

The President Vanishes (1934) was published anonymously and is a pure thriller. *The Hand in the Glove* (1937) features Theodolinda ("Dol") Bonner, who has also worked with Wolfe in other books. Assisted by Sally Colt, she operates her own agency in New York, and Wolfe respects her enough to have invited her to dinner. Tecumseh Fox appeared in three novels: *Double for Death* (1939), *Bad for Business* (1940), and *The Broken Vase* (1941). The most physically active of Stout's detectives, he has no aversion to stretching the law. *Alphabet Hicks* (1940) is the only novel about the colorful title character. Formerly a brilliant graduate of Harvard Law School, he was disbarred in his first year of practice and became a shabby cabdriver. Inspector Cramer has one book to himself: *Red Threads* (1939). *Mountain Cat* (1939) is a mystery novel set in the West; Delia Brand catches the killer.

As a stylist, Stout had only one limitation: he could not write a bad sentence.

STRANGEWAYS, NIGEL (Creator: Nicholas BLAKE). One of the outstanding detectives of England's "Golden Age," Strangeways is Oxford-educated. Although he does not constantly display his erudition, he has used his knowledge of many diverse subjects, including Elizabethan literature, to solve murders. More often, he is content to rely on physical clues and his astute judgment of character to help him. Although he is a private investigator with no official status, Nigel has excellent connections; his uncle, Sir John Strangeways, is assistant commissioner at Scotland Yard.

Nigel has aged as the series in which he appears has progressed, but he has never completely lost the appearance of "an overgrown prep schoolboy." He is 6 feet tall and has shortsighted blue eyes; his sandy-colored hair is forever drooping over his forehead. He falls in love with explorer Georgia Cavendish during the course of *Thou Shell of Death*. After their marriage, they divide their time between a London flat and a house in rural Devon where, in 1938, Georgia becomes aware of a fascist plot against England. In *The Smiler with the Knife*, a book in which Nigel plays a minor role, she deals with this conspiracy in a manner that led Miriam Allen DEFORD to characterize her admiringly as a "female Superman." Her tragic death in World War II is a great blow to Strangeways, whose recovery is slow. He attempts to lose himself in detective work, assisting Scotland Yard's Inspector Blount in many cases and working for British Intelligence. Eventually he forms a liaison with a sculptress, Clare Massinger, with whom he lives and travels for many years. In *The Widow's Cruise*, they sail to Greece and solve a shipboard murder.

CHECKLIST

1935	*A Question of Proof*
1936	*Thou Shell of Death* (U.S. title: *Shell of Death*)
1937	*There's Trouble Brewing*
1938	*The Beast Must Die*
1939	*The Smiler with the Knife*
1940	*Malice in Wonderland* (U.S. title: *The Summer Camp Mystery*)
1941	*The Case of the Abominable Snowman* (U.S. title: *The Corpse in the Snowman*)
1947	*Minute for Murder*
1949	*Head of a Traveler*
1953	*The Dreadful Hollow*
1954	*The Whisper in the Gloom*
1957	*End of Chapter*
1959	*The Widow's Cruise*
1961	*The Worm of Death*
1963	*The Deadly Joker*
1964	*The Sad Variety*
1966	*The Morning after Death*

STRATEMEYER, EDWARD L. *See* KEENE, CAROLYN.

STREET, CECIL JOHN CHARLES. *See* RHODE, JOHN.

STRIBLING, T[HOMAS] S[IGISMUND] (1881–1965). American novelist whose best work deals with life in the South, where he was born (Tennessee) and spent most of his life. His writing career began with adventure stories for PULP MAGAZINES, but in 1931 he began an important trilogy: *The Forge* (1931), *The Store* (1932), for which he won the Pulitzer Prize in 1933, and *Unfinished Cathedral* (1934). His only mystery-detective book, *Clues of the Caribbees* (1929), recounts the humorous adventures of Professor Henry POGGIOLI, philosopher and psychologist.

STRIKER, FRAN. *See* GREEN HORNET, THE.

STRINGER, ARTHUR (JOHN ARBUTHNOTT) (1874–1950). Canadian author. Born in Chatham, Ontario, he was educated at the University of Toronto and at Oxford. Later he became vice-president at Toronto. Among his many books are three interesting collections of short detective stories: *The Under Groove* (1908), *The Man Who Couldn't Sleep: Being a Relation of the Divers Strange Adventures Which Befell One Witter Kerfoot When, Sorely Troubled with Sleeplessness, He Ventured Forth at Midnight along the Highways and Byways of Manhattan*

(1919), and *The Diamond Thieves* (1923), in which Miss Balmy Rymal, acting for a "security alliance," uses her "woman's intuition" and a talent for scenting clues to foil the well-organized plans of a band of desperate criminals.

SUE, EUGÈNE (pseudonym of Marie Joseph Sue; 1804–1857). French novelist. Born in Paris, he was sponsored by Prince Eugène de Beauharnais and the empress Joséphine; he used the prince's name to form his famous pen name. Sue drew heavily on his naval background for several early works, and his interest in painting and medicine is also evident in his writings.

His most important work, *Les Mystères de Paris* (4 vols., 1842–1843), was translated and published in London as *The Mysteries of Paris* in ninety paper-wrappered parts (1844–1846) and then as a triple-decker. Sue was already a highly regarded author in France, and the work, initially serialized in a respectable journal, brought his socialistic views to a wide audience that also became familiar with criminal argot through reading the long book. Much like the real-life François Eugène VICOCQ, the fictional hero of *Les Mystères de Paris*, Prince Rodolphe of Gerolstein, lives incognito among the criminals and lower types of the Paris ghettos, solving mysteries and crimes while exposing and correcting social injustices. Rodolphe appears to have been a prototype for Prince ZALESKI.

Sue's ten-volume *Le Juif Errant* (*The Wandering Jew;* 1844–1845) championed the same social and political causes with a similar blend of sensationalism and melodrama. A change of government drove him into exile in 1852. He died in Annecy.

SUE, MARIE JOSEPH. *See* SUE, EUGÈNE.

SYMONS, JULIAN (GUSTAVE) (1912–). English poet, biographer, criminologist, novelist, and critic. Born in London, Symons has held a number of positions, including secretary to an engineering company and advertising copywriter and executive. After World War II he became a free-lance writer and book reviewer. From 1946 to 1956 he wrote a weekly column, "Life, People—and Books," for the *Manchester Evening News*. During the 1950s he was also a regular contributor to *Tribune*, a left-wing weekly, serving as its literary editor and closely associated with its political views.

Symons founded and edited *Twentieth Century Verse*, an important little magazine that flourished from 1937 to 1939 and introduced many young English poets and also published the works of American poets. Symons has published two volumes of his own poetry, *Confusions about X* (1939) and *The Second Man* (1944).

He has also written critically acclaimed biographies, including a study of his brother, *A. J. A. Symons, His Life and Speculations* (1950), *Charles Dickens* (1951), and *Thomas Carlyle* (1952). A scholar of the mystery-detective genre, he has published *A Reasonable Doubt* (1960), about thirteen controversial murder cases and their disputed verdicts or lack of solution, and edited *A Pictorial History of Crime* (1966), a popular study of wrongdoing published in England as *Crime and Detection . . . since 1840*. His *Bloody Murder* (1972; U.S. title: *Mortal Consequences*), a critically esteemed but often controversial work, traces the history of the detective story from its origins to its transformation into, and replacement by, the modern novel of crime. It received a special award from the Mystery Writers of America (MWA).

Symons is married, has two children, and lives in London. From 1958 to 1968 he reviewed mystery fiction for *The Sunday Times* (London); he now reviews general books for that newspaper. In 1959 it published his *The Hundred Best Crime Stories*, a list of works that had first appeared in his column.

Symons had written his first detective novel, *The Immaterial Murder Case* (1945), and then abandoned it for several years, before he decided to send it to a publisher. It deals with an odd artistic movement called "Immaterialism" and a dead body among a group of statues and boasts two detectives, an amateur, Teak Woode, who is not too bright, and a professional, Inspector Bland, who appears in several subsequent works. A satiric book, it often approaches fantasy in its high-spirited lunacy. Its successor, *A Man Called Jones* (1947), is a rare book that is usually omitted from lists of Symons's works. It features Inspector Bland and was never published in the United States. *Bland Beginning* (1949) tells of Bland's first case and is based on the famous Wise literary forgery case.

Symons, long an advocate of the crime novel, has often attempted to blend the literary values of the conventional novel with the excitement of the thriller. His first crime novel, *The Thirty-first of February* (1950), is a psychological study that starts well, then turns unpleasant, and ends in a shrill and horrendous manner. *The Broken Penny* (1953) is a spy story with a complicated plot and a protagonist who is less than bright. *The Narrowing Circle* (1954) presents the executive editor of *Crime Magazine*, who is cleverly framed for a crime and must prove his innocence. The chief suspect in *The Colour of Murder* (1957) can remember nothing. A long tale told to a psychiatrist by the puzzled young man ends in a courtroom. This novel was judged the best of 1957 by the British Crime Writers' Association (CWA).

Guy Fawkes night and juvenile delinquency are

elements in *The Progress of a Crime* (1960). There are a court trial and a scathing portrait of the police and their methods. This novel was a runner-up in the 1960 CWA awards; it received the MWA Edgar as best novel of 1960. *The Killing of Francie Lake* (1962; U.S. title: *The Plain Man*) is set in the offices of a magazine publishing empire. An editor tries to solve the murder of a colleague. *The End of Solomon Grundy* (1964), a long courtroom novel about a man on trial for murder, has an ending that may shock many readers. *The Man Who Killed Himself* (1967) is about a Jekyll-Hyde type; in his "Mr. Hyde" guise he conceives and executes a perfect crime.

The main character of *The Man Whose Dreams Came True* (1968) is an ambitious but unscrupulous young man whose plans have been unsuccessful. Finally he achieves great success but does not realize that some people are more clever than he is. The experimental *The Man Who Lost His Wife* (1970) was billed by its American publisher as "a novel of suspicion" and avoided overt violence in favor of increasing tension through worry and jealousy. *The Players and the Game* (1972) is set in a business office, and in the mind of one of its characters—a sexual psychopath. It is based on the famous Moors murders of the 1960s. Other Symons titles are *The Paper Chase* (1956; U.S. title: *Bogue's Fortune*), *The Belting Inheritance* (1965), *The Plot against Roger Rider* (1973), *A Three Pipe Problem* (1975), and the nonfiction pamphlet *The Detective Story in Britain* (1962).

Symons has also written many short stories that have been regularly published in *Ellery Queen's Mystery Magazine;* there have been two British paperback collections, *Murder! Murder!* (1961) and *Francis Quarles Investigates* (1965).

T

TATE, ELLALICE. *See* HOLT, VICTORIA.

TAYLOR, H. BALDWIN. *See* WAUGH, HILLARY.

TAYLOR, JOHN M. *See* PIDGIN, CHARLES FELTON.

TAYLOR, PHOEBE ATWOOD (1909–1976). Born in Boston, Miss Taylor is descended from the *Mayflower* Pilgrims. She attended Barnard College in New York City and received a B.A. degree in 1930 before returning to live and write in Massachusetts.

Her literary debut, *The Cape Cod Mystery* (1931), sold 5,000 copies, an extremely large sale for a first mystery. It was the first of twenty-four books about detective Asey MAYO. In these stories Miss Taylor used her intimate knowledge of New England for the settings—Cape Cod communities such as Wellfleet, Quanomet, and Weeset. The dialogue of local characters named Tabitha Sparrow, Phineas Banbury, Aunt Nettie Hobbs, and so on, is convincingly Yankee. Although some of her books emphasize Cape Cod's role as a famed summer resort, most deal with the people who live there after the tourists have gone. *Death Lights a Candle* (1932) takes place during a snowstorm.

Humor is an important element in the Mayo books, and even more so in the eight books Miss Taylor wrote, under the pseudonym Alice Tilton, about Leonidas WITHERALL. Although her last mystery was published in 1951, she has remained very popular with readers. Many of her books, under both names, were reprinted in hard-cover and paperback editions in the late 1960s and early 1970s. Nicholas BLAKE has praised her characterizations and dialogue, and Anthony BOUCHER found her "well-ordered farces" entertaining, if a bit mechanical. He liked her ability to re-create historical moments, for example, the United States in mid-Depression or early World War II.

Phoebe Atwood Taylor.

TAYLOR, TOM. *See* BULLIVANT, CECIL HENRY.

TAYLOR, WENDELL HERTIG (1905–). American teacher and scholar of the mystery novel. A renowned educator in the sciences, Taylor graduated from Princeton and became a researcher for the Du Pont company. He later taught chemistry and the history of science at Princeton and then headed the science department at the Lawrenceville School until his retirement in 1970. He has contributed scientific articles to many journals.

A longtime friend of Jacques BARZUN, Taylor shares his interest in the detective story and joined him in compiling *A Catalogue of Crime* (1971), an extensive guide to crime literature.

TELEVISION DETECTIVES. Detectives on television have been a hardy breed and helped pioneer the medium. In the 1950s mystery stories were regularly used on anthology series—*Suspense, The Web, Hands of Fate, The Whistler, Alfred Hitchcock Presents* (see HITCHCOCK, ALFRED), *The Chicagoland Mystery Players*—and the private investigator, often in trenchcoat with pipe clenched between teeth (tobacco companies were frequent early sponsors), met and dealt with weekly cases. Among the earliest detective programs were *Martin Kane, Private Eye,* which appeared in 1950, and *Rocky King, Detective* (also 1950), featuring a middle-aged and domestic detective who paused during each case to telephone his wife (who was never seen) with details of the investigation.

Many famous investigators from the printed page made at least one thirteen-week transition to the new medium. Ellery QUEEN (detective) was the first, in 1950, settling in for several series of television adventures; he was followed by BOSTON BLACKIE and Flashgun CASEY (in *Crime Photographer*), in 1952, and amateur sleuths Mr. and Mrs. NORTH, in 1953; *The Lone Wolf* (*see* LONE WOLF, THE) and Sherlock HOLMES in 1955; and *The Thin Man* (*see* CHARLES, NICK AND NORA) and Charlie CHAN in 1957. The decade closed with the television debut of Mike HAMMER (1957), Philip MARLOWE (1959), and Michael SHAYNE (1960). In the 1960s a laundered Harry Lime, Graham GREENE's character, appeared in *The Third Man* (1960), and a liberated lady detective was seen on *Honey West* (1965). Roger Moore was the Saint (*see* SAINT, THE) in an hour-long series on network television from 1965 to 1968.

Television was also developing its own investigators, many of whom moved in very colorful circles. The most innovative private eye program of the 1950s was Blake Edwards's *Peter Gunn* (1958); Gunn, played by Craig Stevens, prowled about in an almost surrealist metropolis but could most often be found at a nocturnal jazz club, "Mother's," peopled with eccentrics. No other original television detective was to make so strong an impact on the medium—until Mike Connors appeared in *Mannix*. Stern-jawed and physical, with a black receptionist-friend (Gail Fisher), but not especially friendly toward eccentrics, Mannix began eight seasons of weekly hour-long cases in 1967. Richard Diamond (of *Richard Diamond, Private Eye*) began solving crimes in 1959. He discussed the progress of his cases on the telephone with Sam, who remained unseen (except for her legs, which belonged to Mary Tyler Moore). David Janssen was the star; he later starred in *The Fugitive* (1963–1967) for 120 episodes.

Police procedural dramas have had a strong television following. Although there had been earlier shows involving policemen and plainclothesmen, in 1952 *Dragnet* transferred intact Sergeant Joe Friday (Jack Webb) from the ranks of RADIO DETECTIVES to the visual medium, along with his underplayed, realistic dramatizations of actual Los Angeles police cases (the resulting sentences were also announced), setting standards of realism for police shows to follow. Also in 1952, Reed Hadley's *Racket Squad* documented the swindles and confidence schemes to which the innocent fall prey. Other programs began to explore specialized police activities: Lee Marvin in *M Squad* (1957) was a plainclothesman operating out of Chicago; *Treasury Men in Action*

Batman (Adam West, right) and Robin (Burt Ward) drive out of the Batcave in their specially designed car into a metropolis filled with crime; a scene from the popular TV series. [*ABC-TV*]

(1953) was based on the counterfeiting and tax cases of that federal agency; *Highway Patrol* (1956) and *Harbor Command* (1957) dealt with automotive crimes and water patrols, respectively; and Beverly Garland was a New York City policewoman in *Decoy* (1957).

In 1958, first as a two-part drama in an hour-long anthology program (*Desilu Playhouse*), and then as a long-running (five years), award-winning series, *The Untouchables* presented Robert Stack as G-man Eliot Ness, head of his own incorruptible special unit battling evil against a Prohibition background, mainly in Chicago. Walter Winchell narrated the series, which elaborated on the exploits of the real-life Eliot Ness. Other police units followed: *The Detectives* (1959), a modern Los Angeles department headed by Robert Taylor; the "eight million stories" presented from the perspective of the police in *The Naked City* (1960); and the exploits of the select Metropolitan Squad of Los Angeles (*The New Breed*, 1961), which used modern, scientific crime-fighting methods. In 1961 the detective squads of Ed MCBAIN's *87th Precinct* (*see* 87TH PRECINCT, THE) and the (for television) police-oriented *Asphalt Jungle*, which took its name from the W. R. BURNETT novel, first appeared. Gene Barry was socialite police captain Amos Burke in *Burke's Law* (1963), solving murder cases with a very independent flair; in his fourth and final year, he abandoned the precinct house to become a James BOND-like secret agent.

Even in the 1950s detailed police activities were set in different big cities. *The Lineup* (1954) was drawn from San Francisco files; *Fabian of Scotland*

One of the most popular melodrama players on television, Raymond Burr, after a decade of portraying lawyer Perry Mason, became the crippled Chief Ironside, shot down in the line of duty. [*MCA-Universal*]

Yard (1956) and John Dickson CARR's *Colonel March of Scotland Yard* (1953; *see* MARCH, COLONEL) were but two of the series about crime in London; *N.Y.P.D.* (1967), opening with the flashing of police car lights and the screaming of sirens, followed three plainclothes detectives from the 27th Precinct on cases based on New York files. Confined to a wheelchair, the result of an attempted assassination, former San Francisco chief of detectives Robert Ironside (Raymond Burr) acted as consultant to the department in the long-lived *Ironside* (1967).

In 1968 three long-running police series made their debut: Jack Lord heading a special Honolulu investigative unit, in *Hawaii Five-O,* with jurisdiction over all the islands of the fiftieth state; two police officers on their tour of duty in a Los Angeles patrol car in *Adam 12;* and three youngsters posing as street youths and aiding hippie dropouts for the Los Angeles police in the *Mod Squad.*

Starting in 1971 NBC's *Mystery Movie* began rotating the exploits of several enduring, interesting policemen. Peter Falk is the disheveled, erratic lieutenant of *Columbo,* who doggedly pursues criminals (whose identity is always known to the audience) in the manner of Fyodor Mikhailovich DOSTOEVSKI's Inspector Petrovich, his partial inspiration; *Macmillan and Wife* presents the lighthearted crime chasing of an attractive San Francisco police commissioner (Rock Hudson) and his spirited wife, Sally (Susan Saint James); *McCloud* (Dennis Weaver) is a New Mexico lawman assigned to observe New York City Police Department crime detection methods.

Private eyes also sometimes worked collectively, team spirit being most evident in the late 1950s in such interesting locations as Honolulu (*Hawaiian Eye,* 1959), New Orleans (*Bourbon Street Beat,* 1959), glamorous Beverly Hills (*77 Sunset Strip,* 1958), and Miami Beach (*Surfside 6,* 1960). A somewhat more intelligent team was guided by criminologist Sebastian Cabot in Eric AMBLER's *Checkmate* (1959). Similar scientific investigators operated in the later *Strange Report* (Anthony Quayle, 1968) and *My Friend Tony* (James Whitmore and friend Enzo Cerusico, 1968).

Lawyers are important in television crime, either for the prosecution—as in one of the earliest such programs, *Mr. District Attorney* (1951)—or the defense—as in *Public Defender* (1953). In 1957 Raymond Burr's Perry MASON began his extraordinary television career, defending endless clients. In 1959 the less affluent accused were defended by attorney Macdonald Carey in *Lock-Up* and, in 1963, were often first tracked down and then defended in the unique ninety-minute *Arrest and Trial.* E. G. Marshall and Robert Reed played a father-and-son team for five years on *The Defenders* (1961). The colorful careers of real-life superlawyers inspired *Judd for the Defense* (1967), with Carl Betz as "the most successful lawyer in the world"; courtroom realities shaped the more subdued *Owen Marshall, Counselor at Law* (Arthur Hill, 1971), a compassionate widower.

A lawyer as well as a federal agent, the composite FBI officer portrayed by Efrem Zimbalist, Jr.,

Robert Vaughn is agent Napoleon Solo in the Ian Fleming–created *The Man From U.N.C.L.E.* [*MGM*]

made the hour-long dramas of crime and subversion presented in *The FBI* a singular television success: the program debuted in 1965 and continued on network television until 1974. It is the only such series to have received the blessings and full cooperation of the Bureau's late director, J. Edgar Hoover.

Newspapermen broke many crime headlines in television series programs. Two important journalist sagas began in the early 1950s. *Big Town*, moving from radio in 1950, continued the aggressive reportage of editor Steve Wilson of the *Illustrated Press;* Wilson was portrayed by Patrick McVey and later by Mark Stevens, in an extremely realistic second series lasting until 1955. Jerome Thor's overseas correspondent in *Foreign Intrigue* (1951) wore his trenchcoat in authentic European locales; the program was the first major American television series to be totally filmed abroad (in the following years Thor's assignment was passed to Gerald Mohr and then to James Daly). In 1956 *Wire Service* rotated the investigations of three reporters—George Brent, Mercedes McCambridge, and Dane Clark—employed by newspaper chains, in hour-long dramas. Similarly, for four years the ambitious ninety-minute *Name of the Game* series, which began in 1968, alternated the far-reaching probes of the dynamic editor-publisher of the Howard publishing empire (Gene Barry) and his editors for *Crime Magazine* (Robert Stack) and *People Magazine* (Tony Franciosa), all assisted by an overeager attractive research assistant (Susan Saint James). The popular, lavishly produced program had its origins in a telefeature of the previous year, *Fame Is the Name of the Game*, in which Franciosa and Saint James reported to *Fame Magazine*.

Espionage has been a constant television theme. Beginning in 1953 Richard Carlson impersonated real-life undercover agent Herbert Philbrick for a three-year infiltration of the American Communist party in *I Led Three Lives*. In 1964, from England, *The Avengers* presented (tongue in cheek) the bizarre escapades of dashing, urbane, cane-carrying secret agent John Steed (Patrick Macnee), who, with his female companion, seemed to be forever saving the empire. (Honor Blackman was the heroine of the prototype series, seen only in England; Steed's most popular lady was Diana Rigg—as brisk Mrs. Emma Peel—but when Mr. Peel, long thought dead, returned from a jungle expedition, Steed shared his third and final television year with Linda Thorson as Tara King.) Steed's chiefs were for the most part obscure, but ultimately he reported to a portly, wheelchair-confined, eccentric spy master known only as "Mother." American espionage activity in 1964 was equally lighthearted: Ian FLEMING's *The Man from U.N.C.L.E.* presented American Napoleon Solo (Robert Vaughn) and Russian Illya Kuryakin (David McCallum) as agents of a secret international organization that combated terrorism and subversion and was headed by the elderly, benign Mr. Waverly (Leo G. Carroll). Headquarters was entered from behind the sliding panels at the rear of an ordinary shop. The series lasted four years. In 1965 *I Spy* began chronicling the adventures of an amiable tennis pro (Robert Culp) and his black trainer (Bill Cosby), who were actually earnest agents dabbling in counterespionage around the world. The program—the first to present a black spy as well as a black hero—had a three-year run. Also in 1965, England detailed (for two seasons) the more sober, in fact often grim, exploits of professional spy John Drake (Patrick McGoohan) in *Secret Agent*, also called *Danger Man*. The following year introduced the Impossible Mission Force Special Unit, a team that most often included Peter Graves, Barbara Bain, Greg Morris, Peter Lupus, and Martin Landau, and that very often engaged in worldwide counterespionage tasks, in the seemingly endless tape-elucidated assignments of *Mission Impossible* (seven years). Almost as popular—with a four-year run—was the 1967 series *It Takes a Thief*, in which Robert Wagner was a young master cracksman paroled in the custody of a secret Washington espionage agency, the SIA, and given assignments only a thief could carry out. ("You mean you want me to *steal?*" moaned Wagner at the start of each episode.) Appearing occasionally as Wagner's father was Fred Astaire, "the greatest thief of them all," retired but unreformed.

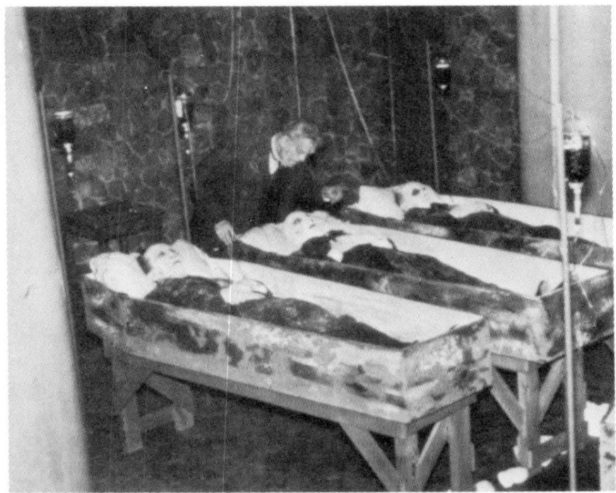

One of the best of the mystery anthology series on television, *Thriller*, had Boris Karloff as host and occasional participant (as here, running a household of living dead) in the melodrama. [*MCA-TV*]

Television detectives of the 1970s have permitted themselves to be far less glamorous than in any previous decade. The overweight private investigator of *Cannon* (portrayed by middle-aged William

The crime-fighting group known as *The Untouchables,* headed by Eliot Ness (Robert Stack, right), blast the Chicago Mafia underworld of the 1930s; note the cut of the clothes.

Conrad; the program debuted in 1971) finds—unlike Nero WOLFE, with whom he shares a love for food—that bulk is no deterrent to mobility, personal involvement, or even an infrequent romantic liaison. Karl Malden is the seasoned policeman of *The Streets of San Francisco* (1971), with young partner Michael Douglas. George Peppard (*Banacek,* 1972) was an urbane Polish-American free-lance insurance investigator with a flair for solving impossible crimes. *Hawkins* (1973) presented James Stewart in the role of Billy Jim Hawkins, who, despite his country accents and ways, was a shrewd, famous criminal lawyer. *The Snoop Sisters* (1973) featured two old maids—Helen Hayes, a mystery writer, and Mildred Natwick—who constantly poked at conveniently neighborly murders. Telly Savalas (*Kojak,* 1973) is a tough, bald-headed cop whose performance in the award-winning telefeature *The Marcus-Nelson Murders,* based on the actual killings of two New York girls, earned the character a series a year later. In another program about a drawn-from-life policeman, *Toma* (Tony Musante, 1973), the detective works under cover in a variety of disguises. And *Police Story* (1973)—created by then policeman Joseph Wambaugh—documented in daringly realistic dramas the temptations and frailities of cops on the job. A spin-off of that show recounted the exploits of the aggressive, good-looking Sergeant Pepper Anderson, portrayed by Angie Dickinson (*Police Woman,* 1974). In private practice, David Janssen is the dour, semidisabled former cop, now a San Diego investigator, of *Harry O.* This low-keyed series (beginning in 1974), is another example of the television detective of the 1970s who eschews the routine image of the past in favor of projecting a solid character.

TEMPLAR, SIMON. *See* SAINT, THE.

TEMPLE, PAUL (Creator: Francis DURBRIDGE). A popular post-World War II radio hero who also battles crime on the British screen and in seven novels, the first being *Send for Paul Temple* (1938).

Films

Calling Paul Temple. Butcher (British), 1948. John Bentley (Temple), Dinah Sheridan, Margaretta Scott, Abraham Sofaer. Directed by Maclean Rogers.

Temple unmasks the killer of a famed doctor's lady patients.

Paul Temple's Triumph. Butcher (British), 1950. Bentley, Sheridan, Jack Livesey. Directed by Rogers.

Temple tangles with "Z," an abductor of atomic scientists.

Paul Temple Returns. Butcher (British), 1952. Bentley, Patricia Dainton, Valentine Dyall, Christopher Lee. Directed by Rogers.

Temple unmasks a master criminal called "The Marquis."

TEY, JOSEPHINE (pseudonym of Elizabeth MacKintosh; 1896–1952). Scottish mystery novelist. Born and brought up in Inverness, Miss MacKintosh graduated from a college for teachers of physical training and taught that subject for a while. However, she spent most of her adult life (her last twenty-eight years) in a small town in a remote part of Scotland, nursing her ailing parents.

Miss MacKintosh began her writing career by contributing verse, short fiction, and sketches to the *Westminster Gazette,* the *Glasgow Herald,* and the *English Review.* Her first book, a detective novel called *The Man in the Queue,* was published in 1929 under the pseudonym Gordon Daviot. She did not write another mystery until 1936, but she did publish two nonmystery novels and then three historical plays. The first play, *Richard of Bordeaux* (1933), starred John Gielgud and established "Daviot's" reputation.

In 1936 she published her second mystery, *A Shilling for Candles,* the first book using the Josephine Tey pseudonym; *The Man in the Queue* was reissued in 1953 under the Tey name. Her next mystery did not appear until 1946. In the interim she published *Claverhouse* (1937), a biography of John Graham, a Scottish leader; *The Stars Bow Down*

(1939), a play based on the Old Testament story of Joseph; and eight one-act plays collected in 1946 as *Leith Sands*. Her subsequent books, beginning with *Miss Pym Disposes* in 1946, were all mysteries except for *The Privateer*, a fictionalized biography of the buccaneer Henry Morgan that was published in 1952 after her death.

The Man in the Queue is the story of the investigation by a slim, elegant Scotland Yard inspector, Alan Grant, of a stabbing that takes place in a line of people waiting outside a London theater. The third Tey book, *Miss Pym Disposes*, is one of only two in which Grant does not appear at all. Its setting is a physical training college. Grant appears only incidentally in *The Franchise Affair* (1948), a somewhat altered account of the famous eighteenth-century Elizabeth Canning case. In it, a young attorney is shaken from the complacency of his comfortable civil practice as he defends a mother and daughter who allegedly held prisoner and mistreated a teen-age girl.

The fifth and sixth Tey mysteries are *Brat Farrar* (1949) and *To Love and Be Wise* (1950).

Grant appears as the detective in the last two Tey books, and the state of his health is pivotal to each. In *The Daughter of Time* (1951) he is confined to bed after having been injured while on a case. Bored, he becomes interested in Richard III, who was assumed by Shakespeare (and others) to have ordered the murder of his nephews in the Tower of London. Convinced of Richard's innocence, Grant attempts to propose another murderer in this unusual historical detective story. Grant is on sick leave in *The Singing Sands* (1952), and close to a nervous breakdown. He travels to the Scottish Highlands to recover. While on the train, he discovers a body and becomes involved in the crime and a Scottish legend in what Anthony BOUCHER called "a study in detection as a method of psychotherapy."

For many years Josephine Tey was known as the mystery writer to be read by people who do not ordinarily read mysteries. Two anthologies of her mysteries were available for years as alternate selections of the Book-of-the-Month Club. Although it is more than twenty years since her death, her works have been continuously in print in both England and the United States.

Films

A Shilling for Candles was the basis for the film *Young and Innocent* (1937), directed by Alfred HITCHCOCK—his favorite among all his British films. The tracking shot across a dance floor to the twitching eye of a musician suspect is still memorable. In 1951 a Tey novel provided the basis for another distinguished British mystery film.

The Franchise Affair. Associated-British, 1951. Michael Denison, Dulcie Gray, Anthony Nicholls, Marjorie Fielding, Athene Seyler, John Bailey, Ann Stephens. Directed by Lawrence Huntington.

A young lawyer reluctantly begins the defense of two spinsters living in a secluded house who are accused by a teen-age girl of holding her prisoner for two weeks.

Television

Miss Tey's mystery about doubles, *Brat Farrar*, was twice used as the basis of American television specials.

THATCHER, JOHN PUTNAM (Creator: Emma LATHEN). The silver-haired vice-president of the Sloan Guaranty Trust Company, though sixtyish and a widower with a married daughter and four grandchildren, is extremely active and fit. He plays three sets of tennis a day and hikes; his journey along the Appalachian Trail in *Pick Up Sticks* is interrupted when he comes upon a dead body.

Thatcher is not only an expert in matters of stocks, bonds, and trusts; he is an excellent judge of human nature—an ability that stands him in good stead in his dealings with such varied personalities as the Sloan's inept president, a Wall Street executive who is an aging playboy, and his own very staid but efficient secretary, Miss Corsa.

In John Thatcher's debut, *Banking on Death*, the amount of money involved, $300,000 from a trust fund, is relatively minor. Millions are at stake, however, in *Accounting for Murder*, in which Clarence Fortinbras, one of the leading auditors in the United States, looks into the shaky financial structure of the "National Calculating Company." He is found strangled—with the cord of his own adding machine. In *Murder Makes the Wheels Go Round*, John Thatcher goes to Detroit to investigate a proposed investment by the Sloan in "Michigan Motors." He attends the special presentation of that company's custom-built limousine to a visiting Arab ruler and discovers a dead body inside the automobile. The Lathen books are often topical. *Death Shall Overcome* centers on the possible acceptance of the first black on the New York Stock Exchange. In *Murder against the Grain* a bank swindle threatens a newly signed Russian-American wheat treaty.

Anthony BOUCHER referred to Thatcher as "one of the very few important series detectives to enter the field in the 1960s—a completely civilized and urbane man, whose charm is as remarkable as his acumen."

CHECKLIST

1961 *Banking on Death*
1963 *A Place for Murder*
1964 *Accounting for Murder*
1966 *Murder Makes the Wheels Go Round*
1966 *Death Shall Overcome*
1967 *Murder against the Grain*

1968 *A Stitch in Time*
1968 *Come to Dust*
1969 *When in Greece*
1969 *Murder to Go*
1970 *Pick Up Sticks*
1971 *Ashes to Ashes*
1971 *The Longer the Thread*
1972 *Murder Without Icing*
1974 *Sweet and Low*
1975 *By Hook or by Crook*

THAYER, LEE (1874–1973). American artist and mystery novelist. Born Emma Redington Lee in Pennsylvania, Mrs. Thayer spent most of her life in the New York City area. She considered herself an artist who wrote as a sideline, mostly for enjoyment. Some of her earliest paintings were on view at the Chicago World's Fair of 1893. She also did pictorial designs for book bindings and dust jackets. She traveled widely and owned a large collection of Japanese art acquired during several trips to the Orient. She was living in retirement in Coronado, a suburb of San Diego, Calif., at the time of her death.

When the book Mrs. Thayer planned as her last, *Dusty Death* (1966), was published, she became the oldest mystery author, age ninety-two, to have published a book. She wrote sixty mystery novels beginning with *The Mystery of the Thirteenth Floor* (1919) but never had a short story published. All but one of her books (*Dr. S.O.S.*, 1925) are about red-headed detective Peter Clancy and his snobbish valet, Wiggar.

THIN MAN, THE. *See* CHARLES, NICK AND NORA.

THINKING MACHINE, THE (Creator: Jacques FUTRELLE). The most cerebral of all detectives, Professor Augustus S. F. X. Van Dusen works for an unnamed college in the Boston area and has more than a score of degrees and honors to his credit. After giving a remarkable demonstration at chess, proving his theory that a man totally unfamiliar with the game could defeat the world champion simply by applying logic and intellect, he was christened by his opponent, who said: "You are not a man; you are a brain—a machine—a thinking machine."

One of the great scientific detectives, a master logician, the Thinking Machine solves cases brought to him by a reporter, Hutchinson Hatch, who also does the legwork in most of the adventures.

Van Dusen is dwarfish in appearance, pale and thin, his shoulders stooped in the usual caricature of a scholar. His most remarkable feature is his huge head (he wears a size 8 hat); he has an abnormally high and broad brow, topped by a shock of yellow hair. His blue eyes constantly pucker into a forbidding squint behind thick glasses. Although irritable and curt, he is not cruel; he is simply too busy to regard the solving of a crime as more than a minor annoyance. Uninterested in the external clues of a case, he merely restates the problem in its simplest form, applies logic, and arrives at a conclusion. His mind, he says, is filled with more important things than crime. At one point, he seriously states (condescendingly) that he would invent an airship but is too busy at the moment (the Van Dusen stories were written when flying was not yet taken for granted).

***The Thinking Machine*, a *Queen's Quorum* and *Haycraft-Queen Cornerstone Library* selection, was first published by Dodd, Mead in 1907. The Kinneys provided the illustrations.**

The professor first appeared at the conclusion of an adventure-crime novel, *The Chase of the Golden Plate* (1906). The best narratives about the eccentric genius are the seven stories in *The Thinking Machine* (1907), reissued as *The Problem of Cell 13* (1917), named for the most famous story of the group, and one of the dozen or so most popular anthology pieces ever written, in which Van Dusen accepts the challenge of two scientific colleagues to "think" himself out of an "escape-proof" cell within a week. The final book about the professor is *The Thinking Machine on the Case* (1908; British title: *The Professor on the Case*), a volume of short connected episodes. "The Haunted Bell" in *The Diamond Master* (1909) is also a Van Dusen tale. Several additional stories survived the author's death in the *Titanic* tragedy; they were published in *Ellery Queen's Mystery Magazine*. A series of stories appeared in newspapers in 1905 and 1906; two of them were published in *Best "Thinking Machine" Detective Stories* (1973), edited by E. F. Bleiler.

THOMAS, ROSS (1926–   ). American publicist and mystery writer. Born in Oklahoma City, Thomas was a cub reporter on the *Daily Oklahoman* when he was a college freshman. He left school to serve in the Army and saw combat in the Philippines at the end of World War II. He returned to the University of Oklahoma and graduated in 1949. He worked as a newspaperman and in public relations in the United States, Europe, and Africa before becoming a mystery writer.

Thomas's first book, *The Cold War Swap,* won the Mystery Writers of America Edgar for best first mystery of 1966. *The Fools in Town Are on Our Side* (1971), *The Porkchoppers* (1972), and *If You Can't Be Good* (1973) deal with corruption in a small Southern city, a large labor union, and the U.S. Senate, respectively. He drew on his experience as publicity director for Chief Obafemi Awolowo of Nigeria for two mysteries about African diplomats, *The Seersucker Whipsaw* (1967) and *The Brass Go-Between* (1969). The latter was published under his pseudonym, Oliver Bleeck, and is the first of three books about Philip St. Ives, a professional intermediary who is paid to ransom stolen objects and kidnapped people.

THORNDYKE, DR. (Creator: R. Austin FREEMAN). The greatest medico-legal detective of all time. Dr. John Evelyn Thorndyke is a forensic scientist and lawyer whose methods are extremely technical and specialized. The precise opposite of Father BROWN and similar intuitive detectives, he does not analyze or examine people closely; he is concerned with things, seeking clues from physical entities that will ultimately serve as irrefutable evidence. He is almost inseparable from his research kit, "the inevitable green case," with its collection of miniature instruments and chemicals. Approaching each case with solemnity and painstaking exactitude, the normally kindly and philanthropic detective attempts to remain emotionally detached, sublimating his wit to become reserved, even secretive. His profound knowledge of such diverse subjects as anatomy, archaeology, botany, Egyptology, and ophthalmology aids his exceptional reasoning powers. Although he does not have a superhuman intelligence, he does possess a scientific imagination—the ability to perceive the essential nature of a problem before all necessary evidence has been accumulated.

Dr. Thorndyke lives at 5A King's Bench Walk in London's Inner Temple with Christopher Jervis, his aide and chronicler, and Nathaniel Polton, his laboratory assistant, butler, photographer, and jack-of-all-trades. Polton is ingenious and has great technical knowledge, but Jervis, who carefully observes and records every detail of a case, inevitably fails to see their significance.

Physically, Thorndyke is the handsomest of all detectives; Freeman gave him every advantage. Tall, slim, and athletic, with a fine Grecian nose and

Dr. John Evelyn Thorndyke, as portrayed by the famous Victorian and Edwardian book illustrator H. M. Brock for *Pearson's* magazine in 1908.

classical features, he also has acute eyesight and hearing and extraordinary manual skills—desirable qualities for a doctor. "His distinguished appearance," wrote Freeman, "is not merely a concession to my personal taste but also a protest against the monsters of ugliness whom some detective writers have evolved. These are quite opposed to natural truth. In real life, a first-class man of any kind usually tends to be a good-looking man."

Although Freeman denied that Thorndyke was modeled after a real person, claiming that "he was deliberately created to play a certain part," he conceded that the character bore some resemblance to Professor Alfred Swaine Taylor (1806–1880), an expert in medical and chemical jurisprudence whose textbooks, notably *Principles and Practices of Medical Jurisprudence* (1865), were read by Freeman as a student.

Two pastiches of Thorndyke have been published recently as pamphlets: "Goodbye, Dr. Thorndyke" (1972) by Norman Donaldson and "Dr. Thorndyke's Dilemma" (1974) by John H. Dirckx.

CHECKLIST

1907 *The Red Thumb Mark*
1909 *John Thorndyke's Cases* (s.s.; U.S. title: *Dr. Thorndyke's Cases*)
1911 *The Eye of Osiris* (U.S. title: *The Vanishing Man*)
1912 *The Singing Bone* (s.s.)
1912 *The Mystery of 31, New Inn*
1914 *A Silent Witness*
1918 *The Great Portrait Mystery* (s.s.; two stories are about Thorndyke)

1922 *Helen Vardon's Confession*
1923 *Dr. Thorndyke's Case Book* (s.s.; U.S. title: *The Blue Scarab*)
1923 *The Cat's Eye*
1924 *The Mystery of Angelina Frood*
1925 *The Puzzle Lock* (s.s.)
1925 *The Shadow of the Wolf*
1926 *The D'Arblay Mystery*
1927 *The Magic Casket* (s.s.)
1927 *A Certain Dr. Thorndyke*
1928 *As a Thief in the Night*
1930 *Mr. Pottermack's Oversight*
1931 *Pontifex, Son and Thorndyke*
1932 *When Rogues Fall Out* (U.S. title: *Dr. Thorndyke's Discovery*)
1933 *Dr. Thorndyke Intervenes*
1934 *For the Defence: Dr. Thorndyke* (U.S. title: *For the Defense: Dr. Thorndyke*)
1936 *The Penrose Mystery*
1937 *Felo de Se?* (U.S. title: *Death at the Inn*)
1938 *The Stoneware Monkey*
1940 *Mr. Polton Explains*
1942 *The Jacob Street Mystery* (U.S. title: *The Unconscious Witness*)
1973 *The Best Dr. Thorndyke Detective Stories* (s.s.; contains first book publication of the novelette *31, New Inn,* an expanded version of which was published in 1912 as *The Mystery of 31, New Inn*)

THURSDAY, MAX (Creator: Wade MILLER). This San Diego private detective is a tall, lean man with a gaunt face. When he first appears, in *Guilty Bystander* (1947), he is a house detective in a cheap hotel and has a history of drinking too much. His former wife, Georgia, goes to him because their small son, whom Thursday has not seen since the divorce, has been kidnapped.

The book marks the rehabilitation of Thursday, who becomes a successful detective despite the hair-trigger temper that makes him reluctant to carry a gun. He is helped in his recovery by his friend Austin Clapp, head of homicide in San Diego, who gives him frequent personal advice. Zachary Scott gave a convincing portrayal of a tortured Thursday in a 1950 film version of this book.

Miller describes Thursday as "a flawed but basically decent human being who clings to his own peculiar ethical code in a corrupt and brutal milieu."

Thursday's other adventures are *Fatal Step* (1948), *Uneasy Street* (1948), *Calamity Fair* (1950), *Murder Charge* (1950), and *Shoot to Kill* (1951).

TIBBETT, HENRY (Creator: Patricia MOYES). A quiet and timid Scotland Yard detective, Tibbett is in his late forties, is slight in stature, and has unmemorable features, mild blue eyes, sandy hair, and pale eyebrows. In short, he might be mistaken for a clerk.

He and his wife, Emmy, live on the ground floor of a decaying Victorian house in London. They enjoy traveling abroad and have recently become proficient in yachting and skiing.

The chief inspector is a conscientious and observant policeman with an occasional flair for intuitive detection. When anything strikes him as being odd, he says: "My nose tells me. . . ." His successes have brought him promotion to chief superintendent.

Tibbett's debut appearance, in *Dead Men Don't Ski* (1959), was warmly welcomed by critic Anthony BOUCHER when it was published in the United States. Set in the Italian Tirol, it concerns a corpse found on a ski lift. The skiing background is well handled by Miss Moyes, who counts the sport among her interests. Similarly, in *The Sunken Sailor* (1961; U.S. title: *Down among the Dead Men*), her interest in a sport—sailing—is integral to Tibbett's investigation into the year-old death of an experienced yachtsman in the harbor on the River Berry in southeastern England.

In *Death on the Agenda* (1962) Tibbett attends an international conference on narcotics in Geneva. He finds himself in the unfamiliar role of chief suspect in a murder case. *Murder à la Mode* (1963), about the murder of a staff member of a fashion magazine, has been favorably compared by many critics to the work of Ngaio MARSH. Boucher stated: "I haven't read a book in at least a decade that reminds me so warmly of those golden days in the nineteen-thirties, when [Margery] ALLINGHAM, [Nicholas] BLAKE, and Marsh were all youthfully reshaping the detective novel."

Falling Star (1964), Miss Moyes's best work, is also notable for its authentic background. Its puzzle concerns an actor who dies while a scene that was not in the script is being filmed. Narrated by one of the film people, the novel stresses characterization rather than puzzle and plot—a tendency in much of her subsequent work.

Johnny under Ground (1965) centers on Tibbett's wife's past, which provides the solution to a current murder problem. *Murder Fantastical* (1967) involves an aristocratic and eccentric English family that has the bad luck to find a murdered bookmaker lying in the driveway with a bullet in his head.

Although *Death and the Dutch Uncle* (1968) starts out with the death of a small-time crook in the bathroom of a third-rate pub, it evolves into a controversy between two emerging African nations. The political ramifications make it necessary for Tibbett to protect the life of an irascible Dutch diplomat in picturesque Holland. *Who Saw Her Die?* (1970; U.S. title: *Many Deadly Returns*) is about a birthday party for an aged and eccentric lady; an uninvited guest—death—also attends. Tibbett suspects foul play, but the medical evidence points to natural causes.

Season of Snow and Sins (1971), narrated by three of the main characters, is set in a small skiing village on the slopes of the Alps. It starts when a pregnant woman kills her unfaithful husband and is convicted of the crime; but the situation becomes more complicated, and the stability of the French government is threatened. *The Curious Affair of the Third Dog* (1973) concerns behind-the-scenes dirty work in the popular English sport of greyhound racing. In *Black Widower* (1975) the action alternates between Washington, D.C., and the Caribbean as a murder occurs in diplomatic circles.

TIBBS, VIRGIL (Creator: John BALL). When Virgil Tibbs, the best-known black detective in fiction, first appeared, Anthony BOUCHER called him "a remarkable individual who may well end up in the great detective category." Born in the Deep South, where his mother still resides, he is visiting in that part of the country when he becomes a murder suspect solely because of his color in *In the Heat of the Night* (1965). He solves the case to preserve his own reputation as well as that of the white police chief who reluctantly works with him.

For ten years Tibbs, who is in his early thirties, has been with the Pasadena, Calif., Police Department. He is its expert on homicide cases, excellent at interpreting clues but equally qualified when physical force is needed. He has studied karate under Nishiyama, who personally awarded him the black belt. He also spent several years studying the highly advanced art of aikido under the late master Isao Takahashi.

He washed dishes and waited on tables in a university dining room while completing his education. Tibbs feels that his color gives him a ready-made "disguise"; early in his career he made an important arrest while pretending to be a bootblack. He assumed, correctly, that his suspect would not hesitate to transact "business," in this case peddling drugs, in the presence of a menial black.

Tibbs is not "hung up" on racial discrimination, feeling that the less attention he gives to it, the less it will be directed toward him. On rare occasions he relaxes, has a drink, and listens to the music of Ravel. These opportunities are few, for Tibbs's dedication to his work leaves him few evenings free, whether he is actively on a case or preparing himself for a court appearance.

Because he views himself simply as a human being who happens to be black, he is able to deal effectively with all people in his community. In *The Cool Cottontail* (1966) he investigates a murder in a widely known nudist resort. In *Johnny Get Your Gun* (1969), a small white boy steals his father's gun, kills a black, and runs away from home. Tibbs must find the boy and prevent an impending race riot. (The facts of this case were somewhat distorted in the hard-cover edition; a more accurate account appears in the Bantam edition under the title *Death for a Playmate.*) The most recent Tibbs novel is *Five Pieces of Jade* (1972).

A tough redneck police captain (Rod Steiger) in a Southern town gradually allows himself to befriend Virgil Tibbs (Sidney Poitier), the black cop from Philadelphia conscripted into using his skills in solving a local murder, in the film *In the Heat of the Night.* [*United Artists*]

Films

Tibbs has solved three cinematic cases, portrayed in all by Sidney Poitier. Ball had no connection with the second or third, neither writing nor approving them.

In the Heat of the Night. United Artists, 1967. Poitier, Rod Steiger, Warren Oates, Lee Grant. Directed by Norman Jewison.

When a prominent citizen is killed in a small Southern town, the red-neck police captain (Steiger) quickly arrests a well-dressed black passing through and is only slightly less suspicious when he learns that his suspect is a homicide detective in the Philadelphia Police Department. Slowly he gives in to tolerance and respect. The film won both the Academy Award and the Mystery Writers of America Edgar for best picture of the year.

They Call Me Mister Tibbs! United Artists, 1970. Poitier, Martin Landau, Barbara McNair. Directed by Gordon Douglas.

Now with the San Francisco Police Department, Tibbs must defend a friend, a crusading minister, against the charge of murdering a prostitute, a crime of which he seems unmistakably guilty.

The Organization. United Artists, 1971. Poitier, McNair, Sheree North, Ron O'Neal, Allan Garfield. Directed by Don Medford.

Again in San Francisco, Detective Tibbs must

unofficially help a gang of well-meaning young vigilantes who want to thwart the very business-like leaders of a nationwide heroin organization by stealing $4 million worth of the drug.

TILLRAY, LES. *See* GARDNER, ERLE STANLEY.

TILTON, ALICE. *See* TAYLOR, PHOEBE ATWOOD.

TOFF, THE (Creator: John CREASEY). The Honorable Richard Rollison, known to the police as "The Toff," is a handsome and romantic gentleman-adventurer.

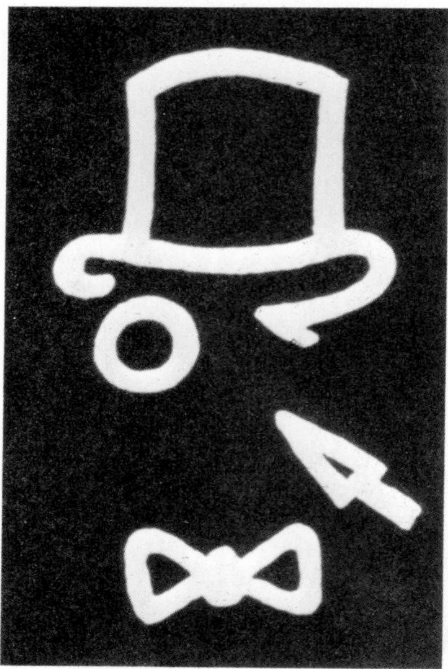

This drawing of the Toff has appeared on more than fifty titles.

The Mayfair playboy has a valet, Jolly, who is faithful, intelligent, and witty. Rollison's patrician aunt, Lady ("Old Glory") Gloria Hurst, is liberal-minded and quite willing to rub elbows with the riffraff of London's East End. Inspector Gryce handles the official investigations in the Toff's adventures. Closely resembling The Saint (see SAINT, THE), the Toff first appeared in *The Thriller* magazine in 1933; the first of his fifty-five book appearances, *Introducing the Toff,* followed five years later.

Films

Two films were fashioned from the elegant Toff, with John Bentley portraying him on both occasions; both were written by Creasey and released in 1952.

Salute the Toff. Nettlefold (British), 1952. Bentley, Carol Marsh, Valentine Dyall (Gryce). Directed by Maclean Rogers.

The Toff investigates a kidnapping and helps a girl who is involved in an insurance swindle.

Hammer the Toff. Nettlefold (British). Bentley, Patricia Dainton, Dyall. Directed by Rogers.

The Toff explores the theft of a secret formula and goes to the rescue of a "Robin Hood" crook.

TOWNE, STUART. *See* RAWSON, CLAYTON.

TRACY, DICK (Creator: Chester GOULD). The first comic strip supersleuth, a plainclothes detective who first appears in 1931 as a civilian (later, he wins a job as an official detective) in a gangster-dominated city that resembles Chicago. He vows to catch the killers of his sweetheart's father. His square-jawed face, with its hawk nose and lean lines, is an idealized conception of the visage of Sherlock HOLMES. A rugged, two-fisted, hard-boiled detective, he is tough enough to handle even the most vicious criminals. The villains with whom he must deal are colorful gangsters whose physical or facial deformities have earned them their names: Pruneface, Flattop (his head resembles an aircraft carrier), the Brow, the Mole (who lives underground), Little Face, B. B. Eyes, the Blank (a faceless killer), Mumbles, and Pear Shape.

Other characters in Tracy's life are Tess Trueheart, his faithful girl friend for eighteen years and then his wife; his adopted son, Junior, a police artist; Chief of Police Pat Patton; Sam Catchem, Tracy's sidekick; Gravel Gertie and B. O. Plenty, two itinerants who are brought together by Tracy and whose union produces a child, Sparkle Plenty; and Diet Smith, the huge millionaire industrialist whose life is saved by Tracy. Some of the gadgets Diet Smith has invented are used by Tracy. When they were first used, the inventions were in the realm of science fiction, but devices such as two-way wrist radios and closed-circuit television are now commonplace.

Probably the second-most familiar detective in the world (only Holmes is better known), Tracy has expressed his philosophy in two succinct, now-famous phrases: "Little crimes lead to big crimes," and "Crime does not pay."

Films

The stylized comic strip hero, with his arsenals of anticrime weaponry, was converted from a plainclothes "dick" to an FBI operative for four serials in the 1930s. Of the Bureau he says: "No criminal can outwit an organization which goes on forever, whose members never sleep." Few familiar faces were carried over from the comic strip, but Ralph Byrd gave the definitive screen portrayal of Tracy.

Dick Tracy. Republic serial, 1937. Byrd, Kay Hughes, Smiley Burnette, Lee Van Atta, John Piccori. Directed by Ray Taylor and Alan James.

Tracy's brother is transformed into a depraved

The name and face of Dick Tracy (originally called Plainclothes Tracy) are probably the most readily recognized of those of any detective in the world after Sherlock Holmes.

criminal by a brain operation performed by a mysterious limping fiend known as both the Spider and the Lame One. From his futuristic aircraft, the *Flying Wing*, the villain tries to collapse the Golden Gate Bridge by using a sonic vibrator.

Dick Tracy Returns. Republic serial, 1938. Byrd, Lynn Roberts, Charles Middleton, Jerry Tucker. Directed by William Witney and John English.

G-man Tracy is assigned to stop the activities of a criminal family—Pa Stark and his five hulking sons—who, while robbing an armored car, have killed a fellow FBI officer.

Dick Tracy's G-Men. Republic serial, 1939. Byrd, Irving Pichel, Phyllis Isley (Jennifer Jones), Walter Miller. Directed by Witney and English.

International spy and anarchist Zarnoff, supposedly executed in the gas chamber, is revived by drugs and continues his frenzied sabotage of American defenses.

Dick Tracy vs. Crime, Inc. Republic serial, 1941. Byrd, Michael Owen, Jan Wiley, John Davidson, Ralph Morgan. Directed by Witney and English.

Tracy is pitted against an invisible adversary, called the Ghost, who is determined to eliminate New York City's mayor and city council for having allowed his gangster brother to be sent to the electric chair; at the end of the first chapter he is about to eliminate New York City altogether by causing (by means of offshore explosions) a tidal wave to sweep in on Manhattan.

Four feature films were then taken from the comic strip, adhering more closely to the source. Tracy is united with many of his friends, including fiancée Tess (omitted from the serials) and the Barrymore-like Shakespearean actor Vitamin Flintheart. The villains, too, are more similar to the grotesque adversaries of the comic strip source. Morgan Conway played Tracy in the first two films.

Dick Tracy. RKO, 1945. Conway, Anne Jeffreys, Jane Greer, Mike Mazurki, Joseph Crehan. Directed by William Berke.

A schoolteacher is stabbed on a lonely street; Splitface (Mazurki), who has vowed to kill the members of the jury who had convicted him of murder years before, is responsible.

Dick Tracy vs. Cueball. RKO, 1946. Conway, Jeffreys, Dick Wessel, Rita Corday, Douglas Walton, Ian Keith. Directed by Gordon M. Douglas.

Cueball, a bald strangler (Wessel), murders a messenger who was carrying a fortune in jewelry and is pursued by Tracy through the dark corners of the underworld. This was Conway's last appearance as Tracy; here and in the preceding film he was an official of the city police.

Dick Tracy's Dilemma. RKO, 1947. Byrd

Morgan Conway, the first Dick Tracy of feature films, is the unsuspecting target of the scarred killer Splitface (Mike Mazurki) in the 1945 film *Dick Tracy*. [*RKO*]

Dick Tracy, here played by Ralph Byrd, is menaced by the notorious Claw in the feature *Dick Tracy's Dilemma.* [*RKO*]

(restored to the role, but no longer an FBI agent), Lyle Latell, Jimmy Conlin, Jack Lambert, Keith. Directed by John Rawlins.

A notorious one-armed killer, "the Claw" (Lambert), whose iron hook replaces a missing hand, engineers a fur robbery and murders a supposedly blind beggar who had been assigned by Tracy to spy on him.

Dick Tracy Meets Gruesome. RKO, 1947. Byrd, Boris Karloff, Anne Gwynne, Edward Ashley, Latell. Directed by Rawlins.

A disfigured escaped convict, "Gruesome" (Karloff), comes into possession of a gas that causes temporary paralysis, and he uses it to rob banks. This was the final Tracy film.

Radio and Television

On radio, Tracy, "protector of law and order," had an active career. The program *Dick Tracy* began on Mutual in 1935 and spanned more than a decade, both as a Monday-to-Friday serial and as a weekly series. Most of Tracy's professional associates and friends (Pat Patton, Chief Brandon, Tess, Vitamin) were represented, and actor Ned Wever was Tracy's most familiar voice. Ralph Byrd played Tracy again in an early half-hour television series, *The Adventures of Dick Tracy.* In 1960 a group of five-minute color cartoons called *The Dick Tracy Show* were produced in which Tracy (the voice was that of Everett Sloane) battled humorous juvenile versions of the comic strip's more famous villains (Pruneface, Flattop), although he left most of the legwork to such newly created cartoon underlings as Hemlock Holmes, Go-Go Gomez, Joe Jitsu, and a police squad called the "Retouchables."

Play

A $500,000 musical, *Dick Tracy,* closed before it got to Broadway in 1970. The adaptation was by Tony Piano; music and lyrics were by Michael Colicchio.

TRACY, LOUIS (1863–1928). English journalist and author of science fiction, fantasy, adventure, and mystery novels. His best-known character is Inspector Furneaux, who appears in many detective novels. Probably his best books are *The Park Lane Mystery* (1924), and *The Albert Gate Affair* (1904; U.S. title: *The Albert Gate Mystery*), which features Reginald Brett, barrister-detective. Tracy's straightforward, uncomplicated style made his easy-to-read fiction very popular in its time, though it is little read today. He also wrote eight novels using the pseudonym Gordon HOLMES, collaborating with M. P. SHIEL on all but the first.

TRAIN, ARTHUR (CHEYNEY) (1875–1945). American lawyer, criminologist, novelist, short story writer, and creator of lawyer-detective Ephraim TUTT.

Born in Boston, the son of Sarah M. (Cheney) and Charles Russell Train, attorney general of Massachusetts for seventeen years, Train graduated from Harvard University and Harvard Law School and then was a lawyer and assistant district attorney. In 1897 he married Ethel Kissam; they had a son and three daughters. His first wife died in 1923. He married Helen C. Gerard in 1926; they had a son.

Train sold his first story in 1904 and produced almost 300 stories and books thereafter. In his autobiography, *My Day in Court* (1939), he wrote: "I enjoy the dubious distinction of being known among lawyers as a writer, and among writers as a lawyer." Members of both professions, he good-humoredly lamented, treated him with condescension.

Although Train's best-known work is about Mr. Tutt, he also wrote some of the first books about true crime in America, nonmystery novels, science fiction, and mystery fiction not involving Tutt, notably his first book, *McAllister and His Double* (1905), a collection of short stories featuring "Fatty" Welch (alias Wilkins) and introducing the scientific detective Monsieur Donaque; *The Confessions of Artemus Quibble* (1911), a series of connected episodes about a New York shyster lawyer; and *Manhattan Murder* (1936), a fast-paced novel about organized crime featuring the Torello mob and its leader, who is known as the "Capone of the East."

TRENDLE, GEORGE W. *See* GREEN HORNET, THE.

TRENT, PHILIP (Creator: E. C. BENTLEY). A famous English artist who has solved some puzzling mysteries and is respected by both the police and Fleet Street, Trent is tall, gangly, and still fairly young. He dresses in rough tweeds that are slightly untidy, as are his hair and short moustache. His face has a quixotic air. Pleasant, friendly, and tactful, Trent is fond of good living. He is curious about any type of crime problem, and his artistic endeavors are frequently interrupted by summonses from an important London newspaper, which considers him an extremely valuable crime journalist, to investigate mysteries.

Trent is very human, in contrast to the infallible type of sleuth personified by Sherlock HOLMES—so human, in fact, that in his first investigation, *Trent's Last Case* (1913; U.S. title: *The Woman in Black*), he not only falls in love with the chief suspect but finds that his solution to the mystery is completely wrong.

The novel concerns the murder of a wealthy financier and the efforts of Trent to solve the problem for his newspaper. Originally entitled *Philip Gasket's Last Case,* and entered in a contest for first novels, the book failed to arouse much interest. Bentley's chance encounter with a representative of the American firm Century Company resulted in overseas publication of the work with two changes: the hero's name was changed to Trent, and the book retitled *The Woman in Black.* Meanwhile, John BUCHAN, a friend of Bentley and a partner in the British publishing firm Thomas Nelson & Sons, Ltd., was instrumental in securing the rights for British publication. This time the book was called *Trent's Last Case,* and subsequent editions on both sides of the Atlantic bore this title.

In his autobiography Bentley stated that the novel had been a conscious reaction against the sterility and artificiality into which much of the detective fiction of the day had sunk. "It does not seem to have been noticed that *Trent's Last Case* is not so much a detective story as an exposure of detective stories . . . . It should be possible, I thought, to write a detective story in which the detective was recognizable as a human being."

Howard HAYCRAFT best summed up *Trent's Last Case* fifty years after publication: "It would be oversimplification to suggest that *Trent* is primarily remarkable for its unremarkableness. Yet the qualities constituting Bentley's chief contribution to the genre are his easy naturalism and quiet humor, which we have long since come to take for granted. Closely related to these is his use of character as a means of detection; often imitated, it has rarely been surpassed. That the detective could be at once brilliantly right and wrong remains one of the novel's achievements; and the ultimate revelation deservedly stands beside Agatha CHRISTIE's *The Murder of Roger Ackroyd* (1926), but without that story's element of trickery."

The widow with whom Philip Trent falls in love is portrayed on the dust wrapper and frontispiece of the first edition of *Trent's Last Case*, published by Nelson in 1913. The first American edition, published the same year by Century, was titled *The Woman in Black.*

Trent's Own Case (1936), Bentley's second detective novel after a silence of twenty-three years, was written in collaboration with Herbert Warner Allen. It concerned the murder of an elderly philanthropist named James Randolph and presented Philip Trent in the role of chief suspect. It met a better fate than that usually received by sequels.

Trent Intervenes (1938) displayed Bentley's ability to write in the short story form. Several stories ("The Genuine Tabard" and "The Sweet Shot") have become anthology favorites, and the volume has also been included in QUEEN'S QUORUM.

Films

Trent's Last Case. Broadwest (British), 1920. Gregory Scott (Trent), Pauline Peters, Clive Brook. Directed by Richard Garrick.

A financier dies mysteriously, and his male secretary, in love with the victim's wife, is framed for murder.

In America, Howard Hawks directed Raymond Griffith as Trent in a 1929 Fox version.

Trent's Last Case. British Lion (British), 1953. Michael Wilding (Trent), Margaret Lockwood, Orson Welles, John McCallum. Directed by Herbert Wilcox.

This film is a very close retelling of the case, with Welles as Sigsbee Manderson, the dead millionaire, seen only in flashback sequences.

TREVOR, ELLESTON. *See* HALL, ADAM.

TREVOR, GLEN. *See* HILTON, JAMES.

TURNBULL, DORA AMY ELLES DILLON. *See* WENTWORTH, PATRICIA.

TUTT, EPHRAIM (Creator: Arthur TRAIN). One of the wisest lawyers in literature, Mr. Tutt is also one of the kindest, handling innumerable cases for which he cannot collect a fee. In the service of justice he often resorts to obscure legal technicalities and loopholes. He has never lost a case.

Born on July 4, 1869, Tutt is equal parts Abraham Lincoln, Puck, Uncle Sam, and Robin Hood. He works in New York City and in his hometown, Pottsville, N.Y., where his unhappy antagonist is Hezekiah Mason, the prosecutor who cannot win a case against the shrewd old lawyer. In Tutt's usual cases a helpless victim is unable to extricate himself from a situation created by the machinations of a wiser—and more evil—person.

Mr. Tutt is the Lincolnesque lawyer who appeared in twelve short story collections. This illustration by Arthur William Brown appeared on the dust wrapper of *Old Man Tutt*, published by Scribner in 1938.

Train describes Tutt as one who "fights fire with fire, meets guile with guile, and rights the legal wrong. He is the Quixote who tries to make things what they ought to be in this world of things as they are, who has the courage of his illusions, following the dictates of his heart where his head says there is no way."

When *Yankee Lawyer: The Autobiography of Ephraim Tutt* (1943) was published, many readers refused to believe that the lawyer who championed the cause of the underdog was a fictional character.

CHECKLIST

1920	*Tutt and Mr. Tutt* (s.s.)
1921	*By Advice of Counsel* (s.s.)
1921	*The Hermit of Turkey Hollow*
1923	*Tut, Tut, Mr. Tutt!* (s.s.)
1926	*Page Mr. Tutt* (s.s.)
1927	*When Tutt Meets Tutt* (s.s.)
1930	*The Adventures of Ephraim Tutt* (s.s.; omnibus)
1934	*Tutt for Tutt* (s.s.)
1936	*Mr. Tutt Takes the Stand* (s.s.)
1937	*Mr. Tutt's Case Book* (s.s.; omnibus)
1938	*Old Man Tutt* (s.s.)
1941	*Mr. Tutt Comes Home* (s.s.)
1943	*Yankee Lawyer: The Autobiography of Ephraim Tutt*
1945	*Mr. Tutt Finds a Way* (s.s.)

TWAIN, MARK. *See* CLEMENS, SAMUEL LANGHORNE.

TWEEDSMUIR, 1ST BARON. *See* BUCHAN, JOHN.

TYRE, NEDRA (1921–   ). American mystery novelist. Born in Georgia, Miss Tyre has worked in a library and as a clerk in a bookstore, advertising copywriter, typist, staff writer, social worker, and sociology teacher.

Her mysteries reflect her life and jobs in the South. The heroine-detective of *Mouse in Eternity* (1952) is a social worker in Atlanta; the book was nominated by the Mystery Writers of America (MWA) as one of the best crime novels of the year. *Hall of Death* (1960) is set in a girls' reformatory in the South. Miss Tyre's nonregional novel *Death of an Intruder* (1953) was described by Frances CRANE as "superbly handled suspense." Among her other mystery novels are *Everyone Suspect* (1964) and *Twice So Fair* (1971).

Many of Miss Tyre's short stories have appeared in the annual anthologies published by MWA, Ellery QUEEN (author), and Alfred HITCHCOCK. "In the Fiction Alcove" (1967) takes place in the library of a Georgia city. "Murder in the Poe Shrine," a prizewinner in *Ellery Queen's Mystery Magazine*'s 1955 contest, is about a murder at the Edgar Allan POE Museum in Richmond, Va.

U

UHNAK, DOROTHY (1933–). American policewoman and mystery novelist. Born in the Bronx, Mrs. Uhnak attended the College of the City of New York for three years before leaving to join the New York City Transit Police Department. She was a policewoman for fourteen years (with time off when her daughter Tracy was born), was promoted to detective second grade, and received the Outstanding Police Duty Medal, the highest award of the department, "for heroism above and beyond the call of duty." Since leaving the police force to write full time, she has earned a degree at the John Jay College of Criminal Justice.

In her spare time Mrs. Uhnak wrote the autobiographical *Policewoman* (1964) before turning to mysteries. The detective in her first three novels is Christie Opara, a young policewoman assigned to the Manhattan district attorney's staff. The first Opara book, *The Bait* (1968), was cowinner of the Mystery Writers of America Edgar as best first novel that year. Mrs. Uhnak's nonseries 1973 novel, *Law and Order,* about three generations of Irish-American policemen, achieved best-seller status.

UNCLE ABNER (Creator: Melville Davisson POST). One of the greatest American detectives, a giant figure of absolute integrity whose strong moral convictions and profound biblical knowledge compel him to serve as the righter of wrongs and protector of the innocent in his Virginia mountain community.

Abner lives in the rugged backwoods during the decades preceding the Civil War, before there were police. He has no official standing and does not seek the job of solving crimes, but he believes that someone must help God administer justice. The evildoers, Abner knows, are perfectly capable of eluding man-made laws, which are vaguely connected with true justice. But the Virginia squire also knows that, ultimately, right must emerge because of the omnipresence of God. In "The Doomdorf Mystery," the first story in *Uncle Abner: Master of Mysteries* (1918), a character says, "It is a world filled with the mysterious joinder of the accident." Abner replies, "It is a world filled with the mysterious justice of God!"

His knowledge of people, and ability to judge their souls, enables him to dissect brilliantly conceived mysteries. Perhaps his finest hour arrives in "An Act of God," in which he proves that a deaf-and-dumb man could not have written an incriminating document because the paper contains a phonetic misspelling.

The austere Uncle Abner, as portrayed by Enid Schantz for the frontispiece of *The Methods of Uncle Abner*. The first edition, limited to 1,500 copies, was published in Boulder, Colo., by the Aspen Press in 1974.

Abner, who often sounds like the earthly voice of God, is seen through the eyes of his nephew, Martin. Squire Randolph generally accompanies him.

The Methods of Uncle Abner (1974) contains a novelette, *The Mystery at Hillhouse,* and three short stories, all originally published in *The Country Gentleman* magazine in 1927 and 1928.

Play

Signature (1945), a play based on "Naboth's Vineyard" (1918), starred Marjorie Lord, Anne Jackson, and Judson Laire as Abner. Written by Elizabeth McFadden, it ran for only two performances on Broadway.

UPFIELD, ARTHUR W[ILLIAM] (1888–1964). English detective story writer; creator of Inspector Napoleon BONAPARTE—one of the most original of all detective characters. Born in Gosport, the eldest of five sons of a draper, he was raised by his grandmother and her sisters. He received his education at a minor public school, where he did well in geography and history but poorly in all other subjects.

He was apprenticed to a surveyor and estate agent and wrote three unpublishable novels that were heavily influenced by Sherlock HOLMES, Nick CARTER, and Sexton BLAKE. He also failed three times to pass tests for professional advancement and at nineteen was shipped to Australia by his irate father. He worked as a cowhand, cook, and sheepherder until war broke out (1914), whereupon he enlisted and fought at Gallipoli and in Egypt and France.

After Upfield returned to Australia, he worked at fur trapping, opal hunting, and gold mining. He also resumed writing. He sent an article on fur trapping to *Wide World* magazine, which bought it and commissioned a series of articles. His thriller *The House of Cain* (1926) was purchased by a London publisher, Hutchinson & Company, which gave him a contract for three more novels. Upfield celebrated his good fortune by getting drunk for a solid month.

The House of Cain, an unusual Upfield mystery in that it does not involve Inspector Bonaparte, starts with the discovery of a murder victim in a hotel room in Melbourne. The narrative shifts to southern Australia, coming to life with exotic details of Australian flora and fauna as the central characters find themselves in a home for murderers that is owned and operated by one of their number, a millionaire.

A chance meeting with an old friend, a half-caste aborigine named Tracker Leon, served as the inspiration for Upfield's famous detective, Inspector Bonaparte, who was substituted for the original white detective in the rewritten version of *The Barrakee Mystery* (1928; U.S. title: *The Lure of the Bush*).

Upfield married, had one son, and lived in Victoria, where he spent most of his life writing the "Bony" stories that made him famous. Much of his material came from his varied and adventurous career; like his sleuth, he was an expert tracker who could read the "book of the bush." Upfield also wrote articles on the history and topography of Australia and headed a group of experts who made a 6,000-mile expedition in 1948 to the northern and western areas of the country for the Australian Geological Society.

Upfield died while he was writing a Bony novel in 1964. *Follow My Dust! A Biography of Arthur Upfield* by Jessica Hawke was published in London in 1957. An original novelist in the mystery fiction field, Upfield had the ability to blend his vivid sense of locale into the fabric of his tales.

VACHELL, HORACE ANNESLEY (1861–1955). English playwright and author of boys' fiction and general novels. Born in Sydenham, Kent, he was educated at Harrow, which was the subject of his most famous book, *The Hill* (1905), a nonmystery about public school life. He wrote more than 100 books and once had three successful plays running in London simultaneously.

His best mystery and detective works are the short stories collected in *Loot: From the Temple of Fortune* (1913); *Quinney's Adventures* (1924), the exploits of an art dealer who matches wits with forgers, thieves, and con men; *The Enchanted Garden and Other Stories* (1929), in which an anonymous detective works on a case called "The Man the Diary Called 'X'"; and *Experiences of a Bond Street Jeweller* (1932), featuring detective Impey. In 1926 Vachell collaborated with Archibald MARSHALL in writing *Mr. Allen* (U.S. title: *The Mote House Mystery*), a novel. His other mystery novels include *The Yard* (1923) and *The Disappearance of Martha Penny* (1934).

The dubious aspects of the world of art and antiques are portrayed in Horace Annesley Vachell's stories of Joe Quinney, a shrewd dealer. This illustration appears on the dust wrapper of the first American edition of *Quinney's Adventures*, published by Doran in 1924.

VALCOUR, LIEUTENANT (Creator: Rufus KING). Valcour was the only son of Henri Jules de la Valcour, who left the Sûreté of Paris to emigrate to the Province of Quebec, Canada, where he joined the Dominion police. When his father dies, young Valcour has to leave Toronto's McGill University, and he accepts employment with a large private detective agency in New York City. After two years he joins the New York City Police Department, where he serves more than thirty years, eventually achieving the rank of inspector; his greatest fame comes while he is a lieutenant.

Valcour learned many of his successful detective techniques from his father. He adopts the "typically French" method of playing upon a suspect's emotional reactions. However, as he grows older, he depends less on intuition and more on clues and logic. A quiet man, he is nonetheless friendly and has a subtle sense of humor. He is intelligent, polite, and physically fit; his only indulgences are Turkish cigarettes, an occasional cigar, and an infrequent Bacardi cocktail. His cases often take him to expensive resorts or wealthy men's yachts. He also spends much of his time on Manhattan's East Side or on exclusive Long Island Sound estates.

CHECKLIST

1929	*Murder by the Clock*
1930	*Somewhere in This House* (British title: *A Woman Is Dead*)
1930	*Murder by Latitude*
1931	*Murder in the Willett Family*
1932	*Murder on the Yacht*
1932	*Valcour Meets Murder*
1934	*The Lesser Antilles Case*

1935 *Profile of a Murder*
1936 *The Case of the Constant God*
1937 *Crime of Violence*
1939 *Murder Masks Miami*

Films

Murder by the Clock. Paramount, 1931. William "Stage" Boyd (Valcour), Lilyan Tashman, Irving Pichel, Regis Toomey. Directed by Edward Sloman.

A scheming woman concocts a plot to kill her husband for the inheritance he has already murdered a relative to obtain.

Love Letters of a Star. Universal, 1936. Henry Hunter, Polly Rowles, Ralph Forbes, C. Henry Gordon (Valcour). Directed by Lewis R. Foster and Milton Carruth. Based on *The Case of the Constant God.*

A rich family is troubled by blackmail, indiscreet letters, and an accidental homicide that Valcour investigates; before he is through, a murder occurs.

VALENTINE, JIMMY. *See* HENRY, O.

VALENTINE, JO. *See* ARMSTRONG, CHARLOTTE.

VALMONT, EUGÈNE (Creator: Robert BARR). The first important humorous detective in English literature and the first of many comic French sleuths.

Appleton used this cover design both for *The Triumphs of Eugène Valmont* in 1906 and for Melville Davisson Post's *The Sleuth of St. James's Square* fourteen years later.

Valmont lives in England, and his fame often forces him to resort to disguises and aliases. Although he is fooled with ease and regularity, he pompously considers the English police inept. His elephantine conceit, elegant clothes, and ever-present wit, as well as many physical characteristics, make him resemble Agatha CHRISTIE's famous Belgian detective, Hercule POIROT. Valmont appears only in *The Triumphs of Eugène Valmont* (1906), which contains one of the most famous and ingenious stories in the genre, "The Absent-minded Coterie."

VANCE, JOHN HOLBROOK (1920–). American author of mystery and science fiction. Born in San Francisco, Vance attended the University of California in nearby Berkeley. He still lives in the Bay area, in Oakland. He served in the merchant marine during World War II and afterward. Before achieving success as a writer, he worked as a fruit picker, cannery worker, carpenter, electrician, rigger, miner, jazz cornetist—to mention just a few of his jobs. His first published story was "The World Thinker," which appeared in *Thrilling Wonder Stories* (Summer 1945). He won Hugos (science fiction achievement awards) for *The Dragon Masters* (1962) and *The Last Castle* (1966). The latter book also earned him the Nebula Award of the Science Fiction Writers of America. With the exception of one short story published under the John Holbrook pseudonym, all his science fiction has appeared under the name Jack Vance.

He has published his mystery fiction under his own name. *The Man in the Cage* won the Mystery Writers of America Edgar for best first novel of 1960. *The Fox Valley Murders* (1966) is the first in a series about Sheriff Joe Bain of fictional San Rodrigo County, somewhere in central California. In his debut, Bain is running for reelection while investigating the connection between a current crime and the murder of a little girl sixteen years earlier.

VANCE, LEIGH. *See* SAINT, THE.

VANCE, LOUIS JOSEPH (1879–1933). American fiction writer and creator of the Lone Wolf, one of the most famous rogues in literature (*see* LONE WOLF, THE).

Born in New York, the son of Lillie (Beall) and Wilson Vance, he initially intended to be an artist and illustrator and studied at the Art Students League. A hack writer for years, Vance produced hundreds of short stories and several indifferent adventure novels until he achieved best-seller status with a series of three mystery novels: *The Brass Bowl* (1907), in which a beautiful young girl becomes a burglar to help a grief-stricken father and meets a dangerous, real-life burglar who coincidentally appears to be the identical twin of a young millionaire; *The Black Bag* (1908), which involves Dorothy Calendar, a young heiress, and a wicked diamond smuggler whose object is her fortune, which consists mainly of a black bag full of valuable jewels; and *The Bronze Bell* (1909), in which an American, innocently duck-hunting on Long Island, is mistaken for a raja and presented with a wonderful Indian bronze box.

In addition to writing about the adventures of the Lone Wolf, who first appeared in 1914, Vance mixed romance and mystery in many of his thirty-five novels, especially *Detective* (1932), *Baroque: A Mystery* (1923), and *The Trembling Flame* (1931), a story of New York gangsters and bootleggers.

Vance's fast-paced crime novels, meticulously written despite their sensational tabloid style, are rarely read today, although some volumes in the Lone Wolf series are not inferior to the books about the Saint (*see* SAINT, THE), Bulldog DRUMMOND, or A. J. RAFFLES, to which they bear some resemblance.

Alan Curtis is a more earthy detective than earlier interpreters of the role in *Philo Vance's Secret Mission*. He has a firm grip on suspect girl friend Sheila Ryan. [*PRC*]

VANCE, PHILO (Creator: S. S. VAN DINE). The most popular detective in literature during the late 1920s and the early 1930s, Vance bears many similarities to the early Ellery QUEEN (detective), to Reggie FORTUNE, and to Lord Peter WIMSEY, notably an affected British accent and speech pattern. Like his creator, he is a dilettante and aesthete who constantly injects his knowledge of the most esoteric subjects, particularly those relating to art, music, religion, and philosophy, into murder investigations.

The aristocratic young amateur detective is asked to help solve murder cases by his best friend, District Attorney Markham. Sergeant Heath of the New York City Police Department initially dislikes Vance because of his pomposity and affectations, his nonchalant and whimsical manner, and his long-winded, pedantic lectures on subjects that have no relation to the matter at hand, but later becomes his friend. Vance appears to be constantly amused, smiling cynically even in the grimmest situations. Like Van Dine, the author and narrator of the novels in which he appears, Vance attended Harvard and several European universities, indulging his thirst for knowledge, particularly of art. His interest in psychology directed him into the field of crime detection, in which he is eager to test his theories about human personalities.

Just under 6 feet tall, slender and graceful, Vance has aloof gray eyes, a straight, slender nose, and a thin-lipped mouth that almost suggests cruelty as well as irony. A disciple of Nietzsche, he is not above killing when it is obvious that the law will be unable to punish a murderer he has tracked down.

There are twelve Philo Vance cases, each with a similar title: *The* ——— *Murder Case,* the missing word being precisely six letters long in all but one of the titles.

The first was *The Benson Murder Case* (1926), in which Alvin Benson is found shot to death in his West 48th Street apartment in New York City. Vance spots the murderer almost immediately but seems to enjoy the plight of Markham and Heath as they employ circumstantial evidence to successively fix the guilt on five different people. This novel was based loosely on the actual 1920 murder of Joseph Elwell.

The "Canary" Murder Case (1927) describes Vance's efforts to solve the murder of a famous blonde Broadway singer, Margaret Odell, who is strangled to death in her apartment. The only entrance to the beautiful entertainer's rooms is through the main hall, in full view of the telephone operator's booth. The suspects are narrowed down to four men known to be enamored of the "Canary."

The Greene Murder Case (1928) is the first Vance case to involve wholesale killings; most of the Greene family is disposed of before it is solved. Vance solves this series of crimes by means of his knowledge of psychology; by his realization that the killer has developed the modus operandi from a German book on criminology, Hans Gross's *Handbuch für Untersuchungsrichter;* and by the process of elimination.

Possibly the best Vance novel is *The Bishop Murder Case* (1929), featuring a series of bizarre murders based on nursery rhymes (the original title was *The Mother Goose Murder Case,* but the editors of the periodical in which it was serialized, *The American Magazine,* feared that readers would think that the story was intended for a juvenile audience). Again the process of elimination is employed; each suspect is murdered in turn, until three remain alive. Finally, Vance switches a poisoned drink intended for him, and the deranged murderer dies.

The remaining novels in the Vance saga are *The*

Scarab Murder Case (1930), *The Kennel Murder Case* (1931), *The Dragon Murder Case* (1933), *The Casino Murder Case* (1934), *The Kidnap Murder Case* (1936), *The Garden Murder Case* (1937), *The Gracie Allen Murder Case* (1938), and *The Winter Murder Case* (1939).

An interesting full-length parody of Vance, *The John Riddell Murder Case* by John Riddell, appeared in 1930. Actually written by Corey Ford, the story involves John Riddell, a book reviewer, found dead in his library. Since his jaws are extended in a yawn, his feet are asleep, and the walls are lined with the best sellers of the previous year, Vance deduces that he was bored to death.

The poet Ogden Nash summed up his reaction to the arrogant, Régie-smoking, g-dropping Vance with this couplet: "Philo Vance/Needs a kick in the pance."

Films

Vance's screen character has ranged, during nearly two decades, from urbane amateur criminologist to tough professional investigator. William Powell's interpretation has been the most outstanding, but many other distinguished actors have done credit to the role. In addition, character actors such as Eugene Pallette (gruff Sergeant Heath of the homicide squad) and Etienne Girardot (irascible police pathologist Dr. Doremus), who appeared in many of the early films, added to the exceptional gloss of the series.

The Canary Murder Case. Paramount, 1929. Powell, Louise Brooks, James Hall, Jean Arthur. Directed by Malcolm St. Clair.

Vance is called upon by Markham (E. H. Calvert) to investigate the strangling of a Broadway musical star, "the Canary," in her locked dressing room.

The Greene Murder Case. Paramount, 1929. Powell, Florence Eldridge, Arthur, Ullrich Haupt. Directed by Frank Tuttle.

In their city mansion, the members of the eccentric Greene family—each of whom seems to hate the others—are being eliminated, one by one.

The Bishop Murder Case. MGM, 1930. Basil Rathbone, Leila Hyams, Roland Young, George Marion. Directed by Nick Grinde and David Burton.

In this film, made by a different studio and starring a different Vance (Rathbone, nine years before he was to become celebrated as Sherlock HOLMES), "the Bishop," a crazed killer, is inspired by phrases from nursery rhymes—an arrow shot in the air, Humpty Dumpty falling off a wall, and so on.

The Benson Murder Case. Paramount, 1930. Powell, Natalie Moorhead, Paul Lukas, William Boyd. Directed by Tuttle. This film uses the title and characters of the first Vance book; the plot is new.

Vance is present at a house party in the country one dark, stormy night; a shot rings out, and the body of Benson, a vicious stockbroker hated by many, tumbles down the stairs.

Paramount on Parade, 1930. Many directors. In this collection of sketches and musical numbers showcasing the studio's talent, Powell, as Vance, and Clive Brook as Holmes, are shot by Dr. FU MANCHU (Warner Oland) in a bizarre comedy skit. The three characters were Paramount properties that year.

The Kennel Murder Case. Warner Brothers, 1933. Powell, Mary Astor, Ralph Morgan, Helen Vinson, Jack LaRue. Directed by Michael Curtiz.

Although Powell had moved to Warner Brothers, the studio acquired a Van Dine novel for him and produced the best Vance film ever made, the perfect screen whodunit. Unpopular dog breeder Archer Coe is found dead inside the locked bedroom of his town house; his skull has been split, and he has also been shot and stabbed. The chief suspect, his quarrelsome brother, is later discovered, also murdered, in a hall closet. Vance uses floor plans and a scale model of the house in his dazzling solution.

The Dragon Murder Case. Warner Brothers–First National, 1934. Warren William, Margaret Lindsay, Lyle Talbot, Dorothy Tree. Directed by H. Bruce Humberstone.

A young member of another strange rich family dives into the dark pool on his estate—the supposedly cursed Dragon Pool—and never surfaces.

The Casino Murder Case. MGM, 1935. Lukas, Rosalind Russell, Donald Cook, Alison Skipworth. Directed by Edwin L. Marin.

Again, various members of an aristocratic family are being eliminated, by an apparently undetectable poison. The particularly cold-blooded murder method involves a deadly eyewash that seeps into the brain.

The Garden Murder Case. MGM, 1936. Edmund Lowe, Virginia Bruce, Gene Lockhart, Benita Hume, H. B. Warner. Directed by Marin.

Several people seem to be deliberately killing themselves: a horseman during a steeplechase race, and a woman who throws herself from the top of a double-deck bus into the busy traffic below.

In 1936 British Paramount produced *The Scarab Murder Case,* with Wilfrid Hyde-White as an American Vance, on holiday in England, becoming involved in murder and archaeology.

Night of Mystery. Paramount, 1937. Grant Richards, Helen Burgess, Ruth Coleman, Roscoe Karns. Directed by E. A. Dupont.

This film is a remake, of lesser quality, of *The Greene Murder Case,* with Richards as a "transitional" Vance—younger, heartier, pipe-smoking.

In 1939 *The Winter Murder Case,* a Twentieth Century-Fox production in which ice skating star

Sonja Henie was to appear in a role with Vance, was scrapped as a screen vehicle when Van Dine died.

The Gracie Allen Murder Case. Paramount, 1939. William, Gracie Allen, Ellen Drew, Kent Taylor. Directed by Alfred E. Green.

Van Dine's friendship with the comedienne led him to tailor this mystery for her. Miss Allen plays herself and helps Vance solve the murder of a convict at a picnic for the workers in a perfume factory.

Calling Philo Vance. Warner Brothers, 1940. James Stephenson, Margot Stevenson, Henry O'Neill, Ralph Forbes. Directed by William Clemens.

Vance is now a secret service operative investigating the death in a locked room of an airplane manufacturer; the film is a lackluster reworking of *The Kennel Murder Case.*

Philo Vance Returns. PRC, 1947. William Wright, Terry Austin, Leon Belasco, Ramsey Ames. Directed by William Beaudine.

Vance, now a tough private eye, heeds the anxiety of a playboy who is later murdered along with most of his six former wives, one of whom expires in a poisoned bubble bath.

Philo Vance's Gamble. PRC, 1947. Alan Curtis, Austin, Frank Jenks, Tala Birell. Directed by Basil Wrangell.

Private investigator Vance is involved by his girl friend in show business and the underworld; phosphorus-coated lipstick figures in the case.

Philo Vance's Secret Mission. PRC, 1947. Curtis, Sheila Ryan, Birell, Jenks. Directed by Reginald Le Borg.

Vance solves a seven-year-old murder when he is hired as technical consultant to a publisher of pulp crime magazines.

Radio

On radio during the 1940s, Vance enjoyed his own weekly mystery series, *Philo Vance* (portrayed by Jackson Beck, later by José Ferrer), with a girl secretary added to his retinue.

VANDERCOOK, JOHN W[OMACK] (1902–). London-born American author of mystery novels. A reporter for the *Baltimore Post* and the *New York Graphic* in the 1920s, he began working for NBC as a radio news commentator in 1940. He spent twelve years as an explorer in Surinam, Fiji, Haiti, Liberia, and other regions and has drawn on his experiences in these exotic settings for the background of his novels about Bertram Lynch, an investigator for the Permanent Central Board of the League of Nations. Lynch's adventures are chronicled by Robert Deane, a professor of medieval history. The locales of the cases are used in the titles of the books: *Murder in Trinidad* (1933), *Murder in Fiji* (1936), *Murder in Haiti* (1956), and *Murder in New Guinea* (1959).

Films

Murder in Trinidad. Fox, 1934. Victor Jory, Heather Angel, Nigel Bruce (Bertram Lynch). Directed by Louis King.

Lynch is sent to Trinidad to investigate a diamond-smuggling case that is baffling even the island's chief inspector—who is soon murdered.

The popular book was made into a film again in 1939; the location was changed to Puerto Rico, and Lynch's place was taken by Mr. MOTO, in *Mr. Moto on Danger Island.* Six years later, the book was again the basis for a film, with Lynch now named Smith.

The Caribbean Mystery. Twentieth Century-Fox, 1945. James Dunn, Sheila Ryan, Roy Gordon, Reed Hadley. Directed by Robert Webb.

The governor of an island in the Caribbean asks Smith, an American private detective, to look into the disappearance of several people near a jungle swamp in which pirate gold was buried long ago.

VAN DER VALK, INSPECTOR (Creator: Nicolas FREELING). After ten years as an inspector in Amsterdam, Van der Valk was made chief inspector of the Juvenile Brigade, a position that allows him to express his compassion for young people in trouble. A leftist intellectual, he hates officialdom, although he is a public employee. He is willing to try unorthodox methods of detection, as in *Criminal Conversation,* in which he poses as a patient to investigate a doctor suspected of murder.

Van der Valk's wife is not only an excellent cook (he is a gourmet) but also a very intelligent and sympathetic spouse who often plays an important part in her husband's cases.

CHECKLIST

1962	*Love in Amsterdam*
1963	*Because of the Cats*
1963	*Guns Before Butter* (U.S. title: *Question of Loyalty*)
1964	*Double Barrel*
1965	*Criminal Conversation*
1966	*The King of the Rainy Country*
1967	*Strike Out Where Not Applicable*
1969	*Tsing-Boom*
1971	*Over the High Side* (U.S. title: *The Lovely Ladies*)
1972	*A Long Silence* (U.S. title: *Auprès de ma Blonde*)

VAN DEVENTER, EMMA MURDOCK. See LYNCH, LAWRENCE L.

VAN DINE, S. S. (pseudonym of Willard Huntington Wright; 1888–1939). American journalist, editor, art critic, and author of detective novels featuring Philo VANCE.

Born in Charlottesville, Va., the son of Annie (Van Vranken) and Archibald Davenport Wright, he

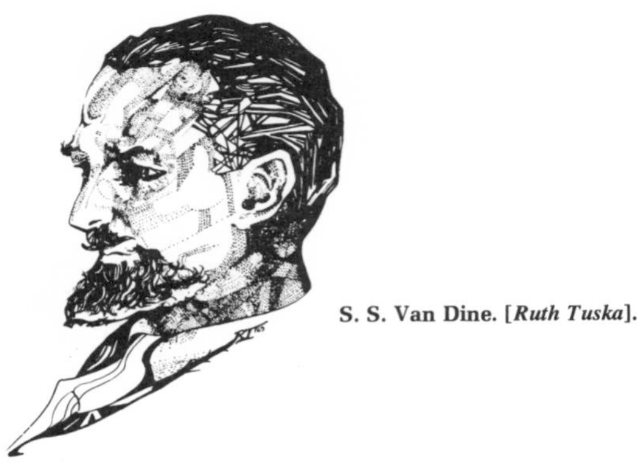

S. S. Van Dine. [*Ruth Tuska*].

was educated at St. Vincent and Pomona Colleges in California and Harvard University and studied art in Munich and Paris.

Wright worked as a literary and art critic for several publications, beginning with the *Los Angeles Times* in 1907. He was editor in chief of *Smart Set,* where he met H. L. Mencken and George Jean Nathan; the three authors collaborated on *Europe after 8:15* (1913), a series of sketches on European night life. Wright's first novel, *The Man of Promise* (1916), received some critical acclaim but little financial reward. In 1907 he married Katharine Belle Boynton; they had one daughter and were divorced in 1930, after which he married Eleanor Pulapaugh.

Never enjoying robust health, Wright had a rigid work schedule as columnist, editor, and aspiring fiction writer and suffered a severe breakdown in 1923, after which he was confined to bed for more than two years with a heart ailment. Forbidden to become excited or to engage in scholarly studies, he read detective novels, amassing a library of more than 2,000 volumes. Believing that he could do as well as the past masters of the form, he decided to improve on their art by writing for a different audience—a more intelligent, better-educated one. Because of his past attempts at serious scholarship (he had written critiques of modern painting, and on Nietzsche for the *Encyclopaedia Britannica*), he feared ridicule if he turned to writing detective novels and thus adopted a pseudonym. Using an old family name (Van Dyne) and the abbreviation of "steamship" as his initials, he outlined three Vance novels and brought them to the greatest of all editors—Maxwell Perkins at Scribner's. Each outline was 10,000 words long and contained every character and plot element necessary to give the prospective publisher a clear-cut concept of the finished work. They were all eagerly accepted. Van Dine then enlarged them to 30,000 words in a second draft, complete except for dialogue, mood, and more complete characterization. The third and final draft was more than twice as long as the second draft and required virtually no editing. His posthumous final book, *The Winter Murder Case* (1939), was published from the second draft.

The books became overwhelming successes, making the previously debt-ridden author wealthy, and his snobbish detective soon became the most popular literary sleuth in the world. Because of all the magazine serializations, book club sales, original editions, reprints, foreign editions, and motion pictures, it is safe to suggest that Van Dine's income was probably one of the largest of any author in the world during the decade preceding his death; yet he left an estate of only $13,000.

Like Vance, Van Dine enjoyed his wealth, living in a luxurious penthouse, dining at the finest restaurants, drinking the costliest wines, wearing expensive clothes, and spending his prodigious income as quickly as possible. Like Vance, too, Van Dine was a sophisticated poseur, able to talk intelligently—and condescendingly—about a wide variety of topics.

Van Dine was the editor of *The Great Detective Stories* (1927), an anthology published under his real name. His introduction to this volume is one of the classics of detective fiction scholarship. His article "Twenty Rules for Writing Detective Stories," which first appeared in *The American Magazine* in 1928, is a complete guidebook for dealing fairly with the reader, even though it is constricting.

Films

Van Dine was one of several famous writers who contributed to *The President's Mystery Story* (Republic, 1936. Henry Wilcoxon, Betty Furness. Directed by Phil Rosen), based on an idea—a legal counsel starts life anew by placing his papers on a corpse—by Franklin D. Roosevelt. Van Dine is also reported to have worked on *Girl Missing* (Warner Brothers, 1933. Glenda Farrell, Mary Brian. Directed by Robert Florey), a drama about gold diggers and murder in Palm Beach. Earlier (1931–1932) he wrote a series of non-Vance minimysteries for Warner Brothers' Vitaphone shorts, featuring Donald Meek and John Hamilton. Among the twelve titles were *The Skull Murder Mystery, Murder in the Pullman, The Side Show Mystery,* and *The Transatlantic Mystery.*

van GULIK, ROBERT (HANS) (1910–1967). Dutch diplomat, scholar, and detective story writer; creator of Judge DEE. Born in Zutphen and educated at the University of Leiden and the University of Utrecht, where he studied law and Oriental languages, he received his Ph.D. degree with honors in 1935. He joined the Dutch Foreign Service, was stationed in the Far East, and at the outbreak of World War II was interned in Japan. He was released in a diplomatic exchange in 1942. He was then seconded to Allied headquarters in Cairo and New Delhi. Meantime, in 1943, he married Frances Shui. After the war he served at the Dutch Embassy in Washington (1946–1947) and later became Minister to Lebanon and Syria (1956–1959) and Malaya (1959–1962). He returned to The Hague and worked at the Ministry of Foreign Affairs (1962–1965) and was then appointed Ambassador to Japan and Korea.

In addition to his series of Judge Dee mysteries, van Gulik wrote, edited, and translated almost twenty works on Oriental languages, literature, and art; some of his titles are *The Lore of the Chinese Lute* (1940), *Erotic Colour Prints of the Ming Period* (3 vols., 1951), *Chinese Pictorial Art as Viewed by the Connoisseur* (1958), and *Sexual Life in Ancient China* (1961). Van Gulik died in Amsterdam.

In 1940 van Gulik found a copy of *Dee Goong An (Criminal Cases Solved by Judge Dee)*, a seventeenth- or early-eighteenth-century Chinese detective story set in the seventh century, translated it, and had it published in a limited edition in England in 1949. Like many other Chinese detective novels of the period, *Dee Goong An* features a magistrate (Judge Dee) who is called upon to solve three interrelated crime problems.

Van Gulik became interested in the character of Dee and the T'ang dynasty and wrote a series of stories about him. The earlier ones were based on true crime cases or incidents in various Chinese detective stories and contained three interrelated cases for the judge to solve. Later, van Gulik varied his formula by inventing his own cases and giving his detective only one problem to solve. In addition to the book-length works about Judge Dee, van Gulik wrote a short story, "New Year's Eve in Lan-Fang" (1958); two novelettes, contained in *The Monkey and the Tiger* (1965); and a collection of short stories, *Judge Dee at Work* (1967), all featuring the judge.

Van Gulik's tales are consistently high in quality and contain real detection; the seventh-century background is an intrinsic part of the narrative that never intrudes on the action and yet is often fascinating and instructive.

VEDDER, JOHN K. *See* GRUBER, FRANK.

VENNING, MICHAEL. *See* RICE, CRAIG.

VICKERS, ROY (1889–1965). English author of detective novels and short stories, the best involving the DEPARTMENT OF DEAD ENDS and Fidelity DOVE. A longtime journalist, court reporter, and editor of *Novel Magazine*, Vickers had limited success as an author in the United States until Ellery QUEEN (author) discovered one of his "inverted" detective stories in an old magazine. "The Rubber Trumpet" was reprinted in *Ellery Queen's Mystery Magazine*, and a collection of "Dead Ends" stories soon appeared, closely followed by several other collections. His earliest books appeared under the pseudonym David Durham, beginning with *The Woman Accused* (1923). He also published crime novels as Sefton Kyle.

Vickers published other story collections in addition to those about Miss Dove and the Department of Dead Ends: *Eight Murders in the Suburbs* (1954), which has two nonseries tales; *Double Image* (1955), which has four nonseries tales; *Seven Chose Murder* (1959); and *The Best Detective Stories of Roy Vickers* (1965; contains the previously uncollected Department of Dead Ends story "Murderer's Duty"; the other stories are reprints). Among his best novels are *The Girl in the News* (1938), which was filmed by Carol Reed in 1940, *She Walked in Fear* (1940), *Murder of a Snob* (1951), *Murder in Two Flats* (1952), and *Find the Innocent* (1961).

VICTOR, MRS. METTA VICTORIA FULLER. *See* REGESTER, SEELEY.

VIDAL, GORE. *See* BOX, EDGAR.

VIDOCQ, FRANÇOIS EUGÈNE (1775–1857). French detective, author of crime books, and a founder of the Police de Sûreté. Born in Arras, the son of a baker, he had an adventurous military career and then turned to crime. He spent a long time in jail and then, in 1809, offered Napoleon his services (mainly as an informer) and became the first chief of the police department. His agents were also former convicts whose practices were highly suspect. His superior forced his resignation, and he went into private business, returning to his official post for a few months before opening a private detective agency in 1832. Continuing to use dubious methods, he was harassed by the authorities, who eventually ruined his practice. He died impoverished.

Fascinated by Vidocq and his career, Honoré de Balzac became his friend and used him as a character (named Vautrin) in several novels.

Vidocq's four-volume *Mémoires* (1828–1829) was a ghostwritten, sensational account of his career, many of the incidents undoubtedly being fiction. It was published in England, also in 1828–1829 and in four volumes, as *Memoirs of Vidocq, Principal Agent of the French Police until 1827; and Now Proprietor of the Paper Manufactory at St. Mandé; Written by Himself* (U.S. title: *Memoirs of Vidocq, French Police Agent*).

VULLIAMY, C[OLWYN] E[DWARD] (1886–1971). English litterateur and mystery novelist. Vulliamy studied art until World War I, when he entered the armed forces and served in France, Macedonia, and Turkey. After the war he pursued a literary career, producing numerous volumes of nonfiction. Vulliamy was noted for his keen wit, which is much in evidence in his fiction. He was a Fellow of the Royal Society of Literature and the Royal Anthropological Society.

Vulliamy, not well known as a mystery writer, was a notable practitioner of the inverted tale and one of the most unusual and individual writers of the genre. His stinging wit and sense of the absurd are of great interest to students of black humor.

Vulliamy's inverted tales are all similar: usually a character stumbles upon what he thinks is the perfect method of committing murder. The victims (and there are more than one per novel) are social parasites, often malicious gossips, whose existences cry out for extinction. The protagonist conceives and executes his first venture with perfect facility. Soon he contemplates further crimes, but his character begins to deteriorate. He makes small blunders—then larger ones, as the gap between sanity and madness narrows. Fate intervenes, and he is apprehended by the police. A long and usually impressive trial follows. The verdict is always a gross miscarriage of justice, but fate once more takes command and sets things right, with an ending full of irony.

The Vicar's Experiments (1932) was published under the pseudonym Anthony Rolls and appeared as *Clerical Error* in the United States. It is considered a minor masterpiece by some, an imitation of Francis Iles (Anthony BERKELEY) by others. Vulliamy's most famous work, it is carefully written and plotted; the wit and satire are kept under tight rein, and little of the author's negativism is present. *Scarweather* (1934), also signed by Rolls, is a straightforward detective story that stresses characterization, social behavior, and description. Written in a graceful style that is at least fifteen years behind its time, it fails because the solution to the crime is obvious to every reader but not to the seemingly intelligent narrator.

Don among the Dead Men (1952) is about a chemist who discovers a poison that leaves no traces. It is not as well balanced as *The Vicar's Experiments*, for the author intrudes much of his own attitude into the narrative. *Cakes for Your Birthday* (1959) concerns the efforts of three not very intellectually gifted gentlemen to dispose of a psychopathic gossip, with disastrous results.

WADE, HENRY (pseudonym of Major Sir Henry Lancelot Aubrey-Fletcher; 1887–1969). English writer of detective stories; creator of Inspector John POOLE.

Born in Surrey and educated at Eton College and New College, Oxford, he married Mary Augusta Chilton in 1911; they had four sons and a daughter.

He served in the Grenadier Guards in both world wars, was wounded twice in active service, was awarded the Distinguished Service Order, and later received the Croix de Guerre. He retired in 1920 and then served as justice of the peace, alderman, high sheriff, and in many other honorary positions in Buckinghamshire.

Constable John Bragg, who is as "inquisitive as a mongoose, unshakable as a bulldog," is featured in Henry Wade's second collection of short stories. This is the dust wrapper of the first edition, published by Constable in 1938.

Sir Henry was the author of the definitive *A History of the Foot Guards to 1856* (1927) in addition to an extended series of detective stories begun in 1926 under the Wade pseudonym, taken from his mother's maiden name.

Of Wade's twenty detective novels, only thirteen have been published in the United States, and his two historically important volumes of short stories never crossed the Atlantic. Only two of his latest works have been printed in paperback editions in the United States, and they, like his other works in England, are out of print.

Wade was a practitioner of the modern British realistic school and a master of the police novel. A staunch advocate of the classical detective novel in its purest form, he also wrote inverted stories that are among the best in the genre.

He can best be compared to Freeman Wills CROFTS, although his police novels and inverted tales never quite achieved the pinnacle of Crofts's *The Cask* (1920). His characterizations were deeper, especially in his later inverted tales, and his personal experience lent realism to his depictions of rural police. His strongly developed sense of irony anticipated that of Richard HULL, and his "ironical criticism of legal procedure" (Dorothy L. SAYERS) anticipated the work of Cyril HARE, Henry CECIL, Raymond POSTGATE, and others.

He accurately limned the changing values of post-World War II England—even more than Agatha CHRISTIE did—in his later novels and did more to explicate the psychology and mores of the English people than any other writer in the genre.

Wade's earliest detective novels, *The Verdict of You All* (1926), *The Missing Partners* (1928), and *The Duke of York's Steps* (1929), which question the entire legal system of Great Britain, have been compared to Crofts's works. The victim in *The Dying*

Alderman (1930), another early work, manages to leave a message as a clue to his murderer before he expires.

The year 1933 marked a turning point in Wade's career, illustrated by two books. *Policeman's Lot,* a collection of thirteen stories (six do not involve Poole) selected for QUEEN'S QUORUM, proved that Wade, like Crofts, could write masterly and incisive short stories. Several have appeared in anthologies, and "The Tenth Round," in particular, is a classic; it also contains hints of thematic material used in later novels. *Mist on the Saltings* (1933) is partly an inverted tale and partly a solid police novel. It anticipates Crofts's inverted story *The 12:30 from Croyden* (1934) and boasts powerful characterizations and superb East Anglian marshland atmosphere.

Heir Presumptive (1935) is a fully inverted novel that details Eustace Hendel's attempts to inherit a large fortune by killing several of his relatives. *Here Comes the Copper* (1938), another collection of thirteen shorts, traces the career of rural constable John Bragg, who is clever enough to rise in his profession and become a member of London's famed CID.

A Dying Fall (1955) poses the problem of whether an unwanted wife who falls to her death from a high balcony has been murdered or has committed suicide. This perceptive view of changing values in postwar England was well received by critics, who praised its characterizations and ironic ending.

Wade's other non-Poole novels are *The Hanging Captain* (1932), *The High Sheriff* (1937), *Released for Death* (1939), *New Graves at Great Norne* (1947), *Diplomat's Folly* (1951), *Be Kind to the Killer* (1952), and *The Litmore Snatch* (1957).

WADE, ROBERT. *See* MILLER, WADE.

WAHLÖÖ, PER (1926–1975). Swedish novelist, reporter, and radio-television scriptwriter. Wahlöö wrote two mysteries alone before he and his wife, poet Maj Sjöwall, collaborated in writing a series about Martin BECK. They met in 1961 while working for different magazines published by the same company. They lived in an apartment in Malmö, in southern Sweden, and because they had two young children, did most of their writing after midnight.

Wahlöö used the crime novel as an instrument to analyze society. His two novels about Chief Inspector Jensen, published under the name Peter Wahlöö, *The Thirty-first Floor* (1966) and *The Steel Spring* (1970), reflect his views on dictatorships and the capitalist system. The Wahlöös' police procedural novels also depict Swedish society, though in terms of individuals, rather than movements.

The style of the Wahlöös has been described as "reportorial . . . spare, disciplined and full of sharply observed detail. . . ." They have admitted to being able to write almost interchangeably and could write alternate chapters simultaneously. Their books, emphasizing slow, patient, and realistic police routine, brought them favorable comparison to Georges SIMENON. In *Roseanna* (1967) Beck investigates the rape-murder of an American girl whose body is found in a Swedish canal. *The Laughing Policeman* (1970), about the investigation of the murder of eight occupants of a Stockholm bus, was awarded the Mystery Writers of America Edgar as best novel of that year. Its locale was shifted to San Francisco when it was filmed in 1973.

WAINER, CORD. *See* DEWEY, THOMAS B.

WALKER, HARRY. *See* WAUGH, HILLARY.

WALLACE, (RICHARD HORATIO) EDGAR (1875–1932). English novelist, short story writer, dramatist, poet, and journalist—probably the most popular "thriller" writer of all time.

Born in Greenwich, the illegitimate son of actress Marie (Polly) Richards and actor Richard Horatio Edgar Marriott (who appeared on the birth records as Walter Wallace), he was adopted by George Freeman at the age of nine days and raised as Dick Freeman, one of eleven children of a fish porter. He learned the truth about his parentage when he was eleven years old and needed birth papers for a job. A year later his formal education ended, and he held a series of odd jobs until he joined the Royal West Kent Regiment at eighteen, later transferring to the Medical Staff Corps. Sent to South Africa, he wrote war poems (later collected in *The Mission That Failed,* 1898, and other volumes) and served as a correspondent during the Boer War for Reuters and South African and London newspapers. In 1900 he returned to England and the following year married Ivy Caldecott; they were divorced in 1918, after

The most famous portrait of Edgar Wallace.

having four children: Eleanor (who died as a child), Bryan, who was also a writer, Patricia, and Michael. Wallace married "Jim," his secretary, in 1921; they had a daughter, Penelope.

Since publishers lacked faith in his work, he founded the Tallis Press and published *The Four Just Men,* his first mystery and best-known work, in 1905. A vast advertising campaign and a unique publicity gimmick—a £500 reward was offered to any reader who could guess how the murder of the British Foreign Secretary was committed—resulted in enormous sales and great financial losses, for there were several correct solutions and everyone had to be paid. In this tale, four (actually three, since one died before the series began) wealthy dilettantes find pleasure in administering justice when the law is unable, or unwilling, to do so. Wallace wrote sequels to *The Four Just Men: The Council of Justice* (1908); *The Just Men of Cordova* (1917); *The Law of the Four Just Men* (1921; U.S. title: *Again the Three Just Men,* 1933); *The Three Just Men* (1925); and *Again the Three Just Men* (1928; U.S. title: *The Law of the Three Just Men,* 1931).

By 1920 Wallace was writing at a prodigious pace, ultimately producing 173 books (more than half involving crime and mystery) and 17 plays. He once dictated an entire novel during a single weekend; on another occasion he plotted six books simultaneously; and he dictated serials at such a furious pace that he never knew what would happen in the ensuing chapters. His output was matched by his popularity. It has often been stated that, in the 1920s and 1930s, one of every four books read in England was written by Wallace, the "King of Thrillers."

This immense popularity earned Wallace a fortune. During the last decade of his life he earned a quarter of a million dollars a year; yet, because of his extravagant life-style, he left enormous debts when he died. He often lost $500 or more a day at the racetrack, but his lack of success at picking horses did not diminish his enthusiasm for the sport. He was a longtime racing editor for newspapers and wrote several books with racing themes and backgrounds. Wallace's books still sell more than a million copies a year, and motion pictures and television programs based on his stories are everywhere.

As might be expected of such prolificacy, much of the writing is slapdash and cliché-ridden, characterization is two-dimensional, and situations are frequently trite, relying on intuition, coincidence, and much pointless, confusing movement to convey a sense of action. The heroes and villains are clearly labeled, and the stock characters—humorous servants, baffled policemen, breathless heroines—could be interchanged from one book to another. The dialogue is convincing, however, with strong elements of comedy at appropriate times, and suspense is effectively created.

Dudley Tennant portrayed a female crook for *Four Square Jane,* a short story collection published by the Readers Library in 1929.

One of the best—and rarest—Wallace books is *The Tomb of Ts'in* (1916), actually little more than a revised version of his *Captain Tatham of Tatham Island* (1909), which was slightly revised in a different way for another publisher in 1916 and issued as *The Island of Galloping Gold.* The main character of *The Man Who Bought London* (1915), Kerry King, is an American millionaire who plans a revolution and forms a gigantic syndicate to buy houses and shops in London as part of his scheme. *The Green Archer* (1923) is a famous story about a man found murdered after having quarreled with the owner of a ghost-haunted castle. The ghost is the Green Archer, and the corpse has a long green arrow in his chest. In *The Crimson Circle* (1922) Derrick Yale, "the amazing psychometrical detective," is pitted against Scotland Yard.

Other popular Wallace characters include Sanders, the commissioner who maintains law and order for the crown in South Africa, assisted by his drawling lieutenant, Bones (*Sanders of the River,* 1911, and others); Oliver Rater, a silent Scotland Yard detective (*The Orator,* 1928); Surefoot Smith, a CID man who hates science and loves beer, and has to deal with an eccentric millionaire in *The Clue of the Silver Key* (1930; U.S. title: *The Silver Key*); James Mortlake, "the Black," a member of U.S. Intelligence who wears black clothing and a black mask (*The Man from Morocco,* 1926; U.S. title: *The Black*); Arthur Milton, "the Ringer," an underworld character who, like the Four Just Men, always gets his man (*The Gaunt Stranger,* 1925; U.S. title: *The Ringer*); financier Tony Braid, known as "the Twister" because he has only one method for extricating himself from difficulties—telling the truth (*The Twister,* 1928); a pretty female crook who steals from people with bloated bank accounts (*Four Square Jane,*

These four short story collections, originally published in paper covers by George Newnes, are among the rarest Edgar Wallace first editions. *Killer Kay* was published in 1930; the others were published in 1929.

1928); a shady character, called "the Squealer," who is in on every major jewel robbery in London—if the robber will not split with him, he tells the police where the culprit can be found (*The Squeaker*, 1927; U.S. title: *The Squealer*); and the benign Mr. J. G. REEDER.

Films

Literally hundreds of screen melodramas have been fashioned from Wallace material. The highlights are given below; the first three are American silent serials.

The Green Archer. Pathé serial, 1925. Allene Ray, Walter Miller. Directed by Spencer Bennet. From the 1923 novel.

A mysterious costumed archer lurks on the grounds of Bellamy Castle, helping a reporter expose the secrets of its recluse millionaire owner.

The Mark of the Frog. Pathé serial, 1928. Donald Reed, Margaret Morris, Frank Lackteen. Directed by Arch Heath. Based on *The Fellowship of the Frog* (1925).

In search of a vanished treasure, a criminal ring headed by the hooded "Frog" terrorizes New York.

The Terrible People. Pathé serial, 1928. Ray, Miller. Directed by Bennet. From the 1926 novel.

An heiress is imperiled by the gang of a criminal who seemingly has returned from the dead.

The Terror. Warner Brothers, 1928. Louise Fazenda, May McAvoy, Edward Everett Horton, John Miljan. Directed by Roy Del Ruth. Warner Brothers' second all-talking feature, the film was based on Wallace's play of 1927.

A Scotland Yard operative goes to an old house in his search for a murderer who mutilates his victims.

The Ringer. British Lion (British), 1928. Leslie Faber, Annette Benson, Lawson Butt. Directed by Arthur Maude. Screenplay by Wallace, from his play, which began a successful London run in 1926; the most frequently filmed Wallace work.

A criminal skilled in disguises eliminates his enemies despite heavy police surveillance.

The Flying Squad. British Lion (British), 1929. Wyndham Standing, Dorothy Bartlam, Bryan Edgar Wallace and Carol Reed (in bit roles as petty crooks). Directed by Maude. From the 1928 novel.

London's motorized police break up a criminal gang.

The Clue of the New Pin. British Lion (British), 1929. Benita Hume, Kim Peacock, Donald Calthrop, John Gielgud. Directed by Maude. From the 1923 novel.

A rich recluse is murdered in an absolutely sealed room.

The Squeaker. British Lion (British), 1930. Percy Marmont, Anne Grey, Gordon Harker. Screenplay and direction by Wallace. The first all-talking British Wallace film, based on the 1927 novel.

London's jewelry thieves are at the mercy of a superfence (actually the head of a benevolent society).

The Menace. Columbia, 1932. H. B. Warner, Bette Davis, Walter Bryon. Directed by Roy William Neill. Based on *The Feathered Serpent* (1927).

A man, sentenced to life imprisonment for the murder of his father, is certain that his stepmother is actually guilty. He escapes.

The Frightened Lady. Gainsborough–British Lion (British), 1932. Norman McKinnell, Cathleen Nesbitt, Emlyn WILLIAMS. Directed by T. Hayes Hunter. Wallace also used this material in a play, *The Case of the Frightened Lady* (U.S. title: *Criminal at Large*).

A titled widow nervously consults the police, fearing that someone in her secret-passage-filled manor, Mark's Priory, is trying to strangle the fiancée of her mad young son (Williams).

King Kong. RKO, 1933. Fay Wray, Bruce Cabot, Robert Armstrong. Directed by Ernest B. Schoedsack and Merian C. Cooper.

Wallace died in Hollywood while working on the original screenplay of this adventure epic.

Before Dawn. RKO, 1933. Stuart Erwin, Dorothy Wilson, Warner Oland. Directed by Irving Pichel. Based on Wallace's short story "Death Watch."

A girl spiritualist, in a trance, tries to find the treasure hidden in a supposedly haunted house.

Mystery Liner. Monogram, 1934. Noah Beery, Astrid Allwyn, Gustav von Seyffertitz. Directed by Neill. Based on Wallace's story "The Ghost of John Holling."

Murders take place on a liner at sea, while an inventor on board experiments with "wireless control of ships."

The Return of the Terror. First National, 1934. Mary Astor, Lyle Talbot, John Halliday. Directed by Howard Bretherton. Loosely based on *The Terror*, the 1927 play.

A man accused of murdering three patients returns to an eerie sanatorium one stormy night.

Sanders of the River. London Film (British), 1935. Leslie Banks, Paul Robeson. Directed by Zoltan Korda. Based on the 1911 novel.

Wallace's tribute to British colonialism centers on efforts to keep peace among savage African tribes.

The Crimson Circle. Wainwright (British), 1936. Hugh Wakefield, Alfred Drayton, Beery, June Duprez, Niall McGinnis. Directed by Reginald Denham. Based on the 1922 novel (there was also a 1922 silent film version).

The victims of a mysterious blackmail gang—and members of the gang itself—are found dead, marked with a red circle.

The Girl from Scotland Yard. Paramount, 1937. Karen Morley, Robert Baldwin, Eduardo Ciannelli. Directed by Robert Vignola. From *The Square Emerald* (1926; U.S. title: *The Girl from Scotland Yard*).

The heroine pursues the mad creator of a death ray.

The Squeaker (U.S. release title: *Murder on Diamond Row*). London-Denham (British), 1937. Edmund Lowe, Ann Todd, Sebastian Shaw, Robert Newton, Alastair Sim. Directed by William K. Howard. Based on the 1927 novel.

Again, London's fences are imperiled.

The Four Just Men (U.S. title: *The Secret Four*). Ealing (British), 1939. Hugh Sinclair, Griffith Jones, Francis L. Sullivan, Frank Lawton, Anna Lee, Basil Sydney, Alan Napier. Directed by Walter Forde. Based on the 1905 novel; previously filmed as a British silent in 1921.

An actor, a producer, a costume designer, and a millionaire join forces to dispense justice privately; they eliminate a member of Parliament who was a traitor.

The climactic moment of the 1940 version of Edgar Wallace's *The Case of the Frightened Lady*, as a strangler stalks Mark's Priory. [*Pennant*]

Dark Eyes of London (U.S. release title: *The Human Monster*). Argyle (British), 1939. Bela Lugosi, Hugh Williams, Greta Gynt. Directed by Walter Summers. Based on the 1924 novel.

Scotland Yard probes the link between the kindly, gray-haired director of a workhouse for blind men and a shady insurance broker.

The Green Archer. Columbia serial, 1940. Victor Jory, Iris Meredith, James Craven. Directed by James W. Horne. Based on the 1923 novel.

Criminals again occupy Bellamy Castle while the masked archer casts his shadow against the walls.

The Door with Seven Locks (U.S. release title: *Chamber of Horrors*). Pathe (British), 1940. Banks, Lilli Palmer. Directed by Norman Lee. Based on the 1926 novel.

Weekend guests at a country house are involved in an attempt to steal a jewel inheritance.

The Case of the Frightened Lady (U.S. title: *The Frightened Lady*). Pennant (British), 1940. Marius Goring, Penelope Dudley Ward, Helen Haye. Directed by George King. Based on *The Frightened Lady* (1932; U.S. title: *The Case of the Frightened Lady*).

Neurotic young Lord Lebanon (Goring) is heard playing the piano wildly as stranglings occur at Mark's Priory.

During the war decade, Wallace received less

attention, and there was only one important adaptation during the 1950s.

The Ringer. London (British), 1952. Herbert Lom, Donald Wolfit, Mai Zetterling, Gynt. Directed by Guy Hamilton.

The Ringer, a master of disguise, will not allow a police cordon to keep him from his vengeance.

In 1959 Germany began a series of Wallace adaptations that became that nation's most popular screen entertainment; in fact, for more than a decade, there was a "Wallace mania." The films are all similar, and familiar—a stock reservoir of players, sets, and even plot elements only slightly rearranged in an endless succession of films. Initially, they remained close to the novels from which they were drawn (including the most faithful *Green Archer* ever filmed, in 1961), but the scenarios soon became heavy and distorted; after almost a hundred films, the specific Wallace inspiration is difficult to detect. These films were produced by Berlin's Rialto, mostly directed by Alfred Vohrer and Harald Reinl (who also specialized in the Dr. MABUSE series of the same period). Joachim Fuchsberger is a recurring hero (often as Scotland Yard's Inspector Higgins, with Siegfried Schuerenberg as his superior, Sir John), and he is frequently photographed in actual London locations. Klaus Kinski is the perennial neurotic suspect-victim–comedy foil.

Among the very best German films are *The Fellowship of the Frog* (1960), in which Graham GREENE's Harry Lime is used (unseen); *The Terrible People* (1960), a somewhat altered version in which the executed criminal returns but the original ending is changed; *Forger of London* (1961), in which a young aristocrat fears that during an amnesia period he became a counterfeiter; the brooding *Inn on the River* (1962), in which a harpoon is the instrument in several murders alongside the Thames; *Curse of the Yellow Snake* (1963), Wallace's tribute to Fu Manchu (*see* FU MANCHU, DR.); *The Indian Scarf* (1963), a wild mix of *The Frightened Lady* (the title refers to the strangler's tool) and an "and-then-there-were-none" theme; and *The Black Abbot* (1963), with its eerie castle setting. The Wallace film craze continued with only slightly lessened vigor into the 1970s, with such blood-curdling titles as *The Mad Executioner, The Phantom of Soho,* and *The College Girl Murders*; a voice identifying itself as Wallace chuckles macabrely under the credits of such films as *Hand of Power.*

A millionaire is found murdered in a locked room in the English Wallace film *Clue of the New Pin.* [*Anglo-Amalgamated*]

In the meantime, England experienced a Wallace film resurrection of almost equal magnitude. In 1960 Jack Greenwood began producing a series of short screen adaptations, all slightly more than an hour in length, for secondary theatrical release, and ultimately for British and American television use, under the umbrella title *Edgar Wallace Mystery Theater.* A bust of the author revolved sinisterly in smoke under the credits. In more than forty films (a few actually the unacknowledged work of other writers, including George Baxt; *see* GARVE, ANDREW), the compact scenarios sometimes overcondensed Wallace's complex stories, but often his characteristic twists and surprises survived the constriction. Some of the highlights of the series are listed below.

The Clue of the Twisted Candle. Anglo-Amalgamated (British), 1960. Bernard Lee (the first of several appearances as Superintendent Meredith of Scotland Yard), David Knight. Directed by Allan Davis. Based on the 1918 novel.

In a room locked from the inside, a millionaire is found murdered; near him are two half-burned candles.

The Malpas Mystery. Anglo-Amalgamated (British), 1960. Maureen Swanson, Allan Cuthbertson, Geoffrey Keen, Ronald Howard. Directed by Sidney Hayers. Based on *The Face in the Night* (1924).

A girl, a former convict, and now secretary to a strange recluse, learns that she is the heir to a fortune—from her long-lost father, who is searching for her.

The Man Who Was Nobody. Anglo-Amalgamated (British), 1961. Hazel Court, John Crawford, Lisa Daniely. Directed by Montgomery Tully. Based on the 1927 novel.

A girl private detective's search for a missing

playboy leads her to the mysterious "South Africa Smith."

Clue of the New Pin. Anglo-Amalgamated (British), 1961. Paul Daneman, Bernard Archard. Directed by Davis. Based on the 1923 novel.

Again, a millionaire is found killed in a locked room, the key to the door on a table near him.

The Fourth Square. Anglo-Amalgamated (British), 1961. Conrad Phillips, Natasha Parry, Delphi Lawrence, Daneman. Directed by Davis. From *Four Square Jane* (1928).

Three valuable jewels are stolen from three London squares, with murder thrown in.

Man at the Carlton Tower. Anglo-Amalgamated (British), 1961. Maxine Audley, Lee Montague. Directed by Robert Tronson. From *The Man at the Carlton* (1931), the title altered so that scenes could be filmed at the newly constructed Carlton Tower Hotel.

The chief suspect in a jewelry theft vanishes, his partner and the police searching for him.

Clue of the Silver Key. Anglo-Amalgamated (British), 1961. Lee (Meredith), Finlay Currie, Patrick Cargill. Directed by Gerard Glaister. From the 1930 novel.

In another "impossible" crime, a bad-tempered blind moneylender is found shot to death.

The Share Out. Anglo-Amalgamated (British), 1962. Lee (Meredith), Alexander Knox, Moira Redmond. Directed by Glaister. From *Jack O'Judgment* (1920).

A shady private investigator tries to clear his past by helping Scotland Yard close in on a large blackmail ring, many of whose members are suddenly murdered.

Number Six. Anglo-Amalgamated (British), 1962. Ivan Desny, Nadja Regin, Michael Goodliffe, Brian Bedford. Directed by Tronson. From the 1927 novel.

Criminals try to ferret out the identity of "Number 6," Scotland Yard's secret agent.

Although the series continued for several more years, less attention was paid to Wallace sources.

Television

In 1959 thirty-nine half-hour television programs were fashioned from *The Four Just Men,* featuring, in turn, the adventures of Dan Dailey, Jack Hawkins, Richard Conte, and Vittorio De Sica, who, as private citizens, corrected injustices in various parts of the world.

Plays

Wallace was quite successful in contributing to England's rich tradition of melodrama theater with such plays as *The Ringer* (1926) and *The Terror* (1927); as late as the 1950s, long after his death, Princess Margaret and Elsa Maxwell participated in a society staging for charity of *The Frog,* which had been adapted from Wallace's *The Fellowship of the Frog* (1925) by Ian Hay. Among Broadway productions, he is best remembered for *Criminal at Large* (a version of the stranglings at the Priory of *The Frightened Lady* of 1932) and *On the Spot,* a popular drama filmed as *Dangerous to Know* (1938). In this play, staged in London in 1930 and on Broadway in 1931, a gangster czar (closely resembling Al Capone) living in a Chicago penthouse is ultimately done in by his wronged Chinese mistress (Anna May Wong). Typically, Wallace wrote the play in four days. It made a star of Charles Laughton.

Joachim Fuchsburger was a constant favorite as the Scotland Yard hero of the English-set German Edgar Wallace melodramas; this one is *Dead Eyes of London.* [*Magna Pictures*]

WALLING, R[OBERT] A[LFRED] J[OHN] (1869–1949). English journalist and author of mystery novels. Born in Exeter, he was the son of the English journalist R. H. Walling. He married Florence Greet, the daughter of a naval officer; they had two sons and two daughters and lived in Plymouth, where for many years Walling was editor of the *Western Independent.* He also wrote travel articles and a biography of Sir John Hawkins.

After he was appointed a magistrate in Plymouth, he developed a strong interest in crime and, though near his sixtieth birthday, began to write mysteries as a hobby. His first book was *Dinner-Party at Bardolph's* (1927; U.S. title: *That Dinner at Bardolph's*). In *The Fatal Five Minutes* (1932), he introduced the suave private investigator Philip Tolefree.

WALLIS, J[AMES] H[AROLD] (1885–1958). American mystery writer. His first work, *Murder by Formula* (1931), is unusual because of the discussion, by several of the characters, of the nature of detective stories; one of them posits the number of characters, murders, and pages that will produce the best example of this type of literature. Wallis follows this advice, and in an epilogue, tells the reader that he has accomplished his goal, but, through some mischance, his narrative falls one page short of the required 300.

Wallis's next-to-last novel, *Once Off Guard* (1942), is a psychological study of a man pursued by his own imagination. It starts with an aging and lonely professor—long sheltered by the academic world—stopping in front of an art dealer's window. Gazing at a lovely portrait, he notices the model directly next to it. Disastrous consequences follow this chance meeting. *Once Off Guard* served as the basis for one of Fritz LANG's best American films, *The Woman in the Window* (1944).

WALTON, FRANCIS. *See* FLYNT, JOSIAH.

WARD, ARTHUR HENRY SARSFIELD. *See* ROHMER, SAX.

"WATERS" (pseudonym of William Russell). English author of detective fiction yellowbacks (fl. mid-nineteenth century). Nothing is known of Russell's life (his name was given incorrectly as Thomas Russell on some early American editions of his books), but his tales about a London police detective are important as the earliest short detective stories by an English author. Told in the first person, the "Waters" adventures first appeared in *Chambers' Edinburgh Journal* beginning on July 28, 1849. The stories were later collected in *The Recollections of a Policeman* and published in New York in 1852 (first English edition: *Recollections of a Detective Police-Officer,* 1856). A second series with the same title appeared in London in 1859. Both volumes were often reprinted in the nineteenth century, undergoing numerous title changes.

Purporting to be the real-life experiences of a London police detective, the cases involved forgers, counterfeiters, thieves, confidence men, and murderers. A member of the Metropolitan Police, "Waters" successfully solves a crime and is promoted to the rank of detective and given two assistants, one of whom is an expert ventriloquist. The success of the first detective yellowbacks inspired a wave of imitators.

Other, similar "Waters" short story collections are *The Game of Life* (1857), *Leaves from the Diary of a Law Clerk* (1857), *A Skeleton in Every House* (1860), *Recollections of a Sheriff's Officer* (1860), *The Experiences of a French Detective Officer: Adapted from the Mss. of Theodore Duhamel* (1861), *Experiences of a Real Detective* (1862; by "Inspector F."), *Undiscovered Crimes* (1862), *Autobiography of an English Detective* (1863), and *Mrs. Waldegrave's Will and Other Tales* (1870).

Russell also wrote novels about the sea and sailors under the pen name Lieutenant Warneford, RN.

WATSON, COLIN (1920–   ). English journalist and author of mystery fiction. Born at Croydon in Surrey, Watson was educated at Whitgift. He was a journalist and newspaper editorial writer in Newcastle upon Tyne and London before he began to write mystery fiction. He is married and has three children.

In 1971 he published *Snobbery with Violence,* an ironic study of detective stories and thrillers, with special emphasis on the attitudes of those who write and read them, in which he condemns such writers as E. Phillips OPPENHEIM, Edgar WALLACE, Sydney HORLER, Agatha CHRISTIE, and Dorothy L. SAYERS for lacking progressive ideas in social, political, and racial matters.

Watson is the author of a series of humorous mysteries about Inspector Purbright and his fictional country town, Flaxborough. Julian SYMONS praised Watson's work, especially *Hopjoy Was Here* (1962), referring to his "unique skill in putting the gifts of a novelist for creating scenes and characters at the service of a comic imagination devoted to crime fiction." In *Lonelyheart 4122* (1967), Purbright investigates murder at Handclasp House, a matrimonial agency.

WATSON, DR. (Creator: Sir Arthur CONAN DOYLE). The faithful friend of Sherlock HOLMES and the chronicler of his adventures. Watson's name has become virtually synonymous with those of the con-

A young, handsome Dr. Watson appears in the series of twenty-five Conan Doyle characters issued as Turf cigarette cards.

Dr. Watson's famous tin dispatch box reveals "something recherché" to Sherlock Holmes. This Sidney Paget illustration originally appeared in the May 1893 issue of *The Strand* magazine, which contained "The Musgrave Ritual."

fidants and "Boswells" of all classic detectives.

Born in 1852, he studied at the University of London Medical School. After receiving his degree, he joined the Fifth Northumberland Fusiliers as an assistant surgeon and saw service in India when the second Afghan War erupted. His orderly, Murray, saved his life when he was wounded by a Jezail bullet at the Battle of Maiwand. Returning to England after months of fever and delirium, he met Holmes, and the two men began to share rooms at 221B Baker Street—Watson setting up practice as a doctor and Holmes becoming the world's first consulting detective.

Assisting Holmes on many of his cases, Watson keeps records of them, which he subsequently has published with the assistance of a literary agent, Sir Arthur Conan Doyle. Watson's intellect, although adequate, is no match for his friend's, but instead of being angry when Holmes laughs at him for being slow in perceiving a clue, he good-naturedly asks for an explanation. He once admits that he is "a whetstone for his [Holmes's] mind. I stimulated him. He liked to think aloud in my presence. . . . If I irritated him by a certain methodical slowness in my mentality, that irritation served only to make his own flamelike intuitions and impressions flash up the more vividly and swiftly." Holmes confesses to a certain dependence on his friend, saying: "I am lost without my Boswell."

Handsome and athletic, if a trifle burly, Watson is a gentle, kind, warm, compassionate, and friendly gentleman. He has a brown moustache, brown hair, and deep-brown eyes that inspire confidence and affection in women. He admires beautiful women, confiding that he has gained knowledge of them on three continents. Often strongly attracted to women involved in Holmes's cases, he marries the lovely and dainty Mary Morstan; their happiness lasts only a few years, however, for she dies of a tragic illness, and he later remarries.

Watson appeared in one work without Holmes, *Angels of Darkness,* an unpublished play by Conan Doyle. The undated manuscript was originally titled *A Study in Scarlet,* the title of the first Sherlock Holmes novel (published in 1887). Kingsley Amis gave Watson a solo adventure on BBC television in 1974.

WAUGH, HILLARY (BALDWIN) (1920–). American mystery writer. Born in New Haven, Conn., Waugh attended schools in that city until 1942, when he received a B.A. degree from Yale University. He served in the Naval Air Forces from July 1942 to January 1946, earning his "wings" as a flier in May 1943. He began writing his first mystery while stationed in the Canal Zone, but it was not published until 1947.

Except for brief periods in New York and Europe, Waugh has lived in New England since being discharged from the Navy. He taught mathematics and physics for one year, and for a year and a half edited a small Connecticut weekly newspaper, the *Branford Review.* In 1971 he was elected, as a Republican, to a two-year term as first selectman (mayor) of Guilford, Conn., but did not seek reelection. He has abandoned all positions that interfere with his main interest, writing fiction.

Waugh was one of the first writers of police procedurals. An early police routine novel with a good twist ending, *Last Seen Wearing* (1952), details an investigation into the disappearance of a Massachusetts college girl. At the time he wrote it, Waugh lived in New Haven, and his future bride, Diana M. Taylor, was a freshman at Smith College. The Waughs have two daughters and a son.

The policemen in *Last Seen Wearing* never became series characters, but Waugh did create two series detectives. One is Fred Fellows of "Stockford," Conn., a patient and thorough rural policeman who is capable of great compassion. In *Prisoner's Plea* (1963), Fellows, acting on his own, reopens a murder case because he believes the personal appeal made by a convicted murderer.

Harsher and more brutal is Waugh's series about New York detective Frank Sessions of Homicide North, introduced in *"30" Manhattan East* (1968). In *The Young Prey* (1969) Sessions investigates the brutal killing of a teen-age girl in Harlem.

Waugh has also written mysteries under the

pseudonyms Harry Walker and H. Baldwin Taylor. As Taylor, he wrote *The Triumvirate* (1966), in which the detective is the editor of a New England newspaper.

WAYNE, ANDERSON. See HALLIDAY, BRETT.

WEBB, CHRISTOPHER. See HOLTON, LEONARD.

WEBB, RICHARD WILSON. See QUENTIN, PATRICK.

WEBSTER, HENRY KITCHELL (1875–1932). American author of popular novels. Webster's mystery fiction has recently undergone critical reevaluation and is now sought, although it has been out of print for more than four decades. Born in Evanston, Ill., he never wandered far. He attended Hamilton College, where he earned a bachelor's degree in 1897 (Hamilton awarded him an honorary L.H.D. degree in 1925). After graduation he spent a year as an instructor in rhetoric at Union College but soon returned to Evanston. In September 1901 Webster married Mary Ward Orth; they had three sons.

Webster collaborated with Samuel Merwin on three successful novels on the theme of railroading, *The Short-Line War* (1899), *Calumet 'K'* (1901), and *Comrade Jim* (1907), as well as several operas. He also edited *The Boy's Herald*, an amateur biweekly, and wrote a volume of verse, published at his father's expense, that was not a success.

Webster's subsequent literary efforts were popular and successful. His fictional contributions to such magazines as *The Saturday Evening Post* and *McClure's* were mainly about the theater and family life. His first mystery was *The Whispering Man* (1908); his second, *The Butterfly* (1914). Copious amounts of fiction followed, including commercial hackwork written under pseudonyms. Under his own name Webster produced a total of thirty-two volumes; one of the most popular was *An American Family* (1918). Toward the end of his life he became a one-man fiction factory and dictated about 20,000 words per week to a stenographer—much in the mystery field.

In commenting on Webster's mysteries, Wendell Hertig TAYLOR wrote, "All are largely concerned with clues and have some amateur detection and, less often, police intervention. The narration is often in the first person; the setting is Chicago or its suburbs in about half the tales. The writing is smooth and competent, and whatever complexities of plot may develop are remembered and neatly resolved at the end. Characterization is excellent; typical of the period is the love-interest which, however, is not allowed to impede the progress of the story. . . . For the most part he avoided violence, preferring to deal with the social tangles provided by the relationships within a large family."

The Whispering Man concerns the efforts of a painter and a lawyer to discover how an alienist was poisoned. *The Butterfly*, about a drama professor and a visiting dancer, is set in a university town, is leavened with humor, and concerns two deaths. Webster's next mystery, *The Corbin Necklace* (1926), is set in a family mansion near Chicago and concerns the whereabouts and the value of a missing necklace.

The Clock Strikes Two (1928) deals with a ninety-year-old tyrant, his scheming relatives, and the solution to the forty-year-old mystery of his granddaughter's death. A chest containing papers that could clear the heroine's father of charges of financial skulduggery is the subject of *The Sealed Trunk* (1929). Incidents such as a long dance-hall sequence and the heroine's abrupt departure might have served as source material for a Cornell WOOLRICH story. *Who Is the Next?* (1931), Webster's best-known work, concerns several murders, amateur aviation, and a charming love story set in a town near Chicago. *The Alleged Great-Aunt* (1935), completed by two friends of Webster, Janet Ayer Fairbank and Margaret Ayer Barnes, probes the relationship between the hero's granduncle and an opera singer and ends in violence and pursuit in the Adirondack foothills.

Webster died while working on a "romance," as he called his mysteries.

WELLMAN, MANLY WADE (1903–). American mystery novelist. The son of a medical missionary, Wellman was born in Portuguese Angola. His brother is Paul I. Wellman, popular American novelist and historian. Manly graduated from the University of Wichita.

Part American Indian himself, he created David Return, a policeman on the reservation of the fictional Tsichah tribe, whom Ellery QUEEN (author) called "the first truly American detective." A story about David Return, "A Star for a Warrior" (1946), won first prize in *Ellery Queen's Mystery Magazine*'s first contest. In 1955 Wellman's *Dead and Gone* won a Mystery Writers of America Edgar as the best fact crime book of the year.

WELLS, CAROLYN (1870?–1942). American anthologist, parodist, and mystery writer. Born in Rahway, N.J., Miss Wells contracted scarlet fever at the age of six and was almost totally deaf thereafter. However, she had a varied education including travel abroad. Her lifelong love of books led her into library work before she discovered writing as a profession. She married Hadwin Houghton, a member of an American publishing family, in 1918; he died a few years later. She lived in New York City for the rest of her life.

After writing sketches and light verse for several

American and British journals at the turn of the century, Miss Wells began the series of anthologies that have probably brought her as much fame as her mysteries have. Her *Nonsense Anthology* (1902) was considered a classic, and her *Parody Anthology* (1904) remains in print today. A popular parodist herself, she wrote *Ptomaine Street* (1921), a full-length parody of Sinclair Lewis, and parodies of Sherlock HOLMES. She also edited many collections of mystery stories.

Of Miss Wells's 170 books, 82 are mysteries. One of them, *The Disappearance of Kimball Webb* (1920), was published under the pseudonym Rowland Wright. Her most famous series detective, the scholarly, book-loving Fleming Stone, appeared in sixty-one of the mysteries, beginning with *The Clue* (1909). He originally appeared in "The Maxwell Mystery," in the May 1906 issue of *All-Story Magazine*. She created ten other detectives, including Kenneth Carlisle, handsome Hollywood star, who gives up his silent-screen career to become a detective; Pennington Wise, a psychic investigator; and Bert Bayliss, socialite private detective.

Miss Wells wrote the first instructional manual in the genre, *The Technique of the Mystery Story* (1913). Her opinion that "the detective story must *seem* real in the same sense that fairy tales *seem* real to children" has been quoted approvingly by Howard HAYCRAFT and others. She inveighed against the use of impossible murder methods, and in her own books bizarre and seemingly supernatural crimes are always given natural explanations.

Many critics have questioned why a writer so prolific and prominent in her own time should be as completely forgotten as Carolyn Wells is today. Although they never explain her initial popularity, Jacques BARZUN and Wendell Hertig TAYLOR find that, although she had ingenious ideas, her powers of execution were poor.

WELLS, H[ERBERT] G[EORGE] (1866–1946). English author of science fiction, satires, and popularizations of history and science. Born in Bromley, Kent, he studied in London and became a teacher and then a journalist and novelist. Wells was a militant exponent of socialism, feminism, and evolutionism, and many of his later books are merely platforms for his social and political theories and are no longer read. His realistic novels were influential in their time but are also seldom read today. His science fiction is still often fresh and exciting, and the pseudoscientific devices and methods he invented were remarkably prophetic. The best known of these works are *The Time Machine* (1895), *The War of the Worlds* (1898), and *The First Men on the Moon* (1901).

Many of his works are borderline mystery and crime fiction, evoking terror and suspense in a variety of ways. *The Island of Dr. Moreau* (1896), *The Invisible Man* (1897), and many short stories fall into this category, notably the title story and "The Hammerpond Park Burglary," a realistic tale of crime, in *The Stolen Bacillus and Other Incidents* (1895); "The Treasure in the Forest" in *The Country of the Blind and Other Stories* (1907); and several pieces in *The Plattner Story and Others* (1897) and *Twelve Stories and a Dream* (1903).

Claude Rains in the title role of *The Invisible Man*. [*Universal*]

Films

Decades after it was written, Wells's unique crime novel *The Invisible Man* was brought to the American screen by Universal Studios; its rich special effects made it a popular success and brought stardom to English actor Claude Rains, who was seen on screen for the first time in the film's final shot.

The Invisible Man. Universal, 1933. Rains, Gloria Stuart, William Harrigan, Henry Travers. Directed by James Whale.

His face bandaged, young chemist Jack Griffin goes to a lonely country inn to work. When villagers disturb him, he runs amok, stripping away his bandages to reveal that he is invisible. One of the drugs with which he has been experimenting causes insanity. He begins a reign of terror, confident that an invisible man can rule the world. But, finally, frozen with cold and hounded by police dragnets, he is shot down.

The popularity of the film inspired other "invisible men," of varying motives and degrees of criminality; none was portrayed by Rains, however. In *The Invisible Man Returns* (1940), English mineowner Geoffrey Radcliff (Vincent Price), unjustly sentenced to be executed for the murder of

Fire and cold bring the Invisible Man to discovery and death. [*Universal*]

his brother, escapes when a chemist friend, Dr. Frank Griffin (John Sutton), makes him invisible. He manages to trap the real killer and becomes visible again. Virginia Bruce suffers no harmful side effects in *The Invisible Woman* (1940), a comedy in which eccentric Professor Gibbs (John Barrymore) advertises for young women to serve as subjects for his chemistry experiments. Jon Hall, in *Invisible Agent* (1942), is the inventor of a process that makes people invisible; he volunteers to parachute unseen into Berlin during wartime. The chemical changes do him no harm. In 1944 Hall portrayed Robert Griffin in *The Invisible Man's Revenge*, in which a madman who wants to terrorize the other members of his family because of a dispute over an estate extracts from recluse scientist Peter Drury (John Carradine) the secret of invisibility. Later, after he has killed the scientist, he too is killed—by Drury's invisible dog. The story was used again as the basis of a comedy film, *Abbott and Costello Meet the Invisible Man* (1951). A young boxer accused of murdering his manager tries to prove his innocence by using a family secret: the ability to become invisible. Claude Rains's picture is seen on the wall.

Television

In 1958 a series of 26 half-hour programs called *The Invisible Man* was produced for British television. Scientist Dr. Peter Brady used his discovery for the good of man and country; he suffered no side effects. In 1975 an invisible man (David McCallum) again became the hunted hero of a television series, *The Invisible Man,* fleeing the U.S. military establishment and the grasping scientific community.

WELLS, TOBIAS. *See* FORBES, STANTON.

WENTWORTH, PATRICIA (pseudonym of Dora Amy Elles Dillon Turnbull; 1878–1961). English author of historical and mystery fiction. Born Dora Amy Elles in Mussoorie, India, the daughter of an English general, she was educated in England. She then returned to India, where, like Kipling, she published her first work in the *Civil and Military Gazette,* the chief newspaper in the Punjab. She married Lieutenant Colonel George Dillon but in 1906 was left a widow with a daughter and three stepsons to raise. She returned to England and began writing to help support herself. In 1920 she married Lieutenant Colonel George Oliver Turnbull and resided at Camberley in Surrey until her death. Her husband helped her with her books and shared her many hobbies, which included reading, gardening, motoring, music, and the theater.

Miss Wentworth's early works were mainly historical fiction. Her first, *A Marriage under the Terror* (1911), was a story of the French Revolution that won a prize of 250 guineas. Her first mystery was *The Astonishing Adventure of Jane Smith* (1923). She is best known for a series of thirty-two novels about Miss Maud SILVER, who first appeared in *Grey Mask* (1928). Miss Silver did not reappear until *The*

Case Is Closed (1937), and in the interim Miss Wentworth wrote almost twenty nonseries mysteries. By the early 1940s Miss Silver was so popular that all subsequent Wentworth books featured her as detective.

Patricia Wentworth was usually as popular with critics as she was with readers. She once said that her aim as a mystery writer was "to portray ordinary, convincing human characters in extraordinary circumstances." Anthony BOUCHER considered *The Fingerprint* (1956), in which an old tyrant is murdered soon after changing his will, typical of "her skill at telling an agreeable, old-fashioned romance in which family dilemmas and love stories are so well delineated. . . ."

WEST, ROGER (Creator: John CREASEY). "Handsome" West has been promoted often in the series of forty-three volumes recounting his police work; he began as an inspector and is now chief superintendent—the youngest ever at Scotland Yard. West has a wife and two sons, who bear the names and personalities of Creasey's own sons, Martin and Richard. In the first adventure about the good-looking policeman, *Inspector West Takes Charge* (1942), and several succeeding volumes, an amateur detective, Mark Lessing, supplies unofficial help.

WESTLAKE, DONALD E[DWIN] (1933–). American mystery novelist. Born in Brooklyn, Westlake grew up in Albany, N.Y. After service in the Air Force, editorial work at a literary agency, and a brief acting career, he published his first mystery in 1960. Divorced and the father of four sons, he lives in New Jersey.

His first five novels were of the hard-boiled school. The second, *Killing Time* (1961), about a corrupt upstate New York town, was favorably compared to Dashiell HAMMETT's *Red Harvest* (1929). *The Fugitive Pigeon* (1965) is the first in a series of humorous novels about unlucky innocents and inept criminals. The "hero" of *The Busy Body* (1966) must dispose of an unwelcome corpse. In *The Spy in the Ointment* (1966) the protagonist is a pacifist enmeshed with bomb-throwing extremists. Westlake's descriptions of the exploits of the fall guy of the title of *God Save the Mark* (1967) earned him the Mystery Writers of America Edgar for best novel.

Dortmunder and his comic associates in Westlake's *The Hot Rock* (1970), *Bank Shot* (1972), and *Jimmy the Kid* (1974) are forever planning "capers" that never come off. More serious (and more successful) is Parker, a professional thief Westlake created under the pseudonym Richard Stark. Featured in sixteen books, Parker resorts to plastic surgery to change his appearance in *The Man with the Getaway Face* (1963), when he is hunted by "the Syndicate." In *The Green Eagle Score* (1967) Parker organizes the robbery of the monthly payroll at an Air Force base.

Under another pseudonym, Tucker Coe, Westlake writes of Mitch Tobin, a guilt-ridden former policeman trying to atone for the act that caused his dismissal.

Films

As Richard Stark, Westlake has contributed tough, grim dramas of the underworld to the screen.

Point Blank. MGM, 1967. Lee Marvin, Angie Dickinson, Keenan Wynn, Carroll O'Connor, Lloyd Bochner. Directed by John Boorman. Based on *The Hunter* (1963).

After his friend shoots him while they are pulling a holdup, leaving him for dead and running off with his wife, a gangster exacts revenge not only on the betrayer but on the entire syndicate.

The Split. MGM, 1968. Jim Brown, Diahann Carroll, Julie Harris, Ernest Borgnine, Gene Hackman, Jack Klugman. Directed by Gordon Flemyng. Based on *The Seventh* (1964).

After stealing half a million dollars from a stadium, members of a gang encounter unexpected problems when they attempt to divide the proceeds.

The films based on works published under the Westlake by-line, however, have been lighter.

The Busy Body. Paramount, 1967. Sid Caesar, Robert Ryan, Anne Baxter, Kay Medford, Jan Murray, Dom DeLuise, Godfrey Cambridge, Marty Ingels, Bill Dana, George Jessel. Directed by William Castle. From the novel of the same name.

Robert Redford (left) and George Segal, clumsy but enthusiastic criminals, break into a suburban jail to help an accomplice break out, in Donald E. Westlake's *The Hot Rock*. [*Twentieth Century-Fox*]

A syndicate collector, blown up at a barbecue, is inadvertently buried in a suit with a million dollars sewn in the lining; but when his coffin is dug up, it is empty.

The Hot Rock. Twentieth Century-Fox, 1972. Robert Redford, George Segal, Ron Leibman, Moses Gunn, Zero Mostel. Directed by Peter Yates.

A representative of an African nation hires a gang of inept former convicts to remove a large jewel, the Sahara Stone, from the Brooklyn Museum.

Cops and Robbers. United Artists, 1973. Cliff Gorman, Joe Bologna, Dick Ward, Shepperd Strudwick. Directed by Aram Avakian. Westlake wrote the screenplay, then based his novel of the same name on the film.

Two New York policemen, unhappy at not sharing enough of the good life, decide to get rich by engaging in one massive robbery: stealing $10 million in pay-to-bearer certificates for the Mafia.

Bank Shot. United Artists, 1974. George C. Scott, Joanna Cassidy, Sorrell Booke. Directed by Gower Champion. Originally written—but not filmed—as a direct sequel to *The Hot Rock*; based on the 1972 novel of the same title.

A master safecracker gathers together a gang to pull off his scheme to rob a bank by simply towing it away.

WESTMACOTT, MARY. *See* CHRISTIE, AGATHA.

WHARTON, ANTHONY. *See* BROCK, LYNN.

WHEATLEY, DENNIS (YEATS) (1897–). English author of historical romances and occult, mystery, and espionage fiction. Born in London, the son of Florence Baker (Lady Newton) and Albert David Wheatley, he was a cadet on the H.M.S. *Worcester* and privately educated in England and Germany. In September 1914 he received a commission in the Royal Field Artillery and later fought at Ypres, Cambrai, and Saint-Quentin. In 1918 he was gassed and invalided out of service, after which he went into the family business as a wine merchant (1919–1931).

His first book, *The Forbidden Territory*, was published in January 1933 and reprinted seven times in seven weeks. The principal characters in this novel became known as "those modern Musketeers" and have since appeared in a number of other books.

Possibly Wheatley's finest achievement is the series featuring Roger Brook, Mr. Pitt's most resourceful secret agent. The twelve volumes cover the main historical events from 1783 to 1815, including the French Revolution, the rise and fall of Napoleon, and the happenings throughout Europe.

Wheatley's other well-known character is Gregory Sallust, a modern secret service agent about whom there are seven volumes dealing with the principal events of World War II in Europe, from September 1939 to May 1945.

His pre-World War II books included an innovative series, called *The Crime Murder Dossiers*, that he produced at the suggestion of J. G. Links. The books consist of cardboard folders containing typewritten sheets; inserted among these pages are photographs of real people, handwritten letters, telegrams, hair, pieces of bloodstained curtain, and so on—all assembled to give the reader an opportunity to solve the crime just as the police would. The titles in the series are *Murder Off Miami* (1936; U.S. title: *File on Bolitho Blane*), *Who Killed Robert Prentice?* (1937; U.S. title: *File on Robert Prentice*), *The Malinsay Massacre* (1938), and *Herewith the Clues* (1939). Publication was discontinued after the war because of rising production costs, and the books are much sought by collectors today.

Wheatley has published over sixty books, most of which are still in print. They have been translated into twenty-nine languages and have sold more than 37 million copies.

WHEELER, EDWARD L[YTTON] (1854?–1885). American author of DIME NOVELS and creator of "Deadwood Dick," a famous outlaw character who appears in thirty-three novels; ninety-seven "Deadwood Dick, Jr." stories are believed to have been

The Deadwood Dick Library reprinted the adventures of Edward L. Wheeler's outlaw; they originally appeared in Beadle's *Half-Dime Library*. The provocative title of this pamphlet is *New York Nell, the Boy-Girl Detective*.

written by another author under Wheeler's by-line. Born in Avoca, N.Y., he spent most of his life in Titusville, Pa. His first "Deadwood Dick" adventure appeared in October 1877, in the *Half-Dime Library*. The young desperado is said to have been based on a real frontiersman, Richard W. Clark.

WHEELER, HUGH CALLINGHAM. *See* QUENTIN, PATRICK.

WHITE, BABINGTON. *See* BRADDON, M. E.

WHITE, ETHEL LINA (ca. 1884–1944). British author of detective novels. Born in Abergavenny, a small English town on the Welsh border, she was raised in Wales, one of a family of twelve. She gave up her job in the Ministry of Pensions to write fiction. Her first published novel, *Fear Stalks the Village* (1932), was followed by more than a dozen mysteries before she died.

Films

Miss White's *The Wheel Spins* (1936) was adapted by Alfred HITCHCOCK into one of his most important British films, *The Lady Vanishes*, in 1938.

The Unseen. Paramount, 1945. Gail Russell, Joel McCrea, Herbert Marshall. Directed by Lewis Allen. Based on *Her Heart in Her Throat* (1942; British title: *Midnight House*).

A newly hired governess is uneasy when her employer, a widower, is suspected of the murder of a mysterious old woman who lived in the vacant house next door.

The Spiral Staircase. RKO, 1946. Dorothy McGuire, George Brent, Ethel Barrymore, Gordon Oliver, Rhonda Fleming. Directed by Robert Siodmak. Based on *Some Must Watch* (1934).

Following the death of a crippled girl, a mute housemaid is warned by her aged mistress that a maniac murderer is ridding the world of the weak and imperfect.

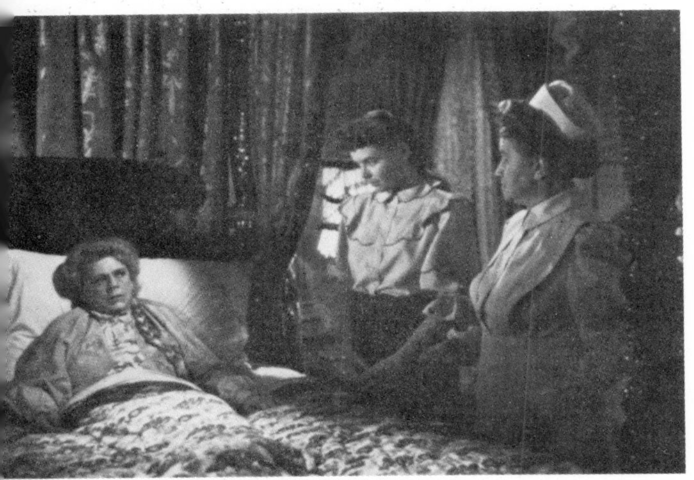

A mute Dorothy McGuire (center) is one of the servants attending imperious, bedridden Ethel Barrymore in a New England community where an unknown killer is eliminating "imperfect" people. *The Spiral Staircase* is based on a work by Ethel Lina White. [*RKO*]

WHITE, WILLIAM ANTHONY PARKER. *See* BOUCHER, ANTHONY.

WHITECHURCH, VICTOR L[ORENZO] (1868–1933). English churchman, author, and mystery writer. A canon of the Anglican Church, Whitechurch lived and worked in the country for many years. Late in life he became honorary canon at Christ Church, Oxford. He was the author of such clerical romances as *A Canon in Residence* (1904), *Concerning Himself* (1909), *A Downland Corner* (1913), and *Mute Witnesses* (1933).

His first effort in the mystery field, *Thrilling Stories of the Railway* (1912), contains fifteen stories, nine of which are from the casebook of Thorpe Hazell, a believer in vegetarianism and exercise and a specialist in railway detection. The volume containing his semihumorous exploits was selected for inclusion in QUEEN'S QUORUM and is now almost impossible to find. *The Adventures of Captain Ivan Koravitch* (1925), another rare collection of short stories, contains more railway mysteries and a spy story.

At the end of his life Whitechurch suddenly became infatuated with the detective story form and dashed off a half-dozen novels without forethought. According to Jacques BARZUN and Wendell Hertig TAYLOR, in *A Catalogue of Crime*, "he was the greatest improviser in the genre—all but one of his stories has distinctive merit."

Whitechurch aired his views on the detective story in the introduction to *The Crime at Diana's Pool* (1927), a tale of a murder that is committed at a lawn party and solved by a policeman and a vicar. He used a clerical setting in *The Robbery at Rudwick House* (1929), which involves stolen snuffboxes and possible impersonation. The book is an early example of the "big caper" novel. *Murder at the College* (1932; U.S. title: *Murder at Exbridge*), Whitechurch's last effort, was written after a protracted illness.

WHITFIELD, RAOUL (1898–1945). American author of hard-boiled detective fiction. Although less remembered than Dashiell HAMMETT, Raymond CHANDLER, Carroll John DALY, and other popular writers for BLACK MASK and other PULP MAGAZINES, Whitfield was one of the most popular and highly paid writers of his time. The many years he spent in the Philippines when he was young provided the background for his Jo Gar stories (published under the pseudonym Ramon Decolta). He sold his first story in 1923, and his output was prolific for the next decade, after which poor health curtailed his activities.

Probably his best-known novel is *Green Ice* (1930), named for the emeralds that cause several murders. Mal Ourney, just released from Sing Sing after serving a term for manslaughter (a crime actually committed by a girl), is determined to make war on the "big shots" of the underworld, those he calls "the crime breeders."

Silver Wings (1930) is a collection of aviation stories (Whitfield had served in the Air Service during World War I). *Death in a Bowl* (1931) and *The Virgin Kills* (1932) are crime novels of the "tough-guy" school.

WHITNEY, PHYLLIS A[YAME] (1903–). American author of juvenile and mystery novels. Born in Yokohama, Japan, of American parents, Miss Whitney lived in the Orient until she was fifteen. After returning to the United States, she lived in Berkeley, Calif., San Antonio, Tex., and Chicago, Ill., where she graduated from high school and worked in bookstores and libraries. She is married to a businessman and lives in northwestern New Jersey. They have one daughter and three grandchildren.

Miss Whitney first gained fame as a writer of juvenile novels, many of which deal with racial, social, and family problems. Two of her books, *Mystery of the Haunted Pool* (1960) and *Secret of the Emerald Star* (1964), have won Mystery Writers of America Edgars as best juvenile mysteries. Her *Writing Juvenile Fiction* (1947) is considered a standard text in the field, and she has taught the subject at Northwestern and New York Universities.

Her first adult mystery, *Red Is for Murder* (1943), is a conventional detective story in which the amateur sleuth is a young girl who works in a Chicago store. Since its publication Miss Whitney has achieved greater success with modern Gothic mysteries aimed primarily at a female audience. The backgrounds for these works are usually based upon her own travels. Critics have approved of her re-creation of the island of Rhodes in *Seven Tears for Apollo* (1963) and rural New Jersey in *The Winter People* (1969), although they suggest that coincidence has been stretched too far in the latter.

WIBBERLEY, LEONARD PATRICK O'CONNOR. See HOLTON, LEONARD.

WILDE, PERCIVAL (1887–1953). American playwright and author of detective novels and stories. Born in New York, he graduated from Columbia University at the age of nineteen. He then reviewed books and sold his first story in 1912. Turning his attention to writing one-act plays for vaudeville, he produced more than 100, most of which were published and were performed in more than 1,300 cities in the United States. He married Nadie Rogers Marckres in 1920; they had two sons. Following service in the Navy during World War II, he worked briefly in Hollywood.

Wilde also wrote highly regarded short stories of crime and mystery. *Rogues in Clover* (1929) is a collection of the adventures of cardsharp Bill Parmelee, who specializes in solving gambling mysteries. *P. Moran, Operative* (1947) is a collection of humorous exploits of a New England detective. A handyman by day and a student of the Acme International Detective Correspondence School at night, "Pete" has a perfect record: no matter how simple the case, he has never been right. Wilde also wrote several mystery novels: *Mystery Week-End* (1938), *Inquest* (1940), *Design for Murder* (1941), and *Tinsley's Bones* (1942).

WILEY, HUGH (1884–). American engineer and author, most of whose books are humorous tales about Negroes or mystery stories about Orientals. Born in Zanesville, Ohio, he left school while still a teenager but went on to build bridges, tunnels, railroads, mines, and power plants as an engineer and contractor. His best work featuring Chinese characters involves James Lee Wong (see WONG, MR.), a popular film detective. His most noteworthy books are short story collections of Oriental intrigue, romance, and mystery: *Jade and Other Stories* (1921), *Manchu Blood* (1927), and *The Copper Mask and Other Stories* (1932).

WILLARD, JOHN A. (1885–1942). American actor and playwright. Born in San Francisco, Willard tried his hand at being a gold miner, reporter, cowboy, art student, aviator, and actor before becoming a pilot in France during World War I. He spent five years in the Latin Quarter of Paris trying to learn to write. In 1912 he made his New York acting debut in *Making Good*. He married Gladys Caldwell in 1915. Among his more successful plays were *The Green Beetle* (1913); *Adventure* (1928), a wild West drama starring Peggy Conway; and *The Murder Game* (1932), which opened in Sharon, Conn.

Willard got the idea for his most famous work, *The Cat and the Canary,* while flying bombing missions in France. It has no relation to the short novel of the same name published in 1908 by Margaret Cameron. When the play first opened in New York (February 7, 1922, at the National Theater), Willard played the role of Harry Blythe (a small part).

Plays and Films

Willard's *The Cat and the Canary,* an old-dark-house melodrama in which devious eccentrics gather for the reading of a will, starred Florence

Danny, the brash young bellhop (Robert Montgomery), is interviewed by the tyrannical Mrs. Bramson (Dame Mae Whitty, in wheelchair) and her spinster niece (Rosalind Russell); neither yet suspects that he is a psychopathic murderer. The 1937 film version of the Emlyn Williams play *Night Must Fall*. [*MGM*]

Eldridge and Henry Hull; it immediately became the inspiration for an entire school of mystery works. Three film versions were made, the first using the skills of a distinguished European director who added Germanic shadows to the sliding panels and claustrophobic terror.

The Cat and the Canary. Universal, 1927. Laura La Plante, Creighton Hale, Gertrude Astor, Tully Marshall, Lucien Littlefield. Directed by Paul Leni.

One sinister night, the relatives of a murdered recluse gather at his passage-riddled home to learn that young Anabel West will inherit his fortune if she can prove that she is sane. A maniac escaped from an asylum is said to be lurking in the house.

The Cat Creeps. Universal, 1930. Helen Twelvetrees, Raymond Hackett, Neil Hamilton, Lilyan Tashman, Jean Hersholt. Directed by Rupert Julian. A remake; again, the heroine is being frightened into insanity.

The Cat and the Canary. Paramount, 1939. Bob Hope, Paulette Goddard, John Beal, Douglass Montgomery. Directed by Elliott Nugent. A remake; the house is now set in the Louisiana bayous.

WILLARD, JOSIAH FLYNT. *See* FLYNT, JOSIAH.

WILLIAMS, (GEORGE) EMLYN (1905–1974). Welsh actor, producer, and playwright. The son of a Mostyn, Flintshire, ironmonger, Williams spoke no English until he was eight. He was attending Oxford when his first play was produced, but his first stage success was with *A Murder Has Been Arranged* (written in 1930). He acted on the stage beginning in 1927 and made his film debut in 1932 in *The Case of the Frightened Lady*. Williams's *George* (1961) is regarded as one of the finest theatrical autobiographies of modern times. His nonfiction *Beyond Belief* (1967) is a compelling chronicle of England's famous Moors murders of the mid-1960s and was a best seller for months. His nonmystery play *The Corn Is Green* (1938), chosen as the best foreign play of 1941 by the New York Drama Critics Circle, was a resounding success on both sides of the Atlantic and a well-received film.

Films

Night Must Fall. MGM, 1937. Robert Montgomery, Rosalind Russell, Dame May Whitty. Directed by Richard Thorpe. Closely adapted from Williams's great stage success, which opened in London in 1935.

The penniless spinster niece of a tyrannical old woman living in a secluded house begins to fear that the brash bellhop who is playing up to her aunt is actually a maniacal murderer who carries about the head of his last victim in a hatbox.

A less successful version of the film, released by MGM in England in 1964, starred Albert Finney, Susan Hampshire, and Mona Washbourne and was, nonetheless, innovatively directed by Karel Reisz.

WILLIAMS, RACE (Creator: Carroll John DALY). The first popular "hard-boiled dick." Williams is a private investigator who is in the business for the thrills and the money. Scores of his adventures appeared in BLACK MASK and *Dime Detective*, two of the most popular PULP MAGAZINES. He has worked in New York, Chicago, and California at various jobs (newspaperman, gambler, insurance investigator, cameraman, undercover man for the racing commission, police detective), but he is always essentially the same heroic figure, living by a strong moral code of right and wrong that is not necessarily identical with the law. Fearless, violent—even brutal—he does what he has to do to administer his idea of justice, including killing scores of individuals. An exceptional shot, he once fired two revolvers at the same time—making only one hole between the eyes of his victim.

Daly described Williams as thirty years old, 5 feet 11½ inches tall, and weighing 183 pounds, with dark-brown hair and black eyes. Men respect and fear him; women admire him—and he them. He is fiercely patriotic, equating criminals with Communists; many of his adversaries are evil foreigners.

Williams's first case was "Knights of the Open Palm" in the June 1, 1923, issue of *Black Mask*. Among the best novels in which he appears are *The Snarl of the Beast* (1927); *The Third Murderer* (1931), about his duel with the Gorgon brothers (two gangsters and one genius who rule a great city); *The Amateur Murderer* (1933); and *Murder from the East* (1935), an adventure-intrigue tale about the mythical country of Astran.

WILLIAMS, (GEORGE) VALENTINE (1883–1946). English journalist and mystery writer. The son of G. Douglas Williams, chief editor of Reuters, he began his career as a journalist and returned to that work frequently, even after his fiction was successful. Dividing his days between England, the French Riviera, and the United States, he acted, lectured, and wrote screenplays in addition to producing more than thirty novels of mystery and espionage.

His best-known characters are "the Fox" (Baron Alexis De Bahl), in *The Fox Prowls* (1939); "Clubfoot" (Dr. Adolph Grundt), in *Clubfoot the Avenger* (1923), *The Mystery of the Gold Box* (1932; British title: *The Gold Comfit Box*), and other books; Mr. Treadgold, a West End tailor and amateur detective, in *Dead Man Manor* (1936) and *Mr. Treadgold Cuts In* (1937; U.S. title: *The Curiosity of Mr. Treadgold*); and Trevor Dene, a bespectacled young genius at Scotland Yard, in *The Clue of the Rising Moon* (1924) and *Masks Off at Midnight* (1934).

Film

The Crouching Beast. Stafford (British), 1935. Fritz Kortner, Wynne Gibson, Richard Bird, Isabel Jeans. Directed by Victor Hanbury. Based on the 1928 novel of the same name.

In the Dardanelles, a mysterious British spy is aided by an American girl in the theft of fortification plans.

WILLING, DR. BASIL (Creator: Helen MCCLOY). Born in Baltimore at the turn of the twentieth century to a Russian mother and an American father, Basil has been described as tall and thin, with alert eyes in an intelligent face and gracefully deliberate gestures. He became interested in psychiatry when he saw "shell-shocked" soldiers during his World War I service and went to Johns Hopkins Medical School upon his discharge. He completed his studies in Paris and Vienna before establishing a New York practice. He married an Austrian refugee, Countess Gisela von Hohenems, after a courtship of several years; they live in suburban Connecticut.

Except for service in World War II (six years in the Caribbean, Scotland, and Japan) he has been medical assistant to Manhattan's district attorney. He solves crimes by acting on his beliefs that "lies, like blunders, are psychological facts" and "every criminal leaves psychic fingerprints, and he can't wear gloves to hide them."

CHECKLIST

1938	*Dance of Death*
1940	*The Man in the Moonlight*
1941	*The Deadly Truth*
1942	*Who's Calling?*
1942	*Cue for Murder*
1945	*The One That Got Away*
1950	*Through a Glass, Darkly*
1951	*Alias Basil Willing*
1955	*The Long Body*
1956	*Two-thirds of a Ghost*
1965	*The Singing Diamonds* (s.s.; British title: *Surprise, Surprise!*; two stories are about Willing)
1968	*Mr. Splitfoot*

WILLIS, GEORGE ANTHONY ARMSTRONG. *See* ARMSTRONG, ANTHONY.

WILMER, DALE. *See* MILLER, WADE.

WIMSEY, LORD PETER (Creator: Dorothy L. SAYERS). The younger son of Mortimer Gerald Bredon Wimsey, 15th duke of Denver, Peter Death Bredon Wimsey was born in 1890. Educated at Eton and Balliol College, Oxford, he starred in cricket and took first-class honors in modern history.

About to wed on the eve of his World War I service, he postponed the wedding because he felt that it would be unfair to any wife if he returned mutilated. He found that he had miscalculated, for the girl he loved married another man. Wimsey attempted to relieve his disappointment by reckless bravery in combat and almost lost his life behind German lines, earning the Distinguished Service Order in the process. He also suffered "a nervous breakdown" as a result of his combat experience and was subject to recurring bouts of headache and nightmare.

Returning from the war to a London flat at 110 Piccadilly, former Captain Wimsey is looked after by Bunter, the loyal sergeant who had served under him. Peter pursues a variety of interests, including history, rare books, and music (he is an expert pianist). His chief interest, however, is criminology, and the witty, eccentric artistocrat soon becomes the leading amateur detective in London.

Wimsey's close family ties are evident in many of his cases. The monocled sleuth takes on the investigation of the nude corpse in a bathtub (*Whose Body?*) at the request of his mother, the Dowager Duchess of Denver. In *Clouds of Witness* he risks his life on three occasions to preserve the family name when his older brother, Gerald, is accused of murder. His flighty sister Mary is a murder suspect involved with a Socialist who attempts to shoot Peter. After an unpleasant experience with quicksand on a Yorkshire fen, Wimsey flies the Atlantic in a storm as his brother's fate is decided by the House of Lords. Eventually, Mary falls in love with Peter's good friend Inspector Charles Parker of Scotland Yard, with whom he works on several cases. In *The Dawson Pedigree* another member of the Wimsey "team," Miss Climpson, is introduced. She is an elderly typist who has pronounced abilities as a detective. Working with other spinsters out of an office financed by Wimsey, she is part of a unique organization of "irregulars."

Miss Climpson figures prominently in *Strong Poison*, in which Peter observes Harriet Vane standing in the dock for murder and determines to exonerate and woo her. Successful in the first objective, he fails at the second, and is rejected by her in this book and again in *Have His Carcase*, in which he solves the murder of the bearded man whose body Harriet discovers while on a walking tour. Although she is attracted to Peter, Harriet is afraid of a permanent liaison with him, partly because she fears that their marriage might be unable to withstand the pressure of the debt she owes him for saving her life.

Rebuffed, Wimsey loses himself in an affair with a beautiful Viennese opera singer and in undertaking a number of delicate missions for the British Foreign Office. He responds quickly, however, when Harriet asks his help, in *Gaudy Night*, in solving a strange puzzle at Oxford that has left a number of female professors in fear. Poison-pen letters, scribbled obscenities, theft, and attempted murder have created a wave of terror at her former college, and Peter's arrival leads to a meeting of minds (and hearts) with Harriet.

Ian Carmichael plays the dashing, sophisticated amateur sleuth Lord Peter Wimsey, in a scene from *The Unpleasantness at the Bellona Club*. The international television series, set in the flapper age, gave Carmichael detailed dramatizations of several Sayers stories and more portrayals of Wimsey than any other film actor.

Married in October 1935 (in *Busman's Honeymoon*), the Wimseys attempt to escape publicity by going to their new home in Huntingdonshire. They find a body on the premises, and, although Peter has no difficulty in finding the culprit, a brief marital crisis occurs because of his customary depression following the execution of a man he has sent to the gallows.

Celebrating the birth of his first son in "The Haunted Policeman" (1938; first book publication in *Lord Peter*, 1972), Wimsey helps the title character solve a mystery about a disappearing house—and the corpse within it. By the time of Lord Peter's final appearance in "Talboys" (written in 1942 but unpublished until 1972, first in a limited-edition pamphlet, then in the second edition of *Lord Peter*), he has three sons and solves a domestic crime involving the oldest. After 1942 nothing is known about Lord Peter, except that at that time he was on a dangerous mission in connection with the war.

CHECKLIST

1923 *Whose Body?*
1926 *Clouds of Witness*
1927 *The Dawson Pedigree* (U.S. title: *Unnatural Death*)

1928 *The Unpleasantness at the Bellona Club*
1928 *Lord Peter Views the Body* (s.s.)
1930 *Strong Poison*
1931 *The Five Red Herrings* (U.S. title: *Suspicious Characters*)
1932 *Have His Carcase*
1933 *Murder Must Advertise*
1933 *Hangman's Holiday* (s.s.; contains four stories about Wimsey)
1934 *The Nine Tailors*
1935 *Gaudy Night*
1937 *Busman's Honeymoon*
1939 *In the Teeth of the Evidence* (s.s.; contains two stories about Wimsey)
1972 *Lord Peter* (s.s.)
1972 "Talboys" (s.s.)

Films and Play

The titled detective has not had an extensive career in films.

The Silent Passenger. Associated British, 1935. John Loder, Mary Newland, Peter Haddon (Lord Peter), Austin Trevor (Inspector Parker), Donald Wolfit, Leslie Perrins. Directed by Reginald Denham. Miss Sayers provided the "theme" for this film under a 1934 agreement with the film company.

The action takes place mostly on the boat train from London to the Channel. A young husband (Loder) tries to avoid being accused of the murder of his wife's blackmailing former lover, whose body (hence the title) is stuffed in his trunk. Another passenger, the eccentric Lord Peter, attended by his valet Bunter (Aubrey Mather), solves the crime in a silly fashion and is called an "insufferable nitwit" by the wife.

The Haunted Honeymoon (British title: *Busman's Honeymoon*). MGM (British), 1940. Robert Montgomery, Constance Cummings, Robert Newton, Googie Withers, Leslie Banks. Directed by Arthur Woods. Based on the play *Busman's Honeymoon*.

A much less eccentric Peter (Montgomery) vows on the eve of his wedding to Harriet Vane, a mystery novelist, to abandon crime solving and lead a more normal life. He purchases the country home at which his bride had spent part of her childhood. After the wedding, the pair, with Peter's faithful butler (Seymour Hicks), drive to the house and find the former owner's body in the cellar. Peter refuses to help Scotland Yard with the case, but when a pretty young girl is accused, he relents.

Miss Sayers had joined forces with Muriel St. Clare Byrne in writing *Busman's Honeymoon*, a three-act "detective comedy," which opened in London just before Christmas in 1936. The 1937 novel, wrote Miss Sayers, was "but the limbs and outward flourishes" of the stage play.

Television

In 1973 the BBC introduced Wimsey to television audiences in two serials that later debuted on the *Masterpiece Theatre* series in the United States (Public Broadcasting Service). Light comedian Ian Carmichael portrays Wimsey as languid but witty, with a wide range of interests in addition to crime solving; he is a bibliophile, music lover, epicure, fashion plate. The series, painstakingly set in 1920s England, dramatized *Clouds of Witness* in five one-hour parts and *The Unpleasantness at the Bellona Club* in four one-hour parts. *The Nine Tailors* and *Murder Must Advertise* were serialized for American viewers during the 1974–1975 seasons.

WINTERTON, PAUL. *See* GARVE, ANDREW.

WITHERALL, LEONIDAS (Creator: Phoebe Atwood TAYLOR as Alice Tilton). Called "Bill" by his friends because of his uncanny resemblance to William Shakespeare, Witherall is a New England prep school headmaster. To supplement his modest pension, he turns to writing thrillers. He also hunts out rare books for "the wealthier and lazier Boston collectors."

Although Witherall seems to be an extremely sober individual, he is drawn into investigating a succession of zany murder cases. In *Beginning with a Bash* (1938), he strives to prove the innocence of a former student whom he encounters, on a below-zero Boston evening, dressed in a gray flannel suit, carrying a bag of golf clubs, and running from the police. This novel originally appeared in *Mystery League* magazine in 1933 as *The Riddle of Volume Four* under the Taylor byline.

Witherall begins his next adventure, *The Cut Direct* (1938), lying in a suburban street, having been hit by a car as he was running to catch a Boston bus. He recovers to solve the case—even though he becomes a suspect himself. He has a penchant for finding dead bodies in unusual places—for example, the corpse in the deep freeze in *Dead Ernest* (1944).

Other Witherall cases are *Cold Steel* (1939), *The Left Leg* (1940), *The Hollow Chest* (1941), *File for Record* (1943), and *The Iron Clew* (1947; British title: *The Iron Hand*).

WITHERS, HILDEGARDE (Creator: Stuart PALMER). A thin, angular, horse-faced spinster detective. Formerly a schoolteacher, Miss Withers has retired to devote her energy to aiding Inspector Oscar Piper (of the New York City Police Department) in solving a long series of murder mysteries that begin with *The Penguin Pool Murder* (1931), in which a body is discovered in a New York aquarium. Other Withers novels include *The Puzzle of the Silver Persian* (1934), *The Puzzle of the Blue Banderilla* (1937), and *Cold Poison* (1954).

Many of the short stories involving Miss Withers were collected by Ellery QUEEN (author) and published in paperback as *The Riddles of Hildegarde*

Withers (1947) and *The Monkey Murder and Other Hildegarde Withers Stories* (1950). She also appears with Craig RICE's John J. MALONE in a collection published by the two authors, *The People vs. Withers and Malone* (1963).

Miss Withers is noted for her odd, even eccentric, choice of hats. She was based on Palmer's high school English teacher, Miss Fern Hackett, and on his father.

Films

The spinsterish Miss Withers was effectively portrayed by Edna May Oliver in a series of RKO pictures; James Gleason, as Inspector Piper, was also well suited to the role of the crusty, unrefined cop who forms an uneasy alliance with the dry, reserved teacher when murder and the fates bring them together. Piper is a bachelor, accustomed to having things his way; the comic badinage and the hints of middle-aged romance that occur in all the films give the series much charm.

The Penguin Pool Murder. RKO, 1932. Oliver, Gleason, Robert Armstrong, Donald Cook, Edgar Kennedy, Mae Clarke. Directed by George Archainbaud. Based on the novel.

On a class trip to the aquarium, schoolteacher Withers spies a corpse in the penguin tank. She becomes an unofficial aide to Inspector Piper and manages a courtroom surprise at the finale.

Murder on the Blackboard. RKO, 1934. Oliver, Gleason, Tully Marshall, Kennedy, Jackie Searle. Directed by Archainbaud. Based on the 1932 novel.

The staff of Miss Withers's public school are being eliminated in the grim old building, the cellar of which is secretly being used as a storage place for bootleg liquor.

Murder on a Honeymoon. RKO, 1935. Oliver, Gleason, Morgan Wallace, Lola Lane, Dorothy Libaire, George Meeker. Directed by Lloyd Corrigan. Based on *The Puzzle of the Pepper Tree* (1933).

On a flight to Catalina Island, a gangster is killed by a poisoned cigarette; Miss Withers and a pair of newlyweds are on board. Later, on the resort island, several more murders occur. This film was Miss Oliver's last appearance as Hildegarde Withers; illness forced her to withdraw from the role.

Murder on a Bridle Path. RKO, 1936. Helen Broderick (a less bony but equally assertive Miss Withers), Gleason, John Carroll, Louise Latimer. Directed by Edward Killy and William Hamilton. Based on *The Puzzle of the Red Stallion* (1936; British title: *The Puzzle of the Briar Pipe*).

Out for a morning walk in Central Park, Miss Withers comes upon the body of a girl supposedly thrown from a horse; she insists that the victim has been murdered. More deaths follow in a gloomy house bordering the park.

The Plot Thickens. RKO, 1936. Zasu Pitts (replacing Helen Broderick as a scatterbrained, more fragile, and less acerbic Miss Withers), Gleason, Lati-

Spinster schoolteacher Hildegarde Withers (Edna May Oliver) helps policeman Oscar Piper (James Gleason) conduct an investigation in the first film of the Withers series, *The Penguin Pool Murder.* [*RKO*]

Police Inspector Oscar Piper (James Gregory) puts ex-schoolteacher-turned-investigator Hildegarde Withers on the trail of a vanished heiress in the telefilm *A Very Missing Person.* Eve Arden plays a somewhat emancipated but not entirely distorted modern Miss Withers. [*Universal*]

mer, Owen Davis, Jr., Richard Tucker. Directed by Ben Holmes. Based on "The Riddle of the Dangling Pearl" (1933).

The death of a girl's escort, shot in a parked car, leads Miss Withers to a museum where another murder occurs and a priceless Cellini cup is stolen from a display that had been thought to be impregnable.

Forty Naughty Girls. RKO, 1937. Pitts, Gleason, Marjorie Lord, George Shelley, Joan Woodbury. Directed by Eddie Cline.

First a press agent and then the leading man of a Broadway musical comedy are murdered, with Inspector Piper and Miss Withers in the audience. The title refers to the show's chorus line. After six films, RKO ended its series.

The team of Hildegarde Withers and Craig Rice's John J. Malone inspired the 1950 MGM film (although Miss Withers became Mrs. O'Malley, a backwoods widow) *Mrs. O'Malley and Mr. Malone* (Marjorie Main, James Whitmore, Ann Dvorak, Don Porter, Dorothy Malone. Directed by Norman Taurog). The action takes place mainly on a New York–bound train; several passengers are murdered, and their bodies vanish. Mrs. O'Malley is aboard because she won the trip in a radio quiz contest.

Television

In 1971 Eve Arden was cast as a less antique Hildegarde Withers, portraying a former schoolteacher turned private investigator in a telefeature entitled *A Very Missing Person* (Universal). A suicide note leads her on a hunt for a missing young heiress. James Gregory is Oscar Piper, and Miss Withers employs a motorcycle-riding, denim-clad male assistant (Dennis Rucker). The film was the pilot for a television series that did not materialize.

WOLFE, NERO (Creator: Rex STOUT). Perhaps the most eccentric of all detectives who have remained human—not lunatic-fringe caricatures—is Nero Wolfe, the elephantine sleuth whose brownstone on West 35th Street in New York serves as his home and office.

He is only 5 feet 11 inches tall, but he weighs a seventh of a ton. He is a gourmand and loathes unnecessary physical activity. "I carry this fat to insulate my feelings," he once admitted. Many years ago he recklessly decided that he was too heavy and set out on an exercise program. For fifteen minutes each day, he threw darts (persistently calling them javelins).

No one—police, criminals, or Wolfe himself—denies that he is a genius. He speaks seven languages (French, Spanish, Italian, Hungarian, Albanian, Bari, and Serbo-Croatian) and has a good knowledge of Latin. His command of English is exemplary and limitless. Anyone who uses words properly, even his enemies, gains his respect. He curses or swears only occasionally; his favorite expletive is "pfui!"

To Wolfe, work is detestable. He keeps his confidential assistant, Archie Goodwin, on the payroll primarily so that Goodwin will prod him to undertake cases, although Archie also serves as secretary, errand boy, bodyguard, bookkeeper, and chauffeur (Wolfe abhors all mechanical devices, especially automobiles, and will do anything to avoid getting into one; he would rather end his own life than step into a taxi, and Archie is the only driver he will trust to take him around the block). All aspects of the private detective business that require travel or physical prowess are handled by Archie. In his spare time, if he does not have a date, Archie chronicles the adventures of his employer.

Wolfe accepts cases only because he realizes that maintaining his luxurious quarters takes money, and that others rely on his income for theirs. In addition to Archie, he must pay Fritz Brenner, the Swiss chef who prepares the epicurean dishes that Wolfe relishes. Fritz could easily work in New York's best restaurant at double his present salary (which exceeds $1,000 a month). While cooking, he wears a chef's hat and apron and will neither talk nor listen to anyone.

Wolfe is reticent about his early years, but William S. Baring-Gould's full-length biography, *Nero Wolfe of West Thirty-fifth Street* (1969), provides the following data (some of which is conjectural): Wolfe and his twin brother, Marko, were born in Trenton, N.J., late in 1892 or early 1893; they are believed to be the illegitimate sons of Sherlock HOLMES and the famous opera singer Irene Adler. The family moved to the Balkans when Wolfe was a tot, and his mother married a man named Vukcic. In his early twenties the adventurous Wolfe worked in the intelligence service of the Austro-Hungarian Empire and later joined the Montenegrin Army. In 1918, when it was nearly wiped out, he walked 600 miles to join the American Army; during his journey, he claims to have killed 200 Germans. He returned to the United States and began his career as a private detective in 1928.

Wolfe quickly earned enough to indulge his whims, which include growing orchids on his roof. Every day he spends two 2-hour sessions with Theodore Horstmann—9–11 A.M. and 4–6 P.M. Archie can remember only five occasions when Wolfe shortened a session because of a case. The rest of Wolfe's schedule is equally structured. He has breakfast in bed or at the table by his window at 8 A.M. He will not speak until he has finished his orange juice, which he will not gulp. When he has read two newspapers, he goes up to the plant rooms in his personal elevator. He lunches at 1:15 and dines at 7:15, but these hours are not rigid if a case is pressing. The remaining hours are for work—if necessary.

He begins work by having Archie report to him. If he requests a full report, Archie can repeat an hour-long, five-way conversation verbatim, including gestures and inflections. Wolfe sits back in his chair, a glass of beer close at hand, and closes his eyes to listen.

Nero Wolfe was selected as one of the greatest detectives of all time and honored on a Nicaraguan commemorative postage stamp.

Wolfe has nearly total control of his emotions, and only Archie can accurately guess what he is thinking. He laughs about once a year; it sounds like a snort. When his eyes are wide open, he is either totally indifferent or very sleepy. When they are nearly closed, forming little slits, he is most alert—and most dangerous. When he is deep in thought, he closes his eyes and compresses his lips, pushing them out and pulling them in in a constant puckering movement.

Ostensibly antagonistic toward women, Wolfe admits, in a moment of candor, that his behavior is merely a defense mechanism. Archie notes that Wolfe seats attractive female clients in the chair that affords him the best view of their legs. More than one has called him handsome. His brown hair is neatly trimmed and brushed; his teeth are so white that they gleam. He dresses conservatively, wearing a suit, tie, and vest year-round. He changes his shirts twice a day; they are almost always yellow, his favorite color, as are his pajamas, which are a somewhat brighter shade.

Wolfe rarely leaves his brownstone, except under extreme provocation or "to meet personal contingencies." Archie does most of the footwork, although Wolfe often uses the services of other private detectives, including Saul Panzer, probably the best free-lancer in the business; "Dol" Bonner; Fred Durkin, who, according to Archie, is "as honest as sunshine, but he isn't so bright as sunshine"; and Orrie Cather, whom Wolfe dislikes. Cather is not smart enough to be cunning, but he happens to look like a trustworthy person and people confide in him.

Wolfe maintains a love-hate relationship with New York's official police, notably Sergeant Stebbins, Lieutenant Rowcliff, and Inspector Cramer, the head of the Homicide Squad, who is intelligent, as

Edward Arnold portrays a jovial, portly Nero Wolfe in this poster collage, with Archie Goodwin (Lionel Stander) in a rare cringing pose in the upper right. [*Columbia*]

he proved in the single case in which he appeared alone (*Red Threads,* 1939), though Wolfe once told him, "Your acceptance of your salary constitutes a fraud on the people of New York and you are a disgrace to an honorable profession."

CHECKLIST

1934 *Fer-de-lance*
1935 *The League of Frightened Men*
1936 *The Rubber Band*
1937 *The Red Box*
1938 *Too Many Cooks*
1939 *Some Buried Caesar*
1940 *Over My Dead Body*
1940 *Where There's a Will*
1942 *Black Orchids* (contains title story and "Cordially Invited to Meet Death")
1944 *Not Quite Dead Enough* (contains title story and "Booby Trap")
1946 *The Silent Speaker*
1947 *Too Many Women*
1948 *And Be a Villain* (British title: *More Deaths than One*)
1949 *Trouble in Triplicate* (three novelettes)
1949 *The Second Confession*
1950 "Door to Death"
1950 *Three Doors to Death* (three novelettes)
1950 *In the Best Families* (British title: *Even in the Best Families*)
1950 *Curtains for Three* (three novelettes)
1951 *Murder by the Book*
1952 *Prisoner's Base* (British title: *Out Goes She*)
1952 *Triple Jeopardy* (three novelettes)
1953 *The Golden Spiders*
1954 *Three Men Out* (three novelettes)
1954 *The Black Mountain*
1955 *Before Midnight*
1956 *Three Witnesses* (three novelettes)
1956 *Might as Well Be Dead*
1957 *Three for the Chair* (three novelettes)
1957 *If Death Ever Slept*
1958 *And Four to Go* (four novelettes; British title: *Crime and Again*)
1958 *Champagne for One*
1959 *Plot It Yourself* (British title: *Murder in Style*)
1960 *Too Many Clients*
1960 *Three at Wolfe's Door* (three novelettes)
1961 *The Final Deduction*
1962 *Gambit*
1962 *Homicide Trinity* (three novelettes)
1963 *The Mother Hunt*
1964 *Trio for Blunt Instruments* (three novelettes)
1964 *A Right to Die*
1965 *The Doorbell Rang*
1966 *Death of a Doxy*
1968 *The Father Hunt*
1969 *Death of a Dude*
1973 *Please Pass the Guilt*
1975 *A Family Affair*

Films

Stout's corpulent recluse was not quite so rotund on the screen, as portrayed by Edward Arnold and, later, by Walter Connolly.

Meet Nero Wolfe. Columbia, 1936. Arnold, Lionel Stander (Archie Goodwin), Russell Hardie, Joan Perry, Victor Jory, Nana Bryant. Directed by Herbert Biberman. Based on *Fer-de-Lance.*

A murder on a golf course, and a second murder nearby, involves Wolfe in a case; he sips beer and tends his indoor garden while Archie does the legwork. The murderer is revealed at a gathering of suspects at Wolfe's home, and there is a hint that Archie may marry a girl (Dennie Moore) who has been chasing him.

The League of Frightened Men. Columbia, 1937. Connolly, Stander, Irene Hervey, Allan Brook, Eduardo Ciannelli, Victor Killian. Directed by Alfred E. Green. Based on the novel.

During their college days ten men hazed a fellow student so roughly that they crippled him for life. When one of the men is later murdered, and the rest receive warning messages, Wolfe is consulted and extracts a large fee from the group.

Radio

The rotund sleuth first appeared in *The Adventures of Nero Wolfe,* a weekly half-hour radio series that began in 1943 and featured Santos Ortega (six years later Ortega, a lean man, portrayed another heavyweight radio detective, Peter Salem). Sydney Greenstreet was the detective in the noteworthy second series. Everett Sloane was Archie Goodwin.

WONG, MR. (Creator: Hugh WILEY). James Lee Wong, a tall, lean, mandarin-like sleuth dressed in a severe black suit and carrying an umbrella or, in his curio-filled Chinatown study, wearing flowing robes, was first transferred from Wiley's stories in *Collier's* to the screen, with Boris Karloff in the role, by Monogram in 1938.

Films

Wong is called into several of his cases by tough, irascible Captain Street of Homicide (Grant Withers), who has grudging respect for the old Oriental's wisdom. Toward the middle of the series, Street acquires a girl friend, a competitive newspaper reporter named Bobby Logan (Marjorie Reynolds).

Mr. Wong, Detective. Monogram, 1938. Karloff, Withers, Maxine Jennings, Evelyn Brent, Lucien Prival. Directed by William Nigh.

Three industrialists are killed by poisoned gas released when a glass receptacle is shattered. Wong suspects that police sirens broke the glass.

The Mystery of Mr. Wong. Monogram, 1939. Karloff, Withers, Dorothy Tree, Craig Reynolds, Lotus Long, Morgan Wallace. Directed by Nigh.

While in China, a rich art collector stole the Eye of the Daughter of the Moon, the largest star sapphire in the world. At a party attended by fellow collector Wong, the man is murdered, and the gem vanishes.

Mr. Wong in Chinatown. Monogram, 1939. Karloff, Withers, Marjorie Reynolds, Peter George Lynn, William Royle, Long. Directed by Nigh.

A Chinese princess, who has been buying airplanes for her homeland, is murdered in Wong's office. Later a dwarf and a vast sum of money vanish. The plot of this film was used again for a 1947 Monogram Charlie CHAN film, *The Chinese Ring.*

Doomed to Die. Monogram, 1940. Karloff, Withers, Marjorie Reynolds, Melvin Lang, Guy Usher. Directed by Nigh.

A millionaire is murdered just after his ship, carrying a vast amount of bonds, is sunk. Since the bonds are owned by the Chinese, a tong war is in the offing.

The Fatal Hour. Monogram, 1940. Karloff, Withers, Marjorie Reynolds, Charles Trowbridge, John Hamilton, Craig Reynolds. Directed by Nigh.

Captain Street's best friend, a detective working on a jewel-smuggling case, is killed. The trail leads Wong to murders committed by remote control.

Phantom of Chinatown. Monogram, 1940. Keye Luke (replacing Karloff as a younger version of the detective, now called Jimmy Wong), Withers (continuing as Captain Street), Long, Paul McVey. Directed by Phil Rosen.

While a famous explorer is presenting a slide lecture about his expedition to the Mongolian Desert, he drinks some water and dies. His last words are about a scroll that may show the location of a vast oil deposit.

WOODS, SARA (1922–). English mystery novelist. Born Sara Hutton, she was educated in Yorkshire. During World War II she was employed in a London bank; later she worked in a solicitor's office. In 1946 she married Anthony Bowen-Judd, an electronics engineer. Since 1957 the couple have lived in Halifax, Nova Scotia, where Miss Woods has been registrar at St. Mary's University.

Although she had long harbored an ambition to become a writer, Miss Woods did not make any serious attempts at writing until she moved to Canada. When her first novel, *Bloody Instructions,* was accepted for its eventual 1962 publication, she was ready with four more novels, which were immediately accepted. All her books have been about English lawyer-detective Antony MAITLAND, and all the titles are lines from Shakespeare. Miss Woods's experiences in a law office have been useful, and she has been praised for her handling of courtroom scenes. In commenting on *Trusted Like the Fox* (1964), about Maitland's defense of a man accused of treason, Dorothy B. HUGHES said that it was "one of the finest law novels in memory."

WOOLRICH, CORNELL (GEORGE HOPLEY-) (1903–1968). American writer of crime and mystery stories whose ability to create an atmosphere of terror has been equaled only by that of Edgar Allan POE. Woolrich was a virtual recluse; indeed, so little is known of his life that *The New York Times* obituary was confused and inept, telling little about his life and neglecting to mention his most famous book, *Phantom Lady.*

Woolrich was born in New York City but spent his early years partly in Latin America with his father, a mining engineer, and partly in New York with his socialite mother. He spent a number of years in Mexico during the revolutions of the second decade of the twentieth century. He enjoyed the excitement of the fighting and the numerous school holidays declared when his town was taken alternately by "Pancho" Villa and Venustiano Carranza. He developed a morbid childhood hobby of collecting the used rifle cartridge shells that littered the streets beneath his window.

While still an undergraduate at Columbia Col-

Cornell Woolrich.

lege, he was confined to bed for six weeks with a foot infection and wrote *Cover Charge* (1926), a well-received romantic novel. The following year *Children of the Ritz*, another romantic novel, won a $10,000 prize offered jointly by *College Humor* magazine and First National Pictures, which produced a film based on the book in 1929. While working on the film script in Hollywood, Woolrich fell in love with and married a producer's daughter, who left him after only a few weeks. He returned to New York and Claire Attalie Woolrich, his domineering mother. He worked at a prodigious pace, rarely leaving their hotel room. His next four novels were all good, if sentimental, love stories, and critics compared him to F. Scott FITZGERALD, who remained one of Woolrich's favorite writers.

His first mystery story appeared in 1934, and thereafter his works were almost exclusively of that type. He produced hundreds of stories in longhand—too many to be sustained by a single by-line. In addition to writing under his own name, he published books as William Irish and two novels as George Hopley: *Night Has a Thousand Eyes* and *Fright*.

The origin of the William Irish pseudonym is disputed. Ellery QUEEN (author) suggests that Whit Burnett, the celebrated editor of *Story* magazine, took the manuscript of a new Woolrich novel to editors at Lippincott, who liked it instantly. Since Simon and Schuster had exclusive rights to the Cornell Woolrich name, a pseudonym had to be invented for a Woolrich work published by Lippincott. Woolrich suggested using the name of a nationality, such as English, French, Welsh, Irish—at which point Burnett stopped him. They then picked an ordinary first name, so that the emphasis would remain on the surname—and "William Irish" was created.

A more likely theory is that Woolrich took the name from a William Irish, a dialogue writer for First National Studios during the time Woolrich was in Hollywood; the credit "William Irish" appeared on three films in the late 1920s. It is probable that Woolrich had some connection with him and remembered the name years later when he needed a pseudonym.

Woolrich's best work appeared before 1950. A diabetic and an alcoholic, he was a bitter, frustrated man who had little desire to live after his mother's death in 1957. He suspected that he was a homosexual and seemed deliberately to antagonize acquaintances. Shortly before he died, he developed gangrene in one leg, and amputation was necessary. Not surprisingly, his funeral was nearly unattended. His estate of approximately $1 million established a scholarship fund at Columbia University in his mother's name.

In 1948 Woolrich won the Mystery Writers of America Edgar for his contribution to the mystery short story. He wrote more than 250 works in this genre, employing virtually every device ever conceived for the creation of suspense.

One of Woolrich's favorite methods of inducing a sense of terror is the movement of time. Each day passes on the calendar, or each second ticks on the clock, until the suspense becomes unbearable. His plots are brilliantly contrived, even though the strong hand of coincidence is too much in evidence on some occasions. Woolrich's style, as unpredictable as the man himself, heightens the suspense of the reader, who never knows whether the terror will ultimately be relieved, or whether it will be even worse when the tale is finished. Sometimes a plot twist allows an apparent victim to escape; at other times, he is doomed; on still other occasions, the prey escapes, only to be replaced by someone else.

The depressing mood of many of Woolrich's stories reflects his own life—intense loneliness and despair dominate the atmosphere. Many of the stories, particularly the early ones, are in the tradition of Dashiell HAMMETT and Raymond CHANDLER—hard-hitting, action-filled adventures of the BLACK MASK school, although far more of his stories initially appeared in *Detective Fiction Weekly* and *Dime Detective* than in the *Black Mask*.

But it is for the subtle story of psychological terror that he will be remembered as possibly the finest mystery writer of the twentieth century—those tales once described by Anthony BOUCHER as "the every-day gone wrong."

Much of Woolrich's best work appeared in his series of "Black" novels. Possibly the best is *Rendezvous in Black*, in which Johnny Marr devotes his life to avenging the death of the girl he loved. Knowing

Franchot Tone (right) and Elisha Cook, Jr., in a sinister moment from William Irish's *Phantom Lady*. [*Universal*]

that one member of a group of men must have been responsible for her death, Marr enters each of their lives, discovers whom they love most, and murders the loved one, so that the man will feel the same grief he does.

In *The Bride Wore Black* a similar tale of vengeance unfolds when a woman sees her bridegroom shot dead on the church steps. She learns the identities of the five men in the car that careened past the church as the shot was fired, and sets out to kill each of them in turn.

The first book under the William Irish by-line was *Phantom Lady*, the now-familiar tale of a race against the clock to save the life of an innocent man condemned to death for a murder (his wife's) he did not commit.

The supernatural does not play a significant role in Woolrich's stories, although it seems to. Ultimately, even the most unnatural events prove to be the result of human effort. Nowhere is this aspect of his work demonstrated more terrifyingly than in *Night Has a Thousand Eyes*, in which a girl and her father are convinced that he is doomed because of a seer's predictions. In few other books does the reader so compellingly "share the agony of the hunted and the terror of the doomed," as Ellery Queen wrote in the introduction to *The Ten Faces of Cornell Woolrich*.

CHECKLIST

1940 *The Bride Wore Black*
1941 *The Black Curtain*
1942 *Black Alibi*
1942 *Phantom Lady* (by William Irish)

Michael Duane tries to help mentally disturbed Lenore Aubert, who has claimed she is being held prisoner by her dead husband's relations, in *Return of the Whistler*, based on a story by Woolrich. [*Columbia*]

1943 *The Black Angel*
1943 *I Wouldn't Be in Your Shoes* (s.s.; by William Irish)
1944 *The Black Path of Fear*
1944 *Deadline at Dawn* (by William Irish)
1944 *After-Dinner Story* (s.s.; by William Irish)
1945 *Night Has a Thousand Eyes* (by George Hopley)
1945 *If I Should Die Before I Wake* (s.s.; by William Irish)
1946 *The Dancing Detective* (s.s.; by William Irish)
1946 *Borrowed Crime* (s.s.; by William Irish)
1947 *Waltz into Darkness* (by William Irish)
1948 *Dead Man Blues* (s.s.; by William Irish)
1948 *Rendezvous in Black*
1948 *I Married A Dead Man* (by William Irish)
1949 *The Blue Ribbon* (s.s.; by William Irish)
1950 "Marijuana" (s.s.; by William Irish)
1950 "You'll Never See Me Again" (s.s.; by William Irish)
1950 *Somebody on the Phone* (s.s.; by William Irish)
1950 *Fright* (by George Hopley)
1950 *Savage Bride*
1950 *Six Nights of Mystery* (s.s.; by William Irish)
1951 *Strangler's Serenade* (by William Irish)
1952 *Eyes That Watch You* (s.s.; by William Irish)
1952 *Bluebeard's Seventh Wife* (s.s.; by William Irish)
1956 *Nightmare* (s.s.)
1958 *Violence* (s.s.)
1958 *Hotel Room* (s.s.)
1959 *Death Is My Dancing Partner*
1959 *Beyond the Night* (s.s.)
1960 *The Doom Stone*
1965 *The Ten Faces of Cornell Woolrich* (s.s.)
1965 *The Dark Side of Love* (s.s.)
1971 *Nightwebs* (s.s.)

Films

Woolrich's mystery works have received varied treatment on the screen, ranging from "B" films to important star vehicles. His first mystery story to serve as the basis of a film had appeared in a pulp magazine.

Convicted. Columbia, 1938. Rita Hayworth, Charles Quigley, Marc Lawrence, Phyllis Clare. Directed by Leon Barsha. Based on Woolrich's short story "Face Work," later "Angel Face."

A nightclub entertainer clears her brother of murdering a gold digger on the very day of his execution.

Street of Chance. Paramount, 1942. Burgess Meredith, Claire Trevor, Sheldon Leonard, Louise Platt, Adeline DeWalt Reynolds, Frieda Inescort. Directed by Jack Hively. Closely based on *The Black Curtain.*

A man, stunned in a street accident, recovers and makes his way home—to learn that he has been absent for a year. During this amnesic period, he discovers, he has been working for a rich man who was murdered on the very day of his accident.

The Leopard Man. RKO, 1943. Dennis O'Keefe, Jean Brooks, Margo, Abner Biberman, James Bell. Directed by Jacques Tourneur. A careful adaptation of *Black Alibi.*

A brash press agent for a Mexican nightclub rents a panther for publicity purposes, but the animal breaks free. Later, three people die, the work, the press agent finally suspects, not of the panther but of a human killer.

Phantom Lady. Universal, 1944. Franchot Tone, Ella Raines, Alan Curtis, Thomas Gomez, Fay Helm. Directed by Robert Siodmak. Based on the novel.

A young architect (Curtis) is accused of strangling his wife; no one believes his alibi, that he was in a theater with a woman (the "phantom lady") he had just picked up in a bar. His faithful secretary (Raines) tries to find the woman, identifiable only by the odd hat she wore.

Mark of the Whistler. Columbia, 1944. Richard Dix, Janis Carter, Paul Guilfoyle, Porter Hall, John Calvert. Directed by William Castle. Based on Woolrich's short story "Chance."

This is the second film in *The Whistler* series, based on the popular radio program, in which an anonymous whistling narrator unfolds macabre mystery tales. A vagrant assumes another man's identity, in order to claim a dormant bank account, and becomes a murderer's target.

Deadline at Dawn. RKO, 1946. Susan Hayward, Bill Williams, Paul Lukas, Lola Lane, Joseph Calleia. Directed by Harold Clurman. Clifford Odets's screenplay changed all elements of the book but the main characters and the time element (the events transpire during a single night).

The lives of a sailor on furlough and a hardened taxi dancer are brought together by the murder of a café hostess.

Black Angel. Universal, 1946. Dan Duryea, Peter Lorre, June Vincent, Broderick Crawford, Constance Dowling. Directed by Roy William Neill. An altered version of the novel.

The wife of a man awaiting execution for the murder of a blackmailing woman enters the milieu of a sinister nightclub in search of the real killer.

The Chase. United Artists, 1946. Robert Cummings, Michele Morgan, Steve Cochran, Lorre, Lloyd Corrigan. Directed by Arthur Ripley. An alteration of *The Black Path of Fear.*

A penniless veteran finds a wallet belonging to a Miami racketeer and is hired as his chauffeur. Soon, he flees to Havana with the gangster's abused wife and, when she is stabbed in a nightclub, is accused of her murder.

Fall Guy. Monogram, 1947. Robert Armstrong, Clifford Penn, Teala Loring, Elisha Cook, Jr. Directed by Reginald Le Borg. From the short story "C-Jag," later retitled "Cocaine."

A man wakes up after a mental blackout to discover that he is covered with blood and accused of the murder of a girl he met at a party and cannot remember.

Fear in the Night. Paramount, 1947. Paul Kelly, DeForest Kelley, Kay Scott, Ann Doran. Directed by Maxwell Shane. From the William Irish short story "Nightmare."

A young man has a nightmare during which he kills a stranger in a room filled with mirrors. A week later, during a family picnic, he chances upon a country house with a mirrored room—and a corpse.

The Guilty. Monogram, 1947. Don Castle, Bonita Granville, Regis Toomey, Elyse Knox, John Litel. Directed by John Reinhardt. From the short story "He Looked Like Murder," later retitled "Two Fellows in a Furnished Room."

A young man returns to the neighborhood where, a year before, a neurotic roomer had killed the twin sister of the girl he loved and pushed her body into an incinerator.

I Wouldn't Be in Your Shoes. Monogram, 1948. Castle, Knox, Toomey, Robert Lowell. Directed by William Nigh. From the short story of the same title. The screenplay was by Steve FISHER.

A down-and-out vaudevillian, unable to sleep, tosses his tap shoes at a cat howling in the backyard of his cheap rooming house; later, a shoe print convicts him of murder. His distraught young wife tries to clear him.

Return of the Whistler. Columbia, 1948. Michael Duane, Lenore Aubert, James Cardwell, Richard Lane. Directed by D. Ross Lederman. From a Woolrich short story, "All at Once, No Alice."

A young man finds the French war widow who had disappeared on the eve of their wedding; she is an inmate in a private asylum, claiming that relatives are after her dead husband's fortune.

The Night Has a Thousand Eyes. Paramount, 1948. Edward G. Robinson, Gail Russell, John Lund. Directed by John Farrow. Freely taken from the novel.

A middle-aged sideshow mentalist tries not to draw upon his ability to predict tragic events; the police keep him from attempting to save the daughter of a friend from doom.

The Window. RKO, 1949. Bobby Driscoll, Barbara Hale, Arthur Kennedy, Paul Stewart. Directed by Ted Tetzlaff. A highly successful version of the 1947 short story "The Boy Cried Murder."

Nobody believes an imaginative small boy when he declares that he has seen a neighborhood couple stab a sailor—no one except the murderers. The film won an Edgar, as the best mystery film of the year, from the Mystery Writers of America (MWA); Bobby Driscoll received a special Academy Award for outstanding juvenile acting.

Because a small boy, while on a tenement fire escape, has witnessed a murder, he too is marked for death in *The Window*, the award-winning screen version of a Cornell Woolrich short story. Here Ruth Roman peers in on Bobby Driscoll. [*RKO*]

No Man of Her Own. Paramount, 1950. Barbara Stanwyck, Lund, Phyllis Thaxter, Richard Denning, Jane Cowl, Lyle Bettger. Directed by Mitchell Leisen. Based on *I Married a Dead Man*.

Fleeing from the man who betrayed her, a woman on a train heading for San Francisco meets a girl who is also seven months pregnant. When the other woman and her husband are killed in a train wreck, the heroine assumes her identity and a new life, until the father of her premature baby finds her and attempts to expose her.

Rear Window. Paramount, 1954. James Stewart, Grace Kelly. Directed by Alfred HITCHCOCK. A lavish color rendering of "It Had to Be Murder" (1942), later retitled "Rear Window" for its first book publication (1944).

A news photographer, convalescing from a broken leg, insists in vain that a murder has been committed in the building he has been observing from the rear window of his apartment. The film was awarded an Edgar by the MWA.

Nightmare. United Artists, 1956. Robinson, Kevin McCarthy, Connie Russell. Directed by Maxwell Shane. A remake of *Fear in the Night* (reverting to the title of the original story.)

In this version, the hero is a jazz musician, and the house with the mirrored room is located outside New Orleans.

The Boy Cried Murder. Universal (British), 1966. Veronica Hurst, Phil Brown, Fraser "Fizz" MacIntosh, Beba Loncar. Directed by George Breakston. A remake of *The Window* (using the title of the original story).

This time, the boy (MacIntosh) "cries murder" on a tourist steamer sailing down the Adriatic coast; accusations continue at a Dalmatian seaside resort.

The Bride Wore Black. Lopert (French: *La Mariée Était en Noir*), 1967. Jeanne Moreau, Jean-Claude Brialy, Michel Bouquet, Charles Denner. Directed by François Truffaut.

When her bridegroom is shot dead on their wedding day, a girl takes revenge on the several men she suspects of his murder.

The Mississippi Mermaid. United Artists (French: *La Sirène du Mississippi*), 1969. Jean-Paul Belmondo, Catherine Deneuve, Bouquet. Directed by Truffaut. Based on the novel *Waltz into Darkness*.

A planter in a French possession in the tropics opens his heart to a mail-order bride; when she disappears with his money, he searches for her.

Television

Woolrich's short stories have been rich sources for half-hour anthology programs on both radio and television. The most important Woolrich novel to be adapted for television was *Rendezvous in Black*, which appeared during the mid-1950s on CBS's *Playhouse 90*, starring Boris Karloff.

WORKER, NORMAN. *See* SAINT, THE.

WRIGHT, ROWLAND. *See* WELLS, CAROLYN.

WRIGHT, WILLARD HUNTINGTON. *See* VAN DINE, S. S.

WYLIE, PHILIP (GORDON) (1902–1973). American author. Born in Beverly, Mass., he attended Princeton and worked at various jobs, including editing *The New Yorker* and writing screenplays for MGM and Universal. He married Sally Ondeck in 1928 (they were divorced in 1937); they had one daughter. In 1938 he married Frederica Ballard.

He wrote potboilers at a prodigious pace (several of them were published anonymously or pseudonymously), and collaborated with Edwin BALMER on several science fiction novels. Wylie was best known for his biting satiric fiction and his mild, pleasant stories about Crunch and Des. His most controversial literary effort was an attack on American mothers in *A Generation of Vipers* (1942), which added the word "momism" to the language.

Wylie's mystery novels are not highly regarded, but they are literate and readable, especially *The Murderer Invisible* (1932), *The Corpses at Indian Stones* (1943), and *Three to Be Read* (1951; contains *The Smuggled Atom Bomb, Sporting Blood*, and *Experiment in Crime*).

Y–Z

YAFFE, JAMES (1927–). American novelist, playwright, scriptwriter, and short story writer. Born in Chicago, Yaffe moved to New York City at an early age. He wrote his first mystery short story when he was only fifteen as part of a "free writing" assignment in a high school English course. Yaffe graduated from Yale, served in the Navy, and spent a year in Paris before launching a full-time writing career. A book of nonmystery short stories, *Poor Cousin Evelyn* (1951), received good reviews. *Nothing but the Night* (1957) is a fictionalized account of the famous Loeb-Leopold trial. *The Deadly Game,* an adaptation of Friedrich Dürrenmatt's *Traps,* was produced on Broadway in 1960. Yaffe has also written television scripts and a number of articles and books on Jewish history.

His successful high school effort, called "The Department of Impossible Crimes," was published in *Ellery Queen's Mystery Magazine* in July 1943, launching a series of six short stories about Paul Dawn and the fictional division of the New York City Police Department that he heads. Yaffe later wrote a series of eight short stories about Mom, a Jewish widow who lives in the Bronx. A true armchair detective, Mom solves cases for her son, the detective, merely by listening to his accounts of the evidence during traditional Friday night dinners. These stories were frequent award winners in the annual *EQMM* contests. "Mom Knows Best" (1952) and "Mom in the Spring" (1954) won third prizes; "Mom Makes a Wish" (1955) and "One of the Family" (1956), a nonseries story about a Jewish matriarch, were second-prize winners.

YATES, DORNFORD (pseudonym of Cecil William Mercer; 1885–1960). English author of adventure and secret service fiction. Yates was educated at Harrow and University College, Oxford, where he was president of the Dramatic Society. He served in both World War I and World War II, rising to the rank of major. He spent his last years in Umtali, Southern Rhodesia.

Yates, who used his pseudonym in both his private life and his literary one, gave up his career as a barrister with the publication of his first novel, *The Courts of Idleness* (1920). He went on to write thirty-three additional books, virtually all of which are fast-paced action thrillers in the vein of those of John BUCHAN and H. C. MCNEILE.

YIN, LESLIE CHARLES BOWYER. *See* CHARTERIS, LESLIE.

YORK, JEREMY. *See* CREASEY, JOHN.

YOUNG, COLLIER. *See* BLOCH, ROBERT.

Z, DEPARTMENT. *See* DEPARTMENT Z.

ZALESKI, PRINCE (Creator: M. P. SHIEL). Probably the most bizarre, erudite, and ethereal detective in literature, Zaleski is an exiled Russian nobleman living in London. He leaves his exotic apartments only once, and Ham, his devoted Ethiopian servant, is filled with grief and fear until his master returns safely. Sitting in semidark solitude, lulled by the "low, liquid, tinkling of an invisible musical-box," he is surrounded by bizarre objects of barbaric beauty—Flemish sepulchral brasses, Egyptian mummies, statues of Brahman gods, gem-encrusted medieval reliquaries, runic tablets.

Author-narrator Shiel brings mysteries to the drug-influenced Zaleski (he uses the "base of the 'bhang' of the Mohammedans"), who solves them by means of his strongly developed intuitive sense, combined with extraordinary powers of concentration and inductive reasoning. Zaleski also has "the unparalleled power not merely of disentangling in retrospect but of unraveling in prospect, and . . . to relate coming events with unimaginable minuteness of precision."

There is never a physical description of the prince; he is as remote and intangible as Shiel's prose style. He studies subjects that are incomprehensible to others and regards his rare excursions into crime solving as unwelcome intrusions, performed only as personal favors to his friend Shiel.

Shiel put Zaleski in perspective when he wrote: "There is no detective but *the* detective and the father of detectives, the 'Dupin' of Poe, of whom this Zaleski is a legitimate son, and the notorious Holmes a bastard son" (an inscription in a first-edition copy of *Prince Zaleski,* 1895; *see* DUPIN, C. AUGUSTE; HOLMES, SHERLOCK; POE, EDGAR ALLAN).

The royal-blooded Zaleski is more arrogant than Dupin and even more learned, his adventures filled with vague references to Greek words, Latin quotations, and obscure mythological figures.

There are only four stories about the prince; three were collected in *Prince Zaleski.* "The Return of Prince Zaleski," an inferior later story, was published in *Ellery Queen's Mystery Magazine* in January 1955, ten years after it was written. Shiel's title was "Lend-Lease."

"The Race of Orven" features the brutal Lord Randolph, who is clearly a dangerous villain. Zaleski, however, refuses to acknowledge Randolph's guilt, saying that "Earls' sons do not, in fact, go about murdering people." The conclusion is deliberately obscure, but it seems likely that Randolph will be brought to justice.

"The Stone of the Edmundsbury Monks" involves attempts to recover a valuable jewel and a missing baronet. After Zaleski examines the nobleman's diary, he accurately predicts the time and place of his death.

An epidemic of apparent suicides, accounting for 8,000 deaths in three weeks, strikes Europe in "The S.S." The urgent need to solve this problem causes Zaleski to take unprecedented action and leave his room, to uncover a secret brotherhood, the Society of Sparta, whose scheme to eliminate the pampering of weakness requires mass murder. The prince finally fathoms their secret and ends their activities, although he does not report any of those responsible.

ZANGWILL, ISRAEL (1864–1926). English novelist, social activist, and author of *The Big Bow Mystery* (1892), for which he is regarded as "the father of the 'locked-room' mystery" (*see* LOCKED-ROOM MYSTERIES).

Zangwill's father was a Russian Jewish refugee who emigrated to London. Raised in a ghetto, Israel Zangwill devoted his life to espousing Jewish causes, in particular, Zionism. He also gave voice to several unpopular opinions of the time, supporting woman's suffrage and referring to the League of Nations as the "League of Damnations."

Edgar Allan POE's "The Murders in the Rue Morgue" (1841) is the first "locked-room" story, but *The Big Bow Mystery* is the first fiction of greater length to use the plot device. Zangwill wrote the novelette in two weeks for the *London Star* the year before it was published in book form. It was reprinted in 1903 in *The Grey Wig,* a collection of stories by Zangwill.

Written as a parody of detective stories, *The Big Bow Mystery* is a clever, if tongue-in-cheek, story of a man who is discovered with his throat cut in a room that has been locked, sealed, bolted, and "as firmly barred as if besieged." The retired Inspector Grodman provides a surprising solution—a solution that Gaston LEROUX must have considered when he wrote *The Mystery of the Yellow Room* fifteen years later.

Films

The Perfect Crime. FBO, 1928. Clive Brook, Irene Rich, Ethel Wales, Carroll Nye, Tully Marshall. Directed by Bert Glennon. Based on *The Big Bow Mystery.*

A famous detective attempts to carry out "the perfect crime" by committing a murder—first poisoning his victim and then cutting his throat—but heeds the pleas of the wife of the innocent young man convicted of his crime.

The Verdict. Warner Brothers, 1946. Sydney Greenstreet, Peter Lorre, Joan Lorring. Directed by Don Siegel. Peter Milne wrote the interesting screenplay, loosely based on *The Big Bow Mystery.*

In gaslit London of the 1890s, a superintendent of Scotland Yard is dismissed for allowing an innocent man to be hanged on circumstantial evidence; he then plots "the perfect crime."

ZINBERG, LEN. *See* LACY, ED.